HANDBOOK
OF WORK, ORGANIZATION
AND SOCIETY

Contributors

Erik Allardt, *University of Helsinki*, Finland
T.J. Atchison, *San Diego State University*
D.W. Belcher, *San Diego State University*
John O. Crites, *University of Maryland*
Louis E. Davis, *University of California, Los Angeles*
Robert Dubin, *University of California, Irvine*
Mitchell Fein, *Professional Engineer*
William H. Form, *University of Illinois, Champaign-Urbana*
Bjorn Gustavsen, *Work Research Institutes*, Oslo, Norway
R. Alan Hedley, *University of Victoria*
Frank A. Heller, *The Tavistock Institute of Human Relations*, London, England
Joan Althaus Huber, *University of Illinois, Champaign-Urbana*
Janez Jerovsek, *University of Ljubljana, Yugoslavia*
Bernard Karsh, *University of Illinois, Champaign-Urbana*
Henry A. Landsberger, *University of North Carolina at Chapel Hill*
Thomas Lupton, *Manchester Business School*, Manchester, England
Alexander Matejko, *University of Alberta*
Martin Meissner, *University of British Columbia*
E. Lauck Parke, *University of Massachusetts, Amherst*
Stanley R. Parker, London, England
Roland J. Pellegrin, *Pennsylvania State University*
Michael A. Smith, London, England
Bjorg Aase Sorensen, *Work Research Institutes*, Oslo, Norway
George Strauss, *University of California, Berkeley*
Curt Tausky, *University of Massachusetts, Amherst*
Thomas C. Taveggia, *Illinois Institute of Technology*
James C. Taylor, *University of California, Los Angeles*
Einar Thorsrud, *Work Research Institutes*, Oslo, Norway
Eric Trist, *Wharton School, University of Pennsylvania*
John Van Maanen, *Massachusetts Institute of Technology*
Theodore D. Weinshall, *Tel Aviv University*, Israel

HANDBOOK
OF
WORK, ORGANIZATION,
AND SOCIETY

Edited by
Robert Dubin

University of California, Irvine

Rand McNally College Publishing Company   •   Chicago

RAND McNALLY HANDBOOK SERIES

Current Printing (last digit)
15 14 13 12 11 10 9 8 7 6 5 4 3 2 1

Copyright ©1976 by Rand McNally College Publishing Company
All rights reserved
Printed in U.S.A.
Library of Congress Catalog Card Number 74–33973

Preface

This is a distinctive Handbook. It is a guide to the future of work, work organizations, and the social systems within which the work will be carried out. The special feature of this Handbook is its treatment of the future. This unique treatment will require some description and explanation.

The simplest way to project pictures of the future of any human activity is to extrapolate from its history. Under present conditions of rapid change in all aspects of life, extrapolation of any lengthy future period may be a certain path to error. Consequently, we have adopted a different approach to confronting the future.

The starting point was to ask a group of imaginative, international scholars, who are deeply knowledgeable about the world of work, to visualize a future that would exhibit fewer of the present disabilities of work. They were asked to base their views of the future on a realistic leap forward from present conditions, guided by a humanistic concern with Man the producer. The intent of such a procedure was to avoid both the errors of extrapolation and of utopia-building. There are already enough of these erroneous contributions existing in the present literature about individuals at work.

The rhetoric employed in this collection of essays has intentionally sought to avoid the declarative style of, "the future will . . ." and "it is predicted that . . ." Rather, the analyses emphasize that the future is *now*, but with much of its shape still shrouded in vague uncertainties. None of the authors wish to be characterized as futurologists, for they are much too concerned with describing what is happening in the present to play the role of seers.

A second feature of the orientation adopted in this volume was to include analyses of industrial systems developed from different value positions than those traditionally buttressing Western capitalism. Technology is nonideological and readily shared across all industrial systems. When man-work relationships differ among social systems, even though similar technologies are employed, we gain important clues about roles played by the social systems. Comparisons among industrial systems should illuminate their differential achievements, and both the universal and unique problems that are affected by social system variables.

From another standpoint, it was also important to bring the social setting of work into strong focus, because in the present and increasingly in the future, work will most likely occupy less of the total life of the citizen. This could mean that a young person will enter the work world with norms and values that may not celebrate work as the center of his or her existence. It might also mean that in the middle and later years of life, workers will envision themselves less as workers and more as consumers. This development will have serious implications for the motivations to work and the nature of the work environment. This Handbook properly contains the word *Society* in its title since almost every chapter makes the social system a central concern for understanding man at work; and a number of chapters have the social system as the organizing principle of their content.

A third intent when developing this volume, was to explore some of the little understood facets of working behavior. It is in these shadowy areas of reality, where the light of knowledge burns dimly, that some of the insights necessary to improve our understanding may well be found. It is a risk for scholars to follow this course of study; it is an uncertain proposition, since the hoped-for insights might never materialize. A fair evaluation of the exploratory work of several of the chapters would be that the ground-breaking efforts have paid off very well.

Still another guide at the developmental stages of this volume, was the mandate to each author to explore individual models and report research in detail. The purpose of this inclusion was to insure that the reader may share a body of ideas and data first-hand, through which he or she will better understand the nature of work. A secondary purpose served by this particular emphasis was to permit the reader to grasp how good theory emerges from the always exciting, and sometimes painful, efforts to make sense out of research data.

The very language utilized by the authors of this volume is indicative of the humanistic orientation of their thinking. We have tried to avoid jargon. Simple ideas are expressed simply, and complex ideas are not made more so by esoteric language. It was the desire of this group of scholars to communicate clearly and effectively both with their professional colleagues and with managers and executives in the business community. Hopefully, the latter might be guided in their executive and managerial functions by the practical, constructive insights contained in this volume.

It will be noted that in almost every chapter, the authors adopt a critical stance toward the conventional "wisdom" of the field. Traditional handbooks honor the traditional "wisdom" and hand it down to the next generation to serve as a guide for action. The emphasis in this volume is to question the conventional thought with the constructive hope that nonconventional thought might prove to be wiser. This theme is perhaps best revealed by the evolution of this book. The editor began with a traditional table of contents, covering usual subjects in more or less accepted, conventional manner. The authors responded by taking the classical subjects and placing them in nonclassical intellectual settings. The editor followed the lead of his authors by rejecting his original outline of subject headings, reducing the number of chapters by almost one-half, and began to see the emergence of an incomplete but fresh and exciting view of people working. There are many components to the working life of an individual. We must view all the components to see how they effect the worker. There may be some material loss of the whole picture if we are driven by scientism to study only small components of reality. The reader will be well advised to consult the subject index to discover the breadth of coverage of the classical subjects of the world of work, rather than depend solely on the twenty-three chapter titles in the table of contents for an exact chronicle of what is in the book.

If we focus in the destiny of industrial man, the conclusion of this volume is that his fate is by no means settled. The world of work is clearly in a state of *becoming*. This state is analyzed repeatedly in the following chapters. Neither despair for the "alienated" worker with his "blue collar blues" nor blind optimism about his potentiality to achieve "self-actualization" are the motifs of this volume. Rather, the present and future can be summed up as a collection of good and bad outcomes. What is "good" (as judged by the explicit values set forth in the chapters) is examined for its characteristics, and what is "bad" is examined just as carefully to discover what can be learned from mistakes. We do not castigate the errors of the past, but instead examine them to determine what action we can take to avoid repetition in the future. Social systems are human inventions for solving problems of living. But they are also sources of problems generated by their own operating characteristics and malfunctions. Only in utopias created inside the minds of visionaries do perfect social systems exist. The real world of society, and specifically the world of work, are now imperfect and will continue to be so. The fundamental optimism of the authors of this Handbook rests on their conviction that improvements can be made in man-work relationships, particularly if a serious search is undertaken to establish a knowledge base for such improvements.

There is a healthy eclecticism represented among the chapters in this volume. The editor deliberately sought conflicting points of view and encouraged their inclusion. If the world of work is, indeed, in a state of *becoming*, then there will surely be controversy about its emergent character. The reader will not find that the authors "sing out of the same prayer book," but there is, nevertheless, an underlying harmonious counterpoint within the ensemble.

This book bears a kinship with two other volumes in the Rand McNally Handbook Series: March's *Handbook of Organizations* and Dunnette's *Handbook of Industrial and Organizational Psychology*. March's volume organized the inchoate field of organization theory, while Dunnette's volume is the most thorough single compendium of knowledge in the area of industrial psychology. Obviously, it would have been a fruitless task to duplicate the contents of these two outstanding volumes. We, therefore, largely avoided covering the areas that are the subject matters of these companion volumes. It is a commentary of the field of human work that there is still much left to be said in the present volume.

There is no one more deserving of the traditional "thank you" for the contribution to this work than the individual authors who created it. This international group of scholars labored with dedication and extraordinary perspicacity to contribute to the collective enterprise. They will each draw individual satisfaction from knowing that their own ideas combine with the ideas of other scholars to produce a synergistic outcome worthy of modern behaviorial science.

Robert Dubin
January, 1976

Table of Contents

PART I

WORK AND LEISURE

INTRODUCTION—PART I

There is usually a hidden agenda underlying the contemporary analyses of work in a modern industrial society. Early students of work assumed that man could be adapted to the conditions of work, and that the managerial problem was to find means for securing the adaptations as rapidly and economically as possible. Thus, the study of jobs focused upon the physiological characteristics of man the "operative" and the technical demands for human labor input into the machine. Making a good fit between the physiological man and the technological machine was considered a triumph of personnel administration. This idea is still widely held.

A second assumption in analyzing work was that workers did, after all, have a psyche, and that this dimension of man needed to be taken into account when designing work environments. Thus we see the genesis of the human relations movement which attempted to manipulate the environment of work to reduce the untoward and sometimes debilitating effects of personnel practices which had failed to take man's psyche into account. Raising work satisfaction was viewed as the key to unlocking human work potential so that it would become a positive contribution to greater output and greater economic gain. Fundamental to the human relations approach was the belief that tools of clinical psychology and sociology could be marshalled to impact directly on the psyche of workers and executives alike.

In an even more contemporary vein, the socio-technical systems analysts see the salvation of the entire social system depending upon pervasive reform of the manner in which the man-machine relationship has heretofore been developed. The hidden agenda of this group of scholars is to produce a revolution in society itself through significant modifications in the organization of the world of work.

There has been relatively little attention directed to the linkages between work and nonwork, perhaps on the assumption that working is so important in an industrial society that it really does not matter what the citizen does with his nonworking time. At best, we characterize the nonwork waking hours as leisure, and assume that each person is quite capable of developing his own leisure activities.

When work organizations turn their attention to leisure, they do so in one of two ways. For executives the prequisites of office often include generous expense accounts, or periodic conventions and "retreats" held in exotic places where it is expected that leisure activities will be combined with business accomplishments. At the worker level, a whole range of company sponsored leisure activities may be provided or even subsidized on the assumption that loyalty and a high level of performance will be the result. At both the executive and worker level, the expected return on company investment in leisure activities for employees is that there will be more efficient working behaviors for the organization than might otherwise be the case.

3

Interesting patterns begin to emerge when work and leisure are viewed as linked in some significant ways. Rather than place a chapter on leisure at the end of a volume dealing with work, where it dangles like a decorative bauble, we have chosen to make it one of the first considerations. We will be able to understand work better when we understand that leisure is, perhaps, its major alternative.

CHAPTER **1**

Work in Modern Society

Robert Dubin

University of California—Irvine

The purpose of this chapter is to review some of the important issues to which attention must be turned in analyzing work in a developed economy. Many of these issues are addressed directly in this volume. It is more important at the beginning of this book to indicate the sorts of problems whose solution is being sought, than to state the solutions that seem most worthwhile. The analysis of individual problems is the subject matter of the following chapters.

Attention will be turned to some of the broad trends in the manner in which work has been conceptualized in the past, and on the basis of which man-machine relationships have been designed. Major attention will also be given to the institutional arrangements of society as that might have an impact on the production institution.

PRIORITY: PEOPLE OR MACHINES

This volume focuses upon complex industrial societies and the characteristic ways in which work is carried out in them. In modern societies, work organizations tend to be large, complex, and costly in their use of all resources, including human resources. The output of such work organizations is goods, services, or both. By way of contrast, there are significant portions of the human race engaged in work basically to sustain life and in a context where "work" is not readily distinguished from other social activities (Richards, 1948). We are not concerned with societies that are still in a state of preindustrial development.

The most celebrated feature of an industrial society is, of course, its technology. In any account of human progress in the Western world, the wonders of technology are always extolled. A good deal less concern is turned toward the people who actually run the wonderful machines. Even in the era of concern with ecology, the impact is often disregarded upon the people closest to polluting machines and industrial processes, the workers.

When examining man as a worker, we are basically concerned with determining whether men at work are continuously and indefinitely adaptive to the conditions under which they work. The general answer up to the present time has been that man was assumed to be infinitely adaptive to whatever conditions are demanded by technology and by organizational processes. We have finally come to the point where serious questions may now be raised as to whether man can be adapted still further to the steadily increasing needs of technology and work organization.

Questions about man's adaptability have inevitably lead to raising alternative questions. These alternative questions are directed to the issue of whether organizations and industrial technologies might have reached such a point of flexibility themselves, that they in turn might be made adaptive to the needs of man (Emery and Trist, 1969).

Thus, in the history of the development of industrial societies, we have reached a critical juncture in the design of sociotechnical environments. We can continue to pursue the refinement of technology and social structures by referring solely or largely to their technical design principles. High-speed processes may be increased in speed; new levels of precision may be obtained in machinery; communications systems can be further elaborated to increase the level of control it is possible to attain over human behavior; and, in general, the technologies of work can be further rationalized to improve the beauty of their technical design and the level of their productive output. This constant perfection of the technical processes is the technocrats' view of further industrial development and it is a road down which much of present social planning proceeds.

The alternative road for future considerations of the technological society is the utilization of technology's fundamental flexibility as a foundation upon which it can be made to adapt to human dimensions and human needs. From this standpoint, we focus on man as the central actor in work and begin to design industrial processes, machines, work operations, and the environments of the work situation so that the essential humanity is retained, and may even be nurtured in the work situation.

The contrast then is between a technocratic view of the perfectability of technology, and the view of technology as a means toward human ends. From the technocratic point of view, the production of goods and services takes consumerism as its human goal. From the standpoint of humane industrialization, the actual processes of *producing* goods and services, as well as their consumption, is viewed as adapting to the needs of man, both individually and collectively. The technocratic view sees man as adapting to technology. The humane industrialism sees technology adapting to the needs of man.

TECHNOLOGY AND MAN

The history of man's relation to machines can be written in two very readily comprehended parts. The first and by far the longest historical period was the one in which there was constant searching to find out how man could be adapted in both his physical and mental capacities to the machines he invented to produce goods and services (Tilgher, 1930). Primitive hand tools, like the hammer and chisel, expanded man's capacity to employ his hands in producing usable goods. He used his mind insofar as he either remembered how to produce the needed goods from his past successes and failures in his work, or after observing an error in his work, he learned what to do to improve. Man was literally harnessed to his machines to provide these services, as a galley slave was chained to his oar.

The same general orientation was visible later in the more sophisticated development of the man-machine relationship. Machine design was oriented toward utilizing the then known capacity of man to use his mind and body as a direct adjunct of the machine. What really had to be known when designing the machines were the various limits or thresholds beyond which man's capacities for production, on the average, ceased to operate. These limits were in the form of reaching distance, strength in lifting, attention span, rate of response to signals, and ability to learn and recall operations at a future time when the various behaviors were demanded by the operating process. These physiological and intellectual limits came to be clearly understood at a very early period in machine design (Munsterberg, 1913; Viteles, 1932). What is today called "human-factors engineering" is simply a more refined attempt to discover the optimum points at which potential work skills can be utilized with the greatest efficiency. We still study the limits and tension cycles of the worker, but we will do it in order to discover some optimal points that yield the greatest sustained attention for the accomplishment of a given task.

To take another example, there is a corresponding focus on the question of whether it is better for an individual to work only an eight hour day even though it is known that man is capable of working more than an eight hour day. The argument rests on the fact that this shorter working day represented an optimal period where more could be accomplished per hour, rather than the worker's limit of working time for a single day. Indeed, today we face the curious phenomenon, that in moving to a four day work week, or even a three day work week, we are willing to re-examine the issue of eight versus more hours a day as a means of fitting a substantial amount of working time into a fewer number of total days. We are now moving toward examining the limits again on the assumption that if we restrict the total number of days in the week that are worked, even though the work day is lengthened, it will yield an optimum output relationship between the working individual and his work.

It is possible to provide further examples of machine design and the design of production processes that have assumed that man was designed to be "operative," rather than "operator." This assumption required some knowledge of the performance capabilities of man the animal and man as the learning and observing being. It is fair to say that this historic epoch in the development of the man-machine relationship is still upon us and that we are not yet fully launched into a new era of rethinking the man-machine relationship.

In the second and still emerging industrial epoch a new conception of the man-machine relationship is becoming apparent. This new conception presumes that technology has reached such sophisticated levels of flexibility that it is possible to consider whether technology and machines should be adapted to human needs and human purposes of working human beings. Using this new view of the man-machine relationship, we start with an image of man and inquire about the compatible ways in which a technology or a machine can be utilized to serve this man. This is a revolutionary viewpoint, for it places man in a new position: on center stage. We then must ask: how might we set this stage with props and scenery and supporting actors (equipment and machinery) so that man is not "upstaged"? This new orientation is inchoate. We know neither its full range of possibilities nor its limitations, but it is worthwhile to consider at least some of the more obvious dimensions.

IMAGES OF MAN

There are many aspects to the images of man that we must consider, while examining the man-machine relationships. From these images we can pose immediate questions about the possibility of satisfying these images in the work situation. Once we know the questions, applied social science will supply us with directions in which to proceed toward their answers.

Man is clearly a creature of habit, learning many behavioral patterns and repeating them throughout most, if not all, of his life (Thomas, 1923). Man is also an open system, constantly receiving new experiences and perhaps even being overloaded with them, especially if he lives in a complex urban-industrial society. Should the work-place be a setting within which the routines are repeated over a working lifetime, or should the work-place be a setting in which new experiences are generated regularly? Perhaps it might even be argued that the work-place, above all portions of the social space of an individual, should be filled with new experiences, because it is in the work-place that new experiences are likely to be disciplined into some kind of utilitarian regularity and routine. So, shall we consider man as merely fulfilling the routine portions of his life at work; or finding his major experiences in the work-place; or perhaps balancing in some way or another the routine with the new experience while working?

Man competes for status and value rewards that are associated either with confirming or improving his status or attaining a position of relatively high status. Will the work-place remain one of the central status-conferring arenas of life as it has been in the past, when a person's occupation and profession were often the only distinguishing features of class, position and status rank? Alternatively, shall the status differentials within work organizations be minimized on the presumption that social-status barriers will be reduced, and individuals will feel more relaxed and be more willing to cooperate with others involved in producing goods and services?

If man is a cooperative animal, we must ask: do we design our work-system so that the opportunities for cooperation are commensurate with man's learned capacity to behave in a cooperative manner? If this is indeed one of the goals in the design of work-places and work processes, then do we know enough about cooperative social behaviors to redesign its more appropriate structures and processes into the work-place? If man is a sociable creature and requires the constant interaction with fellow men who are, to use Mead's happy phrase, "significant others," then how are work situations to be designed so that there is natural opportunity while working to engage fellow men in social interaction?

Man is an *adaptive* animal. We can assume that there is a level of technological imperatives that must always be built into machines and industrial processes. Can we expect an individual to adapt more readily if provided with appropriate means and time periods for relief from strictly technological imperatives like high-level, continuous attention, or working in isolation from other people, or other stressful conditions?

If man is a *responsible* creature, then do there exist opportunities to build individual or group responsibility into the work situation so that this feature of man's social personality may also be realized in the work situation?

If in any group of working people, there is considerable individual variability, then how do we design work situations to adapt to this variable quality of the individuals who fill work positions? In the past, we have tried to fit different types of people to different kinds of jobs by matching job test results with job descriptions. We had presumed that once the fit was compatible, we had taken sufficient account of individual variability. This may no longer be either adequate or optimally desirable from the standpoint of output. It is clearly not desirable from the standpoint of trying to satisfy the opportunities for the expression of individual variability at work.

If man is a *learning* creature, then do we provide the individual worker the opportunity to learn in the work-place? If the answer is yes, does this learning include only that which is job-related, or will it extend beyond that range?

If man is a *choosing* creature, who selects the social settings within which to focus his commitment and central life interest, is it possible either to make the work-place a central life interest, or to insure that the work-place is at least complementary to the various nonwork, central life interests of the individual?

If there are cyclical features in the life-history of man, can we introduce additional cycles to the man-work linkage? We provide daily and weekly working and nonworking time, and introduce short holiday periods and longer annual periods called vacations from work. But we still expect forty-five to forty-eight years of a man's life to be continuously devoted to work, after he once starts in youth and from which he is freed only upon permanent retirement. Is there some possibility that we will want to introduce sabbatical periods of months or years within the larger work cycle so that the time when work is not required is no longer limited to youth or old age?

These various images of man immediately suggest some of the dimensions along which it may be possible to begin varying the nature of the industrial regime. The redesign of the work situation to fit man rather than the attempt to adapt man to the work situation will be a lengthy process and one involving the need to learn a great deal more than we now know about the nature of social organizations and about the relationships between machines and their human operators. However, it is not necessary to invent the new industrialism in one, huge conceptual piece. It will undoubtedly be invented in pieces, and as the pieces prove successful, we will move on to add new parts to the larger design.

SOCIAL INSTITUTIONS

Our attention up to this point has been directed at man's immediate work environment. There is, of course, the larger society that must enter into the analysis. To expand the discussion to the sociology of society as a whole would not be appropriate, and certainly would not be possible within the scope of this chapter. However, there is one feature of modern societies that merits close attention as a basis for better understanding the relationship between production of goods and services and the larger social system. This is the subject of social institutions and their relationships with each other.

In traditional social analysis, the major segments of any society are called its institutions and these are usually designated by characteristic titles like: family institution, governmental or political, religious, production or economic, and educational institutions. The central feature of an institution is that it is a coherent body of functions necessary to the society whose fulfillment is realized in uniform behaviors that are guided by appropriate and institutionally specific values. Institutions also exhibit characteristic structural forms that differ from one institution to another, just as, for example, the kinship system is structurally distinct from business enterprises.

In the analysis of the production institution, as it relates to the full complement of institutions in a modern society, we will find other variables that affect the nature of work and working behaviors. It is to this problem that we must address ourselves.

What impact do the institutions of society have on work? How may institutions serve to encourage or impede changes in the world of work? These are difficult questions to answer, and many of the possible answers are speculative.

Viewed from the perspective of the future, patterns are emerging in developed industrial societies. We will trace these patterns, projecting them beyond the present to capture a glimpse of the interactions among social institutions and work in the world of tomorrow.

FOCAL INSTITUTIONS

Simple societies contain a focal institution, like the family, that dominates the other institutional spheres. The dominance is direct and pervasive. Behavior in the subordinate institutions is significantly derived from position and participation in the focal institution. Work may be performed, for example, only by individuals who occupy designated positions within the familial institution. Who does what work, when, in what manner and amount, cannot be in conflict with the individual's behaviors in his family setting. The political institution may be similarly keyed to the familial institution, with elders and/or males having the right to exercise polity decisions. Such societies are, therefore, able to achieve coherence and unity because behavior in all institutional spheres is congruent with the dominant pattern of behavior associated with the focal institution.

Historians of Western societies have given much attention to identifying the focal institution that has given unity to modern society. Their consensus is that the *production institution* of modern urban-industrial society is focal for all others. This conclusion is impressive for it follows from analyses as disparate as Marxian (emphasizing materialistic conceptions of history) and non-Marxian (emphasizing growth of productive capacity and a market economy).

In industrial societies, even religious institutions are seen as subordinated to the institutions of production. For example, Weber (1930) and Tawney (1926) have shown how religion has evolved its theology so as to be not only supportive of, but even subordinate to the industrial institution. At a more mundane level, social critics have commented on how the family has become subordinate to the demands of work, especially among managers and executives (Whyte, 1956) and how the consumer society, with its particular styles of living, has become a derivative of the manufacture and sale of consumer products (Galbraith, 1958). Moreover, the rather simplistic analyses of the muckrakers and radical critics of American capitalism's great boom periods saw the industrialists greedily assuming social and political power, both in pursuit of their economic goals and as a consequence of achieving them (e.g., Lundberg, 1960).

Recent, more subtle commentary on power elites has also pursued the dominant argument that the center of social power nurtures itself and is sustained by the focal institution of our present society, the production institution, in the form of the "military-industrial complex". Even Keynesian economic arguments (Keynes, 1936), though appearing to suggest the pre-eminence of the governmental institution (with its emphasis on economic development through governmental policies of taxation, public welfare, etc.), are directed toward the more fundamental goal of encouraging and sustaining the production institution. Galbraith (1967) and Boulding (1953), in parallel analyses, have shown how the organizational form of modern urban-industrial society is patterned after the structure of modern industry.

Critics who deny that the production institution is the focal one in urban-industrial society, typically argue that other so-called focal institutions compete for precedence. For example, the whole movement in humanistic psychology, beginning at least with Freud and reaching its climax in the various schools of group dynamics, has attempted to assert that the real focal institution is the company of intimate, face-to-face associates. For a time, the group dynamics movement urged that it, too, was a handmaiden of the production institution by proclaiming the virtues of self-knowledge and interpersonal competence as indispensable to organizational effectiveness and increased productivity (e.g., Argyris, 1957). Lately, however, the emphasis has shifted to a preoccupation with the possibility that intimate group life, as in a commune, is really the focal institution of the society. Creative thought has even been devoted to elaborating and inventing new ways to intensify interpersonal interaction and shared experiencing, through such means as nude encounter groups and sessions with such provocative titles as "Joy, More Joy," "Human Potential," etc. (Howard, 1970; Reich, 1970).

The purpose of this brief and incomplete survey of current analytical schemes for understanding the institutions of society has been to point out the common feature of diverse analytical approaches; they are all anchored in the belief that each society has a focal institution. The focal institution may vary among societies or may change in the history of a given society. At any one time, social unity is dependent upon the integrating consequences of the dominance of a single focal institution.

The focal institution model is an inadequate one. An alternative proposed model has special utility in providing a base for understanding the relations between work and social institutions in the twenty-first century.

MULTI-EQUAL INSTITUTIONS

In seeking answers to the questions concerning the interaction of institutions and work there is an alternative formulation that can be described by the term *multi-equal institutions*. This term emphasizes that there may be several or many institutions having significant impact on behavior that are equally salient for the individual, whether or not these behavioral demands are consistent with each other or made so by the dominance of a focal institution.

A society's major institutions are basically independent of each other and therefore they impinge upon behavior very differently, and in a far more complicated way than has been visualized by advocates of the focal institution concept. Institutions are interacting and essentially *competing* entities. The net effect is to reinforce their mutual isolation—in sharp contrast with the older view that all institutions are dependent upon and subservient to the focal institution. A kind of elegant institutional symbiosis is created, and a modern society becomes institutionally heterogeneous.

There are four characteristics of the institutional structure of a modern urban-industrial society from which may be derived the features of the multi-equal institutional model. These characteristics are: (1) the physical segregation of institutions; (2) the temporal segregation of institutions; (3) the functional segregation of institutions; and (4) the organizational structure of institutional operations. We will examine each of these dimensions in turn.

Physical Segregation

One of the most obvious differences between a primitive society and a modern one is the literal segregation of institutions in space. Evidence abounds of the spatial segregation of institutions from each other. For example, productive activities are separated from family life; in the contemporary world, miles often separate where people live and where they work. But it is equally true that religious functions may be carried on at considerable distance from either productive or familial behaviors. Educational activities have been moved out of the home and are certainly not located, at least during the period of formal education, within the physical boundaries of any other institution. Political action often takes place at centers far removed from the areas affected by the decisions reached. Save for the way in which television has put recreation back into the home setting, a great deal of recreation takes place within its own distinctive physical setting. There are endless examples that make clear the fact that the institutions of a modern, complex society are physically separated and, therefore, segregated from each other.

This sharply contrasts with the image of the primitive tribe carrying out all its institutional activities within a very limited geographic area, and often using the same structures or the same physical locality for a variety of institutional practices. For the participant there was never any sense that physical separation of institutions from each other might suggest their segregation as well.

The citizen of an urban-industrial society needs to move through much space in order to go from one institutional setting to another. The expenditure of effort required could reach such proportions that the individual may choose, given the opportunity, to refuse participation simply because of this fact alone. Thus, one of the consequences for the individual is the fact that the expenditure of energy required literally to move into a new institutional setting may contribute to voluntarism with regard to whether the effort is worthwhile.

Temporal Segregation

The institutions in which modern man participates are also segregated by the time of day, week, or year during which the individual participates in their behaviors. Within the daily cycle, a regular shift of work is followed by a longer period of nonwork during which the individual is more or less free to choose the institution in which he wishes to participate. In the larger weekly cycle, the off-time from work is concentrated in the weekend period. Over the annual cycle, the vacation is a concentrated period of time away from work.

It is characteristic of temporal segregation of institutions that relatively large blocks of time are utilized for participation in any one. There is clearly not a ready movement back and forth among the institutional settings over any short-range time cycle.

The temporal segregation of institutions means that the personnel with whom one interacts in each institutional setting will have relatively little overlap with the personnel of other settings. Thus, one significance of temporal segregation of institutional settings is that interaction takes place with different people as the boundary of an institution is crossed from one into another. This obviously leads to a disjunction among institutions and the assurance that the society as a whole no longer may be characterized as integrated, since participation in its several institutions is distributed among many different individuals.

Furthermore, from the standpoint of individual motivation, the temporal segregation of institutions provides the time frame within which the possibility of deferring gratification may be estimated. For example, vacations and holidays can be anticipated from any moment in time to the time at which they begin. The temporal segregation of institutions provides a very important means for measuring from a given point in time, when the individual will have the opportunity to move into another institutional setting. The deferment of gratification, if it is gratifying to the individual to move from where he is to another institution, can be measured accurately on a time scale.

The relation of time to the deferment of gratification has special meaning not often noted. Usually, it is believed that the deferment of gratification is related to rewards at some real, but indefinitely timed point in the future. However, the rewards of deferred gratifications in moving among institutions can now be calculated precisely as to when they will occur.

The other side of the coin of the rewards produced by the gratifications deferred is the patience that may be inculcated during the deferment period. Thus, if it is clear that family participation, or recreation may be enjoyed at a predictable time in the future, then some of the disadvantageous and unsatisfactory aspects of work may be endured. Consequently the ability of the individual to predict times when movement will occur, from the production institution into others, may make bearable the undesirable features of work itself. Or, even conversely, the deferred gratifications of returning to work after a prolonged absence may have positive consequences for motivation.

Functional Segregation

Functional segregation of institutions simply means that they become increasingly specialized in the performance of narrower and narrower ranges of functions. Productive activities have clearly moved out of the family and home settings, as have education and welfare services. The citizen soldier with his weapon above the fireplace has become the professional or conscript soldier. The family altar in religious services has increasingly been supplanted by the religious edifice and the professional religious ceremony.

Functional specialization has had three consequences for institutions. On the one hand, the greater the degree of functional specialization, the more coherent can be the value system and related behaviors that characterize the institution. Each institution may become an island unto itself, internally consistent with regard to its central values, and reasonably coherent with regard to the behaviors designed to exemplify or achieve these values.

A second consequence of the functional specialization of the institutions is that they become increasingly divergent from each other with regard to values and behaviors. Profit and love may not be reconcilable within a single institution, but separately may be the one goal of the production and the family institutions respectively.

The functional specialization of institutions has also permitted the development of new institutions to serve those functions that are either newly created or separated from institutions that had many functions to perform. Thus, the very specialization of institutions provides the mechanism by which new institutions are born. This is an important source of social change and behavioral innovation. For example, when the welfare and educational functions were taken out of the family institution and each given an institutional identity of its own, the entire social system was restructured through the creation of the two new institutions as well as the modification of one old institution. In a similar way, the welfare capitalism of the 19th and early 20th century in the United States lost much of its relevance when business and industry specialized further on the production of goods and services, and left the institutionalization of welfare activities to collective bargaining or specialized welfare institutions (Commons, 1918).

The effects of institutional functional specialization are to produce a greater coherence in values and behavior over a more limited range of the life-cycle, and with the drawing in of the institutional boundary, to create interstices within which new institutions may develop. Indeed, one of the pervasive evidences of rationality in modern life is the increasing functional specialization of institutions, each with a corresponding purity of values and associated behaviors. The rationality is further exhibited in the relative ease with which it is possible to recognize interstices among institutions and to create new ones to serve emerging functions, or to serve those sloughed off from the specializing institutions.

For the individual, the functional specializations of the institutions in which he participates has two primary consequences. The first is that his whole view of life is neatly compartmentalized into recognizable institutional spheres that have a measurable degree of independence from each other. A man can be a good Christian for one hour on Sunday without feeling any inconsistency between that moment of pious self-image and a rather different world view and pattern of behavior when selling used cars on work days.

The second consequence for the individual increases the level of his autonomy. He is clearly no longer caught up in a dominant institution nor is he required to bring the values of a dominant institution with him into each separate functional institutional setting. To the individual, the world takes on varied sets of values and required behaviors, and with such choices available, the individual achieves his personal independence and behavioral autonomy. Every human act can be justified if it is located in an appropriate institutional setting. The citizen is not puzzled or shocked to find that values of one institution do not carry over into others.

Organizational Structure of Institutions

A very important feature that contributes to institutional segregation is the specialized organizational structure that characterizes some of the most significant institutions. Productive activities are not carried out in general; they are carried out in business organizations. Education is not practiced in the normal daily realm of the society; it is pursued in school organizations. Natural (self-proclaimed) religion is odd; organized religion is characteristic. Battles are fought by organized military units; welfare is distributed by a professional bureaucracy; and scientific research is carried out in highly organized laboratories. The areas of institutional behavior are overlayed with specific organizations that not only fulfill the general institutional functions, but do so through unique organizations. The individual, therefore, engages many times in an area of institutional behavior only provided he becomes a member or a client of an organization.

Organizations not only carry out institutional goals, but have unique organizational characteristics as well. An individual, in order to participate, must meet the organization's special requirements for membership or clienthood. Thus, even within single institutions, behavior is further limited because the individual has to articulate with an organization in order to participate in that particular institution.

Still another feature of the organizational character of institutional behavior is the considerable variability that exists between organizations performing similar institutional functions. A pharmacy and the shopping center drugstore that merchandises drugs as a sideline to its sundries may both perform commercial functions, but certainly do so within quite different value frameworks and require very distinctive personnel to do their respective jobs.

THE CEMENT THAT BINDS

We have emphasized how institutions are isolated from each other. This naturally raises the question of how a society is fused together. The answer to this question lies in a well established distinction utilized by sociologists.

Durkheim (1933), in explaining the basis for social unity, perceived two different bases. First, a broad consensus may exist about the dominant values of a society, and this consensus may provide the weld among all institutions of society. Durkheim called this form of social unity *mechanical* solidarity. He also was well aware, however, of the segregation of institutions from each other, as we have described above. Using a biological analogy, Durkheim saw institutions as organs of the body, society, united through the interdependence of parts to the whole. He called this second form of social unity *organic* solidarity.

Mechanical solidarity, or the consensual basis for social unity, is clearly tied to the focal institutional viewpoint. Values are more readily shared if they are simple and integrated. A focal institution can provide the conditions for achieving consensus over the values of the society, precisely because the values of the focal institution will dominate all other value systems of the society.

How, then, is it possible that social unity can be maintained in a social system characterized by multiequal institutions? Is the interdependence of institutions alone sufficient to bind them together to constitute a social unity? To answer this question, it is necessary to examine two central issues: (1) the meaning of interdependence among functionally specialized institutions; and (2) the grounds for social unity when a high level of functional specialization of institutions has been attained.

Interdependence among functionally specialized institutions is best understood by analogy, once again with biological models. Ecological chains of life specify how food and other resources link to individual biological species, which in turn are interrelated among themselves. Clearly, the resources and species do not operate at a level of consensus about their relations to each other. Nevertheless, the chains of interdependence linking them may be highly complex and when any point in the chain is broken, disaster results.

By analogy, functional specialization and segregation of institutions from each other generate a chain of interdependence so sensitive that any failure of an institution to be effective, or a change in its function, may have consequences upon the other institutions with which it is interrelated. Sociologists have tended to describe these chains of interdependence by calling attention to the "unintended consequences of purposive social action" (Merton, 1949). The unintended consequences are very often located in institutions interdependent with the institution in which the change actually is made. For example, the removal of productive activities from the home as a consequence of significant benefits that resulted from factory production, ultimately led to a middle-class way of life for females that has had measurable consequences in terms of boredom, a sense of purposelessness, and in some cases, deviant individual behavior. A second consequence, at least in the United States, has been the increasing proportion of married women who have become active in the labor force. The movement of the wife and mother into the labor force has, in turn, had unanticipated consequences on the nature of the family life. A third result of this interaction has been the long-time political activity of females seeking equal rights in the labor force as well as in other realms of life. In this highly simplified and obvious illustration, it becomes clear that there may be very pervasive interconnections among institutions so that a change in one often generates one or more responses in the other. The change and response together keep the institutions in balance with each other.

The changes in institutional functions and their unanticipated consequences in other institutions are largely incremental in scope. Fundamental and revolutionary changes are seldom planned, or if planned, seldom produce the anticipated revolutionary consequences. An outstanding example was the introduction of automation into productive institutions. The predicted consequences of automation for family life, leisure, and political behavior have yet to be realized after almost two decades of utilization in industry and commerce (Jaffe and Froomkin, 1968).

We may then think of interdependence among institutions as being characterized at one of two levels. If we view the daily life of the individual, then the interdependence among institutions in which he actively participates is determined by the manner in which he allocates time and energy to its several institutional segments.

On another level, interdependence among institutions is revealed in the ability of a total society to organize the social functions that are necessary for its survival. The institutional structure of a society is fleshed out with sufficient completeness to insure that the essential functions are fulfilled and once fulfilled, that additional desirable functions will also be attended to.

Some degree of consciousness of the interdependence among institutions must be developed at both the individual and societal levels. For the individual, it is necessary that some decisions be made regarding the institutions in which to participate, the order of participation, and the extent of participation. At the societal level, there is similarly some consciousness of what is functionally required by the society to continue its existence. On the societal level, there will also exist conscious allocation of total social resources and citizen time expenditures among the existing institutional spheres. For example, a military draft is clearly a conscious social allocation of citizen time to the military functions.

The individual and collective awareness of institutions may be the foundation for the institution's resistance to change. When an individual participates in an organized institutional setting, or specific social arrangements are made to enact the requirements of an institution, the very acting out of the roles necessitates a behavioral commitment on the part of the individual to the institution. Commitment resulting from participation in an institution ·is strongly maintained (Lewin, 1948). Indeed, the commitment on the part of an individual or society to an existing institution may survive long after the function has been changed or even has disappeared. Within the production institution, there are many relics of earlier institutional practices that are no longer fully functional. For example, in the United States and most of Western Europe, many welfare practices survive in work organizations despite the fact that major welfare functions have been separately institutionalized.

Durkheim's idea of mechanical solidarity in which values are shared across institutions is compatible with the focal institution view of social organization. From the standpoint of the multiequal model of institutions, the unifying bond for a society is the interdependence among institutions. This is Durkheim's idea of organic solidarity. Typically in a modern industrial society, value consensus is achieved rarely, and then usually under conditions of threat to national existence. The daily lives of citizens are lived out among institutions, each with its own differing sets of values. The sense of societal unity is derived largely from the functional coherence and interdependence of its institutions.

It would be beneficial to summarize the discussion up to this point. A contrast has been drawn between a technocratic view of man at work and a view based on humane industrialization. It has been suggested that movement is from the former to the latter in developed economies. However, the rate of change and the specific content of the change is not at all clear. In order better to understand the transformation, a number of images of man have been listed with accompanying questions about how well these images can be realized in the world of work. Finally, some detailed analysis has been presented of the institutional structure of a modern society because it certainly has an impact on the individual citizen.

SOME INTELLECTUAL TRADITIONS IN STUDYING WORK

Before turning to the final section of this chapter in which specific issues relating to work are examined, it would be desirable to examine retrospectively the treatment of some of the analytical problems of the work institution, by different behavioral scientists, engineers, technologists, and creative executives. This review will contain only enough detail to provide a basic knowledge of some of the traditional benchmarks of thought and practice about the world of work since the first Industrial Revolution began.

A classic concern of social analysts has been with the manner in which social status and esteem are determined in a society. The early and persistent conclusion was that social position was largely determined by the work men do. This in turn led to a detailed study of the economic system, with special attention devoted to the productive institution, within which was embedded a large share of all occupations (Smith, 1910; Weber, 1947). Stemming from this broad conclusion have come a host of studies analyzing the status positions of various occupational groups (e.g. Hall, 1969) and the dynamics of the circulation of occupational groups through the status structure (e.g. Weber, 1947). Once the Industrial Revolution was well under way, attention focused particularly on the crucial emergence of the commercial and entrepreneurial middle class (Marx, 1906). Although much of the analysis utilized the term *class* as the referent, it is clear that this term was often a surrogate for occupation. Furthermore, it was recognized relatively early that class labels hardly encompassed the complexity of social distinctions found in emerging industrial societies. Thus, there persisted a line of inquiry regarding occupational structures and their relationship to the distribution of social status in the society (Sorokin, 1927; Dahrendorf, 1959).

There also developed a concern with the impact of occupational position on the behaviors that resulted from the interactions of people who occupy similar and different occupational positions (deMan, 1929). Once the idea of class-grounded social interactions was refined to include interactions among people at different occupational levels, the intellectual roots were established for what later flourished as the study of organizational behavior (Commons, 1918; Warner & Low, 1947). Thus, out of an historical concern with social distinctions in society, there has come a classical stream of intellectual concern with the relations of industry to the class structure of a society.

For a considerable period of time, another tradition of analysis developed which overshadowed the emphasis on the industry-society nexus. This was a kind of pragmatic concern with the compatability between workers and work. Origins of this orientation can be traced to such enlightened industrialists as Robert Owen (Owen, 1830), who early on drew from their practical experience insights about how workers related to their employment (cf. Ure, 1835; Barnard, 1938). The welfare capitalism of late 19th century and early 20th century America was a climactic development of the self-conscious concern with workers in their employment habitat, albeit, this "concern" focused principally on an exploitative goal of getting the most out of workers, without using the real or figurative lash.

Once the pragmatic base was established, it was an easy step to visualize man-work relationships as essentially man-machine relationships. When it became clear that technology had emerged as a dominant feature of industry, problems arose concerning the human animal as a worker and how he could best be related to the machine. This problem was, of course, further compounded with the development of American industrialization. The primary labor supply in America consisted of newly arrived immigrants, largely agrarian in origin, who brought their bodies and willing motivations, and little else, to the factory door (Handlin, 1952).

It is no accident that a Taylor emerged as the spokesman for and ultimately became the "Godfather" of what has come to be called the machine theory of organization (Taylor, 1911). Taylor found it easy to depersonalize the immigrant worker, with whom he could not even communicate in a shared lan-

guage, and to view him largely as a physiological machine. Taylor and his many successors among industrial engineers, motion-and-time study specialists and human-factor psychologists, made a basic assumption that the goal of fitting man to machine was to use optimally only the physiological characteristics of man. On these assumptions, machine design was to be refined until the limits of physiological performance of "operatives" were reached. Men were to be trained to work at physiological capacity by utilizing the "best" or most appropriate physical motions for the machine, and not the man (Gilbreth, 1912).

At a somewhat more subtle level, man was utilized for his ability to perceive and feed back instructions to the machine, or industrial process, as part of a feedback loop controlling the equipment. The act of sensing an ongoing process, the programming of the operator to know the alternative signals (which resulted from his training and experience on the job) to feed back, and the actual feedback of the corrective signals were the characteristically unique features of the human contribution to the industrial process. These three features have, of course, been incorporated in computer controlled technology, so that even these unique contributions of man to the industrial process have now been supplanted.

Thus the analysts move from a purely physiological view to a physiological-plus-mental view of man's contribution to the industrial process. New issues arose as to what the analyst must now consider to be the analytical problems of the man-machine relationship.

New analytical problems appeared when attention was focused on the psychological well-being of man the worker. This focus resulted in what came to be known as the human relations movement, which was supplanted, or at least supplemented, by what is now called the human potential movement. Both of these social movements were concerned with answering the question: "What are the psychological parameters that need to be satisfied in the work situation, and how can they best be satisfied by the redesign of work itself?"

It will be recalled that the human relations movement got its principal start as a result of the classic Western Electric studies which produced the nondirective interview schemes designed to let the worker blow off steam to rid himself of the psychological frustrations of his work (Roethlisberger and Dickson, 1939). The characteristic concern of this study was to adapt man to his work environment by building into that environment a therapeutic device.

At a more advanced stage of development, the analysts began to ask: "Are there things that can be done about the way work is organized, the way people are supervised, and the content of work itself that will reduce the level of frustration, anger, and alienation so that the therapeutic accompaniments of work will become less necessary?" At this advanced level of analysis, a number of new ideas developed that basically evolved from an attempt to describe the features of work and the design that would make a difference in the human response to these features. Thus, by examining some of the extreme forms of industrialization, it was concluded, for example, that the highly segmented and repetitive performance of small tasks, as on the classical assembly lines, was really antithetical to human needs and expectations. The result was that new ideas about job enrichment and job enlargement were developed with the ultimate goal being discovery of the degrees of freedom in the design of the industrial process that would permit individuals to perform related tasks that gave a sense of wholeness and meaning to their work. Much of this theory emerged from the minds of industrial psychologists and industrial social psychologists (e.g., Herzberg, 1966).

Another general development that directly influenced the redesign of work itself focused on the authority and power relations within the work organizations. The issue in this case was posed as one involving close versus general supervision, or alternately as involving strict compliance to orders versus autonomy and its presumed concomitant of initiative. Insofar as there were practical outcomes of this line of inquiry, they resulted in notions about the advantages of true delegation of functions, the development of "flat" versus "tall" organizations, management by objectives, and the belief that there were certain optimal ways in which managers could organize their exercise of power and authority (cf. Argyris, 1964; McGregor, 1960; Katz and Kahn, 1966). Significant efforts were made in experiments carried out in England in the so-called Glacier studies. Demonstrations were conducted, as well, in a number of American corporations, using a wide range of techniques: from sensitivity training to the employment of the managerial grid (as means for retraining the executives and managers to adopt a looser style in the exercise of their authority and power). At a later stage in this very same development, subordinates were subjected to similar kinds of techniques in order to retrain them to accept a delegation of authority and power and presumably to use these delegations constructively.

Still another major development in the redesign of the work situation moved in the direction of substituting group decisions and group process for individual responsibility and individual behavior. Attempts were made, following the work of Lewin (1948), to use the tyranny of the group as a way of insuring that once a group decision had been made, all group members would be coerced into following it and contributing to its successful accomplishment.

All these efforts at the application of new discoveries in social psychology, psychiatry and psychology to the work environment were pursued by applied scientists in these fields with a double-edged claim: (1) that the modifications of interpersonal reactions and/or structural relations would produce desirable outcomes from the standpoint of the individual's adjustment to the work situation; and (2) that the almost inevitable outcome would be a higher level of productivity, which obviously benefits the work organization that adopts such procedures. It is highly questionable whether either of these goals have been attained, which may simply represent the fact that the proponents of the psychological adaptation to the work environment claimed the wrong outcomes for their procedures.

Working at a very different level from the industrial psychologists and psychiatrists, sociologists became concerned with the socialization of individuals to their working environments. Most of the sociological studies focused on the development of an occupational outlook on the part of those in training for technical occupations or professions (e.g., Vollmer & Mills, 1966; Etzioni, 1969). The focus of the analytical attack on the man-work relationship was to determine how a malleable human being evaluates a well prescribed environment, and through socialization to the environment, adapts to it. While the sociological analysis pushed to a high level of sophistication, it was far outstripped by the people who actually applied the concepts: coming largely out of business school orientations, they developed actual programs for training and orientation of workers to their work environment.

The level of the individual in the industrial organization made a considerable amount of difference as to the kind of study carried out. At the workers' level, the main issue centered around psychological adjustment and the corresponding motivation to work effectively. At the managerial level, however, the issues were changed, often not very subtly, to focus on the ability of the manager/executive to remain flexible in his outlook so that he could continue to be innovative in guiding the enterprise or his department. Thus, the research implicitly recognized that there were functional differences between workers and managers, and that at these differing levels of occupations, the relation between man and job were very different indeed.

Another popular direction in which research on work has gone has been the measurement of what has come to be labelled the *alienation* of industrial workers (cf. Marcson, 1970). The general theme here is that the regime of industrial work becomes so onerous that those engaged in it are alienated from the work itself and eventually become alienated from the larger society within which the work is embedded. The alienation theme is more widely believed than it is demonstrated with most researchers equating "dissatisfaction" with "alienation." More recent evidence seems to make it reasonably clear that dissatisfaction and alienation are clearly not the same phenomenon.

In a very different direction is to be found the research dealing with the bases upon which occupational choices are made. Insofar as such choices are usually made at some significant point in time prior to the actual work experience, there is a traceable process, at least in American society, that delineates the sources of influences bearing upon such decisions, and the consequences of that decision, for such subsequent steps toward employment as further education (Crites, 1969; Ginzberg, 1958). For the bulk of the population, however, the decision about the choice of work is clearly made at the time the choice becomes necessary, namely, when the labor market is initially entered. At this point in the beginning of a career, or even in midcourse when jobs are changed, the randomness of actual employment or employment shifts makes it difficult to trace out any patterns of rational choice that may be involved in long-time perspectives on occupational choice (Palmer, 1954).

In another genre entirely, and in renewing the interest in the analysis of occupation and social position, there was a brief vogue in considering the social origins of various classes of participants in the world of work, but especially the social origins of those who made it into or up the ranks of management. These studies showed clearly that the American system was approaching the European system, in that there was an increasing amount of occupational succession within the same social class, particularly in succession to managerial and executive positions (Newcomer, 1955; Warner and Abegglen, 1955). Thus, insofar as social status was related to occupation, it became clearer from the study of the social origins of executives and managers that the social system was selective in providing opportunities for the children of executives and managers to succeed the parental generation. In the western countries of Europe, this was already a very marked development and it now appears that the same phenomenon is to be found in the socialist countries.

Still another line of development, again not particularly pushed by sociologists, but clearly developed by institutional economists and students of business organizations, was the comparative analysis of work organizations (e.g., Harbison and Myers, 1959). This literature produces the general conclusion that culture does indeed affect the nature of work itself and the organizational structure of enterprises within which work is carried out.

Paralleling the comparative analysis of cultural variations in work was the more intensive concern with the impact of industrialization on developing economies, especially as it involved the changing nature of work and the consequences of this for the work force. A principal conclusion that was reached here was that the transition from a peasant to an industrial economy could be made very rapidly in the factory simply by adequate training of agrarian-reared workers in industrial pursuits and in the disciplines required to hold factory jobs. The far more difficult adjustment was the generalized adjustment of the agrarian migrant to the total complex of urban and industrial living outside the factory rather than in it (e.g., Nash, 1958). The concerns here were generated largely by economists interested in the rate of growth of developing economies and the processes by which they move from very low levels to reasonably high levels of industrialism.

In a very different direction, and generated largely out of socialist economies, came the general notion of self-management. The Yugoslav experiments probably were leaders in this regard, although as early as the beginning of the nineteenth century, utopian communities in the United States and their survivors into the twentieth century were precursors of self-management enterprises. The kibbutz of Israel was initiated as an agrarian self-management enterprise and has since developed industrial enterprises that are part and parcel of the kibbutz. The egalitarian philosophy that underlies the notion of self-management has relatively little compatibility with the intricate division of labor required in even reasonably complex enterprises. Most self-management schemes on analysis turned out to be forms of representative democracy, with technical and functional specializations represented in the decision-making body. The American attempts to graft a kind of self-management system onto a highly bureaucratized enterprise form have almost uniformly been failures.

Out of very modest beginnings in the study of coal mining and the organization of a cotton mill in India, several key researchers at the Tavistock Institute (England) began to develop a different view of the man-machine-society relationship. Their point of view came ultimately to be labelled the "socio-technical systems approach" (e.g., Emery and Trist, 1960; 1969). The basic ideas of this approach are quite simple. It assumes that man not only lives in the technical-social world of the factory, but also in the social world outside the factory, and that there must be an appropriate balance between these environments for the individual to be reasonably satisfied and adjusted. This approach further states that within the factory, the design of the technical systems or the technology of work has reached such a level of sophistication that many of the former constraints of a mechanized technology are replaced by the far greater flexibility of an electronic, computer-assisted technology. According to this approach, man can now be taken into account as a partner in production, utilizing the full range of his capabilities, including his social needs. From this standpoint it is concluded that the industrial process can be redesigned, given its many greater degrees of freedom than had formerly existed, so that a beginning might be made to optimize the social dimension of man the worker.

The sociotechnical systems approach places emphasis on the adaptation of work and social environments to man's needs. This contrasts sharply with the earlier views that adapt man to work environments or with the belief that minor tinkering with work environments might do the trick.

There is, of course, basic to the sociotechnical systems notion, the idea that it is possible to lay out parameters of man's social needs so that it might be determined how and when they are satisfied. Beyond this adaptation of environment to human needs is an even larger environmental adaptation problem that lies outside the factory and includes all the rest of the waking hours of man away from work. This nonwork environment is also viewed as far more adaptive now than it ever was, and the sociotechnical systems thinkers perceive the possibility that this environment can also be engineered to maximize the social potentials of men. Thus, the sociotechnical systems analysts view themselves essentially as revolutionaries in the constructive sense; if their prescriptions for the postindustrial world (a term that is a favorite in their lexicon) are followed, then man may be saved from an unknown but clearly unworthy fate.

At the social system level, while assuming a different view of sociotechnical systems, there is a growing concern with the social functions of work and the work institution. For example, in socialist economies and in some capitalist economies (especially Japan and Italy), the work organization becomes the social unit around which housing, recreation, medical services, and education are focused. Thus, the Japanese practice of lifetime employment is accompanied by living quarters, retirement benefits, medical services, and recreational activities, all centered on the work organization and provided through it. In much the same way, in socialist economies, the housing of workers is directly tied to their employment as are their recreational activities, and so forth. In the American experience the rapid expansion of so-called fringe benefits and welfare provisions of collective bargaining agreements have provided private sector supplementation to the Federal Social Security Program. It is estimated, for example, that approximately 30 percent of the total money outlay to employ people is devoted to health and welfare and fringe benefits. These examples highlight the need for more detailed attention than has hitherto been devoted to an analysis of the functions of work institutions as contributing to welfare, education, recreation, and environmental quality.

Viewing the institutional analysis of work from a somewhat different angle and focusing directly on the individual life-cycle, increasing questions are being raised about the location of work in the life-history of the individual. The "normal" procedure now is to complete one's education, enter the labor market, remain in the labor force for about forty-five years, and then retire until death. There is no particular reason why the work might not begin earlier; to be followed by a break after a period of years to return to education; followed by sabbatical leaves from work and so on. A very modest beginning has been made in the direction of variability in the way in which work fits into the individual life-cycle by the so-called "sliding" work day now being employed in Europe. This provides the individual with the opportunity to choose the particular hours of the day when he will work, providing he puts in a minimum number of hours in a week's period. The four day work week as adopted in the United States is a comparable experiment in changing the work-nonwork cycle in the life-history of the individual. But these experiments are only a beginning; a great deal more needs to be done in the analysis of the cycling of work in the life-history of an individual.

The general term "the quality of working life" has come to represent a generalized concern about the worker as a citizen. There are analysts who are beginning to think about the possible impact of work regimes on the total behavior of the worker as a citizen. Following a "spillover" model, several analysts have concluded that if work is dull and demeaning and unstimulating, the worker behaves in a dull and unstimulated way when he leaves work (Meissner, 1971). There is an alternate model, the "compensatory" model, that suggests the undesirable work environment may be more than compensated for by the individual's investment in his nonwork areas of life (Dubin, 1956). A great deal of further research needs to be carried out along these lines to discover whether or not the improvement of the quality of working life will improve the quality of the workers' total life, or whether these two areas of life are relatively independent and unaffected by each other. Part of the work and nonwork problem also becomes involved with the analysis of multiple roles within a complex society. Questions can be raised with respect to the role-congruence among the many roles that the worker plays as citizen.

PLANNING THE INDUSTRIAL FUTURE

If this review of general trends in the thought and research about the man-work relationship is reasonably accurate history, then it would seem clear that the future of the industrial world will not be designed by simply fine tuning the organizations of the past. A major overhaul is required. Indeed, perhaps more changes need to be made than is readily admitted by those who know most about the nature of the industrial institution. This chapter concludes with a statement of problems that must be encountered when planning the future of industrialism. These problems flow from the preceding analysis. They are stated as a challenge more than a prediction, but a challenge that might prove constructive if accepted by those concerned with the industrial institution, as one guide to the planning of the future of the institution.

Meaning of Work

As long as the productive institution was a dominant force in advancing industrial societies, a citizen was defined either as acceptable or unacceptable according to the work, or occupation, of the individual. Social standing was accorded differentially to occupations and professions. Financial rewards for different occupations and types of work also varied and those without paying jobs—the unemployed, the unemployable, children, many women, the elderly, and the infirm—were accorded relatively low social esteem.

The Future Work, Status and Consumerism

The affluent society has introduced a new dimension for evaluating a citizen. A good citizen has come to be identified with being a healthy, active individual who is capable of consuming a wide variety of goods and services (Jones, 1965). The central idea underlying a new definition of the meaning of good citizenship is that of the individual as consumer. The appropriate and significant consumption of goods and services becomes the definition of the good citizen. The idea of a right to consume underlies all demands for societal support of good housing, good health, and good environment. Accordingly, the affluent society, which can also *afford* to be the welfare society, has as important social policy, the provision of goods and services in a manner to insure that the economically disadvantaged may consume at a level satisfactory to accepted notions of equity. In the United States, the growth of welfare activities has also been accompanied by the more recent acceptance of the idea of a guaranteed annual income, the amount and right to which is unrelated to productive work.

If citizenship in the future increasingly comes to be defined in varying degrees of consumerism, then the relationship of the citizen to productive work becomes complicated. It should be recalled that all utopias foresee the possibility that man can be relieved, through a major portion of his lifetime, of the need to engage in productive labor (cf. Bellamy, 1898; Huizinga, 1955). The distinguishing feature among utopian dreams was the manner in which each utopia invented ways to use the waking hours of men no longer required in productive labor. In the more traditional utopian pictures, men were free to engage in the leisure pursuits of the rich (art and literature and music and the other "cultural" activities that improve man's mind and realize his capabilities) since that was the only existing example of nonwork activities. What the traditional utopians did not foresee among the alternatives to working behavior was the possibility that an affluent society, which produces an abundance of goods and services, requires a market constantly capable of consuming these goods and services.

The emerging social system is much more realistically oriented to the consumer problem. We already see that the consumer is becoming the highly esteemed citizen. Indeed, even what Veblen called "conspicuous consumption," (which he viewed as a form of social status one-upmanship) now gets converted into social approval because it moves the goods from the market and keeps the economy going (Veblen, 1918). In addition to being an indicator of acceptable citizenship, the ability to consume and the willingness to do so has also become one of the precious indicators of the state of the American economy, regularly measured by the University of Michigan Survey Research Center in its quarterly survey of consumer buying intentions. The development of a consumer orientation is not limited to capitalist societies, but is also characteristic of socialist societies.

Work and Education

A revision in the meaning of work could have a profound impact upon the educational institution. The present assumption sustaining the educational institution is that during the period when the child is most pliable, and extending through early adulthood for those capable of learning high-level skills, society should devote considerable resources to the socialization of its young citizens for a lifetime of productive work. In all societies, capitalist and socialist, formal education is tied directly to the preparation of the youngster for a productive role in the society. At the most basic level of education, desirable behavior for a worker is reinforced: discipline, regular attendance, obedience to authority, responsiveness to a defined role in relation to rules, and the valuing of self in terms of what is accomplished or produced. Beyond learning the necessary disciplines that make effective transitions into productive work, the students may also learn technical skills requisite to working. These include literacy, the ability to do some arithmetic or mathematics, and low or high levels of technical knowledge ranging from typing to nuclear physics.

The future of work may well revolutionize the educational institution. It is conceivable, for example, that training for a technical skill may be transferred to the work institution itself, where it can be made very specific and pertinent to an industry or occupation and probably can be done more effectively and efficiently than in the educational organization. If the educational institution is to remain in existence, there could follow from this shift in educational content a concern with substituting a new curriculum. Thus, instructing the individual about all the facets of consumerism may well become the central function of the educational institution. This instruction obviously would involve far more than the consumption of physical goods and services, although it has yet to be determined what else this new curriculum would be concerned with.

The daily relationship of children to school could also be radically changed should "how to live" rather than occupation competency be the primary socialization goal of the school institution. This goal may be more effectively achieved if there is a significant period of in-residence instruction as opposed to having the pupil commute every day from home to school and back again. The English middle-class male has been effectively socialized to his role by attendance at boarding "public" schools; the youth in Israeli kibbutzim live a common life with peers in separate quarters during schooling as an important feature of socialization to the collective life of the settlements; and the boarding schools of socialist societies serve similar functions, again providing effective socialization for their participants.

Work and Life-Cycle

Another area in which the shift in meaning of work may have an impact is on the ideas about work-cycles in the life-history of the individual. In the modern industrial world a citizen can typically expect to work approximately 45–48 years, beginning, possibly in late adolescence and extending to the sixth decade of his or her life. The most vigorous periods of the life-cycle have been dominated by the need to work for a living. It would be perfectly conceivable that if citizenship were redefined to include consumerism at its core, work activity will be required to be shifted away from the vigorous period of life. This could be done in large blocks of time. For example, the individual might enjoy the ages 20 to 30 by developing himself as a consumer of nonworking time and then turn attention to making a later productive contribution to the society. Another example might be that the work-nonwork cycle may be based on successive intervals of productive work and freedom from work so that every other year might become the off-time from work. Or, the individual may be given advance opportunities to determine how he proposes to spend his own lifetime by choosing his own schedule of work and nonwork periods. Indeed, the extension of individual liberty may be developed in affording the individual the opportunity to make a personal choice of when he will fit productive labor into his own life-cycle. The "counter culture" of the late sixties and early seventies exemplified personal choice in regards to work and nonwork time within the early adult period.

We may then summarize the impact of the changing meaning of work as possibly resulting in: (a) a shift in the definition of good citizenship from that of being a productive individual to that of being a socially relevant consumer; (b) a significant modification in the function of the educational institution, moving it from a vocational preparation function to the function of socializing for the new society; and (c) a redefinition of work in the life-cycle of the individual.

Organization of Work and Technology

The most obvious characterization of modern industrial and commercial work is that it is based on technology which is rapidly changing. A number of organizational problems stem from this fact. These problems require for their solution distinguishing between types of technological systems, on the one hand, and distinctive forms of division of labor, on the other. There are also issues relating to the linkage with the school institution and concerning the spatial mobility of work organizations that constitute organizational problems. These problems and issues will be discussed in order by illustrating the principle that organizational adaptation as a prominent feature of an evolving humane industrialism.

All technological systems are not the same. We can follow the lead, for example, of Woodward, who distinguished three major types of technological systems labelled respectively, a *batch* production system, a *line* production system, and a *continuous* production system (Woodward, 1965). Each of these systems has very different technological features and associated human systems necessary to make the technological features effective. One of the central design considerations in the new industrialism is to determine whether there is any technological imperative forcing one-way and irreversible development from batch to line to continuous systems. There seems to be an implicit technocratic assumption that such an imperative exists.

This problem can be best illustrated in automobile production. The whole technological design issue has been centered upon turning automobile production into a line production system and moving, in some segments at least, toward continuous production. This has reached the point where not only is the completed automobile the final product of the assembly line, but subassemblies and parts are also produced in the same technological system. This is presumed to be a more efficient way to produce automobiles than the batch system of production, in which recognizable units are produced at a single work station by a group of workers who perform many operations and need and use a variety of task skills to turn out the finished product. When we reexamine the human problems incurred in the production of automobiles, we may now consider a return to the batch system of production: in the Volvo and Saab plants in Sweden, former line production systems for manufacturing automobile engines have been converted to batch production systems in which a group of workers assemble individual engines from start to finish. This redesign of the technology clearly establishes the precedent that it is possible to go from a line to a batch system, and that there is no technological imperative that forecloses such reversibility.

Organizational forms have been invented that are really centered on satisfying the needs of a batch production technology where the final product may be an exceedingly complicated one. What is called "project organization" or "matrix organization" is an organizational structure in which a group of individuals already in the organization are put together in a temporary work system to initiate and carry out a project. Upon completion of the project, individuals return to their permanent positions in the organization. We can think of the project as representing a single product or a single species of product; the project team assembled to initiate and carry out the required output is essentially engaged in batch production.

Thus, there is a genuine possibility of moving back and forth between batch and line production systems, and enough is known about social organization to perceive the differences between these two technological systems with respect to the way in which human beings are organized in relation to them. On the other hand, continuous production systems, like that of oil refining or the operation of a blast furnace, afford little likelihood that they will be modified into a line production system or a batch production system. A continuous production technology may be a very distinctive form of production system, which, when once established, provides fewer opportunities for modification to adapt to human dimensions and human needs than is true of batch or line systems.

The other generalized feature of technological systems is that they produce two basic forms of division of labor. One of these general forms is labelled *specialization* of labor (Dubin, 1958). In specialization of labor, a large number of separate tasks may be performed by the same individual basing his skills in their performance on a substantial body of knowledge learned in schooling or through experience. There is usually a recognizable product that flows from the work of a specialist and a reasonably clear-cut boundary that separates his work from that of surrounding and interrelated specialists. The incumbent of a specialist position as well as those around him know where his work begins and where it ends. It turns out that the vast majority of specialists in modern work organizations are to be found in the ranks of supervisors, managers, and staff people. It is most characteristic that at these levels of an organization, the work is more likely to be specialized on some rational, functional grounds. Accountants perform different tasks from salesmen, and by their functional performance both can be distinguished from production managers, purchasing agents, engineers, and foremen. Specialized positions usually have considerable responsibility attached; a variety in the succession of tasks performed and the time periods over which they are performed; the challenge of meeting unexpected problems and solving them; and the probability that there will be significant change in either single tasks that compose the specialization, or the relations among tasks over the working lifetime of the specialist.

By way of contrast, there is another way to organize the division of labor in a complex operation. In this approach, work is *subdivided* so that a collection of tasks is parcelled out among a number of task performers, each of whom does only a few related tasks as part of the total division of labor. Those occupying subdivided jobs work on relatively short performance cycles, which require only a short learning period and rather simple skills and judgmental inputs. Subdivision of work as the appropriate approach to the division of labor primarily characterizes the worker level of industrial and commercial organizations. When modern industrial work is characterized as "alienating," the referent is almost invariably the industrial worker engaged in subdivided work. It is concluded that this is repetitive and boring work without much challenge and without growth potential or interest that invites commitment to it.

One of the great challenges that faces a production system, depending upon subdivision of work as the basis for its division of labor, is to determine whether subdivided work positions can be converted to specialized work positions. The modern literature that goes under the heading of "job enlargement" or "job enrichment" is precisely directed at this issue (e.g., Herzberg, 1966). However, it is not recognized that a fundamental transformation has to be made in the production system if job enrichment and job enlargement are indeed to be successful. To take finely subdivided tasks and make them coarsely subdivided tasks by putting more work tasks into each position does not transform a technological system of subdivision into anything more than another technological system of subdivision. There is a difference of kind between a specialized system of division of labor and a subdivided one. The real challenge to those who pursue the ideas of job enrichment and job enlargement is to demonstrate when the boundary is crossed between subdivision of work and specialization of work.

WORK ORGANIZATIONS AND JOB TRAINING

With the modern technological equipment found in the plant and office and not in the school classroom, it becomes increasingly difficult to depend on the schools at all levels to produce technically sophisticated workers. The equipment on which to learn is simply not available in the classroom. This is especially true at the common school level of "voc. ed." It is also encountered in highly technical fields, like accounting and engineering, where a newly hired person has to undergo intensive training in the particular operations of his employer, which may differ significantly from what was learned in school.

School skill training changes much less rapidly than does technology in the real world. Work organizations cannot expect, much less demand, that the skill training of their labor forces be done in the educational institution. Indeed, when labor market conditions require the employment of adults who are in the ranks of the "disadvantaged," the irrelevancy of the school institution to the work institution becomes even more marked since higher-level schools have limited age ranges and competence levels for admission.

The simple fact of the matter is that concepts of efficiency and benefits achieved in relation to costs have forced industrial and commercial organizations to provide their workers with technical training as the technology is modified in their own organizations. As technology continues to change and the pace of change has impact over a broader range of industries, the isolation of work organizations from the educational institution may become even greater. Furthermore, there could continue to be significant transfer of technical training to the work organization.

Organizational Mobility

One of the consequences of growing segregation of the production institution is that increased geographic mobility may be possible for work organizations. Improvements in transportation technology have now removed significant limitations on where productive activities may be located. Furthermore, the economics of capital investment in plant and equipment, including tax treatment, has made the requirement of continued utilization of obsolete facilities a less pressing concern in corporate decision-making. Even the invention of lease-back arrangements for physical facilities has given to the corporation a new mobility it never had before in terms of locating its operations geographically.

It is also clear that the vastly increased mobility of the American labor force, and characteristically also of the European labor force, has meant that labor supply is a considerably less limiting factor in plant location than it may have been previously. This, of course, means that the family institution and the production institution are no longer so intertwined that the former acts as a brake on development of the latter. The ties of family will not keep employees from moving to new work locations. By the same token, the movement of an industry to a new location may be accompanied by much greater movement of its employees to retain their employment.

Thus, mobility of industry and commerce with respect to location is enhanced by the isolation and segregation of the production institution. We are not, of course, suggesting that the segregation of the production institution would, by itself, increase mobility with regard to industrial location. However, given the economic and technological considerations that would encourage locational shifts, the segregation of the production institution facilitates that possibility.

Adaptive Responses of Work Organizations

What are some of the adaptive options available to work organizations? First, it is clear that segregation of the production institution provides greater freedom for designing both work and work organizations, which in the future will have greater variability in shape, structure, and function than ever before.

One of the more obvious adaptive responses will see sharp changes in organizational boundaries from their present, rather fixed, positions. A strong trend already is apparent in the increasing use of outside specialists, technologists, and services for carrying out functions that are entirely internal to various work organizations. This is usually done by subcontracting for the services to specialized organizations providing temporary manpower. In addition, of course, many productive organizations also subcontract the manufacture of parts and of assemblies for the products manufactured under their own labels. Very lively and extensive commerce exists across the boundaries of organizations in the purchase of services and goods that are utilized at least initially within the organization. Indeed, this practice has now reached the point where even the facilities, the plants, the equipment, the motor vehicles, and much more may be utilized on a lease-back arrangement rather than owned outright. All such arrangements of subcontracting and lease-back have very good fiscal justification. They also have as one of their functional consequences the explosive expansion of the organizational boundaries so that it becomes increasingly unclear where the responsibilities of any given "organization" may begin or where it ends. The mixture between inside and outside activities may become more and more responsive to changes as the fiscal picture necessitates.

The permeable and open boundary characterizing modern work organizations has profound meaning for the employment relationship. The most obvious implication is that the organization paying the wage and salary bill may not, in fact, be the organization where productive work is actually done. If the payoff for work is the cement that binds an individual to any work organization, then the loyalty of the worker may be to the organization paying wages, and not necessarily to the organization where he or she actually works. These trends may inevitably lead to competing organizational demands for loyalty, commitment, and attachment; and, if so, they also will clearly add to the burdens of supervision and may even require inventing completely new styles of supervision.

A second consequence for the work environment, stemming from the blurring of organizational boundaries, is that variety in a job might be provided merely by moving successively among work organizations. The typist for hire through an organization providing temporary help may, simply by changing offices regularly, have significant variety introduced into his or her work, although technically the actual job operations may remain unchanged. Similarly, the aeronautical engineer who works on a contract basis through an engineering subcontractor may move throughout the industry from company to company adding variety to his or her job, even though specific engineering contributions may be highly standardized. The in-again, out-again character of work performance no doubt enhances the sense of individual autonomy as well as improves the sense of variety in the work performed.

One obvious advantage of open boundaries in work organizations is the ability to determine when to turn over their labor force according to fiscal need without incurring seniority rights and myriad other impediments to manpower flexibility. This, in turn, undoubtedly may generate collective bargaining and social welfare demands for the vesting of retirement and health and welfare benefits in the individual so that no loss of benefits is incurred by moving among organizations.

From the standpoint of the labor market and the availability of labor, the loss of permanent individual attachments as "company people" may generate an even greater emphasis on technical competence and skills as the prime standard for determining who will be employed at any given time, either directly or through a subcontractor. Organizations could become less concerned about whether the young man hired directly from college is the future president of the company, or whether the employee with twenty years of service should be retained as a mark of company loyalty to the employee for his long period of service, even though his skills may no longer be required. The English have used the phrase "meritocracy" to describe the general phenomenon of making paramount the technical performance when judging the competence of employees (Young, 1958). The labor market could well make the merit criterion the standard for hiring and retaining employees.

Another development having relevance for the opening of organizational boundaries is the growing importance of the new corporate form called conglomerates. A conglomerate specifically spreads across a number of different industries and primarily maintains a financial linkage among its respective units. It is not only possible but often probable that managerial and executive personnel will be moved about and among the many separate units comprising a conglomerate. Criteria of skill, ability, and past performance are more likely to determine patterns of executive and managerial mobility than such factors as long service or dedicated devotion to a particular organization.

If the employment contract covers only a narrow portion of the total individual (his technical work performance) it is certain that there will be less room in his life for ideas like loyalty and devotion to company ideals, there is a likelihood that the image of "the organization man" will simply disappear into limbo (Whyte, 1956). Central to the organization man image was the belief that everything in his behavior and personality was bent to fit the organization's demands and needs. This may no longer be necessary and certainly no longer possible with a continuing segregation of the work institutions from other institutions.

It appears likely that considerable revisions will have to be made in the contemporary views with regard to turnover and seniority. Generally, turnover is viewed as a costly process, other than in seasonal industries. Turnover may ultimately come to be valued because it permits a much more rapid reconstitution of a given work organization as the technology, products, and markets of that organization change.

One of the interesting problems in the humane industrialism will be the design of systems with built-in incentives for work. Industry and commerce will certainly require rapid changes in the technological competence in the labor force. Incentives will need to be designed either to recruit those already possessing necessary skills or to "motivate" present employees to develop such skills. It is likely that emphasis will be placed upon awareness on the part of the individual to a constant re-education throughout a good portion of his lifetime. Thus, an organization that guarantees that none of its semiskilled and skilled employees will be doing the same thing five years from now will be able to offer a significant opportunity to those who respond to an incentive of work variety.

In general, it is probable that the new incentives to be developed for work organizations will have a much shorter time perspective than has been characteristic of the past. Some welfare functions now attached to the work organization may become specialized as a welfare institution and separated from the productive organization. Retirement, if it is vested in the individual, may no longer be specified by the organization and the offer of a substantial retirement program will not be a concrete inducement for work. On the other hand, the opportunity to vary the starting time or length of a given work day, or to vary the days of the week in which work is performed could very well turn out to be the sources of considerable incentive value for working.

The final conclusion with regard to the adaptation of the organization to the new condition of work is that far greater imagination will need to be employed in the future than was required in the past to provide incentives for work, the organizational forms, and work and environmental conditions that will continue to make productive work acceptable in the society. The opportunity to use slave labor, as in classical cultures and totalitarian states, or the imperative to work issued by a dominant, central work institution will no longer be a sound basis for insuring an adequate labor supply. The productive institution will remain a coordinate one with other institutions but from within, it will have to develop new ways of organizing work to make work more palatable and sometimes even attractive.

REFERENCES

Argyris, C.
1964   Integrating the Individual and the Organization. New York: John Wiley and Sons.
1957   Personality and Organization. New York: Harper & Bros.

Barnard, C.I.
  1938 The Functions of the Executive. Cambridge, Mass.: Harvard University
         Press.
Bellamy, E.
  1898 Looking Backward. Boston: Houghton Mifflin.
Boulding, K.
  1953 The Organizational Revolution. New York: Harper & Bros.
Commons, J.R., et al.
  1918 History of Labor in the United States. 2 Vols. New York: Macmillan.
Crites, J.O.
  1969 Vocational Psychology. New York: McGraw-Hill.
Dahrendorf, R.
  1959 Class and Class Conflict in Industrial Society. Stanford: Stanford Uni-
         versity Press.
de Man, H.
  1929 Joy in Work. London: Allen & Unwin.
Dubin, R.
  1956 "Industrial workers' worlds: a study of the 'central life interests' of
         industrial workers." Social Problems 3(January):131–142.
  1958 The World of Work: Industrial Society and Human Relations. Engle-
         wood Cliffs, New Jersey: Prentice-Hall.
Emery, F.R. and E.L. Trist
  1969 "The causal context of organizational environments," in F.E. Emery
         (ed.), Systems Thinking. London: Penguin.
  1960 "Socio-technical systems," in C. Churchman and M. Verhulst (eds.),
         Management Sciences Models and Techniques. Vol. 2. London: Per-
         gamon.
Etzioni, A. (ed.)
  1969 The Semi-Professions and Their Organization. New York: The Free
         Press.
Galbraith, J.K.
  1958 The Affluent Society. Boston: Houghton Mifflin.
Gilbreth, F.B.
  1912 Primer of Scientific Management. New York: Van Nostrand.
Ginzberg, E.
  1958 Human Resources: The Wealth of a Nation. New York: Simon &
         Schuster.
Hall, R.H.
  1969 Occupations and the Social Structure. Englewood Cliffs, New Jersey:
         Prentice-Hall.
Handlin, O.
  1952 The Uprooted: The Epic Story of the Great Migrations That Made the
         American People. Boston: Little, Brown & Co.
Harbison, F. and C.A. Meyers
  1959 Management in the Industrial World. New York: McGraw-Hill.
Herzberg, F.
  1966 Work and the Nature of Man. Cleveland: World.
Howard, J.
  1970 Please Touch: A Guided Tour of the Human Potential Movement. New
         York: McGraw-Hill.

Huizinga, J.
　1955　Homo Ludens: A Study of the Play Element in Culture. Boston: Beacon.
Jaffe, A.J. and J. Froomkin
　1968　Technology and Jobs: Automation in Perspective. New York: Praeger.
Jones, P.d'A.
　1965　The Consumer Society. Baltimore: Penguin.
Katz, D. and R.L. Kahn
　1966　The Social Psychology of Organizations. New York: Wiley.
Keynes, J.M.
　1936　The General Theory of Employment, Interest and Money. New York: Harcourt, Brace and World.
Lewin, K.
　1948　Resolving Social Conflicts. New York: Harper & Bros.
Lundberg, F.
　1960　America's 60 Families. New York: Citadel.
Marcson, S.
　1970　Automation, Alienation and Anomie. New York: Harper & Row.
Marx, K.
　1906　Capital. 3 vols. Chicago: Charles H. Kerr.
McGregor, D.
　1960　The Human Side of Enterprise. New York: McGraw-Hill.
Meissner, M.
　1973　"The long arm of the job: social participation and the constraints of industrial work." Industrial Relations 10(October):239–260.
Merton, R.K.
　1949　Social Theory and Social Structure. New York: The Free Press.
Munsterberg, H.
　1913　Psychology and Industrial Efficiency. Boston: Houghton Mifflin.
Nash, M.
　1958　Machine Age Maya: The Industrialization of a Guatemalan Community. Chicago: University of Chicago Press.
Newcommer, M.
　1955　The Big Business Executive—The Factors That Made Him. New York: Columbia University Press.
Owen, R.
　1830　Lecture on an Entire New State of Society. London: Strange.
Palmer, G.
　1954　Labor Mobility in Six Cities. New York: Social Science Research Council.
Reich, C.A.
　1970　The Greening of America. New York: Random House.
Richards, A.I.
　1948　Hunger and Work in Savage Society. New York: The Free Press.
Roethlisberger, F.J. and W.J. Dickson
　1939　Management and the Worker. Cambridge: Harvard University Press.
Smith, A.
　1910　An Inquiry into the Nature and Causes of the Wealth of Nations. New York: E.P. Dutton.

Sorokin, P.A.
  1927   Social Mobility. New York: Harper & Bros.
Tawney, R.H.
  1926   Religion and the Rise of Capitalism. Baltimore: Penguin.
Taylor, F.
  1911   The Principles of Scientific Management. New York: Harper & Bros.
Thomas, W.I.
  1923   The Unadjusted Girl. Boston: Little, Brown and Co.
Tilgher, A.
  1930   Work: What It Has Meant to Men Through the Ages. New York: Har-
         court, Brace and World.
Ure, A.
  1835   The Philosophy of Manufactures. London: Macmillan.
Veblen, T.
  1918   Theory of the Leisure Class. New York: Huebsch.
Viteles, M.S.
  1932   Industrial Psychology. New York: W.W. Norton.
Vollmer, H.M. and D.L. Mills
  1966   Professionalization. Englewood Cliffs, New Jersey: Prentice-Hall.
Warner, W.L. and J.C. Abegglen
  1955   Big Business Leaders in America. New York: Harper & Row.
Warner, W.L. and J.O. Low
  1947   The Social System of the Modern Factory. New Haven: Yale Uni-
         versity Press.
Weber, M.
  1947   The Theory of Social and Economic Organization. New York: Oxford
         University Press.
  1930   The Protestant Ethic and the Spirit of Capitalism. London: Allen &
         Unwin.
Whyte, W.H., Jr.
  1956   The Organization Man. New York: Simon & Schuster.
Woodward, J.
  1965   Industrial Organization: Theory and Practice. London: Oxford Uni-
         versity Press.
Young, M.D.
  1958   The Rise of Meritocracy: 1870–2033: An Essay on Education and
         Equality. London: Thames & Hudson.

Work and Leisure

Stanley R. Parker and Michael A. Smith

London, England

In this chapter we propose to deal with a number of different aspects of the sociology of work and leisure. We first review the ways in which the separate spheres of work and leisure have been treated in sociological analysis. This is followed by a detailed consideration of various definitions of terms, concepts and variables which explicitly or implicitly underlie research in this field. We then bring together some of the summarized results of empirical enquiries into work and leisure patterns. A separate section is devoted to the special features of work which take place in a leisure context. Contributions towards a theory of work and leisure are followed by concluding remarks on the ways in which explanatory frameworks used to study work and leisure relate to those current in sociology generally.

WORK AND LEISURE IN SOCIOLOGICAL ANALYSIS

Work (in its widest sense, including labor) is a basic condition of the existence and survival of human life—it is independent of any particular form of society. This does not, of course, apply to all forms of work. Only some forms are necessary for the production and the reproduction of life; others develop and preserve a particular social institution; while yet other forms of work produce relatively inessential goods and services. The development of civilization corresponds in one sense to the development of the diversity of jobs available and to the expansion of goods and services which are regarded as necessities. At different stages of their social development, societies have had various ways of defining the scope of human work in terms of the goods or services required (Worsley, et al., 1970). But there remains a deeper meaning of work as a value itself that is at least partly independent of its product.

It is only for the last few decades that we have any reasonably objective documentation of the meaning of work for the mass of people. Earlier surveys, such as Henry Mayhew's classic *London Labour and the London Poor*, which covered material conditions, did not extend to explain attitudes regarding those conditions. Thus we have little or no evidence of how "the common man" regarded his work in earlier times. The clues that we have to the various historical meanings of work must be gleaned from philosophical and religious writers of the day and refer to the ideal of work held by the elite. For the rest of the population, the "problem" of the meaning of work did not exist. Throughout history men were what they *did:* a man's work provided him with an identity that was recognized both by others and by himself.

It is worth remembering that to ask men in economically underdeveloped traditional societies why they work is similar to asking them why they try to stay alive (Wax, 1958). To the ancient Greeks, in whose society mechanical labor was done by slaves, work was a curse and nothing more (Tilgher, 1931; Mills, 1956:215). They saw work as brutalizing the mind, rendering man unfit for considering truth or practicing virtue. Like the Greeks, the Hebrews thought of work as a painful necessity, but added the belief that it was a product of original sin. It was accepted as expiation through which man might atone for the sin of his ancestors and cooperate with God in the world's salvation. Early Christians followed this tradition, but added a positive function: work is necessary in order to share what is produced with one's needy brothers. But no intrinsic value was recognized in work—it was still only a means to a worthy end.

The early writings of the Church (and later, the Reformation movement) can give us an accurate glimpse of the "common" man's view of work. As the Church grew closer to accepting worldly standards, it granted fuller justice to labor and its fruits. For Luther, as for Medieval Catholicism, work was natural: it carried with it a penal but also an educational character. With the idea that the best way to serve God was to do most perfectly the work of one's profession, Luther swept away the distinction between religious piety and worldly activity; profession became "vocation" and work was valued as a religious path to salvation. Calvin developed these ideas further: all men, even the rich, must work because it is the will of God. But they must not lust after the fruits of their labor. From this paradox—the command to ceaseless effort, to ceaseless renunciation of the fruits of effort—the power motive and ideological justification of modern business derives. This is the foundation of the Protestant Work Ethic and the abhorrence of idleness and pleasure.

Even since the Renaissance, some scholars had held the view that truly creative work could be a joy in itself. Work was at last considered separately from the religious sphere of influence. The nineteenth century also carried a reaction to these ideas about the religious motivation of work. The early Utopians also had taken a nonreligious view of the role of work in man's life. They saw the need for leisure in the overall development of a man. They sought a limitation of the working day in order that further leisure time might be enjoyed. The nineteenth century socialists, contemporaries and followers of Marx and Engels, though critical of the "idealistic" implications of Utopianism, held views on work and the necessity of leisure which were broadly similar. A century ago, these men formulated opinions concerning the role of work in industrialized society which their followers still hold to this day (Josifovski, 1970): that when work is carried out for the benefit of the society and not for profit, when men are no longer required to work at unpleasant, long, hard and boring jobs for a living, they will have more zeal for their work. The working day will be better organized and require less time for greater output, so the workers will have more free time to spend in more enriching pursuits.

Another view of work comes to us from the anthropologists. The results of many of their studies of primitive communities show that they do not utilize a wage system in which a fixed reward is given for a fixed amount of labor or

CHAPTER **2**

time spent in labor, and in these less industrialized communities it is quite easy to see that the notion of work has been entirely removed from economic considerations.

In our society, participation in work has often been regarded as a duty to one's employer, rather than reward for which material gain can be expected. This view is also noneconomic in nature: psychological or philosophical views of work remain largely unexplored in past literature of the field.

In the preceding paragraphs we have chosen to concentrate on one socio-logical perspective of work—what it has meant to some men during some phases of recorded history. There are, of course, other perspectives, each of which is of some significance in its own right, but which have varying degrees of relevance to the study of work and leisure. A fairly large literature has accumulated on the function and meaning of work to men in different occupa-tional settings in modern industrial societies (Friedman and Havighurst, 1954; Morse and Weiss, 1955; Taylor, 1968). Of rather less relevance to work and leisure are the approaches to work which have, for example, focused on its re-lation to authority structures (Bendix, 1963), stratification and status in work organizations (Parker, 1972), and the study of work activities in specific occu-pations (Caplow, 1964; Krause, 1971).

Leisure

The sociological analysis of leisure has been less developed than that of work and is very largely restricted to modern industrial societies. An historical de-velopment of leisure can be traced (Neff, 1968), but to understand this ade-quately we need to discuss the meaning of leisure and related concepts, which we shall do in a later section. Here we may briefly consider certain more theo-retical issues connected with the sociological study of leisure.

Sociology has not been concerned to any great extent with the subject of leisure. Some sociologists have treated it as a fringe area beyond the bounds of a responsible and respectable discipline. Usually, however, the rejection has been implicit, as though leisure activities and institutions were of only minor significance when compared to the family, education, work, and so on. Certainly the way sociology has developed would seem to confirm the implicit relegation of leisure to the status of an appendage of other social institutions and processes.

In a very particular sense, the reason why few sociologists have treated leisure as a subject in its own right is a question in the sociology of knowledge. The main emphases of interest and research within sociology in general have largely derived from those which the classical social theorists identified. Marx, Weber and Durkheim, each in his own way and with different conclusions, made the economic processes of industrial society the central focus of analysis. The assumption was that the relationship of man to industrial society is best interpreted through the centrality of economic institutions and processes. To some extent, much subsequent analysis has been in this tradition of "standing on the shoulders of giants" without being too careful about where the giants were standing.

The idea that the study of leisure is of marginal significance is fostered by a second tradition in sociology. What is rather simplistically called "the social problems approach" has been and still is a prominent school of thought, par-ticularly in the British context. Committed to humanitarian ideals and with a stress on the usefulness of sociology in describing, interpreting and resolving fundamental problems of human need, this school has led to the neglect of those areas of human behavior where people seem contented with their environment. The enjoyment derived from harmless leisure is one measure of such contentment. It has also been assumed that since leisure is freely undertaken, without the compulsion of need, it is only of concern when it conflicts with the way those needs are met or controlled in society.

While it appears that sociology has ignored leisure in its concern to spell out the importance of economic institutions and processes and in using its insights to identify the effects of these, the subject of leisure has also been discounted for another very basic reason. It is not clear to what existing category of behavior, what institutions, what social processes the concept refers. Many sociologists regard the label of leisure as the rather general title given to all those miscellaneous pieces which cannot be categorized elsewhere. Others suggest that the most useful way of rendering the concept descriptive is to see it as a "spillover" subject—a residual category deriving its content from other spheres, whether of work, the family or community.

Rational Society and Identity-Seeking Culture

Western industrial society has become a rational society in a particular sense of that term. It has been based on the growth of specialized economic and social organization. Separate organizations have emerged which express both the growth of knowledge and the need for predictable behavior on the part of those carrying out organizational demands. One consequence is that man has become "anomic"—exposed to conflicting values and a variety of reference groups. He has become alienated—separated from his "true" identity through the nature of economic organization. Man has become depersonalized because of the demands of the society which he has created.

It could be maintained that this process has its counter-balance in culture, the world of created and constructed meaning: that part of society—whether through literature, art, drama or radical criticism—which probes and questions man's own choices and his relationship to the social world. Sociological analysis is part of this culture. It examines the claims and assumptions on which the organization of society is based. It attempts to see man as a self-aware, decision-making being, with a growing realization of himself as the creator of his own society. The modern stress on the search for identity and authenticity reflects this awareness (Klapp, 1969; Glasser, 1970).

Sociology, then, plays a part in interpreting and changing industrial society. This interpretative and directive function is part of the justification for the study of leisure. To the extent that sociology reflects the growing significance of a leisure-based, identity-seeking culture it goes beyond a descriptive passive analysis. This means moving away from the sterile and narrow formalism of much sociological analysis. Equally, it means trying to avoid the aridity of a simple, fact-gathering approach. Data on leisure (what little there are) need to be interpreted within the critical framework of a culture of which sociology is part; namely, a culture based on individuated self-awareness and man's control over the society he creates. The sociology of leisure, perhaps more clearly than that of work, is in part a recognition of this critical role of sociology in its relation to culture.

DEFINITIONS, CONCEPTS AND VARIABLES

Definitions of Work

To the individual in a modern industrial society, work is usually identified with the means of earning a living. In simpler societies, the relationship between work and such basic necessities as food, clothing and shelter is a direct one for the individual or for a comparatively small group; they consume only what they are able to produce. The evolution of society through various forms of social production and ownership of property progressively breaks down the direct link between individual productive effort and consumption of goods and services. Hard physical labor is less and less required as machines take over more of the tasks of production. Fewer people are needed to produce the basic necessities of life, and the goods and services of what are sometimes called the "leisure industries" account for an increasing proportion of total production and employment.

It will be noticed that we have already used, besides the term *work* itself, four of its synonyms: production, effort, labor and employment. Sometimes the adjective *productive* precedes *work*, but a highly literal interpretation of *productive* is misleading, since the *effort* to produce something is work, irrespective of whether a *product* is the result, and the rendering of services, no less than the production of goods, requires work. The distinction between the terms *work, labor* and *employment* is even more important. Only the last of these terms implies a social relationship, although it is sometimes used in the same nonsocial sense as work, for example, when we say that someone is self-employed. The most common form of employment consists of an employer (individual or corporate body) hiring the working abilities of an employee during set hours. For the employee, these set hours are equivalent of *working time*, and it is relatively easy for him to distinguish this from *nonworking time*, a part or the whole of which may be defined as *leisure time*.

Two other concepts of work and labor (Arendt, 1958:127) have to do with *activity* rather than time. Both are often equated with employment, but while it is true that all employment implies work of some kind, the reverse is not necessarily so. Employment is work in the narrow sense of income-producing activity, but work has a wider biological and physiological meaning of purposeful and sustained action. Whereas employment may be contrasted with idleness or with work that is economically unremunerative or disinterested, work in its broadest meaning is the opposite of rest.

Definitions of Leisure

One of the chief problems of defining leisure is that it is very difficult to take an objective approach to the subject. It is a dubious procedure to ask participants why they engage in activity, since all of us construct our own "reasons" to fit situational expectations and self-images (Kelly, 1972). The way in which someone defines leisure tends to be determined by his view of what it ought to be. There is an element of this subjectivity even in the kind of definition which views leisure as that part of time left over after work and perhaps also after other obligations have been met, because the judgment of where work leaves off and leisure begins is usually a subjective one. Between this kind of definition which concentrates on the dimension of *time*, and the openly "normative" definition which is concerned with the quality of *activity* or being, there is an approach which seeks to combine the two. We may, therefore, conveniently review various definitions of leisure which fall into these three broad groups.

A Temporal Definition of Leisure

The "residual" type of definition of leisure is concerned with the classification of all the nonsleep hours in the day of an individual. The time that is unidentifiable, or unclassified, is termed leisure time. Waking time that cannot be identified and classified is called leisure time. The *Dictionary of Sociology*, in one of its most residual definitions, states that leisure is "free time after the practical necessities of life have been attended to"; and Gross (1961) is equally vague in suggesting that "leisure refers to free time, free, that is, from the need to be concerned about maintenance." Lundberg (1934:2) defines leisure as "the time we are free from the more obvious and formal duties which a paid job or other obligatory occupation imposes upon us." Giddens (1964) is more precise about what leisure excludes, defining it "in a residual fashion, to denote that sphere of life not occupied in working, travelling to work or sleeping," while White (1955) excludes sleeping, eating and working from the realm of leisure. Soule's (1957) concept of unsold time is essentially residual: "What one does in sold time is 'the job'. . . . Time not sold, is 'one's own time,' 'free time is thought of as leisure, no matter what one does with it.'"

Leisure Through Activity

The second group of definitions consists of those that start with a residual approach such as those above, but go on to include a positive description of the content or function of leisure, sometimes adding to a prescriptive element. Space permits mention of only three of these definitions.

> Leisure is . . . the time which an individual has free from work or other duties and which may be utilized for purposes of relaxation, diversion, social achievement, or personal development (Gist and Fava, 1964: 411).

> Leisure consists of a number of occupations in which the individual may indulge of his own free will—either to rest, to amuse himself, to add to his knowledge or improve his skills disinterestedly or to increase his voluntary participation in the life of the community after discharging his professional, family and social duties (Dumazedier, 1960).

> The essential elements of leisure . . . are (a) an antithesis to "work" as an economic function, (b) a pleasant expectation and recollection, (c) a minimum of involuntary social-role obligations, (d) a psychological perception of freedom, (e) a close relation to the values of the culture, (f) the inclusion of an entire range from inconsequence and insignificance to weightiness and importance, and (g) often, but not necessarily, an activity characterized by the element of play. Leisure is none of these by itself but all together in one emphasis or another (Kaplan, 1960:22).

Leisure: A Third View

The third group of definitions consists of those which are wholly prescriptive and normative. They stress the *quality* of leisure by contrasting it with the attributes of work. Many of these definitions have their sources within the spheres of religious thought. The various assumptions and beliefs which lie behind these definitions would take too long to discuss here, though we may briefly note the kinds of attributes which modern (mainly religious) writers think leisure ought to have. The Protestant view of leisure identifies it with qualities of refinement, holding it to be unique because it is often associated with spiritual or artistic values (Anderson, 1961:33). A Catholic view as expressed by Pieper (1952:42) is that leisure "is a mental and spiritual attitude—it is not simply the result of external factors, it is not the inevitable result of spare time, a holiday, a weekend or a vacation. It is ... an attitude of mind, a condition of the soul, and as such utterly contrary to the ideal of 'work.'" From a sociological point of view, the disadvantage of this kind of definition is that it affords no objective criteria for making comparisons. If leisure is to be identified as an attitude of mind or a condition of soul we must ask: *which* attitude of mind and *which* condition of soul?

Finally, it has been suggested that free time is simply a space of time, while leisure is an activity of "state of being" (DeGrazia, 1962:7). But this contrast is not confined to the area of nonwork—it applies also in the work sphere. The two worlds of time and activity are not the domains of work and leisure respectively: both are *dimensions* of work *and* leisure. Unless this two-dimensional property of work and leisure is appreciated, it is impossible to understand that work (or leisure) is a quality of activity that only problematically and not necessarily takes place within a space of time labelled work (or leisure). As Aron (1968:104) remarks, it is the intention, not the activity itself, which determines whether a specified amount of time is to be classified as work or leisure.

Components of Life-Space

"Life-space" is a concept that indicates ways of spending time that people have. In considering the various definitions of work and leisure, it is clear that to allocate all the parts of life-space either to work or to leisure would be a gross over-simplification. It is possible to use the exhaustive categories of "work" and "nonwork," but this still does not enable us to say where the line between the two is to be drawn. Also, important differences exist *within* as well as between these two categories. A number of writers have suggested schemes for analyzing the twenty-four hours in the average person's day into various categories (cf. Parker, 1971:25–27). Instead of examining these schemes in detail, we may put the various categories that have been suggested into five main groups. This should make analysis easier, and it assumes that any differences among the categories in each group are fairly minor.

Work, working time, sold time, subsistence time. As we have already seen, although "work" has a wider meaning than employment, for the purpose of analyzing life-space, it is usually identified with earning a living. If an employee is on piece rates, then it is work, or more precisely the product of work, that he sells; if he is on time rates then he sells so much working time. However, these are both ways of measuring work *and* working time, and differ only in the way the remuneration is calculated. "Subsistence time" lays emphasis on the *purpose* of work to the worker, that is, enabling him and his dependents to subsist.

Work-related time, work obligations. Apart from actual working time, most people have to spend a certain amount of time in travelling to and from the place of work and preparing or "grooming" themselves for work. In some cases, however, at least part of the travelling time may be regarded more as a form of leisure than as work-related—for example, time spent reading newspapers or books, chatting with fellow-travellers, or playing cards with them. Some writers regard as work-related things that would not be done if it were not for work, such as the husband doing a share of his working wife's housework. Voluntary overtime and having a second job may also be regarded as related to the main working time rather than as part of it, as may activities in the no-man's land between work and leisure such as reading on the subject of one's work when at home, attending conferences or trade union meetings which have a social as well as a work side, and so on.

Existence time, meeting physiological needs. This is the first of three "nonwork" groups. We all have to spend a certain minimum of time on sleep and the physical mechanics of living—eating, washing, eliminating, etc. Beyond the minimum necessary for reasonably healthy living, extra time spent on these things may be more like a leisure activity. Eating for pleasure, taking extra care with one's appearance for a party or social occasion, sexual activity beyond the call of purely physiological need are some examples which show that the line between the satisfaction of "existence" needs and leisure activities is not always easy to draw.

Nonwork obligations, semileisure. Dumazedier (1967:14) has coined the term *semileisure* to describe "activities which, from the point of view of the individual, arise in the first place from leisure, but which represent in differing degrees the character of obligations." The obligations are usually to other people, but may be to nonhuman objects such as pets or homes or gardens. Again, the line between obligation and leisure is not always clear and depends to a large extent on one's *attitude* toward the activity: gardening and odd job work around the home can be a chore or an absorbing hobby, and playing with the children can be a duty or a delight.

Leisure: free time, spare time, uncommitted time, discretionary time, choosing time. All the words after *leisure* above describe some aspect of what is meant by leisure. We saw earlier that residual definitions of leisure list it as time free from various commitments and obligations, and that "free" time is best regarded as a dimension of leisure. "Spare" time is a slightly different idea, implying that, like a spare tire, it is not normally in use but could be put to use. "Uncommitted" time suggests lack of obligations, of either a work or nonwork character. "Discretionary" or "choosing" time is perhaps the essence of leisure, because it means time that we can use at our own discretion and according to our own choice.

From a careful study of the various schemes for analyzing life-space, three points emerge:

1. Time and activity are dimensions which are *both* present in all categories of life-space, even where, for the sake of brevity, both are not always stated.
2. Between compulsory activities (in order to live or to earn a living) and freely-chosen ones, some activities have the character of obligations. This applies to both work and nonwork activities.
3. Leisure implies relative freedom of choice, and it is possible to work during one's leisure time.

One important qualification must be made to the above analysis of life-space. In considering the various categories, we have had in mind men in full-time employment. In assuming that all adults work (i.e., are engaged in a full-time paid occupation) we should be right in about 70% of the cases. But a full analysis of life-space would need to take account of minorities who are not in a full-time occupation: the unemployed, the "idle rich" and prisoners. The difference between constrained and freely chosen activities which most employed people experience does not apply—or applies in a different way—to groups such as these.

WORK AND LEISURE PATTERNS

Work Time and Leisure Time

There has been a tendency for the length of the working week to decline in most advanced industrial societies. But second jobs—"moonlighting"—have been increasing (Moore and Hedges, 1971). Earlier retirement (sometimes because of redundancy) and a longer expectation of life are combining to give more nonwork time to many people. Technical developments in some industries are changing the distribution of, as well as shortening the traditional hours of work, involving four- or even three-day working weeks for some (Poor, 1970). But over the labor force as a whole, the early realization of a drastic reduction in the working week seems unlikely. This is because service occupations account for an increasing proportion of the working population and in these occupations—unlike those in manufacturing industry—there is no tendency for the working week to diminish (Carter, 1970).

Unless one uses a purely residual definition of leisure as nonworking time, there is no necessary connection between hours of work and hours of leisure. Few studies have been made of the duration of leisure, no doubt partly because of the difficulty in defining leisure time. A survey of four occupational groups in Britain showed that youth employment and child care employees reported having thirty-three to thirty-four average weekly hours of leisure, and bank and manual workers forty-two to forty-three (Parker, 1972:82). The same survey showed that about three-quarters of certain groups of employees defined leisure as "only the time you feel free to do whatever you like," and the rest agreed with one of two residual definitions. Although clearly it is unrealistic to expect statistics of leisure to approach the precision of statistics of working weeks, there is scope for improving our knowledge of the amount of time people believe they have as leisure.

Leisure of Occupational Groups

The ways in which work and leisure are interrelated at the personal level are partly a matter of the personality characteristics of the individuals concerned, partly a result of cultural or subcultural patterns which influence general behavior norms, and partly a function of the occupation that an individual follows. Personality is of more central concern to psychologists; the cultural influences, although matters of interest to sociologists, would take us outside the scope of this article; but the subcultural influences of occupational experiences *are* relevant to this study.

Data are available on the relation between work and leisure in the lives of people in a wide variety of occupations (cf. Clarke, 1956; Burdge, 1969; Bishop and Ikeda, 1970). Dealing first with the manual group, the decreased physical strain of work has brought about a change in the function of leisure for some manual workers. It has been observed that the work in the steel mills has now become so relatively lacking in strain that the workers leave the plant with a good deal of energy left which carries them readily through their leisure hours (Riesman, 1952). However, in occupations like mining and fishing, leisure tends to have a more traditional role. Tunstall's (1962) study of distant-water fishermen showed that leisure during the time they are ashore fulfills the functions of status seeking and of explosive compensation for physically damaging work.

Something of this violent reaction to work can be seen in the leisure activities of some nonmanual workers. Friedman (1960) quotes a study of the leisure habits of employees at the Postal Cheque Centre in Paris, whose jobs are completely routine: on leaving the office, these clerks are either much more active or, on the contrary, withdraw into themselves, in a sort of apathy. But a different pattern of work and leisure is shown by those nonmanual employees whose work demands more involvement and responsibility. Among professional engineers studied by Gerstl and Hutton (1966:138), 23% said they had hobbies connected with the field of engineering, and as many as 73% claimed work-connected reading as one of their leisure interests.

Heckscher and DeGrazia (1959) concluded from their survey that the way of life of American business executives permits no clear-cut distinction between work and leisure. To counteract the encroachment of work on leisure time, the executive's work is penetrated by qualities which we would ordinarily associate with leisure. On the other hand, Riesman (1952) remarks that the professional and business person is apt to leave his work with a good many tensions created by his reactions to interpersonal situations and so he may have to satisfy his leisure "needs" before he can rise from the level of re-creation to the level of creation. He may move from a job where he is constantly faced with others and their expectations, to leisure pursuits, again in the company of others, where workmanlike performance is also expected of him.

The penetration of the businessman's work into the rest of his life is a function of the demands of the work itself rather than of the culture. This is illustrated by the close similarity of the Japanese businessman's life to that of the American. Vogel (1963:21) reports that in Japan, business is combined with community activities, recreation and personal activities. It is difficult to distinguish working time from leisure time, and the businessman often entertains his clients by a trip to the golf course or a party with entertainment by geisha girls. Vogel also notes that, like successful businessmen, doctors rarely make a sharp separation between work and leisure, partly because to some extent working hours are determined by the arrival or needs of patients. It is the salaried man who makes the sharpest distinction between working time and free time. In contrast to the businessman who mixes business and leisure, and to the doctor whose leisure is determined by the absence of patients, the salaried man generally has set hours so that he can plan certain hours of the day and certain days of the week for himself and his family.

The type of leisure activity chosen may directly reflect the type of work and work situation. Even differences in *style* of a given type of leisure activity may be related to work experience. Thus Etzkorn (1964) notes that "public campground" camping, which is routinized, is practiced more by individuals with routinized jobs, while "wilderness" camping is preferred by individuals in more creative occupations. Blum (1953) goes more deeply into the relation between work and leisure experienced by the typical packing-house worker. This type of worker has a tendency to carry work attitudes on into the weekend in spite of a strong psychological fatigue and desire to get away from work and everything it stands for. Since it is almost impossible to work eight hours intensively and switch over suddenly to a new, creative way of life, workers are pushed into some kind of activity which keeps them occupied without reminding them of their work. Fishing is one of their favorite pastimes. It has elements which are just the opposite of the work process—relaxing, being outdoors, getting

> away from it all—and yet it has elements akin to the work process: It does not require any initiative or attention and, most of all, it allows the psychological mechanisms of busyness to go on. It makes it possible to carry an essential attitude growing out of the work process into the leisure time without making its experience in any way similar to the experience of work ... it eliminates the necessity of a basic change in attitude, of attitude and attention (Blum, 1953).

Also, some French sociologists have done empirical work on the relation between work and leisure. In the preface to the study of pigeon cultivation among miners, Friedmann pointed out that leisure for them does more than merely offer a compensation for the technique of work. It brings professional compensations for work with a limited horizon, emotional compensations for the crudity of social relations in mass society, and social compensations through the success which this leisure-time activity can provide. After quoting this study, Dumazedier and Latouche (1962) note that, far from being a compensation, leisure is more often only an extension of occupational life. However, when one assesses the results of a number of studies of work and leisure, it is clear that the "compensation" theory must be rejected (Argyris, 1973). If individuals tend to experience dependence, submission, frustration, conflict, and short time perspective at work, and if they adapt to these conditions by psychological withdrawal, apathy, indifference, and a decrease in the importance of their worth as human beings, these adaptive activities become more dominant in the person's life, and they will guide his leisure behavior outside the work-place. Individuals will seek leisure activities that are consonant with the adaptive activities.

On the other hand, it is possible for the occupational role to provide opportunities for leisure which extend into working time. In a study of British shipyard workers, Brown (1973) noted that leisure activities such as exchanging stories and playing cards are an integral part of the work context. They are the cement of social relationships in work and the fabric of the occupational culture. Clearly, the opportunities for leisure-like behavior in the work situation vary according to such factors as orientation to work, style of supervision, and the extent to which the work demands full and constant attention. There are signs that occupational sociology is beginning to recognize the subtle interaction of work and leisure (Smigel, 1963; Seligman, 1965; Linder, 1970).

WORK IN LEISURE CONTEXTS

There are two ways in which work may be said to take place in a leisure context: when it constitutes employment in some branch of the leisure industry, and when it takes place as a "voluntary" activity during free time after earning a living. We shall consider these two subjects in turn.

Employment in the Leisure Industries

A substantial and growing proportion of the population is employed in one or another of the leisure industries (Roberts, 1970:ch. 5). These may be taken to include industries providing entertainment, sports and gambling facilities, vacation amenities, materials for hobbies, a considerable part of travel, book production, the care of gardens and pets, and so on. In the field of public enterprise, people employed in running museums, parks and water areas are also in the domain of leisure (Brightbill, 1960:31–36).

The analysis of the occupational roles of people employed in these industries poses some interesting and problematical questions in the study of work-leisure relationships. These questions arise to some extent from ambiguities and contradictory expectations in situations in which one person's pleasure is another's employment, such as the waitress and the customer (Whyte, 1948). The entertainment, vacation and service industries contain a large range of occupations in this category. They are also a growth point in most industrial societies (Briggs, 1960; Landers, 1969).

Certain features are common to all occupational groups: (1) they possess a common, sometimes preclusive subculture based on the acquisition and use of specialized knowledge and techniques (Cannon, 1967); (2) they tend to involve both induction and recognition strategies and rituals which precede the accordance of professional or semiprofessional status to particular employees (Prandy, 1965); (3) they develop ranking systems in which status and skill become part of the wider evaluation of the occupation vis-à-vis others and also in respect to differential rewards within the occupation itself; (4) finally— and this is especially relevant to occupations where work is the provision of leisure—the entertainment, vacation and service occupations tend to have strong normative controls which regulate relationships with customers or clients and enable social distance to be maintained (Goffman, 1961; Wolff, 1964).

It would be instructive to examine these four aspects in relation to several typical leisure occupations. But it is not feasible to discuss the total range of these occupations, since some have been the subject of many studies while others have not been examined at all. We may, however, usefully review what has been said about a small number of typical occupations in this category.

The entertainment industry—and especially the mass involvement in watching and supporting popular sports such as football—suggests that the role of the entertainer may be as important as it is varied. The professional footballer (Riesman and Denney, 1954; Dunning, 1971), the comedian (Bruce, 1966), and the strip-tease artist (Gagnon and Simon, 1968) are all work roles which share certain common features: (1) they give to the person performing them considerable scope for "role style" or personalized performance; (2) the context in which they occur is a fairly "loose" one and this fluidity itself is linked to the emergent nature of the work situation; (3) authority, with its attendant sanctions against stepping too far out of line, is likely to be asserted after the event when the "performance" has finished and the public are not present; and (4) these occupations pose the dilemma of working to *make* others enjoy themselves, this dilemma being expressed through the strains inherent in playing a role which must closely match the expectations of the paying customers.

Certain skills, personal attributes and the exercise of specialized knowledge or techniques, tend to knit occupational groups into fairly well-defined subcultures. The role of the strip-tease artist is a good illustration of this purpose. The need both to excite the sexual fantasies of the customer or "punter" and maintain some sense of self-integrity result in the stripper having to learn how to handle the exacting demands of her occupation. A good stripper will enter into a kind of game with her audience, exciting their interest, provoking them to call to her in a ritualized way to "take it off," while adhering to the norms regulating the degree of physical contact between stripper and audience.

The cohesiveness of an occupational subculture depends not only on the specialized skills of the role and the norms which regulate social relations in the work situation but also on admission and recognition strategies. In the case of the stripper, these are minimal. A process of self-selection tends to occur and strippers recognize the scope they have to perform in their own way to arouse sexual fantasy. Authority is loosely exercised as long as the audience interest in the act is maintained. The general status of the stripper is low, not because the income is usually small but because it is regarded as a morally deviant occupation. It is worth noting that there are other occupations within the leisure industries whose members are said to partake of the culture of a deviant group, a good example being the dance-hall musicians studied by Becker (1963).

Less deviant and often less financially rewarding is the role of the comedian. The village idiot and the strolling player are the historical forerunners of the professional comedian today. The clown and the "patter merchant" in the circus both deal in humor. Success in finding new material is the main factor distinguishing the mediocre from the successful performer. The drive for originality and the idiosyncratic ability to make people laugh tend to preclude the development of a strong occupational subculture. Occupational skill is individualized and stylized and "the act" becomes the basis for occupational status and economic reward.

The tensions in the work role of the comedian are considerable. There is a desire among the audience to laugh both *at* and *with* the performer. The performance itself becomes an identity projection process for both audience and comedian, and humor mediates the tension of working at making people laugh. Some comedians *are* in real life the kind of person around whom their act is woven, and this can create personal problems which sometimes result in premature death under tragic circumstances. The American Lenny Bruce and the British Tony Hancock are examples.

Professional football provides another example of the way in which a public performance—in this case a collective one—constitutes the core of the occupational activity (Loy and Kenyon, 1969; Sage, 1970). Riesman and Denney (1954), in a comparative study of football as an example of cultural diffusion, show how the changing ethnic origins of players on All-Pro American football teams have been accompanied by a shift in the type of popular hero. The work-minded glamour of an all-round craftsman has given way to the people-minded glamour of backfield generals organizing deceptive forays into enemy territory.

Elias and Dunning (1971), writing of football in Britain, see its main attraction as the controlled tension between two subgroups holding each other in balance. The flexible tension-balance that can make the game so exciting to spectators cannot be produced and maintained at just the right level if one side is very much stronger than the other. Also, there are a variety of roles in the game, each requiring different physical and psychological characteristics (Payne and Cooper, 1966). Forwards are more "self-oriented" than defenders; centre-halves are least self-oriented of all. The "striker," the "winger," the "midfield player," the "sweeper," the "full back," and especially the goalkeeper are distinctive in role aptitude and personality, and the range of individuals gaining gratification from football must be wider due to this fact. Additional information on the physical and psychological aspects of American professional football can be found in Mandell (1974).

To be employed in one of the leisure industries may aid the process of upward social mobility, particularly if the occupational role is a public one giving employment also to many other "backstage" workers (Lueschen, 1971). Thus professional football has provided acceptance into the democratic fraternity of the entertainment world where it is performance that counts and ethnic or social origin is hardly a handicap. In some cases, such as professional boxing, coming from a lower socioeconomic background may be a positive advantage, since it has been said with some empirical justification that such people make the best fighters. Weinberg and Arond (1952) point out that boxing, as well as other sports and certain kinds of entertainment, offers slum boys the hope of quick success without delinquent behavior.

Finally, employment in the leisure industries may be a "bridging" occupation (Broom and Smith, 1963), that is, an occupation which provides, through work experience, the conditions and opportunities for movement from one occupation to another. Sometimes this mobility may be more or less forced on the individual because of the short working life in some sports and branches of the entertainment industry. Athletes may become coaches, jockeys may become trainers, and film actors may become directors. Downward mobility may, on the other hand, also occur, as in the case of boxers who become "punchy" or "washed-up."

Working at Leisure

A second way in which work takes place in a leisure context is seen in the various free time creative activities. Ernst (1956:7) quoted figures of Americans then engaged in such work activities; for example, 200,000 people building boats in their cellars and garages, and ten million homes having power tools. Not all these activities may be entirely free of economic considerations, but in many cases they represent a deliberate choice to use leisure time in a productive way, which may be none the less enjoyable for that. Such activities partake of the ideal of craftsmanship, in which there is no split of work and play, or work and culture (Mills, 1956:220).

An example of the way in which a leisure activity might seem to the casual observer to be more like hard work is that of membership in railway preservation societies, popular among a growing minority in Britain. With the coming of new diesel and electric locomotives the old steam trains were taken out of service. Nonprofessionals, however, have acquired many of these visibly more attractive old locomotives and in some cases, the societies concerned have purchased sections of track on which to run these trains for pleasure. The members work hard to keep their engines and track in order—but this is their *chosen* activity, on which they are prepared to spend time and money, and to them it is leisure.

The choice of "serious" activity or taking on obligations to fill at least part of leisure time may be seen in a wide variety of voluntary association membership and office-holding. Again an example from Britain may illustrate this (Parker, 1971:91–98). Local government councils are staffed by paid officials, but they are managed by voluntary elected councilors. These people spend a considerable amount of time on their public duties—an average of fifty-two hours a month according to one survey—but many of them clearly regard it as a fulfilling experience, especially if their jobs are routine. They can find in this "leisure" activity many personal and social satisfactions that may well be lacking both in their paid occupation and in other possible nonwork outlets.

Finally we may turn to the sphere of adult education to find a number of ways of spending time that are manifestly in the sector of work but latently may be more like leisure. Jary (1973) has shown that while the official ideology is that courses in adult education are for extrinsic purposes such as gaining qualifications and learning skills, these courses often function as leisure activities yielding intrinsic gratifications. The popularity of various kinds of social study, in which stimulating discussion with like-minded people forms an integral part, testifies to the fact that for many students this is a freely chosen and even sought after form of leisure occupation.

TOWARDS A THEORY OF WORK AND LEISURE

Types of Work-Leisure Relationships

There are two levels on which we may develop theoretical types of relationships between work and leisure—the individual and the societal. In this section, we deal with the individual and in the following section with the societal. It may be helpful to set out in a table three possible types of relationships between work and leisure in the lives of individuals and the values of the variables which define these types.

TABLE 1
TYPES OF INDIVIDUAL WORK-LEISURE RELATIONSHIPS

	Extension	Opposition	Neutrality
Content of work and leisure	similar	deliberately different	usually different
Demarcation of spheres	weak	strong	average
Central life-interest	work	—	nonwork
Imprint left by work on leisure	marked	marked	not marked

With the *extension* pattern, the similarity of at least some work and leisure activities and the lack of demarcation between work and leisure are the key characteristics. The extreme cases of this pattern are people who are free from the necessity of earning a living but who do work of a kind and in circumstances they choose. Others show a strong *tendency* to extension of work into leisure but also some elements of opposition and/or neutrality. Thus some social workers feel that it is bad for them and for their clients if they are too work-dominated, and their leisure accordingly has some elements of deliberate opposition to work. Having work as a central life-interest is part of the extension pattern. This is because work to someone who sees a continuity between work and leisure is a much more embracing concept than just "the job" or even "the occupation." Work signifies the meaning and fulfillment of life, and in saying that it is also the *center* of life, such people are not necessarily denying the integrated role that leisure plays in it. Also, because of deep involvement in their kind of work, it leaves a relatively great imprint on the rest of their lives— it is often an influence from which they are never really free.

The key aspects of the *opposition* pattern are the intentional dissimilarity of work and leisure and the strong demarcation between the two spheres. The extreme cases of this pattern are those who hate their work so much that any reminder of it in their off-duty time is unpleasant. But paradoxically such people do not in one sense get away from work at all: so deeply are they marked by the hated experience of work that they carry it with them as a kind of negative yardstick by which to judge the pleasures of nonwork. Others have an ambivalent rather than a completely hostile attitude to work—they hate it because of the physical or psychological damage that they feel it does to them, yet they "love" it because they are fascinated by its arduousness or by its dangers (it is "real man's work"). The strain of such work ensures that it is not carried over into leisure, from which it is clearly demarcated. The prediction for source of central life-interest is generally not clear; if work is viewed with unmixed hatred then presumably nonwork is seen as the center of life, but if there is a love-hate relationship to work then either sphere could be seen as central, or perhaps the very opposition and dissimilarity of the spheres render the person incapable of making a comparative judgment.

The third pattern of *neutrality* is only partly defined by a "usually different" content of work and leisure and by an "average" demarcation of spheres. This pattern is *not* intermediate between the other two patterns. The crucial difference between extension and opposition on the one hand and neutrality on the other is that the former denotes respectively a positive and negative *attachment* to work, while the latter denotes a *detachment* from work that is neither fulfillment nor oppression. In the case of extension, the imprint left by work on leisure is a positive one, and in the case of opposition it is a negative one. But people showing the neutrality pattern are neither so engrossed in their work that they want to carry it over into nonwork time nor so damaged by it that they develop a hostile or love-hate relationship to it. Instead, work leaves them comparatively unmarked and free to carry over into leisure the noninvolvement and passivity which characterizes their attitude to work (cf. Wippler, 1969). It is this attitude toward work that makes it likely that their central life-interest will be found in some aspect of nonwork.

Certain occupations, because of the work itself and working conditions involved and because of the impact they make on the participants, are associated with each of the three patterns. Social workers (especially the residential kind), successful businessmen (perhaps they *are* successful because they have little or no time for leisure), doctors, teachers and craft workers often all exhibit the extension pattern. Unskilled manual workers, assembly-line workers, miners, fishermen, oil-rig workers, tunnellers (the last two being "extreme" occupations both in the sense of high pay and physical working conditions) are typical of the opposition pattern. Routine clerical and manual workers, and minor professionals other than social workers probably contain more than their fair share of those with the neutrality pattern.

A number of both work and nonwork variables may be seen to be associated with the three patterns. Studies in the work and nonwork behavior and attitudes of particular occupational groups may be used to suggest values of these variables which seem to be associated with one or other of the patterns. Among work variables, a high degree of *autonomy in the work situation* seems to accompany the extension pattern, and a low degree the neutrality and opposition patterns. Extensive *use of abilities* in work is consistent with the extension pattern, while lack of use of abilities would show up differently in the other two patterns (extension people may be said to feel "stretched" by their work, neutrality people "bored" and opposition people "damaged." Etzioni's (1961) three types of *involvement in work* may be applied to the patterns—extension people are morally involved or committed, neutrality people have a calculative, practical attitude of working only for the money, while opposition people have a sense of alienation from a job they feel forced to do against their will. Having *work colleagues as close friends* is a likely feature of the extension pattern but not of the others. *Work encroaches on leisure time* quite often among the extension people, less often among the neutrality people (and then usually as a means to an end), and hardly at all among the opposition people.

The above types of work-leisure relationships are based mainly on research and theoretical propositions by Parker (1971). They may be compared with other attempts to trace the relationships between types of work and leisure, for example, that of Filipcova (1969):

Kind of work	Relation towards leisure
A. simple work	strong determination mostly in the negative sense
B. "neutral" work	more freedom and neutrality in relation to leisure
C. creative work.	strong determination mostly in the positive sense

Fusion Versus Polarity

The type of relationship between work and leisure spheres is also to be seen at the societal level. On the one hand there is the evidence for and against the proposition that work and leisure are becoming similar to each other, and these "fusion" versus "polarity" hypotheses can be tested against developments in work content, organization and environment. On the other hand, an individual experiences societal fusion as spillover of the work and leisure spheres, and polarity as opposition, or at least differentiation, of them.

Wilensky (1964) cites as evidence of work-leisure fusion the long coffee break among white collar men and women, the lunch "hour" among top business and professional people, card games among night shift employees; and off work, the do-it-yourself movement, spare-time jobs, "customers golf" for sales executives, and commuter-train conferences for account executives. Also, many devices are being invented for creating spaces of free time within the working day and at intervals through the career. In America the sabbatical year is no longer exclusive to academic employees. Some firms are granting twelve months paid holiday after ten years' service and others a quarter-sabbatical after five years. Another type of work-leisure fusion, the integration of sex into work, is noted by Marcuse (1964:74), "Without ceasing to be an instrument of labor, the body is allowed to exhibit its sexual features in the everyday work world and in work relations."

No doubt with such evidence as this in mind, Stone (1958) has asserted that

> more and more we work at our play and play at our work ... our play is disguised by work and vice versa. Consequently, we begin to evaluate our leisure time in terms of the potential it has for work—for us to "do it ourselves," and we evaluate our work in terms of the potential it has for play.

Riesman and Blomberg (1957:83) extend this point by maintaining that leisure now gives status to work rather than the other way around. Young workers look to nonwork activities for a more personal as well as more portable kind of status. They are judged, as it were, "horizontally" by their life-style rather than vertically by their occupation.

Riesman (1953:185) attempts to explain this work-leisure fusion in terms of the "changing American character" from inner-directedness to other-directedness: "The other-directed person has no clear core of self to escape from; no clear line between production and consumption; between adjusting to the group and serving private interests; between work and play." Yet other-directedness is not so much a type of character as a mode of adjustment to technological civilization. The aspect of leisure that is most amenable to fusion with work is mass culture, because it is most subject to social control and therefore can be made most "functional" to the industrial system as a whole. Howe (1948) sees this process of manipulation clearly:

> ... except during brief revolutionary intervals, the quality of leisure time activity cannot vary too sharply from that of the work day. If it did, the office or factory worker would be exposed to those terrible dualities that make it so difficult for the intellectual to adjust his job to himself. But the worker wants no part of such difficulties, he has enough already. Following the dictum of industrial society, that anonymity is a key to safety, he seeks the least troublesome solution: mass culture. Whatever its manifest content, mass culture must therefore not subvert the basic patterns of industrial life. Leisure time must be so organized as to bear a factitious relationship to working time: apparently different, actually the same. It must provide relief from work monotony without making the return to work too unbearable ...

The popular game of bingo is a good example. Bingo has several features which are similar to the work experience of many of those who take part in it: it involves concentration, regulated patterns of physical movement, is supervised by someone else, and allows breaks for refreshments.

There are other observers, however, who take a different view about what has been happening to work and leisure. Dismissing evidence of fusion cited above as peripheral to the main structure of modern industry, they seek to show that work has become more concentrated and active. It may be less arduous physically than it used to be, but its present standards of efficiency require one to key oneself to a higher pitch of nervous and mental effort (Greenberg, 1958:39). The theme of alienation from work is relevant here, since it implies that work as a sphere of human experience is estranged from other spheres such as that of leisure. Under conditions of present society, it is said, the "break in consciousness" between work and socialized play, begun during the industrial revolution, has been completed (Green, 1964:171). Certainly it is arguable that the institution of employment has brought about a fairly sharp distinction between working life and private life, between sold time and unsold time. The "evasion of work," according to Bell (1954:20), is the one characteristic fact about work in the life of a contemporary American:

> Work is irksome, and if it cannot be evaded it can be reduced. In the old days the shadings between work and leisure were hard to distinguish. In modern life the ideal is to minimize the unpleasant aspects of work as much as possible by pleasant distractions (wall colors, music, rest periods) and to hasten away as quickly as possible, uncontaminated by work and unimpaired by its arduousness ...

The ideal may be to split the unsatisfying life of work from the more rewarding life of nonwork, but the extent to which this can actually be achieved seems doubtful. Also, the contrast must be made between leisure as a desired period of time and set of activities, and leisure as a replacement for work. The former is probably on the increase, whereas the latter is not likely ever to predominate (Meyersohn, 1972:208).

The evidence for fusion or polarity of work and leisure at the societal level is thus conflicting, and the theories built on selections of it are not easily reconcilable. Perhaps the whole argument has been confused by referring to different levels—that of society in general and that of occupations and work milieux in particular—each of which requires its own methods of analysis and conclusions. There is the further point that fusion and polarity may not exhaust all the possibilities of relationship between work and leisure. The concepts of fusion and polarity are essentially *dynamic* ones referring to a process of change in a relationship. They also denote symbiotic relationships, in the sense that each side of the relationship is dependent for its form on the form of the other —by a process, as it were, of positive attraction or negative repulsion. This leaves a third possibility that the nature of the "relationship" between work and leisure may be nonsymbiotic, i.e., that work and leisure may each have "lives of their own" and be *relatively* unaffected by each other.

Concerning the future, it has been suggested that there are three probable alternative scenarios (Johnston, 1972; Murphy, 1973). The first is of an automated society in which a small number of people would be responsible for production and distribution of goods, with the remainder of the population limited to consumption. The corresponding ethic would be a takeover by leisure of the intrinsic and personally satisfying aspects of life, with work being accepted primarily for the monetary rewards it brings. The second scenario recognizes the realization and maintenance of a full employment economy, and assumes the maintenance of the work ethic, with a steady flow of appropriately trained persons willing to work. The third scenario (also preferred by the present writers) suggests a gradual reunification of work and leisure into a holistic pattern characteristic of most preindustrial societies. The economic sector would be linked more closely to noneconomic forces, so that nonmaterial cultural values would tend to become the primary determinants of what we produce and consume.

CONCLUSION

After having dealt with our subject from a number of different standpoints— historical, comparative, conceptual, empirical, and theoretical—we shall try to pull the strands together by briefly reviewing the ways in which explanatory frameworks are used in the sociology of work and leisure.

Broadly, two different types of approach may be identified—the interactionist and the structural-functionalist. These two traditions of sociological explanation parallel the distinction in economics between micro and macro models, although there are some differences.

Interactionist models tend to view behavior from the standpoint of the person in the situation. Their focus is on the meaning given by a person to his own actions and the likely anticipated effect of such actions on the behavior of others. Why people make particular choices, the importance of symbolism— especially language—in shaping and mediating such choices, and the way others perceive and react to the choices made, are the questions for discussion and debate. The interactionist framework embraces a number of different emphases.

Role theory tends to stress the more formalized expectations which regulate social relationships and govern the interaction process. *Reference group theory* moves away from a mechanistic approach and seeks to explain interaction on the basis of expectations of reference groups of "significant others." *Exchange theory* focuses on the actual interaction process, and this is seen as a bargaining process in which people negotiate certain social valuables—knowledge, status, etc. *Self-identity theory* treats the self as an independent variable and as the determinant one in shaping behavior: people are said to act so as to express their "real" or "authentic" self.

These four models share the same fundamental problem: examining how the individual relates himself to the social context, which for him is the world of social reality. This, to a large extent, defines the interactionist approach to work and leisure. Work is the activity of man by which he meets the needs of himself and of his society, which affords him a degree of choice in the type of work done, and which provides him with a cultural and subcultural identity—even though this "identity" may assume the negative form of alienation from work. Leisure, by contrast, is seen as the individual's search for authenticity through a "fun" identity. It refers to those choices which express an individual's freedom from the constraints of time-related and situationally-defined obligations.

Structural-functionalist models of explanation are concerned with the ongoing and rather more enduring patterns of social relationships which constitute society. The concern is to describe and analyze the institutions and structures which form discernible patterns of social organization. Here again there is more than one emphasis: interest may focus on the social structure itself or on the functions of that structure. Structuralist explanations tend to stress the historical aspect of institutions—how they have changed over time and, in the context of a total societal model, how changes in one institution relate to changes in others. Functionalist explanations, on the other hand, usually take their starting point from existing patterns and project from these a variety of consequences for the same institutions.

The structural-functionalist view of work is in terms of work organizations, the social purposes they serve, the ways in which they recruit, train, control and motivate individuals, and the optimum conditions for the effective management of group and organizational behavior. Correspondingly, the structural-functionalist approach to leisure examines the functional and instrumental elements of leisure institutions and how these have developed as contexts through which people have expressed their "freely" chosen interests and desires.

In sketching these two explanatory frameworks, our intention has not been to make out a case for either one or the other to be regarded as more appropriate to the study of work and leisure. As Silverman (1970:40) remarks of "systems" and "action" approaches, they stress one side or other of the same coin: society makes man, man makes society. Since both sides have an element of truth, so it appears do both approaches.

REFERENCES

Anderson, N.
1961   Work and Leisure. London: Routledge.

Arendt, H.
1958   The Human Condition. Chicago: University of Chicago Press.
Argyris, C.
1973   "Personality and organization theory revisited." Administrative Science
       Quarterly (18).
Aron, R.
1968   Progress and Disillusion. London: Pall Mall Press.
Becker, H.S.
1963   Outsiders: Studies in the Sociology of Deviance. New York: Free Press.
Bell, D.
1954   "Work in the life of an American," in W. Harper, et al., Manpower
       in the United States. New York: Harper & Bros.
Bendix, R.
1963   "Work and Authority in Industry. Second Edition. New York: Harper
       & Row.
Bishop, D.W. and M. Ikeda
1970   "Status and role factors in the leisure behavior of different occupa-
       tions." Sociology and Social Research: Vol. 54, No. 2.
Blum, F.H.
1953   Toward a Democratic Work Process. New York: Harper & Bros.
Briggs, A.
1960   Mass Entertainment: The Origins of a Modern Industry. Australia:
       University of Adelaide.
Brightbill, C.K.
1960   The Challenge of Leisure. Englewood Cliffs, New Jersey: Prentice-Hall,
       Inc.
Broom, L. and J.H. Smith
1963   "Bridging occupations." British Journal of Sociology. Vol. 14, No. 4.
Brown, R.
1973   "Leisure in work," in M.A. Smith, et al., Leisure and Society in
       Britain. London: Allen Lane.
Bruce, L.
1972   How to Talk Dirty and Influence People. Chicago: Playboy Press. Re-
       print of 1965 Edition in Paper. Chicago: Playboy Press.
Burdge, R.J.
1969   "Levels of occupational prestige and leisure activity." Journal of Lei-
       sure Research. Vol. 1, No. 3.
Canon, I.C.
1967   "Ideology and occupational community." Sociology. Vol. 1, No. 2.
Caplow, T.
1964   The Sociology of Work. New York: McGraw-Hill.
Carter, R.
1970   "The myth of increasing non-work vs. work activity." Social Problems.
       Vol. 18, No. 1.
Clarke, A.C.
1956   "The use of leisure and its relation to levels of occupational prestige."
       American Sociological Review. Vol. 21, No. 3.
DeGrazia, S.
1962   Of Time, Work and Leisure. New York: Twentieth Century Fund.

Dumazedier, J.
   1960   "Current problems of the sociology of leisure." International Social
          Science Journal. Vol. 2, No. 4.
   1967   Toward a Society of Leisure. New York: Collier-Macmillan.
Dumazedier, J. and N. Latouche
   1962   "Work and leisure in French sociology." Industrial Relations. Vol. 2,
          No. 1.
Dunning, E. (ed.)
   1971   The Sociology of Sport. London: Cass.
Elias, N. and E. Dunning
   1971   "Dynamics of sport groups with special reference to football," in
          E. Dunning (ed.), The Sociology of Sport. London: Cass.
Ernst, M.L.
   1956   "New sources of energy, leisure and world culture." Proceedings of
          the International Recreation Congress. New York: National Recrea-
          tion Association.
Etzioni, A.
   1961   A Comparative Analysis of Complex Organizations. New York: Free
          Press.
Etzkorn, K.P.
   1964   "Leisure and camping: the social meaning of a form of public recrea-
          tion." Sociology and Social Research. Vol. 48, No. 4.
Filipcova, B.
   1969   "Information of the theoretical conception of the survey on leisure in
          Ostrava." Society and Leisure, European Centre for Leisure and Edu-
          cation, Bulletin No. 1.
Friedman, G.
   1960   "Leisure and technological civilization." International Social Science
          Journal. Vol. 1, No. 4.
Friedman, G. and R.J. Havighurst
   1954   The Meaning of Work and Retirement. Chicago: University of Chicago
          Press.
Gagnon, J. and W. Simon
   1968   "Sexual deviance in contemporary America." Annals of the American
          Academy of Political and Social Science (March).
Gerstl, J.E. and S.P. Hutton
   1966   Engineers: The Anatomy of a Profession. London: Tavistock Publica-
          tions.
Giddens, A.
   1964   "Notes of the concept of play and culture." Sociological Review. Vol.
          12, No. 1.
Gist, N.P. and S.F. Fava
   1964   Urban Society. New York: Crowell.
Glasser, R.
   1970   Leisure—Penalty or Prize? London: Macmillan.
Goffman, E.
   1961   Encounters. New York: Bobbs-Merrill.
Green, A.W.
   1964   Recreation, Leisure and Politics. New York: McGraw-Hill.

Greenberg, C.
  1958 "Work and leisure under industrialism," in E. Larrabee and R. Meyer-
        sohn (eds.), Mass Leisure. New York: Free Press.
Gross, E.
  1961 "A functional approach to leisure analysis." Social Problems. Vol. 9,
        No. 1.
Heckscher, A. and S. DeGrazia
  1959 "Executive leisure." Harvard Business Review (July).
Howe, I.
  1948 "Notes on mass culture." Politics (Spring).
Jary, D.
  1973 "Evenings at the ivory tower: a sociology of liberal adult education,"
        in M.A. Smith, et al. (eds.), Leisure and Society in Britain. London:
        Allen Lane.
Johnston, D.F.
  1972 "The future of work: three possible alternatives." Monthly Labor Re-
        view 95(May).
Josifovski, J.
  1970 "Work and leisure." Society and Leisure (European Centre for Lei-
        sure and Education). Bulletin No. 1.
Kaplan, M.
  1960 Leisure in America. New York: Wiley.
Kelly, J.R.
  1972 "Work and leisure: a simplified paradigm." Journal of Leisure Re-
        search 4(Winter).
Klapp, O.
  1969 Collective Search for Identity. New York: Holt, Rinehart and Winston.
Krause, E.A.
  1971 The Sociology of Occupations. Boston: Little, Brown & Co.
Landers, P.
  1969 "The growth of leisure industries." I.L.O. Panorama No. 38.
Linder, S.B.
  1970 The Harried Leisure Class. New York: Columbia University Press.
Loy, J.W. and G.S. Kenyon (eds.)
  1969 Sport, Culture and Society. New York: Collier-Macmillan.
Lueschen, G.
  1971 "Social stratification and mobility among young German sportsmen,"
        in E. Dunning (ed.), The Sociology of Sport. London: Cass.
Lundberg, G.A.
  1934 Leisure—a Suburban Study. New York: Columbia University Press.
Mandell, A.J.
  1974 "A psychiatric study of professional football." Saturday Review/World
        (October 5):12–16.
Marcuse, H.
  1964 One-Dimensional Man. London: Routledge.
Meissner, M.
  1971 "The long arm of the job: a study of work and leisure." Industrial Re-
        lations (October).
Meyersohn, R.
  1972 "Leisure," in A. Campbell (ed.), The Human Meaning of Social
        Change. New York: Russell Sage.

Mills, C.W.
   1956   White Collar. New York: Oxford University Press.
Moore, G.H. and J.N. Hedges
   1971   "Trends in labor and leisure." Monthly Labor Review (February).
Morse, N. and R. Weiss
   1955   "The function and meaning of work and the job." American Socio-
          logical Review. Vol. 20, No. 2.
Murphy, J.F.
   1973   "The future of time, work, and leisure." Parks and Recreation (No-
          vember).
Neff, W.S.
   1968   Work and Human Behavior. New York: Atherton Press.
Parker, S.R.
   1971   The Future of Work and Leisure. New York: Praeger.
   1972   "Industry and social stratification," in S.R. Parker, et al., The Sociol-
          ogy of Industry. London: Allen & Unwin.
Payne, R. and R. Cooper
   1966   "Psychology of the good footballer," New Society (July 14).
Pieper, J.
   1952   Leisure: The Basis of Culture. London: Faber.
Poor, R. (ed.)
   1970   Four Days, Forty Hours. Cambridge, Mass.: Bursk and Poor.
Prandy, K.
   1965   Professional Employees. London: Faber.
Riesman, D.
   1952   "Some observations on changes in leisure attitudes." Antioch Review,
          No. 4.
   1953   The Lonely Crowd. New York: Doubleday.
Riesman, D. and R. Denny
   1954   "Football in America: a study of cultural diffusion," in D. Riesman,
          Individualism Reconsidered. New York: Free Press.
Riesman, D. and W. Blomberg
   1957   "Work and leisure: fusion or polarity?", in C.M. Arensberg, et al.
          (eds.), Research in Industrial Human Relations. New York: Free Press.
Roberts, K.
   1970   Leisure. London: Longman.
Sage, G.H. (ed.)
   1970   Sport and American Society. Boston: Addison-Wesley.
Seligman, B.B.
   1965   "On work, alienation and leisure." American Journal of Economics and
          Sociology (October).
Silverman, D.
   1970   The Theory of Organizations. London: Heinemann.
Smigel, E.O. (ed.)
   1963   Work and Leisure. New Haven, Conn.: College and University Press.
Soule, G.F.
   1957   "The economics of leisure." Annals of the American Academy of Po-
          litical and Social Science (September).
Stone, G.F.
   1958   "American sports: play and dis-play," in E. Larrabee and R. Meyer-
          sohn (eds.), Mass Leisure. New York: Free Press.

Taylor, M.L.
  1968   Occupational Sociology. New York: Oxford University Press.
Tilgher, A.
  1931   Work: What It Has Meant to Men Through the Ages. London: Harrap.
Tunstall, J.
  1962   The Fisherman. London: MacGibbon and Kee.
Vogel, E.F.
  1963   Japan's New Middle Class. Berkeley: University of California Press.
Wax, R.H.
  1958   "Free time in other cultures," in W. Donahue, et al. (eds.), Free Time:
         Challenge to Later Maturity. Ann Arbor: University of Michigan Press.
Weinberg, S.K. and H. Arond
  1952   "The occupational culture of the boxer." American Journal of So-
         ciology. Vol. 57, No. 5.
White, R.C.
  1955   "Social class differences in the use of leisure." American Journal of
         Sociology. Vol. 61, No. 2.
Whyte, W.F.
  1948   Human Relations in the Restaurant Industry. New York: McGraw-Hill.
Wilensky, H.
  1964   "Mass society and mass culture: interdependence or independence?",
         American Sociological Review. Vol. 29, No. 2.
Wippler, R.
  1969   Social Determinants of Leisure Behavior. Netherlands: University of
         Groningen.
Wolff, K.H. (ed.)
  1964   The Sociology of George Simmel. New York: Free Press.
Worsley, P., et al.
  1970   Introducing Sociology. London: Penguin.

PART II

WORK AND THE INDIVIDUAL

INTRODUCTION—PART II

There are two central concerns in Part II. The first is to deal with the important issue of adult socialization, and especially the subject of socialization to work. The second concern is the relationship between working and the individual's career.

It has been a relatively recent development to envision the possibility that adults undergo significant socialization when they move into new environments. The Freudian emphasis on the critical importance of early childhood socialization has been such a dominant theme that it acted as a brake on analysis of socialization throughout the life-cycle. We have now broken the grip of the Freudian outlook in order to turn attention to socialization as a continuous process to be found at all stages of life-history.

Of special importance for this volume is the analysis of adult socialization in the world of work. Industry needs particular human skills, and when these are not forthcoming from the labor force, the skills have to be developed on the job. In addition there are values and norms, special to each work organization, that need to be learned so new members will fit in quickly as effective participants. Just as the military socializes citizens to make them become effective soldiers, so does the work organization face the need to socialize its recruits as part of making them productive employees.

One of the payoffs of working is the career that each individual derives from his participation in the world of work. Much of the citizen's status in society is derived from his occupation. For those citizens who value their social position, the choice of an occupation and the move up the occupational ladder are critical to the unfolding of their life-history. Indeed, probably a significant portion of discontent with work may be traceable to unfulfilled expectations about career advancement.

From the standpoint of the work organization, the management and manipulation of careers are important ingredients among the incentives offered for working. The promise of a higher position on the occupational ladder at some future time continues to be a standard incentive to join an organization as employee, and then to work toward the achievement of promotions.

Implicit in the analysis of adult socialization to work and work careers is the notion that the individual is being acted upon in the interests of the work organization. It is presumed that the individual will be adaptive and responsive to the socializing efforts of the organization, and that he will do his share of work, and more, in anticipation of movement up an occupational ladder.

CHAPTER 3

Breaking In: Socialization to Work

John Van Maanen

Massachusetts Institute of Technology

INTRODUCTION

This chapter analyzes an ubiquitous process, organizational socialization. The primary, though not exclusive, focus is upon man's occupational milieu, which, in temporal terms, can only be challenged by the family environment as the locus of adult behavior. For most people, work is more than forty hours out of the week, it is a routinized pattern of actions that largely determine one's way of life.[1] And as Hughes (1958a) has written, "a man's work is as good a clue as any to the cause of his life, his social being and his identity."

In general, social theorists have designated the social and psychological adjustment of men to their work settings as occupational socialization (Moore, 1969). However, as Drucker (1968) points out, the imperatives of industrialization have left western man living increasingly in an "employee society." In fact, Tausky (1970) cites statistical evidence revealing that almost 90% of the labor force in the United States is employed in organizations. Throughout this analysis, the term *organizational socialization* will be preferred to the term *occupational socialization* because it directs attention to the dominant setting in which the process occurs. Although the two socialization processes are often interdependent, the position taken in this chapter is that the characteristics of the socialization setting are far more crucial to the eventual outcomes of the process than are the specific occupational attributes to be inculcated. As Schein (1961, 1962, 1963, 1967, 1968a) has observed repeatedly, the results of "indoctrination" settings are remarkably similar regardless of differences among organizations.

Organizational socialization refers to the process by which a person learns the values, norms and required behaviors which permit him to participate as a member of the organization. Presumably, this process is continuous throughout an individual's career with the organization. Erickson (1950:57) perceptively recognized this dynamic feature of socialization when he noted that

---

[1] This theme of "situational determinism" is a common one in the work-related literature. For example, Porter and Lawler (1968) suggested that a man's work largely explains where he will live, with whom he will associate and even what his children will become.

"identity is never gained nor maintained once and for all." Consequently, a plasticity factor or an adjustment capability of men under most conditions is central to the thesis presented here.[2] As Becker (1964:44) stated:

> A person as he moves in and out of a variety of social settings learns the requirements of continuing in each situation and of success in it.

Related to the postulated learning process, organizational socialization also implies that a man may be forced to relinquish certain attitudes, values, and behaviors. Schein (1968a) succinctly refers to this aspect as the "price of membership." At its best, organizational socialization results in the matching or melding of individual and organizational pursuits. At its worst, the process may lead to rejection by the individual of the expressed requirements of the organization. In the modal case, however, the process may be thought to result in a "psychological contract" mediating the ends of the individual and the constraints and purposes of the organization. In a sense, this "psychological contract" is a *modus vivendi* between the individual and the organization and represents the outcomes of the socialization process. Indeed, such outcomes are critical in the determination of an individual's attachment, productivity and satisfaction with the organization.

At a higher level of abstraction, Brim (1966) has argued persuasively that man has *no* deep personality characteristics which persist over all social situations. Man, therefore, is always in the process of "becoming."[3] This framework implies that the individual constructs "reality" anew each time he encounters a novel behavioral setting.

The available research evidence offers general support for the proposition which claims that the explanations for human nature are located directly in the interplay among phenomenological and social structural variables. Becker and Strauss (1956:262) bluntly state,

> Central to any account of adult identity is the relationship of change in identity to a change in social position.

To date, a major deficiency in organizational socialization research is the overwhelming reliance upon descriptive theories of group and individual change. As Bennis, et al. (1969) pointed out, most organizational socialization theories are similar to "astronomer's models" (i.e., they describe the process

---

[2] One's adjustment to a situation can be viewed as a rule of behavior common to all social settings. Simply stated, this rule requires one to "fit in" (Goffman, 1963). Yet, what "fits in" in one context may be entirely inappropriate in another. Hence, one must learn what is expected of him in a particular setting (or class of settings) if he is not to be *de trop* or "out of place."

[3] My use of the term "becoming" should not be confused with notions such as personality development, individual maturation or self-actualization. True, as settings change, the individual learns new skills (social or otherwise). But, this perspective should not suggest that I have in mind any grand scheme which would permit man to achieve a sort of personal nirvanna in his lifetime. Here, the term must be viewed in terms of its common linguistic usages. Hence, "becoming" simply notes that one "becomes" a doctor, a convict, a "bright young man," or a "devil's advocate" depending largely upon the circumstances which surround him at any particular moment. A terse but valuable statement related to this perspective can be located in McHugh's (1969) work on situational definitions.

in terms of nonmanipulable factors). These descriptive "models" resemble case studies in that they are situationally specific (e.g., professional schools, scientific organizations, fraternities, etc.). Little work has been directed toward the development of predictive socialization models; theories or strategies which are transituationally applicable. This chapter attempts to address the generality problem by drawing together diverse theoretical and empirical considerations into a broadly conceived portrait of organizational socialization.[4]

The analysis begins with a theoretical discussion of the socialization process as a whole, of which organizational socialization is a part. The emphasis in the first section is upon the individual and provides the conceptual framework necessary for a discussion of personal change in adulthood. Section two utilizes Schein's (1968a, b) model of the organization—featuring the related constructs of "boundaries" and "passages"—to describe the setting in which socialization occurs. The third section summarizes much of the relevant literature pertaining to particular phases in the socialization process and discusses the major contingencies which may affect the outcomes of each of these phases. The fourth section outlines several institutionalized methods of organizational socialization and hints at their probable results. Section five encounters the knotty problem of "inefficacious" socialization, stressing the types of dysfunctional outcomes which may result. Finally, section six summarizes the chapter and suggests areas where further research is needed.

I. ORGANIZATIONAL SOCIALIZATION AS ADULT SOCIALIZATION

In the introduction a general interpretation was presented which emphasized continuous social learning as a fundamental characteristic of organizational socialization. In this section, it will be shown that organizational socialization is best viewed as a special division of the more general adult socialization model. As such, the focus will be upon the individual's adjustment to role demands as a way of characterizing socialization through the life-cycle.

Brim (1966) postulates a conception of personality which relates the features of the socialization setting to the consequences for the individual(s) involved. Taking role-acquisition as the central concern of socialization, Brim views personality in terms of a person's perception of self and his behavior in relation to the social organization in which he acts. His conception of "self-other" systems is distinctly sociological and focuses upon learned interpersonal relationships. Hence, the socialization process is seen by Brim (1966:9) as:

> The manner in which an individual learns the behavior appropriate to his position in a group, through interaction with others who hold normative beliefs about what his role should be and who reward or punish him for correct or incorrect actions.

---

[4] Indeed, the proper study of socialization requires the convergence of many disciplines. In general, research in this area leads one ultimately to a consideration of the perennial question of the social sciences; namely, how is social order established and maintained? While this paper does not directly address this question, it is interesting to note that such seminal social theorists as Durkheim, Marx, Weber, Simmel, Freud and Parsons consider socialization processes to be the threads which hold the fabric of society together.

The major factor at all levels of socialization is "taking the role of other" and attempting to determine what the other's response will be toward one's own behavior. This leads to a perspective on personality as a learned set of "self-other" systems which become increasingly complex as the individual is required to learn more and more roles throughout his lifetime.

Using a simple grammatical typology, self-other systems are I-me, they-me, and I-them relationships. At the core of one's personality are the I-me relationships which Brim claims are usually laid down early in one's lifetime. These I-me relationships were generated originally from they-me and I-them relationships. However, the specific they or them is no longer recalled. This is similar to Mead's (1930) conception of the generalized other in which the person generalizes the sources of information derived about one's self. The I-me relationships can be said to represent the individual's self-image or identity.

The implications of such a model are clear. In Brim's (1966:16) words:

> The self-other relationships lead to an individual's appraisal of himself as being good or bad, according to the degree to which he lives up to another's expectation. The importance of the self-appraisal to the individual varies according to the significance of the other person's evaluation of him, which, in turn, is based, in the last analysis, on the degree to which the other controls (or once controlled) rewards and punishments. The consequences of self-appraisal and of perceived adequacies or inadequacies is to increase or decrease an individual's self-esteem.

The maintenance of self-esteem, consequently, occurs via the pursuit of a certain level of competence on an expected task for which the appraiser is either a significant other or one's self. Such tasks are the crucial determinants of one's identity.

As a person moves through the life-cycle, the expectations of others change, new demands are made upon the individual, and behavioral settings shift. For example, such significant others as colleagues at work, teachers, family members and employers subtly (or not so subtly) request the individual to change. To meet these altered or novel claims upon one's identity, the individual must learn to act out new roles. Brim presents an excellent description regarding the nature and content of these implied personal changes in adulthood. Brim (1966:25) notes:

> There are three things a person requires before he is able to perform satisfactorily in a role. He must know what is expected of him, he must be able to meet the role requirements, and he must desire to practice the behavior and pursue the appropriate ends.

The purpose of socialization, then, consists of providing an individual with knowledge, ability and motivation to play a defined role, regardless of whether the target role is father, student, child, prisoner or priest. At the abstract level, this process is accomplished by alterations and extensions of one's self-other systems.

The emphasis on developmental socialization underscores the dictum that there is more difference in the *content* of socialization than there is in the *form* of socialization as the individual moves from childhood to adulthood. Brim outlines several of these changes in content. First, there is a shift in emphasis from values and motives toward a concern for overt behavior. Second, these changes require less of an adaption to new material than they call for a synthesis of old material. Third, there is an increase in specificity as adult socialization aims toward filling roles, positions and statuses. Fourth, there arc fewer I-me relationships in the later stages of the life-cycle. However, Brim notes that the limiting effects of childhood are usually overemphasized. He states (1966:18):

> Not uncommonly, dramatic shifts in identity occur at later states of the life-cycle, since significant persons or experiences may have an unusual impact on a person's appraisal of his own basic characteristics.

The fifth type of change pertains to the individual's development of methods to mediate conflicting demands. Brim calls these methods metaprescriptions and they generally take the form of situationally specific guidelines or roles of action (e.g., when X occurs, withdraw; or, when Y occurs, compromise). Finally, the sixth change postulated is a transformation from idealism to realism. Brim (1966:29) comments:

> As the child matures, he is taught to realize that there is a distinction between the ideal and the real, and learns to take his part in society according to the realistic expectations of others, rather than attempting conformity to ideal norms.

It follows from Brim's model that the extent to which adult socialization attempts are successful is more or less dependent upon preceeding stages. A simple example is given below which is designed to illustrate the progressive characteristic of socialization generally as well as denoting some tactics available to organizations which may influence the outcomes of the process.

In police training academies, a recruit is typically given his service revolver and told how to operate the weapon. The assumptions in this process are implicit and pertain to two critical aspects of the socialization paradigm. The first assumption is that the recruit already possesses the necessary hand/eye coordination and strength to fire the revolver. The second assumption, and perhaps more important to the police organization, is that the recruit desires to participate in the organization and understands and supports the ideology or values associated with the use of the weapon (e.g., it is proper to use the revolver for the protection of one's own life or to prevent a suspected felon from escaping). If the recruit demonstrates that he is unable to operate the weapon, the training program seeks to upgrade his skills. If he is unwilling to spend the time learning this skill, then motivational devices are used to induce the appropriate spirit through the use of special rewards and punishments (e.g., withhold a portion of the recruit's pay, or assign him extra duty). If it appears, however, that education about the values is required, the individual is coached, pressured, or otherwise persuaded to accept the general values of the organization. If the recruit still has problems accepting the values, he is usually dismissed from the organization, although it is conceivable that therapeutic procedures might be instituted to solve this dilemma (e.g., special counseling with the police chaplain). Only in the most extreme case is the recruit assumed not to be motivated toward the appropriate subcultural values. In this case the recruit is immediately dismissed and stigmatized.

While the foregoing paragraph is admittedly a distortion of one aspect of the socialization processes in police organizations, it does suggest that socialization processes can be typified by the extent to which the organization is willing to exert effort in influencing the individual to acquire the knowledge, abilities and motivation required if the person is to play the organizationally assigned role. As will be discussed in the following sections, most organizations are principally concerned with acquainting the participant with the role demands and observing the resulting behavior. Little attention is normally paid to the individual's underlying motivation or his general value structure. On the other hand, some organizations (e.g., total institutions) are characterized by the attention they pay to such latent characteristics as values and motivation (Goffman, 1959; Wallace, 1971).[5] For example, when an army recruit continues to disobey direct orders, he is often sent for what is referred to institutionally as "motivational therapy." Hence, adult socialization settings can be viewed as lying on a continuum from those concerned primarily with overt behavior to those concerned with all facets of the general socialization equation. As will be seen later, most organizations simultaneously occupy different positions on the scale depending upon the centrality (or importance) of a particular role demanded of an organizational participant.

While Brim's notions of personal change provide a useful paradigm for thinking about the underlying processes, his theory is noticeably silent regarding the explicit characteristics of socialization. Relatedly, a more damning criticism can be directed at the unobservable nature of his self-other systems. Like Freud's id, ego, and superego, Brim's I-me, they-me and I-them systems are not subject to empirical verification. They reside solely within the person and, as such, their existence must be taken as an article of faith.

To avoid some of these difficulties, other theorists have directed attention toward the more readily observable aspects of human behavior. For example, cultural values (such as those embodied by Brim's I-me relationships) have been described by Becker and Carper (1956a, 1956b) as entailing only a potential effect upon behavior. In their view, it is the manifest subcultural values which grow around specific roles and identities relevant to a designated setting that are the most important determinants of behavior.

While Brim does not discuss this nuance, it is possible to incorporate this construct into his general theory. By refining the concepts of adult role-learning into smaller sequences and combinations of the numerous adjustments a person makes to others' expectations (e.g., what occurs in face-to-face encounters), one may perceive the larger role (e.g., employee in company X) as composed of the smaller roles one must act out (e.g., "boss" to employee A; "apprentice" to employee B; "colleague" to employee C; and so on). Consequently, when an individual enters a particular socialization setting, he may possess a basic set of self-other relationships pertaining to the values of the larger culture(s)

---

[5] Attempts to modify individual values and motives are, of course, not limited to the so-called total institutions. During the past decade or so, many business firms, public bureaucracies, educational institutions and voluntary organizations have experimented with techniques designed expressly to change participant self-conceptions. For example, proponents of "T-Groups," "Organizational Development," "Consciousness Raising," and "Team Building" unabashedly make use of procedures aimed at modifying certain suppositions persons hold about themselves and others. See Chapter 14, this volume: G. Strauss, "Organizational Development."

in which he participates. However, as he gains experience with the new setting, numerous smaller roles are learned—presumably through the generation of explicit they-me or I-them relationships. Conceivably, the characteristics of the setting may convince the individual to alter some of his core I-me identities which had previously gone unquestioned. For example, Goffman (1959) suggests that when a person consistently fails to receive confirmation for a particular face he presents in a defined situation, the individual may begin searching for a new face which will then provide confirmation of self. Thus, while the general format of Brim's (1966) analysis is sound, its usefulness is increased by the explicit recognition that for the model to be operationalized, it must first be broken down into segments which have meaning in the everyday world.[6]

Within this framework, the tenets of expectancy theory (as postulated by Fishbein, 1961, 1963; Rotter, 1955, 1956; Vroom, 1964; Porter and Lawler, 1968; and Mitchell and Biglan, 1971) provide the needed theoretical linkage between the characteristics of the socialization setting and the consequences for the individuals involved.[7] Essentially, the position taken here is that by tying together expectancy theory with a less eclectic version of Brim's theory of personal change, a serviceable general model of the socialization process will result. Such a model presumably will be subject to empirical tests and be grounded well within the day-to-day environment (work setting or otherwise) experienced by the person.

In simplified fashion, expectancy theory postulates that an individual is motivated to perform a particular role to the extent that the individual visualizes him- or herself capable of performing the role *and* to the extent that the person perceives performance of the role leading to favorable outcomes. In work-settings, the research to date indicates that the values and motives individuals bring with them to organizations are remarkably similar (e.g., Dunnette, et al., 1969; Porter, et al., 1972; Schein, 1962, 1967). The research also indicates that the values and motives considered to be most important by the individual deal largely with the "intrinsic" characteristics of the situation (i.e., in work organizations, such factors as job challenge, the ability to use valued skills, a sense of accomplishment, opportunities to get ahead, etc. are of primary importance—see Herzberg, et al., 1957; Vroom, 1964; Porter and Lawler, 1968; Smith, Kendall and Hulin, 1969). Furthermore, the values and motives one

---

[6] For example, it may be helpful to postulate a distinction between an individual's "hard" and "soft" identities. Hard identities refer to the enduring, relatively obvious "faces" a person presents across all situations (e.g., a priest is generally expected to be thoughtful, attentive and sympathetic, whether he is at a cocktail party or behind the pulpit). Soft identities, however, refer to those relatively short-lived, adjustable "faces" a person presents for specific occasions (e.g., the Machiavellian salesman whose skillful "virtu" enables him to be somber and reliable with some clients, jovial and reckless with others). In Brim's analysis, hard identities are the I-me relationships (one's "character") whereas the they-me, I-them relationships are associated with soft identities (one's "skills"). This perspective has the advantage of focusing attention upon managed impressions created by the social actor as a means of coping with situational demands.

[7] Without delving too deeply into the theoretical issues involved, most approaches to the socialization process suffer from built-in disciplinary biases. Sociologists, for example, stress the structural features of the process which lead to common outcomes, while psychologists emphasize the intrapsychic variables which lead to differential outcomes. Social psychologists, on the other hand, concern themselves with attitude states, often overlooking behavioral elements. What I am attempting to accomplish in this chapter is to integrate these approaches in a manner which neither ignores nor focuses inordinate attention upon either the structural or individual aspects of the socialization process.

brings with him to the work setting (*vis-à-vis* the available rewards) are relatively stable across time (Porter, et al., 1972; Van Maanen, 1972; Schein, 1961, 1962, 1967; Scott, 1965).

From Brim's perspective, these values and motives represent fundamental aspects of the I-me relationships. Their stability suggests a common understanding and acceptance of the larger cultural values upon which one's continuance in the organization depends. Indeed, in most settings, these I-me relationships are indeed crucial if any organizational socialization is to occur. Yet they tell us very little about what actually takes place within socialization settings. What expectancy theory adds to this area of study is the mechanism by which individuals become motivated to perform *specific* role demands— an explanation and delineation of role specific behavior. Therefore, the outcomes of the organizational socialization processes are determined largely by the organization's ability to select and utilize methods which communicate to the participants—in a clear and precise manner—what relevant role behaviors will lead to the available valued rewards.

The manifest subcultural values of the organization (pertaining to the roles surrounding a person's "fitting in") then rest upon latent cultural values (such as one's desire to satisfy the expectations of others). However, these I-me type values have, through experience, been partitioned into more explicit norms like "getting along with one's fellow workers" or "accomplishing something worthwhile." Since these norms were implanted early and reinforced in a positive manner throughout one's lifetime, it should be expected that little change —at least in the short run—would occur in these values. Consequently, most organizational learning depends upon they-me or I-them type relationships and are thus peripheral to one's core "personality."[8] It is these relationships which comprise the manifest subcultural values of the setting. In expectancy theory terms, such relationships represent consensual beliefs regarding activities necessary to gain valued rewards.

In general, the literature concerned with adult socialization appears to support the analysis presented here. Schein's (1968a, b) conception of the individual as an "integrated set of social selves organized around a basic concept of self" is consistent with Brim's self-other systems. Based on extensive research involved with adult socialization, Schein (1968a) feels individuals "construct" social selves which allow them to fulfill various role expectations. Furthermore, he points out that the rules governing behavior are culturally determined, yet there is considerable latitude given in each situation. Sounding much like Brim, Schein (1968b:13) states:

> The changes occurring in a person as a result of adult socialization are changes in the nature and integration of his social self although it is unlikely that the basic character structure will undergo much change.

Another theorist, Caplow (1964:169), defines organization socialization as follows:

---

[8] It is possible, of course, that over time these relationships may become generalized and result in either an extension or shift in one's self-conception. As Brim noted, it is not impossible for one to drastically alter his identity—although such occurrences are relatively rare and can usually be traced to a "climactic" or "catastrophic" event (e.g., divorce, religious conversion, loss of a job, death of a loved one, etc.).

An organizationally directed process that prepares and qualifies individuals to occupy organizational position.

Successful organizational socialization to Caplow provides the individual with: (1) new self-images, (2) new involvements, (3) new values, and (4) new accomplishments. The motivational aspects are largely built into the process via selection or anticipatory socialization (i.e., role preparation which has occurred prior to the individual's formal induction into the organization). In other words, most organizations (especially work organizations) assume the individual possesses a basic desire to participate and a willingness to acquire a new role.

Becker and his associates (1956, 1960, 1961, 1964) view adult socialization from a strong structuralist position. This perspective is perhaps best exemplified by the following quote dealing with socialization settings (Becker, 1964:47):

It is enough to create situations which coerce people into behaving as we want them to and then create conditions under which rewards will become linked to continuing this behavior.

More so than either Brim, Schein, Caplow or the expectancy theory group, Becker stresses the argument that explanations for deep or even superficial "personality" characteristics must be sought in the social structure. Hence, adult socialization consists largely of the person turning himself into the kind of individual the situation necessitates. And the success of this process is dependent upon one's developing knowledge, skills and motivation.[9]

Using the metaphor of a "side bet," Becker (1960) offers an explanation of how consistent behavior emerges from socialization settings. He suggests that socialization settings normally require the individual to invest heavily in certain "counters" (e.g., money, time, public commitment, etc.) which originally were external to the decision to participate. However, the outcome of these "side bets," over time, become tied to the individual's continued participation. Hence, the success of the socialization process—insofar as it is designed to induce consistent behavior in persons—depends upon the size and importance of the "side bets" made by the individual.[10]

At this juncture, our view of socialization—which, in effect, is a partial model of the individual—emphasizes *situational adjustments* made by the per-

---

[9] The "structuralist" position is illustrated by Becker's notions on adult role learning. In his view, the structural setting in which socialization is designed to occur literally defines the nature of the outcomes. For example, if persons are to be processed (i.e., socialized) collectively, the situational adjustments nearly always have the character of "what everyone knows to be true" (i.e., the group develops a consensus as to the approach to be taken regarding reoccurring strains or tensions inherent in the setting). To my mind, the danger of this approach lies in its inability to handle differential responses to a particular socialization setting (i.e., deviant cases). Consequently, individual constructs such as abilities and motivation are necessary for a comprehensive theory of socialization.

[10] It should be noted that "side bets" have differential payoffs. I suspect that it is not so much the size of the original investment that determines the outcome, but rather it is the size of the expected reward or possible loss. Consequently, the larger the payoff, the more motivated (and constrained) the individual.

son to altered or novel settings.[11] Through the manipulation of one's self-other systems, the person makes himself suitable for participation in an organization. Operationally, this means the individual develops a specific set of beliefs that link his activities to the valued rewards in his situation. The perceived attainment of these rewards demonstrate to the person his competence upon which his self-concepts are ultimately based. Whereas varied situations provide opportunity for personal change, commitment processes in these situations constrain and stabilize behavior. Importantly, this perspective on socialization attributes personal change in organizations to the external demands of others placed upon the social actor in various situations throughout the course of his or her "career." It is to this "career" concept that attention is now directed.

Careers

Glaser (1968) notes that occupational careers refer to patterned paths of mobility—where they may take people within a particular occupation. Organizational careers refer to specific routes offered by organizations to their members. As such, the notion of a career implies simply a sequence of activities with a natural history. Becker and Strauss (1956) felt it was useful to visualize organizational careers as a set of "streams" or "escalators." For example, one individual could be characterized as going up or going down a particular escalator. However, individuals may also become "frozen" between escalators and remain in one location for an extended period of time. Furthermore, there are often multiple routes to a particular position. In light of the emphasis placed upon structural variables as determinants of behavior, the concept of organizational careers is quite valuable as a frame of reference for examining personal change.

Schein (1968b) distinguishes organizational careers as a series of separate experiences and adventures through which a person passes during his association with an organization. He sees this process as constituting a major part of adult socialization in organizations. However, Schein (1968b:14) states that the organization views careers differently. He notes:

> To the organization, a career is a set of expectations held by individuals inside the organization which guide their decisions about whom to move, when, how, and at what speed.

Thus careers may be viewed from a number of perspectives. While focusing upon the "entrance" aspect of an individual's career, Merton, et al., (1957:68) noted the interrelatedness of various career perspectives:

> What is considered occupational choice from the standpoint of the individual becomes the process of recruitment from the standpoint of the profession and the allocation of personnel in various occupational statuses from the standpoint of society. What the individual defines as

---

11 This framework suggests that perhaps the more important units of analysis in the investigation of socialization are the smaller encounters, episodes and situations rather than the individual or the organization. By and large, these units have been neglected in most studies. However, for some notable exceptions, see Glaser and Strauss (1965, 1968), Sudnow (1966), Spradley (1970), Humphries (1970), and Manning (1970).

a promising opportunity afforded by the labor market, the profession defines as an acute shortage, the society as an imbalance of occupational distribution.

Clearly, the career concept has many interpretations depending upon the "eye of the beholder." Each interpretation provides a set of expectations regarding a person's career. The degree to which such expectations converge is determined, in part, by the set of experiences both the organization and the individual go through when the person is first introduced to the existing system. The importance of this initial set of experiences in determining how both the individual and the organization will view one's career cannot be understated.

Thus the organizational socialization process—emphasizing the transfer of knowledge, abilities and motivation—necessarily involves the creation of expectations regarding careers. For the individual, these expectations, gleaned from multiple sources in the organization, are crucial inputs to a man's identity and behavior. Focusing upon careers leads to a concern for such variables as timetracks, boundaries, coaches and turning points. As the remainder of this chapter will indicate, these concerns are vital to any account of organizational socialization.

II. THE SETTING: A MODEL OF THE ORGANIZATION

The description of the occupational and organizational milieu of research scientists by Glaser serves as an excellent illustration of the numerous relationships that are involved if one is to avoid oversimplifying the linkages between the individual and the work setting. Glaser (1964:85) states:

> When the scientist affiliates with an organization, he does so within a *set of concentric social units or groups* of which the organization is just one. By joining the *organization*, he locates himself in a *community* of science. The communities of science (clusters of similar research contexts) are roughly graded by the scientific prestige and in turn locate the scientists in the *world* of science. Within the organization, the scientist is placed in another location group, an institute focused on the study of a particular disease or family of diseases, which itself is well known in the community of science. Within the institute he joins a *laboratory* and works in a *section*. Within the section he becomes part of an *informal work group* of professional associates.

Although Glaser's paradigm is situationally specific, it neatly displays the complexity of an occupational environment. This section is concerned with presenting a model of such environments which allows for a description of an individual's career within an organization. Such a model will be shown to have an isomorphic relationship with the conception of organizational socialization which was outlined in the first section. While attention here is directed toward the organization, irrespective of its location along various dimensions in the larger societal context, such considerations as status of the organization, purpose of the organization, interorganizational relationships, and so on may have a major effect upon the form, content and outcomes of the socialization processes. However, discussion of these aspects is reserved for a later portion of this chapter.

A three-dimensional model of the organization focusing upon structural characteristics of the organization has been developed by Schein (1968b). He schematically perceives the organization to be conical in shape with the major variables of the individual's relationship within the work organization representing the three dimensions. The vertical dimension involves the notion of an individual's rank or level within the organization. The radial dimension connotes an assessment of one's centrality within the organization and the circumferential dimension concerns the functional responsibilities of the individual. All organizations are considered to have a somewhat unique structure ("tall," "flat," "bent," etc.) with regard to these dimensions.

Central to this model is the related concept of boundaries as they apply to an individual's career. Since career movement within the organization can occur along any or all of the above dimensions, there are three generic types of boundaries.[12] It is possible, therefore, to view a person's organizational career as a series of boundary passages.

In Schein's view, there are certain structural considerations which are likely to affect the salience and importance of the socialization process. For example, individuals probably are more vulnerable to the organization's socialization efforts just before and just following a particular boundary passage—especially if the person is motivated in a favorable direction toward the shift in level, centrality or function.[13] Or, organizational socialization is likely to be more intense when an individual passes through hierarchical or inclusion boundaries. This latter hypothesis assumes that the organization is most concerned about a member's values and attitudes at the point where it grants more authority and centrality.

Recognizing that organizational socialization occurs at all career stages, the remainder of this chapter will be devoted primarily to a consideration of the individual's *entry* into the organization. Since this crucial passage involves movement across all major types of boundaries, it is of central importance within Schein's scheme. During this "breaking in" period, the organization may be thought to be most persuasive, for the individual has few guidelines—other than what the immediate situation supplies—to direct his behavior and has little, if any, organizationally based support for his "identities" which may be the object of influence. Hence, the initiation of an outsider into the organization is indeed a stressful period (Van Maanen, 1972; Gregg, 1972; Schein, 1968a,b; Kahn, et al., 1964; Becker, et al., 1961).

Some Consequences

A wide range of studies indicate that early organizational experiences are a major determinant of one's later organizationally relevant beliefs, attitudes

---

[12] While these boundaries are conceptually distinct, in practice, they nearly always overlap. Yet, the model is useful for it directs attention to the interplay among dimensions. For example, the organizational practice of promoting persons "up and out" (i.e., promotion to the organizational hinterlands) implies promotion across the hierarchical boundaries may not be accompanied by movement across the centrality dimension.

[13] Some observers note, however, that these periods allow the individual greater freedom from organizational influence. For example, most organizations grant the newcomer a "grace period" during which one's actions are relatively free from censure. Furthermore, in coercive organizations (e.g., mental hospitals, prisons, etc.), initiates and persons about to be released are considered typically to be beyond the purview of the organization (i.e., the least likely persons in the setting to be influenced by the perspectives carried by the majority of others in the institution—see Irwin, 1970; Goffman, 1961; Wheeler, 1961).

and behaviors (Herzberg, et al., 1957; Schein, 1961, 1962, 1965; Berlew and Hall, 1966; Denhardt, 1968; Dunnette, et al., 1969; Vroom and Deci, 1971). The perceptive comments of Hughes (1958a) concerning the early organizational experiences of professional persons are of special interest in this regard. Hughes (1958a:119–120) states:

> The period of initiation into the role appears to be one wherein the two cultures [i.e. professional and organizational] interact within the individual. Such interaction undoubtedly goes on all through life, but it seems to be more lively—more exciting and uncomfortable, more self-conscious and yet perhaps more deeply unconscious—in the period of learning and initiation.

Berlew and Hall (1966) lend further support for this contention by way of an empirical validation of the critical nature of the early organizational learning period. They found that the performance of managers in several industrial organizations was strikingly dependent upon the nature of their induction into the firm. Specifically, the relationship they found was a strong association between early job challenge and later job performance. The conclusion reached by the authors is interesting from the standpoint of its relationship to Hughes' comments. Berlew and Hall (1966:222–223) noted:

> ... the first year is a critical period for learning, a time when the trainee is uniquely ready to develop or change in the direction of the company's expectations. This year would be analogous to the critical period, probably between six and eighteen months, when human infants must either experience a close emotional relationship with another human being or suffer ill effects ranging from psychosis to an inability ever to establish such a relationship ... no organization can afford to treat this critical period lightly.

Some further evidence for the critical nature of the "breaking in" process is presented by Irwin's (1970) excellent study of felon careers. He notes that for a "fish" (i.e., a first offender), the person's long term orientation to imprisonment was strikingly dependent upon very early jailing experiences—the first few weeks "in the joint." To Irwin, the socialization process was characterized by a strand of continuity based upon identities and perspectives acquired during the initial stages of one's incarceration.[14]

The critical nature of the early organizational experience can be related to the developing theory of adult socialization as presented so far in this chapter. When a person first enters an organization, that portion of his life-space corresponding to many of the specific role demands of the organization is blank. Depending upon the neophyte's general values and motivations, he may feel a

---

[14] An insightful analysis of adult socialization processes is provided by Lyman and Scott (1970). They view initiation settings in terms of the manner in which the novice experiences and manages "stagefright." Such "stagefright" occurs precisely because one's claimed identity becomes open to public scrutiny. Like stage actors, individuals in many organizational settings may well experience apprehension regarding their competence to perform adequately in a target role, and, therefore, are receptive to clues originating from others in the environment which may aid them in the social drama. From this position, socialization is viewed in terms of the coping strategies developed by neophytes (e.g., rehearsals, strict adherence to the rules, etc.).

strong desire to define the expectations of others (i.e., the organization, the work group, the supervisor, etc.) and develop constructs relating himself to these expectations. One researcher has called this process building a "mental map" of the organization (Avery, 1968). In most organizations, it can be assumed that the recruit has some *a priori* motivation for membership. Consequently, the new member is extremely receptive to influence while he searches for information and identification models on the basis of which he can change in a manner in which he feels the organization expects him to change. It is the organization's challenge to find the means in which this process may be facilitated.

The stage has now been set for the discussion of some specific outcomes and the related contingencies which are associated with phases of organizational socialization. Up to this point, the concern has largely been with the general framework in which socialization processes may be viewed. Section Three addresses the more pragmatic questions dealing with "when," "how," and "under what conditions" does organizational socialization operate.

III. TRANSFORMATIONS: PHASES AND CONTINGENCIES

While this section deals with the individual's initial passage into the organization, most of the socialization phases and contingencies discussed below are applicable to all "boundary passages" associated with an individual's organizational career. Consequently, the following topics must be considered to have wider implications than application only to the organizational entry processes.

The ensuing discussion is organized around three conceptually distinct problems that the individual about to enter an organization must implicitly or explicitly address. The first problem to be considered revolves around the pre-entry topic of organizational choice. The variables of interest in this portion are linked to an analysis of *anticipatory socialization*. The second problem deals with the notion of entry and embraces a general process labelled *encounter*. The variables examined in this portion are largely structural in nature. The third problem deals with the extent of personal change necessary for continuance in the organization and is called *metamorphosis*. The variables involved in this portion are primarily individual and pertain to the outcomes of the organizational socialization process.[15]

To a large degree, the variables introduced in each problem area are overlapping. Furthermore, these variables are interdependent and often imply a causal ordering. For example, anticipatory socialization influences the individual's perception of the legitimacy of the organizational socialization efforts, which, in turn, influence the degree to which the individual will comply with the organizational directives during later periods of his career. Also, many of the variables must be viewed as affecting the outcomes of all three stages. Thus, the factors which influence organizational choice may also influence the

---

[15] The problematic nature of one's transition from stage to stage in this model can be summarized by likening the process to an obstacle course. In some cases, certainly, the obstacles are relatively easy for persons to surmount and the process goes smoothly for all involved. However, in a number of settings, the obstacles are significant and assume gate-keeping functions (e.g., medical schools, Ph.D. programs, fraternities, recruit selection and training in police departments).

outcomes of the encounter and metamorphosis stages. Consequently, while the three phases are mutually exclusive from a temporal reference point, many of the variables discussed below were placed in a particular stage somewhat arbitrarily.

Choice: Anticipatory Socialization

For the purpose of this analysis, the concept, anticipatory socialization, will refer to the degree to which an individual is prepared—prior to entry—to occupy organizational positions. As such, preparatory learning occurs via the person's family, peers, educational institutions and cultural influences (media, etc.). The results of anticipatory socialization may range from the internalization of broad societal prescriptions (e.g., "a man must work") to specific behavioral guidelines associated with a chosen career (e.g., "doctors must not become personally involved with their patients"). Furthermore, the amount of prior learning and motivation required of a recruit varies across organizations. For example, Wheeler (1966) distinguishes between organizations concerned with developmental socialization and those devoted to resocialization. He suggests that developmental socialization requires that the new members be oriented in a favorable direction toward the avowed purposes of the organization (e.g., business organizations, higher educational organizations, etc.). However, agencies concerned with resocialization make no such assumptions about their new members. Moreover, these organizations exist primarily to correct some assumed deficiency in the person's earlier socialization experiences (e.g., prisons, mental health institutions, etc.).

Merton (1957) regards anticipatory socialization as the process by which persons take on the values of the group to which they aspire. In Merton's view, the process serves two functions. Merton (1957:265) states:

> For the individual who adopts the values of a group to which he aspires but does not belong, the orientation may serve the twin functions of aiding his rise into that group and of easing his adjustment after he has become a part of it.

Merton offers support for the importance of this process by citing evidence from Stouffer's, et al., *The American Soldier* (1949) which found, among other things, that those persons who accepted the official values of the army hierarchy were much more likely to be promoted.

A number of studies have pointed to the importance of "personal characteristics" as a determinant of the success of the organizational socialization process. Kaufman (1960) and Hall, Schneider and Nygren (1971) postulate what they call "identifier types." According to these researchers, identifier types are able to adjust easily to organizational demands. Their study focused upon the interpersonal correlates of goal integration (i.e., the state in which an individual's goals are essentially the same as the organization's) in the Forest Service. The findings of the study indicated that the "identifier type" was the individual who entered the organization with a strong public service orientation, and that the Forest Service was able to successfully screen and select recruits with this personal characteristic. Hence, the socialization process carried on by the organization assumed that the recruits supported and were committed to the service ideology and that this orientation had been implanted through anticipatory socialization mechanisms.

Closely tied to the concept of anticipatory socialization is the consideration of an individual's selection of an occupation. Various attempts have been made to postulate a theory of occupational choice (see Chapter 6). Most of these theories rely upon the perception of the person testing himself against his environment, weighing the factors and alternatives involved in choosing an occupation and finally making a series of conscious choices which determine the direction of his career. In this view, anticipatory socialization is a conscious process in which the individual is viewed as a rational decision-maker. Ginzberg, et al. (1951) hypothesized three phases in the anticipatory socialization or occupational choice process. The first and second phases represented periods in which the individual engaged in fantasy and tentative occupational choices and occurred between the ages of six and sixteen. The process was seen as culminating at the age of seventeen or eighteen when the individual—based on his prior experiences—was able to engage in realistic career choices. Thus, Ginzberg perceived the individual as maturing gradually to the point where action, in the form of occupational choice, was taken. Basic to Ginzberg's theory was his contention that the process was irreversible. He felt that each decision made by an individual regarding appropriate career choices limited the later choices.

Similar to the Ginzberg model of occupational choice, yet more eclectic, is the developmental theory developed by Super (1957). Where Ginzberg stressed choice points at which the individual explicitly selected and acted upon a decision, Super emphasized a continuous process. In Super's view, personal development involves the individual's implementing a self-concept and then testing that concept against reality. This reality-testing process results in the individual's acceptance of aspects of his self-conception which are satisfying (i.e., confirming) and the rejection of other aspects which are not satisfying. While Super's theory is built around chronological life stages, he sees one's self-concept as emerging relatively late in life. Most important, Super (like Ginzberg) feels individuals only make occupational choices which are perceived to be congruent with their particular self-concept. Hence, anticipatory socialization involves the development of self-concepts which direct the person toward the choice of a particular career.

Generally, the theories of occupational choice are consistent with social causation models of career determination. However, while theories of choice emphasize the individual's role in the process, social causation theories stress the structural surroundings in which choice must be made. For example, Miller and Form (1951) view an individual's career as a series of culturally imposed adjustments. They view the anticipatory socialization process as providing the individual with a set of expectations regarding his appropriate location within the occupational strata. Furthermore, they note that while personal motivation and effort are necessary, the crucial determinants of one's occupational level and choice exist independently of the individual and are found in the class structure of society. Indeed, Miller and Form (1951) tend to feel that by the time race, nationality, class, family and area of residence have been played out, not only has the range of occupational choice been severely restricted but so have work expectancies. Dalton (1951) provides some support for this contention when he found that organizational membership (and organizational promotion) correlated highly with such factors as race, political

and social affiliations, and religion. Certainly, if we were to study only social and economic variables, we would be forced to admit that for the vast majority of people in the world, occupational choice does not exist. It does occur, however, within industrialized societies, but research into choice factors can only be considered valid providing the social context is spelled out and the results are not given wider significance.

Related to the above are various differential theories which regard anticipatory socialization as an intrapsychic process. These theories postulate a direct relationship between early childhood experiences and later occupational choice. Roe (1956) suggests that the keys to behavior are those stimuli to which a person automatically or unconsciously directs his attention. Depending upon his early learning, a person develops individual interests which he will retain throughout life. Kubie (1958) notes that it is the subtle balance between conscious and unconscious forces which determines one's career pattern. More recently, Zaleznik, Dalton and Barnes (1970) utilize Kubie's idea of conscious and unresolved conflict to explain differences in managerial adjustment and behavior in a research organization.[16]

The position taken in this chapter is that anticipatory socialization occurs primarily through social interaction with persons who are significant to the individual and is not confined to the period of early childhood. Yet, anticipatory socialization becomes increasingly more role specific as an individual acquires certain values, attitudes, interests, skills and knowledge. Furthermore, anticipatory socialization becomes more important to the individual as he nears boundary points. This position is consistent with the Becker, Greer, Hughes and Strauss (1961) criticism of the pervasive gradualism approach taken when viewing the socialization process. In *The Student Physician*, Merton, et al. (1957) argued that as a student passed through medical school, he progressively comes to view himself as a professional. Fox (1957) noted that the student undergoes a process of learning wherein he gradually assimilates the required traits he will later need to play the role for which he is being prepared. Taking issue with this stand, Becker, et al. (1961:420) found little evidence of such a process occurring in the medical school they examined. They state:

> ...students do not take on a professional role while they are students, largely because the system they operate in does not allow them to do so. They are not doctors and the recurring experiences of being denied responsibility make it perfectly clear to them they are not. Though they occasionally engage in fantasy and play at being doctors, they never mistake their fantasy for the fact, for they know that until they have graduated and are licensed they will not be allowed to act as doctors.

Consequently, anticipatory socialization cannot fully account for the behavior of individuals in organizational settings. Yet its influence is well documented and may—depending upon the role for which an individual prepares—

---

[16] Regardless of the source of these models stressing early childhood learning in the organizational socialization process, all theorists more or less view anticipatory socialization as an imperfect and unfinished process. If it is to be meaningful, it must be accompanied by social and structural support from the organization. In other words, a basic compatability must be perceived by the individual between his strongly held belief systems and his target role within the organization.

aid or hinder an individual's adjustment to the organization demands.[17] Just how realistic and pertinent such preparation is to the individual becomes subject to a severe test when he or she encounters an organization for the first time as a participating member.

Entry: The Encounter

When an individual enters an organization as a newly recruited member, he is likely to experience what Hughes (1958b) calls a "reality shock." The extent to which the shock affects the outcome of the organizational socialization process depends largely upon the extent to which the person has correctly anticipated the various expectations of the organization. If the individual's expectations are accurate, the process merely provides for reaffirmation. However, if the novice enters the organization with expectations which are at variance with the role requirements of the organization, the socialization process must first involve a destructive phase (analytically similar to the Lewinian concept of unfreezing) which serves to detach the individual from his former expectations. The various contingencies upon which this destructive phase rests are examined in this subsection.

Basic to any discussion of the encounter period is the fundamental difference between making and implementing occupational or organizational choice. As Vroom and Deci (1971), Porter and Lawler (1968), Berlew and Hall (1966), Dunnette, Avery and Banas (1969) have pointed out, most of the individual's learning that occurs prior to entry in work organizations serves to reinforce and amplify unrealistic expectations. Hence, disillusionment is a likely outcome once the person actually enters the existing organization. In many cases, anticipatory socialization sharpens the positive features of the organization and dulls the negative features. For example, recruiting procedures seek to present the organization in its most favorable light. Consequently, the encounter period is likely to be an extremely trying period for the individual.

The following discussion considers the various factors which mediate the individual's initial experience with the organization. The analysis is organized according to environmental, organizational, relevant group, task and individual characteristics which may be expected to influence both the form and content of the socialization process.

Environmental factors. It is assumed generally that most people act consistently in society because they hold broad cultural values which inform and constrain their behavior (Becker, 1960). As noted, cultural values are conventional understandings shared by all—or at least most—of the participants in

---

[17] It should be pointed out that I have somewhat neglected an aspect of the pre-entry phase in the above discussion. This aspect is perhaps best illustrated by Caplow (1964:177). He noted: "Few organizations are exempt from that spontaneous chauvinism that makes the candidate with conforming traits look more talented than the outsiders."

Thus, to some degree, all organizations try to insure the inclusion of only the "right types" (via psychometric tests, experienced interviewers, organizational prerequisites and even nepotism). Hence, the ability of the person to present the "appropriate face" during the selection process determines his or her opportunity to move inside the organization. Quite clearly, his or her success depends upon the extent to which the aspiring member has anticipated correctly the expectations and desires of the organization.

society. These values refer to general prescriptions concerning appropriate social behavior. Such cultural values are perhaps the cornerstone of most organizational socialization efforts. However, cultural values are subject to gradual change and may slowly intrude upon the effectiveness of the process. For example, Starling (1968) notes the difficulty the armed services are having with their traditional socialization techniques. He notes that such techniques were geared for recruits who valued symbolic rewards. However, as the military increasingly takes on characteristics of large scale, technological business organizations, the traditional modes of securing minimal performance are no longer functional. Cultural prescriptions require monetary rewards in such organizations, rather than honorific rewards. Furthermore, cultural imperatives which have been supportive of the military are slowly eroding. Hence, broad societal values can and do influence the relevancy of the organizational socialization process.

Other contingencies, such as the characteristics of the community in which the organization is located, impinge upon both the content and outcomes of the socialization process. Hulin (1968) argued that the prevalent economic conditions (job opportunities, pay levels, etc.) establish the frame of reference against which workers evaluate their positions and organizations. Crowther (1957) found organizational withdrawal associated in a positive direction with the number of job alternatives. Blauner (1964) and Glaser (1964) found much the same situation in the industries they examined. Finally, Denhardt (1968) found regional norms concerning the exercise of authority may run counter to efficient organizational practices. Hence, if the socialization process is effectively to integrate new members into the organization, such regional norms must be taken into account.

The status of the organization and/or occupation within the social structure has also been shown to influence the socialization process. It has been observed that the higher the status of the organization/occupation, the more likely the new member will be motivated toward full acceptance and approval Hence, the higher the probability that the novice will be receptive to organizational influence attempts (Moore, 1969; Abramson, 1967; March and Simon, 1958).

The relationships among organizations within the social, economic, or political spheres may also influence the socialization process. If, for example, "raiding" is common practice within an industry, the organizations may well intensify their indoctrination efforts in an attempt fully to infuse their new employees with a strong sense of loyalty. At the same time, new members may be more resistant to such socialization efforts in light of the available alternatives.

To conclude, it is apparent that environmental conditions do influence the organizational socialization process. Yet, for the most part, these factors are relatively stable and beyond the immediate day-to-day control of either the organization or the individual.

Organizational factors.   Ultimately, the ability to influence the behavior, values and attitudes of its newly hired members depends upon the extent to which the organization can control the sources and amounts of the rewards valued by the new members. As will be noted, regardless of settings, some rewards are inevitably beyond the grasp of the organization's control. This segment discusses the organizationally-determined characteristics of the socialization process. The emphasis is upon the different types of organizations and selected structural properties dealing with the socialization process.

Etzioni (1961) suggests a typology of organizations which focuses upon the nature of member compliance with the demands of the setting. Viewing socialization as the process by which individuals acquire the requisite orientation for the satisfactory performance of a role, Etzioni sees the process as stressing various forms of participant compliance which depend upon the particular type of organization. He postulates three types of organizations, each emphasizing a different form of compliance. *Normative* organizations are characterized by a high moral commitment of their members to the mission of the organization. These organizations stress "expressive" socialization aimed at insuring that the individual's values, attitudes and motives are congruent with the mission. While normative organizations may be dependent upon outside agencies for support (e.g., educational institutions), they must still develop some internal mechanisms for the socialization of their members. On the other hand, *utilitarian* organizations emphasize "instrumental" socialization—aimed primarily at controlling only the overt behavior of the members. Values, attitudes and motives are considered largely irrelevant providing the new member's behavior is in the organizationally defined direction. Hence, utilitarian organizations orient their socialization procedures toward supplying novices only with the knowledge and behavior required of the specific role they are to perform. Finally, Etzioni perceives *coercive* organizations as most concerned with obedience. The organizational socialization process is punishment-centered and, as such, is conducive to an alienating form of individual compliance.

Although every organization contains a mixture of the normative, utilitarian and coercive characteristics, Etzioni's typology is useful in assessing the direction and intensity of the organizational efforts. Normative organizations, because of the reliance and concern with the values, attitudes and motives of their members, are likely to be most concerned with the socialization of their new participants. Hence, these organizations usually have time-consuming and intensive socialization methods. Utilitarian organizations, stressing behavior, are concerned primarily with teaching explicit skills which are instrumental in the accomplishment of organizational goals. Finally, coercive organizations rarely engage in much formal socialization. The socialization that does take place in such organizations is determined largely by the informal group and is based upon a subcultural value system which often runs counter to the value system expressed publicly by the organization.

Another useful organizational classification has been developed by Blau and Scott (1962). In their conceptualization, organizations can be differentiated according to the prime beneficiary principle of *cui bono* (i.e., who benefits). They distinguish four types of organizations using this criterion. Each type of organization faces a different problem which has implications throughout the organization—and the socialization process as well.

Still other useful classifications have been developed utilizing various criteria by Parsons (1960), Weber (1947), Barnard (1938), Berle and Means (1932). Each of these typologies depends upon certain assumed functional relationships between the organization and the larger environment and has direct implications upon the socialization processes utilized by the organizations.

A slightly different manner in which to classify organizational settings relies on the concept of "total institutions." In Goffman's (1961) view, total institutions have close to absolute control over their individual members. Given that all organizations exercise some power over their participants, it is possible to type organizations according to the degree of control they have over their membership. Consequently, the main issue is not which organizations are total, but rather how much totality does each display.

In strong total institutions, such as the army, persons are socialized normally by harsh methods. Shiloh (1971) suggests that initiates to these organizations are "profaned" by a standardized series of abasements and degradations. The organizational machinery is directed toward the classification of the initiates. As the socialization process progresses, tests of obedience are administered under tight supervision. These tests are considered necessary if the individual is to learn a new role.

Wallace (1971) points out that for the new member in organizations resembling total institutions an entirely separate social world comes into existence. In Etzioni's terms, coercive organizations are the most like total institutions. Virtually all facets of an individual's life are controlled within these organizations. However, normative organizations, such as schools or the church, also demand rigid adherence to an institutionalized way of life. For example, professional schools traditionally sequester their trainees in settings similar to total institutions. Even utilitarian organizations, when they require great amounts of overtime work or when work is performed in isolated settings, can sometimes approximate total institutions.

The extent to which the organization attempts to control a member's non-organizational life-space is another important dimension having implications upon the organizational socialization process. For example, the wife or husband of a new member may play a large role in the individual's acceptance into the organization. Janowitz (1960) notes that the etiquette and ceremony surrounding military life serve to instruct both the officer and his wife in the appropriate behavior for all phases of the life-cycle. Hence, some organizations require the recruit to learn a new style of life. Such learning places the members in a community (or subculture) whose claims over their daily existence exceed their official duties. Socialization into such organizations is generally harsh and attempts to force the novice to break old patterns and relationships. The new member is expected to emerge from the organizational socialization process with a strong identification with the collectivity. Moore (1969:879) notes that in such organizations, the process invariably involves suffering.

> The initiate is put through a set of tasks that are difficult and unpleasant. Success comes to most, but failure is a realistic possibility. However, the suffering is shared and a fellowship is formed.

The existence of danger in an occupation or organization is another characteristic having implications for the socialization process. Janowitz (1964) and Van Maanen (1972) note that organizations involved in the performance of crucial life-death functions develop far-reaching claims over the participant's life. In such organizations, a sense of solidarity is required when the members are preoccupied with potential danger. Consequently, the organizational socialization process is likely to be more intense and stress values appropriate to the inculcation of such solidarity.

Caplow (1964) states that all organizations, to some degree, have a core of expectations about the proper attitudes, values and motives to be held by their members. He labels this set of expectations the normative system. Violations of the norms run from trivial to serious. The more pervasive the normative system, the more important the organizational socialization process. According to Caplow, the normative system is based upon an organizational ideology. This ideology serves the dual function of linking the organization to wider purposes and reinforces the member's commitment to the organization by reference to a common cause. The ideology, if accepted by the new member, creates a sort of psychological barrier prohibiting the individual's desertion of the organization. Consequently, a prominent goal of the organizational socialization process is to gain the new member's acceptance of the normative system and corresponding ideology. However, the extent to which organizations attempt to develop such acceptance varies greatly.

The above discussion illustrated some of the broad dimensions affecting the socialization process along which organizations may be expected to differ. A complete listing would be impossible, for the potential number of variables is infinite. At this point, attention is now turned to a set of structural variables influencing the organizational socialization process. Again, the listing is far from inclusive. However, the purpose is to highlight certain structural considerations which are likely to have important consequences when an individual first encounters the organization.

One of the more salient aspects of the organizational socialization process is the formality for the setting (Brim, 1966; Wheeler, 1966; Cogswell, 1958). Is the newcomer's role as "learner" specified or unspecified? If unspecified, much learning takes place via the informal organization. Generally, the more formal the setting, the more stress there is upon influencing the newcomer's values and attitudes, and the more severe the socialization process (Dornbush, 1955).[18] Formality also appears to emphasize status specialization (i.e., preparing the recruit to occupy a particular status in life) rather than role specialization (i.e., preparing the recruit to perform a specified task in the organization), although the two are often complementary (Wheeler, 1966).

The length of the formal socialization period is often a good indication of the organization's desire to influence deep or surface characteristics of the recruits. Hughes (1958a:36) states:

> In general, the longer and more rigorous the period of initiation, the more culture and techniques are associated with it.

Consequently, the more drawn out the formal socialization process, the greater the likelihood that organizationally desired outcomes (e.g., traits, etiquette, skills, etc.) will become imbedded within the neophytes as motives and values (i.e., personal characteristics). Furthermore, the length of the indoctrination process influences the degree to which bonds of cohesion and commitment may be formed (Becker, 1964; Kanter, 1968).

An important structural characteristic involved in organizational socializa-

---

[18] Just as formal structure appears to indicate stress for the individual, unstructured situations may also induce personal anxiety. Left to his own devices, the individual may well feel a strong desire to define his role within the organization. Most often, these laissez-faire situations increase the effectivness of the informal group *vis-à-vis* the formal organization in the socialization of its members (Blake and Mouton, 1961; Roy, 1955; Lewin, 1952; Roethlisberger and Dickson, 1940; etc.).

tion is whether recruits are processed individually or collectively. A number of studies have demonstrated that a collective setting (if it remains intact for some length of time) provides a new member with strong social support for forming and adopting group perspectives.

Evan (1963) noted that a helpful condition increasing the likelihood of successful organizational socialization is the formation of recruit peer groups. Specifically, he hypothesized that the level of recruit peer group interaction would be negatively associated with the level of early turnover. Empirically confirming his hypothesis, Evan noted that peer groups can perform the function of reducing strain and alleviating tension, thus easing the person's passage into the organization. Bruckel (1955) found a similar phenomenon when he examined the differences between individual and team replacement in army combat units. Furthermore, as Becker (1960) has noted, collective perspectives arise only when individuals are able to consider themselves in a similar situation facing similar problems. Hence collective socialization settings which literally put individuals "in the same boat" are effective mechanisms of encouraging the development of group solutions to the contextual problems of everyday life in the organization.

Becker (1964) suggests that when a "cohort" group experiences the socialization program together, the outcomes are likely to be more uniform than if they had been processed individually. In the collective case, individual changes in attitudes, values and motives are made and based upon a group consensus. Becker (1964:48) states:

> As the group shares problems, various members experiment with possible solutions and report back to the group. In the course of collective discussions, members arrive at a definition of the situation and develop consensus.

On the other hand, the collective character of such solutions allows the recruit group to deviate more from the standards set by those doing the socializing than would be possible by an individual. Hence, the group pattern provides the recruits with a basis for resistance. This topic will be further explored in the discussion of relevant group factors.

Another important structural aspect concerns the serial or disjunctive patterns of organizational socialization. If the new member has been preceded by others who have been through the same situation and can instruct him about the setting, the pattern is considered to be serial. However, if the new member is not following in the footsteps of predecessors, the pattern is disjunctive. Wheeler (1966) feels the greatest danger of the serial pattern is stagnation. For example, if the organization is characterized by low morale, the serial socialization pattern risks contaminating the new individuals with similar attitudes. However, the disjunctive pattern has problems as well. By leaving the individual to his own resources, the organization risks increasing that individual's anxiety and may complicate the outcome of the socialization process.

Certain organizations possess selection devices which reduce the importance of the socialization process. For example, some organizations select only those individuals who have already assimilated the proper attitudes, values and motivations required for membership. Scott (1965) found little evidence of attitudinal or behavioral change throughout a person's fraternity career. Since the fraternities were successful in selecting only those recruits who possessed the characteristics relevant to the particular role prior to initiation, the socialization process was primarily one of reaffirmation.

Glaser and Strauss (1971) have noted that the rate of passage through organizational boundaries—such as the boundaries crossed at entrance—are of deep concern to all organizational participants. Furthermore, a "sentimental order" about "when things should happen" is developed, through experience, by the organization or group and is transmitted to newcomers. If these expectations about scheduling and movement are unfulfilled, the organization and individual will perceive the socialization process to be working improperly. Hence, these "timetables" provide the organization, relevant group and individual with a set of criteria for evaluating the socialization process (Roth, 1963).

The above set of variables is only representative of the wide range of structural characteristics that can be expected to influence the socialization process. For example, the organization may desire to create homogenous or heterogeneous results among the new members and this objective will certainly affect the form and content of the socialization process. Additionally, the reward and hierarchical structures may influence the process. All that was hoped to accomplish in this subsection was to outline certain basic, yet often overlooked, organizational factors influencing organizational socialization.

Before continuing, the interdependency of the socialization variables listed above must be recognized. For example, recruit composition logically influences the formality of the organizational socialization setting and the length of the formal indoctrination period. Additionally, a process which is both serial and collective can be expected to differ in important ways from a process which is disjunctive, yet collective. Hence, the complexity of the organizational factors cannot be overstated.

Relevant Group Factors

This discussion is somewhat related to the structural considerations outlined briefly in the preceding section. Organizational socialization is sometimes both formal and collective, but not in every case. Consequently, the emphasis here is upon contingencies which lie outside the control of the formal organization— although the organization may capitalize upon their presence.

Virtually all organizational members are part of a smaller group context which constitutes a key source of learning. The group to which a recruit is first assigned possesses and transmits to a new member a set of collective understandings which represent an esoteric system of values. Thus, the influence of the group on the recruit—regardless of setting—has direct implications for the outcomes of the organizational socialization process.

Roy (1952, 1955) has dramatically shown that in some organizations a worker will not be taught the necessary skills and secrets of his relevant work group until he is accepted as trustworthy by his fellow workers. The acceptance process may be rapid or slow depending upon the nature and secrets of the particular group.

Once the member is accepted, the relevant group may be viewed as cushioning the impact of the "reality shock" accompanying the individual's encounter with the organization. Generally, these groups are supportive and help the individual interpret the role demands dictated by the organization. Hughes

(1958b) notes that the colleague group helps the newcomer to determine what constitutes a mistake both in the group and within the organizational context. At the same time, if the new member is approved, the work group will defend the newcomer's right to make mistakes. Blau (1955) found that a system of colleague consultation existed in some public service bureaucracies and these systems generated stable social bonds which determined both an old and a new member's standing within the group. Clearly, the group within the organization in which the individual is a member plays a significant role in organizational socialization. The following discussion is aimed at examining some of the more crucial variables associated with the group influence process.

The general literature in social psychology contains impressive evidence for the influence of groups upon the attitudes and performance of its members (Asch, 1951; Newcomb, 1958, 1961; Sherif and Sherif, 1956; Cartwright and Zander, 1960). Newcomb (1966) suggests three conditions which may facilitate the socialization of the new member into the group. Presumably, the power of the group's influence upon the initiate is determined by the degree the following three conditions are satisfied:

1. Size of the group—smaller groups are generally more influential.
2. Homogeneity of the group—homogeneous groups are generally more influential.
3. Communicative isolation—isolated groups are generally more influential.

Related to Newcomb's factors of influence is the distinction between primary and secondary groups first postulated by Cooley (1922). Essentially, a primary group is characterized by regular, face-to-face interaction among all members in which affective bonds develop. A secondary group (any group which does not meet the face-to-face criteria) is considered to be diffuse in its influence upon its members. Intrinsic to this consideration is the notion that people come to be more and more like those who surround them. Shibutani (1962) suggests that deliberately or unconsciously, each person performs for some type of audience and that each person also takes into account the expectations of others. The group within which a person interacts on a daily basis within the organization then must constitute a major audience—at least in temporal terms—for the individual actor. Hence, part of the organizational socialization process involves the individual's continual adjustment to the demands of the various subgroups in which he participates within the social system.

Recalling Becker's (1964) discussion of situational adjustments, the term "reference group" is used here to signify the group whose perspective is used by the novice as a frame of reference for defining his organizational experiences and expectations. To an individual, a reference group is an audience—shared, real or imagined—to whom certain values are assigned. More importantly, this audience is the one before which the individual is trying to maintain or increase his standing. However, an individual may have many reference groups. Shibutani (1962:138–139) notes:

> For any individual, there are as many reference groups as there are channels of communications in which a person regularly becomes involved.

Consequently, from the organizational perspective, the problem of socialization becomes partially one of making sure that the new member selects appropriate reference groups. Merton (1957) suggests that new persons select reference groups on the basis of aspirations. Similarly, Festinger (1957) perceives personal attractiveness to be the primary consideration in an individual's selection of a reference group.

What is often missed in the discussion of the influence of reference and/or colleague groups is that the members of such groups are rarely perceived as equals by the recruit. Moore (1969) indicates that it is the role of the significant other that induces a new member to share the group's attitudes and beliefs. The significant other provides the affective component needed for personal change. As Shibutani (1962:141) states:

> Those who feel they have been treated by another with affection and consideration usually regard their personal obligations as binding.

Strauss (1968) sees the "coach" as the significant other for some organizational initiates. The coach (or in some cases, coaches) is one who takes—either formal or informal—responsibility for seeing that a recruit is properly groomed, instructed, advised or cared for during the "breaking-in" period. He notes that the coach's role is to develop a new identity for the learner by guiding him along a series of noninstitutionalized steps leading to full organizational membership. And the affective relationship that develops between coach and learner is the key to the success of the process.

Additionally, Brim (1966) considers both the affective and the power relationships which bind individuals to one another as the basis for personal change. Yet, Brim feels that in adult socialization the affective relationship is neutralized—compared to the strength it had in child socialization. Furthermore, in adult socialization, Brim notes that the power relationships are equalized. To the extent that one or both of these conditions do not hold, Brim feels that deep personal change is possible.

Dornbush (1955) observed that the "union of sympathy," which recruits developed in the Coast Guard Academy, served as a buffer against the extreme suppression and regimentation accompanying their training. Consequently, as Becker (1964) noted, where there exists a common set of problems all shared by a group (i.e., "in the same boat"), subcultures are likely to develop. These subcultures influence the organizational socialization process by providing individuals with social support and help them to navigate a path through the boundary passage process.

Lortie (1968) suggests that entrance into some occupations (e.g., college teaching) requires a person to experience a "shared ordeal." Such experiences provide the newcomer with a set of colleagues and dramatize for him the worth of such relationships. Essentially, the ordeal may be viewed as a part of the organizational socialization process and is designed to test the capacity of the neophyte. Using the rhetoric of puberty rites, Lortie (1968:255) states:

> Those who endured and passed the tests imposed by the elders changed subjectively—the gap they had felt between themselves and adults narrowed appreciably. Candidates who shared the trial with others changed more than those who went it alone; sharing added to the impact of the experience.

Up to this point, the implicit assumption has been that the individual's important reference groups, significant others and subculture are, in all cases, related intimately to the organization. Nothing could be further from the truth. For example, Dubin (1956) inferred from his data that for three of every four industrial workers, the workplace was not a "central life interest." Furthermore, only 10% of his sample reported that their important primary social relationships occurred in the work organization. In a later study, Tausky and Dubin (1965) found that career perspectives were "anchored" to set positions often established independently of the work organization. To explain work behavior, Dubin (1956) argues persuasively that for many workers, adequate social behavior occurs in organizational settings because it is mandatory, not because it is important to him. Schein (1974) makes a similar argument when referring to certain managerial careers. Social experiences which are capable of changing the person can only occur in primary relationships which are valued by the individual. Hence, the implication is that in many organizations, the only areas in which the socialization process can reasonably be expected to influence the individual are the surface dimensions concerned only with overt behavior.

A discussion of relevant group considerations is not complete without examining the question of conflicting loyalties. This topic is important because it is apparent that the manner in which newcomers perceive their social roles and positions is a major influence on the organizational socialization process. Gouldner (1957, 1958) suggests that expectations about roles can either be manifest or latent. The manifest roles are regarded by the organization as relevant in the given situation, whereas the latent roles rarely are recognized fully by the organization. Following Merton's (1957) analysis of community leaders, Gouldner postulates that organizations (particularly professional organizations) are populated by a mix of two types of employees. At one polar position is the "cosmopolitan" who is more committed to his specialized role than he is to the organization itself. At the other extreme is the "local" whom Gouldner depicts as more committed to the organization than to his specialized role. For the cosmopolitan, his reference group is located outside the organization. Hence, socializing the new cosmopolitan member to organizational norms or values that differ from those of his reference group is bound to be difficult. On the other hand, a new member with a local orientation can be viewed as highly susceptible to organizational influence efforts.

Becker and Greer (1966) qualify Gouldner's analysis by noting that latent identities will not affect the new member unless they are in some way mobilized (i.e., made salient). For example, latent identities may be irrelevant in a particular setting, hence, do not play a part in the socialization process. However, there is evidence to indicate that the individual's latent identity may conflict with his organizationally defined role and produce a set of problems for both the individual and the organization (Gouldner, 1957, 1958; Bennis, et al., 1958; Kornhauser, 1962; Glaser, 1964; Wilensky, 1964). For example, Burchard (1954) found that military chaplains were torn between the cross-pressures of professional and organizational norms. Thus, the new member's resolution of this dilemma has serious consequences for the outcomes of the socialization process.

It should be noted, however, that the conflicting loyalties question does not necessarily involve an either-or solution. In many cases, the individual may learn to adjust both to the set of demands arising from his participation in the organization and the set of demands arising from an outside reference group related to the person's latent identity. Avery (1968) found that through a process he labelled enculturation, professional scientists were able to transform themselves into industrial researchers by connecting their technical competence to that of the organization in a manner which was mutually satisfying. Consequently, as Avery points out, the local-cosmopolitan dichotomy is an oversimplification. Yet the socialization process must explicitly recognize the importance of latent identities if the organization is to successfully integrate new members with strong cosmopolitan predispositions.

This brief discussion was not concerned with the direction of the group's influence upon the individual (i.e., in ways approved by the organization, or ways not approved). The intention here was simply to establish support for the proposition that an individual is likely to be influenced by various groups both inside and outside the organization. Whether or not this feature of the socialization process is congruent with the specific organizational expectations and objectives is the subject of a later section.

Task Factors

It is not uncommon for many work organizations to experience an extremely high turnover rate among their newly employed members. Studies investigating withdrawal in work organizations nearly always emphasize task factors as one of the major causes for this turnover. Schein (1962, 1963, 1968b) suggests that one of the primary reasons for a new member's organizational disillusionment (and perhaps his subsequent withdrawal) is receiving, upon encounter, an assignment which is either too easy or too difficult. Both types of assignments upset and disconfirm some of the major assumptions a new person holds about himself or herself. If a person's motivation to belong is not sufficiently strong to induce the personal changes that allow the individual to adjust to the situation, if able, he or she will leave the organization. For example, Saleh, Lee and Prien (1965) noted that 12.5% of a sample of nurses resigned because of their specific assignments. The researchers reported that the jobs assigned to the nurses who remained with the organization were characterized by variety, autonomy, role-clarity and feedback. Schein (1961, 1962, 1965), Dunnette, et al. (1969), Guest (1960) and others have observed that certain tasks appear to carry with them an alienating feature which exists for virtually all types of persons. Hence, the nature of the specific task plays a crucial role in the outcomes of the organizational socialization process and, to some degree, this factor is independent of other characteristics of the setting (e.g., environmental, organizational, relevant group and individual). The following is a brief attempt to delineate certain features of tasks which are likely to effect the organizational socialization process.

Porter and Lawler (1968) maintain that intrinsic job satisfaction is directly affected by job design factors. Furthermore, they feel that certain job design factors can lead to better performance and provide the member with a certain level of satisfaction (see also, Hackman and Lawler, 1971). One of these job design factors is the amount of control an individual is able to exercise over his assigned task. Schein (1962, 1968a) also noted that one of the major problems many individuals face when adjusting to the demands of the organization is to obtain a level of autonomy relating to the performance of one's assigned task. Part of the problem is located in the question of how much participation in decision-making (concerning one's own functions) a new member is allowed during his adjustment period. While this variable may be more crucial later in an individual's career, the extent of voluntarism during the socialization process can be expected to influence the recruit's organizationally relevant attitudes. Vroom (1960) and March and Simon (1958) have both noted that participation in the decisions which relate to the individual's job can be expected to raise the amount of identification and satisfaction the person receives from his organizational membership.

Job design factors which emphasize and require continual changes may have a negative effect upon the socialization outcomes. Melbin (1964) found that forced assignment changes increased frustration among workers. He felt that the pressure to perform in unfamiliar settings reduced the probability that the individual would become integrated into the organization system. On the other hand, settings which leave a new member with the same task may face stagnation problems with the participant becoming restless and bored—particularly if the task is learned easily and consists of much routine. Thus, it appears that some type of balance is required if the socialization process is to accomplish its purposes.

Another job design aspect involves the amount of responsibility and challenge associated with a particular task. As noted previously, Berlew and Hall (1966) felt that this variable was indeed a prerequisite for successful socialization.

Some systematic evidence has been compiled by Hackman and his associates which indicates that five so-called "core" dimensions of work tasks are critical *vis-à-vis* one's satisfaction and performance in the organization (Hackman and Lawler, 1971; Hackman and Oldham, 1974; Hackman, 1969). The dimensions include: *skill variety* (the degree to which the job requires one to use different skills or perform different activities); *task identity* (the degree to which the job requires the individual to complete an entire process); *task significance* (the degree to which the job has a perceivable impact on others, either inside or outside the organization); *feedback* (the degree to which the individual receives information from significant others as to the effectiveness of his work); and *autonomy* (the degree to which the job provides one with freedom, independence and discretion in scheduling and carry-out work assignments). According to theory, at least, jobs ranked high on these dimensions will provide strong internal motivation for anyone assuming such a job.

The new member's performance (as judged by the member himself and the organization) on the assigned task is linked also to socialization outcomes. Becker, Geer and Hughes (1968) found that students who were doing poorly in college (from a GPA perspective) often stopped working altogether. Hence, the organizational socialization process broke down when, as the authors stated, "the students decided not to throw good money after bad." Korman (1968) and Locke (1965) found a similar phenomenon in industrial settings. Basically, the principle is simply that task success leads to task liking and both are related positively to high self-esteem. Korman (1968:485) states:

All things being equal, individuals will choose, adjust their behavior to, and find satisfying, those behavioral roles which will maximize their sense of cognitive balance or consistency. This implies that individuals will tend to find most satisfying those jobs and task roles which are consistent with their self-cognitions.

Some tasks, on the other hand, simply do not have the potential of supplying the individual with rewarding experiences. Roy (1960) observed that on certain isolated jobs, the "game of work" could not be played, the task being far too dull. Consequently, in such situations, extrinsic considerations (e.g., work group, supervision, pay and security) are of more importance to the individual than intrinsic considerations. Such task features are often implied in the role for which the new member is being prepared. As Centers and Bugental (1966) pointed out, members at the higher organizational levels place greater emphasis upon the intrinsic factors since the task itself is generally richer and more rewarding than tasks assigned to members at lower levels. Thus, members at lower levels are forced to emphasize the extrinsic factors associated with their assignment. Attention is now turned to these extrinsic features.

The Ohio State University and the University of Michigan leadership studies have demonstrated clearly the importance of the supervisor's behavior as affecting the satisfactory adjustment of the individual to organizational demands. Lewin (1952), Likert (1961), McGregor (1960), Fiedler (1958) and many others have stressed supervision as a critical variable that influences all facets of organizational behavior. Essentially, as Fleishman, Harris, and Burtt (1955) concluded, the consideration (i.e., friendliness, trust, respect, etc.) a supervisor shows for his new subordinates largely determines his ability to influence them. This is consistent with the preceding discussion which emphasized the affective requirements involved in personal change. Hence, the organizational socialization process should proceed more smoothly if the leadership climate displays a high degree of consideration.

The degree to which the role expectations are defined to a new member may also play a major part in the organizational socialization process. As Weitz (1957) concluded, the degree to which an individual is given a clear picture of his job duties prior to actually performing the task may often determine whether or not the individual will leave or stay with the organization. Kahn, et al. (1964) suggested that role clarity is dependent upon the speed at which the organization is changing, the degree of organizational complexity and the overall communications philosophy of the organization. All three of these contingencies are likely to affect the organizational socialization process.

Finally, overriding many of these concerns, the technology employed by the organization can be expected to aid or hinder the socialization process. Guest (1955) referred to technology as the "neglected factor in labour turnover studies." However, the work of Blauner (1964), Woodward (1965), Chinoy (1955), Roy (1953, 1955) and others has gone a long way to correct this neglect. The basic hypothesis suggested by these researchers is that the more redundant a worker's task (e.g., the assembly line) the more difficult it is for an individual ever to adjust to the "immediate task." In fact, Guest (1955) considers that the "work itself" is the single most important source of an individual's dissatisfaction. Consequently, the organizational socialization process must occasionally deal with alienating types of role specifications and must attempt to provide a new member with alternative means of organizational reward.

Individual Factors

The following discussion touches briefly on some influences upon the encounter phase of organizational socialization resulting from personal characteristics of the new members. However, most of the individual factors have been covered elsewhere since they are related inherently to other aspects impinging upon the process. For example, the importance of membership to an individual was discussed in the previous section. Individual commitment and investment were covered in the organizational factors portion of this section. Consequently, the following attempts to gain closure upon the Entry Encounter phase of socialization by considering a set of individual variables which have been ignored thus far.

As Brim (1966) noted, much socialization in adult life is self-initiated and not merely a response to the demands of others. Yet, this self-initiated socialization has its roots in the expectations of "significant others" whether they are present or not. For example, the sensitivity group movement assumes that most people are motivated to seek at least some change in themselves. However, as Maslow (1954) suggested, personality differences may well be at the base of such self-initiated changes—even those which will allow the person to "self-actualize." Thus, personality differences should be expected to influence the outcomes of the organizational socialization process. For example, Porter (1961, 1962, 1963) found that personal differences were linked to felt needs of the individual *vis-à-vis* the organization. Several studies examining the effects of college environments on students have postulated that personality characteristics exert a pervasive influence on an individual's perceptions and reactions to the environment (Heath, 1964; Brown, 1962; Stern, 1962; Trow, 1962).

Of the extrinsic job features, one's pay is probably the most discussed—by theorists, as well as the job holders themselves. Yet, as Adams (1963a, b, 1965) notes, it is not the absolute level of pay one receives for his efforts that is expected to influence one's behavior. Rather, it is the perceived "equity" of pay *vis-à-vis* others performing similar tasks within the organization that is important. In other words, if a new member feels he is treated fairly by the organization (i.e., as well as his relevant peers), pay is unlikely to effect the socialization process. It is only when his paycheck is perceived to fall below what others "in the same boat" are receiving that it becomes an obstacle in the process.[19]

After reviewing the literature concerning organizational withdrawal, Porter and Steers (1972) concluded that the available evidence indicates that those individuals who leave the organization manifest personality characteristics near

---

[19] While pay *per se* cannot be considered a socialization devise, the ability of the organization to reward new members differentially according to the degree each displays the appropriate characteristics may have far reaching consequences. As Lawler's (1971b) recent work attests, pay is the most important of the so-called extrinsic rewards. Within our theory, pay may be viewed as providing an individual with "feedback" as to his competence. Furthermore, in many situations, one's pay may be his only source of evidence by which to assess his importance to the organization. Herzberg's (1966) two-factor theory not withstanding, pay means different things to different people and the extent to which it influences the socialization process may properly be viewed as a personal variable—although group perspectives often increase or decrease its saliency (e.g., union settings). To some, pay may be a major source of individual identity. To others, it may have little effect on self-definitions.

the polar extreme of the various continua (e.g., anxiety, aggressiveness, self-esteem, etc.). The implication for the socialization process is that new members clustering near the middle of the various personality dimensions will be more susceptible to the organizational socialization process in terms of the outcome, remaining with the organization.

Schein and Ott (1962) noted that the attitudes one holds about the legiti-macy of the organization's attempt to influence certain behavior may determine the boundaries of the socialization outcomes. Their study, an attitude survey, re-vealed that the more job-related the area of influence, the more it was con-sidered legitimate for the organization to attempt influence. However, while individual differences within subgroups existed, most differences were discovered among subgroups. For example, the subgroup consisting of labor leaders re-ported the fewest areas of legitimate organizational influence, while industrial managers reported the most. With this finding in mind, Schein and Ott (1962: 689) concluded:

> ... The social ethic that Whyte (1956) worries most about is most likely to be found among managers who, of course, are in the best po-sition to implement it.

This implies that the individual's perception and the organization's per-ception (as represented by managers) of areas of legitimate influence may be a source of tension and possibly a major obstacle in the socialization process. It also suggests that conflict models, emphasizing role negotiation, may be a fruitful frame of reference for the study of some socialization settings.

The adage about the impossibility of teaching an old dog new tricks does not appear to apply to the socialization of older persons into organizations. A number of studies demonstrate that older workers are more likely to identify with the organization and value their membership (Minor, 1958; Ley, 1966; Palmer, 1962; Farris, 1971). The problem with most of the above studies is that they were concerned with turnover and not devoted explicitly to the socializa-tion process itself. One study, however, which examined this aspect found turn-over among older recruits in public service agencies higher during the early phases of socialization (e.g., formal training period) than among the younger recruits. Yet, after six months with the organization, older members had a lower turnover rate than their younger counterparts (Downs, 1967).

Up to this point, little attention has been paid to the underlying nature of the attitude variables involved in organizational socialization. The next portion considers several theories of attitude change. Emphasis is placed upon factors which are likely to secure a newcomer's continuance with the organization.

Continuance: Metamorphosis

The focus in this section is on what Becker, et al. (1961) called the "final per-spective." This perspective consists of solutions the new member has worked out regarding the problems he or she has discovered during the first encounter with the organization.

Porter (1971) notes that during the encounter phase, the organization has three tactics available to induce new members to change. First, the organization may reinforce and confirm the new member's behavior by providing rewards. Additionally, the organization may punish the recruit by withholding rewards or providing various negative reinforcements. The punishment approach is designed to "extinguish" certain characteristics which the organization deems inappropriate for the prescribed role the new member is expected to play. Finally, the organization may do nothing. This tactic literally ignores certain characteristics and behaviors of the new member. All three strategies are associated typically with the organizational socialization process. According to Porter, success of any of these strategies depends upon the individual's motivation to belong and the extent to which the organization possesses the ability to administer the valued rewards or relevant punishments to the neophytes.

Moore (1969) suggests that most new members in work organizations have sufficient motivation to perform their assigned role. Thus, the problem of continuance revolves largely around the reward and punishment processes. This is similar to Schein's (1968a) view of organizational socialization as being a reaffirmation process in most cases.

Kelman (1958) notes that there are three underlying processes which the individual engages in when he adopts new responses. Each of the three affect the continuance of the induced response by manipulating various aspects of the individual's expectations and self-conceptions. The individual may accept organizational demands because they enable him to gain specific rewards and avoid certain punishments. Kelman calls this process compliance. At another level, a person may accept influence because he desires to establish or maintain a satisfying, self-defining relationship with another person or group. This process is labelled identification. Finally, the individual may accept organizational influence because the content of the induced behavior—the ideas and actions of which the behavior is comprised—is intrinsically rewarding. This process is referred to as internalization.

Kelman suggests that it is possible to view the three processes developmentally. For example, when a new member first encounters the organization, he accepts role demands primarily because of the explicit rewards involved. However, he gradually begins to associate with other members of the organization and selectively develops positive affective bonds for certain others. Yet these relationships are contingent upon certain behaviors manifested by the new member. Finally, the neophyte finds that simply the performance of these behaviors is rewarding and, furthermore, their performance is congruent with his evolving value system. Hence, the organizational socialization process may be seen as most influential when the outcome provides the new member with a set of internalized role specifications.

This analysis is useful from the standpoint of categorizing a new member's response to influence attempts. However, it merely describes particular mental and/or behavioral states. Kelman says little about the actual process by which individuals experience the "need" to change and then change in desired directions. Also, Kelman's work is of limited value when discussing the kinds of changes in attitudes, beliefs and values which are thought to be central or deep and involve one's self-identity.

Schein (1964b) describes a process of personal change which overcomes certain deficiencies in Kelman's analysis. Using Lewinian terminology, he suggests that an unfreezing process is required because some persons enter socialization settings at odds with the organizational expectations. Hence, the organization must prove to the individual that parts of his "previous self" are no longer of value to him. The organization may accomplish this by deliberately or accidentally creating a series of "upending" events which disconfirm some of the new member's assumptions about the situation. The intensity of these upending events vary widely, yet they serve to motivate the new member to search for new responses based upon his new information.

In general, the most serious "upending" events revolve around the individual's failure to receive confirmation of self. This situation is likely to produce the most significant personal changes in a new member. Disconfirmation may, however, only involve certain organizationally related expectations, producing only mild readjustments in the individual's cognitive structure. Regardless of level, disconfirmation induces a sort of guilt anxiety or inadequacy feeling within the individual. Consequently, since this state is uncomfortable, he is motivated to seek what Schein (1968a) calls "psychological safety" by rearranging his expectations or, at a more profound level, his self-image.

The novice acquires new learning from a variety of sources. For example, peers, coaches, institutionalized rewards and punishments, etc. provide the new member with multiple stimuli from which he can select relevant information. Schein (1968a) states that when a single source is used, cognitive reorganization is achieved via identification. However, when multiple sources are used, the change is assisted by "scanning" the relevant information. Both mechanisms are present in most settings, although the various sources vary in both saliency and credibility.

Schein's conception of the metamorphosis process is indebted heavily to various congruity theories arising from studies examining attitude change and structure (e.g., Festinger, 1957; Lewin, 1952; Heider, 1953; Osgood and Tannenbaum, 1955; Fishbein, 1961; McGuire, 1968). These theories are essentially variations on a theme involving what Newcomb (1958) called a "strain toward consistency." Attitudes are viewed as predispositions to respond in a particular way to a specified class of objects (Rosenberg, et al., 1962). At a very general level, the theory postulates that attitudes are mediating states which exert a direct and dynamic influence on behavior. Attitudes are viewed as composed of cognitive, affective and conative states associated with knowing, feeling and acting, respectively. Attitudinal responses to influence may fall into one or all of these states. Attitude change is perceived as primarily a social influence process relying on communications. Lasswell (1948) states succinctly that the variables in the process are "who says what, to whom, how, and with what effect?" The cornerstone in the theory is that a person holding conflicting attitudes is in an uncomfortable mental state and is motivated to reduce the tension by altering his attitudes. Thus, the person is viewed as striving to adjust his attitudes so that they will be in maximum harmony.[20]

---

[20] Another view of the personal change process is presented by the so-called ethnomethodologists. From their perspective, all social settings provide ample opportunities to examine socialization processes. For example, to Goffman (1963, 1967), each social encounter requires the participants to discover what behavior is appropriate (or will be tolerated) in the situation. Such discovery assumes that the person "gleans" information from the situational properties which are more or less obvious in the setting (e.g., the bodily appearances of others, personal accounts given by others, the time of day, and so on). Indeed, Goffman feels that all social situations have norms of propriety which regulate the behavior of those present. Furthermore, because of the everyday nature of these microsociological settings, the moral

Often of importance to the continuance phase of socialization are symbolic transitional events. These *rites de passage* may be formal or informal, but they demonstrate to the initiate that he has been granted full-fledged membership and aid in developing a new member's sense of belonging (Blau, 1955). Such transitions may involve the giving of title, extra rights, or the sharing of information which previously had been withheld. Thus, these events celebrate a sort of individual metamorphosis. They signify that the member now has the skills, knowledge, and motivation to occupy a particular role.

Transition rites provide a temporal reference point which allows the individual to say, "I am not what I used to be." *Rites de passage* are then formal turning points and signify what Caplow (1964) calls a "change of soul." For example, at times of initiation and graduation, explicit recognition is given to the members' new status and such events serve to separate him from his former equals.

In some organizations, the symbolic transition to full-fledged membership may occur long after the person has entered. In other organizations, the rituals of passage may occur much sooner. Yet regardless of when the rites are held, transitions take time. As Barnard (1938:7) stated: "There is no instant replacement, there is always a period of adjustment."

IV. METHODS OF SOCIALIZATION

The manner in which a new member fits into the status order, the social networks and the activities of the work organization is crucial if the initiate is to acquire simultaneously the attitudes, behaviors and values appropriate for participation. Within certain broad limits (e.g., financial, legal, cultural, etc.), the organization has many options available regarding the choice of methods by which to "break in" its members.

Child (1954) discussed the socialization process from the perspective of reward and punishment. He indicated that behavior may be influenced by arranging and controlling rewards so that every additional increment of effort displayed by the learner is associated with a commensurate increment in reward. However, in organizational settings, it is common to tie the most potent sanctions to the achievement of some minimal standard of performance. Consequently, new members are willing to settle for this minimal level of reward and ignore the relatively smaller additional rewards to be gained from the further investment of effort.

Each method of organizational socialization discussed below varies in the amount of effort required of a recruit. Furthermore, the ability of the organization to reward and punish the recruit in the various activity aspects of his

---

norms which govern these situations are often overlooked as the determinants of behavior.

Without arguing for or against a particular unit of analysis for the study of socialization, the position taken here is that it is the additive nature of such "minisocialization" encounters which are important to organizations. Personal change attributed to a search for "psychological safety," consequently, occurs only after a number of situations have convinced an individual that his "present self" is unworthy—or after a particularly catastrophic encounter. Additionally, while individual attitudes may gloss over specific characteristics of change settings, they provide good approximations as to the consequences of the various settings provided by organizational membership.

For a further discussion of the ethnomethodological perspective, see: Turner (1974); Sudnow (1972); and Garfinkel (1967).

life-space is differentially distributed. Hence, the minimal levels of effort and performance required and displayed by a new member in the organizational setting are linked intrinsically to the mode of socialization.

The following discussion lists five modes of organizational socialization. Each is viewed from the perspective of its likely outcomes. It is felt that this listing is sufficiently general to include all the major approaches available to organizations.[21]

Training

This mode of socialization is at times difficult to separate from the education method to be discussed next. For the purposes here, training will be related to the instrumental goals of socialization (Etzioni, 1961). The training process is skill-oriented and directed toward imparting the abilities and knowledge necessary for the new member to perform a designated organizational role. Furthermore, training should be thought of as that portion of skill-related socialization that occurs within the organization or work group in which the new recruit is to participate.

The problem with the above definition is that training programs are never limited to their nominal objectives. Caplow (1964:173) states:

> Organizations that conduct training programs conceive of them as imparting skills, but analysis of any particular training program always shows it to be concerned with the communication of values, the development of an ambiance, the rejection of prior affiliations and the development of an appropriate self-image.

If a training program is to influence behavior, it must affect the participants' motivations, response capacities, self-images, and/or role prescriptions (Lawler, 1971a). Thus the training program may provide different influences for persons with different entering characteristics. For example, for those new members with sufficient motivation, the training program will largely consist of instrumental activities (i.e., the learning of role prescriptions and response capacities). For others, it may be a more expressive process designed to change

---

[21] Quite clearly, much socialization which occurs in organizations results from the informal interaction among the participants. Indeed, the "trial and error" mode of socialization occurs frequently in organizations. For example, Caplow (1964) notes that the founders of any organization are necessarily socialized in this manner. Furthermore, much of the learning a newcomer experiences in the organization is of the nonprogrammed variety—regardless of the form and content of the designed socialization process. As a rule of thumb, this method of socialization has been relied upon when experience demonstrates to organizational decision-makers that most neophytes adjust to situational demands without formal direction. For the most part, such a strategy implies that the informal networks which exist within the organization provide the newcomer with sufficient guidelines to meet the organization's minimal requirements.

In this section, however, I concentrate upon the more defined socialization techniques available to the organization. While the "trial and error" mode may certainly be the conscious choice of the organization, it implies no special effort in which to modify the attitudes, knowledge or motivations of newcomers.

the individual's motivation and self-image. Fine (1970) referred to these targets of expressive socialization as "adaptive" skills. He suggested that such skills provide the new member with the ability to cope with the organizational demands for conformity. In other words, training may have to provide a new member with a baseline of social attitudes and abilities which allow him to perform specific role-related skills required by the organization.

The interpretations of others or evaluations of an individual's performance during the training phase may have lasting effects on the person's later career. Those recruits who are assessed as the "right" type for the organization may be in the best position for later advancement. Those trainees who are perceived as having an "attitude problem" may well have future difficulties within the organization. Hence, if a new member is unable to present a "face" which conveys the message that he has no need of expressive socialization, he may find that his success or failure to learn the specific role of his work makes little difference to his organizational future. While it is clear that organizations vary regarding the expressive content of their training programs, all organizations at least require that the new member demonstrate the "proper attitude"—which ranges from a simple criterion, such as "being on time" to far more elaborate criteria, such as "speaking the organizational line." In general, the longer the period of training, the more emphasis is placed upon development of the "proper attitudes" in new members.

In recent years, some relatively new techniques have been developed to promote "planned change" in organizations. Under various semantic disguises (e.g., organizational development, team building, and sensitivity training), these techniques seek to increase organizational effectiveness by affecting employee attitudes (Strauss, 1975 [Chapter 13, this volume]).[22] Essentially, these training strategies focus upon both latent and manifest interpersonal problems and attack such problems by open confrontation conducted normally under the leadership of an experienced "trainer" or "consultant." As such, these techniques rely heavily upon the principles of group dynamics as postulated by Lewin (1938).

Some critics of these new techniques claim they are merely dressed up traditional training tactics (e.g., role-playing, guided discussions, case studies, etc.). Strauss (1975), however, notes that because of their emphasis upon the "here and now," organizationally-wide objectives, structural implications, two-way communications, and feedback, these more recent modes of training can be distinguished from their historical predecessors.

The effectiveness of these training devices is difficult to gauge. Yet it does seem clear that they, at least, may bolster morale. Unfortunately, research in this area is enormously difficult—as is research directed toward measuring the effectiveness of any of the socialization/training techniques (see Section Five).

---

[22] The placement of these techniques within this subsection—rather than the education subsection which follows—was made on the basis that most of these programs are conducted on an in-house basis. Furthermore, while there are some real differences among each of these training modes (i.e., sensitivity training is not synonymous with organizational development), their goals are quite similar and, hence, are lumped together here. Finally, the treatment afforded these techniques in this section does not reflect their prevalence within organizations. Yet, since these techniques are rarely utilized during the "breaking in" process, only an abbreviated consideration is presented.

Education

This mode of socialization refers to the systematic teaching of values and skills required for participation in an organization. However, it specifically refers to those learning experiences which occur outside the organization in which the individual will eventually participate.[23]

Generally, the scope of the educational process is broader than the role requirements of a particular organization. Caplow (1964:172) states:

> The educational institution prepares its students not for a particular socializing experience, but for a vast number of such experiences with similar requirements.

Socialization into the so-called professional organizations relies extensively upon this method. Abramson (1967) notes that professional education creates strong identifications. In fact, he feels that an individual's sense of identity becomes intimately tied to his professional role. Recently, Miller and Wager (1971) found that a professional's role orientation (i.e., local, cosmopolitan, mixture, indifferent) was dependent upon the length and type of education he received prior to joining an organization (i.e., the length and type of education was determined by the type of degree the person held [M.A., M.S., or Ph.D.]). Not surprisingly, they found that the longer and more "scientific" an individual's education, the more likely he was to assume a cosmopolitan role orientation upon entering the organization. While the purpose here is not to delve deeply into the concerns of professionalization, it should be recognized that the professional school is a major socializing institution.

The educational method combines both instrumental and expressive goals of socialization. Organizations are generally most concerned with the expressive outcomes of the educational mode, limiting their concern for the instrumental outcomes to some minimal level (Schein, 1962; Becker and Strauss, 1956). Yet, as Etzioni (1961) observed, instrumental socialization usually becomes more salient and important as the individual nears the end of the educational process. As the person reaches the terminal point, he is assumed to have internalized the values, attitudes and motives since he has proved his desire to become an organizational member by virtue of his tenacity.

Whether education can truly be regarded as an organizational socialization technique depends partially on the degree to which the organization influences the particular educational institutions. However, all educational organizations must respond and adjust to the prevailing climate outside their boundaries. Furthermore, organizations consciously set prerequisites for membership. Thus, the degree to which these selection criteria are associated with an individual's educational attainment determine the extent to which the organization utilizes the educational method of socialization.

---

[23] To some degree, both training and educational modes may be viewed as the "first wave" of socialization. The "second wave" occurs when the newcomer is actually placed in his designated organizational position. Where the "first wave" emphasizes general skills and attitudes, the "second wave" stresses specific behaviors and idiosyncratic nuances within the organizational setting. Inkeles (1969:152) describes this phenomenon as follows: "The second wave in the socialization process occurs where and when the individual learns the detailed role contents which are socially necessary to behave in a previously acquired disposition and where the new dispositions and social skills couldn't have been learned earlier."

Apprenticeship

This method of socialization is similar to the training method in that it takes place within the organization. However, the responsibility for transforming the new member to full status is delegated to selected experienced organizational members. Such a mode of socialization is frequently used (although not exclusively) in graduate schools, craft guilds, police departments, business organizations, etc. Caplow (1964) suggests that the practice is common whenever the incumbent is viewed by the organization as being the only member capable to form his own successor. He notes that this is often the case in the upper levels of bureaucratic systems.

Since the delegation of responsibility is to only one member of the organization, that member may be viewed as a role-model which the new participant is expected to emulate. The one-to-one situation is likely to lead to an intense, value-oriented socialization effort, with the outcomes dependent upon the quality of the affective relationship which may (or may not) develop. In cases of high affect, the socialization process works well and the new member is likely to internalize fully the values of the particular role he is to play. However, when there are few affective bonds between the two individuals, the socialization process is likely to be incomplete and may lead to inefficacious results. This implies that while role-skills may be transferred, confirmation of full acceptance into the organization depends upon the judgment of the experienced member regarding the recruit's conformity to the older member's expectations. Ultimately, these expectations are embedded within the values and norms of the particular organization. Clearly, in such socialization settings, there is no middle ground—either the new members fail or succeed. Consequently, apprenticeship must be viewed as an expensive mode of socialization for failures cannot easily be rescued. Training, because of its ease, efficiency and predictability, has tended to replace apprenticeship in the modern organization—except for those positions considered of high importance (Caplow, 1964).

Becker and Strauss (1956) and Hughes (1958a) use the notion of sponsorship to discuss the apprenticeship mode of socialization.[24] Describing the interdependence of careers within organizations, they point out that during a new member's early organizational experiences, he must be more concerned with satisfying the expectations of his sponsor than with satisfying the expectations of the organization (although the two sets of expectations may be closely related, if not the same). The ability of the new member to satisfy organizational demands influences his sponsor's stature within the organization. If the new member is perceived as doing well, the role of the sponsor in the process is likely to be minor. However, if the recruit is perceived as proceeding poorly, the sponsor's role is likely to become much more active.

Debasement Experiences

This mode of socialization is most frequently encountered in "resocialization" organizations. As noted, resocialization organizations aim to destroy old and

---

[24] The organizational practice of nepotism is somewhat akin to apprenticeship. Although nepotism cannot analytically be considered a socialization technique *per se*, it does imply that the nepotist assume some responsibility for his new member (Caplow, 1964). However, the inculcation of values and attitudes appropriate to the organization takes place in the family (or other primary groups of which both the nepotist and protégé are members).

create new behavioral predispositions in their new members (Wheeler, 1966). Goffman (1961:14) noted that such settings process a neophyte through a "series of abasements, degradations, humiliations and profanations of self." The object of such a process is to force the new member to relinquish his previous roles by depriving the person of his incoming self-image. Porter (1971:15) stated:

> This method refers to dramatic experiences the individual undergoes that have the effect of detaching him from his previous attitudes and ways of thinking about himself and substitution of a more humble self-view that will permit easier application of organizational influence.

The experiences created in these settings (deliberately or accidentally) serve to deprive the new member of control over his own activities and make it difficult for him to resist the organizational directives. Features of this mode include: standardization of appearance, removal of any outside identifying devices, punishments for slight deviations of organizational rules, minute subjection to routine events calculated to embarrass or demean, and verbal profanations.

While debasement experiences are used more intensively in resocialization settings, all organizations, to some degree, utilize this method. Consistent with the preceding sections of this chapter, the learning of new responses to situational demands usually requires the abandonment of the old responses. Debasement is often the most effective mode of demonstrating to the new member the need to acquire new responses. The problem with this tactic is its intrinsically alienating character. If the potential rewards of "learning the ropes" are not of sufficient worth to the person, if able, he will leave the organization. Hence, the extent to which this mode is utilized depends, in part, upon the ability of the organization to hold the new members captive.

Cooptation

This method of socialization refers to a two-step process in which the new member is first admitted into the organization and then absorbed into a particular subculture within the organization. The sequence is indeed quite common. The work of Selznick (1949), Dalton (1959), Wheeler (1961), and Avery (1968) all demonstrate the pervasiveness of this phenomenon.

Cooptation has been defined by Selznick (1949:13) as

> ... the process of absorbing new elements into the leadership or policy determining structure of an organization as a means of converting threats to its stability or existence.

Often, cooptation is used as an organizational tool for the absorption of a particular collective subculture into the larger culture. By tying the subcultural (and individual) expectations and interests to the larger system, the organization is presumably able to check deviancy. Leeds (1964) describes a process by which a previously nonconforming enclave is given legitimacy. Hence, the subcultural goals become linked to the organizational goals. Such "protest absorption" works with individuals or groups. For example, an innovative, yet rebellious new member may be allowed to implement his plans, and in this way the organization shows him that the success of his ideas depends upon the success of the larger system.[25]

The "methods of socialization" list could be expanded. However, the differences between added strategies and the ones named above would be slight and provide little more of substance to this discussion.[26] Attention is now focused upon cases where the socialization efforts fail or where the effort produces outcomes which have dysfunctional consequences from the organization's perspective. Such considerations are discussed under the heading "inefficacious socialization."

V. INEFFICACIOUS SOCIALIZATION

When dealing with socialization outcomes which differ from certain organizational objectives, researchers have exhibited some conceptual and terminological confusion. On one hand, individuals who are not integrated successfully into the organization are often stigmatized as socialization failures. Yet, even in the case of early withdrawal from the organization (both voluntary and involuntary), it is likely that a certain amount of learning and personal change did occur.[27]

On the other hand, the socialization process is often deemed unsuccessful if it produces the overconforming member. White (1956) referred to such

---

[25] It should be emphasized that the use of co-optation as a method of organizational socialization rarely occurs at the "breaking in" stage. Normally, this technique is reserved for those members with at least some organizational history. Indeed, most neophytes are hardly in a position to be absorbed into leadership roles within the organization. Furthermore, to be a candidate for co-optation, one must be labelled a nonconformist and such labelling takes time. However, in some cases, co-optation is used as an entering socialization mode. For example, as a result of some fundamental changes in the delegate selection rules, the 1972 Democratic National Convention represented a large scale co-optation process in which former "deviant" amateurs became professionals in one fell swoop. Or, as another example, certain programs in the so-called War on Poverty relied extensively upon co-optation as a means of attaching indigenous "street" leaders to the means and ends of the intervening Federal agency.

[26] Some observers postulate an additional socialization technique labelled "conversion" (Porter, 1971; Caplow, 1964; Schein, 1961; etc.). To these researchers, conversion occurs as a result of some traumatic experience and results in the person's alteration of deeply felt attitudes and values. The argument normally made for distinguishing conversion from other modes of socialization is that it occurs rapidly, involves one's self-concepts and is usually self-initiated. The position I have taken here rejects this distinction and notes that even in religious conversions a strong social element is almost always present (Gregg, 1972; Strauss, 1968). Furthermore, for conversion to "stick," it generally must be supported by some or all of the listed socialization techniques.

[27] For example, a neophyte may enter the organization with the appropriate abilities for successful participation. However, during his initiation period, he discovers that his *a priori* expectations and values regarding the organization are at variance with the reality of membership and the person withdraws from the system. Clearly, both attitude and behavioral changes have occurred. Assuming the member entered the organization with some motivation to participate, the decision to leave represents perhaps a dramatic shift in the individual's values, norms and behavior patterns.

Similarly, those persons involuntarily severed from the organization have also been exposed to the various influences of the socialization process. What is rarely recognized in these situations is that the perceived failures may have been a consequence of the socialization process itself (e.g., trainer-trainee relationships as generating self-fulfilling prophecies; debasement experiences which create traumatic, sometimes immobilizing individual reactions, etc.). Furthermore, involuntary dismissal from an organization is itself a powerful socialization influence.

outcomes as "regrettable socialization." Another researcher coined the term "institutional automaton" to refer to the overconforming member (Dubin, 1959). In such cases, the process results in an organizational member who adheres ritualistically to the existing norms, values and behaviors communicated to him during his socialization experiences. Such outcomes may be even more dysfunctional to the organization than the so-called socialization failures.

For the purpose of this chapter, the term "inefficacious socialization" is used to refer to the process which fails to produce outcomes which are in the managerial interests of the organization. Importantly, this definition casts both overconformity and underconformity under the same analytical rubric.

It is important when discussing inefficacious socialization to keep in mind the type of organization involved. What is inefficacious to one organization may well be success to another. As noted, utilitarian organizations differ from normative organizations in that they typically require only compliance to a set of minimum behavioral demands. For example, Dubin (1951) suggested that in most work settings, it does not make much difference to a firm whether its employees are motivated by "lust," "greed," or "love." All that is important is that they are motivated. For such organizations, socialization techniques which are concerned with a new member's motivational bases may prompt inefficacious outcomes.

As indicated, organizations make varying demands upon entering members. However, in all organizations, the knowledge, acceptance and fulfillment of certain requirements are necessary if a new member is to be granted continuing membership. Schein (1968a) distinguishes three sets of role behaviors in terms of their necessity *vis-à-vis* the organization's goals. His model is psychosocial in that it places extensive reliance upon the neophyte's perception of the situational requirements.

Socialization processes, according to Schein, are most concerned with securing a new member's acceptance of role-behaviors which are "pivotal" to the organization's mission. Such pivotal behaviors are essential if the person is to perform at a minimally acceptable level. Therefore pivotal role demands are aimed normally at task-related behavior. Next, Schein notes that socialization processes may induce or make salient certain "relevant" role-behaviors. These behaviors are considered by the organization to be desirable, but not absolutely necessary for organizational participation. They generally involve matters of decorum and have little to do with an individual's ability and willingness to perform an assigned role. Finally, Schein suggests that socialization processes may induce certain "peripheral" role behaviors. While these behaviors may be inculcated or reinforced by certain structural aspects of the organizational processes, they must be viewed as ultimately undesirable and as interfering with the organizational goals. Peripheral role-behaviors may be task- or decorum-directed, yet regardless of orientation, such behavior is regarded as dysfunctional from the organization's perspective.

To Schein, outcomes of socialization processes can be seen in light of the above role demands. Drawing heavily from Merton (1957), he notes that three basic responses can characterize socialization outcomes.[28] The first is "rebellion."

---

[28] In Merton's (1957) justly acclaimed work, he distinguishes four modes of "deviant" adjustments ranging from innovation to rebellion. Each mode is based upon one's acceptance or rejection of cultural goals and institutional means. Complimentary to the discussion here, Merton views deviancy in terms of overconformity and underconformity to these goals and means.

This outcome refers to a new member's rejection of all organizational demands. Hence, either the individual convinces the organization to alter its role demands or the person leaves the organizational setting (either he quits or is dismissed). The second type of response involves the new member's acceptance of the pivotal demands, but also involves the neophyte's rejection of most relevant and peripheral role-behaviors. This type of response is labelled by Schein, "creative individualism." The third response is called "conformity." This type of outcome involves the new member's acceptance of all role demands—pivotal, relevant and peripheral. Since all organizations, in the long run, require innovation and change, the results of conformity as a socialization outcome tend to be suboptimal, causing stagnation.

It must be emphasized that these three responses to the organization's socialization efforts fall roughly on a continuum. The extremes of rebellion and conformity represent end points from the organization's perspective. Within this framework, socialization processes may be classified according to their likely outcomes. Some organizations, such as prisons, produce rebellion in their new members as the modal response.[29] Other organizations, such as professional schools, produce conformity as the modal response. While most organizational socialization processes deliberately attempt to avoid creating extreme responses, the line separating inefficacious socialization from its counterpart is often difficult to maintain. As Porter (1971:19) states

> ...it is often hard for both the individual and the organization to discern when a person is exhibiting enough individualization to contribute something new and valuable to the total collectivity, on the one hand, and when one is going so far in this direction, on the other, that he is in danger of tearing down a reasonably well functioning system, rather than building it up.

Consequently, the encouragement of "creative individualism" is problematic. Some insight into this perplexing issue is provided by Dubin (1959). He suggests that innovation in organizational settings must be viewed as deviant behavior because such behavior requires, at least, partial rejection of the organizational values, goals or institutional routines.[30] Within Schein's model, such outcomes are functional and may lead to the development of "creative individualism." Thus organizational socialization processes which do not have sufficient flexibility to tolerate deviant cases are likely to produce conformity or rebellion as modal response categories.

---

[29] Schein displays a certain amount of definitional confusion when he fails to specify the type of role-behaviors which characterize the "rebel" response. Since the rebel does *something* in reaction to his situation, his role-behavior in my view must be seen as peripheral. Even if the novice does nothing but "sit on his hands," this so-called act of rebellion must be recognized as a role-behavior. In this sense, the rebel is analytically similar to the "conformist," for it is the peripheral role-behaviors which are likely to create organizational problems.

[30] Dubin's (1959) analysis of deviant behavior lists fourteen types of deviant adaptations in social action. While only a few of these adaptations would be considered inefficacious outcomes as defined in this chapter, his discussion illuminates several useful concepts related to the general organizational socialization process. For example, unlike Schein, Dubin distinguishes between active and passive rejection. Active rejection implies that the person attempts to substitute his own values, norms or behaviors for those values, norms and behaviors demanded by the organization. Passive rejection merely means the individual rejects certain values, norms or behaviors without attempting to replace them with others of his own. Thus active rebellion may have far different consequences for the organization than passive rebellion.

This notion of tolerable levels of deviancy brings into question some of Schein's observations concerning inefficacious socialization. First it becomes clear that both creative individualism and rebellion are deviant responses to an organization's socialization efforts. The difference between them is actually a matter of degree. Furthermore, the boundary between creative individualism and rebellion is in large part dependent upon environmental contingencies (e.g., when economic conditions are good, the organization can tolerate more "rebels" than when economic conditions are poor).

Second, Schein's portrait of the rebel as having virtually no serviceable value to the organization ignores an important sociological observation. Essentially, as Durkheim (1938) noted long ago, deviance often performs a needed function by drawing people together in a posture of indignation. The rebel therefore may provide a focus for organizational feelings by drawing attention to the values which constitute the "collective conscience" of the organization.

Third and related closely to the above qualification, deviancy must be viewed as a labelling process undertaken by certain organizational participants. In other words, deviancy is not a property inherent in a particular activity, rather it is an external property conferred upon certain behavior by members of the organization who come into contact with it. In a sense, behaviors which are labelled deviant define the contours of the organization. Furthermore, we must treat deviant behavior from several levels of analysis; for what is deviant at one level (e.g., to one's cohort of peers) is not deviant at another level (e.g., to the organization). This distinction suggests that Schein's pivotal, relevant and peripheral role-behaviors are not meaningful unless their specific organizational referent is denoted.

Finally, Schein's emphasis upon organizationally defined peripheral behavior somewhat obfuscates the individual's perspective toward his target roles. In general, the range and variety of individual role preferences exceed those roles provided by the organization. Colloquially, we speak of such situations as "fitting a square peg in a round hole." Since the individual cannot alter the organizational complex at will, the limitation of role-behaviors to the pivotal set is likely to be extremely confining to the person. It is probably correct to say that few persons find their organizationally defined mold fully suitable in all respects, and for many, such a mold is appropriately comparable to a strait jacket.

Within this framework, socialization settings can be classified according to the degree they allow for differential (or deviant) role-behaviors on the part of the neophytes. Clearly, socialization processes which systematically ground out all individual efforts at modifying pivotal role behaviors are as dysfunctional to the long range interest of the organization as processes which promote a cornucopia of anarchistic role-behaviors. Consequently, contrary to Schein's view, some peripheral role-behaviors are undoubtedly functional (both to the individual and to the organization at large).[31]

---

[31] To be fair to Schein's work, he does postulate a sort of reverse socialization process called "innovation" which attempts to account for differential role responses. In brief, he claims the "innovation" process coexists with the socialization process with the same person typically being influenced and, in turn, exerting influence. Basically, this concept requires the person be regarded as struggling to maintain some degree of self-control over the situation so that the organization may better satisfy his needs.

The problem with this twin process idea is the difficulty inherent in distinguishing

With these qualifications in mind, several examples of inefficacious socialization (from the organization's perspective) are presented below. These illustrations deal with the extent to which organizational socialization processes are designed (intentionally or unintentionally) to develop newcomers to fill pivotal, relevant or peripheral role demands. These cases are believed to be sufficiently common; to have rather wide applicability across institutional settings.

Obsolete socialization involves providing the new member with social learning in an area which was once functional to the organization, but has since been abandoned. In other words, pivotal roles have been altered without the necessary changes occurring in the socialization process. Caplow (1964:190) suggests that changes in the organization may have retroactive effects upon the completed processes of socialization. He states,

> After members have been induced to accept certain values, it may happen that the organization itself abandons them. What was once adaptively useful becomes an obstacle to adaption. Successful socialization sometimes lures the recruit into a situation he finds progressively less satisfying with the passage of time.

Another problem arises when a new member's socialization into the organization is carried on without reference to his other role requirements outside the organization. Since an individual always has difficulty satisfying all demands placed upon his various memberships, role strain is likely to develop (Goode, 1960). The individual's response may be an attempt to manipulate the situation to some acceptable level of strain or to set limits upon the degree to which he will allow the organization to penetrate his life-space. Both of these response influence the outcomes of the socialization process. Hence, success of the process depends in part upon the sensitivity exhibited by the organization to the new member's other obligations. If the organization is extremely insensitive, the new member is likely to assume peripheral role-behaviors calculated to minimize role strain and may force the individual to adopt an extreme location on the response continuum (rebellion or overconformity). For example, these considerations are inherent in the local-cosmopolitan issue discussed in a preceding section. If the organization attempts to force the new member into adopting the local orientation, it may lose his participation, or result in an overconforming member who no longer will contribute innovative suggestions developed from a cosmopolitan orientation. Some organizations—particularly the more coercive total institutions—attempt to overcome role strain by providing a new member with only one relevant role and setting—each one defined solely by the organization.

A loss of idealism occurring with the socialization process has been postulated by a number of researchers (Merton, 1957; Stouffer, 1949; Schein, 1961, 1962; Becker, et al., 1961). In fact, Caplow (1964:199) stated that much of the socialization experience results in the individual's "progressive abandonment of the organization's major values." Furthermore, it is viewed as the

---

whether or not a particular outcome is attributable to innovation or to socialization. Furthermore, innovation attempts may be viewed as originating within and stimulated by the socialization efforts. Hence it seems pointless to confuse an already murky area with another process.

gradual development of cynicism toward the organization's proclaimed objectives. A new member learns that the organization's goals which he first encountered (and which are communicated to the outside environment) cannot justify his activities within the organization. This realization is likely to be disturbing to a recruit. To compensate, he adopts peripheral behaviors—such as rejecting the organizational values. However, as noted previously, such loss of idealism is a very general process. Schein (1962) states that accepting the emotional reality of organizational life always involves the reconciliation of expectations and actual experience. As Dubin (1959) suggests, a "levelling of aspirations" helps many individuals cope more meaningfully with their life chances.[32]

This brief discussion has suggested that if the socialization process is to avoid inefficacious outcomes, it must, among other things, deal with questions of obsolescence, role strain and a loss of idealism. If the process is not attuned sufficiently to these considerations, peripheral role adjustments will be made by the entering members. Consequently, all socialization efforts must build in dynamic reassessment devices that gauge short- and long-run effects, both intended and unintended.

To conclude this section, a partial outcome typology is suggested. This classification is believed useful for depicting an individual's mode of adjustment to his organizational setting. The typology is partial because it rests upon only two general features of organizational socialization—the degree to which the individual satisfies the expectations of his relevant group; and the degree to which the individual satisfies the expectations of the formal organization.[33] A complete typology would include other sets of expectations which arise in socialization settings, including those of the new member himself. However, this systematic outcome grouping has wide applicability since the expectations of the group and the organization are two of the more salient socialization demands to which the novice must quickly adapt. More importantly, this classification scheme dramatically illustrates the differential meanings accorded to pivotal, relevant and peripheral role demands.

The "teamplayer" refers to the individual who conforms to both group and organizational expectations. To a large degree, this mode of adjustment implies that the expectations and objectives of one's own group are in accord with the organizational expectations and objectives. Such modes of adjustment are frequently found in the teamplayer's metaphorical source, the sporting world (e.g., professional football players are expected to be teamplayers re-

---

[32] In a sense, such a phenomenon can be viewed as a sort of institutionalized cognitive dissonance process. Hence, individuals (especially at the lower organizational levels) begin to recognize that their aspirations are unlikely to be fulfilled and devalue such expectations accordingly. One purpose of the socialization process (particularly the informal or nonprogrammed portion of the process) is to provide the individual with information upon which he can somewhat accurately appraise his "life chances" within the organization. For some excellent discussions of this process, see: Chinoy (1955); Cyert and March (1963); Caplow (1964); Vroom (1964); Vroom and Deci (1971).

[33] In many organizational settings, the relevant group to which one belongs is preoccupied with avoiding the focused attention of higher-ups in the organization (or "outsiders" in general). These groups are called "teams" by Goffman (1959:104). In "Goffmanesque," a team is "A set of individuals whose intimate cooperation is required if a projected definition of the situation is to be maintained." Consequently, in such organizations, the individual's adaptation to situational requirements involves learning how to adjust to formal requirements in a manner which maintains the team definitions.

TABLE 1
A PARTIAL TYPOLOGY OF INDIVIDUAL ADJUSTMENT
WITHIN ORGANIZATIONAL SETTINGS

	Level to which the Person Satisfies the Expectations of:	
Mode of Adjustment	The Relevant Group	The Organization
"Teamplayer"	Acceptable	Acceptable
"Isolate"	Unacceptable	Acceptable
"Warrior"	Acceptable	Unacceptable
"Outsider"	Unacceptable	Unacceptable

gardless of whether they are defensive or offensive specialists). By the same token, the industrial worker who satisfies the organizationally defined production quotas without violating the informal restrictions of his cohorts is a teamplayer. In general, the teamplayer adjusts to allow both organizational overseers and the members of his relevant group to claim, "he's on our side."

The "isolate," however, is the person who satisfies only the expectations of the organization—he does not fulfill the demands of his relevant group. Ratebusters afford us excellent illustrations of this adjustment mode (Roy, 1953). More often than not, the organizational parvenu falls into the isolate category. For example, persons protected by "good connections" in the organization often fall within this class (e.g., the army private who "pulls soft duty" to the chagrin of his peers).

The "warrior," on the other hand, is a participant who engages in a running battle with the organization at large—with the rules, policies, management, structure, etc. Protected to a certain degree by his relevant group, the warrior may be the union steward, the dissident professor, the haughty clerk or the iconoclast senator. While the warrior may be a thorn in the organization's side, such individuals are fully supported and accepted by their peers. Situations marked by union contracts, strong institutional norms and civil service regulations are ripe for developing warriors because of the relative freedom individuals possess *vis-à-vis* organizational punishments.

Finally, there is the "outsider." He is the individual who fails to meet the expectations of either the group or the organization. Normally, such participants find their organizational membership shortlived. In some cases, however, the outsider acquires support for his deviant position and moves into the warrior or isolate classifications (or, in the extreme, he converts the entire organizational system, becoming a teamplayer in the process).

Within the scope of this section, the above typology denotes that socialization which is efficacious to the group may sometimes be inefficacious from the organizational perspective. Schein's conception of role-behaviors is a helpful device for understanding this classification of organizational socialization outcomes. The position assumed in this section argues that the determining factor of a particular adjustment mode is the degree to which relevant or peripheral role-behaviors interfere with pivotal role-behaviors (pivotal from either the group or organizational frame of reference—or both). For example, warriors and isolates exist because what is pivotal from the group's (or organization's) perspective is merely relevant from the organization's (or group's) perspective. For the teamplayer, pivotal role demands overlap the group and organization. He need not adopt relevant or peripheral role-behaviors to satisfy particular expectations.

This abbreviated paradigm hints that relevant or peripheral role-behaviors arise because the group and organization may differ as to the definition of pivotal role behaviors. To the group, behaviors which help the collectivity reach valued goals or protect certain privileges may be pivotal. To the organization, such behaviors are inappropriate because they have little relationship to the organization mission. For example, in police departments, the conflict between patrolmen and the "brass" over ticketing rates (pivotal role expectation *vis-à-vis* the organization; peripheral role expectation *vis-à-vis* the patrolmen) often force patrolmen to assume either a warrior- or isolate-like stance in regard to this issue. Teamplaying in the situation is prohibited since pivotal role demands differ.

To conclude, this discussion says little about the processes which characterize each outcome. While each adjustment may be thought of as a predictable state, there is little empirical evidence at the present time to establish anything resembling a comprehensive theory. Furthermore, these adjustment modes are ideal concepts. Indeed, it is unlikely that any pure cases of the categories exist. For example, the teamplayer is probably acceptable to the group because he is at crucial times a warrior, helping the group fend against the organization. At other times, he may well be an isolate, playing up to the organization at the expense of the group. Thus the teamplayer is able to balance these different expectations in a manner which is acceptable to both audiences.

VI. CODA

As the length of this chapter indicates, the topic has involved a multitude of interrelated considerations. Basically, this chapter represented an attempt to isolate and thus highlight the more conspicuous of these considerations. In this section, a brief summary statement is presented which indicates the range of the previous discussion. Following this cursory review, some remarks will be directed toward the specification of certain areas requiring further research.

Summary

The foregoing discussion has been based upon the premise that an individual's socialization into the organization is a continuous process carried on by a variety of sources both inside and outside the formal membership boundaries. Furthermore, the socialization process was viewed as providing the recruit with a sort of organizational *Weltanschauung*—consisting of unique norms of conduct, esoteric sets of values and an outlook toward the organization which is shared with other participants.

Organizational socialization was viewed as a special case of a larger research area labelled adult socialization. The focus was upon a person's adjustment to both specific and generalized role demands considered necessary for participation in generalized social settings. The individual's personality system was defined to consist of a set of self-other relationships which become in-

creasingly complex as the person ages and moves in and out of an assortment of roles.

It was suggested that the individual's movement into organizational environments entails boundary passages across several dimensions. Each of these dimensions possesses a certain set of characteristics which, when related to a person's prior experiences, motivations, values and expectancies, help determine the ease or difficulty associated with linking the individual to the organization.

The transformation from nonmember to member was perceived as a three-stage process. First, the preentry problem of choice was viewed generally as being contingent upon the degree of anticipatory socialization experienced by the individual and the perceived structural surroundings in which the organization was located. Second, a person's entry into the organization was seen as involving an encounter often associated with a reality shock. However, the impact and outcome of the encounter phase was considered to be mediated by the interplay among environmental, organizational, relevant group, task and personal variables. Third, it was proposed that if the individual was to continue with the organization, he must undergo some type of metamorphosis. However, the intensity and depth of individual change was regarded as situationally determined and dependent upon both organizational and individual characteristics.

Consequently, in some organizations, the socialization process is like "passing through the mirror ... [to create] ... the sense of seeing the world in reverse" (Hughes, 1958a; Davis, 1968). In other organizations, the socialization process does not involve such profound change. However, the assumption that guided the discussion throughout this chapter was that some sort of "deformation professionale" process was common to all organizations.

This chapter stressed that the content of various socialization processes was more important and diverse than the forms in which the process occurred. Although, for purposes of clarification, several general socialization techniques were discussed and related to their outcomes.

Finally, inefficacious socialization was analyzed in terms of outcomes which do not contribute to the overall success of the organization. While inefficacious socialization was viewed as providing for individual adjustments, such adjustments were suboptimal from the organizational perspective—although not necessarily dysfunctional *vis-à-vis* the neophyte.

New Directions

As noted, the interest in childhood socialization has a rich and historical past while adult socialization has only just begun to excite scholarly attention. Only recently have scholars questioned the assumption that the major determinants of behavior are established irrevocably in childhood. Despite this lengthy period of neglect, the newborn interest in adult socialization has produced much theoretical speculation. Furthermore, the literature abounds with research reports describing adult changes.

The problem is simply that there is minimal empirical validation for the growing number of conceptual models. Even the available descriptions of adult change have little to say about the underlying phenomenon which would explain such alterations. For example, the relationships between status passages and changes in personal identity (critical to most theories of adult change) have received only slight empirical attention. Similarly, the process by which identical settings produce different impacts on individuals has not been investigated systematically. Fundamentally, it is the relationships among the characteristics of socialization settings and the changes in personal identity which demand further consideration and empirical examination.

Turning specifically to organizational socialization, a large part of the available literature is devoted to what can be referred to as the "training and development dustbowl." Although the tremendous jump in training budgets during the past decade reflects, in part, a strong belief that programs can be constructed readily which will successfully integrate new members into the organizational system, such programs usually rest upon speculative assumptions devoid of theoretical input. Additionally, very little work has been directed toward the evaluation of the short and long range effects of such programs (Strauss, 1975). Unfortunately, it appears that most training programs are more often based upon passion rather than upon reason. As Lawler (1971a:34) stated:

> By and large, the training and development literature is voluminous, nonempirical, nontheoretical, poorly written and dull. It is fadish to the extreme.

Research in the training area must consequently be devoted to developing testable theories outlining the critical variables and their interaction effects, as well as developing the ability to assess accurately the outcomes of these specialized socialization experiences.[34]

As I indicated in Section Five, the area labelled "inefficacious socialization" is burdened with conceptual and methodological problems. Indeed, while some lip service has been paid to the functions of deviant modes of individual adaptations within organizations, such outcomes have not generated much empirical research. Furthermore, we know very little about the types of deviant definitions which exist in organizations at various levels of analysis. Nor do we have data regarding the ceremonial confrontations between the deviant and the offended. In a figurative sense, at least, organizationally acceptable and unacceptable behaviors meet during such confrontations, and it is during this meeting that the line between the two is drawn. Therefore, these "degradation ceremonies" may provide a very interesting setting from which to observe the definitional properties of inefficacious socialization.

Schein (1965) notes that most studies of individual adjustment to organizational demands have discovered little change. However, he points out that these studies have concentrated predominantly upon broad, widely held cultural values which tend to remain stable regardless of the contextual situation. What is required is research which aims at beliefs, attitudes and motivations unique to a particular feature of social settings. Consequently, social settings and their corresponding structures can be related comparatively to both the methods and outcomes of the organizational socialization process.

---

[34] In practice, research on training involves a number of problems. Aside from the criteria problem faced in all types of evaluative research, the multiplicity of variables involved in training programs creates havoc for the researcher interested in designing scientifically valid experiments. Yet as Argyris (1970) has argued, just because research is difficult is no reason to avoid trying.

Unmistakably, longitudinal study designs are a prerequisite if the organizational socialization process is to be understood adequately. Far too much research has been conducted cross-sectionally without insuring the proper controls needed to measure personal changes attributable to the socialization process. Furthermore, most career studies do not look beyond the decision to engage in a formal course of study or to accept a particular job. However, as noted in this chapter, there is growing support for the contention that the early organizational socialization process is a major factor involved in a person's later career.

Regrettably, there is little evidence available to determine the relative importance of the various characteristics of the organizational socialization process. Hence, research questions need to be addressed toward the various contingencies upon which outcomes of the process depend. For example, at present, it is difficult to assess which organizational factors outweigh certain relevant group factors in the determination of the socialization outcomes. Furthermore, little is known about the relative long range effects of the various methods of socialization. Consequently, little advancement in the comprehension of the process can be expected until the variables of organizational socialization are investigated in a comparative fashion.

Throughout this chapter, socialization has been viewed as an interactive process carried on largely between the individual and the organization. This perspective suggests that a conflict model may provide an excellent analytic tool by which to view the socialization processes. Indeed, the organization may be viewed as a negotiating environment in which the individual (and his allies) is pitted against the socialization agents. Such an approach would postulate a game analogy, the results of which could be cast in terms of zero sum or non-zero sum outcomes. Furthermore, this frame of reference would feature certain power variables which are so noticeably lacking in most of the research to date. Perhaps viewing the entire organization as an "ecology of games" could encompass all boundary passages and provide a fruitful framework for building a comprehensive theory of organizational socialization.

Finally, it was mentioned that organizational socialization may occur as a gradual process or as a result of a climactic event. Most studies have been devoted to the examination of developmental socialization sequences where changes are both programmed and expected. The other pole of this continuum has largely been ignored. Little is known about the characteristics of swift socialization or of the individual or organizational factors which facilitate such occurrences. It is probable that many organizations depend upon these "baptism-by-fire" situations as a mechanism of socialization. For example, many police recruits are not considered fully integrated into the department until they have experienced certain "street" episodes (e.g., making an "on view" arrest, engaging in a "tavern brawl," etc.). The examination of such turning points across organizations is likely to result in fruitful findings both in terms of the socialization processes and of the culture of the organization itself.

In conclusion, this chapter has presented a framework for the numerous concerns embodied in the term "organizational socialization." The purpose was to crystalize the amorphous shapes of the various approaches to the socialization process and to emphasize the prominant role the process plays in the social drama of "breaking in."

REFERENCES

Abramson, M.
 1967 The Professional in the Organization. Chicago: Rand McNally.
Adams, J.S.
 1963a "Toward an understanding of inequity." Journal of Abnormal and Social Psychology 67:422–436.
 1963b "Wage inequalities, productivity and work quality." Industrial Relations 3:261–275.
 1965 "Injustices in social exchange," in L. Berkowitz (ed.), Advances in Experimental Psychology. Vol. 2. New York: Academic Press.
Argyris, C.
 1970 Intervention Theory and Method. Reading, Mass.: Addison-Wesley.
Asch, S.
 1951 "Effects of group pressures upon the modification and distortion of judgment," in H. Guetzkow (ed.), Groups, Leadership and Men. Pittsburgh: The Carnegie Press.
Avery, R.W.
 1968 "Enculturation in industrial research," in B.G. Glaser (ed.), Organizational Careers: A Source Book for Theory. Chicago: Aldine Publishing Co.
Barnard, C.
 1938 The Functions of the Executive. Cambridge, Mass.: Harvard University Press.
 1948 Organizations and Management. Cambridge, Mass.: Harvard University Press.
Becker, H.S.
 1960 "Notes on the concept of commitment." American Journal of Sociology 65:32–40.
 1964 "Personal changes in adult life." Sociometry 27:40–53.
Becker, H.S. and J.W. Carper
 1956a "The development of identification with an occupation." American Sosiological Review 61:289–298.
 1956b "The elements of identification with an occupation." American Sociological Review 21:341–348.
Becker, H.S. and B. Geer
 1958 "The fate of idealism in medical school." American Sociological Review 23:50–56.
 1966 "Latent culture: a note on the theory of latent social roles." Administrative Science Quarterly 5:304–313.
Becker, H.S., B. Geer and E.C. Hughes
 1968 Making the Grade: The Academic Side of College Life. New York: Wiley.
Becker, H.S., B. Geer, E.C. Hughes and A. Strauss
 1961 Boys in White: Student Culture in Medical School. Chicago: University of Chicago Press.
Becker, H.S. and A. Strauss
 1956 "Careers, personality and adult socialization." American Journal of Sociology 62:404–413.

Bennis, W.G., K.D. Benne and R. Chin (eds.)
  1969 The Planning of Change. Second Edition. New York: Holt, Rinehart and Winston.
Bennis, W.G., N. Berkowitz, M. Affinito and M. Malone
  1958 "Reference groups and loyalties in the out-patient department. Administrative Science Quarterly 2:179–192.
Berle, A.A. and G.C. Means
  1932 The Modern Corporation and Private Property. New York: Macmillan.
Berlew, D.E. and D.T. Hall
  1966 "The socialization of managers: effects of expectations on performance." Administrative Science Quarterly 11:207–223.
Blake, R.B. and J.S. Mouton
  1957 "The dynamics of influence and coercion." International Journal of Social Psychiatry 2:117–132.
  1961 The Managerial Grid. Jennis Springs, New Mexico: HRTL Laboratory in Management Development.
Blau, P.M.
  1955 The Dynamics of Bureaucracy. Chicago: University of Chicago Press.
Blau, P.M. and W.R. Scott
  1962 Formal Organizations. San Francisco: Chandler Publishing Company.
Blauner, R.
  1964 Alienation and Freedom. Chicago: University of Chicago Press.
Brim, O.G.
  1960 "Personality development as role learning," in I. Iscoe and H. Stevenson (eds.), Personality Development in Children. Austin: University of Texas Press.
  1966 "Socialization through the life cycle," in O.G. Brim and S. Wheeler (eds.), Socialization After Childhood. New York: Wiley.
Brim, O.G., D.C. Glass, D.E. Lavin and N. Goodman
  1962 Personality and Decision Processes: Studies in the Social Psychology of Thinking, Stanford, Calif.: Stanford University Press.
Brown, D.
  1962 "Personality, college environments and academic productivity," in N. Sanford (ed.), The American College. New York: Wiley.
Bruckel, J.E.
  1955 "Effects on morale of infantry team replacement systems." Sociometry 18:129–142.
Burchard, W.W.
  1954 "Role conflicts of military chaplins." American Sociological Review 19:528–535.
Caplow, T.
  1954 The Sociology of Work. New York: McGraw-Hill.
  1964 Principles of Organization. New York: Harcourt, Brace and World.
Carper, J.W. and H.S. Becker
  1957 "Adjustments to conflicting expectations in the development of identification with an option." Social Forces 36:212–223.
Cartwright, D. and A. Zander (eds.)
  1960 Group Dynamics: Research and Theory. Second edition. Evanston, Ill.: Row, Peterson.

Centers, R. and D.E. Bugental
  1966 "Intrinsic and extrinsic motivations among different segments of the
        working population." Journal of Applied Psychology 50:193–197.
Child, I.
  1954 "Socialization," in G. Lindzey (ed.), Handbook of Social Psychology.
        Reading, Mass.: Addison-Wesley.
Chinoy, E.
  1955 Automobile Workers and the American Dream. New York: Random
        House.
Clausen, J.A. (ed.)
  1969 Socialization and Society. Boston: Little, Brown and Co.
Cogswell, B.
  1958 "Some structural properties influencing socialization." Administrative
        Science Quarterly 14:111–124.
Cooley, C.H.
  1922 Human Nature and the Social Order. New York: Charles Scribner
        and Sons.
Crother, J.
  1957 "Absence and turnover in the divisions of one company, 1950–1955."
        Occupational Psychology 41:137–141.
Cyert, R.M. and J.G. March
  1963 A Behavioral Theory of the Firm. Englewood Cliffs, New Jersey: Pren-
        tice-Hall.
Dalton, M.
  1951 "Informal factors in career achievement." American Journal of Sociol-
        ogy 56:61–77.
  1959 Men Who Manage: Fusions of Feeling and Theory in Administration.
        New York:Wiley.
Davis, F.
  1968 "Professional socialization as subjective experience: the process of doc-
        trinal conversion among student nurses," in H.S. Becker, B. Geer,
        D. Reisman and R.T. Weiss (eds.), Institutions and the Person. Chi-
        cago: Aldine Publishing Co.
Denhart, R.B.
  1968 "Bureaucratic socialization and organizational accommodation." Ad-
        ministrative Science Quarterly 13:218–229.
Dornbush, S.
  1955 "The military academy as an assimilating institution." Social Forces
        33:316–321.
Downs, S.
  1967 "Labour turnover in two public service organizations." Occupational
        Psychology 35:51–57.
Drucker, P.
  1968 The Age of Discontinuity. New York: Harper & Row.
Dubin, R. (ed.)
  1951 Human Relations in Administration. Englewood Cliffs, New Jersey:
        Prentice-Hall.
  1956 "Industrial worker's worlds: a study of the 'central life interests' of
        industrial workers." Social Problems 3:131–142.

1959   "Deviant behavior and social structure: continuities in social action." American Sociological Review 24:332–344.

Dubin, R., R.A. Hedley and T.C. Taveggia
  1975   "Attachment to work," in R. Dubin (ed.), Handbook of Work, Organization and Society. Chicago: Rand McNally College Publishing Co.

Dunnette, M., R. Arvey and P. Banas
  1969   "Why do they leave?" Minneapolis, Minnesota: University of Minnesota. Unpublished paper.

Durkheim, E.
  1950   The Rules of Sociological Method. Eighth Edition. New York: The Free Press.

Erickson, K.
  1966   Wayward Puritans. New York: Wiley.

Ericson, E.H.
  1950   Childhood and Society. New York: W.W. Norton and Co.

Etzioni, A.
  1961   A Comparative Analysis of Complex Organizations. New York: Free Press.

Evan, W.M.
  1963   "Peer group interaction and organizational socialization: a study of employee turnover." American Sociological Review 28:436–440.

Farris, G.F.
  1971   "A predictive study of turnover." Personnel Psychology 24:127–141.

Festinger, L.
  1957   A Theory of Cognative Dissonance. Stanford, Ca.: Stanford University Press.

Fiedler, F.E.
  1958   Leader Attitudes and Group Effectiveness. Urbana, Ill.: University of Illinois Press.

Fine, S.A.
  1970   "Three kinds of skills: an approach to understanding the nature of human performance." Unpublished paper.

Fishbein, M.
  1961   "An investigation of the relationships between beliefs about an object and the attitude toward that object." Technical Report No. 6, University of California, Los Angeles. Contract No. 233, Office of Naval Research.
  1963   "An investigation of the relationships between beliefs about an object and the attitude toward that object." Human Relations 16:223–229.

Fleishman, E.A., B. Harris and H.E. Burtt
  1955   "Leadership and supervision in industry." Columbus, Ohio: Ohio State University Press.

Fox, R.C.
  1957   "Training for uncertainty," in R.K. Merton, G.G. Reader and P.L. Kendall (eds.), The Student Physician. Cambridge, Mass.: Harvard University Press.

Garfinkel, H.
  1967   Studies in Ethnomethodology. Englewood Cliffs, New Jersey: Prentice-Hall.

Ginzberg, E., S.W. Ginzberg, W. Axelrod and J.L. Herna
  1951   Occupational Choice: An Approach to a General Theory. New York: Columbia University Press.
Glaser, B.G.
  1964   Organizational Scientists: Their Professional Careers. New York: Bobbs-Merrill.
Glaser, B.G. (ed.)
  1968   Organizational Careers: A Sourcebook for Theory. Chicago: Aldine Publishing Co.
Glaser, B.D. and A.L. Strauss
  1971   Status Passage: A Formal Theory. Chicago: Aldine Publishing Co.
  1965   The Awareness of Dying. Chicago: Aldine Publishing Co.
  1968   Time for Dying. Chicago: Aldine Publishing Co.
Goffman, E.
  1959   The Presentation of Self in Everyday Life. Garden City, New York: Doubleday and Co.
  1961   Asylums. Garden City, New York: Doubleday.
  1963   Behavior in Public Places. New York: Free Press.
  1967   Interaction Ritual. Chicago: Aldine Publishing Co.
Goode, W.J.
  1960   "A theory of role strain." American Sociological Review 25:185–196.
Goslin, D.A. (ed.)
  1969   Handbook of Socialization Theory and Research. Chicago: Rand Mc-Nally College Publishing Co.
Gouldner, A.
  1954   Patterns of Industrial Bureaucracy. New York: The Free Press.
  1957   "Cosmopolitans and locals: toward an analysis of latent social roles—I." Administrative Science Quarterly 2:281–306.
  1958   "Cosmopolitans and locals: toward an analysis of latent social roles—II." Administrative Science Quarterly 2:444–480.
Gregg, R.
  1972   "Getting it on with Jesus: a study of conversion." Doctoral Dissertation. Los Angeles: University of Southern California.
Guest, R.H.
  1955   "A neglected factor in labour turnover." Occupational Psychology 29.
  1960   "Work careers and aspirations of automobile workers," in W. Galenson and S.M. Lipset (eds.), Labor and Trade Unionism. New York: Wiley.
Hackman, J.R.
  1969   "Nature of task as determiner of job behavior." Personnel Psychology 22:435–444.
Hackman, J.R. and L.W. Porter
  1968   "Expectancy theory and predictions of work effectiveness." Organizational Behavior and Human Performance 3:417–426.
Hackman, J.R. and E.E. Lawler
  1971   "Employee reactions to job characteristics." Journal of Applied Psychology 55:259–286.
Hackman, J.R. and G.R. Oldham
  1974   "The job diagnostic survey." Technical Depot Number 4. Department of Administrative Science. New Haven, Conn.: Yale University.

Hall, D.T., B. Schneider and H. Nygren
  1971   "Interpersonal factors in organizational identification." New Haven,
        Conn.: Yale University, unpublished paper.
Heath, R.
  1964   The Reasonable Adventurer. Pittsburgh: University of Pittsburgh Press.
Heider, F.
  1953   The Psychology of Interpersonal Behavior. New York: Wiley.
Herzberg, F.
  1966   Work and the Nature of Man. New York: World.
Herzberg, F., B. Mausner, R.O. Peterson and D.F. Capwell
  1957   Job Attitudes: Review of Research and Opinion. Pittsburgh: Psy-
        chological Service of Pittsburgh.
Herzberg, F., B. Mausner and B. Snyderman
  1959   The Motivation to Work. Second Edition. New York: Wiley.
Hodgeson, R.C., O.J. Levinson and A. Zaleznik
  1965   The Executive Role Constellation: An Analysis of Personality and Role
        Relations in Management. Cambridge, Mass.: Harvard Business School.
Hughes, E.C.
  1958a Men and Their Work. Glencoe, Ill.: The Free Press.
  1958b "The study of occupations," in R.K. Merton, L. Broomand and L.
        Cotrell (eds.), Sociology Today. New York: Basic Books.
Hulin, C.L.
  1968   "Effects of changes in job satisfaction levels on employee turnover,"
        Journal of Applied Psychology 52:122–126.
Humphries, L.
  1970   Tearoom Trade. Chicago: Aldine Publishing Co.
Inkeles, A.
  1969   "Society, social structure and child socialization," in J.A. Clausen (ed.),
        Socialization and Society. Boston: Little, Brown and Co.
Irwin, J.
  1970   The Felon. Englewood Cliffs, New Jersey: Prentice-Hall.
Janowitz, M.
  1960   The Professional Soldier: A Social and Political Portrait. New York:
        Free Press.
Janowitz, M. (ed.)
  1964   The New Military: Changing Patterns of Organization. New York:
        Russell Sage Foundation.
Kahn, R., D. Wolf, R. Quinn, I. Snoek and R. Rosenthal
  1964   Organizational Stress: Studies in Role Conflict and Ambiguity. New
        York: Wiley.
Kanter, R.M.
  1968   "Commitment and social organization: a study of commitment mecha-
        nisms in utopian communities." American Sociological Review 33:499–
        516.
Kaufman, H.
  1960   The Forest Ranger. Baltimore: Johns Hopkins Press.
Kelman, H.C.
  1958   "Compliance, identification and internalization: three processes of atti-
        tude change." Conflict Resolution 2:51–60.

1969   "Processes of opinion change," in W.G. Bennis, R.D. Beene and R. Chin (eds.), The Planning of Change. Second Edition. New York: Holt, Rinehart and Winston.

Korman, A.
1968   "Task success, task popularity and self-esteem as influences on task liking." Journal of Applied Psychology 52:61–73.

Kornhauser, W.
1962   Scientists in Industry: Conflict and Accommodation. Berkeley: University of California Press.

Kubie, L.S.
1958   Neurotic Distortion of Creative Process. Lawrence, Kansas: University of Kansas Press.

Lasswell, H.
1948   Power and Personality. New York: Norton.

Lawler, E.E.
1971a   "Organizational design." New Haven, Conn.: Yale University. Unpublished paper.
1971b   Pay and Organizational Effectiveness. New York: McGraw-Hill.

Leeds, R.
1964   "The absorption of protests: a working paper," in W.W. Cooper, H.J. Leavitt and M.W. Shelley (eds.), New Perspectives in Organizational Research. New York: Wiley.

Lewin, K.
1938   The Conceptual Representation and Measurement of Psychological Forces. Durham, North Carolina: Duke University Press.
1952   "Group decisions and social change," in G.E. Swanson, T.M. Newcomb and E.L. Hartley (eds.), Readings in Social Psychology. Second Edition. New York: Holt, Rinehart and Winston.

Ley, R.
1966   "Labour turnover as a function of worker differences, work environment and authoritarianism of foremen." Journal of Applied Psychology 50.

Likert, R.
1961   New Patterns of Management. New York: McGraw-Hill.

Locke, E.A.
1965   "The relationship of task success to task liking and satisfaction." The Journal of Applied Psychology 41:313–319.

Lortie, D.C.
1968   "Shared ordeal and induction to work," in H.S. Becker, B. Geer, D. Reisman and R.S. Weiss (eds.), Institutions and the Person. Chicago: Aldine Publishing Co.
1959   "Layman to lawman: law school careers and professional socialization." Harvard Educational Review 29:426–438.

Lyman, L.M. and M.B. Scott
1970   A Sociology of the Absurd. New York: Meredith.

Manning, P.
1970   "Talking and becoming: a view of organizational socialization," in J.D. Douglas (ed.), Understanding Everyday Life. Chicago: Aldine Publishing Co.

March, J.G. and H.A. Simon
  1958   Organizations. New York: Wiley.
Maslow, A.
  1954   Motivation and Personality. New York: Harper & Row.
Matza, D.
  1969   Becoming Deviant. Englewood Cliffs, New Jersey: Prentice-Hall.
McGregor, D.
  1960   The Human Side of Enterprise. New York: McGraw-Hill.
McGuire, W.I.
  1968   "The nature of attitudes and attitude change," in G. Lindzey and E. Aronson (eds.), Handbook of Social Psychology. Reading, Mass.: Addison-Wesley.
McHugh, P.
  1969   Defining the Situation: The Organization of Meaning in Social Interaction. New York: Bobbs-Merrill.
McNeil, E.B.
  1969   Human Socialization. Belmont, California: Cole Publishing Co.
Mead, G.H. (edited by C.W. Morris)
  1930   Mind, Self and Society. Chicago: University of Chicago Press.
Melbin, M.
  1964   "Organizational practice and individual behavior: absenteeism among psychiatric aids." American Sociological Review 17:126–139.
Merton, R.K.
  1945   "Bureaucratic structure and personality." Social Forces 23:405–415.
  1957   Social Theory and Social Structure. Revised Edition. Glencoe, Ill.: The Free Press.
Merton, R.K. and A.S. Kitt
  1950   "Contributions to the theory of reference group behavior," in R.K. Merton and P.T. Lazarfeld (eds.), Continuities in Social Research: Studies in the Scope and Method of "the American Soldier." Glencoe, Ill.: The Free Press.
Merton, R.K., G.G. Reader and P.L. Kendall (eds.)
  1957   The Student Physician. Cambridge, Mass.: Harvard University Press.
Miller, D.C. and W.H. Form
  1951   Industrial Psychology. New York: Harper & Row.
Miller, D.C. and L.W. Wagner
  1971   "Adult socialization, organizational structure and role orientations." Administrative Science Quarterly 16:116–139.
Minor, F.J.
  1958   "The prediction of turnover of clerical employees." Personnel Psychology 11:116–123.
Mitchell, T.R. and A. Biglan
  1971   "Instrumentality theories: current uses in psychology." Psychological Bulletin 76:432–454.
Moore, W.E.
  1963   Social Change. Englewood Cliffs, New Jersey: Prentice-Hall.
  1969   "Occupational socialization," in D.A. Goslin (ed.), Handbook of Socialization Theory and Research. Chicago: Rand McNally.

Newcomb, T.M.
   1950   Social Psychology. New York: Dryden Press.
   1958   "Attitude development as a function of reference groups: the Benning-
          ton study," in E.E. Maccoby, T.M. Newcomb and E.L. Hartley (eds.),
          Readings in Social Psychology. Third Edition. New York: Holt, Rine-
          hart and Winston.
   1961   The Acquaintance Process. New York: Holt, Rinehart and Winston.
Newcomb, T.M. and E.K. Wilson
   1966   College Peer Group. Chicago: Aldine Publishing Co.
Osgood, C.E. and P.H. Tannebaum
   1955   "The principle of congruity in the prediction of attitude change." Psy-
          chological Review 62:42–55.
Palmer, G.L.
   1962   The Reluctant Job Changer. Philadelphia: University of Pennsylvania
          Press.
Parsons, T.
   1951   The Social System. New York: Free Press.
   1960   Structure and Process in Modern Society. New York: Free Press.
Porter, L.W.
   1961   "A study of perceived need satisfactions in bottom and middle manage-
          ment jobs." Journal of Applied Psychology 45:1–10.
   1962   "Job attitudes in management: I. Perceived deficiencies in need fulfill-
          ment as a function of job level." Journal of Applied Psychology 46:375–
          384.
   1963   "Job attitudes in management: II. Perceived importance of needs as a
          function of job level." Journal of Applied Psychology 47:141–148.
   1971   "Adaption processes." University of California, Irvine. Unpublished
          paper.
Porter, L.W. and M.M. Henry
   1964   "Job attitudes in management: V. Perceptions of the importance of
          certain personality traits as a function of job level." Journal of Applied
          Psychology 48:31–36.
Porter, L.W. and E.E. Lawler
   1968   Managerial Attitudes and Performance. Homewood, Ill.: Irwin.
Porter, L.W. and F.E. Smith
   1970   "The etiology of organizational commitment: a longitudinal study of
          initial stages of employee organizational relations." University of Cal-
          ifornia, Irvine. Unpublished paper.
Porter, L.W. and R.M. Steers
   1972   "Organizational, work and personal factors in turnover and ab-
          senteeism." Technical Report No. 11. University of California, Irvine.
Porter, L.W., J. Van Maanen and W.J. Crampon
   1972   "Continuous monitoring of employees' motivational attitudes during the
          initial employment period." University of California, Irvine. Unpub-
          lished paper.
Presthus, R.
   1962   The Organizational Society. New York: Vintage Press.
Roe, A.
   1956   The Psychology of Occupations. New York: Wiley.

Roethlisberger, F.L. and W.I. Dickson
  1940 Management of the Worker. Cambridge, Mass.: Harvard University
        Press.
Rosenberg, M.J., C.I. Hovland, W. McGuire, R.P. Abelson and J.W. Brehm
  1962 Attitude Organization and Attitude Change. Englewood Cliffs, N.J.:
        Prentice-Hall.
Roth, J.
  1963 Timetables. New York: Bobbs-Merrill.
Rotter, J.B.
  1955 "The role of the psychological situation in determining the direction
        of human behavior," in M.R. Jones (ed.), Nebraska Symposium of Moti-
        vation. Lincoln, Nebr.: University of Nebraska Press.
  1966 "Generalized expectancies for internal versus external control of rein-
        forcement." Psychological Monographs 80:1–28.
Roy, D.C.
  1952 "Quota restriction and goldbricking in a machine shop." American
        Journal of Sociology 57:426–442.
  1953 "Work satisfaction and social reward in quota achievement: an analysis
        of piecework incentives." American Journal of Sociology 60:321–332.
  1955 "Banana time: job satisfaction and informal interaction." Human Orga-
        nization 18:158–168.
Saleh, S.D., R.J. Lee and E.P. Prien
  1965 "Why nurses leave their jobs—an analysis of female turnover." Person-
        nel Administration 28:25–28.
Schein, E.H.
  1961 "Management development as a process of influence." Industrial Man-
        agement Review 2:59–77.
  1962 "Problems of the first year at work: report of the first career panel re-
        union." Office of Naval Research. MIT Cont. No. 1841(83).
  1963 "Organizational socialization in the early career of industrial manag-
        ers." Office of Naval Research. MIT Cont. No. 1841.
  1964a "How to break in the college graduate." Harvard Business Review
        42:68–76.
  1964b "The mechanisms of change," in W.G. Bennis, E.H. Schein, W. Steel
        and D.C. Berlow (eds.), Interpersonal Dynamics. Homewood, Ill.: The
        Dorsey Press.
  1965 Organizational Psychology. Englewood Cliffs, New Jersey: Prentice-
        Hall.
  1967 "Attitude change during management education." Administrative Sci-
        ence Quarterly 11:412–417.
  1968a "Organizational socialization." Industrial Management Review 2:37–45.
  1968b "The individual, the organization and the career: a conceptual scheme."
        Cambridge: Massachusetts Institute of Technology. Unpublished paper.
  1974 "Career anchors and career paths: a panel study of management school
        graduates." MIT Working Paper 707-74. Cambridge: Massachusetts In-
        stitute of Technology.
Schein, E.H. and J.S. Ott
  1962 "The legitimacy of organizational influence." American Journal of So-
        ciology 6:682–689.

Schein, E.H., W.R. McKelvey, D.R. Peters and J.M. Thomas
   1965   "Career orientations and perceptions of rewarded activity in a research
          organization." Administrative Science Quarterly 9:221–236.
Schneider, B., D.T. Hall and H.T. Nygren
   1969   "Individual differences and job characteristics as correlates of changing
          organizational identification. New Haven, Conn.: Yale University. Un-
          published paper.
Scott, W.A.
   1965   Values and Organizations. Chicago: Rand McNally and Co.
Selznick, P.
   1949   TVA and the Grass Roots. Berkeley: University of California Press.
   1957   Leadership and Administration. Evanston, Ill.: Row, Peterson and Co.
Sherif, M. and C.W. Sherif
   1956   An Outline of Social Psychology. New York: Harper & Row.
Shibutani, T.
   1962   "Reference groups and social control," in A.M. Rose (ed.), Human
          Behavior and Social Processes. Boston: Houghton Mifflin.
Shiloh, A.
   1971   "Sanctuary or prison—responses to life in a mental hospital," in S.E.
          Wallace (ed.), Total Institutions. Chicago: Aldine Publishing Co.
Slocum, W.A.
   1966   Occupational Careers: A Sociological Perspective. Chicago: Aldine
          Publishing Co.
Smith, B.L., H.D. Laswell and R.D. Casey
   1946   Propaganda, Communications and Public Opinion. Princeton, New
          Jersey: Princeton University Press.
Smith, P.C., L.M. Kendall and C.L. Hulin
   1969   The Measure of Satisfaction in Work and Retirement: A Strategy for
          the Study of Attitudes. Chicago: Rand McNally.
Spradley, J.P.
   1970   You Owe Yourself a Drunk: An Ethnography of Urban Nomads. Bos-
          ton: Little, Brown and Co.
Starling, J.D.
   1968   "Organization and the decision to participate." Public Administrative
          Review 52:72–89.
Stern, G.G.
   1962   "Environments for learning," in N. Sanford (ed.), The American Col-
          lege. New York: Wiley.
Stouffer, S.A., E.A. Suchman, L.C. DeVinney, S.A. Star and R.M. Williams
   1949   The American Soldier: Adjustments During Army Life. Princeton, New
          Jersey: Princeton University Press.
Strauss, A.
   1959   Mirrors and Masks. Glencoe, Ill.: The Free Press.
   1968   "Some neglected properties of status passage," in H.S. Becker, B. Geer,
          D. Reisman, and R.S. Weiss (eds.), Institutions and the Person. Chi-
          cago: Aldine Publishing Co.
Strauss, G.
   1975   "Organizational development," in R. Dubin (ed.), Handbook of Work,
          Organization and Society. Chicago: Rand McNally College Publishing
          Co.

Sudnow, D.
   1966   Passing On. Englewood Cliffs, New Jersey: Prentice-Hall.
Sudnow, D. (ed.)
   1972   Studies in Social Interaction. New York: Free Press.
Super, D.E.
   1957   The Psychology of Careers. New York: Harper & Row.
Tausky, C.
   1970   Work Organizations: Major Theoretical Perspectives. Itasca, Ill.: F.E.
          Peacock Publishers, Inc.
Tausky, C. and R. Dubin
   1965   "Career anchorage: managerial mobility motivation." American. So-
          ciological Review 30:725–735.
Thibaut, J.S. and H.H. Kelley
   1959   The Social Psychology of Groups. New York: Wiley.
Trow, M.
   1962   "Student cultures and administrative action," in R.L. Sutherland (ed.),
          Personality Factors on the College Campus. Austin, Texas: Hogg
          Foundation for Mental Health.
Turner, R. (ed.)
   1974   Ethnomethodology. London: Penguin.
Van Maanen, J.
   1972   "Pledging the police: a study of selected aspects of recruit socialization
          in a large urban police department." Unpublished doctoral dissertation,
          Irvine: University of California.
Vroom, V.H.
   1960   Some Personality Determinants of the Effects of Participation. Engle-
          wood Cliffs, New Jersey: Prentice-Hall.
   1964   Work and Motivation. New York: Wiley.
Vroom, V.H. and E.L. Deci
   1971   "The stability of post-decisional dissonance: a follow-up study on the
          job attitudes of business school graduates." Organizational Behavior
          and Human Performance 6:36–49.
Walker, C.R. and R.A. Guest
   1952   Man on the Assembly Line. Cambridge, Mass.: Harvard University
          Press.
Wallace, S.E. (ed.)
   1971   Total Institutions. Chicago: Aldine Publishing Co.
Weber, M. and T. Parsons (ed.)
   1947   The Theory of Social and Economic Organization. Translation by A.D.
          Henderson and T. Parsons. New York: The Free Press.
Weitz, J.
   1957   "Job expectancy and survival." Journal of Applied Psychology 40:346–
          361.
Westley, W.A.
   1968   "The informal organization of the army: a sociological memoir," in
          H.S. Becker, B. Geer, D. Reisman and R.S. Weiss (eds.), Institutions
          and the Person. Chicago: Aldine Publishing Co.
Wheeler, S.
   1961   "Socialization in correctional communities." American Sociological Re-
          view 26:699–712.

1966   "The structure of formally organized socialization settings," in O.G. Brim, Jr. and S. Wheeler (eds.), Socialization After Childhood. New York: Wiley.

White, W.H., Jr.
1956   The Organization Man. New York: Simon and Schuster.

Wilensky, H.
1964   "The professionalization of everyone?" American Journal of Sociology 70:137–150.

Woodward, J.
1965   Industrial Organization. London: Oxford University Press.

Zaleznik, A., G.W. Dalton and L.B. Barnes
1970   Orientation and Conflict in Career. Boston: Harvard University Graduate School of Business Administration, Division of Research.

CHAPTER **4**

Work and Careers

John O. Crites

University of Maryland

INTRODUCTION

Were it not for man's unique symbolic capacity to visualize the "merely possible" (Shoben, 1957) ; and his facility for inventing and using tools with which to control and change the environment (Smith, 1962) ; and his creativity in embellishing and interpreting the world of his private perceptions (Barron, 1958), "work" and "career" as distinctively human phenomena would be unknown. In contrast to even the most advanced infrahuman species, man possesses the peculiar capability for performing various mental, physical and social tasks which are subsumed by the terms work and career. By engaging in these enterprises man enjoys not only the rewards which stem from accomplishment and mastery, but also suffers the pain which results from failure. Early in the history of his labors, if not from the very beginning, he found to his disappointment that work was a two-edged sword: it often occasions as much (if not more) frustration and anxiety as it does elation and satisfaction. Man discovered that his work created problems as well as solved them. Particularly in contemporary society, with its massive organizational aggregates, its frenzied tempo of economic activity, and its emphasis upon achievement, man has been increasingly confronted with problems of work and career adjustment, the complexities of which often seem to defy satisfactory resolution.

How the worker attempts to adjust to these problems—the uninteresting job, the poor pay and long hours, the hypercritical supervisor, the unfulfilled ambitions of youth—can be conceptualized in many different ways (e.g., Korman, 1970; Lawler, 1970). A model which has been adapted from adjustment and experimental psychology (Shafer & Shoben, 1956; Underwood, 1949) has considerable value for synthesizing (and expanding) what is known about the dynamics of vocational adjustment (Crites, 1969). This model is graphically portrayed in Figure 1. The process of vocational adjustment can be viewed as comprised of several interrelated components. The first of these is *motivation* (1), the needs and drives which are the mainsprings of the worker's behavior and which are routinely filled or reduced unless *thwarting conditions* (2) intervene. The latter may encompass either frustrations, due to external obstacles posed by environmental constraints and restrictions, and/or conflicts, generated

131

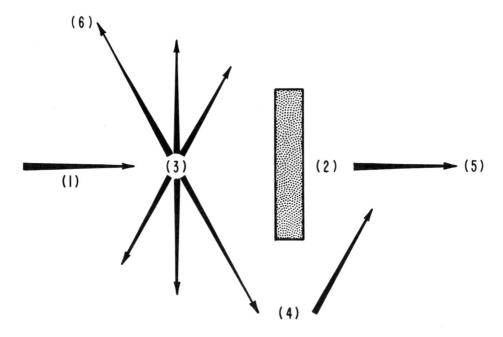

FIGURE 1.   A model for the process of vocational adjustment (Crites, 1969).

by internal competition among antagonistic response tendencies. When frustrated/conflicted, the worker experiences tension or anxiety, and he tries to reduce or eliminate these states of discomfiture by *adjusting* (3) to the situation. To the extent that his behavior is effective (4) he will achieve greater or lesser job success and satisfaction (5), the two principal components of overall vocational adjustment, as the outcomes of his efforts. If his coping mechanisms are ineffectual (6), however, he will continue to be tense or anxious and will be vocationally maladjusted.

Presumably, this process of vocational adjustment has the same components and formal characteristics at all points-of-time during the work-life, although its substance most likely changes as the worker grows older. Thus, the materialistic needs of youth, for example, may give way to the altruistic values of maturity, just as the frustrations of "getting ahead" early in one's career are transformed into the conflicts of "getting along" when on the threshold of retirement.

Assuming its applicability and usefulness for organizing and explicating theory and research on vocational adjustment (Crites, 1969), the above model can serve as a convenient frame of reference for the phenomena discussed in this chapter: *work* and *careers*. To reflect the various components represented in the model, four major programs of theory and research, along with others of lesser scope but possible promise, have been selected for presentation and evaluation in this chapter. These theories are: (1) Herzberg's (1959) two-factor theory of *Work Motivation*, and the empirical findings which have accumulated on it; (2) Lofquist (1969), Dawis (1968), Weiss (1964), and others' studies of *Work Adjustment*; (3) Sewell, Haller, et al.'s (1969, 1970) analyses of *Career Paths*; and, (4) Super's (1957) longitudinal investigation of *Career Patterns*.

A summary of the theory and research generated by each of these approaches precedes a critical comment on what can be concluded from then concerning the nature of work and career. A final section surveys several more circumscribed and recent formulations of how and why man adjusts to his vocation as he does.

HERZBERG'S TWO-FACTOR THEORY

Not since the Western Electric Hawthorne studies (Roethlisberger & Dickson, 1939) during the era of the Great Depression, has a program of theory and research on work motivation had an impact equivalent to that of Herzberg's (1959) analysis of why men work. Adopting an inductive approach to this age-old problem, he and his associates (Herzberg, Mausner, Peterson, & Capwell, 1957:7) first undertook a comprehensive survey of the accumulated opinions and results on "job attitudes," from which they drew this conclusion:

> The one dramatic finding that emerged in our review of this literature was the fact that there was a difference in the primacy of factors, depending upon whether the investigator was looking for things the worker liked about his job or things he disliked. The concept that there were some factors that were "satisfiers" and others that were "dissatifiers" was suggested by this finding.

To test this hypothesis Herzberg, Mausner, and Snyderman (1959) conducted a study of 200 accountants and engineers, in which they used the "critical incident" technique (Flanagan, 1954) to gather interview-derived data on the factors and attitudes that differentially affect job satisfaction. In general they found that *Achievement, Recognition, Work itself, Responsibility*, and *Advancement* contributed to satisfaction, whereas *Company Policy* and *Administration, Supervision-technical, Salary, Interpersonal Relations-supervision*, and *Working Conditions* fostered dissatisfaction, depending upon whether they constituted positive or negative factors in the work *milieu*. Herzberg and his co-workers (1957) interpreted these findings as confirmatory of a "two-factor" or motivator-hygiene theory of work motivation, in which they proposed that:

1. Job satisfaction and dissatisfaction are two separate, independent continua, not opposite ends of a bipolar dimension of liking/disliking for one's work.

2. Motivator factors (e.g., *Achievement, Recognition*, etc.) increase job satisfaction, and hygiene factors (e.g., *Company Policy* and *Administration*) increase job *dis*satisfaction, but the obverse effects do not obtain, except possibly for a factor like *Salary* which is related to both job satisfaction *and* dissatisfaction.

Generalization of the Two-Factor Theory of Work Motivation

More recently, Herzberg (1966) has elaborated upon his theory by casting these propositions into the broader context of "the nature of man" and extrapolating implications for both the individual's vocational adjustment and the organization's philosophy of labor relations. His view of man in general, and the worker, in particular, is twofold: In one view, he postulates that the human organism is bound biologically to the animal kingdom. Man strives to avoid pain and to maximize physical pleasure: he seeks to reduce his hunger, satisfy his sexual needs, protect himself, be warm and sheltered, etc. He accomplishes these ends primarily by structuring and restructuring the environmental context within which he works and lives. In short, he minimizes job dissatisfaction by pursuing what Herzberg (1966) has termed the *hygiene* factors: better Company Policy and Administration, higher salary, improved working conditions, and more satisfactory Interpersonal and technical supervision. Herzberg's other view of man and the worker observes that the individual is motivated in both life and work activities to fulfill his uniquely human potentialities. There is a definite need on the part of the individual to achieve psychological growth. This growth is much more than simply the avoidance of pain. It involves self-actualization along several different dimensions: *understanding more* about the world within which one lives; *recognizing more relationships* among categories of knowledge; *being creative* in the use of one's capabilities; *behaving effectively* in ambiguous situations; *maintaining a sense of individual beliefs and values,* in spite of the pressure to conform to custom and convention; and striving for *honesty and truth in human endeavors,* rather than specious status achieved through sham and charade. In one's work, these attributes and qualities of psychological growth can be acquired to the extent that the so-called *motivator* variables are present: *Achievement, Recognition,* the *Work* itself, *Responsibility* and *Advancement.*

The implications of Herzberg's dualistic concept of human nature contrast sharply with traditional theories of motivation, which have been predicated upon the assumption that job satisfaction and dissatisfaction are the opposite ends of a continuum and that overall satisfaction is a function of the ratio of the two. Thus, a worker may be more or less satisfied with his job, depending on how dissatisfied he is with it. Herzberg (1966) is proposing, however, that because different factors ellicit reactions of satisfaction and dissatisfaction (namely, motivators and hygienes, respectively), satisfaction and dissatisfaction are two separate continua. This distinction is represented diagrammatically in Figure 2, where it can be seen that traditional theory (A) has viewed satisfac-

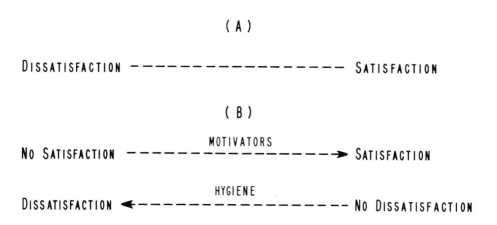

FIGURE 2.   Traditional and two-factor concepts of job satisfaction and dissatisfaction.

tion and dissatisfaction on the same dimension, with an intermediate "neutral" point, whereas two-factor theory (B) hypothesizes that there are two independent dimensions, with unrelated points of origin. As Whitsett and Winslow (1967:394) observe:

> The opposite of satisfaction is *no satisfaction*, while the opposite of dissatisfaction is *no dissatisfaction.*... This is different from traditional thinking of satisfaction and dissatisfaction as simple opposites...

Herzberg and his associates belabor this point because its full import has not always been grasped. Inappropriate tests of two-factor theory have been made with instruments designed to measure satisfaction-dissatisfaction as bipolar, rather than as two distinct continua, and the erroneous conclusion has been drawn that the data are not consistent with the theory (see "Comments" section later in this chapter). It is critical, therefore, in testing Herzberg's (1966) theory to articulate both conceptually and operationally the distinction he makes between job satisfaction and dissatisfaction.

If a two dimensional as opposed to a bipolar concept of work motivation and satisfaction is assumed, a taxonomy of the possible general and vocational adjustment behaviors in which it is possible for the worker to engage can be derived. Herzberg (1966:86–90) enumerates and defines these as follows (Figure 3 represents them graphically):

1. The paragon of job adjustment is the *healthy* motivator seeker who avoids pain and achieves psychological growth.
2. The *unhappy* motivator seeker moves toward psychological fulfillment but unsuccessfully avoids pains.
3. The *unfulfilled* motivator seeker successfully avoids pain, but fails to realize his personal potentialities.
4. The *unhappy* and *unfulfilled* motivator seeker suffers the consequences of neither avoiding pain nor accomplishing self-actualization.
5. The *maladjusted* hygiene seeker manages to avoid pain but does not even attempt to attain psychological growth. As the Figure indicates, he is not on the mental health (motivator) continuum.
6. The *mentally ill* hygiene seeker is also absent from the health dimension, but in addition he has not been able to avoid pain.
7. The *monastic* hygiene seeker similarly stands on only the hygiene continuum, but he denies that avoiding pain is important to him. Herzberg (1966) cites as examples the no-talent beatnik, the sacrificing mother, and the severe disciplinarian.

Obviously, these types of adjustments which can be sought in life and work vary in degree, since the mental health and illness dimensions are continua. They represent the possible combinations of the two basic sources of work motivation in Herzberg's theory: the external, job contextual situation in which the individual works, and the internal, job content stimuli which give impetus to the individual's efforts to become more than he is.

Research in Two-Factor Work Motivation

If one mark of the usefulness of a theory is its heuristic value, then the utility of Herzberg's conceptualization of work motivation is unquestioned. It has

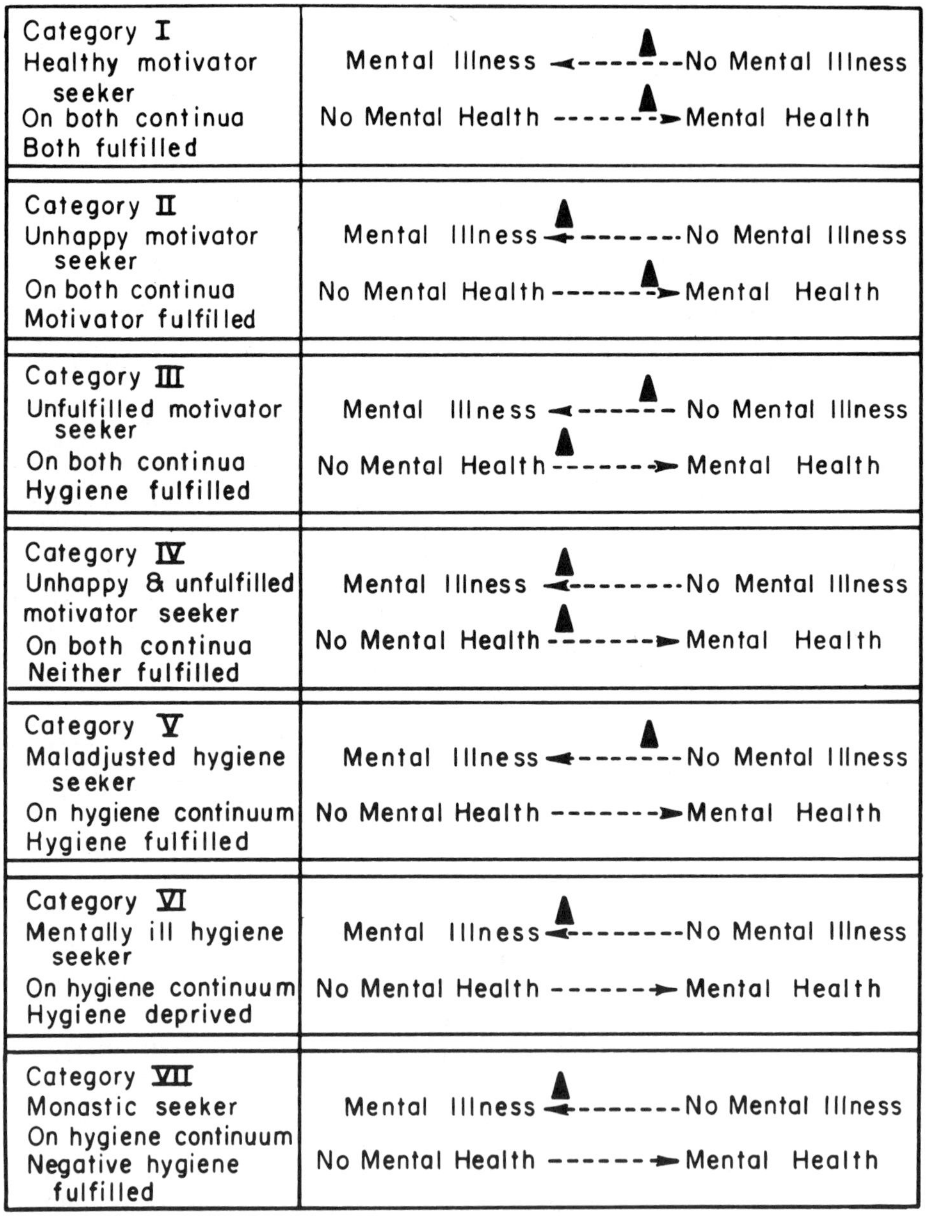

Category I Healthy motivator seeker On both continua Both fulfilled	Mental Illness ◄-------No Mental Illness No Mental Health ------►Mental Health
Category II Unhappy motivator seeker On both continua Motivator fulfilled	Mental Illness◄-------No Mental Illness No Mental Health------►Mental Health
Category III Unfulfilled motivator seeker On both continua Hygiene fulfilled	Mental Illness ◄------ No Mental Illness No Mental Health------► Mental Health
Category IV Unhappy & unfulfilled motivator seeker On both continua Neither fulfilled	Mental Illness ◄-------No Mental Illness No Mental Health--------►Mental Health
Category V Maladjusted hygiene seeker On hygiene continuum Hygiene fulfilled	Mental Illness ◄-------No Mental Illness No Mental Health -------►Mental Health
Category VI Mentally ill hygiene seeker On hygiene continuum Hygiene deprived	Mental Illness◄-------No Mental Illness No Mental Health ------► Mental Health
Category VII Monastic seeker On hygiene continuum Negative hygiene fulfilled	Mental Illness◄-------No Mental Illness No Mental Health ------► Mental Health

FIGURE 3. Adjustment continua as defined by motivators and hygienes.

generated a host of studies to test and extend its basic proposition, the total number being approximately 35 at last count. It is not possible to summarize and evaluate these here, nor is it necessary since several excellent reviews are already available (Vroom, 1964; Burke, 1966; House & Wigdor, 1967; Whitsett

& Winslow, 1967; Crites, 1969). Because the findings on Herzberg's theory have been both confirmatory and nonconfirmatory, however, the conclusions drawn from these reviews have often been conflicting, and there has ensued what has been called the "Herzberg Controversy." No attempt will be made to resolve the controversy but only to present the pros and cons of it in order to clarify the issues which are being debated. Ultimately, the fate of Herzberg's (1966) theory will be determined by its viability over time—the extent to which it gains long-term acceptance in understanding work motivation.

Criticisms of motivator-hygiene theory and research have focused upon many presumed flaws in Herzberg's hypotheses and methodology, but most of them can be categorized into three types of shortcomings discussed by House and Wigdor (1967).

Methodological bounds of the theory.   Opponents of the Herzberg theory (e.g. Vroom, 1964, 1966) point out that it may be specific to the methods he used to formulate it. Hulin (1966:435) comments, for example, that: "Unfortunately, those studies which appear to indicate the basic tenability of the theory use the same method by which the theory was derived." In other words, it is argued that if the theory is confirmed only by the methods initially used to construct it, then it is an artifact, not a model, of reality.

Faulty research foundation.   A related contention is that the data collected to test Herzberg's propositions are contaminated by the investigator's knowledge of the theory as he interviews subjects with the critical incident technique. Scientific investigation requires that the hypotheses and procedures be completely independent. Apparently this was not the case in Herzberg's original study or subsequent ones modelled after it.

Inconsistency with previous evidence.   It has been observed that, although one implication of Herzberg's statements about the relationship of motivators to satisfaction is that highly motivated and satisfied workers should produce more, there is no evidence from either past or present research to substantiate such an expectation (House and Wigdor, 1967). On the contrary, the accumulated findings indicate little or no correlation between satisfaction and productivity (Brayfield and Crockett, 1955; Crites, 1969).

Herzberg (1966:130) has acknowledged that his theory "may be technique-bound," but he does not agree that it "necessarily discredit(s) the theory." Also, he rejects the criticism that bias in the "storytelling" technique has influenced results, concluding that it would "obscure the motivation-hygiene theory rather than enhance it" (Herzberg, 1966:130). He states that such issues should be settled on the basis of the available evidence, however, and then proceeds to review and interpret it as highly favorable to his theory. From an analysis of ten different studies, he states that "the predictions from the theory were wrong in less than 3% of the cases" (Herzberg, 1966:125). Similarly, Whitsett and Winslow (1967:410–411) observe:

> It would appear, because of the numerous misinterpretations of the M-H theory, the general weaknesses in methods and the frequent misinterpretations of results, that, taken as a group, the studies reviewed offer little empirical evidence for doubting the validity of the theory.

> We conclude that the theory has clearly retained its utility and viability.

These reviewers legitimately point out that in several studies investigators have attempted to test Herzberg's theory with measures of *overall* job satisfaction which are wholly inappropriate to assess the hypothesized *independent* continua of job satisfaction and dissatisfaction. Moreover, Whitsett and Winslow (1967) note that there are probably just as many methodological drawbacks to some of the questionnaire and test measures of motivator and hygiene factors as there are to the critical incident interview procedure. Finally, Whitsett and Winslow (1967) reanalyzed some studies of M-H theory, and contend that the findings have been misinterpreted by critics as being contrary to M-H theory, rather than either supportive or inconclusive.

Comment

That there are merits to the arguments on both sides of the "Herzberg Controversy" is obvious, but they have usually been obscured by the subjectivity of the opposed positions. If a more dispassionate consideration of the issues involved can be undertaken, however, it may serve to identify lines of future inquiry. Consider first the formal characteristics of Herzberg's theory. It was constructed in an intuitive, rough-and-ready way; it does not conform to the canons of the philosophy of the science of constructing theories. It is not surprising, therefore, that it has been misinterpreted, as Whitsett and Winslow (1967) maintain. Nor is it unexpected that, due to its lack of rigor, it sometimes "catches the data however they fall." Thus, Hulin (1966:436) correctly observes that salary, for example, has been used as a "catch-all" explanatory concept of M-H theory:

> if pay acts as a dissatisfier, as the theory would predict, no discussion is presented. If it acts as a satisfier as well as a dissatisfier, the claim is made that pay contains elements of recognition and achievement which are satisfiers. Therefore, it *should* act in both directions. This may well be true, but if it is, then pay should always act as both a satisfier and a dissatisfier (italics in original).

If M-H theory were more structured, it would not only facilitate its correct interpretation but it would make its "boundary conditions" more explicit. One of the legitimate contentions of the Herzberg defenders has been that tests of the theory, particularly those which have yielded negative results, have not evaluated it fairly. The use of measures of overall satisfaction, for example, clearly violates one of the basic propositions of the theory. If the boundary conditions are to be realized, experimentally independent assessments of satisfaction and dissatisfaction (as two conceptually different variables) must be made. Furthermore, it should be recognized that an "experimentum crusis," such as that attempted by Ewen, Smith, Hulin, and Locke (1966), is not logically possible because both traditional and M-H theory are predicated upon different assumptions (Cohen & Nagel, 1934).

Methodologically, the foremost problem to be solved is to devise some procedure for quantifying the variables in Herzberg's theory which remain faithful to it but at the same time are psychometrically sound. The critical-incident technique unfortunately confounds the hypothesis-testing with the data-collecting phases of the research process and consequently increases the possibility of obtaining results favorable to the theory. It also fails to provide for experimental independence among the variables in the defining operations, since they are all quantified from the same interview data. The "paper-and-pencil" approaches which have been used by some investigators in place of Herzberg's original "storytelling" technique are also open to serious criticisms. Herzberg objects to these techniques because they do not assume the subject's frame of reference and they present the subject with stimuli selected by the experimenter. Actually, the results that are available on the controversy between the idiographic and the nomethetic approaches to measurement problems (as posed by the Herzberg theory) indicate that findings are much the same whichever method is used (Oppenheimer, 1966). What is needed is an instrument which conforms to the accepted standards for psychological tests (American Psychological Association, 1966) as well as meets the specifications of M-H theory: that it should treat satisfaction and dissatisfaction as separate dimensions. Furthermore, to transcend the objections that Herzberg's theory is method-bound, the multitrait-multimethod model of convergent and discriminant test validation (Campbell & Fiske, 1959) might be used concurrently with data collected on one sample of subjects, that would utilize several different measuring devices. If there were no "methods" factor which emerged from the analysis, any one of the techniques could be selected to test M-H theory with the confidence that the results would not be dependent upon the methodology.

Until some or all of these theoretical and methodological problems are satisfactorily solved, there would appear to be insufficient reason to entertain seriously the several "revisions" of Herzberg's theory which have been proposed as substitutes for it. A brief summary of them may be of interest, however, because they are closely related to Herzberg's thinking about work motivation and represent extensions of it in different directions. On the premise that much of the controversy surrounding M-H theory has been occasioned by its imprecise statement, Lindsay, Marks, and Gorlow (1967) have cast it into symbolic terms and specified the hypothesized functions as follows:

$$S = f(M + e)$$
$$DS = f(H + e)$$
$$P(M,N) = 0$$

where S is satisfaction, DS is dissatisfaction, M is motivator, H is hygiene, and e is error. The formulae indicate that satisfaction and dissatisfaction are functions of motivators and hygienes, respectively, and that the latter variables are unrelated. Lindsay, et al. reject this model, however, and test a linear theory based upon the traditional assumption of bipolar satisfaction/dissatisfaction: $S = aM + bH + cMH + e$, where a, b, c, and e are parameters. Taking a more conciliatory tact, Soliman (1970) has proposed that one- and two-factor theories of work motivation are not contradictory, if the need-satisfying potential of the environment is introduced as what appears to be a "moderator" variable. Thus, he hypothesized that, if the environment is need-satisfying, then motivators are more potent than hygienes as sources of job satisfaction, whereas if the environment is not need-satisfying, then hygienes are more important motivators in producing job dissatisfaction. This conceptualization is little more than the application of Maslow's (1954) general theory of motivation to work, however, as articulated more explicitly and comprehensively by Wolf (1967), who postulates that both motivators and hygienes can act as both satisfiers and dissatisfiers depending upon the extent to which higher and lower level needs are being fulfilled. Wolf (1967) extrapolates several research implications from his formulation, which seem to have greater promise for advancing knowledge of work motivation in the future than they do for further exacerbation of the "Herzberg Controversy."

WORK ADJUSTMENT

A more comprehensive approach than Herzberg's, to the problem of how and why men relate to their work, and one which encompasses most of the Model of Vocational Adjustment, is the Work Adjustment Project of the Industrial Relations Center at the University of Minnesota. Under the leadership of Lloyd H. Lofquist and his principal associates, Rene V. Dawis, George W. England, and David J. Weiss, this long-term investigation of work adjustment is the most prolific and productive which has ever been undertaken. Also referred to as the Minnesota Studies in Vocational Rehabilitation, because of its initial emphasis upon the job placement problems of disabled workers, the project was broadened in scope several years ago to include normal workers as well. Conceptually, it is an outgrowth and elaboration of the Matching Men and Jobs approach (Crites, 1969) which was implemented so effectively in the Minnesota Employment Stabilization Research Institute (Paterson & Darley, 1936) during the Depression years. But it has gone beyond the "dustbowl empiricism" of the earlier program, which was tied closely to the applied problem of placing and training the unemployed, and has attempted to integrate in a meaningfull manner, theory and research. A long series of monographs has reported the ongoing work of the project, which is too lengthy and detailed to summarize here, but an overview of what has been accomplished can be gained from Lofquist and Dawis' (1969) book *Adjustment to Work* and from selected monographs in the series.

The Theory of Work Adjustment

Lofquist and Dawis (1969:45) state that the central principle of work adjustment theory is that of correspondence—the "harmonious relationship between individual and environment; suitability of the individual to the environment and of the environment for the individual; consonance or agreement between individual and environment; and a reciprocal and complementary relationship between the individual and his environment." Stated more succinctly, the individual is adjusted to his work according to the extent of his correspondence. Correspondence in turn, is a function of the degree of "fit" between a man and his job.

If a worker has the appropriate abilities to perform the duties and tasks of a job at a minimally acceptable level, and if his needs are filled as a result of his job performance, then he is considered to be vocationally adjusted. The principal criteria of the latter are, then, the individual's *satisfactoriness* and his *satisfaction*. By satisfactoriness is meant the worker's externally evaluated success on the job—how well he is doing as judged by his employer or fellow-workers. In contrast, satisfaction is defined as the worker's subjectively experienced liking/disliking for what he is doing, and as such, may or may not be related to his satisfactoriness, depending upon the interactive effects of any number of other variables (Crites, 1969).

Taken together, satisfactoriness and satisfaction predict *tenure*, which is the length of time a worker spends on his job. More generally:

> *The levels of satisfactoriness and satisfaction observed for a group of individuals with substantial tenure in a specific work environment establish the limits of satisfactoriness and satisfaction from which tenure can be predicted for other individuals* (Lofquist and Dawis, 1969:47; italics in original).

This hypothesized relationship between satisfactoriness and satisfaction, on the one hand, with tenure, on the other, is depicted graphically in Figure 4.

Projected over time, there are two major classes of variables which work-adjustment theory postulates as antecedents to job satisfactoriness and satisfaction: abilities and needs. These attributes or characteristics of the individual are defined broadly as follows (Dawis, Lofquist, and Weiss, 1968:9 [italics in original]).

> *Abilities are basic dimensions of response capability generally utilized by the individual. Needs are preferences for responding in certain stimulus conditions which have been experienced to be reinforcing.*

More specifically, the concept of abilities refers to the individual's basic capacities to perform a variety of tasks, that might involve eye-hand coordination or spatial visualization, rather than the particular skills demanded by one or a limited number of job functions. Similarly, the concept of needs implies generalized conditions of the individual which motivate a wide range of behavior, not just responses to one situation.

In work adjustment theory, abilities and needs are viewed as constituting the *work personality*, which is ultimately related to, and implemented in, the work environment. Before correspondence is effected, however, i.e., prior to occupational entry, a long period of "individuation" of the work personality takes place during which abilities and needs develop from relatively rudimentary forms to highly complex traits. Figure 5 traces this process from the preschool years to the advent of employment and shows how the interaction of maturing sets of abilities and needs with social, educational, and prevocational experiences eventuates in a stable work personality. Thus, personal development through childhood and adolescence is seen as a prelude to work adjustment in the adult years.

Utilizing the postulate of correspondence and the concepts of abilities, needs, satisfactoriness, and satisfaction, the Work Adjustment Project staff has formulated a theory of work adjustment comprised of the following propositions (Dawis, et al., 1968:9–10):

> Proposition I. An individual's work adjustment at any point in time is indicated by his concurrent levels of satisfactoriness and satisfaction.
> Proposition II. Satisfactoriness is a function of the correspondence

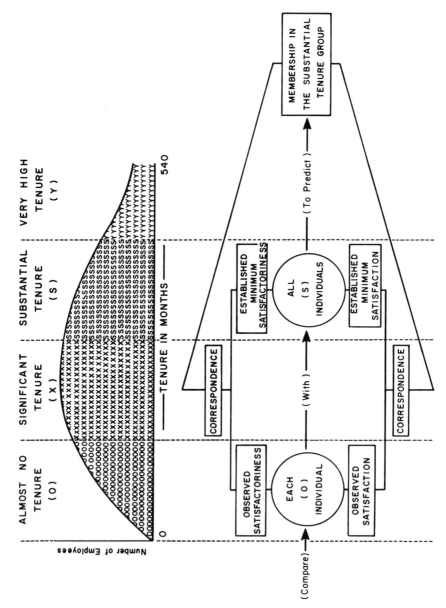

FIGURE 4.   The relationship of satisfactoriness and satisfaction to tenure.

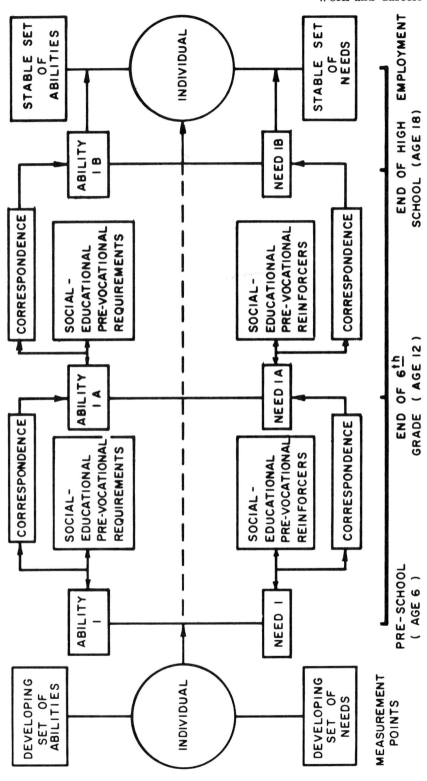

FIGURE 5.   Individuation of the work personality.

between an individual's abilities and the ability requirements of the work environment, provided that the individual's needs correspond with the reinforcer system of the work environment...

Proposition III. Satisfaction is a function of the correspondence between the reinforcer system of the work environment and the individual's needs, provided that the individual's abilities correspond with the ability requirements of the work environment...

Proposition IV. Satisfaction moderates the functional relationship between satisfactoriness and ability requirement correspondence.

Proposition V. Satisfactoriness moderates the functional relationship between satisfaction and need-reinforcer correspondence.

Proposition VI. The probability of an individual being forced out of the work environment is inversely related to his satisfactoriness.

Proposition VII. The probability of an individual voluntarily leaving the work environment is inversely related to his satisfaction.

Combining Propositions VI and VII, we have:

Proposition VIII. Tenure is a joint function of satisfactoriness and satisfaction...

Proposition IX. Work personality-work environment correspondence increases as a function of tenure.

These propositions have constituted the conceptual framework within which the research of the Work Adjustment Project has been conducted.

Research on the Work Adjustment Theory

Before tests of the work adjustment theory could be undertaken, however, it was necessary to devise measures of the concepts or variables which entered into the hypothesized relationships stated in the propositions. The instruments which were constructed, with the exception of one that was already available, are briefly described below:

Abilities. The General Aptitude Test Battery (GATB), which had been developed independently by the United States Employment Service, was selected as a multifactor battery of tests to assess Intelligence, Verbal Aptitude, Numerical Aptitude, Spatial Aptitude, Form Perception, Clerical Perception, Motor Coordination, Finger Dexterity, and Manual Dexterity. Normative data on the GATB also provided the necessary ability requirements for a variety of occupations.

Needs. The Minnesota Importance Questionnaire (MIQ) was constructed to measure 20 different work-related needs, including Achievement, Compensation, Recognition, and Working Conditions.

Occupational Reinforcer Patterns (ORP's). The extent to which reinforcers are present in occupations and their magnitude assessed by the Minnesota Job Description Questionnaire (MJDQ), which is comprised of scales parallel to those in the MIQ and the Minnesota Satisfaction Questionnaire. The MJDQ is completed by supervisors, who rank the reinforcer characteristics of the jobs under them.

Satisfaction. The Minnesota Satisfaction Questionnaire (MSQ) asks a worker to rate, on a bipolar scale, his degree of satisfaction/dissatisfaction with each of 20 items which sample the same dimensions as in the MIQ.

Satisfactoriness. There are four Minnesota Satisfactoriness Scales (MSS) which have been derived through item and factor analyses from a set of 29 questions about a worker's job performance. These scales are: promotability/ competence; personal adjustment; conformance; and, general satisfactoriness. Extensive research on these instruments indicates that their psychometric characteristics are acceptable and that they can be used with confidence in tests of the work adjustment theory.

Such tests have been conducted on Propositions I through IV thus far, and the findings are generally consonant with the hypotheses. Using a large sample of slightly more than 2,000 men distributed in six different occupations (janitors and maintenance men, assemblers, machinists, office clerks, salesmen, and engineers), the following results were obtained:

Proposition I. One of the principal implications of this proposition is that, if satisfactoriness and satisfaction are complementary aspects of work adjustment, then they should be relatively independent. And the data substantiated this expectation, the highest canonical correlation for any occupational group being .31 for assemblers. As discussed below, however, this relationship may be moderated by other variables, such as level of ability.

Proposition II. Support for one aspect of this proposition has been garnered from data which establish that there are positive (although low) correlations between abilities (GATB) and satisfactoriness (MSS).

Proposition III. Two of the relevant variables in this proposition are needs and satisfaction, which were found to be moderately highly related to each other. In a "double cross-validation" multiple regression analysis, most of the Rs (multiple correlation coefficient) were in the 50s and 60s, although some ranged as low as —.09 and as high as .92.

Proposition IV. Preliminary findings on the role of satisfaction as a moderator of the relationship between abilities and satisfactoriness are suggestive but not conclusive. Lofquist and Dawis (1969:66) conclude that higher rs (zero-order correlation coefficient) from the moderated regression support the proposition, yet they do not report significant tests for the differences between these and the unmoderated rs.

It is clear from this brief summary of research on the work adjustment theory that the findings to date are fragmentary and incomplete. Considered *en toto*, however, they are encouraging and generally substantiate the usefulness of the approach taken by the Work Adjustment Project.

One additional study which not only is relevant to the work adjustment theory but also to the longstanding interest in the relationship of satisfactoriness (or success) to satisfaction has been reported by Carlson (1969). Using Lawler's (1966) multiplicative model: job performance = f(ability × motivation), he inferred that the degree of "fit" (correspondence) between a worker's abilities and those demanded by his job will act as a moderator of the relationship between satisfactoriness and satisfaction. More specifically, the hypothesis is that these variables will be more highly related, the greater the correspondence is between actual and required abilities.

The measures used to quantify satisfactoriness and satisfaction were somewhat different than those developed subsequently by the Work Adjustment Project, but they seem to be conceptually, if not empirically, equivalent to them. Abilities were assessed with the GATB, and correspondence of scores from this battery with Worker Trait Requirement ratings were calculated for each cognate ability dimension. These were then summarized for three types of abilities (cognitive, perceptual, and motor) and for total correspondence, with high, average, and low levels within each.

For each type and level of ability-job correspondence in samples of blue- and white-collar workers, correlations were obtained between satisfactoriness and satisfaction. All but two of the resulting six rs were significant ($= .05$ level) in the high correspondence groups; none were significant at the average and low correspondence levels. Thus, the evidence from this study lends considerable support to the supposition that agreement between abilities and job requirements acts as a moderator of the relationship between satisfactoriness and satisfaction. As Carlson (1969:168) observes, a worker should be both satisfied and successful when he has "the ability required by his job tasks."

Comment

Work adjustment theory represents a refinement and sophistication of its precursor, the "Matching Men and Jobs" approach (Crites, 1969). Whereas the latter was characterized by an ultra-pragmatic, "dustbowl" type of empirical orientation, the current commitment of the Minnesota vocational psychologists is to a functional model of conceptualization and investigation, in which there is an inductive-deductive relationship between theory and research (Marx, 1963). The Work Adjustment Project staff has attempted to formulate theoretical propositions which are based upon previous findings and which serve to generate predictions of new findings. Thus, their theory of work adjustment meets at least two of the canons usually stipulated by philosophy of science for theory construction: it has both subsumptive and heuristic value. It is also internally consistent, that is, its propositions are logically interrelated, and they can be combined to deduce testable hypotheses. Moreover, work adjustment theory is parsimonious: it consists of an economical set of propositions, none of which appears to be superfluous to the explanatory task. If there is a shortcoming in this theory, it is probably more substantive than it is formal. The theory pays lip service to the concept of vocational development, but it does not embrace and incorporate in its propositions the idea that vocational behavior changes systematically over time from lesser to greater maturity. The consequence is that work adjustment theory has a static quality about it; it does not deal with the behavioral events which intervene between the predictors (abilities and needs) and criteria (satisfaction and satisfactoriness) of work adjustment. Work adjustment theory is closer to the older tradition of the two-point-in-time prediction model than it is to contemporary multi-point-in-time longitudinal analyses of vocational development.

It is unfortunate, too, that there is almost no emphasis in the Work Adjustment Project upon laboratory research, despite the use of such concepts as reinforcement which have been drawn from experimental psychology. Work adjustment theory would lend itself, however, to more highly controlled investigation than field-correlational studies, particularly as it pertains to the role of needs in adjustment to work. Weiss, Dawis, England, and Lofquist (1964:6) observe, for example, that the operational definition of needs:

> implies a measurement procedure in an experimental setting, where various classes of stimulus conditions can be presented experimentally to an individual and the reinforcement values of these stimulus conditions measured as an index of need strength.

Similarly, the ways in which workers respond to different work environments might be studied in the laboratory, where the latter can be more readily manipulated than on the job. To illustrate, Lofquist and Dawis (1969:67–69) have delineated two possible *modes of vocational adjustment* (cf., Crites, 1969: 404–406), the *active* and *reactive*, which workers may use in coping with the environments in which they work. If workers were exposed to standardized "work adjustment problems" in the laboratory, and their solutions to these problems measured, it might considerably advance our knowledge of which coping mechanisms are the most effective under which conditions. Work *personality styles*, ranging along a continuum of rigidity-flexibility (Lofquist and Dawis, 1969:68), might be identified which could then be related to ability and need reinforcer systems. Such a line of inquiry might serve to fill in the substantive lacunae in the work adjustment theory and better fit it to the dynamic processes of vocational development.

CAREER PATHS

The concept of "career" is implicit in both Herzberg's two-factor theory of work motivation and Lofquist, et al.'s work adjustment theory, particularly the latter, but it is not made explicit in either. In fact, the term *career* is not used in the formal statements of these two theories. Yet, the concept of career is not a new one; its history dates back at least as far as Davidson and Anderson's (1937) classic study of occupational mobility in the late thirties, and more recently, its theoretical and heuristic value has been increasingly recognized in occupational sociology (Miller & Form, 1964) and vocational psychology (Crites, 1969) alike.

What the notion of career introduces to the analysis of work behavior which less dynamic conceptualizations do not is the dimension of *time*, and the interrelationship of events along it. More specifically, career refers to the sequence of variables which have preceded a worker's current position in the occupational hierarchy. These variables may include previous positions, which can be measured by tenure and their level in the stratification system, as well as a variety of sociopsychological background and status factors, such as father's occupation and son's educational attainment. The relationships among these variables can be traced both graphically and mathematically, and the resulting "career paths" can describe the movement (mobility) of a worker through time from the antecedent conditions of his family and school to the current circumstances of his occupational station in life.

Theory of Career

The definition and delineation of career paths through time is a special case for application of the principles of path analysis to behavioral phenomena (Land, 1969). In recent years, increasing interest has been aroused in the use of path analysis as a model and method for studying time-related events which may be considered as causally connected to each other (Blalock, 1964, 1967, 1968; Duncan, 1966; Werts, 1968). Without elaborating upon the theory and technique of this approach, both of which have been thoroughly explicated elsewhere (e.g., Land, 1969), the logic of path analysis can be illustrated by reference to Figure 6, which presents Blau and Duncan's (1967:170) proposed model of career paths. First, some of the conventions used in drawing the paths should be defined: the bidirectional (two-headed) curved line connecting X and V indicates that these variables affect each other and that they probably have common causes which have not been measured; the straight lines denote a direct influence of one variable upon another, such as shown between U and Y; and the lines with no origins, e.g., the one leading to W (first job), represent "the residual paths, standing for all other influences on the variable in question, including causes not recognized or measured, errors of measurement, and departures of the true relationships from addivity and linearity . . ." (Blau & Duncan, 1967:171). Second, the numerical values alongside the lines in the

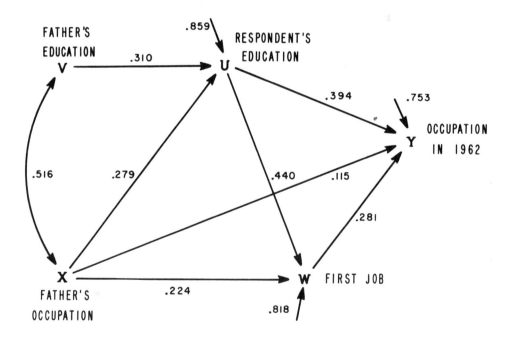

FIGURE 6.   A social structural model of career paths.

diagram are path coefficients, which can be calculated in raw score form from the equation

$$X_1 = a + (c_{12}X_2) + (c_{13}X_3) + \ldots + (c_{1n}X_n) + (c_{1a}X_a)$$

(Land, 1969:8). These coefficients resemble partial rs, except that some variables in the system from which they are derived may be unmeasured or hypothetical. Sometimes zero-order rs are also used in analyses of career paths. In either case, however, the notation is the same, with the first subscript designating the "dependent" variable and the second the "independent" variable.

The first model of career paths to be proposed was that of Blau and Duncan (1967), as shown in Figure 6. Based upon data from a large representative sampling ($N = 20,700$) of men 20 to 64 years of age in 1962, it is what might be termed a *social structural* model of career process and attainment. It posits as antecedents the education and occupation of the worker's father, which not only fix the initial level of the career path but which presumably influence directly and indirectly subsequent events in the system. Thus, father's occupation is hypothesized as having both a direct effect upon first job, and through it, an indirect influence upon later jobs. More proximate in time are the effects of the worker's educational level and his initial job upon his current employment, and so on with the other career path variables, including the sizeable contribution of those which have not as yet been incorporated into the model (the "residual" paths). And these "effects" are seen as causative. Contrary to accepted interpretations of correlation coefficients as indices of covariation and not causation, path coefficients are interpreted *as if* the variables in a model are causally related one to another. Blau and Duncan (1967:166, 168, *et passim*), for example, make such statements as these:

> A basic assumption in our interpretation of regression statistics—though not in their calculation as such—has to do with the causal or temporal ordering of these variables.

> The respondent's (worker's) education, U, is supposed to follow in time—and thus to be susceptible to causal influence from—the two measures of father's status.

The career paths model of Blau and Duncan, then, is assumed to be a network of *causal* connections between one set of variables which has temporal priority over another set.

Similarly, Sewell and others (Sewell, Haller & Portes, 1969; Sewell, Haller & Ohlendorf, 1970; Woelfel & Haller, 1971) have formulated models of career paths based upon the assumption of causation, the principal differences being substantive rather than formal. Whereas the Blau and Duncan model might be characterized as social structural, Sewell's is avowedly *social psychological*, as can be discerned from the graphic representation in Figure 7. Although several variables in the two models are roughly equivalent, namely, Educational Attainment, Socioeconomic Status, and Occupational Attainment, only the last is defined operationally in exactly the same way. Sewell, et al. have added Mental Ability as a major "input" variable, which has been demonstrated as a strong

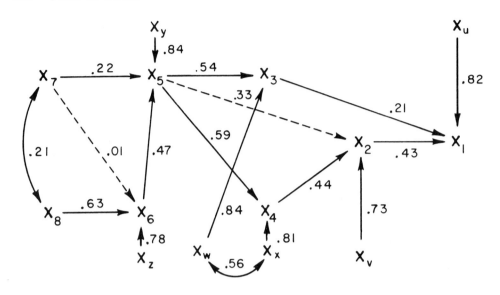

X₁   OCCUPATIONAL ATTAINMENT

X₂   EDUCATIONAL ATTAINMENT

X₃   LEVEL OF OCCUPATIONAL ASPIRATION

X₄   LEVEL OF EDUCATIONAL ASPIRATION

X₅   SIGNIFICANT OTHERS' INFLUENCE

X₆   ACADEMIC PERFORMANCE

X₇   SOCIOECONOMIC STATUS

X₈   MENTAL ABILITY

FIGURE 7.   A social psychological model of career.

correlate of occupational level (Crites, 1969), and they have incorporated four so-called "intervening" variables—Significant Others' Influence, Levels of Educational and Occupational Aspiration, and Academic Performance—into the network as career paths which link the worker's background to his vocational behavior. Sewell, et al. (1969:83) also reason, that one's cognitions and motivations (including, among others, knowledge, self-concept and aspirations) are developed in structured situations (including the expectations of others), and that one's actions (attainment in this case) are a result of the cognitive and motivational orientations one brings to the action situation, as well as the factors in the new situation itself.

In other words, it is proposed that the effects of the independent variables (Mental Ability and Socioeconomic Status) upon the dependent variables (Educational Attainment and Occupational Attainment) are *mediated* by the intervening variables (Significant Others' Influence, Levels of Educational and Occupational Aspiration, and Academic Performance).

Research on Career Paths

The basic findings on Blau and Duncan's (1967) model of career paths are given in Figure 6. With the exception of r_{xv}, which is a zero-order correlation, the numerical values are path coefficients as defined previously. If the latter have been properly estimated, and if the causal connections in the model fit reality reasonably well, then the path coefficients should be close approximations of the product-moment correlations among the several variables. And such was the case, according to Blau and Duncan (1967:173), who report the differences were small, not larger than .001 correlation points. They note that the results support certain expected sequences of relationships, such as $r_{wu} >$ $r_{wx} > r_{wv}$. That is, the worker's first job is more strongly correlated with his educational attainment than with either his father's education or occupational status, and it is more closely associated with the latter than the former. Similarly, education is more highly related to second job than it is to the first (.596 vs. .538), although the difference is most likely not significant (see below for a discussion of this point). Overall, the input variables contribute approximately 26% of the variance in educational level, 33% in first job, and 42% in current job. Thus, despite the seemingly large coefficients for the "residual" paths, the model would appear to have considerable explanatory power for the dependent variables specified in it. With respect to the "unexplained" variance in the model, Blau and Duncan (1967:175) contend that:

> The relevant question about the residual is not really size at all, but whether the unobserved factors it stands for are properly represented as being uncorrelated with the measured antecedent variables.

That this assumption is a tenuous one for the Blau and Duncan model is apparent from Sewell's findings on the relationship of Mental Ability to each of the other predictor variables, such as Socioeconomic Status, and to the dependent variables of interest. In the social psychological model, which includes Mental Ability, it is correlated significantly with SES ($r = .21$) as well as all other variables in the system. In fact, despite the salience attributed by Sewell, et al. (1969) to Significant Others' Influence and the other "intervening" variables, it would appear that it is the more strictly psychological "power" variables, namely, Mental Ability, Academic Performance, and Educational Attainment, which account both directly and indirectly for the major portion of the variance in Occupational Attainment. Educational Attainment alone contributes 27% of the common variance to Occupational Attainment, and Educational Attainment in turn is correlated .48 and .40, respectively, with Academic Performance and Mental Ability. Sewell, et al. (1969:89) properly conclude that:

> What we have here, then, is a plausible causal system functioning primarily to explain variation in educational attainment. This, in turn, has considerable effect on occupational attainment.

They go on to add that:

> The same set of variables adds a small but useful amount to the explanation of occupational attainment variance beyond that contributed by its explanation of educational attainment.

This conclusion is not empirically substantiated, however, with appropriate data on the significance of the difference between the multiple regressions of the predictor variables on Occupational Attainment with and without Educational Attainment.

In a large-scale replication of the 1969 study, Sewell, Haller and Ohlendorf (1970) have obtained results which corroborate the interpretation of Mental Ability and Academic Performance, especially the latter, as more important factors in the social-psychological model than Significant Others' Influence. From this second set of findings, they concluded that: "academic performance has effects on aspirational and attainment variables that are not mediated by significant others' influence" (Sewell, et al., 1970:1025).

As a consequence of this empirical evidence, which was fairly uniform across samples from residential areas varying in size from villages to large cities, the Sewell model is reduced, by-in-large, to Mental Ability, Academic Performance, and Socioeconomic Status as the most potent predictors of later Educational and Occupational Attainment. Stated differently, it has not been demonstrated that such "intervening" variables as Significant Others' Influence contribute unique variance to the prediction of the dependent variables, either directly or indirectly. Yet, Sewell, et al. (1970:1024–1025; et passim) are reluctant to accept this conclusion. They observe that both of their studies confirm "the critical role of significant others' influence in the status attainment process"; only with qualifications do they concede that "significant others' influence is perhaps slightly less important than was previously reported." They do suggest, however, that the search for mediating variables might include age at marriage, help and encouragement of one's spouse, number of dependents, spacing of offspring, and such personality characteristics as need for achievement.

Comment

On a conceptual level, the career path models of Blau and Duncan (1967) and Sewell, et al. (1969, 1970) have much to commend them. They provide ready frames of reference for specifying the expected relationships among a set of variables, and they direct research to test the hypotheses generated by the network. There is no gainsaying the obvious heuristic value of such an approach to theory construction (Marx, 1963).

If any issue can be taken with career path analysis, it is the cogency or legitimacy of assuming causal connections among the variables in a career model. From one standpoint (Brodbeck, 1957, 1963; Dubin, 1969) at least, the concept of causality in behavioral theory and research has little or no utility. Not only does it amount to a hypothetical construct, which by definition connotes unanalyzable surplus meaning (Bergman, 1957), but it cannot be given empirical specification. Only if an exhaustive enumeration of the antecedents to an event could be made would it be possible to identify the probable "cause" of an event through a process of control and elimination (Cohen & Nagel, 1934). And, estimating the variance contribution of residual paths only begs the question, since these variables are unknown. It can be argued, therefore, that the most which can be inferred from a career path model are systematic relationships in which "independent" variables have *temporal priority* (but not necessarily causality) over "dependent" variables. Viewed from this logical position, imputing causal properties to antecedent conditions serves no useful purpose either theoretically or methodologically.

On an empirical level, several observations pertinent to the analysis of career path data are appropriate. First, comparative statements concerning the relative magnitudes of correlation coefficients and the respective contributions of "independent" variables to the total variance in "dependent" variables are made both by Blau and Duncan (1967) and by Sewell, et al. (1969, 1970) without benefit of tests for statistically significant differences. That the numerical value of one r is greater than another, for example, does not mean that it is *significantly* greater; the difference between them may simply be due to chance sampling fluctuations. Thus, to state that the correlation between first job and education ($r = .538$) is greater than the correlation between the former and father's occupational status ($r = .417$), as Blau and Duncan (1967:169) do, without testing for the reliability of the difference, is misleading. Second, the data in Blau and Duncan's study were largely retrospective and hence subject to all of the sources of bias which are inherent in these kinds of data. In this regard, the follow-up data gathered by Sewell and his associates are to be preferred, although they were influenced to an indeterminate degree by nonrespondents. Lastly, it is noteworthy that neither design is longitudinal, in the sense that data are collected on the same sample of subjects at several different points-in-time. The advantages of such data, among others, are that changes in the independent and dependent variables, as well as the relationships between them, can be plotted from one occasion to another as the individual develops throughout the school and work years (Crites, 1969; Super & Bachrach, 1957).

CAREER PATTERNS

In contrast to career path analyses, the study of career patterns has generally been longitudinal (Super, Crites, Hummel, Moser, Overstreet & Warnath, 1957; Crites, 1965; Gribbons & Lohnes, 1968), the pioneer investigation being the Career Pattern Study (CPS) conceived and directed by Donald E. Super at Teachers College, Columbia University, since 1950. This twenty year study of career patterns was designed to follow-up at periodic intervals a group of male adolescents from the time they were in ninth grade until they reached the middle years of their work lives at approximately age thirty-five. The plan was to collect not only traditional trait-and-factor data on the subjects, but also data on what the CPS researchers have termed *vocational maturity*. This concept, as is true of many others in CPS, was extrapolated from developmental psychology, which has been adopted as the most relevant theoretical frame of reference for career patterns, and refers to "the degree of development, the place reached on the continuum of vocational development from exploration to decline" (Super, 1955:153).

The basic assumption underlying the concept of vocational maturity is that vocational behavior changes in a systematic way as the individual grows older—that earlier behaviors are developmentally revised in order to cope with the increasingly difficult and complex tasks of later life. In normal vocational development, the individual acquires the appropriate coping mechanisms apace with his progress through the several stages of the choice and career years. In delayed and impaired vocational development (Lo Cascio, 1964), however, the individual's behaviors are inappropriate or not adequate enough to cope effectively with the developmental tasks of his vocational life stage.

Theory of Career Patterns

The total span of vocational development is subdivided into five stages: (1) growth, (2) exploration, (3) establishment, (4) maintenance, and (5) decline (Super, 1957). These stages closely correspond to the periods which are usually delineated in general development: childhood, adolescence, early adulthood, late adulthood (sometimes called "maturity"), and senescence. They can be defined by either one of two principal sets of criteria: the behaviors which are typical of a given age-range, or the tasks which are usually encountered at a particular time in life. Following Havighurst (1953), the CPS theorists have preferred the latter and have attempted to enumerate the vocational developmental tasks which define each vocational life stage (Table 1). This enumeration is not an exhaustive one, but with emendations made in a later analysis (Super & Bachrach, 1957; Super, Starishevsky, Matlin, and Jordaan, 1963), it is reasonably comprehensive, especially during adolescence and adulthood, which have been the foci of CPS research. During the adolescent years, the most important task faced by the future worker is choice of a vocation. This process involves a progressive narrowing down of the vocational alternatives which are viable in terms of reality factors and then the specification of the goals which the individual intends to pursue. When a vocational choice has been made and acted upon, typically by first obtaining the necessary training and then seeking full-time employment, the exploratory stage of vocational development comes to an end and the Establishment Stage begins.

This transition from school to work does not mean however, that there are no longer decisions to make. On the contrary, as Super, Kowalski, and Gotkin (1967) have made clear, the neophyte worker is often confronted with a confusing array of career alternatives from which he must choose those which will presumably maximize his chances for satisfaction and success later on. In the first instance, he must decide how he is going to find a job—through the newspaper, a placement service, personal contacts, etc. And, should he apply for positions in person or by letter—or how should he present himself? Also, what

TABLE 1
VOCATIONAL DEVELOPMENTAL TASKS AND LIFE STAGES AS DELINEATED
IN THE CAREER PATTERN STUDY
(Super and Bachrach, 1957 :44)

Preschool Child
    1. Increasing ability for self-help
    2. Identification with like-sexed parent
    3. Increasing ability for self-direction

Elementary School Child
    1. Ability to undertake cooperative enterprises
    2. Choice of activities suited to one's abilities
    3. Assumption of responsibility for one's acts
    4. Performance of chores around the house

High School Adolescent
    1. Further development of abilities and talents
    2. Choice of high school or work
    3. Choice of high school curriculum
    4. Development of independence

Young Adult
    1. Choice of college or work
    2. Choice of college curriculum
    3. Choice of suitable job
    4. Development of skills on the job

Mature Adult
    1. Stabilization is an occupation
    2. Providing for future security
    3. Finding appropriate avenues of advancement

Older Person
    1. Gradual retirement
    2. Finding suitable activities or skills to occupy time
    3. Maintaining self-sufficiency insofar as possible

type of work setting would he prefer: large corporation, small business, government agency, or self-employment?

Once on the job, a decision may have to be made between further training, such as an apprenticeship, and regular work, or whether to pursue additional education at night or by correspondence courses. With the shortened work week, an individual may choose to hold a second job as well as the one he originally entered. And if there is a conflict between them, e.g., he likes the work of his second job better but gets higher wages in the first, he will probably have to choose which one he wants to keep. He may also have to make a decision about military service: whether to take his chances in the draft, enlist for a specified length of time, retrain for an exempted occupation, become a conscientious objector, etc. What may have seemed to him the end of the choice process, when he decided which occupation to enter, has only been transformed into one of adjusting to the new tasks of the Establishment stage in vocational development.

How the young worker adjusts has been the subject of intensive analysis by the CPS Staff (Super, et al., 1963; Super, et al., 1967). Five discernible coping behaviors for the developmental tasks of the Establishment Stage have been identified: (1) floundering, (2) trial, (3) instrumentation, (4) establishment, and (5) stagnation. Conceptual or "literary" definitions (Underwood, 1957) of each of these aspects of career patterns are (Super, et al., 1967:i, 9–12):

1. *floundering:* "movement to a position which is not logical as a next step from the position being vacated, for which the subject lacks required aptitudes, interests, and preparation, or for which he is no better suited than for the position being vacated."

2. *trial:* "movement from one related job to another, the next job having some characteristics of the preceding job but lacking others...a zeroing in on a field of activity."

3. *instrumentation:* "action which enables, or is designed to enable, the subject to prepare for or enter a regular adult occupation which is appropriate for him."

4. *establishment:* behavior "which achieves stability in an occupation in which the subject can function as a normal adult ..."

5. *stagnation:* "staying in a position or in an occupation longer than is appropriate."

There are two differentia which run through these definitions of coping behaviors: one is the appropriateness of the movement from one position to another, in terms of the characteristics of the positions, and the other is appropriateness of the worker for a position, in terms of his characteristics and its requirements. Thus, to the extent that an individual's coping behavior results in an orderly progression from one job to another (*trial*), for which he is qualified (*instrumentation*), and in which he eventually stabilizes (*establishment*), it can be inferred that he is successfully mastering the tasks of the Establishment stage in vocational development.

Research on Career Patterns

To collect data on the coping behaviors and nascent career patterns of young adult workers, CPS followed-up their original groups of eighth and ninth graders (Super & Overstreet, 1960) in 1962 and 1963 when these subjects were approximately age twenty-five. Using questionnaires, semistructured interviews, and work histories, four classes of variables were defined (see Table 2): (1) vocational coping behaviors, (2) scaled career behaviors, (3) career statistics, and (4) occupational behaviors and outcomes. The last category was included in order to test the distinction proposed by Super (1961) between *career* and *occupation*, the former being a developmental concept and the latter a cross-sectional or time-bound one. Through the persistent efforts of the CPS staff, remarkably high percentages of the original groups were followed-up: 89% of the eighth graders and 94% of the ninth graders.

Concerning the coping behaviors of these new entrants into the world-of-work, it was found by Super, et al. (1967:v–6) that: "In both samples, the majority of subjects were judged to be stabilizing, operating in a positive way at age twenty-five; over half of each sample had reached this status directly by a majority of positive moves. Of those subjects whose modal behavior had been negative or floundering, about one-half in each sample had none-the-less reached a positive status by age 25." Similarly, the findings on the other career and occupational behaviors indicated that at least a modicum of progress was being made by the CPS groups toward establishing themselves in their chosen lines of work. There was some evidence, however, such as the less than optimal correspondence of their abilities with those required by their jobs, which suggested that some of them were still trying to "find themselves" and that their careers were only beginning to stabilize.

TABLE 2
CRITERIA OF VOCATIONAL ADJUSTMENT INVESTIGATED BY THE CAREER
PATTERN STUDY AT AGE 25
(Super, et al., 1967:ii, 13–14)

Vocational Coping Behaviors
1. Floundering
2. Trial
3. Instrumentation
4. Establishment
5. Stagnation

Scaled Career Behaviors
1. Equity Change
2. Movement Realism
3. Goodness of Fit: Abilities
4. Goodness of Fit: Interests
5. Relation to Goal
6. Status Improvement: Occupational
7. Status Improvement: Educational
8. Career Development Total (sum of 1, 2, 5, 6, and 7)

Career Statistics
1. Number of Moves
2. Number of Times Unemployed
3. Number of Months Unemployed
4. Number of Months Self-Supporting
5. Educational Level Attained
6. Educational Level Comparison
7. Educational Success: College Grade-Point Average
8. Career Satisfaction, Self-Estimated
9. Career Success, Self-Estimated
10. Career Establishment, Self-Reported
11. Attainment of High School Leaving Vocational Goal

Occupational Behaviors and Outcomes
1. Occupational Level Attained
2. Position Success, Self-Estimated
3. Position Success, Employer Rated
4. Occupational Success, Self-Estimated
5. Position Satisfaction, Self-Estimated
6. Occupational Satisfaction, Self-Estimated
7. Occupational Satisfaction, Self-Reported
8. Utilization of Assets, Self-Reported
9. Opportunity for Self-Expression, Self-Reported

It was found that the conceptual distinction between career and occupation was *not* substantiated by the data on six different clusters of behavioral criteria at age twenty-five: (1) career satisfaction, (2) self-improvement, (3) job getting and holding, (4) economic self-sufficiency, (5) early establishment, and (6) occupational satisfaction. From the intercorrelations of these variables, Super, et al. (1967:p. iv–8) concluded that:

The first and second (clusters) are largely career but partly occupational in composition. The fifth is largely occupational but includes one career criterion (stabilizing vs. floundering behavior). The fourth also seems partly career and partly occupational in nature, but having just two components is less easy to classify. The third and sixth are rather clearly career in their composition, for they involve progress or events over a period of time. Thus the logical career-occupational dichotomy is not well supported empirically, for four clusters are entirely or largely made up of career criteria, one is largely but not purely occupational, and one is a mixture of doubtful balance.

In contrast, the interrelationships of the career development scales were generally low and nonsignificant. Only change in Equity, defined as the carry-over of pay rate, worker benefits, etc., from one position to another appeared to be systematically related to other career behaviors in both the original eighth and ninth grade samples. It was highly correlated for example, as would be expected theoretically, with Realism of Reasons for a Move. These are only a few of the findings on the interrelationships of the coping behaviors which CPS is investigating in the early Establishment stage. In general, the results have indicated that such variables can be measured and that they are related not only to each other (although not as highly as might be desired) and to other variables of interest.

The latter include two broad classes of predictors and correlates of young adult career patterns: (1) measures of vocational maturity obtained earlier in the subjects' vocational development and (2) sociopsychological-educational status indices during the school years and also after occupational entry. Preliminary analyses of both types of variables have been made but only those on the status indices are presently available for reporting. They reveal that such variables as intelligence, parental occupational level, grade-point-average, and level of vocational aspiration in junior and senior high school are good (rs in 30s and 40s) predictors of career and occupational behaviors at age twenty-five.

Also related to career and occupational behaviors were correlates on which data were gathered at the time of the follow-up. These included parental occupational level, family social mobility, cultural participation, independence, adjustment, and marital status; only parental occupational level and cultural participation were related consistently to the criteria, however, with the greatest number of significant correlations being found for cultural participation. This variable is defined as the extent to which an individual makes use of cultural resources, such as clubs, museums, travel, and books; it was correlated positively ($r = .34$) with intelligence in the ninth grade. Thus, the implications of these findings seem to be twofold according to Super, et al. (1967:viii, 3, 5; et passim) : first, indices of status in adolescence and early adulthood have some validity as predictors and concomitants of career behavior in the latter period; and, second, criteria of vocational development at the onset of the Establishment stage are predictable.

Comment

The Career Pattern Study (CPS) represents a unique approach to the study of work and career. Theoretically, it has been cast into a developmental framework (Super, et al., 1957) which is dynamic, in that it stresses the changing character of careers as workers grow older. It incorporates the concept of vocational life-stages to denote the periods or phases which occur in the work-cycle from its advent at the time of occupational entry to its termination with retirement. And, possibly most important, it recognizes the interrelationships of vocational development and other aspects of development, e.g., intellectual, physical, and social (Super, 1955). In concept, then, CPS is probably the most comprehensive conceptualization of careers which has as yet been proposed (Super & Bachrach, 1957).

Empirically, however, it suffers from the lack of rigor which is so often a shortcoming of ground-breaking research (cf., Ginzberg, Ginzburg, Axelrad, and Herma, 1951). Although CPS has been remarkably successful in achieving a high percentage of follow-up data on its subjects, the Ns for many of the analyses which have been made, e.g., intercorrelations of variables, are sometimes smaller than would be desired statistically. Correlation coefficients based upon samples less than 125 degrees of freedom, for example, often have such wide confidence intervals that their values vary considerably upon replication. Likewise, small Ns are not sufficient for the establishment of norms, but if CPS is viewed as a *survey* research project (Crites, 1969), then these restrictions are relatively unimportant.

CPS's contribution to a greater understanding of career patterns might be viewed as the identification of salient variables, such as the coping behaviors of the Establishment stage, and the formulation of hypotheses concerning their relationships to other sociopsychological-educational variables. More focused, large-scale research hopefully will investigate some of the problems defined within the broader scope of the Career Pattern Study.

Other Theory and Research

In addition to recent systematic surveys of work and career (Osipow, 1968; Crites, 1969), there have appeared during the last decade several more intensive analyses of these phenomena which have viewed them from multifaceted frames of reference, as well as collections of readings which have made otherwise inaccessible primary sources readily available. Cutting across the choice and career years is a volume of reprints of Ginzberg's (1966) papers on *The Development of Human Resources*, which treat such diverse yet interrelated topics as "Work and Freedom," "Career Plans," "Personality and Performance," and "Human Potential and American Democracy." Of similar scope but different orientation are Neff's (1968) sociopsychological review of *Work and Human Behavior*, the major parts of which are "Work and Society," "Work and the Individual," "Clinical Issues," and "Some Contemporary Problems," and Slocum's (1966) sociological perspective on *Occupational Careers*, which ranges in subject matter from "The Meaning of Work" to "Career Patterns and Strategies."

In a more empirical vein, there is Gribbons and Lohnes' (1968) summary of their longitudinal investigation of *Emerging Careers*, which was inspired by Super's Career Pattern Study and which elaborates upon it by developing *a priori* measures of readiness for vocational planning and by studying females as well as males. Also of interest is the decision-making model of *Career Development* proposed by Kroll, Dinklage, Lee, Morley, and Wilson (1970), which attempts to explicate the relationships of self-evaluation and commitment to career choice. Two sides of the same coin are represented in Kornhauser's (1965)

Mental Health of the Industrial Worker and Simons' (1965) *Work and Mental Illness,* in which the authors deal with the complex problem of the interrelationships of personal and vocational adjustment. Finally, there are two anthologies of articles relevant to work and career which bring together many of the more significant theoretical and empirical papers in the area: Hershenson and Roth's (1970) *The Psychology of Vocational Development: Readings in Theory and Practice* and Zytowski's (1968) *Vocational Behavior: Readings in Theory and Research.*

SUMMARY AND CONCLUSIONS

This chapter has reviewed four major contemporary approaches to the conceptualization and study of work and career. Herzberg's motivator-hygiene or two-factor theory *of work motivation* has had a catalytic effect upon research dealing with this component of the vocational adjustment process. Not only has it challenged the traditional concept of job satisfaction as a unidimensional variable, but it has been generalized to apply to a phenomenon as comprehensive as mental health. Distinguishing between motivators and hygienes as sources of satisfaction and dissatisfaction, respectively, has had a pervasive impact upon the psychology of work.

Less spectacularly but no less significantly Lofquist, et al.'s (1969) long-term investigations of *work adjustment* have proven the value of persistent programmatic research. The measures of motivation (needs), satisfaction, satisfactoriness (success), and occupational ability and reinforcer patterns which have issued forth from this project would alone be enough to commend it, but it has also produced a viable theory of work adjustment which is continually being tested. And, the confirmatory findings on it attest once again to the theoretical usefulness as well as the intuitive appeal of the Matching Men and Jobs approach in vocational psychology.

Probably the most exciting conceptual and methodological innovation in the study of careers in recent years, however, has been the application of *path analysis* to hypothesized relationships between sociopsychological antecedents and later educational-occupational attainment, as exemplified in the research of Blau and Duncan (1967) and of Sewell, et al. (1969, 1970). It is conceivable that this logical-statistical technique might also be used with data such as those gathered on *career patterns* by Super and his associates, who have been conducting a 20-year longitudinal study of the vocational choice and adjustment of two groups of male subjects from early adolescence to midadulthood.

Each of these approaches to work and career has made its unique contribution, but would the contribution not have been greater if the discourse among them had been less indifferent? Herzberg asked the subjects in his original study of work motivation to recall incidents from their past, but nowhere throughout his writings does he acknowledge that longitudinal data might be preferable to retrospections, or that the worker's subjective evaluation of motivators and hygienes may change as he develops vocationally. Similarly, the Work Adjustment Project pays lip service to vocational development concepts in its theory, but it has not used any measures of these variables or even collected longitudinal data on satisfaction and satisfactoriness. Sewell, et al. have conducted one follow-up of their 1957 sample, and may have others contemplated, but they have not interpreted their findings within a framework of vocational development. Yet, their data lend themselves to such a conceptualization and might be more meaningful if related to a dynamic developmental model as well as a static sociopsychological one.

The Career Pattern Study has drawn most heavily upon developmental principles and longitudinal designs in its work, and it has systematically included such sociological variables as father's occupation and other indices of status characteristics. If it has neglected any variable of significance, it is work motivation. Not only Herzberg's procedures but also other methods for assessing why people work (Crites, 1961) were available at the time of the last CPS follow-up, and, if they had been used, might have provided data on a variety of problems, e.g., whether variations in the motivation to work differentiate between stabilizing and floundering career patterns. Perhaps in future theory and research on work and career the most useful concepts from several different approaches can be incorporated into a logical and methodological framework which is truly multidisciplinary.

One last observation concerns the research setting in which most investigations of work and career have been carried out: almost without exception they have been conducted in the field and not in the laboratory. Yet, if there is a portent for the future, it would seem to be the increased incidence of laboratory experiments in the study of work and career phenomena. The choice to enter the laboratory, which is an alien environment to many occupational sociologists and vocational psychologists, may be less one of preference than one of necessity. For it has become clearer and clearer that certain issues cannot be settled by field-correlational research, in which extraneous variables are largely uncontrolled and often uncontrollable. Had the move to the laboratory been made earlier, where the experimenter has greater control over the independent and dependent variables, controversies such as that which has raged over Herzberg's theory for the last ten years or more might now be resolved. In any case, an experimental research strategy has much to recommend it: not only can variables be directly manipulated and appropriate controls instituted, but more explicit models must be formulated, so that unequivocal predictions can be made. It is not enough to invoke vaguely defined hypothetical constructs to account for the data; their explanation must rest upon intervening variables which are linked to both the stimulus *and* response sides of the behavioral equation.

REFERENCES

American Psychological Association
    1966   Standards for Educational and Psychological Tests and Manuals. Washington, D.C.: American Psychological Association.
Barron, F.
    1958   "The psychology of imagination." Scientific American (199):151–166.
Bergmann, G.
    1957   Philosophy of Science. Madison, Wisconsin: University of Wisconsin Press.
Blalock, H.M.
    1964   Causal references in Nonexperimental Research. Chapel Hill, North Carolina: University of North Carolina Press.

1967 "Path coefficients versus regression coefficients." American Journal of Sociology (72):675–676.

1968 "Theory building and causal inferences," in H.M. Blalock and A.B. Blalock (eds.), Methodology in Social Research. New York: McGraw-Hill.

Blau, P.M. and O.D. Duncan
1967 The American Occupational Structure. New York: Wiley.

Brayfield, A.H. and W.H. Crockett
1955 "Employee attitudes and employee performance." Psychological Bulletin (52):396–424.

Brodbeck, M.
1957 "The philosophy of science and educational research." Review of Educational Research (27):427–440.

1963 "Logic and scientific method in research on teaching," in N.L. Gage (ed.), Handbook of Research on Teaching. Chicago: Rand McNally.

Burke, R.J.
1966 "Are Herzberg's motivators and hygienes really unidimensional?" Journal of Applied Psychology (50):317–321.

Campbell, D.T. and D.W. Fiske
1959 "Convergent and discriminant validation by the multitrait–multimethod matrix." Psychological Bulletin (56):81–105.

Carlson, R.E.
1969 "Degree of job fit as a moderator of the relationship between job performance and job satisfaction." Personnel Psychology (22):159–170.

Cohen, M.R. and E. Nagel
1934 An Introduction to Logic and Scientific Method. New York: Harcourt, Brace and Co.

Crites, J.O.
1961 "Factor analytic definitions of vocational motivation." Journal of Applied Psychology (45):330–337.

1965 "Measurement of vocational maturity in adolescence: I. attitude test of the vocational development inventory." Psychological Monographs 79(2, Whole No. 595).

1969 Vocational Psychology. New York: McGraw-Hill.

Davidson, P.E. and H.D. Anderson
1937 Occupational Mobility in an American Community. Stanford, Calif.: Stanford University Press.

Dawis, R.V., L.H. Lofquist and D.J. Weiss
1968 A Theory of Work Adjustment. Revised Edition. Minneapolis: Industrial Relations Center, University of Minnesota.

Dubin, R.
1969 Theory Building. New York: Free Press.

Duncan, O.D.
1966 "Path analysis: sociological examples." American Journal of Sociology (72):1–16.

Ewen, R.B., P.C. Smith, C.C. Hulin and E.A. Locke
1966 "An empirical test of the Herzberg two-factor theory." Journal of Applied Psychology (50):544–550.

Flanagan, J.C.
1954 "The critical incident technique." Psychological Bulletin (51):327–358.

Ginzberg, E.
  1966   The Development of Human Resources. New York: McGraw-Hill.
Ginzberg, E., S.W. Ginzberg, S. Axelrod and J.L. Herma
  1951   Occupational Choice. New York: Columbia University Press.
Gribbons, W.D. and P.R. Lohnes
  1968   Emerging Careers. New York: Teachers College Press.
Havinghurst, R.J.
  1953   Human Development and Education. New York: Longmans, Green.
Hershenson, D.B. and R.M. Roth
  1970   The Psychology of Vocational Development: Readings in Theory and
         Practice. Boston: Allyn Bacon.
Herzberg, F.
  1966   Work and the Nature of Man. New York: World.
Herzberg, F., B. Mausner, R.O. Peterson and D.F. Capwell
  1957   Job Attitudes: Review of Research and Opinion. Pittsburgh: Psycho-
         logical Service of Pittsburgh.
Herzberg, F., B. Mausner and B.B. Snyderman
  1959   The Motivation to Work. New York: Wiley.
House, R.J. and L.A. Wigdor
  1967   "Herzberg's dual-factor theory of job satisfaction and motivation: a
         review of the evidence and criticism." Personnel Psychology (20):369–
         390.
Hulin, C.L.
  1966   "Review of Herzberg's *Work and the Nature of Man*." Personnel Psy-
         chology (19):434–437.
Komhauser, A.
  1965   Mental Health of the Industrial Worker. New York: Wiley.
Korman, A.K.
  1970   "Toward an hypothesis of work behavior." Journal of Applied Psychol-
         ogy (54):31–41.
Kroll, A.M., L.B. Dinklage, J. Lee, E.D. Morley and E.H. Wilson
  1970   Career Development. New York: Wiley.
Land, K.C.
  1969   "Principles of path analysis," in E.F. Borgatta (ed.), Sociological Meth-
         odology. San Francisco: Jossey-Bass.
Lawler, E.E.
  1966   "Ability as a moderator of the relationship between job attitudes and
         job performance." Personnel Psychology (19):153–164.
  1970   "Job attitudes and employee motivation: theory, research and practice."
         Personnel Psychology (23):223–238.
Lindsay, C.A., E. Marks and L. Gorlow
  1967   "The Herzberg theory: a critique and reformulation." Journal of Ap-
         plied Psychology (51):330–339.
Lo Casio, R.
  1964   "Delayed and impaired vocational development: a neglected aspect of
         vocational development theory." Personnel and Guidance Journal
         (42):885–887.
Lofquist, L.H. and R.V. Dawis
  1969   Adjustment to Work. New York: Appleton-Century-Crofts.

Marx, M.H. (ed.)
  1963   Theories in Contemporary Psychology. New York: Macmillan.
Maslow, A.H.
  1954   Motivation and Personality. New York: Harper.
Miller, D.C. and W.H. Form
  1964   Industrial Psychology. Second Edition. New York: Harper.
Neff, W.S.
  1968   Work and Human Behavior. New York: Atherton.
Oppenheimer, E.A.
  1966   "The relationship between certain self constructs and occupational preferences." Journal of Counseling Psychology (13) :191–197.
Osipow, S.H.
  1968   Theories of Career Development. New York: Appleton-Century-Crofts.
Paterson, D.G. and J.G. Darley
  1936   Men, Women and Jobs. Minneapolis: University of Minnesota Press.
Roethlisberger, F.J. and W.J. Dickson
  1939   Management and the Worker. Cambridge, Mass.: Harvard University Press.
Sewell, W.H., A.O. Haller and A. Portes
  1969   "The educational and early occupational attainment process." American Sociological Review (34) :82–92.
Sewell, W.H., A.O. Haller and G.W. Ohlendorf
  1970   "The educational and early occupational status attainment process: replication and revision." American Sociological Review (35) :1014–1027.
Shaffer, L.F. and E.J. Schoben, Jr.
  1956   The Psychology of Adjustment. Second Edition. Boston: Houghton Mifflin.
Shoben, E.J., Jr.
  1957   "Towards a concept of the normal personality." American Psychologist (12) :183–189.
Simmons, O.G.
  1965   Work and Mental Illness. New York: Wiley.
Slocum, W.L.
  1966   Occupational Careers. Chicago: Aldine.
Smith, K.U.
  1962   Work Theory and Economic Behavior. Bloomington, Ind.: Foundation for Economic and Business Studies.
Soliman, H.M.
  1970   "Motivation-hygiene theory of job attitudes: and empirical investigation and an attempt to reconcile both the one- and two-factor theories of job attitudes." Journal of Applied Psychology (54) :452–461.
Super, D.E.
  1955   "The dimensions and measurement of vocational maturity." Teachers College Record (57) :151–163.
  1957   The Psychology of Careers. New York: Harper.
  1961   "Some unresolved issues in vocational development research." Personnel and Guidance Journal (40) :11–14.

Super, D.E. and P.B. Bachrach
  1957 Scientific Careers and Vocational Development Theory. New York:
         Teachers College Bureau of Publications.
Super, D.E., J.O. Crites, R.C. Hummel, H.P. Moser,
P.L. Overstreet and C.F. Warnath
  1957 Vocational Development: A Framework for Research. New York:
         Teachers College Bureau of Publications.
Super, D.E., R.S. Kowalski and E.H. Gotkin
  1967 Floundering and Trial After High School. New York: Columbia Uni-
         versity Teachers College.
Super, D.E. and P.L. Overstreet
  1960 The Vocational Maturity of Ninth Grade Boys. New York: Teachers
         College Bureau of Publications.
Super, D.E., R. Starishevsky, N. Martin and J.P. Jordaan
  1963 Career Development: Self-Concept Theory. Princeton, New Jersey:
         Educational Testing Service (College Entrance Examination Board).
Underwood, B.J.
  1949 Experimental Psychology. New York: Appleton-Century-Crofts.
  1957 Psychological Research. New York: Appleton-Century-Crofts.
Vroom, V.A.
  1964 Work and Motivation. New York: Wiley.
Vroom, V.H.
  1966 "Some observations regarding Herzberg's two-factor theory." Paper
         presented at the American Psychological Association Convention, New
         York (September).
Weiss, D.J., R.V. Dawis, G.W. England and L.H. Lofquist
  1964 The Measurement of Vocational Needs. Minneapolis: Industrial Re-
         lations Center, University of Minnesota.
Werts, C.E.
  1968 "Path analysis: testimonial of a proselyte." American Journal of So-
         ciology (73):509–512.
Whitsett, D.A. and E.K. Winslow
  1967 "An analysis of studies critical of the motivator-hygiene theory." Per-
         sonnel Psychology (20):391–416.
Woelfel, J. and A.O. Haller
  1971 "Significant others, the self-reflexive act and the attitude formation
         process." American Sociological Review (36):74–87.
Wolf, M.G.
  1967 "The relationship of context factors to attitudes toward company and
         job." Personnel Psychology (20):121–132.
Zytowski, D.G.
  1968 Vocational Behavior: Readings in Theory and Research. New York:
         Holt, Rinehart and Winston.

PART III

WORKING BEHAVIOR

INTRODUCTION—PART III

The actual working behavior of people in industry and commerce is a most obvious target for study because of high visibility and ready access. There is, however, a limited number of studies that are concerned with good description of what people actually do when they are working. Even in the field of motion and time study, the analyst deliberately limits his attention to the technologically determined behaviors.

The society of the shop floor is a very rich environment full of many objects and opportunities for social interaction. Furthermore, in the working life time of the employees there will very often be major transformations of the technologies with which they work. This simply adds variety to an already full environment. Perhaps we can attribute some of the neglect of behavioral scientists, who have failed to use their skills in observing working behavior, to their preoccupation with questionnaire instruments. The amount of information which we still lack about actual working behavior is one of the disgraces of behavioral science.

In the first two chapters of Part III attention is directed at some of the typical behaviors to be found in a factory. It is particularly notable that an entire chapter is devoted to language behavior. The continuous use of language is such an obvious feature of any human group that it is likely to be taken for granted, and as a result, analytically ignored. When we do accept the responsibility to study this behavior, an improved sense of the variety in the social life of the work-place emerges. Man apparently tunes each environment in which he participates to his own needs, and in the process may make that environment a little more bearable.

Some notion of the complexity of the work environment is revealed when a search is made for the features of work that are salient to workers. The entire subject of the attachment to work requires a great deal more research before we can arrive at firm conclusions. But even in the present state of our ignorance we are discovering that the work environment is truly "in the eye of the beholder." We may eventually discover that each employee creates an image of his work organization and his work station that is built upon his expectations as much as it is upon the reality "out there." The perceived work organization may be the more important reality than the "true" organization. This, of course, makes the analysis of work even more complicated for it becomes necessary to take into account the perceived reality as well as the observed reality.

The last chapter of Part III is devoted to the analysis of a highly bounded work environment, the school classroom. This chapter tells us a good deal about the complexities of work encountered daily by the school teacher. Even in the work-cycle of the professional, there exist many contingencies that make it unlikely that each work day will be like the previous one.

The analysis of working behaviors is an important field of inquiry that needs an infusion of analytical interest and research effort not yet forthcoming. Perhaps as the idea gains currency that the technology and work environment are readily adaptable to human needs, we will then be oriented toward finding out what that environment is like. It is obvious that if the environment must be adaptive in relation to people, we will have to know what the environment is now, in order to know the directions in which to change it.

CHAPTER 5

Shop Floor Behavior

Thomas Lupton

Manchester Business School
Manchester, England

INTRODUCTION

There is a class of persons in industrial societies who are variously denoted "industrial operatives," "payroll," "hourly paid" or simply, "manual workers" or "workers." I shall refer to them as workers, and as I proceed I will clarify, if clarification be needed, what it is that distinguishes this class of persons from other classes denoted as, for example, "managers," and "white collar" workers.

The deceptively straightforward question, "when workers are at their jobs, why do they behave the way they do?" has generated a flood of books and articles. This chapter is an introduction and guide to literature that does exist. To encompass the whole of it here would be impossible. We shall remain mostly at the research end of a spectrum that stretches from carefully conducted research to books full of resounding moral imperatives. However, the boundaries between research, diagnosis, and prescription are blurred in the social sciences, so we shall inevitably be referring occasionally to a different question, "are workers behaving as managers and social scientists think they *ought* to behave, and if not, what is to be done."

Any attempt in the text to refer to, and to footnote every published authority, would make it virtually unreadable. I have therefore divided the chapter into two parts.

In Part I, I discuss ideas about the causes and consequences of worker behavior, omitting direct references altogether. The books and articles to which the reader should refer if he wishes to explore further, are listed in Part II and their relationship to various parts of the text is explained. It is thereby hoped that the reader will more easily follow the complex strands of argument, and having done so, become interested in contributing to or evaluating the debate.

PART I

Approaches to the Study of the Shop Floor

On-the-job behavior of workers is notoriously difficult to observe accurately and fully, and to record faithfully. Any set of observations, however closely focused, must exclude some activities and events. What is excluded, and what is included, is related to the method of observation the investigator prefers, and the time and other resources available to him. It is also related to the way he defines the problem to be investigated. Sometimes, a problem may be defined in ways that make possible the use of a preferred or familiar method of data-collection and analysis. An example or two at this point will help to underline some differences in observing the same social interactions.

Industrial engineers are trained observers of the behavior of workers while on the job. Their motives for making and recording observations of behavior are entirely of a practical nature: they wish to assemble enough information to assess whether or not changes should be made in the organization, and if so, what the changes will be.

Psychologists are also trained in the art of observing behavior. It would be most unusual to find a psychologist standing by a worker with a stopwatch and clipboard, recording the exact times taken by the worker to complete his or her specifically assigned task. More likely, the psychologist would be asking the worker, on an individual basis (and probably temporarily away from the job) questions designed to elicit their attitudes about matters relating to their work: the payment system; the behavior of supervisors and industrial engineers; the working conditions; the promotion prospects; and the characteristics of the job itself. In many cases, the psychologist's sample might cover a wide range of enterprises and industries. In these studies, he might replace the direct interview with a postal-type questionnaire, designed to elicit similar information, thus making wider comparisons possible as well as saving the psychologist time and money. Such questionnaires might ask the subject to respond to: "what kinds of job contexts and job designs seem to promote a favorable attitude toward the job on the part of the worker, a high level of motivation to pursue the organization's objectives, opportunity for personal development, and commitment to cooperation in the tasks of the enterprise?" The sociologist also might utilize the interview as a method of collecting information for his study, but more often than not he tries to observe behavior directly, either by working on the particular job for a period (participant observation), or as a direct observer. In either case, his observations would probably include a description of the cliques and factions among the workers; a record of the criteria used to judge and sanction their behavior; details about who works with whom; who defers to whom; how newcomers are inducted; who leaves and the reason for turnover. The sociologist might be seeking to show how these data might help explain the observed response to the payment system, to the supervisory and managerial controls, and to opportunities in the labor market.

The foregoing examples of differing methods for studying working behavior differentiate too strongly between the way industrial engineers, psychologists, and sociologists define their problems and gather and order their data. Psychologists have been known to observe, sociologists to interview, and both to simulate experimentally. Industrial engineers are not uninterested, either, in the attitudes and social relationships of workers. However, the three different modes of problem definition and the methods of investigation give a rough framework for the organization of this chapter. The distinction is also a fairly good guide to the difference in the way inferences as to chains of causation of worker behavior on the shop floor are drawn from data.

Typically, workers operate machines, process materials, assemble components, service and maintain equipment, drive cranes and fork-lift trucks, issue tools and parts from stores, and other similar activities. Managers usually do none of these things; they make plans, devise administrative control procedures, issue instructions, make decisions, set objectives and targets, and check results. Foremen and supervisors are employed to ensure that at the point of operation, the plans are adhered to, the targets met, the instructions followed. The need for plans, targets, budgets and other controls originates in a requirement that certain organizational objectives be met: for example, a six-month sales target or monthly production target. These targets, in their turn, arise from a managerial commitment to organizational profit, and to other means that will enable the organization to survive, develop and grow. The decisions of upper management rest finally on their interpretation of the state of the organization's environment, regarding the strategy and tactics of competitors in the product or client market, and the availability of resources or, more generally, the constraints and opportunities as they perceive them.

Machine Theory of Shop Floor Behavior

A simple, mechanistic viewpoint that sometimes characterizes the approach of the industrial engineer leads to some obvious conclusions as to what goes wrong in the behavior of workers, why the dysfunctional behaviors occur, and what can be done by management to correct the situation. This line of reasoning assumes that if there are any problems for management about behavior (workers falling short of the targets set up for them as individuals, or combining to enforce [low] group standards of quantity and quality of production or service), then this below average performance must arise from either misunderstanding, or incompetence, or malice, or any combination of these. The worker's own best interests are surely not served, so the argument goes, if as a result of his behavior, the costs of making the product or providing the service are increased to an uncompetitive level. At best, the outcome will be that the surplus left for distribution after costs have been met will be less than it could possibly have been. At worst, the worker's job is at serious risk. If for a given wage, therefore, the worker limits his output, it must be because:

1. management, by design or default, has allowed him discretion to vary his output, and
2. he cannot understand the connection between his own behavior; variation in the cost of the product or service, and his own economic interest.

On this line of argument, the responsibility for limitation of output rests not with workers, but with managers and supervisors. The problem would never arise if:

1. managers made clear to workers, in detail, what was required of them and the method prescribed by management to meet that requirement,
2. workers were selected and trained appropriately and effectively, for the job, and
3. the precise relationship between the rewards offered for the contributions expected were closely defined.

Given these conditions, the worker would be relieved of the need to try to understand the complex and lengthy connection between his own behavior and the fortunes of the enterprise as a whole. That connection would now find its expression in a managerially planned inducement-contribution equation, made visible continuously and closely to the worker and intimately influencing his behavior. Such improvements in management, so the reasoning goes, would remove misunderstanding about the nature of the effort-reward equation. Since the discretion left to the worker to decide what he will do, when he will do it, and by what method, is also minimized, the scope is therefore reduced for malicious or subversive influences on the worker's behavior, and the costs of bowing to such influences will now be painfully apparent to him. In any case, it has sometimes been claimed that "soldiering" is demoralizing, so that by making such behavior difficult and unrewarding management is affecting much more than a cash improvement in the worker's position; it is enhancing his self-respect.

Critique of the Industrial Engineers Approach

There are two broad lines of criticism to calling in industrial engineers to handle problems in work-place behavior. The first accepts the assumptions about the nature of individuals and organizations that lies behind it and examines the argument in detail. The other criticism, a more fundamental and general line of attack on the position will be introduced, more appropriately, at a later stage.

For the engineer to handle effectively problems of work-place behavior he will have to:

1. describe the job a worker has to do, and the method to be employed, in terms that exclude alternatives,
2. ensure that the worker is physically and mentally equipped to do the job and properly trained,
3. plan in such a way that the tools, machinery, and materials for the job are at hand when required,
4. specify concretely the universally best method of doing the job so that the scope for improvement by the worker is strictly limited (otherwise the minimum-discretion rule is breached),
5. state the time required by a properly selected and trained worker to complete the job as specified,
6. define the appropriate cash and other rewards for completing the job as specified in terms that break no rational disagreement.

As one can see, it is an awesome task to analyze a job completely. The degree of difficulty that is experienced in describing a job completely and accurately, and in getting agreement on that description, is related to the time the job takes to complete, its complexity, and the skills and aptitudes it calls on. This may be relatively easy, for example, for a short-cycle, repetitive bench-assembly job of the kind commonly found in light manufacturing, which requires nimble fingers, good eyesight, high resistance to boredom, and little more. By way of contrast, consider the job of a skilled mechanic employed on the maintenance and repair of a complex piece of machinery. Not all the parts of that job are in any way repetitive; some, probably most, are quite lengthy and complex. The skills required are partly mechanical, partly diagnostic, partly intuitive. It would seem obvious that in this case there is more scope for disagreement as to how much time is required and what method might best be employed. Such jobs require that the craftsman have discretion to decide, when confronted with the problems the job presents, how to go about solving them, leaving room for disagreement between management and the operator about how that discretion had best be used. It is not always possible, even if it were desirable, or acceptable, to design the work-place and the jobs in it to eliminate worker discretion entirely, although moving conveyor-type operations approximate this condition, with, as we shall see later, consequences that are held by some to be undesirable.

The design of a work-place and its jobs, however it is tackled by the managers and engineers responsible, gives rise to another kind of problem. Having done the best they can to define the skills and aptitudes required, managers then have to select from the persons available in the labor market those who already have the required attributes or can be trained to acquire them. The reader will have noticed that, if there is no one unique solution to the job design problem, which is usually the case (although some technologies and products impose tighter limits than others), then the availability of a suitable or a potentially suitable labor force might exert an influence on the design of the job. In any case, there is a problem of assessing suitability or potential by reference to skills, aptitudes, intelligence, as well as to personal characteristics. Although much progress has been made in the development of techniques of personnel selection, the chances are still high that even where these techniques are used, efficient compatability will not occur between the job and its incumbent, so that the job poses no practical difficulties, but also so that the worker will carry it out without getting unduly bored, irritated, dissatisfied, or fatigued and in consequence, unproductive. Even putting aside the quality of the worker's relationships with those persons with whom his job brings him into contact, there is likely to be in any given work-place a greater or lesser degree of "poor compatability" between the workers and their jobs.

The task of keeping down the cost of a unit of output or service clearly is high in the manager's scale of priorities, and this influences the matters just discussed, namely, the design of the job, and the "fit" of the worker to the job. The design of the job, if it is to be economical, must also minimize waste of time due to workers being held up by lack of parts and materials, waste of materials due to faulty workmanship, lack of availability of equipment of tools, machine breakdowns, absence of service personnel, and so on. It is useful for the industrial engineer to distinguish between two aspects of the work-place technology: *first,* the physical layout of the machines, benches, handling equipment, and the tasks as designed for the workers, and *second,* the administrative procedures for ensuring that the materials, tools, equipment, and men are in the right place at the right time, and that the machinery and equipment works well. This second aspect will be referred to as the *work flow administration.* In situations where the product requires that large numbers of component parts be made or purchased and then assembled to make a complex mechanical or electrical product, and where the product changes frequently according to the general dictates of taste and fashion or the specific requirements of particular customers, it is generally acknowledged that there will be great difficulties with work flow administration. To the extent that this is the case, the strength of managerial control over worker behavior diminishes, since another source of worker discretion is created, namely "unproductive time."

There are limits then, to the scope for managerial control over worker behavior and these arise from intrinsic difficulties about job design, job description, and work flow administration. The extent of these difficulties is determined by factors such as size and technology, and the skill of management in planning and controlling production. But however skilled the management of production, however good the specification of the job and the selection and training of the workers and the quality of personal supervision, there will still be some room for the exercise of judgment by the worker, and for worker-selected criteria to guide that judgment, neither of which are easily accessible to control by management. Attempts by management to gain access to those areas of judgment, and to influence the criteria chosen, by formal planning and control, are likely to be increasingly costly to administer.

Human Relations: The Discovery of the Working Group

The ideas about worker behavior that were considered above, rest upon a conception of organization that stresses the existence and value of a distinction between policy makers, executives, supervisors and workers. The policy makers are seen as defining objectives; the executives make, and carry responsibility for, plans at various levels of detail to set subobjectives and manage their accomplishment and coordination; and the workers, under supervision, manipulate machines and materials to give effect to the plans. If the plans are well conceived, then the achievement of the objective rests finally upon how well workers perform the duties assigned to them.

As we have seen, there are technical difficulties involved in making the plans, and in influencing worker behavior to ensure their success. To the extent that these technical problems remain unsolved, the worker has a choice as to how he will use the residue of discretion left to him. Unless there are some other managerial influences upon that choice, workers might choose to act in ways that frustrate managerial plans and objectives. Logically then (or so it would seem) the problem becomes one of how to influence the worker so that he exercises his discretion in ways that serve the objectives of the enterprise as management has defined them.

The "scientific managers" hardly attempted to explain why workers indulged in behavior that was apparently contrary to their own best interests and the efficiency of the organization. That workers were allowed enough range to behave in such a manner was no more to managers than a reflection of the failure of management to devise proper controls.

Unless the factors are understood that move workers to behave, as it seems, contrary to their own and the organization's interests, it is difficult to determine what influences might redirect their behavior into more constructive channels. This is how the problem was originally posed in the work we shall now discuss. It is as well to preface that discussion by repeating that the social scientists who first tackled the explanation of worker behavior were working within the same frame of reference as the scientific managers, and with much the same questions in mind—questions about how to direct behavior toward organizational efficiency, as that is defined by management. The adequacy of the framework and the mode of questioning will be examined later. For the moment, we are interested in the extent to which understanding may be found *within* that framework.

Imagine a department, one of many in a large manufacturing company, in which there are some machines for molding metal parts, and some work benches where those parts, together with other premolded parts, delivered by other departments in the factory, are assembled and will be delivered to another department where still further assembly operations will take place. The layout of the machines and work benches in the first room was certainly not arranged randomly. The engineer responsible for the design would have had in mind savings in transport and handling costs of various alternative layouts, and the elimination of unnecessary movements by workers in search of tools and materials. Also, he would have considered the balance of the flow of work from machine to assembly area and vice versa, and from assembler to assembler, in order to keep the machines fully loaded, and the workers fully occupied. Having considered all these variables, he would probably have drawn up a detailed set of instructions for each job, and a time to be allowed for the completion of it, taking into account the probability of late delivery of components, substandard materials, etc. Then, assuming a supply of machinists and assembly workers can be found, capable of following his instructions and trained to complete the work within the designated time period, the engineer will have set some targets for the output of completed components from the workroom, to which the work schedules of other departments in the manufacturing system are related.

It is also likely that the industrial engineer and his colleagues will have taken the further step of offering additional cash incentives to motivate each worker to complete his particular task in less than the time allowed, or to exceed some individual target number of parts produced per hour or day; and to motivate individuals as part of the work team, to cooperate wholeheartedly so that the collective output is enhanced.

In this imagined assembly room, there will certainly be a small office or desk for the foreman, probably positioned so that he can see everything that goes on. The foreman will be expected to encourage the workers to work well, remove any unanticipated obstacles to high performance as it occurs, and keep individual and group records of the relationship of performance to the target.

The department described above is similar to a large number of examples that have been observed closely by social scientists who were interested in explaining, and generalizing from, the behavior they have observed. These social scientists have found that not only does the performance of workers in many cases fall short of target; it also exhibits regularities other than, and far removed from, those planned for and envisaged in the designs of the engineers.

For example, in an engineering department carrying out mainly bench-assembly operations, targets were set by the management, and cash incentives were offered to the individual workers to meet or exceed the targets. Cash incentives were also offered to groups of workers for meeting and exceeding group targets for completed assemblies. The work groups were observed to set *their own* output targets, and these were below those set by management. Individual workers expected their fellow workers not to exceed the targets set by their group. Failure to meet these expectations was a signal to the rest of the group to punish the offender by social ostracism, by verbal reminders, or by mild physical punishments. Success was rewarded by gestures of approval that temporarily or permanently enhanced the standing of the successful individual in the working group.

In this, as in most of the cases reported, it was not as if the targets set by management were particularly onerous. They could have been achieved without undue physical fatigue, but were not.

A further example: In a machine shop in the maintenance department of a steel mill, monetary rewards were offered to those who could achieve and exceed performance targets. Some of these targets, as experience had indicated, were easy to achieve, some were difficult. Too frequent or too much success in exceeding easy targets was regarded by the work group as an open invitation to management to make them more difficult. The work group therefore sanctioned an infrequent and controlled exploitation of the "easy" jobs. There were times when it was not expedient to strive too hard to meet the difficult targets. The group perceived it to be in its interest to encourage its members, in most cases, to relax their effort in order to demonstrate that these targets ought to be made easier to achieve. The accepted norm of behavior came to be a pattern of working where occasional great gains on "easy jobs," were balanced by low rewards when no attempt had been made to achieve "hard job" targets, leading to a predictable and equitable distribution of effort and reward in the group.

Another example of observed behavior exhibits similar patterns. Detailed reports by social scientists from other manufacturing plants describe how work groups establish and enforce conventions regarding the manner in which individuals ought to report their performance to management. The accepted practice in these cases is that "windfall" gains that result from exploiting easy performance times not be reported as such. The unreported "windfall" hours are "saved," and reported as time spent on difficult tasks, where in fact little or nothing had actually been gained. The "windfall" time also was used to compensate for the diminished opportunity to earn that was due to unanticipated and uncontrollable work flow interruptions. This practice of "banking" or "cross-booking" is defended by workers on the ground that it irons out fluctuations in their earnings, conceals from management the existence of "slack" performance standards, thus giving the workers a degree of flexibility in setting a reasonable schedule (to them) and continuing the apparent overall relationship between effort and reward.

In order to maintain group influence over the level of individual earnings, it is necessary, as many studies have shown, that "banking" be supplemented by group influence over the procedure for setting work standards on new jobs, and on the procedures for allocating jobs among individuals. In short, working group influence on the reward-effort relationship has been observed to rely for its effectiveness, in many cases, on being comprehensive in its scope.

The reader may be encouraged by these brief accounts to examine the detailed published reports of worker behavior, as listed in the bibliographical section (Part II) of this chapter. The reader will certainly be enlightened, instructed, even amused. Our immediate concern in this section of the text is to explain behavior. We have therefore described only what seemed necessary in order to explain what seems puzzling. Before one jumps too hastily to the conclusion that all work-places everywhere are similar to the examples cited above, it should be pointed out that there are reported cases of work-places where there is little, if any, attempt at group control over the individual work performance. The examples cannot be cited as representative behavior of conveyor or machine-controlled work either, nor do they report impeccably designed and comprehensive administrative controls. What *is* reported is the existence of a wide range of potential influence, but minimal actual influence. The puzzle here is not only why workers group together to establish their own output norms, and even enforce them on some individuals, but why, in some instances, they do not establish work-control groups, even when the opportunity exists.

Naturally enough, "systematic soldiering" or "restriction of output" by the work-group has attracted attention and it is in this area that we may begin our inquiries. Later we shall address ourselves to related and even less tractable mysteries, namely, what kinds of persons in what sorts of situations seem to be associated with the behavior usually referred to as "limitation of output"; and how, if at all, do the persons and situations differ where there is no limitation of output. Initially, let us consider restriction of output. The discussion will lead us naturally into an examination of persons and situations associated with restrictive behaviors.

A Possible Explanation for "Limitation of Output"

Consider for a moment, this explanation of "limitation of output," and evaluate its credibility (after Maslow [1945]).

Workers (they are only human) have needs like everyone else. A human being needs to have others: recognize him both for what he is and for what he is capable of; show him approval or disapproval, praise or blame. In other words, a person needs to feel socially visible, that he somehow "belongs." He needs also to locate himself in "social space"; to know, who his superiors are, and why, and from whom, legitimately to expect deference. Stability and predictability in social relationships, and security, *i.e.*, knowing and approving of what is likely to happen next, are also strong human needs. The individual certainly needs scope and encouragement to exercise his talents and competences, and needs the opportunity to discover unsuspected potential and to develop it; he needs freedom to criticize, to comment, to participate.

The extent to which these needs find their expression in behavior, e.g., in frustration at the absence of means to satisfy them, or satisfaction when opportunity abounds, is related to what extent the more pressing needs for physical survival have been met. Men who are hungry and cold are unlikely to take time off from gathering food and keeping warm to complain that their "higher order needs" remain unsatisfied. In other words, "Prestige don't fill your belly."

The setting in which the individual has lived his life is also relevant to the needs he perceives, and expresses in his behavior. The familial and social class structure, and the educational and political milieu which the individual has experienced equips him with values with which to judge his own behavior (what to feel guilty about, what to be proud of) and the behavior of others (what to condemn, what to praise), and endows him with rights, and assigns duties to him.

An explanation of limitation of output that results from the theory about human needs (as outlined above) is that these human needs might be frustrated by: the physical layout of the work-place; the procedure for work flow administration; and the managerially contrived system of reward or punishment for completion or failure to complete, set within certain times. If these human needs are frustrated to any great extent by managerial attempts to control behavior in ways that are inconsistent with the fulfillment of these needs, manipulation, by workers or by the work group, would result in order to create a set of conditions in which these needs would be satisfied. The outcome of that manipulation might result in performance levels unsatisfactory to management; hence the managerial epithet "limitation." For the group, however, the outcomes might be regarded as highly satisfactory; as a successful mode of protection against attempts to deprive the individual members of security, predictability, opportunity, status, and so on. More positively, the satisfaction might arise from a feeling that the workers are exerting some control in the work-place, and are actually participating in the creation of conditions necessary for their own need satisfaction. Also, the group may confer status upon the individual worker.

Needless to say, managerial judgments about limitation of output can be judged irrational from a social system viewpoint. Having ignored most of the needs of workers in the design of the work-place, by giving priority to technological considerations, the responses of workers to create a social organization to fulfill some needs within the technological restrictions, ought to be recognized for what it is by management, rather than condemned. Furthermore, if management had been successful in designing the technical work situation, the range of worker need satisfaction might have been diminished even more. This could result in either complete withdrawal from the situation by the workers, so as to escape intolerable frustrations, or if other employment was not readily available, to exert more energy and ingenuity in the creation of social situations to escape those frustrations, further exacerbating the conditions of restriction of output and other behaviors viewed negatively by managers.

A management unaware of worker's needs, or aware of them to some extent but unable to imagine how to incorporate them into the design of work-places and reward systems, might decide, in the face of competition, to press for the results they expected, by exerting tighter administrative controls, by imposing oppressive personal supervision and the like, and by so doing, simply compound the effects they had striven so mightily to avoid.

There is a tragic aspect to all this. Managers will undoubtedly feel frustrated in their failure to plan and control. It might well appear to them as if they have failed to demonstrate technical competence, and that the legitimacy of their authority is being called in question. That frustration could well be aggravated by ignorance as to its causation. From this experience might come a tendency to attribute the limitation of output behavior of workers to the influence of malicious antimanagement persons or imported antimanagement ideas. Since continued attempts by management to change the behavior in directions consistent with its original design will be technically inadequate (we have noted already the inherent inadequacy of the technical apparatus, work measurement, performance setting, scheduling and control of production) and socially unacceptable, then its hypotheses about malicious ideas and persons will seem to be amply experienced and confirmed. Equally, the workers will view managers as continually and somewhat perversely attempting to frustrate their natural impulses, or their culturally sanctioned beliefs about right and proper behavior, and as a result be seen as either malicious or insensitive. Since management and workers are locked in circular chains of *ex post facto* reasoning about their own behavior and the behavior of their opponent, then the only course open to them is to take up positions where formal bargaining can occur, about the most obvious measurable aspects of the reward system: performance standards and pay. Conflict, rather than cooperation, becomes characteristic of the relationship, and levels of performance well below the potential of the system become a permanent attribute of it, accompanied also by less than optimum satisfaction of human needs.

Prescriptions of the "Human Relations" School

Certain clear general prescriptions for improvement are often derived from the arguments of the "human relations" school. Like the prescriptions of the industrial engineers, they relate to the design of the work-place, but they include much more in that design. The responsibility of management for efficient work flow administration, for sound selection and training procedures, and well designed systems of wage payment is not denied. What should be noted is that these by themselves will not necessarily cause workers to be moved to direct their best efforts to the goals of the organization as these are defined by management. The plan for work-place design must also include, therefore, other items such as style of supervision, and the amount of discretion allowed to the worker.

The style of supervision favored by the Human Relations School is defined as follows. *First*, the supervisor works actively to involve workers in the discussion of matters such as the plan to meet the departmental targets of cost, quality and quantity; *second*, workers are helped out of difficulties with their work rather than punished for getting into those difficulties, and are taught how to avoid them in future; *third*, the supervisor will make sure that worker frustrations arising for the worker from shortcomings in management oganization will be promptly dealt with, if possible. In short, the supervisor sets out to create a situation where the chief expectation of the workers is that they will be helped and supported, not harried and punished, and he does this by being free with information, by listening carefully, and by encouraging suggestions for improvement, acting on them quickly if possible, and explaining patiently the reasons why certain suggested action is not possible. With this style of supervision, the workers should cease to perceive the environment in which they work as hostile, punishing, and frustrating. If this were the case, the reasons why they might adopt an attitude of less than full commitment to the organization's goals will have largely disappeared. Therefore, one might expect that there would be no need for workers to establish protective output norms, and to "bend" the systems of managerial control to maintain these norms. More positively, workers might even be disposed, in consequence, to release more active commitment and put it at the disposal of management.

An examination of the literature of the "Human Relations" School reveals differences in emphasis regarding the relative significance of a style of participative supervision as a contributor to job-satisfaction (i.e., satisfaction of human needs at work) and commitment, although such supervisory style would always rate as being of some significance. The design of the job itself, as well as the design of the supervisory and administrative context within which the job is done, is heavily stressed in some prescriptive writing. In the Human Relations School, the argument for stressing job-design is that the design of the job-context should be largely an attempt to remove worker frustrations and obstacles to worker needs and to provide a supportive context. If management and industrial engineers focused more on job design, jobs would become more interesting and challenging and would result in a more positive personal commitment to that job on the part of the worker. However, there are some proponents of this view who argue that in working conditions where the jobs are repetitive, have a short time-cycle, are paced by machines, and require little skill and only surface mental attention, the returns in improved worker commitment due to job satisfaction (which is a direct result of a participative supervisory style) might be very small. This might lead to managerial and supervisory disillusionment.

One solution to this problem is elemental. When designing the layout of a work-place, the engineers could choose a method of completing the assigned task which would allow workers the opportunity, and provide them with the skills, to transfer with some frequency from one job to another (e.g., as the standby man or utility man does in assembly line work). This is a process that has been described as "job enlargement." Another alternative is that they could assign each worker a job (or jobs) which would be absorbing and challenging in itself (job enrichment). As a result, the commitment of workers to the goals of the organization would follow directly and positively from the commitment of each individual to his own job. A participative style of management would bear greater fruit, would indeed be indispensable, in such a context. One can easily see how the worker with a challenging, interesting job would respond positively to supportive and participative direction, and negatively to attempts at detailed control. Of course, it is also essential that they perceive their rewards as equitable.

Both the industrial engineers and the human relations theorists accept the organization's goals from the outset. This acceptance implies that the designers feel that the goals should be accepted by the workers as well. If the workers are not committed to these goals, then something must be done about: the targets that are set, the work flow administered, the payment system designed, the performance standards set, the job allocation; the "largeness" and "richness" of the jobs, etc., so that the quality of interpersonal relationships within the working group will enhance commitment, satisfaction, and efficiency. Both sets of theorists/prescribers are stating, however tacitly, claims that their analyses and prescriptions are generally applicable to any work-place.

The most accurate test of any general theory concerned with the causes of worker behavior, would seem to be the practical test, where changes in the organization were made in the direction indicated by the theorists, and precise records were kept which would enable the suggestions made by the theorists to be compared with the actual observed outcomes. Such tests have, in fact, been made. They have been inconclusive, in the sense that the suggestions seem to work out in some situations and not in others, for reasons the theorists themselves cannot explain. It would appear, therefore, that even if the objectives are considered desirable, namely, to increase commitment to organizational goals through job satisfaction, then the path toward those objectives might have to differ from one work-place to another, because of the influence of variables not considered by either the industrial engineers or the Human Relations School. So let us consider another approach, which treats the organization as the unit of analysis rather than the individual, and which makes the design of the work-place contingent upon the special circumstances of a particular case. Let us call this the contingency approach to the explanation of worker behavior and the design of work-places.

A Contingency Approach

The argument over the cause of worker behavior (limitation of output) that we have just discussed, views the solution to lie with the individual worker. Each worker was assumed to have needs that must be fulfilled. It was concluded that if the needs are met then the workers will behave cooperatively and, as a result, productively. If not, they will behave defensively, and will direct their resourcefulness and their energies to combatting the forces that frustrate their needs; hence they will appear to be actively uncooperative and unproductive, or to have lapsed into apathy.

It is possible (although it is not often done) to combine an explanation of worker behavior (such as those discussed above) that begins with the individual and his characteristics as the unit of analysis, with one that considers the organization and *its* characteristics as the starting point. This combination, although more complicated, offers a more convincing explanation of worker behavior. There are many reasons why this should be so, and they will emerge in what ensues; but one of them stands out. "The job context," to which we have referred, and which, it is claimed, can be changed to engender greater worker motivation and satisfaction, is itself influenced by certain salient characteristics of the organization: technology, and work-flow administration in their relation to its product market and labor market. These characteristics could act as limits on the extent to which the "job context" could be designed or redesigned to produce the desired effects on worker motivation and satisfaction. As a matter of practical management then, the attempt to change worker behavior to make it corresponds more nearly to that perceived by management as necessary to bring about the simultaneous satisfaction of needs and the pursuit of managerially defined ends, is likely to be more complicated than it at first appears, and in some cases greatly so. The "malleability" of the job context will differ from work-place to work-place, and from organization to organization. As a consequence, although we may seek, and eventually find a general explanation of worker behavior, the steps that might be taken to change it, whatever the end in view, would be *contingent* upon the circumstances of a particular case. It is necessary now, as a prelude to the further elaboration of this point, to explain what is meant by "considering the organization as the unit of analysis."

Organizations and Individuals

Organizations can be described as assemblages of buildings, plant, and machinery, brought together with the intention of transforming "imports": raw materials, components, ideas, knowledge, competences, skills, and procedures, into a product or service which is then "exported." Unless the exports are disposed of on terms that allow further imports to be obtained, and to maintain and improve the fixed plant and machinery, the competences, etc., will cease and the system will run down. Put another way, organizations exist in, and adapt to, an environment. In the sort of manufacturing organizations to which we have referred throughout this chapter, the environment will include other organizations that compete for the favors of the consumer; the consumers themselves, and potential customers; individuals who have competences the organization needs; and other organizations that have knowledge the organization can use. Also in the environment are the suppliers of credit, the suppliers of raw materials and components, trade unions and so on. Without making specific reference to the place of the individual and the group in the organization, it is possible to suggest what we might call the "logic" of manufacturing organizations.

For convenience let us focus on an already existing organization and assume it transacts with a *product market*. The nature of that market is, we shall suppose, explored by specialists whose task it is to gain knowledge of the behavior of competitors and the strategies of competitors, and make that knowledge available to the organization. Other specialists will decide what is to be done in the light of that knowledge, regarding the terms on which it is possible to "export" what products, at what prices, and in what quantities. These decisions give rise to a requirement that plant, machinery, materials, administrative procedures, and human competences, be deployed to get the products made and disposed of so that a surplus will be earned which at least ensures the organization's survival. In summation, a logical choice is made from all sets apparently available of that set of *production arrangements* thought to be most appropriate to cope with the product market environment, given certain objectives. It should be noted that:

1. there is no unique and obvious set of production arrangements that goes with any state of the product market environment. There is room for choice, but there are also situationally determined limits on the extent of that choice. These limits may be tight or loose;

2. the existing set of production arrangements may narrow the range for choice in the product market; or there may be lags before plant, machinery, etc. can be adapted, added to, or diminished, in order to meet a desired sales target.

If technology is to be defined to include not only plant and machinery but also the work flow administration, as we previously defined that term, then we can use "technology" as a substitute term for "production arrangements." Clearly, the next logical step is to specify a set of requirements for work to be done in order to activate the technology, and produce the products at the cost, in the quantities, and of the quality required, by the sales plan. These *job requirements* are, as it were, a set of interrelated job descriptions. They state that the organization requires work to be performed through individual jobs but they do not name the persons to fill the jobs; merely the skills and other characteristics required. The requirements for cooperation in work are also in large part specified in the job requirements; the manning tables for example, and the job descriptions; the physical layout of the work-place; the arrangements for moving work from one place to another; all influence job requirements. In short, the technology and the job requirements set more or less strict limits on the behavior and relationships of *whatever persons may happen to be called upon to do the jobs required*. In short, the structure and definition of job positions is influenced greatly by technology; obvious examples being vehicle assembly by moving conveyor and the bench assembly of small engineering components. The technology is, in its turn, influenced by the organization's structure and its relationships with its markets. For example, the machinery, the way it is used, and the administration of the flow of work in a custom tailor workshop is obviously related to the fact that every suit is being made to a customer's specification. Some other product market conditions require that manufacturing firms engage in the production of small batches of custom-built products, combined with longer runs of standard lines, and this has consequences for the type of machinery used, the procedures chosen for scheduling and controlling production, the methods of cost control, the structure of job grades, the system of wage payment and so on.

The literature is replete with detailed illustrations of the close connection between product/technology and job structure. There are also examples of the connection between structure and behavior. Most of the examples of "limitation of output" of the classic group control type are taken from manufacturing, particularly job and batch manufacture. In some other settings of product/technology, behavior is different where group influences on the level of output is minimal, or nonexistent, sometimes because technology banishes choice (as in the assembly line case). There are, however, reported examples where product/technology offers range but "the will to control" is absent for other reasons. This tends to be the case in some sectors of the garment trade, where women workers predominate: where the demand for the product is subject to marked seasonal fluctuations; where trade unions are weak; where small firms predominate and are clustered in certain localities; where the "trade" has been long established; and where the labor market is highly visible.

Although almost all studies of workers attribute the behavior observed *in some degree* to the product/technology/labor market, it would be mistaken on that account to assert that the causes of *all* observed behavior at work may be attributed to the product/technology/labor market, just as it would be mistaken to attribute it *all* to the presence or absence from the job-design or job context, of need-satisfying attributes. In our terminology, the *job requirements*, which are derived from the *technology* (as broadly defined) which are the result of the way the needs of consumers, and the behavior of competitors, are interpreted, are a significant part of the job context—but not the whole of it by any means.

A worker comes to the job having already formed ideas, opinions, values, and having expectations as to which of his needs his work ought to be *satisfying and expressing* and in what way. Some of these ideas, values, etc. he will already hold in common with his workmates, especially if there is a distinctive local working-class culture, as there is in certain traditional coal, steel, and textile communities. The *job requirements* are examined and eventually selected by the workers for their compatibility with these common ideas, expressed needs and expectations, and if there is discrepancy then an attempt may be made individually or in concert to adjust the job requirements. "Limitation of output" represents such an adjustment but it is not the only possible one. The worker can adjust to the job; and the job can adjust to the worker. Ideas, needs, and expectations can be adjusted to the job requirements, as may happen under economic conditions that foster high unemployment, when workers are easily replaced. A third, less likely possibility, is that managers, having observed symptoms of dissatisfaction, such as high absenteeism and labor turnover, may alter the technology and/or derive a new set of job requirements which are more compatible with the existing worker needs, values and expectations. But even if that expedient were adopted, the range for alteration may be, in certain cases, limited by its possible effects on the quantity, quality, and delivery of the product. It may not be so limited, in which case one might expect the successful results reported in some experiments in job enrichment and job enlargement, namely a sharp improvement of satisfaction and motivation with consequent improvements in efficiency. Some of these results, it may be noted, concern supervisory, technical and managerial employees. The chances of success with these groups is of course greater, because the structuring of job requirements is in general less influenced by product/technology, although in specific cases, such as salesmen and Research and Development (R & D) scientists, the influence of the product market, or the state of knowledge in particular fields, might in some circumstances exert a strong influence on job requirements and these could run counter to personal and professional values and expectations.

The result of having included both the individual and the organization in a model that attempts a general explanation of worker behavior can be shown in a simple diagram—as in Figure 1.

Figure 1 shows product market conditions (box 1) influencing (arrow A) technology (box 2). The "ch" on the left of arrow A denotes the assumption that for any one set of product market conditions there will be some choice among technologies, within some limits on the range of choice. How tight these limits are will differ from organization to organization.

Technology (box 2) is assumed to influence (arrow B) the job requirements (box 3). Again there are limits to the choices among sets of job requirements that may be devised as appropriate for a particular technology, and again these limits will differ from one technology to another.

Job values and expressions (box 4) describe the set of ideas, prejudices, modes of thought, etc. that the worker brings with him to the job, and learns on the job, and his expectations as to what will be required of him. They also include his characteristic personal "style." All these values and expressions influence (arrow C) the way workers interpret job requirements, and singly, or in concert, carry them out. Arrow C also indicates the effect of

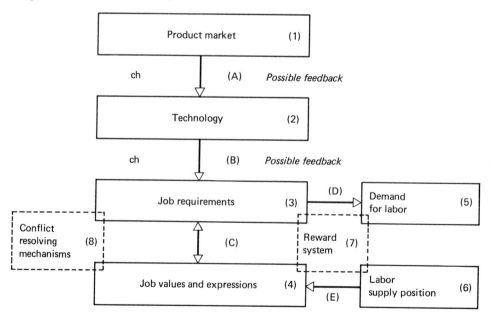

FIGURE 1.   Causes of worker behavior.

the formal demands of the job on individual values and expressions. There are two heads on arrow C to denote this reciprocal relationship.

All organizations are assumed to have mechanisms for resolving conflict (box 8) between job requirements and job values and expressions, e.g., bargaining and consultative procedures. The conflicts arise because job requirements change in response to product market and technological changes, and job expressions and values change in response to changes in labor markets (arrows D & E, boxes 7 & 8), as well as through wider societal changes—e.g., in education, and in social and geographical mobility. The reward system (box 7) also acts as a conflict-resolving mechanism when labor market conditions disturb the relationship between box 3 and box 4.

It can be clearly seen from Figure 1 that the choices made along arrows A and B may create difficulties in the adjustment of job requirements to job values and expressions; difficulties that may put severe strains on the reward system (in given labor market conditions) and on the mechanisms for resolving conflict. In that case, the organization might find itself unable to meet product market demands regarding price, quantity and delivery.

The industrial engineers response to this situation might be to alter the technology/work flow administration within the limits of the product plan so as to press job values and expressions into conformity with a more tightly defined set of job requirements. Such action is based on the assumption that the job values and expressions are misguided or mistaken, or incongruent with an assumed common purpose, probably setting up further strains along arrow C. The "human relations" practitioner would attempt to change the job requirements to correspond to some postulated set of universal job values and expressions in the confident expectation that the technology is always malleable.

If the system of relationships shown in Figure 1 is valid, then the job context (boxes 1 and 2) that was thought to be so crucial to need satisfaction, may not be completely open to alteration, in order to satisfy social and psychological needs. To attempt an alteration of the technology and the job requirements with need satisfaction in mind, might succeed at the expense of the product market and of the labor market. To repeat, the scope for alteration is contingent on the circumstances of the organization. It is a matter for investigation, not for assertion. If there is anything in the hypothesis that says that low productivity occurs when needs are not satisfied, and if there are product market and technological obstacles to the restructuring of the job context in order to satisfy certain crucial needs, it may well be that the mechanisms of conflict resolution should be made more effective, or the reward system attended to.

As the conventional wisdom would have it, "limitations of output" could consequently turn out not to be the result of unsatisfied needs, or poor industrial engineering, and it might not be something to be remedied. It may be, in these circumstances, the most effective mechanism of adjustment in the production system given certain conditions in the product/technology/labor market complex. It could also be regarded as a "do-it-yourself" method for satisfying certain needs and aspirations at work, which might result in a benefit to the management (e.g., low labor turnover and absence). Equally, the lack of "will to control" output is also susceptible to explanation using the same analytical method.

Attempts on the part of industrial designers to elaborate, to quantify, and to use variants of the "model" shown in Figure 1 have so far been encouraging. The model has been used to explain and to predict labor turnover, to design reward systems, to decide upon the best possible combination of elements in a worker's pay packet, if the inflation of unit labor costs is to be minimized, and to describe the process by which organizations "die."

CONCLUSION TO PART I

The path that has been taken by successive investigators and theorists towards more convincing, and practically useful ways of explaining shop floor behavior may seem to those who have followed it thus far, to have led managers toward unnecessary complicated theoretical models and greater practical difficulties. The open sociotechnical system perspective would have the investigator of shop floor behavior observing: the decisions of marketing men; the design of products, technical processes and administrative procedures; the structure and style of managers and supervisors; the demand and supply situation in the labor and product markets; the expectations, attitudes and beliefs of workers; the machinery of bargaining and consultation; and the system of nonmonetary and monetary rewards. All these variables would also be assumed to be connected in some way; whether closely or remotely, directly or indirectly, simply or complexly. Because the state of the variables, and the connections among them, differ from organization to organization, one would be led to expect differences of some degree between one organization and another in the state of the system and its parts. Therefore, if a manager, for example, wished to respond intelligently to environmental change, or to initiate internal change, it would seem that there is no one universally most efficient way of doing it. Each situation would have to be explored in all its complex details to arrive at a viable program for response or innovation. The expectation that some exhortation, plus a little work study, or a profit-sharing scheme or some job enrichment, or a little participative supervision, would automatically, and generally always improve matters in any organization, is, as we can now see, mistaken. New and complex diagnostic observational and personal skills would seem to be required to replace ready-made partial and packaged universalistic solutions.

Among such skills should be an understanding of what has been described as the workers' job values and expressions, without prejudging the values; and an appreciation of the consequences of worker behavior. Such an appreciation would at least mean that less of the consequences (pleasant or unpleasant) would be unanticipated. It could also mean that management might learn to respond to values and expressions of values as they are manifested by workers, and, to become more resourceful at finding ways of shifting the technical/managerial superstructure in order to satisfy those values, expectations, and expressions, without jettisoning their own personal and organizational aims.

At present, this observer sees few signs of this, but it would be beneficial to remember how recent the limited acceptance of the notion that technology is linked to structure/behavior, and structure/behavior to the rate of change in an organization's environment. It would be beneficial to note as well, that the development of a model that utilizes and combines variables previously held to be the separate and sole property of economists, psychologists, and sociologists, and that defines them, is a formidable interdisciplinary task, which many discipline specialists in the social sciences have little motivation to contribute to, or even positively disapprove of. One should also bear in mind that the practical administrator may find the prospect of learning to work with such complex models very intimidating.

One must settle for slow, patient work, and consequent steady progress in research and theory in the sure knowledge that meanwhile, prescriptive universalistic procedures for explaining and changing shop floor behavior will be cheerfully and somewhat uncritically accepted.

PART II: BIBLIOGRAPHICAL INFORMATION

The Literature on Shop Floor Behavior

This part has been written as a guide to the reader who wishes to explore further the interpretations, controversies and comments expounded in Part I, and to better enable the reader to draw his own conclusions. The list of books and articles as represented here is not by any means complete. A single criterion for the selection was employed: what material the interested reader will need if he is to understand the main themes in the subject matter. The specialist will undoubtedly find gaps in the literature as presented: a significant research study overlooked, or some general text missing that he would prefer to see cited. His own particular biases will only serve to expose mine. However, I am confident that if the reader will follow the references given, he will find them to be accurate signposts leading into the heart of the subject matter.

I have employed a sevenfold classification of the literature. The lists of references, numbered 1 to 7, roughly follow the order of the presentation of ideas in Part I, and this order represents again (somewhat roughly) the history of ideas about worker behavior. I did not intend that the history of worker behavior is to be considered as a process in which schools emerge, flourish, dominate the field, decay and disappear. Some of the ideas which are now explicitly worked out in the later books and articles under the headings, "sociological studies," or "psychological studies" may be found, for example, in the work of the early industrial engineers. The sociologists and the psychologists certainly anticipated much that is now classified under the heading "Open Sociotechnical System" analysis.

The boundaries between the seven sections are fairly arbitrarily drawn. I personally find it difficult to draw clear lines between academic disciplines in the social sciences; some find it easy and will wish to move a book or article from one category to another. They are welcome to do so.

The reader who has carefully followed the concepts presented in Part I, will not be surprised at the degree of emphasis accorded the ideas of engineers and psychologists; but the reasons for it will bear a brief repetition. The engineer by his design of machines, shop layouts, and control procedures, imposes limits, often unknowingly, on: the freedom of the worker to order his relationships with others in ways that the worker and others find congenial; on the psychological and pecuniary rewards offered for his contribution; and on what that contribution is, or ought to be. The psychologist is naturally interested in the response of the individual to the situations he finds himself in, and the effects on his job performance, his attitudes to managers and supervisors and so on. For these reasons, an attempt to explain worker behavior and more especially to influence it, would be incomplete unless the work of engineers and psychologists were taken into account.

In Section One, "The Industrial Engineers," I have avoided taking the reader too far into the technical development of motion and time study, production scheduling and control and so on. Works have been included that set out, clearly and authoritatively, the ideas about the causes of worker behavior that underly the design of the procedures for the investigation, measurement, and design of work-places, and the techniques employed to influence worker behavior.

Many of the references in all sections carry an implicit criticism of industrial engineering. For Section Two, "Critique of Industrial Engineering," work has been chosen which set out explicitly to criticize the ideas and techniques of the industrial engineers, some by later industrial engineers criticizing earlier ones, some by social scientists.

Some economists, but not many, have interested themselves in the effect of the administration of the work-place, and the payment system on the regulation of the supply and demand for the resource "worker effort." Section Three, "The Economists Work," refers to some sources of research and opinion. The role of economists is not dealt with explicitly in Part I.

The investigation of worker behavior by psychologists has enjoyed a long and distinguished history. Much of it has had a highly practical bias, especially the earlier work on the influence of the physical setting of work on the bodily and mental health of workers, and hence on their morale and performance. This is still a lively trend in psychology, hence Section Four has had to be quite lengthy to do justice to the massive output of the psychological school.

Some might think that the distinction between the psychological work and sociological work on the one hand, and what is described as "Human Relations" on the other, is somewhat forced. It has been made in that section on the grounds that what I have called "Human Relations" work, is, like "Industrial Engineering," a body of ideas, procedures, and tools whereby managers may influence worker behavior in directions consistent with the managers' aims. The psychological and socialogical work cited is biased toward explanation rather than managerial prescription. In some cases, the distinction has been difficult to make. The sociological work is listed in Section Five, the Human Relations work in Section Six.

In recent years, a merging of the psychological and sociological perspective has taken place within a wider "open systems" framework. Some ideas from the "human relations" school have also been encompassed by this new approach, and it certainly takes full account of the technical and administrative setting of work. Witness the use of the term "sociotechnical system" to describe the work-place. Much more work in organizational design is going on using this approach than I have included in Section Seven. I have referred only to those researchers who have focused their attention in some part on the shop floor.

1. The Industrial Engineers

Taylor (1947), Gantt (1919), and Gilbreth (1917) are generally regarded as pioneers in the development of procedures for the measurement and control of the work of manual workers, and routine clerical employees. Most later work is elaboration and refinement, with little change of aims and assumptions; but it has had to come to terms with advances in psychology and sociology, and to adapt to changes in size and technology. The works by Barnes (1949), Abruzzi (1952), Maynard, et al. (1948), and Shaw (1952) exemplify these trends.

Industrial engineers have also created an extensive literature on the design and management of financial incentive payment systems. The short book by Currie (1963) is a recent defense and elaboration of this position.

2. Critique of Industrial Engineering

Much of the sociological and psychological writing listed in Sections Four, Five, Six, and Seven is implicitly critical of industrial engineering mainly on the grounds that industrial engineer approach rests on inadequate, even harmful, assumptions about human nature and organization. The works listed in this section are more specific in their critical approach to aspects of industrial engineering. Industrial engineers, like Rodgers (1957) and Abruzzi (1956), challenge from within some of the assumptions, and the objectivity and accuracy claimed for some procedures. Hoxie's (1915) book reflects many early general anxieties as to the effects of the procedures on workers. Barkin (1948 through 1957), Gomberg (1944) and Crawford (1954) reflect later attempts by trade union leaders at well informed critical comment and suggestion. Brown (1962) like Kingsland (1949) is a manager considering the moral and administrative case against piecework. Lupton (1957) is a specifically sociological critique of the assumptions underlying much of industrial engineering practice.

3. Economic Studies of Worker Behavior

The relation between the industrial worker effort expended and the financial rewards accruing to him would seem to be an area suitable for supply and demand analysis, with the wage (or increments of it) being regarded as the price for effort (or increments of it). The idea is taken up briefly by Marshall and developed among others by Sargant-Florence (1924). Baldamus (1961), Berhend (1957) and Ross, et al. (1958) are in this tradition. Kerr, et al. (1957) is critical of the industrial sociologists for their lack of methodological rigor and their managerial biases. Robertson is rare among labor economists in his detailed concern with shop floor behavior; Robinson (1970) is a critic of the assumptions of economic theory as to the effects of labor markets on worker behavior; and Roy (1952) examines the economic assumptions of cash payment-by-results. Most economists who have interested themselves in worker behavior have been influenced by psychology and sociology. Baldamus (1961) and Berhend (1957) particularly have published works that might just as easily be included under the heading sociology or psychology.

4. Psychological Research and Comment

It would be impossible to comment in detail on all the books and papers included in this highly selective list, but certain themes may be noted, and trends observed. The early work in Britain of the Industrial Health Research Board and the Medical Research Council leaned heavily toward the study of the effects of physical conditions on the health and performance of workers. Later, British psychologists in this tradition focused on the study of supervisory behavior, long working hours, payment systems, family background, size of group, and so on, as factors that might influence worker behavior—particularly "pathological" behavior such as excessive absence, sickness, and turnover, or "healthy" symptoms such as high productivity and job satisfaction. Reference to much of this work may be found in Myers (1926) and in Marriott (1968).

Since the Hawthorne experiments, psychological work in the U.S. has been very concerned with the relationship of group structure, culture, and size of the group to the productivity and morale of individuals. It has been difficult to distinguish between some psychological work, and what I have called "Human Relations," but I have included those works that seemed mostly directed toward the advance of theory or research method in this section, and those which, although reporting research in some cases, are concerned mainly to effect improvements in management.

Maslow's (1943) "needs" theory had to be included because of its influence on managerial theory and practice; Gomberg (1957) turns up again, this time as a commentator on the *uses* of psychology.

5. Human Relations—Research and Comment

Herzberg's two factor theory of motivation has been widely accepted, much as has Maslow's "hierarchy of needs" theory, as a sufficient general explanation about men at work, by practitioners, and as a justification for making changes. McGregor's (1960) is a popular prescription for the production of high productivity and job satisfaction, drawn largely from findings of psychological research and theory.

Tannenbaum's (1966) small book charts the progress of the research (much of it done in the United States at the Social Science Research Center, University of Michigan, Ann Arbor) on group size, cohesiveness, leadership, and productivity. Mann and Hoffman (1960) is a well-known work in that idiom.

Likert's (1961, 1967) (also of the Ann Arbor group) two books are fine, persuasive prescriptive writing, setting out, with impressive research backing, the set of general conditions that must be present if productivity and satisfaction are to be maximized.

The Hawthorn experiments are represented by Roethlisberger and Dixon (1939), and Whitehead (1936). Whyte (1952) who was associated with later "participant observer" studies of worker behavior, is represented in this section, somewhat arbitrarily, by a well-known Harvard Business Review article.

6. Sociological Analysis of Worker Behavior

Many of the works in this section describe and analyze in close detail the behavior of workers, usually of work groups. Many of them were carried out by sociologists acting as "participant observers," for example, Roy (1954), Lupton (1963), and Cunnison (1966). Others use the more usual combination of observation and interview, for example, Goldthorpe (1968), Scott, et al. (1963),

Walker, et al. (1952), Zaleznik, et al. (1958). Bolle de Bal (1962) summarizes and comments on more recent European work particularly regarding the effects of payment systems. These books and papers have been grouped together because of their distinctively sociological bias. That is to say, they are seeking, like Sayles (1958), for example, to explain the behavior of the workers they observe by referring much more to structural factors such as technology, social class, the structure of formal authority, and reward systems, than to individual states of mind; although the Goldthorpe (1968) work is much more within the "action" frame of reference.

The selection covers a number of different types of workers: Chinoy (1955) and Walker (1952) wrote on automobile workers; the Banks (1960, 1963) and Scott, et al. (1963), on steelworkers; dock workers are represented in the Liverpool University study (1954) supervised by Woodward; garment workers by Cunnison (1966); engineering workers by Lupton (1963) and Klein (1964), shoe operatives by Horsfall and Arensberg (1949).

7. Open Sociotechnical Systems

Many of the works listed in this section are the result of empirical research carried out from the Tavistock Institute of London. The features that distinguish this from the psychological, sociological, economic, and engineering work discussed in the text are:

1. its refusal to be confined within the bounds of a single academic discipline.
2. its recognition of the influence of technology on the structuring of work relationships, on role definition, and hence on behavior.
3. its avoidance of technological determinism and its stress on the mutual interdependence of the psychosocial factors on one hand and the technical and economic ones on the other.
4. the treatment of the production or service unit as open to influence from its environment, and interest in the development of models of the environment, and organization-environment transactions.
5. its "action" orientation, i.e., a belief that the social researcher has obligations to work with the subjects of his research, to define objectives, and to use data and theory to derive programs for change.

The works selected exemplify all the above distinctions in one way or another. Jaques' (1951) work with the Glacier Metal Company is an excellent example of the "action" orientation. Rice's (1956, 1963) works also exemplify the "methods of action research" but Rice works more self-consciously with an open-systems model. The work by Trist (1951) and his colleagues in coal mines is concerned with the minutely detailed exploration of the relations of mutual dependence of the psychosocial and technical variables at the coal face in conditions of technical innovation, and their results on morale and satisfaction at work. Millward's (1968) article is a detailed analysis of the impact of some features of family *rites de passage* on the behavior of certain family members in the work setting.

Lupton and Gowler (1969) attempt to use the open sociotechnical systems model as a basis for the development of technical procedures for choosing pay systems and structures appropriate to the circumstances of particular situations.

REFERENCES

The Industrial Engineers

Abruzzi, A.
   1952   Work Measurement. New York: Columbia University Press.
Barnes, R.M.
   1949   Motion and Time Study. New York: Wiley.
Currie, R.M.
   1963   Financial Incentives. London: British Institute of Management.
Gantt, H.L.
   1919   Organizing for Work. New York: Harcourt, Brace and Howe.
Gilbreth, F.B.
   1911   Motion Study, a Method for Increasing the Efficiency of the Workman.
          New York: Van Nostrand.
   1912   Primer of Scientific Management. New York: Van Nostrand.
   1917   Applied Motion Study: A Collection of Papers on the Efficient Method
          to Industrial Preparedness. New York: Sturgis and Walton Co.
Lowery, S.M., H.B. Maynard and G.S. Stegemerten
   1940   Time and Motion Study. London: McGraw-Hill.
Maynard, H.B., et al.
   1948   Methods-Time Measurement. London: McGraw-Hill.
Shaw, A.G.
   1952   The Purpose and Practice of Motion Study. Manchester and London:
          Harlequin Press.
Taylor, F.W.
   1947   Scientific Management. New York: Harper and Brothers.

Industrial Engineers: Criticism

Abruzzi, A
   1956   Work, Workers and Work Measurement. New York: Columbia Uni-
          versity Press.
Barkin, S.
   1948   "Labor's attitude toward wage incentive plans." Industrial and Labor
          Relations Review 1(July):553–573.
   1953   "Concepts in the measurements of human application." Industrial and
          Labor Relations Review 7(October):103–118.
   1954   "Diversity of time-study practice." Industrial and Labor Relations Re-
          view 7(July):537–549.
   1957   "The bench-mark approach to production standards." Industrial and
          Labor Relations Review 10(January):222–236.
Brown, W.
   1962   Piecework Abandoned. London: Heinemann.
Crawford, J.
   1954   The Attitude of Trade Unions Towards Modern Management Methods.
          London: British Institute of Management.
Dalton, M.
   1951   "Economic incentives and human relations," in L.R. Tripp (ed.), In-
          dustrial Productivity. Madison, Wisc.: Industrial Relations Research
          Association.

Gomberg, W.
  1948   A Trade Union Analysis of Time Study. Chicago: Science Research As-
         sociates.
  1955   A Trade Union Analysis of Time Study. Englewood Cliffs, New Jersey:
         Prentice-Hall.
Hoxie, R.
  1915   Scientific Management and Labor. Washington, D.C.: U.S. House of
         Representatives.
Kingsland, K.W.
  1949   "Does piecework restrict output?" Time Study Engineer 4(May) :146–
         149.
Lupton, T.
  1957a Money for Effort. London: H.M.S.O.
  1957b "A sociologist looks at work study." Work Study and Industrial En-
         gineering 1(February) :43–48.
Rodgers, D.A.
  1957   "Predetermined motion-time standards: a history and evaluation."
         Work Study and Industrial Engineering 1(April) :147–162.
Rodgers, W.
  1955   "The accuracy and use of time study." Operational Research Quarterly
         6(March) :16–19.
Rodgers, W. and J. Hammersley
  1954   "The consistency of stop-watch time study practitioners." Occupational
         Psychology 28(April) :61–76.

   ### Economic Studies of Worker Behavior

Baldamus, W.
  1961   Efficiency and Effort. London: The Tavistock Institute.
Behrend, H.
  1957   "The effort to bargain." Industrial and Labor Relations Review 10
         (July) :503–passim.
  1959   "Financial incentives as the expression of a system of beliefs." Edin-
         burgh: Social Sciences Research Centre. Reprint Series No. 1. Reprinted
         in British Journal of Sociology 10(June) :137–147.
Dawson, J.P., P. Sargant-Florence, B. Gray and N.S. Ross
  1958   Productivity and Economic Incentives. London: Allen and Unwin.
Kerr, C. and L. Fisher
  1957   "Plant sociology: the elite and the aborigines," in M. Komorovsky
         (ed.), Common Frontiers of the Social Sciences. Glencoe, Illinois: The
         Free Press.
Robertson, D.
  1960   Factory Wage Structures and National Agreements. Cambridge: Cam-
         bridge University Press.
Robinson, D. (ed.)
  1970   Local Labor Markets and Wage Structures. London: Gower Press.
Roy, R.H.
  1952   "Do wage incentives reduce costs?" Industrial and Labor Relations Re-
         view 5(January) :195–208.

Sargant-Florence, P.
  1924   The Economics of Fatigue and Unrest. New York: Holt and Company.

Psychological Research

Barrett, J.H.
  1970   Individual Goals and Organizational Objectives: A Study of Integration Mechanisms. Ann Arbor: Institute for Social Research, University of Michigan.
Berkowitz, L.
  1954   "Group standards, cohesiveness and productivity." Human Relations 7(November):509–519.
Blum, M.L. and J.G. Naylor
  1968   Industrial Psychology: Its Theoretical and Social Foundations. New York: Harper and Row.
Brenton, R.
  1971   "Output norms and productive behavior in non-cooperative work groups: a simulation study." Simulation and Games 2(March):45–72.
Campbell, H.
  1952   "Group incentive payment schemes: the effects of lack of understanding and group size." Occupational Psychology 26(January):15–21.
Davis, N.
  1944   "Some psychological effects of women workers of payment by the individual bonus method." Occupational Psychology 18(April):53–62.
Fletcher, L. and J.R. Simon
  1962   "The relationship between method of payment and incidence of psychosomatic disorders." Occupational Psychology 363:140–145.
Ford, R.N.
  1969   Motivation Through the Work Itself. New York: American Management Association.
Gomberg, W.
  1957   "The use of psychology in industry: a trade union point of view." Management Science 4(July)348–370.
Great Britain. Industrial Health Research Board
  1936   Sickness, Absence and Labour Wastage. London: H.M.S.O. (Reprint No. 75).
  1944   A Study of Variations in Output. London: H.M.S.O.
  1945   A Study of Certified Sickness Absence Among Women in Industry. London: H.M.S.O.
  1950   Researches on the Measurement of Human Performance. London: H.M.S.O. (Special Report No. 26).
Great Britain. Medical Research Council
  1937   Fatigue and Boredom in Repetitive Work. London: H.M.S.O. (Report No. 77).
  1942   Hours of Work, Lost Time and Labour Wastage. London: H.M.S.O. (Emergency Report No. 2).
Handyside, J.D. and M. Speak
  1953   "Raising job satisfaction: a utilitarian approach." Occupational Psychology 27(April):89–97.
  1964   "Job satisfaction: myths and realities." British Journal of Industrial Relations 2(March):57–65.

Lawler, E.E., III
1971 Pay and Organizational Effectiveness: A Psychological View. New York: McGraw-Hill.
Mace, C.A.
1950 "Advances in the theory and practice of incentives." Occupational Psychology 24(October):239–244.
Marriott, R.
1949 "Size of working group and output." Occupational Psychology 23 (January):47–57.
1951 "Sociopsychological factors in productivity." Occupational Psychology 25(January):15–24.
Marriott, R., S. Wyatt and R. Deverley, et al.
1956 A Study of Attitudes to Factory Work. London: H.M.S.O.
Marriott, R., S. Wyatt and D. Hughes
1943 A Study of Absenteeism Among Women. London: H.M.S.O.
Maslow, A.H.
1954 Motivation and Personality. New York: Harper and Bros.
Myers, C.S.
1926 Industrial Psychology in Great Britain. New York: The People's Institute Publishing Co.
Norse, N.C. and E. Reimer
1956 "Experimental change of a major organizational variable." Journal of Abnormal and Social Psychology 52(January):120–129.
Schacter, S., et al.
1951 "An experimental study of cohesiveness and productivity." Human Relations 4:229–238.
Shimmin, S.
1958 "Worker's understandings of incentive payment systems." Occupational Psychology 38(January):37–47.
1962 "Extra-mural factors influencing behavior at work." Occupational Psychology 36(July):124–131.
Shimmin, S. and G. De la Mace
1964 "Individual differences in overtime working." Occupational Psychology 38(January):37–47.
Shimmin, S., C. Williams and L.J. Buck
1959 Payment by Results: A Psychological Investigation. London: Staples Press.
Vernon, H.M.
1954 Industrial Fatigue and Efficiency. London: Staples Press.
Wyatt, S.
1934 "Incentives in repetitive work: a practical experiment in a factory." Industrial Fatigue Research Board. (Reprint No. 69.) London: H.M.S.O.
1953 "A study of output in two similar factories." British Journal of Psychology 44(February):5–17.

Human Relations: Research

Herzberg, F., B. Mausner and B. Snyderman
1959 The Motivation to Work. New York: Wiley.

Likert, R.
   1961   New Patterns of Management. New York: McGraw-Hill.
   1967   The Human Organization. New York: McGraw-Hill.
Mann, F.C. and L.R. Hoffman
   1960   Automation and the Worker. New York: Henry Holt and Co.
McGregor, D.
   1960   The Human Side of Enterprise. New York: McGraw-Hill.
Roethlisberger, F.J. and W.J. Dixon
   1939   Management and the Worker. Cambridge, Mass.: Harvard University
          Press.
Tannenbaum, A.S.
   1966   Social Psychology of the Work Organization. London: The Tavistock
          Institute.
Whitehead, T.N.
   1936   The Industrial Worker. Cambridge, Mass.: Harvard University Press.
Whyte, W.F.
   1952   "Economic incentives and human relations," Harvard Business Review
          30(March-April):73–80.

   Sociological Analysis

Banks, J.A.
   1963   Industrial Participation, Theory and Practice. Liverpool: Liverpool
          University Press.
Banks, O.
   1960   The Attitudes of Steelworkers. Liverpool: Liverpool University Press.
Blumberg, P.
   1969   Industrial Democracy: The Sociology of Participation. New York:
          Schocken Books Inc.
Bolle de Bal, M.
   1958   Relations humaines et relations industrielles. Bruxelles: Institut de
          Sociologie, Solway.
   1962   Les modes de rémunération et les sciences sociales du travail en Grande-
          Bretagne. Bruxelles: Université libre de Bruxelles, Institut de So-
          ciologie.
Chinoy, E.
   1952   "The tradition of opportunity and the aspirations of the automobile
          workers." American Journal of Sociology 57(March):453–459.
   1955   Automobile Workers and the American Dream. Garden City, New
          York: Doubleday.
Collins, O., M. Dalton and D. Roy
   1946   "Restriction of output and social cleavage in industry." Applied An-
          thropology (Summer):1–14.
Cunnison, S.
   1966   Wages and Work Allocation. London: The Tavistock Institute.
Dalton, M.
   1948   "The industrial 'rate-buster': a characterization." Applied Anthro-
          pology 7(Winter):5–18.
Dennis, H., B. Henriques and C. Slaughter
   1956   Coal Is Our Life. London: Eyre and Spottiswoode.

Dubin, R.
   1956   "Industrial worker's worlds: a study of the central life interests of industrial workers." Social Problems 3(January):131–142.
   1958   Working Unions—Management Relations. The Sociology of Industrial Relations. Englewood Cliffs, New Jersey: Prentice-Hall.
Dubin, R., G.C. Homans, F.C. Mann and D.C. Miller
   1965   Leadership and Productivity, Some Facts of Industrial Life. San Francisco: Chandler Publishing Co.
Faunce, W.A.
   1968   Problems of an Industrial Society. New York: McGraw-Hill.
Goldthorpe, J., et al.
   1968a The Affluent Worker: Industrial Attitudes and Behavior. London: Cambridge University Press.
   1968b The Affluent Worker: Political Attitudes and Behavior. London: Cambridge University Press.
   1969   The Affluent Worker in the Class Structure. London: Cambridge University Press.
Golembiewski, R.T.
   1965   "Small groups in large organizations," in J.G. March (ed.), Handbook of Organizations. Chicago: Rand McNally College Publishing Co.
Horsfall, A. and C. Arensberg
   1949   "Teamwork and productivity in a shoe factory." Human Organization, 8(January):13–25.
Katz, F.E.
   1968   Autonomy and Organization: The Limits of Social Control. New York: Random House.
Klein, L.
   1964   Multiproducts Ltd., Department of Scientific and Industrial Research. London: H.M.S.O.
Klein, S.M.
   1971   Workers Under Stress: The Impact of Work Pressure on Group Cohesion. Lexington: University Press of Kentucky.
Landsberger, H.A.
   1958   Hawthorne Revisited. Ithaca: Cornell University.
Liverpool University, Social Research Series
   1954   The Dock Worker. Liverpool: Liverpool University Press.
Lloyd, W.W. and J.O. Low
   1951   The Social System of the Modern Factory. New Haven: Yale University Press.
Lupton, T.
   1963   On the Shop Floor. Oxford: Pergamon Press.
   1964   "Workshop behavior," in M. Gluckman (ed.), Closed Systems and Open Minds. Edinburgh: Oliver and Boyd.
Mathewson, S.B.
   1934   Restrictions of Output Among Unorganized Workers. New York: Viking Press.
Meissner, M.
   1969   Technology and the Worker: Technical Demands and Social Processes in Industry. San Francisco: Chandler Publishing Co.

Mills, T.M.
    1967 The Sociology of Small Groups. Englewood Cliffs, New Jersey:
          Prentice-Hall.
Roy, D.
    1952 "Quota restriction and goldbricking in a machine shop." American
          Journal of Sociology 57(March):427–442.
    1953 "Work satisfaction and social rewards in group achievement: and
          analysis of piecework incentives." American Sociological Review 18
          (October):507–514.
    1954 "Efficiency and 'the fix': informal intergroup relations in a piecework
          machine shop." American Journal of Sociology, 60(November):255–
          266.
Sayles, L.R.
    1958 The Behavior of Industrial Work Groups. New York: Wiley.
Scott, W.H., et al.
    1963 Coal and Conflict. Liverpool: Liverpool University Press.
Scott, W.H., J.A. Banks, A.H. Halsey and T. Lupton
    1956 Technical Change and Industrial Relations. Liverpool: Liverpool Uni-
          versity Press.
Tausky, C.
    1970 Work Organizations: Major Theoretical Perspectives. Itasca, Ill.: F.E.
          Peacock Publishers.
Touraine, A.
    1965 Workers Attitudes to Technical Change. Paris: O.E.C.D.
Walker, C.R. and R.H. Guest
    1953 Man on the Assembly Line. Cambridge, Mass.: Harvard University
          Press.
Zaleznik, A., C.R. Christensen and F.J. Roethlisberger
    1958 The Motivation, Productivity, and Satisfaction of Workers: A Predic-
          tive Study. Cambridge, Mass.: Harvard University Press.

Open Sociotechnical Systems

Bowey, A.M. and T. Lupton
    1970 "Productivity drift and the structure of the pay packet." Journal of
          Management Studies 7(May, October):157–171, 310–335.
Cooper, R. and M. Foster
    1971 "Sociotechnical systems." American Psychologist 26:467–474.
Davis, L.E. and R.N. Taylor
    1972 The Design of Work. London: Penguin.
Gowler, D.
    1969 "Determinants of the supply of labour to the firm." Journal of Man-
          agement Studies 6(February): 73–95.
Jaques, E.
    1951 The Changing Culture of a Factory. London: Routledge.
Jaques, E., A.K. Rice and J.M.M. Hill
    1951 "The social and psychological impact of a change in method of wage
          payment." Human Relations 4(April):315–340.
Lupton, T. and D. Gowler
    1969 "Selecting a wage payment system." Research Paper Number III,
          London: Engineering Employers Federation.

Miller, E. and A.K. Rice
   1967   Systems of Organisation. London: Tavistock Publications.
Millward, N.
   1968   "Family status and behavior at work." Sociological Review 16(February):149–164.
Mumford, E.
   1970   "Job satisfaction—a new approach derived from an old theory." Sociological Review 18(March):71–101.
Rice, A.K.
   1951   "The use of unrecognised cultural mechanisms in an expanding machine shop." Human Relations 4(May):143–160.
   1958   Productivity and Social Organisation. London: The Tavistock Institute.
   1963   The Enterprise and Its Environment. London: The Tavistock Institute.
Rice, A.K., J.M.M. Hill and E.L. Trist
   1950   "The representation of labour turnover as a social process." Human Relations 3(November):349–372.
Trist, E.L. and K. Bamforth
   1951   "Some social and psychological consequences of the longwall method of coal-getting." Human Relations 4(February): 3–38.
Trist, E.L., et al.
   1963   Organisational Choice. London: The Tavistock Institute.

General

Alderfer, C.P.
   1972   Existence, Relatedness and Growth: Human Needs in Organizational Settings. New York: Free Press.
Argyris, C.
   1964   Integrating the Individual and the Organization. New York: Wiley.
Bendix, R.
   1963   Work and Authority in Industry: Ideologies of Management in the Course of Industrialization. New York: Harper Torchbooks.
Blauner, R.
   1964   Alienation and Freedom. Chicago: University of Chicago Press.
Brown, E.K.
   1967   "Research and consultancy in industrial enterprises: the Tavistock industrial studies." Sociology 1(January):33–60.
Brown, J.A.C.
   1964   The Social Psychology of Industry. London: Penguin Books.
Caplow, T.
   1954   The Sociology of Work. Minneapolis: University of Minnesota Press.
Cartwright, D. and A. Zander
   1968   Group Dynamics: Research and Theory. New York: Harper & Row.
Crozier, M.
   1964   The Bureaucratic Phenomenon. Chicago: University of Chicago Press.
Dubin, R.
   1958   The World of Work. Englewood Cliffs, New Jersey: Prentice-Hall.
   1974   Human Relations in Administration, with Readings. Fourth Edition. Englewood Cliffs, New Jersey: Prentice-Hall.

Dufty, N.F. (ed.)
1969   The Sociology of the Blue-Collar Worker. Leiden: Brill International
       Studies in Sociology and Social Anthropology, V. 9. Reprinted from
       International Journal of Comparative Sociology 10, No. 1–2.
Freidmann, G.
1955   Industrial Society. Glencoe, Illinois: The Free Press.
Golden, C.S. and H.J. Ruttenberg
1942   The Dynamics of Industrial Democracy. New York, London: Harper
       & Brothers.
Goodrich, C.
1920   The Frontier of Control. New York: Harcourt, Brace, and Howe.
Herzberg, F.
1966   Work and the Nature of Man. Cleveland: World.
Homans, G.C.
1961   Social Behavior: Its Elementary Forms. New York: Harcourt, Brace
       and World.
Hugh-Jones, E.M. (ed.)
1958   Human Relations in Modern Management. Amsterdam: North Hol-
       land Publishing Co.
Kahn, R.L.
1958   "Human relations on the shop floor," in E.M. Hugh-Jones (ed.),
       Human Relations in Modern Management. Amsterdam: North Holland
       Publishing Co.
Katz, D. and R.L. Kahn
1966   The Social Psychology of Organizations. New York: Wiley.
Lupton, T.
1971a Management and the Social Sciences. International Edition. London:
       Penguin Books.
1971b Wage Payment Systems. London: Penguin Books.
Marriott, R.
1968   Incentive Payment Systems: A Review of Research and Opinion. Sec-
       ond Edition. London: Staples Press.
Mayo, E.
1933   The Human Problems of an Industrial Civilization. New York: Mac-
       millan.
1945   The Social Problems of an Industrial Civilization. Boston: Graduate
       School of Business Administration, Harvard University.
McGregor, D.
1960   The Human Side of Enterprise. New York: McGraw-Hill.
Porter, L.W., E.E. Lawler and J.R. Hackman
1975   Behavior in Organizations. New York: McGraw-Hill.
Schein, E.H.
1965   Organizational Psychology. Englewood Cliffs, New Jersey: Prentice-
       Hall.
Shimmin, S.
1959   Payments by Results. London: Staples Press.
Tannenbaum, A.S.
1966   Social Psychology of the Work Organization. London: The Tavistock
       Institute.

Thompson, J.D.
  1967   Organizations in Action. New York: McGraw-Hill.
Vernon, H.M.
  1954   Industrial Fatigue and Efficiency. London: Staples Press.
Viteles, M.S.
  1954   Motivation and Morale in Industry. London: Staples Press.
Vroom, V.
  1964   Work and Motivation. New York: John Wiley and Sons.
Vroom, V. and E.L. Deci, (eds.)
  1970   Management and Motivation: Selected Readings. New York: Penguin.
Whyte, W.F.
  1955   Money and Motivation: An Analysis of Incentives in Industry. New
         York: Harper.
Woodward, J.
  1958   Management and Technology. London: H.M.S.O.
  1971   Industrial Organisation. Behavior and Control. Oxford: Oxford Univer-
         sity Press.

CHAPTER **6**

The Language of Work

Martin Meissner

University of British Columbia

This chapter is concerned with the communication practices of industrial workers at work. In the perspective of social ecology, it examines communication as observable activity adapted to its environment—the technology and organization of production. This environment contains the demands, opportunities, and constraints to which communication practices respond.

Communication among workers has both technical and social functions. It is instrumental to the purpose of getting work done. It is also expressive, the stuff of which social relations are made and maintained for their own sake. It takes both verbal and nonverbal forms, and some technical environments give prominence to communication by gestural signs, technical signals, and material objects, often to the exclusion of speech.

A major part of this chapter is focused on production workers—the women and men whose job it is to transform and move industrial products. The first section begins with the identification of the properties of the technical and organizational environment which influence workers' communication. It emphasizes the multiplicity of channels through which communication flows in the work-place, and provides a classification of its major forms. In order to understand the nature of communication at work, and how its different forms are related, it is useful to know how much of it there is, and how rates of communication are distributed. The discussion then turns to the functions and uses of communication, and the system of references through which utterances become meaningful.

These dimensions of the communication system are then put to use in an analysis of the relation of technology and communication. The analysis demonstrates how verbal and nonverbal communication rates are influenced by mech-

I am grateful to John Bryan, Edward Harvey, Alan Hedley, Gerald Merner, Stuart Philpott, and Peter Wiebe, for the pleasure of their cooperation and competent help; to Robert Dubin, for his enthusiastic interest; and to Margot Meissner, for critical contributions to the sense and justice of my work.

I had the benefit of continued support from the Institute of Industrial Relations of the University of British Columbia, and a year of full-time concentration on research at the International Institute for Labour Studies in Geneva, with the assistance of the Canada Department of Labour.

anization and the constraints of time, space, and function, and by work-group size and noise.

The second section deals with the activities of foremen. An assessment of the available data indicates that the major part of a foreman's job *is* communication, and describes the role which communication plays in the composition of activities. It shows the extent of communication in authority relations—with subordinates and superiors—in comparison to contacts with other foremen, the technical staff, and outsiders. Special attention is directed to relations between foremen and their workers, and to a neglected segment of these relations, namely those which involve workers who exercise supervisory functions *below* the foreman level. Foreman communication is also part of the technical and organizational environment, and the analysis shows the effects of this environment on foremen's communicative relations.

Much of the analysis is quantitative, dealing with major distinctions among means of communication, and with variations in frequencies and time used. The relative neglect of the actual content of communication will be made up in the third section through examples of language use, and meanings and detailed forms of expression. It includes the description of a sign language, and of joking and obscenity at work. These descriptions bring into view the relative wealth and poverty of articulation in the communication practices of people who work for a living.

The focus and treatment of this chapter is relatively uncommon in industrial sociology. It draws on varied sources from several countries, and relies in large part on data from my first-hand research. It is also a comment on the problems of method and measurement in this research field, and the selective effect which choices of method have on the scope and quality of our understanding.

COMMUNICATION AMONG WORKERS

The Technical and Organizational Environment

Communication among workers takes place in a *purposeful* organization, where principal activities are directed toward the goal of material output, a goal which is not the worker's own. It occurs within a *technical* organization in the design of which workers have no part, while being its first-hand users and themselves instruments. Through differentiated *task* organization, workers become parts of the production process in the allocation of their activities according to function, time, space, and number. Differentiated tasks are coordinated through the organization of *authority relations*, that is, a boss who can tell the worker what to do.

Communication at work is deeply embedded in a complex environment. It is this very embeddedness which gives the language of work its character, and tends to select and bring to the fore particular properties of communication behavior. The following paragraphs provide an outline of the technical dimensions of industrial tasks, and the sense in which they constitute constraints on communication.

An obvious and often recognized property of the production process is mechanization, or the extent to which component operations are performed by machines rather than people. Explications of the dimensions of mechanization and related properties of production technology have been developed in detail by several authors (Marx, 1867; Touraine, 1955; Bright, 1958; Hammer, 1959:5–15; Woodward, 1965:36–44, 268–274; Meissner, 1969:13–25, 158–170). For the purpose of understanding worker communication, the importance of mechanization lies in the fact that it describes a relationship between person and machine. Attention to this relationship tells us that all other activities are conditioned by the primary requirement that the workers interact with their machines, tools and work pieces. The conditioning mechanisms are a number of crucial constraints through which the worker's activities are fitted into the production process.

Spatial constraints make it possible for tasks to be performed at the right place. They become expressed in requirements for staying in one place for continuous manipulation of the controls of production machinery, or for moving between machines or work pieces. Spatial task allocation results in different distances between workers. Spatial confinement and distance will create varying opportunities for access to other workers and result in different forms and rates of communication.

Temporal constraints assure that tasks and task elements will be performed at the right time and thus synchronized with the rhythm of production. That rhythm has its source in requirements for coordination of worker activity with machine cycles and activities of other workers. Temporal constraints take the form of production speed and pacing by machine or production process. Time required for physical work activity will budget, as it were, the continuity and amount of communication.

Differentiated task assignments produce further constraints in the form of functional relations. In the typically complex arrangements of modern production organizations, some jobs are connected through dependence of tasks and sequence in a work flow. The tasks of other workers are independent from each other, with functional dependence shifting to the higher level of interdependence between entire departments. Task allocation is also intimately related to the number of workers performing the same job and to the number of workers in a work group or section under the supervision of a foreman. Communicative requirements and opportunities will depend on whether workers share tasks, perform dependent tasks, and find themselves in groups or sections of varying size.

Authority relations set limits to workers' activities, mainly through anticipations of the powers a foreman can exercise, and through dependence on the foreman in the case of unprogrammed events. However, a foreman's activities are highly segmented, and constrained by technology and organization, thus limiting worker surveillance and foreman-worker communication. Coordination is a function of supervision, but a great deal of coordination of work components is built into the production process or accomplished by the workers themselves. Finally, the activities of both workers and foremen are subject to technical constraints which are likely to affect their relationship. The constraints of authority are then more likely to take effect indirectly through job assignments than directly through active supervision.

In order to understand the nature of communication among workers, it is important to see it in its technical and organizational context. The purpose of a mill, mine, logging operation, warehouse, repair shop, or dockside and ship, is to get work done. Most of the time when work is in progress, workers are actually working, and they do not talk much. They do, however, communicate a great deal and display striking ingenuity in meeting the communicative requirements of the job and of maintaining expressive relations with others, often both at the same time. The forms which communication takes, and the rate at which these forms are used, are adapted to the work environment characterized by the constraints of mechanization, time, space, function, number, and authority.

Forms of Communication

Work in kinesics, semiotics, and nonverbal communication tells us that all activity must be taken to have potential communicative significance (Birdwhistell, 1952:6; Birdwhistell, 1968; Morris, 1955:190; Ruesch & Kees, 1959). In the research literature of industrial sociology one finds the assertion that, of course, nonverbal communication must be taken into account (Homans, 1950:101; Horsfall & Arensberg, 1949:91; Atteslander, 1954:28, and 1956:69), and careful observations of cooperative manual work reveals a multitude of communications in the form of gestures and technical signals, or mediated by work pieces and machinery. Yet, none of the empirical reports make an attempt to classify types of communication or even to indicate which kinds were taken into account and which were not. The bulk of the systematic, quantitative data refer to speech and a smattering of gestures which happen to be parts of ongoing verbal exchanges. One nonindustrial study gave a simple reason: "Our analysis is restricted to verbal conversation because that is the portion of the interaction most easily reported by an observer" (Watson & Potter, 1962:247).

Where the industrial ethnographies describe nonverbal communication, they curiously tend to focus on tactile and object communication, the forms most removed from "language." Roy described how conversational occasions were introduced as a daily event, by Ike switching off the power on Sammy's machine; by "surreptitiously extracting (a banana) from Sammy's lunch box;" and by one opening a window and the other closing it again (1960:161–162). An ingenious system for equalizing output rates and pay in a shoe factory was reported by Horsfall. It consisted of a set of objects which represented certain types of shoes which differed in the amount of work they required. When it was time for one work group to process a rack of suede shoes, for example, the rack was exchanged for an old cardboard box; or a scraper was handed over in return for a rack of wedge sandals; always in the same sequence from one of the four production lines to the next (Horsfall & Arensberg, 1949:88–90). The practice of "binging," or hitting another person on the upper arm, was described by Roethlisberger and Dickson (1939:421–423). They also reported how co-workers annoyed a supply man by spitting on materials he was about to stamp with an identification number; joggling his arm when stamping; holding up his hand truck; or tickling him (p. 489). My own records contain accounts of playful throwing of a rotten avocado in a produce warehouse; the repeated blowing of powerful steam whistles to harass a tardy relief operator in a sawmill; and turning a large lumber-carrying roller case on and off to prevent the same relief man from stepping over it. In contrast to these expressive communications, a steel-mill study described how three operators of a blooming mill coordinate the very rapid and intricate set of remotely controlled movements of the work piece and equipment, feeling the vibrations through the handles of their controls, and recognizing the flash of the ingot emerging from the invisible side of the roll stand (Popitz, et al., 1957a:56–59).

A full identification of all forms of communication would take us far afield from the available data of industrial research, and only those forms accessible to simple observation will be dealt with. One classification has been proposed by Buehler and Richmond (1963). A previous formulation and use of the following categories can be found in Meissner (1969:33–37, 209–233).

Speech. The most obvious form of communication consists of speech accompanied by vocal variation and face and body movement. The extent to which speech and body movement are congruent or go their separate ways, in frequency, temporal extension, and signification, is almost entirely unknown, and the determination of speech as the central part of this communication is all that can be dealt with.

Gestural signs. Industrial work is one of the settings where body movement as communication occurs regularly *in the absence of speech.* The conditions under which that is the case will be pointed out later. The clearest type is the manual gesture, often in combination with facial expression and corresponding body posture and positioning. Attention has been drawn to the cultural basis of gesture (Effron, 1972; Hall, 1959; Krout, 1935; Labarre, 1947). The dominant element of the "culture" of the factory is the production process and its requirements and constraints. Within it can be found expressive gestures, and signs facilitating necessary cooperation, which are foreign to the home, office, store or university. Technical gestural signs frequently signify numbers and movement or relative positioning of work piece and equipment. These develop sometimes into entire, though small, sign systems. Occasionally, technical and expressive gestures form the components of an industrial sign language. One such language will be discussed in a subsequent section.

In the observation of gestures it is useful to make a distinction between several types. The first belongs to a relatively standardized sign system or sign language which tends to be unique to an industry or a particular type of technical operation. The second consists of gestures brought into the work place from the customs of the community. A third type is created on the spot, in pantomimic or chiromimic form (the last term has been suggested by Kroeber, 1958). Following are examples of each of these. Directions given to overhead crane operators, truck drivers, and railroad men (Spier, 1959:43) tend to be of the first type, with a short dictionary of one-handed or bimanual signs, and corresponding to those used in basketball or at boards of trade (New York Times, October 4, 1963). An example of the second would be both hands in a fist, with thumbs outstretched and pointing up, as if sticking behind imaginary lapels, to signify "boss" or "bossy." One example of the third type took place in a sawmill, when a slab of wood cut off the side of a log was moving along a roller case. This slab had the remainder of a branch sticking up from it, perhaps two feet long and three inches in diameter. As it passed by the roller-case operator, he banged his pickeroon (a small pick-like tool) against the steel rolls to attract attention, then formed a circle with both hands stretched and curved, palms down and thumbs bent back, around the branch stub, moving his hands jointly up and down quickly several times, with a grin on his face.

Signals. Another major form of communication in industry is mediated through specially designed electric or mechanical channels. These signals may involve pushing buttons to turn on colored lights or pulling a rope to blow a steam whistle. Their signification range can be extended by the number of times the signal is given, the time at which it is given in relation to some other event, and through variations in color or pitch. Although rare in communication among workers, the specially designed channel can of course be combined with language communication in speech or writing, through telephone, public-address system, or remote-writing equipment. Walker has described the use of a public address system for purposes of work and fun, by the operators of an automated tubing mill (Walker, 1957:45–46). Much more extended signal channels can be found in automated plants where an adjustment made by an operator on one of the controls is transmitted into the actual production process and then appears as a change on a dial or chart scanned by another person (Meissner, 1969:222–223).

Objects.   An important form of communication in industry is the movement of objects, consisting of work pieces and equipment whose "messages" are received by sight, hearing, touch, smell, or temperature. It tends to occur most often where work is highly mechanized. As suggested in the examples given above, object communication can have technical or expressive relevance. As a form of delayed communication, it can also have utility as information for social control, as suggested by the wealth of information available to janitors in the garbage (Gold, 1952, 1964). Cases can frequently be observed, but have rarely been reported in the literature, where the movement of objects is the sole communication channel between workers whose tasks are technically connected and require closely timed coordination. Examples can be found in the analysis of types of cooperative systems by Popitz, et al. (1957a). For routine work-piece movement to meet standard definitions of communication applied to relations between workers, it is important to identify those processes where such movement is controlled or set in motion by a worker, and the recognition of movement or arrival of a work piece if responded to by another. Thus, the movement of car bodies on a continuously moving auto assembly line does not constitute communication between workers on the line.

Complex forms and sources of meaning.   The above classification has identified four major forms of communication which are prominent in industrial work: speech, gestural signs, technical signals, and objects. Several of these forms are frequently combined into multichannel communication, and an utterance of one type often depends on another type for its meaning. A gesture and the manipulation of an object may go together to form a single utterance, as shown in several of the examples. Gestural signs may be generated from technical signals, and then elaborated: In one Canadian sawmill, four whistle blows call for the millwright, and five for the foreman. In the manual sign language in use in that mill, a hand sign indicating "five" tells other workers that the foreman is coming, while the sign for "4½" refers to the lead hand, who ranks between millwright and foreman.

Utterances frequently do not only signify something in the immediate context to which the recipient is intended to respond, but also constitute the symbolization of something else which is often not found in the current environment. Many sexual implications of technical terms illustrate this process when, for example, "cock" or "nipple" designate equipment parts. Similarly,

English speech is not part of the immediate context of sawmill workers' communication, but becomes the source of an analogue: grasping the biceps of the other arm, as a symbol of "weak," is intended to signify "week."

Explorations in non-work settings illustrate the possibilities for comprehending communication at work in greater depth: the study of material contexts and objects and persons in space (Hall, 1966; Ruesch & Kees, 1959:87–159; Sommer, 1969; Watson, 1970); the examination of tactile communication as the basis for language learning (Frank, 1957); and the interpretation of object symbolization in children (Kubie, 1934; Erikson, 1940). Examples of corresponding interpretations applied to work settings can be found in the accounts of: the spatial ecology of restaurants (Whyte, 1949; Goffman, 1959); the significance of incontinence in mental hospitals (Stanton & Schwartz, 1954); historical changes in the meaning of protective work clothes among steel rollers (Verry, 1955); taken-for-granted elements of communication between taxi drivers and dispatchers (Psathas, 1967); a full enumeration of sexual meanings in the names of industrial tools (Thomas, 1951); and sexual expressions in oil fields (Haslam, 1967).

As a newcomer or outsider, an observer will find much communication in work places incomprehensible, and will be unable to communicate on an equal footing. The reasons why can be summarized as follows. Communication at work is not only accomplished through *speech* and its nonverbal adjuncts, but also through body movement and gestural *signs*, as well as *signals* transmitted through technical channels, and *objects* in motion. It relies on touch, smell, sight and sound. It draws for the make-up of its expressions on *symbolic sources* often not found in the working environment. It depends on the *context* of the technical means of production and the shared experience of accumulated daily events, to the extent that even apparent inaction communicates: A machinist simply standing beside a large work piece, to be set up in a boring mill, communicates to the overhead crane operator to come and pick up the piece.

Rates of Communication and Their Distribution

The preceding account of forms of communication suggests that communication at work, as elsewhere, is a multichannel system. When adding to that characteristic the consideration that the context of technical and social organization is always active, communication at work is *continuous*, and the notion of rate of communication is only meaningful when specific channels are selected for counting.

Social interaction means communication (Homans, 1950:101) and is an important focus of sociological research. It is a peculiarity of the field that it has not produced the basic data for one of its more important theoretical problems, namely the distribution of frequencies. The data which are available tend to be limited to very special circumstances. The work stimulated by Bales' (1950) development of an observation method applies to voluntary groups in free discussion or therapy, and its most common environment is the small-groups laboratory. Even where communication frequencies form the main data, they tend to be reported without the time base necessary for the calculation of rates and without the basic distributions (for examples see Stephan, 1952, and several contributions to Hare, et al., 1965:358–387, 427–433). Other studies of rates and distributions of communicative activities were concerned with children (Arrington, 1938; Barker, 1963); the handicapped (Lubow, et al.,

1969) ; or a surgeon (Richardson, 1966). If we take seriously the importance of the context in which communication at work is embedded, little of this already meager information lends itself to inferences about the behavior of industrial workers.

There are some data on the communication amounts of managers, summarized by Dubin (1962), and of industrial foremen (to be dealt with in a separate section of this chapter). Basic data for workers are scarce. The Hawthorn studies, classic of industrial sociology, included over five years of continuous observation of a group of six women. Recognition of the importance of social interaction was emphasized by many references to the fact that the workers were frequently reprimanded, and even threatened with dismissal, for talking too much. Still, the record of data for this crucial variable was unsystematic and unreliable, according to Whitehead (1938:106). Impressions of the rate of verbal communication in the room are given by the following statements: "Seven persons sat in the room each day, and an average of at least one person was talking continuously" (p. 106); "Operator 1a, 2a, 3, and 4 laughed and talked about 75% of the day, or more than ever before" (p. 111). A second part of these studies involved 6½ months of continuous observation of the men in the Bank Wiring Room, and it was meant to describe the "Social Organization of Employees." The report contains no information of actual interaction rates (Roethlisberger & Dickson, 1939:377–548), even though "the observer kept a daily record of significant happenings in the observation room, of conversations of the employees, and of his impressions" (p. 406). In the same tradition of intensive field work, several studies were carried out which involved lengthy periods of observation (Zaleznik, 1956; Zaleznik, et al., 1958; Lombard, 1955). Only one of these included data of interaction rates: "The field workers spent some two weeks in which they recorded every fifteen minutes during the day who was talking with whom regardless of what was being said" (Zaleznik, et al., 1958:21). The actual counts of interactions within and outside the group of workers in each of four departments were reported (p. 172), but without the number of times at which counts were taken in the systematic time sampling. These studies suggested the usefulness of communication rates for describing and comparing social interaction, but did not account for their distribution. Following is a summary of research describing the quantitative distribution of communication at work and some conclusions one might draw from it.

The quantitative study of social interaction in natural settings has its origin primarily in Chapple's development of observation techniques (1939, 1940). Other partly quantitative work was stimulated by Barker (1963), including Soskin and John's (1963:261) data of proportions of talking time in a few episodes around one man. Both of these important methodological developments produced little quantitative data, and there are only a few studies of rates of communication in work places.

In his "verbal conversation records," Horsfall covered 120 periods of fifteen minutes each, thirty for each of the four production lines of seven workers in the bottoming department of an American shoe factory (Horsfall & Arensberg, 1949:99). The reported unit of analysis was an "event" for which one "initiation" was recorded for one worker, and one "response" for another, each counted as an "act," even though the event may have been a continuing exchange of several utterances between the two workers. A recalculation of the data gives a mean frequency per worker per hour of 20.9 acts. Of these, 12.5 were intrateam contacts ranging from 25.2 to 4.8. The distribution is shown in Figure 1, as generated from the intrateam interaction matrix (Horsfall & Arensberg, 1949:104).

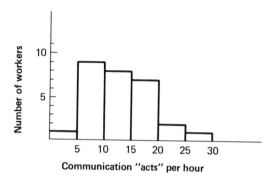

FIGURE 1. Distribution of hourly communication rates of 28 shoe workers. Horsfall, 1949: 103–104. (Observation period 7.5 hours)

Miller (1958) carried out similar observations using the same definitions. In addition, however, he wanted to take into account those interactions initiated, as it were, by the work process. Without identifying it as such, he introduced a form of "object communication." He observed each of four cooperative teams making glass products during eight hours of observation time, in periods of twenty minutes each. There were six workers in three of the teams, and five in the fourth team, for a total of twenty-three workers and ·thirty-two hours of observation. Ignoring "situational" (nonverbal) interactions and counting only intrateam communication, the mean hourly frequency per worker was 19.3, with a range from 32.9 to 5.8. The distribution is shown in Figure 2 (Miller, 1958:41–42).

Blau (1954:338) reported an average rate of 8.3 "contacts" per hour for the sixteen officials of an American government agency, with a rate of 5.1 between members of the group. These figures compare with Horsfall's rates of 20.9 and 12.5, and with Miller's intra-team rate of 19.3.

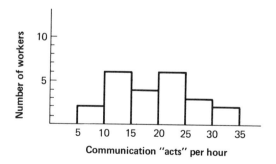

FIGURE 2. Distribution of hourly communication rates of 23 glass workers. Miller, 1958: 41–42. (Observation period 8 hours)

For fourteen workers on three machines of a German steel tubing mill, Stieber (1956:85–86) found a mean interaction rate of 16 per hour by seemingly the same unit of count. These were about two-thirds verbal and one-third part of a sign language, and included communication with outsiders of a team. Stieber further indicated that communication tended to be higher during disturbances in the production process. Also, "when formal interaction frequency rises, informal interaction declines, and vice versa. When verbal frequency increases, nonverbal frequency goes down, and vice versa" (p. 86).

In my study of 156 Canadian workers in a wide variety of production operations, the rate of speech per worker per hour was an average of 27.9 of which 6.8 involved contacts with outsiders to the work group. The rate of gestural signs was 11.4 including .9 with outsiders. The unit of count in this case was an utterance emitted or received, counting as one unit all continuous communicative expressions of one person ending with the beginning of communication from a partner or a clear temporal break. The frequency would thus tend to be higher than in the studies just referred to. The frequency distributions are shown in Figures 3 and 4.

We can now examine two important features of these data. The first is the proportion of communication with "outsiders" to a work group, and the second the shape of the frequency distributions. Table 1 is a summary of the data just reviewed. It indicates that, in situations of low levels of mechanization,

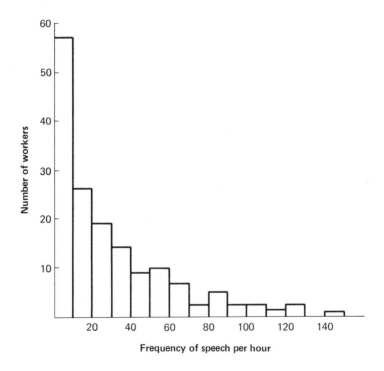

FIGURE 3.   Distribution of verbal communication rates of 156 production workers. Observation period 60 minutes.

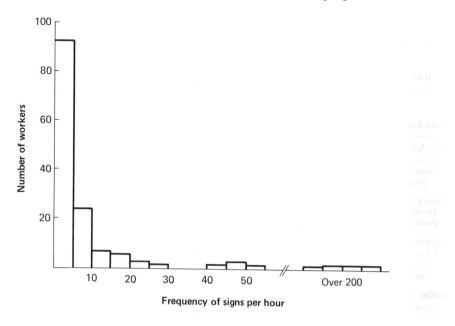

FIGURE 4. Distribution of gestural sign communication rates of 156 production workers. Observation period 60 minutes.

from one-fourth to two-fifths of the communications relate members of the work group to nonmembers. This finding suggests a relatively high degree of permeability of these groups. If the meaning of "group" implies boundaries defined by greater interaction of members with each other than with outsiders, these work groups approach the state of very open, relatively unbounded interaction systems. High proportions of outward communication also limit the applicability of findings from experimental groups which tend to be sharply bounded by experimental *fiat*.

Figures 1, 3, and 4 indicate an apparently common property of the distribution of communication. The reported distributions are skewed, with most cases concentrated toward the low communication frequencies. They are based on incidence counts and show the distribution for a *group* of individuals. Arrington (1938:290) reported the distributions for *individual* children in kindergarten and first year of school over a number of sampled five-minute periods, many of which "were J-shaped, with positive skewness and a piling up of scores at the low frequency end of the scale." Chapple (1939:60) reported the *durations* of individuals talking, and the "frequency distributions showed a characteristic asymmetry, the curve being definitely J-shaped." Distributions of contact durations of two individuals in a rehabilitative work shop shown by Lubow, et al. (1969:310, 316) have the same shape.

One of the conditions which contribute to skewed frequency distributions is the length of observation time. Longer periods shift the mode to the right. For example, the data in Figures 1 and 2 are based on 7½ and 8 hours of observation per individual, and those in Figures 3 and 4 on sixty minutes.

TABLE 1
RATES OF COMMUNICATION WITH WORK-GROUP MEMBERS AND OUTSIDERS

Data Sources	Hourly Rate Per Worker		Percent With Outsiders
	Total	With Outsiders	
Horsfall (1949) 28 workers in shoe bottoming room Participation in interaction events (verbal)	20.9	8.4	40%
Blau (1954) 16 officials in government office Participation in contacts (verbal)	8.3	3.2	39%
Stieber (1956) 14 workers on steel tubing mill Participation in contacts (verbal and gestural)	16.0		
Miller (1958) 23 workers in glass-working teams Participation in interaction events (verbal)	19.3		
Zaleznik (1958) 45 workers in machine-shop and assembly departments Verbal interactions			29%
Meissner 156 workers in 37 manufacturing operations Utterances emitted and received (verbal and gestural) by level of production-line mechanization			
No production line (45)	45.8	15.8	34%
Unmechanized production line (23)	34.7	8.8	25%
Machine feeders and operators on mechanized production line (47)	32.8	2.7	8%
Remote-control production line (41)	42.0	3.8	9%

Skewed distributions of both frequencies and durations would indicate that most people in an observed situation communicate infrequently, and that most communications are short. In eight periods of observation of three therapy groups, Talland (1957) counted the number of sentences or their equivalent for each turn when an individual spoke. The average number of sentences per "turn" for the 152 observed individuals ranged from 1.0 to 3.3, with a mean of 1.9. This finding suggests that a person will rarely put more than three sentences (or shorter sentence equivalents) into one turn of speaking to another person, and most of the time only two. In the constraining conditions of industrial work, the ratio would be even lower. Nonverbal expressions tend to take less time than speech, with the effect that each turn of communicating would be shorter still.

These characteristics of communication rates can tell us that workers do not talk often and, when they do, they are likely to make it short. They put into question the assumption of strong sociability norms prevalent in American industrial sociology, and may justify the critique of its "romanticism of group formation" (Popitz, 1957a:42). The American literature rarely mentions workers who may positively prefer *not* to have personal contacts with their coworkers. When the description reveals cases of low contact rates, they become identified as isolates or deviants, and when whole groups show little communication, little is made of the fact. (One exception is the finding of Dubin (1956: 136) that in his sample of 491 workers in three American factories "only 9% ... prefer the informal group life that is centered in the job.")

The incidence of preferences for being left alone on the job has been more fully identified in European research. Baumgarten (1947:19–25) interviewed thirty Swiss machine-shop workers. The twenty-five workers who articulated their views gave four types of assessments: (a) ten workers preferred to work alone; (b) the preference of four workers depended on the number or the personal characteristics of people with whom they would have to put up; (c) seven felt that the presence of coworkers was useful in their work; and (d) only four indicated an unqualified liking for people which extended to those with whom they worked together. An interview by Popitz (1957b:39) of a German blast-furnace lift operator revealed a fully developed preference for an isolated job:

> The nice thing here is that we work independently. I have nothing directly to do with anyone, and nobody butts into my work....I hardly ever talk with (the workers at the top and bottom of the lift). I keep my room clean. I would have to sweep up the dirt that others bring in; they wouldn't do that. I keep to myself....I don't bother about the others. They have their work, and I have mine. That way we get along best with each other.

For French industrial workers, Sainsaulieu found a variety of reasons for the limitations in personal communication on the job (Sainsaulieu and Kergoat, 1968). Even though there was the usual *camaraderie* to pass the time, these workers felt that, after all, they had no choice with whom they worked. They saw little chance to understand the other person in depth. They tended to take the point of view of coworkers as an undifferentiated and hostile block. They also felt that they lacked elegance in verbal expression.

Crozier (1964:35) also pointed out that most of the women working in a French government agency found acquaintances, but did not seek friends at work. From interviews with 229 English workers, Goldthorpe, et al. (1968:53) concluded that these workers "show no great concern over maintaining stable relationships with any particular set of workmates." 45% of these men had no close friends from work, and 31% had more than two. Just under half of those with friends at work extended their contacts to visiting and outings (p. 62). Putting together the communication rates of North American studies with these European findings, one may ask if workers are quite as gregarious as "human relations" writers have implied. Analytically, this raises the question of the functions of communication at work, the subject of the following section.

The Functions of Communication at Work

Some communication can be said to be an end in itself. It is produced, as they say, "for the hell of it." Its expressive or purpose-free character is indicated in terms like "bullshitting," "fucking the dog," or "horsing around." Other communications facilitate work in a direct way, enabling workers to do their job and to coordinate their activities according to the requirements of the technical system.

In the literature of industrial sociology one cannot miss the distinction between "formal" and "informal" activities. "Formal" is intended to refer to compliance with stated or explicit rules. "Informal" refers to a response to implicit social norms usually located within the work group, and describes unofficial, if not surreptitious, behavior. However, many official rules are far from explicit, and researchers' attention to informal work-group norms has tended to be limited to those concerning desirable rates of production. The distinction between formal and informal activities has depended on an identification of organizational goals, on the one hand, and of social consequences on the other (such as maintaining stable relationships within, and boundaries around the group). This involves the common problem of functional explanation where the number of potential factors which contribute to maintaining preferred states is typically large (Stinchcombe, 1968:84), and somewhat indeterminate. However, the properties of a production process as a functioning system tend to be obvious and can be interpreted with a certain amount of engineering knowledge. The outcome of the process is clear, and one can impute to many events the characteristic of being necessary or not necessary to that outcome.

Even very tightly designed industrial operations depend on some degree of voluntary discretion on the part of workers. A focus on interpersonal communication will lead one to recognize a special area of discretion, namely those technical circumstances which require that two or more workers order their actions cooperatively in order to make the required result possible. In this collectively discretionary area, the means of coordination is communication. A central example of coordination can be found in the temporal order of actions, through synchronization or sequentialization.

Wherever the output of a production operation cannot be attained without coordination of workers' activities, one would expect to observe communication with the function of accomplishing coordination. Among the various means, speech appears to be preferred for technical purposes. This preference may have two reasons. Although it is not the most efficient, it is cheap because it is already fully developed, and it is available to almost all participants. Among the main forms described above, it is also perhaps the most redundant, and therefore most reliable. Speech redundancy is increased when used in its usual multichannel context of nonverbal corrolaries. When technical constraints inhibit speech, there will be other forms to meet technical requirements, and these other forms entail the cost of learning, and of incomprehensibility to the uninitiated, including supervisors and managers. In most industrial circumstances, workers adapt their necessary communication practices to the limitations of the technical environment, and develop communication channels from whatever resources are readily available. But when such worker-developed forms are inadequate or impossible, adaptation becomes organizational, and technical channels are deliberately installed to meet the demands of the production system. These are the signal channels described above.

In many industrial work places, communication can be observed which can be interpreted without much difficulty as serving no direct technical function. The social organization of production is dominated by the technical requirements of getting work done, and it is in that sense that all technically "unnecessary" communication can be regarded as expressive, even though it may be instrumental to some other, personal and social purpose. The incidence of expressive communication, sometimes even in the most unlikely industrial settings, is interpretable from two assumptions. The first is the belief in the tendency of humans to develop social relations readily, to reinforce and maintain them, and to elaborate them into complex patterns, far beyond the necessities of survival. The second assumption has been put as a "need for symbolization" and for the "symbolic transformation of experience," in excess of what is merely practical (Langer, 1948:45–49).

In the abstract, the differential recognition of instrumental and expressive communication is conventional. When it comes to operations productive of data, it is problematic. When the data are so microscopic as to deal with single utterances as units, the difference becomes tenuous. One of the reasons for the difficulty is the multichannel quality of much communication. Another lies in the fact that a unit of communication has multiple uses, functions, and referents.

The idea that a word has different meanings is, of course, readily understood. But situational conventions limit their variability in use, and users would tend to treat the problem as one of deciding whether it is one or the other. The possibility that an utterance would communicate, at the same time, several quite distinct meanings is less obvious, because we tend to pay attention selectively and take the rest for granted. Some of the additional meanings are taken for granted because we assume that they do not vary. For example, one of the meanings of an utterance in a common language is that the speaker is a member of that language community. Between two members of that community, that meaning is taken for granted as unchanging.

Let us call a unit of communication a sign, and its "meaning" a referent, that is, something to which the communication refers. To an observer of communication in industry, a number of its features are unfamiliar, including the technical context, the nature and prevalence of channels in use, and so forth. The referents of the observed signs can then not be taken for granted. The following few paragraphs contain a classification of the possibilities. They include examples from an industrial sign language which are intended to illustrate why it is important to recognize these distinctions when it comes, for example, to deciding whether a piece of communication is technically *necessary* or *expressive*.

Morris (1955:71–88, 95–111) and Seboek (1962) have identified several classes of referents of a sign and of corresponding usages or functions. Their analyses have suggested to me the following categories.

1. A sign or utterance communicated between two persons may signify, or designate, some third person or object. Much technical communication between workers would give primacy to this type of referent. A head sawyer giving the sign for "2" directs the attention of the "setter" to the log on his carriage and to the controls. The "meaning" of the sign is interpretable through the setters response of making the log move forward by two inches.

2. The production of a sign can be taken "as itself a sign of some state of the producer" (Morris, 1955:71). An inexperienced sawmill worker will

signify, by the very fact of producing a technical hand sign, that he has finally mastered the language. By a subfeature of his sign he may indicate that he is angry.

3. A sign may describe a state of the receiver. The repetition or very deliberate production of a hand sign can tell an inexperienced relief man that the head sawyer feels he is a "dumb clod" who does not know better.

4. An utterance, by its form or its very production, tells about the nature of the relationship between the communicators. A specialized sign known only to two workers may suggest that they have known each other for some time. Incomplete or sloppy sign formation implies that A trusts B to respond correctly.

5. Expressions have always metacommunicative referents, by implying rules of sign formation, interpretation, and syntax, and by indicating the nature of the channel in use and the means of sifting information from noise.

6. The particular composition of common-language words is usually regarded as arbitrary. But in sign languages there are often identifiable sources of signs, in the sense that the sign is a symbolization of a source referent which is different from what its communication signifies. In the sawmill workers' sign language, for example, touching the ear lobe with the index finger is a symbol of "ear," but this gesture signifies "year." Similarly, rubbing index finger and thumb in the area slightly above and to the right of the mouth is a symbol of "moustache," but signifies "man."

Upon recognition of the multichannel, multifunction nature of communication, the distinction between technical and social, instrumental and expressive, uses of communication between workers becomes a matter of assigning primacy or greater importance to one or the other of the many elements and properties of observed activity. Because communication at work is socially motivated and technically constrained, the distinction becomes important in attempts to explain variations in communication rates.

The practical problems of sorting technical designation from social expression lie in the fact that both functions are sometimes accomplished in one utterance, and that familiarity and skill produce differences in redundancy. An important piece of machinery in a sawmill is a lift arm, called a dog, which pivots around a pin on one end. In order to tell the next man that the pin has broken, a worker will stick his right index finger into his left fist, and then move both hands as if breaking a stick. The first part of this composite sign can be elaborated into a simultaneous joke by moving the index finger in and out of the left fist several times—a modification of the ancient *mano in fica* (Critchley, 1939:82). Redundancy appeared in the repetition of numerical signs directed to a relief man, and in signs produced by a relief man, which were not observed by the regular operator. Are these communications technically necessary?

Difficulties of empirical determination aside, technical communication between workers serves the functions of the production system designed to convert and move material products. It enables workers to perform acts, and manipulate work pieces and equipment, in the required temporal and spatial order, and to change effort and select task elements to make up for variations in the performance of other workers. Technical communication tends to be designative and prescriptive, that is it will point to specific objects external to the communicators themselves and tell the recipient what to do. It tends to include feedback for corrective changes in work activity.

Nontechnical communication serves expressive functions. It meets the need for symbolization and reduction of boredom. It has the consequence of maintaining relations of influence and exchange; identifying and protecting the boundaries of a group; and teaching newcomers local customs.

One of the less noticed functions of communication is keeping a work group and its members in touch with other work groups and the larger organizational environment. Workers are officially related with other parts of the organization through their foreman and other higher-ups. A number of reports have demonstrated that supervisors communicate not only with superiors and subordinates, but also maintain frequent lateral relations. It was indicated above that work groups have relatively high rates of communication with outsiders. That fact suggests that workers maintain "external relations" of their own, and many work-group descriptions provide a wealth of incidental information on the nature of these relations.

In my interview study of subsample of 206 industrial workers in sawmills, a plywood mill, a pulp and paper mill, and logging operations on Vancouver Island, 66% said they get to talk to people other than their immediate workmates while they are actually working. 87% indicated that they talk to fellow workers before work begins, and a third give themselves more than ten minutes for that purpose. Workers manage to maintain contact with outsiders to their work group while they work, before work starts, and possibly during breaks as well. What other communicative links are there?

There are both particular places and jobs which serve as centers or carriers of information and gossip. In a steel mill, the control room from which an operator regulates the flow of hot air to the blast furnace attracts other workers, especially when it is cold outside (Popitz, 1957a:170). The tool crib in large machine shops brings workers from different sections together (Roy, 1954:259). There are also special jobs which require their incumbents to move from work place to work place and enable them to carry news from group to group. Roy (1960:162) likened the arrival of the pickup man to that of a daily passenger train in an isolated town, and described how the pickup man brought news of impending layoffs or changes in production orders, and "bits of information on plant employees told in a light vein." Similar links are formed by apprentices (Merk, 1963) and window dressers and porters in a department store (Bradney, 1957:182, 184).

A related type of communication channel can be found between workers within a section who may be unable to maintain direct communication. The channel is formed by workers who perform special functions which bring them into contact with various work-group members. Examples include: relief workers who substitute temporarily for those who want to leave a production line, as the "utility men" on auto assembly lines (Walker & Guest, 1952:73); the "burner spellman" on a seamless tubing mill (Walker, 1957:11); and inspectors, time checkers, and set-up men in machine shops (Roy, 1954: 258).

Other centers of cross-group information exchange can be found in the longshoremen's hiring hall (Philpott, 1964; Woodward, 1956:58–84), or among printers looking for work (Lipset, Trow & Coleman, 1956:127–129). Construction foremen's notebooks contain the names of potential work-crew members and represent another intergroup connection (Myers, 1946).

One of the more important functions served by these communicative connections between work groups is to carry information concerning job security, and to protect workers from external interference. Information about changes in production orders, expected layoffs, accidents, changing performance standards, and impending inspection, tends to be transmitted effectively, and these channels are used to protect the workers' own standards of performance and output equalization (Roy, 1954; Horsfall & Arensberg, 1949; Bensman & Gerver, 1963).

Technology and Communication

At the beginning of this chapter, I have identified the major dimensions of the technical and organizational environment in which communication at work is embedded. I have described the main forms which communication among workers can take, and then examined rates of communication and their distributions. Finally, the functions of communication in the work-place were considered.

We can now put these directions of inquiry together and ask how the technical environment influences rates of communication in its different forms. The relative effectiveness with which these forms of communication serve technical and social functions will help interpret the direction of influence of the dimensions of technology.

The main source of data in the following analysis was a project of direct observations of 156 Canadian workers while actually working, in thirty-seven production operations of twenty-eight firms. Both technical characteristics and communication rates were uniformly recorded by a number of observers. A secondary source of data was a subsample of 206 workers from a sample-survey interview study of adults working for pay in a Canadian industrial community. This subsample was restricted to men, wage earners, union members, below the level of foreman, who worked in logging, saw mills, a shingle mill, a plywood mill, a pulp and paper plant, and large-scale transportation and loading operations (Meissner, 1971).

In the "observation project" we concentrated only on work in central production operations. The "interview project" includes, in addition, persons who worked in inspection, maintenance, or transportation. Both studies cover a wide range of technological variation, from muscle work to very advanced mechanization, but little automation in the sense of self-regulating and integrated processes. The foundation of both projects was a previous study of systems of cooperation and communication among industrial workers (Meissner, 1969, 1970).

Mechanization. By definition, the machine component in the production process becomes greater as mechanization increases. The person-performed remainder must be fitted into the process, in order to get work done as technically designed. More control over events is built into production machinery with greater mechanization, and the workers' choices of action are reduced. Among the various means of verbal and nonverbal communication, ordinary speech amplified by corresponding body movement facilitates social conduct most fully. It is most variable, makes use of many channels, and requires the greatest degree of flexibility and choice. The constraints associated with greater mechanization, however, reduce variability and choice, and one would expect that the frequency of verbal communication declines with advancing mechanization.

Speech is the preferred mode of interpersonal communication, and nonverbal communication without speech is less desirable. It would therefore be expected that the rate of verbal communication will be higher than rates of nonverbal communication when there are few external restrictions and, particularly, when work is not mechanized.

The events of production processes are coordinated through communication. As mechanization increases, the requirement becomes more demanding for communication which coordinates workers' activities effectively. A sign of this requirement is the fact that in automated systems, communication is routinely accomplished in built-in feedback devices. At the various levels of mechanization, it is the human operators themselves who communicate. However, the availability of speech decreases with mechanization, and speech becomes less effective when greater mechanization demands more speed and precision. As a consequence, one would expect rates of nonverbal communication to increase with greater mechanization, to the extent that it serves technical functions.

Communication between workers also serves nontechnical functions. Particularly, it is a respite from the instrumental demands of production (as in joking), and these demands increase with more mechanization. Speech combined with gesture has greater expressive potential, but is limited by mechanization. To the extent that it has expressive possibilities, nonverbal communication would substitute for speech as mechanization increases.

Table 2 contains mean hourly frequencies of verbal communication, and the average frequencies of three types of nonverbal communication: gestural "signs," the "signals" transmitted through technical channels, and communication through "objects." It shows four degrees of "mechanization of production line," that is, of the process by which work pieces are moved between work stations. This dimension determines whether or not there is a sequence of work in a production line, and if there is a line, the extent of its mechanization. "Dead line" identifies manual movement of work pieces in a physically predetermined sequence, as on an unmechanized roller conveyor. On a "machine-feeding line" work pieces move through continuously running conveyors or the push from the output of automatic machines. It is typically occupied by

TABLE 2
MECHANIZATION OF PRODUCTION LINE AND FREQUENCIES OF COMMUNICATION

Mechanization of production line	(N)	Mean hourly frequency of communication by			
		Speech	Signs	Signals	Objects
No line	(45)	43.4	2.4	.7	23.5
Dead line	(23)	33.5	1.2	.0	112.1
Machine-feeding line	(47)	29.7	3.2	.4	359.4
Remote-control line	(41)	5.5	36.5	11.2	466.2

Note: Tables 2–5 contain frequencies of communication emitted and received by each worker. They include communication with outsiders to the work group.

machine feeders and unloaders; machine operators who set up and monitor a machine and sometimes help feeding or unloading; and workers on the line, packing, labelling, or stacking work objects. On a "remote-control line" most workers are removed from direct contact with work pieces, but they control work-piece movement into and between machines by levers, push-buttons, and foot pedals.

Table 2 shows that the average hourly frequency of verbal communication (speech) at the lowest level of production-line mechanization is higher than the frequencies of three types of nonverbal communication combined. It also indicates that verbal communication declines with advancing mechanization, and that all forms of nonverbal communication increase.

In addition to mechanization of product movement, there is also mechanization of the individual task. Most simply, one can distinguish jobs which involve hand work, and work with manually controlled hand tools, from jobs in which a worker operates a machine. One would expect that task mechanization would have effects on communication similar to those of mechanization of production line.

Table 3 shows the relative effect of both production-line mechanization and mechanization of individual tasks. In that table, communication by gestural "signs" and technical "signals" have been combined. The table indicates that there is a major reduction of verbal communication only when both types of mechanization are high, and that there is a large jump in the rate of nonverbal communication by signs and signals only under the same joint condition. The main effect on communication by "objects," however, comes from production-line mechanization alone.

TABLE 3
JOINT EFFECTS OF MECHANIZATION OF PRODUCTION LINE
AND MECHANIZATION OF TASK

Mechanization of Task	Mechanization of Production Line				Difference
	Low*	(N)	High	(N)	
Mean frequency of speech					
Hand work	39.8	(49)	25.9	(49)	− 13.9
Machine operation	40.6	(19)	9.1	(39)	− 31.5
Difference	+ .8		−16.8		− 17.6**
Mean frequency of signs and signals					
Hand work	1.6	(49)	7.7	(49)	6.1
Machine operation	4.6	(19)	44.7	(39)	40.1
Difference	3.0		37.0		34.0**
Mean frequency of object communication					
Hand work	72.0	(49)	440.7	(49)	368.7
Machine operation	5.7	(19)	369.5	(39)	363.8
Difference	−66.3		−71.2		− 4.9**

* "Low" mechanization of production line includes "No line" and "Dead line"; "High" mechanization includes 'Machine-feeding line" and "Remote-control line."
** The difference of the differences is a measure of interaction effect. In the case of speech and of communication by signs and signals, a large part of the effect is due to the simultaneous occurrence of a high level of mechanization of both production line and individual task.

Temporal and spatial constraints on communication. As mechanization increases it becomes necessary to fit workers' activities more tightly into the production process, and to constrain their choices of action. The most obvious dimensions of this constraint are time and space. Temporal constraints consist of work speed and pacing by machine or production line. Spatial constraint on an individual's activity has its source in confinement to a single working location.

The components of a worker's task are bounded by an operation cycle. When speed increases, less time is available in each cycle for communication. Normal conversational expressions become less probable because they take more time than is available, while a hand sign, light signal, or the movement of an object tend to be quicker. Greater speed would tend to make coordination more crucial and would require greater use of nonverbal means of communication.

A task paced by machine or production line ties activities to the operation cycle, and requires more focused attention. It takes attention away from conversation partners, and makes it less likely that facial expressions and gestures can aid verbal communication.

When a task confines a worker to a specific narrow location, it is not possible to walk to someone else and talk. Spatial confinement is often more easily overcome by nonverbal communication.

Table 4 describes the effects of these constraints on rates of communication. Spatial confinement, machine pacing, and greater work speed, markedly reduce verbal communication and increase the rate of communication by the three nonverbal means.

In Table 5, the joint effects of production-line mechanization and technical constraints are being assessed. In that table, spatial confinement, pacing, and work speed were combined in a simple index, where a "high" degree of constraint combines the extreme condition on all three components. The table shows that a relatively high rate of verbal communication occurs only if both

TABLE 4
SPATIAL CONFINEMENT, PACING, WORK SPEED, AND COMMUNICATION FREQUENCIES

Technical constraints	(N)	Mean hourly frequency of communication by			
		Speech	Signs	Signals	Objects
Spatial confinement					
Not confined	(70)	40.1	2.9	1.2	57.1
Confined	(86)	17.9	18.3	5.0	414.5
Pacing by machine					
or production line					
Not paced	(50)	42.9	2.6	.6	28.5
Paced	(106)	20.8	15.6	4.5	360.5
Number of work cycles					
per hour (cycle duration)					
12 cycles p. hr. or less					
(5 min. or longer)	(31)	42.9	1.8	1.0	2.4
13–240 cycles p. hr.					
(15 sec.–5 min.)	(64)	28.1	3.7	2.7	99.0
over 240 cycles p. hr.					
(under 15 sec.)	(61)	20.0	24.4	5.0	545.8

TABLE 5
JOINT EFFECTS OF MECHANIZATION AND SPATIAL AND TEMPORAL CONSTRAINTS

Confinement, Pacing, and Speed	Mechanization of Production Line				Difference
	Low	(N)	High	(N)	
Mean frequency of speech					
Low	43.0	(59)	20.6	(23)	− 22.4
High*	20.6	(9)	17.7	(65)	− 2.9
Difference	− 22.4		− 2.9		19.5**
Mean frequency of signs and signals					
Low	2.7	(59)	13.0	(23)	10.3
High	1.0	(9)	28.1	(65)	27.1
Difference	− 1.7		15.1		16.8**
Mean frequency of object communication					
Low	36.1	(59)	110.3	(23)	74.2
High	167.8	(9)	514.9	(65)	347.1
Difference	131.7		404.6		272.9**

* The category of "high" constraint by confinement, pacing, and speed includes workers who are confined to their work station, whose work is paced by machine or production line, and whose work speed is higher than sixty operation cycles per hour. The "low" category includes work where one or more of these conditions is not in force.
** The difference of the differences is a measure of interaction effect. For all three types of communication, the interaction effect is considerable, and it is the combination of both mechanization and spatio-temporal constraints which makes the main difference.

mechanization and constraint are low. Similarly, relatively high rates of nonverbal communication are found most predominantly where both mechanization and constraint are high.

This examination of the joint effects of mechanization and the constraints of time and space has indicated that only their *combination* makes a clear difference in rates of communication. As mechanization progresses, workers are more and more relieved of the physical burdens of work, but they pay the price of reduced freedom of movement and choice of timing. In the process they have far less chance to talk, but they make up for the loss in a limited way by increased reliance on nonverbal means of communication.

One may ask if the results shown so far, of the effects of technology on workers' communication, are not limited to the particular locations, industries, and data-gathering methods of the observation study. Two other studies lend themselves to a comparable, though more limited, analysis. The first is the "interview project" already mentioned, which contained three questions about social interaction while work is in progress. Table 6 shows the effects on social interaction, according to these three questions, of machine pacing, spatial confinement, and the difference between work in production and work in maintenance or transportation. The table indicates that the proportion of workers who can talk during their work declines consistently with higher technical constraints. This finding corresponds with the data in Table 4 obtained by direct observation in different locations and industries.

A third set of data comes from a study by self-administered questionnaire of several thousand industrial workers in Britain (Hedley, 1971; Dubin, et al., 1975). Table 7 compares the data of these three studies, regarding the effect of pacing and spatial confinement on the proportions of workers who can

TABLE 6
TECHNICAL CONSTRAINTS AND SOCIAL INTERACTION WHILE WORKING (Interview study)

Social Interaction While Working	Machine Pacing		Technical Constraints Spatial Confinement		Constraints of Work Type	
	Low	High*	Low	High**	Low	High***
1. "While you are actually doing your work, do you get to talk to other people, besides the ones you work with?"						
Can talk to other people (percent)	79	49	79	59	84	53
2. "How many people can you talk to while you are working?"						
Can talk to one or more (percent)	88	70	87	72	87	74
3. "What do you talk about? Do you only talk about work, or only about other things? What do you talk about most?"						
Talk about something (percent)	91	72	90	75	92	76
(N = 100%)	(114)	(92)	(101)	(105)	(86)	(120)

* Paced by machine or production line.
** Confined to fixed position or small area.
*** High = work in central production process; Low = work in maintenance or transportation.
Note: Forming an index of constraints (where "high" is a high value on all three indicators) and of social interaction (where "high" is a positive answer on all three questions) has the following results:

	Percent "high" interaction	(N)
Low constraint	67	(133)
High constraint	36	(73)

Percentage difference d = − 31; chi squared = 17.5; p = .00005

talk during their work with fellow workers. It shows a consistently negative effect of temporal and spatial constraints on verbal communication. The results vary, however, by the method of obtaining data. From direct observation at the work-place, to interviews in workers' homes, to questionnaires ticked off by workers themselves, there is increased distance from the recorded events; greater reliance on workers' interpretations; and reduced specificity of information. As a result, the proportions of workers counted as talking on the job increases, and the difference made by technical constraints becomes smaller. Even with these procedural differences, these are several sets of consistent results for a variety of industries, places, times and research methods, and they correspond with the findings of earlier case studies (Meissner, 1969:229, 231).

The data discussed to this point describe characteristics of *individual* workers and their communication with anyone around them at work. They have dealt with the pacing and speed of an individual task, and the spatial confinement associated with it. We now turn to an analysis of communicative relations in *pairs* of workers. Taking the pair as the unit of analysis makes it possible to assess the effects of constraints which describe technical *relations* between two workers.

The identification of relevant pairs is not problematic when a relatively small work group has clear boundaries in architecture, functional relations and work-flow interruptions, and the territory of a supervisor. But on an extended production line, particularly where line segments form a complex system, the

TABLE 7
EFFECTS OF PACING AND CONFINEMENT ON VERBAL
COMMUNICATION IN THREE STUDIES

Measures of Verbal Communication	Constraints of Pacing and Confinement*			Overall Effect
	Low (not paced, and mobile)	Medium (paced or confined)	High (paced and confined)	
	(N)	(N)	(N)	
1. OBSERVATIONS of 156 Vancouver production workers, sixty minutes of direct observation				
Observed talking (%)	76 (62)	40 (20)	36 (74)	−40
2. INTERVIEWS of 206 Vancouver Island manual workers, "How many people can you talk to while you are working?"				
Talk to one or more (%)	88 (88)	87 (39)	67 (79)	−21
3. QUESTIONNAIRES filled out by 2257 British workers** "I can talk to the people around me when I'm working"				
Yes (%)	93 (337)	82 (682)	77 (1238)	−16

* Indicators of pacing and confinement were as follows:
Pacing "high":   1. Observation study: Paced by machine or production line and work cycle of one minute or less
                 2. Interview study: Paced by machine or production line ("Do you decide on your own work speed or what determines how you use your time?")
                 3. Questionnaire study: Yes ("My job requires that I work at a certain speed.")
Confinement "high":   1. Observation study: Confined to own work station.
                      2. Interview study: Confined to single position or small area ("Do you have a fixed work place, or do you move around during your work?")
                      3. Questionnaire study: No ("I can move around the factory while doing my job.")
** Data kindly supplied by R. Dubin, A. Hedley, and T. Taveggia.

nature of a work "group" is more open to question, and the selection of worker pairs in them requires additional criteria. In previous research, attention has been drawn to "floating groups" on assembly lines, where there is a unique "group" for each worker, and successive overlap between the groups of adjacent workers (Walker & Guest, 1952:72; Zaleznik, 1956:121; Meissner, 1969:217).

In such a system it would not be meaningful to include all possible pair relations in the analysis, because a very large number of pairs would have only the remotest technical relation and no possible communication. For the data of my observation study, a pair of workers was taken into account in the analysis only when at least: (1) the two workers could see each other, or (2) the two tasks were directly functionally dependent, or (3) the two work stations were directly connected by work flow, with no others intervening.

The previous individual data included communication with outsiders to the group. Analysis of pairs restricts data to communication between workers in a pair, and thus to members of the work group. Consequently, the communication rates shown will be lower.

We have so far identified spatial confinement as one dimension of spatial constraint. Another dimension is the distance between the work stations of two workers. One would expect that verbal communication decreases with greater distance, and communication by nonverbal means would increase to the extent that these means are capable of overcoming distance.

Figure 5 shows the effect of distance on the proportion of worker pairs who were observed to communicate with each other by the four means of communication. The proportion of workers in pairs who talked to each other in sixty minutes of observation time consistently declines from 65% in distances of twenty-five feet or under, to 13% where their distance is over fifty feet. In contrast, communication by technical signals and objects increases monotonically with distance. Proportionate use of gestural signs increases in the lower distance range, and decreases again where distances are greater, suggesting that sign communication is sensitive to greater distances where visibility of detail becomes impaired.

The limitations of distance for verbal communication can be overcome at least to some extent, if workers are not confined to their work stations and can move closer to a communication partner. The relative influence of distance and

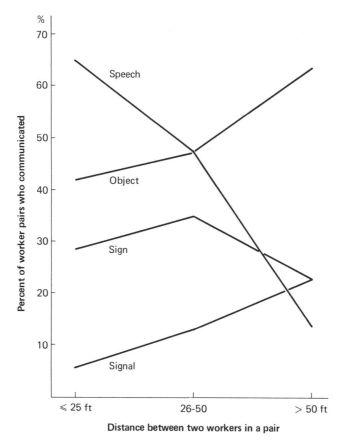

FIGURE 5. Distance and incidence of four types of communication in 251 pairs of production workers during 60 minutes of observation.

spatial confinement on verbal communication is described in Figure 6. Both dimensions of spatial constraint have an independent, additive effect. As a way of describing the magnitude of the consequences of the two factors combined, only 5% of the workers talk to each other who are confined to fixed positions which are more than fifty feet apart, and 80% who are near each other *and* can move around.

Communication by speech and gestural signs requires visibility, and visibility is influenced by distance and confinement. Verbal communication also requires favorable conditions of audibility, and noise would tend to reduce the *effective* distance for communication. In Figure 7, distance and confinement have been combined in a three point index. In the cases of "low" constraint the distance is twenty-five feet or less and at least one of the two workers is not confined. "High" constraint includes distances of over twenty-five feet and confinement of both workers. Noise was measured on a crude four-point scale, and "noisy"

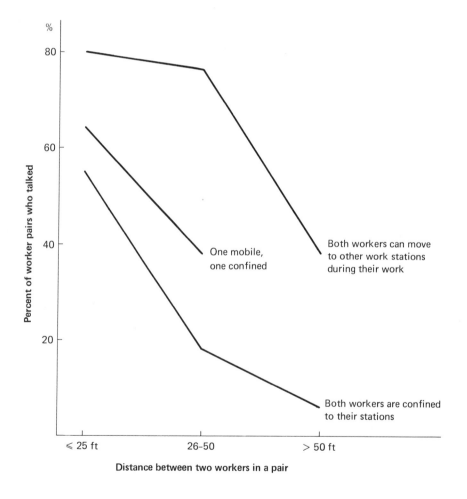

FIGURE 6. Distance, spatial confinement and incidence of verbal communication in 251 pairs of production workers during 60 minutes of observation.

in Figure 7 includes the cases with the highest noise level, while "quiet" refers to the cases with the remaining, relatively less noisy three values on the scale.

According to Figure 7, the effects of noise and spatial constraint interact: spatial constraints make a great deal of difference in quiet circumstances; but where it is noisy, there is much less verbal communication to begin with, and spatial constraints make less of a difference.

Constraints of function. Mechanization describes the balance between the task components performed by workers and those performed by machinery. Pacing and speed describe a relation between the worker's task and the machinery on which it is performed. Spatial confinement describes a relation of worker and work station, and distance a spatial relation between the work stations of two workers. When considering communication between two workers, it becomes also important to take account of the functional relations between their tasks and work stations, because they form the basis for necessary and voluntary cooperation and the communication facilitating it.

Modern industrial work is characterized by the allocation of tasks in varying degrees of differentiation. Differentiated task allocation has consequences for relations between tasks on several dimensions. As tasks are distributed for the accomplishment of a common outcome, some tasks become *dependent* on

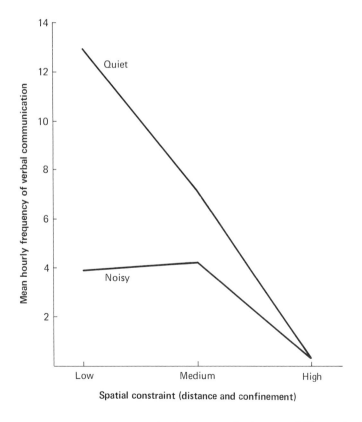

FIGURE 7.   Spatial constraint, noise, and verbal communication rate of 251 production workers.

the performance of other tasks. When operations must be performed in sequence, work stations will be connected by *work flow*, often facilitated through the mechanization of work-piece movement. The degree of task differentiation and mechanization will influence the probability that two workers perform the *same* or *different tasks*, and the *number* of workers in a work group.

Following is an examination of the effects on communication between two workers; of work flow between their work stations; interdependence of their tasks; the differentiation of their tasks; and number of workers in their group.

The dimensions of functional relations form complex patterns. Workers unconnected by work flow can be independent and perform (1) *separate* tasks, or their tasks can be mutually dependent in a (2) *team* relation of simultaneous cooperation. When a worker's task succeeds that of another worker in a work flow, the performance of the second task can be directly dependent on the performance of the first, in a (3) *tandem* relation of sequential cooperation; or they can be relatively independent, because the performance of one task is (4) *contingent* upon a third task which intervenes in sequence between the two. These four categories of combinations of work-flow and dependence will be applied to the following analysis.

For technical reasons one would expect functionally dependent pairs to communicate more frequently, because dependent tasks tend to require cooperation facilitated by communication. At the same time, dependent pairs without work flow (teams) are less subject to technical constraints, and would be more likely to communicate verbally. Work flow between the work stations of sequentially dependent pairs (tandem) tends to mean increased technical constraints and more reliance on nonverbal means.

In Table 8 we find that verbal communication is highest for "team" relations, and nonverbal communication for "tandem" relations. Nonverbal communication is concentrated in pairs related by both work flow and direct functional dependence, and is quite low in all other cases. Verbal communication is least in pairs in "contingent" work flow relations, that is, between workers who are functionally more distant from each other.

Where work is connected by work flow, tasks tend to be highly differentiated, with each worker performing a different segment. (This fact has been

TABLE 8
WORK FLOW, TASK DEPENDENCE, AND COMMUNICATION
BETWEEN WORKERS IN A PAIR
(Observation study)

Functional connection between two tasks*				Mean hourly frequency of communication by		
Work flow	Dependence of task		(N)	Speech	Signs & Signals	Objects
No flow	Dependent	(team)	(26)	19.8	1.5	.5
No flow	Independent	(separate)	(38)	7.1	.5	.2
Flow	Dependent	(tandem)	(120)	5.8	7.4	150.7
Flow	Independent	(contingent)**	(67)	2.1	1.1	24.6

* The tasks of two workers in a pair are connected by work flow if work pieces move from one to the other, directly or with other tasks intervening. They are dependent when one task can only be performed if the other has been, or is being, performed, with no other tasks intervening.
** "Contingent" pairs include workers in a work flow sequence between whose tasks at least one other task intervenes; their functional relation is mediated by, or contingent upon, the performance of other tasks.

expressed in the title of Friedmann's book: *Le travail en miettes*—"work in bits," Friedmann, 1956.) Among the pairs in the observation data connected by work flow, only 5% involve two workers doing the same task. In contrast, 80% have the same tasks in "teams" of dependent tasks not connected by work flow. Thus, pairs with different tasks are unusual in "team" relations (dependence and no work flow), and pairs with the same tasks are unusual in "tandem" relations (dependence and work flow connection).

In the different combinations of work flow and dependence of tasks, task differentiation has varying effects on communication. In the two "unusual" conditions just mentioned, verbal communication tends to be higher than in their corresponding more "usual" condition. In Table 9 we find that verbal communication in "team" pairs is higher when the two workers perform different tasks (a rate of 27.8 as against 17.9), suggesting that their coordinative requirements are greater and demand more communication. The same effect can be seen in "tandem" pairs for *nonverbal* communication which, in these cases, is the technically more important and effective means (a rate of 7.8 versus 1.5). However, in the "unusual" condition of tandem pairs with un-

TABLE 9
TASK DIFFERENTIATION, WORK FLOW, TASK DEPENDENCE
AND COMMUNICATION IN PAIRS
(Observation study)

Work flow and task dependence		Mean hourly frequency of communication by							
		Speech				Signs & Signals			
		Two tasks same	(N)	Two tasks differ	(N)	Two tasks same	(N)	Two tasks differ	(N)
No flow									
Dependent	(team)	17.9	(21)	27.8	(5)	1.3	(21)	2.0	(5)
Independent	(separate)	11.3	(17)	3.8	(21)	.9	(17)	.2	(21)
Flow									
Dependent	(tandem)	17.7	(6)	5.2	(114)	1.5	(6)	7.8	(114)
Independent	(contingent)	3.3	(3)	2.0	(64)	.0	(3)	1.2	(64)

	Differences between means of*	
	Speech	Signs & Signals
Work flow		
—no other factors controlled	− 7.8	4.3
—with task dependence controlled	−10.2	3.7
—with task dependence and differentiation controlled	−12.0	3.0
Task dependence		
—no other factors controlled	4.4	5.5
—with work flow controlled	6.0	4.9
—with work flow and task differentiation controlled	6.3	5.0
Task differentiation		
—no other factors controlled	−9.9	3.7
—with work flow controlled	−9.9	3.6
—with task dependence controlled	−8.2	3.1
—with work flow and task dependence controlled	−6.4	3.3

* With other factors controlled for, the weighted average difference between mean frequencies is shown.

differentiated tasks, verbal communication is highest (17.7) in comparison with all other work-flow connected pairs (5.2; 3.3; 2.0). These cases are "throw-backs" in technological development, where workers perform relatively heavy manual work in a highly mechanized context (an example is a pair of workers in a rolling mill who transfer hot-rolled reinforcing bars from one roll stand to another by use of long tongs.) Task differentiation makes little difference for verbal communication in "contingent" pairs where the level of communication is low to begin with. Finally, "separate" pairs have nothing by way of work flow or dependence to connect the two workers. Performing the same task, however, is the only thing they have in common, and that fact makes for more verbal communication between them (11.3) than if their tasks are different (3.8).

In these complex combinations of functional relations and their effects, it is useful to ask what difference each condition makes when the others are "held constant." The bottom of Table 9 shows the difference (positive or negative) between mean communication rates for each of the three dimensions of functional constraints in worker pairs. In each case, the first row of two figures indicates the difference associated with that factor with no other dimensions controlled for. Then the other factors are introduced as controls, where the figures are weighted average differences. The last line under each factor indicates the independent effect which that factor has on the rate of speech and of signs and signals.

Each of the three factors makes an independent difference. In addition, we find that the effects of work flow and dependence on speech increase as the other factors are introduced as controls (from -7.8 to -12.0 for work flow, and from 4.4 to 6.3 for dependence), while the effect of task differentiation is decreased as other factors are controlled (from -9.9 to -6.4). Finally, work flow and differentiation affect verbal communication negatively and nonverbal communication positively. Task dependence tends to *increase both* verbal and nonverbal communication.

Functional relations between jobs have tended to be lumped together in the research literature, and have even been combined with social interaction (Sayles, 1958:69–76; Meissner, 1969:253–254). The above results suggest that the dimensions of functional relations and different means of communication need to be distinguished. Particularly, work flow constitutes a connection between work stations, and dependence a relation between tasks, and these have a differential effect on communication which is a relationship between workers.

When task differentiation has reached the point, at high levels of mechanization, where each task is performed by only one person, a new development occurs which constitutes a form of reintegration of functions, by means of technical changes. Our observation study contains data from five sawmills in British Columbia, all of them highly mechanized operations in which the huge logs of the Pacific Coast are converted to lumber. At the core of these sawmills are a number of technical functions which must be performed in order to cut logs into shapes which, through further processing, become standardized timber or lumber. These functions include: setting the log in position on a carriage for cutting; cutting logs into large slabs on a head rig; guiding these slabs onto a roller conveyor; shifting them to a chain conveyor; cutting the edges off the slab; controlling movement away from the edger; and cutting up scrap pieces and controlling their movement to a chipper or burner. The five sawmills can be ordered such that these functions are progressively combined in fewer tasks through the relocation of operating controls. For example, the job of the setter is being eliminated by adding a number of hydraulic controls to the levers and push buttons of the head sawyer. The number of persons performing the common bundle of functions varies from seven to three in these five mills, as indicated in Table 10.

TABLE 10
TECHNICAL CHANGE IN SAWMILLS: EFFECTS OF REINTEGRATION OF TECHNICAL FUNCTIONS ON NONVERBAL COMMUNICATION

Sawmill	Number of workers Performing Task Bundle	Hourly Frequency of Communication per Worker by		
		Signs	Signals	Signs & Signals
Mill 1	7	121	28	149
Mill 2	6	78	0	78
Mill 3	5	7	15	22
Mill 4	3	3	3	6
Mill 5	3	5	1	6

We focus here on communication by manual signs and technical signals, and observe how the rate of these forms of communication is reduced as functions are combined (there is hardly any verbal communication and much routine communication through work objects in these operations). Table 10 contains communication rates *per worker*. It shows that the number of signs and signals emitted and received declines from 149 per hour when seven workers perform a set of tasks, to six per hour in the two mills where the same task bundle is performed by only three workers. As the number of technical functions controlled by one worker increases, the attention requirements become more demanding and there is less time for communication; more coordination is built into the machinery and less communication is necessary; distances between workers increase as fewer of them are spread over the same equipment-occupied space; and the size of the work group is of course reduced. The combination of these changes explain the reduction in nonverbal communication rate.

Group size.   In verbal conversations, the average frequency of participation per member tends to decrease the greater the number of members of a group (Thomas and Fink, 1965:527–528; Bales and Borgatta, 1965:498). In ordinary conversation groups, one person often communicates to several others, and there tends to be relatively equal access to other members. The technical constraints of industrial work limit access to some other work-group members and favor two-person communication. In our observation data, the number of utterances directed to more than one other worker was extremely small and had no effect on the results.

Figure 8 shows the effect of work-group size on the frequency of verbal communication of individual workers with anyone (including outsiders), and of pairs of workers with each other (and therefore excluding outsiders). Communication decreases the greater the number of workers in the group. This finding is less pronounced for the individual data where the effect of number

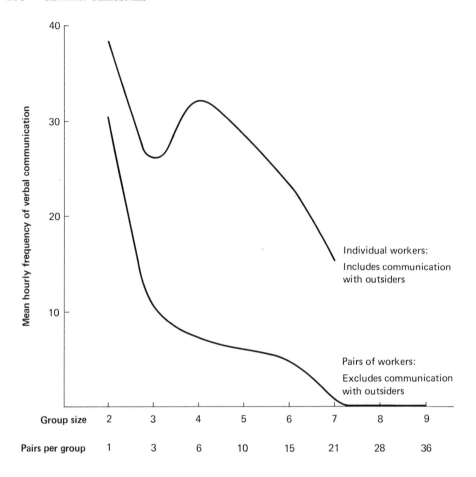

FIGURE 8. Group size and verbal communication; 156 individual workers and 251 pairs of workers.

is modified by inclusion of communication with outsiders. The effect is clear and monotonic for pairs.

The data shown above for five sawmills already suggested that nonverbal communication frequency is higher in the larger groups, and that effect was associated with functional reintegration of tasks. The same relation holds for all the observation data, except that the differences made by group size are smaller and more irregular. The general direction of effect is shown in Table 11 by grouping group sizes. This finding is similar to those shown for other constraints: Verbal communication decreases with group size, and frequency of communication by nonverbal means increases.

Noise. Much industrial work is dominated by the noise of high-speed motors, rumbling conveyors, banging sheet metal, the screech of cutting tools, the whine of saws, explosive bursts of flame from smelters or welding rods. If one

TABLE 11

GROUP SIZE AND VERBAL AND NONVERBAL COMMUNICATION (Observation project)

Type of data	Number of workers in the group	(N)	Mean hourly frequency of communication by		
			Speech	Signs & Signals	Objects
Individual workers:	2–3	(48)	29.0	7.6	197.6
communications with	4–5	(83)	29.2	13.8	247.8
all others (including	6 & more	(25)	21.4	31.2	383.6
outsiders)					
Pairs of workers:	2–3	(35)	13.4	2.2	65.5
communication between	4–5	(136)	6.7	3.8	74.2
two workers (excluding	6 & more	(80)	3.1	5.4	92.0
outsiders)					

Note: Workers on production lines often form "floating" groups, where the composition of the group varies from person to person. In these data, the "group" of an individual worker includes another person in the section under observation when the two workers can see each other or when they are directly connected by work flow or task dependence. The "group" of a pair includes the two workers in the pair and each other person in the section under observation with whom at least one of the two is related by one of these criteria of visibility or technical connection of their tasks.

were to ask why, in some work-places, workers depend primarily on nonverbal communication, an obvious answer may well be that it is too noisy to talk. However, matters are not so simple. Our observations include newspaper-press operators who can cite chapter and verse on the relation between press-rpm. and decibel level and know at what point ear drums will burst. In fact, they whisper into each other's ears to protect their ear drums, and the average verbal communication rate for these five men is 17.6 per hour, while the frequency of communication by signs and signals is 10.2. A second case is a shop where cylindrical tanks are fabricated from sheet metal. The average rate of speech of these men is 39.2 per hour, and there is no communication by signs and signals.

Both of these operations were rated as "very noisy" during our observations, and yet the principal form of communication was verbal. There can be no question that noise will tend to reduce verbal communication and increase the use of nonverbal means. But in view of these two examples, additional factors are required to explain differences in the rates of nonverbal and verbal communication more fully.

Tables 12 and 13 indicate the relative effect of noise and each of the three sets of technical constraint we have examined before. The effect of noise on verbal communication is greater when work is technically least constrained than when technical constraints are high. The differences by noise in the last column of Table 12 become smaller with increasing constraints of time (pacing and work speed), space (distance and confinement), and function (work flow and dependence). Conversely, noise has less effect on nonverbal communication where technical constraints are low (Table 13).

If one were to argue that the effects of technical constraints can be explained by noise, one would expect that the differences made by each of the technical constraints would disappear when noise is introduced as an additional factor. What we find instead in Table 12 is that the differences by temporal, spatial and functional constraints tend to increase somewhat (from the overall difference shown on the left) in relatively more quiet working conditions, and

TABLE 12
JOINT EFFECTS ON VERBAL COMMUNICATION BETWEEN TWO WORKERS IN A PAIR OF
NOISE AND THE CONSTRAINTS OF TIME, SPACE AND FUNCTION (Observation project)

Constraints	Overall mean	(N)	Quiet	(N)	Noisy*	(N)	Difference by noise
Pacing and work speed							
Low temporal constraint	9.8	(96)	12.1	(69)	3.9	(27)	− 8.2
High temporal constraint	4.4	(155)	6.4	(86)	2.1	(69)	− 4.3
Difference	− 5.4		− 5.7		− 1.8		
Distance and confinement							
Low spatial constraint	10.9	(75)	13.0	(57)	3.9	(18)	− 9.1
Medium spatial constraint	6.3	(126)	7.4	(86)	4.2	(40)	− 3.2
High spatial constraint	.2	(50)	.2	(12)	.3	(38)	.1
Difference Low–High	−10.7		−12.8		− 3.6		
Work flow and dependence							
No flow—Dependent	19.8	(26)	22.0	(23)	2.7	(3)	−19.3
—Independent	7.1	(38)	7.3	(36)	4.0	(2)	− 3.3
Flow—Dependent	5.8	(120)	8.3	(63)	3.0	(57)	− 5.3
—Independent	2.1	(67)	2.4	(33)	1.8	(34)	− .6
Weighted average difference							
by work flow	−10.2		− 9.8		− .6		
by task dependence	6.0		9.2		1.1		

* Noise was crudely measured on a four-point scale, from quiet to very noisy. In the above dichotomization, "noisy" contains the pairs of workers in the most noisy situations, with the highest value on the scale; "quiet" combines the remaining three less noisy values on the scale.

are reduced substantially at a higher level of noise. Similarly, the effects of technical constraints on nonverbal communication shown in Table 13 increase with noise, and virtually disappear in quiet conditions.

As in previous analyses we find here an interaction effect. Nonverbal communication tends to be most frequent when a high noise level is combined with a high degree of constraint, and the combination of quiet and low constraint produces the highest frequencies of verbal communication.

FOREMEN'S COMMUNICATION

From the mid-1940s, articles began to appear with titles like "The man in the middle" (Gardner and Whyte, 1945), "Master and victim of double talk" (Roethlisberger, 1945), "Marginal man of industry" (Wray, 1949), and "Member of two organizational families" (Mann and Dent, 1954). They depicted the foreman as a person between two lovers (and their families to boot), who is exposed to conflicting demands for attention and loyalty. A study of auto assembly foremen appropriately coined the term "shock absorber" (Walker, Guest and Turner, 1956:24). The circle of foremen's companions was enlarged with the discovery of their "horizontal" relations (Simpson, 1959; Jasinski, 1956).

Meanwhile, some empiricists wanted to know "what a foreman really does" (Guest, 1956:478) and, instead of interpreting expectations, found out with whom foremen actually talk and how much, by observing their activities first-

TABLE 13
JOINT EFFECTS ON COMMUNICATION BY SIGNS AND SIGNALS BETWEEN TWO
WORKERS IN A PAIR OF NOISE AND THE CONSTRAINTS OF
TIME, SPACE, AND FUNCTION
(Observation project)

| | Mean hourly frequency of signs and signals | | | | | | |
Constraints	Overall mean	(N)	Quiet	(N)	Noisy	(N)	Difference by noise
Pacing and work speed							
Low temporal constraint	1.5	(96)	.5	(69)	4.3	(27)	3.8
High temporal constraint	5.6	(155)	.6	(86)	12.0	(69)	11.4
Difference	4.1		.1		7.7		
Distance and confinement							
Low spatial constraint	.6	(75)	.5	(57)	.8	(18)	.3
Medium spatial constraint	6.3	(126)	.6	(86)	18.5	(40)	17.9
High spatial constraint	3.8	(50)	.0	(12)	5.0	(38)	5.0
Difference Low—High	3.2		− .5		4.2		
Work flow and dependence							
No flow—Dependent	1.5	(26)	1.0	(23)	4.7	(3)	3.7
—Independent	.5	(38)	.1	(36)	8.5	(2)	8.4
Flow—Dependent	7.4	(120)	.7	(63)	14.9	(57)	14.2
—Independent	1.1	(67)	1.1	(33)	1.9	(34)	1.6
Weighted average difference							
by work flow	3.7		− .1		3.9		
by task dependence	4.9		.6		12.1		

hand. Others discovered that the number of workers whom foremen supervise varied with the continuity with which products moved through operations (Woodward, 1965:62), and that the communication practices of foremen were affected by production technology (Lipstreu and Reed, 1964).

This section examines the composition of activities and tells us where the foremen's communication fits into these activities; how much of it there is; with whom it takes place; and to what extent the records of activities vary according to work-place and method of obtaining data. Having looked at communication among rank-and-file workers in the previous section, it is interesting to focus on the communication between foremen and workers. How much of the foreman's communication is addressed to subordinates, and what chances does each worker have of talking with the foreman? In this context, a few factors are introduced as important: the exercise of supervision below the foreman level; the foreman's span of control; the time the foreman spends in the vicinity of the workers; and the technical constraints which limit the workers' chances to communicate.

In the preceding analysis of workers' communication, a number of dimensions of the technical and organizational environment were identified as important influences. The foreman works in the same environment, but the relevant characteristics of that environment differ, in correspondence with pronounced differences between the jobs of production workers and foremen. By looking at communication within the activity structure of foremen, we will consider the effects of the constraints and demands of the foreman's work-place. Workers'

preferences about amount of contact with foremen, and the problems of ambivalence in these preferences, are a matter of further interest.

A substantial part of the following analysis relies on data from Merner's
(1970) study of fifty-eight foremen in nineteen production plants in Vancouver.
He recorded the activities of each foreman for four periods of thirty minutes,
spreading these periods over the working day. The fifty-one foremen included
in the analysis were salaried, not union members, and considered the first-line
supervisors of management. Seven "working foremen" were omitted. They
were paid hourly wages, were covered by union contract, and spent substantial
parts of their day in manual work. Foremen were selected from a sample of
manufacturing firms representing four types of production technology (unit,
batch, mass, and process production; Woodward, 1965). The tables are the
result of my own analysis of the data which were kindly made available by
the author.

Communication and the Foreman's Activities

The foreman's job is communication, more so than supervising in the sense
of "overseeing," and it is predominantly concerned with production. This conclusion is consistently supported by the data from studies of eleven kinds of
production operations in Canada, Britain and the United States, as shown in
Tables 14 and 15. In the data obtained by continuous observation (Table 14),
the time which foremen spend in direct communication with others ranges
from one-third to one-half of the working day. With paperwork included as
communication, the proportion goes up to a range of 43% to 55%.

The proportions for communication in the study of English firms by
Thurley and Hamblin (1963) are consistently lower, but still constitute the
largest category (Table 15). The differences between the sets of data in the
two tables can be due to differences in research method, and the actual behavior of foremen who might be more tight-mouthed in Britain than in North
America. In Thurley and Hamblin's time sampling, the nature of an activity
was determined at randomly selected points in time. An average of 7% of
the time, they could not find the foreman, and 11% of the time they found
him taking a break which did not include "personal" activities. One could
imagine that communication took place during a good part of these times
which would raise the communication percentage. Six brewery foremen seem
to have taken enormous breaks, amounting to an average of more than one
and one-half hours a day.

Time taken up by sociable conversation is small indeed, as shown at the
bottom of Table 14, a surprising observation in a period of "human relations"
and sensitivity training. In contrast, around half of the foremen's time is spent
in activities concerning production. Communication is the major activity of
foremen, and production their principal concern. Grossly simplifying the data,
about half of the time foremen are talking and half of the time they are doing
other things. About half of their talking and half of their other activities have
to do with production.

Activity distributions are shown separately according to type of production technology in Tables 14 and 15. Within the study by Merner, the study
by Thurley and Hamblin, and between the two studies by Yanouzas and Guest,

TABLE 14
FOREMEN'S TIME BUDGETS OF ACTIVITY IN DIFFERENT PRODUCTION TYPES
(Observation)

Production type	Unit (piece by piece)	Batch (inter- mittent)	Mass (contin- uous)	Process (flow)	Batch (job lot)	Mass (auto ass'y)
Source	Merner	Merner	Merner	Merner	Yanouzas	Guest
Foremen (N)	14	20	8	9	15	56
Obs. time each	2 hrs.	2 hrs.	2 hrs.	2 hrs.	45 min.	8 hrs.
ACTIVITIES	%	%	%	%	%	%
Communicate with						
own workers	15	12	11	8		
straw boss(es)	10	5	5	14		•
subordinates	25	17	16	22	18	23
other foremen	7	6	3	6	1	6
superiors	4	2	3	7	5	5
staff	6	12	7	6	7	7
others	5	6	3	1	5	9
Communicate (subtotal)	47	43	32	42	36*	50*
Paper work	8	21	11	12	9	5
Manual work	7	16	14	2	10	16
Walk	23	15	23	24	14	7
Stand, oversee, rest, etc.	15	6	19	20	31	22
Total time**	100%	101%	99%	100%	100%	100%
Sociable conversation	4	3	1	3	5	10
Activities concerning production	55	51	47	40	48	42

* In Guest's and Yanouzas' reports there is a discrepancy between percent of time spent in "contact" with others and percent of time spent in communication activities, where contact time was greater than communication time. The breakdown by categories of other persons was therefore proportionately reduced.
** The base figure for the percent distribution is in each case the number of observed foremen multiplied by the time each foreman was observed.
Sources: Guest, 1956; Yanouzas, 1964; Merner, 1970.

differences in proportion of communication time appear associated with type of technology.

In Merner's data, several items of communication first decline with more advanced technology, and then increase again in process technologies. They include the overall communication, communication with subordinates, communication with strawbosses (chief operators, lead hands, assistant foremen), communication with other foremen, and sociable conversation. In correspondence with Woodward's finding, the span of control in Merner's cases changes in the opposite direction. From operations where work pieces move sporadically piece by piece, to those where they move occasionally in batches, to continuous work-piece movement, the average number of workers per foreman increases slightly from 27.5 to 28.2 to 33.6. It goes down to 12.1 in continuous-flow process operations.

The percentage of foremen who have a chief machine operator or similar position to help in supervision increases over the full range of technologies (sporadic piece-by-piece movement 8%; occasional batch movement 15%;

TABLE 15
FOREMEN'S ACTIVITIES IN DIFFERENT PRODUCTION TYPES (Time Sampling)*

Activities	Packaging Small batch 19 foremen	Shoes** Large batch 4 foremen	Electronics Mass production 24 foremen	Brewing	
				Cleaning vessels 6 foremen	Process production 16 foremen
Communication	31%	36%	27%	27%	20%
Paperwork	13	8	12	16	9
Inspection	16	10	20	3	10
Manual work	13	17	7	3	13
Walk	5	9	16	11	21
Stand & supervise	3	1	2	—	1
Not seen	6	10	6	13	8
Break	12	7	6	21	14
Personal	1	2	6	6	4
Total time	100%	100%	102%	100%	100%

* Source: Thurley and Hamblin, 1963, pp. 18–19, 39.
** Three small-department foremen were omitted, because they appeared to be "working foremen," that is, substantially involved in manual work.

continuous work-piece movement 25%; flow process 89%). The proportion who are aided by charge hands or an assistant foreman, however, declines (71%, 55%, 50%, 0%). At the same time, there is a decrease in the proportion of time spent talking to nonsupervisory workers, and in activities concerning production. The proportion for communication of the English foremen in Table 15 also tends to decline through a comparable range of technologies.

The explanation of these differences is not a simple matter. For communication with subordinates, it depends on such factors as the availability of different types of supervisory assistance below foreman level, the span of control, and technical constraints on workers' communication. For time spent on production matters and talking to other foremen, an explanation would draw on information about functional dependence between operations under different foremen, and other conditions.

A check on the consistency of the above relations between technology and communication consists of a comparison between Yanouzas' (1964) and Guest's (1956) studies which represent the difference between small batch and mass production technologies. For most of the items mentioned, the direction of the difference is the opposite of that noticed in the other two studies: proportions in overall communication, talking with other foremen, talking with subordinates, and sociable conversation, are greater in the auto assembly plant than in the job-lot operation.

As interesting as the differences between these activity distributions is their general uniformity. In Table 16, the results of the four studies included in Tables 14 and 15 are summarized. By combining the Guest and Yanouzas studies, each of the first three columns represent data from a relatively broad range of technologies. Data from a report about three conveyor-belt supervisors in the garment industry are added, in order to indicate the extent to which activity distributions differ when based on time use in comparison to incident counts.

TABLE 16
FOREMEN'S ACTIVITIES BY METHOD AND COUNTRY

Activities	Merner*	Guest** & Yanouzas	Thurley*** & Hamblin	Treinen****	
	Canada	USA	Britain	Germany	
	51 foremen	71 foremen	69 foremen	3 conveyor-belt chiefs	
	4 x ½ hour observation each	45 min./8 hr. observation each	2–6 week sampling period	3¼ hours observation each	
	Continuous time recording	Continuous time recording	Random time sampling	Continuous time recording	Incidence count
	%	%	%	%	%
Communicate with—					
subordinates	20	21			
other foremen	6	4			
superiors	4	5			
staff	9	7			
others	4	7			
Communication	43	44	27	39	39
Paperwork	14	7	12	1	1
Manual work & inspection	10	13	24	29	26
Walk	20	11	13	7	21
Stand, oversee	6	{ 27 }	2	11	11
Rest, not in area	7		22	13	2
	100	102	100	100	100

* Merner, 1970, from data supplied by the author.
** Guest, 1956, p. 482, and Yanouzas, 1964, pp. 248–249; simple average of the percent figures of the two studies.
*** Thurley and Hamblin, 1963, pp. 18–19.
**** Treinen, 1956, p. 80; recording of both time taken and number of incidents, permitting a comparison of two methods (see also Atteslander, 1956, pp. 69–70).

The distributions of communication activities in the Canadian and American studies are strikingly similar. Time spent talking with subordinates is 20% and 21%, and overall communication time 43% and 44% respectively. If one assumes some communication time hidden in Thurley and Hamblin's residual category, the overall proportions of time spent in communication are well within the same neighborhood in all these distributions. Most of the items in the two distributions from Treinen's report are the same, suggesting that incidence counts can produce results comparable to time-use data. This similarity depends on uniformity in duration of incidents between the activity categories. Treinen's time per incident of communication is about thirty-three seconds, and for an incident of walking it is about nine seconds. This difference explains why the two proportions for walking are so different. However, each of these supervisors is responsible only for work along one conveyor seventy-five feet long. Many foremen would cover much larger areas and their time for an incident of walking would be greater. The opposite difference occurs in Treinen's residual category which includes primarily "leaving the room" and small amounts of "doing nothing." Being out of the room counts as one incident, and activities during that time are not differentiated. The time taken, however, is nearly five minutes per incident. A reanalysis of Treinen's data also indicates that the duration of an incident of communication between the supervisor and a worker is greater when it is initiated by the supervisor and when it is personal rather than work-related.

Is the foreman's communication limited to what the observers in these studies identified as such? Workers in some technical settings must rely on nonverbal means of communication. One might expect foremen to be similarly affected to some extent, and to make use of gestures in communicating with their workers. Gestural signs are exceedingly short in duration. They would certainly escape count by the time-sampling method employed by Thurley and Hamblin. Most of them would be missed in the methods by which duration is recorded, because an observer running along with a busy foreman cannot employ the precision necessary to record the second or less it often takes for an incident of sign communication. Even the five-second unit of Treinen's recording method would be too long for most items of nonverbal communication. I would conclude that important parts of the foremen's communication might be included under other categories, such as walking, and the total amount underestimated.

A great deal of the effectiveness of authority in working relations does not lie in what the boss actually says. Foremen who inspect a faulty work piece, who appear around the corner and walk past, who stand and watch, *do* communicate with their workers. Some workers prefer foremen who do not breathe down their necks, and some workers feel troubled when the boss is not around much. To the first, the foremen's presence communicates distrust; to the second, their absence communicates neglect. I have observed a plant superintendent in a concrete-block plant who absentmindedly picked up a small piece of broken brick while talking to the foreman. As soon as he had left, the foreman ordered a half-hour of overtime for the entire crew to clean up the plant. Nothing had been actually said about it.

This section began with a reference to the dual relation of foremen with their workers and their boss, and to the discovery of horizontal relations with other foremen. The data reviewed so far suggest that matters are more complex. Foremen typically communicate in substantial amounts with at least six major categories of people (some of these have been described for auto-assembly foremen by Jasinski, 1956). These categories, and the amounts of communication directed to them, are described in Figure 9. The data in that picture now take total communication time as the base (rather than the entire working time, as before).

The smallest amount of communication (9%) brings foremen into contact with their superiors, that is even less than the time given to talking with outsiders. The largest proportion is addressed to workers who are not performing supervisory functions (28%). A significant amount of time is spent talking to workers who assist the foreman in supervision. These "strawbosses" include chief machine operators, lead hands or charge hands, and assistant foremen. They absorb 40% of the communication with all of the foreman's subordinates. The average span of control in these cases is twenty-six. Consequently, an average of only 1% of the foremen's communication can be taken up by each nonsupervisory worker ("worker X" in Figure 9). Relations with other fore-

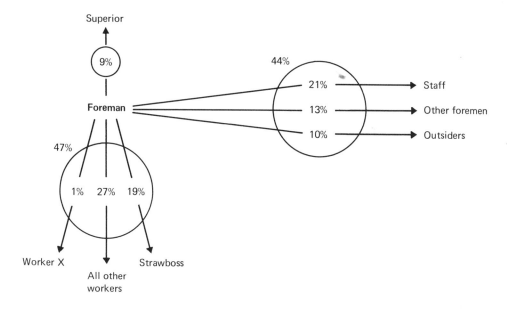

FIGURE 9.   Percent of communication time of 51 foremen in vertical and nonvertical relations.

men consume 13%, leaving as much as 31% for relations which are neither vertical nor horizontal.

In the development of modern organizational forms, many functions earlier performed by foremen have been taken over by specialists in technical staff positions. The fact that over one-fifth of the foremen's communication time brings them into contact with staff personnel suggests that the differentiation of specialized functions has created varied relations of dependence for foremen. If one considers that much of the foremen's paperwork involves communication with staff departments, the magnitude of relations with them becomes even greater.

Most foremen's job description would not very likely provide for relations with outsiders, that is, talking to people who are not employees of the organization, or former employees, or workers from other parts of the plant. And yet, we find here that as much as 10% of the time during which a foreman communicates with someone, it is one of these "outsiders." The fifty-six auto assembly foremen in Guest's (1956) report devote an average of 18% of communication to "others."

The division of labor in industry has created highly segmented jobs for production workers, where each man or woman performs only a small part of the work. The job of the foreman is segmented in a different sense. The image created by the preceding descriptions is one of incredible complexity. While production workers may go through the *same* activities hundreds of times a day, the days of foremen are composed of hundreds of *different* incidents which take, on average, less than a minute, and often only a few seconds (Guest, 1956:480). Their activities are a response to constant demands from many people, in markedly different work roles, who look for solutions to an enormous variety of problems. Their major response to these demands is verbal, that is, the articulation on short order of questions, answers, instructions, encouragements, explanations. Much of the remainder of their time they are in motion, walking, scanning their territory for problems and responding to demands for attention.

Under these circumstances, what happens to the foremen's relations with their workers, the people they are supposed to supervise? Jasinsky (1956:134) has suggested that managers considered those foremen more effective who spend more time in contact with people other than their subordinates. Turner (1955: 12) described an association between workers' frequency of contact, and the degree to which they felt they got along well with their foreman, suggesting that from the workers' perspective the better foremen spend more time in contact with their workers. Finally, beginning with the large-scale program of therapeutic interviewing between supervisors and workers at Western Electric (Roethlisberger and Dickson, 1939:189–376), foremen have been encouraged and trained to maintain good "human relations" with their subordinates. An entire research literature has been devoted to the effect of supervisory style on work satisfaction and productivity, perhaps in "the endearing belief that actions defined as good ought to make a big difference" (Homans, 1965:57–58; for a re-evaluation of this issue see Dubin, 1965).

Communication Between Worker and Foreman

For some condition to take effect, there must be exposure to that condition. Within the structure of activities of foremen, what chances are there for workers to be exposed to communication with their foreman? This question is approached in two ways: (1) by examining the data of the foremen's activities, in order to see how much of their time ends up in contact with each worker (Table 17), and (2) by looking at the reports which workers give in interviews of how often their foremen talk to them during a working day (Table 18).

Very few reports contain all the information necessary for making this assessment. In addition to Merner's (1970) study of fifty-one Canadian foremen, there is information about one foreman on an American auto assembly line, and three conveyor-belt supervisors in a German garment factory. From these reports, I have taken the number of workers per foreman (span of control), and extracted the number of minutes in an hour during which foremen talked with their subordinates. In two reports there was also information by which the number of incidents of foreman–worker communication per hour could be determined.

On the average during an hour of working time (Table 17), each worker gets a half minute of communication with the foreman, which corresponds to a little under the 2% allocated to our "worker X" in Figure 9. During an eight-hour working day, it amounts to approximately four minutes. In this respect, the data from three different studies, in three different countries, are remarkably uniform, with daily average contact times of 3.7, 4.4, and 4.0 minutes.

Judging by the two quite limited studies dealing altogether with four supervisors, the time taken for each incident of foreman–worker communication is somewhere between one-half and three-fourths of a minute. The number

TABLE 17

COMMUNICATION OF FOREMAN WITH EACH WORKER (Three Observation Studies)

	51 foremen Many industries (Merner)	1 foreman Auto assembly (Walker, et al.)	3 conveyor-belt chiefs Garments (Treinen)
(a) Average number of minutes during which each foreman talks with workers per hour	12 min.	11 min.	20 min.
(b) Average number of workers per foreman (span of control)	26 workers	20 workers	40 workers
(c) Average number of incidents during which each foreman talks with workers per hour	(no data)	14 incidents	36 incidents
Number of minutes per hour in which *each* worker communicates with foreman (a/b)	.46 min.	.55 min.	.50 min.
Time each worker spends talking with foreman in eight-hour day	3.7 min.	4.4 min.	4.0 min.
Average time per incident of foreman-worker communication (a/c)		.78 min.	.56 min.
Average number of times each worker talks to foreman in eight-hour day $\left(\dfrac{8c}{b}\right)$		5.6 times	7.2 times

Sources: Merner, 1970; Walker, Guest, and Turner, 1956, p. 86; Treinen, 1956.

of times during a day when foreman meets worker, averages between six and seven, that is, less than once an hour.

The other way of getting an idea of how much contact workers have with their foremen is shown in Table 18, by information from two interview surveys of American auto-assembly workers, and one of Canadian workers in technologically quite varied wood products plants. Between one-fifth and one-third of the auto workers get to talk to their foremen *once a day* or less, and 15% of the Canadian workers *less than* once a day. Only 25% and 33% of the auto workers communicate with their foremen once an hour or more, and 14% of the Canadian workers more than once an hour. The average frequencies shown in Table 17 lie between these two extremes, and so does the mode in the three interview studies, suggesting that there is about the same basic contact rate throughout the several studies and industries.

Verbal communication between worker and foreman is infrequent and short. A relatively small proportion of workers talk with their foreman every hour or more, and about as many do so only once a day or less. If one considers that a substantial part of many foremen's communication with subordinates is absorbed by strawbosses (Table 14 and Figure 9), the rate of verbal contact becomes smaller yet. What chances, then, for the foreman's "good

TABLE 18
COMMUNICATION OF WORKERS WITH THEIR FOREMAN (Three Interview Studies)

Source of data	Question asked	Answer categories	Percent
Turner, 1955, pp. 11–12 (American auto assembly workers, "Plant Y")	"In an average day, how often do you and your foreman talk together?"	Once a day or less	33%
		Between twice a day and under once an hour	42
		Once an hour or more	25
		(N)	(178)
Walker, et al., 1956, p. 93 (American auto assembly workers, "Plant X")	"In an average day, how often does the foreman talk with you?"	Once a day or less	21%
		Between twice a day and under once an hour	46
		Once an hour or more	33
		(N)	(180)
Meissner (Canadian worker's in wood products plants)	"How many times in a day does your boss talk to you?"	Less than once a day	15%
		Once or twice a day	28
		Between three times a day and once an hour	43
		More than once an hour	14
		(N)	(196)

"No answer" cases omitted.

human relations" or supervisory style, if exposure to occasions for exercising them is so slight?

The human touch of foremen can be expressed when they get a chance for personal conversation unrelated to the work at hand, particularly when they are the ones who initiate it. Table 19 contains data by which one can assess what difference it makes for the length of an encounter between supervisor and worker when the conversation originates from the worker or the supervisor, and when it is about work or personal matters. An incident of communication initiated by the supervisor takes eight or nine seconds longer, and when it does not concern work it lasts ten or eleven seconds more. Between a work-related incident taken up by a worker, and a non-work related encounter started by the supervisor, the difference is nineteen seconds. In fact, the du-

TABLE 19
DURATION OF COMMUNICATION INCIDENTS BETWEEN SUPERVISOR AND WORKER
BY CONTENT AND INITIATION (Duration in seconds) *

Initiation of Interaction	Content of Communication				Differ- ence
	Work	(Number of incidents)	Non- work	(Number of incidents)	
Initiated by worker	23	(112)	33	(90)	10
Initiated by supervisor	31	(267)	42	(113)	11
Difference	8		9		

* Calculated from data for three regular conveyor-belt supervisors in garment factory in Treinen, 1956, p. 80. The observation period was three and one-quarter hours each.

ration of the second type is almost twice that of the first. In this setting, the proportion of private communications is relatively large—40% of these supervisors' communication time (it ranged from 8% to 20% in other data shown in Table 14). And yet, the length of these "conversations," and the difference made by their sociable character, are incredibly small. The quality of "human relations in industry" seems to depend on a split-second difference.

Two factors constitute simple and relatively obvious conditions of exposure of workers to communication with their foreman. One of them is the amount of time the foreman spends in the vicinity, because it is during that time that the opportunity for contact exists. The other condition consists of technical constraints which limit the worker's opportunity to talk with anyone, including the foreman. Figure 10 clearly illustrates the joint effects of these two factors, for the subsample of 206 workers in my interview study. Proportionally few workers under conditions of high technical constraint have

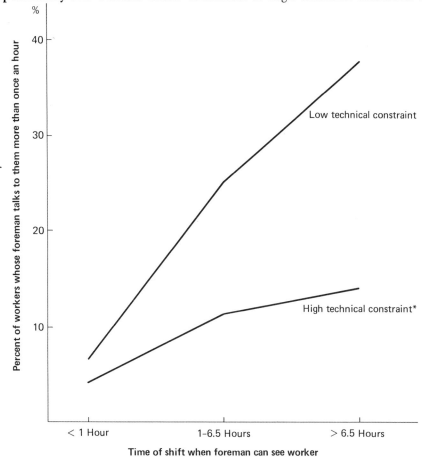

* High constraint = paced by machine or production line, *and* confined to single position or small area, *and* working in production rather than in maintenance or transportation.

FIGURE 10. Technical constraint, foreman's time in worker's vicinity, and worker-foreman communication. 196 workers; nonresponse omitted from total of 206. (Interview study.)

regular verbal contact with their foreman, and the amount of time the foreman spends where he can see them makes comparatively little difference. Workers who are free from one or more of these constraints are distinctly more likely to talk with their foreman, but only if the foreman spends a sufficient amount of time near them. The foreman's availability makes a great deal of difference only when workers have the technical opportunity to communicate verbally.

Technical constraints, however, do not only mean restrictions on workers' verbal communication. They can substitute for supervision to the extent that they are requirements built into the production machinery which regulate work speed, location and functional coordination between tasks. In that sense one can argue that technical constraints not only limit the opportunity for worker-foreman contact, but also its necessity. The production process can be a much more severe boss than most foremen would ever be.

In addition to its technology, industrial organization has other adaptive devices through which the functions of foremen are fitted to varying requirements, including communication with production workers. The first is differentiation of their task with the consequence of allocating parts of the job to the technical and service staff, and we have seen in Figure 9 that 21% of foremen's communication takes place with staff personnel. The second is another form of task differentiation, namely the allocation of supervisory functions to subordinates in positions of chief operator, lead hand or charge hand, and assistant foreman. Figure 9 has indicated that foremen talk 19% of the time with these strawbosses. The third consists of variations in the span of control, that is, the number of workers under the foremen's supervision.

Span of control and the availability of different kinds of supervisory assistance are related. For whatever reasons the number of workers under a foreman is relatively large, it is compensated for by greater reliance on subsupervisors with some scope of responsibility. Table 20 indicates that the greater the span of control, the greater the probability that foremen have under them lead hands or assistant foremen to help them supervise. In fact, none of the foremen with fewer than fourteen workers (the lower quartile in this distribution) had such assistance, and all the foremen with forty or more workers did (the upper quartile). The smaller the number of workers, the greater is the chance that the foremen had no supervisory assistance at all, or that they had to rely on the quite circumscribed help of machine operators.

The span of control has received considerable attention in the research

TABLE 20
FOREMEN'S SPAN OF CONTROL AND SUPERVISION BELOW FOREMAN LEVEL

Span of control		Supervision below the level of foreman			
Number of workers	Mean	None	Chief machine operator	Lead hand or asst. foreman	(N = 100%)
6–13	9.5	38	62	0	(13)
14–19	16.8	31	38	31	(13)
20–39	28.1	25	8	67	(12)
40 & over	49.7	0	0	100	(13)

Source: Merner, 1970, from data supplied by the author (51 salaried, nonunion foremen).

and management literature, but control from below the so-called first line of supervision has not even been mentioned, although it appears to be an important mechanism of adaptation to variation in span of control. How much of this form of delegation of authority is there? Of the fifty-one foremen in Merner's study, 14% had chief machine operators with responsibility for the other workers on their machine. In 18% of the cases there were hourly-paid lead hands in charge of a crew not limited to a piece of machinery. 7% had an assistant foreman who either shared the foreman's entire territory or had complete charge of part of it, subject to the foreman's overall direction (Merner, 1970:12). In a study focused on foremen, these were jobs whose supervisory functions were positively identified by the foremen. There are likely to be additional workers on whom other workers depend for directions, as in the relations between maintenance journeyman and helper; sawyer and spotter; rigging slinger and chokerman; or catskinner and helper.

In my interview study in an industrial community on Vancouver Island, we approached the problem of the distribution of authority from two directions. First we asked respondents if they supervised anyone and the answers are shown in Table 21, according to the respondent's own position. Of the workers whose jobs did not involve supervisory duties as a strawboss (lead hand, charge hand, etc.) or foreman, 17% indicated that they did, indeed, supervise the work of others. Most of this kind of supervision dealt with one or two other workers.

We also asked "What is the position of your boss?" and "Who tells you what to do?" in order to distinguish between official designation of authority and the most immediate source of directions. As shown in Table 22, 22%

TABLE 21
SUPERVISION BELOW FOREMAN LEVEL (Interview project)

"Is there anyone working under your supervision?" Number supervised	Foreman %	Strawboss %	Worker %
No one	—	—	83
1–2	—	—	13
3–4	—	—	2
5–9	7	36	2
10 or more	93	64	—
(N = 100%)	(14)	(11)	(195)

TABLE 22
SOURCE OF DIRECTIONS AT DIFFERENT RANKS (Interview project)

"Who tells you what to do?"	Foreman %	Strawboss %	Worker %
Manager, superintendent	86	18	9
Foreman	—	82	57
Lead hand	—	—	22
Worker	—	—	5
Dispatcher	7	—	1
No one	7	—	7
(N = 100%)	(14)	(11)	(195)

of the nonsupervisory workers receive directions from a strawboss, and 5% from another rank-and-file worker. A small proportion of both strawbosses and workers take orders from above the foreman level. One foreman and thirteen workers told us that "no one told them what to do," and one foreman and one worker were given instructions by a dispatcher.

Altogether there are more chiefs and fewer Indians than one might expect. Most foremen are "first-line" supervisors only as occupants of the last rank of management, signified by a monthly salary and a desk, but not by immediacy of contact with production workers. Communication channels tend to increase when there are more subordinates, but the potential increase in demands becomes buffered through additional nodes of communication. We can now examine the combined effects of numbers and nodes, and consider the consequences of other dimensions of the foreman's technical environment.

The Technical Environment of Foreman Communication

The principal job of the industrial worker is the manipulation of work objects, and communication is only one of the means of accomplishing it. Technical constraints affect the worker's communication in deterministic fashion—when constraints increase, verbal communication goes down—and there is limited, direct and relatively simple compensation for restrictions on communication—nonverbal communication substitutes for verbal communication.

The foreman's main job is communication and a major part of it is directed to subordinate workers. This job is so crucial to getting work done that potential threats to the coordinative functions served by the foreman's communication are compensated for by changes affecting the structure of communication channels, rather than by different means of communication. These adaptive devices include the span of control, communication with strawbosses and the production technology itself.

One function of supervision is coordination of tasks within a section of the work organization. Another is coordination with other sections, technical services and superiors. As the rate of production, spatial dispersion of workers, and internal dependence of tasks increase, one would expect foremen to spend more time talking to workers in their section, in order to meet the increased demands for internal coordination. However, two factors intervene before this happens. In compensation for the potentially greater demands, the number of workers (span of control) tends to be smaller and communication with strawbosses (chief operators, lead hands, and assistant foreman) increases.

The first three columns of figures in Table 23 show the *difference* in percent of time spent by foremen in various activities, between a sporadic and continuous rate of production, spatial concentration of workers in one room and dispersion over several rooms or floors, and the degree to which tasks are dependent and vulnerable to breakdowns. It shows that the amount of time spent talking with nonsupervisory workers *decreases* with increasing demands, but that communication with strawbosses *increases*. Taken together, the two differences tend to cancel each other out, with the result that the overall amount of time spent talking to subordinates of both kinds remains the same.

Would one not, however, expect communication with subordinates to increase rather than, in balance, to remain the same? The expectation is met, if strawbosses are seen as amplifiers of the foremen's communication. While

TABLE 23
EFFECTS OF TECHNICAL CONSTRAINTS, SUPERVISORY ASSISTANCE, AND SPAN OF
CONTROL ON FOREMEN'S ACTIVITIES (Differences in percent of time spent)

Activities	Rate of pro- duction	Spatial dis- persion	Internal depen- dence	External depen- dence	Superv. assist. controlling for: Span of control	Span of control controlling for: Superv. assist.
Communicate with						
own workers	− 3	− 5	− 3	+ 7	− 3	+ 6
strawbosses	+ 3	+ 4	+ 3	0	+ 6	− 3
subordinates	0	− 1	0	+ 7	+ 3	+ 3
other foremen	− 1	+ 1	0	+ 3	+ 1	− 1
superiors	+ 2	+ 3	+ 3	0	+ 1	− 2
staff	− 4	− 2	− 4	− 3	+ 3	0
others	− 3	+ 1	− 1	+ 4	+ 4	− 6
All communication	− 6	+ 2	− 2	+11	+12	− 6
Paperwork	− 5	− 5	− 3	− 9	+ 7	−10
Manual work	− 5	−12	− 8	− 1	− 9	+17
Walk, stand, oversee	+ 5	+ 8	+ 4	+ 5	− 4	+ 2
Rest	+11	+ 7	+ 9	− 6	− 6	− 3
Sociable talk	− 1	+ 2	+ 2	0	0	− 2
Production talk	− 8	− 1	− 4	+14	− 5	+ 8
Average span of control	− 9	− 8	−10	− 2	+ 9	+15

Source: Merner, 1970, from data supplied by the author.
Note: The breakdown of the categories at the top of this table is shown on the left side of Table 24.

they reduce the number of channels through which foremen communicate directly, the number of final recipients (the workers) is increased. The same amount of additional communication with strawbosses would tend to increase the amount which reaches the workers, as it is mediated and distributed by the strawboss.

The second mechanism which tends to compensate for greater demands on foremen can be seen in the upper part of Table 24. This table shows time in minutes for a two-hour observation period (instead of the percentages of Table 23), and it shows the dimensions of constraint on the left. Here we can see again the reduction in time spent talking with nonsupervisory workers associated with increased internal demands on the foreman, in the first column. It then shows a reduction in the span of control related to increased demands in rate of production, spatial dispersion, and internal dependence. As a result of the decreased number of workers, the potential negative effect on *each* individual worker's contact with the foreman is cancelled out, that is, the difference in communication per worker nearly disappears or becomes positive (in the case of internal dependence). The column on the far right of Table 24 shows what the difference would be in the time which foremen spend talking to all nonsupervisory workers, if there had been no difference in span of control. A large part of the difference made by these first three sets of constraints is counterbalanced by the difference in span of control.

A third source of balance lies in the technical constraints themselves. As

TABLE 24
TECHNICAL CONSTRAINTS, SUPERVISORY ASSISTANCE, SPAN OF CONTROL AND
COMMUNICATION BETWEEN FOREMEN AND NONSUPERVISORY WORKERS
(in minutes per two-hour observation)

Constraints	(N)	Talk to *all* workers	Span of control	Talk to *each* worker	All workers (span of control controlled for)
Rate of production					
Occasional unit or batch	(34)	15.7	27.9	.56	
Continuous work flow	(17)	11.3	22.3	.51	
Difference		− 4.4		− .05	− 1.5
Spatial dispersion					
All workers in one room	(23)	17.7	30.5	.58	
More than one room	(28)	11.5	22.4	.51	
Difference		− 6.2		− .07	− 1.8
Internal dependence (work stations affected by breakdowns)					
Less than one-fourth affected	(34)	15.4	29.5	.52	
One-fourth or more affected	(17)	12.0	19.1	.63	
Difference		− 3.4		+ .11	+ 2.9
External dependence (connections with other foremen's sections)					
Independent or buffered	(35)	11.6	26.7	.43	
Dependent or not buffered	(16)	20.1	24.6	.82	
Difference		+ 8.5		+ .39	+10.1
Supervisory assistance and span of control					
Chief operator or none					
—span of 6–19 workers	(22)	11.7	12.4	.94	
—span of 20 or more workers	(4)	24.3	28.8	.84	
Difference		+12.6		− .10	
Lead hand or assistant foreman					
—span of 6–19 workers	(4)	12.8	17.3	.74	
—span of 20 or more workers	(21)	15.3	41.5	.37	
Difference		+ 2.5		− .37	

we have shown earlier, a more advanced production technology works by imposing greater spatial, temporal and functional constraints on workers. One would expect that these worker-level constraints are related to the foremen's constraints being discussed here. Technical constraints on worker activity have two consequences: they reduce opportunities for verbal communication, and they form a partial substitute for supervision by built-in regulation of the performance and coordination of tasks. An additional sign of this kind of "supervision by machine" is the fact that fewer foremen have lead hands or assistant foremen at the more advanced levels of technology, and rely more on machine operators for subsidiary supervision.

So far, we have dealt with the foremen's internal coordination problems and discovered a delicately balanced system composed of variations in technical demands, span of control, relations with workers performing subsupervisory functions, and its effects on the amounts of time a foreman spends talking to nonsupervisory workers, and to each of them in particular. Rate of production, spatial dispersion and internal dependence, have additional effects. They tend to increase time spent talking to superiors, and decrease communication with the technical and service staff. They also decrease time spent with paperwork and manual work, and increase walking, standing and overseeing, and time off recuperating.

We can now turn to a problem of external coordination signified by functional dependence of the operations of a foreman with those of other foremen. In the fourth dimension shown along the top of Table 23 and down the side of Table 24, a distinction is made between (1) foremen whose sections are independent from other sections or where work-flow connections are buffered through storage, and (2) foremen whose sections are functionally connected with others and not protected by buffers in the work flow. Solutions to problems of external dependence cannot be delegated to a strawboss. They might be referred to a common superior or, most likely, will be handled by negotiation with other foremen. Table 23 indicates that time spent talking with other foremen increases with external dependence, but that communication with superiors remains unchanged. Time communicating with strawbosses is also not affected, but talking with nonsupervisory workers increases markedly. Furthermore, the entire amount of time in communication increases, and so does the part of it concerned with production problems. These increases are made up for by a decrease in communication with staff personnel, paperwork, and personal time off.

These data suggest that functional dependence with other operations create special requirements for coordination. These are being met by more communication with other foremen, but not with higher levels of authority or with supervisory assistants. They are also being met by increased communication with production workers, perhaps because the performance of their work affects technical relations with other departments directly.

Unlike the conditions of internal coordination previously discussed, external dependence does not evoke balancing mechanisms through reduction in the span of control or rechanneling of communication through strawbosses. Instead, its demands must be met by reducing other parts of the foreman's own activities. The main resource to this end is the foremen's personal time off, indicated by a 6% reduction when there is greater external dependence. In contrast, an increase in personal time is associated with each of the three conditions which make greater demands for internal coordination.

As can be seen in Table 24, the foremen's span of control does not adjust to demands for external coordination (the average number of workers declines by only two). As a result, the average time spent communicating with each nonsupervisory worker virtually doubles (from twenty-six to forty-nine seconds in a two-hour period).

Having recognized the functions of span of control and supervisory assistance in balancing the demands on the foremen's communication, it is useful to examine what the relative effects of these two factors are. The two columns on the right of Table 23, and the bottom of Table 24, indicate the difference made by each of the two conditions, while controlling for the effects of the other. With the number of subordinates held constant, the foremen obviously communicate more with strawbosses (including chief machine operators) when they have the help of lead hands or an assistant foreman (Table 23). At the same time, the amount of communication with nonsupervisory workers declines—the difference being absorbed by strawbosses. When the number of workers increases (holding supervisory assistance constant), foremen talk less to strawbosses and more to workers. Relative to each other, the effect of the two factors is balanced, both resulting in the same increase in overall communication with all subordinates (a percent difference of three in each case).

Time spent in all other communication activities (including paperwork) increases when foremen have more supervisory assistance, and all noncommunication activities decline. Having help in supervision of workers makes time available to attend to the demands of others in the organization. The effect of a greater span of control is generally the opposite (when supervisory assistance is controlled for). It requires increased attention to communication with workers, and more walking, overseeing, and manual work.

A greater number of workers requires more time of the foreman to talk to them, but lead hands and assistant foremen tend to absorb these additional demands. In Table 24 it can be observed that the span of control doubles communication with all nonsupervisory workers, when the foreman has little supervisory assistance—with a difference of 12.6 minutes in two hours. When he has more help, however, the effect of a greater span of control is substantially reduced—to a difference of 2.5 minutes.

When the foreman has little supervisory help, a greater number of workers is not much reflected in reduced communication with *each* worker, because the foreman devotes more time to all of them taken together. The average time of talking with each worker is reduced by only one-tenth of a minute. But if there are lead hands or an assistant foreman, and the span of control increases, they absorb a large part of the additionally required communication with workers (transmitting and amplifying it), and the foremen's time for each worker is halved.

Both workers and their bosses adapt their behavior to those constraints and demands of their technical environment which impinge on their different jobs. One set of constraints affects the balance between a worker's verbal and nonverbal means of communication and the rate of communication with other workers. Another set of constraints affects the distribution of the foremen's activities and their communication with a variety of other people. The technical environments of both have consequences for their communication with each other. An important difference between the two is that there are organizational adaptations which compensate for demands on foremen which would threaten their ability to perform their coordination functions. Workers, in turn, must make do, and some of them even take on some supervisory functions.

What effects do varying rates of contact between foremen and workers have on the way workers feel about their foremen? In a study of American auto workers, Turner (1955:12–13) demonstrated a positive relation between frequency of contact and the degree to which workers felt they got along well with the foreman. But there were substantial exceptions. Of the men who rarely talked with the foreman (once a day or less), 34% indicated they got along fairly well, and gave as their reason that the boss did not interfere with them. 22% of the men whose foremen talked to them often (at least once an hour) did not think much of their relationship because their foremen gave them too much trouble. Among a sample of "affluent workers" in Britain, 54% said they got on well with their foremen because they left them alone and did not interfere (Goldthorpe, et al., 1968:66; for strong reactions to supervision in coal mining, see Goldthorpe, 1959, and Jantke, 1953:228; for foremen with unpleasant reactions to talking among workers, see Jasinski, 1956:25). Perhaps the distribution of these comments is an empirical indication of ambivalence towards authority, whose causes in industrialization have been examined by Erich Fromm (1941).

EXPRESSIVE STYLES

Organization and technology select channels and frequency of communication in industry, but the production worker shapes its style and content. More often than not, workers are left to their own devices in developing and maintaining communication systems which are frequently essential to production, and nobody else is much concerned whether they have the means for personal expression and interpersonal relations. The style of both instrumental and expressive communication is the workers' own creation. It is concrete, direct, in important parts nonverbal, and close to the essentials of life. For the community—the home, school, office, and most of social research—it is invisible and esoteric, and less subject to its controls of prurience.

The first part of this chapter has made much of nonverbal communication, and particularly the language of gestural signs. One may well ask how it looks and works in practice. This question is answered by the description of a unique case—a full-blown industrial sign language in sawmills on the Pacific Coast of Canada.

The preceding analysis has selected communication as activity, without much attention to content. From industrial ethnographies and a few descriptions of language use, it is possible to piece together a picture of some of the things which occupy workers in their conversation. Ways can be suggested in which content and style are addressed to the problems of working in industrial production.

Our analysis has implied sharp limitations on verbal language use in industrial work. Limits on articulateness can be considered more broadly, as coming from both work and class experiences, as well as the implications they have for the nature of the worker's social life on and off the job.

The Sign Language of Sawmill Workers[1]

Most of the central operations in a modern sawmill are remotely controlled by a number of sawyers and control-panel operators. The dominant operation is performed by the head saw, or head rig, which determines much of the rate

---

[1] This account is the result of an inquiry into the communication of sawmill workers carried out in cooperation with the anthropologist Stuart Philpott and the sociologist Alan Hedley. Off and on during a period of two years we made our observations in three large sawmills. Alan Hedley produced comprehensive descriptions of the technical processes and communication frequencies and content. Stuart Philpott provided field notes, a dictionary, and records of usages of the sign language. Drawings for a complete dictionary were made by Diana Philpott. The sign language pictures (Figure 12) shown in this section were redrawn for this chapter by Nicolai Meissner.

and quality of output and sets the pace for subsequent work. In the mill to which our main sign language description applies (see Figure 11), the head sawyer controls the placement of the log (often several feet in diameter and up to forty feet long) on to a carriage on rails, and the movement of the carriage. The carriage is run past a huge, continuously running band saw (the head rig) which cuts slabs of wood (cants) off the log, and then returned for the next cut. The "setter" sits on the carriage and controls the position of the log, making up for the taper of the log and advancing it for each successive cut by the required thickness of the next cut. Both head sawyer and setter cooperate in placing and rotating the log from time to time. The head sawyer controls the "dog," which rotates it, and the setter controls the "dogs" which clamp it down once placed. In passing, the two men face each other, and the head sawyer gives instructions to the setter by signs, for each cut and every time the log is positioned or rotated. We counted an average of 293 cutting cycles, and a sign-communication rate of 315 per hour between the two.

The tail sawyer stands to the side of the head sawyer's operating cubicle, also facing the setter. He cannot see the head sawyer and does not communicate directly with him. With a pickeroon he sometimes guides the cants cut from the log as they drop on the roller conveyor, and gets scrap pieces out of the way. The roller conveyor is controlled by the leverman who regulates work-piece flow along the roller conveyor or across to the edger. He also operates a cut-off saw occasionally, and receives light signals from the head sawyer indicating the direction into which work pieces are to be sent.

Few men in the central operations of the mill have freedom of movement, and these are the ones in manual contact with work pieces or scrap wood. The machine and control operators cannot talk to each other while the mill is running, and they communicate through observation of work objects and a sign language. The language was most fully developed in one of the three mills in which we carried out extensive observations. Its more intense and interesting use took place around the head rig.

A triangle is formed by the head sawyer on one side, the tail sawyer and leverman on the other, while the setter moves back and forth about five times a minute, first facing the head sawyer and then the other two men. The setter sits higher up on his carriage and has a relatively fuller view of the mill than the others. The head sawyer depends particularly on the setter for news about events elsewhere, and for relaying jokes from the tail sawyer or leverman.

These workers, together with a relief man and the men from the head rig of an adjacent second mill, tended to rotate jobs to some extent by spelling each other off for coffee or smoke breaks. Much of our information came from observations and lunch-room conversations with men from this group who contributed, we believe, much to the elaboration and maintenance of the sign language. Most of them had worked together for several years.

The language is most centrally used for technical purposes, to make the very rapid coordination of work possible. It must be executed and understood very quickly, particularly between head sawyer and setter. Learning it effectively takes time. One setter seemed to be conversing more incessantly than most. We were told that he had finally mastered the language after five or six months on the job, and that he was now overdoing it a bit. Between men familiar with each other, a head sawyer often signed with casual, minimal motions while resting his hand on a control knob. In another mill we saw a

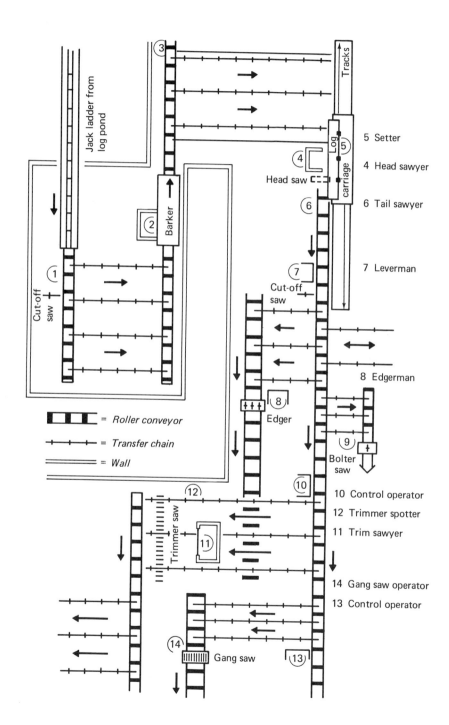

FIGURE 11.   Sawmill

head sawyer form each sign twice and very explicitly to a vacation-substitute setter, and remark, "The guy is a little stupid, he can't remember the signals." Two men by themselves at the other end of one mill had developed a subversion so private that others could only partly understand it. These examples suggest that effective learning, and the more elaborate use of the language, depend on the characteristics of the men involved.

The sign language appeared to be used more fully, particularly for non-technical purposes, between men (1) whose tasks were functionally connected by the work process; (2) between whom technical communication was neces-sary (as between head sawyer and setter); (3) who worked together for several years; (4) who had similar job statuses; (5) who had the same age, education, or ethnic background; (6) who had a high degree of technical competence which allowed them not to have to pay all their attention to the work; and (7) who were extroverts, that is, willing "to make a bit of a fool of themselves," as one sawyer told us.

For example, in one mill there was little more than technical communica-tion between an older high-status head sawyer, and a young replacement setter. In another mill, prominent communication links tended to follow an ethnic distinction. In the third mill, an important group of sign communicators was held together by some younger men who had completed high school in the same area.

The idea that you have to "make a bit of a fool of yourself" suggests important features of sign language use. When you meet these men in the lunch room or coffee shop, they are relatively grey and expressionless. In the mill they suddenly come alive. In addition to requiring clear execution of the signs, the conversational uses of the language would not "come off" without (1) the imagination to think up a fitting sign and to put it into the context of a funny expression; (2) corresponding forceful facial expressions and often mouthing of words that make a general reference specific; and (3) behav-ing like an actor in a medium for which a mill worker would appear to be least prepared.

The core of the language is a system of numbers. When I first asked about it, someone tore a page for me from a notebook in use in the industry which had the basic number signs printed on it, in crudely drawn pictures. For out-siders, and in the view of management, that was more or less all there was to it. In the cooperation between head sawyer and setter, number signs in-dicate by how many inches the log is to be moved forward for the next cut. Even for that purpose alone it is a relatively sophisticated system.

There are unique signs for the numbers from one to twelve. Numbers from thirteen to twenty can be formed by the numbers three to ten held horizontally and drawn across in front of the body. Twenty-five is a five drawn downward. Usually the additional motion for higher numbers is omitted be-cause it is contextually implied to the nearest ten. Fractions are signified by the direction of quick movement of the basic number sign: quarters forward; halves sideways; and eighths down. Because there is only one possibility for halves, a number like "5½" is "five" flicked sideways. Fourths and eighths require additional specification. The fraction "¾" is "three" with fingers flicked forward, and a downward jerk of "three" means "⅜." One head sawyer formed "1¼" by bending his index finger which signifies "one" when held up straight.

Because number signs form the technical core of the language, they are put to many other uses. Some conversations are started by asking for the time and getting an answer often deliberately and ridiculously wrong. There are many exchanges about sports events which allow talking about the results (and the bets placed on them) in numerical terms. Some number signs have multiple meanings: "two" for engineer, "four" for millwright, and "five" for foreman, corresponding to blows on the steam whistle as call signals. "4½" refers to the strawboss who ranks a notch below the foreman. A fist with thumb sticking out, with the back of the hand turned to the viewer, indicates "seven." Moved sideways, it can mean "off" or "go" as well as "7½."

In addition to numbers in the technical vocabulary, there were names for all the major pieces of equipment and several special signs for use in particular operations. Some of these had also multiple and sometimes simultaneous uses, such as the sign for "pin" which also signified "fuck." Similarly, the sign for "a little bit" (rubbing index finger and thumb together) tells the setter to advance the log a little more. It also refers to sexual intercourse, as in this sequence of signs:

I—think—I—go—home—get—a little bit.

After an exhaustive search, we recorded 127 single signs, some of which were combined to form seventeen "compounds." We also noticed thirteen less formalized conversational gestures or on-the-spot inventions, for a dictionary of 157 signs. In addition there were many variations on numbers, and forty signs had more than one distinct meaning, resulting in a total repertory of over 200 items. The main groups of items signify work and other objects; persons at work and at home; quantities; evaluative and descriptive qualifiers; and activities. While these would correspond to the nouns, adjectives and verbs of ordinary speech, the language does not vary tenses, and contains no signs for articles, conjunctions, or auxiliary verbs.

The combination of two signs to form a compound expression contains fascinating features. The three sample sentences in Figure 12 contain two examples. The colloquial expression for pregnant is "knocked up," formed by two simple and obvious signs. A worker who gets fired from his job, gets his walking papers, and the signs are "walk" and "paper." Similarly, "new" (rubbing the upper arm with a flat hand) and "paper" make "newspaper." But the sign for "new" also means "nice," yet no one in the mill would form the combination "nice paper." A comparable limitation applies to the signing of "sister," as follows. The index fingers of both hands are put side by side, pointing forward, to indicate "same," "even" (as in even bet), or "brother." The sign for "woman" is shown in the third sentence in Figure 12. The sequence—woman-brother—is the sign for "sister." However, the reverse sequence would not be used to say something like "the same woman." (In fact our conversational attempts were unsuccessful in part because we tried to form compositions of this sort.) Other combinations include Friday (fish day), Sunday (pray day), Tuesday (two day), payday (money day), and bank (money house).

The sawmill sign language is not much constrained by rules and is open to instant innovation. Any sign is admissible as long as it works, that is, can be understood. Consequently we found both ordinary conversational gestures (shrugging shoulders, shaking head, or spreading hands apart with palms down for "all over"), and on-the-spot inventions. The latter include the sign for "house" (two hands making a pointed roof) turned on its side for "points" as

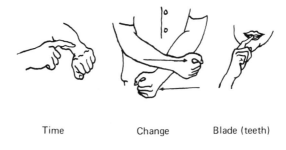

| Time | Change | Blade (teeth) |

"It's time to change the saw blade!"

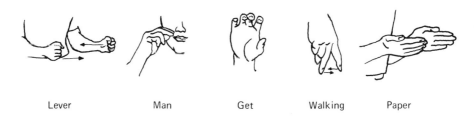

| Lever | Man | Get | Walking | Paper |

"The leverman got fired"

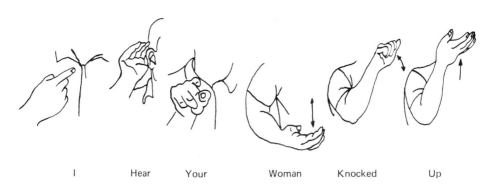

| I | Hear | Your | Woman | Knocked | Up |

"I hear your wife is pregnant"

FIGURE 12. Examples from the sawmill worker's sign language.

in: *my-car-break-down—I-get-new-points*. Others include the motion of pulling down pants (in a friendly "You (are) full (of) crap"); tracing the letter "C" for a Calgary sports team; or a scooping motion for "more."

As in ordinary speech, many signs have several meanings, and the interpretation relies on context. Two examples involve transformations from English speech sounds. Grasping the biceps of the other arm signifies "weak" but is most commonly used for "week." Grasping the lobe of the ear is the sign for "year." A few signs have different, though related, meanings in different mills. One fist above the other, hit together two or three times, says "stopped" in one mill, and "fix it" in another. Good, bad and sick are related. Patting the stomach with a flat hand is "good;" circular rubbing of the stomach is "bad"; and making the circle with the index finger is "sick."

Persons are identified either by a number (according to whistle signals mentioned already), by job (leverman, edgerman, etc.), or by ethnic identity. Drawing a circle above the head indicates a turban for "Sikh" in one mill, and a circle of thumb and index finger in front of the mouth for "spaghetti" is the reference for Italian in another mill. In order to make a sign specific which could refer to several people, the signer can either mouth the name or point in the direction with his thumb. Pointing is generally used quite frequently.

Questions begin with the sign for "question" which is, depending on distance: raised eye brows, backward jerk of head, fist raised to above shoulder height and back of hand to viewer, or open hand facing the viewer. This generalized interrogative can also mean "how." Other questions start by pointing at the wrist for "What time is it?" or "How long?" or "When?". The sign for relative height (high or low depending on position) is also used for "How much?" and the letter "Y" borrowed from the alphabet of the deaf stands for "Why?" in one mill.

A look at conversation around the head rig will give a flavor of communication at work. In the three-way relations with the setter in the middle, the tail sawyer (or the leverman) would start with some outrageous gestural remark to the setter during the moment he was in view. The setter would tell the head sawyer on the way back, who in turn gave his contribution to the setter for transmission to the other two on coming up-front again, and so forth, with everyone bursting into laughter or broad grins.

Because the head sawyer could see only a small area, the setter reported to him events elsewhere in the mill which he could see from his more prominent position. When an executive toured the plant with one younger and two older women, the setter signed the following sequence on one pass: *big-shot-over there* (pointing)-*three-women*. On the following pass he continued: *one-woman-twenty-five-figure* (outlined with both hands)-*just right*. He then drew a rectangle with his index finger and pointed to the head sawyer's operating cubicle, wanting to liken the woman he described to the calendar nude behind the sawyer. This message came through only after a second try, and on a fourth pass he finished with: *she* (pointing)-*my-girl-friend*.

This conversation network also served technical functions. The head sawyer once gave a light signal to the leverman which would have resulted in sending a work piece to the wrong destination. He told the setter: *I-push button-wrong-tell-lever-man*. The setter transmitted the message successfully to the leverman, allowing him to retrieve the piece by reversing the rolls and sending it to the right place, all in a matter of seconds.

Many exchanges involve terse joking. They include expressions like "you crazy old farmer," "you prick," "you cunt," or "you're full of crap," all made with the friendliest of intentions. The foreman gets more than his share of attention: *boss-fucking-around-over there* (pointing); *I-fix-boss-tomorrow-night.* There is also much attention to time—quitting time, lunch time, coffee time— and the relief operator plays an important part in it. Once a setter signed "time (for a) smoke," but his relief man had not arrived. When he finally came, the setter made a great hissing noise with the block-moving hydraulics and clapped his hands sarcastically, suggesting "Good of you to show up!" Another time, two men with access to steam whistles got together alternately blowing them (they can be heard well beyond the mill) to remind the relief man. When he finally turned up and tried to step over a roller conveyor, an operator (who could only see him through a suspended mirror) kept moving the conveyor back and forth, leaving the relief man with his foot in mid-air.

In short, the sawmill workers' sign language is an unusually elaborate adaptation to the exigencies of a mechanized production technology. It is kept alive by the technical necessity of communication for the purpose of rapid coordination, and by similarities in the characteristics of workers and job rotation for relief purposes. It is open to constant innovation, but limited in repertory and acceptable combinations. It requires relatively exuberant acting, and willingness to go out on a limb. Its important nontechnical uses involve jokes created to break the routine of repetitive and demanding work.

A Sense of Humor

The description of the sawmill workers' sign language contained the main characteristics of communication at work which are of interest in this section: (1) the argot of a specialized occupation; (2) an imagery which draws on a few major symbolic sources; (3) names of jobs and persons; and (4) joking. In a short section of this chapter, it is hardly possible to do justice to the esoteric vocabularies which are unique to many specialized occupations. Being merely technical, many of them are intended to confine terms to single meanings, and would be of little interest to the readers of this handbook. However, the fascination of some working languages, argots, and styles of communication lies in the hidden dimensions of the symbolic community of people compelled to work together, and it is their very ambiguity which gives us the sense of its overt humor, and can reveal its covert tragedies.

Argot and analogies.   Analogies are a central method in the formation of expressions in manual work. They are amusing when unexpected images are applied to the tools and processes of work, and to the people doing it. The few available listings have a tendency of becoming outdated by technical change, and come from some of the more isolated occupations or those with long traditions. A few examples include the printers' "dead horse," the recomposing of type already printed (Jacobs, 1962); the loggers' "whistle punk" who gives signals when a tree is coming down, and "widow maker" for tree branches which might unexpectedly break off to drop on the "fallers and buckers" (with initial letters sometimes reversed) (see Bergren, 1966, and Holbrook, 1962, for short loggers' dictionaries). Safecrackers perform a "jam shot" or "gut shot" designed to open a "can" (safe) which "drinks" the "grease" (nitroglycerin) set off by a "knocker" (detonator), but the "can" can also be "peeled," "un-buttoned," or "punched" (Letkemann, 1973:57–79).

Selected images: sex, body and animals. A substantial part of the vo-cabularies of manual occupations and industries draws on a few major sources of imagery. The names of animals invoke a veritable industrial bestiary. Steel production has its sows and pigs, where pig iron is a standard designation. All manner of dogs stop or hold objects or run along conveyor chains, and are equivalent to cats in the German steel industry (Popitz, 1957a:86). Generally, "dog" suggests gripping power, and "bull" indicates strength (Boone, 1949:32), in equipment like bulldozer and bull pump, and in persons like bull bucker and bull of the woods (Holbrook, 1962:236–237). In the oil fields, a "rabbit" is an obstruction in a pipe or a device to remove it; a "whale" or "wildcat" a producing well; and a "bird dog" a geologist (Boone, 1949). A "king snipe" was the boss of a track-laying crew in logging and a "cat skinner" a tractor driver (Holbrook, 1962:237–239). In railroad work, "frog" stands for a cross-over plate or rerailing implement; a "donkey" is a section man; a "hog" a locomotive run by a hog head or hog jockey; a "rabbit" a derail iron; and a "monkey house" a caboose (Cottrell, 1940:117–139; Spier, 1959). "Monkey wrench" and "grease monkey" have become commonly used terms.

Body parts constitute a simple and direct source for the description of many instruments of work: knuckle, elbow, belly, head, toe, or ass end. The shapes and functions of many tools, equipment parts and work pieces are dis-tinguished as male or female, or by other direct or indirect sexual analogies. The following examples describe practices in Britain which were enumerated and interpreted by Thomas (1951). Many technical objects, one fitting into the other, are simply called female or male, including clutches, pipe fittings, shafts and bushings, and electric plugs and receptacles. Trade cataloges list hermaphrodite callipers which can measure both inside and outside dimensions, and "bastard" files and flanges. Grease fittings are nipples, and well-fitting flanges "kiss all around." Sexual origins can be seen in nuts, cocks, jacks, or couplings. An example of the reverse relation was suggested by Thomas (1951), in that "tool" is a common word for penis.

The general, nontechnical employment of sexual and excretory (and some-times sacred) expressions seems to be pronounced in industrial work. Whether its incidence, despite contrary impressions, is really different from any other setting, has been put into question implicitly by at least one, and somewhat limited, study: Cameron (1969) reported word counts which were systematically sampled by a number of students, and found the principal English four-letter words ranked well within the fifty most frequently used words in American restaurants, stores, a clinic, telephone conversations in homes, a party, and in student groups. However, the question of comparative emphasis and frequency is not settled by these findings, and they may indeed be greater in industry than elsewhere, just as the same observation has been made among soldiers (Elkin, 1946:419).

There may well be differences between the languages of industrial coun-tries so that speakers of English put more weight on sex in dirty words, and degrade both themselves and others in their most tender aspects (Sagarin, 1962), but the main verbal and nonverbal equivalents of "four-letter words" are near-universal currency. Yet, social research in industry has either been scrubbed clean beyond recognition, or its practitioners have listened and watched with only one ear and one eye. Supposedly "disinterested" inquiry has revealed one of its "interested omissions."

Names of jobs and persons. In earlier periods of industrialization, expressions like "the mass," "the proletariat," or "the working class," have implied the namelessness of persons working for a living. However, individual namelessness has become, as it were, more personal. In common naming practices at work, a woman or man is identified by a *category* which denies personal uniqueness or common humanity, and sometimes both. Beyond a supervisor's completely depersonalized "Hey you!" (a practice mocked in the film "The Man on the Assembly Line," National Film Board of Canada), workers' names refer to sex, race, or ethnic origin. The reverse process occurs when such a category is degradingly applied to a piece of machinery, a practice which is curiously equivalent to the use of animal names for working equipment. In sawmills, logs are still turned by either a "nigger" or a "dog," and according to Cottrell's probably outdated dictionary (1940), railroaders called a part on top of a locomotive "nigger-head," and a foreign car a "zulu car." Intermittent contract work in logging is "gyppo," joining the common term of being "gypped" in maligning Gypsies. The reduction of functions described before, in Table 10, contains a case where a worker has literally been replaced by a "dog," a manual task having been designed into a simple piece of machinery of a type normally called "dog."

Even in personal conversation, technical function or ethnic origin frequently replace a personal name. The description of the sawmill sign language contains a number of examples, where persons are named through a mixed task-and-sex classification, such as leverman, edgerman, etc., or an ethnic tag like "spaghetti" or the sign for "turban." An ethnic label like "Frenchy" is as common as a simple physical category like "Red" or "Lefty." The incorporation of categories of sex, race, and ethnicity into "joking" makes for destructive humor. It often occurs in combination, and includes "woman" as a man's derogation. Relevant incidences have been described by Roy (1960:163), Zaleznik (1958:157) and Lantz (1958:145), and older discussions of "humor" in American racial conflict are found in Burma (1946) and Barron (1950).

While they are of a different source and administrative function, job categories and occupational titles are also part of the language of work. They display, and possibly maintain, pervasive sexual prejudices. A corporation has a chairman for its board of directors, and a charwoman for its floors and toilets. "Nurse" is only thinkable as a man's job when it is pointedly called "male nurse." The titles of foreman and journeyman automatically assign authority or skill to men (see also Geselle, Meister, Vormann, contre-maître). Through names like chambermaid, bonne, femme de chambre, Putzfrau, and Krankenschwester, jobs of personal and menial service are assigned to women. Adult status is accorded to the salesman, while the salesgirl remains permanently juvenile, together with entire collections of jobs, such as office girls: Robinson Crusoe's "Man Friday" turned into the girl fridays of modern offices. While the order of suffixes is never reversed, some men also suffer the symbolic fate of immaturity as a bellboy, busboy, and garçon. After making a valiant attempt with "charworkers," and turning bellboys into "bellmen," even the occupational listing of the census cannot find alternatives for fishermen, repairmen, sectionmen, trackmen, furnacemen, or policemen. Developments in production methods and fashions may no longer justify keeping tailors and dressmakers, hat makers and milliners, and barbers and hair dressers in their respective places. The Renaud automobile works prepared a list showing the composition of its foundry personnel in 1919, which included such jobs as core makers, moulders, welders, maintenance workers, etc., and at the end of the list: women (Touraine, 1955:73). Men had differentiated functions, but women only their gender.

What is represented in names corresponds to functions. After the single most careful examination of women's tasks in industry, Guilbert came to the conclusion that women's jobs are the most segmented, repetitive, and constraining even among the unskilled industrial jobs (Guilbert, 1966:190–195). The managers whom Guilbert questioned about their reasons for assigning different jobs to women and men were remarkably straightforward: they said about one type of job only done by men that "it is skilled work which cannot be done by women"; and another could only be done by women, because "it requires a great deal of resistance to monotony" (Guilbert, 1966:250–369).

The job category which applies to a larger number of persons than any other is "housewife." When asked what they do, people often say, "Oh, I'm *only* a housewife." According to labor statistics and important parts of the feminist literature, they are not "working" or, in French, not "active." The inequity of the "nonworking" and "inactive" labels should be seen in the perspective of working hours. In comparative time budgets from twelve countries, the hours of work of housewives without paid jobs, as a percentage of the job and job-related hours of men, range from a low of 99% in Belgium, and 100% in the USA, to a high of 133% in the Soviet Union (Szalai, 1972:583–593).

In different ways, categories as names deny personal uniqueness or do not allow a full share in the status of a human person. To be called "Red," instead of Robert, reduces Robert's complex characteristics to one, and makes it easier to ignore the others. When Robert is called "leverman," nothing personal is left—the person is reduced to a segmented technical function, a confirmation in personal conversation of the "use of human resources." When ethnicity or sex define the name, injury is added to reduction. A feminine tag for technical functions reduces social value, and contains justifications for lower pay. The tag "housewife" denotes "not working" and "not active," and the *value* of housework is set to zero, even when its *hours* are at least equal to the hours of "working" men.

Perfunctory relationships, joking and ritual. While obscenities at work have been all but ignored in social research, joking among industrial workers has had its share of attention. From observations of American machine shop and assembly workers, Zaleznik (1958:157) concluded that "joking was the common denominator around which many of the workers' interactions took place." "Joking relationships" in an English department store have been described by Bradney (1957). An analysis of patterns of "person-focused joking" in a work shop has been provided by Lundberg (1969), and Sykes (1966) told the story of an entire system of intersex joking relationships among several hundred women and men in a Glasgow printing plant. Sykes' report may also contain a reason why the neglect of obscenity may have been only apparent: joking in at least this case included gross obscenities, as a device for regulating sexual distance.

I am not certain whether the mere utterance of an obscenity is not often taken as joking, if for no other reason than that people laugh, however uncomfortably. I would apply the same question to other types of events which have been mentioned earlier in this chapter under "Forms of Communication." They included hitting others on the arm, spitting, tickling, and quarrels over open and closed windows. Donald Roy's justly famous "Banana Time" (1960) told us of daily and hourly occasions and conversational themes, repeated every day. Similar qualities can be seen in my observations in sawmills, such as the frequent questions about what time it was, and the only apparent uncertainty induced by the good possibility that the answer would give a ridiculously wrong time. An important quality of these rituals was revealed by Roy, when the entire system of occasions and themes collapsed because Roy, a participant but relative newcomer, inadvertently questioned one element which had been taken at face value: it is the perfunctory nature of the occasions on which workers communicate with each other in these repetitive and predictable ways.

Conduct appropriate to the reported joking relationships in industry seems to have the same perfunctory quality. Ritual interactions, communication in joking relationships, and what passes for joking more generally, appear to correspond in a number of ways with the characteristics which Bernstein (1973) has called a "public language" and a "restricted code." In comparison with its alternatives, this form of conduct is less capable of expressing tender feeling, a characteristic which is obvious in view of the dominant sexual content and its invariably crude form. It is "tough" and tends to discourage the experience of shame. It puts emphasis on solidarity and is a poor medium for individuation (Bernstein, 1973:62–77). The perfunctory character of communication among workers has been pointed out by Sainsaulieu and Kergoat (1968) and Treinen (1956:74). In contacts with supervisors, it is often enhanced by a desultory or defiant style (but rarely joking), as described for American railway workers (Spier, 1959:59), French bakery employees (Sainsaulieu, 1965:169), and British and German coal miners (Goldthorpe, 1959; Jantke, 1953).

Why do joking and other perfunctory forms tend to dominate communication in industrial work? A plausible answer might be found in the "joking relationship" which has been of long-standing interest to social anthropologists: through an analogy between industrial employment and marriage, the anthropologists' explanation might be extended to the world of industry.

Industrial employment and marriage have certain similarities. They both produce occasions for joking, as well as perfunctory social interaction, and both begin with high expectations and have consequences not bargained for. For example, even when a woman is free to choose her husband, she does not choose her brother-in-law. Compelled by resources tied to kinship, her brother-in-law is obligated to interact with her, and to do so with propriety. He may also see in her a potential sexual property (in some societies it could be his turn to marry her after his brother's death). The ensuing joking relationship often carries sexual connotations and constitutes the "solution" to the conflict between propriety and sexual potential.

Industrialization has created "free labor," a condition according to which a man is free to choose his job, but does not choose his co-workers. Compelled by the necessity of earning a living, and the technology and organization of the work-place, he is obliged to share resources and cooperate with people he was not free to choose. One might argue by analogy that the joking so common to industrial work-places has the function of controlling the reactions to conflicting demands which these circumstances make on the quality of social relations on the job.

Like other devices which regulate enforced but tenuous relationships, joking is a perfunctory form of social interaction. Pursuing the analogy of marriage and industrial employment may suggest the reason. Marriage turns out to be a lifetime contract for the (unpaid) labor of a woman whose inducement to enter it is romantic love. The inducement to work in employment is an anticipation of social worth and the promise of work satisfaction, but work turns into a lifetime of labor. Work satisfaction and romantic love are "instruments of production," that is, devices for committing "human resources" to use, in the production of goods for public markets or in the production of private services for men in the household.

The hidden injury (term adapted from Sennett and Cobb, 1972) in both circumstances is that the inducement device has made commitment *voluntary*, to a virtually inescapable condition of being used as a resource. Through exercising their freedom of choice, industrial workers and married women give up their freedom of choice. The injury is so severe and permanent that it cannot be expressed unambiguously, or admitted in personal terms: consistently large proportions of industrial workers indicate in questionnaires that they are "satisfied" with their work; and many married women continue to express their belief that they scrub the floor as an expression of love to their husbands. In personal contact, you cannot tell your husband that he is exploiting your love, as you would rather not tell your fellow worker that you did not choose his company and do not cooperate with him for personal reasons. Economic dependence makes it impossible to leave the relationship, even when changing partners, at work as at home. The result? a form of communication which depersonalizes the dilemma, and which does not require individual articulation of hidden injuries and emphasizes the solidarity of circumstance in place of differentiated empathy. Marital conversation or nagging takes on a perfunctory code which serves functions that correspond to those of obscene joking, ritual, and desultory relationships at the work-place.

When married women take jobs for money, there is "No Exit," all doors are closed. Overworked, underpaid and undervalued, confined to menial tasks and personal service at home and on the job, they may, as some reports suggest (Mumford, 1959; Sykes, 1966), participate in obscene joking, but more likely as a matter of defense against male presumption and dominance than for fun. For them, joking at work is not funny, except in a self-destructive sense, because they are the victims of symbolic fun at their expense (Weisstein, 1973). Their perfunctory cover does not stretch far enough to keep their hidden injuries under wraps.

A Touch of Class

Comparisons of the quality and extent of articulation have been made between social classes. Selecting extremes of income and education, differences were assessed in the way in which people described the events of a community disaster in an American city (Strauss and Schatzman, 1955; Schatzman and Strauss, 1955). Lower-class respondents tended to offer a direct, concrete, single-line narrative told from their personal perspective. Higher-class people could do as well in direct and concrete reporting, and also displayed an ability to take the listener's point of view; to account for the perspective of other participants in the event; and to identify the relevance of organizations and entire categories of people. Lower-class accounts were particularistic, and their sequence was guided by connections between unique events, rather than a more inclusive view of complex relationships.

Comparing the characteristics of language use of English middle-class and lower working-class people, Bernstein (1959, 1960, 1964, 1973) argued that persons in different classes come to adopt linguistic codes which are not a function of intelligence but of class culture. Middle-class people communicate in an "elaborated code," and lower working-class people in a "restricted code." According to Bernstein, a restricted code discourages "individually differentiated cognitive and affective responses" and "the verbalization of tender feeling," and elicits " 'tough' responses either through vocabulary or through expressive style" (1959:316, 319). Bernstein (1964:56) further states that working-class speech is

> characterized by a reduction in qualifiers, . . . more concrete than abstract propositions, . . . a code which does not help the user put into words his intent, his unique purposes, beliefs and motivations, . . . where changes in meaning are more likely to be signaled nonverbally than through changes in verbal selections . . .

Although these selections of lower-class Americans and lower working-class Britons coincide only partly with the category of "industrial workers," the findings correspond with the views expressed by French factory workers. In an impressive study of observations and interviews, Sainsaulieu and Kergoat (1968) examined the quality of personal relationships among workers; their scope of articulation; and their image of work. According to these workers, communication in depth is an impossibility, and all attempts of really getting to know the others in the work place are useless. The "Other" is a rigid block with which one's "Self" collides, but without being able to do anything about it. Relationships lack reciprocity and remain superficial: "Entre nous, on plaisante, mais on ne parle pas beaucoup." The authors suggest that this is a "universe without nuances," ideas are juxtaposed as right or wrong, and discussion is not a matter of rapprochement but of selecting those with whom one is in agreement. As in the other two studies reviewed above, this report points to difficulties in verbal expression, limited vocabulary, and dependence on brief and conventional gestures (Sainsaulieu and Kergoat, 1968:788–789).

Comparable problems of verbal control were implied in diary records of observers in German coal mines (Jantke, 1953:227–232). Interviews with German steel workers revealed that only a little over half could provide meaningful answers about the sources of technical changes in the mill. The answers of others revealed either grotesque conceptions or helplessness in coping with the question (Popitz, 1957b:53).

The first section of this chapter has indicated the limitations on verbal communication imposed by the technical constraints of the production process. This last review of research findings suggests that working-class upbringing and experience also limits the scope and complexity of verbal articulation. The effects of both are mutually reinforcing: technical constraints and social isolation on the job result in reduced social participation away from work (Meissner, 1971).

However, the analysis of technical constraints, the description of sign language use, the assessment of expressive styles, and the review of language coding by social class, have all pointed to greater reliance on nonverbal means of expression. They have demonstrated the potential for innovation, elegance, humor, and frankness, in the development and application of instrumental and expressive codes which represent adaptations to making a living by manual work.

These differences in the coding and communication of experiences constitute, I believe, a dilemma for the worker who must cope with the expectations inherent in the literacy which dominates the larger social environment. They also create a dilemma for social researchers in industry who must cope with a communication system for which they are ill equipped. As an example of the first, we experienced difficulties in interviews with Canadian production workers in a question designed to determine amount of formal schooling. However we phrased the question, many workers expressed regret (and sometimes hostility) of not having had enough education, and one said bruskly "Just put down I've had a *good* education."

The second problem, concerning research in industry, is revealed in unreconciled differences in findings concerning workers' satisfaction with their work. In a study employing self-administered questionnaires, nearly three-fourths of over three thousand industrial workers in Britain checked off "very satisfied" or "satisfied" in answer to the question "How do you feel about your job?" (Hedley, 1971:43). Reports of extended direct observations in industrial work-places, however, bring into view not only workers' habitual griping, resentment of the boss, or ingenious arrangements for "beating the system" of controls, but also profound contempt of their work and anxiety over their place in it. A man in a concrete-pipe plant told me, "They should show this place on TV, so the mother can tell her kids 'if you don't do your homework, that's where you're gonna end up!' " A French worker contemplated, looking through the factory window over a nearby graveyard, "Là, au moins, t'es pas emmerdé par le travail" (Sainsaulieu & Kergoat, 1968:794).

Faced with a questionnaire or formalized interview, workers have to cast their responses in a literate code. It is the code in which they communicate with persons who do not share their experience. As their work, good or bad, is a crucial source of their worth in the eyes of others, how can they say that it is no good? By contrast, the social researcher as observer is forced to interpret the code of the work-place, its style of expression and mode of interpretation, where workers communicate in terse jokes, gestures, and through the machinery of production. Two images of the world of work will remain until one universe of discourse is explicitly and sensitively mapped into the other.

SUMMARY

I have argued in this chapter that communication at work is embedded in an environment of technology and organization, and that it cannot be understood without recognition of this environment as both a contextual resource and a constraint. I have described the dimensions of the technical organization of production and demonstrated that rates of verbal and nonverbal communication respond in opposite direction to the constraints of time, space, function and number. I have shown that the effects of these constraints are only partly cumulative and mostly interactive. The analysis was predicated on the recognition of the multichannel and multifunctional nature of communication, and that nonverbal communication plays an important part in many industrial work places.

The examination of activities of foremen has shown that communication is the principal component of supervision. The foreman's job is highly segmented and responds to a multiplicity of demands. It brings the foreman into contact with a wide diversity of other people. Under these conditions, the opportunity of each worker to communicate directly with the foreman is slight. A great deal of worker-foreman communication is absorbed by strawbosses, whose supervisory functions constitute one of several mechanisms by which demands on the foreman's communication activities are modified. Another important mechanism is the span of control. Differences in the number of subordinates, and in communication with workers who carry out supervisory functions below foreman level, are adaptations to technical requirements for internal coordination. External coordination is accomplished by more communication with other foremen and with workers, and not by greater contact with superiors or strawbosses. It is balanced by a reduction in noncommunicative activities and personal time.

In the final section, concerned with expressive styles at work, I have described the structure and uses of an industrial sign language, and the character of language use among production workers. These descriptions have contrasted elaborations in gestural styles and humor with limitations in verbal articulation. Together with the earlier analyses, this contrast puts into focus the problematic requirement for social researchers in industry and other outsiders, to match their code of communication with the language of work.

REFERENCES

Arrington, R.E.
   1938   "An important implication of time sampling in observational studies of behavior." American Journal of Sociology (43):284–295.
Atteslander, P.M.
   1954   "The interactio-gram." Human Organization 13(No. 1):28–33.
   1956   "Die Erforschung der Aufsichtsfunktion in Arbeitsgruppen durch das Interaktiogramm." Kölner Zeitschrift für Soziologie und Sozialpsychologie (8):64–73.
Bales, R.F.
   1950   Interaction Process Analysis. Reading, Mass.: Addison-Wesley.
Bales, R.F. and E.F. Borgatta
   1965   "Size of group as a factor in the interaction profile," in A.P. Hare, et al. (eds.), Small Groups. Revised Edition. New York: Knopf.
Barker, R.G. (ed.)
   1963   The Stream of Behavior. New York: Appleton-Century-Crofts.

Barron, M.L.
   1950   "A content analysis of intergroup humor." American Sociological Review (15) :88–94.
Baumgarten, F.
   1947   Zur Psychologie des Maschinenarbeiters. Zürich: Rascher.
Bensman, J. and I. Gerver
   1963   "Crime and punishment in the factory." American Sociological Review (28) :588–598.
Bergren, M.
   1966   Tough Timber: The Loggers of B.C.—Their Story. Toronto: Progress Books.
Bernstein, B.
   1959   "A public language." British Journal of Sociology (10) :311–326.
   1960   "Language and social class." British Journal of Sociology (11) :271–277.
   1964   "Social class, speech systems and psycho-therapy." British Journal of Sociology (15) :54–64.
   1973   Class, Codes and Control. Vol. I: Theoretical Studies Towards a Sociology of Language. St. Albans: Paladin.
Birdwhistell, R.L.
   1952   Introduction to Kinesics. Louisville: University of Louisville.
   1968   "Communication," in International Encyclopedia of the Social Sciences. Vol. 3. New York: Macmillan.
Blau, P.M.
   1954   "Patterns of interaction among a group of officials in a government agency." Human Relations (7) :337–348.
Boone, L.P.
   1949   "Patterns of innovation in the language of the oil field." American Speech (24) :31–37.
Bradney, P.
   1957   "The joking relationship in industry." Human Relations (10) :179–187.
Bright, J.R.
   1958   Automation and Management. Boston: Harvard Business School.
Buehler, R.E. and J.F. Richmond
   1963   "Interpersonal communication behavior analysis." Journal of Communication (13) :146–155.
Burma, J.H.
   1946   "Humor as a technique in race conflict." American Sociological Review (11) :710–715.
Cameron, P.
   1969   "Frequency of words in various settings." Pacific Sociological Review (12) :101–104.
Chapple, E.D.
   1939   "Quantitative analysis of the interaction of individuals." Proceedings of the National Academy of Science (25) :58–67.
   1940   "Measuring human relations." Genetic Psychology Monographs (22) : 3–147.
Cottrell, W.F.
   1940   The Railroader. Stanford University Press.

Critchley, M.
  1939   The Language of Gesture. London: Arnold.
Crozier, M.
  1964   The Bureaucratic Phenomenon. Chicago: University of Chicago Press.
Dubin, R.
  1956   "Industrial workers' worlds: a study of the 'central life interests' of
         industrial workers." Social Problems (3):131–142.
  1962   "Business behavior behaviorally viewed," in G.B. Strother (ed.), Social
         Science Approaches to Business Behavior. London: Tavistock.
  1965   Leadership and Productivity. San Francisco: Chandler.
Dubin, R.; A. Hedley and T.C. Taveggia
  1975   "Attachment to work," in R. Dubin (ed.), Handbook of Work, Orga-
         nization and Society. Chicago: Rand McNally College Publishing Co.
Effron, D.
  1972   Gesture, Race and Culture. The Hague: Mouton.
Elkin, F.
  1946   "The soldier's language." American Journal of Sociology (51):414–422.
Erikson, E.H.
  1940   "Studies in the interpretation of play." Genetic Psychology Mono-
         graphs (22):557–671.
Frank, L.
  1957   "Tactile communication." Genetic Psychology Monographs (56):209–
         255.
Friedmann, G.
  1956   Le travail en miettes. Paris: Gallimard.
Fromm, E.
  1941   Escape from Freedom. New York: Holt, Rinehart & Winston.
Gardner, B.B. and W.F. Whyte
  1945   "The man in the middle: position and problems of the foreman."
         Applied Anthropology (Human Organization) 2(4):1–28.
Goffmann, E.
  1959   The Presentation of Self in Everyday Life. Garden City, New York:
         Doubleday.
Gold, R.
  1952   "Janitors versus tenants." American Journal of Sociology (57):486–493.
  1964   "In the basement: the apartment-building janitor," in P.L. Berger
         (ed.), The Human Shape of Work. New York: Macmillan.
Goldthorpe, J.H.
  1959   "Technical organization as a factor in supervisor-worker conflict." Brit-
         ish Journal of Sociology (10):213–230.
Goldthorpe, J.H., et al.
  1968   The Affluent Worker: Industrial Attitudes and Behavior. London:
         Cambridge University Press.
Guest, R.H.
  1956   "Of time and the foreman." Personnel (32):478–486.
Guilbert, M.
  1966   Les fonctions des femmes dans l'industrie. La Haye: Mouton.
Hall, E.
  1959   The Silent Language. Garden City: Doubleday.
  1966   The Hidden Dimension. Garden City: Doubleday.

Hammer, M.
  1959 Vergleichende Morphologie der Arbeit in der Europäischen Automobilindustrie. Basel: Kyklos; Tübingen: Mohr.
Hare, A.P.; E.F. Borgatta and R.F. Bales (eds.)
  1965 Small Groups. New York: Knopf.
Haslam, G.W.
  1967 "The language of the oil fields." Etc.: A Review of General Semantics (24) :191–201.
Hedley, R.A.
  1971 Freedom and Constraint: A Study of British Factory Workers. Ph.D. dissertation. Eugene: University of Oregon.
Holbrook, S.H.
  1962 The American Lumberjack. New York: Collier.
Homans, G.C.
  1950 The Human Group. New York: Harcourt, Brace.
  1965 "Effort, supervision, and productivity," in R. Dubin (ed.), Leadership and Productivity. San Francisco: Chandler.
Horsfall, A.B. and C.M. Arensberg
  1949 "Teamwork and productivity in a shoe factory." Human Organization 8(No. 1) :13–25. Also, in A.H. Rubenstein and C.J. Haberstroh (eds.), Some Theories of Organization. Homewood, Ill.: Dorsey-Irwin.
Jacobs, P.
  1962 "Dead horse and the featherbird: the specter of useless work." Harper's Magazine 225(September) :47–54.
Jantke, C.
  1953 Bergmann und Zeche. Tübingen: Mohr.
Jasinski, F.J.
  1956 "Foreman relationships outside the work group." Personnel (33) :130–136.
Kroeber, A.L.
  1958 "Sign language inquiry." International Journal of American Linguistics (24) :1–19.
Krout, M.H.
  1935 "The social and psychological significance of gestures." Journal of Genetic Psychology (46) :385–411.
Kubie, L.S.
  1934 "Body symbolization and the development of language." Psychoanalytic Quarterly (3) :430–444.
Labarre, W.
  1947 "The cultural basis of emotions and gestures." Journal of Personality (16) :49–68.
Langer, S.K.
  1948 Philosophy in a New Key. New York: Mentor Books.
Lantz, H.R.
  1958 People of Coal Town. New York: Columbia University Press.
Letkemann, P.
  1973 Crime as Work. Toronto: Prentice-Hall.
Lipset, S.M., M.A. Trow and J.S. Coleman
  1956 Union Democracy. Glencoe, Ill.: Free Press.

Lipstreu, O. and K.A. Reed
1964   Transition to Automation. Boulder: University of Colorado Press.
Lombard, G.F.
1955   Behavior in a Selling Group. Boston: Harvard Business School.
Lubow, B.K., et al.
1969   "An empirical approach to work behavior, interaction and rehabilita-
        tion." Human Organization (28):303–321.
Lundberg, C.C.
1969   "Person-focused joking." Human Organization (28):22–28.
Mann, F.C. and J.K. Dent
1954   "The supervisor: member of two organizational families." Harvard
        Business Review (32):103–112.
Marx, K.
1947   Das Kapital (1867), Vol. I, Chapters 12 and 13. Berlin: Dietz.
Meissner, M.
1969   Technology and the Worker: Technical Demands and Social Processes
        in Industry. San Francisco: Chandler.
1970   "Workers and work: meanings and methods of research." Bulletin of
        the International Institute for Labour Studies (7):293–314.
1971   "The long arm of the job: a study of work and leisure." Industrial
        Relations (10):239–260. Also, in W.F. Mann (ed.), Canada: A Socio-
        logical Profile. Toronto: Copp Clark.
Merk, G.
1963   "Lehrlinge als Informationsträger im Betrieb." Kölner Zeitschrift für
        Soziologie und Sozialpsychologie (15):270–276.
Merner, G.B.
1970   Technology and Supervision. Unpublished M.A. thesis. Vancouver:
        University of British Columbia.
Miller, F.B.
1958   " 'Situational' interactions—a worthwhile concept?" Human Organiza-
        tion 17(No. 4):37–47.
Morris, C.
1955   Signs, Language and Behavior. New York: Braziller.
Mumford, E.M.
1959   "Social behavior in small work groups." Sociological Review (7):
        137–157.
Myers, R.R.
1946   "Interpersonal relations in the building industry." Applied Anthro-
        pology (Human Organization) 5(No. 2):1–7.
New York Times
1963   "Old Chicago Board of Trade feels new excitement." New York Times
        October 4.
Philpott, S.
1964   "The union hiring hall as a labor market." British Journal of Indus-
        trial Relations (3):17–30.
Popitz, H., et al.
1957a Technik und Industriearbeit. Tübingen: Mohr.
1957b Das Gesellschaftsbild des Arbeiters. Tübingen: Mohr.
Psathas, G. and J. Henslin
1967   "Dispatched orders and the cab driver: a study of locating activities."
        Social Problems (14):424–443.

Richardson, F.L.W.
  1966 "Recollecting vs. 'live' recording: organizational relationships of a surgeon." Human Organization (25):163–179.
Roethlisberger, F.J.
  1945 "The foreman: master and victim of double talk." Harvard Business Review (23):283–298.
Roethlisberger, F.J. and W.J. Dickson
  1939 Management and the Worker. Cambridge: Harvard University Press.
Roy, D.
  1954 "Efficiency and the 'fix'." American Journal of Sociology (60):255–266.
  1960 "'Banana time': job satisfaction and informal interaction." Human Organization 18(Winter):158–168. Also, in W.G. Bennis, et al. (eds.), Interpersonal Dynamics. Homewood, Ill.: Dorsey.
  1974 "Sex in the factory: informal heterosexual relations between supervisors and work groups." In C.D. Bryant (ed.), Deviant Behavior: Occupational and Organizational Bases. Chicago: Rand McNally College Publishing Co.
Ruesch, J. and W. Kees
  1959 Nonverbal Communication. Berkeley: University of California Press.
Sagarin, E.
  1962 The Anatomy of Dirty Words. New York: Lyle Stuart.
Sainsaulieu, R.
  1965 "Pouvoirs et stratégies de groupes ouvriers dans l'atelier." Sociologie du Travail (7):162–174.
Sainsaulieu, R. and D. Kergoat
  1968 "Milieu de travail et modèle d'action." Analyse et Prévision–Futuribles (6):781–807.
Sayles, L.R.
  1958 Behavior of Industrial Work Groups. New York: Wiley.
Schatzman, L. and A. Strauss
  1955 "Social class and modes of communication." American Journal of Sociology (60):329–338.
Sebeok, T.A.
  1962 "Coding in the evolution of signalling behavior." Behavioral Science (4):430–442.
Sennett, R. and J. Cobb
  1972 The Hidden Injuries of Class. New York: Knopf.
Simpson, R.L.
  1959 "Vertical and horizontal communication in formal organizations." Administrative Science Quarterly (4):188–196.
Sommer, R.
  1969 Personal Space. Englewood Cliffs, New Jersey: Prentice-Hall.
Soskin, W.F. and V.P. John
  1963 "The study of spontaneous talk," in R.G. Barker (ed.), The Stream of Behavior. New York: Appleton-Century-Crofts.
Spier, J.
  1959 "The railroad switchman." Berkeley Journal of Sociology 5(No. 1):40–62c.
Stanton, A.H. and M.S. Schwartz
  1954 The Mental Hospital. New York: Basic Books.

Stephan, F.F.
  1952 "The relative rate of communication between members of small groups." American Sociological Review (17):482–486.
Stieber, H.W.
  1956 "Interaktionen—Ausdruck der sozialen Organisation einer Arbeitsgruppe." Kölner Zeitschrift für Soziologie und Sozialpsychologie (8): 83–89.
Stinchcombe, A.L.
  1968 Constructing Social Theories. New York: Harcourt, Brace & World.
Strauss, A. and L. Schatzman
  1955 "Cross-class interviewing." Human Organization 14(No. 2):28–31.
Sykes, A.J.M.
  1966 "Joking relationships in an industrial setting." American Anthropologist (68):188–193.
Szalai, A. (ed.)
  1972 The Use of Time: Daily Activities of Urban and Suburban Populations in Twelve Countries. The Hague: Mouton.
Talland, G.A.
  1957 "Rate of speaking as a group norm." Human Organization 15(No. 4): 8–10.
Thomas, E.J. and C.F. Fink
  1965 "Effects of group size," in A.P. Hare, et al. (eds.), Small Groups. Revised Edition. New York: Knopf.
Thomas, M.
  1951 "Sexual symbolism in industry." International Journal of Psychoanalysis (31):128–133.
Thurley, K.E. and A.C. Hamblin
  1963 The Supervisor and his Job. London: HMSO.
Touraine, A.
  1955 L'évolution du travail ouvrier aux Usines Renault. Paris: Centre National de la Recherche Scientifique.
Treinen, H.
  1956 "Eine Arbeitsgruppe am Fliessband: Sozialstruktur und Formen der Beaufsichtigung." Kölner Zeitschrift für Soziologie und Sozialpsychologie (8):73–83.
Turner, A.N.
  1955 "Interaction and sentiment in the foreman-worker relationship." Human Organization 14(No. 1):10–16.
Verry, M.
  1955 Les laminoirs Ardennais: déclin d'une aristocratie professionelle. Paris: Presses Universitaires de France.
Walker, C.R.
  1957 Toward the Automatic Factory. New Haven: Yale University Press.
Walker, C.R. and R.H. Guest
  1952 The Man on the Assembly Line. Cambridge: Harvard University Press.
Walker, C.R., R.H. Guest and A.N. Turner
  1956 The Foreman on the Assembly Line. Cambridge: Harvard University Press.
Watson, J. and R.J. Potter
  1962 "An analytic unit for the study of interaction." Human Relations (15): 245–265.

Watson, O.M.
  1970   Proxemic Behavior: A Cross-Cultural Study. The Hague: Mouton.
Weisstein, N.
  1973   "Why we aren't laughing anymore." Ms. 11(November):49–51, 88–90.
Whitehead, T.N.
  1938   The Industrial Worker. 2 vols. Cambridge: Harvard University Press.
Whyte, W.F.
  1949   "The social structure of the restaurant." American Journal of Sociology (54):302–310.
Woodward, J.
  1956   The Dock Worker. Liverpool: Liverpool University Press.
  1965   Industrial Organization: Theory and Practice. London: Oxford University Press.
Wray, D.F.
  1949   "Marginal man of industry, the foreman." American Journal of Sociology (54):298–301.
Yanouzas, J.N.
  1964   "A comparative study of work organization and supervisory behavior." Human Organization (23):245–254.
Zaleznik, A.
  1956   Worker Satisfaction and Development. Boston: Harvard Business School.
Zaleznik, A., C.R. Christensen and F.J. Roethlisberger
  1958   The Motivation, Productivity, and Satisfaction of Workers. Boston: Harvard Business School.

CHAPTER **7**

Attachment to Work

Robert Dubin

University of California—Irvine

R. Alan Hedley

University of Victoria

Thomas C. Taveggia

Illinois Institute of Technology

INTRODUCTION

The purpose of this chapter is to raise the broad question: To what features of their work do workers become attached? In this period of history when alienation from work is so fashionable an intellectual concern, it may seem bizarre or archaic to focus on such an issue. Nevertheless, at the risk of being considered gauche for even asking such a question, we will elaborate a set of positive answers indicating that there are many sources of attachment to work.

The idea of attachments to work underlies all theories of motivation to work, and is a central concern of the analysis of work satisfaction. Organizational programs designed to reduce turnover, increase loyalty, improve individual productivity, or attract workers to expanding organizations are grounded in assumptions about person-work linkages. Indeed, there are scarcely any considerations of the relations between people and work that do not take into account work-centered features that attract people. Even the most doleful mourners for the alienated fate of the modern industrial worker can point to the work features which, if they were added to or restored to the work situation, would reduce or eliminate alienation. It would be impossible to catalog

The authors have cooperated since 1968 in the study of attachments to work. In that year Dubin organized a research team for a year's study of this subject in Great Britain, with Hedley and Taveggia serving as research officers on the study. We devised the first work attachment inventory which was employed in the study of over 3,000 industrial workers in Great Britain. Subsequently Dubin continued the study of work attachments among American firms. Some of the data from these studies are set forth in the last section of this chapter.

the numerous times that job enlargement, job enrichment, self-pacing, autonomy, decision participation, Muzak, "gliding time," fringe benefits, pay levels, supervisory consideration, and the like have been put forth as the features of work whose manipulation will increase employee commitment and even productivity. What is missing in such analyses is any sort of systematic treatment of total work environments in a search for a broad view of their features that attract participants to them.

Few would disagree that the work institution is one of the most important social institutions in industrial societies. However, considerable disagreement exists as to the significance of this institution for those who participate in it (Dubin, 1973). Many social scientists assume that this is the single most important sector of social experience for its participants. Others argue that work is but one among many important sectors in which people participate in industrial societies. The former view sees the totality of man's social life centering around and deriving from his participation in work, while the latter view sees man moving from one sector of social life to another, developing distinct attachments to each (Goodwin, 1972).

CENTRAL LIFE INTERESTS AND WORK ATTACHMENTS

These divergent views were first systematically and empirically juxtaposed in the senior author's theory and research on the central life interests of industrial workers (Dubin, 1956). Following the lead of general sociologists like Emile Durkheim, it was proposed that individuals in western, industrial societies would not find in their work and work-place an overall central life interest; a central life interest being operationally defined as an "... expressed preference for a given locale or situation in carrying out an activity."

In addition to predicting that work would not represent a preferred arena for social participation in general, the central life interest theory nevertheless predicted that employees would develop strong bonds of attachment to impersonal features of their work environments. Specifically, it was predicted that organizational and technological work features would represent important sources of work attachment for most employees, but that employees would not be attached to work by virtue of primary social relationships with fellow workers on the job.

The reasoning here is clear-cut. The work setting occupies such a significant segment of the person's waking hours that the individual inevitably becomes attached to conditions and objects experienced in the work environment. But, the work-place is not congenial to the development of intimate and primary social relationships. Thus, informal relationships will not constitute a significant source of work attachment.

These predictions were corroborated in their original test in 1952–1953 among a sample of 491 industrial workers employed in three plants in midwestern United States. Eighteen replication studies were subsequently undertaken to provide a more comprehensive test. These studies were done in five different countries, among both rural and urban workers, in diverse organizational settings, and among workers in a variety of occupations. Altogether, a grand total of over 9,000 employees representing extremely varied sociocultural, organizational and occupational settings are represented in these researches.

In Table 1, we present the results of these studies bearing on the predic-

TABLE 1
PERCENT JOB ORIENTED BY CENTRAL LIFE INTEREST RESEARCH, 1956–1972

	N	Percent Work Oriented			
		Total	Formal	Technical	Informal
Dubin, 1956*	491	24%	61	63	9
Corrie, 1957	592	70	96	82	34
Orzack, 1959	150	78	91	87	45
Ranta, 1960	203	85	94	87	52
Ima, 1962	406	14	62	54	5
Kremer, 1962	120	24	80	71	2
Nelson, 1962	230	24	67	69	12
Dubin, 1965	226	44	80	72	24
Parker, 1965	343	28	—	—	—
Brown, 1968	475	26	—	—	—
Goldman, 1968	501	43	88	80	15
Latta, 1968	349	12	34	62	8
Maurer, 1968	111	54	76	87	5
Bowin, 1970	384	41	84	73	11
Endo, 1970	457	82	92	90	32
Starcevich, 1971, 1973	518	47	85	80	18
Taveggia, 1971	2298	26	—	—	—
Dubin and Porter, 1974	945	16	—	—	—
Muhammed, 1973	377	23	—	—	—

* See references at the end of the chapter.

tions regarding overall central life interests and attachments to formal, technical, and informal work experiences, respectively. The first conclusion contained in these data is that employees vary considerably in the extent to which they locate their overall central life interests in work. In another place (Dubin, Taveggia, and Hedley, 1975), we suggest that this variation in overall central life interests is attributable, at least in part, to variations in the occupational and organizational settings within which these studies were conducted. That is, the "climate" or "milieu" within which these people worked seems to have significantly affected their overall orientations to work.

Most pertinent to the present discussion are the results of these studies bearing on attachments to formal, technical and informal work experiences. As indicated in Table 1, organizational and technological work features were significant sources of work attachment for over two-thirds of the respondents from eleven of fourteen studies presenting comparable data. Furthermore, informal social relationships constituted a significant source of work attachment for less than one-third of the employees represented in eleven of these fourteen studies. Thus, while many employees become attached to impersonal work features, few are attached to work by virtue of their social relationships with fellow workers.

We feel these results are clear in suggesting that employees develop strong bonds of attachment to work, irrespective of whether they locate their overall central life interests in work. It is equally clear, however, that these results are merely suggestive of classes of work-place conditions and objects that might represent significant sources of work attachment. A thorough understanding of the ways in which people become linked to work requires more detailed investigations of the full range of potential sources of work attachment as in a recent study by Ronan (1970).

We assume this task of describing the features of work environments as sources of work attachment. In order to do so we draw a very sharp distinction between these work environment features and the characteristic human responses to them. We will deal with large systems found in the work-place, such as the employing organization or work groups; with work-place objects (e.g., technology) and human conditions (e.g., autonomy); and with payoffs (e.g., money, status) derived from working. We will *not*, in this analysis, treat the characteristic human responses to these features of work.[1] In short, we will be limiting our attention to the *sources* of work attachments and will not consider the human reactions to them.

We initiate the discussion with a brief analysis of the nature of linkages between persons and their environments of behavior. There follows a summary of coordinate theoretical models of man-environment linkages that have been set forth as explanatory models of working behaviors. The bulk of the chapter is then devoted to a presentation of attachments to work.

MAN-ENVIRONMENT LINKAGES

In an ordered and relatively stable environment, man can readily regulate his relationship to it by moving in a deliberate cycle from one activity, and from one activity setting, to another. The ability to articulate such a man-environment linkage is enhanced by the institutional arrangements which clearly locate social behavior in specific institutional settings. The flow of experiences is also made easy by the fact that much of what is done in a simple society with a deliberate tempo is required social behavior necessary to meet the creature comforts and even survival of its citizens. Under the circumstances of a carefully monitored relationship to his environment, the person may engage in each sequence of activities out of the requirements of necessity, and feel linked to each activity, and through it to its relevant environment. Indeed, the citizen of such a society probably does not exhibit consciousness of the bonds that link him to its institutions, and would be nonplussed by the question: "Why did you do that?"

Self-consciousness about the linkage of man to his environment comes when alternatives for behaving are available. In a society in which stimuli for action abound, the discipline of deliberate tempo and life-sustaining necessity are no longer sufficient means for monitoring the cycle of personal activities (Hughes, 1958:11–22). Additional mechanisms need to be developed to achieve orderly relationships between man and a complex environment (Moore, 1963). Complexity of environment derives from two essential features: (1) when there are many more stimuli inputs in each behavior setting than is true under simpler conditions; and (2) when the opportunity to make choices introduces voluntarism in the responding behavior.

The world of action then divides itself into behavior realms in which there are necessary activities to be carried out, and behavior settings for which the

---

[1] In a forthcoming volume entitled *Central Life Interests and Work Attachments*, Dubin elaborates the analysis of this chapter, with special attention to the social psychology of the characteristic human responses to work attachments, viewed from the standpoint of the person.

chosen behavior is a matter of voluntary selection (Dubin, 1959). The intro-duction of the opportunity for voluntary choice of behaviors represents one of the important developments in the unfolding freedom of man. It is precisely because there are some behavior areas in which choices can be made that there develops a positive affect about the opportunity for such choices, or the objects toward which such chosen behaviors are directed. Thus, the intro-duction of decisions, and therefore voluntarism, into the situation of action becomes the opportunity to establish positive affective bonds between actor and environment.

The other side of the coin of voluntarism is that the prescribed or neces-sary behaviors in those areas where no choices exist may be tolerated, provided there are other areas in which choice of behavior may be exercised. The para-dox of modern industrial work—that necessary technical behaviors (e.g., machine pacing, short cycle repetition of work operations, etc.) grow apace and can be tolerated at the same time that the dignity of the man on the job and his autonomy in certain job-related behaviors persists—may be explained by the balance between necessary and voluntary areas of behavior. Assembly line work can be tolerated in automobile factories if the pay is high and, especially, if the pay rates have been negotiated with the employer through the collective and, consequently, voluntary action of unionized workers.

We are, therefore, proposing a law. Attachment is made to those parts of the social environment in which choices for personal action exist. The environ-ment, defined in operational terms, refers to any portion of the life-space of the person with which he interacts in behavioral terms. This may be an in-stitution, an industry, the locale of residence, the work group, the equipment and machinery with which work is accomplished, or even parts of the worker's own body. The search for linkages between persons and their work will, therefore, center upon those aspects of the work environment, broadly con-ceived, in which some voluntarism exists with regard to their own working behaviors. These points of attachment to work may vary in the work-life history of individuals so that we may anticipate that over the complete working life-cycle, there may be different points of attachment. This, of course, suggests the desirability of longitudinal studies to tease out such life-cycle changes.

There are two central dimensions to our approach. The environments within which people work are composed of myriad objects, each one being a potential object to which the individual may become attached. An attachment, once established, involves some sort of reaction on the part of the individual.

The environment as a collection of objects can be broadly characterized as the objective world. This objective world is composed, first of all, of objects that may be apprehended through the senses, and that includes all the senses, for the world of work involves seeing, hearing, feeling, smelling, and tasting in at least some of the jobs that produce the goods and services of society. In addition, there are other objects which are not apprehended by the primary senses but which nevertheless elicit responses from the person. This category in-cludes those objects that only become so when passed through the mind and emotions of the person. For example, the notion of "beauty" of a product, although visible to the craftsman and his audience, does not become "beauty" until so labelled in the mind of the beholder. If the beholder happens to be the craftsman, he may react to his definition of beauty in his output by taking pride in his own workmanship. This more abstract notion of objects, as exemplified in "beauty," must also fall within the range of the objective world we wish to take into account as the environment of work.

The reaction of an individual to an object of his work environment is necessary for a relationship to be established between the person and the objective environment. This reaction, in turn, has several possible dimensions. It may be an intellectual reaction involving evaluational or judgmental operations on the part of the person. The reaction may also be emotional, involving affective responses within the individual. Finally, the reaction may be strictly behavioral, involving muscular responses to the stimulus of the environmental object, as when the lathe operator "automatically" actuates the control lever to start the cutting tool moving across the turning metal blank.

In this chapter, we make a major analytical step to identify objects of the work environment to which individuals might respond. We begin by examining some of the main trends in the literature to identify classes of such objects and to illustrate the connectedness of the ideas basic to this chapter with those already in the literature.

COORDINATE MODELS AND THEORIES

What is proposed here is a developmental advance from earlier and contemporary theorizing about man's attachment to work. Very briefly, we will present some of the main trends to illustrate the linkage of the ideas here presented with those already current.

In the area of work satisfaction, studies have repeatedly shown that people with high skill and complex jobs are more satisfied with their work than less skilled persons with routine jobs to do (Blauner, 1969; Herzberg, et al., 1957:20–23). From these findings, it is typically concluded that interesting work is work which is varied, and so may demand decisions regarding timing, cycling, and sequence of the various job operations. Clearly, in more complex work, there must be decisional areas in which the worker, or the technician, or the scientist, or the executive has opportunities for decisions about his own work. These findings have caused theorists to focus upon what may be called the "work behavior mix" as the central feature of work to which attachment is made. The managerial policy outcome of this line of reasoning has been to propose a general program of "job enlargement" as a way of enhancing people's attachment to work (and often claiming that greater work satisfaction, increased personal effort and productivity, heightened loyalty, etc., will also result) (Hulin and Blood, 1968).

Quite a different line of development, stemming from the work of Lewin (1948), focused attention upon the colleague group as providing the most potent reinforcement for individual behavior. It was shown in some of Lewin's early and classic studies that group consensus was vital in achieving individual conformity to a given course of behavior. Lewin then turned his attention to theorizing about the condition for securing group agreement about what needs to be done. Once the group consensus was achieved, the individual member was under extreme pressure (as Sherif [1935] and Asch [1951] demonstrated in their classic experiments) to conform to the chosen behavior, or perhaps, more charitably put, was reinforced in making the group decision his own. The Lewinians needed only to look back in the literature on restriction of output in industry to realize that their point had long since been established, although the outcome was negative with respect to management productivity goals (Mathewson, 1935). The policy implication flowing from the Lewinian idea about what attached men to their work was to urge a sharing of decision-making with regard to at least some aspects of the work performance and work goals (Coch and French, 1948). The history of participative management, of course, predates the experiments of Lewin that gave some empirical base to the earlier notions (see, for example, Carey, 1942).

To take another example, an examination of the incentive payment systems in modern industry reveals very clearly that their designers believed that man's attachment to his work is through the financial payoffs it provides. The much reviled "economic man" was an unwilling worker whose linkage to work was as a means to the end of securing the currency with which to become a consumer (Taylor, 1911). The designers of work incentive schemes are most interested in the attachment men have to the cash equivalent of their work. The policy conclusion they urge is that the prospect and achievement of financial payoff bears a positive relationship to attachment to work (Schein, 1965).

Another more recent tradition in the analysis of work has stemmed from the psychoanalytic theories, and, in particular, those features of the theories that emphasize the restrictive and proscriptive character of social organization. This tradition emerged in the work of McGregor (1960), Argyris (1964), and Bennis (1966), among others, who viewed the social situation of work as generally suppressing the opportunity for "self-actualization." In this view, the worker is concerned with self and the realization of his own perceived skills, abilities, and qualities, whatever they may be. So long as the work situation provided for the realization of these skills, abilities, and qualities (and according to the theorists, it usually did not), there would be congruence between self and work, and therefore, between self and organization. There would follow an enhancement of attachment of self to organization. Presumably flowing from this came increased dedication, devotion, loyalty, or at least as a bare minimum, increased productivity and self-satisfaction. Obviously, this way of viewing man at work sees his attachment to work being made through self. At the level of managerial policy, the conclusions become very murky indeed. Short of a return to a modern form of "cottage industry" in which each worker goes off on his own to do his "thing," it is difficult to see how the work situation can be so designed that it provides maximum "self-actualization" for all, or even a majority, of its participants. Perhaps the net effect of this particular line of analysis has been to argue: (1) that the self is an important point of attachment to work, and (2) that individuality should be tolerated, even in the work situation.

The analytical scheme proposed by Likert (1961, 1967) suggests still another dimension along which attachment to work develops. His is a model based on influence and its relationship to organizational distance. An individual feels himself part of the work situation to the extent that he can perceive some degree of his own influence on those who make decisions regarding that work situation. Thus, work attachment is to an authority structure, or, more generally, to the organization structure, and the amount of this attachment or linkage is measured by the degree to which the individual, from his working position, feels he can influence the exercise of authority over his own work.

The policy prescription that flows from the Likert viewpoint is that the authority structure should be as flat as possible and that in many situations, authority can devolve upon the worker himself. This latter conclusion is described under the broad rubric of autonomy.

These examples are sufficient to illustrate the point we wish to make, namely, that the proposal to examine the linkage between the person and his work is a general concern. All modern theories of working behavior that deal with motivation, work satisfaction, or the condition of lack of attachment to work, popularly described as alienation, share a common concern with trying to specify the most important sources of man-work linkage.

What is different in what we are proposing is that instead of a monistic theory of attachment to work, or even an hierarchical theory as in the Maslowian (Maslow, 1954) or, in the foreshortened form, the Herzbergian varieties (Herzberg, et al., 1959), we are proposing an eclectic theory of work attachment which attempts to span the many dimensions of work to discover whether each provides to the individual an opportunity for attachments to work.

SOURCES OF ATTACHMENT TO WORK

The following discussion arises out of our search of the empirical liteature for those objective features of the work environment to which workers become attached. We were particularly interested in those research reports dealing with the various boundaries of the world of work, for it was here that we anticipated that most of these aspects of work would be brought out into bold relief. For example, young people about to enter the labor force have been questioned concerning the features of work they hope to have incorporated into their new jobs (Super, 1962), as have older workers about to retire been asked what features they will miss upon taking up a life of leisure (Friedmann and Havighurst, 1954). Similarly, workers engaged in collective bargaining or open conflict with their employers are forced by their situation to give serious consideration to those aspects of work to which they are attached (Stieber, 1960; Gouldner, 1965).

The following areas of research were thought to have potential utility in providing an empirical base for an initial typology of attachments to work:
1. job satisfaction and worker morale studies;
2. occupational and social mobility surveys;
3. industrial relations and collective bargaining research;
4. worker motivation investigations;
5. organizational case studies;
6. experimental technical and social change studies;
7. occupational choice and retirement studies;
8. studies of industrialization in developing areas.

Needless to say, we did not attempt an exhaustive survey of the research in these categories. We did, however, wish to take a sampling of this voluminous literature, for it was here we believed that the linkages between men and their work would be most apparent for the simple reason that in each of these areas of research, in some way or other, the nature of work itself is a focus of attention. Not all of these studies were immediately relevant to our objective, but the search did suggest a broad classification of work which was helpful in locating specific work attachments.

Initially, we identified various *systems of the work environment*, ranging from the self system to industry as a system, as being possible sources of work attachment. We mean by system that there is some form of interdependence among the components composing the system, and that the system as a whole may be recognized by the fact that it has a defined boundary. The self is an obviously essential system of work while most work environments involve several other systems of organization which can include the work group, the company, the union, the craft/profession, and the industry.

Among the six systems mentioned, only the "self" may prove puzzling, since it might be difficult to comprehend how the person may relate to himself as a system. The person is clearly a complex system. Such terms as "self-respect" and "self-image" make clear that the person is an object to himself under a variety of circumstances.

Two related features of a work environment which are also possible sources of work attachment are the *objects* in that environment and the *human conditions* that characterize it. There is no difficulty in understanding the class called objects since they have physical existence and can be apprehended through the senses. Two of the principal objects of the work-place are the technologies of work and the products of labor.

The human conditions of the work-place require some more extended description. The term "human" is used advisedly. It is intended to distinguish certain conditions of the work setting from what are usually called "working conditions." Working conditions are the basic creature comforts that are provided to make a work-place habitable. Adequate working conditions meet standards of expectation regarding physiological comfort. The human conditions of work, on the other hand, focus on the portions of the work environment that generate responses in the higher human faculties. When a work regime is described as "boring" or "frustrating" the description utilizes intellectual and emotional dimensions as the responding features of the person. In this sense, the work regime properly lies in the realm of human conditions as distinct from working conditions. We can then define the "human conditions" of work environments as the complex work regime features that have special impact on the higher human faculties.

Finally, work environments contain within them a number of physical and social *payoffs* which can serve as additional sources of attachment to work. Most of us are so tuned into the idea of reward for behavior that it is scarcely necessary to explain what is meant by the payoffs for working. The worker gives his labor and in return receives rewards that he considers somehow commensurate with his input of work.

What is so typical about work is that the return to the worker is seldom solely one payoff, such as money. Other payoffs, as obvious as the perquisites surrounding a job, as subtle as the authority attached to a position, or as complex as the work career of an individual, may act as inducements contributing to a person's attachment to work.

As an initial summary of what can be retrieved from the literature, Table 2 sets forth the sources of work attachment grouped under the three major headings just discussed. The subsequent discussion will follow the order of the listing in Table 2.

We summarize attachments to work as the linkages that persons develop to features of their work environments. When work features are evaluated as important for whatever reason by persons who experience them, then these features of the work environment have a subjective linkage function for such persons. The importance of the work features may be either positive or negative. Under the circumstance where the evaluation is negative *and* where this negative evaluation results from insufficiency of that particular work feature, then we count this as an attachment to work. Thus, low wages may be negatively important to workers and a raise in wages would not make them less of a source of work attachment even if pay then takes on positive importance to the workers.

SYSTEMS OF THE WORK ENVIRONMENT

We follow the outline of Table 2 in presenting the sources of attachments to work.

Self

The world of work is one arena in which the self finds expression (Hughes, 1958). Indeed, working in such an important part of the definition of the self that the kind of work an individual does has long been taken as the most prominent measure of the individual's standing or status in the society (e.g., Weber, 1947; Edwards, 1938; Warner, 1941–59). This is illustrative of the centrality that occupation has as a critical feature of self-image, reflecting the evaluations others make of one's place in the occupational structure. Indeed, in socialist countries, occupational status may be decisive in determining political and social standing, if not survival itself, as has been demonstrated in

TABLE 2
ATTACHMENTS TO WORK

Sources
I. Systems of the Work Environment
Self
Work Group
Company
Union
Craft-Profession
Industry
II. Work-Place Objects and Human Conditions
Technology
Product
Routine
Autonomy
Personal Space/Things
III. Payoffs
Money
Perquisites
Power
Authority
Status
Career

the recent cultural revolution of the Peoples Republic of China, and the periodic purges of entire classes of intellectuals, technicians and managers that have characterized other socialist countries.

Aside from the evaluative ascription made by others of an individual's work, there is an internalized aspect of the work a person does. A self-evaluation occurs regarding ability, competence, and effectiveness in the work world. Clearly, with self as the object, each individual comes to some self-image about work performance. This has been demonstrated repeatedly. It has been shown that complexity of tasks performed is positively related to a "sense of self-worth on the job" (Argyris, 1959). Working from the expectancy theory of Vroom (1964), Korman (1968, 1970) has suggested that persons in work situations employ a self-consistency strategy so that their choice of work, their performance, and their satisfaction level will be in work roles that are consistent with their self-images. In earlier works, Korman (1966, 1967, 1969) had shown that the same principle of self-consistency applied in the very choice of an occupation, with particular emphasis on the role that self-esteem plays as a moderator of occupational choice. In several tests of Adams' equity theory of wages (Adams, 1963, 1964) it has been found in experiments that when individuals are overcompensated on a task, and are fed back this negative evaluation by the experimenter, they respond by feeling a sense of devalued self-esteem (Wiener, 1970; Andrews and Valenzi, 1970). It seems clear that self-image in its various dimensions is one product of the work situation in which the person operates.

Another line of inquiry deals with the "fit" of personality and work. Maslow (1954) has set forth the need hierarchy, at the apex of which is "self-actualization." This idea has been repeatedly applied to work environments to measure whether they provide opportunities for self-actualization, with Argyris (1964) concluding that most work settings do not. It has been shown that men seem to seek self-actualization at work more than women (Centers and Bugental, 1966) but that this need is poorly satisfied even among managers (Ivancevich, 1969). On the other hand, studies have shown that individuals whose personalities "fit" their work situation have high satisfaction and liking for their work (Tannenbaum and Allport, 1956), and that given mobility options at work, individuals will gravitate to supervisors with whom they have personality compatibilities (Mullen, 1966). Studies of birth order and occupational choice make use of the idea that birth order and personality are linked with the result that individuals of a particular birth order have a higher than chance frequency in some occupations (e.g., lawyers are first born at higher than chance frequencies [Very and Prull, 1970]).

Some negative relationships between features of self and work have been set forth in the literature. Illustrative is the contention that too much individual creativity may be disruptive of an organization (Strother, 1969); that self-estrangement may be an outcome for hourly paid workers in highly bureaucratized work settings (Bonjean and Grimes, 1970); and that level of job dissatisfaction may have some subtle self-destructive consequences since there is a positive correlation between level of job dissatisfaction and death rates for coronary disease (Sales and House, 1970).

This sampling of the literature about work makes abundantly clear that an important object of attachment to work is the self. Within the self system, there are several distinctive subsystems that may provide the nodes through which such linking occurs. This is a complex area of work attachment and needs the benefit of a strong infusion of self and personality theories, as we move from descriptive to more analytical studies.

Work Group

A significant body of industrial research has focused on the work group. Early studies of restriction of output located the informal work group as the social unit effecting the output lag (Mathewson, 1935; Collins, et al., 1946). The systematic focus on the work group was elaborated in the Western Electric studies (Roethlisberger and Dickson, 1939) where horseplay, restriction of output, and what Dubin (1958a) has called "nonformal" behavior were observed. Subsequent descriptive studies have shown that the group of work colleagues promotes a sense of individual satisfaction at being part of a skilled and integrated work unit (Walker, 1950); develops standards for judging individual performance (Blau, 1955); promotes a sense of job security by controlling work pace (Sykes, 1960; Horsfall and Arensberg, 1949); provides nonwork preoccupations to relieve the strain of monotonous tasks (Roy, 1959); and through group pressures and sanctions secures from their members adherence to informal group norms (March and Simon, 1958).

At a more analytical level, a number of distinctive functions of work groups have been elaborated. One very central function is to provide for sociability in the work setting. Katz (1965) has suggested that the work roles of members of complex organizations are so prescribed that there exists a substantial amount of behavior within the organization, but outside the work tasks, where considerable individual autonomy is possible. In this realm of autonomy, informal groups are formed with distinctive subcultures (Baur, 1963) that become reference groups for their members (Jackson, 1959), pursuing sociability as a central group function (Felton, 1966). Over-specification of work tasks, however, may create effective barriers to informal group formation, with adverse effects throughout many aspects of the total work organization (Jasinski, 1956).

Another major function of the work group is to provide a base for feelings of solidarity with other persons in the work setting. In relating group performance to the perception of pressure for output, it has been found that the greater the cohesiveness of work groups, the higher is their self-perception of their work status (Seashore, 1954). Work group solidarity has been shown to diminish identification with formal work leaders in Yugoslavian socialist factories (Rus, 1966), with males exhibiting higher levels of solidarity than females (Kranjc-Cuk, 1968), while level of specialization of work tasks in a Polish socialist factory was positively related to the work team solidarity (Gniazdowski, 1969). In a large Indian factory, displaced Hindus from East Pakistan had higher measured work group solidarity than any of the Indian work groups (Bose, 1958), suggesting a possible ethnic base for work group cohesion. That work group solidarity has significant consequences is revealed in a study of changes in a stereotype about foremen in which it was concluded that individuals did not change their attitudes until the change received informal group support (Sykes, 1964).

Informal groups have additional functions including the socialization of new workers (Evan, 1963; Chadwick-Jones, 1964); the development of collaboration and coordination beyond prescribed work task routines (O'Brien, 1968); and the nurturing of morale (Ferrarotti, 1960; Dan-Spinoiu, 1969).

There has been continuing attention given to the power of work groups, especially in thwarting managerial expectations and directions. Various types of work groups behave differently with respect to management (Sayles, 1958) and different levels of resistance to management have been described among Parisian factory workers (Sainsaulieu, 1965). The problem of potential or actual conflict with management is particularly acute in socialist enterprises so that it is not surprising to find studies of this phenomenon by socialist scholars. Thus, in a study of a Polish engineering plant, it was observed that regulation of output and rhythm of work were determined by the social norms of informal work groups (Doktor, 1962), while another study in the construction industry showed the existence of group norms for time of reporting to work and intensity of effort (Doktor, 1966). On the other hand, it has also been pointed out that in a highly automated production line that manufactures automobile engines, the shift to automation significantly reduced the opportunity for effective work group solidarity by reducing the number of social contacts per day and reducing the number of workers having informal contacts (Faunce, 1958a). That this is not a bar to strong collective action is evidenced by the bitter labor struggle that developed between the General Motors Corporation and its union at the Lordstown factory, a highly automated assembly plant.

In a number of complex ways, the individual finds in his work group a multifaceted source of linkage with work. The essential interaction is with other people, but a limited number of other people with whom the individual associates, usually because of task complementarity, but with whom are developed social relations above and beyond task requirements. These associations are powerful ties that link the individual with the work setting.

Company

We use the term *company* to mean any organization in which work is accomplished. Since most productive work in industrial societies is carried out in organizations, it is not difficult to make the assumption that some features of organizations must be sources of attachment to work. Indeed, the most common response made to the question: "What do you do for a living?" is the answer: "I work for XYZ Company." At least for the purpose of identifying publicly one's work, the employing organization serves as the most commonly employed label.

Research has indicated, however, that it is seldom the employing organization as a whole that is the object of work attachment for the individual (Shister and Reynolds, 1949; Wickert, 1951; Ross and Zander, 1957; Purcell, 1960). It is desirable to examine in some greater detail individual features of organizations that serve the linking function.

A general sense of belonging somewhere in the world of work emerged from a factor analysis of views about work among a group of engineers and scientists (Strauss, 1966). This sense of belonging or affiliation has been given theoretical elaboration (Levinson, 1965) as the substitute for losses the individual suffers during early experiences in friendships, support and family continuity. As if to give some confirmation to this notion, a study of worker attitudes in the Italian iron industry reveals that they viewed their employing organization as a "great mother," the source of personal favors and the solver of personal and family problems (Baglioni, 1969). This would conform to managerial expectations under conditions of paternalism, but other studies have shown that at least some workers have strong negative reactions to such paternalism (Dubin and Wray, 1953).

In an extensive study covering service and sales organizations and voluntary associations, Indik (1965) concluded that the amount of communication up and down the authority structure and involving the individual is the mechanism that binds the individual to the organization. In an earlier study of a telephone company, the bonds of organization were set forth as essentially social-psychological ones (Bakke, 1950), with the congruence of individual and organizational goals being central. Vroom (1960) pursued the goal congruence notion in a study of electronics employees and concluded that individuals tend to attribute their own attitudes, opinions and goals to groups and organizations toward which they have positive attitudes, thus confirming the social psychological nature of individual-organizational goal congruence. In a study of a voluntary association, it was found that individual commitment to specific values of an organization is distinct from commitment to the organization as a whole (H.P. Gouldner, 1960), giving further support to the idea that linkage with the organization is probably only to portions of its totality.

In a recent study of scientists working in a private laboratory, it has been found that sheer investment of personal energy is one source of attachment to the organization (Sheldon, 1971). However, in a study of members of Yugoslavian works councils, it was not established that their high level of investment in work raised the level of attachment to the organization (Obradovic, 1970), although in an earlier study of a Yugoslavian factory, it was found that identification with the enterprise increased the higher an individual advanced up the authority structure of the organization (Kolaja, 1961). Among a large number of employees in the TVA, it was found that identification with this government agency depended upon the presence of opportunities to satisfy symbolic motivational states in the individual (M.E. Brown, 1969). Working with his previously established distinction between cosmopolitans and locals as organizational members, A.W. Gouldner (1958) found four distinctive categories of locals: (1) the dedicated—true believers in the organizational ideology, (2) bureaucrats who are loyal to the organization *per se*, (3) homeguards who are loyal for various personal reasons, and (4) elders whose advanced age makes them immobile and hence negatively committed to the organization.

The evidence seems very clear that the organization does provide a source of attachment to work. However, it is also clear the organization as a whole is such a complex system that attachment to it for any individual will be made to only limited features of the system. The further exploration of these features of the organization awaits further developments in organization theory that expands the dimensions along which organizations are conceptualized.

Union

In many work organizations, the employees are represented by a union. The very existence of unions and their ability to hold members can be taken by itself as evidence that they are additional sources of attachment to work. The proportion of the total labor force to be found in unions varies among countries, as does the proportion of blue and white collar employees who are union members. In the United States, for example, only about one-quarter of employed persons are in unions, and they are largely concentrated among blue collar workers (Lipset, 1967; Bruner, 1962). For a significant portion of the labor force, therefore, the union does not constitute a source of work attachment.

The collective bargaining agreement, and what it represents in the form of wages, hours, and working conditions, is the most obvious feature of the union's activities toward which members feel attachment. Some scholars have suggested that unions are the focus of social and political attachments as well (Form and Dansereau, 1957; Schlag-Rey, Ribas and Feaux, 1959; Hoshikawa, 1962). Where national unions and union federations have political bases, as in France, Italy, Britain and Germany, the political role of unions for their members may become equal in importance to the economic role. It has also been suggested that fellow union members become a reference group, and in the process add another linkage of the individual to the work setting (Spinrad, 1960).

A closer look at the functions of unions reveals that they play a central role in handling day-to-day grievances of their members *vis-à-vis* management. In this function, unions both develop and sustain membership attachment (Dubin, 1958b; Sinha and Pai, 1963). Some unions, such as printers, have broad control over their occupation so that entry into the trade and performance in it is dependent on close and continuous ties with fellow unionists within the local union (called the Chapel among printers) which becomes a very strong tie to the work situation (Lipset, Trow and Coleman, 1956; Sykes, 1960, 1967). Among the building trade unions in the United States, a high level of job control coupled with personal recruitment of friends and relatives to the occupation has added an ethnic and racial bond among union members that further enhances attachment to the work environment (University of Chicago Law Review, 1970).

Generally, the day-to-day participation of workers in union activities is low (Rose, 1952; Sayles and Strauss, 1953; Peck, 1963; Perline and Lorenz, 1970; Seidman, et al., 1958; Tagliacozzo and Seidman, 1956). It has been pointed out that during these periods of low participation, the workers express a stance of dual linkage with both union and company (Miller and Rosen, 1957; Purcell, 1960). This lack of daily participation does not mean, however, that the attachment to the union is eliminated, for a tense bargaining situation or a strike will mobilize intensive collective action. The study of strikes reveals the strength of attachment workers feel toward their unions and, through the collective action, toward their jobs, which they protect with picket lines (Hiller, 1928; Chaumont, 1962; Maurice, 1965; Dubois, 1970).

The strongest attachment to work through the union is typically found among union officers (Jenkins, 1962). At the local level among shop stewards there is usually both a working and a union role performed by each individual with the union role centered on handling grievances. The grievances are almost exclusively work-centered so that stewards have a reinforced attachment to work through handling grievances. It is not uncommon for stewards to be chosen by management for promotion to supervisory positions (a phenomenon characteristic in Europe as well as the United States [Flanders, 1963]) which adds another element of attachment to work through the union. At higher levels of union officialdom, holding union office tends to become a career, with the obvious implication this has for attachment to work in the union rather than in industry.

A labor union turns out to be a complex system which in a number of different ways links its members with their work. This is a function of unionism that is perhaps better recognized in socialist economics than in capitalist countries. Indeed, in socialist countries unions may have only a minor role in collective bargaining but perform a major function in managing the labor force and providing the bureaucracy through which social benefits tied to the work-place are administered.

Craft-Profession

Attachment to work through a craft or a profession focuses attention upon the performance characteristics of an occupation. Where task behaviors are distinctive and are based on an extensive body of knowledge, often secured through formal education or apprenticeship, this combination of factors may provide the basis for attachment to a craft or profession (Dibble, 1962). The congerie of task behaviors and knowledge is carried with the individual regardless of where the occupation is practiced so that attachment to the craft-profession is likely to take precedence over attachment to a particular work organization. Early craftsmen were actually itinerate workers, and medicine and law are still designated as "independent professions" even though they are increasingly practiced in corporate settings. When a profession has the aspect of a "calling" or vocation (as in medicine, the priesthood) the professional ethic and way of life may be pervasive (Caplow, 1964).

The powerful hold that craft-profession may have upon the individual is related to the extensive preparatory period of training and socialization that precedes assumption of the occupational role (Hall, 1948; Becker and Carper, 1956; Kornhauser, 1962). Indeed, it has been demonstrated that the academic socialization of scientists is a blockage to their resocialization to industrial values when they are employed in industry (Abrahamson, 1964), although a subsequent study of scientists and engineers in an aerospace company disputes the existence of such conflict and suggests that schooling does prepare for industrial employment (Miller, 1971).

The detailed study of scientists and engineers in industry reveals what Marcson has called "colleague authority," the opportunity to be self-governing within the realm of professional performance (Marcson, 1960; cf., Rourke, 1960; Goss, 1962; Vollmer and Mills, 1966; Miller, 1967; Abrahamson, 1967). The failure to achieve professional career expectations within private employment may give rise to cynicism and insurgency against the organization (McKelvey, 1969). However, one way to reconcile the professional and organizational roles was revealed in a study of a Polish factory where engineers and technicians played the roles of experts and advisors with marked satisfaction (Sicinski, 1964). The argument about the conflict between the professional and bureaucratic roles has been elaborated to contend that professionals create their own distinctive social organization which cannot be understood within the framework of bureaucratic theory (Bucher and Stelling, 1969).

Among craftsmen, various studies have indicated the high awareness of their special skills and knowledge which becomes highly visible when the craft is in jeopardy due to automation or standardization and rationalization of work processes (Mann and Hoffman, 1960; Sheppard, Ferman and Faber, 1960; Friedmann, 1961; Killingsworth, 1963; Durand, 1965; Shostak, 1969). Rottenberg (1963) has even argued that workers whose skills have been made obsolete demand severance pay as compensation for their personal investment in the acquisition of their skills.

The practice of a craft or profession entails a long preparatory training and socialization period as well as distinctive behaviors while working, both complex systems linking persons with their work. The underlying demographic shifts in the labor forces of industrialized nations make clear that an increasing proportion of the working population falls within the craft-professional category.

Industry

An industry may provide a significant point of attachment for those employed in it. The features of industries which constitute the sources of attachment may vary. Such features as strategic importance, universality, exclusiveness, inherent danger, challenge, novelty, or profitability may constitute the bases for attachments of workers to them (Cottrell, 1939; Archibald, 1947; Walker, 1950; A.W. Gouldner, 1954; Liverpool University, 1956; Horobin, 1957; Blauner, 1964; Hollowell, 1968; Dennis, et al., 1969; Sykes, 1969). These notable features of industries may decline over time as happened in the U.S. railroad industry (Cottrell, 1951), or they may be only short-lived as in war-time military industries (Archibald, 1947).

A sense of industry identification also arises as a result of special features that isolate particular industries, or their employees. Some industries have remote and isolated sites as in mining, for example (A.W. Gouldner, 1954; Horobin, 1957; Dennis, et al., 1969), while other industries are just as distinctive because they have no fixed site, as in transportation where employees move over great distances as part of their daily work (Cottrell, 1939; Hollowell, 1968). Furthermore, some industries are wholly isolated along with the living community surrounding them, as in company towns, so that attachment to the industry is reinforced throughout the local community (Walker, 1950). In some industries, the special work schedules, such as continuous operations, simply preclude social relations outside of work with any but work mates and their families (Aris, 1964).

Several mechanisms lend support to attachment to an industry, including occupational inheritance. Among dockworkers in Liverpool, 75% were sons of dockworkers (University of Liverpool, 1956), while in Soviet logging in the Karelians there were generations of workers who knew nothing but work in that industry (Pimenov, 1963), and a study of the forestry industry in Japan also found kinship an important determinant of who worked in the industry (Bennett, 1958). The kinship ties turned out to be an important basis for recruiting workers to the pipeline construction industry and reinforcing their attachment to the industry once in it (Graves, 1970). It has been found that workers from particular industries constitute a distinctive subculture in an area and remain "outsiders" to the surrounding community so that the primary identification of the workers remains with their segregated industry, a condition found in a French steel plant set in the agricultural department of Mayenne (Cloitre, 1962).

Intrinsic characteristics of industries as well as their special conditions and mechanisms of social relations contribute to making the industry itself a source of work attachment. Indeed, it has been concluded that the growing specialization of occupations that are peculiar to individual industries has produced a trained incapacity of workers to be employed in any but the industry utilizing their special occupation, thereby making their work attachment to the industry even stronger (Dubin, 1958a).

WORK-PLACE OBJECTS AND HUMAN CONDITIONS

Attention now turns to a consideration of other aspects of the work environment. The examination centers first on *technology* and *product* as two of the most obvious and pervasive features of the work-place. Then we will analyze *routine* and *autonomy* as human conditions characteristic of work, with each providing in distinctive ways their own means of linking people with their work. Finally, in this general section, we will examine *personal space* and the personal possessions that characterize the work station of every employed person.

Technology

The most general relationship of persons to the technology of getting work done is grounded in the skilled and knowing utilization of the technical ideas and/or equipment and processes employed in the work. The common way to view technology is to associate the term exclusively with equipment and machines. However, technical ideas are equally important, and in some rare instances, are the total technology employed (e.g., the technology of the psychiatrist). On the other hand, technology need not be complicated to warrant that designation, for in many jobs involving simple equipment and ideas, their proper employment requires a learned skill and experience (e.g., a janitor mopping a floor [Taylor, 1911]).

It has been suggested that in modern industry the development of mass production technologies has tended to transfer to machines and industrial processes the skills formerly exercised by workers and thereby reduced or eliminated the opportunity for workers to feel attached to the technical operations they have mastered (Vroom, 1964). That conclusion rests on the belief that workers lose their autonomy in relation to work, a point we will analyze in a succeeding section. That is not the same thing as asserting that the job simplification and job subdivision accompanying mass production reduces the possibility of developing a sense of attachment to the simplified work operations. In addition it should be noted that only a small percent, estimated at less than 5% (Blauner, 1969), of workers in modern industry work on high speed, continuous assembly lines. Furthermore, it has been shown that automation, with the opportunities it affords for the worker to control entire systems of complex machinery, with much less physical effort, actually enhances the development of strong attachments to the technology (Walker, 1957; Faunce, 1958a; Mann and Hoffman, 1960; Blauner, 1964; Daniel, 1969).

One of the strong operational tests of worker attachment to technology comes when technology is changed. Many studies have reported serious worker opposition to technical change (Mann and Hoffman, 1960; Shils, 1963; Somers, et al., 1963; Scott, 1965; Touraine, et al., 1965; Blitz, 1969). These and similar studies indicate that the factor of attachment to craft-profession is operative since workers report a feeling of loss of developed skills as one basis for opposition to the technological change. A much quoted study of changes in coal mining technology demonstrates that the technology ruptured the fabric of social relations and work group structure and thereby loosened the work attachment through the work group (Trist and Bamforth, 1951).

In an interesting experiment, ground controllers trained to employ simple operating criteria, continued to do so on aerial intercept tasks even when the conditions of the simulated situation required the employment of complex criteria for successful intercept of planes (Briggs and Johnston, 1966). The implication of this study is that persons become imprinted with their learned technical skills and continue to apply them to work tasks even when they are not appropriate. Perhaps this is the deep reason why workers opposed technological change because of their attachment to the technology in which they are skilled. This conclusion is strongly supported by the results of an important longitudinal study by Walker (1957) in which he analyzed the consequences of the introduction of a semi-automatic process to replace a multi-stage manufacturing process for producing seamless steel pipe. It was found that the features of the new technology most strongly opposed by the workers making the transition were warmly praised by the same workers several years later. Clearly, the work attachment to the old technology was transferred to the new technology.

The importance of technology as a source of work attachment is beyond question. The idea of technology as "the enemy," which has been a theme since the Luddite workers rose up and smashed the power looms at the beginning of the industrial revolution, is clearly a less useful way to evaluate technology than to see it as a source of linkage between persons and their work.

Product

In traditional thinking, the product of labor is viewed as central to attachment to work. Almost all definitions of work are made in terms of the production of goods and services—an outcome or a product. It is not surprising that this view is so common since the model from which it is derived is that of the creative artisan, artist, and intellectual who is, after all, recognized only through his creative output (Dubin, 1958a; Blauner, 1969). For all those who produce a complete product, doing the finishing work and much of what precedes, the product itself is the embodiment of the creative process, and indeed, often carries the mark or signature of the individual creator (as in sterling and porcelain marks, authors' names and artists' signatures).

It is analytically more difficult to view a complex product, to which many individuals have contributed, as still being able to claim each individual's attachment to "my" product. It has been suggested that by surrounding the product with prestige such identification may result (Perrow, 1961). It has also been suggested that at least among engineers in industry, the product orientation that can be developed by using project management or matrix organization structures is highly conducive to developing enthusiasm and identification with output goals (Kaufman and Ritti, 1965). Perhaps the major answer to the issue of identification with a complex product that results from the effort of many workers lies in the nature of what Woodward (1965) called unit production. The contributing workers can see the "unit" grow in place as they add their work to it. Thus, workers who construct a skyscraper or a bridge can take satisfaction in "their" structure, just as shipyard workers can feel attached to the ship they send down the ways. There is a wide range of products manufactured on a unit production basis, ranging from tiny sophisticated electronic instruments to diesel locomotives, to which a large and skill diversified group of workers can simultaneously feel attached.

Obviously, when the linkage is lost between what one does and the ultimate product in which the labor was invested, the opportunity to develop an attachment to product is also lost. It has been repeatedly asserted that this occurs in much of modern industrial production, commercial operations, and clerical work (industry: Walker and Guest, 1952; Chinoy, 1955; Blauner, 1964; Durand, 1965; commercial and clerical work: Worthy, 1950; Mills, 1951; Lockwood, 1958; Hoos, 1961; Scott, 1965). Not only do complex products get manufactured and assembled in many parts and places, but often clerical operations are also subdivided so that clerks do only a small part of the total operation. Perhaps the most extreme instance of disengagement from product occurred when identification with the product was deliberately suppressed in the American Manhattan Project for the production of the atom bomb where, for security reasons, only a few persons at the top of the organization knew what the product was on which thousands expended their energies.

It is understandable that one of the targets of attack on modern work systems is the fact that attachment to product has been obliterated by the logic and structure of work operations. This may be an overstated negative case, however, for it assumes that only the final product is the object to which identification can be made. Is a casting, to be machined, to be assembled into an engine, to be incorporated into a finished automobile, identifiable enough that its production may occasion attachment to the casting itself? This is a possibility that long ago was recognized by a brilliant participant observer of work around the world (Williams, 1925). The final answer is not yet in as to what is the minimum recognizable product that can constitute an object of work attachment.

Routine

For some people, the very routineness of an environment is a source of attachment to it. Routine involves the high probability that when an individual reenters a given environment, he will do just about what he did the last time he was in that environment. The daily round of life is lived in many such environments. That the work environment is a member of the class of routine environments has been established many times (e.g., Barrier, 1962; Masuda, 1966; Hulin and Blood, 1968). The rationalization of industrial production has as one of its central elements making work operations routine.

Theorists who have dealt with the idea of routine as characterizing an environment have either focused on the characteristics of the environment, or its selective features that are attention-compelling for those who live or work in it. Thus, Merton has suggested that the kind of individual he calls a "ritualist" is one who values "safe routines and . . . institutional norms (Merton, 1957: 149), while Dubin (1969) has suggested that there are several kinds of ritualists, depending on the special features of their behavior setting.

When the term "bureaucrat" is used in a pejorative sense, it usually refers to an individual who does a job in a routine, unvarying way. There are many bureaucrats in work organizations, public and private, who merit the pejorative definition of their orientation. Central to this orientation is the individual's attachment to work routines. Indeed, it has been demonstrated in a study of welfare and health organizations that the actual structure of the organization is related to the routiness of the work performed so that those doing more routine work are more highly centralized and formalized (Hage and Aiken, 1969). Thus, structure may actually reinforce attachment to work routine.

A good description of the function of routine in the work setting is provided in a study of the meaning of work (Friedmann and Havighurst, 1954; 190) :

> Our studies of the significance of work in the lives of people underline for us the importance of an activity that fills the day, gives people something to do, and makes time pass. Sheer passing of time seems to be an important value of work. Work is admirably designed to provide this value, since it usually requires orderly routines. Even people who dislike their work as dangerous, unpleasant, or monotonous often recognize the value of the work routine to them and cannot imagine how they would fill the day if they were to retire.

This study covered five different occupational groups and the general findings have been replicated (e.g., Heron, 1962). An experimental study utilizing unskilled workers demonstrated that significant improvement in productivity could be attained on a monotonous, routine metal grinding operation simply by feeding back information on individual output without any change in the task itself (Hundal, 1969). In another study, focused on turnover, absenteeism and transfer, often believed to be the negative responses to routine work, it was found that differential rates were not explainable by the repetitive character of the work being performed, but were related to company and work situation characteristics (Kilbridge, 1961). These two studies lend support to the Friedmann-Havighurst conclusions.

There have been several interesting attempts to discover the dynamics of attachment to routine aspects of environments. For example, it has been suggested that autoarousal occurs while doing monotonous tasks and this self-stimulation may substitute for external stimulation (Murrell, 1969). A related idea is that substitution of social interaction, itself having routinized characteristics, displaces feelings of monotony and fatigue on routine jobs (Roy, 1959). It has even been found that the growth of business mergers within the European Common Market has been violently disturbing to routine operations within business firms and that this has produced pronounced incidence of insomnia, panic, fugue, suicidal ideas, and other complaints among individuals affected, suggesting that psychosomatic linkages to routinized work may exist (Vidart, 1967).

Clearly, abundant evidence exists that routine is not universally valued, and that, for example, the mental health of industrial workers doing routine and repetitive jobs is lower than the mental health of other workers (Kornhauser, 1965). This suggests that there may be special personality types to whom routine work is acceptable, if not attractive. For such individuals, routine work is another source of attachment to the work environment.

Autonomy

The organization of work operations into a job usually lies somewhere between two poles. At one pole is the complete specification of work behaviors, and the level of skill input required to perform the job. At the other pole is the specification only of an outcome or a product, with the individual left free to work out the necessary means to the output. The individual who works at the "freedom" pole has maximum autonomy, while the person working at the other pole has no autonomy. In real situations, the actual job lies somewhere between these poles. Research scientists in industry are to be found close to the "freedom" pole (Misshauk, 1970), while continuous assembly line operatives are near the opposite pole. While the focus of autonomy has been on job operations, it should not be forgotten that all behavior is surrounded with opportunities for expression of autonomy. For example, a long term, participant observer study of routine work in a French factory revealed that joking and laughter were an important means for expressing individual autonomy completely outside the job tasks (Frisch-Gauthier, 1961).

It is apparent, then, that autonomy in the work situation is the opportunity to make decisions about one's own working and other behaviors. A number of studies have demonstrated positive relationships between level of work-place autonomy and general job satisfaction (e.g., Shepard, 1969). However, there has been a tendency to equate autonomy with increased responsibility so that in the name of autonomy, analysts have urged job enlargement and job enrichment. Such analysts have concluded that subdivision of work has deprived workers of job autonomy and consequently, by enlarging jobs this autonomy would be restored (Bass and Leavitt, 1963; Conant and Kilbridge, 1965; Shepard, 1970; Borgatta and Ford, 1970).

The linkage between autonomy and job enlargement/job enrichment is not nearly as direct as has been assumed (MacKinney, et al., 1962; Hulin and Blood, 1968; Hulin, 1971). The issue turns on the willingness of individuals to accept the added responsibilities thrust upon them. For example, it has been concluded on the basis of a review of the research literature that workers accept control and autonomy only to the degree that some benefits are a payoff (Trahair, 1969). In an experimental study, delegation of freedom to solve a problem was not accepted by the subjects, a result previously observed among industrial managers (Maier and Thurber, 1969). In a study of twelve Polish factories, it was found that the typical foreman simply served as a transmitter of orders from above and saw to their proper execution, although opportunities for autonomy existed (Pomian and Bursche, 1963). Perhaps we can understand the reluctance to accept responsibility by noting that in a study of supervisory job redesign the increased responsibility for product completion and quality required a great deal of auxiliary sociotechnical system redesign, including the elimination of goal conflicts and disincentives for the supervisors (Davis and Valfer, 1966). For these supervisors, it was necessary that the benefits outweigh the costs before the additional responsibilities were accepted. This phenomenon was revealed in the long-time experiment in the Glacier

Company in England where the retrospective view of the results by the managing director made clear the strong unwillingness of subordinates to accept the autonomy that was literally thrust upon them by the experimental procedures (W. Brown, 1960).

Obviously, there must be a wide range in the amount of autonomy that individuals seek in their work. Part of fitting people to jobs usually takes this variability into account. Thus, attachment to this feature of work may be disturbed if there is either too little autonomy, or too much autonomy accorded to the individual in his work, relative to the individual's own needs for autonomy.

Personal Space/Things

It is interesting that the social science literature dealing with working does not give any attention to the functions of personal space and possessions in the work environment. We have found no significant literature dealing with these topics so we fall back on our own collective observations of people at work as a basis for the analysis of personal space and possessions as sources of attachment to work.

There is absolutely no reason to believe that the citizen, when he enters the work-place, ceases to have a sense of territoriality or possessiveness. An individual work station "belongs" to its occupant whether it is a desk, a welding booth, or the driver's seat of a truck. To take possession of this work-space is signaled by actually introducing personal possessions into it, or by rearranging it to taste. The higher up one moves in the hierarchy of an organization, the greater is the sense of possessiveness of personal space with the occupant giving "his" work-space the unique touch of personally selected decor and displayed memorabilia. Names on doors or desks or even work benches and equipment serve to post the privacy of the territory. One of the constant irritations in multiple shift operations is the bickering between shift occupants of the same work station who accuse each other of various failures to preserve the integrity of the space.

The sense of connection with things may be even stronger than the linkage with work-space. The machine an individual works with is "his" machine, even though it may be interchangeable with many others in the shop. A typist has "her" typewriter and is reluctant to permit its use by others. Truck drivers, bus drivers, and taxi drivers will have strong preferences for their particular vehicle and insist upon continuous assignment to it. Hand tools and work equipment, even when company issued, are treated as precious possessions, often with the claim that they uniquely "fit" their user and would be spoiled if used by anyone else. The list is almost endless of the things that are viewed possessively in the work environments of people.

The importance that individuals assign to place and things in their work environment may be simply interpreted as signifying that the person does literally have a place in the organization. There is nothing more obvious to signal this than the assigned work station to which the individual repeatedly returns and which is given a personal touch of decor and possessions to confirm this unique place.

We find that personal space and things do constitute a source of attachment to work. It remains to be seen how strong the attachment to work is through work-place and things. We know of no work environment we have ever observed where this source of work attachment does not exist.

PAYOFFS FOR WORKING

The most universally believed idea about linkage to work is that the payoffs received are the most general and strong attachments to the work setting. The generality of money pay in cash economies, and payment in kind in barter economies, seems to be sufficient confirmation of the power of the payoff attachment to work. Our goal, therefore, in this elaboration of work attachment through payoffs for working, is to suggest some additional kinds of rewards besides money, as well as to indicate how various kinds of payoffs function as sources of attachment to work.

Money

It is almost self-evident that money functions to attach people to their work. Given even a moderately complex economy, money wages and salaries are developed as a means for valuing and rewarding the work and contributions of those who produce goods and services (Dubin, 1958a; Caplow, 1964; Moore, 1969). The crucial point to recognize is that pay received for work is meaningful only when used to purchase consumer needs. The phrase, "to earn a living" is a happy, shorthand way to express the linkage between working and pay for effort. Thus, the link to work through the financial payoff received for working is really a link with the larger society.

If any further confirmation is needed that money earned from working is almost entirely utilized for consumption, we need only look at the American economy. Personal savings constitute only about 6% of individual income, on the average. Consumer credit, on the other hand, is about three times as great as the amount of personal savings. Thus, it is clear that the working population spends more than it earns, and that part of future earnings is even spent for present consumption.

The universality of money payoff for working is readily recognized. Even when experiments are made to modify the social system to reduce the significance of money as a source of work attachment, money and what it purchases for the citizen remains a dominant feature of working. In socialist economies, wages and wage differentials still play decisive roles, as demonstrated for example by studies of working behavior in Hungary (Hethy and Mako, 1971), Rumania (Desmireanu and Weiner, 1962) and the Peoples Republic of China (Hoffman, 1964).

The attractiveness of money for work is revealed by the fact that work involving extraordinary working conditions is generally paid more, on the presumption that this will lure otherwise reluctant workers to such jobs. It usually does. Dangerous work, unusual hours (including second and "graveyard" shifts), physically stressing work, exceptional isolation, or any other non-normal condition of work is likely to carry with it some added pay.

Money income for working is used in the management of work organizations to encourage increased output, and to differentiate among classes of employees in accordance with the contributions to the organization. Typically, piecework, in some form or other, is employed to encourage increased output, for which more wages are paid. While this is a phenomenon of the factory, it is not uncommon in commercial operations where sales commissions are the form that piecework takes. It has been pointed out that managers may be ambivalent about piecework because it makes the employee only interested in money, at the same time being essential because the workers are only interested in money (Klein, 1964). The phenomenon of holding two jobs simultaneously ("moonlighting") may be taken as further evidence that money income does encourage output (Wilensky, 1963).

The use of money to differentiate the level of contribution to the enterprise has been institutionalized in job evaluation, which is designed to establish some summary judgment about the relative contribution made by all jobs and positions in an organization. One of the consequences of such comparative schemes is that they call into play an evaluation of the justice of the unequal distribution of the rewards for working. The confirmation of the justice of unequal distribution has been labelled "distributive justice" by Homans and this has given rise to what is called equity theory in industrial psychology (Adams, 1963, 1964). Insofar as the individuals in the organization believe the differential payoffs of various jobs are equitable, they tend to view the entire system of pay as a just one. This, of course, is an important basis for institutionalizing the money reward system for working, thereby supporting the institution of which it is a part. Marx, for example, concluded that the sense of distributive justice was always outraged in a capitalist system, and that such outrage would provide one of the engines for moving workers to revolt against the system.

All advanced economies, regardless of social system, depend on work effort being induced by money income. Furthermore, all advanced social systems are exchange economies so that the money earned from working becomes the means for buying a living. Under such conditions it is obvious why money is a central source of attachment to work.

Perquisites

Perquisites are features of work that are payoffs for working almost entirely utilized in the work environment (limousine service and country club membership [or Dachas] provided by the organization for executives are exceptions as to where they are utilized). Perquisites of work may range from features of the work environment contributing to creature comforts to aspects of the work setting that have considerable intrinsic value to the individual. For example, a secretary with a luxuriously furnished private office enjoys exceptional creature comforts as well as clearly marked personal space and privacy. The military man's opportunities to purchase a wide range of goods at substantial savings in the PX store, live in government subsidized housing, and enjoy free medical services, is an example of high intrinsic value attaching to perquisites, as is the airline hostess's free flight travel for self and family.

Personnel activities of business organizations often include organized recreation and sports programs which come to be viewed as employment perquisites (Neer, 1957). In the Soviet Union, and in most socialist states, health care, housing, sports and recreation are work-based in the opportunities to enjoy them and represent a very central feature of the perquisites of socialist work (Valchev, 1969).

The primary function of perquisites is to provide forms of payoffs for working that could also be provided by each individual for himself. The perquisites are substitutes for what the individual could buy with his own money or provide for himself in some way (Dubin, 1958a). It is the practice in western industrial societies to incorporate (in collective bargaining agreements) what have come to be called "fringe benefits": generally, perquisites that become institutionalized when incorporated in the collective agreement.

The analysis of perquisites for working is surprisingly sparse. Except for the areas of personnel management (e.g., Lester, 1954), and collective bargaining, there has been very little serious attention given to the subject (Vollmer, 1960). It has been pointed out that conflicts regarding perquisites of a job are most likely to occur when the tasks comprising jobs are changed or revised (Hughes, 1958). Some analysis has been devoted to the problems of unique, individual perquisites versus perquisites available to a class of employees (Katz and Kahn, 1966). "Privilege pay," the opportunity afforded to initiate interaction with those in positions of higher authority (the "open door," for example) has been analyzed as a significant perquisite of work (Dubin, 1958a); as has the role of perquisites in managerial paternalism (Dubin and Wray, 1953).

Perquisites are almost never recaptured by the organization, once accorded to employees (Vollmer and McGillivray, 1960). Considerable industrial strife was generated in India, for example, over the problem of bonuses, which had become a practice in Indian industry after World War I, and which was called into question by a decision of the Indian Supreme Court in 1966 (van den Bogaert, 1968). This very "permanence" of perquisites, once granted, is perhaps sufficient evidence that they constitute still another universal source of attachment to work.

Power

The idea of power as a human relationship has been conceptualized in a variety of ways. In spite of this difficulty, this concept is very important to understand for it aids the analysis of organizational behavior. The concept covers a wide spectrum of human behavior, ranging from the power of children over their parents to the power of a dictator over a nation. We mean by power something very simple: the importance of the contribution that an individual makes to a system of division of labor (Dubin, 1962; Mumford and Ward, 1965; Pennings, Hickson, Hinings, Lee and Schneck, 1969; Hickson, Hinings, Lee, Schneck and Pennings, 1971). This view of power is coordinate with a widely held definition that power is the ability to carry out a course of action regardless of opposition to it (i.e., it is the power to do something [Weber, 1947]).

However power is viewed, it is a relational notion linking individual power-holders to other persons (Emerson, 1962). There then arises the question as to whether there is some point in the hierarchy of positions in a work organization, below which its members are powerless. The answer is clearly no so long as the members perform functions in the organization (Weber, 1947; Dubin, 1962). It has been demonstrated, for example, that even such lowly participants as typists and hospital attendants have power in their respective organizations because they have access to and control over information, work flow, and their own tasks that are necessary to the performance of tasks by others (Mechanic, 1962). Some analysts have argued that power resides only in the managerial levels of an organization, and that power is, therefore, only a payoff for working to a limited segment of the organization's personnel

(Barnard, 1938; Dalton, 1959). More recently, analysts have contended that the total amount of power in an organization is variable and expands with the addition of new functions in it (Kahn and Boulding, 1964; Lammers, 1967).

The idea that persons are power seekers has been an analytical concern of many social scientists (e.g., Cartwright, 1959; Kahn and Boulding, 1964; Zald, 1970). It has been shown that individual's power need (n Power) does not differ among middle managers of government and private organizations (Guyot, 1962), but that in one comparative study of two different business firms, the amount of n Power possessed by members was differentially rewarded with promotion because of the differing values characterizing the two organizations (Andrews, 1967). Attempts have been made to classify the types of organizational power possessed by individuals, and the conditions under which each is attained (e.g., French and Raven, 1959; Etzioni, 1964; Blau, 1964).

An influential school of thought has identified power or control as the ultimate payoff in the continual struggles among individuals, factions, and organizational subunits (March, 1962; Long, 1962). Several studies of power struggles have highlighted how the power payoff, if won, serves to explain much of the behavior that occurs in organizations (Dalton, 1959; Zald, 1962; Seiler, 1963; Hedley, 1970; Perrow, 1970).

When new functions are introduced in work organizations, as with the advent of automation, technical staffs and experts, through their specialized functional contributions, develop accretions of power without struggling for it (Karsh and Siegman, 1964). Indeed, it has even been suggested that a good measure of power distribution in a bureaucracy is the number of staff members associated with a line executive because of the functional importance of such personnel (Kaufman and Seidman, 1970). Perhaps one of the conditions that facilitates the flow of power to specialist roles is the general satisfaction that other participants feel for the work system as a whole (Ås, 1961). It has also been pointed out that there is experimental evidence to support the conclusion that when nonexperts participate with experts in decision-making, this will increase the power differential between the participants, providing another condition that obviates the appearance of a power struggle (Mulder, 1971).

Power is such a pervasive feature of human interaction in work organizations that not even ideology or organizational structural arrangements can shift its locus readily. In repeated studies of workers' councils in Yugoslavian factories, it has been found that neither the national socialist ideology (Kavcic, Rus and Tannenbaum, 1971), nor the worker council structure (Rus, 1970) were instrumental in shifting much power to the worker side and away from managers and experts.

Since all modern work organizations involve more or less intricate systems of division of labor, power will characterize these systems. Power is necessary for the functioning of such systems, and it is sought by its participants because it places others in a situation of dependence upon the self. This is a widely sought payoff for working.

Authority

Authority may be defined as the legitimate right to make decisions determining the behavior of others (Simon, 1947). Obviously, the structure of authority of a work organization will not extend to the lowest levels of the organization, and is generally limited to those who occupy supervisory and managerial positions (Barnard, 1938; Drucker, 1946; W. Brown, 1960). The position descriptions of supervisors, managers, and executives always include the imperative that the occupants make decisions, including the areas of decision and the personnel who will be affected by such decisions.

Central to the idea of authority is the complementary idea of compliance. Authority is effective only if subordinates respond in a compliant manner. This in turn rests on their perception that the decision affecting them is legitimate, and that it has issued from a legitimate source. It has been found that the degree of legitimacy of decisions is positively related to the degree that it affects job-related behaviors (Schein and Ott, 1962). It has also been found in a study of a marine industry that an open and consultative type of leadership has the effect of "sucking in" subordinates into deference to authority and consequent compliance with it (Denhardt, 1970). A social psychological interpretation of compliant behavior interprets workers who have low status in the community as entering the organization as workers with a status deficit and compensating for this by identification with and submission to authority (Grosof, Gross, Yeracaris and Hobbs, 1970). In a critique of Barnard's idea that subordinates' failure to accord compliance is a major limitation on the authority holder, it has been suggested that in bureaucracies there are coercive aspects of authority that are independent of subordinates' consent (Wells, 1963).

One of the interesting aspects of authority relations is the nonreciprocal perceptions of authority among authority holders and their subordinates. Self-perception of the amount of authority possessed and the perceptions of others often do not coincide (Peabody, 1963; Bates and White, 1961). While this failure of congruent perception of authority is not the sole condition leading to conflict, it is one situation from which conflict is likely to result. The contest to control positions of authority or to enter them from a staff position is another important source of organizational conflict (Dalton, 1959).

We can take the fact that people struggle to gain authority in work organizations as evidence that this is one of the payoffs widely sought, and consequently one of the attachments to work.

Status

Status is the comparative rank accorded to individuals according to some standard of measurement. The important point is that whatever measuring standard is used, it results in distributing individuals into hierarchically arranged ranks. Thus, status distinctions may be grounded in any feature or attribute about which comparative judgments exist for sorting out members of a group. In the work setting, skill, seniority, performance, job titles, loyalty, interaction style, and a host of other characteristics and attributes are utilized to establish the status rankings of individuals. Even unusual features of work, such as work shift, may become status distinguishing (Bohr and Swertloff, 1969). It is also important to note that the conferring of status in the work situation may either have its source in the formal organization, or in the informal work group (Robertson and Rogers, 1966).

Status has an important function as a payoff to the individual. Except for those persons at the very bottom of the status structure, all others have a higher status with respect to at least some of their fellow workers. This relative ranking is the payoff function that conferred status has for the individual, called "scalar status" by Barnard (1946).

Barnard, in his pioneering analysis of status in work organizations, discussed the marks of status. He pointed out that the organization confers these status marks upon the individual in the form of differentiating designations (e.g., head office personnel), titles, insignia, work-place furnishings, and behavior (e.g., deferential treatment).

The essential characteristic of all behaviors based on status evaluations is that it produces two basic forms of human interaction: relationships of equality and relationships of inequality (Dubin, 1958a). Two people interacting with reference to their identical status relate to each other as equals. They are status peers and their interactions are significantly determined by the mutually recognized fact of their identical status. Two persons occupying different status positions relate to each other as unequals. If they agree on the relative difference in their standing, then the individual of higher status is defined as superior to the one of lower status and is usually accorded some deference by the latter. If their respective status evaluations do not agree, then discordant behavior may be engaged in, and the relationship may be fraught with conflict. It has been found in an extensive study in Holland, for example, that the frequency of negative work behaviors (e.g., absence from work) are more strongly associated with negative status self-perception than they are with work satisfaction (Gadourek, 1965).

Insofar as the status system is legitimated, and consequently accepted by those who are subject to evaluation in it, the social relations deriving from the system are also viewed as legitimate. There are some kinds of relationships that are not status grounded but depend on the work flow, and although the individuals interacting may have nonreciprocal relationships they do not overlay those relationships with status considerations while interacting (e.g., surgical nurse and surgeon) (Blau, 1959). Status relations, because of their very simplicity, lend themselves well to mathematical formulations (Harsanyi, 1966) and to rather precise allocations of insignia and indicia of rank, as in the hierarchy of square footage of floor space allotted to individuals in each rank of an organization.

It has often been found that there is a positive correlation between the status of an occupation and the level of job satisfaction (Inkeles, 1960; Blauner, 1969). It has been suggested that individuals whose occupations are highly ranked receive gratifying social acknowledgement of their skill and performance because of their high status and consequently express high levels of job satisfaction (Blau and Duncan, 1967).

Next to money, status is probably the most systematized form of payoff for working to be found in organizations. Status is pursued as a reward for working (the proverbial key to the executive washroom), and obviously is a strong source of attachment to work.

Career

Attachment to work through an individual's career focuses attention upon the working life history of the person as a salient feature of his work experience. A career is a series of connected stages of an occupation or profession through which he begins work, until he retires. It has been suggested that the selection of a line of work from a career perspective is related to the individual's self-image (Super, 1969; Osipow and Gold, 1967); and that the linkage with self-image persists if the individual actually does find a career, since workers with careers have a much more active participation in their nonwork social life (Wilensky, 1961). Insofar as the individual perceives his work as a career, he possesses a perspective within which he is able to: (1) know where his present job is in relation to the career line, and (2) knows how much further he needs to progress to "top off" his career. Thus, the career turns out to be important as a means of orienting a person's present work to his entire working life history. This is a particularly strong influence in professions (Westby, 1960), and has an important bearing on satisfaction with pay raises since they tend to be evaluated as marking stages in a career (Hinrichs, 1969).

In an earlier study of work careers, five general stages of career progression were described along with six distinct types of career orientation (Miller and Form, 1964). This analysis showed that the strongest attachments to career were found among persons at higher occupational levels, and this was attributed to the fact that such individuals felt they had significant control over the type and rate of career progression.

It is notable that career perspectives are distinctive for different occupations and professions. Among engineers, for example, it has been found that about 66% of their working time is spent in administrative rather than technical tasks, with little of the training for engineering preparing for the administrative work (Zelikoff, 1969). The length of a career line may not be highly correlated with the incentives offered for moving from the bottom to the top of the career. If the organizational objective is to hold individuals at their present career stage, then a wide pay rate range may be provided at each step so that merit increases may be earned without moving to a higher career step. If mobility is the goal, then the pay rate range will be narrow to encourage upward striving by offering more pay only when a career advance has been achieved (Dubin, 1958a). Furthermore, whether the full range of mobility is sought by the individual depends on the "career anchorage" of the person (Tausky and Dubin, 1965). Persons anchoring their career perspective on the top of a career ladder may continue to respond to incentives for advancement, while those who anchor their career perspective on the beginning step of their career and feel they have already made satisfactory progress may no longer be "strivers" to move further up the career line. The downward career anchorage may explain refusal to strive for promotion found in the steel industry (Walker, 1950) and in a study of contrasting perspectives of executives and supervisors (Coates and Pellegrin, 1957). However, in process industries where there is a high responsibility demand on the worker, but a short career line, the question of the motivational "pull" of career has been displaced by the attractions of guaranteed life-long employment (Blauner, 1964).

An interesting transformation of career perspective occurs when some form of working life tenure of employment is provided. The individual is likely to make a career out of organizational membership rather than his special work (Dubin, 1958a). This is characteristic of Japanese industry, of employment in government bureaus, and academic employment. In academic institutions, for example, it is possible to recruit administrators from among academics who give up their intellectual pursuits to take on very difficult and often more demanding positions of managers of academic enterprises. Such career shifts are possible because the individual is able to make membership in the organization his career.

Work histories of many persons in the labor force do not accord with socially recognized careers. This applies especially to women (Saleh, Lee and Prien, 1965; Farmer and Bohn, 1970). Indeed, it has been estimated that only about one-third of employed persons work in career-type occupations and professions (Wilensky, 1960). Furthermore, enforced job changes through lay-off and unemployment may destroy career perspectives of individuals who thought they were in an established career (Aiken and Ferman, 1966).

For individuals who see their work as a career, there are strong and long-time bonds established that link such persons to their work.

MULTIPLE WORK ATTACHMENTS

It is clear from the previous discussion that we have been addressing single sources of attachment to work. No consideration was given to the possibility or extent of multiple attachments to work that, working together, may increase the strength of linkage between the person and his work. Obviously, there are seldom instances where only a single work attachment is operative. It would be beyond the purpose of this chapter to examine this issue in any detail.

The analytical issues posed by multiple work attachments are clear. It is important to know: (1) what the frequency distribution of multiple work attachments is (e.g., is the average number three or five or ten?); (2) what are the typical combinations of multiple work attachments; and (3) what is the relative strength of work attachment of given multiples and given combinations (eg., do three "strong" work attachments have greater potency than five "weak" ones?).

Furthermore, it would be a significant contribution to our knowledge of the dynamics of labor markets to know the special work attachments that characterize individual occupations and professions. The same kind of knowledge about social classes, or ethnic and racial groups, or males and females would improve our understanding of the characteristics of industry and commerce. Obviously, the design of personnel management programs in work organizations would be advanced with better knowledge about work attachments, and especially would we be able to improve the design of incentive systems for working. There are a number of additional issues that we hope will be tackled from the standpoint of work attachments.

WORK ATTACHMENTS IN THE UNITED STATES AND GREAT BRITAIN

We have done several major studies of work attachments among industrial workers in Great Britain and the United States. The data are far more extensive than those we will present here. What follows is a simplified summary of some of the broad findings we have made that are intended to illustrate one approach to measuring work attachments as well as to give a few general findings.

Our method of measuring work attachments was to list a series of brief phrases describing work and the work environment. The respondent was instructed to chose any such statements that he considered to be important, for whatever reason, with respect to his own work. Each statement was to be considered by itself without reference to answers on other statements. We thus ended up with a list of chosen items for each respondent, indicating the work features of importance to him.

In the original study in Great Britain, we used a list of 124 statements which was revised in the subsequent American study to include 94 statements, all of which had been in the original list. We base this report of the study on the shorter list. The study in Great Britain covered six manufacturing firms located in the Midlands, to West Country, Scotland and Wales. The American study covered a telephone company and a large bank, each having many branches, located in California.

This particular report combines the results of the two studies in a single analysis since an exploratory effort of this sort is designed to determine whether the empirical domain corresponds to the theoretical domain we have set forth above. We are not claiming that the data from either country is representative of the working populations of those countries. We do claim that our data represent somewhat over 3,500 industrial and clerical workers, male and female, who have their own ideas of what they consider important in their work and which we believe we have captured in our measure of work attachments.

The items used to measure work attachment were designed by the authors after an intensive review of the literature, utilizing our own industrial research experience. We grouped the items under subjct heads, such as "company" and "union" and "fellow workers" and under each heading there were items that fitted into several of our analytical work attachment categories. Thus, there was no cueing of the respondent regarding the analytical categories we were seeking to study.

In the following tables, the work attachment items are grouped under the appropriate work attachment category described above. This is an initial step of the analysis and we believe that these are the appropriate assignments of the various work attachment items. They are, however, our interpretations of what we think was the underlying factor represented by each work attachment item.

All the comparisons in the following tables are based on the rank order of each item for the particular population group. This was determined by making a distribution of the frequency with which each item was chosen by that group, utilizing the rank order so generated. Our comparisons in the tables are then the result of comparing rank orders. We focus attention on only those items where there is a difference of at least ten ranks between the two groups being compared. This is shown in the last column of each table under the heading "Rank Difference." Obviously, then, there were many items of work attachment where the differences were less than ten ranks which do not show up in any of the tables. Especially notable is the relative absence of "money" items. This is due entirely to the fact that money items, and especially "take home pay," had the highest frequency of any items chosen, exceeding 90%. Thus, the absence of an item from the tables should not be interpreted as meaning that such items are unimportant—it means only that there is a minimum rank difference on such items in the comparisons being made.

Within each table, the analytical work attachment categories are listed in the order of the number of work attachment items found in each. Where there is an equal number of items in two or more categories, the categories are listed in accordance with the relative rank of the items contained in each. Within each analytical category, the items are listed by their rank in the first column. Finally, where there is only one item in an analytical category, such categories are listed according to the rank of their respective items in the first column. Thus, the *order* of listing in each table is a rough measure of the relative importance of analytical categories and work attachment items.

Central Life Interests and Work Attachments

It will be recalled that an individual's central life interest (CLI) is measured by the locale preferred for carrying out activities. The measuring instrument takes activities that are equally likely to occur in both a work and nonwork setting and asks the respondent to choose which is his preferred location for the activity (Dubin, 1956). We secured comparable measures for CLI for all respondents in our studies and were thus able to classify each individual as to whether his CLI was a job or a non-job one. We scored a third category of individuals who were ambivalent about their CLI, and this group is not included in our present analysis.

The data on the work attachments of workers according to their central life interests are shown in Tables 3 and 4. The first notable result to observe is that a total of forty-seven, or exactly one-half of the ninety-four work attachment items are distinctively valued by workers with one or the other CLI orientation. This means that a very high proportion of the items used have special significance for a given CLI orientation.

For individuals who view work as the central institution of their life, it is clear from Table 3 that their work attachments are consistent with this outlook. The "self" items are positive and outgoing; the "power" items are contributory to the work setting; there is positive concern about the "products," "company," "craft-profession," "autonomy," and "career." Even the "technology" is represented by essentially positive items. The picture that emerges is that workers with a central life interest in work have eight major sources of attachment to work, each of which has positive significance, when contrasted with workers with a non-job orientation in CLI.

The contrast is made even sharper if we examine the detail of Table 4 where the results indicate the preferences of non-job oriented workers. All of the "self" items are narsissistic in focus; "routine" is emphasized as are "perquisites," while "autonomy" items feature withdrawal from rather than advance toward the work setting. The "work group" items are oriented away from work effort while "personal space/things" and "money" items are also concerned with non-output matters. Even "company" and "technology" are viewed in terms of modernity rather than utility or output. The overall image of non-job oriented workers is that they are attached to their work by being concerned with limiting their self-investment and seeking routinized work operations with significant preferences for payoffs of several sorts.

Remembering that the central life interest and work attachments were

TABLE 3
WORK ATTACHMENT ITEMS RANKED HIGHER BY WORKERS WITH A CENTRAL
LIFE INTEREST IN JOB THAN THOSE WITH A NON-JOB ORIENTATION

Work Attachment Item	Rank Among Job-Oriented Workers	Rank Among Non-Job-Oriented Workers	Rank Differences
Self			
Supervisor's confidence in me	5	33	28
Skill required to do my job	41	55	14
Contributing something to society	56	69	13
Personal contacts with managers	64	85	21
Power			
Responsibility in my job	11	43	31
Teaching new employees	48	78	30
The influence I have with my fellow workers	59	82	23
Product			
Products (services) company provides	25	51	26
Usefulness of products (services) of firm	34	66	32
Value of product (services)	43	74	31
Company			
Firm's reputation	32	58	26
Knowing what goes on in the firm	38	52	14
Firm's profits	58	68	10
Craft-Profession			
Creating new methods to do my job better	35	71	36
Inventing new ways to do my job	42	56	14
The things I do on my job	62	84	22
Autonomy			
Challenging or interesting work	7	22	15
Chance to use what I have learned	22	48	26
Career			
Chances for advancement and promotion	9	47	38
Having a job as a way of life	78	88	10
Technology			
How well my equipment works compared to others	54	79	25
Importance of equipment and methods in operations	55	75	20
Average number of items chosen	42	34	

measured by different instruments, it is highly significant that workers who see their work as a CLI have positive linkages with work while those whose institutional attachments are outside of work have negative attachments to the same work settings. Perhaps these findings, more than any other we will report, make sense out of the fact that a large proportion of working people do effective work even though they are linked to their work through negative work attachments. These are not the popularly labelled "alienated" workers. Their interests lie outside of work, and yet they have important work attachments which clearly defy the possibility of the workers being alienated. Perhaps it is time to discard the alienation notion of explaining very little, if anything, about orientations toward work.

TABLE 4
WORK ATTACHMENT ITEMS RANKED HIGHER BY WORKERS WITH A CENTRAL
LIFE INTEREST IN NON-JOB AREAS THAN THOSE WITH A JOB ORIENTATION

Work Attachment Item	Rank Among Non-Job-Oriented Workers	Rank Among Job-Oriented Workers	Rank Difference
Self			
Hours I work	4	27	23
Being left alone to do my work	7	44	37
How far I have to travel to work	19	51	32
Time for personal needs	35	82	47
How hard I have to work	44	74	30
Physical work I do	54	79	25
Thinking about other things when I'm working	76	94	18
Routine			
Knowing tasks in advance each day	32	66	34
How supervisors give orders	37	49	12
Knowing enough to get by	60	89	29
Perquisites			
Holidays and vacations	5	28	23
Whether firm provides sports and entertainment	64	86	22
Company facilities	65	75	10
Autonomy			
Controlling work speed	50	60	10
Controlling the number of things I do	57	69	12
Number of supervisors	67	85	18
Personal Space /Things			
Cleanliness of work area	9	26	17
How clean facilities are kept	17	36	19
Work Group			
Talking to others while working	30	80	50
Together we have some control over how work is done	34	50	16
Money			
Method of payment	36	70	34
Pay compared to other firms	39	52	13
Company			
How modern the firm is	23	61	38
Craft-Profession			
Doing my job my own way	38	65	27
Technology			
How modern equipment and methods are	53	68	15

Age and Work Attachments

To gain some notion of the relationship between age and work attachments we contrasted a young group of workers with an older group. The young group was between twenty and thirty years of age, while the older group ranged from fifty to sixty in age. The data are shown in Tables 5 and 6.

It will be noted that the items in Table 5 that distinguish older from younger workers have a general aspect of passivity in relation to work. The number of distinctive work attachments is relatively small, and they spread out over eight work attachment categories with no concentration in any single

TABLE 5

WORK ATTACHMENT ITEMS RANKED HIGHER BY OLDER THAN BY YOUNGER WORKERS

Work Attachment Item	Rank Among Workers 50–59 Years Old	Rank Among Workers 20–29 Years Old	Rank Difference
Routine			
Being familiar with my job	11	21	10
Knowing tasks in advance each day	25	58	33
Company			
How modern the firm is	23	47	24
Size of firm	68	81	13
Self			
Attention I have to pay to my work	33	43	10
Physical work I do	59	73	14
Career			
Length of service with firm	39	72	33
Having a job as a way of life	72	87	15
Personal Space /Things			
Convenience of my job to work area	18	29	11
Power			
Whether my fellow workers depend on the work I do	42	63	21
Autonomy			
Controlling the number of things I do	53	67	14
Perquisites			
Whether firm provides sports and entertainment	66	78	12
Average number of items chosen	40	38	

category. These older workers gave special emphasis to "routine" and to the physical and attention demands on the "self." There seems to be some linkage to "career" as representing long service with the company as well as having a job as a way of life.

The younger workers have a sharply contrasting set of work attachment preferences. The "work group" is an important source of attachment to work as are the challenging and variety aspects of "autonomy." They are concerned with the quality of "technology" and see the chance for promotion as a "career" dimension. The creative aspect of "craft-profession" is emphasized as is the contributory aspect of "power" in teaching others. It seems clear that the younger workers, in comparison with older workers, are optimistic and forthcoming in relation to their work environments.

The work attachment contrasts between older and younger workers accord with expectations about how age will affect the aspects of work chosen as important by each age group. The older workers seem to see themselves as resting easy in the harness while the younger workers are going toward their work with expectations of dynamic linkages to it.

Length of Service and Work Attachments

Ordinarily there is a fairly high relationship between age and length of service, providing workers remain in the company of their first employment.

TABLE 6
WORK ATTACHMENT ITEMS RANKED HIGHER BY YOUNGER THAN BY OLDER WORKERS

Work Attachment Item	Rank Among Workers 20–29 Years Old	Rank Among Workers 50–59 Years Old	Rank Difference
Work Group			
Chances to meet new people	34	65	31
Talking to others when working	45	70	25
Getting together off the job (with fellow workers)	62	88	26
Autonomy			
Challenging or interesting work	12	30	18
Variety in my work	20	35	15
Technology			
How well equipment and methods do the job	22	32	10
Quality of equipment and methods	36	46	10
Career			
Chances for advancement and promotion	19	52	33
Company			
Knowing what goes on in the firm	42	54	12
Craft-Profession			
Creating new methods to do my job better	46	69	23
Product			
Usefulness of products (services) of firm	48	60	12
Power			
Teaching new employees	59	74	15

But the labor force is mobile, and with each new job the worker starts his length of service record over again. Since we had a large enough sample to include individuals who had changed employers, we gave separate consideration to the relationship between length of service and work attachments. To make appropriate contrast, we compared workers with less than one year of service with those who had more than ten years of service. These data are shown in Tables 7 and 8.

The long service employees give higher ratings to "power" items, "perquisite" items, "company" items, "craft-profession" items, "routine" items, "personal space/things" items and "career" items than do short-term employees. Furthermore, "perquisites," "company," "routine," "personal space/things" and "career" do not appear as categories of work attachment among those preferred by the short-term employees.

The short-term employees give higher rankings than long-term employees to "work group" items and "autonomy" items, neither of which category is in the preferred listing for long-service workers. The attention of short-service employees is focused on finding a place in the organization as revealed by the "career" items and the "craft-profession" items they rank higher than do long-service employees, as well as their distinctive emphasis on "work group" attachments.

The major contrast between long-service and short-service employees is in the distinctiveness of the categories of work attachment each group ranks

TABLE 7
WORK ATTACHMENT ITEMS RANKED HIGHER BY LONG SERVICE
THAN BY SHORT SERVICE WORKERS

Work Attachment Item	Rank Among Over 10 Years Service	Rank Among Less Than 1 Year Service	Rank Difference
Power			
Responsibility in my job	20	35	15
Whether my supervisor does his job	48	58	10
Influence I have with fellow workers	72	83	11
Perquisites			
Company benefits	3	13	10
Job security	8	26	18
Company			
How the firm is run	22	32	10
Firm's profits	55	68	13
Craft-Profession			
Skill required to do my job	42	52	10
Creating new methods to do my job better	54	65	11
Routine			
Being familiar with my job	14	24	10
Personal Space / Things			
Convenience of my job to work area	18	29	11
Career			
Length of service with company	31	85	54
Average number of items chosen	40	39	

TABLE 8
WORK ATTACHMENT ITEMS RANKED HIGHER BY SHORT SERVICE
THAN LONG SERVICE WORKERS

Work Attachment Item	Rank Among Less Than 1 Year Service	Rank Among Over 10 Years Service	Rank Difference
Work Group			
Chances to meet new people	27	70	43
Talking to others when working	49	64	15
Whether my friends work here	81	93	12
Career			
Chance to learn more than one job	6	23	17
Chances for advancement and promotion	25	44	19
Power			
Relations with my supervisor	12	27	15
Craft-Profession			
Training required for my job	48	62	14
Autonomy			
Controlling work speed	50	63	13
Perquisites			
Whether firm provides sports and entertainment	63	79	16

higher than the rating of the other group. It appears that as service with a work organization increases, the sources of work attachment shift from one set of categories to another. This shift may have important implications for the manner in which length of service is treated in company policies.

Sex and Work Attachments

The several studies had a significant number of female workers involved. Almost the entire group of women workers in Great Britain were factory workers while most of the female sample members in the United States were clerical workers. In Tables 9 and 10 are presented the data showing the work attachments of males and females.

The males give preference to categories of work attachment, and items within categories, that seem to fit the image of the male factory worker. There is a pronounced emphasis on "craft-profession," "perquisites," "technology," and "career," none of which are emphasized by the females. Furthermore, the "self" item denotes the self as contributing rather than having to exert effort, as among the females. The male worker is still viewed as the primary bread winner so that the categories rated higher by males seem to reflect this expectation.

Among the female workers the categories of "work group," "routine," "product," "personal space/things," and "company" are uniquely selected and do not show up among the males. The work group is a sociability dimension of work and clearly this work attachment category is a major one for women

TABLE 9
WORK ATTACHMENT ITEMS RANKED HIGHER BY MALES THAN BY FEMALES

Work Attachment Item	Rank Among Males	Rank Among Females	Rank Difference
Craft-Profession			
Doing my job my own way	37	51	14
Inventing new ways to do my job	45	62	17
Creating new methods to do my job better	49	65	16
Perquisites			
Job Security	7	18	11
Company facilities	60	70	10
Technology			
Quality of my equipment and methods	36	50	14
Importance of equipment and methods in operations	64	78	14
Career			
Chances for advancement and promotion	27	40	13
Autonomy			
Chance to use what I have learned	30	42	12
Work Group			
Together we have some control over how work is done	33	44	11
Self			
Contributing something to society	57	68	11
Average number of items chosen	43	35	

TABLE 10
WORK ATTACHMENT ITEMS RANKED HIGHER BY FEMALES THAN MALES

Work Attachment Item	Rank Among Females	Rank Among Males	Rank Difference
Work Group			
Chances to meet new people	28	61	33
Talking to others when working	45	59	14
Getting together off the job (with fellow workers)	64	82	18
Whether both men and women work here	71	87	16
Whether my friends work here	81	92	11
Self			
How far I have to travel to work	19	34	15
Skill required to do my job	42	58	16
How hard I have to work	52	67	15
Routine			
Knowing tasks in advance each day	33	52	19
Knowing enough to get by	66	81	15
Product			
Products (services) company provides	34	48	14
Value of products (services) of company	59	69	10
Personal Space/Things			
Cleanliness of work area	7	19	12
Company			
Firm's reputation	41	53	12
Autonomy			
Controlling work speed	48	65	17

workers, reflecting, perhaps, the social image of women as nonpermanent members of the labor force.

As with length of service, the distinctiveness of categories of work attachment is the major contrast between male and female workers. This may suggest that personnel policies designed to equalize the treatment of males and females in the proper pursuit of justice may need to be supplemented with policies that provide differential treatment to accord with the sex differences in sources of work attachment.

Country and Work Attachments

We conclude this examination of work attachments among workers in our several studies by comparing the results obtained in Great Britain with those secured in the United States. There are substantial differences between the two countries that are set forth in Tables 11 and 12.

An important fact about the two tables is the number of work attachment items that distinguish between the workers in the two countries. There is a total of forty-seven different items listed in both tables, exactly half of the total number of items, and coincidently, the same number of distinctive items found when we examined differences in CLI orientation. The conclusion is that there are many grounds for believing that the work attachments are distinctive in different cultures.

Consider the following listing as a way of summarizing the data of the two tables.

Characterizations of British Workers' Attachments to Work	Characterizations of American Workers' Attachments to Work
SELF—"inner directed" orientation; preoccupied with physical effort and personal needs and conveniences.	SELF—"other directed" orientation.
WORK GROUP—solidarity with and emphasis on collective action.	WORK GROUP—like-mindedness.
CRAFT/PROFESSION—independence.	CRAFT/PROFESSION—inventiveness and skill.
AUTONOMY—concern with excessive supervision.	AUTONOMY—work-oriented uses of autonomy.
COMPANY—its organizational characteristics.	COMPANY—its social standing and internal operations.
PRODUCT—its social significance.	PRODUCT—its utility.
PERSONAL SPACE/THINGS—cleanliness.	PERSONAL SPACE/THINGS—convenience.
Unique Features	*Unique Features*
PERQUISITES—company-related, off-job features.	POWER—having responsibility for work, and influence on others.
ROUTINE—pre-knowledge of work and output expectations of company.	TECHNOLOGY—quality of equipment.
	CAREER—possibilities of advancement.
	STATUS—public respect for own work.

These characterizations are clearly different in two respects. For those work attachment categories where each group has preferred work attachment items, these are clearly different in their content. Thus, the "self" as an object of work attachment has a different meaning for British workers than it has for the American workers. It will also be noted that each group has distinctive work attachment categories that characterize it. "Perquisites" and "routine" are work attachment categories for which British workers express a higher preference than American workers, while the latter has a higher preference for "power," "technology," "career," and "status" features of work attachments.

The data of the comparisons of workers in the two cultures gives content to the obvious fact that the cultures are distinctive. We now have some idea of how they differ in the manner in which workers in each culture view their linkages with their work.

Empirical Study of Work Attachments

The data presented on the measurement of work attachments provide convincing evidence that it is possible to apprehend this phenomenon. In a crude but

TABLE 11
WORK ATTACHMENT ITEMS RANKED HIGHER BY WORKERS IN GREAT BRITAIN
THAN BY WORKERS IN THE UNITED STATES

Work Attachment Item	Rank Among Workers in Great Britain	Rank Among Workers in United States	Rank Difference
Self			
Hours I work	5	21	16
Being left alone to do my work	7	31	24
How far I have to travel to get to work	19	43	24
Attention I have to pay to my work	27	52	25
Time for personal needs	42	66	24
How hard I have to work	46	76	30
Physical work I do	63	78	15
Being left alone by the people I work with	77	89	12
Work Group			
How I stand with my fellow workers	26	37	11
Together we have some control over how work is done	31	47	16
Talking to others when working	44	62	18
Personal Space / Things			
Cleanliness of work area	8	26	18
How well facilities are kept	18	33	15
Perquisites			
Holidays and vacations	4	25	21
Whether firm provides sports and entertainment	56	92	36
Company			
How modern the firm is	20	65	45
Size of firm	70	81	11
Routine			
Knowing tasks in advance each day	25	74	49
Knowing enough to get by	65	87	22
Product			
Importance of product (services) to country	34	46	12
Craft-Profession			
Doing my job my own way	38	58	20
Autonomy			
Number of supervisors	71	83	12
Average number of items chosen	37	41	

effective way we have learned from the responses of workers about some of the complexities of the ties that link them to their work. We are convinced that with refined instruments we can learn even more.

It is desirable to repeat the caution that these data be interpreted in the manner in which they have been presented. The organizing criterion was to contrast the ranking differences for any work attachment item between two groups being compared. The result is that we have tried to make statements limited to the conclusion that one group preferred an item by a significant amount more than the other group. This does not indicate whether the preference ratings was at the top or bottom of the range of ratings. For example, in Table 11 British workers rank "being left along to do my work" as seventh and "time for personal needs" as forty-second in their over-all preferences. Each of these items is rated twenty-four ranks lower by the American workers. It is quite another analytical problem to deal with the absolute rankings rather than the

TABLE 12
WORK ATTACHMENT ITEMS RANKED HIGHER BY WORKERS IN THE
UNITED STATES THAN BY WORKERS IN GREAT BRITAIN

Work Attachment Item	Rank Among Workers in United States	Rank Among Workers in Great Britain	Rank Differences
Power			
Helping others to do their job	17	29	12
Responsibility in my job	20	39	19
Teaching new employees	53	76	23
The influence I have with my fellow workers	64	80	16
Craft-Profession			
Creating new methods to do my job better	30	78	48
Skill required to do my job	40	55	15
Inventing new ways to do my job	48	58	10
The things I do in my job	61	84	23
Autonomy			
Challenging or interesting work	4	30	26
Variety in my work	15	33	18
Chance to use what I have learned	29	43	14
Product			
Products (services) company provides	28	51	23
Usefulness of products (services) of firm	35	68	33
Value of product (services)	44	72	28
Technology			
Quality of equipment and methods	32	49	17
How well my equipment works compared to others	57	82	25
Importance of equipment and methods in operations	59	75	16
Self			
Supervisor's confidence in me	14	24	10
Contributing something to society	51	67	16
Company			
Firm's reputation	38	53	15
Knowing what goes on in the firm	39	50	11
Personal Space/Things			
Convenience to work area	11	40	29
Career			
Chances for advancement and promotion	13	47	34
Status			
Respect from my family and friends because of my job	34	62	28
Work Group			
Whether the people I work with like the same things I do	84	94	10

rank differences. For example, the rank order correlation between the total rankings of the British and American sample was 0.58, indicating enough lack of similarity in rankings that we turned immediately to the rank difference analysis presented here.

WORKERS' ATTACHMENTS TO THE WORLD OF WORK

We have followed the classic procedure of drawing on our own observations and hunches to reach a belief that the linkages persons have to work are complex and variable. We did an extensive search of the empirical literature with the focus on attachments to work. The result was that we found a significant body of description that permitted us to sort out and organize the ideas about work attachments into analytical categories. The obvious next step was to move into the field to see if we could find evidence that the categories were real. This we found, and in the process reorganized, amplified, and came to a better understanding of our analytical scheme.

There are a host of applications of what is now known about attachments to work. There is obviously much more to be done in the way of additional research. We hope the applications will be made and the research undertaken.

We no longer believe that there is an economic man, or a psychological man, or a sociological man who does the work of the world and who is to be reached through his pocketbook, or his psyche, or his social relations, in order to motivate his work effort. We think the working man is a whole man—he is simultaneously an economic, psychological and sociological person. It is only when the whole man idea is taken seriously that we can perceive that there are multiple attachments to work.

REFERENCES

Abrahamson, M.
  1964 "The integration of industrial scientists." Administrative Science Quarterly 9(September):208–218.
  1967 (ed.) The Professional in the Organization. Chicago: Rand McNally.
Adams, J.S.
  1963 "Wage inequities, productivity and work quality." Industrial Relations 3(October):9–16.
  1964 "Effects of wage inequities of work quality." Journal of Abnormal and Social Psychology 1(July):19–25.
Aiken, M. and L.A. Ferman
  1966 "Job mobility and the social integration of displaced workers." Social Problems 14(Summer):48–56.
Andrews, I.R. and E.R. Valenzi
  1970 "Overpay inequity or self-image as a worker: a critical examination of an experimental induction procedure." Organizational Behavior and Human Performance (5):266–276.
Andrews, J.D.
  1967 "The achievement motive and advancement in two types of organizations." Journal of Personality and Social Psychology (6):163–168.
Archibald, K.
  1947 Wartime Shipyard. Berkeley: University of California Press.
Argyris, C.
  1959 "Understanding human behavior in organizations: one viewpoint," in M. Haire (ed.), Modern Organization Theory. New York: Wiley.
  1964 Integrating the Individual and the Organization. New York: Wiley.
Aris, S.
  1964 "The future of shift work." New Society 2(January):8–10.
As, D.
  1961 "Rate setting and balance of power in the industrial company." Tidsskrift fur Samfunnsforskning 2(June):103–116.

Asch, S.E.
   1951   "Effects of group pressure upon the modification and distortion of
          judgments," in H. Guetzkow (ed.), Groups, Leadership and Men:
          Research in Human Relations. New York: Russell and Russell.
Baglioni, G.
   1969   "The workers' attitude and labor in the iron industry." Studi di Socio-
          logia 7(January–June):21–55.
Bakke, E.W.
   1950   Bonds of Organization. New York: Harper & Bros.
Barnard, C.I.
   1938   The Functions of the Executive. Cambridge: Harvard University Press.
   1940   The Nature of Leadership. Cambridge: Harvard University Press.
   1946   "The functions and pathology of status systems in formal organiza-
          tions," in W.F. Whyte (ed.), Industry and Society. New York: McGraw-
          Hill.
Barrier, C.
   1962   "Continuous production, division of labor, and the adaptability of the
          organization." Cahiers d'Etude L'Automation et des Sociétés Indus-
          trielles (3):19–79.
Bass, B.M. and H.J. Leavitt
   1963   "Some experiments in planning and operating." Management Science
          (9):574–85.
Bates, F.L. and R.F. White
   1961   "Differential perceptions of authority in hospitals." Journal of Health
          and Human Behavior 2(Winter):262–267.
Baur, E.J.
   1963   "The spontaneous development of informal organization." Hospital
          Administration 8(Summer):45–58.
Becker, H.S. and J. Carper
   1956   "The elements of identification with an occupation." American Socio-
          logical Review (21):341–347.
Bennett, J.W.
   1958   "Economic aspects of a boss-henchman system in the Japanese forestry
          industry." Economic Development and Cultural Change 7(October):
          13–30.
Bennis, W.G.
   1966   Changing Organizations. New York: McGraw-Hill.
Blau, P.M.
   1955   The Dynamics of Bureaucracy. Chicago: University of Chicago Press.
   1959   "Social integration, social rank and processes of interaction." Human
          Organization 18(Winter):152–157.
   1964   Exchange and Power in Social Life. New York: Wiley.
Blau, P.M. and O.D. Duncan
   1967   The American Occupational Structure. New York: Wiley.
Blauner, R.
   1964   Alienation and Freedom: The Factory Worker and His Industry. Chi-
          cago: University of Chicago Press.
   1969   "Work satisfaction and industrial trends," in A. Etzioni (ed.), A So-
          ciological Reader on Complex Organizations. New York: Holt, Rine-
          hart and Winston.

Blitz, H.J. (ed.)
   1969   Labor-Management Contracts and Technological Change: Case Studies
           and Contract Clauses. New York: Praeger.
Bohr, R.H. and A.B. Swertloff
   1969   "Work shift, occupational status, and the perception of job prestige."
           Journal of Applied Psychology (53):227–229.
Bonjean, C.M. and M.D. Grimes
   1970   "Bureaucracy and alienation: a dimensional approach." Social Forces
           48(March):364–373.
Borgatta, E.F. and R.N. Ford
   1970   "A note on task and situational factors in work orientation and satis-
           faction." Journal of Psychology (74):125–130.
Bose, S.K.
   1958   "Group cohesiveness and productivity." Psychological Studies 3(Jan-
           uary):20–28.
Bowin, R.
   1970   "Career anchorage points and central life interests of middle-managers."
           Eugene: University of Oregon. Unpublished Doctoral Dissertation.
Briggs, G.E. and W.A. Johnston
   1966   "Influence of a change in system criteria on team performance." Jour-
           nal of Applied Psychology (50):467–472.
Brown, D.R.
   1968   "Alienation from work." Eugene: University of Oregon. Unpublished
           Doctoral Dissertation.
Brown, M.E.
   1969   "Identification and some conditions of organizational involvement."
           Administrative Science Quarterly 14(September):346–356.
Brown, W.
   1960   Exploration in Management. London: Heinemann.
Bruner, D.
   1962   "Why white-collar workers can't be organized," in S. Nosow and
           W.H. Form (eds.), Man, Work, and Society. New York: Basic Books.
Bucher, R. and J. Stelling
   1969   "Characteristics of professional organizations." Journal of Health &
           Social Behavior (10):3–15.
Caplow, T.
   1964   The Sociology of Work. New York: McGraw-Hill.
Carey, H.H.
   1942   "Consultative supervision and management." Personnel 18(March):
           286–295.
Cartwright, D. (ed.)
   1959   Studies in Social Power. Ann Arbor: Institute for Social Research,
           University of Michigan.
Centers, R. and D.E. Bugental
   1966   "Intrinsic and extrinsic job motivations among different segments of
           the working population." Journal of Applied Psychology (50):193–
           197.
Chadwick-Jones, J.K.
   1964   "The acceptance and socialization of immigrant workers in the steel
           industry." Sociological Review 12(July):169–183.

Chaumont, M.
  1962   "Strikes, unionism, and worker's attitudes." Sociologie du Travail 4
         (April–June) :142–158.
Chinoy, E.
  1955   Automobile Workers and the American Dream. New York: Random
         House.
Cloitre, Y.
  1962   "The religious life of the steel workers of Port-Brillet." Archives So-
         ciologiques de Religion 7(January–June) : 87–104.
Coates, C.H. and R.W. Pellegrin
  1957   "Executives and supervisors: contrasting self-conceptions and concep-
         tions of each other." American Sociological Review (22) :217–221.
Coch, L. and J.R.P. French, Jr.
  1948   "Overcoming resistance to change." Human Relations (1) :512–532.
Collins, O., et al.
  1946   "Restriction of output and social cleavage in industry." Applied An-
         thropology (5) :1–14.
Conant, E.H. and M.D. Kilbridge
  1965   "An interdisciplinary analysis of job enlargement: technology, costs,
         and behavioral implications." Industrial and Labor Relations Review
         (18) :377–395.
Corrie, W.S., Jr.
  1957   "Work as a 'central life interest': a comparison of the Amana Colony
         worker with the non-Amana Colony worker in a given industrial set-
         ting." Iowa City: University of Iowa. Unpublished Doctoral Desserta-
         tion.
Cottrell, W.F.
  1939   "Of time and the railroader." American Sociological Review (4) :190–
         198.
  1951   "Death by dieselization: a case study in the reaction to technological
         change." American Sociological Review (16) :258–265.
Dalton, M.
  1959   Men Who Manage. New York: Wiley.
Daniel, W.W.
  1969   "Automation and the quality of work." New Society (May 29) :833–
         836.
Dan-Spinoiu, G.
  1969   "'Morale' in groups of industrial workers." Revista de Psihologie
         (15) :229–243.
Davis, L.E.
  1957   "Job design and productivity: a new approach." Personnel 33(March) :
         418–430.
Davis, L.E. and E.S. Valfer
  1966   "Studies in supervisory job design." Human Relations (19) :339–352.
Denhardt, R.B.
  1970   "Leadership style, worker involvement and deference to authority."
         Sociology & Social Research 52(January) :172–180.
Dennis, N., et al.
  1969   Coal Is Our Life: An Analysis of a Yorkshire Mining Community.
         London: Tavistock.

Desmireanu, I. and P. Weiner
  1962   "Changes which took place in the working and living conditions of the working people in the industrial region of resita in the years of people's democracy." Rumanian Journal of Sociology (1) :141–164.
Dibble, V.K.
  1962   "Occupations and ideologies." American Journal of Sociology (62) : 229–241.
Doktor, K.
  1962   "Research on behavior and opinions of workers in a Polish factory." Polish Sociological Bulletin 3(July–December) :113–116.
  1966   "The conformism of workers—a case study." Sociologie du Travail 8 (January–March) :77–89.
Drucker, P.F.
  1946   The Concept of the Corporation. New York: New American Library.
Dubin, R.
  1956   "Industrial workers' worlds: a study of the 'central life interests' of industrial workers." Social Problems (3) :131–142.
  1958a   The World of Work. Englewood Cliffs, New Jersey: Prentice-Hall.
  1958b   Working Union Management Relations. Englewood Cliffs, New Jersey: Prentice-Hall.
  1959   "Industrial research and the discipline of sociology," in Proceedings of the Eleventh Annual Meeting. Madison, Wisc.: Industrial Relations Research Association.
  1962   "Business behavior behaviorally viewed," in C. Argyris, et al. (eds.), Social Science Approaches to Business Behavior. Homewood, Ill.: Dorsey-Irwin.
  1965   "Central life interests of German industrial workers." Paper presented before the Annual Meetings of the American Sociological Association, Chicago, Illinois.
  1973   "Work and non-work: institutional perspectives," in M.D. Dunnette (ed.), Work and Non-Work in the Year 2001. Monterey, Ca.: Brooks/ Cole.
Dubin, R. and L.W. Porter (Directors)
  1974   "Individual-organization linkages." Research project sponsored by the Office of Naval Research, University of California, Irvine. Unpublished data provided courtesy of the project.
Dubin, R., T.C. Taveggia and R.A. Hedley
  1975   "Central life interests: a cumulation." Technical Report No. 28, Individual-Organizational Linkages, ONR research project, University of California, Irvine.
Dubin, R. and D.E. Wray
  1953   "Case study 2: metal products," in M. Derber, et al. (eds.), Labor Management Relations in Illini City. Vol. I. Urbana, Ill.: University of Illinois Press.
Dubois, P.
  1970   "The methods of mobilization in the working class." Sociologie du Travail 12(July–September) :338–344.
Durand, C.
  1965   "Fragmentation of work and the maintenance of occupational autonomy," in A. Touraine, et al. (eds.), Workers' Attitudes to Technical Change. Paris: OECD.

Edwards, A.M.
   1938   A Socio-Economic Grouping of the Gainful Workers of the United States. Washington D.C.: U.S. Government Printing Office.
Emerson, R.M.
   1962   "Power-dependence relations." American Sociological Review (27): 31–41.
Endo, C.M.
   1970   "Career anchorage points and central life interests of Japanese middle-managers." Eugene: University of Oregon. Unpublished Doctoral Dissertation.
Etzioni, A.
   1964   Modern Organizations. Englewood Cliffs, New Jersey: Prentice-Hall.
Evan, W.M.
   1963   "Peer-group interaction and organizational socialization: a study of employee turnover." American Sociological Review 28(June):436–439.
Farmer, H.S. and M.J. Bohn, Jr.
   1970   "Home-career conflict reduction and the level of career interest in women." Journal of Counseling Psychology (17):228–292.
Faunce, W.A.
   1958a   "Automation and the automobile worker." Social Problems 6(Summer):68–78.
   1958b   "Automation in the automobile industry: some consequences for in-plant social structure." American Sociological Review 23(August): 401–407.
Felton, G.S.
   1966   "Psycho-social implications of the coffee break." Journal of Human Relations (14):434–449.
Ferrarotti, F.
   1960   "The sociology of labor and of union life: some basic needs." Rassegna Italiana di Sociologia 1(January–March):71–75.
Flanders, A.
   1963   "The importance of shop stewards." New Society 1(February):13–15.
Form, W.H. and H.K. Dansereau
   1957   "Union member orientations and patterns of social integration." Industrial and Labor Relations Review (2):3–12.
French, J.R.P. and B. Raven
   1959   "The bases of social power," in D. Cartwright (ed.), Studies in Social Power. Ann Arbor: Institute for Social Research, University of Michigan.
Friedmann, E.A. and R.J. Havighurst
   1954   The Meaning of Work and Retirement. Chicago: University of Chicago Press.
Friedmann, G.
   1961   The Anatomy of Work. New York: Free Press of Glencoe.
Frisch-Gauthier, J.
   1961   "Laughter in work relationships." Revue Française de Sociologie (2): 292–303.
Gadourek, I.
   1964   Absences and Well-Being of Workers. Assen, Holland: van Ghorcum and Co.

Gniazdowski, A.
  1969   "Solidarity within small work teams." Studia Socjologiczne (33):225–248.
Goldman, D.R.
  1968   "Career anchorage points and central life interests of middle-managers." Eugene: University of Oregon. Unpublished Doctoral Dissertation.
Goodwin, L.
  1972   Do the Poor Want to Work? A Social-Psychological Study of Work Orientations. Washington, D.C.: Brookings Institute.
Goss, M.E.W.
  1962   "Administration and the physician." American Journal of Public Health 52(February):183–191.
Gouldner, A.W.
  1954   Patterns of Industrial Bureaucracy. New York: Free Press.
  1958   "Cosmopolitans and locals: toward an analysis of latent social roles." Administrative Science Quarterly 2(March):444–480.
  1965   Wildcat Strike. New York: Harper & Row.
Gouldner, H.P.
  1960   "Dimensions of organizational commitment." Administrative Science Quarterly 4(March):468–490.
Graves, B.
  1970   "Particularism, exchange and organizational efficiency: a case study of a construction industry." Social Forces 49(September):72–80.
Grosof, E.H., L.Z. Gross, C.A. Yeracaris and W.C. Hobbs
  1970   "Anchorage in organization: a dialectial theory." Social Forces 49 (September):81–90.
Guyot, J.F.
  1962   "Government bureaucrats are different." Public Administration Review 22(December):195–202.
Hage, J. and M. Aiken
  1969   "Routine technology, social structure, and organizational goals." Administrative Science Quarterly 14(September):366–377.
Hall, O.
  1948   "The stages of a medical career." American Journal of Sociology (52):327–336.
Harsanyi, J.C.
  1966   "A bargaining model for social status in informal groups and formal organizations." Behavioral Science 11(September):357–369.
Hedley, R.A.
  1970   "Organizational objectives and managerial controls: a study of computerization," in J. Woodward (ed.), Industrial Organization: Behaviour and Control. London: Oxford University Press.
Heron, A.
  1962   "Preparation for retirement: a new phase in occupational development." Occupational Psychology (36):1–9.
Herzberg, F., et al.
  1957   Job Attitudes: Review of Research and Opinion. Pittsburgh: Psychological Service of Pittsburgh.
  1959   The Motivation to Work. New York: Wiley.

Hethy, L. and C. Mako
   1971   "Production remuneration in an Hungarian enterprise." Sociologie du
          Travail 13(January–March):25–37.
Hickson, D.J., C.R. Hinings, C.A. Lee, R.E. Schneck and J.M. Pennings
   1971   "Strategic contingencies theory of intra-organizational power." Admin-
          istrative Science Quarterly 16(June):216–229.
Hiller, E.T.
   1928   The Strike. Chicago: University of Chicago Press.
Hinrichs, J.R.
   1969   "Correlates of employee evaluations of pay increases." Journal of
          Applied Psychology (53):481–489.
Hoffmann, C.
   1964   "Work incentives in Communist China." Industrial Relations 3(Febru-
          ary):81–97.
Hollowell, P.G.
   1968   The Lorry Driver. London: Routledge and Kegan Paul.
Hoos, I.R.
   1961   Automation in the Office. Washington, D.C.: Public Affairs Press.
Horobin, G.W.
   1957   "Community and occupation in the hull fishing industry." British
          Journal of Sociology (8):343–356.
Horsfall, A.B. and C.M. Arensberg
   1949   "Teamwork and productivity in a shoe factory." Human Organization
          (8):13–25.
Hoshikawa, S.
   1962   "The structure of Habatsu (Clique) in a trade union." Japanese So-
          ciological Review 13(August):53–64.
Hughes, E.C.
   1958   Men and Their Work. Glencoe, Ill.: Free Press.
Hulin, C.L.
   1971   "Individual differences and job enrichment—the case against gen-
          eral treatments," in J. Maker (ed.), New Perspectives in Job Enrich-
          ment. New York: Van Nostrand Reinhold.
Hulin, C.L. and M.R. Blood
   1968   "Job enlargement, individual differences, and worker responses." Psy-
          chological Bulletin (69):41–55.
Hundal, P.S.
   1969   "Knowledge of performance as an incentive in repetitive industrial
          work." Journal of Applied Psychology (53):224–226.
Ima, K.
   1962   " 'Central life interests' of industrial workers: a replication among
          lumber workers." Eugene: University of Oregon. Unpublished Masters'
          Thesis.
Indik, B.P.
   1965   "Organization size and member participation: some empirical tests
          of alternative explanations." Human Relations (18):339–350.
Inkeles, A.
   1960   "Industrial man: the relation of status to experience, perception, and
          value." American Journal of Sociology (66):1–31.

Ivancevich, J.M.
  1969   "Perceived need satisfactions of domestic versus overseas managers."
         Journal of Applied Psychology (53) :274–278.
Jackson, J.M.
  1959   "Reference group processes in a formal organization." Sociometry 22
         (December) :307–327.
Jasinski, F.J.
  1956   "Technological delimitation of reciprocal relationships: a study of
         interaction patterns in industry." Human Organization 15(Summer) :
         24–28.
Jenkins, P.
  1962   "Unions: what makes the leaders tick?" New Society 3(October 18) :
         9–12.
Kahn, R.L. and E. Boulding (eds.)
  1964   Power and Conflict in Organizations. New York: Basic Books.
Kaplan, H.R. and C. Tausky
  1972   "Work and the welfare Cadillac: the function of and commitment to
         work among the hard-core unemployed." Social Problems (19) :469–
         483.
Karsh, B. and J. Siegman
  1964   "Functions of ignorance in introducing automation." Social Problems
         12(Fall) :141–150.
Katz, D. and R.L. Kahn
  1966   The Social Psychology of Organizations. New York: Wiley.
Katz, F.E.
  1965   "Explaining informal work groups in complex organizations: the case
         for autonomy in structure." Administrative Science Quarterly 10(Sep-
         tember) :204–223.
Kaufman, H.G. and R.R. Ritti
  1965   "Product identification and morale of engineers." Journal of Indus-
         trial Psychology (3) :68–73.
Kaufman, H. and D. Seidman
  1970   "The morphology of organizations." Administrative Science Quarterly
         (15) :4.
Kavcic, B., V. Rus and A.S. Tannenbaum
  1971   "Control, participation, and effectiveness in four Yugoslav, industrial
         organizations." Administrative Science Quarterly 16(March) :74–87.
Kilbridge, M.D.
  1961   "Turnover, absence, and transfer rates as indicators of employee dis-
         satisfaction with repetitive work." Industrial and Labor Relations Re-
         view 15(October).
Killingsworth, C.C.
  1963   "Cooperative approaches to problems of technological change," in
         G.G. Somers, et al. (eds.), Adjusting to Technological Change. New
         York: Harper & Row.
Klein, L.
  1964   "Operators' attitudes to piecework." New Society 16(July) :11–13.
Kolaja, J.
  1961   "A Yugoslav workers' council." Human Organization 20(Spring) :27–
         31.

Korman, A.K.
1966   "Self-esteem variable in vocational choice." Journal of Applied Psychology (50):479–486.
1967   "Self-esteem as a moderator of the relationship between self-perceived abilities and vocational choice." Journal of Applied Psychology (51): 65–67.
1968   "Task success, task popularity, and self-esteem as influences on task liking." Journal of Applied Psychology (52):484–490.
1969   "Self-esteem as a moderator in vocational choice: replications and extensions." Journal of Applied Psychology (53):188–192.
1970   "Toward an hypothesis of work behavior." Journal of Applied Psychology (54):31–41.
Kornhauser, A.
1965   Mental Health of the Industrial Worker: A Detroit Study. New York: Wiley.
Kornhauser, W.
1962   Scientists in Industry: Conflict and Accommodation. Berkeley: University of California Press.
Kranjc-Cuk, A.
1968   "Characteristics of working groups." Poklicno Usmerjanje (17):395–401.
Kremer, D.H.
1962   "A comparative study of the 'central life interests' of a group of workers—retail department store workers." Unpublished paper presented to the Faculty of Commerce and Business Administration, University of British Columbia.
Lammers, C.J.
1967   "Power and participation in decision-making in formal organizations." American Journal of Sociology (73):201–216.
Latta, L.H.
1968   "Occupational attitudes of over-the-road truck drivers: an exploratory survey." Unpublished Thesis, Department of Management, Michigan State University.
Lester, R.A.
1954   Hiring Practices and Labor Competition. Princeton, New Jersey: Princeton University, Industrial Relations Section.
Levinson, H.
1965   "Reciprocation: the relationship between man and organization." Administrative Science Quarterly 9(March):370–390.
Lewin, K.
1948   Resolving Social Conflict. New York: Harper & Bros.
Likert, R.
1961   New Patterns of Management. New York: McGraw-Hill.
1967   The Human Organization: Its Management and Value. New York: McGraw-Hill.
Lipset, S.M.
1967   "White collar workers and professionals: their attitudes and behavior toward unions," in W.A. Faunce (ed.), Readings in Industrial Sociology. New York: Appleton-Century-Crofts.
Lipset, S.M., M. Trow and J. Coleman
1956   Union Democracy. Glencoe, Ill.: The Free Press.

Lockwood, D.
  1958 The Blackcoated Worker. London: Allen and Unwin.
Long, N.E.
  1962 "The administrative organization as a political system," in S. Mailick
        and E.H. VanNess (eds.), Concepts and Issues in Administrative Be-
        havior. Englewood Cliffs, New Jersey: Prentice-Hall.
McGregor, D.M.
  1960 The Human Side of Enterprise. New York: McGraw-Hill.
McKelvey, W.W.
  1969 "Expectational noncomplementarity and style of interaction between
        professional and organization." Administrative Science Quarterly (14):
        21–32.
MacKinney, A.C., P.F. Wernimont and W.O. Galitz
  1962 "Has specialization reduced job satisfaction?" Personnel (39):8–17.
Maier, N.R. and J.A. Thurber
  1969 "Problems in delegation." Personnel Psychology (22):131–139.
Mann, F.C. and L.R. Hoffman
  1960 Automation and the Worker: A Study of Social Change in Power
        Plants. New York: Henry Holt.
March, J.G.
  1962 "The business firm as a political coalition." Journal of Politics (24):
        662–678.
March, J.G. and H.A. Simon
  1958 Organizations. New York: Wiley.
Marcson, S.
  1960 The Scientist in American Industry. New York: Harper & Row.
Maslow, A.H.
  1954 Motivation and Personality. New York: Harper & Bros.
Masuda, K.
  1966 "Fatigue and monotony in Japanese industry." Studia Psychologica
        (8):275–285.
Mathewson, S.B.
  1935 Restriction of Output Among Unorganized Workers. New York: Viking
        Press.
Maurer, J.G.
  1968 "Work as a 'central life interest' of industrial supervisors." Academy
        of Management Journal (11):329–39.
Maurice, M.
  1965 "Determinants of militantism and union action of workers and tech-
        nicians." Sociologie du Travail 3(July–September):254–272.
Mechanic, D.
  1962 "Sources of power of lower participants in complex organizations."
        Administrative Science Quarterly (7):349–364.
Merton, R.K.
  1957 Social Theory and Social Structure. Glencoe, Ill.: Free Press.
Miller, D.C. and W.H. Form
  1964 Industrial Sociology: The Sociology of Work Organizations. New York:
        Harper & Row.
Miller, G.A.
  1967 "Professionals in bureaucracy: alienation among industrial scientists
        and engineers." American Sociological Review (32):755–767.

1971 "Adult socialization, organizational structure, and role orientations."
      Administrative Science Quarterly 16(June):151–163.
Miller, G.W. and N. Rosen
1957 "Members' attitudes toward the shop steward." Industrial and Labor
      Relations Review 10(July):516–531.
Mills, C.W.
1951 White Collar. New York: Oxford University Press.
Misshauk, M.J.
1970 "Importance of environmental factors to scientist-engineers." Personnel
      Journal (49):319–323.
Moore, W.E.
1963 "The temporal structure of organizations," in E.A. Tiryakian (ed.),
      Sociological Theory, Values, and Sociocultural Change: Essays in
      Honor of Pitirim A. Sorokin. New York: The Free Press of Glencoe.
1969 "Changes in occupational structures," in W.A. Faunce and W.H. Form
      (eds.), Comparative Perspectives on Industrial Society. Boston: Little,
      Brown.
Muhammed, J.
1973 "Organizational attachment." Unsponsored research project, University
      of British Columbia. Unpublished data provided courtesy of the
      project.
Mulder, M.
1971 "Power equalization through participation?" Administrative Science
      Quarterly 16(March):31–39.
Mullen, J.H.
1966 "Personality polarization as an equilibrating force in a large organiza-
      tion." Human Organization 25(Winter):330–338.
Mumford, E. and T. Ward
1965 "How the computer changes management." New Society 6(Septem-
      ber):6–10.
Murrell, K.F.
1969 "Laboratory studies of repetitive work: IV. Auto-arousal as a de-
      terminant of performance in monotonous tasks." Acta Psychologica,
      Amsterdam (29):368–378.
Neer, D.L.
1957 "Industry." Annals American Academy of Political and Social Sciences
      313(September):79–82.
Nelson, H.E.
1962 "Occupational self-images of teachers: a study of the occupational
      involvements and work-role orientations of Michigan industrial edu-
      cation teachers." East Lansing: Michigan State University. Unpublished
      Doctoral Dissertation.
Obradovic, J.
1970 "Participation and work attitudes in Yugoslavia." Industrial Relations
      9(February):161–169.
O'Brien, G.
1968 "The measurement of cooperation." Organizational Behavior and Hu-
      man Performance (3):427–439.
Orzack, L.H.
1959 "Work as a 'central life interest' of professionals." Social Problems (7):
      125–132.

Osipow, S.H. and J.A. Gold
  1967   "Factors related to inconsistent career preferences." Personnel and
          Guidance Journal (46) :346–349.
Parker, S.R.
  1965   "Work and non-work in three occupations." Sociological Review (13) :
          65–75.
Peabody, R.L.
  1963   "Authority relations in three organizations." Public Administration
          Review 23(June) :87–92.
Peck, S.
  1963   The Rank and File Leaders. New Haven, Conn.: College and University
          Press.
Pennings, J.M., D.J. Hickson, C.R. Hinings, C.A. Lee and R.E. Schneck
  1969   "Uncertainty and power in organizations." Mens en Maatschappij 44
          (September–October) :418–433.
Perline, M.M. and V.R. Lorenz
  1970   "Factors influencing member participation in trade union activities."
          American Journal of Economics and Sociology 29(October) :425–437.
Perrow, C.
  1961   "Organizational prestige: some functions and dysfunctions." American
          Journal of Sociology 66(January) :335–341.
  1970   "Departmental power and perspectives in industrial firms," in M. Zald
          (ed.), Power in Organizations. Nashville: Vanderbilt University Press.
Pimenov, V.V.
  1963   "Proizvodstvennyĭ Byt Lesorubov." Soviet Sociology (2) :13–20.
Pomian, G. and K. Bursche
  1963   "The role and social position of foremen in industrial works." Polish
          Sociological Bulletin (1) :93–94.
Porter, L.W. and E.E. Lawler, III
  1965   "Properties of organization structure in relation to job attitudes and
          job behavior." Psychological Bulletin (64) :23–51.
Purcell, T.V.
  1960   Blue Collar Man: Patterns of Dual Allegiance in Industry. Cambridge,
          Mass.: Harvard University Press.
Ranta, R.R.
  1960   "The professional status of the Michigan Cooperative Extension Ser-
          vice." Madison: University of Wisconsin. Unpublished Doctoral Dis-
          sertation.
Robertson, L.S. and J.C. Rogers
  1966   "Distributive justice and informal organization in a freight warehouse
          work crew." Human Organization 25(Fall) :221–224.
Roethlisberger, F.J. and W.J. Dickson
  1939   Management and the Worker. Cambridge, Mass.: Harvard University
          Press.
Ronan, W.W.
  1970   "Relative importance of job characteristics." Journal of Applied Psy-
          chology (54) :192–200.
Rose, A.M.
  1952   Union Solidarity. Minneapolis: University of Minnesota Press.

Ross, I. and A. Zander
  1957 "Need satisfactions and employee turnover." Personnel Psychology
        (10) :327–338.
Rottenberg, S.
  1963 "Property in work versus property in jobs: a reply." Industrial and
        Labor Relations Review 16(January) :284–288.
Rourke, F.E.
  1960 "Bureaucracy in Conflict: Administrators and Professionals." Ethics
        70(April) :220–227.
Roy, D.F.
  1959 "Banana time: job satisfaction and informal interaction." Human Or-
  –60   ganization 18(Winter) :158–168.
Rus, V.
  1966 "Socijalni Procesi I Struktura Moci U Radinoj Organizaciji." Socio-
        logija (8) :95–112.
  1970 "Moc I Struktura Moci U Jugoslovenskim Preduzecima." Sociologija
        (12) :191–207.
Sainsaulieu, R.
  1965 "Pouvoirs et strategies de groupes ouvriers dans l'atelier." Sociologie
        du Travail 7(April–June) :162–174.
Saleh, S.D., R.J. Lee and E.P. Prien
  1965 "Why nurses leave their jobs—an analysis of female turnover." Per-
        sonnel Administration (28) :25–28.
Sales, S.M. and J. House
  1970 "Job dissatisfaction as a possible contributor to risk of death from
        coronary disease." Proceedings of the Annual Convention of the
        American Psychological Association (5) :593–594.
Sayles, L.R.
  1958 Behavior of Industrial Work Groups. New York: Wiley.
Sayles, L.R. and G. Strauss
  1953 The Local Union: Its Place in the Industrial Plant. New York: Harper
        & Bros.
Schein, E.
  1965 Organizational Psychology. Englewood Cliffs, New Jersey: Prentice-
        Hall.
Schein, E.H. and J.S. Ott
  1962 "The legitimacy of organizational influence." American Journal of So-
        ciology 67(May) :682–689.
Schlag-Rey, M., R. Ribas and V. Feaux
  1959 "Union members and their unions: investigation of the knowledge,
        opinions, and religious persuasion of unionized workers concerning
        their unions." Tijdschrift voor sociale wetenschappen (7) :155–181.
Scott, W.H.
  1965 Office Automation: Administrative and Human Problems. Paris: OECD.
Seashore, S.E.
  1954 "Group cohesiveness in the industrial work group." Institute for So-
        cial Research.
Seidman, J., et al.
  1958 The Worker Views His Union. Chicago: University of Chicago Press.

Seiler, J.
  1963   "Diagnosing interdepartmental conflict." Harvard Business Review
         (41):121–132.
Sheldon, M.E.
  1971   "Investments and involvements as mechanisms producing commitment
         to the organization." Administrative Science Quarterly 16(June):143–
         150.
Shepard, J.M.
  1969   "Functional specialization and work attitudes." Industrial Relations
         8(February):185–194.
  1970   "Functional specialization, alienation, and job satisfaction." Industrial
         and Labor Relations Review (23):207–219.
Sheppard, H.L., L.A. Ferman and S. Faber
  1960   Too Old to Work—Too Young to Retire: A Case Study of a Permanent
         Plant Shutdown. Special Committee on Unemployment Problems of
         U.S. Senate, Washington, D.C.: U.S. Government Printing Office.
Sherif, M.
  1935   "A study of some social factors in perception." Archives of Psychology
         (27):No. 187.
Shils, E.B.
  1963   Automation and Industrial Relations. New York: Holt, Rinehart and
         Winston.
Shister, J. and L.G. Reynolds
  1949   Job Horizons: A Study of Job Satisfaction and Labor Mobility. New
         York: Harper & Bros.
Shostak, A.B.
  1969   Blue-Collar Life. New York: Random House.
Sicinski, A.
  1964   "Expert—innovator—adviser: certain aspects of the differentiation of
         roles in a factory." Polish Sociological Bulletin (1):54–66.
Simon, H.A.
  1947   Administrative Behavior. New York: MacMillan
Sinha, D. and M. Upendra Pai
  1963   "Motivational analysis of union-membership." Indian Journal of Social
         Work 23(January):343–350.
Somers, G.G., et al. (eds.)
  1963   Adjusting to Technological Change. New York: Harper & Row.
Spinrad, W.
  1960   "Correlates of trade union participation: a summary of the literature."
         American Sociological Review 25(April):237–244.
Starcevich, M.
  1971   "An analysis of the relationship between the dual-factor theory of
         motivation and central life interests of employees." Oklahoma City:
         University of Oklahoma. Unpublished Doctoral Dissertation.
  1973   "The relationship between the central life interests of first-line man-
         agers, middle managers, and professional employees and job char-
         acteristics as satisfiers and dissatisfiers." Personnel Psychology (27):
         107–115.
Stieber, J.
  1960   "Non-wage aspects of collective bargaining." Business Topics (Spring):
         26–34.

Strauss, G.
1966   "Psychology of the scientist: XXI. Growth and belonging perceptions as factors in the behavior of engineers and scientists." Perceptual & Motor Skills (23):883–894.

Strother, G.B.
1969   "Creativity in the organization." Journal of Cooperative Extension 7 (Spring):7–16.

Super, D.E.
1962   "The structure of work values in relation to status, achievement, interests, and adjustment." Journal of Applied Psychology (46):231–239.
1969   "Vocational development theory: persons, positions, and processes." Counseling Psychologist (1):2–9.

Sykes, A.J.M.
1960   "Unity and restrictive practices in the British printing industry." Sociological Review 8(December):239–254.
1964   "A study in changing the attitudes and stereotypes of industrial workers." Human Relations 17(May):143–154.
1967   "The cohesion of a trade union workshop organization." Sociology 1 (May):141–163.
1969   "Navies: their work attitudes." Sociology (3):21–35.

Tagliacozzo, D.L. and J. Seidman
1956   "A typology of rank-and-file union members." American Journal of Sociology (61):546–553.

Tannenbaum, A.S. and F.H. Allport
1956   "Personality structure and group structure: an interpretive study of their relationship through an event-structure hypothesis." Journal of Abnormal and Social Psychology 53(November):272–280.

Tausky, C.
1969   "Meanings of work among blue collar men." Pacific Sociological Review (12):49–55.

Tausky, C. and R. Dubin
1965   "Career anchorage: managerial mobility motivations." American Sociological Review (30):725–735.

Taveggia, T.C.
1971   "The necessity of work: an empirical study of British factory workers." Eugene: University of Oregon. Unpublished Doctoral Dissertation.

Taylor, F.W.
1911   The Principles of Scientific Management. New York: Harper.

Taylor, L.
1968   Occupational Sociology. New York: Oxford University Press.

Touraine, A., et al.
1965   Workers' Attitudes to Technical Change. Paris: OECD.

Trahair, R.C.
1969   "Dynamics of a role theory for the worker's judgment." Human Relations (22):99–119.

Trist, E.L. and K.W. Bamforth
1951   "Some social and psychological consequences of the longwall method of coal-getting: an examination of the psychological situation and defenses of a work group in relation to the social structure and technological content of the work system." Human Relations (4):3–38.

University of Chicago Law Review
  1970   "The building trades." The Review 37(Winter) :328–358.
University of Liverpool, Department of Social Science
  1956   The Dock Worker: An Analysis of Conditions of Employment in the
         Port of Manchester. Liverpool: University Press of Liverpool.
Valchev, A., et al.
  1969   "Novata Sistema Na Stopansko R'Kovodstvo V Promishlenostta V
         Sotsialnokhigienna Svetlina." Sotsiologicheski Problemi (1) :42–49.
Van den Bogaert, M.J.
  1968   "The bonus question in India: from ex cratia payment to industrial
         claim." Economic Development & Cultural Change 17(October) :50–64.
Very, P.S. and R.W. Prull
  1970   "Birth order, personality development, and the choice of law as a
         profession." Journal of Genetic Psychology (116) :219–221.
Vidart, L.
  1967   "A current aspect of psychoneurotic states of a reactional type due
         to concentration of business enterprises: 'The Merger Syndrome.'"
         Annales Medico-Psychologiques (2) :437–440.
Vollmer, H.M.
  1960   Employee Rights and the Employment Relationship. Berkeley: Uni-
         versity of California Press.
Vollmer, H.M. and P.J. McGillivray
  1960   "Personnel offices and the institutionalization of employee rights." Pa-
         cific Sociological Review 3(Spring) :29–34.
Vollmer, H.M. and D.L. Mills (eds.)
  1966   "Professionals and complex organizations," in Professionalization. En-
         glewood Cliffs, New Jersey: Prentice-Hall.
Vroom, V.H.
  1960   "The effects of attitudes on perception of organizational goals." Hu-
         man Relations 13(August) :229–240.
  1964   Work and Motivation. New York: Wiley.
Walker, C.R.
  1950   Steeltown: An Industrial Case History of the Conflict Between Progress
         and Security. New York: Harper & Bros.
  1957   Toward the Automatic Factory: A Case Study of Men and Machines.
         New Haven, Conn.: Yale University Press.
Walker, C.R. and R.H. Guest
  1952   Man on the Assembly Line. Cambridge, Mass.: Harvard University
         Press.
Warner, W.L.
  1941   Yankee City Series. 5 Vols. New Haven, Conn.: Yale University Press.
Weber, M.
  1947   The Theory of Social and Economic Organization. New York: Oxford
         University Press.
Wells, L.M.
  1963   "The limits of authority: Barnard revisited." Public Administration
         Review 23(September) :161–166.
Westby, D.L.
  1960   "The career experience of the symphony musician." Social Forces 38
         (March) :223–229.

Wickert, F.R.
  1951 "Turnover and employee's feelings of ego-involvement in the day-to-day operation of a company." Personnel Psychology (4) :185–197.
Wiener, Y.
  1970 "The effects of 'task- and ego-oriented' performance on two kinds of overcompensation inequity." Organizational Behavior & Human Performance (5) :191–208.
Wilensky, H.L.
  1960 "Work, careers, and social integration." International Social Science Journal (12) :543–560.
  1961 "Orderly careers and social participation: the impact of work history on social integration in the middle class." American Sociological Review 26(August) :521–539.
  1963 "The moonlighter: a product of relative deprivation." Industrial Relations 3(October) :105–124.
Williams, W.
  1925 Mainsprings of Men. New York: Scribners and Sons.
Woodward, J.
  1965 Industrial Organization. London: Oxford University Press.
Worthy, J.C.
  1950 "Organizational structure and employee morale." American Sociological Review (15) :169–179.
Zald, M.N.
  1962 "Power balance and staff conflict in correctional institutions." American Sociological Quarterly (7) :22–49.
  1970 (ed.) Power in Organizations. Nashville: Vanderbilt University Press.
Zelikoff, S.B.
  1969 "On the obsolescence and retraining of engineering personnel." Training & Development Journal (23) :3–14.

CHAPTER **8**

Schools as Work Settings

Roland J. Pellegrin

Pennsylvania State University

The primary aim of this chapter is manifestly to analyze schools as work settings, an objective we shall pursue in its diverse phases. We have, in addition,
two additional objectives closely related to one another: to contribute to the
understocked storehouse of knowledge about discrepancies between empirical
realities in organizational settings and the institutionalized contexts in which
organizations are embedded; and to contrast real life conditions with organizational models developed by analysts of social systems. Thus we hope to
add to the existing knowledge about organizations in general, in accordance
with our conviction that an urgent current task for social scientists is to conduct empirical research about operational conditions in organizations. Such
work, we believe, is indispensable for furthering organizational theory.

The existing state of knowledge about educational systems restricts the
potential scope of our analysis. Periodically scholars have called attention to
the lack of comprehensive and systematic studies of schools as organizations
(Gross, 1956:62–67; Bidwell, 1965:972; Lortie, 1969:2). Not only has the knowledge base been meager, but sources providing satisfactory and relevant empirical
data are few and widely scattered. Given this rather disheartening situation, one
welcomes the appearance in recent years of a number of research reports and
analytical summaries of literature that have made important contributions to
our knowledge about the organization of the school. These publications make

I am indebted to numerous colleagues and graduate students in the Center for the
Advanced Study of Educational Administration at the University of Oregon for their efforts
to improve my understanding of schools as organizations. Except for Max G. Abbott and
W.W. Charters, Jr., whose assistance has been especially helpful, I shall not identify these
scholars by name; they are many, and my ability to identify the contributors of specific insights is, alas, frustrated by a defective memory.

Some of the research of the author and his colleagues reported herein was conducted as
part of the research and development program of the Center for the Advanced Study of Educational Administration at the University of Oregon, a national research and development
center which is supported in part by funds from the National Institute of Education, Department of Health, Education, and Welfare. The opinions expressed in this paper do not necessarily reflect the position or policy of the National Institute of Education, and no official
endorsement by that agency should be inferred.

it seem feasible and worthwhile to attempt a summary of what is known about schools as work settings.

We are limited in our consideration, of course; we cannot deal with schools in all their infinite variety. Although it is no doubt true that "school is school, no matter where it happens" (Jackson, 1968:vii), it is also the case that there are important differences (as well as subtle and often surprising similarities) in schools within various social and cultural contexts and from one level to another within the educational system of a given society. Accordingly, we shall focus our discussion on American schools, and more precisely, on public elementary schools because they have been most intensively, systematically and recently researched. The work of the author of this chapter and his former colleagues in the Center for the Advanced Study of Educational Administration at the University of Oregon (to which we shall refer at various points in this analysis) has also been directed mainly toward the elementary school level.

A further limitation of our presentation is that it is concerned mainly with commonplace, traditional, or conventional types of elementary schools that dominate the American scene—those characterized by a relatively simple division of labor and the self-contained classroom. This is not to say that other organizational forms are not emerging for the elementary school. There is, in fact, considerable experimentation under way involving both radical and modest changes in organizational structures and processes. (An excellent study of "open-space" elementary schools was published by Meyer and Cohen, 1970; for a report on another type of school with unconventional organization, see Pellegrin, 1969). These innovative designs, however, affect relatively few schools so far; furthermore, it is still much too early to say whether or not these experiments will be successful in institutionalizing significant modifications in instruction or in the behaviors of school personnel.

The discussion that follows reflects our choice of critical factors that should be examined in a brief analytical treatment of schools as work settings. The analysis of a work setting requires an examination of the organizational and institutional contexts in which an occupation is practiced. In studying these contexts, we shall develop certain themes while covering several main topics or content areas. Our thematic emphases are given to: (1) the discrepancies between institutionalized structures and operational conditions, (2) the effects of legal and bureaucratic controls upon the instructional duties of the teacher, and (3) the consequences of an ill-defined teaching technology and the exigencies of the classroom situation for instructional behavior. In anticipation, we can say that the teacher is, in terms of his legal and organizational statuses, officially an employee without specified powers or authority. Despite an abundance of controls intended to constrain his behavior, he retains considerable autonomy in his job performance.

In developing these themes and spelling out some of their implications, we shall deal with the following topics. First to be discussed is the nature of the teaching occupation, with emphasis given to the professional and nonprofessional characteristics of the instructional role. This will be followed by an analysis of educational organizations as social systems, where we shall scrutinize the allegedly bureaucratic features of schools and school districts. Next, we summarize basic characteristics of the classroom as a work environment. Then we examine in some detail the critical factors of power, constraint, and autonomy as they relate to the work situations of teachers. The division of labor of the school is then discussed, with special emphasis given to the task structure of teachers and interdependence in work activity. The teaching role and the technology of teaching are given brief attention, and the analysis ends with some concluding observations.

THE OCCUPATIONAL AND ORGANIZATIONAL CONTEXTS OF TEACHING

Insight into the occupational context in which teaching is carried on is essential for understanding the nature of schools as organizations and the working situation within which instruction is conducted. There is much to be said about the social background of teaching (see Charters, 1962:715–813) and the history of the occupation that we cannot go into in this presentation. We shall accordingly outline but a few of the pertinent facts about teaching in the past and present in the United States.

As many writers have indicated (see, for example, Lortie, 1969:16 ff.), teaching in America as an occupation has been profoundly affected by its history. While schools and ideologies pertaining to education evolved differently in the various sections of the country, a concern for schooling as an indispensable means of socializing children eventually became widespread. Despite regional and local variations, schools had certain critical characteristics in common. They were established and supported at the local community level within an ideological framework of "layman control." During the Colonial Period and for several decades thereafter, no criteria for eligibility to teach, with the exception of minimum literacy, were established. Most early teachers were males; teaching in Europe being traditionally a man's occupation, despite the fact that teaching was regarded as relatively easy work that did not tax "the full strength of a man" (Lortie, 1969:17). Especially in elementary teaching, which was believed to require little academic knowledge and for which potential recruits were in relatively ample supply, teachers were poorly paid and offered unattractive working conditions. For many, teaching became an occupational pursuit which could be followed temporarily and often on a part-time basis until more long-lasting career plans materialized.

In the decades following the establishment of the republic, state school systems began to emerge in response to the widespread commitment to the importance of public schooling. During the Civil War and the years following it, women largely replaced men in elementary teaching, being attracted by salaries and working conditions which were deemed unrewarding for men (Lortie, 1969:17). By the end of the nineteenth century, as the nation experienced rapid population growth, heavy immigration, and continued demands for universal schooling, teaching provided a more or less livable income and secure status for many thousands of women.

In recent decades there have been several changes in the institutional setting of the occupation. In this century the superintendency, principalship, and other administrative and specialist positions have become institutionalized. Teacher organizations, notably the National Education Association (NEA) and the American Federation of Teachers (AFT), have become prominent features of the educational scene. Tenure arrangements have become widely established, and salaries of elementary and secondary teachers have been equalized and improved to some extent. "Entry standards rose to require college attendance, and certification machinery was constructed" (Lortie, 1969:19).

Elementary teaching continues to be characterized by a number of conditions that reflect the historical developments cited above. The framework of local, lay control and its accompanying ideology persist. Teachers remain poorly paid in comparison with other allegedly "professional" occupations. In recent decades the overwhelming majority of teachers in elementary schools have been women, a fact that reflects social and cultural conditions as well as economic ones. While many occupations and professions exceed teaching in both prestige and income, it is well worth noting that teaching has attracted many women simply because until quite recently they had few career alternatives. At present and in the future, new occupational opportunities for women promise to change this situation. If careers in higher paying and prestigious occupations become available to large numbers of women, the attractiveness of elementary school teaching in terms of social status and income will lessen for them. Most women now teaching, however, entered the labor force when attractive alternative careers were quite limited. The social status and income of teachers, therefore, drew many more women than men into the field.

The preponderance of women in elementary school teaching is also related to the fact that the occupation requires less than a lifetime commitment, making it possible for teachers to pursue the occupation intermittently while dropping out for a greater or lesser period to explore other job alternatives or, in the case of women, to play the traditional roles of housewife and mother. For many who have taught intermittently, the occupation has proved attractive because continuous participation in it has not been required in order to maintain one's qualifications in the field.

The typical career pattern for women teachers in recent decades was described by Charters (1967:184). In the usual case, the teacher accepted her first teaching position immediately after receiving the bachelor's degree, taught some two to four years, resigned her position to bear and rear children, and then returned to teaching some ten to fifteen years later when her youngest child was old enough to go to kindergarten. Those who returned to teaching at this stage usually remained in the occupation and were employed in the same school system until retirement age.

Intermittent employment of teachers has caused considerable interest in "survival rates" among scholars in education, and high turnover has been of special administrative concern. The typical career pattern has resulted in a situation in which the likelihood that a teacher will stay on the job is increased with age. As Charters (1967:192) has indicated, "The older a teacher is when you hire him, the longer he will stay." Indeed, movement from one school system to another is relatively rare, and often occasioned by the transfer of the teacher's husband. Long tenure in a given school district, it might be observed, does little to enhance the cosmopolitan orientations of teachers.

There is relatively little differentiation within teaching ranks. Teacher salaries tend to be tied to training and years of experience (seniority) rather than to function or position (Bidwell, 1965:977). There is, therefore, little vertical mobility to be experienced as a reward for high quality job performance. Opportunities for upward mobility are limited almost exclusively to an administrative career, where salaries are based upon administrative rank and promotion is achieved through movement to higher positions in the hierarchy. For those who remain teachers, there is no such thing as a promotion. Improving one's situation consists of becoming more firmly established in one's school, and, as Becker (1952:560–561) has shown, often takes the form of transferring to another school in the same district which serves a clientele of higher social and economic status.

Teaching: Profession, Semiprofession, or Job?

Whether or not teaching is a profession is an issue of considerable importance in education. There is, to be sure, a great deal of talk about professionalism among educationists. There has been an extensive professionalization movement sponsored by the National Education Association since 1946 (Lindsay, 1961). Professionalization has been a major theme at many conferences and meetings of administrators and teachers, and almost innumerable essays on the subject have appeared in education journals. Despite this interest, practically all effort has been directed toward increasing "professionalism"; it is usually assumed in these discussions that education *is* a profession and that future efforts should be directed toward making educators more professional. Professionalization itself has seldom been subject to systematic analysis or questioned in relation to existing occupational conditions (an exception is Lieberman, 1956). Nor is there much empirical research on the extent to which teachers approximate the professional model in behavioral or attitudinal characteristics, and virtually no one has raised the issue of whether or not the professional model is a viable one for improving instruction. It is, of course, possible for professionalization efforts to produce deleterious consequences for an occupation's capacity for serving the needs of its clients (Taylor and Pellegrin, 1959:110–114).

The criteria to be employed in assessing the extent to which an occupation approximates a "true" or "full-fledged" profession have been extensively discussed (for a summary of this literature, see Hall, 1969:Ch. 4). In these presentations it is customary to identify the structural and attitudinal correlates of professionalism and the stages occupations go through in moving toward professional status. These analyses are often abstract and somewhat arbitrary; identifying the essential criteria of professionalism is by no means a simple matter, and subjective judgment enters into selecting and assigning priority to them.

Because we are mainly interested in professionalism as it relates to work behavior, we shall not review the literature on correlates and stages of professionalism (discussed in Hall, 1969:78–91). Our reason for not using "correlate-stage" analysis is simply that this approach tells us relatively little about the actual implementation of structural correlates or attitudes in the performance of job activities. As an alternative, we shall employ our knowledge of the classical literature on the professions to identify the "essential components" of a professional model. These components represent the conditions under which an occupation would approximate realization of a "true" profession. Each of these components will be briefly stated and then discussed in relation to the job of teacher. Our presentation is supplemented by the only comprehensive and systematic empirical research on teacher professionalism that has been published (Simpson, 1969; Simpson and Simpson, 1969).

Knowledge base. A profession has a strong knowledge base, embodying abstract and theoretical principles as well as the foundations for technical expertise.

Education has a weak knowledge base and the technology of teaching is seriously deficient. The main problem lies not so much in the content of instruction, which comes mainly from fields other than education itself, but in the technology of teaching. We shall examine this matter in more detail in a later section of this chapter. Here we shall but call attention to the lack of a systematic, codified technology that is universally known to practitioners, and discuss some of the factors that account for this deficiency.

There is, first of all, no substantial research tradition in education that might have led to the accumulation of a satisfactory knowledge base;

> The general intellectual atmosphere in education is one which gives scant emphasis to the development of a research orientation to one's work, or to the development of a scientific attitude. It goes almost without saying that teachers and administrators rely on precedent and common sense much more than they do on research findings as justifications for their practices (Pellegrin, 1965a:71).

Moreover, there is widespread ignorance in the profession of what research can contribute to the field, accompanied by a thorough lack of appreciation of the role that theory plays in the development of a discipline (Griffiths, 1964: 96). Consequently, work activities in the schools are heavily based on tradition and precedent; they are, as Griffiths (1959:5) has said, "value bound" and "practice oriented." All of these factors pose major barriers to innovative educational practices (Carlson, 1965:5).

Commitment. The work of the professional practitioner constitutes a career to which he has a continuous lifetime commitment. This career commitment is indispensable; without it, the practitioner lacks (1) the personal discipline to master the complex knowledge base of his field, and (2) the intrinsic commitment to work which makes it possible for him to meet the exacting standards of his profession.

As we have already noted, a large proportion of the teaching corps lacks a continuous lifetime commitment to teaching as a career. In many cases, the career pattern involves temporary and intermittent employment. An intrinsic commitment to the teaching profession is often lacking. The situation is further aggravated by other conditions we have previously recognized. The lack of a teaching hierarchy leads to the abandonment of the classroom for administrative work as a means of achieving upward mobility. A related consequence of temporary and partial commitments to the profession is the instability and high turnover to which we have already referred.

Collegial controls. Collegial controls provide the principal constraints on professional behavior; within the framework of these constraints, the practitioner has considerable discretionary authority—that is, he is highly autonomous in his work behavior. In view of the fact that professions deal with matters critical to societal welfare, the autonomy of the individual practitioner is possible in the final analysis only because stringent collegial controls exist and are enforced.

In education, collegial controls over work behavior are few and extremely weak. The principle of autonomy for the individual practitioner is almost universally misunderstood among educators; when teachers speak of autonomy, they are talking about freedom from restraints, with no collegial controls whatever. The control of teacher behavior is entrusted to administrative superiors rather than to the colleague group (Abbott, 1965:51).

In the case of teachers, control of the schools by laymen is in many ways fundamentally antithetical to professional autonomy. Layman control of local schools is considered to be an important structural constraint on teacher behavior by many authorities. (An interesting analysis of how local control structures, ideologies, and institutional arrangements affect the American teacher, and a comparison with different institutional conditions in England, are presented in Baron and Tropp, 1961:546–549.) Interestingly, the ideology of local, lay control of the schools is so firmly entrenched in American culture and tradition, and even in the thinking of educators themselves, that teachers and administrators rarely oppose (at least in public) institutionalized arrangements for local control. Instead, in seeking to mitigate the constraints these arrangements produce, teacher "militants" cast their demands in a completely different context of discussion. Rather than proposing formal or legal changes in the governing structure of education, teachers press for improvements in teacher status (including, of course, income), amelioration of working conditions, and, more recently, betterment of the instructional capabilities of schools.

License and mandate. The professional is formally and publicly acknowledged as an authority in his areas of competence. The public defers to his expertise; in some professions, practice is restricted by law solely to members of the profession in question. This, as Hughes (1958:78–87) has explained in a classic analysis, means that the professional has a "license and mandate" to exercise his professional skills.

As Simpson and Simpson point out, in analyzing this matter in relation to semiprofessions (in which they include teaching), the public does not grant a license or mandate to practitioners in these fields because it "does not feel that they have any just claim to specialized esoteric knowledge" (1969:198). Not only does the general public deny a mandate to teachers, but it is also denied them by their own administrative superiors, who often lack confidence in the professional abilities of their staff.

It should be emphasized that public sentiment is also undoubtedly influenced by the fact that teaching does not merely involve imparting objective knowledge to students; there is, in addition, the important matter of socializing children into "approved" value orientations and behavior patterns. While the public tends to defer to acknowledged expertise in technical or factual matters, deference to the values of others is an entirely different matter.

Affective neutrality. The professional practitioner's orientation toward his clients is characterized by affective neutrality. This orientation contrasts sharply with emotional involvement with the client and his problems. Professionals assume that only through affective neutrality can practitioners adequately serve the *needs*, as opposed to the whims or desires, of their clients. Many professionals also believe that affective neutrality protects their fiduciary obligations; this belief is based upon the assumption that emotional involvement threatens one's fiduciary relationship to the individual client as well as one's responsibilities in serving society.

The dominant orientation among teachers, especially in the elementary school, is in direct opposition to affective neutrality. This generalization needs qualification; norms pertaining to distributive justice (especially in evaluating student performance) are strongly held by most teachers. On the whole, however, what teachers primarily stress is a close, "warm," sympathetic relationship with the individual student. It is taken for granted by the vast majority of teachers that only such a relationship makes it possible to know the student well enough to meet his individual learning needs. This feeling is so strong among teachers that the possibility of emphasizing a relationship dominated by affective neutrality is rarely discussed.

Furthermore, departure from the norms of affective neutrality may be increasing in American education. Current educational thinking, which insists that there is a pressing and critical need for educational reform, sees the amelioration of instruction in the classroom as achievable in large measure through "humanizing" the educational process and developing close and informal ties with individual students. Current educational philosophies emphasize and defer to values and goals of disadvantaged populations. To the extent that these philosophies should become implemented in schools, meeting such objectives might take priority over serving the cognitive educational needs of students.

Perhaps as an alternative to affective neutrality, teachers stress a service orientation and the contribution that their profession makes to society. This, we believe, serves as a substitute for relationships of affective neutrality in the minds of teachers, and is a sort of functional alternative to the affective neutrality concept. In his research, Hall found that while teachers ranked low in relation to several components of the professional model, they ranked very high in their service orientation. In fact, of all the professions he studied, teachers ranked highest in this regard (Hall, 1969:84).

Simpson (1969) analyzed in depth the components of a professional model in his excellent and systematic study of professionalism among elementary teachers. He obtained data on a wide range of matters relating to professionalism from several thousand teachers and students in teacher preparatory programs. His basic conclusion is that education is simply not a profession. While he correctly emphasizes that teaching "offers opportunities for professionalism among individual teachers if they are professionally inclined" (p. xiii), he found little evidence that the vast majority of teachers exhibit attitudes and behaviors that are compatible with professionalism. His justifications for his conclusions are quite similar to our generalizations about teaching in relation to the components of the professional model. In general, Simpson found low commitments to abstract knowledge and individual autonomy, and weak colleague controls. In his sample population, there was typically a low instrinsic commitment to work and to the knowledge relating to it. Internal motivation to work in accordance with professional standards was weak and unevenly distributed among teachers. He also discovered that functionally specific, universalistic, and affectively neutral orientations were subordinated to those that emphasized service to society, a humanitarian attitude toward students, and emotional involvement with the client. Such orientations he views as the antithesis of professionalism.

Why teachers fail to meet the necessary conditions of professionalism is a matter that Simpson examines in considerable detail. He attributes his finding, that teaching is not a profession, primarily to the fact that it is a predominantly feminine occupation. Feminization of the teaching role, aptly described in the classic study by Waller (1932:50) several decades ago as "the assimilation of the teacher to the female character ideal," has marked consequences for the participation of teachers in educational as well as other community affairs (Carson, et al., 1967:55–56). Even in high schools, where a slight majority of teachers are men, feminine attitudes toward social participation dominate the orientations of practitioners (Zeigler, 1967:Ch. 1).

Simpson (1969:xii) sees the feminization of the occupation as detrimental to professionalization in several respects. For one, "the primacy of family rather than work role orientations among women keeps them from being professional in outlook or behavior." Simpson's (1969:xii) data show that few women teachers are committed to lifelong teaching careers, and that

> ... the large number who aspire to stop work and be full-time housewives are the least professional teachers. Women teachers, like other women semiprofessionals, are characterized by compliant predispositions, a desire for friendly work atmospheres, an orientation to humanitarian service rather than to technical expertise, and a lack of colleague reference groups and collegial authority orientations. All of these characteristics make teachers less professional than they would otherwise be.

He adds that "these characteristics of the occupation and of the prevailing beliefs about it help to explain why schools are in many ways run like bureaucracies rather than organizations staffed by autonomous professionals" (p. xiv).

Simpson (1969:9) devotes considerable attention to the question, what is teaching if it is not a profession? He concludes that teaching is just a job for many teachers, "something they do to earn money or fill time but to which they have little intrinsic professional commitment." He finds that, typically, teachers "want primarily a pleasant, easy, sociable work situation, and these features of a job are more important to them than is the encouragement the job gives them to enlarge their knowledge and apply it in professional ways." Relationships on the job are valued "more for the ease of sociability they afford than for the professional stimulation they provide." Lortie (1961:3–4), in his study of teacher work values similarly found that sociability assumes extremely high priority in informal teacher rules for interaction with one another.

Deviations from the professional model have led to the characterization of teaching as a semiprofession. In an extensive analysis, Simpson and Simpson (1969) have identified the dominant features of the semiprofessions. They stress some characteristics we have previously mentioned as associated with teaching—for example, the weak knowledge base, the achievement of mobility through substitution of an administrative career for professional practice, a low commitment to task performance, and the feminization of these occupations. Additionally, they point out that the work organizations of semiprofessions tend to be organized along bureaucratic lines to a greater extent than is the case with organizations dominated by professionals. Semiprofessional organizational patterns are characterized by bureaucratic controls rather than by the control of autonomous groups of colleagues which one finds in established professions. Moreover, semiprofessions lack autonomy in their work, being told "what to do and how to do it." To a greater extent than professionals, semiprofessionals are held accountable for their performance, not only to superiors, but to outsiders. Their work organizations have numerous rules governing not just their central work tasks, "but extraneous details of conduct on the job." Finally, in organizations staffed by semiprofessionals, hierarchical rank and the differentiation of units by level in the organization receive great emphasis and attention (Simpson and Simpson, 1969:196–198).

Schools as Social Systems—Bureaucracies or Quasi-Bureaucracies?

In describing the characteristics of educational organizations, many writers have been impressed by the similarities of schools to the bureaucratic model. Indeed, some have alleged that schools surpass the limits of bureaucratic control and regulation. Thus, for example, Moore (1967:6) tells us

> ...it must be emphasized that any teacher in urban schools is simply part of a larger organization that conforms by and large to the pattern of bureaucracy developed in Western governments and business corporations.

He sees the teacher as not on "an official or policy-making level in this bureaucratic organization. He is an executor of policy decided from above. Just like the student, he is one of the managed, not a manager" (p. 6). Later, he adds that "the teacher in the urban schools is more often simply a task master, giving out tasks that were in turn set by bureaucratic supervisors" (p. 7). This view, of course, misrepresents to some degree what the bureaucratic model implies; the conditions he refers to approximate an authoritarian and highly controlled setting operated by administrative decree rather than in terms of established rules and regulations basic to the model of bureaucracy. The theory of bureaucracy, despite its emphasis on rules and procedures, allocates considerable authority to functionaries in recognition of their expertise in their areas of competence. Notwithstanding, this exaggerated view of "bureaucracy" and constraints in the school is also encountered in other works (see, for instance, Eddy, 1969:25–26, 35–36).

At the same time, school systems and individual schools are clearly embedded in a formal and legalistic context that embodies definite bureaucratic features (the ensuing discussion follows Lortie, 1969:3–4). To begin with, school systems function under the constitutional authority of the state, which delegates powers to local school boards. These boards "hold the vast majority of specified powers in public schooling" (p. 3); indeed, school boards have legal responsibility over all aspects of school affairs, although some powers may be delegated to the office of the superintendent. The superintendent's job, however, is to implement policies established by the school board, not to initiate them.

Interestingly, no specific powers are allocated legally to any of the superintendent's subordinates, including teachers.

> In legal and formal terms the occupants of other school offices are almost nonexistent.... Principals, apparently heads of visible and discrete units, direct subunits which possess no official policy-making powers or independent fiscal resources.... Teachers ... are officially employees without powers of governance.... The formal and legal al-

location of authority in school systems is monolithic, hierarchical, and concentrated; official powers are focused at the apex of the structure (Lortie, 1969:4).

Other bureaucratic characteristics of school systems have been described by Bidwell (1965:974) as follows: There is "a functional division of labor," manifested in "the allocation of instructional and coordinative tasks to the school-system roles of teacher and administration"; staff roles are defined as offices, with recruitment conducted "according to merit and competence"; there is legally based tenure and "functional specificity of performance"; offices are ordered in a hierarchical fashion, "providing an authority structure based on the legally defined and circumscribed power of offices, a system of adjudication of staff disputes by reference to superiors, and regularized lines of communications"; and the schools are "operated according to rules of procedure, which set limits to the discretionary performance of officers by specifying both the aims and modes of official action."

Thus there is no denying that the formal, legal, or official framework embodies certain primary bureaucratic characteristics. At the same time, examination of organizational characteristics makes it quite clear that nonbureaucratic features are also endemic in schools. A major purpose of this chapter is to describe how the structural bureaucratic features of schools are subverted under actual operating conditions. At this point, however, we shall but list some of the salient features of schools that modify the formal bureaucratic context we have described above.

Despite bureaucratic strictures, there is a noteworthy "structural looseness" in schools and school systems, characterized by a "looseness of articulation between sub-units" (Bidwell, 1965:977). Not only are schools largely self-contained organizational units, but the same is usually true of individual classrooms (Bidwell, 1965:976). Further, while employment is based "upon technical competence and constitutes a career" (Abbott, 1965:44), this is wholly true for the administrative but not the teacher component. It is also the case that, even within a given school system, individual schools develop through time their own structural and cultural elements that deviate in significant ways from those of other schools (Shipman, 1968:25). There are also obvious contradictions between the official employeeship status of the teacher and the professional claims of the teacher fraternity, as noted by Lortie (1969:2) and by Corwin (1966), who, in a major study, explored the conflicts attending professionalization efforts in the bureaucratic context of the high school.

As Lortie (1969:9) has indicated, efforts at bureaucratization are also impeded by the "unrationalized nature of teaching technique." Further, the interaction patterns of teachers and students in the classroom, dominated by the exigencies of interpersonal relations, serve as "countervailing forces to bureaucratic operations" (Bidwell, 1965:991).

Miles (1965:57–61) has identified additional characteristics of schools that frustrate the implementation of bureaucratic procedures. He notes that schools are characterized by output ambiguity, intensified by a lack of goal clarity; input variability, owing to differential characteristics of staff and students; vulnerability to the demands of a variety of publics inside and outside the school; role performance invisibility, particularly of teachers; and a division of labor low in interdependence. All of these comments add real pertinence to Lortie's admonition (1961:2) that "To say that the public school is a bureaucratic institution is to leave much unexplained."

THE CLASSROOM AS A WORK ENVIRONMENT

There are basic classroom characteristics which set the tone for the work activity of the school. In a perceptive analysis of the classroom environment, Jackson (1968:5–17) emphasizes that the school abounds in routine occurrences. Teacher and student alike engage in repetitive events. The environment itself tends to be standardized in nature and physical setting. The atmosphere is permeated by social intimacy which Jackson feels is "unmatched elsewhere in our society." Indeed, he says, "Even factory workers are not clustered as close together as students in a standard classroom." School, in short, is where students learn to live in crowds. It is a "fairly stable environment—one in which the physical objects, social relations, and major activities remain much the same from day to day, week to week, and even, in certain respects, from year to year." It is also an evaluative setting, in which the student learns to have his activities judged by strangers.

The teacher as well as the student is affected by these realities. One learns from Jackson (Ch. 1) that the teacher is the manager of routine, enforcer of standardization in environment, ringmaster who prevents social intimacy from turning into chaos, evaluator of an often heterogeneous population, and one who teaches the hard lessons of delay, denial, interruption, social distraction, and power—while simultaneously dispensing praise and reproof.

One of the most critical things about the classroom environment, and indeed about the teaching occupation itself, is the apparently simple fact that teaching occurs in a group situation. In great contrast to members of professions that deal with the individual client or, at most, small groups of clients, the teacher characteristically works with large groups of students. "No other profession has to exercise its particular skills with large groups, many of whom may be unwilling clients" (Shipman, 1968:128).

The teacher is therefore a manager of group or crowd behavior (see Jackson, 1968:Ch. 1). Interaction is frequent, intense, and rarely interrupted for a substantial period of time. Almost incredibly, Jackson found in "one study of elementary classrooms that the teacher engages in as many as 1,000 interpersonal interchanges each day" (1968:11). The handling of interaction pressures is in itself a major task of teaching, one requiring major effort that might otherwise be directed toward the achievement of other goals. While as yet little studied and poorly understood, the "interaction press" faced by the teacher during the work day is certainly one of the critical factors in instruction.

Intensity of interaction is related to a like phenomenon in the classroom—the chronic "busyness" of the class setting. Conant, whose detailed observations in elementary school classrooms we shall discuss later, was struck by the fact that activity dominates the school day; there is virtually no leisure time. "There simply is no time to relax even if one wanted to, in class situations where twenty to thirty busy children are present" (1971:36). Jackson (1968:119–120), who also stresses the busy nature of classroom activity, says that there is an

> ... *immediacy* of classroom events ... that anyone who has ever been in charge of a roomful of students can never forget. There is a here-

and-now urgency and a spontaneous quality that brings excitement and variety to the teacher's work, though it also may contribute to the fatigue he feels at the end of the day.

The busy nature of classroom activity and the high frequency of interaction are important contributors to the fatiguing nature of the occupation. Indeed, popular conceptions notwithstanding, fatigue is one of the chronic burdens of teaching. Webb, in fact, refers to this fatigue as residual: "That is, it is not significantly dispelled by the normal rest or recreation periods (a night's sleep or a weekend's relaxation) and is therefore cumulative" (1962: 267). Industrial studies, Webb informs us, conclude that residual and cumulative fatigue attends jobs that are noisy and tedious.

Another distinguishing characteristic of the elementary classroom setting is the teacher belief that constant activity is a necessity; without it, waste of time and disciplinary problems will develop. The teacher feels constant pressure to keep the class engaged in some kind of activity. Something must be going on—otherwise negative consequences will develop. This emphasis on continuous activity undoubtedly has unforeseen consequences. For one thing, the emphasis on continuous activity "drives out" educational planning. One is reminded at this point of the reference by March and Simon (1958:185) "to Gresham's Law of planning"—that is, "Daily routine drives out planning." In view of the fact that modern educational theory emphasizes the critical significance of planning, chronic deficiencies in it may at least in part be attributed to the activity pattern of the school day.

The tensions and strains of managing classroom activity are often intensified by the reluctance and resistance of the student population. Public schools have virtually no control over the selection process; that is, they take on all comers as clients. As Carlson (1964:268) has noted, schools are "domesticated" service organizations in which "neither the client nor the organization enters the relationship voluntarily." In any event, a small but significant proportion of the student body (which presumably varies in size from one school to another) simply does not like to attend school (Jackson, 1968:Ch. 2). This situation does little to improve interaction pressures or to mitigate the necessity for teachers to maintain constant activity in the classroom.

Another characteristic of classrooms to which we wish to direct attention at this time is that their activity is heavily influenced by time pressures and scheduling. This, in turn, does little to alleviate activity and interaction pressures. "Adherence to a time schedule requires that activities often begin before interest is aroused and terminate before interest disappears" (Jackson, 1968:16).

POWER, CONTROL AND AUTONOMY

Literature on control and decision-making structures and processes in education is often misleading, contradictory and ambiguous. One reason for this state of affairs is the tendency to confuse legal and bureaucratic structures with real-life conditions. Perhaps even more important, however, is the fact that discussions of power and decision-making have been dominated by a community power structure perspective that examines educational policy formulation and political activity at the level of the community or the school district as a whole.

These writings provide a perspective on power and decision-making that directs the reader's attention almost exclusively to political and bureaucratic constraints and controls. There is little said about decision-making in the school, and even less about the classroom level.

Adequate insight into matters of power and control requires some basic distinctions among types and levels of decisions. There are, first of all, *resource allocation* decisions, which determine the extent of support for education and the kinds and amounts of resources to be made available to the school district. Secondly, there are *resource utilization* decisions, which determine how resources will be distributed to schools and classrooms after they are obtained. These again are made primarily at the district level, but to a lesser extent in the individual school. Finally, there are *resource implementation* decisions, which determine how available resources will be used in practice, under operational conditions. These decisions are made at the school and, particularly, classroom levels. We now turn attention to these different types and levels of decisions.

The Control of Resource Allocation and Utilization Decisions

There is a sizeable literature on resource allocation decisions in education. Undoubtedly such decisions are an integral part of the political process in most communities. At the same time, there is evidence (Pellegrin, 1965b, 1968) that educational matters are subordinated in priority and emphasis to economic and governmental affairs, at least as far as the top figures in the community "power structure" are concerned. That is, economic and governmental concerns exert stronger claims than educational ones on the time and effort of the "community elite." This fact alone goes a long way in explaining the difficulties educators have in obtaining what they consider adequate resources.

The educational power structure consists of disparate elements of the community—a few high ranking "general influentials" (when issues involving high economic stakes arise), a number of second and third echelon "influentials," school board members and high administrative officials (particularly the superintendent and his top aides), highly motivated citizens committed positively or negatively to educational programs, and even "powerless" people who temporarily assume vital roles during educational controversies. In general, however, the dominant figures in resource allocation decisions are those school board members and high-ranking administrators whose concern with educational questions is long-lasting and persistent. In such decisions, teachers and most principals play very minor roles, and, furthermore, show little interest in participation in such matters (Carson, et al., 1967:Ch. 2). While this situation is changing in some places, our generalization is undoubtedly correct for the vast majority of communities.

Resource utilization decisions are almost exclusively in the hands of persons holding the highest positions in the official educational hierarchy—that is, the local education "establishment." Specifically, these decisions are dominated by occupants of the top echelons in the school district office, with some participation by school board members and a small number of lesser administrative officials at the level of the school. Teachers have some representation on committees concerned with a few resource utilization decisions, but altogether their role is a minor one.

The Influence Structure at the Level of the School

Educators employed at the district and school levels have ambiguous and conflicting views about whether or not official policies dealing with vital instructional matters even exist in their communities. They vary a great deal in their perceptions of the locus of decision-making authority for policy formulation. They believe official authority for policy decisions and actual decision-making prerogatives are dispersed or diffused—that is, "shared" by various categories of educators and laymen. At the same time, the vast majority of the staff members of the school see operational decisions as being made primarily at the school and classroom levels.

The above generalizations and the findings presented below emerge from the Organizational Attributes Project, a comprehensive study conducted from 1967 to 1970 by the author of this chapter and colleagues in the Center for the Advanced Study of Educational Administration at the University of Oregon. Our data are drawn from an intensive analysis of eighteen elementary schools in the eastern, midwestern, and northwestern regions of the country. Special emphasis was given in this research to an investigation of influence, esteem, decision-making, and constraints at the levels of the school and classroom.

We now begin an analysis that deals with power, controls, and constraints at the school and classroom levels, examining at the same time the context in which resource implementation decisions are made. In this section the school "as a whole" is our context for analysis; in the next section, we shall focus on the classroom.

Let us start out by looking at the "influence structure" of the school. We use the term "influence" synonymously with "power" to refer to the ability of an individual or group to affect the decision-making process, to the part played in determining the outcomes of problems or issues. "Influence structure" refers to the relative influence of members of the organization, which can be roughly measured by a ranking of its personnel. The data we obtained required respondents to list the most influential persons in the school; influence structure was determined by simple tabulations of frequency of nominations.

It is quite clear that when we consider matters of school-wide import, influence is a function of position in the official hierarchy of the school. The conventional school, with its simple principal-teacher hierarchy, has an influence structure that is dominated by the principal. Influence is attached to positions; the principal's position confers influence. In some larger schools, where lesser administrative or quasi-administrative jobs exist, influence also "flows" to these positions.

Looked at from another perspective, influence flows away from rather than toward the teacher. As far as influence at the level of the school is concerned, teachers have difficulty in overcoming the structural constraints which impede their ability to become influential. Only rarely do even one or two teachers receive as many as one-third of the number of influence nominations received by the principal.

Further light on the influence structure of the school is provided by data on "esteem structure." Here we devised questions to measure the evaluation placed by group members upon the role performance of individuals; a view of the esteem structure was obtained by ranking individuals by means of a procedure identical to that used to identify the influence structure.

Once again the principal dominates the rankings. While he does not do so to the extent that he does in the influence structure, it is clear that esteem, like influence, is closely correlated with official position. What seems really significant here is the way the organizational structure of the school affects the influence and esteem of individuals *regardless of their abilities or other personal characteristics.* Thus in matters that pertain to the educational program of the school as a whole, the merit of ideas seems less important than their source. The position of the teacher in the school structure provides few opportunities for exercising building-wide influence. School level decisions, then, are largely the province of the principal and, if the school is large enough to have them, his administrative subordinates.

This is not to say that teachers are totally without influence in certain matters affecting the school as a whole. There is, after all, an informal power structure among teachers, and it does constrain the principal to some extent. The situation, however, seems to be a bit curious. While informal alliances of teachers can initiate actions to change organizational structure (Kimbrough, 1964:254), their efforts are usually directed toward reinforcing or establishing procedures designed to protect the "integrity" of the classroom. In matters of power and control, the real province of the teacher, as well as his main sphere of concern, is not the school, but, as we shall now see, the classroom.

Influence and Decision-Making at the Instructional Level

We now examine what is surely the most crucial of instructional decision-making contexts—the teaching–learning situation, more often called the classroom environment. The question that now concerns us is, what control does the teacher have over work decisions that affect him?

We obtained data (Organizational Attributes Project, 1967–1970) on the teacher's role in certain kinds of basic, recurrent, decision-making matters concerning instruction. In a series of questions, we asked each teacher to indicate the part he plays in the decision-making process with regard to the following activities: choosing teaching methods used in the classroom, determining the scope and sequence of subject matter content, selecting instructional materials other than textbooks, deciding on pupil promotion, and scheduling classroom activities. For each of the five activities, the respondent was asked to indicate if he had (1) complete autonomy to make the decision himself, (2) final power to make the decision after receiving suggestions and recommendations from others, (3) power to make the decision within certain limits, (4) power to share the decision with other persons in a group or committee, or (5) no voice in making the decision (i.e., the decision is made by others). When the respondent chose any but the first alternative, he was asked to identify the other persons involved in the decising-making process and the positions they occupied. In addition, we asked our study population to specify the "limits" when Response 3 was chosen. Tabulations of responses to these questions, together with identifications of the persons or limits mentioned when one of the last four responses was chosen, provide us with considerable information concerning the autonomy of teachers and restrictions on their discretionary behavior, as seen by teachers themselves. We also asked principals and central office personnel these same questions concerning the decision-making prerogatives of the teacher.

With the partial exception of personnel in three schools in our sample that had adopted an unconventional organizational structure embodying collaborative collegial decision-making, it is clear that teachers feel highly independent in making these critical educational decisions. Let us consider Responses 1 (complete autonomy) and 2 (final power subject to suggestions and recommendations from others) as representing "considerable control" over one's work situation. For the item on teaching methods used in the classroom, the proportions of teachers reporting considerable control ranged from 66% to 94%. (In the three innovative schools referred to above, 88% indicated considerable individual or collegial control.) The other four decision-making items deal with matters one would especially expect to be affected by school and district rules and procedures. Nonetheless, teachers reported that they held considerable control over these matters. The lowest proportion of teachers in any set of schools reporting considerable control over any item was 37%, while the highest was 83%.

Even these findings, however, exaggerate the force and scope of the constraints on teachers. When we examined the replies of teachers who chose Response 3 (power to make the decision within certain limits), we found that the numbers of persons limiting the teacher's discretionary behavior were few, there were not many constraints specified, and the limits described were usually not severe. These data are consistent with the fact that but a very small number of teachers (none at all in most schools) said that they had no voice in making these decisions (Response 5). It is also instructive to note that principals and central office personnel attribute only slightly less autonomy to the teacher than teachers themselves do.

In summary, we have dealt in this section with five matters that are critical in controlling the teaching–learning context. We have found that at this level of analysis teachers have considerable influence in making important instructional decisions. This finding varies markedly from (1) our previous findings about teacher influence at the school and school district levels, and (2) commonplace conclusions in the literature that teachers are passive figures, dominated at work by the bureaucratic apparatus or other constraining forces. The key to understanding the situation is the realization that in classroom-related matters teachers have power regardless of their lack of legally or organizationally sanctioned authority. Our empirical evidence indicates that the teacher plays a highly significant role in decisions precisely at that critical juncture where teaching and learning take place—in the instructional situation.

The Control of Work Behavior

The legal and bureaucratic structures of school systems notwithstanding, definitive policies and procedures—to the limited extent that they exist and are known to personnel—are irregularly and partially enforced. Further, "It appears that school systems, when contrasted to other organizational systems, feature a relatively high proportion of low-constraint decisions, particularly as far as teachers are concerned" (Lortie, 1969:12). When goals are set, there is a "range of tolerated possibilities" (Lortie, 1969:13). High-constraint decisions deal primarily with resource utilization questions (e.g., reports concerning money and property, procedures for disciplining students, and student records). Lortie (1969:14), points out that rules and regulations are sometimes "soft" and sometimes "hard." Hard rules deal with "cost and efficiency" as well as property and materials, while soft rules are found

> ... where thorny issues of instructional policy are at stake—the exact aims of a particular class, the best way to present specific material, and general rules in regard to the conflict between distributive justice and the needs of an individual student.

The administrative controls and constraints imposed by central office personnel and the principal fall largely in the hard rule sphere. As Corwin (1966: 78) has noted, close surveillance is impeded by the sheer complexity of modern organizations, as well as by certain professionalization claims of personnel. The administrative official most directly responsible for controlling the school program, the principal, spends most of his time and effort in enforcing hard rules, performing routine duties, and engaging in public relations (Organizational Attributes Project, 1967–1970). It is rare for principals to devote much energy to instructional matters, regardless of their desire to do so. Given the pressures of the principal's duties, experienced teachers are left pretty much to their own devices (Meyer and Cohen, 1970:7). The demands on the principal to perform managerial functions often cause him to neglect his supervisory responsibilities relating to instruction (Charters, 1962:781).

The relative isolation of the classroom teacher also militates against the enforcement of controls and constraints. In performing work tasks, teachers rarely interact with one another. Thus "it follows that the organization not only fails to control the teacher's behavior, but also cannot modify, improve, or encourage the teaching process" (Meyer and Cohen, 1970:5). The teacher in the traditional elementary school, therefore, is far from being a highly controlled bureaucratic employee; indeed, "the closest thing to a routine bureaucratic employee turns out to be the child!" (Meyer and Cohen, 1970:6).

With which important constraints do teachers have to contend? In general, they are the constraints posed by hard rules and other basic facts of life with regard to working conditions, materials, and facilities. The lists of these in the literature are almost endless, and we shall mention but a few—scarcities and inflexibilities of curriculum materials, equipment, and supplies (of critical importance in the total scheme of things), written records of remarkable detail and variety, limitations on the use of facilities and curriculum enrichment materials, and standardized rules and procedures for student behavior that are enforced school-wide (see Corwin, 1965:241–242; Eddy, 1969:25–27).

In our own research (Organizational Attributes Project, 1967–1970), we asked teachers to identify the strongest constraints that impeded achievement of their primary instructional objectives. The following constraints were chosen by substantial proportions of teachers (listed in order of choice): lack of time, the difficulty or complexity of instructional tasks, conflicts with lesser duties, lack of resources, and the reactions of their students. Conversely, the following constraints were deemed strongest by infinitesimally small proportions of teachers: the reactions of parents, official school district policies and procedures, reactions of other teachers, reactions of the principal, and reactions of central office personnel. While we would not claim either that the constraints we had the respondents rank are trivial or that teachers are objective and systematic analysts of existing constraints, we believe our data show that, in the eyes of teachers, relatively low constraint is exerted by legal, bureaucratic, collegial, and public policies, procedures, and pressures.

Constraints on work behavior vary, of course, in different types of schools and school–community situations. Constraints increase as schools and school systems become larger and more complex, new layers of authority are added, multitudinous rules and regulations are devised, and staff and student populations become more heterogeneous (Corwin, 1966:447; Lortie, 1969:42). It is undoubtedly true that the quantity as well as the extent of enforcement of rules and regulations is greatest in large schools in metropolitan areas with disadvantaged minority student populations. (Note the schools studied in Eddy, 1967, 1969; Moore, 1967.)

If we focus our attention on autonomy rather than on the external control over work behavior, it is apparent that autonomy is enhanced by what Bidwell calls the "structural looseness" of school systems and by the fact that each school is largely a "self-contained organizational unit" in which teachers and administrators "enjoy broad discretionary powers" (1965:976). As we have said, autonomy manifests itself above all in teacher control over instructional decisions and classroom activities. Meyer and Cohen (1970:5–6), who made careful observations in elementary classrooms, are enormously impressed by the extent to which the teacher dominates classroom activity. They further tell us that "teaching proceeds in an organizationally uncontrolled manner," with the teacher doing most of the "controlling, directing, and evaluating, as well as doing most of the talking in the classroom." This critically important conclusion is consistent with the views of Lortie (1969:14), who concludes that "Indications are that that which is most central and unique to schools—instruction—is least controlled by specific and literally enforced rules and regulations."

In terms of ideology, it is clear that most teachers are virtually obsessed with guarding their prerogatives over individual autonomy. Lortie (1961:3) has characterized these strongly held, informal expectations in terms of what he calls the "autonomy-equality" pattern. Concern for "freedom from interference," considered so desirable by teachers, is a vital component of teacher ideology (Meyer and Cohen, 1970:7). Noninterference is also, perhaps inappropriately, viewed by teachers as a manifestation of their desire for professionalism, noninterference with the individual being confused with collegial controls which characterize a "true" profession. In any case, while teachers may relinquish control over the affairs of the school as a whole and the school system, they are more concerned about their autonomy in the classroom situation than they are about any other educational matter (Carson, et al., 1967:Ch. 2). In their study of teacher participation in school decision-making in Canada, Simpkins and Friesen (1969:15), discovered that the desire of the teacher to control classroom management is so strong that the individual teacher wishes "to protect this jurisdiction in classroom decision-making from the authority exercised both by his colleague group and by those in administrative positions."

To summarize, the empirical evidence concerning the control of work behavior deviates drastically from the views of those who see the teacher as a puppet dancing to the music of external constraints. Instead, our findings reinforce the conclusions of those scholars who see important zones of autonomy for the teacher (Lortie, 1969:10–15; Bidwell, 1965:975–976).

If legal and bureaucratic constraints were to limit teacher classroom behavior severely, we could logically expect that conditions such as the following would exist: (1) policies and procedures would be clearly identified and known to teachers; (2) influence structures would allow teachers few decision-making prerogatives; and (3) the behavior of teachers in the classroom would be uniformly patterned, reflecting the constraints under which they operate. The empirical findings we have presented above cast much doubt upon the existence of the first two hypothetical conditions in the typical elementary school. In our later discussion of the division of labor, we shall similarly raise doubts about the third condition. We believe that the teacher has considerable autonomy at the classroom level, despite the fact that there may be no "legitimate" organizational or legal arrangements that grant him such autonomy. Obviously, in studying any occupation or profession, we have to make a crucial distinction between its control over legal, institutional, or organizational arrangements, on the one hand, and its control over the actual work setting and behavior at work on the other.

The Control of Student Behavior

Much of what we have already said in this chapter demonstrates that maintaining control over the work situation is a basic concern of the teacher. Why is this so? The answer to this question, we believe, is found through examining the problems teachers face in trying to control student behavior, which the teacher views as indispensable for maintaining a manageable instructional setting or environment.

The priority teachers give to maintaining order and control over the classroom has been noted by a variety of observers. "Within the classroom, the importance of maintaining order and adult authority is viewed as crucial by the teacher" (Eddy, 1967:146). The same point is emphasized in a widely read analysis recently published by Silberman (1970:122): "The most important characteristic schools share in common is a preoccupation with order and control." Four decades ago, the same theme occurred repeatedly in Waller's analysis of teaching. Speaking of the school as "a despotism in a state of perilous equilibrium," he dealt at length with the techniques used by teachers for maintaining "a stable social order" (1932:10 and *passim*).

Order and control over student behavior are intimately tied to the teacher's instructional objectives. As a societal agent entrusted with socializing the young, the teacher is not only involved in instructing children concerning "proper" values, but in preparing his students to live in a societal system of ordered relationships. "The orderliness of the school is intended to facilitate the educational task of enabling the pupil to make the transition into the modern world" (Eddy, 1967:159). Shipman (1968:6–14), in reaching similar conclusions, has also pointed out that the teacher's success in this regard is essential in preparing students for vertical social mobility. Teachers believe that complying with authority is something the student must learn in order to function effectively in other settings as an adult. Jackson (1968:32) has observed that "The transition from classroom to factory or office is made easily by those who have developed 'good work habits' in their early years." Jackson adds:

> So far as their power structure is concerned classrooms are not too dissimilar from factories or offices, those ubiquitous organizations in which so much of our adult life is spent. Thus, school might really be

called a preparation for life, but not in the usual sense in which educators employ that slogan (p. 33).

Lortie (1961:11–12) in speaking of the use of sanctions in the classroom, says that teachers "must maintain order and enforce discipline while simultaneously maintaining an acceptable state of distributive justice. The ability to control the class is the *sine qua non* of standing in the group, for without it, no instruction can occur." Order and control in the classroom, therefore, are primary objectives in the eyes of the teacher for other than trivial reasons.

Under the circumstances that prevail, there are ample reasons why teachers guard their classroom autonomy zealously. The key fact is their belief that external pressures and constraints will disturb the precarious balance of classroom order. There are several dangers that threaten this balance.

(1) Education at the local level is politically vulnerable. The teacher fears public, especially parental, reactions and pressures, and every teacher knows that the one certain way to get into trouble with parents (and administrators) is to be charged with lack of order and discipline in the classroom. Control of the classroom "makes for a good assessment as a teacher" (Webb, 1962:268). Anxiety about such complaints is so great among teachers that a primary criterion they use in evaluating their principal is the extent to which he can protect them from outsiders who try to undermine their control of the classroom (Becker, 1953:245; Shipman, 1968:49).

(2) As we have previously said, educational policies and procedures are often vague and unknown to the teacher. Furthermore, the teacher works in an environment in which the normative expectations that others (colleagues, administrators, parents, and the public) hold for him are unclear and often inaccurately perceived by him, a situation amply documented by Foskett (1967, 1969).

(3) Teacher authority in the classroom is tenuous, owing in part to the "interaction press" we have previously described. Additionally, at the present time the customary bases of teacher authority—traditional, rational-legal, and professional—are being eroded, while charismatic authority (always rare in any occupation) is assuming increasing importance (see Shipman, 1968:123–134).

(4) To a greater or lesser extent, depending on the characteristics of the student clientele, the teacher contends with various student resistances and the countervailing influences of the student subculture (Bidwell, 1965:990). This matter relates, in turn, to the ever-present problem of capturing and holding student attention as required for instruction. "It is only because teachers wish to force students to learn that any unpleasantness ever arises to mar their relationship" (Waller, 1932:355). Capturing and maintaining student attention are by no means simple matters (Jackson, 1968:Ch. 3).

(5) Teachers therefore seek workable techniques for maintaining order and control. In part, they try to achieve this objective by means of a proliferation of rules and procedures that circumscribe student behavior (Corwin, 1965: 27). They also develop normative and coercive controls, depending on student characteristics in the specific situation at hand (Shipman, 1968:103–109). Techniques for maintaining social distance between teacher and pupil are many (Shipman, 1968:52); maintaining social distance as a means of preserving order and control is a matter of such import that Waller (1932:Ch. XVII) devoted an entire chapter to its discussion.

We conclude that existing institutional and organizational structures of school districts and schools force teachers into a preoccupation with autonomy as a means of maintaining classroom order and control. It is possible that as long as the present division of labor and the isolated classroom persist, "freedom from interference" will be a primary goal of teachers.

THE DIVISION OF LABOR

Surprisingly little research has been conducted on the division of labor within the school. In part, this inattention results from deficient application of organizational theory in conceptualizing the operational basis of educational organizations. Additionally, the general acceptance of the existing simple division of labor, especially in elementary schools, accounts for the lack of scholarly interest in the subject.

The customary division of labor of the elementary school gives primacy to two positions, those of the teacher and principal. New positions added in recent decades in response to increases in school size and complexity have consisted mainly of increments at the administrative and specialist (e.g., librarians, counselors, psychologists) levels. The idea of developing specialized teaching capacities has grown slowly. To a considerable extent, the lack of specialization reflects an ideological commitment to a holistic conception of the teacher role which insists that all teachers should instruct in all basic content areas (Pellegrin, 1969:7–8). (The exceptions are in "support" areas such as art, music, and physical education, where specialists are employed if resources permit.)

The division of labor of schools and school systems has a temporal basis (school year, term, etc.) and is tied to what Bidwell calls "the age-grade placement of students."

> This close correspondence of school grades and age-grades is not typical of other times and places, suggesting that it arises as school systems become routinized, so that students must be moved through the system in batches and cannot be assigned to school grades individually on the basis of achievement (Bidwell, 1965:975).

Thus grade level assignments are based almost exclusively on chronological age, the achievements or abilities of the students being subordinated to age as criteria for assignment. The latter become the basis for placement in tracking systems, to the extent that a school district or school has them. Quite clearly, such a division of labor is designed to achieve certain primary goals—"mass processing" of students at "reasonable" cost—but does not easily serve other important goals, such as the individualization of instruction.

There are, of course, certain advantages in such a system. It facilitates multiplication of units—schools and classrooms. The standardization of organizational structure permits accommodation to a rapid population growth and provides educational opportunities to massive populations (Silberman, 1970: 14–15). There are also substantial economic advantages to replication of standardized organizational forms.

These gross features of the division of labor give a general perspective on the work organization of the school. Only recently has research sought to discover the characteristics of the division of labor of teaching under operational conditions. In the following discussion, we shall examine two aspects of this division of labor—the task structure of teaching and interdependence in work behavior.

The Task Structure of Teaching

Two recent studies have examined the work behavior of the teacher. (The first is that of the author and his colleagues we have discussed at various points in this chapter. The following materials are drawn from Pellegrin and Stehr, 1971.) Our data deal with teacher reports on the most important tasks they perform in their work. The second study involves detailed and systematic observations of teacher behavior during the school day (Conant, 1971).

It is usually taken for granted that there is considerable uniformity in the work behavior of teachers. In testing this assumption empirically in the Organizational Attributes Project, we administered a questionnaire to the teachers of the eighteen schools in our sample which required that the respondent prepare a job description in which he identified and described the main sets of tasks or dimensions of his job and state the nature and extent of his dependence on other persons in performing his work. Job dimensions were identified and tabulated for respondents by school, type of educational organization or program, school district, and region. The various dimensions are categorized into broad task areas, using terminology commonly employed by professionals in the field of education.

Examination of these task areas provides a general view of the task structure of the elementary teacher. The task areas, and the proportion of all tasks falling into each, are as follows: instructional activities, 25.0%; management, 19.7%; planning, 16.5%; evaluation, 14.1%; supervision-discipline, 10.1%; special instruction, 4.5%; public relations, 3.4%; meetings, 3.3%; professional development, 1.7%; and miscellaneous or other tasks, 1.7%.

While various insights into the role of the elementary teacher may be obtained by careful examination of these task area distributions and by more detailed analyses of subcategories and individual tasks, the point we wish to make in this context is that such tabulations give us but a gross picture of the task structure and tell us little about task uniformity and variation. The latter subject is illuminated considerably, however, when we compare task categories, subcategories of tasks, and individual tasks for the teachers in our sample schools. Significantly, there is much uniformity in these distributions from one region or school district to another, and even between sets of experimental and conventional schools within a given district. There is, on the other hand, considerable variation from one school to another, regardless of location or type. Thus, for example, we find in one school district that the percentage of all tasks listed that fall into the instructional activities category is 45.3 in one school and 17.2 in another. Two schools in the same region with the same basic educational organization and program vary considerably in the proportions of tasks in the management category; one had 15.0% of all tasks in this category, while another had 31.4%. To cite but one more example, two schools with the same basic organization and program in the same district have large variations in tasks in the meetings category, the proportions being 0.0% and 8.3%. When we compare subcategories of tasks from school to school, variation increases; and when individual tasks are examined, even greater differences appear among schools. The greatest interschool variation is found when the smallest schools are compared.

These findings lead us to a critical conclusion—namely, that the greatest differences in task structures exist among individual teachers. Whether we examine task categories, subcategories, or highly specific individual tasks, we find that the greatest variation is among teachers—even teachers instructing the same grade in the same school. Study of job descriptions prepared by individual teachers reveals not only that certain important individual tasks are not considered among the main tasks or job dimensions of a particular respondent, but even critical subcategories or entire categories may be omitted by a given teacher. What seems indispensable in teaching is that all teachers engage in *some* kinds of instructional activities and evaluation, with perhaps minimal attention given to management and supervision-discipline. In all these task categories, however, the precise nature (and conceptualization) of specific tasks varies drastically from one teacher to another.

Thus, if one regards the position of the teacher as calling for the performance of a narrow and well-defined set of role behaviors, he is likely to be surprised by the wide variety of tasks carried out by those who teach. The fact is that the position of teacher does not consist of a limited number of well-defined, agreed-upon sets of roles, behaviors, or tasks. With the exception of instruction itself, there is little agreement as to what the main dimensions of the job are; nor, we discovered in examining responses to other questions directed to respondents, is there high consensus concerning the importance of a given task or the amount of time devoted to it. A task to which one teacher devotes considerable time and energy may be virtually ignored by another teacher whose official position in the division of labor is virtually identical to that of the first. To the extent that teachers engage in common activities, the commonality apparently grows largely out of the general expectation that each will teach students and that they will all deal with like content and use similar materials. In any case, behavioral uniformities do not arise from common conceptualizations of their roles as teachers. There is simply too much variation in task performance and emphasis for these conceptualizations to provide a great deal of commonality of behavior.

It is accurate to say that schools employ persons to perform a variety of general and amorphous *functions*, that the system does not operate so as to insure that all these functions will be performed, and that, in any event, the specific tasks carried out in connection with these functions are highly variable. Even when we focus on main sets of tasks or job dimensions, as we did in this research, we find a surprising lack of core work behaviors shared by incumbents of similar or identical positions.

Instead, we note highly variable task identification and performance from one individual to another. Our interpretation is that this variability is made possible because there is little task uniformity induced or enforced by organizational or professional prescriptions. Given that situation, educational functions are translated into tasks and specific work behaviors by the individual teacher. This translation results in the prevalence of what might be termed *idiosyncratic specialization*—i.e., specialization based on the knowledge, objectives, interests, etc. of the individual teacher rather than on organizationally or professionally planned and prescribed commonalities of behavior.

In light of the above discussion, one sees irony in (and derives amusement from) the conclusions of those writers who tell us that teacher behavior is virtually prescribed by the bureaucratic apparatus, and then go on to describe job performances of highly variable quality by teachers within a given school.

Conant's (1971) study involved systematic observations of teacher work behavior in elementary schools, including some in which aides were employed to assist the teacher with routine as well as other tasks. Being unable to find published empirical data on what teachers do during the work day, he constructed activity categories by examining the literature on teaching and discussing the tasks of teachers with educators. In addition to the category he called "instruction," which he defined very broadly (or charitably) to include almost any activity that could be instructional in nature, he identified a variety of other categories—routine tasks (clerical, materials handling, monitoring, etc.), nonlearning activities (opening ceremonies, announcements, discipline, etc.), out of class time (personal and free time, intervals between classes, etc.), planning activities, evaluation activities, administrative activities, and others (pp. 30–31).

When his observations were completed, he discovered that classroom activity was highly concentrated within his first two categories. On the average, for teachers without aides instruction took up 27.9% of the work day (33.1% for teachers with aides). Routine work occupied teachers without aides 43.5% of the day (teachers with aides, 38.6%). Nonlearning activities consumed 11.8% of the work day of teachers without aides and 9.6% of the day for those with them. Out of class time accounted for 15.1% of the day for teachers without aides (with aides, 14.5%). All other categories of activities, including planning and evaluation, took up but a small fraction of the work day (p. 33). Indeed, if one adds up the percentages reported above, he finds that the four categories of activities account for 98.3% of the work day of teachers without aides and 95.8% of the work day of those having these assistants.

Conant concluded that "Teachers who worked in conventional, single-teacher classrooms had little daily time to teach" (p. 3). During the teaching day, teachers without aides devoted an average of ninety-two minutes to instruction, as compared with 109 minutes for those who were assisted by aides (p. 3). On the other hand, teachers without aides gave an average of 144 minutes to routine work, while those with aides spent 127 minutes on such activity (p. 33).

Thus the average teacher with an aide did not materially increase the time he devoted to instruction. The provision of aides simply did not free the teacher from his customary work patterns, even though the opportunity to be so freed was clearly available. That this finding has general validity is supported by other research. In one study it was discovered that when teachers are given virtually complete freedom to alter their work situation, they typically fail to depart significantly from their established routines (Gross, et al., 1968: *passim*). Another scholar concluded that "even when free to guide their own activities, teachers seldom suggest distinctly new types of working patterns for themselves" (Brickell, 1964:503). Along these lines, a startling discovery of Conant is that the addition of aides to the classroom division of labor resulted in more exposure of children to instruction, but mainly because much teaching was done by the aides—who were employed primarily for other purposes.

It is noteworthy that such critical tasks as planning and evaluation are conducted hurriedly and are not provided for during the work day. Presumably these tasks are performed by teachers during nonwork time. The essential point, however, is that such tasks are organizationally uncontrolled and unsupervised, and are undoubtedly subject to "idiosyncratic performance." The individual teacher has great discretion in determining how much nonwork time and effort will be spent on tasks that are not an integral part of his work day.

Our basic conclusion concerning the task structure of teaching is that diversification is a central principle in the division of labor (see Katz, 1964:428–455). The data also serve to reinforce our basic conclusion that teachers face few strong constraints over their instructional activities.

Interdependence in Work Behavior

Variations in task structure could possibly be interpreted to mean that a complex division of labor exists at the school level, and that tasks omitted by one teacher are performed by other teachers, specialists, administrators, or other personnel. The prevalence of the self-contained classroom in most elementary schools, however, argues against this conclusion. In order to examine the matter in more detail, we obtained data on the nature and extent of patterns of interdependence perceived by respondents (see Pellegrin and Stehr, 1971). These questions on interdependence were asked: (1) "List the names of those persons both within and outside your school (other than students) upon whom you depend *most heavily* in order to perform your job effectively"; and (2) "Who are the persons listed above, if any, whose job is so closely related to *yours* that you believe the two jobs *must* be performed collaboratively in order for either of you to perform his work effectively?" We term responses to the first question "dependence relationships" and to the second question "essential relationships."

Tabulations of answers to these questions reveal that the average number of dependence relationships listed by teachers in the conventionally organized schools in our sample varies between 2.8 and 6.7 (the mean number being about 4), and the average number of essential relationships ranges from 0.0 to 2.5 (mean number, approximately 1). The extent of interdependence is, therefore, limited, especially as indicated by responses to the second (and more critical) question. Further analysis of the data indicates that the scope of interdependence is similarly limited, being confined mainly to the school principal and other teachers of the same grade in one's school.

An additional question was posed in order to obtain data on the types of interdependence that exist between teachers and other persons. Here the respondent was asked to specify how his job "tied together" with those of the persons listed in answers to the two questions stated above. These data show that the types of relationships specified by teachers consist primarily of those that deal with the provision of resources (facilities and materials), psychological and social support, advice, and exchange of ideas. It is quite rare for *task* interdependencies to be mentioned. Our evidence therefore indicates that interdependence is restricted or limited and that variations in the task structures of teachers are not easily explainable in terms of the division of labor of the school.

The low degree of complexity in school organization produces, then, few planned and prescribed patterns of interdependence between the teacher and incumbents of similar or related positions. Existing interdependencies are limited in scope, voluntary, and individualistic in nature. For these reasons, it is appropriate to refer to such interdependencies as "casual" rather than as embedded in the organizational structure of the school.

THE TEACHER ROLE AND THE TECHNOLOGY OF TEACHING

We have said enough about teaching to conclude that, as Sexton (1967:74, italics in original) has phrased it, "the classroom teacher's role is quite *un*defined and *un*standardized." There is a lack of systematic teaching technology; "The subjects teachers themselves believe useful in teaching (e.g., child psychology) are primarily the property of others" (Lortie, 1969:24).

Considerable insight into the technology of teaching is provided by Jackson (1968:Ch. 4), who interviewed fifty reputedly outstanding teachers concerning various aspects of their work. He found that they had no technical vocabulary, derived either from their own or related fields, to use in describing their tasks or objectives. Their discussions of their work were characterized by conceptual simplicity, largely devoid of elaborate words or ideas. Their view of causality was "uncomplicated," and classroom events were subjected to intuitive rather than rational analysis. Alternative teaching practices were viewed with an opinionated rather than an open-minded stance. The use of abstract terminology was limited and narrow in scope. A tendency to accept existing educational conditions, rather than express concern for their improvement, was interpreted by Jackson to reflect the teacher's identification with the events of the moment and an emotional attachment to the work situation. Altogether, interest in innovation was "mild" and restricted to minor amelioration of educational "givens," i.e., existing conditions (pp. 119–148).

The factors that underlie the undeveloped teaching technology have in part been mentioned in other contexts of our analysis. There is the weak knowledge base on which practice rests, together with the lack of a professional and scientific literature which is credible to the teacher. This factor is closely linked to a widely held ideological commitment to the notion that teaching is basically an intuitive art not greatly amenable to improvement through rational study.

It is also important to note the work behavior of teachers is learned in large part not through the formal training they receive, but through their own socialization experiences over the years as students and their exposure to other teachers (Howsam, 1967:69–70; Lortie, 1969:10, 26). It is also true that the teacher's work objectives are often very general and vague; for this reason, teaching under existing conditions may well require diffuse rather than specific task behavior (Wilson, 1962:22–25), owing to the variability of objectives, the complexity of socialization functions and the heterogeneity of student populations, and other problems such as gaining student attention and maintaining classroom control.

Jackson (1968:159) has also pointed out that "Despite a half century of research and the development of several sophisticated theories, the teacher's classroom activities have been relatively unaffected by what the learning theorist has to say." The same can also be said of the contributions made by other scholars to knowledge about educational organization and instruction.

In the final analysis, the individual teacher learns the essential techniques useful to him in practicing his craft largely on his own, mainly through his experiences in the classroom. What untold thousands of teachers have learned independently is not preserved, systematized, and codified, and hence not transmissible. To cite a case in point: one of the most important and stressful tasks facing any teacher, as we have observed, is learning to cope with the complex problems of managing group behavior in the classroom. This is not even a coherent subject of study in teacher training courses, usually being approached indirectly as well as unsystematically. Here as elsewhere, what other teachers have learned about the matter is usually lost (Lortie, 1969:29).

The eventual result of all this is that each experienced teacher develops his own teaching technology, at least partly idiosyncratic in nature. Once he has developed a technology that he considers successful for him, he changes his behavior very reluctantly, for reasons we have alluded to in our earlier discussion of classroom order and control.

CONCLUDING COMMENTS

In this analysis we have tried to demonstrate that the teacher holds a legally established employeeship status that delegates little specific authority to him. He plays a passive role in resource allocation and utilization decisions and in matters pertaining to the program of the school as a whole. These facts have obscured the vital role played by the teacher in influencing that most crucial of decision-making contexts, the teaching–learning environment. We discovered that teachers exercise considerable autonomy and discretion in their work behavior, and that maintaining this autonomy and discretion is so important to them that it affects the instructional process in significant ways. It was also shown that the division of labor of the school is simple, but that the tasks performed by individual teachers are highly variable. Furthermore, organizational rigidities are perpetuated by the teacher's desire to maintain control over the precarious balance of the classroom. Preoccupation with routine and classroom control detracts from efforts to increase the time allocated to instruction itself. All of these conditions impede the development of a systematic and sophisticated teaching technology.

These basic findings, it should be noted, have critical implications for organizational theory in that they raise serious questions about the effectiveness and limits of legal and bureaucratic controls in constraining and directing work behavior. In the present case, we find that educational policies at the state, community, and school levels are designed to produce uniformities in the instructional process. At first glance, we see an abundance of controls covering the job behavior of teachers. Probing further, however, we find that the plethora of constraints does not have a determining impact on instructional behavior. Nor is there, either in ideology or practice, a set of collegial controls that might direct job performance. Instead, the pressures of the classroom situation militate against external controls and lead to highly autonomous and variable classroom performances by teachers. The teacher is much concerned with maintaining his autonomy, and is reinforced in striving toward that goal by deficiencies in teaching technology, the ecology of the school, and certain myths of professionalism that justify noninterference with the individual practitioner. While some of these conditions are perhaps unique to schools and teaching, our analysis points to important limits of bureaucratic controls over work behavior. The subject, we believe, merits further attention in other organizational and occupational contexts.

In this presentation we did not have the space—nor was it our purpose—to draw out the practical implications of our findings for improving the organization and operation of the schools and the instructional process. Suffice it to say that we believe that an important key to educational reform lies in fundamental alterations of the organizational components of schools and the structural conditions that limit possibilities for enrichment of the educational process.

The discrepancies between the institutionalized contexts of teaching and operational realities in the schools are considerable and significant. We believe that research in other occupational and organizational settings will discover similar discrepancies that will further our knowledge of empirical conditions at work and lead to improvements in organizational theory.

REFERENCES

Abbott, M.G.
1965 "Hierarchical impediments to innovation in educational organizations," in M.G. Abbott and J.T. Lowell (eds.), Change Perspectives in Educational Administration. Auburn, Alabama: Auburn University School of Education.

Baron, G. and A. Tropp
1961 "Teachers in England and America," in A.H. Halsey, J. Floud and C.A. Anderson (eds.), Education, Economy, and Society. Glencoe, Illinois: The Free Press of Glencoe.

Becker, H.S.
1952 "The career of the Chicago public school teacher." American Journal of Sociology 57(March):470–477. Reprinted in R.L. Pavalko (ed.), Sociology of Education. Itasca, Illinois: F.E. Peacock Publishers, 1968.
1953 "The teacher in the authority system of the public schools." Journal of Educational Sociology 27(November):128–144.

Bidwell, C.E.
1965 "The school as a formal organization," in J.G. March (ed.), Handbook of Organizations. Chicago: Rand McNally.

Brickell, H.M.
1964 "State organization for educational change: a case study and a proposal," in M.B. Miles (ed.), Innovation in Education. New York: Bureau of Publications, Teachers College, Columbia University.

Carlson, R.O.
1964 "Environmental constraints and organizational consequences: the public school and its clients," in D.E. Griffiths (ed.), Behavioral Science and Educational Administration. The Sixty-third Yearbook of the National Society for the Study of Education. Chicago: The National Society for the Study of Education.
1965 "Barriers to change in the public schools," in R.O. Carlson, et al., Change Processes in the Public Schools. Eugene, Oregon: Center for the Advanced Study of Educational Administration, University of Oregon.

Carson, R.B., K. Goldhammer and R.J. Pellegrin
 1967   Teacher Participation in the Community: Role Expectations and Behavior. Eugene, Oregon: Center for the Advanced Study of Educational Administration, University of Oregon.

Charters, W.W., Jr.
 1962   "The social background of teaching," in N.L. Gage (ed.), Handbook of Research on Teaching. Chicago: Rand McNally.
 1967   "Some 'obvious' facts about the teaching career." Educational Administration Quarterly 3(Spring):183–193.

Conant, E.H.
 1971   "A cost-effectiveness study of employment of nonprofessional teaching aides in public schools." Final Report. Project No. O.E. 8-0481. Washington, D.C.: Bureau of Research, Office of Education, U.S. Department of Health, Education, and Welfare.

Corwin, R.G.
 1965   A Sociology of Education. New York: Appleton-Century-Crofts.
 1966   Staff Conflicts in the Public Schools. Final Report. Cooperative Research Project No. 2637. Washington, D.C.: Bureau of Research, Office of Education, U.S. Department of Health, Education, and Welfare.

Eddy, E.M.
 1967   Walk the White Line: A Profile of Urban Education. Garden City, New York: Doubleday.
 1969   Becoming a Teacher: The Passage to Professional Status. New York: Teachers College Press, Columbia University.

Foskett, J.M.
 1967   The Normative World of the Elementary School Teacher. Eugene, Oregon: Center for the Advanced Study of Educational Administration, University of Oregon.
 1969   Role Consensus: The Case of the Elementary School Teacher. Eugene, Oregon: Center for the Advanced Study of Educational Administration, University of Oregon.

Griffiths, D.E.
 1959   Research in Educational Administration: An Appraisal and a Plan. New York: Bureau of Publications, Teachers College, Columbia University.
 1964   "The nature and meaning of theory," in D.E. Griffiths (ed.), Behavioral Science and Educational Administration. The Sixty-third Yearbook of the National Society for the Study of Education, Part II. Chicago: The National Society for the Study of Education.

Gross, N.
 1956   "Sociology of education, 1945–1955," in H.L. Zetterberg (ed.), Sociology in the U.S.A.: A Trend Report. Paris: UNESCO.

Gross, N., J.B. Giacquinta and M. Bernstein
 1968   An Attempt to Implement a Major Educational Innovation: A Sociological Inquiry. Report No. 5, Center for Research and Development on Educational Differences. Cambridge, Mass.: Harvard University.

Hall, R.H.
 1969   Occupations and the Social Structure. Englewood Cliffs, N.J.: Prentice-Hall.

Howsam, R.B.
  1967 "Effecting needed changes in education," in E.L. Morphet and C.O. Ryan (eds.), Planning and Effecting Needed Changes in Education. Reports Prepared for the Third Area Conference. Denver: Designing Education for the Future.
Hughes, E.C.
  1958 Men and Their Work. Glencoe, Ill.: The Free Press.
Jackson, P.W.
  1968 Life in Classrooms. New York: Holt, Rinehart and Winston.
Katz, F.E.
  1964 "The school as a complex formal organization." Harvard Educational Review 34(Summer):428–455. Reprinted in R.L. Pavalko (ed.), Sociology of Education. Itasca, Ill.: F.E. Peacock Publishers, 1968.
Kimbrough, R.B.
  1964 Political Power and Educational Decision-Making. Chicago: Rand McNally.
Lieberman, M.
  1956 Education as a Profession. Englewood Cliffs, N.J.: Prentice-Hall.
Lindsay, M. (ed.)
  1961 New Horizons for the Teaching Profession. Washington, D.C.: National Commission on Teacher Education and Professional Standards, National Education Association of the United States.
Lortie, D.C.
  1961 "Craftsmen and colleagueship: a frame for the investigation of work values among public school teachers." Paper presented at the Annual Meetings of the American Sociological Association.
  1969 "The balance of control and autonomy in elementary school teaching," in A. Etzioni (ed.), The Semi-Professions and Their Organization. New York: Free Press.
March, J.G. and H.A. Simon
  1958 Organizations. New York: Wiley.
Meyer, J. and E. Cohen
  1970 The Impact of the Open-Space School upon Teacher Influence and Autonomy: The Effects of an Organizational Innovation. Stanford, Calif.: Stanford Center for Research and Development in Teaching, Stanford University.
Miles, M.B.
  1965 "Planned change and organizational health: figure and ground," in R.O. Carlson, et al. Change Processes in the Public Schools. Eugene, Oregon: Center for the Advanced Study of Educational Administration, University of Oregon.
Moore, G.A., Jr.
  1967 Realities of the Urban Classroom: Observations in Elementary Schools. Garden City, New York: Doubleday.
Pellegrin, R.J.
  1965a "The place of research in planned change," in R.O. Carlson, et al. Change Processes in the Public Schools. Eugene, Oregon: Center for the Advanced Study of Educational Administration, University of Oregon.

1965b "Community power structure and educational decision-making in the local community." Occasional Paper Series. Eugene, Oregon: Center for the Advanced Study of Educational Administration, University of Oregon.

1968   "Community organization and the decision-making process: a search for perspective." Occasional Paper Series. Eugene, Oregon: Center for the Advanced Study of Educational Administration, University of Oregon.

1969   "Some organizational characteristics of multi-unit schools." Working Paper No. 22. Madison: Wisconsin Research and Development Center for Cognitive Learning, University of Wisconsin.

Pellegrin, R.J. and N. Stehr
1971   "Idiosyncratic specialization and casual interdependence in elementary school teaching." Paper presented at the Annual Meetings of the Pacific Sociological Association.

Sexton, P.C.
1967   The American School: A Sociological Analysis. Englewood Cliffs, N.J.: Prentice-Hall.

Shipman, M.D.
1968   The Sociology of the School. London: Longmans, Green.

Silberman, C.E.
1970   Crisis in the Classroom: The Remaking of American Education. New York: Random House.

Simpkins, W.S. and D. Friesen
1969   "Teacher participation in decision-making." The Canadian Administrator 8(January):13–16.

Simpson, R.L.
1969   The School Teacher: Social Values, Community Role, and Professional Self-Image. Final Report. Cooperative Research Project No. 5-0451. Washington, D.C.: Bureau of Research, Office of Education, U.S. Department of Health, Education, and Welfare.

Simpson, R.L. and I.H. Simpson
1969   "Women and bureaucracy in the semi-professions," in A. Etzioni (ed.), The Semi-Professions and Their Organization. New York: Free Press.

Taylor, M.L. and R.J. Pellegrin
1959   "Professionalization: its functions and dysfunctions for the life insurance occupation." Social Forces 38(December):110–114.

Waller, W.
1932   The Sociology of Teaching. New York: Wiley.

Webb, John
1962   "The sociology of a school." British Journal of Sociology 13:264–272.

Wilson, B.R.
1962   "The teacher's role—a sociological analysis." British Journal of Sociology 13:15–32.

Zeigler, H.
1967   The Political Life of American Teachers. Englewood Cliffs, New Jersey: Prentice-Hall.

PART IV

WORK ORGANIZATIONS

INTRODUCTION—PART IV

Of the many possible features of work organizations that need analysis, two have been selected for special attention. The man-technology-organization relationships have always been crucial, but not always understood. The incentives offered and the compensation received for working are universal features of work organizations, and they, too, are not always understood. Hopefully, our explorations of these two features will further understanding.

We are now entering an area where there is lively debate and controversy. The debate is reflected in the differing positions presented by the authors of the several selections. As we move ahead to resolve some of the differing ideas, and the controversies they generate, we will be making progress in understanding how work organizations operate.

Technology and pay are so vitally important that they deserve even more space than is allotted to them in this volume. There is, nevertheless, a depth of coverage in these chapters that exposes some of the crucial issues whose resolution is a high priority task for behavioral scientists.

CHAPTER **9**

Technology, Organization and Job Structure

by Louis E. Davis and James C. Taylor

Graduate School of Management
University of California-Los Angeles

INTRODUCTION

We are living in a period of rapidly increasing and wrenching social and technological change. Organizations and job structures are changing in response to these changes and because of our increased knowledge of the behavior of organizations and individuals. Changes discernible in our environment are more than sufficient to show that western industrial society is in transition from one historical era to another. The environmental characteristics of the emerging era will lead to crisis and massive dislocation unless adaptation occurs. The structures of most purposeful organizations, based as they are on industrial era concepts, are growing increasingly dysfunctional because they stand at the confluence of changes involving technology, social values, economic environment, and the practices of management.

Purpose

The nature of changes in the various American societal environments in the 1970s are not only massive in that they are creating environments for organizations essentially different in kind but are subtly misleading as well in that they are inducing a comforting familiarity by the apparent similarity of outcomes. Given the evolving postindustrial era, it is our purpose to aid in developing a new appreciation of the relationships between technology, the work organization, and job structure, based on assessments garnered from research and "state-of-the-art" innovations, with special attention given to changes in the technological environment.

A New Appreciation of Technical and Social Systems Interaction

In order to form a new understanding of the relationship of technology to organization and job structure, the existing dominant appreciation needs to be made explicit. The present view, carefully nurtured for the past 150 years, is that of technological determinism, and it is dangerously simplistic. This position has been reified in a spate of recent pronouncements, some by those seeking to show that although technical and social systems are changing, all is still the same, and other pronouncements by those predicting impending doom (e.g., Ellul, 1964). Technological determinism maintains that technology evolves according to its own internally derived logic and needs, quite independent of social environment and culture. Further, it holds that to use technology effectively and thus secure its benefits for society, its development and application must not be inhibited by any considerations other than those determined as relevant by its developers—the engineers or technologists.

Technological determinism has generally been invoked to support the organizational and institutional status quo, usually of the *industrial* era type. The claim is made that organizational structure and behavior is predetermined by technology and unalterably locked into its needs. Therefore, given the negative consequences of a substantial number of technical developments, the impending doom of society as we know it is predicted. While it has been shown that there are some correlations between technology and work organization structure (Woodward, 1958) and organizational process (Burns and Stalker, 1961), there are choices available based on social system values and assumptions. Additionally, it should be part of our new understanding of the technological-organizational relationship to see that this unalterable determination of technological form is both misleading and defeatist. It is well known that of the many technological alternatives considered in any instance, technical systems planners put forth only one as a solution. The new appreciation should caution us to examine the design process of production technology itself to see which social system planning and psychosocial assumptions were considered in the design of various technical system alternatives. Further, we need to know what economic, social and technical factors are included in the decision process of selecting a technological alternative.

In the design and development of technology, we are dealing with the application of science to invent technique and its supportive artifacts (machines) to accomplish transformations of objects (materials, information, people) in support of certain objectives. The invention of technique may involve engineering to an overwhelming extent, but in part it also involves social system design. It is difficult to isolate the influence of these two interacting factors on the invention of technique. If, then, we look at work, we can see two sets of antecedent determinants that constrain the choices available for design of tasks and job structure. First, there are the social choices already contained within the technological design; second, there are the social choices contained within the organization design undertaken to use the technology. Our present appreciation is that one rarely finds technological determinism, in the pure sense of technological or scientific variables, exclusively determining the design or configuration of a technical system. On the contrary, most frequently we find that technical system designs incorporate social system choices, either made intentionally or included accidentally, either casually or as the result of some omission in planning. In this sense, engineers or technologists can be called social system engineers, and they are crucial to evolving new organization forms and job structures.

The interdependence of social systems planning and technology design leads us to the position that it is impossible at present to draw many cause-

and-effect or even correlative conclusions about the causal effects of technology on the structure and process of organizations and jobs. Yet, today, in study after study, we are confidently offered such conclusions, despite the fact that the researchers did not undertake appropriate analysis of the technological systems to ascertain incorporated psychosocial purposes and assumptions. The rare examination (Davis, Canter and Hoffman, 1955) of decision rules and precepts underlying technical production system design should alert us to the trap of the self-fulfilling prophecy. As subjectively indicated, it appears that all production technologies, whether designed or selected, include social system choices. Social system requirements derived from scientific and empirical bases, from values, or from commonly held assumptions can be and are directly designed into technical systems or their applications (Boguslaw, 1972). There are innumerable instances in which psychosocial assumptions indirectly or subconsciously become part of a technical system design. It is unknown to what extent psychosocial requirements or assumptions are wholly ignored in the design or choice of a technical system (particularly a work system), except insofar as the designer inevitably carries with him and expresses the values and assumptions of his culture.

TECHNOLOGICAL ALTERNATIVES AND SOCIAL SYSTEM CHOICES, SOME CASES

There are many technological alternatives and psychosocial system choices that are made as part of the design of a technical system. This can be seen by examining some cases which can be fitted into a 2×2 matrix of inclusion of psychosocial effects, as follows:

		Manifestations of Psychosocial Effects	
		Considered	Not Considered
Levels of Psychosocial Effects	System	II	I
	Job (Task)	III	IV

The cells in the matrix show cases where psychosocial effects (or assumptions) were: I, not considered in system design or planning; II, considered in system design or planning; III, considered in job (or task) design or planning; and IV, not considered in job (or task) design or planning.

Cell I illustration. An illustrative case where psychosocial system effects were ignored or not considered in the technical system design concerns the design of a new technology for distribution of petroleum products that required changing an existing network of depots.

For many years, British road laws had limited heavy goods vehicles to eighteen tons and twenty m.p.h. in maximum speed. By 1968, after a period of less than ten years, maximum legal weight had increased to thirty-two tons and permitted speed had increased to the posted road maximum. These legislative changes happened to coincide with increases in market demand for domestic and commercial petroleum products, which were distributed mostly by road transport. The increased demand from the marketplace, coupled with increased competition, led British petroleum distribution companies to adopt the larger, faster vehicles, newly permissible under the law, as quickly as possible. In a study of one of these companies, it was noted that the change of vehicle type was in turned linked (of necessity) to changes in size and location of the vehicle terminals. The company changed from a large number of small distribution depots, each having customers within a radius of fifteen to twenty miles and a maximum of twenty to thirty drivers, to a small number of large terminals, each with customers in a radius of fifty to seventy-five miles and up to two-hundred and fifty drivers.

Such changes in terminal size and location would not always result from more productive equipment, but in this case they did. The larger, faster vehicles introduced were far more productive in proportion to the demands of the increased share of the market for any one company, given the increased competition. By decreasing the overall number of vehicles and increasing their range, the company in this case opted to use the technology to couple the moderate net increase in demand with a considerable increase in the amount of product that could be moved and the speed with which it was transported.

With these changes in vehicle type and terminal size, the individual driver's job changed little—the vehicle cab remained the same, as did the product or service he performed. The organizational structure of the terminals also changed little. From the driver's point of view, however, other changes of importance took place. In the smaller depot he knew and was known to the manager and the other workers and lived in the small town where he had grown up. However, in the larger terminal he was moved to a larger town or city and became something approximating that faceless cipher, the worker in a large factory. The informal ties of the smaller place were effectively broken and were replaced with more formal bureaucratic controls, and the driver's work-place, as a consequence, was much different. It seems implausible to attribute this marked change in the social system to a conscious decision on the part of the lawmakers who were responsible for the change in the legislation. It is difficult to see how the legislators who designed the laws or the managers who saw themselves as being literally forced to implement the changes, could have had in mind that the transition of the truck drivers into alienated factory hands (the psychosocial result of the increased bureaucratization) would serve that industry. Not having examined the consequences in a scenario, we may assume that the managers either estimated no consequences or saw themselves in the grip of technological determinism. This is not to say that the managers did not have choices with regard to social system design that would reduce this alienation—they did—but their failure to choose was more out of ignorance of the manifold effects, than based upon their explicit human assumptions.

Cell II illustration. An illustrative case where psychosocial system effects were considered in technical system design concerns a quite highly automated chemical fertilizer plant.[1] In this instance, the designers, both engineers and social scientists, following the concepts of sociotechnical systems, set about analyzing and designing the technical system and the social system jointly. This permitted a focus on the interface between these interacting but independent systems, so that not only could social system effects of the technical system be considered but also the reverse. The focus on the interface stimulated the development of a new means of technical system analysis that would indicate the kind, timing, and location of variances being imposed on the prospective social system and therefore the kind of regulation and control the social system would be required to undertake if the technical system remained unchanged.[2]

In addition, this experience demonstrated that neither the technical system nor the social system could be "optimal" in its own right. Both systems were modified from original ideals and the technical system was "degraded" when judged exclusively by engineering considerations. What took shape at Norsk Hydro was an "optimal" joint sociotechnical system. Significant for future systems design or redesign were the evolution and testing of a new means of carrying on such design: a "joint action committee" consisting of technical, managerial, supervisory, worker, and union representatives, plus external competence in the form of a social science consultant (Holte, 1971).

To satisfy the joint needs of economic operation of a highly sophisticated new technological development and of "democratization of the work-place," the question was asked whether jobs could be designed solely on the basis of the blueprints of the factory before it was built or staffed. In that way, as the physical plant was going up, the designer could begin to prepare the organization and the jobs and skills of the people who would man the plant when it was finished.

Prior to the focus on social systems design, the engineers had designed the plant so that the work to be done (monitoring, diagnosing, and adjusting, since no physical work was done in the plant other than maintenance) would be carried out in three monitoring or control rooms. The equipment was so sophisticated that it required only one man in a control room, which would have required nine men for three work shifts. Other, miscellaneous functions brought the total work force to sixteen men, excluding maintenance workers.

Based on analyses of the technical system, undertaken by the sociotechnical consultants provided for the joint action committee, the planners made a decision to avoid a situation in which people would work in isolation. To put more than one man in a control room, however, would have been economically inefficient. Therefore, totally new jobs were created by combining the maintenance and control functions. As the completed Norsk Hydro plant now operates, at least two men are based in each control room, one leaving it alternately to perform maintenance tasks. They support each other, and the new job design also brings feedback from the plant by means other than the control room instruments. For the company, the new job design meant that maintenance men had to learn chemistry, and chemical operators had to learn maintenance skills.

---

[1] The design of the Norsk Hydro chemical fertilizer plant in Eidanger, Norway, 1966–67, its implementation, and the follow-up development of the operating organization were all part of the Industrial Democracy Program, underway in Norway for the last ten years. See Thorsrud and Emery (1969); see also, Thorsrud, Sørensen and Gustavsen, Chapter 10, this volume.

[2] For the original treatment see Engelstad (1972).

Totally different jobs were developed than had ever existed before. They were not derived from previous job histories in the company. These jobs came out of analysis, theory, and specific consideration of their social effects rather than out of past practice. And in the plant's six years of operation, it has been very successful.

Cell III illustration. The following anecdotal case illustrates the Cell III configuration, in which particular psychosocial effects operating at the individual worker, or job level are considered by technical system planners. A set of parallel operating automated machines for filling and capping aerosol spray cans was installed in a midwestern consumer goods plant. The machines were arranged some fifty to seventy-five feet apart, with one operator assigned to each machine. Empty cans and the product with which the cans were filled were delivered periodically to each machine by a tender.

With two exceptions, the process was completely automated, so that the cans, after being dumped into the hopper by the tender, were turned right side up, moved into the machines, filled, capped, and packed into cartons.

The major human (i.e., nonautomated) intervention, in terms of sheer time and effort requirements, was the insertion of a small plastic tube and attached plastic cap into the large holes at the top of the upright cans which passed, before capping, on a circular conveyor in front of the operator. The second human intervention, and the primary task or *raison de être* for the human operator, was a large "stop button" placed on a post directly before the operator. In the event of perceptible trouble anywhere in the machine, the operator could press the button, stopping the machine, and either rectify the problem himself or obtain help. In this case, the machine design had not included the sophisticated sensing devices necessary for the machine either to self-correct in the event of trouble or to transmit those signals to a remote monitoring station where another person or group could have done the machine supervision. In order to have human eyes and ears constantly on duty at each machine in the event of trouble, humans were designed or "built into" the machines as replaceable parts, to do the isolated, tedious, and unnecessary task of inserting tubes, which could easily have been done by the machine. This decision was clearly a considered one, in which the psychosocial task of inserting tubes into cans was developed simply because the primary task of sensing and diagnosing required human eyes and ears; and by hiring those, one also acquired a set of hands.

Cell IV illustration. The situation represented by Cell IV, where psychosocial effects at the task level, although extant, are not considered in advance, is in our estimation the one most frequently found in industrial settings. Rather than describe a specific instance, we will simply refer to two general cases.

The first case is that of the assembly line manufacture (e.g., Walker and Guest, 1952) in which the technological demands for material transfer are considered to the exclusion of the psychosocial task demands, which are at once monotonous and inexorably onerous. The psychosocial assumptioons about people working at repetitive, machine paced jobs are present of course, even if technical system planners have not directly considered them. There is a veritable folklore to the effect that repetitive assembly line work is desired by workers and suited to limited human capacities and aspirations, which makes comfortable the exclusion of other psychosocial alternatives.

The second case concerns key punch operation in electronic data processing (e.g., Hoos, 1960a). In this instance, again, the individual task is designed with the machine in mind; i.e., human elements doing some machine tasks and machine elements doing some tasks, without direct consideration of the psychosocial task demands of monotonous work, which demands considerable attention and accuracy.

Other illustrative cases in Cell IV are legion, and it can be seen from these how the position of technological determinism has emerged so strongly. If we take the position that psychosocial assumptions are not considered in Cells I and IV because they do not need to be, we have technological determinism; but the changing values of western workers (cf., Davis, 1971a) and the results of these changes suggest that even in assembly line and key punch jobs, psychosocial needs must be considered or the "human elements" will not perform and will become even more unreliable than originally assumed.

The Emerging Post-Industrial Era

The urgency implicit in the new understanding of the relationship between psychosocial assumptions and technological choices arises because the dominant and long-held assumptions about people at work are being called into question by a growing segment of all who work in western societies. Established values and long-held expectations are beginning to change.

The values of a society and its institutions evolve slowly, in response to social and physical conditions and to the society's conceptions of its environment. It is the emergence of some new values and the change in the relative importance of others that leads to the recognition that we are witnessing the evolution of a new epoch, the post-industrial era.

The emergence of the post-industrial era is stimulated by an ever-increasing rate of change in organizations and institutions and by changes in technology. The latter contribute to changes in values not only by evoking new social systems and roles for its members (for this is, if anything, a minor effect) but also by stimulating the rising level of expectations concerning material, social, and personal needs, and by providing the wealth to support the continuously rising level of education that western countries provide, which is changing the attitudes, the aspirations, and the expectations of major segments of society (Bell, 1967; Heilbroner, 1972).

The seeming ease with which new (automated) technology satisfies society's material needs, coupled with the society's provision of subsistence-level support for its citizens, has stimulated a growing concern on the part of groups and individuals about their relationship to work, its meaningfulness, and its value —a growing concern, that is, for the quality of working life (Davis, 1971c).

In the U.S., questioning the relationship between work and satisfaction of material needs is widespread through the ranks of university students, younger industrial workers, women, and minority unemployed. For industrial workers, there is a revival of concern with the once-buried questions of alienation from work, job satisfaction, personal freedom and initiative, and the dignity of the individual in the work-place. Although on the surface the frequently expressed concern is over the effects of automation on job availability and greater sharing in the wealth produced, there are indicators—restlessness in unions, their failure to grow in the nonindustrial sectors, and their image as "establishment"—that, in the U.S., there is a changing field that stems from the increasingly tenuous relationship between work and fulfillment of material needs.

Changes in Technology

The continued change in technology, from simple technique of modifying or transforming a material by human effort with the use of elementary tools to the present increasing application of automated, computer-aided production systems, has provided driving impetus during the past 150 years for changes in our society, its organizations, its occupations, and its jobs. Technological change has contributed to continued urbanization through mechanized food production; it has also contributed to rising personal income levels, to growth of leisure availability, and so forth. Our particular focus is its effects on organizations, jobs, work, and workers.

In the preceding discussion, technology was defined as technique, and its artifacts in the form of tools and machines—usually based on an underlying science—developed to transform objects (materials, information, people) in support of certain objectives. Less evolved techniques may exist as tricks of the trade and craft skills (and special tools), acquired by a worker, doctor, or teacher through training and experience. Technique, where completely evolved, may exist as a program located in a machine or a person by training. Which it is depends both on the state of underlying science and on how self-contained the technique is relative to its own tools and machines; i.e., to what extent human or social system intervention is required to accomplish the transformation to a stated set of outcomes. Man once had three roles to play in any production technology, two of which can now be preempted by machines. Man's first role, as an energy supplier, is now virtually nonexistent in western industrial societies. His second role, as a guider of tools, is more and more being transferred to machines, as part of a continued process of mechanization. Man's third traditional role is the only one that remains in advanced technology or automation: man as controller and regulator of a working situation or system and as a diagnoser and adjuster of difficulties.

For reasons partly scientific and partly economic, the inexorable movement in the development of technology is from simple technique and tools to mechanization and then to automation. Mechanization is that state of development in which machines absorb the power and tool guidance components from men. Although many transformation tasks can be performed by machines, in mechanization the regulation activities are left to men. Regulation tasks performed by men are inspection, feedback, decision, and change. What strikes us most frequently is that most technologies are developed to an incomplete state of mechanization, leaving some tasks—sometimes highly skilled ones, but frequently simple "mechanical" tasks or parts of tasks—to be performed by "human elements of the machine." Some of these tasks are central to the transformation, and here the machine is the adjunct to the man. Too frequently it is the other way around: the machine is central and man is the adjunct to the machine. In automation (the sophisticated end of the scale of technological development), routine activities are absorbed into the machine, and the machine can perform many if not all of the regulation activities: inspection, feedback, decision, and change under stable conditions.

The advancing state of development of technology is having a variety of effects on society, organizations, and jobs, which we will examine. Two of the effects of advancing technology are producing secondary effects on organizations and jobs; namely, changes in occupations and in employment. The change in occupations is partly the consequence of the shift from occupations associated with manufacturing and farming to ones associated with general and personal services. It is also partly the consequence of the shift within the production of goods and services from blue collar to white collar occupations. Additionally, in automated production, many of the blue collar jobs are made up of activities—tasks—generally no different than those performed in white collar jobs.

The change in employment is another effect raising particular concerns for society at large and for internal organization structures and jobs within companies. In goods production, and to a lesser extent, in services, the continued development of technology has led to reduced manpower per unit of output. In the U.S. so far, the burden of readjustment to displacement largely falls on the individual, whether it means finding new employment, moving to a new location, or learning new skills or a new occupation. The consequent resistances to technological change generated through protective work rules, labor-management contracts, and other practices inhibit the development of new organizational forms and jobs that have the potential for meaningful and satisfying roles. The resistances are so extensive that there is considerable confusion over what can be called the jobs-numbers argument. It is frequently difficult to distinguish whether the job issues that are raised concern job content and structure or whether they concern the number of positions affected; i.e., the employment effect. The data presented in our review, while overlooking the numbers or employment issue, is not to be taken as a denigration of the importance of this issue for society and the need to reconsider priorities as concerns work and roles for its citizens.

A number of studies assert that although automation is decreasing the demand for labor, the manner in which industry is approaching automation makes the spectre of sudden mass unemployment less likely to become a reality in the near-to-mid-range future. It is this argument that leads us to the position that the immediate and crucial effects of post-industrial technology in organizations concern the design of jobs and work rather than job displacement and leisure (Theobald, 1965; Beaumont and Helfott, 1964; Crossman, 1966).

Characteristics of New Technology

Technologies developed during the industrial era have powerfully affected the organization of work. These began with a number of developments in England about 150 years ago: (1) men and animals were replaced as the essential power sources for carrying out work; (2) the nature of the new power source required that groups of men be brought together around it, giving rise to the factory system; (3) some elements of men as workers (i.e., some of their skills) were displaced into mechanical tools and devices; (4) men and machines had to be coordinated; and (5) the foregoing changes provided new opportunities to organize or "rationalize" the ways in which men worked.

The central property of industrial era technologies is that they are *deterministic:* what is to be done, how it is to be done, and when it is to be done are all specified. Cause-and-effect relationships are known, and most, if not all, actions can be prescribed to obtain the desired results. Among the driving forces in the continuing development of production technology has been the attempt to specify (or program) more and more processes completely.

Organizations evolving out of the design processes of allocating tasks to men and machines and developing a guiding and regulating superstructure reflected both the *deterministic* technology and the values and beliefs of western industrial society. A new kind of specialization of labor was introduced, in which jobs were deliberately fractionated so that unskilled people could do them. In 1825, after some 20 years of experience with fractionating jobs, Charles Babbage reported this social innovation in his book, *The Art of Manufacture*, which is still relevant today. In about 1890, F.W. Taylor rediscovered what Babbage had begun 100 years earlier and created an approach called "scientific management," which can be called the "machine theory of organization" and is the present basis of industrial organization throughout the western world (Davis and Taylor, 1972).

Most present production organizations are based to a large degree on the machine theory of organization, in which interdependence between tasks and between individuals is controlled by special managerial arrangements, systems of payment, and the like. Such organizations have large superstructures or hierarchies designed to coordinate the elements in which work is done, join them together, counteract variances arising both within the elements and within the socio-organizational links created by its members, and adjust the system to changes in input or output requirements. In such organizations, learning, planning, coordinating, and controlling are functions exercised within the superstructure; transformation tasks, most of which are programmable, are performed at the worker levels. Under such organizational arrangements, management is reinforced in its beliefs that workers are unreliable, interested only in external rewards, and regard their work as a burden to be set aside at the first possible opportunity. Largely, this is a self-fulfilling prophecy. What saves the day is that the organizational system can continue to operate—rickety though it is—as long as the technology can be maintained as deterministic and social expectations for a humane quality of work-life are not too widespread.

The most striking characteristic of the new sophisticated, automated technology is that it absorbs routine activities into machines, creating a new relationship between the technology and its embedded social system. Men in the new, emerging automated systems are interdependent components required to respond to *stochastic*, not deterministic, conditions: they operate in an environment whose "important events" are randomly occurring and unpredictable. Sophisticated skills must be maintained, although they may be called into use only infrequently. This technological shift disturbs long-established boundaries between jobs and skills and between operations and maintenance. Additionally, the new technology requires a high degree of commitment and autonomy on the part of workers in the automated production processes (Davis, 1971c)—a commitment and autonomy that derive from the role required of man as a regulator of a working situation or system, an adjuster of difficulties. This role requires skills related to regulation—skills in monitoring and diagnostics and skills in the adjustment of processes (Davis, 1962). In this sense, blue collar work takes on white collar attributes and supervisory attributes in relation to machines and process, rather than to people. Man is involved in transformation processes in his role as monitor of stochastic dislocations. His contribution to the outcome is that of variance absorber, dealing with and counteracting the unexpected. He provides interventions that are nonprogrammable. His relationship to the process shifts out of the mainstream; he is "on standby," and is concerned primarily with start-up operations and with reducing downtime by anticipating faults and developing strategies for corrective action. The required degree of autonomy at the work-place is likely to be in serious conflict with the assumptions and values held within the bureaucratic technostructure (Galbraith, 1967).

In production systems, stochastic events have two characteristics: unpredictability as to time and unpredictability as to nature. For economic reasons, they must be overcome as rapidly as possible, which imposes certain requirements on those who do the work. First, the workers must have a large repertoire of responses, because the specific intervention that will be required in any one instance is not known. Second, they cannot be dependent on supervision for direction because they must respond immediately to events that occur irregularly and without warning. Third, they must be committed to undertaking the necessary tasks on their own initiative.

These requirements create a very different world, in which the organization is far more dependent on the individual (although there may be fewer individuals). From the point of view of the organization, the chain of causation is:

1. If the production process collapses, the economic goals of the organization will not be met.
2. If appropriate responses are not taken to stochastic events, the production process will collapse.
3. If the organization's members are not committed to their functions, the appropriate responses will not be made.
4. Commitment cannot be forced or bought; it can only arise out of the experiences of the individual with the quality of life in his working situation, i.e., with his job.
5. Therefore, automated industries tend to seek to build into jobs the characteristics that will develop commitment on the part of the individual. The major characteristics are those of planning, self-control, and self-regulation; that is of autonomy (Davis, 1966).

Opportunities Presented by New Technology

Not only is technology changing, but it is doing so at a very high rate. This is reflected in the rate of introduction of both new products and new processes or techniques which are growing in sophistication—being more highly science-based. The high rate of change has consequences for organization and job structure. On the product side, frequent new developments are leading to the growth of shorter production runs and the consequent need for adaptability of organization and workers to more changes. On the production side, there is the phenomenon of more sophisticated machines and simpler manual activities embedded within automated complex production processes, which blurs the boundaries of jobs and organization units as conventionally conceived.

Advanced technology presents us with a number of opportunities to develop new, more humane organizational forms and jobs providing a high quality of working life.[3] First, although it poses new problems, highly sophisticated

---

[3] For a report of cases and description of methods and requirements for design of jobs see Davis and Taylor (1972).

technology possesses an unrecognized flexibility in relation to social systems. There exists an extensive array of configurations of the technology that, within limits, can be designed to suit the social systems desired.

Secondly, the new technology both increases the dependence of the organization on the individual and on groups and requires more individual commitment and autonomous responsibility in the work-place. These requirements for mutual dependence and independence provide opportunities to redress past deep-seated errors in social organization and member's roles. Such opportunity may now be at hand to overcome alienation and provide humanly meaningful work in sociotechnical institutions.[4] The development, over a period of nearly twenty years, of a body of theory (Emery, 1969) concerned with the analysis and design of interacting technological and social systems permits a research-based examination of the organization and job design in complex environments. Advanced technology and its mismatch with conventional industrial organization have further stimulated this examination. The diffusion of knowledge about applications of these theories is itself changing the environment of other organizations. The concepts were first developed in Britain (Emery and Trist, 1960) and followed by developments in the United States (Davis and Taylor, 1972) and recently in Norway, Holland, Canada, and Sweden. They are far from having come into common practice. Their most comprehensive application is taking place in Norway, and their most extensive application is taking place in Sweden, on a national scale, as a basis for developing organizational and job design strategies suitable to a democratic society.

TECHNOLOGICAL EFFECTS ON JOB CONTENT AND STRUCTURE

Studies: Some Problems

The above-noted position that psychosocial assumptions are involved in nearly every technological design or application complicates a review of the existing empirical literature dealing with technology and work, because most of that literature reflects the assumptions of technological determinism. Given considerable variance among the results of the accumulated studies, it may appear cavalier for us to discuss at least some of this variation on the basis of the psychosocial assumptions that might have been considered by the designers or implementers of the particular technology under study. Nonetheless, we are constrained to do so, because we feel strongly that psychosocial assumptions are included and will continue to be included implicitly or explicitly.

Another issue, which we believe will aid in explaining a portion of the variation among the extant empirical results, is the conceptualization and measurement of the technology itself. The empirical literature dealing with the incidence and general effects of "modern technology" in plant and office is based, at least indirectly, on one or another of the multitude of classification schemes devised by various researchers to distinguish variations in technology. In some studies, investigators studied only one case, describing in considerable detail the technology and jobs at hand (e.g., Trist and Bamforth, 1951; Walker, 1957). For example, the investigators often describe exactly what they mean

---

[4] To this end, directions that may be taken are suggested by Fromm (1968, Chapter 5); similarly, strategies for grasping the present opportunity are suggested in Emery (1967).

when they say "automation," or "mechanization." Even though we as readers may not agree with the designations, we at least have sufficient information about the technology and can label it ourselves to suit our own classifications. In other studies, attempts have been made to develop relatively objective and quantitative measures of technological sophistication, which were subsequently used in empirical study (e.g., Bright, 1958a; Turner and Lawrence, 1965; Taylor, 1971b). Even though we as readers may not agree with the criteria used, we at least know what instrument was employed and could use it to attempt replication of the results.

By far the largest number of reports on technology and work, whether theoretical or empirical, rely on more gross categories of technology. Empirical studies here claim to note differences between more and less sophisticated technology (e.g., Goldthorpe, et al., 1968; Mann and Williams, 1960) without additional description; more theoretical papers propose ways of classifying technology but never measure it directly (e.g., Perrow, 1970; Cooper, 1972). In empirical studies of this third type, the reader, never being really certain what the technology did, cannot replicate the results with another "sophisticated technology" in another industry, nor can he compare various studies in which technologies are described in the same way. The results of this type of empirical study will not always be comparable, not only because what is called "automation" by one researcher in one country or industry may be called "traditional mechanization" by another researcher or by the reader but also because of the methodological problem of definitive classification, which forces a discrete distribution. Discrete simplex classification by definition assigns cases that might be considered in the interstices between traditional industrial techniques and automation into either one of those classifications or the other; it can also include cases in one category which may be valid assignments, but which also make very different demands on workers. In the more theoretical papers that develop new classification schemes for prior empirical studies, the errors of omission by the original authors are frequently further augmented in the new classifications.

A final problem, which must be recognized when dealing with discontinuities among the empirical studies of technology and work and with the noncomparability of results, is derived from misassessment related to transitional needs of a new technology. In these instances, some workers have job demands characteristic of the system as it will finally be, whereas other workers have job demands that are transitional; that is, temporary in relation to the ultimate stable system. For example, a machine or process may be fully automatic, but transitional tasks may be maintained, even though they are redundant. This may be done because of management's concern regarding layoffs, or to insure against the unknown by providing transitional roles during the initial start-up phase or, finally, because of management's inability to forecast the necessary social organization in advance. In any event, this type of job is likely to have different characteristics from the jobs in the ultimate system. Even if these transitional jobs are in themselves not disruptive or dehumanizing to the job occupants, they are likely to be disruptive of the system by virtue of comparison and distributive justice.

Some transitional jobs of a more long-term nature are created via conscious, usually cost-related decisions in which people perform as parts of machines or parts of the technical system until it becomes economically feasible to eliminate these worker performed tasks. A popular example of this type of transitional job is that of keypunch operator. Relatively simple changes in computer input form would drastically reduce the number of keypunch jobs, which are repetitive, fractionated tasks that will exist until the diffusion of this technological development.

Automation and Skills

Automated, computer-aided production systems are bringing about crucial changes in the relationship between technology and the social organization of production. In an early study of a new semiautomated automobile engine assembly plant (Faunce 1958, 1959), it was found that the new work required more constant and careful attention, that workers were responsible for a larger share of the production process, but that they had less control over the work pace in the semiautomated plant. It was also learned that the proportion of skilled job classifications was higher: almost 25% of the jobs were of the skilled type or required an apprenticeship. As a result, pay was also higher.

Bright, in a study from the same period (1958a), concluded that, under partial automation, the skill levels of workers increase to a point; the skill requirements then decrease as more sophisticated levels of automation are achieved. Bright's study involved interviews with management and some employees and examination of records in thirteen plants selected as different and outstanding examples of automation, mostly in the metal-working industry. He found that training and education increased with automation, to a point at which measurement is added to the system; then mental effort in decision-making dropped off. Bright contends that findings of increased mental strain (e.g., Faunce, 1958; Walker, 1957) are a function of too little automation (that is, a transitional state) rather than too much. The sole aspect that increases with the level of automation is operator responsibility. In the Ford Motor Company's automated engine plant in Cleveland (similar to the one in Faunce's 1958 study) the operating staff and the managers were quoted by Bright (1958a: 181) that

> In the plant *as a whole*, automation reduces training requirements because less skill, less dexterity, less knowledge and care are required of the worker. (Italics added.)

The difference in conclusion between Bright and Faunce, based on a similar if not the same plant at the same time, suggests that the increased skills by traditional definition were found in maintenance functions and not in production jobs.

Friedmann (1955, 1964) discusses a set of several new skill requirements of automation. The set includes the worker supervising the workline and intervening only when stock is exhausted (1955), when the unexpected happens, when changes are made, or when something goes wrong with the machine (1964). This is very similar to the responsibility component of the job that Bright refers to as the only job demand that consistently increases with rising technological level. For Bright (1958b), this increase in demand included responsibility for a larger span of the line and responsibility for a higher caliber of duties (e.g., maintenance of quality control).

Other reviews of early automation such as Van Auken (1959) on the effects of automation on skills, as traditionally defined, provide conflicting and inconclusive results.

Crossman's 1960 survey of a number of British firms to determine the effects of automation on skills concluded that continuous-flow production plants have a common pattern of skill requirements in work that "... comprise control—monitoring and making adjustments to secure good yield and quality—and communication—logging instrument readings and reporting to their members of the operating team" (1960:57).

Burack (1969) has also noted that in more modern technology, traditional concepts of skill are often not applicable. He postulates that the aptitudes required in advanced production technology include (a) high attention to the work process or instruments, (b) rapid response to emergency situations, (c) ability to stay calm in a tension producing environment, and (d) an early detection of malfunctioning or of conditions leading to it.

Gardell (1971) has recently surveyed the relationships between technology and mental health in two mass-production and two continuous-process plants in Sweden. He reports a "U" shaped distribution curve of many of the discretionary and skill characteristics involved in work, on a three-point scale ("handicraft," "machine-controlled repetitive," and "process monitoring") of mechanization. Among the characteristics found higher for handicraft and process monitoring than for machine-controlled repetitive jobs were responsibility for equipment (quality and quantity) freedom for social contact, decision-making power, and variation in tasks. On the other hand, control over work methods, planning of work sequence, and control of work pace were found to be no greater in process monitoring tasks than in the repetitive work tasks in his sample.

Hazlehurst, Bradbury, and Corlett (1969) compared the skill requirements of numerically controlled (NC) and conventional machine tools for eight pairs of jobs in four companies. They conclude that while NC tools reduce physical effort, demand for motor skills, and the number of decisions an operator is required to make, these new machines involve an appreciable increase in demand for perceptual skills (machine monitoring and controlling) and conceptual skills such as interpretation of drawings, instructions, and calculations.

These authors also note that although the results reported above are reasonably clear in the sample they observed, the skill profiles derived reveal that the profile configurations for the NC jobs frequently have more in common with the jobs they replace than with other NC machines. The authors ascribe part of this variance in skills profiles to managerial assumptions, in the following quotation

> Some companies regard NC machines as highly specialised, to be treated in ways related to their particular characteristics, while others regard NC as normal machine tools and subject them to the same work programming, planning and loading systems as conventional machines. Policy decisions about the number of hours per day the machines are to be worked, supervisory training, number of men per machine, whether to use setter/operators or operators, and so on, depend upon the depth of understanding by managers of the machines' fundamental characteristics, and how managers decide to use NC to deal with their

own products and circumstances. All these decisions affect the job skills demanded of operators (Hazlehurst, et al., 1969:177–178).

This conclusion is not dissimilar to one reported in a study by Wedderburn and Crompton (1972) in which three continuous process plants in the same company and location were surveyed for worker perceptions of their jobs, work group, supervision, management climate, and organizational structure. In two of the plants, similar technological changes resulted in similarly titled jobs being quite different in intrinsic interest and demands as experienced by the workers. The authors report that this difference can be accounted for by planned changes in the supervisory system in one plant which acted at cross purposes with the otherwise facilitating effects of the technological change on job requirements (p. 114).

In the later studies, these suggestions that managerial discretion in decision-making can intervene between technology and skill requirements, at least provide some evidence for the fact that implementation of technical systems involve psychosocial assumptions juxtaposed with technical efficiency.

Among the most extensive studies of the effects of computers on office workers is that of Ida Hoos (1960a, 1960b, 1961), who in 1957 undertook a two-year study of nineteen organizations in the San Francisco area. She interviewed people closely associated with the computer at all levels in each company. Fifteen of the companies she studied had more than five-hundred clerical employees and had an average of only nineteen computer programmers each and no plans for increasing that number. Displaced by the computers were account clerks, bookkeepers, file clerks, ledger clerks, and their supervisors (1960a). They were replaced by keypunch operators, in the main, in jobs involving little if any upgrading and average salaries of the new jobs compared poorly with the old ones. In analyzing these new jobs, Hoos found that they were simple, repetitive, monotonous, requiring high accuracy and speed. Simplification and routinization made work measurement easier, and subsequently increased the use of work measurement. Most interviewed employees considered their previous job more interesting and less physically constraining. Electronic Data Processing (EDP) led to: a recentralization and integration of specific functions, to the regrouping of entire units, and to transferring many of the supervisor's duties to the computer. Hoos concluded that unlike factory automation, which has been said to enhance intrinsic interest in the job by integrating functions so that workers are not assigned to fragments of the production process, office automation has splintered job content into minute, highly repetitive units suitable for processing by the computer (1961).

Other authors of early studies support that conclusion. Stieber (1957), citing a Labor Department study, reported that computer installations led to little upgrading or enlarging of jobs. Referring to a study of employee reactions to EDP, he found that 15% felt the computer greatly changed the work; of those noting change, less than one-half felt variety increased. Faunce (1968) maintains that current development of EDP is increasing the number of semiskilled operators. Office automation, he says, may better be called a major advance in mechanization of information processing. Only improving the input-output system will lead to true office automation. He likens precomputer office work to the earlier craft or handicraft period, in that the equipment (e.g., typewriters) did not have skills built into them. Now that machines have built-in skills, the operators become semiskilled.

Hardin used before-and-after questionnaires of workers in two studies of office automation in a medium sized insurance company, in which a computer had been installed (1960a, 1960b). He found in the first study that people in departments affected by EDP liked the changes and did not see them as major. In his second study (1960b), he reported that four aspects of the job increased; namely, accuracy requirements, importance of job, work interest, and job security.

Another study (Jacobson, Trumbo, Cheek, and Nangle, 1959) used the same data from Hardin's first study of an insurance company. General results reported by these researchers are similar to Hardin's. They found that two-thirds of all employees claimed that they had experienced no change. Of those who reported change, the types of change most frequently cited were variety, amount, and the interesting nature of work. Those who reported more variety attributed it mostly to the computer. The computer was also slightly more likely to be credited with decreases in the amount of work and slightly less likely to be credited with decreases in supervision.

A later study by Crossman and Laner (1969) revealed that partial computerization of the check processing and account posting in a bank increased aggregate skill demands on direct workers on the order of 9%, while substantially reducing direct labor man-hours needed by some 47%. The same technological change increased skill demands on indirect labor (supervision, maintenance, services, and supplies) 41%, while reducing indirect labor man-hours needed by 61%. The dramatic increase in indirect labor skills, it must be noted, is affected by the inclusion of the computer manufacturer's field representative, who was classified as very highly skilled. Because indirect labor accounts for only 10 to 15% of the work force in this case, the net effect of increased skill for all workers as a function of the technological change amounts to about 26%.

A longitudinal study by Mann and Williams (1959, 1960, 1962); Mann, (1962) was made of the effects of a computer on an accounting division in a large utility company. Three questionnaire surveys took place over an eleven year period, the first being conducted some five years before the computer was installed, the second just before the computer installation was announced to the company, and the third about five years afterward. Company responses of eighty-eight people whose jobs were highly integrated into EDP and of eighty people whose jobs were independent of it, showed that for the integrated jobs, the job-grade increased slightly and significant job enlargement took place. Mann and Williams caution, however, that these changes may not necessarily follow in other cases. In this instance, EDP required shift work for white collar office workers. The new jobs had conditions of significantly lower tolerance for error, and workers' and supervisors' feelings of autonomy decreased. Much of the work was rationalized; rules and regulations were substituted for individual decision-making. Significantly greater interdependence of work groups was required, and individual responsibilities were more obvious and easily evaluated. The researchers concluded that work in the plant and in the office is becoming more alike; that is, jobs are more important, require more responsibility, and are more demanding. The jobs do differ, however, in that office jobs involve fewer duties than factory jobs. In the Mann and Williams study, white collar employees in the new work environment had more interesting and challenging jobs than before, but the greater exposure to risk and the tighter performance standards negated the attractive aspects of job content. Centralization of control and decision-making followed integration of the system. Autonomy and flexibility were reduced. Supervisory tasks ceased to exist and lead clerks were eliminated, which the researchers say leads to loss of self-direction and motivation.

Eva Mueller (1969), in an empirical study of the impact of general technological advance on a cross section of the U.S. labor force, found that workers with several years' experience on a job reported a tendency for machine changes to result in greater speed, skill and planning/judgment/initiative requirements, with a diminution in physical effort. Although the degree of technological advance is unclear, and the definitions of job requirements are cursory, these results tend to confirm those of the studies reported earlier.

Worker Autonomy and Discretion; and the Redefinition of Supervision

Dubin has long maintained that technology is the most important single determinant of what people do at work (1958). He postulates that management under systems of high technology is becoming more concerned for things and machines and less concerned for people (1958). Dubin believes that democratic management may prove costly in high technology where errors are made in the process operations (1965). He goes on to say that

> ...there is reason to believe that worker autonomy may be relevant to batch- or unit-production technologies, but probably not to mass-production technologies and almost certainly not to continuous-process technologies (Dubin, 1965:30).

As evidence for this position, Dubin cites Woodward's (1958) findings that (a) process production technology has more levels of management than either mass production or unit production, and (b) the ratio of managers and staff personnel to employees is also greater in process production. Dubin cites Woodward's findings that process production firms also have the lowest span of control in first-line supervision (1:15), although in this case mass production has the highest span of control (1:45), and the span of control for unit production is also small (1:25).

These data are used as evidence that a tall, centralized organizational structure such as Woodward found in the process technology is inexorably linked to regimented, authoritarian management style, close supervision or lack of autonomy. Woodward, in fact, specifically refutes this with other more anecdotal evidence she later presents (cf., 1965:64–67, 115). The conclusion that continuous process manufacturing is not a suitable technology for exercise of worker autonomy, or flexible or adaptable human work systems is patently at odds with reports (as yet unavailable in English language publications) from a number of Norwegian firms, showing autonomous (leaderless) groups operating automated process plants making pulp, paper, and chemical fertilizer (Gulowsen, 1971; Quale, 1968; Ødegaard, 1967). Similar North American reports are available for aluminum and consumer products manufacture (Archer, 1975; McCullough, 1975).

Woodward's results are reasonably similar to those reported by Harvey (1968), in which the contention is made that "specific technologies" (quantity production of a small range of products) were frequently associated with formalistic, more centralized organizations not unlike the mechanistic model of Burns and Stalker (1961). Granting this, then Dubin's point also seems reasonable. It must be noted, however, that Harvey's product or output classification is described by the Aston group (Hickson, Pugh, and Pheysey, 1969) as more like organization charter or purpose than technology, therefore, making his results less valid evidence for the case at hand. Faunce (1958) claims to have observed (not quantitatively measured) close supervision, at least during down-time and perhaps with regard to increasing production as well. Gruenfeld and Foltman (1967), in a study of indirect automation in a foundry, also report observing increased close and punitive supervision of first-level supervisors by top management.

The whole issue of whether technology has any real effects—autocratic or democratic—was challenged in studies and reports in which the effects of technology on organizational behavior were seen to be reduced by introducing culture as a mediating variable (e.g., Blood and Hulin, 1967; Dubin, 1965; Hulin and Blood, 1965; Turner and Lawrence, 1965). Their reports suggested that although there might be a tendency to develop a universal system of management adequate to the demands of high technology, strong cultural forces may have operated against it.

Cultural determinism. The evidence for this position of cultural determinism is not unequivocal. In an early cross-cultural study of steelmaking, Harbison, Kochling, Cassell, and Ruebmann (1955) reported that although greater mechanization and higher levels of technology were associated with closer supervision in the companies they studied, they found no evidence for cultural differences overriding technological forces in job design or in the proliferation of more general organizational structure of middle management or staff groups. They observed the work processes and studied the records of one West German steel firm and compared it with one American steel firm. Although both firms employed similar numbers and produced a broad line of products, they were different from each other in process, machinery, ores, product mix, products, and output. The American firm used a "higher level of technology." The authors report the ratio of management people to all employees was higher in the American firms (1:11) than in the German one (1:17). They also found that the span of control at first-line supervision was higher in the American firm (1:15) than in the German one (1:45). They found that the proportion of highly skilled workers was much higher in the German firm than in its American counterpart. Their data indicated that the American trend was to transfer supervision from leadmen to foremen, with much investment in the technical training of the foremen. Finally, with the greater labor-saving and skill-saving machinery in the American firm and more technical supervision as well, the level of production skill necessary in traditional terms was lower. Harbison, et al. found, however, that jobs in the American firm were being reclassified upward because of the improved and different technology. They concluded from these data, and other observations, that technological development in the steel industry requires supervisors with higher training and more of them, as well as more technically trained special staff personnel. The authors provide apparent support for the proposition that the greater the mechanization of operations, the greater the need for close supervision and the less the dependence on skilled craftsmen in the traditional sense.

More recently, the evidence in support of the cultural determination position has come into question (e.g., Davis, 1971c), and some studies have begun to re-analyze and test the earlier ones. For example, Susman (1972) has reviewed the Turner and Lawrence (1965) findings and concluded that religion and the contemporary national political scene played at least as great a role in attitudes toward enlarged jobs as did rural residence as opposed to urban residence. Susman further presents data from his own study in which he controls for both industry and technology and finds no differences in employee response to enlarged jobs among rural-bred rural residents and urban-bred urban residents.

That we are now in a period of massive reassessment of values (Yankelovich, 1974) and that urban centers are increasingly transmitting values to the rest of the country may be leveling the regional and rural-urban differences that were noted and assumed to be valid not more than a decade ago. The case of the Lordstown, Ohio auto assembly plant (*Newsweek*, February 7, 1972) is relevant in that auto assembly technology seems at least as alienating to young, primarily rural workers as it is to the older, unionized urban workers of Detroit.

An interesting point can be made from the postulate that close supervision is the production management of the future (e.g., Dubin, 1965). The point seems to be that supervision becomes increasingly "closer" and more highly skilled, until industry returns once more to the craft notion that the supervisor is simply the most skilled of the workers; and if work groups continue to decrease in size, they may eventually be considered either leaderless groups —"groups of supervisors"—or autonomous groups of workers. Thorsrud and Emery (1969) report that in the Norwegian developments, semiautonomous groups of competent workers supervise processes and exclude the need for the "supervisory" role at the work level. In Dubin's terms then:

> As technology tends toward continuous-process manufacture there will be a shift of control of product quality and quantity from workers to supervisors and management personnel (1965:15).

But who are supervisors as distinguished from workers? Bright (1958a) and Dubin (1965) indicated that the supervisor will become more in control of output—not necessarily a supervisor of people, but of machines. The emerging issue now seems to be what is supervision in relation to advanced technology.

An English study by Thurley and Hamblin (1963), reported by Dubin (1965), revealed that supervisors under conditions of advanced technology devoted much attention to meeting schedules, planning sequences of operation, and overcoming blockages to continuity of production. They maintained quality by checking the product, not the people. They also spent much time checking machinery. Dubin concludes that these men are supervising technical processes and that for them, people are incidental.

The early finding of Harbison, et al. (1955), that more technically trained foremen were needed and that remaining nonsupervisory jobs were being upgraded, introduces the element of worker skill into the phenomenon of closer supervision and smaller supervisory control spans. It appears that what Harbison, et al. meant by higher skills is what Burack (1969), Bright (1958b), and Friedmann (1955, 1964) discuss as automation's new skill requirements of machine and process supervision.

Williams and Williams (1964), in a study of the effects of numerically controlled machine tools, found that marked changes occurred in the decision-making structure. Information was collected from an employee and management sample of 146 people in thirty-three user firms. Numerically controlled equipment is important in the study of technological effects on the work-place because it alone, of the types of automation of durable goods manufacturing, is a possible alternative for small firms as well as large ones and for technologically diffuse (i.e., producing a wide range of products) as well as specific type firms in Harvey's sense (1968). Most other forms of automation are feasible only when the demand is large for a specific product or process. Williams and Williams (1964) found that pressures for output, low downtime, and responsibility for errors in operation increased for workers, but that supervisors became ineffective in identifying errors when they approached workers punitively. Additionally, horizontal communication increased at all levels, and vertical communication decreased at the bottom of the organization because of the higher skills and technical knowledge required by the operators. High operator skill was required because of the danger of downtime caused by incompetent operating. As technical skill increased at the worker level, they found that supervisory duties became less technical and more administrative (control of boundary conditions) and "human relating." They concluded that potential is high for first-line supervision. Basic supervisory decisions were moved to higher levels and supervision ceased to be a training ground for higher management.

It seems apparent that even though the pattern of actual supervisory activities differs from one industry or plant to another, the trend with advanced technology is in the direction of supervisors doing less in the way of traditional management—supervising behaviors of others, attending to selection or training functions, and the like—and more in the direction of acting as a facilitator, boundary controller, and communications link for the work group or becoming more technically skilled operators themselves. This takes us back to the general observation that at higher levels of technology (automation), conventional notions of work and skills no longer apply. Workers, individually or in groups, supervise machines or processes, so that the conventional notion of supervision is no longer applicable. An indication of the evolving supervisory role in these instances may be seen in the study of supervisory job design by Davis and Valfer (1966), in which supervisors of autonomous workers spontaneously assumed boundary-regulating activities to keep long-range disturbances from interfering with the work of their groups.

It is interesting to note that although the similarity of white collar automation to blue collar machine-tending factory work seems reasonable, little mention has been made of significant differences noted in supervision. Supervision in white collar automation has not been studied as extensively as supervision in factory automation. It is difficult, therefore, to tell whether white collar supervision is becoming closer, more pressureful, more helpful, or coming more to control boundary conditions.

Englestad (1972a) reports an organizational design study in Norway, which highlights the problem of assessing technological effects on worker autonomy and supervision. This case, involving the implementation of a semiautonomous group structure in a pulp and paper mill, relates managements' insistence on maintaining a newly developed foreman role with strong internal group controls in spite of the fact that the researchers warned against its use with a technology where process control and monitoring were the primary tasks. Worker autonomy and discretion were achieved in some measure, but the company itself decided to eliminate the foreman role for this type of work after four years of implementation (Englestad, 1972b).

The studies available to date do not lend unqualified support to the notion that higher levels of technology will in some way lead to increased autonomy and worker discretion. Again, we need to indicate that the organizational requirements or potential of higher-level technology must be separated from management ideology in considering the humanization of work. Davis (1971b) indicates that higher-level technology is setting the requirement for commitment and self-direction at the work-place, which would seem to be the base for work that satisfies human needs.

Increased pressure, close supervision, and decreased horizontal communication do not fit under the rubric of today's "enlightened management" (e.g., Argyris, Likert, McGregor). Many of the early empirical studies linking technology with blue collar and white collar supervisory and worker behavior have generally been poorly controlled, and most have attempted to generalize from severely limited data. There are optimistic utterances similar to the conclusions we drew from Dubin's position above (Drucker, 1955; Strauss and Sayles, 1960; Faunce, 1968) that perhaps the worker will pace the machine rather than it pacing him; that he will determine what it does and will be restored to the position of being his own boss, as craftsmen were in an earlier day. Fairly early studies that tend to support this position are Walker (1957), Mann and Hoffman (1960), Trist, et al. (1963), Blauner (1964), and Woodward (1965). These researchers tend to find that structural changes in the work group, supervision, and control systems, associated with technological advance, can also be defined as "humanizing."

Mann and Hoffman (1960) studied two power plants, one using more traditional technology and having a history of poor-to-average labor relations, the other using new and automated (continuous-process) technology. The authors found that 85% of the workers in the new plant said they had much more responsibility in their new jobs. An analysis of the correlates of increasing job responsibility in the new plant indicated that although increased responsibility may be offered as a means of overcoming some of the morale-oriented defects of overspecialization of jobs, it needs to be coupled with an opportunity for workers to use what they consider to be their talents. Although it was found in both plants that supervisory human relations skills were related to how satisfied the employees were with their supervisor, no relationship existed between employee reports of perceptions of either human relations skills or technical skills and reports of closeness of supervision. The researchers conclude that closeness of supervision may be appropriate to certain situations and that this behavior is independent of the supervisor's skills. They did not report that closeness of supervision was different in the two plants, but they did find that management philosophies differed in the two plants. In the newer plant, control rested in the hands of the supervisors rather than the superintendent, who in the newer plant provided a review function rather than a decision-making function with respect to immediate problems of the worker. Their data suggest that since technical complexities of automation can eventually be handled by the workers, the supervisor's job will be to concentrate more on directing employee activities and meeting employee needs. The supervisor will be less concerned with technical production problems, and more concerned with personnel management.

Automation and Work Group Behavior

Mann and Hoffman (1960) also found in their study that automation affects work group structure and behavior. In centralizing operating control in two areas in the newer plant, many of the isolated jobs that existed in the older plant were eliminated. The men in the newer plant were able to spend a greater proportion of their time in the company of other men. These authors found that men in the newer plant differed significantly from those in the older plant in their increased feelings about their opportunities to elicit help from others in their work group. There was also a tendency for more of the men in the newer plant to say that they were really a part of a work group and that their jobs were no more or less important than those of their peers. Mann and Hoffman concluded that centralization forced increased substantial contact among operators in the newer plant, which in turn created identification with the group and with the common objectives and tasks of its members. These results are at variance with those of Faunce and may suggest a difference between continuous-process technology and semiautomated transfer technology.

A four-year study of one work group (three shift crews) in a semiautomated steel tube mill (Walker, 1957) provides data suggesting that the differences among many of the studies cited above are reconciled over time. Walker studied about thirty workers (three shift crews of originally eleven, later nine men each) from shortly after the new mill was installed until it had been in operation for four years. The effects of the new technology on the work group were (a) a reduction in group size from about seventy over three shifts to about thirty, with eventual production increases of 400%; (b) an increase in distance between work stations, with face-to-face communication being replaced by a public address system; (c) the number of levels of supervision reduced from four to three; (d) work roles highly interdependent because of the integrated process; (e) intra-group status differences reduced, and lead men and assistant lead men eliminated; and (f) a new foreman role including information transmission up the line as well as down. Effects variously noted in the studies above have included: distance between work stations (Faunce); elimination of lead men (Harbison, et al., 1955); decreased span of control (Harbison, et al., 1955; Harvey; Woodward).

Walker also found that, not unlike Faunce's results, the workers originally had less communication with one another because of the increased distances and unfamiliar PA system, and more contact with their foreman and superintendent. They saw relations with management, however, as good, and they welcomed the increased contact. Two years later, workers said that group communication was much increased but contacts with management were less frequent and were accompanied by pressure, tension, and bad feelings. After three and one-half years, contact with management was still low, although the earlier hostility toward supervision had disappeared. During this time, however, the men complained that not enough participation in decisions about structure was allowed them. It seems clear that what structurally might be considered close supervision cannot be construed as autocratic and pressureful manage-

ment. Both Mann and Hoffman and Walker found that although new technology may initially create constraints in the direction of foremen closely
supervising machine operations and breakdowns, the behavioral effects of
these constraints are not necessarily resented by the workers; rather, they are
frequently welcomed. In fact, the behavior and actions of the supervisors may
engender greater feelings of responsibility and greater participation in immediate, specific, work-related decisions. Walker's data showed further that such
closeness of supervision can well be reduced over time—even with a small
span of control—as the operation of the work group becomes smoother and
more efficient. Findings by Marrow, Bowers, and Seashore (1967) tend to confirm this. Two years after technical-structural change in a pajama factory
(which included a decreased span of control), supervision was seen as more
diffuse, coming from more sources and less close than it had been.

Walker found that intragroup status differences were reduced and that
work roles became more interdependent under the advanced technology he
studied. Mann and Hoffman found that the new technology provided conditions
for enhanced intragroup cooperation and acted to reduce differences in perceived intragroup role importance. Are these data representative of the effects
of technology on work group structure and behavior? There seem to be two
factors that may condition the relationship: (1) a particular configuration of
certain elements in advanced technology; (2) conscious advance planning for
social system change, by management or others.

Evidence for the first point is contained in a review of thirty-nine case
studies of organizational behavior (Meissner, 1969). These cases were assigned
to eight categories of technological reduction of human effort, which was rated
as high or low in three types of technological demands based on: (1) attention
requirements, (2) interrelated characteristics of work flow and functional dependence, and (3) spatial relations between work stations. Differences in organizational behavior patterns of communication, influence, cooperation, and
status relations were then analyzed in terms of the labor-saving aspects and the
demands of technology. The conclusion reached was that neither reduction of
human effort nor any of the three types of technological demands would by
itself predict organizational behavior as measured. Only the combination of
technology and technical demands explained the variation of the behavioral
differences.

Bright (1958a), Hanke (1965), and Trist, Higgin, Murray, and Pollock
(1963) advance the thesis that the extreme division of labor typical of earlier
stages of mechanization gives way in advanced technology to a functional synthesis of formerly separated occupations. There are fewer work roles, and they
are less narrowly specialized than in a previous era. This role diffusion then
gives rise to informal if not formal changes in work organization. The smallest
increment in production organization is no longer one job, but a set of jobs.

The second and more indirect effect of technology on work group structure
and functioning is the emergence of "composite or autonomous groups" (Trist,
et al., 1963:78; Thorsrud and Emery, 1969), or "integrated, autonomous divisions" (Thompson, 1967). Composite groups are not the inexorable outcome
of advanced technology any more than close but helpful supervision initially may
be. The point in both cases is that to produce maximum system efficiency
requires jointly optimized social and technical systems. Among the characteristics of composite or autonomous groups are multiskilled workers, member

responsibility for allocating all roles, group incentive payment, and a task definition involving continuity. With conventional division of labor and work groups, technical progress in production is disrupted by the disturbances that a fragmented social system induces. The composite case is more efficient because of the more continuous activity pattern arising from an integrated work group.

Trist, et al. (1963) seem to be confirming what Walker and Mann and Hoffman found: that groups tend to become more cohesive and their role structure more equalitarian under conditions of higher technology. Trist and his colleagues at the Tavistock Institute studied technological change and subsequent changed and unchanged social systems in British coal mines (Trist and Bamforth, 1951; Herbst, 1962; Trist, et al., 1963) and textile mills in India (Rice, 1958, 1963) to determine the subsequent effects on productivity and worker commitment. The Tavistock people have experimented extensively in field settings over a period of twenty years. Their data regarding worker behavior are not systematically quantified, although they have been able to measure subsequent productivity.

In an experiment in a six-month-old automated weaving shed in India, Rice (1958) replaced the previous organizational arrangement with autonomous work groups. Nine old jobs were replaced with three new ones, group incentive pay was introduced, and new work groups were organized. The new groups were internally structured and led, with fewer exployees reporting to one supervisor. It was found that assigning work groups to a number of looms markedly increased output levels over that under the older system of division by function, in which interaction patterns were not regular, jobs were not interrelated, and workers could not be held responsible for their production. Trist and Bamforth (1951) experimentally developed a similar autonomous group structure in coal mines in which a more advanced technology had previously been installed. In that case, however, mine managers had coupled the advanced technology with fractionated tasks and individual incentives. Trist and Bamforth found that the productivity levels that management had anticipated under the new technique—but had not realized under their social system change—were achieved once autonomous group functioning was instituted.

In a later study, Trist, et al. (1963) described a similar study, using experimental controls (i.e., installing autonomous groups in five different but matched mines representing three mining techniques) and reported similar results. They found that partial mechanization with unfavorable local tradition and experience was a poor situation for trying to institute composite or autonomous group structure and that increased mechanization, regardless of local tradition, was the best situation for introducing autonomous group structure.

Trist, et al. (1963) conclude that increasing technology can lead to a number of very different supervisory and work group arrangements, but that composite- or autonomous-group functioning seems to have the best results. The group structure, however, must be consciously installed if it is to succeed.

Interestingly, the Tavistock results differ from reports of earlier studies of advanced technology in showing that larger ratios of worker to supervisor can be successfully used with increased worker authority. Trist, et al. (1963) point to their data revealing favorable performance (which, in this case, implies favorable worker responsibility and commitment) resulting from autonomous groups of fifty persons. They claim that relatively large primary groups are capable of sustained self-regulation and maintenance. They add that industrial management has not believed this, and that the small group theory in social psychology has not helped.

Thorsrud (1968) studied the results of installing autonomous group structure in organizations and concomitantly improving their production technologies in various degrees, as part of the Norwegian Industrial Democracy Program. He found that the change in the social system was more productive as a function of the extent of the technological change. Thorsrud's finding lends support to the notion by Trist, et al. that extensive technological change provides a better climate for development of autonomous groups. Thorsrud's data (Thorsrud and Emery, 1969) on worker attitudes are of a more quantitative nature than those of the British group, but his findings are as yet unpublished in English.[5] He attempted, as far as it was possible in each organization, to install the same autonomous group system. His first case was a wire drawing department in a steel mill where the technical change was minor, consisting of the installation of gang controls to allow group operation. The second case was a metal fabrication department of an electrical product firm with a technological change in production representing an increment in advance over the wire plant. The third case was a pulp and paper plant that incorporated an unspecified stepwise increment in technological advance over the fabricating plant. The fourth case was a totally automated new chemical fertilizer plant. After the change in each case, Thorsrud measured resultant productivity, company earnings, costs, and employee attitudes. He found improvements in all of these with autonomous group functioning.

In discussing autonomous groups, the Tavistock Institute investigators describe a supervisory role different from and broader than the traditional one. The sort of supervision required for a group that controls the production process is the control of boundary conditions such as maintenance, supply, external planning, and the like (Emery, 1959; Emery and Marek, 1962; Rice, 1963). This is similar to the emerging supervisory role observed by Walker in the steel tube mill (1957), by Mann and Hoffman in power plants (1960), and by Marrow, et al. in apparel manufacturing (1967).

How far a work group is capable of responsible autonomy and is able to adapt itself in correspondence with ongoing conditions indicates the extent to which its social structure is appropriate to the demands of the work situation. Herbst (1962), using Rice's and Trist's research as the basis for an analysis, suggests that the difference between autocratic management and autonomous work organization lies not in the amount of control exercised by the supervisor but in applying control to external factors affecting internal stability. If the technology is such that worker actions are difficult to observe, and the quality and quantity of output are easily supervised, and if the relations between the actions and output are a matter of skill, or are best known to the operators, then control will best be applied by the specification of quality and quantity of output rather than requiring and enforcing a specific activity or behavior.

When technology makes it easier to evaluate results, then it is easier to supervise on the basis of results, and autocratic management of work activities

---

[5] Editor's note: For a discussion of the experiments, see Thorsrud, Sørensen and Gustavsen; Chapter 10, this volume.

is less likely. Woodward (1965), in a case study of technical change, having rationalized control system manifested throughout the process organization in the sample, reported that there was more delegation and decentralization at the work-place in process industries than in mass-production industries. These trends were associated with an increasing ability to predict results and to control the physical limitations of production. Friction between management and supervision was low because computers were used to schedule and evaluate the work in terms of output. More of these machine-made decisions were accepted over decisions made by management production planning staff because output measures became the "law of the situation."

A comparison between an industry that is highly automated and one that is not demonstrates these differences very clearly. In the oil-refining industry, the tasks that remain to be performed by workers are almost entirely control and regulation, and the line between supervisor and worker is tenuous. The construction industry, on the other hand, still retains prominent roles for man as a source of energy and tool guidance, and supervision (often at several levels) mediates all system actions. Industrial relations officers in the oil industry are proud of their "advanced and enlightened" personnel practices. These practices may indeed be accurately described as enlightened, but they were not adopted for the sake of their enlightenment. They were adopted because they were, and are, a necessary functional response to the demands of process technology.

In two studies of different refineries, Susman (1970a, 1970b) and Taylor (1971a, 1971b), it was found that relatively self-supervising work groups developed in this continuous process technology to an extent not evidenced in other industries having less sophisticated technologies. In the case of Taylor's research, it was also found that groups with more sophisticated technology were also more amenable to change in the direction of even greater autonomy and self-direction, which suggests that the original assumptions of managers and production system planners were such that they greatly undervalued the self-direction capabilities of their workers.

Here is the point at which both the social and the technological forces can be seen working toward the same end, for "job characteristics that develop commitment." Thus requirements that promote the economic goals of the highly automated organization are exactly those that are beginning to emerge as demands for "meaningfulness" from the social environment: participation and control, personal freedom, and initiative.

Nor is this linking of the two threads confined to industries that are as highly automated as oil refining and chemicals. Most industries are neither all automated nor all conventional; they utilize a mix of the two modes of production. If an industry has some employees whose enhanced jobs were designed to meet the requirements of automated technology, then the enhanced quality of their work-life is visible to all the employees of the organization and creates demands by all employees for better, more meaningful jobs. It becomes very difficult to maintain a distinction in job design solely on the basis of a distinction in technological base.

Several recent publications argue against the position stated earlier: that work in automated technology is shifting from single jobs to a set of jobs (or group of performed activities). The first of these publications (Goldthorpe, Lockwood, Bechhofer and Platt, 1968) involves a comparative survey of British companies representing several different levels of technological sophistication. From the evidence of the Goldthorpe, et al. survey, it was concluded that in automated lathe operation, as well as continuous process operations, social interaction and group relations are less frequent than in more traditional industrial technology; as well as involving lower skill levels, as traditionally defined.

Turning to our earlier discussion of the influence of social system assumptions on design of a technical system, we can offer a possible explanation for the absence of any meaningful group structure in automated operation noted by Goldthorpe, et al. If the managers and technical system planners in this case imposed job and organizational structure which flow from the assumption that people (or parts of people) are merely parts of the machine or process, then whatever potential the technology could provide for formation of group activities would be negated.

It seems reasonable to speculate that whereas management may tolerate changing some psychosocial assumptions toward higher individual worker responsibility in more automated systems, it is likely to offer more resistance to changing its assumptions about devolution of commensurate authority and reductions in supervision of worker behavior. This is an issue referred to by the Norwegian investigators as imposing the "managerial authority structure" regardless of the "work authority requirements."

In a literature review paper (Cooper, 1972), a number of earlier studies are reclassified in terms of the author's technological scheme. Cooper finds that although group-performed activities are particularly important in an automated process system, they may constitute a transitional stage in technological development in oil and chemical industries; in any event, they were not found to the same degree in other forms of advanced automatic production. Even though Cooper evaluates prior research on its own assumptions, as it were, of technological determinism, he concludes on the note that we must go beyond the traditional view that task content is largely determined by technology. If viable organizations and jobs are to be developed in relation to the opportunities provided by advanced technology, then it becomes mandatory that appropriate psychosocial considerations are introduced in the design of technological systems.

Structural and Organizational Behavior Concomitants of Technology

Limited direct and consistent evidence is available for the proposition that fundamental differences in organizational form or type are related to technology. The controversy, centering in whether technologically advanced industrial organizations are becoming more or less bureaucratized or more or less autocratic, rages in general theoretical terms. Most available evidence used is segmental, its ambiguity attested to by its use by advocates on both sides. The problem surrounding the various definitions of technology has been noted above, and will be assumed to introduce additional contamination into the evidence used on both sides.

Janowitz (1959), discussing technical advances in a military organization, Litwak (1961), looking at conflict patterns in bureaucratic organizations, and Touraine, Durand, Pecant, and Willener (1965), assessing the European experience in automation, all conclude that positive involvement of lowest-level persons, coordination among work groups, and horizontal informal communication are required when the situation (technologically created) becomes complex. Although their definitions of technological complexity vary and rely on a small amount of impressionistic data, it is interesting that the conclusions are so similar.

Thompson and Bates (1957), comparing a hypothetical mine, manufacturing plant, hospital, and university, also comment that higher technological complexity and development is associated with more organizational improvisation, more need for subunit integration, and more cosmopolitan attitudes on the part of employees. Technological specialization, they say, is associated with decreased organizational flexibility in goal definition and response to the market. Thompson (1967) later simplifies this by saying that assembly line or "long linked" technologies operate best under the machine theory organization of scientific management; that single technique or "mediating" technologies are best suited for a bureaucratic organization; and that multiple-technique, or "intensive" technologies are most likely to operate in a different sort of organization from the other two.

Burns and Stalker (1961:vii), after interviewing over 300 managers and observing organizational processes in more than ten plants, conclude that:

> When novelty and unfamiliarity in both market situation and technical information become the accepted order of things, a fundamentally different kind of management becomes appropriate.

This new kind of management, which Burns and Stalker call "organic," is adapted to unstable conditions. Jobs lose much of their formal definition, being continually redefined by interaction with others participating in the task. Interaction is as much horizontal as vertical, and omniscience is no longer imputed to the head of the concern. These authors set this system against the older or more traditional system that they call "mechanistic." A mechanistic system is characterized by problems or tasks being broken down into specialties; technical methods, duties, and powers attached to each functional role are precisely defined by role prescription. Interaction tends to be vertical in the mechanistic system. In short, this system has a great deal in common with the bureaucracies described by Weber. Little empirical, quantified data are available for support of these assumptions, although the authors' broad experience and ability to compare the companies they observed and to relate it anecdotally are evident in their conclusions.

Another study, and one which is felt by its author to be complementary to the findings of Burns and Stalker, is that of Joan Woodward (1958, 1965). Unlike the Burns and Stalker study, Woodward's study of the structural concomitants of technology concentrates on organizational shape rather than control process, is more quantified, and her sample is larger and more representative. Woodward studied 100 manufacturing firms that employed more than 100 persons each, in Southeast England. After determining little relationship between organizational size and organization structure, Woodward developed a scale of technology to match with structure. Using the technological classification scheme of "unit production," "mass production," and "continuous-process production," she found direct positive relationships between this scale and the number of levels in the management hierarchy, and between the ratio of managers and staff to other personnel. She found negative relationships between her technology scale and both the ratio of wages to costs and the ratio of direct to indirect workers. She also found, as previously noted, that the span of control of first level supervision was largest in mass production and smallest in continuous-process. Finally, she found that more process production firms hired college graduates in both line and staff (1965). Although these were quantified results, Woodward used few statistical tests to assess her data. From this and other less quantified observational data, she concludes that classical bureaucratic methods of management have little relevance for other than mass production firms. Unit production and process firms, compared with mass production firms, have quite different organizational structures. The organization of production is most important for both ends of the technology scale, since situational demands impose themselves more rigidly and obviously at the extremes than at the middle of the scale. In discussing similarities between the top and bottom of her technological scale, Woodward finds that organization at both ends of the scale of technical complexity is more flexible and less subject to formal specification than it is in the middle part of the range.

Automation in the office, it is claimed, does not affect management structure and functioning by its changes in the way work is done in the production process. Computers and EDP do affect management structure, however, by changing the requirements of decision-making. Routine decisions will be made by machine and a greater centralization will follow (Anshen, 1962).

Blauner (1964) also states that organizational form is related to technology. His four classes of technology, he says, are found in four different kinds of organizations. Blauner's findings seem to be less in agreement with Woodward's conclusion regarding similarities between the two extremes in her technological scale discussed above. It would seem that Woodward's classification of unit or small batch production could accommodate either Blauner's pre-bureaucratic traditional organization or postbureaucratic organic organization, depending on whether the firm was craft-based or science-based.

Very tentative conclusions, based on a paucity of data, would be that more modern technologies are associated with flexibile, adaptive, more formless organization like that described as organic by Burns and Stalker or with bureaucracy based on a consensus and sense of industrial community.

Perrow (1970:90) has similarly postulated that continuous process production can be best served by a bureaucratic organizational structure. Although he provides no evidence of his own, Perrow draws on several studies—notably Woodward's study of 100 plants—for support of this position.

Harvey (1968), however, provides data more specifically the converse of this point. That is, the greater the technological advance in the direction of specialization, the greater the organizational rigidity. Harvey comes to this conclusion using data from a study of the records and managerial beliefs in forty-three industrial organizations, classified as technically specific, technically intermediate, or technically diffuse. This classification was operationalized as the number of reported product changes in a previous ten-year period (ranging from one to eight changes in the "specific" category, twenty to forty-three changes in the "intermediate" category, and seventy-two to ninety-five changes in the "diffuse" category). Separating the firms by technical class, Harvey found direct observable relationships between this tricotomized continuum of diffuse-intermediate-specific and the number of specialized subunits, the number of levels of authority, the ratio of managers and supervisors to total personnel, and program specification (job specification, flow chart delineation of output process, and formal specification of communication channels). Since his sample of organizations is non-probable, Harvey did not apply statistical tests to his data, but these seem reasonably clear in their outcome. He concludes that organic management appears more typical in the technologically diffuse organization, which is more likely to include Woodward's unit or small batch production firms rather than continuous-process plants. In checking his data against contaminants, Harvey indicates no effects were apparent for geographical location, worker culture (within the U.S.), or firm size. Since, as Schon (1967) has suggested, craft industry is usually too small to affect technological innovation easily, Harvey's technologically diffuse organizations must include craft and larger science-based firms as well. His intermediate firms, he states, have a certain amount of product change (for example, model change in auto manufacturing), and the sub-units most involved in product change and development tend to be the most unstructured. Other subunits—for example, personnel, marketing, and routine production—tend to be more structured and formal. Since Woodward did not study subunit specification, Harvey's finding that technologically specific firms had greater numbers of functional subunits cannot be said to refute her conclusions, although the increased degree of program specificity surely indicates that Woodward's data should be reanalyzed, taking product change into account. The differences between Harvey's findings and those of Woodward may also reflect an inadequate sampling of firms for either or both studies.

As noted previously, Harvey's technology classification is seen by the Aston group more as a measure of organizational purpose than of type of technology. Taking this perspective, the relationship obtained between product specificity (a contextual element of organizational purpose or charter) and structural rigidity is consistent with relationships found by Pugh, Hickson, Hinings, and Turner (1969).

The Aston group (Pugh, Hickson, Hinings, Macdonald, Turner, and Lupton, 1963) have long studied and considered the structural effects of a number of variables—organization size and technology among them. Following nearly a decade of work in the area, including a conscious attempt to utilize the "factorial approach" of systematic, cross-sectional, and comparative study, Pugh and Hickson (1972) conclude that although technology and organizational size are both related to organizational structure, in general, size is a better predictor.

Hickson, Pugh, and Pheysey (1969), testing the proposition of technological imperative in control strategy aspects of organizational structure, conclude that: "...variables of operations technology (equipping and sequencing of activities in the work flow) will be related only to those structural variables that are centered on the work flow." This effect is more organizationally persuasive in smaller organizations than in larger ones, where managers and administrators are buffered from the technology by staff departments and formalized communication channels and procedures. Child and Mansfield (1972) note that "technology" theorists such as Woodward and the "size" theorists such as Pugh are primarily concentrating on different (and complementary) aspects of organizational structure. Furthermore, in consonance with the position taken in the present papers, they posit that ideology and perceived interests are likely to influence the attempts of organizational decision-makers to manipulate the interactions between technology and structural aspects involving processes of bureaucratic control. A continuation of the Child and Mansfield position states that

> ...variables which have often been regarded as independent determinants of organizational structures are...seen to be linked together as multiple points of reference for the process of strategic decision-making (Child, 1972).

The reported phenomenon of increased organizational rigidity with increased technology has some support from a study by Scott, Banks, Halsey, and Lupton (1956). In studying a North Wales steelworks plant that had experienced three major technological changes in twenty years (changes, in effect, from batch production to almost full process production), they found that with later innovations the organization became more formal and systematic in order to deal with new problems of coordination and control, as was the case with technological effects on work group tasks.

The empirical evidence for technological effects on organizational structure is not only conflicting, but in even greater disarray than the results presented earlier for jobs and group effects of technology. This is not surprising, for at least two reasons. The first is that the available studies (e.g., Burns and Stalker, Woodward, Thompson, Blauner) utilize fairly gross, unquantified comparative judgments of degree of technological sophistication at the organizational level. Such gross categorization of technological sophistication makes comparison difficult and replication impossible.

The second possibility for disparate conclusions regarding technological effects on organizational structure involves the considerable resistance to changing psychosocial assumptions operative at the system level. We have noted earlier that whereas management may be less willing to allow modification of group structural arrangements and more tolerant of individual job and task changes, it is likely to resist even more strongly any attempts at changing organizational form or control structure, since such modifications come even closer to touching the organizational life-space of managers themselves.

SUMMARY AND CONCLUSIONS

We have taken a new look at technology in the organizational setting based on our new appreciation that technology design implicitly or explicitly includes certain psychosocial assumptions. The review of a wide range of studies provides some direct evidence that there is considerable flexibility in the design of technology, which challenges the widely accepted notion of technological determinism.

We have taken this position that the psychosocial assumptions related to postindustrial technology are at present the most crucial (and the most useful) elements to meaningful change in organizations. The position translates into action in the sphere of designing jobs and larger social systems in organizations by taking into consideration emerging values towards people and work in joint consideration with extant potentials of the technology. This implies a recognition that nearly all technology is designed by exercising certain assumptions about people and work. In almost every case in the past, these have been industrial era psychosocial assumptions.

This review has dealt with studies of technological effects on job and skill requirements, on worker autonomy and supervision, effects on group relations, and finally, effects on organizational structure. As we go from the specific topic area of jobs and skills to the more diffuse topic area of organizational structure, agreement among results of studies diminishes.

The study of changes in job and skill requirements when technology changed from conventional manual to numerically controlled machining provides direct evidence for questioning acceptance of technological determinism. The results indicated that the determinants for different skills are related to how management decided to utilize the numerically controlled machines. Additional evidence for managerial discretion intervening between technological and job requirements is described by Wedderburn and Crompton in their study of jobs and work in three continuous process factories owned by the same parent company.

Direct evidence of managerial intervention in worker autonomy and supervision comes from Engelstad's (1972b) case of the Norwegian pulp and paper mill. In this case, overt managerial resistance to the changing of supervisory roles to fit opportunities created by the new technology is clearly shown. Evidence that managerial psychosocial assumptions can effect relations between technology, group structure, and behavior is provided in several studies. Trist, et al. (1963) stated that although autonomous group functioning may be best used with sophisticated technology, they make a strong appeal that this social system must be planned. In their studies, in fact, two alternative managerial schemes for employing the same technologies showed that each had different effects on skills, jobs, and work group relations. Taylor's study of an oil refinery leads to the conclusion that management originally underestimated worker or employee potential for self-managed groups. Cooper, in his review article, counsels the inclusion of managerial discretion as an important variable in sociotechnical analysis.

In the area of organization structure, little direct evidence is available so far, since it has not been looked for, for establishing managerial discretion as an important variable conditioning the relation between technology and organization. John Child, however, in reviewing the work of the Aston group and Joan Woodward's research program, like Cooper, suggested that ideology and the perceived interest of organizational decision-makers may well influence interactions between technology and structural aspects.

The remaining studies reviewed neither directly support the technological determinism model (which most of them were meant to do), nor do they directly support the decision-maker intervention model. In the former case, methodological limitations of measuring technology, at a minimum, create enough inconsistency across studies to obviate any monolithic support for technological determinism. At the same time, these inconsistencies might in themselves provide indirect evidence for the latter model in that managerial discretion may account for some of the inconsistencies noted.

We have presented evidence that although vastly different social systems have been associated with similar technologies, these within-technology differences typically have been less than the differences among technologies. This, we reason, is probably as much a function of the dominant social values extant at the time of a technology's introduction as it is of the constraints of the technology itself. If, for example, designers considered workers to be "parts of machines" by virtue of the values of the culture at that time, then this would have an effect upon all the similar technological installations of the period. Dramatic changes in technology over the past twenty years have been associated with a general shift toward jobs, work, and organizations, which are different from those that preceded them and which reflect the changing value patterns of society as well as of technological designers specifically. Such value shifts occur slowly, however, and are by no means universal. That many engineers and managers continue to operate with industrial era assumptions about people at work is obvious. One element in evidence of the shift is the greater degree of agreement among results of studies reporting new skill level demands of automation for individual workers, compared with lower agreement among results of associations between automation and psychosocial effects at the work group level and at the organizational system level. This we believe can be explained by greater tolerance on the part of managers and engineering designers for psychosocial changes affecting the lower levels of the organization and the individual worker, and by less tolerance for psychosocial changes with general effect on the organization as a whole or upon higher organizational levels.

If we accept the fact that technology design also involves social system design, and if psychosocial assumptions in the technology are revealed, the consequences of our review result in rendering the findings of studies of the effects of changes in technology more ambiguous. We have, therefore, weakened the cause-and-effect linkages stated by many of the authors in the studies reviewed.

Starting with the position that psychosocial assumptions are a part of technical system design, we see the effects of technology in the light of a self-fulfilling prophecy. By this we mean that the observed effects on workers and on organizations of technology reflect the assumptions held by the designers of the technological systems about men and social systems. Hypotheses held about the nature of man embedded within a technical system are operationalized in the design of the technical system. It is in this sense that we are referring to a self-fulfilling prophecy. For example, when assumptions are held that a system is comprised of reliable technical elements and unreliable social elements, then in order to provide total system reliability, the technical design must call for parts of people as replaceable machine elements to be regulated by the technical system or by a superstructure of personal control. On the other hand, if the system designers' assumptions are that the social elements are reliable, learning, self-organizing, and committed elements, then the technical system will require whole, unique people performing the regulatory activities. Experience has shown that in the latter case such a technical system design produces effects markedly different than the former.

We, therefore, have no alternative but to consider technical systems and social systems to be joint systems with elements of one system residing in the other. The consequence then is that in designing organizations or jobs, these two subsystems have to be jointly optimized if we are to see a mutually effective organization or job result.

The conceptualization of correlated sociotechnical systems has been supported by the experiences in action research where researchers are forced to accept the complexity of the field as an outgrowth of a triple responsibility to: (1) the created system, (2) science, and (3) the greater social good rather than merely to science alone. Such researchers have been forced to accept the reality of how technology is designed, and how decisions about technological alternatives get to be made. From these experiences have developed the learning or appreciation that is central to this review. Future research must go beyond the limited focus of positivistic science, yet at the same time lend itself to the descriptions of the real world complexities long experienced in applied science. What is called for is an end to the acceptance of technology as given and of unidimensional concepts or effects. One important variable stressed in this report is the interaction of the decision-maker's discretion in both the design of technologies and the organization of jobs based on the assumptions about people. That the inclusion of this variable increases analytic complexity and reduces elegance in research design is accepted as necessary if we are going to develop useful, causal models in organization behavior and design.

REFERENCES

Anshen, M.
   1962   "Managerial decisions," in J.T. Dunlop (ed.), Automation and Technological Change. New York: The American Assembly, Columbia University.

Archer, J.
   1975   "Achieving joint organizational, technical and personal needs: the case of the Sheltered Experiment of Aluminum Casting Team," in L.E. Davis and A.B. Cherns and associates, Quality of Working Life Cases. New York: The Free Press.

Beaumont, R.A. and R.B. Helfgott
   1964   Management, Automation and People. New York: Industrial Relations Counselors, Monograph No. 24.

Bell, D.
   1967   "Notes on the post-industrial society (I and II)." The Public Interest, Nos. 6 and 7.

Blauner, R.
   1964   Alienation and Freedom. Chicago: University of Chicago Press.

Blood, M.R. and C.L. Hulin
   1967   "Alienation, environmental characteristics and worker responses." Journal of Applied Psychology (51):284–290.

Boguslaw, R.
   1972   "Operating units," in L.E. Davis, J.C. Taylor (eds.), Design of Jobs. London, Baltimore: Penguin.

Bright, J.R.
   1958a Automation and Management. Boston: Division of Research, Harvard Business School.
   1958b "Does automation raise skill requirements?" Harvard Business Review No. 36 (July):85–98.

Burack, E.H.
   1969   "Industrial management and technology theory and practice." Unpublished. Chicago: Illinois Institute of Technology. Spring.

Burns, T. and G.M. Stalker
   1961   The Management of Innovation. London: Tavistock.
Child, J.
   1972   "Organizational structure, environment and performance: the role of strategic choice." Sociology (6):1–22.
Child, J. and R. Mansfield
   1972   "Technology, size and organizational structure." Sociology (6):369–393.
Cooper, R.
   1972   "Man, task and technology." Human Relations (25):131–157.
Crossman, E.R.F.W.
   1960   Automation and Skill. London: H.M.S.O.
   1966   "Automation, skill and manpower predictions." Seminar on Manpower Policy and Program (September) U.S. Department of Labor.
Crossman, E.R.F.W. and S. Laner
   1969   "The impact of technological change on manpower and skill demands: case-study data and policy implications." Berkeley: University of California. Research Document Department of Industrial Engineering (February).
Davis, L.E.
   1962   "The effects of automation on job design." Industrial Relations (2)1:53–71.
   1966   "The design of jobs." Industrial Relations (6)1:21–45.
   1971a "The coming crisis for production management: technology and organization." International Journal of Production Research (9):65–82.
   1971b "Readying the unready: post-industrial jobs." California Management Review (13)4:27–36.
   1971c "Job satisfaction research: the post-industrial view." Industrial Relations (10):176–193.
Davis, L.E., R. Canter and J. Hoffman
   1955   "Current job design criteria." Journal of Industrial Engineering (6)2:5–11.
Davis, L.E. and J.C. Taylor (eds.)
   1972   The Design of Jobs. London, Baltimore: Penguin.
Davis, L.E. and E.S. Valfer
   1966   "Studies in supervisory job design." Human Relations (19)4:339–352.
Davis, L.E. and R. Werling
   1960   "Job design factors." Occupational Psychology (34)2:109–132.
Drucker, P.F.
   1955   The Practice of Management. London: Heinemann.
Dubin, R.
   1958   Working Union-Management Relations. Englewood Cliffs, New Jersey: Prentice-Hall.
   1965   "Supervision and productivity: empirical findings and theoretical considerations," in R. Dubin, G.C. Homans, F.C. Mann and D.C. Miller (eds.), Leadership and Productivity. San Francisco: Chandler Publishing Co.
Ellul, J.
   1964   The Technological Society. New York: Knopf.
Emery, F.E.
   1959   "Characteristics of sociotechnical systems." London: The Tavistock Institute of Human Relations. Unpublished Manuscript.

1967   "The next thirty years: concepts, methods and anticipations." Human Relations (20):199–235.

Emery, F.E. (ed.)
1969   Systems Thinking. London, Baltimore: Penguin.

Emery, F.E. and J. Marek
1962   "Some sociotechnical aspects of automation." Human Relations (15): 17–25.

Emery, F.E. and E.L. Trist
1960   "Sociotechnical systems," in C. Churchman and M. Verhulst (eds.), Management Sciences, Models and Techniques. Vol. II. London: Pergamon.

Englestad, P.H.
1972a   "Sociotechnical approach to problems of process control," in L.E. Davis and J.C. Taylor (eds.), Design of Jobs. London, Baltimore: Penguin.
1972b   "Abstract of the Hunsfos case of the Norwegian Industrial Democracy Project." Oslo: Work Research Institutes. Unpublished.

Faunce, W.A.
1958   "Automation in the automobile industry." American Sociological Review (23):401–407.
1959   "Automation applied to the automobile industry," in H.B. Jacobson and J.S. Roucek (eds.), Automation and Society. New York: Philosophical Library.
1968   Problems of an Industrial Society. New York: McGraw-Hill.

Faunce, W.A., E. Hardin and E.H. Jacobson
1962   "Automation and the employee." Annals of the American Journal of Political and Social Science (340):60–68.

Friedman, G.
1955   Industrial Society. Glencoe, Ill.: The Free Press.
1964   The Anatomy of Work. Glencoe, Ill.: The Free Press.

Fromm, E.
1968   The Revolution of Hope: Toward a Humanized Technology. New York: Harper & Row.

Galbraith, J.K.
1967   The New Industrial State. Boston: Houghton Mifflin.

Gardell, E.
1971   Produktionsteknik arbetsglädje (with English Summary). Stockholm: Personaladministrative rådet.

Goldthorpe, J.H., D. Lockwood, F. Bechhofer and J. Platt
1968   The Affluent Worker: Industrial Attitudes and Behavior. Cambridge: Cambridge University Press.

Gruenfeld, L.W. and F.F. Foltman
1967   "Relationships among supervisor's integration, satisfaction and acceptance of a technological change." Journal of Applied Psychology (51): 74–77.

Gulowsen, J.
1971   Selvstyrte Arbeidsgrupper. Oslo: Tanum.

Hanke, H.
1965   "Wissenschaftlich-technische revolution und berufsausbildung." Berufsbildung (Berlin). 19(1):3–5. Also in I.L.O. Automation Abstracts (93) 2(February, 1966).

Harbison, F.H., E. Kochling, F.H. Cassell and H.C. Ruebmann
   1955   "Steel management in two continents." Management Science (2):31–39.
Hardin, E.
   1960a "Computer automation, work environment and employee satisfaction:
          a case study." Industrial and Labor Relations Review (13)4:559–567.
   1960b "The reactions of employees to office automation." Monthly Labor Re-
          view (83):925–932.
Harvey, E.
   1968   "Technology and the structure of organizations." American Sociolog-
          ical Review (33):247–259.
Hazlehurst, R.J., R.J. Bradbury and E.N. Corlett
   1969   "A comparison of the skills of machinists on numerically controlled
          and conventional machines." Occupational Psychology (43):169–182.
Heilbroner, R.L.
   1972   "The future of capitalism: the future of industrial organization."
          World (12 September):27–30.
Herbst, P.G.
   1962   Autonomous Group Functioning. London: Tavistock.
Hickson, D.J., D.S. Pugh and D.C. Pheysey
   1969   "Operations technology and organization structure: an empirical re-
          appraisal." Administrative Science Quarterly (14):378–397.
Holte, J.B.
   1970   "Experiments in cooperation." Co-partnership, No. 542:31–38.
Hoos, I.R.
   1960a "When the computer takes over the office." Harvard Business Review
          (3)4:102–112.
   1960b "Impact of automation on office workers." International Labor Review
          (82):363–388.
   1961   Automation in the Office. Washington, D.C.: Public Affairs Press.
Hoppe, R.A. and E.J. Berv
   1967   "Measurement of attitude toward automation." Personnel Psychology
          (20):65–70.
Hulin, C.L. and M.R. Blood
   1968   "Job enlargement, individual differences and worker responses." Psy-
          chological Bulletin (69):41–55.
Jacobson, E., D. Trumbo, G. Cheek and J. Nagle
   1959   "Employee attitudes toward technological change in a medium size in-
          surance company." Journal of Applied Psychology (43):349–354.
Janowitz, M.
   1959   "Changing patterns of organizational authority: the military establish-
          ment." Administrative Science Quarterly (3):473–493.
Litwak, E.
   1961   "Models of bureaucracy which permit conflict." American Journal of
          Sociology (67):178–179.
McCullough, G.
   1975   "The effects of changes in organizational structure: demonstration in
          an oil refinery," in L.E. Davis, A.B. Cherns and associates, Quality of
          Working Life Cases. New York: The Free Press.
Mann, F.C.
   1962   "Psychological and organizational impact," in J.T. Dunlop (ed.), Auto-

mation and Technological Change. New York: The American Assembly, Columbia University.

Mann, F.C. and L.R. Hoffman
1960 Automation and the Worker. New York: Henry Holt and Co.

Mann, F.C. and L.K. Williams
1958 "Organizational impact of white collar automation." Industrial Relations Research Association Proceedings.
1960 "Observations on the dynamics of change to electronic data processing equipment." Administrative Science Quarterly (5):217–256.
1962 "Some effects of changing work environment in the office." Journal of Social Issues 18(3):90–101.

Marrow, A.J., D.G. Bowers and S.E. Seashore
1967 Management by Participation. New York: Harper & Row.

Meissner, M.
1969 Technology and the Worker. San Francisco: Chandler Publishing Co.

Mueller, E.
1969 Automation in an Expanding Economy. Ann Arbor, Michigan: Survey Research Center, Institute for Social Research.

Newsweek
1972 "The bullet biters." (February 7):65–66.

Ødegaard, L.A.
1967 Feltforsøk ved NOBØ fabrikker. Trondheim, Norway: Institute of Industrial and Social Research.

Perrow, C.
1970 Organizational Analysis: A Sociological View. Belmont, California: Wadsworth. Also, London: The Tavistock Institute.

Pugh, D.S. and D.J. Hickson
1972 "Causal influence and the Aston studies, letter to the editor." Administrative Science Quarterly (17):273–276.

Pugh, D.S., D.J. Hickson, C.R. Hinings, K.M. Macdonald, C. Turner and T. Lupton
1963 "A conceptual scheme for organizational analysis." Administrative Science Quarterly (8):189–315.

Pugh, D.S., D.J. Hickson, C.R. Hinings, C. Turner
1969 "The context of organizational structures." Administrative Science Quarterly (14):91–114.

Quale, T.U.
1967 Etterstudier ved NOBØ fabrikker. Trondheim, Norway: Institute of Industrial and Social Research.

Rice, A.K.
1958 Productivity and Social Organization, the Ahmedabad Experiment. London: Tavistock.
1963 The Enterprise and Its Environment: A System Theory of Management Organization. London: Tavistock.

Schon, D.A.
1967 Technology and Change. New York: Delta Books.

Scott, W.H., J.A. Banks, A.H. Halsey and T. Lupton
1956 Technical Change and Industrial Relations. Liverpool: Liverpool University Press.

Stieber, J.
  1957 "Automation and the white collar worker." Personnel (34):8–17.
Strauss, G. and L.R. Sayles
  1960 Personnel: The Human Problems of Management. Englewood Cliffs, New Jersey: Prentice-Hall.
Susman, G.I.
  1970a "The concept of status congruence as a basis to predict task allocations in autonomous work groups." Administrative Science Quarterly (15): 164–175.
  1970b "The impact of automation on work group autonomy and task specialization." Human Relations (23):567–577.
  1972 "Worker's responses to job enlargement by location of childhood and current residence." University Park, Pennsylvania: The Pennsylvania State University. Unpublished paper.
Taylor, J.C.
  1971a "Some effects of technology in organizational change." Human Relations (24):105–123.
  1971b Technology and Planned Organizational Change. Ann Arbor, Michigan: Institute for Social Research.
Theobald, R.
  1965 Free Men and Free Markets. New York: Doubleday.
Thompson, J.D.
  1967 Organizations in Action. New York: McGraw-Hill.
Thompson, J.D. and F.L. Bates
  1957 "Technology, organization and administration." Administrative Science Quarterly (2):325–343.
Thorsrud, E.
  1968 "Industrial democracy project in Norway 1962–1968." Oslo: Work Research Institute. Unpublished paper.
Thorsrud, E. and F. Emery
  1969 Mot En Ny Bedriftsorganisasjon. Olso: Tanum.
Thurley, K.E. and A.C. Hamblin
  1963 The Supervisor and His Job. London. H.M.S.O.
Touraine, A., C. Durand, D. Pecant and A. Willener
  1965 A Worker's Attitudes to Technical Change. Paris: O.E.C.D.
Trist, E.L. and K.W. Bamforth
  1951 "Some social and psychological consequences of the longwall method of coal-getting." Human Relations (4):3–38.
Trist, E.L., G.W. Higgin, H. Murray and A.B. Pollock
  1963 Organizational Choice. London: Tavistock.
Turner, A.N. and P.R. Lawrence
  1965 Industrial Jobs and the Worker. Cambridge, Mass.: Harvard University Press.
Van Auken, K.G.
  1959 "Personnel adjustments to technical change," in H.B. Jacobson and J.S. Roucek (eds.), Automation and Society. New York: Philosophical Library.
Walker, C.R.
  1957 Toward the Automatic Factory. New Haven, Conn.: Yale University Press.

Walker, C.R. and R.H. Guest
  1952   The Man on the Assembly Line. Cambridge, Mass.: Harvard University
          Press.
Wedderburn, D. and R. Crompton
  1972   Worker's Attitudes and Technology. Cambridge, England: Cambridge
          University Press.
Williams, L.K. and B.C. Williams
  1964   "The impact of numerically controlled equipment on factory orga-
          nization." California Management Review 7(2):25–34.
Woodward, J.
  1958   Management and Technology. London: H.M.S.O.
  1965   Industrial Organization: Theory and Practice. Oxford: Oxford Uni-
          versity Press.
Yankelovich, D.
  1974   The New Morality: A Profile of American Youth in the 70's. New
          York: McGraw-Hill.

CHAPTER **10**

Sociotechnical Approach to
Industrial Democracy in Norway

Einar Thorsrud, Bjørg Aase Sørensen and Bjørn Gustavsen

Work Research Institutes, Oslo, Norway

PART I—SOCIOTECHNICAL STUDIES

Why did the concept industrial democracy become central to our research? The answer is very simple. We, as social scientists, were invited by national union and management representatives to study industrial democracy and to help do something about it. We were given ample chance, in collaboration with the "sponsors," to explore alternative meanings of industrial democracy. We were convinced that this key concept was meaningful enough for those involved, that it might lead them to act in new ways if new alternatives became available. This led to planning two phases of research and development. The first concentrates on the experience gained with formal systems of participation through representative arrangements. The second deals with field experiments with sociotechnical changes to improve the concrete conditions for direct, personal participation. Results of the first phase were published in Norwegian in 1964 and in English in 1969 (see Emery and Thorsrud, 1969a). Results of the second phase have only been published in Norwegian (see Thorsrud and Emery, 1969, English translation forthcoming). What follows below is in part a condensation of the report of the second phase.

This chapter does not follow the usual social science handbook style. The three authors try to represent a larger group of social scientists who have collaborated actively with representatives of trade unions and employer's organizations and with all levels of different company organizations over a number of years.

Part I, written by Einar Thorsrud, outlines the problem area to be covered by the Industrial Democracy Program, and its major postulates regarding participation, job demands and enterprises as systems. A brief description of the stepwise strategy used in the research and development is followed by a report of four field experiments.

Part II, written by Bjørg Aase Sørensen and Einar Thorsrud, contains selected data from a larger comparative study of local industrial environments in Norway. The attitudes of workers toward different types of jobs and different aspects of participation are contrasted with some experimental and traditional types of plants.

Part III, written by Bjørn Gustavsen, summarizes an empirical study of company boards and their functioning process under different environmental conditions. The role of boards and new forms of work organization is discussed in relation to industrial democracy.

421

THE INITIAL CONDITIONS OF THE INDUSTRIAL
DEMOCRACY PROGRAM

First, the Industrial Democracy (I.D.) Program aimed primarily at the development and testing of *alternative organizational forms and their impacts upon employee participation* on different job levels. Major emphasis was placed on the concrete conditions for personal participation, including technological factors structuring the tasks, the work roles and the wider organizational environment of workers. A project within the program could not be limited only to the level of the workers, since major changes in any work system cannot be sustained without correlative changes eventually at all levels of the organization. It seemed important, however, to focus initially on the workers' level for two reasons. First, it is on this level that the lack of participation and involvement is most widespread. Second, jobs are currently designed on workers' level so that it is very difficult to achieve basic changes in the control systems and in participative relationships on the supervisory and other levels. Jobs are often so narrow and meaningless that supervisors and higher levels of management are forced into control and coordination of every detail. Such direct "top-down" control, in itself, causes frustration rather than participation, leaving little energy and time for constructive long term improvement.

Partly Autonomous Work Groups

These work groups came to be an important aspect of our explorations of alternative forms of organization. The individual has his limitations as a building block in organizational design, for technological reasons (Blauner, 1964). Process control and information handling cannot be dealt with entirely on an individual level. There were also a number of psychological and social reasons for exploring the potential usefulness of autonomous work groups in this particular context. Team work has always been an important part of the Norwegian work culture. Theoretical reasons for considering groups as essential to participation have been listed in a series of studies following Lewin's (1935) early experiments with group climate.

A major feature of the I.D. program has been the active engagement of researchers in effecting social change. With the present rate of change in technology, resulting in the change in the social aspects of industrial life, any alternative structure of organization might become obsolete almost before it could be established. The answer to this dilemma might be to build a great deal of reorganizational flexibility into existing organizations themselves. So the I.D. program has become an attempt to establish self-sustaining processes of organizational learning.

In what respect then, is the I.D. program different from other organization change efforts? It is related to the tradition initiated by Lewin (1935) and developed further in the U.S. in 1950–60 at The Institute for Social Research at the University of Michigan (Mann, 1957). Furthermore, it is strongly influenced by the work done during the 1940s, 1950s, and 1960s by the Tavistock Institute of Human Relations in England (Trist, 1968). But the I.D. program is different from the Michigan and Tavistock studies mainly because the institutional involvement went far beyond that of the single project in one or a few work organizations. Within the Norwegian cultural framework, it was possible in the 1960s to establish a set of starting conditions for large-scale social change over a period of at least ten years. The strategy of change was based on leadership and support from trade unions and employers associations and eventually from government. The role of successive field experiments as a way of testing and demonstrating new principles of organization was crucial in our early strategy. It included four major steps: (1) information, (2) involvement, (3) commitment and (4) joint social action. (Further explanation is given in a later section on our stepwise strategy of research and development [see also Thorsrud, 1970, 1972a].) This stepwise strategy had a parallel in agricultural change programs (Emery and Oeser, 1958). In retrospect, it might subsequently have caused problems in diffusion (Herbst, 1974b).

A long term program of this size demanded research resources beyond what was available in Norway. The collaboration with the Tavistock group was vital. Links to Sweden, Holland, and the U.S. were also important.

The relations established between the researchers and the researched can be classified according to Churchman and Emery (1966) who have distinguished three major roles for social scientists working with organizations: the academic, the servant and the collaborative roles. The research roles of the I.D. project clearly fall into the third category. The project satisfies two basic conditions stated by Churchman and Emery: first, the research was guided by some set of values that included the values of the researcher and the researched, and second, a governing body, able to sanction this inclusive set of values. A sanctioning body, the Joint Research Committee, was set up by the Trade Union Council and the Employers' Association, the two institutions which shared the financing of the project until the government came in on a tripartite basis. The value problems can perhaps best be considered when we have reported the cumulative research work.

Only one point had to be made clear in advance. The researchers, as well as people from collaborating organizations and institutions, had to be prepared to accept the fact that their own values (as well as those of any future participants) might be subject to change as the program progressed. It was clear in fact that the program itself might generate entirely new values, and as a result would have to affect the power structure if results of some importance were to be achieved in practice. For this reason, it was necessary at every major step to let both researchers and the researchees participate actively together in formulation of the goals of their joint effort. They had to agree on what conditions of the organization had to be changed and on the criteria to be used in evaluating the outcome of whatever changes might be achieved. (For further discussions of research strategy, see Thorsrud [1970, 1972a, 1972b]. For the reflections of other researchers who have been involved, see Herbst [1974a, 1974b], Qvale [1973] and Gulowsen [1973].)

Some Postulates Regarding Participation and Job Needs

The joint research committee agreed that the problems of industrial democracy had to be approached within a wider institutional framework, but it concluded that the company or the enterprise would be the primary unit of investigation. This point of departure followed from the analysis of the current debate in Norway of the issues we were to investigate (Emery and Thorsrud, 1969:4–16). A different frame of reference might have been relevant if we had not worked within the context of existing Norwegian industrial conditions: a long tradition of achieving social justice through labor-management cooperation on the basis of strong unions and management associations. We were encouraged by the labor-management organizations to go beyond representative forms of participation. Before doing so, we concluded from our exploration of representative systems in Norwegian industry, that these would be *complementary* to conditions for direct personal participation in the workplace. We also stressed the point, that *three different but interdependent levels of representation* would have to be observed (Emery and Thorsrud, 1969a: 26–30):

1.   political representation of social class; in Norway, mainly within the context of the parliamentary system, supplemented by a network of different organizations and institutions,
2.   *occupational* representation—in our case, mainly through unions integrated on the national level by a strong Trade Union Council,
3.   *employee representation* on the company level, to promote the interests of individuals in a particular contract situation.

In other countries, like Western Germany and Yugoslavia, where we surveyed the literature on participation, codetermination, etc., representation on these three levels would be quite different than it was in Norway. Consequently, the whole basis for democratization of work organizations would be different.

The first year of the I.D. program (1963) was spent in building institutional support for the main experimental phase and in the development of a research strategy. Simultaneously, we explored the experiences abroad and in some leading Norwegian enterprises with regard to representative employee participation on the board level. The results are discussed elsewhere (Emery and Thorsrud, 1969) and we shall here repeat only some key points:

1.   There seemed to be a need for extending the areas of negotiation within the firm, to improve conditions in democratization. Works Councils and the like are potentially able to handle many problems in the concrete work situation. If unable to do so, they can translate such problems to be dealt with by the trade unions or professional associations.
2.   The Norwegian experience was that the benefits of representational systems can be realized only if they are matched by an effective management, recognizing that the success of an enterprise depends on how it works as a sociotechnical system (not only as a technical system). Systematic personnel programs and appeal systems would be important aspects of such management.
3.   If democratization was to mean more than extended consultation and negotiation, there was a need to transfer real managerial power to the employees. Our study indicated that this would *not* start effectively on the management level under existing Norwegian conditions. It would have to start at a level where a larger proportion of employees are able and willing to participate.

In order to explore the basic conditions for increased involvement and participation, we went over the literature and found a considerable amount of work done as far back as the Gestalt experiments in the late 1920s (Lewin, 1935). Combining what we found in the literature with field experiences in British coal mines (Trist, et al., 1963), Indian textile industry (Rice, 1958) and in American industry (Davis, 1957, 1960), we started to formulate a series of job design criteria (Emery and Thorsrud, 1969:105–106). These were to be used as guidelines in field experiments. They were supposed to cover the main psychological requirements that pertain to the content of jobs (taking for granted that wages, hours, safety, security, etc. would be covered by negotiated contract or similar agreement). Six basic psychological needs were formulated as a result of our exploration.

Psychological Job Needs

1. The need for the content of a job to be reasonably demanding or challenging, in terms other than sheer endurance, and to provide a minimum of variety,
2. The need to learn while on the job and to continue the learning process (which involves known standards and feedback of results),
3. The need for some minimal area of decision-making, involving responsibility that the individuals can call their own,
4. The need for some minimal amount of social support and recognition in the work-place,
5. The need for the individual to be able to relate what he does and what he produces to his social life,
6. The need to feel that the job leads to some sort of desirable future (beyond simply promotion in a status hierarchy, e.g., personal growth and vertical career development).

These requirements are not confined to operators on the factory floor, nor is it possible to meet them in the same way in all work settings. Complicating matters further, is the fact that these needs cannot always be judged from questionnaires or other methods relying on conscious expression (e.g., on a job where there seems to be no chance of learning, a worker will soon "forget" his need to learn).

The six requirements did not imply that we were going to work primarily on a psychological or motivational level of analysis. Nor did we intend them to constitute our entire model of man or human nature. They represent a minimal set of criteria according to which we could design and evaluate jobs in concrete technological settings. (A set of hypotheses for task structuring on individual, group and organizational levels were also formulated [Emery and Thorsrud, 1969:103–105].)

It will become clear in later parts of this chapter, how psychological job needs were linked to other aspects of organizational change that are necessary if major improvements are to be achieved and sustained in people's control over their own work situation and their participation in decision-making.

Some General Postulates About Enterprises as Systems

The company was the primary unit of investigation in the main phase of the I.D. project. Therefore we needed a conceptual frame of reference from which we could start our analysis of the concrete conditions under which participation on a company level would occur. Characteristics of sociotechnical systems had been analyzed theoretically by Emery (1959) and had been summarized in a more general framework by Emery and Trist (1960). The experience they had gained together with colleagues at Tavistock and empirical studies in the U.S., enabled them to develop some basic postulates about enterprises as open systems (Trist and Bamforth, 1951; Jacques, 1951; Rice, 1958; Herbst, 1961; Selznick, 1949; Blau, 1955; and Gouldner, 1954). During the 1960s, while our field work proceeded, more work was done by the Tavistock group to understand enterprise environment relations (Emery and Trist, 1965, 1972). In the same period, there was a general breakthrough of systems thinking in organizational research (e.g., Emery, 1969).

We do not pretend to have worked out our frame of reference for each field experiment according to the level of conceptualization reached in the publications referred to above. Nor did we pretend to have discussed with the joint research committee on the national level or the action committees on company level all models available. But we made it clear before each major step of our research that alternative models existed. We stressed the critical difference between (1) scientific management models, (2) a sociotechnical systems model and (3) human relations models. The second model and the implications involved in utilizing it were explored in realistic terms for each major step of project development on national and company levels.

We did not structure our research problems according to a preconceived "Grand Theory." Whatever the research group (and its wider professional network) possessed in terms of theory, it was not utilized to its greatest extent in every field experiment. The requirements of the situation and the capacity of research workers involved presented many limitations.

Our conceptual framework of the firm developed gradually as we struggled with our problem area. When we made our analysis of the first experimental plant in 1964, the postulates published five years later by Emery were used implicitly in our study. The following formulations are excerpted from Emery's introduction to systems thinking (1969). We have chosen to present them in a somewhat different form than his. This may distort some of Emery's intentions, but it will better represent the understanding of the senior research workers when they operated in the field, when they worked with managers and other members of collaborating organizations. These formulations listed below, functioned as guidelines for our researchers in explaining in concrete terms, the organizational phenomena dealt with in the experimental field situation.

1. The *goals* of an enterprise can be understood as special forms of interdependence between the enterprise and its environment. (The environment is represented in terms of easily measured inputs and outputs on the one hand [e.g., raw materials or outputs of certain products] and on the other hand, in much more intangible interdependencies [such as the common values of collaboration organizations].)

2. The enterprise as an open system, will strive for a steady state in relation to its environment by maintaining its growth rate on an optimal level and by maintaining constancy of direction in its goal orientation. (Growth can be defined not only in terms of measurable expansion but also in terms of achieving the same level with less effort, with greater precision or under greater variability; or it can also mean differentiation to achieve something new.)

3. The *variations* in the input of supplies and the output of viable products that the enterprise must cope with in a complex environment depend upon the *flexibility* of its technology and upon the degree of

self-regulation in its organization. Commitment to a *mission* and a *distinctive competence* will also increase the ability of the enterprise to adjust effectively the variations in its environment.

4. The steady state of an enterprise as a system in relation to its environment, cannot be achieved by any permanent form of input-output rates, internal change mechanism or environmental contact. *Leadership* and *commitment* of members are basic conditions for maintaining a steady state. The goals and values that direct the activities of members must be clearly defined; enough to maintain unidirectedness and growth. Commitment of members must be strong enough for them to respond to external requirements in the form of self-regulation. (The impact of such regulatory mechanisms in an enterprise like cost control, computerized planning, etc. must be viewed in terms of its contribution to self-regulation.) The measure of the efficiency of self-regulation, of whether the system is healthy, is to be found in the capability of the enterprise to fulfill the tasks arising from its goal. (A good record of performance, e.g., high profits, would not in itself exclude the possibility that potential capacity had in fact been reduced.)

5. The task of management is primarily governed by the need to match the actual and potential capacities of the enterprise to the actual and potential requirements of the environment. In other words, the *primary task of management is the boundary control* of the enterprise. To the extent that the manager has to coordinate internal variances in the organization, he will be distracted from his primary task.

6. An enterprise can only achieve the conditions for steady state if it allows its members a measure of *autonomy* and *selective interdependence*. The autonomy of members will enable them to make choices and to exercise control over their own work situation and will tend to increase their commitment. Internal coordination of organizational components through self-regulation will put limitations on autonomy of individuals and consequently on their commitment. These limitations can be overcome to some extent by allowing members of an organization a degree of selective interdependence. This is clearly illustrated by the way professionals relate to each other within the context of their organizations. It is less obvious on the level of rank-and-file workers.

A Stepwise Strategy of Research and Development

Our theoretical formulations above, concerning the enterprise and psychological job needs, may be more meaningful if we describe our research strategy as it unfolded in the early stages of the I.D. program some ten years ago.

1. *A joint national committee* was organized to represent labor and management, and was the first step taken in 1962. Its purpose has been to assist the researchers in planning, initiating, carrying out and evaluating the research.

2. *The choice of experimental companies* was left to the joint committee according to criteria set out by the researchers: size, location, type of technology, level of management-labor relations, and the company's potential ability to influence its own branch of industry.

3. *A systematic analysis of the company* was made to get an outline of the critical relations between company and environment, i.e., product markets, raw materials, financial situation, relations to research and education to the labor market and community institutions.

4. *The choice of experimental sites* within the companies was made in collaboration with management and shop stewards. We wanted a site with a boundary fairly well defined and also well placed for subsequent diffusion of results.

5. *Establishment of local action committees*, with representatives of operators, supervisors and management has proved to be of crucial importance for continued experimental changes.

6. *Sociotechnical analysis* of the experimental sites was undertaken in cooperation with action committees and company specialists. Major aspects of the analysis were:
   • variations in inputs and outputs of departments;
   • estimates of relative importance of differing variations;
   • establishing the primary tasks of departments;
   • description of work roles, status recruitment and training;
   • analysis of communication networks;
   • analysis of attitudes to work (related to job needs 1–6) ; and
   • analysis of the system of remuneration, wages, bonuses, etc.

7. *Company policy* was studied in concrete terms with respect to management practices (job allocation, training, incentives, etc.) and with respect to markets (materials, technical competence, labor, capital and products). How and by whom policy is made, has been important because experiments have usually involved questions of company policy.

8. *Programs for experimental change* were drafted in cooperation with personnel in the experimental departments and with company specialists. The action committees played a major role in formulating and presenting the programs. Typical features of change programs were changes in task structures, information and control systems, salary systems, etc. These changes are clearly illustrated in the four summaries of our experiments which follow later in this chapter.

9. *Institutionalization of a continued learning and organizational change process* is the final stage of each development project. Gradually the change process, and the responsibility for it, must shift from the action committee to the management and shop stewards or be otherwise assigned to formal parts of the work organization in terms of standing committees, etc. This can only be accomplished by incorporating the lessons of the experiment in the philosophy or style of management, thus making appropriate organizational changes.

10. *Diffusion of results* has been an objective of all the experimental studies undertaken in the I.D. Program. It has been clearly understood by the experimental companies that they would be carrying a certain responsibility to help the results of the research gain recognition within the industry. The central joint committee assumed a major responsibility for the diffusion process, together with the researchers, but it was obviously going to be necessary for the experimental plants to act as demonstration sites. Gradually, the researchers would have to take less responsibility for the diffusion of results and would be re-

quired to concentrate mainly on reanalysis and reformulation of the hypotheses and principles that formed the basis of these experiments.

The research strategy had to vary considerably according to local conditions (as we shall illustrate in the summary of the field experiments). Although these are presented separately, it should be kept in mind that they were actually four highly interdependent developments during the first years of the I.D. program.

BRIEF SUMMARY OF FOUR FIELD EXPERIMENTS

In each of the four cases we shall deal very briefly with the following aspects:
- general background condition of the enterprise;
- key characteristics of the experimental department;
- experimental changes;
- major results and constraints and
- diffusion on company level and on other levels.

THE FIRST FIELD EXPERIMENT (WIRE DRAWING MILL 1964–65)

Background Conditions of the Firm

- The experimental site (wire drawing) was part of a nationally well-established steel mill in a large city.
- Stable sales market and good profit margins had existed for ten years.
- Largely unskilled men came from the rural countryside and the merchant marine into routine jobs on two shifts in most departments. Some departments had mainly skilled and semiskilled men from a tight labor market.
- The tradition-bound firm was facing restructuring, but neither management nor union felt a great need for basic changes at the worker's level.

Key Characteristics of Experimental Department

- "Natural selection" took place among recruits, two-thirds adapted to routine work in approximately one and one-half years. But these were not enthusiastic volunteers for collaborative experiments.
- The major variations in the primary task (batch processing of wire) turned out to be caused by the quality of the raw materials used, and consequently the variations were outside the control of the experimental groups.
- Unpredictable variations between very high and very low work efforts were caused by "the one man–one machine system" where mutual help was impossible.
- Little interdependence existed between men on individual piece rates, who were earning a good wage.

Experimental Changes

- Individual job allocation was changed to group work-systems with job rotation between five to six men on six to seven benches (this was the main structural change).

- Operators learned additional techniques (multi-skills) through job rotation and a group trainee was to enter each group.
- Individual piece rate system was changed to fixed base rates plus group bonus on output.
- Minor technical changes facilitated local control.
- A local repairman was on direct call for the groups according to their needs.
- Clarification of group responsibilities as well as feedback of results was arranged.
- The foreman was supposed to move from internal coordination and local discussion of pay to departmental planning and boundary control.

Results and Constraints

- Members of experimental groups universally preferred the new system and reported greater job interest, more variety and greater group involvement. Learning, decision-making and job perspective mostly remained unchanged. (See section on psychological needs, this chapter.)
- A productivity increase of 20–25% caused major problems in wage structure and blocked diffusion in spite of group initiative for prolongation of the new system (the experimental groups were "too effective").
- Departmental evaluation concluded that new job design principles were clearly related to democratization but had to be introduced under less time pressure and integrated in management and trade union practice.
- The research group failed to induce continued organizational learning, even though related projects started in other parts of the company.
- Prearranged time limits of too short a duration resulted in poorly established experimental conditions and only two weeks of controlled experiment.
- The novelty of the exercise was too great for management and union, thereby limiting their utilization of the results to systematically institute policy changes.

Diffusion

- The joint national committee agreed after evaluation that new principles had proved valuable in spite of unfavorable conditions. Follow-up and continued experiments were encouraged.
- As a result of the diffusion, new experiments were introduced in new firms in two other industries.
- No direct diffusion took place in the same industry within the succeeding two years, when experiment number three began.

The major diffusion took place in terms of contacts between those involved in the first experiment and those in later experiments. This was basic to our strategy of change and to the whole I.D. program. The experiments should be viewed as successive steps in an institutional learning and change process on different levels of companies, industries and trade unions in Norway. Within this frame of reference, a partly unsuccessful developmental experiment can be very rewarding from a social action point of view as well as from a social science viewpoint. The report from the first field experiment became a standard introduction for new experimental firms.

Preliminary Conclusions from the First Experiment

Management and the local union never perceived the experiment as *their own*, but rather as an exercise carried out in loyalty to institutions on the national level. The company and the shop stewards did not experience any pressing need to utilize the experimental results. For management, conditions were rather good as they were, at least in most other departments, and no one could guarantee that the new system would not bring new problems along with the rather striking benefits that had been demonstrated. The exposure of an illogical piece rate system and a gross suboptimization of the previous man–machine system was a threat to the prevailing management philosophy. An even greater threat (or embarassment) was the fact that workers could organize and control their work better than the engineers had been able to.

The experiment was continuously viewed as a physical experiment particularly by the dominant group of industrial engineers. The researchers' model of a learning and growth process based on necessary and sufficient conditions for change was branded unscientific and routinely dismissed. Changes in worker behavior and attitudes were explained by engineers in economic terms or as Hawthorne effects.

The researchers' basic assumption regarding new forms of work organization had been sufficiently corroborated for them to be tested further under different conditions. When the same principles were shown to operate in traditional work groups already existing in other departments, and when results came from new experiments, renewed interest appeared in the first firm. Regarding the division of work, payment systems, and control systems, the basic assumptions of management (and partly those of the union) were clearly in conflict with the new ideas demonstrated by the experimental groups. The research group had insufficient time and personnel resources to work through with all parties the lessons to be learned. The researchers' experience with this particular type of social change process was limited. The collaborative partners on the company level had insufficient motivation and leadership capacity for integrating their new experience into current practices and policies. Nor had they gained sufficient trust in the researchers, their methods and the results reported. In spite of these findings, the partners on the company level invited the research group back for new experiments.

SECOND FIELD EXPERIMENT (PAPER AND PULP PLANT 1965–69)

Background Conditions of the Firm

- Experimental site (chemical pulp processing) was part of an old and fully integrated paper and pulp factory in a rural area, where the manufacturing industry was well integrated with primary industries and local culture as a whole.
- Sales, raw materials and finance markets were unstable and new technology favored larger firms operating in the same world market.
- The stable labor market was integrated with other industries and local

institutions and the labor-management relations were good but somewhat paternalistic.
- The tradition-bound firm with new management was under pressure for change, for technological and financial as well as social reasons.

Characteristics of Experimental Department

- Batch production on continuous shift was highly dependent on effective control and coordination of subsystems within and between departments.
- Variation measurement, information handling and control were critical for maintaining standards of quality and full production capacity.
- Specialized work roles left room for considerable autonomy for the majority of thirty operators in a tradition-bound status and contract system. Differentiated base rates existed with a bonus for quantity.
- A strong drive to tighten up technical and supervisory control had recently been started and some reduction in manpower was expected as part of a drive to overcome major problems following a business recession.

Experimental Changes

- Partly autonomous shift groups replaced the segmented role system. (This was the basic structural change.)
- Improvements were worked out in input and output measurements, and production standards were clarified.
- A new information room was built and data-handling between work stations and shifts was improved.
- Some decentralization of maintenance and technical service was planned.
- Supervisors and production management roles were redefined in the direction of boundary maintenance and away from internal coordination and control.
- Junior operators were trained for a multiple-role system and for limited job rotation.
- A new bonus system was set up to encourage continuous learning related to quality control. (Learning results were fed back on both the group and individual levels.)
- Shop stewards were to promote information and participation programs across shifts and departments.
- Management assumed special responsibilities of a technical nature and some guarantees were given regarding payment and manpower. (The last two points were important in order to transfer the ownership of the experiment to management and shop stewards.)

Results and Constraints

- Consecutive phases of system analysis, departmental information, group involvement and effective experimentation were followed by a period of stagnation.

- Partial fulfillment of experimental conditions led to cumulative learning on operator level, improving yield and quality of processing.
- A great number of local initiatives originated on the shop floor through the departmental committee to improve information, stability of processing, safety and "house keeping." (Forty main changes were introduced in two weeks.) The summer vacation was handled according to a local plan based on increased rotation among operators and a minimal number of temporary replacements.
- Internal communication and teamwork increased significantly on the operator level.
- Attitudes toward the new system were divided and a polarization occurred when further integration of processing and services dragged out and when the foremen turned against the new system. A new role for the foremen in the emerging situation was not developed early enough. After nearly a year of preparation and six months of rapid development and change, a year-long stagnation set in until new projects were begun in a neighboring department.

Diffusion

Diffusion within the company took place when a new project was started in the paper plant. Little research and other help came from outside. Foremen problems were dealt with as part of a new policy for increased autonomy to be introduced in all units.

Experimental projects were terminated as such and transferred into institutionalized labor-management programs. Management control systems were decentralized and service departments were given supportive instead of directive roles.

Diffusion across company boundaries occurred in terms of new institutional links to financial systems, to regional authorities and to the forestry industry. New sales policies developed as distinctive competence was sharpened, based on the improved capacity to switch rapidly between short runs of quality products.

Improvements in employer-union relations were significant: local union impact on the national level was strengthened mainly in educational and bargaining policy. Diffusion occurred on the regional level to the local industry and trade unions and to a new experimental company in the service industry (a new hotel where the director of the paper plant was a board member).

Little transfer occurred from the project company to other companies in the same industries, but considerable impact was observed in vocational training policy and in the area of organizational design in the process industries in general.

The major diffusion of results took place in terms of contact and mutual backing between experimental companies and unions involved in developmental experiments in different parts of the country.

The project had some impact upon development in an international oil company and was helped forward itself by a field visit from an experimental company in England. Some diffusion took place from the project company to firms in Sweden and Denmark.

Preliminary Conclusions from Second Field Experiment

The same basic principles of work organization were as effective in a complex chemical process technology as in a more primitive technology as found in the wire drawing mill.

The greater success in the second experiment could partly be explained in terms of a more integrated and active local culture around the paper and pulp company and in a greater need for and a higher capacity to pioneer in organizational change among top management and union leaders. Reorganizational capacity was built into the company structure on many levels. (A detailed case history and analysis of this particular experiment was written up by P.H. Engelstad [1974], and its personal and social consequences were explored by Elden and Engelstad [1973].)

The major breakthrough in the second experiment occurred after long periods of sociotechnical analysis and information diffusion on the shop floor and among management. Involvement on all levels took place in planning for the change (approximately one year). When a local action committee took over the experiment from the researchers, joint action for change was released. Considerable resistance occurred among foremen and production management and among some operators who previously held protected, high status jobs.

The company assumed responsibility, in close cooperation with local union and organizations on national levels, for transferring experimental lessons into new policies and practices. A five to ten year program of change was envisaged and has been monitored at varying levels.

THE THIRD FIELD EXPERIMENT (METAL FABRICATION 1965–71)

Background Conditions

- The experimental plant was small, employing one-hundred people. It was a subsidiary to a nationally well established firm in sheet metal products.
- Growing national and international market in home heating equipment, steel furniture and component parts for the automotive and other industries, had created increased sales over a ten year period. (Long term sales policy was dependent on outside agents.)
- This company enjoyed a stable labor market which supported a small village with manufacturing firms. It was also in a favorable position in relation to decreasing primary industries.
- There were peaceful but paternalistic labor-management relations in the mother firm located in a nearby city.

Key Characteristics of Experimental Department

- The entire production cycle was geographically and functionally separated from other departments and from the mother firm which supplied raw materials, specifications, technical service and sales. Localities were old and the equipment was simple, if not primitive.
- The department was a small unit, comprised of thirty people, mostly young women, in narrow, semi-skilled and unskilled jobs in pressing,

painting, assembly and packing operations. One person was trained and assigned to one job. Tayloristic job design for which the speed of manual operations paid on piece rates (as determined by Method-Time-Measurement or MTM) was critical for output.

- A close, informal, social network existed inside and outside the plant among people with recent employment in primary industries and housework. This culture was in rather sharp contrast to the philosophy and practices of technocratically oriented production management. Still considerable autonomy existed because of the distance to the mother firm.

Experimental Change

- Already existing tendencies to organize the production process according to work-groups was further developed.
- Training of all operators for more than one job took place and variations in work flow were approached in partly autonomous groups.
- Training of "contact men" began in each of the three groups (of approximately ten people) to coordinate variations between groups and to plan production in consultation with group members and the planning assistant in the office.
- The wage system was changed to fixed base rates plus departmental bonus on total output of products within given quality standards.
- Effective feedback of results was set up in quantitative and qualitative terms.
- To some extent, the local production engineer changed his attention from internal coordination and daily trouble shooting to boundary control of materials, specifications and small investment decisions.
- Partial decentralization of maintenance occurred and minor technical changes were introduced to increase group autonomy.

Results and Constraints

- After six months of information-gathering, sociotechnical analysis and collaborative preparation for change, a group system was established on the basis of a ten week controlled experiment. The group system spread afterwards to the neighboring departments of the experimental plant (total: one-hundred workers). No assistance was extented by researchers or by the main company in this diffusion process.
- Productivity increased approximately 20% during the experiment, with an additional 10% in each of the next two years.
- Earnings increased approximately 15% during the experiment and increased further about 10% in each of the next two years, after which periodic local bargaining set new income levels.
- The quality control system was slightly improved and standards well maintained.
- Turnover and absenteeism continued to be below average for the industry and region.
- The time perspective of the workers increased from two and one-half hours to two and one-half months, two years later.
- Authority of the production manager shifted to some degree towards

boundary control of departments but rather unstable relationships with
top management remained to cause some anxiety.

- Attitudes toward a group system were positive among 90% of the
operators. Significant improvement was experienced in job variation, in
learning, participation in decisions, and in collaborative relations generally.

- No basic changes were observed in management philosophy above plant
level.

- Some constraints existed on the trade union side, since results of experiments raised serious questions regarding the policies and practices of the mother firm collaborating closely with the local union.

Diffusion

Only limited diffusion occurred from the experimental plant to the main plant.
When a new and larger plant was built to take over from the experimental department, a similar group system (with no supervisors) was introduced among
the 300 to 400 workers (extended to 500 in 1974).

Limited diffusion occurred in the mechanical industry in Norway and in
the metal workers union while more impact was observed in Sweden where a
number of experiments were started after visits by study groups to the second
and third experimental plants.

The major impact on trade unions took place in terms of increased opposition to Taylorism in wage and control systems. Little influence was noticed in
the national Iron Workers Union (the bargaining agent in this plant) in terms
of decentralized bargaining and local developmental work, although this was
requested by shop stewards of the experimental plant.

This experiment became a very important part of information programs
and experiments in other companies and industries, mainly in Sweden. T.V.
teams and other reporters from several European countries visited the field
site. Those who were directly involved in the experiment had some concern
for the exaggerated publicity as long as more basic changes had not taken place
in the production control system and in the top management philosophy of the
mother firm.

A more detailed case history of this experiment was written up by the
field worker L. Ødegaard and reported by Thorsrud and Emery (1969). A
follow-up study was written up by T. Qvale (1974). More extensive conclusions
from this field experiment will be drawn at the end of this chapter.

THE FOURTH FIELD EXPERIMENT (FERTILIZER PLANT 1967–)

This experiment was undertaken by a large chemical manufacturing firm in
collaboration with the chemical workers' union and the research group. It
should be judged primarily as an exercise in diffusion of new principles of
work organization. The field site was part of a corporation with technologically
advanced plants spread over the country, buying its raw materials and selling
its products and technical capabilities in the world markets.

After a year of preparations and experiments in one new and one old fertilizer plant, top management and the union agreed that similar projects should

be started in several different plants. The following main changes were introduced in the first plant:

- Partly autonomous shift groups were established instead of specialized, segmented work roles. Four job levels based on competence in broad areas of operations were to be learned mainly by in-plant training.
- Further integration of processing and services took place initially by inclusion of all housekeeping and some maintenance in shift groups.
- Status hierarchy was reduced by two levels, one unskilled and one supervisory. An information system was built to cut across formal role and status structures and across specialist departments.
- A new wage system was based on fixed rates according to four levels of competence plus a plant bonus based on two major production vari-ables: improvements in quality and reduction of waste-pollution. After two years of experimentation, the first national contract was signed with a guarantee of continuous learning opportunities for all workers.
- Specialist and service departments were to be reorganized to encourage autonomy on individual, group and departmental levels. For some func-tions, like training, this did occur and, to a certain degree, also for rationalization. (Cost control, research and other services remained less decentralized, which seemed to slow down local developments.)
- A new philosophy of management was initiated, emphasizing participa-tion in decision-making on all levels. The new philosophy was not effectively worked through and some stagnation occurred.
- The efficiency of the new work-system could be evaluated in terms of improved production regularity and significantly reduced cost. The atti-tudes of production operators toward the new system were positive, while a large minority of skilled tradesmen were skeptical. Most sig-nificant in the context of the I.D. Program was the increased continu-ous learning, more participation in decision-making and the flattening of the status hierarchy.

As an exercise in diffusion the following experiences can be observed:

- The transfer and further development of new principles took place from field experiments in other branches to a "sheltered" area of a technologically advanced corporation. The strategy agreed upon by the joint national committee and the sponsoring institutions proved effective on the plant level but less so on corporate and trade union levels. Two out of four new company projects failed to get off the ground during the next three years. Responsibility for diffusion was placed in the formal bodies for labor-management participation, but did not result in effective joint action.
- Major barriers were observed among supervisors and middle manage-ment who felt that traditional roles were threatened. Alternative ones were not presented at an early stage of change. (After two years of stagnation, a two-year program was set up to establish alternative roles in lower- and middle-management, and extensive retraining was ar-ranged, covering several hundred supervisors and first-line managers.)
- Another constraint on change was the ineffective introduction of new principles in management services and specialist functions. The research group did not take an active role in this process of institutionalization,

which was probably a strategic error. A systematic evaluation of project results and corresponding training programs in the corporation may now (1974) be correcting this error. These programs can only be effective if based on policy clarification down the line of the corporate structure.

- Necessary changes in trade union policy will mainly depend on further commitment of national unions to extend their bargaining to new areas, e.g., to include in their contracts educational rights and principles for the use of new control systems. The models for doing this exist in the experimental plants. Another constraint is the slow process of decentralizing several aspects of contract bargaining to plant level.

- A great number of national and international labor- and management-groups have visited the fertilizer plant and facilitated informal diffusion of information. A great number of "grass roots" experiments have been reported, particularly in Sweden, based on information from the fourth field experiment.

AUTONOMY ON GROUP LEVEL AND ON OTHER LEVELS

As we have reported from the four field experiments, increased autonomy has been achieved partly through the development of autonomous work groups. It is important to note, that we have not limited ourselves to an approach which would necessarily lead to group-based work organizations. The six psychological job needs and the more specific hypothesis for restructuring jobs (Emery and Thorsrud, 1969:103–105) explicitly stated criteria applicable on an individual level—as well as on group and organizational levels. Many examples in the field experiments exist where individual jobs have been redesigned. However, the sociotechnical analysis and the suggestions for change as they come from those involved in all the four work-places, have led to a concentration of activities on the group level. The stepwise change process has always included compromises between individuals and groups. We could report a number of examples where individual operators, skilled tradesmen or privileged specialists, both in terms of job rewards and autonomy, had to adjust to role changes supportive to groups of unprivileged members. There were also many instances where groups were not allowed to organize their work in ways optimal for their autonomy, but suboptimal on some other level of the work organization.

Internal coordination of organizational components through self-regulation will (as stated in our postulates about enterprises as systems) put limitations on the autonomy of individuals. However, the higher the level of competence and knowledge of individuals, the easier it is to allow selective interdependence to members of an organization. This means in practice, that when groups increase their autonomy they will usually take over marginal tasks from specialists, who in turn can concentrate on higher-level tasks with a longer time perspective. The specialists may depend upon their membership in professional groups for their role definitions, or they may enter composite work groups. In the fourth field experiment, we could see role changes in both directions. Skilled mechanics and plumbers in some cases joined composite operator groups. Some personnel specialists joined decentralized groups of production management. Work-study specialists did the same for periods of time. The use of project organization will probably increase when partly autonomous groups or composite work groups are used systematically as parts of decentralized work organizations.

Job enlargement or job enrichment as developed by Argyris (1957), Guest (1957), Herzberg (1966), Mayers (1970) and others, begins from a motivational point of view on the individual level. No doubt, this approach may also be useful to achieve the previously stated objectives of the I.D. Program. However, the individual approach has its limitations within many types of technologies. It also seems to leave untouched major areas of decision-making on the supervisory and managerial levels that had to be included in the I.D. Program. Ford (1973) reports after long experience with job enrichment experiments, that "mini-groups" and "nesting of jobs," and the configuration of related tasks, may be the next big step forward.

The second and the third experiments led to work organizations without supervisors of the traditional type. The fourth experiment led to the development of four alternative supervisory roles, all of them leaving more decision-making to the level of partly autonomous work groups. In all the experiments, managerial roles were planned to change from internal to boundary control. Where stagnation has occurred in the experimental plants, these types of changes have not been sufficiently radical to reinforce the self-sustaining learning and growth process toward increased autonomy on lower levels of the organization. A lot more has to be learned about the new leadership required by the types of organizations emerging from such experiments as we have described. Emery has discussed this elsewhere (1967) and makes it clear that we have to be concerned with complex situations demanding more than simple decisions about means-ends relations. Most importantly, management decisions are not of this nature. They are decisions regarding values made in the face of incalculable risks. Development of institutional leadership as discussed by Selznick (1957) and others will be a critical issue in the next decade, if systems management is to include real sharing in decision-making between higher and lower levels of work organizations.

A Measure of Work Group Autonomy

Gulowsen (1971), building on Herbst (1962) and on a number of field studies, has developed a measure of autonomy on the group level. The criteria he has used may give further insight into the characteristics of the changes introduced in the field experiments summarized in this chapter. Gulowsen used a very simple scale for the grading of each criterion. A score of (+) was given when the group or individual members could make the decision either without interference or in cooperation with outsiders, (−) was used when they could not and (0) when the criteria were irrelevant for the groups. Sorting the workgroups according to how many of the criteria of autonomy they achieved, and sorting the criteria according to how many groups satisfied them, a matrix (Figure 1) was generated, showing that these criteria form a Guttman scale (Gulowsen, 1972).

Gulowsen indicated that his data may be insufficient for conclusions to be drawn, but his approach no doubt can open an important field of research. A major point is to improve the operational criteria of autonomy. When that is done, it will be easier to carry out comparative studies and accumulate theory on the basis of empirical studies.

Criteria

Groups	The group has influence on its qualitative goals	The group has influence on its quantitative goals	The group decides on questions of external leadership	The group decides what additional tasks to take on	The group decides when it will work	The group decides on questions of production method	The group determines the internal distribution of tasks	The group decides on questions of recruitment	The group decides on questions of internal leadership	The group members determine their individual production methods
	1a	1b	6b	2c	2b	3	4	5	6a	7
The logging group	−	+	+	+	+	+	+	+	+	+
The coal-mining group	−	+	+	+	+	+	+	+	+	+
The electrical panel-heater group	−	+	+	+	+	+	+	+	+	+
Alfa Lime Works, oven group	−	−	−	+	+	+	+	+	+	+
Alfa Lime Works, quarrier group	−	−	−	+	+	+	+	+	+	+
The rail-spring group	−	−	−	−	−	0	+	+	+	+
The ferro-alloy group	−	−	−	−	−	−	+	+	+	+
The galvanizing group	−	−	−	−	−	−	−	−	−	+

FIGURE 1.   A matrix for measuring work group autonomy. Gulowsen (1972).

If we use Gulowsen's data, we can see that the groups in our third field experiment (sheet metal/electrical panel heater department) rank among the three highest in terms of autonomy in a sample of eight. At the bottom of the list is a galvanizing group in the company where we made our first experiment. This group made decisions regarding only the working methods of individual members. Another group in the same company ("the rail spring group") ranks sixth, making the same type of decisions (plus three more) regarding group leadership, recruitment and distribution of tasks among members. These examples illustrate how we can make comparisons between groups with different degrees of autonomy. Gradually we should be able to refine this method and use it in the follow up of field experiments and other studies.

SOME PRELIMINARY CONCLUSIONS FROM THE FOUR FIELD EXPERIMENTS

When the report from the first four field experiments was published in Norway (Thorsrud and Emery, 1969) a newly established council for participation in industry took over the organized diffusion of results. The trade unions and employers organization sponsored this council jointly and agreed that the preliminary results and the principles followed in the experiments deserved further testing on a broad scale in Norwegian industry. During 1970 and 1971, a number of new experiments were started, only a few of which were directly influenced by the research team. Compared with the development in 1968 and 1969, it seems as if management of most companies were unable to follow-up effectively toward a new philosophy and practice of management. It can be no surprise to anyone who knows the inertia of traditional management structures, that it will take time to have widespread application of principles and practices suggested by the developmental experiments.

A second reason for a slower diffusion than what was expected from the pattern up to 1970, is particularly important from a social science point of view. The cautious detailed scientific approach to the early experiments appears to have created the view that job redesign required the heavy involvement of social science experts. The supply of social scientists in Norway was not adequate to meet these expectations. We have to reconsider whether the social science contribution need be so large. In fact, the development in Sweden has shown that the diffusion has occurred on a rather broad scale with very little direct involvement of social scientists (for further discussion of diffusion problems in democratization, see Herbst [1974b]).

The diffusion of sociotechnical experiments from industrial manufacturing into Norwegian shipping, is a clear indication that the new approach has come to stay. The diffusion into vocational and other aspects of education corroborates this trend. These two and other extensions of new concepts of organization are described in the Work Research Institute's catalog of programs and projects (Arbeidspsykologisk Institutt: Prosjekter 1964–1972, to be published in English in 1975). On the other hand, the rather slow diffusion in the manufacturing industry and the slow diffusion of new policies from the National Trade Union Council through the upper levels of national unions, represent some very real problems. The level of trade union activity on the local level has been significantly improved in the experimental sites. Union membership has increased as well as the involvement of shop stewards in formal bodies of representative participation. Significant extension has taken place in the issues covered in local and central collective bargaining. Most important perhaps, are the new contracts signed in the largest of the experimental companies, where the workers' right to continuous learning has been guaranteed through the collective bargaining process. Also important is the tendency among participants of the field experiments to influence the types of systems to be introduced in planning and control in the companies. In spite of all this, many trade union officials find it difficult to adapt to the strong demands for increased autonomy and for local initiative in company affairs as well as in the formulation of policies and practices of the trade unions themselves. In recent policy statements from trade union councils in both Norway and Sweden, where the participative experiments have become part of public debate of democratization in general, the message is this: the trade union movement will pursue further democratization in industry along three lines of action:

1. Extension of the system of collective bargaining to strengthen the voluntary arrangements for information, participation and local problem-solving in labor-management relations (i.e., works councils—long es-

tablished in Norway). Further influence on educational matters, on systems of supervision, on personnel management and on the introduction of new systems of rationalization, planning and control are important issues of trade union policy.

2. Extension of local experiments with new forms of work organization, including partly autonomous work groups, job enlargement and similar arrangements (but now possibly following a more participative design strategy such as pioneered by Emery and Emery [1974]).

3. Changes in the formal structure of company organization, if necessary, through corporate law. (E.g., the law passed January 1, 1973 placing worker representatives on the boards of directors of all companies with more than 200 employees.)

The diffusion of new organizational ideas in management seems to go in the same direction as indicated by the first two points above. Disagreement occurs when it comes to formal, legal changes to be established without complementary improvements in the concrete conditions for participation in the work-place.

PART II—THE ATTITUDES OF WORKERS IN DIFFERENT LOCAL ENVIRONMENTS AND DIFFERENT TYPES OF JOBS

The Industrial Democracy Program chose the company as the major unit of experimentation and analysis. However, it was made clear that other levels of analysis and social change were endemic to the solution of the problems of democratization. Other social scientists would go much further and claim that the general societal structure outside the company is more vital to the employees than their day-to-day job situation. Looking at companies as open systems, we would agree that some environments like the one in our second experiment (paper and pulp company) are much more open to the kind of changes we have introduced than companies in other environments. Firms situated in urban areas characterized by social disintegration would be much less open. The same might be true for companies in rural areas, more or less dominated by a single company, and by its special type of technology and social structure. To test some of these assumptions, we have made representative surveys in a number of companies in different environments. The analysis of the data is not completed but some of the results can be reported.

Some major characteristics of the four companies from which we report survey results are listed in Table 1. The first of these firms is our second experimental company. In the cement firm, which is known to have a very good industrial climate, some experiments had been run by the company itself. A sort of "gang" system and group production bonus had been introduced. This system was similar to traditional group work in mining and construction work, in forestry and farming. The metal manufacturing firm was one of the companies wanting to initiate sociotechnical experiments based on our research report. We acted as an outside resource group but were not able to establish the initial conditions for involvement and commitment necessary to get experimental changes off the ground. The metal processing company has not undertaken any experimental work of the type we have been involved in, but have lately been applying some ideas from the I.D. Program.

TABLE 1
MAJOR CHARACTERISTICS OF FOUR COMPANIES

	Paper and Pulp	Chemical Process	Metal Processing	Manufacturing
Number of employees	800	800	2,000	400
Location	Rural area with variation in industries near small city.	Rural area with mixed industrial structure near small city.	Dominating plant in an isolated community.	Industrial area in an Oslo suburb.
Type of technology	Process control chiefly concerned with quality and change between type of product.	Process control chiefly concerned with maintaining quantity level.	Process quantity depends chiefly on process quality control.	Batch production; control chiefly concerned with shift of product and scheduling.
Payment system	Differentiated base rates and departmental quality bonus.	Fixed rates and group production bonus.	Differentiated base rates and production bonus.	Individual piece rates.
Complaints concerned with physical environment	Gas and noise in some areas.	Noise, dust and draft in many areas.	Heat, gas and noise in some areas; chemical burn and poison hazards.	Noise in many areas, machine accident hazards.
Finance and market stability	Instability in financing, in input and output markets.	Stability in financing and in output markets.	Stability in financing and slight instability in output markets.	Stability in financing and instability in output markets.
Ownership	Limited company with no single group in control. The company is an "institution" in the local community.	Part of a national industrial group with a few financial institutions as strong share holders. The company is an "institution" in the local community.	Government 50% and international group 50% (after 1968). The company is acting as a "provider" of the local community.	Privately controlled, limited company. The company is struggling for a viable share of the labor market.

General Job Satisfaction in the Four Companies

A survey covering social and occupational backgrounds, task and social structure of the work situation, physical working conditions and private and community conditions was undertaken. One-hundred different items were covered in questionnaires, usually with five or more alternative answers for each item. A stratified sample of approximately eighty workers were covered in each plant.[1]

One item among a number of questions related to satisfaction and complaints regarding work, was phrased in the following way: "How do you eval-

---

[1] For further details, see Bjørg Aase Sørensen (1972).

uate (like) your job in general?" The response to this question is tabulated below in Table 2.

TABLE 2
GENERAL JOB SATISFACTION

	Paper & Pulp		Cement		Metal Processing		Metal Manufacturing	
	Skilled	Unskilled	Skilled	Unskilled	Skilled	Unskilled	Skilled	Unskilled
Satisfied with the job	85%	81%	85%	62%	58%	44%	75%	43%
Dissatisfaction with the job	15%	16%	10%	36%	45%	54%	25%	45%
No response— do not know	0%	3%	5%	2%	7%	2%	0%	12%
Total in percent	100%	100%	100%	100%	100%	100%	100%	100%
Total	14	66	55	21	14	50	34	12

There are some striking features in Table 2 which correspond with case material we have from our field sites.

Satisfaction Variances

The variations in general job satisfaction corroborates the data from our case material, showing gross differences between the views of the people living in the community surrounding the paper and pulp plant and the views of the people residing in the community surrounding the metal manufacturing plant. In the paper and pulp company with the highest level of job satisfaction, we found a situation where life outside of work plays quite a meaningful part of a person's total life-space. As Table 2 shows, job satisfaction at the paper plant is not limited to the skilled workers. At this plant, unskilled people from agriculture, seafaring and other nonrelated types of industrial manufacturing, acquired relatively secure, well adjusted employment in the paper mill. We found as many reasons for job satisfaction at the paper plant as there are indicators of job satisfaction. The voluntary turnover is usually very low, thus contributing stability to the work-place (although at the time of our study, nearly 200 people had left the company within three years, due to a recession in the industry). The private homes of the workers, which they have built and own themselves, show a steadily improving standard of living. The work itself has always demanded something more from the workers than mere physical endurance, thus improving the self-esteem of the workers. The status system of the company does not dominate the local environment, but rather is complementary to it: the assistant acid boiler might well be the leader of a religious group in the community; the chief engineer might play second violin in a small orchestra; the trade union chief shop steward always has a strong link with the local Labor Party, usually a majority in the community council; and the administrative director might be a member of the board of the nearby college or of the new hotel. All these factors contribute to increasing interests outside the work-place, which in turn contribute to greater job satisfaction and greater output.

This is a summary of our data from the local community surrounding the paper and pulp mill. The industry has lived through a difficult period in an international market, in spite of its handicaps in size and technology.

The metal manufacturing plant represents a contrast to the paper and pulp mill in most respects mentioned. This is reflected in our case material and corroborated by the subjective evaluation of management when they compare the situation in their main plant today with the situation some twenty years ago. They are reminded of this contrast in culture because they still have a small subsidiary where much of the culture has survived.

The cement factory had much of the same work and community culture as that of the paper and pulp mill. Management and union leaders reported the same positive experience from reestablishing something like partly autonomous work groups. This represented a deviation from scientific management, breaking with the traditional one-man, one-job principle. Job satisfaction as well as productivity and earnings are reported to have improved. It should be stressed that this plant has not been part of the Industrial Democracy Program although some mutual learning has taken place between this plant and experimental plants.

The metal processing plant represented a case of almost total domination of a surrounding local culture. It was part of industrial reconstruction after World War II and one of the important sources of income in Norway's foreign trade. It was also one of the most technologically structured work organizations developed in Norway in the early 1950s. Today, different trends in organizational thinking are beginning to have an impact upon company structure, but the technology still dominates. The fractional task and role structure is strong, the control system is rigid and the lack of social integration in the local community is likely to continue for quite some time.

Variations in Job Satisfaction Between Skilled and Unskilled

In the metal processing plant one would expect, following Blauner (1964), that the process technology would contribute to a higher job satisfaction rate than in the batch production technology of the metal manufacturing plant. We did not find this to be true, although we might assume that some of the high job satisfaction in the cement plant and in the paper and pulp mill can be accounted for by their process technology. The skilled workers at the metal processing plant have a lower job satisfaction level than skilled workers in all the other plants. We would tend to explain this as a general effect of fractionated and disintegrated work culture and local culture, but the work environment (pollution, gas, noise, etc.) provides for an additional explanation. The skilled workers in the aluminum plant have a higher job satisfaction rate than the unskilled, as we would expect. The same holds true for the metal manufacturing firm. In the latter instance, we found that the skilled workers had been able to maintain a somewhat privileged situation, often at the expense of the unskilled workers. This was reflected even in their work-life in terms of meaningful jobs and in their living conditions in the community.

Is this difference on job satisfaction between skilled and unskilled workers unavoidable in modern industry? In the paper and pulp mill, we find very little difference between skilled and unskilled in terms of job satisfaction. We cannot explain this finding in any other way than by pointing to the fact that in this mill, unskilled as well as skilled workers have experienced significant improvements in their task and role relations during the experimental period. This seems to be corroborated if we look at the difference between skilled and unskilled workers in the cement factory. Here they have not experienced the effects of a sociotechnical change of the same type as in the experimental paper and pulp mill. So-called unskilled workers in modern industry are not necessarily condemned to meaningless jobs.

It is important to note that the survey of workers' job satisfaction was carried out in the paper and pulp mill at a time when the consequences of a new type of work organization were not yet experienced by employees in all departments. We would expect the general job satisfaction to improve further when this is the case. However, we would not be surprised if the skilled workers experienced relatively less improvement since they may feel that the unskilled workers are getting more than their fair share of job improvements. This we found to be the case during some phases of experimental change in our fourth field experiment in the chemical industry. This last remark should be taken as a warning that we do not think that survey data alone, such as those we are presenting here, should be taken as proof of basic changes in attitudes toward jobs, or as strong indicators of reasons for such changes. The data we have presented here are supported by our case material from the plants and their environments.

These remarks about attitude surveys stem from more than merely our methodological orientation. More important is our experience that attitudes of employees surveyed in terms of job satisfaction may tend to be quite negative during phases of change. When people are personally involved in basic changes in their work situation, as we have seen in our sociotechnical experiments, they are impatient to achieve important goals. They are dissatisfied with major problems which might earlier have been perceived not as *their* problems that they could do something about. Many of them might have expressed greater job satisfaction before they believed something could be done to improve their lot (Emery and Thorsrud, 1968).

Interpretation of Democratization in Different Plants

Since the sociotechnical experiments were part of the Industrial Democracy Program, it seems important to check the opinions of workers when they have been involved in experimental change and when they have not. In our representative survey, this was done in the form of the following question: "*What do you mean by the concept of industrial democracy?*"

They could choose between one or more of seven alternative answers. The responses have been tabulated in Table 3.

The noteworthy factors in this table are perhaps those indicating that among workers in the paper and pulp mill who have been involved in experimental change, we find the largest percentage of employees who have a different perception of what industrial democracy means. To workers in this company, the concept has a meaning in both the traditional sense and in terms of improved conditions for personal participation. The great majority of them, some 64% of the skilled and some 50% of the unskilled, put the greatest emphasis on the concrete conditions for personal participation (direct representation). In the mechanical metal manufacturing plant, only 12% of the skilled and 18%

TABLE 3
MEANING OF INDUSTRIAL DEMOCRACY

	Paper & Pulp		Cement		Metal Processing		Metal Manufacturing	
	Skilled	Unskilled	Skilled	Unskilled	Skilled	Unskilled	Skilled	Unskilled
Direct influence on the job itself and the planning related to it (direct representation)	21%	8%	19%	11%	8%	23%	0%	0%
Direct influence on the job itself and autonomous work groups (direct representation)	43%	42%	14%	28%	14%	23%	12%	18%
Direct influence on the job itself, autonomous work groups and representation on boards (indirect representation)	29%	12%	19%	11%	36%	19%	50%	20%
Other definitions— mainly board representation	7%	20%	10%	7%	14%	14%	0%	21%
Do not know; no response	0%	17%	38%	34%	28%	21%	38%	41%
Total in percent	100%	100%	100%	100%	100%	100%	100%	100%

of the unskilled assign major importance to this particular alternative. In this same metal manufacturing plant, 50% of the skilled and 20% of the unskilled define industrial democracy in the traditional way (indirect representation), while close to 40% of skilled and unskilled workers assign no particular meaning to the concept.

PART III—THE BOARD OF DIRECTORS, COMPANY POLICY AND INDUSTRIAL DEMOCRACY*

Introduction

The sociotechnical approach was initially (around 1950) directed at problems on the operator-group level in mining and industrial manufacturing. The main

* I am indebted to a number of people who have helped me with the study. I will not give a long list of names here, but mention just one: Fred Emery whose ideas about how to set about the task of describing board behavior were of a tremendous help. Concerning this Part III in particular, I would like to express thanks to William H. McWhinney and Benjamin R. Aston who have given valuable comments.—Bjørn Gustavsen

contributions on this "school" are still on this level of problems and organization, but we are moving toward higher system levels and new types of problems. When moving away from work situations on the industrial shop floor, the term "sociotechnical" tends to become somewhat misleading because "technical" is easily associated with technology, which does not carry the same meaning, for example, at the top management level as it does at the shop floor level. What characterizes the sociotechnical approach is the weight placed on *tasks* as the basis for understanding and controlling social structure on any level, irrespective of the role of technology in the constitution of the task.

The following is a summary of an empirical study exemplifying the use of a sociotechnical approach to the analysis of problems not only at group level, but at the level of the enterprise as a whole. The study refers to boards of directors in industrial companies in Norway, delimited in such a way as to include the approximately two hundred larger ones as the basic population.[2] It was the Industrial Democracy Project's phase A (reported upon in Thorsrud and Emery, 1969) which brought us into contact with problems concerning the governing bodies of enterprises and such questions as the roles of different types of bodies, the formation of company policies, and the role of capital and professionalization in society. In 1964, a broader and more comprehensive study of these problems was launched, a study which was not completed until 1971 (Gustavsen, 1972).[3] The chief aim of the study was a further clarification of the role of boards of directors in industrial companies, but the boards were to be seen in the light of a context made up not only of the enterprise and its immediate surroundings, but also society at large.

The Problems

The points of departure were the following four questions:
1. What degree of control do the boards exert over the companies?
2. What characterizes the content of the decisions made at board level?
3. What degree of freedom do the boards have; can they to a large extent define their own roles or are they primarily instruments for something outside themselves, e.g., the interests of shareholders, of capital in general, or the like?
4. What is the basis of (a given level of) control over the companies on the part of the boards; is it educational and experiential prerequisites (cf., the idea of "professionalization" as put forward by Burnham

---

[2] The law on companies where members' liability is limited by shares, has marked similarities from country to country. International trade has called for a relatively high level of standardization, but this does not mean that differences do not occur. As this is not the place for a discussion in depth of legal aspects, I will just mention the point. It can be added that the board of directors in Norwegian company law is closer to *Aufsichtsrat* and "Supervisory Board" than *Vorstand* and "Managerial Board." Another point to be mentioned is that Norwegian company law makes no distinction between public and private companies; they are subject to the same legal requirements.

[3] The following is a concentrated and highly simplified presentation of some of the main results of the study. As the report in Norwegian runs to 450 printed pages, it should be clear that the following is not a sufficient basis for evaluating the methodology, theoretical framework, etc., of the study. An abbreviated English translation has been planned for quite a while, but hitherto neither time nor other resources for attacking this task have been available.

[1941]) ; is it something else, or is there no need for any special qualifications at all?

Points of departure. The first part of the investigation was a series of relatively unstructured interviews with board members, managing directors, bank managers, etc., where the main object was to gain some knowledge of the field. These interviews were used as the basis of a *typology* of boards.

To construct a typology, a model of cases or issues for decision at the top level of the company was needed and was drawn from the framework put forward by Simon (1947). The influence or power of the board becomes a question of the number of elements taken up for evaluation/decision, and the amount of redefinition made, and new inputs given by the board.

The minimum board is characterized by considering only those issues which the law explicitly demands that the board decide upon, and actually not providing much new input even for these elements.

The board of consultants is characterized by exerting influence over such elements that might fall within the professional competence of the board, i.e., in law, economics or the like. An alternative, resulting in a board of the same general type, is that the managing director brings up before the board only those issues where he experiences a need for emotional support, for example, because of the "loneliness at the top."

The supervisory board considers those aspects of the individual cases or issues which have a bearing on the more general developmental trends in the environment of the company, with a view to initiating corrections to the present course of action if it is perceived to be necessary. Such a board seems rather passive when one looks at the enterprise from a day-to-day perspective, but this gives a somewhat false picture.

The limited policymaking board is characterized by being interested in much the same types of elements as the supervisory board, but provides more input for the decisions. Such a board will often be relatively strongly engaged in such areas as financing, general aspects of market strategies and the like, while, for example, personnel policy, the technological aspects of investments, etc. will be left to the managing director and his staff.

The policymaking board considers such a broad set of elements in relation to all areas of decision-making that it can be said to make the policy of the company in general.

The managerial board holds an even more prominent position in relation to the company than does the policymaking board, in that it takes upon itself decisions about those issues which are ordinarily handled by the managing director and his staff.

There are also things common to all the boards, among them being the elements of a setting or role, determined by legal requirements. As a point of departure, the principal role of the board as set forth by Thorsrud and Emery (1969) was taken as given: that the board has to do with the management of the enterprise as wealth or capital.

We had, then, on the one hand a set of general and rather broad normative requirements, and on the other a series of actual behavioral forms. To explore further the factors determining what role the board actually comes to play, case studies of five different boards/companies were conducted. The studies were of an historical kind, and covered the period from 1954 to 1968.

Space does not allow for more than a brief sketch of some aspects of one of the cases.

A Case: The Beta Company

In the period from 1954 to 1968, the Beta Company[4] experienced an increasingly problematic situation. One illustration is profits/losses over time, as pictured in Figure 2, on the basis of the annual balances.

Initially, in 1954, the board played the role of a minimum board. Both board and management considered the situation to be good: in 1954 there was a 30% return of owners' capital; the return on working capital as a whole was 15%; external financing amounted to about 50% of the total capital; the level of liquid assets as measured by "banker's ratio" was 1.9, very close to the ideal norm of 2.

There were, however, some clouds appearing over the horizon. The rather bright general situation of the enterprise was greatly due to the after-effects of the Second World War, to which had been added the general world boom created by the war in Korea. Beta exported most of its products, and was dependent upon a world market where a large number of producers operated. The main customers, however, were located in Europe.

During the 1950s, the effects of the wars wore off, and the relationship between market demands and production capacity slowly but steadily changed

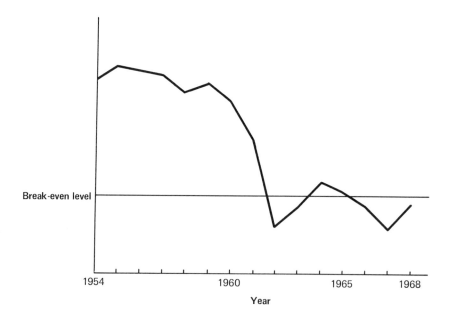

FIGURE 2. The relationship of gross profit to break-even point in the Beta Company, after depreciation but before taxes and capital reinvestment.

---

[4] The Beta Company is the paper and pulp company whose production plant was the site of one of the experiments of the industrial democracy project.

to the disadvantage of the producers. When the prices came under downward pressure—which happened in 1957–58—one would expect a decrease in investments within the industry. In actual fact, the opposite happened, for two reasons: one was the idea of reducing costs per unit through increasing the scale of production, a rather common philosophy at the time. The other was more specialized and involved the raw material situation. In the late 1950s, possible shortages of wood as a raw material had the effect of accelerating investment programs in many companies. These companies tried to secure for themselves a "home base" of suppliers sufficiently large to meet the possible needs of a more distant future. A further critical factor entering the picture in the late 1950s, was the formation of the European Common Market. For the products of Beta, there had been differences in the duties imposed on exports to the various countries which formed the Common Market; in 1960 the duties were harmonized on the basis of the highest of the previous duties, an occurrence which worsened the problems of European producers outside the Common Market.

In 1962, the situation had become critical in the view of the board and the managing director. The board adopted a policy parallel to the one followed by many other companies within the industry: to increase capacity with the aim of reducing costs per unit produced. To finance the program, large loans had to be raised and the board was confronted with a critical choice. Could it take the risk of drawing in the capital needed if there was a probability of losing it? The board had to engage itself in the evaluation of the market situation and the medium and long term development of the industry. It went one step up the control scale and became a supervisory board.

The investment program was accepted and put into effect. As one can see from Figure 2, it had the effect of turning the tide, but for a short time only. In 1964–65 the decline set in again, and in 1965 it was again clear that another basic policy decision was called for. The board was strengthened by adding a new member with special competence within the industry. Another large investment program was no longer possible; it would not be possible to raise a sufficient amount of capital on the assets of the company. After a thorough working-through of the situation, it was agreed that if the company was to survive, no aspect of it could be taken for granted. One had to question every aspect of it from the types of raw materials to the types of market and product. Such a total evaluation was made, and elements of a new enterprise were constructed as a policy goal. The board again changed character, moving from supervisory to limited policymaking in that it actively went into the development of policy in such areas as raw materials and markets. It was also during 1965 that the board decided to participate in the industrial democracy project, and consequently became the participating company in the second field experiment of Part II, this chapter. This was part of the "loosening up" of the board in its explorations of new features of the enterprise.

Preliminary conclusions. This and other case studies suggested the following conclusions:

1. The board's role seems to be linked to the policy issues faced by the company and may change as the seriousness or breadth of issues change. The board must be seen as part of a system of roles for the formation of company policy.

2. The policy generated by the members of the policymaking system seems to vary with the situation of the company.

Given these two points, the important question became how to define and classify the "situations" which seem linked in some way to board behavior. The framework for description and classification of organizational environments developed by Emery and Trist (1969) was used as a point of departure.

The case studies showed, however, that environmental differences alone were not sufficient basis for giving a tentative explanation of differences in board behavior. It was also necessary to take into account characteristics of the resources of the companies. Among these characteristics, the dimension "rigidity-flexibility" emerged as important: the ability of the enterprise to meet external changes without having to change the composition of its concrete resources. A description and classification of "situations," then, called for a conceptual scheme taking into account external as well as internal factors. At the one extreme are enterprises with a relatively high level of flexibility of resources, which are confronted with a relatively placid environment. At the other extreme we find enterprises with highly rigid resources which are confronted with highly complex environments where turbulence might occur.

There is a need for a general term to characterize the "environment of the board"; in the Norwegian language, the English term *problem-situation* suggested itself, a term that is rather awkward, but nonetheless accurate. The extremes are called respectively, simply and highly complex problem-situations.

This framework allowed for the presentation of the basic results of the case studies (Table 4) in the following form (again I repeat the highly simplified character of this presentation).

TABLE 4
THE RELATIONSHIP BETWEEN PROBLEM-SITUATION,
COMPANY POLICY AND TYPE OF BOARD

Characteristics of the Problem-Situation	Company Policy	Type of Board
Simple	Rationalization, removal of bottlenecks; "trimming", etc.	Minimum board
	Larger steps to increase capacity and the like, but without any change of the basic characteristics of the company	Supervisory board
Highly complex	Evaluation and change of the basic characteristics of the company (its character in the terms of Selznick [1957])	Limited policy-making board

Follow-up

There was a follow-up study of twenty companies in addition to the original five case studies, with the twenty selected so that each four had problem-situations as close as possible to one of the case companies. This made for five groups of companies with five units in each group, the problem-situation of each group ranging from simple to highly complex.

The following dimensions were included in the follow-up study:

1. Reasons why issues are, or are not, brought up before the board.

2. To what extent and for what reasons the board takes the initiative to bring up issues for consideration and decision.
3. To what extent and within what fields the board contributes information to the decisions of the company.
4. The level of control over the company exerted by the board.
5. To what extent special restrictions and the like are put upon the managing director (to what extent the board acts as a "house of lords").
6. To what extent the board adopts a broad perspective in its decisions.
7. The educational background and types of experience of the board members.
8. The external contacts of the board members, and how and to what extent they are used.

Some of these dimensions were further split up into variables, and in relation to all dimensions/variables, item lists were constructed. In the analysis, indices were constructed from the lists of items.

On the basis of the case studies, the hypotheses concerning dimensions 2, 3, 4 and 6 above, were that the scores indicating the activity level of the board would increase in accordance with increases in the level of complexity in the problem-situation of the company. In relation to dimension 5, the hypothesis was the opposite; dimensions 7 and 8 will be taken up later in the chapter.

Roughly, the hypotheses were borne out by the follow-up and thereby strengthened. Here space allows us to look more closely at only one of the dimensions, and we will select no. 4—level of control in general.

Problem-Situation and Control

The results for the twenty-five companies are presented in Figure 3; the values along the y-axis are sums of scores on ten of the thirteen items which were used in the questionnaire.

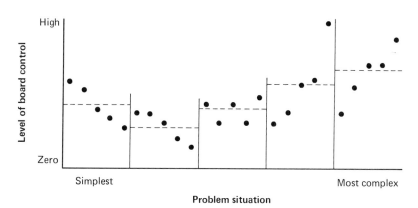

FIGURE 3. The level of control exercised by the company board in relation to the complexity of the problems handled.

Note: The companies are grouped into five categories of problem situations, ranging from the simplist to the most complex. Broken lines are the within-group mean values. The level of board control score is the sum of 10 items' scores, for each of which the amount of board control was determined on a three point scale of high-, medium-, and low-zero.

We shall use these data to go a little further into one point. Some aspects of Figure 3 are highlighted if we denote the averages for each group with points and draw two least-square lines (Figure 4).

This indicates that variations in the problem-situation have two effects: the line which is rising towards the right indicates the connection which is discussed above: the more critical the problem-situation, the higher the level of influence from the board; the other line can be taken to indicate that simple problem-situations, which call for very little activity on the part of the board, can be utilized to engage in other types of activity than those which emerge from the need to cope with a given problem-situation. We can put forward the following tentative hypothesis: the less critical the problem-situation, the greater the degree of freedom at the board level. This seems to be an aspect of a more general truth about organizations; when it does not take much to cope with the external conditions, a series of different organizational structures and types of decisions are possible without the survival of the company being endangered.

The Prerequisites for Functioning as a Board Member

Dimensions 7 and 8 (above) refer to the prerequisites for functioning as a board member. In general, there are the following three possibilities:

1. There are no prerequisites which must be fulfilled; loyalty towards certain goals—e.g., the growth of the shareholders' capital—is sufficient.
2. Conditions concerning education and experience must be fulfilled.
3. Conditions of a social character must be fulfilled, e.g., in terms of contacts with other board members, bank managers, state authorities, etc.

We are touching here upon an old field in the discussion of the relationships between companies and society, where the question of professionalization of managerial roles has played an important part (see Berle and Means [1932]; Burnham [1941]; Galbraith [1967]). This also involves the question of connec-

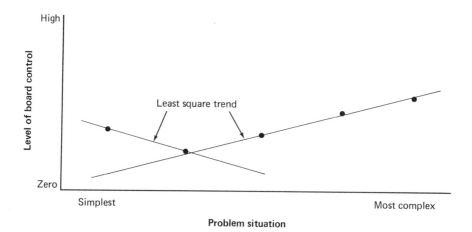

FIGURE 4. Mean score of the company boards on the level of control exercised over problem situations of varying difficulty.

tions between those who manage capital and the society in which they operate, a question discussed by Mills (1956), Baran and Sweezy (1968) and others.

Two major empirical findings emerged in the data from the twenty-five companies: (1) that there was no connection between educational and experiential prerequisites fulfilled by the board members and the problem-situation of the enterprise; and (2) there was a connection between the problem-situation and contacts external to the company: the more complex the problem-situation the better the contacts and the more active the use of them by board members.

With regard to dimensions 4, 7 and 8, the questionnaire contained two main questions: one referring to the board as it actually was, the other to what sort of board the managing director would like to have if he alone had the option of picking a board. This made it possible to calculate the differences in scores on "is" and "ought" for all units on all three dimensions and correlating the differences. The results are depicted in Figure 5.

The figures are correlation coefficients (Spearman's rho) calculated on the basis of the scores of the twenty-five units on the variables mentioned in the text.

Together with other data, which would be impossible to analyze here, this suggests that external contacts are the more important prerequisites at board level. This, again, raises a series of new questions and perspectives of which only some will be discussed.

Functions of External Contacts

The first question to arise is why external contacts might be of paramount importance. The point of departure is that the board is directly concerned with the control of an open system, which means that it must deal first and foremost with aspects of transactions between the company and its environment. The case material suggested at least two specifications of this.

1. The need for information about such things as what other companies, governments, etc., are planning to do. We cannot go into this point in depth in this chapter, but it is beyond doubt that a high level of information exchange actually exists between companies, and between companies and government agencies.

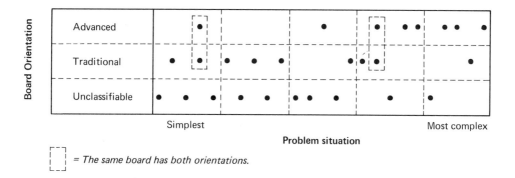

FIGURE 5.   Orientation of the company board in relation to complexity of problems handled.

2. The need to be able to influence the acts of other companies and other organizations. The exchange model seems to apply to this aspect; today company A promises not to interfere with company B's plans, while B promises the same to A tomorrow. Such a system can work since exchanges take place over time: the individual actor, board or company sometimes gives but sometimes takes.

This suggests the question of the relationship between enterprises in terms of competition and cooperation; a topic well known in economic theory but also appearing in more sociologically oriented analyses of enterprises and/or industrial society. Within our framework, this problem belongs primarily to a certain range of problem-situations: those where the disturbed-reactive environment appears. In such environments, it does not seem as if unlimited competition is the optimal relationship between enterprises. At least a certain degree of "co-respective" behavior (Schumpeter, 1947) seems to be advantageous to all concerned. Even though both empirical investigations and deductive reasoning point to limitations on competition occurring in the disturbed-reactive environment, two important questions are still relatively open. The first refers to the level of co-respective behavior: where does the balance between competition and cooperation actually lie? Different points of view have been put forward, from the rather loose norm of mutual consideration suggested by Perrow (1970) to the bloc theory of Baran and Sweezy (1968). The second question refers to situations other than those generated by a disturbed-reactive environment; the possible functions of "co-respective" behavior under other conditions than intercompany competition are much less discussed in theory.

With respect to the second question, we found that external contacts are a factor of *general* importance and not restricted to problem-situations where the disturbed-reactive environment is present. The usefulness of such contacts in a turbulent type of environment is fairly obvious; the external contacts we observed included not only other companies in Norway and abroad, but also other types of organizations and state authorities. In general, it seems as though a superstructure in the form of a social network emerges in relation to industry as a whole under conditions of disturbed-reactive environment; a network, which, when it is established, becomes of great importance to the emergence and handling of more complex problem-situations.

When a general network encompassing a large number of enterprises is brought into existence, it can, under certain circumstances, promote the emergence of turbulence. On the other hand, the network can also prevent the emergence of turbulence because it increases the companies' possibilities for controlling the environment through joint action. As far as we have been able to judge for the situation in Norway and areas with which Norwegian companies interact strongly, the second outcome has been more important than the first.

With respect to the degree of co-respective or coordinated action among the companies of Norway, we have limited data. If we compare interlocking board membership among Norwegian companies with what obtains in Sweden, it is clear that there is less of this phenomenon in Norway. On the other hand, there are strong employer associations among Norwegian companies through which limited but effective coordination among companies is achieved in collective bargaining and in relation to the government regarding labor policies.

THE QUESTION OF INDUSTRIAL DEMOCRACY

The problem of industrial democracy is one of the more special issues of relevance to the boards, but an issue of particular interest to the Work Research Institute. One of the chief reasons behind the general study of boards was to be able to further our research and experiments within the field of industrial democracy.

When the issue of industrial democracy is raised with reference to boards, there are two sets of problems emerging as particularly important. One refers to employee representation on the board level, the other refers to the role of the board in relation to such forms of work organization as we have tried to develop through the Industrial Democracy program in Norway (see Parts I and II, this chapter). We will examine both of these problems.

The Role of the Board and New Forms of Work Organization

We have as yet no strong empirical data linking such things as changes in board role to changes in shop floor organization. We know for example that changes have taken place at lower organizational levels and at the board level simultaneously—the Beta company treated earlier in this chapter is an example—but we have not conducted any systematic study of the relationships between these two processes and consequently are limited to less systematic impressions from individual cases and to deductions from theoretical points of departure. We hope, though, to expand this field in the years to come, because it is a chief link between representative systems as solutions to the problem of industrial democracy and such solutions as increasing workers' control over factors in their work assignments.

Some main points, however, can be summarized. The role the top governing bodies choose to play is highly important for the forms of work organization that develop at the level of the shop floor. This point needs to be emphasized: the model of the organization upon which the experiments are built is a model of the enterprise as a whole. The need to operate from a total system perspective has been verified through all the Norwegian experiments. What, then, does this mean with reference to the role of the board?

We can summarize experience and deductions up to now in the following three areas:

1. The board—and top management in general—must take care of such tasks as are commonly called boundary control and not engage in the regulation of internal processes, beyond what is necessary from a boundary control perspective.
2. The top management must be supportive in relation to the shop floor developments.
3. The management of the enterprise must be socially responsible.

Boundary control. The need for top management to take care of the boundary conditions follows from different points of departure, and is well recognized today. This means that any exploration in depth is unnecessary here. I will mention just one point: if top management develops an inward-directed orientation, they will usually force the rest of the managerial hierarchy to do the same, resulting in decreasing possibilities for autonomy as one approaches the shop floor. As suggested in the earlier discussions in this chapter, the possibilities for developing an inward-directed orientation on the part of top management will depend upon circumstances, particularly the type of problem-situation with which the enterprise is confronted. The danger of inward-directedness occurs first and foremost in enterprises where the problem-situation is—or is perceived as—relatively simple, resulting in simple boundary control tasks. The freedom from difficult boundary control problems can be utilized to take over the control of internal processes on a detailed level.

Supportive management.   The need for supportive management of the enterprise is more critical and important today since it is not so clearly recognized. It is still widely believed that developments at the shop floor level can take place relatively independently of managerial developments at the top level. This, however, is quite clearly not the case; but we are as yet not able to present a complete set of requirements for supportive management. First we have, of course, the very simple fact that any development whatsoever on the shop floor is dependent upon the enterprise remaining financially solvent. Theoretically more important is that having to manage "crisis situations" and/ or "crisis policies" is not particularly well suited for furthering the development of autonomy on the shop floor. Since developing autonomy at all levels is a difficult learning process with a long term perspective, the enterprise as a whole must take on some of the important characteristics of learning environments. The squeeze and tension generated by crises are usually not compatible with the conditions for long term learning processes.

A more positive way to examine supportive management orientation is from the standpoint of the concept of "organizational slack." Learning and development is a process which by itself is in need of resources; if the aim is to make a more radical break with traditional ways of organization, the process will usually cost more than it returns in benefits in the initial phase, measured according to conventional cost-benefit criteria. One must, for example, have the freedom to experiment, and if this freedom is to be real one must have the freedom to fail now and then. The point is that the enterprise must be managed in such a way as to provide for the necessary resources and freedom. This is no simple requirement when one takes into consideration that the resources might have to be forthcoming for years.

Another important consideration has to do with evaluating development programs aiming at increasing autonomy on the shop floor. There are two issues here: (1) what criteria are used and (2) what time perspectives to apply. Quite a few companies seem intent on evaluating solely in terms of short or medium term productivity increases on the part of operators. Autonomy is perceived as a gift "granted" the operators, for which they have to pay in productivity terms. This is, of course, not a particularly progressive approach to the industrial democracy issue. This issue has ultimately to do with commitment to values, and shop floor autonomy is no exception. This means that a broad set of criteria must be used and a long term perspective applied. Autonomy must usually function within a productivity framework, and is often —particularly through learning—correlated to productivity, but democratization in its own right must be the primary consideration.

Social responsibility.   The third of the general requirements for capital management is that it should be socially responsible. One approach to this aspect can be the models of man to be used at the different steps of the thinking about work organizations (see Chapter 1, "Work in Modern Society," this volume). Our models have progressed from the mechanical man image to the social man, and from the social man to the self-actualizing man. It emerges increasingly more clearly, however, that one will also have to take an account of *political man* in future thinking about organizations. It is reasonable to believe that enterprises are moving toward a situation where a certain level of consensus among all important groups in the organization on the general role of the enterprise will be a prerequisite for the trust and confidence, which will be more necessary in order to work with more advanced forms of organizations than the controlling-type, conventional structure upon which most enterprises depend today. One interpretation of socially responsible capital management is that it should invest in forms of production, products, and services that at least meet some minimum standards of quality and will contribute in a positive way to the solution of some of the more pressing social problems of industrial societies. It is quite clear that a relatively large number of enterprises in our Western world have already fallen below such standards. For an enterprise to remain below standards, it would in all likelihood be in the process of maintaining an alienated relationship with its employees, thus enabling the employees to avoid responsibility for the acts of the enterprise.

Employee Representation in the Governing Bodies of Companies

We turn now to the other aspects of the democratization problem: the question of employee representation in the governing bodies of the enterprises, including the directing board. As part of the Norwegian Industrial Democracy program, this consideration was made the object of a study in the early 1960s. Since the report from this study is available in English (Thorsrud and Emery, 1969), we will in this connection just state the main conclusions of this study.

In general, employee representation did not emerge as a particularly successful way for taking care of the interests of the employees. The role of the representatives tended to develop in one of two directions: either they tried to act like "establishment" board members; or they became rather passive. These developments were not the results of strong disagreements concerning how to decide, but rather the result of a dilemma concerning what *issues were relevant* for decision-making on the board level. The traditional role of the board required it to consider issues with a bearing on the allocation of capital, while the employee representatives wanted to bring up personnel matters for settlement at board level. Unless the employee representatives could force the board to consider certain types of issues new to the board, they found it very difficult to function as representatives. These conclusions had a rather limited empirical basis, however: there had been only a handful of state owned industrial companies that practiced board representation since the late 1940s.

Even though previous experience with employee representation did not seem to be an unqualified success, such a system was still introduced in Norway from the beginning of 1973. In companies employing at least fifty persons, the employees were given a one-third representation on the board; minimum two members. In companies employing at least 200, there was established a new body—the company assembly—which was to have at least twelve members (of whom the employees are to elect one-third). In the larger companies, board representation was not specifically declared in the law, but it was presupposed in the motives that such a representation would be granted the employees by allowing the worker representatives in the company assembly to elect a number of board members in proportion to their share of the company assembly members. This has been followed up in practice: companies employing 200 or more have board representation as well as a company assembly made up of one-third employee representatives. Initially, this system was applicable to companies within industry and mining. It will be successively expanded to cover trade, transport and other fields.

This system raises a number of questions. One question to be considered as the point of departure for some reflections in this chapter is how the development will be regarding the above-mentioned conflict between the traditional (past) role of the board and representation of employee interests. This question is worth commenting on, because broad representation as a solution to the problems of industrial democracy is presently being discussed and analyzed in various countries all over the world. This chapter allows space for only a few remarks.

If we assume that there might be a conflict between the traditional role of the board and the special interest of employee representation, there are—in principle—two ways of solving the conflict: one can redefine the role of the board or one can redefine the basis for employee representation.

No open position was taken on this issue when the law about employee representation passed the Norwegian parliament. Nor could such an explicit treatment of a rather complex political problem be expected. In the documents and debates preceeding the passage of the law, some remarks were made that could be interpreted to lean toward the view that the representative system is intended to produce new general board members; that is, people who can play the role of an ordinary board member but at the same time contribute to new types of investment decisions and company policies in general. These remarks, then, indicated that one solution to the conflict is to abolish the thought that the representatives are to pursue the more concrete specific interests of the employees in the given company.

The pointers in the direction of the above solution are not many, however; the majority opinion indicates that the idea is representative of concrete employee interests.

One way to approach the problem concerning the fate of this system is to query if there are important new or different conditions, compared to the situation at the time of the first study. Some conditions are clearly different.

First, the system is now general; not limited to a few state owned companies. It received broad political backing when it passed the Parliament. On board representation, the decision was actually unanimous; there were more disagreements concerning the company assembly. That the system is general, means that various elements can now support each other and that an apparatus for the education and training of the employee representatives can be established—and has in fact been established.

Second, the general situation of Norwegian industry has undergone changes. Norway has felt the impact of the global changes in priorities with the increases in emphasis on energy, raw materials, food and space. Access to resources has now become relatively more important, with a corresponding reduction in dependence upon market strategies. Access to resources is to a large extent a problem of a political or semipolitical nature. The dominant political force in Norway is the Social Democratic movement, with the Labor Party in the center. This means that employee representatives—who usually belong to the same political party—are often just as well equipped to act as "gatekeepers" to important elements in the environment as the "ordinary" board members.

Third, changes are taking place concerning the financial system and the finance institutions. In the future, relatively more of the capital for investment will be under the control of the state (oil revenues), and the banks will be brought under a stronger state influence. This will also influence the "gatekeeper" and "watchdog" issue, in favor of the employee representatives.

Fourth, there are various trends that eventually might mean improved possibilities for a new industrial policy on the national level, and consequently also on the level of the individual company. Ecological consciousness and populistic political tendencies are relevant in this connection, the same holds for the degree of freedom on the national level that stems from the rise of prices on the international energy, raw materials and semi-finished goods-markets, that are typical of the Norwegian export structure. These and other trends might lead to the emergence of a new type of industrial policy calling for new types of policy makers.

These points will have most of their possible effects in the long run. It might be, however, that some effects are felt already. We have some data concerning "here and now" experiences with the new system, because for a while the Work Research Institute has been in charge of a new research program within this field. Under the policy guidance of a steering committee made up of representatives from the Ministry of Labour, The Federation of Trade Unions and the Employers Confederation we are trying to find out what happens in the introductory phase that is now emerging. Since there are no reports that have as yet been cleared for official use, there is not much we can say. The general impressions gained up to now seem, however, to be that the system generally receives a positive evaluation from both sides: employee representatives as well as the shareholder-elected board members—and for that matter, managing directors. The reasons for this concurrence, though, are somewhat different. The representatives seem to feel that they get something done: they feel that they bring up new issues and generally get something out of the system. To a degree, this might be due to the fact that new situations are often experienced in a more dramatic light than real circumstances call for, but it is probably also due to the fact that something is actually done; the system seems to afford some real payoff as well. Turning to the other board members and to the managing directors of the companies, the emerging satisfaction with the new system seems to be caused by the possibilities for sharing the responsibility for decision-making with the employees through their representatives. It seems as if the companies today operate in much more troubled and politically difficult waters than they did only a few years ago, and that there is a real need to have interest groups like the employees involved in the decisions if one does not want to experience difficulties when trying to carry out the decisions. However this may be, the new system seems to be evaluated as a reasonable success. It appears that some of the changes in general conditions must have made themselves felt, since the new system has been received in a politically balanced and mature way by both sides of the controversy.

REFERENCES

Argyris, C.
1957 Personality and Organization. New York: Harper & Row.
Baran, P. and P. Sweezy
1968 Monopoly Capital. London: Pelican Books.
Berle, A.A. and G.C. Means
The Modern Corporation and Private Property. New York: Macmillan.
Blau, P.
1955 The Dynamics of Bureaucracy. Chicago: University of Chicago Press.
Blauner, R.
1964 Alienation and Freedom. Chicago: University of Chicago Press.
Burnham, J.
1941 The Managerial Revolution. New York: John Day.
Churchman, C.W. and F.E. Emery
1966 "On various approaches to the study of organizations," in J.R. Lawrence (ed.), Operational Research and the Social Sciences. London: Tavistock.
Davis, L.E.
1957 "Towards a theory of job design." Journal of Industrial Engineering (June) :305–309.
Davis, L.E. and R. Werling
1960 "Job design factors." Occupational Psychology (April) :108–132.
Elden, J.M. and P. Engelstad
1973 A Preliminary Evaluation of the Hunsfos Experiment. AI Doc 38/73. Oslo: Work Research Industries.
Emery, F.E.
1959 "Characteristics of socio-technical systems." Document 527. London: Tavistock.
1967 "Some characteristics of enterprises and their leadership." Manpower and Applied Psychology (2) :26–34.
1969 Systems Thinking. Harmondsworth, Middlesex, England: Penguin.
Emery, F.E. and M. Emery
1974 "Participative design." Canberra: Australian National University. Mimeographed.
Emery, F.E. and O.A. Oeser
1958 Information, Decision and Action. Melbourne, Australia: Melbourne University Press.
Emery, F.E. and E. Thorsrud
1969 Form and Content of Industrial Democracy. London: Tavistock (Published in Norway in 1964).
Emery, F.E. and E.L. Trist
1960 "Socio-technical systems," in C.W. Churchman and M. Verhulst (eds.), Management Sciences: Models & Techniques. Oxford, England: Pergamon.
1965 "The causal texture of organizational environments." Human Relations (18) :21–32. (Reprinted in Emery [1969])
1969 "The causal texture of organizational environments," in F.E. Emery, System Thinking. London: Penguin.
1972 "Towards a social ecology." London and New York: Plenum Press.

Engelstad, P.H.
  1974 "The Hunsfos case of the Norwegian Industrial Democracy Program
        from 1964–1973." AI Doc. 2/1974 (March). Oslo: Work Research In-
        stitutes.
Ford, R.N.
  1969 Motivation Through the Work Itself. New York: American Manage-
        ment Association.
  1973 "Job enrichment lessons from A.T.&T." Harvard Business Review
        (January).
Galbraith, J.K.
  1967 The New Industrial State. London: Hamilton.
Gouldner, A.W.
  1954 Patterns of Industrial Bureaucracy. Glencoe, Ill.: Free Press.
Guest, R.H.
  1957 "Job enlargement." Personnel Administration (20):9–16.
Gulowsen, J.
  1971 Selvstyrte arbeidsgrupper. Oslo: Tanum.
  1972 "A measure of work group autonomy," in L.E. Davis and J.C. Taylor,
        Design of Jobs. Harmondsworth, Middlesex, England: Penguin.
  1973 "Organization design in industry—towards a democratic sociotechnical
        approach." Personnel Review 2(2):30–37.
Gustavsen, B.
  1972 Industristyret. Oslo: Tanum.
Herbst, P.G.
  1962 Autonomous Group Functioning. London: Tavistock.
  1974a Socio-technical Design: Strategies in Multidisciplinary Research. Lon-
        don: Tavistock.
  1974b "Some reflections on the work democratization project." AI Doc 13/
        1974. Oslo: Work Research Institutes.
Herzberg, F.
  1966 Work and the Nature of Man. New York: Harcourt, Brace and World.
Jaques, E.
  1951 The Changing Culture of a Factory. London: Tavistock.
Lewin, K.
  1935 A Dynamic Theory of Personality. New York: McGraw-Hill.
  1951 Field Theory in Social Science. New York: Harper.
Mann, F.
  1957 "Studying and creating change: a means to understanding social orga-
        nization." Industrial Relations Research Association Publication, No.
        17.
Mayers, M.S.
  1970 Every Employee a Manager. New York: McGraw-Hill.
Mills, C.W.
  1956 The Power Elite. New York: Oxford University Press.
Nichols, T.
  1969 Ownership, Control and Ideology. London: Allen and Unwin.
Perrow, C.
  1970 Organizational Analysis: Sociological View. London: Tavistock.
Qvale, T.U.
  1973 A Norwegian Strategy for Democratization of Industry. AI Doc. 14/
        1973. Oslo: Work Research Institutes.

1974   The Nobo Case of the Norwegian Industrial Democracy Program. Oslo: Work Research Institutes.

Rice, A.K.
1958   Productivity and Social Organization. London: Tavistock.

Schumpeter, J.A.
1947   Capitalism, Socialism and Democracy. New York: Harper.

Selznick, P.
1949   T.V.A. and the Grass Roots. Berkeley: University of California Press.
1957   Leadership in Administration: A Sociological Interpretation. New York: Harper.

Silverman, D.
1970   The Theory of Organizations. A Sociological Framework. London: Heinemann.

Simon, H.A.
1947   Administrative Behavior. New York: Macmillan.

Sørensen, B.A.
1972   "Industrien som Levevei." Mimeographed. Oslo, Norway: Work Research Institutes.

Tannenbaum, A.S.
1966   Social Psychology of the Work Organization. Belmont, California: Wadsworth Publications. London: Tavistock.

Thorsrud, E.
1970   "A strategy for research and social change in industry: a report on the Industrial Democracy Project in Norway." Social Science Information 9(5):65–90.
1972a   "Complementary roles in action research." Working paper for Arden House conference on the Quality of Working Life, New York. (To be included in a forthcoming publication edited by E.L. Davis and J.C. Taylor of the Quality of Work Life Program, Institute of Industrial Relations, University of California, Los Angeles.)
1972b   "Policy-making as a learning process," in A.B. Cherns, R. Sinclair and W.I. Jenkins (eds.), Social Science and Government. London: Tavistock.

Thorsrud, E. and F.E. Emery
1969   Mot en ny bedriftsorganisasjon. Oslo: Tanum.

Trist, E.
1968   "The professional facilitation of planned change in organizations," in Management and Motivations. Penguin Modern Management Readings. Harmondsworth, Middlesex, England: Penguin.

Trist, E., et al.
1963   Organizational Choice. London: Tavistock.

Trist, E. and K.W. Bamforth
1951   "Some social and psychological consequences of the Longwall method of coal-getting." Human Relations 2(4):3–38.

CHAPTER **11**

Motivation for Work

Mitchell Fein

Professional Engineer, New Jersey

1. MOTIVATIONAL FACTORS

Managers all over the world have long sought the secret of how to release the motivation genie. The payoff from increased productivity of human work would be enormous. But judging from practices in industry and the tumult of action and reaction between workers and management, the genie remains locked in his magic urn.

The subject of motivation receives increasing attention from management in this country. In a study of motivation concepts and practices conducted by The Conference Board (formerly, NICB), Rush (1969) found that of 302 companies, 80% had an interest in the behavioral sciences. More than three-fourths of the firms sent their executives to outside courses and seminars dealing with behavioral science concepts. There is undoubtedly great intellectual interest in behaviorists' proposals among managers. But Rush's (1969) study shows that very few companies have put the behaviorists' proposals into practice in operating their plants, particularly in relations with workers.

Popular Behavioral Motivation Concepts

The general notion in industry regarding motivation is that managers must motivate their employees. Actually, it works the other way around: motivation results from the urge *within* a person to do something, to accomplish a task, to reach a goal. At most, managers can provide a climate which will nourish the growth of motivation within workers. Equally, if not more important, is the perception the workers have of the working climate and their readiness to view management's goals as in their own best interests.

Many able and dedicated behaviorists are engaged in research on human behavior to provide an understanding of how people react as they do, with the ultimate aim of enabling people to live more fulfilling lives. Industrial behaviorists propose that the fulfillment process will pay handsome dividends to industry in more effective operating organizations and increased productivity.

Rush's (1969) study of managers' views of behavioral science showed that Douglas McGregor stood out as the behaviorist who had most influenced managers' opinions, followed by Frederick Herzberg. Though their teachings are differently oriented, there is a broad base common to their theories. Each must be considered separately and, at times, together.

McGregor is best known for his Theory X and Theory Y concepts, which were generally taken by managers as McGregor's version of two opposing styles of managing. But as McGregor (1967:79) continually tried to clear up, "Theory X and Theory Y are *not* managerial strategies: they are underlying beliefs about the nature of man that *influence* managers to adopt one strategy rather than another. McGregor proposed that in a climate of trust and respect, employees would be encouraged to become involved in their work and accept the goals of the organization as their own. This would lead to increased productivity.

McGregor drew inspiration from Maslow (1954), whose theory of personality and motivation stems from his humanist and idealized concepts of human behavior. Maslow's famous "Hierarchy of Needs" (1954) postulated that man aspires through a succession of needs, starting with his basic subsistence, up through safety, belongingness and love, esteem, and finally to self-actualization. Maslow reasoned that a hungry man is motivated to food and bodily needs but, once these are achieved, he no longer strives for them. The logical extension of his needs-motivation theory is the maxim that "a satisfied need is no longer a motivator of behavior." Maslow contended that all humans have the capacity to climb through the motivational hierarchy but cautioned that some people will never aspire past their lower needs.

Maslow (1965:ix) conceptualized man with the capability of striving to higher aspirations, of finding fulfillment in creative tasks. His idealism is epitomized as the human striving in a "... culture that would be generated by 1,000 self-actualizing people on some sheltered island where they would not be interfered with," which he called Eupsychia. Maslow longed for his utopian concepts to reach the whole human species and thus, improve the world. It is obvious why Maslow's humanism and idealism caught the attention of the behaviorists. Here were concepts which, if they could be made operational, could shake the world.

Job Involvement Needs

An insight into McGregor's reasoning can be gleaned from an excerpt from his writings:

> Management often asks, "Why aren't people more productive? We pay good wages, provide good working conditions, have excellent fringe benefits and steady employment. Yet people do not seem to be willing to put forth more than their normal effort." It is unnecessary to look far for the reasons. Consideration of the rewards typically provided the worker for satisfying his needs through his employment leads to the interesting conclusion that most of these rewards can be used for satisfying his needs *only when he leaves the job.* Wages, for example, cannot be spent at work. The only contribution they can make to his satisfaction on the job is in terms of status differences resulting from wage differentials ... Most fringe benefits ... yield needed satisfaction only when the individual leaves the job. Yet these, along with wages, are among the major rewards provided by management for effort. It is not surprising, therefore, that for many wage earners, *work is per-*

ceived as a form of punishment, which is the price to be paid for the various kinds of satisfaction away from the job. (1960:39–40)

McGregor contends that since workers' physiological and safety needs are well provided by social legislation and management, the motivational emphasis of workers has shifted to their social and egoistic needs. He maintains that

> Unless there are opportunities *at work* to satisfy these high level needs, people will be deprived; and their behavior will reflect this deprivation. Under such conditions, if management continues to focus its attention on physiological needs, the mere provision of rewards is bound to be ineffective, and reliance on the threat of punishment will be inevitable. Thus one of the assumptions of Theory X will appear to be validated, but only because we have mistaken effects for causes. (1960:40–41)

McGregor's main thesis is that workers have a need to find fulfillment *at their work*. If this does not occur, he predicts workers will be deprived, resulting in a work force which is negatively inclined to management's goals. Some workers might even become mentally ill. We do not need large-scale studies to learn that workers do not identify with management's goals. But is McGregor correct in pinpointing the cause? On what grounds does McGregor base his conclusions that workers must find fulfillment at work? His writings offer no proof of this contention. In an early article, in discussing the basis for his concepts of motivation, McGregor says, "... I will draw heavily on the work of my colleague, Abraham Maslow of Brandeis University. His is the most fruitful approach I know." But several years after McGregor wrote *The Human Side of Enterprise*, Maslow (1965:55) questioned the validity of McGregor's concepts:

> ... a good deal of the evidence upon which he bases his conclusions comes from my researches and my papers on motivation, self-actualization, etc. But I of all people should know just how shaky this foundation is as a final foundation. My work on motivations came from the clinic, from a study of neurotic people. The carryover of this theory to the industrial situation has some support from industrial studies, but certainly I would like to see a lot more studies of this kind before feeling finally convinced that this carryover from the study of neurosis to the study of labor in factories is legitimate.

Maslow's warning to the behaviorists that his concepts required further experimentation has not been heeded by the behaviorists during the past fifteen years since he postulated them. In a study hypothesising work behavior, Korman (1970) questions Maslow's concepts which have served as the basis for the thinking of McGregor and other behaviorists:

> ... this theoretical approach has gained great popularity in many management and psychological circles. One wonders why, however, since so far as the writer is aware, *it has only been tested once as a theory of performance in an industrial context, and that test provided little or no support* (italics in original).[1]

---

[1] The test referred to by Korman was by D.T. Hall and K.E. Nougaim. For an examination of Maslow's need hierarchy in an organizational setting, see Hall (1968).

Herzberg's theories parallel McGregor's in basic ways, also stemming from concepts of a hierarchy of needs and self-actualization. Herzberg is most popularly known for his two-factor theory of motivation-hygiene, which postulates that satisfaction and dissatisfaction are not opposite ends of a continuum. He contends the opposite of satisfaction is *no* satisfaction. In the reverse, the opposite of dissatisfaction is *no* dissatisfaction. Herzberg proposed that motivation was encouraged by satisfiers, which he defined as job content factors: achievement, recognition, work itself, responsibility, advancement and growth. The job context factors he labeled as dissatisfiers were: company policy and administration, supervision, working conditions, interpersonal relations, salary, status, job security, personal life.[2] Herzberg contends that only the satisfiers are motivators. He defined the dissatisfiers as maintenance factors, because their presence is needed to maintain a person's level of performance; more will not add to performance but less will lower it. Herzberg also referred to the dissatisfiers as hygiene factors.

Equally important to Herzberg, as it was to McGregor, is the concept that motivation will result from workers' involvement in performing meaningful work. But Herzberg goes further; he states that working conditions, salary, job security and other dissatisfier-maintenance factors will not act as motivators even if they are improved. These behaviorists propose that motivation hinges on the extent to which workers are meaningfully involved in their work. If this concept is valid, then there must be radical changes in industry in relations between workers and the production process.

Job Dissatisfaction

Some behaviorists believe that increasing mechanization in industry creates an environment which stultifies workers and robs them of their creativity and vitality. Gellerman (1963:93) proposes that "Management's greatest task, if it is to stop the trend toward the dehumanization of work and tap man's creative potential more fully, is to fashion this environment into a stimulus, not a suppressor." Other behaviorists, including Argyris, Kornhauser, Likert and Whyte, regard division of work as leading to job dissatisfaction, monotony, boredom and ultimately to reduced performance.

The HEW (1973) sponsored study, *Work in America*, found that the primary cause of dissatisfaction of white and blue collar workers stemmed from the nature of their work:

> . . . significant numbers of American workers are dissatisfied with the quality of their working lives. Dull, repetitive, seemingly meaningless tasks, offering little challenge or autonomy, are causing discontent among workers at all occupational levels.

The study reports that the discontent of women, minorities, blue collar workers, youth, and older adults would be considerably less if these Americans had an active voice in decisions at the work-place that most directly affect their

---

[2] For an overview of Herzberg's theories, see Rush's (1969) NICB study. For Herzberg's research and theories, see Herzberg (1966) and Herzberg, Mausner and Snyderman (1959).

lives. "The redesign of jobs is the keystone of this report . . ."; work must be made more meaningful to the workers.

But a contrary study on the trend of job satisfaction in the United States from 1958 to 1973, conducted by the U.S. Department of Labor (1974), found that:

> In spite of public speculation to the contrary, there is no conclusive evidence of a widespread, dramatic decline in job satisfaction. Reanalysis of fifteen national surveys conducted since 1958 indicates that there has not been any significant decrease in overall levels of job satisfaction over the last decade.
>
> There is no convincing evidence of the existence of a direct cause-effect relationship between job satisfaction and productivity. In reality, the contribution of job satisfaction to productivity is probably indirect and more likely to be reflected in reductions on the "cost" side of the corporate ledger than in increases on the output side. These indirect benefits are associated with reductions in turnover, absenteeism, alcohol and drug abuse, sabotage and theft—all of which have been linked to some degree with job dissatisfaction.

The percentage of satisfied workers, based on seven national surveys, rose from 81% in 1958 to 90% in 1973. The Gallup organization found a relatively consistent level from 1963 to 1973, averaging 88.8%. The very high levels of worker job satisfaction, confirmed over fifteen years by reliable studies, are completely opposite to the dire predictions of the school of behaviorists which proposes that jobs must be changed to raise job satisfaction.

A study by Form (1973) reported that:

> Three areas of work satisfaction were studied for four operations which varied in amount of worker control. Respondents were auto workers in four countries which varied in extent of industrialization. Most workers believe that their work integrates their lives, they prefer to work in the industrial sector, and they report that their jobs are satisfying. Nowhere did assemblyline workers dwell upon monotony.

He also states that:

> . . . this study shows that auto workers, both in countries where industry is recent and where it is not, generally feel the same way about working, factory life, and the job. Some differences do appear with increasing industrialization, but they are relatively small. Machine work does not make workers more unhappy at any industrial stage. Nor do workers heed the lament of the intellectuals that the monotony of the job drives them mad.

A study by psychiatrists Siassi, Crocetti and Spiro (1974) of worker dissatisfaction in a large automobile plant found that 95% reported themselves as satisfied with their work. They cautioned that:

> To impute boredom, alienation, anomie, or the seeds of mental illness to another man's work or existence is a hazardous thing. To some blue

collar workers, the social scientist's preoccupation with books, dry articles, tables of statistics, and obsessive academic discourse must seem more boring, more alienating, more fraught with anomie, than his own existence. That worker might provide excellent evidence that the lonely, dissatisfied social scientist has a much higher rate of surveyed mental illness, psychiatric utilizations, and suicides than any UAW population.

A reliable index of things which dissatisfy workers and which they want is readily seen in their demands at the bargaining table. Nowhere are there demands for enriched work. Yet many behaviorists propose that workers' apathy and hostility to managements' goals will be lessened and even removed by making work in offices and factories meaningful to workers. They counsel that this can most effectively be accomplished by establishing opportunities for workers to participate in their work and by restructuring work through job enlargement and enrichment.

Participation

Participation and involvement of employees in their work are among the most frequent suggestions by behaviorists and management theorists of ways to improve human performance and organization effectiveness. Of the several approaches to create meaningful work, participation seems the easiest to institute, since all that need be done by management is to create a fertile environment and for workers to participate in. No new machines need be purchased, no production process must be changed, no costs are incurred. All that need be done is to change workers' and managements' attitudes. But as experiences have proven over the past thirty years, participation in the full sense as conceived by the behaviorists is practically not attainable.

The management and behavioral literature treats participation broadly, as Schregle (1970:117) discusses in an article:

> Workers participation has become a magic word in many countries. Yet almost everyone who employs the term thinks of something different. There are people who feel that workers participation is the panacea for solving most labor-management relations problems and that it will even become the underlying concept of the future society. Some people use the term as a synonym for what they call industrial democracy. Still others use it as the battle cry for uprooting the present system of ownership and management of the economy. Again, for others it is more a tool of applied psychology to be used to counteract the dehumanization of industrial work. Still others employ the term "participation" with regard to specific procedures, for instance the consultation machinery in an enterprise, negotiation over problems of displaced workers, or profit sharing.

Since participation has assumed major importance in the development of more effective managing strategies, it is vital that managers are assured of the validity of the participation concepts. Are behaviorists on solid ground when they propose that participation by workers will benefit workers, improve production effectiveness and on the whole benefit society? To establish participation requires that management and employees *both* desire it. Moreover, for participation to be of any value to management and meaning to workers, workers must have the capability to participate. The following sections test participation concepts in various ways against significant worldwide experiences over the past thirty years.

Attitude of managers toward participation.   To determine how managers feel about the value of worker participation and the concepts and approaches used by managers in their work, Haire, Ghiselli and Porter (1966:16, 21) conducted a study covering 3600 managers in fourteen countries, from West Germany to Japan, including the United States. One of their significant findings was that, on the question of worker initiative and leadership, "In each country, in each group of countries, in all countries taken together, there is a relatively *low opinion* of the capabilities of the average person ..." Yet, on questions of the managers' own attitudes to managing, "... these managers felt that participative, group-centered methods of leadership are more effective than traditional directive methods."

Obviously, the managers were preaching en masse what they were not practicing! As a group, they had low opinions of workers' capabilities in relation to initiative and leadership—the essentials for effective participation. Yet surprisingly, they also believed that the participative methods were more effective than the traditional methods. In studying this seeming contradiction, Haire, et al., (1966:24) explained it as due to "universal lip service throughout middle and upper levels of management," to the exhortations of the behavioral scientists; meaning that managers said what they thought was expected of them, but managed "realistically." The preponderance of Theory Y concepts in the management literature of the past ten to fifteen years has made an impact on managers. Intellectually they accept participation as the future way of managing. But in the present they do not or cannot implement it on the plant floor.

A large scale experience with participation.   Behaviorists' proposals that participation of employees in their work is natural is extended by Myers (1968) to: "... people are responsible and creative when given the opportunity!" Managers are urged to revamp their managing styles to develop a climate in their plants and offices which will encourage workers to participate.

Just such a situation prevailed early in World War II. An insight to the attitude of workers toward involvement can be obtained from what can be considered the largest experiment ever conducted on participation. At the beginning of the war, when material was desperately needed, a broad participation program was organized by the War Production Board for implementation in all plants in the nation. Though the program was hastily conceived and poorly organized at the beginning, 5,000 labor-management committees were established. Participation and involvement had the full support of the government and the official backing of unions and management. Most importantly, it had the wholehearted support of the leadership in the strong industrial unions. Despite the tremendous efforts put behind the labor-management committees and the all-out publicity, the committees failed in their major goal to involve workers in production and to raise productivity through participation. The workers had every incentive to participate. Our nation was in great danger. The men at the front desperately needed the material. But the labor-management committees only attracted small numbers of workers in the plants. Perhaps one-third to one-half of the committees were paper statistics that were never met. The committees mainly spurred bond drives, blood bank contributions, raised morale, and reduced absenteeism. This conclusion was shared by all who reported on the workings of the labor-management committees (D. de Schweinitz, 1949; E. Dale, 1949; F.S. McElroy and A. Moros, 1948; International Labor Office, 1948; and Bureau of National Affairs, 1951).

At the end of the war, no effort was made in industry to extend the labor-management committees. Management saw no value in participation leading to increased productivity. Undoubtedly, many managers were apprehensive that continuing the committees might dilute management's control of the plants. But significantly, workers and unions also showed no desire at all to extend the committees or any other form of participation.

In my experiences with participation and labor-management cooperation, I found that much of the enthusiasm for participation generated during the World War II period was based on individual plant successes, most often resulting from the efforts of highly motivated individuals in management and labor who wanted labor-management cooperation to succeed. Even where there were effective committees, great masses of the workers did not get involved. In most of the plants, the committees were ineffective and not involved in production.

Participation experiences abroad.   Derber (1970:131–132) reports on studies he made of participation in England, Israel and Australia: "Recent developments in workers' participation in management reflect a wide and persistent gap between rhetoric and action." He writes:

> . . . I found few signs of managers who were ideologically convinced of the value of extensive workers or union participation in decision-making . . . the managers have been presented with little clear evidence that participation will really produce increases in productivity, efficiency, and profitability—their major institutional objectives.

In regard to workers, Derber (1970:133) further states that:

> The substantial American and English literature on worker attitudes toward their jobs, their supervisors, and their companies has tended recently to cast doubts on the validity of the theses propounded by Maslow, Likert, and McGregor that, once workers have satisfied their primary physiological, economic, and social needs, they would actively seek self-expression, self-actualization, and creativity in the work-place.

A significant Derber (1970:135) finding is that:

> At the shop level, the chief problem of participation seems to be motivation. If monetary incentives are absent, workers tend to lose interest in decision-making apart from what is required to perform their jobs. If they combine an interest in decision-making with ability, they will often be drawn into the supervisory ranks or become union shop stewards or officers.

Derber (1970:135) sees developments in recent years relating to participation in management as:

I am impressed by the uncertainties, the shifting tides of thought, the atmosphere of experimentation. At the level of participation *theory*, there is more rather than less doubt. A few years ago in the United States, optimistic theories like those of McGregor and Likert regarding workers needs and desires for self-actualization seemed to be sweeping the field; today they are regarded as psychologically inadequate and faulty.

Participation in West Germany is substantially different from practices in other countries. Known as "codetermination," it was established by law in 1951, supported by labor and management. Hartmann (1970:143) reports that: "Opinion polls (in West Germany) reveal that there are serious obstacles to the popular acceptance of codetermination." A study of all employees of West Germany showed that codetermination was eighth on a list of workers' preferences, behind such things as full employment, improvement of pensions, higher wages and better education.

De Schweinitz (1966) made a study of labor-management committees operating in Sweden, England and West Germany, with the cooperation of unions, management and government officials. Her report shows these committees were constituted to handle labor-management relations on a broader basis than usual. The preponderance of cases reported handled by the committees involved "bread and butter" union matters: job security, working conditions, etc. Unions were sometimes opposed to permitting employees to participate in cost-reduction efforts. There was a wide divergence of opinions among employees and management representatives on the role and function of the committees. Where committees operated, consultation between management and labor was largely effectual in creating harmonious relations and reducing tensions. De Schweinitz's European experiences did not indicate that worker involvement in the production process was desired by workers.

A report by Obradovic (1970) on workers' participation in Yugoslavia is most interesting, because worker participation in that industry is fostered by law and in the spirit of the economy. Obradovic studied workers in twenty Yugoslav factories to determine whether workers who have participated as members in worker management councils have different attitudes toward work than do those who have not. The study tested worker attitudes toward six dimensions of jobs: general work satisfaction, work alienation, satisfaction with wages, satisfaction with working conditions, perception of promotional opportunities, feeling of control over how the job is performed. Obradovic (1970:169) reports:

> My findings fit no fixed pattern. Perhaps the most important finding is that participation in self-management should not be overemphasized as a source of satisfaction. Even participants ranked participation no higher than fifth in their list of desired job characteristics, and participants felt more alienated than nonparticipants.... This failure of participation to generate satisfaction may be due to a variety of reasons: Dubin's thesis that work is not a central life interest, the frustrations and headaches that come from trying to administer an industrial bureaucracy, the present situation in workers' councils, factors inherent in the Yugoslav culture, etc.

In reporting on attempts by the Histadrut-controlled enterprises in Israel to institutionalize workers' participation, Rosenstein (1970:169) writes: "It is generally agreed that the implementation of participation to date has been quite limited and the results by and large discouraging." This is significant because Histadrut is both a powerful trade union and a major economic entrepreneur. Histadrut controls the activities of nearly fifty national trade unions with 700,000 members, and is responsible for about 24% of the national employment and 23% of the net national product. Histadrut's aims since early in the 1920s were to create enterprises in which workers and management would have congruent goals. Rosenstein (1970:174) reports that in 1945, Joint Production Committees (JPC) were introduced to provide a formal framework through which workers could participate in the management of the enterprise and to increase productivity. He states:

> These early committees were not intended to benefit employees economically; for this reason they were only reluctantly accepted by the workers. The initiators of the JPC program, assuming that the workers were altruistically eager to be more productive, sought to satisfy workers' self-interest in psychological terms. This erroneous assumption is probably the main reason why the early JPCs failed to solve the basic problems of low productivity and poor work discipline. JPCs were introduced on a national scale in Israel in the early fifties, and they have gradually spread to all three sectors of the economy. Over the years, their emphasis has been shifted from workers' involvement in management to increases in productivity through piece-work. What was originally conceived as a participation scheme has turned into an incentive program from which both the enterprise and its employees could derive financial gains.

Significantly, Rosenstein found that: "Where incentive schemes are not practical the councils have either withered into disuse or have never been established" (p. 175).

Rosenstein (1970:181–182, 186) further reports that the "Plant Council" program that was initiated in 1956 ended in 1961 without establishing a community of workers or creative worker identification with the enterprise. From 1961 to 1968 there were discussions in Histadrut to obtain workers participation in central management of the organizations. Despite all efforts, Rosenstein (1970) found that:

> The hope that a program would cause an improvement in the work atmosphere in the enterprises, or that it would cause workers to identify more with their work-place, has not materialized. . . . There is much evidence to support the conclusion that as long as material rewards are not an integral part of a participation program, it will not be effectively implemented (p. 181–182, 186).

Strauss and Rosenstein (1970:197, 198, 199) take a critical view of workers' participation:

> "Participation" is one of the most overworked words of the decade. Along with "meaningful" and "involvement" it appears in a variety of forms and contexts. . . . Participation in many cases has been introduced from the top down as symbolic solutions to ideological contradictions. . . .

especially in the countries with strong socialist parties, they found that:

> In general the impetus for participation has come more from intellectuals, propagandists and politicians (sometimes all three combined) than it has from the rank-and-file workers who were supposed to do the participating.

Strauss and Rosenstein (1970:213) further state that:

> A ... major reason for the failure of many participation schemes is their tendency to place emphasis on psychological rewards exclusively. Those plans which have elicited the most worker interest are those which gave the promise of improving the workers' material rewards.

Worker participation in Poland has met with varied impediments and low success since the end of World War II, when it was started. The International Institute for Labor Studies (1968:219) states that: "... (a) serious obstacle (was) lack of a system of economic incentives which would tie the workers' interest closely and directly to that of the undertaking ..."

A report of the International Institute for Labor Studies (1968:184) from India states that:

> The Indian experience provides little encouragement to those who would like to see a greater and speedier development of participative managerial practices. The government's efforts to promote such practices by means of works committees have not been notably successful. ...

A recent study by Obradovic (1975:32–44) on the extent to which workers participate when given the opportunity, provides data gathered in meetings of workers' councils in twenty companies in Yugoslavia:

> The findings indicate that deliberations in these councils are largely dominated by high-level managers and technical experts, most of whom are members of the League of Communists and have better than average educations—with the result that the rank and file members participate less actively than theory might suggest.

Technically by law in Yugoslavia, managers may not be members of workers' councils, though they can attend meetings and speak. Obradovic found that

> rank and file workers who become council members are more alienated from their work than those who merely view its operations from afar; those who are actually present at the proceedings recognize how limited their real power is.

Participation in the United States.   The predominant theme of U.S. participation advocates is that workers should receive psychological income from its adoption. But a study of the U.S. literature reveals relatively few companies which have successfully employed participation in this form. Companies using Scanlon Incentive Plans use participation tied to financial rewards. The prime example in the literature of participation without incentives is Texas Instruments. This case is discussed in a later section.

Workers and unions in the U.S. have not, to my knowledge, advocated that management establish participation programs. In the few cases reported in the literature, the initiative and support came solely from management. Judging from the literature, participation has proportionately fewer proponents in the U.S. than abroad.

The Future of Participation

Participation failures in all countries, including the U.S., stem primarily from *lack of worker interest*. Despite the strong pleas by behaviorists that participation is needed as an antidote to the dehumanization of the work-place, workers show few signs that they perceive participation as a psychological need. The growing trend to humanize relations between workers and managers should not be mistaken for greater adoption of Theory Y participation concepts. Though managers intellectually accept participation and Theory Y concepts as preferable to Theory X, managing on the plant floor overwhelmingly follows Theory X precepts. There are no reports to show that Theory Y participation has made any inroads on the plant floor.

When our nation was in grave danger during World War II, only small numbers of workers showed an interest in participation, despite an almost perfect environment in which workers were given every encouragement for involvement. Why should workers now be more inclined to participate than they were during a period when all conditions were ideal from every view?

Participation is always proposed as a goal of *management*. Workers will not identify with management's goals when they perceive management's goals as not in their best interests. Can it be that workers see participation as a need of management and not their own?

Job Enlargement and Enrichment

Participation is based on workers' intellectual acceptance of involvement. It reflects workers' attitudes to their work and to management's goals. Job enlargement and enrichment requires that management take definite steps to change the production process, to restructure the performance of work in the plant. It gets down to basic philosophic questions and engineering considerations of how work should be performed. But even if management takes the necessary steps to establish job enlargement, for the process to bear fruit, it must be viewed as desirable from workers' views.

Job enlargement has received wide support as a way to create more meaningful work. Hulin and Blood (1968) review the job enlargement thesis as:

> One of the most pervasive and dominant themes which exists in the attempts of industrial psychologists to provide guidelines and frameworks for the motivation of industrial workers is the notion of job enlargement. Job enlargement is a concerted attempt to stem and even reverse the current trends among industrial engineering programs toward job simplification and specialization. The attack on job specialization and job simplification has a long and impressive history going back nearly two hundred years to the writings of Adam Smith.

For a time there was a movement to rotate jobs as a way that made work more interesting. But it was demonstrated in numerous plants that one-third to three-fourths of the employees prefer working on a single job which they master well, rather than rotating their jobs. Friedmann (1964) reports that workers in Europe responded similarly. Rotation causes all sorts of problems for managers in training, balancing manpower loads, and maintaining quality. Behaviorists are now agreed that job rotation does not add meaning to work in the sense that they are aiming for.

As more studies were conducted on ways to create meaningful work, behaviorists agreed that job enlargement which added more of the same kind of work to a job (this would occur if an assembler put on an increasing number of different parts) accomplishes little in making the job more fulfilling to the employee. Herzberg (1968:59) labels job enlargement which builds up job size as horizontal enlargement, "the adding of nothingness to nothingness." He claims that meaningful work can only come from job enrichment, a vertical loading of new responsibilities to the job to typically include some of the following:

A. Removing some controls while retaining accountability
B. Increasing the accountability of individuals for their own work
C. Giving a person a complete natural unit of work (module, division, area, and so on)
D. Granting additional authority to an employee in his activity (job freedom)
E. Making periodic reports directly available to the worker himself rather than to the supervisor
F. Introducing new and more difficult tasks not previously handled
G. Assigning individuals specific or specialized tasks, enabling them to become experts

Herzberg (1969:61, 72) states that

> ... job enrichment seeks to improve both the task efficiency and human satisfaction by means of building into people's jobs, quite specifically, greater scope for personal achievement and its recognition, more challenging and responsible work, and more opportunity for individual advancement and growth.

The article describes a study of the effects of job enrichment on a number of jobs. The study concludes that:

> From the evidence now available, it is clear that results are not dependent on any particular set of circumstances at the place of study. The findings are relevant *wherever people are being managed.* (emphasis added)

This study to test Herzberg's (1969:63) hypothesis regarding enrichment included the following types of employees: laboratory technicians in an R & D Department; sales representatives in three companies, design engineers, production foremen, engineering foremen. It is interesting to note that the laboratory technicians were titled Experimental Officers who "... were professionally qualified people but lacked the honors or doctorate degrees possessed by the scientists." The authors undoubtedly reported their findings accurately. But were the employees in the studies representative of blue collar employees in factories? The findings of this study were not necessarily "relevant wherever people are being managed," but relevant wherever people are being managed who are typical of those in the study. Blue and white collar workers have different aspirations and goals from managerial employees—who made up the entire population of this Herzberg study. Workers and managerial employees may react differently under the same circumstances.

McGregor and Herzberg propose that when workers are given opportunities to increase the complexity and responsibility of their jobs, they will derive greater satisfaction from their work and will respond by increasing their performance levels. But a study by Turner and Lawrence (1965) did not support the hypotheses that increasing the skill content of jobs will raise the job satisfaction of workers on these jobs. They found that workers who came from small towns responded differently from workers who came from the large cities. Cultural backgrounds and attitudes toward work greatly affected how workers reacted to the work in the factory. Hulin and Blood (1968:48) also found that increasing job size is not related to job satisfaction. They believe that workers from large cities

> ... could be considered to be alienated from the "work" norms of the middle class (... a belief in the intrinsic value of hard work, a belief in the work-related aspects of the Protestant ethic) and integrated with the norms of their own particular subculture.... Simply because blue collar workers do not share the work norms and values of the middle class does not mean they have no norms.

Hulin and Blood (1968:50) believe that:

> The case for job enlargement has been drastically overstated and overgeneralized.... The argument for larger jobs as a means of motivating workers, decreasing boredom and dissatisfaction, and increasing attendance and productivity is valid only when applied to certain segments of the work force—white collar and supervisory workers and nonalienated blue collar workers.

This thesis is supported by a large-scale study of job enlargement practices in industry by Schoderbeck and Reif (1969:58), who found that of the plants that use job enlargement, three-fourths use it to improve the jobs of supervisors. My experience in numerous plants has been that the lower the skill levels, the lower the degree to which job enlargement can be established to be meaningful to the employee and management.

Sirota and Greenwood (1971:60) found that:

> Job autonomy appears in the literature under a number of labels— e.g., "participative management," "consultative management," "democratic management"—and is assumed to be a major goal of most employees. But this emphasis on autonomy may be little more than a projection of the theorists' own goals that stem from their own professional environments. Our data suggest that in some work environments—especially those with tasks that are routinized and predictable —high degrees of autonomy may be neither desired nor appropriate.

Myers' job enrichment program at Texas Instruments incorporates the basic philosophy of McGregor and Herzberg. In discussing the TI program, Myers states (1968:9): "The informed manager no longer needs to be convinced of the merits of job enrichment ... the desirability of job enrichment is no longer in question. ..." But Myers' enthusiasm for job enrichment is not shared by industry's managers. Schoderbeck and Reif (1969:42) polled 276 companies at random from the *Fortune* list of 500 of the largest industrial companies, plus the largest in transportation, insurance and utilities in the United States, and found that 80% of the companies did not use any type of job enlargement. Of the 20% reported using job enlargement, many were not using job enrichment as viewed by Myers and Herzberg, but the adding of additional tasks.

Notwithstanding managers' disbelief in the values of job enlargement or job enrichment, Myers (1968:9) continues: "... the quest now is for definitions and implementation procedures." But it is at definitions and implementation that everything breaks down for the manager. The first question is: Job enrichment for whom? For a porter, a punch press operator, an electronics assembler doing highly repetitive work, a screw machine set-up man, a Class A Maintenance Mechanic, a quality control group leader, a supervisor? It makes a great difference as to the type of work performed, the capability of the employee to make contributions and the workers' cultural background. What generates the potentials for exercise of creativity—the nature of the job or the person on the job? Actually it is a combination of both. Katz and Kahn (1966:389) found that:

> The motive of self expression depends primarily on objective attributes of the job itself. As the job increases in complexity, variety and responsibility, the individual has increased opportunity to express his skills and abilities in performance on the job.

This is confirmed by Patchen (1970:233). In general, the higher the skill requirements of a job, the greater is the need for ingenuity and initiative. In all probability, a creative person will move up the skills-ladder into a job which affords him opportunities for self-expression. Greater proportions of people in skilled jobs will become involved in creative opportunities than will people in low level jobs.

It is usually found that where workers have the ability to make useful contributions in low level skilled jobs, such workers, either when given the opportunity or when they create the opportunity, will advance to higher skilled jobs. Managers know from long experience with the job bidding process for job advancement in plants that relatively few workers choose to advance to higher skills, even though they have the opportunity through seniority to bid on jobs. The more skilled jobs such as Group Leader, Set-up Men and other such jobs often go unfilled. Kornhauser's (1965) studies of the automobile workers in Detroit found that, though workers groused about their jobs as boring, lacking challenge, and beneath their dignity, very few made any real attempts to upgrade themselves through job bidding, on-the-job training, or through other ways. Managers would be extremely pleased if workers strove to advance themselves through the skill levels. The ideals of Maslow's self-actualizing man fit perfectly into both managers' and behaviorists' concepts of managing. But unfortunately, in the true life of the plant, over a period of time people rise to a skills level commensurate with their abilities and their desire for advancement. Managers know from experience that job enrichment is possible only for some jobs. Few jobs can be altered to include the vertical enlargement responsibilities suggested by Herzberg (1968:62), (who also recognizes this limitation) when he says: "Not all jobs can be enriched, nor do all jobs need to be enriched." But this is in contradiction to the basic writings of Herzberg and his associates which state, in fact and by inference, that all jobs should be enriched and that all workers will gain from enrichment.

Herzberg (1968:62) then continues with a statement which is misleading and not supported by experiences in industry:

> If only a small percentage of the time and money that is now devoted to hygiene, however, were given to job enrichment efforts, the return in human satisfaction and economic gain would be one of the largest dividends industry and society have ever reaped through their efforts at better personnel management.

When a manager in a top position of a company reads the latter statement, his reaction will depend on his knowledge of the plant. The farther away he is from operations, the more it will appeal to him. The manager in the plant recognizes the contradictions and limitations of the two statements which the non-operating manager may not perceive. When the operating manager checks the types of responsibilities needed for meaningful job enrichment against the jobs in his plant, he finds that few jobs have the potentials for enrichment. In most plants, relatively few workers are in jobs that can be enriched. What about the great numbers of workers who will not be included? If widespread benefits are to be derived from job enrichment, they are most needed for workers in the low-level jobs, where boredom and routine are highest. The work of skilled workers already has challenge and interest built into the jobs, requiring judgment, ingenuity and initiative. Adding job enrichment responsibilities in some cases may only be gilding the lily. What are managers to do with the low-skilled workers who make up the great majority of the work force? That is the nub of the problem confronting managers. That is one reason why so little is done in plants to implement the behaviorists' suggestions. When tested in the plant, Herzberg's enrichment proposals do not operate as he predicts because they can mainly be applied only to the wrong people—those that do not need it, at least to the degree that the low skilled workers do.

Further enriching the skilled workers may produce an undesired effect: it may increase the gulf between the skilled and unskilled workers and create new problems for managers. As it is, in many industries, the needs of skilled and unskilled workers vary and find different expressions in the negotiation of union contracts. The skilled workers are the elite of the plants. Because they usually have higher seniority, they have greater rights, longer vacations, work more days during the year, and receive a higher share of overtime and other benefits. If the skilled workers take on additional job enrichment responsibilities, which border on the fringes of management responsibilities, the skilled may become more associated with management in the eyes of the unskilled, thereby creating a wider split between the two groups. This can create additional managerial problems.

Work Simplification as Job Enrichment

Work simplification is recommended as a way to create more meaningful work involvement and job enrichment. To understand work simplification fully, one must review the background and development of the technique. The forerunners in the development of participation and job enlargement concepts in American industry were industrial engineers and engineering educators: Lillian M. Gilbreth, Allan H. Mogensen, David B. Porter and Erwin H. Schell. They proposed in 1937 that human work productivity could be raised by harnessing the creativity of workers, rather than relying on a few engineers. The major emphasis was on training employees in work simplification principles so that they could become improvement experts in the jobs around them. Mogensen and his associates visualized that once workers were trained in work simplification and they saw the extent to which they could improve productivity through their ingenuity, they would participate in the improvement process. Vital to the process was the creation of plant-wide enthusiasm and involvement. Though they lacked the language and rationale of the behaviorists, the engineers proposed the same type of participation and involvement suggested by Herzberg and Myers twenty years later.

Work simplification was received warmly by industrial engineers before World War II, but implementation in the plant was rarely as Mogensen had proposed. Work Simp, as it came to be called, became another label for the process of making methods and procedures improvements.

In 1942, at the start of World War II, I was asked by an engineers union to prepare a work simplification manual to be used in the war production plants and especially by the Labor Management Committees established under the War Production Board. This manual was endorsed by Phillip Murray, President of the CIO, and supported by all unions. Though many thousands of copies were distributed, work simplification concepts of worker involvement in the planning and development of new and improved production techniques did not catch hold either in labor or management circles during the war period.

Mogensen's work simplification training conferences at Lake Placid, N.Y., and Sea Island, Georgia, have been attended by about 500 companies during the past thirty years, including some of the foremost companies in the country. The sessions are always oversubscribed with enthusiastic management followers of WS. Auren Uris (1965:113) writes glowingly of WS: "Employees who are trained in WS techniques, because of personal involvement, accept and identify with the company's desire for efficiency, waste reduction and so on." Uris lists companies which use WS, citing the huge savings these companies made. But he fails to state that all (except two) of the companies only trained their supervisors in WS, not workers, and that the savings were made by the supervisors: Detroit Edison Co., Manufacturing Division of the Mobil Oil Co., Rochester Gas & Electric, Procter & Gamble, American Viscose Division of FMC. The two companies that involved workers were Texas Instruments and The Maytag Company, but Uris also did not mention that Maytag pays substantial bonuses to its employees who suggest improvements. Of all the companies mentioned, only TI's workers were involved in improvements with no reward to themselves. A study of WS installations showed that less than 25% involved workers to any appreciable extent.[3] Most companies organized their WS programs to involve employees from first-line supervision and higher. Managers twisted Mogensen's concept of involving all employees into involving only management personnel and sometimes skilled crafts.

The basic concepts of WS understandably caught the imagination of Herzberg, McGregor, Myers and other behaviorists. Here was an approach custom-made to their proposals on how to create meaningful work and an environment of job enrichment. But experiences in numerous plants have shown that most companies using WS involve higher-skilled workers and supervisors. Relatively few companies use WS for the entire work force.

Job Enrichment in Practice

The management literature frequently discusses two companies in the forefront of job enrichment practices. American Telephone & Telegraph's (ATT) experiments conducted by Ford were designed to develop an insight to the effect of meaningful work on workers' attitudes. Ford (1969:50) states that: "What is predicted in these studies is that deep satisfaction for more employees will result from a systematic effort to load jobs with motivators named by Herzberg." The experiments developed by Ford (1969:188) were well conceived and suited to the types of work selected. As to results: "Of the nineteen studies, nine were rated 'outstandingly successful,' one was a complete 'flop' and the remaining nine were 'moderately successful.'" Ford states that the studies do not represent a cross section of the Bell System.

Since no manufacturing jobs were included in the studies, it is difficult, if not impossible, to interpolate the results for industrial applications. Care must be used in drawing inferences from the ATT experiments to other plants and offices. For example, the case frequently cited in the literature of the success achieved with the ATT stockholder correspondents happens to involve types of work where employees can take on enlarged tasks and execute all of it within their own responsibility. But this is not an example of work typically found in an office.

The results of ATT's experiments were judged mainly on two criteria: (1) measurement of turnover as an indicator of employee satisfaction and (2) a customer service index, a measure of customer satisfaction. While employee turnover represents a cost, in the overall scheme of a highly repetitive manufacturing plant, it may not be as important as viewed at ATT. Besides, as Vroom (1964:262) and others have found, there is no necessary correlation between job satisfaction and job performance. A manager with profit and loss responsibility may hesitate to establish an improvement program such as Ford designed for ATT and use their criteria for measuring results. If ATT's customers do not like their prices or service, they cannot very well shop across the street at a competitor. Before managers establish meaningful work programs they must be assured a tangible return on investment.

Texas Instrument's (TI) job enrichment program is widely cited as an outstanding success in creating meaningful work and in demonstrating the viability of McGregor's and Herzberg's concepts. TI's management was con-

---

[3] Discussions and correspondence with officers of the International Work Simplification Institute, not published.

vinced in 1952 of the value of Mogensen's concepts of work simplification, and concerted efforts were made to establish a program to enlist employees in improving their jobs. The original plans envisioned involving all TI's employees in work simplification and job enrichment. But even at an early stage it was apparent that not all employees desired enrichment. After years of experimenting with training approaches, management selected as the most fruitful method the formation of teams of employees working in their own production areas and receiving training and guidance from leaders they selected and from their supervisors. Texas Instruments' management was probably more dedicated to job enrichment than any other company in the world. They earnestly backed their managing philosophies with millions of dollars of efforts. After fifteen years of unrelenting diligence, management announced, in its 1968 report to the stockholders, its program for "increasing human effectiveness," with the objective: "Our goal is to have approximately 10,000 TI men and women involved in team improvement efforts by the end of 1968 or 1969." Since TI employed 60,000, the program envisioned involving only 16% of its work force. The total involved was actually closer to 10%.

E.R. Gomersall, of TI, acknowledges that TI's job enrichment program involves a lower number of employees than management would like. But he ascribes the low number to other causes than lack of interest. He states:

> TI's motivation program is taking a different vector than was originally planned. To begin with, TI's original program was not sized for TI's geometric growth. What has seriously interfered with TI's training plan has been the normal turnover of employees and the rapid growth of TI from 8,000 to 60,000 employees in ten years. If we assume that TI has a normal national annual turnover rate of 36% and that it takes three to five months to train a new employee to a skill level where he can meaningfully participate in a work improvement program, then a very large proportion of the work force will not become involved because they are too busy learning a new job and keeping up with their daily responsibilities. TI still conducts formal work simplification courses for supervisors and highly motivated employees. Most of the job enrichment and job improvement training is given right on the job by supervisors who act as instructors.[4]

Gomersall's explanation for the changed direction taken by TI's job enrichment program is unquestionably valid and understandable. It matches my experiences in numerous other plants. But I still wonder, if there were no turnover at TI, would much larger numbers of employees have become involved in their job enrichment program? Comparing the low percentage involvement of TI's employees against the enormous and dedicated efforts of management casts serious doubt on the viability of job enrichment as a need of workers. Workers at TI seem to react the same way to participation, job enrichment and motivation through the work itself as do workers all over the world, reported by Derber, Obradovic, Rosenstein, et al. Rosenstein's (1970:174) conclusions are worth repeating: "The hope that a (participation) program would cause an

---

[4] E.R. Gomersall, manager, Group Management Systems, Semiconductor-Components Group, Texas Instruments, Incorporated; in discussions and correspondence with the author, August 1970.

improvement in the work atmosphere in the enterprises, or that it would cause workers to identify more with their work-place, has not materialized."

A number of prominent cases, including General Foods Company in Topeka, Kansas, Texas Instruments Company cleaning and janitorial employees, Polaroid Corporation, are discussed in an article by Fein (1974a), in which it was found that:

1. What actually occurred in the cases was often quite different from what was reported to have occurred.
2. Most of the cases were conducted with hand-picked employees, who were usually working in areas or plants isolated from the main operations and thus did not represent a cross section of the working population. Practically all experiments have been in nonunion plants.
3. Only a handful of job enrichment cases have been reported in the past ten years, despite the claims of gains obtained for employees and management through job changes.
4. In *all* instances the experiments were initiated by management, never by workers or unions.

An analysis by Fein (1973a) of the *Survey of Working Conditions*, conducted by the Survey Research Center of the University of Michigan, found that two errors had been made in the survey, which reported that workers hold interesting work as their first need, pay as fifth and job security seventh. The SRC had lumped all subjects into one group and averaged the data. When the data was separated by Fein into occupation groups, pay and job security came up to the top for the unskilled blue collar workers.

A research project supported by the National Science Foundation, headed by Katzell and Yankelovich, Fein, Ornati and Nash (1975) in which the author is involved, in analyzing over 300 studies in the United States has found that:

1. Studies show that different people react differently to job changes.
2. There is a relationship between job skills and attitudes to job enrichment. The higher the skill, the greater the desire for enlarged jobs.
3. The data does not show a clear positive relationship between job changes and productivity.
4. A program for job changes (JE) showed no appreciable results—if there were no other changes in working conditions, pay, or other changes in attitude by management. In other words, if job enrichment is treated mechanically, do not expect results.
5. There is no correlation between job satisfaction and motivation.
6. The common thread that ties productivity to satisfaction is motivation. When motivation is based on the attainment of rewards, job satisfaction is the byproduct (at least over the long haul). When attainment of rewards is based on productive behavior, higher productivity will result (all other things being equal). In other words, wage incentives will motivate to increased productivity.

Is Job Enrichment Morally Justified?

When job base rates are established in industry and offices, the money value of a job is determined by the skill and effort needs of the job. Many companies in this country determine job rates through formal job evaluation plans. The procedure always followed is: (1) the preparation of a job description delineating the principal requirements of the job and then (2) evaluating the job against one of the recognized point evaluation plans. Never do production jobs contain the requirement in the job description that the job incumbent is required to use judgment and initiative in developing improvements in the job and in reducing costs. Whenever a job requires that an employee exercise judgment, the point rating scale provides substantial points for the judgment factor, which often rates higher than any other factor.

When management establishes a job enrichment program to involve its employees in job improvements, it violates a basic principle of job evaluation. Employees are encouraged to work at higher skill levels than those for which the job was evaluated. The universal principle followed in relations between management and employees is that employees are only required to perform tasks of a skill level commensurate with those listed in the job description. When additional skill requirements are added, the job is always reevaluated. On what grounds does management violate this principle and encourage work of a higher skill level without properly compensating the employee?

Additional moral and ethical considerations are found in Fein (1973b). In discussing TI's program, behaviorist Wass (1967) stated that: "The problem still remained what it was in the beginning—how to get both the first-line supervisor and the employees to recognize that the task of suggesting improvements was an integral part of their jobs." Wass is correct with respect to the supervisors. But how can management ask employees to take on responsibilities which are not part of their job and for which they are not compensated?

Behaviorists claim employees receive considerable satisfaction from improving their jobs. Wass (1967) describes the reactions of Toy Wynn, a typically involved and motivated TI employee, after she had suggested an improvement:

> And what did the originator of an improvement receive for her efforts? Not any money, as one might expect, except through the company's employee profit-sharing plan as savings in operation costs affected profit margins, a long-term consequence. No, the reward was intangible. Toy Wynn had the stimulation of looking at her job as something she could improve for her own benefit and for the company's. She had the fun of shepherding a suggestion through team discussions and before the supervisor. And she had the satisfaction of being recognized by the supervisor and her peers for having come up with a good idea.

In defense of TI's policy, when their managers consider employees for merit increases or promotions, participation in work simplification is a plus for the employee. The fact that an employee receives a psychological lift from job enrichment does not justify management's not compensating him for his skills and ingenuity. Some employees resist job enrichment on the grounds that management benefits at their expense.

Management's Stake in Job Enrichment

From the inception of job enrichment concepts, management saw the huge potentials for cost savings which could be generated. Most interesting were the prospects that these savings could be gained at little cost to management. TI's job enrichment program is based on the philosophy "... that *company* goals could best be served by providing opportunities for employees to achieve their *personal* goals" (see, Myers, 1964:73). In discussing ways to help employees achieve their goals, Myers (1964:86) recognized that: "Paradoxically, satisfying motivation needs is not only the more realistic approach for satisfying personal goals...but it is also less expensive."

If Herzberg's job content factors (recognition, achievement, the work itself, etc.) will motivate workers, TI's policy, from management's view, is preferred to using money as a motivator. Giving employees the opportunity to participate in meaningful work costs nothing.

2. THE ROLE OF MONEY IN WORK

The aspect of Herzberg's two-factor theory that most attracted managers' attention was his formulation that money is *not* a satisfier, that a lack of money will dissatisfy but an increase will not motivate. What music this makes to a manager's ears. Increased money will not motivate! Job involvement and fulfillment will motivate. If this works, the savings to industry could be enormous due to stopping increases in pay which are not getting the intended results. If Herzberg's concept that money is not a motivator had worked as he predicted, the management literature would have reported it boldly. The lack of success stories at least testifies to management's inability to get it to work. We must consider, briefly, the reasons people work; what is the motivating force behind the worker?

Why do people work? Neff (1968:142) poses it as:

> At first glance, it may seem silly to ask this question at all, since the answer appears self-evident. People work for money. Although the obvious answer is far from complete, it should not be ignored. While modern students of work motivation often appear to be arguing that work behavior is influenced by many motives in addition to monetary reward (Vroom, Herzberg), it would take a very wild variety of special pleading to maintain that these other motives will operate effectively in the total absence of monetary recompense. For economic reasons, the other motives for work may be of greater interest to employers of labor than the strictly monetary motive. An industrialist will be pleased indeed to learn how he can secure increased output without increasing his wage bill. Nevertheless, the monetary rewards consequent upon work constitute one of the primary motives governing the work behavior of the employee. In the modern industrial society, whether capitalist or communist, money is the essential medium of exchange and the prerequisite for material existence. While the love of money may be the root of all evil, money is also the chief means by which people estimate the quality and quantity of their work.

Leavitt (1964:206) goes a step further:

> ...of all the ways of setting up a wage situation that encourages hard work, the one that industry has formalized most is the money-incentive system. Money incentives have come to occupy a central place because money is a common means for satisfying all sorts of diverse needs in our society and because money may be handled and measured. Money is "real"; it is communicable. Many other means to

need-satisfaction are abstract and ephemeral. Moreover, money incentives fit with our culture's conception of what work means, with the definition of work as nonsatisfying and restrictive activity given by people in exchange for means like money. The means thus allow the earner to satisfy his idiosyncratic needs off the job.

Haire, et al. (1963) called pay the most important incentive in our society. Porter and Lawler (1968:96) support the conclusion that it is a major incentive.

There is no question that people work for money, more precisely for the things for which money can be exchanged. However, there is question as to whether money acts as a motivator. Will it activate the motivational motor within a person and keep it running? Opsahl and Dunnette (1966) examine the principal thinking on the subject and suggest money plays a larger role in motivation than is generally believed, but that more study is required to produce definitive answers. But even in the absence of clear-cut evidence for or against money as a motivator, let us examine in a commonsense fashion the world around us. While it may be intellectually stimulating to discuss the operation of motivation on some idyllic South Sea Island, more useful results will be obtained from examining the role of money in our society.

Money in Society

Again, why do we work? In the simplest terms: to eat, to exchange our skills and efforts for the things and services we can obtain only by earning the money paid for work. When a professor considers changing to a new university, unquestionably the salary of the new job is a key determinant. While some changes are made for prestige and improved facilities at work, few changes are made with reductions in pay. The question of work load for academicians is frequently a sore point between them and their administrators. At one college, the professors refused to take on extra teaching loads. But when extra pay was offered, not one professor refused to take on an extra load.

A study by Bureau of Labor Statistics (BLS) of moonlighting showed that one out of five public school teachers held two or more jobs, higher than for any other occupational group. When the study group was asked why they held extra jobs, two-thirds answered, "We are able to live better" (see, H.W. Guthrie, 1969).

In discussing compensation practices, Dunnette (1969) suggests: "It should be clear to any observer that in spite of ... confused comment to the contrary, people do behave as if they value money highly. Executives strive mightily to advance to high paying jobs...." A survey by D.A. Weeks (1972:36) of The Conference Board on the pay practices for salesmen shows that there has been a significant growth in the last decade in the use of pay incentive compensation, to where from two-thirds to three-quarters of companies used some form of incentive. Managers increasingly believe that the potential of increased earnings will motivate salesmen to improve their performance. In studies of top executive compensation in this country, Fox (1974:11) of The Conference Board finds that 74% of the top three officers of manufacturing companies are paid on an incentive basis, with the median bonus equal to 40% of their base wages. Porter and Lawler (1968:60) found that top management executives attached as much and sometimes more importance to their pay level as to the amount of autonomy, esteem or social need fulfillment they received from their work. In discussing manager motivation, Myers (1966:58) says that: "Motivation is highest among top management." Why, then, offer incentives to top management? If, as Herzberg claims, work itself can serve as a motivator for workers, why will it not serve even more so as a motivator for executives?

In the operation of a corporation, the person who stands most to benefit from profit is the shareholder, who frequently has nothing to do with the company other than that he holds a piece of paper indicating his interest. The shareholder has the least loyalty to the company, yet he stands most to benefit from its operations. The manager, who in Myers' view has the highest motivation, is among the highest paid in the corporation and most of the time receives bonuses for extra performance. The worker, who occupies the lowest rung of the ladder and who stands least to benefit from the corporation's prosperity, is expected by behaviorists to be motivated primarily by his work, not by money. When managers find that workers do not identify with their work, or with managements' goals, then some behaviorists suggest that what is needed is the restructuring of the work so that it becomes interesting and meaningful for workers. Then they will respond and be motivated to increase their performance and to identify with management. In my opinion, there is no logical support for this expectation. Of all those whom industry supports and benefits, from the stockholders on down through management levels to the workers, the workers benefit the least. They are treated as "hired hands," paid by the hour, and rarely have income security. Is it logical to expect that workers will be motivated by meaningful work alone; that money will *not* motivate to a sufficient degree? The answers to the above-posed questions lie hidden in the analysis of the general relationship between the management and the worker; a relationship founded upon mutual misunderstanding of roles and role-fulfillment and resulting in distrust, dissatisfaction and unmotivated activity.

3. IDENTIFYING A MAJOR PROBLEM BETWEEN EMPLOYEES AND MANAGEMENT

There are serious problems between management and workers that stifle motivation. That most work is not meaningful is not one of them. Managers generally believe that the major problem to be solved in order to raise productivity is workers' lack of a will to work and their opposition to productivity improvements. The behaviorists' solution is to create meaningful work and involve employees in their work. But the problem remains unsolved because managers and behaviorists have been tilting at symptoms. Workers' lack of a will to work and their opposition to productivity improvement are not problems to be solved but *symptoms* of the problem. The true problem is that *management and workers are not motivated in the same direction; they have different goals, aspirations, needs and expectations.*

Let us examine this formulation. What do management and workers each want? Management strives for increased productivity, higher profits, an improved competitive position in the marketplace, strengthened finances, and a more effective organization. While labor's interests are also served by these objectives, in daily relations between management and labor in the plant, the short-term interests of the workers come to the fore and control their relations with management. Workers primarily want wage increases, greater security, shorter working hours and improved fringe benefits. Though reduced productivity and increased costs actually erode their security, the effect of these factors is too indirect to enter significantly into their considerations. Workers voice concern for the welfare of their employer and his ability to stay in business, but when confronted by daily issues, they fall back on their subjective interests. Many managers know from bitter experience that demonstrating with hard facts to their employees that competitors are way out in front usually brings no improvement in productivity. Pleas of poverty when negotiating renewal of a labor agreement often fall on deaf ears at the bargaining table. Managers understandably view their day-to-day relations with employees as a constant struggle to maintain productivity and to hold the line against the erosion of management's prerogatives. But as long as managers' strategies are based on countering symptoms, they cannot solve their basic problems. An approach to a solution becomes apparent when management understands the issues which are important to workers. Why do they act as they do? What are they trying to protect? Why do they oppose management? A look into any plant discloses a simple fact of life that is crystal clear to the workers: in practically all plants and offices, *if the workers do anything to raise productivity, some of them will be penalized*. This situation is created by the system in effect in our country wherever workers are employed. If employees increase production, reduce delays and waiting time, reduce crew sizes or cooperate in any way, less overtime will be available or some employees will be displaced. If a truck driver stops for fewer coffee breaks during his trip, he might bring his truck back within eight hours and lose overtime. If the men in the Shipping Department did not permit goods to pile up on the shipping dock until late in the afternoon, they would lose their overtime. If the typists in a clerical pool increase their output, some will be released. If the employees in the plant raise their productivity, the plant will require fewer employees. But the workers will receive no financial benefits, nor can they be persuaded that increased company profits will benefit them in the future. What employee will voluntarily raise his production output, only to be penalized for his diligence?

Let us consider the "exempt" employees, the executives, administrators, professional and salesmen.[5] Have you ever heard of a manager who worked himself out of his job by superior performance? Have you ever heard of a salesman whose security was threatened because he sold too much? Or of an engineer who caused the layoff of other engineers because he was too creative? These employees can usually anticipate rewards for their creativity and effectiveness. When workers excel and raise productivity, the company benefits and management is pleased, but the workers do not benefit. To the contrary, in the short run, their economic interests are *threatened*; some suffer loss of income. When "exempt" employees are more effective, they cover themselves with glory; their economic security is *enhanced*, not threatened. Ironically, the relationship between workers and management actually provides workers with the incentive *not* to cooperate in productivity improvement.

---

[5] Exempt as broadly defined by the regulations of the Fair Labor Standards Act.

When managers state that workers oppose productivity improvement on the plant floor, they are correct. But when managers claim that this attitude of the workers is their problem, they are not correct. The workers' attitude is not the problem, but a *symptom of the problem*. The problem is that management and workers are not motivated in the same direction; they have different goals, aspirations and needs. The closer the goals of each can be brought to the other, the more effectively will the organization serve the needs of both.

Goals of Workers

Behaviorists have counseled that managements' main efforts should be directed toward getting employees to identify their interests with the company's. McGregor (1967:136) proposes "...that the task of management is to create relationships...such that the members of the organization perceive that they can achieve their own goals best by directing their efforts toward the goal of the enterprise." As Simon (1957:218) puts it: "Identification is the process whereby the individual substitutes organizational objectives...for his own aims as a value-indices which determine his organizational decisions." Workers, however, view their interests from their own perspective, which McClelland and Winter (1969:22) formulate as:

> Since a man's actions are guided largely by his own perception and evaluation of the situation, any incentive or disincentive must be perceived as such by him in order for it to have its fullest and most appropriate effect. A man's maximization of interests over time is always with respect to the situation as he perceives or processes it.

So many managers are unsuccessful in their attempts to convince workers that their best interests lie in identifying with management because they do not honestly evaluate the situation. Workers do not join with management as they would root for the local baseball team. McClelland and Winter (1969:22) caution: "We cannot understand a man's actions until we understand his perceptions." That is the key to a solution.

H.M.F. Rush (1969:27), in paraphrasing Argyris, perceives workers' aspirations as:

> Since his human needs are more urgent and more relevant to the individual, his first concern is their realization—*not* the realization of the organization's needs, if the organization's objectives are perceived as taking precedence over personal needs. If the individual perceives that organizational objectives are placed before his personal needs, the psychological energy he possesses may be directed toward personal dissatisfaction, apathy, conflict, tension, or overt subversion of the organization's objectives.

McGregor's and Herzberg's proposition that workers must find fulfillment through involvement in their work can in reality be reformulated as: fulfillment for workers will come from their identification with management's goals. But under the conditions prevailing today in industry, that is just not achievable. Realistic managers know they cannot sell workers the concept that if they accept management's goals they will be rewarded by warm personal feelings of accomplishment. Let us examine a case in the literature showing how incorrectly identifying the cause of a problem leads to failure in solving it. M. Sorcher (1969) of General Electric says that "... shop employees are poorly motivated.... Their goals and ideals are often incompatible with those of management."

In discussing ways to change workers' attitudes, he suggests, "... that merely adding responsibility to an employee's job may not be effective in motivating him unless he were receptive to taking on more responsibility. In fact, added responsibility could be seen as an additional burden." To create worker receptibility to added responsibility, Sorcher suggests that what is needed is "stewardship," which he defines as "... having pride in doing the work properly, maintaining sustained alertness for job improvements in all aspects of job-related functions and a willingness to accept responsibility for related tasks...." Sorcher wants workers to identify with management's objectives. Let us consider several pertinent questions: Why should a worker take on these responsibilities? *Cui bono?* If a worker does not get these feelings of "stewardship" of his own volition, why should he respond to management's suggestions? If he felt the need for involvement, he would not need any stimulation; he would be doing what comes naturally. Apparently, workers in Sorcher's case do not see identification or stewardship as in their best interests. Sorcher's conclusion that workers' goals and ideals are often incompatible with those of management is, in my opinion, correctly formulated. But when he searches for causes, he seems to miss the most powerful force which keeps workers and management apart: they have different goals, aspirations and needs. Workers will not accept concepts which they do not perceive as in their best interests. In writing on the subject, J.K. Galbraith (1967:151) states that a worker has "... no illusion that he can adapt the goals of the organization to his own."

Gellerman recognizes the enormous potentials for increased productivity which may be gained if workers would accept management's goals. He proposes that it is management's responsibility to develop managing strategies which will encourage workers. Gellerman (1969:45) states that present managing methods are based on a "cost control" approach which restricts behavior. He suggests that: "An alternative strategy for behavior management is emerging from the behavioral sciences: instead of merely restricting costly behavior, it seeks to *encourage actions which add to productivity and efficiency.* We can therefore refer to it as a *value adding* behavioral strategy." Gellerman (1969:50) sees workers' goals in the same terms as did Sorcher of GE: "... that most people will invest more effort and ingenuity in their work if it is made completely *theirs*—if they can recognize in it a unique and significant contribution of their own." Gellerman (1969:46) suggests that managers will encourage workers with: "... the strategy of (Gellerman's) approach (which) is to increase opportunities for value-adding behavior to occur. Some of its more common tactics are participative management styles, job enrichment, chains of two-way communication 'loops' and programs for employee advancement and development." (Italics in original.) The theme of Gellerman's essay (1969:51) is that if "... management gives up some of its power to restrict behavior in exchange for a hoped-for increase in value-adding behavior," and workers are encouraged to take on greater responsibilities, the results will be value-adding. But he completely omits the view of workers. The overwhelming evidence in practically every plant is that workers *do not* accept management's goals. Will they change their attitude when management gives up some of its power to restrict behavior?

Gellerman, McGregor, Herzberg, and other behaviorists who share common views base their concepts on the proposition that workers must find fulfillment in their work, otherwise they will be deprived. This myopic middle-class concept of workers' views leads behaviorists to nonoperational concepts. Managerial strategies for workers must meet with workers' goals and aspirations. And when they do not, workers will simply ignore management's goals. Management will suffer the consequences. But when this occurs, we cannot blame the workers for not cooperating. What is wrong in the plants is that managers are not attuned to workers' goals and as a result both go in divergent ways. Lest American managers think their workers are different, Sirota and Greenwood (1971: 60) found that there is considerable similarity in the goals of employees around the world.

Workers' Attitudes Toward Their Work

The typical attitudes of mass production workers to their jobs is revealed in a study by Wild (1970:161) of 2,159 female workers and 236 female exworkers in seven electronics plants in the United Kingdom:

> Aspects of the actual work done were undoubtedly the major source of overall job dissatisfaction, the difference between overall-satisfied and overall-dissatisfied being particularly marked in this area. The dissatisfied workers typically described their work as depressing, uninteresting, providing no sense of achievement, making little use of their abilities, and having little variety. Opposite views were expressed by those workers who were satisfied with their jobs, namely, they found their work to be interesting, not depressing, giving a sense of achievement, and making use of their abilities.

The study found that 21.0% of current employees were on the overall dissatisfied with their jobs and 79.0% were on the overall satisfied. 35.6% of the previous employees were in the overall dissatisfied category. Wild's conclusions are particularly noteworthy:

> There is little doubt that job enlargement would be welcomed by, and beneficial for, those workers who expressed dissatisfaction with their present jobs. Hence, as remedial action for the minority of workers, job enlargement is completely justified. However, since the majority of operatives display a lesser need for self-actualization, the general and indiscriminate enlargement of jobs is unlikely to result in a significant modification of workers' behavior.

When a behaviorist studies the highly repetitive work performed in the typical factory, he is disturbed at the prospect facing the worker who, perhaps for the rest of his life, will endlessly perform the same type of work. Transforming a human being into a machine with no feeling toward his work is a horrible thought to the behaviorist. Yet, on innumerable occasions when I have asked workers how they feel about the monotony, repetition and boring nature of their jobs, I invariably received answers which indicated the worker does not perceive his role in society in the behaviorists' image. Though not nearly all workers hate their work, very few love it. If workers were asked to pick the work they would like, few would show a preference for the work they are doing. Most view it as a necessary way to earn their livelihood. Many philosophically point to other less desirable work and console themselves that their jobs are not as bad as others. Workers do not look upon their work as fulfilling their existence.

Anthropologist Liebow (1970) makes the point, with regard to menial and dirty jobs, that:

> It is very easy to overestimate the extent to which such jobs are despised because they are dirty or hard and to underestimate the extent to which they are despised because they pay so little money. There is little that is intrinsically bad about being a janitor or trash collector. What is so bad about them is that in such jobs you cannot earn a living. Where the pay for garbage and trash collectors approaches a living wage, as in New York City, there is intense competition for the work that is elsewhere shunned and accepted only as a last resort. . . . That these jobs tend also to be dead-end jobs is probably true, but perhaps we make too much of this also. The job of the lathe operator, the assembly-line worker, the truck driver, the secretary, these tend to be dead-end jobs too, but they are not bad jobs because of it. Not everyone in our society is career-oriented. We have a large and relatively stable working-class population which does not aspire to moving up a career ladder. The working man who earns a living and supports his family by doing work that everyone agrees is socially useful does not necessarily want to become a foreman, or plant manager, or office executive. If he is dissatisfied, it is probably because he wants more of what he has, and wants to be more certain of keeping what he has, not because he wants something different. So would it be, perhaps, with jobs that are presently considered menial, dead-end jobs. If a man could earn a living at these jobs, they would not be dead-end. They would be much like other jobs—a job.

McGregor and Herzberg maintain that unless workers find fulfillment in their work, they will be deprived. But the ultimate test of a concept is how it is perceived by those who are to operate with it. How do they react to it and what are the consequences growing out of their reactions? Suppose workers took the behaviorists seriously and became deeply involved in their work. Consider the feelings of a worker who accepts that fulfillment in his life will come from being an appendage to a machine or from performing a highly repetitive assembly operation. Behaviorists recognize that such thoughts could be devastating, which is why they propose that work be enriched. Workers, however, do not look upon their work as fulfilling their existence. Their reaction to work, as a rule is the opposite of what the behaviorists predict. It is only because *workers choose not to find fulfillment in their work* that they are able to function as healthy human beings. By rejecting involvement in work which simply cannot be fulfilling, workers save their sanity. Workers would indeed become mentally ill if they took the behaviorists' proposals to heart. The factory workplace is abhorrent to the self-actualizing person. Behaviorists find it next to impossible to conceive that workers would reject involvement, opportunities to enrich their work, to get away from the deadening monotony of the repetitive work. Yet this is precisely what occurs in plants where low-skilled workers are given opportunities to move into work which is enriched. Persisting in the position that workers do not know what is good for them, but that behaviorists do, leads to futile experiences.

I am not negating people's need for creative activity, for fulfilling their lives. Rather I propose that fulfillment may not be possible at the work-place if the work is of a nature which offers the worker little satisfaction. Such workers' self-actualization needs will be fulfilled in activities which the worker freely chooses in his leisure time. Here he can get involved in activities which interest him, which fit his cultural and economic background and where he can do as he pleases. The modern office or factory is often highly regimented and leaves little room for initiative or expression. Workers desiring fulfillment from their work will find opportunities to express themselves.

Having considered the workers' perceptions of their jobs, we now must advance to a deeper consideration of the workers' values. It is the values of the worker which influence his perceptions of and attitudes toward the work-place. The values of the worker are one of his measurements of job satisfaction/motivation. Let us examine briefly the value system of the worker.

Values: Money or Fulfillment—Which Is More Important?

Some models: incentives. Behaviorists see the huge potentials for human progress which are possible through motivation, exemplified in the ultimate form by Maslow's self-actualizing man. The tremendous enthusiasm and will to work shown by the members of the kibbutzim in Israel has attracted the attention of outstanding behaviorists in this country who have formed the American Council for the Behavioral Sciences to study motivation in the kibbutz. Conditions of life on the kibbutz, particularly in the initial establishment of the collective, are far worse than those prevailing in other parts of Israel, but that does not deter people from joining a kibbutz. The kibbutzim are probably the only places in civilized cultures where the maxim followed is: from each according to his ability, to each according to his needs. Reports show that there is no shirking of even the simplest and dirtiest of details. Everyone works very hard and without thought of material recompense. Data on the kibbutzim are now being gathered by behaviorists. Undoubtedly their reports will show that the inhabitants of the kibbutzim are all idealists, highly motivated to reach their goals. To them, huge obstacles and personal deprivation mean nothing. Only the ultimate goal has meaning. Can it be that the secret of the kibbutzim's success is that these collectives are structured after Maslow's Eupsychia and that the inhabitants of the kibbutzim are all highly motivated, self-actualizing people?

Model: wage incentives. Every revolution for social progress is carried on the shoulders of highly motivated men. The American Revolution was led by zealots motivated by desires to free the Colonies from tyranny. The revolt in Russia was against tyranny. The leadership of the Russian Revolution was grasped by Lenin and a highly motivated group who then attempted to restructure their economy following Marxist-Socialist principles.

Marx (n.d) wrote against what the factory was doing to workers' jobs:

> It becomes a question of life and death for society . . . to replace the detail worker of today, crippled by life-long repetition of one and the same trivial operation, and thus reduced to the mere fragment of a man, by the fully developed individual, fit for a variety of labours,

ready to face any change of production, and to whom the different social functions he performs are but so many modes of giving free scope to his own natural and acquired powers.

Yet when the leaders of the revolution were faced with real-life problems of operating industry, Lenin (1921) overlooked Marx's pleas and introduced piecework (and Frederick W. Taylor's concepts) with the statement:

> The possibility of socialism will be determined by our success in combining Soviet rule and Soviet organization or management with the latest progressive measures of capitalism. We must introduce in Russia the study and teaching of the Taylor System and its systematic trial and adoption.

Wage incentives have been used more extensively in the Soviet Union than in any capitalist country. Bergson (1964:110–112) reports the following percent of total workers in industry as working on incentive: 1928, 57.5%; 1936, 76.1%; 1953, 77.0%; 1956, 72%; 1961, 60%. The reduction in recent years was "... partly because piece work previously had been introduced where it was inappropriate and partly because, with changes in technology, it often ceased to be appropriate where it once had been." Wage incentive coverage in the United States is reported by BLS at a level of 26–27% from 1948 to 1968 (Stelluto, 1969; Lewis, 1960).

Despite the very wide use of incentives in the Soviet Union, in the early 1930s, production lagged and workers showed little interest in identifying with their work. Dobb (1966:464) reports that to overcome worker resistance:

> In 1930, ... Stalin ... spoke of the campaign for what was known as "socialist competition" in reaching production targets as the beginning of "a radical revolution in men's views of labor, transforming labor from an unworthy and painful burden, as it was formerly considered, into a matter of honor, a matter of glory, a matter of valor and of heroism.

About 1935 saw the birth of the Stakhanov movement. Dobb (1966:468) states that:

> When the Stakhanov movement began to develop, it was commonly discounted as a propaganda-façade. ... The methods used in the main introduced no new principle and it is true that few of them will surprise students of American Scientific Management. As Ordzhonikidze, Commissar for Heavy Industry, said at the time: "There is nothing strange, nothing bewildering in all this. ... Correct division of labour, correct organisation of the work-place, correct arrangement of the technical process—there you have the secret of the Stakhanov movement."[6] What was novel about it was that it represented a movement to rationalise working methods that arose from the initiative of individual workers themselves; and as such its achievements came as a definite surprise to the management of industry. What in other countries has

---

[6] From a speech at the Plenum of the Central Committee of the Communist Party of the C.P.S.U., December 21, 1935.

generally been devised by functional foremen and efficiency engineers, often in the teeth of relentless hostility from ordinary workers, was now being initiated by workers themselves. Moreover, it was an emphasis on rationalising working methods or technique and not on greater effort on the worker's part as previous campaigns of shock-brigades and socialist competition had very largely been. It showed a concern with quality, and not an attention to quantity alone. It was a product of thought and not merely of good intention—moreover, of thought about his job from what for most workers was an entirely new angle.

This simple description of Stakhanovism reveals it to American managers and industrial engineers as essentially the same as the work simplification principles developed in this country. In reality, the Russian industrialists implemented this technique about two years before such programs were initiated in the U.S. Mogensen and his associates announced Work Simplification (WS) in 1937. Notice how the phraseology and appeals of the Russians are so similar to those proposed by some western behaviorists. The Soviet leaders introduced Stakhanovism with one big difference: money incentives. Dobb (1966:479) reports that: "Many Stakhanovites trebled or even quadrupled their earnings within the space of a few months." The increased earnings in plants created new problems for the authorities by dislocating the structures of earnings, costs and prices, but that is an irrelevant fact.

Whether in this country or in the Soviet Union, involvement by workers in their work, whether accompanied by money incentives or not, always seems to attract only a small proportion of the workers. In the Soviet Union in August 1936, out of 19,000 workers at the Kaganovitch ball-bearing works in Moscow, 2,000 were Stakhanovites. In Texas Instruments in 1969, about 15%–20% of the workers got involved in their work simplification and job enrichment program. Wild (1970) found that job enlargement would be welcomed by and beneficial to 21% of the workers in his study. Wherever one turns, the magic number of involved workers comes up as 15%–20%. Why? Can it be that this percentage is about the proportion of self-actualizers in the worker population, whether in capitalist or communist countries?

It may well be that intuitively workers see the issue of work fulfillment as against their interests. They see it as a form of exploitation, of obtaining work from them without recompense. Could that be what it really is? When Wass (1967) described how a typical worker at Texas Instruments feels at TI when she is involved in their work enrichment program, he also presented the principal aspect of the program to which workers are opposed:

> And what did the originator of an improvement receive for her efforts? Not any money, as one might expect. . . . No, the reward was intangible. Toy Wynn had the stimulation of looking at her job as something she could improve for her own benefit and for the company's. She had the fun of shepherding a suggestion through team discussions and before the supervisor. And she had the satisfaction of being recognized by the supervisor and her peers for having come up with a good idea.

Workers do not come to work for fun. And they do not want to see management benefit at their expense. However, that is exactly what happened to Toy

Wynn. She gave TI increased productivity and received no pay for it. Her only recompense was the mental stimulation she received from having her supervisors tell her she had done a good job and from the satisfaction of having been creative.

When Russian managers were confronted with worker resistance to increased productivity in the 1930s, their first response was wage incentives as a motivator. This was followed by a worker involvement program based on work simplification principles, but reinforced very heavily with wage incentives. Stakhanovism appealed to the 20% high achievers' fulfillment needs. All workers were given opportunities to increase their earnings. As shown in the experiences of the prior years, wage incentives alone were not enough. The realistic Russian leaders knew that patriotism and work involvement appeals alone would surely fail. Both were needed. The Russian workers in 1935 were undoubtedly less sophisticated than Americans are today. Are we to believe that Russian workers needed money incentives to urge them on, though their nation was in peril, and that American workers will raise their production for the sheer love of their work? As Derber, Obradovic, Rosenstein, et al. found, wherever involvement programs did not incorporate the factor of material rewards, the program failed.

Herzberg states that money is an hygienic factor; when pay is too low it will be resented, but increased earnings will not motivate. To what worker is he referring? The self-actualizers in the Israeli kibbutzim? The small number of "eager beavers" in the American plants? He is certainly not talking about the great masses of blue and white collar workers in this country and abroad, including the Communist countries.

When Kornhauser (1965:268) studied workers in Detroit factories to determine what they really wanted most in life,

> ... their answers overwhelmingly specify financial and material goals and wishes for security, family welfare, health and happiness. There are strikingly few expressions of interest in personal achievement, self-development, and self-expressive activities; even fewer references to altruistic aims or desires to participate in collective efforts to help others or to work for the improvement of society.

To answer the question, "Money or fulfillment, which is more important?" obviously, each worker must make the choice for himself. Where involvement is desired, managers should make it available in the jobs which are amenable to self-expression. Friedmann (1964) clearly perceives the problems regarding the attempts to create involvement through the introduction of job enlargement and enrichment when he suggests that

> ... we must not give way to tempting illusions. These new movements, whatever their importance and however excellent their effects, are far from affording a universal solution to our problems ... there are still today millions of jobs which cannot be revalued in such ways, and this will continue to be the case for a long while yet. The work that millions of men and women do every day for a living neither enriches their lives nor acts as a balancing factor. Such people can only look for true satisfaction and the means of self-realization in leisure-time activities, more particularly in the "free time" which is progressively

increased as the working week is shortened. It is the time spent away from work, as Marx (and Hegel before him) saw, that should constitute the "true realm of freedom" for mankind.

Finally, to answer the question, "which is more important, money or fulfillment," we must ask, "Important to whom?" The case for management's interests is academic without first considering workers' needs.

An indication of workers' need priorities is seen in a Wall Street Journal (1971) article: "About 6500 workers at General Electric Company's Appliance Park facility (Louisville, Kentucky) here were off the job as a result of a strike over a back-pay claim of $35 by a former employee who left the company almost two years ago."

Why is it that workers have no difficulty in determining what they want in their demands to management? And why is it that humanizing the work-place is never a demand of workers at the bargaining table? Why have workers never demanded opportunities to *find fulfillment at work* which McGregor and Herzberg find is absolutely essential to their mental health? Are workers so infantile and bashful that they need behaviorists to frame their bargaining demands? Kornhauser (1965:279) meets the question squarely on what workers should find desirable and who decides: "... people must decide for themselves; it is not for the 'experts' to prescribe what men *should* want." Judging by what they demand and what they do not, workers have made it clear to management that they do not need fulfillment from the work itself. They do not view the behaviorists' issues as in their best interests. I cannot presume to speak for workers. But the evidence at the work-place, in the factories and offices, wherever blue collar and white collar workers work, is that workers by and large prefer material returns for their labors and skills. Most of all, they want secure pay.

Expectations vs. Realities

Emphasizing that workers' dissatisfaction stems from uninspiring and unfulfilling work may have obscured a more basic cause. The blue collar workers' blues may in fact be more a reflection of the plight of workers' overall lives than of the eight dreary hours they spend on the job. Rosow (1971:28) believes that:

> American workers expect that steady, full-time, conscientious job performance will pay off in an acceptable quality of life for themselves and their families. Instead, millions of workers are getting increasingly frustrated by a system they think is not giving them a satisfactory return for their labor:
>
> • The legitimate, basic needs of their families have grown beyond the capability of their take-home pay, even though their pay has increased.
> • They are unhappy with their jobs but see no way of breaking out.
> • Their total life patterns are less than satisfactory.
>
> ... These dissatisfactions constitute three very basic pressures that could be called the economic squeeze, the work-place squeeze, and the sociopsychological-environmental squeeze. Caught in this bind—in

varying degrees—are persons who are members of families whose incomes are above the poverty line but below what is required to meet moderate family budget needs.

... These workers are not at the fringes of our economic system. They are at the center, with family incomes between $5,000 and $10,000 a year. There are some twenty million families comprising about eighty million individuals in that income bracket. Some are caught in the squeeze only temporarily. But studies show that, given current economic conditions, many are permanently trapped—or seem to be—in this kind of vise.

A combination of factors is working to create increasing worker dissatisfaction:

- The educational level of the worker population is rising, especially among the new workers; they expect more out of life.
- Blacks and minority groups are refusing to accept lower standards of living.
- Workers producing the nation's goods are increasingly frustrated by not being able to purchase the products they make.
- Workers in lower paying industries see the discrepancy between their working conditions, benefits and wages, compared to basic industries such as steel and auto, and there is increasing dissatisfaction.

Being caught in a dead-end or uninteresting job is one thing. But then not earning enough for a decent standard of living creates frustration which inevitably is manifested as job dissatisfaction. What would workers' reactions be to these jobs if they and their families could live good lives? Will job enrichment create more fulfilling lives for the breadwinners of the twenty million families described by Rosow?

With increasing attention to the four-day work-week, fulfillment off the job takes on far greater promise. Two days off in seven may not allow sufficient room for diversion of interests. Three days in seven is almost half the week. But if workers' standard of living does not rise, the increased free time away from the job will cause even greater frustration when workers see more clearly how they are boxed in and unable to break out of their stultifying job-home cycle. It is natural for most to vent their frustrations on their work because it is the workplace and all it stands for, which is holding them back from living the life they wish. The blacks and minorities, in addition, vent their anger on the community which they see as additionally imprisoning.

Basic Errors of Behaviorists

One of McGregor's (1960:41) basic assumptions in formulating his motivation concepts was that, "The high standard of living created by our modern technological know-how provides adequately for the satisfaction of physiological and safety needs." Events all around us prove the error of this premise. It was not valid in 1960 when McGregor wrote his book nor is it true today. Quite conceivably other behaviorists made the same error.

Behaviorists recognize the differing needs of low and high achievers. But the motivational plans and strategies they propose are slanted to the high achievers. The absence of proposals suited to the needs of the great majority of the work force suggests that the upward striving of the high achievers is the most desirable goal for all workers. It appears that all management need do is to provide job enrichment and involvement opportunities, and eventually workers will move toward management's goals. The hard realities of life in plants all over the world, even under the most favorable conditions, demonstrate the fallacy of this reasoning.

What I have tried to show by various citations and experiences is that the concepts of work-fulfillment proposed by Herzberg and McGregor apply only to an elite minority of workers. The percentage of workers who would benefit from such work-fulfillment programs is small. In my opinion (supported by the existing field data), this includes only about 15% to 20% of the blue collar work force. These behaviorists' concepts have little meaning for the other 80% to 85% of the work force. Contrary to their proposals, the majority of workers seek fulfillment outside of their work.

Behaviorists who continue to press upon management variations on a non-operational theme commit a most serious error: what about the harm that comes to workers and management in plants which adopt their nonoperational proposals? Where workers view managements' actions as opposed to their interests, they may take counter measures. Yet the managers' strategies may have been designed with the best of intentions, guided by behaviorists' counsel. How are workers to distinguish between one management which knowingly uses behavioral theories to exploit workers and another management which unknowingly and in good faith pursues similar practices?

Even when managers do not institute behavioral proposals, harm may be done through the confusion caused in management circles, as now exists. Behaviorists cannot duck their responsibilities by proclaiming that management has the responsibility of making the behavioral theories operational, as Herzberg (1966:171) did in his book:

> What recommendations can be made in industry in order to carry out the ideas propounded in this book? I am tempted to reply that if I had the answers, I would program them and make a living in a much easier way than by writing books. And in truth, this *is* the task of those who are responsible for the management of organizations, and not the task of psychological critics. In fact, it is this area of management that has been most bankrupt in creativity.

What are the consequences to society if behaviorists furnish management with information and procedures designed to increase productivity at the workers' expense? As Kelman (1968:21, 22) puts it, what if "... the worker is being manipulated so that he experiences a sense of participation and involvement which is not reflected in the reality of his position in the industrial organization?" Kelman admits this possibility and goes on to suggest that: "In response to this criticism it can be argued that, considering the overall lack of satisfaction in industrial work, it is a net good to give the worker some sense of participation and involvement in the work situation, to give him at least a limited opportunity to make choices and thus find some meaning in the job." But even with such rationalized good intentions, behaviorists and managers must tread carefully and not assume the right to make decisions regarding what is good for workers and what they should want out of life.

Lest managers think that all behaviorists agree with Herzberg's two-factor theory of motivation, there are numerous behaviorists who oppose it. Unfortunately, the management literature over the past ten years has been overwhelmingly pro-Herzberg. The behavioral literature has carried a number of articles disputing Herzberg's concepts based on studies conducted by other behaviorists (Ewen, Hulin, Smith and Locke, 1966; Graen, 1966, 1968; Hulin and Smith, 1967; and Graen and Hulin, 1968).[7]

This chapter suggests that some of the prominent psychologists have made basic errors when they proposed that:

1.   Workers have a need to find fulfillment in their work.
2.   Workers will identify with management's goals when management adopts managing strategies which will offer workers greater participation and identification with their work.
3.   Work can be restructured and enriched so that it is fulfilling to workers.
4.   Enriched work will increase a worker's will to work.

As demonstrated, only a minority, about 15% to 20% of the worker population, responds to these concepts. These behaviorists also greatly miscalculated the economic motive for working and the extent to which fulfillment at work will substitute for cash in the pay envelope. Each worker views identification with his work from his own perspective and needs. Identification is not like food which can be made more and more appealing by fancy dressings. The proposals of McGregor, Herzberg, Myers, Sorcher and Gellerman make some sense to those who practice and benefit from work fulfillment. But they fall on the deaf ears of those who do not identify with their work. The achievers identify with their work naturally and without conscious thought. Despite all sorts of impediments in the plant, including social pressures from others around them not to cooperate with management, they find ways to identify. But the 80% to 85% of the work force that does not find fulfillment on the job continues not to identify, regardless of how encouraging an environment management creates in the plant.

4. PRECONDITIONS TO RAISING THE WILL TO WORK

The environment surrounding the work-place critically affects the formation of an employee's attitude regarding identification with his work and with acceptance of management's goals. Behaviorists and management writers counsel that work conditions and management policies should promote employees' feelings of "belonging" to the organization, of identity with management.

A most critical component of the work environment is job security and continuity of income. The threat of job termination stops everyone dead in his tracks. The most highly motivated person wilts to nothingness when faced by layoff. Reduced employment affects the morale of everyone in the organization. Even when employment is stabilized and the threat of further reductions passes, fears and memories linger. Managers' strategies for managing seldom take into account employees' apprehensions, let alone the havoc wrought on workers' lives by layoffs. Changes in employment levels in a company are usually handled on the basis of cold statistics, on the needs of the corporate machine for more or fewer pairs of hands. What happens to feelings of identity and loyalty when employees see their increased productivity contributing to their layoff? It is hard

---

[7] These five articles may be obtained as Reprint Series No. 196, "Job Satisfaction: Models, Methods and Empirical Results," from the Institute of Labor and Industrial Relations, Bulletin of the University of Illinois, at Champaign-Urbana. No. 33, 66(February):1969.

to conceive of a manager who would cooperate in designing his own job out of existence, as might occur when several managerial jobs are combined and one person is no longer required. When managers consider their own job security, they quite expectedly have empathy for J.F. Lincoln's truism that: "No man will willingly work to throw himself out of his job, nor should he." Yet managers do not extend this obvious logic to their work force.

Managing strategies are sometimes based on expecting employees willingly to raise their productivity as production changes are instituted. More often management expects some resistance and feels its way along, developing improvised approaches to cope with opposition. Employees' reactions vary depending upon past relations with management, employment conditions in the area, the strength and resources of the company and many other related factors. When cutbacks occur, employees' attitudes reflect their concern for continued income. The fear of loss of income increases or diminishes with changing economic conditions and with the strength of the employer. For some workers this fear diminishes with promotion or a high position on the seniority list. Insecurity, however, touches all workers to some degree. It is usually thought of as resulting from a downturn in the economy. But substantial job loss can occur from other less dramatic causes: hardships for a single company which loses out to its competitors, or pressures on one industry by other industries and by foreign competition. Jobs can be lost through mechanization, as occurred in the steel and metalworking industries. As technological advances in the graphic arts industry are put into practice, these result in considerable displacement of workers. Some industries are being supplanted by others as, for example, leather by plastics, with reductions of tannery workers. Some products are now almost entirely made abroad in low labor rate countries. The list is endless.

Job security is an essential precondition to enhancing the will to work. While the idea is not new that economic insecurity is a restraint on the will to work, its effect is often minimized by managers, behavioral scientists and industrial engineers involved in productivity improvement.

The relationship of job security to motivation can be seen in the propositions that:
1. A relatively high level of economic security for workers in a given plant is an essential precondition for fostering the will to work. Only when this has been established can the various motivational theories have any chance of success.
2. Workers must be motivated to achieve a high level of productivity.
3. Increased economic security without positive motivation will only raise costs, not productivity.
4. Workers will respond to motivational inducements in direct proportion to their economic security.

In short, the productivity of workers will be highest when they are motivated and when they have no fear of working themselves out of their jobs.

The Need to Increase Job Security

Job security is as vital to productivity improvement as advanced technical processes and new equipment. Managers must view job security not only in the social sense of how it affects workers' lives, but as *absolutely essential to high-level productivity*. Managers have historically considered job security as a union demand, to be bargained as are other issues. This has been a tragic error, because whenever job security is lacking, labor productivity is restrained. Para-doxically, job security must be established as a demand of *management*. Where managers experience opposition by workers to productivity improvement, it is because the managers have failed to assure the workers against loss of income. Argyris (1965:259) cautions that "...if the restriction of output is due to the employees' fear of the loss of their jobs if they produce too much, then it is the organization's responsibility to meet the problem realistically." Fears of techno-logical displacement can be removed in only one way: by guaranteeing that dis-placed workers will be protected. Responsible unions in this country do not oppose mechanization, but often object to the way it is introduced.[8] The AFL–CIO Research Department has produced a guide to unions suggesting that the impact of mechanization be cushioned by the following approaches: (1) pro-tecting job rights through attrition clauses; (2) easing job changes by advance notice; (3) using SUB (Supplemental Unemployment Benefits) to close the wage-loss gap; (4) protecting the transfer rights of displaced workers; (5) using severance pay to cushion job termination; (6) quickening the trend toward early retirement; (7) investigating the shorter work week (see Oswald, 1969). Every proposal is a form of income protection, either while working or later in retirement. Numerous companies have had success with their improvement pro-grams when job protection was developed in advance. When the Allan Wood Steel Company started its modernization program in 1965, it encountered worker opposition on its new 110-inch mill to an extent that the new mill was a loss rather than a gain. Resistance stemmed from fear of layoffs from increased productivity. Management and the union solved the impasse by a cost-savings sharing plan and by liberalizing their job security plan.

The agreement reached in 1961 on the West Coast waterfront between the International Longshoremen's & Warehousemen's Union and the industry asso-ciation is a milestone of cooperation in which both benefited. During contract negotiations in July 1966, both parties agreed that results of their pact have exceeded original expectations and that cargo on the West Coast moved at an average hourly pace of .875 tons in 1965, up from .627 tons in 1959 before the pact went into effect. In the same period labor costs per ton fell to $6.16 from $6.39 despite a 35% increase in wages and benefits since 1959. A report on the 1966 contract negotiations in the *New York Times* (1970) stated: "It reverses the popular concept of labor union men who fear machines and automation, and outlines a union insistence that machines be employed 'whenever feasible and practical.'" What managers would give to hear their union say this to them!

Insuring Effective Job Security

In the mid-1940s, many unions, and especially the United Automobile Workers, made the guaranteed annual wage their prime objective because of the heavy

---

[8] The AFL–CIO, in its annual convention in 1958, proclaimed that:
"Unions in the United States are not opposed to and do not stand in the way of technological improvement. They well recognize that technological advance and the resulting increasing productivity are needed to enable improvements in the standard of living. The union concern about the manner in which technological change is introduced is unfortunately sometimes mistaken for resistance to the change, when in fact it is not. If a union has not been informed and consulted about a major change or if it finds that worker problems have not been taken into account, it may quite understandably be critical and resentful of the procedure, and seek needed corrective steps, even though it does not object to the technological change itself."

unemployment expected after the war. During the 1950s, though business levels were high, there were serious misgivings in the national unions about techno-logical displacement of workers. Even the skilled tool and die makers in the automotive industry were apprehensive of their job security because of the radical development in machine tool technology. The guaranteed annual wage gave way in 1955 to the plan negotiated by the UAW with Ford, later known as the Supplemental Unemployment Benefits (SUB) plan. During the past fifteen years, SUB has proven to be the most effective way of assuring income for workers. SUB is defined as: a private plan of employment benefits whose eligi-bility or benefit requirements are linked directly with the public program of unemployment insurance (UI). The essence of SUB is that a worker on layoff receives payments in addition to unemployment insurance, depending on the plan, of amounts that can approach his regular take-home pay. The most aston-ishing thing about SUB plans is the low cost to management. The SUB plans in the rubber, steel and auto industries cost about $.10 per hour.[9] For several cents per hour, management can establish a plant environment in which fears of lay-off are greatly reduced. Actually SUB becomes not a cost, but a catalyst to de-creased production costs. Since SUB plans are funded, management is assured that its SUB costs are limited to its agreed contribution.

Worker Views on Job Security and SUB

Workers' views on job security vary with the industry and their past history of steady employment. Becker's (1968:54) study found that:

> ...the average employee ranks many other objectives higher than a program of unemployment benefits. Just as the fear of unemployment is the main explanation of why SUB has appeared where it has, so the absence of that fear, felt as an immediate threat, is the main explana-tion of the lack of SUB in most labor contracts. The fact that the threat of unemployment at any one time and place is limited is probably the chief reason why SUB plans ten years after birth still cover less than 4% of the industrial force.

Becker's study covers up to 1967. In a study made in 1965 of the seventy-five larger unions which were considered the most likely to be interested in SUB, Becker (1968) found that the majority of the unions rated SUB low on their scale of values. The most usual reason given for SUB's low ranking was the absence of a serious threat of unemployment to the bulk of their membership. But with the softening of the economy during the past year and greatly in-creased layoffs, workers are now more receptive to SUB. The difficulty union leaders have had in selling SUB to workers parallels the original resistance of workers to pensions when weighed against cash in the pay envelope. The younger workers' reaction to pensions was summed up by: "Why should we pay to retire the old geezers?" as if they would never get older. The outlook of the older workers to SUB is the same: "Why should we pay to protect the low seniority workers?"

---

[9] For a thorough presentation of SUB plans from the beginning through 1967, see J.M. Becker (1968).

When workers think of job security, they usually visualize layoffs due to a downturn in the economy or to seasonal trends. They often do not consider increased productivity as a threat in the *immediate* period for which they need income protection. For total income security, all causes must be covered:

- Economic downturn in industry or in a particular company.
- Short term layoffs due to shortage of orders, lack of materials or technical difficulties.
- Increased worker productivity which makes possible reduced work-force.
- Technological, equipment and process advances reducing manpower requirements.

A new twist to SUB.   A most unusual thing has occurred in plants utilizing SUB. Unions are now asking that layoffs occur in *inverse seniority*, with the highest seniority employees going first. By inverting seniority and giving the senior employees a choice, a layoff under SUB becomes a reward, not a penalty! For working diligently and working himself out of a job, a worker is rewarded by time off with pay. In the plant without job security, workers stretch out the last job if they do not see the next job ahead of them. They will not work themselves out of their job. But with SUB, they can go ahead and not worry about a layoff. In fact, they may welcome it. When workers stretch out their job, though it is hidden from view, it is reflected in costs. Under SUB the stretch-out may be avoided.

Managers oppose inverse layoffs because it drains off the most experienced men in the plant. Union leaders recognize the problems that can be caused and offer arrangements to ameliorate the impact. But getting the older men out of the plant has its benefits: younger men can be trained faster to upgrade their skills. Very often, the lower grade operators often go for twenty years or more without the opportunity to become first class operators because the spot ahead is filled by a senior man. Another possible advantage yet to be tested is whether, having tasted time off with pay, the older employees might be more receptive to early retirement. There could be many resulting benefits both to employer and employees.

Inverse seniority layoffs should be the option of each person. Some may prefer to work; others may choose time off with pay. There is a hitch to the layoffs that workers will consider. To be eligible for state unemployment insurance, they must be available for work at their skills, if offered it by the unemployment office. In large scale layoffs, the probability is that other jobs are not available. The situation will vary depending upon industry and locale.

Management Views of SUB

Since management needs job security to remove the impediments to increased productivity, the pressure for job security must come from management even if workers do not press the issue. Where job security is not established and there is an economic downturn or technological advances which displace workers, these workers will take steps to protect their job security by various tactics, all of which reduce productivity.

The benefits to management from SUB are:

- Resistance by workers to technological advances is reduced.

- There will be less tendency to stretch jobs out when work backlogs are low.
- Establishment of proper work crew sizes will be facilitated.
- The domino-like effect caused when workers bump others with less seniority, which often seriously disrupts production and raises costs, could be reduced.
- Costs are raised when workers on layoff accept employment with other companies and new workers later must be trained. A worker on layoff covered by SUB will be more likely to remain available for recall.

When considering SUB, managers overlook the fact that the costs of SUB are *borne by the workers, not management!* In contract negotiations, the total of wage increases and benefits is usually considered as a package. Whether the workers choose SUB or the equivalent of a cash wage increase, it does not appreciably affect the wage package cost. Management gets nothing in return for a wage increase. But SUB creates potentials for sizeable cost savings. Employees understand they pay the cost of SUB. During periods of high employment several years ago when SUB funds reached their funded peak before the end of a year, and management could therefore stop contributing to the fund, unions raised demands that the companies continue SUB payments into the employees' pay envelopes. Employees felt the entire contribution belonged to them as part of the pay package.

If workers and management benefit substantially from SUB, why is SUB not more widespread in industry? The best opinions I have solicited from union and management circles reduce to the following:

- Workers have not called for SUB for the same reasons that many people are not inclined to repair their roof when the sun is shining. There has also been a split between the lower seniority workers on one side and the older ones and skilled crafts on the other. But this can be removed by inverse seniority layoffs.
- Managers' main fear is that opening the door to job security may lead to all sorts of horrible things and eventually to the guaranteed annual wage. Such management fears are not solidly grounded. SUB is really an extension of state and federal unemployment insurance that has existed since the late 1930s. In this sense, SUB is not new. While it is difficult to foretell the future, the probability is high that 95% SUB is close to the millenium of job security. New frills will be added, but these should be low in cost.

The Future of Job Security Programs

The study of a subject's past and present has traditionally given impetus to a consideration of its future. There is usually always some apprehension and anxiety about such glimpses of things to come. This is certainly true of the field literature of job security. In a study of potential changes in employee benefits, a panel of experts predicted that pressures for income security benefits in the future would come primarily from labor. The panel believed that by 1976 we would see the beginning of some form of guaranteed employment, with the impetus primarily from labor with support by the government. Crystal-balling the year 1985, the panel sees various employee benefit plans meshed together: "We have translated at least part of our capacity for economic production into *security.* The 'rugged' individual who wants to take his wages in cash instead of guarantees against adversity has almost passed from the scene" (in Gordon, 1969:51).

Whether or not individual managers concur in these predictions, the trend certainly is in this direction. A critical problem of the present that might serve to jeopardize the future of job security is the high unemployment rate. Those most affected are the minority groups recently brought into industry. If industry does not protect their job security, the government may have to take appropriate steps. Industry has much to gain by keeping SUB as a private benefit plan.

Removing Blue Collar Stigmas

Another area of income security receiving increasing attention is the disparity in wage payment methods between white and blue collar workers, which was highlighted by the National Commission on Technology, Automation and Economic Progress. The Commission (1966:91) suggested that the old status distinction and social stigma be removed by paying factory workers by the week, as are white collar workers, instead of by the hour. Some leading companies such as IBM, Texas Instruments, Motorola and others pay all their employees by the week and report no problems. Management is rather pleased by the workers' response. In the first step of a major transformation of the wage system of France, Peugeot and Renault, two of the largest industrial enterprises, announced a changeover from hourly pay to monthly salaries for all their factory workers. The late President Pompidou's committee of experts, which had planned the change, set this as a goal to increase the dignity of workers and make factory jobs more attractive. The *New York Times* report (1970) said that the differences that existed between hourly-paid workers and those paid on a monthly basis "constitute an obstacle to the development of a dynamic industrial society, disadvantage workers, and keep away from the manual trades an important part of the active population."

In many plants, managers could pay workers by the week without increasing costs. It is not scheduling problems which hold them back as much as their outdated concepts of workers as "hired hands." It is precisely this thinking which the Commission counsels feel should be changed. Pay by the week is not nearly as radical as it sounds, since on the average it is two and one-half days call-in pay. If the week is from Monday to Friday, when told on Friday to report the following week, the worker has five days guaranteed. On Monday it is four and on Thursday only one. The average for the week is thus two and one-half days. Handling absence and lateness depends on company policy and does not affect the principle of a weekly paycheck. Though many plants have four or eight hours call-in pay practices, practically no plant manager schedules only one day in advance. Most managers know the work load far ahead and schedule their plant for at least a week or more. Managers who have responsibility for planning may want one day call-in pay because of the apparent protection it gives them, but this is illusory. Any layoffs are costly to management; smooth production is usually most efficient. Effective forecasting and scheduling techniques have been developed which make it possible to accurately anticipate weekly manpower needs.

Granted, obtaining a constant flow of orders is no simple task. In some companies, such as those producing parts and servicing other plants, it is very difficult. Regardless of the circumstances, workers must be convinced that management is doing everything possible to insure them against loss of income and jobs. What bothers workers is seeing management make gross errors, use poor judgment or, worst of all, not evidence any real interest in their security.

What Does Management Get From Job Security?

When workers see that management is considerate of their apprehensions and secures their income, and if they believe they can go all out and not endanger their job security, the entire climate in the plant will have been changed; a major obstacle to productivity improvement will have been removed. Just picture the reaction of the employees and the union when management insists that job security be established, without waiting for prodding by the employees! Even hardened antimanagement employees would respond in kind in their attitude and concern for management's problems. But if security becomes a gain of the union, forced out of reluctant managers, a tremendous psychological lever will have been lost by management.

Job security creates a new plant environment; it removes the fear which nurtures resistance to productivity improvement. But job security alone will not raise productivity. It only creates an *opportunity* for improvement which management must exploit. Managers must understand the quality of the new plant environment and develop new plans and strategies for managing which provide a means to motivate the employees. Unless positive steps are taken to motivate these secured workers, the huge sums spent for improved economic security will bring no appreciable benefits to management. (Some management strategies for increasing the will to work will be discussed in detail in later Section 5 of this chapter.) Secure workers, even happy workers, are not necessarily highly productive if management does not provide the motivation and leadership. From numerous discussions I have had with managers and union leaders in plants with SUB, it is my opinion that the benefits obtained by management through increased job security are directly in relation to workers' perception of management interest in their welfare. SUB will enhance job security regardless of how it is initiated. Secured workers will not resist changes in productivity improvement to the extent they did with no job security. Some managers have established job security through SUB and did not recognize that a vital change had been made in the employee-employer relationship in their plants and they did not get the benefits from job security which were possible. Their security plans may have bought some peace on the plant floor, but the value of the job security plan was largely lost.

Summary

Management's plans cannot succeed when they are based on obtaining increased productivity without protecting the income security of its employees. When employees' economic interests are threatened, especially in the extreme where they are faced with unemployment resulting from increased productivity, they will turn their full efforts toward protecting their security. Even where, through the use of considerable mechanization, management is able to pace production mechanically, the employees will introduce all sorts of impediments which must act to reduce productivity. Job security is a necessary precondition to raising the will to work and reducing employees' resistance to increased productivity. Before any plans are introduced to raise productivity, management must first remove the most serious impediment—job insecurity. For its own self-interest if for nothing else, management must secure the economic interests of its employees so that restraints on productivity will be reduced.

5. DEVELOPING RATIONAL STRATEGIES TO INCREASE THE WILL TO WORK

The greatest obstacle to increasing the will to work is the adversary-relationship between labor and management. Workers see increased productivity as detrimental to their income and job security. Managers see relations with workers in the traditional ways as remaining win-lose. Their opposing views create a formidable block to mutual understanding of each other's needs and dampen efforts to find ways of solving productivity problems. Workers will want to raise productivity only when relations between management and labor are such that workers see identification with management and increased productivity as in their best interests. Management plans to get employees to identify with management are continually turned down by the workers. Before we consider the actual strategies for increasing the will to work, we must examine worker behavior in relation to management goals.

Regardless of managers' approaches to managing, they should clearly understand the nature of the forces which shape their positions and those of their employees. Managing strategies to increase the will to work must be designed to deal with relations in the plants as they are, not as managers would like to see them. Too frequently managers base their plans on their own perception of workers' needs, dooming in advance any possibility of success. Some behaviorists do worse; they propose that workers "ought" to do certain things, neglecting whether workers will in fact act as the behaviorists predict.

Traditional Managing Philosophy

Philosophies for managing blue and white collar workers are based on the premise that workers are generally unsympathetic to managements' goals and, if given the choice, will perform at a lower productivity level than management believes is reasonable and considerably lower than they are capable of achieving. This is evidenced by managements' jealous guarding of their rights and prerogatives. They are convinced that productivity is reduced as management's rights are diluted by limitations on management's right to manage.

Managing policies therefore require that management establish work performance criteria and continually press workers to perform to standard. Compliance is most frequently obtained by instituting control procedures to monitor performance and determine substandard variances which managers then attempt to correct. Traditional managing theory places full responsibility on management for managing and maintaining effective operations. Management does not expect assistance from workers in raising productivity; they ask only that workers do not oppose them.

Conflicting Worker and Management Goals

Management's primary productivity goal is more units of output with fewer man hours of input, and with lower requirements for capital equipment and investment. Workers have little if any desire to assist in attaining management's goal. Each worker views this goal in terms of how it affects his own interests.

The need to coerce workers to perform to production standards stems from the adversary-relationship between management and workers, which arise from basic differences between them (developed earlier in this chapter). Management and workers are not motivated in the same direction; they have different goals, aspirations and needs; if workers do anything to raise productivity, some of them will be penalized. Ironically, the relationship between workers and management actually provides workers with the incentive *not* to cooperate in productivity improvement. Without realizing it, all most companies offer their employees for raising productivity is the opportunity to reduce their earnings and job security. No wonder workers oppose productivity improvement.

Motivation: Cause or Effect?

The key to motivating the low achiever is in developing an environment at the work-place which each worker perceives as in his own best interests. Motivation through the work itself is rejected by the noninvolved employee. There must be another way. There is one company that seems to have found that way for *all* of its employees. The questions are: "Is it cause or effect? Are these all 'turned-on' employees because management carefully screens and hires only high achievers and the high level drive in the plant further weeds out the nonconformers? Or is it that management has developed a managing strategy which appeals to all its employees so that they accept management's goals?" This company is an enigma. Very little is known about its inner operations except that the will to work of the entire work force down to the lowest skills is not matched anywhere in the world. No behaviorist has studied this unusual work-force, though its management has extended invitations to other managers to emulate its successful policies. The company most atypical of industry is The Lincoln Electric Company. Its employees' earnings are probably the highest in the world. Their man-hour productivity is unsurpassed. Over the years, Lincoln's competitive drive to market better products at lower prices has resulted in management decisions at some of the largest companies in this country to get out of the welding business.

I visited the Lincoln plant and talked to its management. With their co-operation, I toured the plant and, at my choice, talked to workers and supervisors. One worker reported earning $25,000 last year. Another earned $18,000 and bragged of his $58,000 home. Most unusual is Lincoln's employees' identification with their work. At one work station, I saw a worker operate five different machine tools to produce a rotor shaft from a blank; he operated a tape controlled engine lathe, a tracer lathe, two small milling machines, a hydraulic press, and he performed all his own inspections; he made a finished part to close tolerances ready for assembly. I saw another worker make finished gasoline tanks: he took two tank halves, soldered on the fittings, submerged arc welded the two halves into the completed assembly, pressure tested the tank, repaired it if necessary, sprayed it in a paint booth, and delivered a finished tank to the main assembly line. Many parts and subassemblies are made by "one man shops" where a complete subassembly job is performed as it might be by a small subcontractor. Each man does all his own set-ups, his own inspection, and is responsible for his production. Foremen do not have to supervise their employees.

Each man is practically his own supervisor. These employees participate in their work to a far greater extent than visualized by psychologists in their writings. The key to this participation is that the employees *want* to do it; there is no holding back. A manager from the outside would drool on witnessing Lincoln employees at work.

Lincoln's high productivity is not new; it has gone on quietly and continuously since 1934 in Cleveland, one of the major centers of American industry. Let us examine what goes on and why. In 1934, the late James F. Lincoln laid the basis for Lincoln Electric's future development through initiating a program he later called Incentive Management. Stemming from deep convictions that employees would respond sympathetically to management's goals only when they perceived management's goals as compatible with their own, Lincoln established its management's philosophy on the concepts that:

1. Each employee's job security must be fully protected; his raised productivity must not penalize him.
2. Employees must see their increased productivity and identification with management's goals reflected in increased take-home pay and enhanced job security.
3. Increased productivity and reduced costs are passed along to Lincoln's customers to strengthen the company in the marketplace and thereby further enhance job security.
4. Management would continue to plow back earnings to develop the plant and Lincoln's position in the market.

James F. Lincoln (1961:36) firmly believed that management must comprehend the apprehensions and aspirations of workers, which he expressed as:

> The greatest fear of the worker, which is the same as the greatest fear of the industrialist in operating a company, is lack of income. The policy of industrial management is controlled by a program that will in the opinion of management assure continuous profit. All industrial plants are controlled by this need. The wage earner has the same necessity and a more personal one than has the industrialist. That necessity also controls his actions. The industrial manager is very conscious of his company's need of uninterrupted income. He is completely oblivious, evidently, of the fact that the worker has exactly the same need. The worker's fear of no income is far more intense than the industrialist's, since his daily bread and that of his family depend on his job. The industrialist would not miss a meal if his company should run at a loss for a length of time equal to that for which the worker was laid off because of lack of orders.
>
> In spite of these facts, the industrialist will fire the worker any time he feels that he can get along without him. The worker has no control over his future. His need of continuous income is far more urgent than that of management, yet he has no recourse. Only management is responsible for the loss of the worker's job. Only management can follow and develop a program that will bring in orders. The worker can't. Management, which is responsible, keeps its job. The man who had no responsibility is thrown out. Management failed in its job and had no punishment. The wage earner did not fail in his job but was fired. No man will go along with such injustice, nor should he. This is still true, in spite of custom which completely sanctions such procedure.

Lincoln (1951:170) again states:

> It is management's duty to make the worker secure in his job. Only so can the worker feel that he can develop the skill and apply the imagination that will do his job more efficiently, without fear of unemployment from the progress he makes. If a man is threatened with loss of his job by a better way of producing, which eliminates the need for his service, he cannot do his best.
>
> This attitude that the unprotected worker has toward progress will limit his usefulness to the company. There may even be no conscious effort on the part of the worker to hold back progress. However, in his subconscious mind there is the fear of the consequences that come from job elimination unless there is assurance that if the job he is doing is eliminated for any reason there will be another one equally attractive awaiting him. Only so can any man cooperate to the full both by mind and body in the progress so necessary in a free country.
>
> Only management can protect the worker in matters of this kind. The fact that the usual management will fire the worker when he runs out of work has had more to do with production limitation than any other circumstances. No man will willingly work to throw himself out of his job, nor should he.

In 1934, at the depths of the depression, Lincoln went to his workers with a proposition that management was prepared to share with their employees the fruits of their combined efforts, if the workers would identify with the company's goal to produce better products at lower prices. Lincoln's simple approach won the workers' acceptance and at the end of 1934, management distributed a bonus equal to 26% of their annual pay. The best proof of what has occurred since then is that a substantial bonus has been distributed every year. The bonus for 1972, totalling $19.1 millions was shared by 2,150 employees, ranging from below the President to the lowest level employee.[10] For the past several years, the annual bonus has equaled or exceeded the total amount of the employees' annual pay.

Lincoln's greatest emphasis was on the establishment and maintenance of credibility and integrity with their employees and customers. The employees' confidence in management is borne out by their continuing efforts to improve productivity. The policy toward pay is simple: pay is directly based on work output. All production work is on incentive with no guaranteed minimum.

Lincoln's attitude to job security and earnings is unmatched. Basic wages, which are in line with Cleveland industry, have been adjusted continuously since 1936 according to the area cost of living. All employees, after two years of employment, are guaranteed fifty-two paychecks a year equal to at least thirty hours pay. A retirement plan of 5.8%, paid by the company, vests at fifteen years, providing for retirement at age sixty or sixty-five.

The work pace at Lincoln is probably faster than in any other plant. Yet the waiting line to get in to Lincoln is inexhaustible. Why have no other companies followed Lincoln's principles? Perhaps one reason is Lincoln management's attitude to its employees and to its stockholders, with reference to who

---

[10] The annual bonus is actually shared in proportion to each employee's total annual pay and according to a merit rating plan for all employees.

creates the company success. Data on the sharing of the fruits of their labors tells the story: in 1972, with annual sales of $137,389,000, management distributed stockholder dividends of $5.181 million and bonuses to management and employees of $19.1 million. Even when the dividends are converted to pretax dollars, the employees received far more than the stockholders. Not many companies distribute this amount of money to their employees with the firm conviction that it is theirs because they earned it. The profits and value added of Lincoln Electric are enormous by any standards, but especially in view of the keen competition in the industry. Before distributing dividends and profit sharing, management first sets aside a portion of profits to reduce product prices and to improve quality. Next they put aside a portion for capital improvement and corporate use; then come dividends and last is profit sharing.

The management which took a giant step forward in relations with its employees has created a labor-management team which is unbeatable in its industry. With the highest employee earnings in the world, Lincoln is the largest in its industry, sells its products at the same or only slightly higher prices than in 1934, has created a healthy climate in the arc welding industry in the U.S., experiences little if any foreign competition, and exports its products to all parts of the world in competition with low cost foreign labor.

Are Lincoln Electric's Experiences Transferrable?

Lincoln Electric has been visited by many skeptical managers over the years, yet there are no reported successful emulations. From my discussions with managers who considered Lincoln's approach, and from researchers in management and the behavioral sciences, the principal impediment seems to have been that managers did not have the courage to recommend to their boards of directors that they approve adoption of the seemingly "radical" concepts of Lincoln.

Neglecting the Lincoln experience may have cost our economy dearly. The present severe wage-cost-price squeeze can only be overcome by sharply increased productivity. If the Lincoln experiences can be established in other companies, huge productivity increases can be accomplished *without the expenditure of a cent.* Unleashing the will to work does not require new equipment or plant facilities—only the desire of workers to reach goals. There is no power in the world to match the zeal of dedicated and motivated people.

Perhaps there are lessons to be learned from the Japanese, whose productivity and industrial progress is outstanding in many ways. The U.S. Dept. of Labor (1971:9) reports:

> The approach to employee's compensation in Japan is quite different from that in the United States. Unlike the United States, where wages are related to job evaluation and worker performance, in Japan labor compensation is part of a system of "lifetime" employment in large part embodying a "wage-for-age" principle. The Japanese employer is involved in many aspects of the employee's life, providing many amenities beyond the workers' cash earnings, such as housing, recreational and vacation facilities, loans for education of children, gifts for marriages and births, and "condolence" gifts in the event of family disaster or death. The employee, whose whole life is centered on the enterprise, looks to the employer to become "involved" and responds to the em-

ployer's business objectives with a dedication that is probably unmatched anywhere else in the world.

Peter Drucker (1971:115) believes the Japanese system is no more perfect than any other system:

> But the basic principle which the Japanese have evolved—not by planning rationally, but by applying traditional Japanese concepts of mutual obligation to employment and labor economics—seems to make more sense and works better than the expensive patchwork solutions we have developed that do not come to grips with the problem itself. Economically, it might be said, we have greater "security" in our system—we certainly pay more for it. Yet we have not obtained what the Japanese system produces, the psychological conviction of job and income security.

Workers generally dislike paternalism. But when their employment relationship permits a week old stockholder greater rights to company profits and progress than a thirty year employee, then perhaps some of what is labelled as paternalism may in fact be the levelling of equities. Some of the deep rooted restraints on productivity which stem from the employment relationship practices will be lessened as employees see that management is considerate of their needs.

Managing Styles for Blue and White Collar Employees

Union-harassed managers often complain that the union is trying to take over and run their plant. Nothing could be further from the truth. Neither the employees or the union want to have anything to do with managing the plant. *They are mainly concerned with protecting their income and job security.* They want to continue receiving full pay checks so they can feed their families.

The rationale of the stretch-out creates workers' ethics and morals on the plant floor which managers sometimes construe as workers trying to run the plant. Taking unauthorized material from the plant is stealing, which the employees and the union do not countenance; violation is grounds for immediate firing. "Making money with a pencil," sometimes practiced under wage incentives, is in the gray area. Falsifying production counts or time records can result in dismissal. But stretching out a job so that it lasts several times longer than it should does not disturb workers' consciences. Taking unauthorized material is stealing, but consuming unauthorized time many times the value of the material is not stealing in the workers' view. The stretch-out is practiced by every worker at some time in all countries, including those in the Socialist bloc. Managers who came up from the ranks have short memories of what they did as workers.

In hundreds of plants and offices, complaints by managers that workers and unions were eroding management's prerogatives could often be traced to instances when management established unsound work practices which deteriorated over the years. When management later tried to pull back on a "good thing" a group of workers enjoyed, management's action was resisted. The workers' position was not primarily antimanagement; rather it was proworker. There is a sharp difference, though a manager may not see it.

It is sometimes thought that behaviorists' proposals for employee involvement are associated with loosened management control over its operations. This is not so. Experiences reported in the literature show that managing styles are often flexible, with greater autonomy allowed in the skilled jobs. Freedom to redesign work tasks and to participate in job decisions does not bring loosened organizational controls nor freedom outside of the job. To do otherwise would be to invite disorganization and possible reduced effectiveness of the overall operation.

A casual reading of the literature describing Texas Instruments' (TI's) job enrichment program may lead the reader to believe that Texas Instruments is loosely run, with employees working as they please and doing their own "thing." In conversations with Gomersall of TI, he emphasized that their job enrichment program would have been short-lived were it not for the excellent managing skills and the close control exercised over their manufacturing operations. TI's industrial engineers and managers employ the gamut of modern engineering and managing techniques. The degree of autonomy permitted in specific jobs varied with the complexity of the work and the ability of the employees to make decisions regarding the work.

Behaviorists' views on the need for control in managing can be seen in the case histories of Harwood Manufacturing Corporation, which has been identified in the behavioral and management literature as a classic example of how participative management will encourage superior performance from workers and create a more harmonious and motivating environment. When Harwood purchased the Weldon Company in 1962, and all sorts of traditional business problems were encountered, Harwood management moved into Weldon and restructured it in its own image. The complete case history of Weldon is described by Marrow, Bowers and Seashore (1967:ix, 33):

> ... reports an extraordinarily successful improvement of a failing organization through the introduction of a new management system. An unprofitable enterprise was made profitable, and a better place to work, in the short span of two years. Many managers and students will want to know how this was done.

Harwood management made

> ... a business decision to undertake a participative approach to the salvaging of the Weldon enterprise.

Though Harwood's management was devoted to the participative approach to managing, nowhere in the book is there any evidence that the changeover in management practices introduced job enlargement or enrichment, nor is there mention that Weldon's workers participated to any appreciable extent in creating improvements in work methods and systems. Management's efforts seemed to have been concentrated on revising the management organization, eliminating the former one-man rule of the company, and raising productivity. The major improvement in plant productivity was obtained from a straightforward, conventional, industrial engineering program established by a firm of consulting engineers. A rise in productivity of thirty percentage points was obtained, measured by operator productivity, from 85% of standard to

115%. Marrow, et al. (1967:181–182) report that management improvements were created as follows:

> ...the earnings development program with individual operators was the most potent of the steps undertaken, contributing perhaps eleven percentage points of the total gain of thirty points. Next in influence were the weeding out of low earners...and the provision of training for supervisors and staff in interpersonal relations, each contributing about five percentage points to the total gain. The group consultation and problem resolution program with operators appears to have contributed about three percentage points. The balance of six percentage points can be viewed as arising from miscellaneous sources or from a combination of the several program elements.

The industrial engineers' section of the Weldon case history reports that the fundamental goal selected for concentration and agreed upon by all in management as the problem of first priority was raising employee earnings which were based on an incentive plan. The goal was reached in one year (see, Marrow, et al., 1967:77). This section reads as a typical case of resurrecting a disintegrated incentive plan.[11] Some of the engineers' efforts were spent in "...three to four hour production studies of the operator to estimate her performance potential" (Marrow, et al., 1967:77). The engineers encouraged the operator to convert to more effective methods and to raise her skill. "An operator was helped in this manner until an outcome was apparent, until her earnings increased or she was deemed unlikely to change" (Marrow, et al., 1967:82). During this period, "...an effort was made to get rid of the remaining employees with chronically low production records and histories of frequent absence" (Marrow, et al., 1967:179). The success achieved in raising productivity at Weldon seems to have been obtained by using conventional Theory X practices on the plant floor. The approach followed was what any competent manager would have employed.

Harwood-Weldon management designed its management organization on participative principles. But the managing style with respect to the production employees seemed to be quite firm; behaviorists might label it authoritarian. Particularly interesting is that this case history involves a behaviorist's wearing two hats: manager and behaviorist. Alfred J. Marrow, originally president of Harwood and later chairman of the board of Harwood-Weldon Corporation, has considerable standing as a social psychologist. This study involved a number of psychologists from the Institute for Social Research at the University of Michigan. When viewed in perspective, managing styles to direct the Weldon work force seem to reflect more closely the nature of the work and the capabilities of the work force than the managing philosophies of management. Though management in a plant may be basically Theory X minded, the implementation of their policies on the operating level may not be materially different from a participative minded management under the same work-worker conditions.

---

[11] For a full discussion of the problems encountered with disintegrating wage incentive plans, see M. Fein (1971). Copies available from American Institute of Industrial Engineers, 25 Technology Park, Norcross, Georgia 30071.

Pay by Performance as a Motivator

What brings the worker to the work-place? The same motivator that brings the manager to work: pay. How many managers would continue on their jobs without it? Pay is the common denominator that brings all people to work. It seems useless to debate whether money is first or fourth on value scales for workers or executives. No one works without it.

If pay moves people to work, then it seems reasonable that pay can also serve as an incentive to increased motivation to work and to improved work performance. Management seems convinced that money incentives are effective for salesmen, since about 75% work on some form of incentive. Managers themselves look favorably on money incentives for themselves. Yet studies (L.E. Lewis, 1960, 1964, 1965–67; and G.L. Stelluto, 1969) of the prevalence of wage incentives for manufacturing in this country show that from 1945 to 1968 about 26% of the work force was on incentive. The prevalence of incentives in England was about 33% in 1961 (National Board for Prices and Incomes, 1968: 76–78). Surprisingly (or not) the Soviet Union makes the widest use of incentives; Bergson (1964:110) reports that about 60% of Russian workers are on incentive. Practically all Soviet managers work against goals and incentives.

In their annual study of executive compensation of 1100 companies listed on the New York Stock Exchange, Peat, Marwick, Mitchell & Company, an international accounting firm, found that in 1970, the top executives received bonuses of 49.2% of their base salaries and that:

> One of the most significant findings of the PMM & Co. survey was the fact that bonus-paying companies achieved better profit performance than non-bonus companies. Firms with *formal* incentive plans had an average pretax return on investment of 16.8% compared to only 11.7% for those companies without bonus plans. After-tax profits followed the same pattern, 8.6% to 6.0% (reported in Brindisi, Jr., 1971:52).

PMM & Co. believed this to be one of their most significant findings. Companies which paid their top executives bonuses earned on the average 43.6% more profit than did the non-bonus paying companies. It appears that incentive pay motivates executives to superior performance. Yet on the question of pay for workers, most executives seem to believe that pay by the hour is sound and that equitable wages will encourage employees in plants and offices to respond favorably to managements' goals. But "equitable" no longer has meaning; witness the sharply escalating wage increases. Unless there is a clear relation between earnings and productivity, increased earnings will just make for more satisfied employees, not increased productivity.

One way of raising productivity is to offer employees financial incentives for improved results. The entire question of wage incentives should be re-examined in the context of present-day labor-management relations and knowledge of human behavior. Different forms of incentives should be developed to suit the needs of companies and employees. All sorts of new possibilities become obvious when stereotyped beliefs are discarded. Most important, the plans must benefit *both* management and employees and not undermine employees' job security. Managers must not misinterpret employees' increased productivity when working under incentives as increased identification with managements' goals. Employees who were not sympathetic to management before incentives remain so after. The desire for increased earnings will motivate employees to move in a direction parallel to managements' goals, but for entirely different reasons from those which motivate management to achieve these goals: increased productivity. It is the results that matter, not the reasons that prompt them.

Designing New Management-Labor Relationships

An ideal relationship would have both management and labor moving in parallel directions toward the same or equivalent goals. The motives of the parties are not as important as that the thrust of their efforts is in parallel directions. Through a simple change from the typical situation in goals and relations between employee and employer, both parties will pull in the same direction, each for its own valid reasons. The change can best be shown by an illustration. Assume a company of 125 employees on the average manufactures a single product in quantities of 500 a day. The average labor cost is 2.0 hours per unit $(125 \times 8 \div 500)$. Suppose the manager proposes to the employees that since his product cost is 2.0 hours per unit, he is prepared to share increased productivity with the employees, say on a fifty-fifty basis, calculated weekly. With cooperation between the employees and management, the total production at the end of the week is raised to 3,000 units, the labor value of which is $3000 \times 2.00 = 6000$ hours. Since a total of $5 \times 125 \times 8 = 5000$ hours was expended, the value of the increased production is the difference between the output and the input, equal to 1,000 hours. The employees' share is 500 hours, calculated as increased pay. Now consider what has occurred: previously the manager was interested in the production count into the warehouse and the labor hours expended, but the employees were not. Under the sharing plan the employees are also interested in the same measurements. Productivity gains are measured the same for the employees as for management. Reduced productivity reduces the employees' share. Before implementation of the plan, only management gained or lost as productivity changed. Under the sharing plan, both gain or lose in exactly the same way. Here is a relationship in which both forces move in parallel directions toward the same or equivalent goals, each for its own reasons.

This form of incentive plan is not new. Variations of it were used back in the 1920s in American industry and abroad. In the late 1930s and after World War II, Joseph Scanlon, the perceptive and universally respected Research Director of the United Steelworkers of America and later on the faculty of the Massachusetts Institute of Technology, popularized the sharing plan which came to bear his name. Scanlon breathed life and meaning into his plan far beyond the narrow way in which sharing plans previously operated. McGregor (1959:89) perceived the potentials as:

> The Scanlon Plan (is) a philosophy of organization. It is not a program in the usual sense; it is a way of life—for the management, for the union, and for every individual employee. Because it is a way of life, it affects virtually every aspect of the operation of the organization. In this fact lies its real significance.

Many articles in the 1950s foretold success for the Scanlon plan. In the ten years Scanlon was at MIT until his death in 1956, a number of Scanlon Plans were instituted. Lesieur and Puckett (1968), who took over Scanlon's work, report that in 1959 there were about fifty to sixty plants using the plan. In 1968 about 180 companies used the Scanlon Plan and from 300 to 500 plants were using some version of the plan.

Despite the potentials of the Scanlon Plan, it did not win the broad support from management that its enthusiasts anticipated. This occurred because of two main reasons:

1. Practically all published reports of Scanlon Plan installations highlighted the labor-management committees which were established. Managers are wary of such committees, because they seem to give the workers a greater voice in managing the operations. This alone is enough to scare off most managers.
2. There is a major flaw in the way productivity standards are set which was readily discerned by operating managers, who were often more experienced with work measurement than were the Scanlon Plan supporters.

When Scanlon Plans or conventional wage incentive plans break down, it is inevitably because the work measurement process proves defective, either in its original design or in its administration. Most Scanlon Plans measure work output as a ratio of payroll dollars to sales volume dollars. Since the ratio does not remain constant with changes in technology, product, or production process, the ratio is not a valid measurement of work output. Moreover, the sales value of a product may change due to market conditions and other factors beyond the control of the employees. This unsound means of measuring productivity change usually causes Scanlon Plans to start degenerating in several years, depending on the magnitude of the changes which are made. However, a recent article by Lesieur describes the case histories of three companies which have operated with the Scanlon Plan for from fourteen to seventeen years to the satisfaction of management and the employees (see Lesieur and Puckett, 1969: 109).

Sharing plans hold great promise. A most important feature is that it makes possible a new relationship between management and labor in which both are provided with incentives to move in parallel directions. The very nature of the plan creates goals which each can accept as beneficial to them. Descriptions and details of such plans, called Improved Productivity Sharing Plans (Improshare), are described in another publication (Fein, 1974b).

Profit Sharing as a Motivator

The efficacy of profit sharing as a motivator to increased productivity and reduced costs cannot be proven from available data because it is impossible to obtain before and after statistics where profit sharing has been employed. Even if data were to show that profit sharing companies were more profitable than comparable nonprofit sharing companies, there would be no way of isolating the effect of profit sharing on profit against other factors which affect profit, including the most important: the quality of management. At best, the opinions of managers can be used to shed light on the value of profit sharing as motivator to increased productivity.

Profit sharing is becoming more popular in this country. A large scale study by Metzger (1966:26) of companies with 500 and less employees showed that about one out of five companies has either a cash, deferred or combination profit sharing plan. A study by the Research Institute of America (1969:25) showed about one in three companies used profit sharing. Metzger (1966:122) further states that:

> Managements usually establish cash profit sharing plans as "production incentive" programs and aim their profit sharing communication activities in the direction of productivity increases, quality improvement and the like. Deferred plans, on the other hand, are frequently set up as substitutes for fixed benefit pension plans and managements have "retirement security for employees" almost exclusively in mind.

Metzger's study showed that profit sharing managers considered cash payments as more effective in creating productivity consciousness in employees than deferred income.

Most profit sharing plans are used as deferred income in conjunction with retirement plans. A Conference Board study of profit sharing in manufacturing companies with 250 and over employees, for blue and white collar employees, showed 17% had cash plans, 62% had deferred plans, and 21% had combination plans. Data for nonmanufacturing companies was very similar (see Conference Board, 1964:110). The Metzger (1966:30) study of companies of 500 employees or less showed 65% of the companies used cash plans. Smaller companies' managers seem to prefer cash to deferred income. Metzger (1966:10) presents the essence of profit sharing philosophy as:

> ... profit sharing means much more than mere "money sharing"—it means "sharing the caring" in the business. Profit sharing is a way of developing an atmosphere in which employees want the business to succeed as much as management does. A profit sharing partnership evolves out of which flows appropriate information-sharing, responsibility-sharing, participating, a sense of belonging, and the like; money sharing then becomes the essential outward sign and vital cohesive force of the partnership. A climate of cooperation is created conducive to the growth of both human beings and profits.

Profit sharing ideals cannot be realized, however, when management does not follow through with practices which workers view in their best interests. Healy (1965:49) discussed this point in the unsuccessful American Motors Corporation profit sharing plan:

> The most significant conclusion from the American Motors experience thus far is that a *profit sharing or progress-sharing plan, by itself, is unlikely to produce a "new" relationship.* When it stands alone, it becomes a "gimmick." There must be accompanying day-to-day efforts to improve the relationship and change the attitudes. (Italics in original)

In discussions I had with Metzger, he emphasized that many companies with profit sharing fail to see clearly that management bears the responsibility to implement policies and practices which will encourage employees to increasingly accept management's major goal: profit. Too frequently, managers treat profit sharing mechanically and expect a magic turnabout in employees' attitudes merely on the announcement that a profit sharing plan has been established.

The attitudes of profit sharing managers to direct incentives showed up most interestingly in Metzger's (1966:215) study: 9.8% of the nonprofit sharing companies employed individual incentive, production or sales bonuses, while 69.5% of the profit sharing companies employed incentive practices in addition to profit sharing. *Seven times as many profit sharing managers used incentives as did nonprofit sharing managers.* Unfortunately the data do not show which came first; profit sharing or incentives. Did managers first employ incentives and then find that the environment at the work-place was lacking, which they believed could be improved by profit sharing? Or did they first adopt profit sharing and then find that it did not provide individual employees with sufficient motivation to urge them to higher productivity? This data can be interpreted in several ways:

- Profit sharing managers are generally incentive-minded and they believe in sharing productivity increases through direct incentives in addition to overall profit sharing.
- Profit sharing managers believe in the efficacy of direct incentives to a far greater extent than do nonprofit sharing managers.
- Profit sharing is not as effective when used alone as when it is used with direct incentives.
- Profit sharing managers see the need to change the environment at the work-place. By giving workers a piece of the action, they strive to make them more receptive to management's goals.

The highest paying cash profit sharing plan in this country is at Lincoln Electric; their employees now receive about 105% of their annual pay in profit sharing bonuses. Lincoln employees work all year on piece work, the oldest form of wage incentive. Each employee strives to increase his weekly earnings by increased productivity. Together, all employees work toward reducing costs and increasing profits so that their share of profits will increase. Management and employees make Lincoln's profit sharing plan work to everyone's benefit. Lincoln's customers also benefit by improved products at lower prices. The shareholder's dividends are fairly stable but their equity grows constantly as management plows back capital each year to improve the plant. Would Lincoln Electric's productivity be as high, or would their profit sharing plan work as well without piece work? There is no data available to answer the question. But the plant and its employees are living proof that a combination of factors is working to produce what I believe is the highest productivity level of any plant in this country.

In my discussions with Metzger, he made a strong point that the most effective results will be obtained from combining direct incentives and profit sharing as a systems incentive program for the entire organization; individual and group incentives for the narrow interests at the work-place and profit sharing to create organization-wide interests and teamwork. Using both types of incentive strengthens each and helps to overcome inherent shortcomings.

Why the Low Use of Incentives?

A study by Fein (1973c) of 400 companies showed that companies which used work measurement for their operations had 14.6% higher productivity than companies that did not measure their work; companies that used wage incentives had 42.9% higher productivity than companies that used only work measurement and 63.8% higher than companies with no work measurement. Wage incentives unquestionably motivate workers to higher output. Since only about 26% of the nation's manufacturing work force is on incentive, it appears that most managers prefer to manage without incentives. The more obvious reasons for not using incentives do not require discussion: some operations are not suited to incentives; highly mechanized or process-controlled operations are not appreciably affected by workers. Many managers claim they can operate more effectively without incentives and maintain as high a productivity level as could be accomplished with incentives. But studies (Fein, 1973c) show that where incentives can work, employees will always produce at higher levels with incentives.

Some reasons. A major reason advanced by some managers who do not employ incentives is that they believe incentives will create conditions which will erode their rights to manage. Perhaps that is how it appears to some managers with incentives. But what more probably occurs in their plants is that workers on incentive are more outspoken on production problems which interfere with their ability to earn incentive pay. Employees on incentive often take on some supervising responsibilities to maintain their raised productivity, particularly where supervisors are inept. While it is obviously unsound to allow incentives to bolster weak supervision, management often encourages employees to exercise greater initiative. After years of working in this sort of environment, it is little wonder that employees on incentive are more independent and vocal regarding production problems than are employees in day work plants.

Another management reason for not using incentives is that they place managers in the limelight of workers' criticism. Management can make the most stupid errors and if these do not affect workers' income security, they are not concerned. But if workers' income is affected, management quickly hears from their critics. When on incentive, workers become sensitive to management actions and decisions. Some of the most serious incentive disputes arise when management cannot maintain production flow because of such things as material shortages, engineering difficulties and equipment problems. Some managers cannot or will not tolerate criticism from their work force. Many managers prefer their work force to be mute on production problems. One way to accomplish this is to avoid incentives.

Still another reason for the low utilization of incentives for workers is that experiences show that over a period of time, wage incentive plans often run away and earnings outdistance productivity. Workers and unions are usually blamed for the disintegration. In examining hundreds of incentive plan installations for causes and effects of failures, I invariably found that the disintegration was due to management incompetence in one form or another. Reports on the operation of wage incentive plans for workers frequently stress problems encountered, but such reports usually do not correctly pinpoint the causes of the problems and why the plans went wrong. A full discussion of the design and operation of incentive plans, and ways to prevent degeneration, is contained in Fein (1971). In my opinion, sound incentive plans can be operated practically forever.

Developing Rational Managing Strategies (a Summary)

One might question the validity of the various issues I have raised by pointing to the tremendous material gains made in this country, despite the restraints on the will to work. But how much more would be accomplished if workers performed their tasks with the ardor managers only dream of! Yet the dream can be fulfilled if managers will honestly evaluate the overall relationship between workers and management and establish conditions and relations which workers will see as beneficial to them or at least as not operating to their disadvantage. All approaches to increasing the will to work must start with equity bases which offer employees real stuff they can touch, not ephemeral slogans. Management must see that the present relations lead to wasteful practices and increased costs. Developing managing strategies which will raise workers' will to work is not difficult. Most needed are managers with the fortitude to break with past archaic practices and establish relations in their plants which workers will see as benefitting them. This does not require giving away the proverbial company shirt. On the contrary, management will benefit greatly from a new environment in which workers sympathetically view management's problems as also affecting them.

A program to meet workers' and management's needs will consider the following:

- The concept that the work itself must become the end for which work is performed is rejected by about 85% of the work force.
- Attempts to enrich work so that it becomes meaningful to most workers have low possibility of success. Production technology in the advanced industrialized countries has reduced the need for skilled craftsmen in the production process, with the bulk of work highly mechanized and routinized, requiring low skills and limited judgments. These jobs cannot be meaningfully enriched. The production process cannot be reversed without tremendously increasing product costs, which no one would tolerate. Proposals that jobs be enriched with additional responsibilities and skills are made through sheer ignorance of the production process.
- What is really demeaning about low level skill jobs is that workers in these jobs cannot earn enough to achieve a level of living to which they aspire. The work itself is not demeaning.
- Income and job security are most highly prized by workers. These are the preconditions for fostering the will to work, without which no motivational plan can fully succeed.
- Job security creates a new plant environment; it removes the fear which nurtures resistance to productivity improvement. But job security will not raise productivity. It only creates an opportunity for improvement which management must exploit.
- In practically all plants, relations between employee and employer are such that if employees cooperate in raising productivity, some employees' interests are damaged.
- The employment relationship between workers and management must be restructured so workers have a real stake in the progress of the enterprise. While the individual employee's work may still lack mean-

ing, the environment in the plant may engender group and plant-wide involvement of a new sort which will be beneficial to employees and management.

- Management should develop financial incentive plans to give employees an opportunity to benefit from their increased productivity and contributions. In most work situations, individual and small group incentives will promote the highest productivity. Plant-wide incentive plans prove less effective as the group size increases. In addition to incentives at the work-place, there should be opportunities to gain from overall increased productivity and progress of the enterprise.
- Opportunities for involvement in the work should be available to workers who desire it. These achievers are an important segment of the work force and they should be given every encouragement.
- Various restraints on the will to work should be pinpointed and removed.
- Management must design its programs to suit the needs of workers and not make value judgments about what workers should want, how they should react, or what is good for them.

This chapter does not propose the creation of strifeless work environments. On the contrary, I believe competition and challenge bring out the best in people. But the thrust of the competition must be constructive and improve workers' interests. Management must aim toward creating a new environment at the work-place so that more workers will be interested in their work. Most people now work to eat, not because they want to or because they have a stake in the outcome of their work. Much work is performed in an environment of coercion, largely through the threat that failure to perform will result in dismissal. Further depressing the scene is the Damocles' sword of layoffs, seasonally or due to management's failure to produce sales. In all, the environment at the work-place does not raise the will to work.

Management should encourage management-labor relationships which give their employees real reasons for involvement in the enterprise. Management need not relinquish its rights needed to manage the company. By more equitably distributing the progress and profits to its employees, management stands to gain far more than it gives up. I foresee far-sighted managers more fully accepting their responsibilities to their shareholders, employees, customers, and the public, and developing relationships within the company which will enhance everyone's interests. Competition from increased productivity in these companies will inevitably force traditionally managed companies to reconsider their policies.

REFERENCES

American Federation of Labor and Congress of Industrial Organizations (AFL–CIO)
  1958   "Collective bargaining report." Washington, D.C., Department of Research, Vol. 3, No. 4–5.
  1969   "Labor looks at automation." Washington, D.C., Department of Labor (January).
Argyris, C.
  1965   Integrating the Individual in the Organization. New York: Wiley.

Becker, J.M.
  1968   Guaranteed Income for the Unemployed: The Story of SUB. Balti-
          more: Johns Hopkins University Press.
Bergson, A.
  1964   The Economics of Soviet Planning. New Haven, Conn.: Yale Univer-
          sity Press.
Brindisi, L.J., Jr.
  1971   "Survey of executive compensation." World. Published by Peat, Mar-
          wick, Mitchell and Co. 5(Spring):53–56.
Bureau of National Affairs
  1951   "Plant labor-management committees." Washington, D.C., U.S. Govern-
          ment Printing Office (June).
Conference Board (formerly, NICB)
  1964   "Personnel practices in factory and office: manufacturing." Studies in
          Personnel Policy No. 194.
Dale, E.
  1949   "Greater productivity through labor-management cooperation." Amer-
          ican Management Association. Research Report No. 14:17–18.
de Schweinitz, D.
  1949   Labor and Management in a Common Enterprise. Cambridge, Mass.:
          Harvard University Press.
  1966   "Labor management consultation in the factory." Honolulu, Hawaii:
          University of Hawaii. Unpublished paper.
Derber, M.
  1970   "Crosscurrents in workers participation." Industrial Relations No. 2,
          9(February):123–136.
Dobb, M.
  1966   Soviet Economic Development Since 1917. New York: International
          Publishers.
Druker, P.F.
  1971   "What we can learn from Japanese management." Harvard Business
          Review 49 (March–April):115.
Dunnette, M.D.
  1969   "Compensation: some obvious answers to unasked questions." Com-
          pensation Review of the American Management Association 1(1):8–15.
Ewen, R.B., C.L. Hulin, P.C. Smith and E.A. Locke
  1966   "An empirical test of the Herzberg two-factor theory." Journal of Ap-
          plied Psychology 6(50):544–550.
Fein, M.
  1942   "Producing for victory: a labor manual for increasing war produc-
          tion." Report written for the International Federation of Architects,
          Engineers, Chemists and Technicians. New York: Congress of Indus-
          trial Organizations (CIO).
  1971   "Wage incentive plans," in H.B. Maynard (ed.), Industrial Engineer-
          ing Handbook. Third Edition. New York: McGraw-Hill.
  1973a   "The real needs and goals of blue color workers." The Conference
          Board Record (February):26–33.
  1973b   "The myth of job enrichment." The Humanist (September–October):
          30–32.

1973c "Work measurement and wage incentives." Industrial Engineering, American Institute of Industrial Engineers (September) :49–51.

1974a "Job enrichment: a reevaluation." Sloan Management Review 15(Winter) :69–88.

1974b "Rational approaches to raising productivity." American Institute of Industrial Engineers, Norcross, Georgia 30071. WM and ME Monograph No. 5.

Ford, R.N.
1969   Motivation Through the Work Itself. New York: American Management Association.

Form, W.
1973   "Auto workers and their machines: a study of work, factory and job satisfaction in four countries." Social Forces, University of North .Carolina Press 52(September) :1–15.

Fox, H.
1969   "Top executive compensation." Conference Board Report No. 640. New York: The Conference Board.

Friedmann, G.
1964   The Anatomy of Work. Paperback Edition. London: Heinemann.
n.d.   "De la Soviétique a l'U.R.S.S." Unpublished.

Galbraith, J.K.
1967   The New Industrial State. Boston: Houghton Mifflin.

Gellerman, S.
1963   Motivation and Productivity. New York: American Management Association.
1969   "Behavioral strategies." California Management Review 12(Winter) : 45–51.

Gordon, T.J.
1969   A Study of Potential Changes in Employee Benefits. Middletown, Conn.: The Institute for the Future.

Graen, G.B.
1966   "Addendum to 'An empirical test of the Herzberg two-factor theory.' " Journal of Applied Psychology 6(50) :551–555.
1968   "Testing traditional and two-factor hypotheses concerning job satisfaction." Journal of Applied Psychology 5(52) :366–371.

Graen, G.B. and C.L. Hulin
1968   "Addendum to 'An empirical investigation of two implications of the two-factor theory of job satisfaction.' " Journal of Applied Psychology 4(52) :341–342.

Guthrie, H.W.
1969   "Teachers in moonlight." Monthly Labor Review, U.S. Department of Labor, Bureau of Labor Statistics (February) :28–31.

Haire, M.E., E. Ghiselli and L.W. Porter
1963   "Psychological research in pay: an overview." Industrial Relations (3) :3–8.
1966   Managerial Thinking: An International Study. New York: Wiley.

Hall, D.T. and K.E. Nougaim
1968   "An examination of Maslow's need hierarchy in an organizational setting." Organizational Behavior and Human Performance 3(February) : 3–35.

Hartmann, H.
  1970 "Co-determination in West Germany." Industrial Relations 9(February):137–149.
Healy, J.J. (ed.)
  1965 Creative Collective Bargaining: Meeting Today's Challenge to Labor-Management Relations. Englewood Cliffs, New Jersey: Prentice-Hall.
Herzberg, F.
  1966 Work and the Nature of Man. Cleveland, Ohio: World Publishing Co.
  1968 "One more time: how do you motivate employees?" Harvard Business Review 46(January–February):53–62.
  1969 "Job enrichment pays off." Harvard Business Review 47(March–April):61–78.
Herzberg, F., B. Mausner and B. Snyderman
  1959 The Motivation to Work. New York: Wiley.
Horne, G.
  1966 The New York Times (August 8).
Hulin, C.L. and M.R. Blood
  1968 "Job enlargement, individual differences and worker responses." Psychological Bulletin 69(January):41–55.
Hulin, C.L. and P.C. Smith
  1967 "An empirical investigation of two implications of the two-factor theory of job satisfaction." Journal of Applied Psychology 5(51):396–402.
International Institute for Labor Studies
  1968 "Worker's participation in management in Poland (No. 2)." Geneva, Switzerland: Bulletin No. 5(November).
International Labor Office
  1948 "Labour management co-operation in United States war production." Studies and Reports, New Series No. 6.
Institute of Labor and Industrial Relations
  1969 "Job satisfaction: models, methods and empirical results." Bulletin of the University of Illinois, Report Series No. 196, Champaign-Urbana. No. 83, 66(February).
Kelman, H.C.
  1968 A Time to Speak on Human Values and Social Research. San Francisco: Jossey-Bass, Inc.
Katz, D. and R.L. Kahn
  1966 The Social Psychology of Organizations. New York: Wiley.
Katzell, R., D. Yankelovich, O. Ornatti, M. Fein and A. Nash
  1975 Work, Productivity and Job Satisfaction. An Evaluation of Policy-Related Research. National Science Foundation, Research Applied to National Needs Grant No. 55H, 73–07939 AO1.
Korman, A.K.
  1970 "Toward an hypothesis of work behavior." Journal of Applied Psychology 1(54):36.
Kornhauser, A.
  1965 Mental Health of the Industrial Worker. New York: Wiley.
Leavitt, H.J.
  1964 Managerial Psychology. Revised Edition. Chicago: University of Chicago Press.

Lenin, V.
  1921   "Scientific management and the dictatorship of the proletariat," in
         J.R. Commons. Trade Unionism and Labor Problems. Also found in
         Lenin's Collected Works, Vol. 7.
Lesieur, F.G. and E.S. Puckett
  1968   "The Scanlon Plan: past, present and future," Proceedings of the
         Twenty-First Annual Winter Meeting. Industrial Relations Research
         Association. Chicago, Illinois. December.
  1969   "The Scanlon Plan has proved itself." Harvard Business Review
         47(September–October):109–118.
Lewis, E.L.
  1960   "Extent of incentive pay in manufacturing." Monthly Labor Review,
         U.S. Department of Labor, Bureau of Labor Statistics (May).
  1964   "Wages and related benefits." U.S. Department of Labor, Bureau of
         Labor Statistics, Bulletin 1345–83 (June).
  1965   "Personal correspondence with Bureau of Labor Statistics." Un-
         published.
Liebow, E.
  1970   "No man can live with the terrible knowledge that he is not needed."
         New York Times Magazine (April 5).
Lincoln, J.F.
  1951   Incentive Management. Cleveland, Ohio: Lincoln Electric Co.
  1961   A New Approach to Industrial Economics. Old Greenwich, Conn.:
         Devin-Adair.
McClelland, D.C. and D.G. Winter
  1969   Motivating Economic Achievement. New York: Free Press.
McElroy, F.S. and A. Moros
  1948   "Joint production committees." Monthly Labor Review, U.S. Depart-
         ment of Labor, Bureau of Labor Statistics (January, August).
McGregor, D.
  1959   "The Scanlon Plan through a psychologist's eyes," in F.G. Lesieur, The
         Scanlon Plan. Cambridge, Mass.: MIT Press.
  1960   The Human Side of Enterprise. New York: McGraw-Hill.
  1966   Leadership and Motivation. Cambridge, Mass.: MIT Press.
  1967   The Professional Manager. New York: McGraw-Hill.
Marrow, A.J., D.G. Bowers and S.E. Seashore
  1967   Management by Participation. New York: Harper & Row.
Marx, K.
  n.d.   Capital. Translation from the German. Vol. 1. New York: E.P. Dutton.
Maslow, A.H.
  1954   Motivation and Personality. New York: Harper & Row.
  1965   Euphysician Management: A Journal. New York: Irwin.
Metzger, B.L.
  1966   Profit Sharing in Perspective. Evanston, Ill.: Profit Sharing Research
         Foundation.
Myers, M.S.
  1964   "Who are your motivated workers?" Harvard Business Review
         42(January):73–88.
  1966   "Conditions for manager motivation." Harvard Business Review
         44(January–February).

1968   "Every employee a manager." California Management Review 10(Spring):9–20.

National Board for Prices and Incomes
1968   "Payment by results system." Report No. 65, H.M.S.O.(May).

National Commission of Technology, Automation and Economic Progress
1966   "Technology and the American economy." 1(February).

Neff, W.S.
1968   Work and Human Behavior. New York: Atherton.

New York Times, The
1970   March 28.

Obradovic, J.
1970   "Participation and work attitudes in Yugoslavia." Industrial Relations 9(February):161–169.
1975   "Workers' participation: who participates?" Industrial Relations No. 1 14(February). Published by the University of Illinois.

Opshal, R.L. and M.D. Dunnette
1966   "The role of financial compensation in industrial motivation." Psychological Bulletin, 2(66).

Oswald, R.
1969   "Adjusting to automation." AF of L–CIO Research Department, Washington, D.C. Publication No. 144. January.

Patchen, M.
1970   Participation, Achievement and Involvement on the Job. Englewood Cliffs, New Jersey: Prentice-Hall.

Porter, L.W. and E.E. Lawler III
1968   Managerial Attitudes and Performances. Homewood, Ill.: Irwin.

Research Institute of America
1969   "Fringe benefits for rank-and-file employees."

Rosenstein, E.
1970   "Histadrut's search for a participation program." Industrial Relations No. 2 9(February):170–186.

Rosow, J.M.
1971   "Toward a brighter blue collar." Manpower, U.S. Department of Labor (March).

Rush, H.M.F.
1969   "Behavioral science, concepts and management applications. Studies in Personnel Policy No. 216, The Conference Board (formerly, the NICB).

Schoderbeck, P.P. and W.E. Reif
1969   Job Enlargement: The Key to Improved Performance. Ann Arbor: University of Michigan Press.

Schregle, J.
1970   "Forms of participation in management." Industrial Relations 9(February):117–122.

Siassi, I., G. Crocetti and H.R. Spiro
1974   "Loneliness and dissatisfaction in a blue collar population." Archives of General Psychiatry, American Medical Association 30(February): 261–265.

Simon, H.A.
1957   Administrative Behavior. New York: Macmillan.

Sirota, D. and J.M. Greenwood
  1971   "Understand your overseas work force." Harvard Business Review
         49(January–February) :53–60.
Sorcher, M.
  1969   "The effects of employee involvement on work performance." Per-
         sonnel Planning and Research Practices, Corporate Employee Rela-
         tions, General Electric Company, New York.
Stelluto, G.L.
  1969   "Report on incentive in manufacturing industries." Monthly Labor
         Review, U.S. Department of Labor, Bureau of Labor Statistics
         9(July) :49–53.
Strauss, G. and E. Rosenstein
  1970   "Workers participation: a critical view." Industrial Relations 9(Febru-
         ary) :197–214.
Turner, A.N. and P.R. Lawrence
  1965   "Industrial jobs and the worker." Harvard University Division of
         Research. Unpublished Paper.
Uris, A.
  1965   "Mogey's work simplification is working new miracles." Factory Man-
         agement (September).
U.S. Department of Health, Education and Welfare
  1973   Work in America. Report of a Special Task Force to the Secretary
         of Health, Education and Welfare. Prepared under the auspices of
         the W.E. Upjohn Institute for Employment Research. Cambridge,
         Mass.: MIT Press.
U.S. Department of Labor, Bureau of Labor Statistics
  1971   "Employee compensation in Japan." No. 3, 16(March).
U.S. Department of Labor
  1974   Job Satisfaction: Is There a Trend? Manpower Research Monograph
         No. 30, GPO, Stock Number 2900-00195:1–5.
Vroom, V.H.
  1964   Work and Motivation. New York: Wiley.
Wass, D.L.
  1967   "Teams of Texans learn to save millions." Training in Business and
         Industry (November).
Wall Street Journal, The
  1971   (April 16) : 6.
Weeks, D.A.
  1972   Compensating Salesmen and Sales Executives. Conference Board
         Report Number 579. New York: The Conference Board: 36.
Wild, R.
  1970   "Job needs, job satisfaction and job behavior of women manual
         workers." Journal of Applied Psychology 2(54).

CHAPTER **12**

Job Enrichment, Need Theory and Reinforcement Theory

Curt Tausky and E. Lauck Parke

University of Massachusetts, Amherst

INTRODUCTION

Judging from the number of conferences, books and articles on "humanizing" the work-place, the redesign of highly fractionated, monotonous tasks into enriched jobs seems to be an idea whose time has come. In practice, however, the number of American workers actually experiencing extensive job redesign programs is relatively small. Of a total civilian labor force of 85 million, it has been estimated (Report of a Special Task Force to the Secretary of Health, Education and Welfare, 1973:103) that only 3,000 workers have been involved in extensive schemes of job enrichment. Nonetheless, it may be anticipated that despite the small number of American workers currently affected by such programs, this number will grow over time; it also appears that much the same could be said about European job enrichment programs (Dowling, 1973; Mire, 1974; Paul, Robertson and Herzberg, 1969).

The reason why such programs may be extended to more work-places is, first and foremost, that they seem to yield desirable results. Nearly all of the published cases indicate that turnover and absenteeism are reduced, while quality and often quantity of output are increased.[1] The employees evidence enhanced work satisfaction, reflected in decreased turnover and absenteeism, which in turn reduces organizational costs for recruitment and training.

Job enrichment, however, runs quite against the grain of standard industrial engineering conceptualizations of how jobs should be designed. Adam Smith's (1937) portrayal of the advantages of an extreme division of labor among pin makers is an example of this approach to job design.

> One man draws out the wire, another straights it, a third cuts it, a fourth points it, a fifth grinds it at the top for receiving the head; to

---

[1] Overviews of cases and results can be found in: Report of a Special Task Force to the Secretary of Health, Education and Welfare (1973), Davis and Taylor (1972), Maher (1971), Foulkes (1969) and Rush (1971). For an appraisal of unpublished, unsuccessful job redesign efforts, see Hackman (1974).

make the head requires two or three distinct operations; to put it on is a peculiar business, to whiten the pins is another; it is even a trade by itself to put them into the paper; and the important business of making a pin is, in this manner, divided into about eighteen distinct operations.... But though they were very poor, and therefore but indifferently accommodated with the necessary machinery, they could, when they exerted themselves, make among them about twelve pounds of pins in a day. There are in a pound upwards of four thousand pins of a middling size. Those ten persons, therefore, could make among them upwards of forty-eight thousand pins in a day.... But if they had all wrought separately and independently ... they certainly could not each of them have made twenty, perhaps not one pin in a day....

Definitions and Distinctions

Before proceeding, let us at this point define some terms which are often confused: (1) Job rotation—the movement by a worker from one work station to another, either every few hours or day to day; the tasks remain designed as they were, but the worker shifts among a limited set of tasks. (2) Job enlargement—the tasks stay as they were, but a limited set of tasks are grouped together into a job, thus providing the worker more variety at his work station; this sort of variety is sometimes referred to as "horizontal loading." (3) Job enrichment—this is sometimes referred to as "vertical loading," because the tasks then involve the elements of variety plus complexity and discretion. Variety, we noted, has to do with the number of operations to be performed, complexity involves the sequence, timing and coordination of the variety, and discretion incorporates the decisions required to deal with complexity. Vertical loading of a task, however, requires a bit more flesh than the bare bones we noted; in a fundamental sense it resembles the vertical integration of a firm. A series of operations that come before and after a single task are grouped together so that the overall task has a discernible unity. For example, instead of simply feeding a machine, the worker with an enriched job would perform "set up," feed the machine, and then inspect the output, accept, reject or repair the output, and if necessary, adjust or even perhaps repair the machine. Thus, variety, complexity and discretion are joined in the design of enriched jobs.

Does this mean Adam Smith was mistaken in 1776, and present-day industrial engineers are still wrong about the efficacy of a minute division of labor? Yes, in the sense that "larger" tasks have been shown to be as productive and frequently more productive than highly fragmented tasks, at least among contemporary American workers; no, in the sense that there are limits, though very unclear, to enriching jobs. The limitations arise from the amount of discretion required to perform a task. The greater the task complexity confronting a person, the more knowledge of appropriate responses he must have in order to exercise discretion properly. To the extent that the task involves "routine variety," the proper responses can be learned relatively quickly through training. To the extent "nonroutine" variety occurs, the training must be lengthier, hence more costly of time and money to the employee, the company, or both. Nonroutine variety, for example, of the sort a mechanic or doctor might confront, requires a lengthy training which enables them to have in memory, or know how to search for, a "correct" response to infrequent events. Thus, the amount of variety in a job must be matched by an equal amount of discretion, and the knowledge appropriate to exercising that discretion. Our job distinctions in the world of work basically involve the reduction of variety in order to make the knowledge required to deal with that variety accessible. It is costly in time and money for a plumber to learn how to respond to the tasks performed by the electrician.

As long as job enrichment involves routine variety, the responses to which can be quickly learned, there is no outstanding reason why such a program cannot succeed. But, to stretch variety in a manner that requires discretionary response to nonroutine events presents a serious problem. Nearly all published cases of job enrichment actually involve routine variety; the tasks incorporate a degree of complexity—but rarely so much that the worker cannot respond to task variety in a way which is familiar to him. It is clear that the amount of training and on-the-job thinking markedly increase for jobs where nonroutine events must be dealt with. These costs are recognized in the analysis of whole organizations (Galbraith, 1973; Thompson, 1967:57) for example, the contrast between mass production and job shops, and appear to present a similar limitation on the design of jobs *per se*.

Enriched job designs apparently run counter to traditional notions of task structure. However, because enriched tasks incorporate mainly routine variety, the break with traditional engineering concepts, though highly significant, is not nearly as complete as may appear at first glance. Nevertheless, there is evidence to indicate that even from an industrial engineering standpoint, job enrichment has advantages. Consider that if a person completes a whole component and tests it himself, rather than utilize an assembly-line production method, the transfer time of the incompleted assembly between work stations is decreased, and "balance delay" time is saved (the idle time of some workers whose tasks take less time than other tasks on the assembly line). For instance, Kilbridge's (1960) analysis of a pump assembly production line disclosed that a six-man assembly line completed one pump in 1.77 minutes; the job was restructured and each man completed a pump in only 1.49 minutes. Each worker then went on to test "his" pump. It should also be noted that the traditional assembly line is highly vulnerable to disruption from absenteeism. By designing tasks so that single workers, or small groups of workers, complete a whole or significant part of an assembly, the production process becomes much more flexible. At worst, total output may suffer slightly from absence of workers, but the production process continues. Additionally, it is much easier to add persons or groups if more output is needed, than to rebalance an entire assembly line. Dowling (1973) states that the major impetus in the Volvo and Saab facilities to undertake job redesign apparently stemmed from severe absenteeism problems. It was felt that job enrichment might not only make the work more attractive, and thereby reduce absenteeism, but also that the assembly line method of production was overly vulnerable to disruption from absenteeism, whereas production carried out by a number of small work groups would be less seriously affected by absenteeism.

As we saw, although job enrichment only partially questions the conventional wisdom of industrial engineering in regard to job design, traditional task designs are clearly open to serious criticism. The evidence simply does not support the premise that the smallest job is the most productive. However, job enrichment *does not*, on close examination, challenge certain hoary management principles but rather sharpens them. The concepts of accountability and pay for amount produced, are not diminished with job enrichment. We will return to this theme below.

In the remainder of this chapter we (1) present two alternative theoretical frameworks—need theory and reinforcement theory—each of which may be used to interpret workers' behavior under job enrichment conditions. (2) We then turn to a series of cases in quite diverse organizational settings, but which all share the structural feature that organizational participants are held responsible and accountable for their activities. (3) Finally, we suggest that reinforcement theory promises to be more useful in explaining and predicting employee's reactions to job enrichment programs than alternative explanations grounded in need theory.

THEORIES OF MOTIVATION

Content and Process Theory

Campbell, et al. (1974:85–95) suggest that the various approaches toward explaining motivation in work organizations may be usefully distinguished as either content or process theories.

Content theories, from an organizational point of view, are retrospective. They attempt to specify the content of what energizes people, the specific things which motivate them, for example, security, recognition, achievement and challenge. Such motives, drives, or needs are brought by people into the work organization. The prevailing structures of organizations are then viewed by content theorists as satisfactory if they foster satisfaction of the hypothesized needs, or as is more often the case, as unsatisfactory if the structures impede satisfaction of the hypothesized needs. From this point of view, the "needs" are givens and organizational structures must be adapted accordingly or there results a continuous friction between persons and organizations which reduces the effectiveness of both. If, however, organizational structures can be devised which match "needs," the problem of motivating people largely disappears. For example, if school-age children are deemed to have curiosity, then the classroom should provide learning materials which match the children's particular curiosities. Structural elements, such as tests and grades, should not be required "to motivate" the children.

In contrast to this approach to motivation are process theories. They attempt to explain and describe *how* behavior is maintained, altered or stopped. The emphasis is on the structural features—including other people—of ongoing work situations, particularly those characteristics of organizations which can be managed or administered in order to elicit particular behaviors from participants. Thus, attention is given to pay, promotion, prestige and peer group pressure. The core conception is that people pursue certain goals (e.g., promotion or pay increase) and that in order to gain the desired goals, those behaviors which are perceived to yield the goal will be enacted. The motivation process in this light is viewed as an exchange between the individual and his social environment. Particular behaviors, verbal or physical, are exchanged for things of value proffered in the situation; the motivation to work toward organizational objectives, then, is viewed as a process whereby the individual exchanges his time, energy and know-how for a valued "reward" that the organization offers.

Content theories emphasize the adaptation of structures to fit needs, whereas process theories urge the adaptation of organizational inducements in directions which produce valued payoffs for participants *if* they contribute toward organizational goals.

Need Theory

Content theories of work motivation have been well received academically, and recently a number of popularizing books for managers and the general public have emerged (Report of a Special Task Force to the Secretary of Health, Education and Welfare, 1973; Jenkins, 1974). In this literature the perspectives of several major theorists recur. They attempt to specify what people's needs are in relation to their work and, for the most part, view contemporary organizational structures as need-frustrating rather than need-satisfying. In this section we will show the "needs" that have been formulated by Maslow, Herzberg, McGregor, and Argyris.

Abraham Maslow. Nearly all modern need theorists acknowledge the influence of Maslow on their thinking, and this is markedly true for the need theorists presented here. Maslow developed an intuitively engaging conceptualization of man as motivated to action in the effort to satisfy his needs. Motivation, in this framework, refers to seeking for what is lacking; therefore, a need which has been satisfied cannot continue to motivate action in the direction of fulfilling that need until the need is again unsatisfied.

According to Maslow (1954:80–98), needs exhibit a hierarchical pattern:
1. Physiological (hunger, thirst, sex, sleep);
2. Safety and security (protection of the physical self and life-style);
3. Belongingness and love (affection);
4. Self-esteem, esteem by others (self-approval, approval by others, prestige);
5. Self-actualization (the need to become what one is potentially, to become more and more that which one is capable of becoming).

If the "lower-order" physiological needs are unsatisfied, the organism will be dominated by these needs and all other needs will remain dormant. It is then meaningful to characterize a person as hungry, for example, because thoughts of food dominate consciousness. Maslow (1954:83) tells us that when food has satisfied his need, "at once higher order needs emerge, and these, rather than physiological hungers, dominate the organism. And when these in turn are satisfied, new and higher needs emerge, ... the basic human needs are organized into a hierarchy of relative prepotency."

One particular implication of Maslow's theory has become embedded in need theory, turning it in a different direction than alternative views. From the need hierarchy perspective, satiation with the lower-order physiological, safety and security needs is possible, and so it is, on up to but not including self-actualization. What this means is that there is in people some sense (of indeterminate origin) of what constitutes "enough" prestige, or, perhaps more interestingly, enough pay, so that the self-actualization need becomes dominant. According to the theory, people can then *not* be motivated by more pay or promotion but only by more interesting work which fosters self-actualization; indeed, their consciousness will not revolve entirely around more pay or prestige because these needs, once satisfied, become dormant. This is precisely the conclusion drawn by need theorists from Maslow's work. Thus, the material payoffs an organization could use will not motivate today's workers because they have attained, for the most part, sufficient lower-order need satisfaction; societal affluence, when shared by employees, requires, for motivational reasons, structures which satisfy the higher-order self-actualization needs.

Let us consider a few examples. Argyris (1962:75) has argued that organizations which stultify higher-order needs produce the consequence that, among other things such as gold bricking and rate setting, employees will engage in "... requesting increased material rewards almost regardless of the financial state of the organization, and demanding programs that guarantee their job security." Argyris (1960:153) further suggests they will display a "... desire for unionization...." McGregor (1957:88) mentions in this regard "... unreasonable demands for economic benefits." Herzberg, as will be seen, insists that pay cannot serve as a motivator at all. The widely read Report of a Special Task Force to the Secretary of Health, Education and Welfare (1973:10–13) makes a distinct point of informing the reader that pay is down on the list of important employee wants. Another recent popular work by Sheppard and Herrick (1972:10–11), cautions that "Interesting work, enough help and equipment to get the job done, enough information to get the job done, and enough authority to do their jobs—all were very important to more workers than was good pay."

Students of work motivation, then, whose writings bear the conceptual imprint of Maslow, characteristically mute the role of extrinsic rewards such as wages. The reason merits restatement: if all lower-order needs are deemed to be adequately satisfied, then the highest-order need for self-actualization will predominate. As Maslow (1943) put it, "A musician must make music, an artist must paint, a poet must write, if he is to be ultimately happy. What a man can be, he must be." Presumably, the push from self-actualization needs, rather than the pull of extrinsic rewards, also applies to motivating workers in business and industry; they will strive for greater competency and exert heightened work effort if their jobs are so designed that individual abilities and knowledge are given room for growth on challenging tasks.

Frederick Herzberg. Although Herzberg's conclusions regarding work motivation are similar to Maslow's, his framework is formulated differently. Herzberg's major concern has been the relationships among work satisfaction, dissatisfaction and motivation. To explain the relationships he found among these variables, Herzberg developed a two-dimensional theory of workers' responses to their tasks and the work setting.

In this perspective, different sets of variables are related to the separate dimensions of work satisfaction and work dissatisfaction. The satisfaction variables he terms "motivators," and the dissatisfaction variables "hygienes." Based on his research, Herzberg found that satisfaction is related to variables encompassing (a) *job content*—the task itself, achievement, recognition, autonomy, advancement in knowledge and acquisition of new skills; whereas dissatisfaction is related to variables comprising (b) *job environment*—salary, security, working conditions, relationships with superiors, peers and subordinates, and status of the job.

According to Herzberg (1959, 1966), the job content and job environment variables have different consequences. The job environment may be perceived as positive, but if the job content is viewed negatively, the worker will not be dissatisfied, but neither will he be satisfied. Conversely, if job content factors are favorably perceived, the worker will be satisfied, but if job environment factors are unfavorable, dissatisfaction will also occur. Satisfaction and dissatisfaction are here conceptually distinguished as responses independently determined by separate sets of conditions, rather than as two poles on a single continuum.

The job content factors are in this model the "satisfiers" as well as the "motivators." The theory postulates, then, that the work itself influences workers' satisfaction, which in turn influences their level of effort on the job. It is pertinent that the subtitle to Herzberg's (1968) article, "One More Time: How Do You Motivate Employees?" answers: "Not by improving working conditions, raising salaries, or shuffling tasks."

Douglas McGregor.   McGregor has described two types of managerial perspectives on what constitutes the "job of managing," and the assumptions about subordinates' personalities associated with each of the management outlooks. These descriptions of personality are contrasting conceptions of man held by managers and in part account for the kinds of organizational structures presently extant.

The first, Theory X, represents the conventional view of management and personality, according to McGregor. The second, Theory Y, can be seen as conceptual kin to Maslow's theory. Theory X states:

1. Management is responsible for organizing the elements of productive enterprise—money, materials, equipment, people—in the interest of economic ends.
2. With respect to people, this is a process of directing their efforts, motivating them, controlling their actions, modifying their behavior to fit the needs of the organization.
3. Without this active intervention by management, people would be passive—even resistant, to organizational needs. They must be persuaded, rewarded, punished, controlled—their actions must be directed. . . .
4. The average man is by nature indolent—he works as little as possible.
5. He lacks ambition, dislikes responsibility, prefers to be led.
6. He is inherently self-centered, indifferent to organizational needs.
7. He is by nature resistant to change.
8. He is gullible, not very bright, the ready dupe of the charlatan and the demagogue (McGregor, 1957:22–28, 88–92. Theory X is shown on p. 23).

Theory Y was formulated by McGregor (1957:88) as an alternative conception ". . . of the task of managing people based on more adequate assumptions about human nature and human motivation." Theory Y states:

1. Management is responsible for organizing the elements of productive enterprise—money, materials, equipment, people—in the interests of economic ends.
2. People are *not* by nature passive or resistant to organizational needs. They have become so as a result of experience in organizations.
3. The motivation, the potential for development, the capacity for assuming responsibility, the readiness to direct behavior toward or-

ganizational goals are all present in people. Management does not put them there. It is a responsibility of management to make it possible for people to recognize and develop these human characteristics for themselves.

4. The essential task of management is to arrange organizational conditions and methods of operation so that people can achieve their own goals best by directing *their own* efforts toward organizational objectives (Theory Y is shown in McGregor, 1957:88–89).

McGregor notes that the application of Theory X is based on control by the carrot and stick technique, whereas Theory Y is based on self-direction. The consequences of Theory X, McGregor (1957:88) suggests, are that people respond with "...indolence, passivity, resistance to change, lack of responsibility, willingness to follow the demagogue, unreasonable demands for economic benefits." Alternatively, McGregor (1957:92) states that the application of Theory Y "...will not only enhance substantially...[our] materialistic achievements, but will bring us one step closer to the 'good society.'"

Chris Argyris. Argyris (1960:8–9; 1973) approaches the issue of what people need in their work from the point of view of personality development. He suggests that in our culture the characteristic mode of personality development is from an immature to mature state through changes in these aspects of the self:

1. From passivity to activity (doing for oneself rather than having others do it for one);
2. From dependence to independence (from seeking direction to preferring autonomy);
3. From shallow interests to deep interests (finding satisfaction and rewards in doing something for its own sake rather than as a means to some other end);
4. From accepting subordination to desiring equality or superiority to peers (seeking at least an equal voice in determining one's activity);
5. From lack of control to self-control (ability to direct oneself without external control).

Because work organizations are typically hierarchically patterned, Argyris maintains they are rigid and authority-bound. Hence, the structure of organization is in conflict with the needs of mature personalities—the personalities of participants are forced back to a prior, less mature stage of development. The potential of people, their readiness to self-actualize, is stifled by the demands made upon them to behave like children who are not allowed to think for themselves, control themselves, or pursue longer-range goals without close direction from superiors.

The solution suggested by Argyris is to redesign authority and jobs in such a manner that mature personalities are necessary in all organizational posts. Such restructuring would result in enhanced individual satisfaction and motivation, and therefore increased productivity.

Conceptual and Methodological Problems

In the literature on work motivation, several images of man have risen to prominence and then waned. First, *economic man* was popularized by Frederick Taylor (1947). In this model, man pursued the maximum possible economic gain; he obeyed authority without question and did not reject routinized work if an economic incentive was provided. Without such an incentive, he "soldiered," in Taylor's terminology.

Partly in reaction to this perspective, *social man* entered the literature subsequent to the Hawthorne (Roethlisberger and Dickson, 1961) experiments. In Likert (1967), for example, the emphasis shifted to the human relationships of the work-place. Friendliness among peers, cohesive work groups, and supportive, considerate, democratic supervision replaced money as the factors which were suggested to improve satisfaction and productivity.

The most recent emergence is that of the *self-actualizing man* for whom neither money nor favorable human relationships are of ultimate primary concern. Need theorists present an image of man to whom job involvement is a desirable state, and self-actualizing on the job a preferred condition. This preferred condition, however, is often blocked by an inappropriate match among self-actualizing needs and the constricted task structure of the work-place. Both satisfaction and productivity suffer as a result of this mismatching; conversely, both would likely increase with better matching. These predicted gains in satisfaction and performance follow from the image of man embedded in need theory.

Here lies a basic problem. How did the need theorists arrive at a description of man for whom self-actualizing at work is the primary need once the lower-order needs are satisfied? Essentially, intuitively. This in no way disparages Maslow's or other need theorists' observations, but we believe it must be concluded that self-actualizing man is a hypothetical construct *intuitively formulated*.

This is certainly an appropriate initial step in theoretical development. The model when put to test may then confirm or disconfirm the initial formulation. But here more serious problems for the theory emerge. First, it should be noted that there is scant evidence to substantiate the view that a need hierarchy, as described by Maslow, exists (E. Lawler III, 1973:34–38). Nor is the evidence favorable to Herzberg's framework.[2]

Second, there is the problem that even if future research among a population confirmed the dominance of self-actualization needs, this would not resolve the following questions: (a) the motivational impetus of self-actualization on the job, and the core issue, (b) how do needs originate.

What is required to resolve question (a) above, is the following: Locate workers who, on empirically grounded psychological measurements, evidence self-actualization needs corresponding to Maslow's formulation. Enrich these workers' jobs, while holding other factors constant, for example, pay, supervision, working conditions, and so forth. And then assess what the consequences are for productivity, compared to a control group with a different pattern of needs but operating under identical conditions. Finally, vary factors such as pay, while holding job enrichment constant, to determine how the group with salient self-actualization needs responded in terms of performance. Unfortunately, this sort of research has not been conducted. In published cases of job enrichment in ongoing work organizations, a host of variables are altered jointly, making it virtually impossible to untangle the performance consequences of salient self-actualization needs.

---

[2] For a review of research, see: Dunnette, Campbell and Hackell (1967); Vroom (1964: 126–129) and House and Wigdor (1967).

Thus, demonstrating the occurrence of the need for self-actualization would not be adequate. It is also necessary to establish its consequences for *on-the-job* effort. The reason for this is that a very considerable amount of research has shown that satisfaction at work is but slightly related to the degree of effort exerted at work. One extensive review of the literature by Vroom (1964:183) finds a median correlation of .14 among work satisfaction and work performance; such a result would account for less than 2% of the variance of performance. Vroom (1964:186) comments:

> ...the median correlation of .14 has little theoretical or practical importance.... Obtained correlations are similar for analyses based on individuals and groups and do not seem to depend, to any appreciable extent, on the occupational level of the subjects or on the nature of the [performance] criterion (objective or ratings) employed.

Brayfield and Crockett (1955:408) in an earlier review of the satisfaction-performance relationship concluded: "...there is little evidence in the available literature that employee attitudes of the type usually measured in morale surveys bears any simple—or for that matter, appreciable—relationship to performance on the job" (Kahn, 1956; E. Lawler III and Porter, 1967). Even though a job's features may closely correspond to what is desired by an individual, and therefore satisfy him, there is little evidence to support the conceptual linkage with work effort.

Origin of needs. Turning now to the issue of how needs originate, there are two possible explanations to account for the origin of needs: (1) genetic, and (2) social learning processes.

With the exception of Argyris (1960:8), who carefully notes that "in our culture" people tend toward mature personalities, Maslow, Herzberg, and McGregor are either silent on the origins of needs, or imply a genetic determination. For example, Maslow (1965:1) mentions self-actualizing "highly-evolved individuals"; and again (1965:47), in commenting on people's responses to fragmented, routinized tasks: "There *is* no other human, reasonable, intelligent way to respond to this kind of profound cutting off of half of one's growth possibilities than by getting angry or resentful or struggling to get out of the situation."

There is no intention here to demonstrate that need theorists claim a genetic origin of self-actualization needs. We would only emphasize their silence on this subject, and that phrases which imply genetic origins can be found. However, if the argument is that the self-actualization need is innate, it cannot be proven. Because people grow up in social surroundings, whatever is innate is buried beneath layers of socialization, probably irretrievably. Lawler (1973: 40) notes in a review of Maslow and other need theorists: "No conclusions have been reached ... about whether needs are innate or learned because these questions don't seem to be answerable at this time." The hereditary origin of self-actualization needs, if that is what is proposed, is an extraordinarily shaky foundation for development of a theory of motivation because it is beyond empirical confirmation.

If, however, the need theorists propose social learning processes as the locus of the origin of self-actualization needs, the argument is on an entirely different footing because it can then be empirically evaluated. The questions now become: Do people learn to value work as self-development? Do they learn a definition of "enough" money, prestige, or authority so that increased mastery of a work task is valued *for its own sake* rather than as a means to the end of gaining additional extrinsic rewards?

The evidence indicates that socialization practices do not exhibit in workers' responses to jobs anything approaching unanimity of satisfaction with complex jobs, or unanimous dissatisfaction with less complex jobs. This is perhaps not surprising. But recognition of it is a significant step away from the presumption that repetitive jobs are universally dissatisfying.

Let us review a few examples. Our recalculation of Sheppard and Herrick's (1972:29) data indicates that work dissatisfaction, or "the blues" as they term it, occurs among 51% of the workers engaged on the most fragmented, repetitive tasks; conversely, 49% of these workers do not evidence the blues. According to their own data, then, nearly half of the men working on the dullest jobs cannot be described as exhibiting the blues. Turner and Lawrence (1965:50) found a nearly identical relationship. They constructed an overall task index composed of job variety, autonomy, interaction, learning time, responsibility, task identity and cycle time, and related the overall index scores to a measure of job satisfaction. Among the workers on jobs with the least variety, autonomy, etc., 50% were dissatisfied and 50% were not; among those with the most complex jobs, 39% were dissatisfied. Walker and Guest's (1952:54) earlier study classified automobile assembly workers according to whether they found their work "very or fairly interesting," or "not very or not at all interesting," and related this to the number of operations performed. Among the men engaged on the most repetitive tasks (one operation), 33% were reported to find their work very or fairly interesting; among those performing the most operations (five or more), 69% found their work to be interesting.

Blauner's (1964:84, 116) review of previous studies shows that among unskilled automobile workers, 49% felt the jobs "are too simple to bring out the best abilities," but 51% did not feel this way; 61% also defined their jobs as monotonous "most or all of the time," 39% did not. The U.S. Manpower Administration released a report (U.S. Department of Labor, 1974:16) which indicates that in employees' ratings of a variety of job factors, 57% of blue collar, and 69% of white collar, employees rated "I have an opportunity to develop my special abilities" as "very important" to them; conversely, 43% and 31% did not rate the development of "my special abilities" as "very important." Hulin's (1971) review of the literature on satisfaction with enriched jobs also indicates the substantial variability of people's reactions to the job itself. Overall, it is difficult to detect a time trend in these data. This suggests that orientations to the nature of work tasks exhibit a persisting variability which should not be ignored.

The recent literature (notably, Turner and Lawrence, 1965; Hulin and Blood, 1968; Katzell, Barrett and Parker, 1961; Susman, 1973) on responses to work tasks emphasizes a social learning process as the basis of differential reactions to work tasks. The major explanatory "background variable" has been urban and rural residence. Workers with rural or small town backgrounds are found to be more concerned with autonomy and variety, whereas urban workers are more "instrumentally" oriented. The latter prefer that job which provides the greatest economic payoff for the least psychological and physical involvement with the work.

Summary of the Need Theory

The model of man incorporated in the need theories reviewed above, suggests that self-actualization emerges as a dominant concern unless blocked by lack of satisfaction of lower-order needs, and that self-actualization needs, once emerged, provide the motivational impetus to work effort on properly designed tasks. Work is then performed for its own sake.

It was indicated that these assertions rest essentially on intuition rather than evidence. There are scant data to support the conception of a need hierarchy as formulated by Maslow, and from which other need theorists derived their conceptions of work motivation. Additionally, well-designed research has not been conducted to determine the motivational impetus of complex tasks among job-holders for whom self-actualization is salient. Job enrichment programs characteristically introduce a host of variables, thereby confounding analysis of the consequences of separate variables.

It was also indicated that the interpretation of the origins of higher-order needs is unclear. If such needs are innate, as is sometimes implied by need theorists, empirical confirmation of these needs is presently impossible; the effects of socialization cannot be undone to recover the original unsocialized needs. If, however, the interpretation of the origin of higher-order needs is by way of social learning processes, the evidence does not support the importance of such needs among workers in a universalistic fashion. Some display satisfaction with a complex job, others do not.

The intriguing difficulty with theory grounded in intuitive, untested premises about man is that the imagery shifts across time, no doubt influenced by the social ambiance of the theorist, which in turn accepts some imagery while ignoring others. The theorist is limited only by his imagination, and lacking empirical demonstration, there is no compelling reason the theorist's audience will be swayed to accept or reject a theory except on grounds of ideology, or perhaps the optimism or pessimism about man implied by the theory. For instance, there is scant reason provided in the empirical literature on work motivation not to substitute Freud's view for Maslow's. Freud (1962:27) commented: "The great majority of people only work under the stress of necessity, and this natural human aversion to work raises most serious social problems." It is well to keep in mind that economic man and social man were once as attractive as contemporary self-actualizing man.

As was seen earlier, the literature on job enrichment programs indicates that they yield desirable results. However, since empirical research shows substantial variation on workers' interests in enriched jobs, and the lack of a significant relationship among work satisfaction and work performance, it appears that need theory cannot adequately explain the positive results achieved with enrichment programs. In the following section, reinforcement theory is presented as an alternative explanation to that proposed by need theory in regard to work behavior and performance on enriched jobs in particular.

REINFORCEMENT THEORY

Psychologists have written about work motivation using the labels *instrumentality* theory and *expectancy* theory, while sociologists dealing with similar ideas have used the term *exchange* theory. All of these labels refer to the process of evoking behavior by means of some sort of "reward" provided for appropriate behavior. The reward is termed *reinforcement,* and provides a handy label for this perspective.

In the previous section the term need was used to refer to such things as physical security and self-actualization. Another way to convey this idea is to think in terms of *outcomes.* People desire to obtain from their social environments certain outcomes, such as security or complex work tasks; the outcomes which are sought may be said to satisfy certain needs. But the question still remains, what needs energize the seeking outcomes? The biology of human organisms may appear to be the most likely locus of needs, but is in fact not very helpful for social theory.

Drives such as hunger, sex, and security undoubtedly energize behavior, yet the nearly infinite variety of ways different populations satisfy these drives points to a necessarily more social explanation. As Dubin (1974:82) put it:

> We observe first that specific drives, like sex and hunger, result in wide variations of behavior for their satisfaction. Peoples around the world eat quite different foods, prepared in a bewildering variety of ways, using eating utensils in many forms. Even when hungry, some peoples will not eat certain foods tabooed by their customs. We observe, second, that the same people can be trained, educated, conditioned, or coerced into changing the form in which they satisfy their hunger, for example. These two observations ... call attention to an important consideration. ... The social environment gives to the individual sets of preferences or values which constitute the goals toward which the instinctual drives are expressed. Furthermore, the social environment is the source of norms of behavior which draw the line between good and bad, right and wrong, legitimate and illegitimate.

To illustrate, assume that self-actualization is, like hunger, an empirically established drive. What outcomes are then related to this drive? Conceivably, anything from becoming a better and better extortionist to a more accomplished embezzler, lover, musician or machinist. Only when the social circumstances of people's backgrounds and ongoing situations are introduced into the analysis does it become possible to make predictions about the specific outcomes individuals will seek to attain. This is less a slighting of biology than it is a recognition of the limitations of attempting to predict from biology. Some people, after all, become celibates denouncing sex, and some renounced life and went to the Roman lions.

From the point of view of reinforcement theory, work itself is an outcome that is neither inherently attractive nor repellent. It depends on the positive reinforcements and the penalties contingent upon working or not working. Consider for a moment W.H. Lewis' (1957:157) rendition of a day in the life of a country squire in the eighteenth century:

> If the squire was in moderately easy circumstances he spent his time as such men have probably spent it from the beginning of things: hunting, shooting, fishing, quarreling, dicing and drabbing, all day in the saddle, retailing his day's adventures before the kitchen fire of an evening, or towsing Lisolette in the barn; riding out on a non-hunting morning to look at his fields, or to call on a neighbor with whom he

happened to be on speaking terms, and killing the day with a dinner lasting three or four hours.

Now let us contrast this with Best's (1972:211) view of nineteenth century Britain:

> ...all respectable early Victorian citizens were expected to fill six days a week with work...; the merely amusing or relaxing, the utterly uneducational, was deprecated as feeble.... [For men of all stations] leisure should be devoted to self-improvement, not self-indulgence.

Neighbors, friends and family in the social settings of the country squire and the respectable mid-Victorian citizen praised, approved and condemned some behaviors and not others. It is very difficult to interpret such diversity of behavior without recourse to reinforcement as an explanatory scheme.

The implications of reinforcement theory extend to all sphere of behavior. Educators, for instance, would not use the concept of growth or development to explain learning. Rather, they would seek explanation of learning in the changing expectations among parents, teachers, and peers toward the child. That the child's world of praise for new behavior has changed is, from this viewpoint, more accurate than assuming inherent developmental processes which are evoked by presenting the child with curiosity-stimulating materials (Skinner, 1974:184–185). Particularly in low-income areas, where peers and family may not reinforce learning behavior, education theories which look to the child itself as the locus of interest in learning are highly suspect.

Prevalent Theories

Taking an example from the organizational literature, consider the concept of "participation." As it appears in the literature it has minimal explanatory utility. But if specific and valued reinforcements can be determined to occur with participation, then explanation is on much firmer ground. Thus, prestige from association with higher status managers, paid time off from work, and an enhanced feeling of security from exercising greater control over the work environment, may all serve as reinforcements to the activity of participation. Participation, as such, tells us only that some amount of time is utilized for interaction. If this is a desirable activity, there will be some specifiable reinforcements to the participants which occur as outcomes of the activity.

Work organizations are able to utilize people because of two related reasons. First, the organization can make valued rewards contingent upon employee's job performances. Reinforcements such as job security, pay, promotion, prestige and authority can be offered in exchange for participants' contributions to the organization. Second, people come to the organization after having learned to value at least some of the rewards the organization proffers. The process of learning what the outcomes to be sought are, is identical to the subsequent process whereby behavior is motivated once the individual has joined the organization.

The process by which family and peer groups influence a youth's conception of valued outcomes is that approval and other more tangible rewards (an allowance, or use of the family car, for instance) are made contingent upon meeting the expectations placed upon him. The process whereby the individual provides appropriate behavior in exchange for valued rewards continues in organizations. As Dubin (1974:82–83) notes, "Without this notion of exchange between the person and the social system in which he operates, motivation would lie beyond social control and the managers of organizations would be helpless to channel motivations or to modify the level at which they operate."

Shown below are three models of reinforcement. The first, Homans' exchange theory, and the second, Vroom's instrumentality-valence model, assume as given variables the rewards people seek. The last, Lawler's expectancy theory, takes into account the variability of important outcomes to people.

George Homans' exchange theory. Homans (1961: Chapter 4) offers several propositions as the nucleus of his exchange theory. Although Homans formulated these propositions to explain informal social interaction, they have a wider applicability. Homan's core propositions subsequently examined in Blau (1967) and Emerson (1972) are:

1. If in the past the occurrence of a particular stimulus in a situation has been the occasion on which a man's activity has been rewarded, then the more similar the present stimulus and situation are to the past one, the more likely he is to repeat the activity.

2. The more often within a given period of time a man's activity rewards the activity of another, the more often the other will repeat the activity.

3. The more valuable to a man the activity of the other is, the more often he will repeat the activity rewarded by the activity of the other.

Homans' propositions are useful as an overview of the exchange process because they indicate (1) the manner in which desirable outcomes are learned, and (2) the way in which outcomes are gained.

The question may be asked, How can outcomes be initially learned if there is no reward already desired? The answer must assume some innate desirable outcomes. Among these are physiological wants, and the need for approval. Quite early on, approval-seeking provides an important motivational influence to meet others' expectations. Operant conditioning (Homans' first proposition) as discussed by Skinner (1974:181) assumes that "Interpersonal contact is frequently a matter of approval ('prestige') or censure, some forms of which are probably effective for genetic reasons. . . ." This is certainly not a new notion originating with the social sciences. Another form of the same idea is the biblical aphorism, "all is vanity."

Having learned a set of preferred outcomes, Homans describes how people go about attaining them. The core idea in this and all other reinforcement theories is the presumption that *behavior is a function of its consequences.* The consequences represent the outcomes sought (positive reinforcement) or avoided (negative reinforcement) because they are unpleasant (aversive). The decision to engage in activity x rather than y is from this perspective interpreted as an assessment by the actor of the consequences contingent upon engaging in x instead of y. Additionally, any activity has a "cost." The cost is the rewards foregone by not engaging in an alternative activity to the present one. For instance, if a student studies he foregoes beer drinking, t.v., etc.; by appearing for work, recreation is sacrificed by the workman; if a man courts one girl, he cannot simultaneously by trying his luck with another.

It may be obvious that the order of preferences is critical to the choices

made. Is the outcome to be gained from studying more valued than the pleasures of beer drinking? Is the outcome from showing up for work more valued
than recreation? Since any chosen activity also has its cost side, as we have
shown, reinforcement theory would suggest that the outcomes should be meaningful for a choice among preferences. Let us illustrate. Because studying does
require foregoing other rewards, strengthening the consequences contingent
upon studying or not studying nudges the choice of activity toward studying if
the overall preference of the student leans more toward passing the course than
toward recreation. Similarly for the worker. If no significant consequence results from choosing a day off over a day at work, why not opt for recreation?
Usually, of course, at least for most manual workers, a day's pay must be foregone. However, it is quite realistic to suggest that the preference for attendance
at work could be tilted more strongly in that direction by providing an additional pay increment for no days absent over a week or month. This has indeed
been attempted with persuasive results (Lawler, 1973:108). Because behavior is
a function of its consequences, a person who prefers outcome x rather than y,
will choose the activity leading to that outcome if choosing another activity
would mean foregoing outcome x. For instance, if high wages require highly
productive activity, and if high wages are an important outcome for a person,
he will not choose the activity of low productivity or absenteeism if that means
he will not obtain high wages. If the activity chosen makes no difference for
income, there is no reason to expect high productivity; the gains from high
productivity will not outweigh the costs of additional mental or physical effort.

The image of man in this line of reasoning is that of a being who pursues
goals in a reasonably rational manner by assessing the results which follow
from alternative activities. Behavior is motivated by the outcomes which follow
from an activity, and socially learned sets of preferences channel the selection
among alternative outcomes.

Victor Vroom's valence-instrumentality theory. Vroom (1964:6) usefully defines motivation as the "process governing choices made by persons ...
among alternative forms of voluntary activity. We specifically exclude from the
realm of motivated behavior reflexes ... as well as responses mediated by the
autonomic nervous system such as salivation or heart rate." He notes that his
approach, like other reinforcement theories, builds upon Thorndike's (1911:
244) Law of Effect:

> Of several responses made to the same situation, those which are ac-
> companied or closely followed by satisfaction to the animal will, other
> things being equal, be more firmly connected with the situation, so
> that, when it recurs, they will be more likely to recur; those which are
> accompanied or closely followed by discomfort to the animal will,
> other things being equal, have their connections with that situation
> weakened, so that when it recurs, they will be less likely to occur. The
> greater the satisfaction or discomfort, the greater is the strengthening
> or weakening of the bond.

Vroom distinguishes between historical and ahistorical explanations of behavior. From an ahistorical standpoint, behavior at a given time is viewed as
depending only on contemporaneous events. From an historical point of view,
behavior is dependent on events occurring at an earlier time. Ongoing reinforcements are thus viewed from an ahistorical perspective as the explanation

of behavior, whereas from an historical standpoint the problem is to determine the way in which a person's present behavior is affected by the past situations he has experienced and the responses he has made to them.

Vroom's major interest has been the development of an ahistorical explanation of motivated behavior. In his model, Vroom uses the terms valence and instrumentality. Valence refers to affective orientations toward particular outcomes, or what we previously referred to as preferences among outcomes. Vroom points out, however, that an outcome may have high valence for a person, and yet have little value to that person. This is the case when an outcome is not in itself anticipated to be satisfying on the basis of its intrinsic properties, but is anticipated to be associated with other outcomes which are valued. The first outcome therefore has *instrumental* value because it leads to other associated outcomes. Vroom (1964:16) comments that "People may desire to join groups because they believe that membership will enhance their status in the community, and they may desire to perform their jobs effectively because they expect that it will lead to promotion." Another term important in this framework is *expectancy*, defined by Vroom (1964:17) as "a momentary belief concerning the likelihood that a particular act will be followed by a particular outcome." Beliefs about outcomes may be developed through personal experiences, or vicariously by learning from other people "what to expect." Lastly, the key term in Vroom's model is *force*. This concept refers to how valences and expectancies combine to determine choices. The strength of force is defined as the product of valences and expectancies. Expectancy assumes values ranging from zero (no likelihood is anticipated that an act will be followed by an outcome) to $+1$ (indicating certainty that the act will be followed by an anticipated outcome). Valence ranges from $+1$ (indicating maximally attractive outcome) to -1 (indicating maximally unattractive outcome). The notion of product, a multiplicative relationship, is important because it states that if either expectancy or valence is low, the force of choice to perform the activity will be low.

The theory may be written like this: Force $= \Sigma(E \times V)$, indicating that the products for all outcomes are added to determine force. Lawler's (1973:46) illustration of this is apt:

> ... it means that tying a valent reward, such as pay, to a desired behavior, such as good performance, will not be enough to motivate the desired behavior. Pay can be highly valued and can be seen as closely related to performance; but if negative consequences, such as feeling tired, or being rejected by a work group, are also perceived as related to good performance, there may be no motivation to perform....According to Vroom, a person will be motivated to perform well in a situation only if performing well has the highest $E \times V$ force in that particular situation. Performing well can have a strong force, but if performing poorly has a stronger force, the person will not be motivated to perform well.

Vroom (1964:Chapters 4–8) has applied this theory to a book-length discussion and assessment of a large number and broad range of studies in the organizational literature. It appears that the model has considerable utility.

Lawler's expectancy model. This model has the advantage of being neither historical nor ahistorical; it combines both approaches to explain motivated behavior in work organizations. As the label of the theory implies, expectancy theory emphasizes people's beliefs about what will occur, while also taking into account what has occurred.

Lawler (1973:49) notes that the expectancy model is based on four points that his previous reading of research on human motivation suggests are valid. These are:

1. People have preferences among the various outcomes that are potentially available to them.
2. People have expectancies about the likelihood that an action (effort) on their part will lead to the intended behavior or performance.
3. People have expectancies about the likelihood that certain outcomes will follow their behavior.
4. In any situation, the actions a person chooses to take are determined by the expectancies and the preferences that person has at the time.

Expectancy here refers to the person's estimate of the probability that he can accomplish his intended performance, which Lawler labels an $E \rightarrow P$ (effort→performance) expectancy. Additionally there are $P \rightarrow O$ (performance→outcomes) expectancies: the beliefs held by a person about the probability that his performance will result in a particular outcome. Both $E \rightarrow P$ and $P \rightarrow O$ expectancies range from zero (the performance cannot be accomplished or the outcome will not result) to $+1$ (subjective certainty that he can accomplish the performance or attain the outcome). Motivation is thus the product of the $E \rightarrow P$ and $P \rightarrow O$ expectancies. As stated by Lawler (1973:51),

> ... the model suggests that a person's motivation to perform in a particular way will be influenced by expectancies about trying to perform in that way, his expectancies about the outcomes associated with performing at that level ... and the attractiveness of the outcomes involved. These factors combine to produce a motivational force to perform in the specified manner.

The determinants of $E \rightarrow P$ expectancies suggested by Lawler are the present situation, past experience in similar situations, communication from others, and self-esteem. It is interesting to note that two of these factors point back in time toward a person's history—past experience and self-esteem—and two concern the ongoing situation. In this manner the model combines historical and ahistorical elements.

The determinants of $P \rightarrow O$ expectancies may be summarized as past experience in similar situations, communication from others, the present situation, and attractiveness of outcomes (highly valued outcomes are subjectively viewed as more likely to occur from a performance). Again, both the biography and present situation of an individual are incorporated in the model.

Motivation, then, involves an assessment of the probability of attaining alternative outcomes, where some outcomes are preferred over others, and an assessment of the likelihood that one is capable of performing adequately to achieve the various outcomes. Lawler (1973:52–53) summarizes:

> In organizations, people are often forced to choose among a number of behaviors that are relatively attractive. Simply stated, the expectancy model predicts that people will choose to behave in whatever way has the highest motivational force. ... In the case of productivity, this means people will be motivated to be highly productive if they feel

they can be highly productive and if they see a number of positive outcomes associated with being a high producer. However, if for some reason they will receive approximately the same outcomes for being less highly productive, they probably will be low producers. Managers often ask why their subordinates are not more productive. They seem to feel that people should be productive almost as if it is a question of morality or of instinct. The expectancy approach suggests asking a rather different question: Why should people be productive in a given situation? People are not naturally productive (or nonproductive). Thus, managers who wonder why their people are not more productive should start by comparing the rewards given to good performers with the rewards given to poor performers. Time after time, no real difference is found when this comparison is made. Thus, the workers' perception of the situation is that the good and the poor performers receive the same treatment, and this view is crucial in determining motivation.

Lawler's (1973: Chapters 4–7) application of the model to the literature on behavior in work organizations suggests it is perhaps the most promising reinforcement model.

Summary of the Reinforcement Theory

Common to the reinforcement theories reviewed here is the emphasis on exchange. People are influenced by their social surroundings in the process of learning preferred outcomes. In this manner, preferences among outcomes are channeled by a person's past experiences in situations and his responses to them. Once learned, the preferred outcomes are sought in ongoing situations. People perform in ways appropriate to others' expectations in current situations in exchange for valued outcomes. Whereas need theory emphasizes the push from a set of given higher-order needs as the primary motivational mechanism, reinforcement theory points to the pull of valued rewards.

Reinforcement theory appears to be able to explain a wide range of human behavior, including the lack of involvement in regularized work. No givens of specific human behaviors are assumed. It is a matter of the groups in which socialization has taken place, and a person's current situations.

The following section reviews a number of experimental cases in which reinforcement principles have been applied. Organizationally appropriate behaviors were successfully elicited upon the introduction of these principles.

REINFORCEMENT PROGRAMS

Much of the systematic experimentation using reinforcement methods to influence behavioral performances has taken place in mental hospital and public school settings. As the following cases illustrate, organizationally appropriate behaviors were elicited by rewarding those performances which approximated an administratively determined standard. In this manner, the probability that organizational standards would be achieved was increased, in some cases dramatically.

Ney and his associates (1971) applied reinforcement techniques to twenty schizophrenic boys who exhibited an inability to communicate and function in normal social settings. The program was designed to develop behaviors which were considered necessary for normal social interaction. By reinforcing successive approximations of normal behavior, the reinforcement techniques were able to move the boys' progress along from simple to more complex forms of social behavior. For positive reinforcers, Ney used candy and verbal praise; punishments (negative reinforcement) included such things as the therapist turning his back to a boy who acted improperly. Ney concluded that the reinforcement technique was more effective than conventional forms of therapy for obtaining desired behavioral changes.

Studying young adult males with histories of sexual deviance, Abel, Levis and Clancy (1970) found it possible to completely suppress deviant sexual responses by applying shock treatments whenever a subject responded inappropriately; subjects were rewarded for verbalizing normal sexual fantasies by having the shock removed. After ten training sessions, the subjects expressed fewer deviant sexual fantasies and showed less interest in deviant questions on a personality inventory; at the same time they responded acceptably to tape recordings of normal sexual fantasies. Eighteen weeks after the termination of experimental treatments, only one incident of overt deviant sexual behavior had been reported.

Also of interest is a study conducted by Atthowe and Krasner (1970:89–96) on the behavior of elderly chronic schizophrenics in a Veterans Administration Hospital. This token economy experiment was aimed at reducing the apathetic, overly dependent or annoying behaviors of patients who required constant custodial care. Every major aspect of the patients' hospital life was included under the reinforcement program; attaining tokens became dependent upon the patient's performance of specific behaviors. Subsequently, tokens could be used to purchase such items as cigarettes, money and passes as well as other ward privileges. Atthowe and Krasner noted that after the start of the experiment there was a marked decline in inactivity and apathetic behavior; more patients began going on passes, drawing weekly cash and using the ward canteen. Patients' participation in group activities increased from an average of 5.8 to 8.5 hours per week when tokens were awarded for attendance. During the experiment social interactions and communication increased and the number of infractions in carrying out the morning routine dropped from a weekly average of seventy-five to nine. The researchers concluded that the token reinforcement technique was very successful in eliciting therapeutically appropriate forms of behavior among this patient population.

Studies involving the use of reinforcement principles applied to children in the classroom are fairly numerous; as in mental hospitals, the results are promising. For example, Wagner and Guyer (1971), studying students with specific learning disabilities, used reinforcement techniques to increase each student's span of attention and thus reduce disruptive classroom behavior. A token economy was established in which each student could exchange the teacher's initials for items such as caps, toys or crayons. Initials were amassed by attending to a series of assigned tasks, each of fifteen minutes' duration. Results indicated that the differences between pre and postexperimental attention spans and behavioral ratings were statistically significant beyond the .01 level.

McIntire (1970) attempted to increase the mathematics and spelling scores of 5th and 6th grade students by offering access to a special projects room as a reward. When the reward was given for mathematics and spelling improvements, students' scores increased in both areas. However, when the reward was systematically decreased for spelling performance on tests and homework, students' scores on spelling concomitantly decreased. McIntire concluded that school performance can be improved when the proper rewards are present as contingencies.

Recognizing that the usual rewards of stars, grades and teachers' attention often do not effectively elicit appropriate behaviors among disruptive and aggressive children, O'Leary and Becker (1970:182–187) created a token system for such cases. They studied seventeen nine year-old students who frequently expressed inappropriate behaviors such as temper tantrums, fighting, crying and disruptive laughing. When the token system began, every student received a token booklet in which the teacher would record ratings of the student's behavior during lessons. While placing the ratings in the booklet the teacher verbally praised any improvements in the child's behavior, while ignoring deviant behavior. Students exchanged tokens earned for rewards of candy, pennants, comics, perfume and similar items. It was reported that in the eight most serious cases, disruptive behavior decreased from a daily average of 80% of classroom time to 15% during the experiment; among the remaining students, inappropriate behavior decreased from a daily average of 76% to 10%.

In a similar study, Hall and his associates (1968) examined three inexperienced Kansas City teachers with severe behavior control problems in their classrooms. The intent was to improve the study behavior of thirty 6th graders, twenty-four 1st graders and thirty 7th graders, most of whom exhibited disruptive classroom behaviors. Rewards included teacher's attention, between period breaks and a classroom game; students were punished by reprimands and demerit marks placed by their names on the blackboard. The results indicated that study behavior increased from 44% to 72% of the study period time in the classroom for 6th graders, from 51% to 82% for 1st graders, and from 47% to 76% among 7th graders. It was concluded that reinforcement techniques were an effective teaching method.

Breslaw (1973) confronted with student apathy at a college with an open admissions policy, reported that reinforcement techniques can be used to increase class attendance, completion of required readings, written assignments and expressed interest in the subject matter. The point system she used in lieu of the traditional grading system allowed students to amass points toward a given grade in several different ways. At all times students knew their point totals and what had to be accomplished to earn the grade desired in the course; class attendance, acceptable book reviews and performance on quizzes and examinations were rewarded with points, whereas late assignments received no points. Breslaw reported that the library circulation of reading materials for her course tripled over previous terms, class attendance increased and examination results revealed that a majority of the students had read and understood the assigned materials. As a result of this experience, Breslaw concluded that reinforcement techniques are a valuable method for improving academic performance in an open admissions setting.

In contrast to mental hospitals, the major problem in school settings is that there are often many conflicting and disruptive reinforcers available to students. In order to overcome this problem, researchers have attempted to either isolate the student from the disruptive setting or bring elements of the larger environment, such as parents, into the experiment.

To examine the effects of isolation, Phillips and his associates (1968, 1973) studied Achievement Place, an experimental setting in Lawrence, Kansas. Eight 12 to 16 year old boys, formerly judged delinquent and lagging academically, together with two "parents," set up housekeeping away from the usual family ties in a home-style rehabilitation center. During the day, boys attended a local school. Teachers provided a report card on each student's behavior and daily performance. Using a token economy, "parents" rewarded each youth for a good report card and socially appropriate behavior in Achievement Place. Two years after attendance at Achievement Place, 90% of the boys were in a regular school compared to 9% among a control group of boys with reformatory experience; additionally, the Achievement Place boys had higher grade averages. Phillips concluded that this type of treatment center could be a very effective, economical way to rehabilitate delinquents.

In order to include parents in the reinforcement process, Cantrell and his associates (1969) incorporated reward contingencies into written contracts between parents and their children. Parents specified the behaviors they wanted the child to express and the rewards they would pay the child for these behaviors, then the contract was given to the child. Students thus earned points which could be exchanged for money or preferred activities when they exhibited approximations to the desired behaviors. In two illustrative cases, Cantrell reported that one student's grades improved in three subjects by one letter grade and by two letter grades in another subject; the other student, a school-phobic child, willingly attended school after only eight school days subsequent to use of the reinforcement technique.

As a result of reported successes with reinforcement techniques, school systems are beginning to attempt to take advantage of such methods (Goodall, 1972). However in the business world, despite the rather impressive gains which seem to have accrued to those companies that have applied reinforcement techniques, there are only a handful of organizations overtly experimenting with principles of reinforcement.

Industrial Applications

Edward Feeney (*Business Week*, 1972) of Emery Air Freight appears to be one of the first managers who actively took up reinforcement ideas and aggressively attempted to apply them to a business organization. In 1967, Feeney initiated a programmed learning course for sales personnel; this was based on the Skinnerian idea of step by step learning and frequent feedback and reinforcement. After one year of using the method, it was reported that sales increased by 28% compared to the previous year's increase of 11%. When similar techniques of immediate feedback and positive reinforcement for appropriate behavior were applied to the customer service department, speed in handling customers' queries greatly improved. Prior to introduction of these techniques, the customer service department answered only 30% of the queries within ninety minutes, whereas after implementation of Feeney's reinforcement program, 95% of customers' queries received a response within ninety minutes.

When reinforcement techniques were applied to the containerized shipment operation, use of containers jumped in some locations from 45% to 90% in a single day; the cost savings of such usage was substantial. Employees in the containerized shipping departments were informed that they were expected to strive for the use of containers in 90% of the shipments. A continuous container-use record, tallied daily, was clearly visible to supervisors and regional managers. Feeney attributed the impressive results to the positive reinforcement of supervisors' praise for each worker's daily performance relative to the standard.

Another manager who found reinforcement techniques useful in industry is Daniel Grady (*Business Week*, 1972) of Michigan Bell Telephone. Experiencing serious absenteeism problems with telephone operators, Grady decided to apply reinforcement concepts in a pilot project. Attendance records were put on a weekly rather than a monthly basis, and supervisors were instructed to praise good attendance. Grady reported that as a result of this program absenteeism fell from 11% to 6.5% per week. The program was then expanded to a thousand Detroit telephone operators. Again absenteeism declined, from 7.5% to 4.5% per week.

In a somewhat different type of application, Schneier (1973) found reinforcement techniques useful in training hard-core unemployed men in the boxing of metal bedframes. A step by step reinforcement technique gradually brought each new trainee's speed and accuracy up to desired levels. As reinforcement, the trainee who executed a step properly received verbal praise and points were placed on a chart next to his machine; the points were later converted into money. Schneier noted that the reinforcement system worked well as a training device and as a method for reducing turnover among the trainees.

Coordination in organizations inherently involves means for integration of individuals' behavior with organizational ends. As in the preceding illustrative cases, it is likely that an underlying process of reinforcement is present when such integration occurs. To the observer, the reinforcement process may be evident, resembling the cases above, or more opaque, as in job enrichment.

JOB ENRICHMENT PROGRAMS

Although successful cases of job enrichment are usually considered to illustrate the application of need theory, it is also possible to offer an alternative interpretation: Job enrichment programs indicate the application of reinforcement theory. The cases of job enrichment reviewed below suggest this alternative interpretation. Two important features of organizational control appear in these programs, indicating that they may be realistically viewed as the application of reinforcement methods. Accountability for performance, and associated material reinforcements for performance which meets a specified standard, are characteristically incorporated into programs of job enrichment.

AT&T

Confronted with problems of employees' productivity, errors, absenteeism and turnover, AT&T initiated a series of job enrichment programs. In one experiment, reported by Ford (1973), selected clerks compiling directories for Indiana Bell Telephone were given the opportunity to compile and verify a whole section of a directory without having their work rechecked for accuracy. This change led to a reduction of the work force by one-third, since checkers were no longer needed. Ford stated that the performance improvements which occurred stemmed from the ego-enhancing autonomy and responsibility given each worker. However, the enrichment program also served to identify each worker's performance. Previously, it was unclear as to who had committed a clerical error because a number of people worked on each section of a directory. After enrichment, the accuracy of all entries in a section of a directory were directly traceable to a specific employee. Visibility of results simultaneously increased the worker's accountability for his performance and alerted management to performances either above or below standard expectations. In the words of Ford (1973:98):

> The trouble with so much work processing is that no one is clearly responsible for a total unit that fails. In Indianapolis, by contrast, when a name in a directory is misspelled or omitted, the clerk knows where the responsibility lies.

In another AT&T experiment, delayed processing of installation and repair orders and high turnover of service-order typists led to a reorganization. Initially, service representatives answered incoming service requests and passed them on for processing by service-order typists in a typing pool. The first attempt at enrichment regrouped service representatives and gave them responsibility for specific geographic areas; typists remained in a pool. With this arrangement, the turnover of typists increased and the percentage of orders completed on time fell below 40%. Next, the desks of typists were shifted into a "wagon wheel" arrangement with the service representatives at the center. Typists were now also given specific geographic responsibilities. Ford stated that the "wagon wheel" arrangement of desks and responsibility for geographic areas increased people's feelings of participation and importance, thus accounting for the 63% increase in the number of service orders processed on time and the decline in turnover among typists. However, it is important to note that the job enrichment program has now made a specific employee accountable for delays that were previously of anonymous origin. In addition to this, when the service order typists were moved into the "wagon wheel," they were promoted to a higher pay scale. Commenting on the issue of pay, Ford (1973:106) himself notes,

> Trouble can be expected, of course, if the economics of increases in productivity are not shared equitably.... An employee who takes the entire responsibility for a whole telephone directory, for example, ought to be paid more.... Job enrichment is not in lieu of cash.... ˮ

Motorola

Concerned with motivational development and the involvement of workers in shop floor democracy, Motorola embarked on its TEAM program (Top Effort At Motorola). Hill (1972) states that at their 3,500 employee Schaumburg plant, work teams were created to analyze past achievements and failures, suggest improvements and set performance goals. Each team elected a group leader, a secretary, a captain for quality, and a captain of attendance. Minutes of each group meeting were sent to the manager of motivational development for review to insure that the group was functioning properly. In departments where TEAM was used, productivity increased by 25%, attendance improved, and product rejects fell. It was also reported that detailed attendance and quality records were kept and that peer pressure was applied to team members who were frequently absent; teams requested that poor performers be laid off first if necessary. With its focus on job improvement, the company claims to look beyond the paycheck. However, Hill (1972:45) states "... as a non-union company, it also takes care to ensure that pay and benefits do not fall behind what the rest of industry is paying."

In another program, Motorola expanded the assembly-line jobs in its Pageboy II receiver plant. Each worker's task now involved the complete assembly of the eighty component parts in a Pageboy unit, and the repair of units found defective by quality-control personnel. The worker's name was placed on each assembled unit; the worker also packed with each unit a mimeographed letter that described the unit and specified the person who assembled it. Although 25% more workers were now needed to produce the same number of units, these costs were offset by increased quality and reduced inspection and repair costs. Assembling an entire unit may enhance a worker's sense of pride and self-esteem, however, the attachment of a worker's name to the completed unit presents a clear gain in accountability compared with the anonymous assembly line.

Gaines

Experiencing high absenteeism, indifference to productivity, inattention to equipment maintenance, and product waste in their conventional plants, General Foods built a new pet food plant designed to be operated by autonomous work groups. Walton (1972) reported that each team had seven to fourteen members and was given extensive responsibility and control over the allocation of work among team members as well as decisions concerning entrance into the group. Despite estimates by industrial engineers that one hundred and ten employees should man the facility, less than seventy people were actually used to successfully operate the plant. Additionally, less quality-control rejects were experienced, lower absenteeism and fewer safety problems occurred in comparison to conventional plants in the same company producing similar products. Reports attribute the marked success of this enrichment program to the creation of a work-setting which provided challenging jobs, opportunities for personal growth, and participation in decision making. However, management was initially highly selective in obtaining the labor force, accepting seventy applicants out of 600 (Strauss, 1974:46), and the pay system was very different from that in other plants. Pay was related in the new facility to the number of jobs a worker was able to perform, with an approximately 50% difference in pay between a man who could do only one job and the worker who could perform any job required in the whole facility. In addition to this, the informal group pressure for each worker to show up for work was apparently very potent—since no substitute worker was called in. Since the work team was accountable for a specific block of tasks, and each team member's performance affected the distribution of effort within the group, performance of one's fair share of the tasks became a matter of overt concern and intervention within the group. Walton (1972:77) mentioned in this regard "excessive peer group pressure." Due to worker unrest with the allocation of pay and subsequent company concern, Walton (1974:156) further states, "In mid-1973, they were exploring group bonus schemes as vehicles for additional rewards."

Corning Glass

In 1965 Corning Glass enriched its assembly-line jobs in the manufacture of hot plates in their Medfield, Massachusetts instrument plant. Jenkins (1974) explains that after enrichment, each of the six former assembly-line workers assembled a complete hot plate, performed quality-control checks, and participated in the design of production improvements and the scheduling of work hours. Additionally, the workers who assembled and tested the units placed their initials on the completed hot plates.

In regard to the initials, management noted that the initialling allowed the employees to "identify" with their work, but that the initials were also used to "reference" customer complaints. It was reported that after implementation of the program, product rejects dropped from 23% to 1%. It appears clear that in this case, as in the Motorola program, the individual worker's accountability for the quality of performance was greatly increased by associating a worker's name with the specific product he or she produced.

Early success with the hot plate project led to the expansion of the enrichment program to cover a total of ninety production workers, all of whom were involved in the assembly of instruments for the bio-medical industry. As in the hot plate case, assembly lines were removed, authority and responsibility were distributed downward, and each worker completely assembled and tested the particular products he produced. The expansion of the enrichment program was based upon the "whole-job-concept," in which each worker was given a distinct area of responsibility and expected to perform up to set standards. In regard to the success of the program, one observer (*U.S. News and World Report*, 1972:50) commented: "All of the Medfield plant's workers have specific responsibilities to live up to. They are rewarded for success and held accountable for failures." Management had changed the structure of the pay system in order to base it more directly on merit. Additionally, appraisals are now apparently made not only of managerial personnel, but also of hourly workers (Walton, 1974:156).

Maytag

Success with previous job improvement programs prompted Maytag to embark on a series of job enrichment programs shortly after World War II. One of the fifteen implemented programs reported on by Biggane and Stewart (1972), involved the assembly of the control panel for a new line of push-button automatic washers. Previously, this type of work was performed by workers on an assembly-line, with quality control checks after the unit left the conveyer; defective units were repaired by a special service group. In the enriched situation, each control panel was completely assembled, checked for quality and repaired if necessary by a single worker. An increase in quality and a reduction in inspection costs resulted. It has been reported that these improvements were due to the worker's identification with the wholeness of his contribution to the product and his sense of achievement. It should be noted, however, that under the enriched program, each worker placed his identification number on each completed unit; moreover, these new jobs were classified in a higher pay grade than ordinary assembly jobs.

Polaroid

Following the managerial philosophy of President Edwin H. Land, Polaroid instituted its "pathfinder" program of job-changing in 1959. Foulkes (1969) discusses this program that was designed to provide factory workers holding repetitive jobs with a more worthwhile work-life. Workers on routine factory jobs in production, assembly, or inspection were allowed to apply for half-time transfers to more challenging research, clerical, quality control and engineering positions. By 1963 more than one hundred employees had experienced different jobs. The company considered the program a success because it had provided workers with a challenge and management with a lesson in administration and training. In addition it had prepared workers for promotion by allowing them to develop in skill and ability, and low employee absenteeism and turnover benefited management. Additionally, recruitment for factory jobs became easier after initiation of the program. An important consideration, however, is that potential participants, in addition to being well screened for suitability, were guaranteed that they would not lose financially if they joined the program. As Foulkes (1969:39) notes, "Because many of the participants were at the top of the rate range for their old job, this program would permit them to reach a rate higher than would have been possible otherwise." A disadvantage indicated by management was that employees tended to join the program only if they saw it as the best possible route for advancement; workers seemed unwilling to settle for half old and half new work.

Donnelly Mirrors

Concerned with the issue of productivity, Donnelly Mirrors experimented throughout the 1960s with various plans for sharing responsibility with their employees. Efforts were made to involve workers in a wide range of decisions about the setting and attainment of production and cost goals. The 460 plant employees were formed into production groups, each group having specific responsibilities. Workers inspected their own work and were encouraged to recommend cost-saving improvements. *U.S. News and World Report* (1972:51–52) tells of a 1970 plan whereby workers could collectively grant their own salary increases—provided that they increased production or reduced costs enough to pay for the agreed increases. The program has been reported as successful since Donnelly has reduced its prices despite increased costs and wages. It should be pointed out that although workers were on a salary, group bonuses (which were central to the program) were contingent upon increased production. In this regard, Walton (1974:157) states:

> . . . management related the size of the annual increase in base pay to (a) collective judgment about the feasible magnitude of cost reductions over the next year and (b) collective commitment to achieve the cost reductions that would pay for the increase.

Hence each worker's bonus was dependent upon how well his entire group performed on productivity increases and cost reductions. Again performance of one's fair share of the work would seem to be a critical point and reports of group pressure to perform bear this out.

Texas Instruments

Impressed with the research of Maslow, Herzberg and McGregor, Foulkes (1969:56–96) reported that Texas Instruments pioneered in the area of job enrichment. Feeling that workers wanted to participate in the planning and control of their jobs and that workers should be involved in these activities, the management of Texas Instruments initiated a number of programs. In a 1966 experiment to implement McGregor's Theory Y, the manager of one department instituted natural work groups and conducted a problem-solving and goal-setting meeting with production operators. The manager sought to identify why goals had not been met in the past by asking workers to participate in suggesting how improvements could be made. Additional meetings on performance were conducted by the foremen and involved sub-groups or individuals. It was reported that output goals for the final three months of 1966 were exceeded, and that in 1967, when scrap loss also became a goal, improvements and savings were experienced. It seems, however, that operators' accountability increased with the program since supervisors' graphs were now used to show them how many units had been shipped. Foulkes (1969:76) describes: "In addition, the supervisors established individual tally sheets so that each operator knew how much he was contributing to the overall goal."

Rush (1971:39–45) describes still another experiment which arose out of the company's dissatisfaction with the janitorial work being performed by outside contractors. Management felt that part of the problem was the low status of janitorial jobs and the lack of involvement of outside contract workers in the affairs of Texas Instruments. A decision was made to establish the company's own cleaning staff on a pilot basis. The ensuing job enrichment program encompassed these changes: (1) wages of cleaning personnel were increased from $1.40 per hour to $1.94 per hour, equal to the minimum rate for Texas Instrument production workers; (2) from minimal fringe benefits to inclusion in profit sharing, sick leave, paid vacations, and insurance programs; (3) cleaning technology and equipment were improved; (4) more stringent selection of employees; (5) better training; and (6) teams were formed in which workers participated in the planning and control of their work. Janitorial workers were hired from the ranks of the existing cleaning contractors and given extensive training and coaching on the program. The emphasis was on job improvement, including individual and team development; weekly team meetings were held to identify problems, goals, and the methods for attaining them. After monitoring the program for more than two years, the company reported that the cleanliness rating had increased by 20%, the number of workers required to do the job had dropped from one hundred and twenty to seventy-one, quarterly turnover had fallen 91%, and annual cost savings averaged $103,000. Consequently, the program was expanded to cover all cleaning functions within the plant.

The personnel department attributed success to such factors as employees having had a voice in planning, problem-solving, and goal-setting, thorough training in job requirements, the provision of adequate equipment, and worker freedom to develop independently their strategies for doing the job. In addition, however, it is interesting to note that specific areas of cleaning responsibility were assigned to individuals and that management committees inspected and rated the job sites weekly (Weed, 1971:55–77). Rush (1971:45) states: "The company assigned the job and let it be known that the employees were expected to have high performance and above-average cleanliness." Not only did the workers receive significantly higher pay and benefits than they had been receiving from the outside contractors, but also their accountability for the performance of specific cleaning tasks was increased substantially.

Arapahoe Chemicals

Further reports by Rush (1971:32–39) and Jenkins (1974:209–210) show that problems of long laboratory delays, delayed scheduling of production, dissatisfied customers, and low productivity led Arapahoe to review the operating role of its chemists. Finding discontent and resistance among many of its most competent scientists, management introduced an enrichment program designed to increase their involvement, participation and productivity. Prior to the program, a chemist had a narrow range of responsibility and control over each customer's order assigned him. After enrichment, each chemist was assigned responsibility for the research of a customer's entire project including the ordering of raw materials, estimation of costs, pilot testing and setting of completion schedules; objectives set by the chemist were reviewed by a management planning committee for approval. The company reported the success of the program, noting faster processing of customers' orders, increased productivity, reduced turnover, and increased morale. Concerning the planning committee, Rush (1971:35) states that "The costs and the time schedule finally agreed upon become concrete objectives, with established benchmark intervals, against which the chemist measures his progress and against which management evaluates his performance." Hence under the enrichment program a single chemist is held accountable for the success of a customer's order; in the past such clear accountability did not exist.

Job enrichment was also applied to production workers when a customer demanded that management reduce the price of his future orders by 10%. Plant personnel were summoned to a participative problem-solving meeting and confronted with the issue of increasing productivity by 10% to maintain profits. The participative involvement produced useful suggestions on possible modifications to production bottlenecks; implementation of the workers' ideas led to the necessary productivity increase. Management suggested that participation and the delegation of responsibility to the workers led to their increased involvement and subsequent production improvements. However, the workers' suggestions did not go financially unrewarded. In the words of Rush (1971:37): "These suggestions merited the maximum award under the company's already existing suggestion plan. At the end of the year actual savings will be reviewed for possible additional rewards."

Weyerhaeuser

Weyerhaeuser instituted a pilot job enrichment project in 1968. Underlying the program was McGregor's Theory Y. Rush (1971:55–60) states that the pilot "I Am" plan (I am manager of my job) was established in a typical paper production plant on the east coast, involving three hundred employees. Work teams were formed and trained in problem-solving and decision-making. Once production objectives had been set and communicated by the plant's top management, work groups established specific methods, schedules, and responsibilities for attaining these objectives. The company indicated that the productivity of this plant, after implementation of the program, exceeded the productivity of other plants of similar size. As in other cases, however, accountability and pay seem intertwined with successful job enrichment. Rush (1971:59) notes that in Weyerhaeuser's pilot project,

> The company measures effectiveness on a group basis; and each work group evaluates itself as a group, as well as the contributions of each of its members, against its goals and objectives. Since wage rates are negotiated by the bargaining unit, base pay scales are predetermined for each job classification. However, the bargaining contract provides for additional compensation for work groups that are high producers.

CONCLUSIONS

The foregoing cases cut across two bodies of literature that are conventionally treated as dissimilar: reinforcement research involved with mental hospitals, schools and business firms, and literature on work settings with job enrichment programs. We suggest that in these physically divergent settings, a similar reinforcement process occurs through which behavior appropriate to organizational ends is elicited. We attempted to indicate with a sampling of job enrichment studies those features of each case that served to increase accountability, thus linking an individual's performance more directly to contingencies of reinforcement such as job security and pay.

We have noted that individuals' inherent needs are often invoked to explain behavior in organizational contexts; productivity increase or quality improvement in the enriched situation are then assumed to be the consequences of satisfying workers' needs for autonomy and task complexity. If people have learned to value autonomy and complexity in their work, then work satisfaction may indeed be enhanced by the presence of these factors in the work setting. Nevertheless, to understand the quality and quantity of performances, it is important to examine the consequences employees face as a result of their performances. Satisfaction with work is one thing, the degree of effort exerted is quite another; these are different aspects of responses to a task, and should be conceptually distinguished. As was seen previously, satisfaction is but slightly related to performance. Upon reflection, there seems to be little reason to expect a stronger relationship unless one assumes that workers are grateful for satisfying work, which leads to a feeling of obligation to behaviorally express thanks with improved performance. This does not appear to be a persuasive argument. A more promising alternative is to consider the consequences resulting from work performance.

Unless employment is guaranteed, or alternative employment or nonwork income is available, the performance requirements for keeping the job—and perhaps getting a pay raise or promotion—cannot be easily ignored. If the worker does not want to forego the overarching reinforcements associated with keeping the job, he must at least meet the minimum performance levels established by management. Consider that in job enrichment programs, work standards and accountability are characteristically designed into the situation, as at, for example, Texas Instruments which utilizes accountability and quite precise work standards for its enriched cleaning service jobs. When such is the case, to hold the job requires that the scheduled, specified tasks be accomplished. In published studies of enriched jobs, there is nearly always a statement about the quality and quantity of production before and after the introduction of enrichment. It may reasonably be assumed that either implicit or explicit standards— explicit in most cases since feedback to the worker is usually integral to the job enrichment program—are present, known to the workers, and central to the managerial decision to continue a program of enrichment. Given accountability, only one assumption need be introduced, namely, that the benefits of the current job are salient to the worker; no further assumptions about higher-order needs are required.

An alternative explanation of successful job enrichment programs thus appears to be that the accountability characteristically present in these programs provides a fundamental mechanism for maintaining organizationally relevant behavior. From the perspective of the reinforcement paradigm, theories which by *fiat* locate in people a spontaneous impulse to contribute effort in behalf of organizational ends, offer wishful conceptualizations of human motivation.

REFERENCES

Abel, G.G., D.J. Levis and J. Clancy
   1970   "Aversion therapy applied to taped sequences of deviant behavior in exhibitionism and other sexual deviations: a preliminary report." Journal of Behavior Therapy and Experimental Psychology 1(March): 59–66.
Argyris, C.
   1960   Understanding Organizational Behavior. Homewood, Ill.: Dorsey and Irwin.
   1962   "The integration of the individual and the organization," in C. Argyris, et al., Social Science Approaches to Business Behavior. Homewood, Ill.: Dorsey and Irwin.
   1973   "Personality and organization theory." Administrative Science Quarterly 18(June):141–167.
Atthowe, J.M., Jr. and L. Krasner
   1970   "Preliminary report on the application of contingent reinforcement procedures (token economy) on a 'chronic' psychiatric ward," in R. Ulrich, T. Stachnik and J. Marby (eds.), Control of Human Behavior. Vol. 2. Glenview, Ill.: Scott, Foresman and Co.
Best, G.
   1972   Mid-Victorian Britain. New York: Schocken Books.
Biggane, J.F. and P.A. Stewart
   1972   "Job enlargement: a case study," in L.E. Davis and J.C. Taylor (eds.), Design of Jobs. Baltimore: Penguin Books.
Blau, P.M.
   1967   Exchange and Power in Social Life. New York: Wiley.

Blauner, R.
1964   Alienation and Freedom. Chicago: University of Chicago Press.
Brayfield, A.H. and J.H. Crockett
1955   "Employee attitudes and employee performance." Psychological Bul-
        letin 52(September):396–424.
Breslaw, E.
1973   "Behaviorism in the classroom." Change 5(April):52–55.
Business Week
1972   "Where Skinner's theories work." (December 2):64–65.
Campbell, J., et al.
1974   "Theories of organization," in R. Dubin (ed.), Human Relations in
        Administration. Fourth Edition. Englewood Cliffs, New Jersey: Pren-
        tice-Hall.
Cantrell, R.P., et al.
1969   "Contingency contracting with school problems." Journal of Applied
        Behavior Analysis 2(Fall):215–220.
Davis, L.E. and J.C. Taylor (eds.)
1972   Design of Jobs. Baltimore: Penguin Books.
Dowling, W.F.
1973   "Job redesign of the assembly line: farewell to blue-collar blues?" Or-
        ganizational Dynamics 2(Autumn):51–67.
Dubin, R. (ed.)
1974   Human Relations in Administration. Fourth Edition. Englewood Cliffs,
        New Jersey: Prentice-Hall.
Dunnette, M.D., J.P. Campbell and M. Hackell
1967   "Factors contributing to job satisfaction and job dissatisfaction in six
        occupational groups." Organizational Behavior and Human Perform-
        ance 2(May):143–174.
Emerson, R.M.
1972   "Exchange theory, part I: a psychological basis for social exchange,"
        in J. Berger, M. Zelditch and B. Anderson (eds.), Sociological Theories
        in Progress. Boston: Houghton Mifflin.
Ford, R.N.
1973   "Job enrichment lessons from AT&T." Harvard Business Review 51
        (January—February):96–106.
Foulkes, F.
1969   Creating More Meaningful Work. New York: American Management
        Association.
Freud, S.
1962   Civilization and Its Discontents. Translation by James Strachey. New
        York: Norton.
Galbraith, J.K.
1973   Designing Complex Organizations. Reading, Mass.: Addison-Wesley.
Goodall, K.
1972   "Shapers at work." Psychology Today 6(November):53–57.
Hackman, J.R.
1974   "On the coming demise of job enrichment." Department of Admin-
        istrative Sciences, Technical Report No. 9. New Haven, Conn.: Yale
        University.

Hall, V., et al.
1968 "Instructing beginning teachers in reinforcement procedures which improve classroom control." Journal of Applied Behavior Analysis 1(Winter):315–322.

Herzberg, F.
1966 Work and the Nature of Man. Cleveland: World Publishing Co.
1968 "One more time: how do you motivate employees?" Harvard Business Review 46(January–February):53–62.

Herzberg, F., B. Mausner and B. Snyderman
1959 The Motivation to Work. New York: Wiley.

Hill, R.
1972 "The team effort at Motorola." International Management. 27(February):43–45.

Homans, G.C.
1961 Social Behavior: Its Elementary Forms. New York: Harcourt, Brace and World.

House, R.J. and L.A. Wigdor
1967 "Herzberg's dual factor theory of job satisfaction and motivation: a review of the evidence and criticism." Personnel Psychology 20(Winter):369–389.

Hulin, C.L.
1971 "Individual differences and job enrichment: the case against general treatments," in J. Maher (ed.), New Perspectives in Job Enrichment. New York: Van Nostrand Reinhold.

Hulin, C.L. and M.R. Blood
1968 "Job enlargement, individual differences and worker responses." Psychological Bulletin 69(January):41–55.

Jenkins, D.
1974 Job Power. Baltimore: Penguin Books.

Kahn, R.L.
1956 "The prediction of productivity." Journal of Social Issues 12(Spring):41–49.

Katzell, R.A., R.S. Barrett and T.C. Parker
1961 "Job satisfaction, job performance and situational characteristics." Journal of Applied Psychology 45(April):65–72.

Kilbridge, M.D.
1960 "Reduced costs through job enlargement: a case." The Journal of Business 33(October):357–362.

Lawler, E.E. III
1973 Motivation in Work Organizations. Monterey, California: Brooks/Cole.

Lawler, E.E. III and L.W. Porter
1967 "The effect of performance on job satisfaction." Industrial Relations 7(October):20–28.

Lewis, W.H.
1957 The Splendid Century. New York: Doubleday.

Likert, R.
1967 The Human Organization. New York: McGraw-Hill.

McGregor, D.
1957 "The human side of enterprise." The Management Review 46(November):22–28, 88–92.

McIntire, R.
  1970 "Spare the rod, use behavior mod." Psychology Today 4(December):
        42–46.
Maher, J. (ed.)
  1971 New Perspectives in Job Enrichment. New York: Van Nostrand Rein-
        hold.
Maslow, A.
  1943 "A theory of human motivation." Psychological Review 50(July):
        381–382.
  1954 Motivation and Personality. New York: Harper.
  1965 Eupsychian Management. Homewood, Ill.: Irwin and Dorsey.
Mire, J.
  1974 "Improving working life—the role of European unions." Monthly La-
        bor Review 97(September):3–11.
Ney, P.G., A.E. Palvesky and J. Markely
  1971 "Relative effectiveness of operant conditioning and play therapy in
        childhood schizophrenia." Journal of Autism and Childhood Schizo-
        phrenia 1(July):337–349.
O'Leary, K.D. and W.C. Becker
  1970 "Behavior modification of an adjustment class: a token reinforcement
        program," in R. Ulrich, T. Stachnik and J. Marby (eds.), Control of
        Human Behavior. Vol. 2. Glenview, Ill.: Scott, Foresman and Co.
Paul, J.W., Jr., K. Robertson and F. Herzberg
  1969 "Job enrichment pays off." Harvard Business Review 47(March–
        April):61–78.
Phillips, E.L.
  1968 "Achievement place: token reinforcement procedures in a home style
        rehabilitation setting for 'pre-delinquent' boys." Journal of Applied
        Behavior Analysis 1(Fall):213–223.
Phillips, E.L., et al.
  1973 "Behavior shaping works for delinquents." Psychology Today 7(June):
        75–79.
Report of a Special Task Force to the Secretary of Health, Education, and
  Welfare
  1973 Work in America. Cambridge, Mass.: MIT Press.
Roethlisberger, F.J. and W. Dickson
  1961 Management and the Worker. Cambridge, Mass.: Harvard University
        Press.
Rush, H.M.F.
  1971 Job Design for Motivation. New York: National Industrial Conference
        Board.
Schneier, C.
  1973 "Behavior modification: training the hard-core unemployed." Person-
        nel 50(May–June):65–69.
Sheppard, H.L. and N.Q. Herrick
  1972 Where Have All the Robots Gone? New York: The Free Press.
Skinner, B.F.
  1974 About Behaviorism. New York: Knopf.
Smith, A.
  1937 Inquiry into the Nature and Causes of the Wealth of Nations. Edited
        by Edwin Cannan. New York: The Modern Library.

Strauss, G.
   1974   "Job satisfaction, motivation and job redesign," in G. Strauss, R.E. Miles, C.C. Snow and A.S. Tannenbaum (eds.), Organizational Behavior: Research and Issues. Madison, Wisc.: Industrial Relations Research Association.
Susman, G.I.
   1973   "Job enlargement: effects of culture on worker responses." Industrial Relations 12(February) :1–15.
Taylor, F.
   1947   Scientific Management. New York: Harper and Row.
Thompson, J.D.
   1967   Organizations in Action. New York: McGraw-Hill.
Thorndike, E.
   1911   Animal Intelligence. New York: Macmillan.
Turner, A.L. and P.R. Lawrence
   1965   Industrial Jobs and the Worker. Soldier's Field, Boston, Mass.: Division of Research, Harvard School of Business.
U.S. Department of Labor
   1974   "Job satisfaction: is there a trend?" Manpower Research Monograph No. 30, Washington, D.C., U.S. Government Printing Office.
U.S. News and World Report
   1972   "The drive to make dull jobs interesting." 73(July 17) :50–54.
Vroom, V.
   1964   Work and Motivation. New York: Wiley.
Wagner, R. and B. Guyer
   1971   "Maintenance of discipline through increasing children's span of attention by means of a token economy." Psychology in the Schools. 8(July) :285–289.
Walker, C.R. and R. Guest
   1952   The Man on the Assembly Line. Cambridge, Mass.: Harvard University Press.
Walton, R.E.
   1972   "How to counter alienation in the plant." Harvard Business Review 50(November–December) :70–81.
   1974   "Innovative restructuring of work," in J.M. Rosow (ed.), The Worker and the Job. Englewood Cliffs, New Jersey: Prentice-Hall.
Weed, E.D., Jr.
   1971   "Job enrichment 'cleans up' at Texas Instruments," in J. Maher (ed.), New Perspectives in Job Enrichment. New York: Van Nostrand Reinhold.

CHAPTER **13**

Compensation for Work

D.W. Belcher and T.J. Atchison

San Diego State University

INTRODUCTION

Organizations, despite the high level of technology, still rely primarily upon human resources for the accomplishment of organizational goals. Unlike other resources, the human resource is relatively mobile and reactive. Thus constant energy expenditure by the organization is required to maintain and develop this resource. This energy is the compensation to the employee for his work.

Despite its obvious importance, study of the field of compensation has been described as fragmentary and inadequate (Belcher, 1960; Haire, et al., 1963). Two reasons seem to lie behind this neglect. First, it is more difficult to study phenomena which are basic than those which are peripheral. Compensation strikes so close to the individual and to the organization that it is hard to. study it in any sort of dispassionate way. Both the individual and the organization resist the behavioral scientists' intrusion.

Second, the subject of compensation is complex. It is difficult to separate the study of compensation from the study of organizations. The boundaries of the subject are not neat and clean. Exactly what should be included and excluded in an analysis of compensation for work is not at all clear.

Our research in this field and particularly for this chapter leads us to believe that although much remains to be done, more than a modest amount is known about compensation for work. New conceptual approaches of the last few years provide a useful framework for the study of compensation. These concepts and studies based upon them have added to understanding. But while most of the behavioral sciences are proceeding to work on various aspects of the compensation process, there is little coordination among them. The majority of writing in this field is still descriptive, with very little conceptual or research base. Furthermore, much of the material which is useful in discussing compensation is derived from studies which had as their major purpose some other behavioral phenomenon.

The following pages represent an attempt to fit as much of this material as possible within a framework which seems to us at this time to be most applicable to analyzing the subject of compensation. Once this conceptual framework has been developed each of the parts is examined in terms of what we know and what we need to know. From this method of analysis some inferences concerning the effectiveness of current compensation practice and changes which seem likely in the future become visible.

EXCHANGE AS A BASIS FOR ANALYZING COMPENSATION

The economist has had an advantage in analyzing compensation because he had a ready model. He always used the model of exchange. Employment to the economist is simply the exchange of time, effort, and ability for payment in money or in kind. Given the purposes of the economist, this model has served well. It has not been faultless, however. The labor economist in particular has found that many phenomena surrounding compensation cannot be analyzed in terms of this simple model.

Early behavioral scientists found the economist's model of the employment exchange inadequate. The human relationist in particular felt that the simplicity of this model left out important variables. He proceeded to throw out exchange as a model for examining the employment relationship and to focus upon satisfaction and motivation. Disenchantment of the human relationist with the exchange model was basically a result of the belief that motivation and satisfaction of the individual in the employment relationship were more than a matter of money. It was also noted, but never quite followed through, that the individual brought more to the job than simply his time, effort, and ability.

The economic model was most useful in describing the employment exchange as it emerged from the industrial revolution. It was a close fit with the ideology of the early industrialists (Bendix, 1956). Industrialism was aided by the values of individualism and materialism (Peters, 1968). Individualism encourages a relationship between employers and employees which is narrowly defined and basically economic in nature.

The economic model was not a good explanation, however, of preindustrial employment relationships. The master-serf relationship, for example, was much more encompassing, including social and political considerations along with economic ones.

Nor can the relationship between man and organization in modern society be adequately described in economic terms. Perhaps the most useful partial model is still the economic one. But in a society in which guaranteed income is under consideration, the employment relationship is only partially explained in economic terms. In addition, the individual expects to gain certain social values from his relationship to the organization. A job has a certain status attached to it. It permits interaction with other people. It provides a sense of achievement and an opportunity to realize one's potential capabilities. On the organization's part, much more than time, effort, and ability is expected. At least as important to the organization are: acceptance of responsibility, willingness to accept change, concern for quality, cooperation with other employees and other organization units, and flexibility in meeting changed demands. Particularly as the professional and managerial ranks of organizations grow, the need for commitment is greatly expanded.

In recent years there has been a resurgence of interest in exchange by behavioral scientists. Sociologists and psychologists both have become interested in the concept of exchange and of viewing behavior as exchange. (See particularly Homans, 1961; Blau, 1967; Adams, 1963; Gergen, 1969.) The study and conceptualization of exchange have expanded the scope of items considered in the exchange relationship, and have examined exchange as a process. This new conceptualization of exchange has provided a good model for analyzing compensation for work.

An advantage of using exchange theory as a vehicle for studying compensation is that all three of the major disciplines involved in compensation—economics, psychology, and sociology—have used and studied exchange theory as it relates to compensation. Another advantage is that exchange theory views compensation more broadly than has been traditional. In this way exchange theory is extremely helpful in identifying both knowledge and gaps in knowledge about various aspects of compensation.

THE EXCHANGE MODEL OF COMPENSATION

The remainder of this section develops the model we employ to analyze compensation for work. The applicability of exchange theory to the employment exchange is shown. Then the parts of the exchange process are delineated.

The Actors

Exchange is a two-party game. The parties to the exchange may be two individuals, an individual and a group, or two groups. Ordinarily the employment exchange is a relationship between an individual and a group. Where a union is involved the exchange takes on the aspect of a group-to-group relationship. The exchange may also take on the aspect of an individual-to-individual relationship when superior-subordinate relationships are considered.

The parties to the exchange need not be equal. Indeed, in most situations, one party or other to the exchange has more power (Blau, 1967). However, both parties must be able to influence the other party to some degree. Each party to the exchange must be giving something and receiving something of value to him. Thus, exchange is a positive-sum game. When it is not perceived as a positive-sum game, exchange does not take place.

Exchange as a Double System

Exchange can be conveniently viewed as a double input-output system. Each party to the exchange is contributing something to the exchange in return for which he receives something of value to him. That is, for a given input on his part he receives some output. This is a double input-output system because what is the input for one party is the output of the other, and vice versa. At first glance, the employment exchange seems to be a closed system which consists of two completely interdependent subsystems. In fact, exchange is not a closed system but an exceptionally open system as the following explanation will show.

First, the exchange process is a perceptual one. Each party to the exchange views what he considers to be his and the other party's contributions to, and outcomes from, the exchange. The result of this dual perceptual field is that the two parties may not view the exchange in the same manner. There can be a considerable difference in perception and still an exchange will take place.

This lack of congruence is not only inevitable but desirable. If both parties were to put the same value upon a particular input or output exchange would not take place (March and Simon, 1958). An exchange becomes possible only because the two parties place different values on the same item. That is, each party wants what the other party has and, therefore, must enter into an exchange in order to gain it. In such a situation people tend to undervalue what they have and to overvalue what the other person has.

A further condition for lack of congruence occurs when one party or the other sees something in the exchange that the other party does not. In order for a factor to enter the exchange at least one party must recognize that the factor is present and consider it relevant (Adams, 1965). The closer the two parties come to considering the same factors as relevant, the higher the probability that the exchange will be regarded as "fair" by both parties. However, the different perceptual fields of the organization and its managers, on the one hand, and its employees and their unions, on the other, suggest that the factors involved in the employment exchange are likely to be seen quite differently unless special efforts are made to specify and agree upon them.

Specificity and Time in Exchange

Two very important factors in any exchange are the degree to which the terms of the exchange are specified and agreed upon by the two parties, and secondly, the time period over which the exchange extends. These two factors tend to be interrelated. In exchanges of short time duration the tendency is for the terms to be well known to both parties. Exchange in which the time period between giving and receiving is great or which involves continuing exchange over time tends to be ill-defined (Whyte, 1969:148). Quite often in social exchange one is never sure how he is going to be repaid for some act of social giving, or when he is going to be repaid (Blau, 1967).

The conditions of the employment exchange are not well spelled out. Some aspects are usually quite clear. Such things as hours of work and sometimes production standards, on one side of the exchange, and pay rates and benefiits on the other side, are examples of parts of the exchange which may be clearly spelled out in advance. The parts clearly specified are usually those involved in the economic aspects of the employment exchange. On the other hand, much of the employment exchange is quite unspecified. On one side of the exchange there may be such things as loyalty, commitment, and certain behavior norms expected by the organization. On the other side of the exchange are expectations of individuals concerning status, achievement, and recognition. The discrepancy regarding these unspecified expectations may be quite great. The high turnover of new college graduates in industry can be viewed as a case of discrepancy between the parties to the employment exchange (Schein, 1964).

Even less defined than the items in the employment exchange is the time perspective. Again the economic variables are most likely to be time-defined. People tend to get paid at specific intervals of time for having worked a standard period of time. Pensions are awarded for a certain time period spent in the organization. In certain instances, particularly in the construction industry, people are hired for just certain projects or jobs, at the end of which their employment is terminated. For the most part, however, the employment exchange continues in some sort of indefinite manner. It is a continuing exchange where, when both parties are reasonably satisfied, it remain in force. Also it is never quite clear when the scales have been balanced in the employment exchange. The economic model would assume that on each pay day the scales had been balanced with the exception of deferred benefits. In some, but probably few situations, this is the extent of the employment exchange. In most cases, however, there are long-range expectations. An employee who has been with the organization for a long period of time expects to be treated differently from one who has just been hired. People tend to build up an expectation of something more over time. The professional may not expect immediate recompense for his current sixty-hour week but see this as the road to advancement two or three years hence (Ritti, 1968). On the other side of the exchange, the manager may be lenient today with the expectation that when emergencies arise employees will increase their organizational commitment (Blau, 1963).

It is this lack of specificity that makes the subject of compensation so challenging. When the economic model of the employment exchange can be assumed, the subject can be handled with a certain quantitative precision. But as the varying expectations of the parties and various social factors enter into the exchange, the subject becomes a matter for interdisciplinary study. Such integrated studies have not yet been forthcoming.

The Exchange Process

The employment exchange may be divided into a number of parts. For convenience, these parts are viewed from the standpoint of one of the participants, that of the employee. The individual engages in the employment exchange in order to gain some rewards by making contributions to the organization. The individual makes a comparison of these contributions and rewards which has an effect upon his attitudes and behavior.

Rewards.   Rewards are what the individual receives from the exchange. The importance of the exchange to him depends upon the degree to which he wants or needs the items which are available to him. Almost any item the individual needs or desires can be a reward. As pointed out above, the necessary condition is that it be recognized by him as relevant. Any particular exchange may have from one to many possible rewards. The more rewards available the more likely the exchange will be binding and important to the individual.

The employment exchange is a good example of an exchange in which there are many highly important rewards available. Working provides not only monetary gains but a number of other important rewards. In particular, working provides a major way in which the individual finds his place and status in society. Often the importance of the employment exchange in satisfying human needs is overemphasized. One gets the impression from reading the behavioral science literature that the employment exchange provides the central life interest of all who work. Of course, it cannot (Dubin, 1958b:261).

Contributions.   Contributions are what the individual provides in the exchange—his investments and costs. The possible contributions are as numerous as the rewards, and again must be recognized and viewed as relevant to be part of the exchange. Contributions then are the price the employee pays for participating in the exchange.

In the employment exchange there is always a commitment of the individual's time and effort and certain of his abilities. But organizations usually require many more kinds of contributions than they recognize. Also individuals have perceptions of the abilities they wish to contribute to the exchange.

Because it has been assumed that the contribution required from employees was work, and employees expected to work, contributions have not been carefully studied. But work has not been defined (Drucker, 1973). It is apparent that organizations want many kinds of contributions and different contributions from different employee groups. It is also apparent that different employee groups have different ideas about their contributions to organizations.

The comparison process. The comparison process involves relating rewards and contributions to each other and to some criterion. It is a crucial part of the employment exchange with both behavioral and attitudinal consequences in that the comparisons determine whether the exchange will be made or continued, and also its fairness.

The comparison process involves a number of complexities. The time lag between rewards and contributions and the lack of specificity of both, complicates comparisons. Power differentials between the parties may permit one party to take advantage of the other. Expectations, in ill-defined situations, may be quite different for both parties and both may diverge from reality.

Equally troublesome is the problem of units. Neither rewards nor contributions reduce to common units and a direct comparison between rewards and contributions is difficult. In some situations, such as a wage incentive plan, a specific reward is apparently associated with a particular contribution. But even in this situation the association is illusory and in the typical employment exchange, direct associations are absent.

Another problem faced in the comparison process is the lack of a common standard of fairness. Equity seems derived from expectations which are determined partially by social norms and partially by previous experience in other exchanges.

The lack of a definite standard suggests that the two parties to the employment exchange may be using different criteria and that criterion selection is unstable. There may be a strain toward organizations' selecting other organizations and employees other employees as standards, thus comparing with units most like themselves. This means that organizations are making external, and employees internal comparisons. But both parties in an unstructured situation could be expected to select the criterion most advantageous to themselves.

Availability of information should affect the comparison process and criteria selection. The amount and quality of information from various sources would seem to be important variables.

Results of the Exchange Process

The final part of the model focuses on the output of the exchange process. As mentioned previously, results are both behavioral and attitudinal. The exchange is made or continued and adjudged as fair or unfair.

The exchange is likely to have its primary effect on behavior. If both parties value the rewards to be obtained from the exchange more than the contributions they must make, the exchange will take place. If the exchange is perceived as unfair, either party may search for a better one, attempt to change the terms in his favor by increasing rewards or decreasing contributions, perceptually increase rewards or reduce contributions, or change to more acceptable criteria of equity. The more choices are perceived to be limited, the more likely the latter will be followed. If, however, the exchange is perceived as fair, the individual is more likely to be committed to the organization, to define contributions in the broadest possible manner, and to seek opportunities to make contributions beyond the minimum requirements of the exchange.

The behavioral and attitudinal results of the exchange process are usually assumed to be interdependent and equivalent. However, because some employment exchanges are made which one party perceives as unfair and other exchanges are not made although both parties perceive them as fair, the assumed equivalence between behavior and attitudes needs further study.

This model of the employment exchange is used as a framework for analysis of compensation for work. The following sections present our analysis employing each part of the model.

THE EXCHANGE PROCESS: REWARDS

Rewards for work include all those things that the employee receives as a consequence of the employment exchange. In systems terms, they represent inputs to employees from the organization in exchange for outputs from employees in the form of contributions. To the organization, rewards represent outputs to employees in exchange for inputs from employees in the form of employee contributions. To both, outputs must exceed inputs if the systems are to survive and achieve their goals. Thus employees must perceive their rewards as greater than their contributions and organizations must perceive rewards provided employees as less than employee contributions.

This definition suggests that rewards may be of various kinds. It also suggests that organizations may be supplying a greater variety of rewards than they are typically aware of. Organizations are, of course, aware that they are providing economic rewards and that these economic rewards are limited by organization resources. They may or may not be aware that they are providing many other kinds of rewards and that not all of them are limited by organization resources.

What We Know: A Survey of the Literature

A good deal is known about the rewards employees receive from the employment exchange. It is known, for example, that the variety is almost endless. Employees receive economic rewards (pay and benefits) but they also receive a large number of noneconomic rewards.

Types of rewards. Psychologists have distinguished many of these rewards in studies of job satisfaction. A very careful study of job satisfaction research resulting in a standardized instrument to measure job satisfaction has reduced rewards to five types: characteristics of the work, pay, promotions, supervision, and co-workers (Smith, Kendall, and Hulin, 1969). Most job satisfaction studies distinguish a greater variety of rewards. The factors employed by Herzberg (1966) are probably representative of the rewards which job satisfaction research has shown to be forthcoming from the employment exchange.

These factors are: recognition; achievement; possibility of growth; advancement; salary; interpersonal relations with superiors, subordinates, and peers; technical competence of supervision; responsibility; company policy and administration; working conditions; the work itself; personal life; status; and job security.

Sociologists have also pointed out various noneconomic rewards from work. Dubin (1958a, 1958b), for example, distinguished power pay (a job of greater importance, exclusive jurisdiction over a job), authority pay (promotion, more authority), status pay (giving the individual higher status), and privilege pay (giving employees opportunities for informal relationships with people of higher authority). His recent work on sources of attachment to work extends the list of possible rewards from the employment exchange to over 100 items (see Chapter 4). The variety of rewards from the employment exchange is immense. Anything an employee perceives as a reward from employment must be so classified.

The reader may note that all rewards are conceived to be positive. It is, of course, possible to point to negative rewards or punishments such as boredom, danger, or discomfort which may be conceived as outputs from employment. We prefer to classify such factors as contributions of employees to the exchange.

Some knowledge exists of the manner in which employees learn what rewards to value. Dubin (1958b:215; Van Maanen, 1972) has shown how the early socialization process serves to internalize the rewards appropriate for particular activities and how the specific work organization builds upon these societal foundations while teaching the individual the rewards specific to that institutional setting. Reference groups (Hyman and Singer, 1968) either within the organization or without have a strong influence on desired rewards.

Reward preferences. Different employee groups are known to differ in the rewards they value. Caplow's (1954) study of the characteristics of sociological labor markets shows how diverse labor markets (bureaucratic, industrial, craft, professional, common labor, unique services) imply quite different preferred rewards. Nealey (1963) found that benefit preferences and pay versus benefit preferences vary by demographic groups. Lester (1967) in a review article found employee preferences for benefits growing over time. Atchison and Belcher (1971, and unpublished studies) have examined the reward preferences of a number of different groups (white collar, production, skilled employees, and engineers in one organization; managers in a government organization; professional football players; administrators, teachers, clerical workers, and bus drivers in a public school). Results suggest that some rewards are highly valued by some occupational groups but not others and other rewards are highly valued by some demographic groups but not others. For example, young unmarried women place a high value on a social life at work; football players highly value leisure time; and engineers place a high value on assignments with heavy responsibility.

The general conclusion from studies of rank-and-file employees in the United States is that job security, opportunities for advancement, interesting work, and interesting co-workers are valued highly and that financial rewards are fifth to eighth in importance (Campbell, et al., 1970:364). A compilation of forty-nine studies of the relative importance of pay shows that it ranked from first to ninth position, with an average rank of three (Lawler, 1971). Managers, however, are usually found to prefer high pay over job security and benefits (Mahoney, 1964; Andrews and Henry, 1963).

The relative importance of different rewards to employee groups is still unsettled. It is obvious that employees expect to be paid but that economic rewards while necessary are not sufficient. Vroom (1964:32) suggests that the relative value of economic and noneconomic rewards can probably only be settled by an experiment which no organization is likely to try: discontinue all economic rewards and see how many employees continue to work. The statement: "Deep down, everyone assumes that we mostly work for money" (Haire, et al., 1963) is widely accepted. A psychological study which attempted to determine the importance of particular rewards for total job satisfaction found that pay loomed large in all employee groups studied, although the mix of important rewards varied from group to group (Hinrichs, 1968).

Organization practices. If employees are receiving such a wide variety of rewards, organizations are providing them. Organizations, however, do not seem to be aware of the range of rewards they are offering. Campbell, et al. (1970:62) found that organizations rely on money, promotions, and status symbols as rewards for managers but focus primarily upon the former. They found that only a few organizations were aware that interesting jobs might have been rewards.

Organizations obviously differ in the kinds of rewards they provide and emphasize. Etzioni's (1961) analysis of organizations shows that coercive, remunerative, and normative organizations emphasize different types of rewards. Churches obviously have different rewards than business organizations. Organizations also are constrained in the amounts of rewards they can provide. All organizations are limited by organization resources in the amount of economic rewards available. Most other rewards are also limited by organization resources.

But oganizations of all kinds act as if the employment exchange is entirely an economic transaction. They act as if only economic rewards are being exchanged for purely economic contributions. In addition, in many organizations the prevailing belief is that additional contributions are always available for more monetary rewards. For example, compensation in most organizations means pay. Fringe benefits are administered separately from pay, except for executives. Promotions are treated as an aspect of manpower planning. Job design is not a responsibility of the personnel department. Thus, rewards are treated on a fragmented basis and only pay appears to be regarded as the central reward.

Careful analysis of organization practice, however, suggests that while following an economic ideology, most organizations rely heavily on custom and tradition. Wage or salary surveys, a common practice by organizations of all kinds, while collecting information on an economic variable, are actually a device for maintaining customary relationships. Dunlop's (1957) "wage contours" (organizations exchanging wage information) are heavily based upon custom. Lipset and Trow (1957) have translated the economists' "coercive comparisons" into reference group theory. The manner in which surveys are typically used (Groenkamp, 1967) suggests that rather than being a source of economic information, they represent a ceremonial to convince employees that the organization is keeping up with the market. In fact, if Robinson's (1967) finding in Great Britain that earnings vary widely between organizations is more broadly applicable, using wage surveys as economic indicators would be dysfunctional to organizations. Benefit surveys, another common practice, typically exchange not benefit costs but prevailing practice. For obvious reasons unions encourage such surveys. Use of prevailing practice benefit surveys encourages continuing customary relationships.

Job evaluation, in widespread use in the United States and in growing use in Europe (National Board for Prices and Incomes, 1968), while simulating economic forces to develop an internal pay structure, actually relies heavily on tradition and employee acceptance. Even plans heavily keyed to the labor market (Pasquale, 1969) represent a combination of tradition, employee acceptance, and customary relationships (from wage surveys).

Salary ranges, common practice especially for white collar and managerial employees, represent in theory an economic transaction of more pay for more economic contribution (performance). In practice, however, they represent more pay for either seniority (Slichter, et al., 1960:605) or previous experience (Fogel, 1965), neither of which is necessarily an economic contribution.

Wage incentive plans probably represent the strongest example of an apparent economic transaction actually representing both tradition and ideology (Behrend, 1959). In theory, wage incentives represent an economic transaction of more pay for more economic contributions (effort). In practice, wage incentive plans often represent the power of tradition and a management myth while resulting in less effort, resistance to change, and industrial relations problems (Corina, 1970).

A much discussed but apparently seldom followed organization practice holds promise for both broadening organization perspective on rewards and providing employees with the rewards they value. The so-called "cafeteria" plan permits employees to choose the package of rewards they seek from the employment exchange (Schuster, et al., 1971). Although typically limited to pay and benefits, there appears to be no reason why the package of potential rewards could not be extended.

Studies of rewards.   Organizations should not be blamed for their narrow focus on rewards. Rewards in the broader sense discussed here have not been carefully studied. Economists have quite understandably focussed on wages and benefits. Psychologists have been interested in job satisfaction and motivation but only recently have they become interested in organizations and in organization reward programs. Sociologists have only recently begun to apply their concepts to organizations and organization reward practices. Perhaps of equal importance has been management ideology. Until very recently management was certain that the employment exchange was a purely economic transaction.

Economic studies.   Economists have made many studies of rewards because of their conception of the employment relationship as an exchange transaction. From their studies of labor markets (Reynolds, 1951) and of collective bargaining, labor economists are aware that organizations provide other rewards as well as economic ones. They tend to define wages as encompassing all of the clauses in a labor agreement and the actual administration of these clauses (Taylor, 1957). In their study of wage determination under collective bargaining, the influence of custom and power is as evident as economic forces (Ross, 1948). But even though labor economists by the nature of their data become part-time sociologists and political scientists, they confine their analysis of rewards to wages and benefits (Taylor and Pierson, 1957). Study of the institution of collective bargaining undoubtedly encourages this narrow view in that labor leaders act as if rewards from the employment exchange are principally economic.

Economic studies of wages have contributed a great deal to the understanding of wage-making forces and the effects of wage decisions at the level of the economy and at the level of the organization (Livernash, 1970). Separate analyses have been made of wage levels and wage structures although advancing knowledge has shown the interdependence of the two.

Wage level determinants at the level of the economy have been found to be numerous. The real wage level (money wages divided by cost of living) is strongly influenced by productivity and perhaps unions (Brown and Browne, 1968). The money wage level, however, has been found to be subject to at least some influence from the following factors: (1) bargaining, (2) both product and labor markets, (3) profits, (4) unemployment, (5) productivity, (6) competition and (7) price trends (Eckstein and Wilson, 1962; Perry, 1966; Eckstein, 1968; Brown and Browne, 1968). The influence of unionism has been particularly difficult to trace but a detailed study of one company's records shows a marked effect of unions on both real and money wages (Ozanne, 1968). However, the influence of unionism remains controversial (Weintraub, 1963; Rees, 1962; Lewis, 1963).

A stable relationship between money wage changes and unemployment at the level of the economy was found by Phillips (1958). This so-called Phillips curve has encouraged a good deal of wage research and controversy. The weight of evidence supports the existence of the relationship but it is imprecise and complex (Livernash, 1970). The Phillips curve implies as much about the effects of national wage levels as about wage determination. It suggests that national goals of full employment, rising wages, stable prices, and collective bargaining may be incompatible.

Benefit levels have been studied by economists (Mabry, 1973). Benefits in the United States have been increasing at a rate such that the total economic package grows at about double the rate of wages (Livernash, 1970). Growth of the benefit package constitutes a continuing change in the form of economic rewards for work (Bauman, 1970). The U.S. Chamber of Commerce in a continuing series of studies on benefit costs has traced the benefit costs of a group of identical firms over the years. The benefit costs of these firms have increased from 16% of payroll in 1947 to 31.7% in 1969 (Chamber of Commerce, 1970). A 1970 study predicted that benefit costs will amount to 50% of payroll by 1985 (Gordon and LeBleu, 1970). Pay for time not worked, premium pay for time worked, and health and security benefits have shown the greatest expansion. The United States stands alone in the degree it has provided benefits and security arrangements by private means.

Economic studies of the wage structure at the level of the economy have found a high degree of stability with only modest changes in industrial, occupational, and regional differentials over time (de Wolff, 1965). A long-term narrowing of occupational differentials has been found (Keat, 1960), and some narrowing of regional differentials (Segal, 1961), but earlier predictions that all differentials would narrow over time (Taylor and Pierson, 1957) are not supported.

The wage structure has been shown to be influenced by profit levels and competitive characteristics of industries (de Wolff, 1965). In all countries similar industries experience similar wage and employment changes. Custom and tradition blend with market forces to influence the wage structure (Reder, 1958). However, institutional differences between countries have almost no effect on the wage structure (Johnson, 1962).

Studies of the benefit structure show great variation by industry, region, and size of firm (Chamber of Commerce, 1970). Large firms and unionized firms have higher benefits, but wage levels and benefit levels are not correlated (Reynolds, 1951). Variations in benefits highlight the discrepancy between employees covered and not covered and this relative deprivation would seem to increase pressures for public welfare and retirement benefits.

Attempts to determine the effects of collective bargaining on the wage structure have been studied through wage patterns. The strength of patterns has been found to vary over time. There are many types and degrees of variation. The influence of the pattern loses its clarity beyond the particular industry, the jurisdiction of the particular union, and national product markets (Seltzer, 1961; Carpenter and Handler, 1961). A study of patterns in six industries found economic, political, and power variables in operation (Levinson, 1966).

One of the effects of the wage structure that has interested economists is its influence on the allocation of labor. Although competitive theory postulates a relationship between relative changes in wages and employment, no strong relationship has been found. Job vacancies rather than relative wages are the major influence on labor allocation, except at the extremes. There are, however, relationships between wages and employment for certain groups such as salaried and professional employees (de Wolff, 1965).

Economists have also studied wages at the level of the organization. Much of the economists' research on the general wage level and structure has implications for wage decisions in organizations. Wage level determinants within organizations have been found to be: collective bargaining, conditions in product and labor markets, wage criteria and customary relationships (Taylor and Pierson, 1957). Wage determination under collective bargaining involves sociological and psychological variables as well as economic ones. Economic variables prescribe broad limits within which behavioral and institutional variables operate.

Benefit levels are also influenced by economic variables. The influence of collective bargaining is shown in the advantage of union workers over nonunion workers in benefits (Davis and David, 1968). While to the employer wages and benefits are interchangeable in that both involve wage costs, unions sometimes do and sometimes do not consider them to be wage equivalents (Ross, 1957).

Wage structure determinants in organizations include job evaluation, product and labor market conditions as they affect the organization, and collective bargaining. Some unions insist on job evaluation, some unions insist on bargaining job rates, and some unions appear quite uninterested in the internal wage relationships in organizations. The influence of collective bargaining on wage structures in organizations in the United States has been carefully studied (Slichter, et al., 1960) and the findings show a reasonable accommodation between the parties.

Dunlop's (1957) formulation relating wage rates of jobs to each other and to the market through job clusters, key rates, and wage contours (organizations which exchange wage information) represents a reasonable abstraction of wage structure determination in organizations. Both job clusters and wage contours are strongly influenced by custom as well as economic considerations (Livernash, 1957).

Effects of wage structure changes in organizations have been studied. As in wage structure determination, a wide latitude exists for organizations and institutional forces that is at least as influential as economic forces (Lester, 1957).

Economists have also studied payment practices in organizations. Rate ranges have been found in practice to be a method of rewarding length of service. Wage incentive plans in practice may be quite unsuccessful or successful in terms of economic criteria but are continued or even expanded for sociological reasons (Mangum, 1962).

Psychological studies. Psychologists have studied rewards as sources of job satisfaction and motivation. Job satisfaction studies have served to delineate a number of rewards from work and differential employee preferences for these rewards (Smith, et al., 1969).

Psychological research on motivation has sought to determine how rewards operate and which rewards motivate. Such work has served to show that motivation is complex and the number of separate motivation theories suggests that much remains to be learned.

One psychologist has observed that all rewards follow the law of diminishing returns and that it is necessary to find out both if a particular reward serves to motivate and, if so, within what range (Haire, 1959). A recent review of organization practice shows that organizations do not consciously use rewards other than money to motivate employees (Campbell, et al., 1970). An excellent review article published in 1966 (Opsahl and Dunnette) found several studies concerning theories of the role of money and a substantial number concerned with the behavioral consequences of financial compensation. A comprehensive 1971 study compiled and analyzed psychological research and theory on pay importance, pay as a motivator and pay satisfaction (Lawler, 1971). Among subjects which have been studied are incentive plans, effects of pay secrecy, pay and performance relationships and pay histories. All show potential effects on employee behavior.

Psychological studies of wage incentive plans show that installation of such plans usually results in greater input, lower costs, and higher wages (Viteles, 1953; Lawler, 1971). But the conditions associated with these results have not been isolated. Few studies have been made of the effects of wage incentive plans by psychologists.

Lawler (1967) has studied the effect of secret pay policies and finds that secrecy reduces the motivation of managers. Haire (1965) has studied career pay histories in organizations for evidence of the relationship between pay and performance and interprets his findings as showing little relationship. A statistical study of pay curves over time yields inferences of past salary policies and suggestions for future policies (Haire, et al., 1967).

A number of psychological studies have shown the effects of perceived relations between performance and pay. Individuals who perceive higher productivity as a means to higher pay perform more effectively (Georgopolous, et al., 1957; Porter and Lawler, 1968; Lawler, 1971). But apparently money does not operate as an incentive on repetitive, destructive, boring, or disliked work. There is some evidence that relating pay to performance may serve to reduce the value placed upon intrinsic rewards (Deci, 1972).

Some studies have been made of pay preferences—the form in which individuals desire their pay. Mahoney (1964) found that managers want their pay in salary. Nealey (1963) found that individuals differ demographically in their preferences for pay versus benefits. One study developed a scaling technique that permits measurement of preferences by attaching a monetary equivalent to each reward (Jones and Jeffrey, 1964). Lawler (1971) has assembled the studies on the importance of pay to separate employee groups.

Perhaps the largest volume of psychological studies of pay in recent years has been concerned with equitable payment. From the viewpoint of the psychologist, the purpose of these studies has been to determine the effects of perceived over- and under-reward. Quite a large volume of experimental studies has appeared over the past few years and some review articles summarize and interpret the results to date (Lawler, 1968; Pritchard, 1969; Goodman and Friedman, 1971).

The model on which these studies are based is called equity theory. In simple terms, the theory suggests that employees seek equitable rewards for what they have contributed to the job. Homans's (1961) theory of distributive justice and Jaques's (1961) theory of equitable payment represent early formulations. The most careful statement of the equity theory was made by Adams (1963), who conducted several experiments.

In general, laboratory studies based upon equity theory tend to show that underpayment results in decreased output, and overpayment in increased output, except under incentive payment arrangements where overpayment results in improved quality rather than quantity. Attempts to ferret out what actually occurs in the experiments is made difficult by the complexity of the variables. These studies make clear that many rewards and contributions are perceptually present even in apparently simple exchanges and that we need to know a great deal more about how they operate and change.

An area where little psychological research has been done but which is likely to expand in the future is in designing reward systems in terms of operant conditioning (Skinner, 1967). Some interesting examples have involved designing rewards to improve attendance (Nord, 1972; Lawler and Hackman, 1969).

Sociological studies.   Until quite recently sociological contributions to the understanding of rewards from the employment exchange consisted of studies in other areas that could be applied to problems of organizations. The following are not meant to be exhaustive. Rather, they are suggestive of the manner in which sociological concepts have been and can be applied to the employment exchange.

As noted previously, Dubin (1958b) has shown how the individual learns the rewards to expect from the employment exchange through the socialization process. Etzioni (1961) has shown how organizations differ in the kinds of rewards they emphasize.

Studies of the social stratification process (Tumin, 1967) have much to say concerning who gets what rewards in organizations. Although to our knowledge the application has not been made, it would seem that the principles of social stratification could be used to test organization reward structures.

The studies of the sociology of occupations (Caplow, 1954; Hall, 1969) have shown the different rewards sought by separate occupation groups. Perhaps more importantly, they suggest how the division of labor in society may differ from the division of labor in specific organizations, the strains thereby produced, and the mutual adjustment process.

Sociological studies of groups in organizations show the power of groups in influencing reward preferences and in providing rewards. Reference group theory seems a useful but relatively untapped resource for understanding reward preferences and how they develop and change (Lipset and Trow, 1957; Hyman and Singer, 1968).

Also previously mentioned was Homans's (1961) theory of distributive justice as the trigger of equity theory. Homans's work and Blau's (1967) conception of social exchange provided the conceptual foundation of the model of the employment exchange utilized in this chapter.

Sociologists have also studied pay systems in organizations. A number of sociological studies have investigated the operation of incentive plans and have shown a number of latent consequences (Dalton, 1948; Collins, Dalton, and Roy, 1946; Roy, 1952; Whyte, 1955). These studies have not only shown the possibility of restriction of output under incentive plans but have shown the other rewards available in organizations that may be unintentionally altered by incentive plans.

In Europe, industrial sociologists have studied rewards for work from a broader perspective than has been used in the United States. Lupton has been concerned with developing and testing a model for evaluating payment systems in organizations that employ sociological as well as psychological and economic variables (Lupton, 1969, 1970). Corina (1970:121) has shown how reward systems in organizations must respond to social pressures as well as economic ones.

One of the currently most discussed rewards—job design—which has resulted in much experimentation (especially in Europe) owes much to the work of sociologists (Emery and Thorsrud, 1969; Davis and Taylor, 1972). Developing cohesive work groups and building jobs and organizations in terms of interactions required by the work flow represent applications of sociological research which long antedated present terminology (Sayles, 1973).

What We Need to Know

The knowledge that the typical organization employs diverse occupational and demographic groups and that these groups have distinguishable reward preferences suggest that we need to know the reward preferences of these groups. We need to know, for example, what rewards are desired from their employers by top management, middle management, lower management, various categories of professionals, white collar workers, craftsmen, and blue collar industrial workers. We also need to know how reward preferences differ demographically; limited evidence suggests that certain age, sex, and marital status groups have a high preference for specific rewards regardless of occupation. It is not being suggested that pay will be absent from any of these schedules, but it is suggested that the value of pay as a reward differs substantially for different groups and that it is important for an organization to know the reward preference schedule for each group.

It is also important for organizations to become aware that they have potentially a large arsenal of rewards. Studies suggest that organizations are providing rewards that they are not aware of providing. This suggests that organizations must search out the rewards that they have available and decide which of these they are prepared to provide each employee group. The latter decision includes the limits to be placed upon rewards. Obviously every organization has only limited economic resources. But there may be limits on noneconomic rewards as well, probably largely dictated by custom.

Organizations in their search for potential rewards are constrained by the expectations of society. In the past, society's evaluation of reward legitimacy was closely correlated with organization type (Etzioni, 1961). It seems quite likely that this evaluation is changing so that the rewards employees want and that organizations can offer will be considered legitimate (Selznick, 1969).

At present a useful taxonomy of rewards would seem to be: (1) extrinsic rewards—those rewards that the organization consciously provides its employees, (2) intrinsic rewards—those rewards that employees provide themselves because organization climate permits them to do so and (3) other rewards that the organization provides its employees without organization awareness (Belcher, 1974).

Some implications of the state of our knowledge regarding rewards from the employment exchange may need emphasis. If the rewards that employees expect and want from the employment exchange are incompletely known and organizations are only partially aware of the rewards that they provide employees, the total reward side of the employment exchange remains unspecified. Collective bargaining in this context must also be thought of as having the function of specifying the reward side of the exchange. But unions as well as employing organizations are influenced by custom and tradition and are organizations which have been defined as "political institutions operating in an economic environment" (Ross, 1948). The evidence does not suggest that unions have been any more diligent in seeking out the needs and desires of employee groups (beyond the economic ones) than employing organizations have been; constraints of time, energy, and organization reality probably prevent them from it. Thus it may be said that more knowledge exists on the rewards side of the exchange because wages have been long and carefully studied and because collective bargaining primarily seeks the specification of wage and benefit rewards. But the total rewards available from the employment exchange remain quite unspecified.

CONTRIBUTIONS

Contributions include all those things that the employee brings to the employment exchange and for which he expects rewards. In systems terms, they represent outputs from employees to the organization in exchange for inputs from the organization in the form of rewards. To the organization, contributions represent inputs from employees in exchange for outputs to employees in the form of rewards.

This definition suggests that contributions may be of many kinds (from physical attractiveness to professional skills), of many levels (from mere physical presence to total commitment), and either positive (acceptance of responsibility) or negative (sabotage). It also suggests that organizations may be receiving a greater variety of contributions than they are typically aware of, and that employees and organizations may not agree on what the contributions should be.

What We Know: A Survey of the Literature

Much less is known about the contribution side of the employment exchange than about rewards. Organizations assume that employee contributions consist of labor service or work. While aware that the organization requires many different kinds of labor services, organizations assume that contributions are primarily work, and that more contribution means more or better work. Because organizations assume that contributions are limited to labor services (while presenting the public with a highly decorative receptionist and attempting to secure total commitment from managers), little attempt is made to specify the contributions when the employment exchange is initiated. Nor is any attempt typically made to determine what contributions the employee wants to make to the employment exchange.

Economic definitions of contributions.   Economists assume that employee contributions to organizations are labor services. Economic wage theory has employed the concept of "units of labor" in which labor services are expressed as multiples of units of common labor (Clark, 1899). The abstraction "units of labor" does not specify units of measurement but the convention is to assume the least common denominator is an hour of unskilled labor and that an hour of skilled labor is some multiple of this basic unit (Cartter and Marshall, 1972). Economists are of course aware that organizations employ many different kinds of labor services, but labor supply for purposes of analysis is assumed to consist of units (typically hours) of productive service.

Labor economists seem to recognize that collective bargaining represents a method of specifying employee contributions as well as rewards. Characterizing collective bargaining as a system of industrial jurisprudence (Slichter, 1941:1–2) or as a method of rule-making (Dunlop, 1958) implies employee contributions. Labor agreements appear to imply a number of employee contributions: (1) willingness to work under specified conditions, (2) acceptance of jobs and job assignments, work rules, organization policies and practices, (3) willingness to follow specified dispute settlement procedures, (4) acceptance of technological change, and (5) (sometimes) willingness to cooperate in solving organization problems. However, because the emphasis of labor economists has been on the reward side of the employment exchange, the contribution side has not been well delineated.

Behrend's (1957) study of the effort bargain underlying wage determination in both union and nonunion situations focuses on effort as a contribution. Her suggestion that effort is the pertinent measure of labor supply to both organizations and employees represents an example of the type of insight that may be latent in studying contributions to the employment exchange.

Dunlop's (1957) reformulation of wage theory focuses wage-making forces within organizations on key jobs. This implies that employee qualifications for key jobs are pertinent contributions.

Thus, economists have not focused on the contribution side of the employment exchange. Their concept of labor supply probably hides more than it reveals about contributions. Units of labor are too abstract to be operational.

Hours worked and job requirements include many unidentified contributions. Effort is an important contribution but only one of many. Economists typically assume that organizations measure the contributions they require and base rewards on the results of these contributions (productivity).

Organization practices.   Organization practices with respect to pay provide some information on the contributions that are recognized and rewarded by organizations. For example, the organization's first criterion of contributions is the job to which the employee is assigned, and the second is performance on the job. Thus, the employee attributes required by jobs are the first contributions recognized, and measured by the organization, and the performance for the organization is the second (Belcher, 1974).

Job evaluation is the term applied to the process of rating the relative content of jobs in terms of required contributions. The formal process of job evaluation dates back to about 1925 (Lott, 1926). Today, either a formal or an informal process of job evaluation probably is universal in organizations.

Organizations appear to view job evaluation as a method of simulating economic forces attenuated by organizational boundaries. Economists view job evaluation as an influence on internal wage structure and study the conditions under which the resulting internal wage structure fits or conflicts with the labor markets (Hildebrand, 1963). Psychological studies of job evaluation have been concerned with measurement problems—rating scale construction, rater judgment and bias, and empirical description of job clusters (Champoux, 1971). Sociologists view job evaluation as a method of ranking jobs in organizations (Dubin, 1958b), an example of the process of the social stratification process within organizations.

Formal job evaluation plans have isolated important contributions. Most of them recognize responsibility, skill, effort, and working conditions with the items subsumed under these headings numbering about 100 (Belcher, 1974). For example, skill is often measured by education and experience; mental effort is often differentiated from physical effort; responsibility of various kinds is usually delineated. An implication is that the typical organization recognizes responsibility, skill, effort, and willingness to accept certain working conditions as contributions of employees to the employment exchange.

The similarity of job evaluation in organizations and the ranking of roles in the social stratification process should not go unnoticed. Nor should the similarity of the contributions involved be overlooked. Two of the three criteria of differential evaluation of jobs and social roles (trained skills and abilities, and the personal characteristics required by the role) (Tumin, 1967) are identical.

The usual approach to testing the validity of job evaluation is to determine the degree of organization, union, and employee acceptance (Belcher, 1974). This approach implies that the contributions recognized by the organizations are those the employees and unions also consider relevant. Job evaluation has been dubbed by Munson (1963) as "a procedure for writing employee preferences into company policy." To achieve this result employees have sometimes been assigned the task of evaluating jobs (Chambliss, 1950; *The Executive*, 1970). Unions often participate in job evaluation and a hidden advantage of job evaluation might be that it makes bargaining more of a communications process (Corina, 1970).

Utilizing employee inputs in the job evaluation process places the focus upon definitions of contributions held by organization members, rather than on external or market considerations. The extreme of this internal viewpoint is the approach of Jaques (1961), which essentially ignores economic considerations and concentrates on the norms of equity internal to the individual. Jaques develops a global measure of job level—time span of discretion (the longest period of time an employee is permitted to exercise discretion without review of his actions by his supervisor). Time-span of discretion centers upon the decision-making aspects of jobs and undoubtedly subsumes quite a number of contributions which individuals consider relevant.

Application of the time-span approach has been limited (National Board for Prices and Incomes, 1968). One difficulty has been that operationalizing Jaques's instructions on how to measure time-span is unclear (Jaques, 1964, 1967). Atchison was able to measure the time-span of engineers and scientists in a small study (Atchison and French, 1967). Richardson (1971) reports measuring both time-span and "felt-fair pay" in a large organization and finding very high correlations between them, indicating that time-span includes many of the contributions employees use in determining equity. But whether time-span can be reliably measured is still controversial (Strauss, 1970).

If job evaluation is assumed to be a process in which the organization and its employees agree on contributions to the employment exchange, then situations where job evaluation is not accepted may be evidence that the contributions implied by job evaluation may not be considered relevant. For example, the difficulty quite often encountered in applying job evaluation to engineering and scientific jobs (Sibson, 1974) may be evidence that these employees consider other contributions more relevant. Some organizations employing large numbers of engineers and scientists use maturity curves (a graph plotting salaries against age or years of relevant experience) instead of job evaluation (Torrence, 1962; Lee, 1969). This practice implies that age and experience, whether or not required by jobs, are relevant contributions of engineers. Difficulties encountered in using job evaluation for some kinds of jobs and use of methods involving other kinds of contributions may indicate that organizations are broadening their perception of relevant contributions and differentiating between employee groups in contributions. Drucker (1973) has suggested the military system which differentiates an individual's job from his rank in the organization as a solution for the compensation of professionals.

As mentioned above, the second measure of contributions to the employment exchange recognized by the organization is performance on the job. Two practices are common in organizations to reward performance on jobs—both rate ranges and incentive plans.

Rate ranges probably apply to at least one-half of wage and salaried workers in the U.S. (Fogel, 1965). The majority of office workers in almost all areas of the U.S. and the majority of plant workers in many areas work under ranges (U.S. Department of Labor, 1970). Management and professional employees typically work under pay plans employing ranges.

Organizations assume that ranges exist to recognize the performance contributions of individuals. But studies of organization experience with rate ranges show that practically all employees move regularly to the top of ranges whether progression is based upon length of service or merit (Slichter, et al., 1960). A recent study found the same situation existing for managers—only about one-fifth of thirty-three firms made any effort to tie payment directly to the achievement of performance goals (Campbell, et al., 1970). A series of studies of managerial pay curves (Haire, et al., 1967) brought the authors to the conclusion that pay increases for managers do not depend upon performance but rather appear to follow a random curve. These findings suggest that if rate ranges are evidence of contributions to the employment exchange, the contribution is not performance. Rather the evidence suggests that the contribution implied by ranges is length of service.

An analysis of rate ranges (Fogel, 1964), however, suggests that they constitute recognition, by organizations, of: (1) quality differences among workers (measured by experience), (2) performance differences when such differences are highly correlated with length of service, (3) cultural expectations of individual pay progress, and (4) employee expectations of reward for length of service. These conclusions imply that the contributions evidenced by ranges are skill as measured by experience, length of service, and performance where the learning curve correlates performance and time on the job. The cultural expectations do not seem to imply a separate contribution but a belief that all contributions increase in value over time.

Incentive plans are employed by organizations throughout the world. Although only a minority of workers in the U.S. work under incentive plans and coverage remains fairly stable, in Europe and the developing countries, worker coverage is much greater (Corina, 1970).

Incentive plans imply that the major contribution of employees to the employment exchange is effort (Behrend, 1957). Analysis of the operation of incentive plans suggests that the effort bargain is difficult to obtain and subject to constant day-to-day revision. These analyses further suggest that potential gains in effort are obtained at a high cost in other contributions: (1) willingness to accept change in technological methods; (2) willingness to save time; (3) concern for quality and optimum utilization of materials and equipment; (4) cooperation with other employees and other organization units; and (5) flexibility in meeting changing demands (Corina, 1970; Marriott, 1968; and Slichter, et al., 1960; Whyte, 1955). Part of the difficulties of operating incentive plans may be attributable to employee resentment of being evaluated on the basis of a single contribution (effort), and in part to the employee's recognition that other contributions required by the organization are unrewarded.

Our previous analysis of organization practice would seem to raise serious doubts about the feasibility of reducing contributions to the employment exchange to one common denominator. Employees appear to have a number of contributions that they consider relevant and want explicitly considered.

Studies in equity theory. Adams's (1965) formulation of equity theory offers the most complete list of potential contributions to the employment exchange: education, intelligence, experience, training, skill, seniority, age, sex, ethnic background, social status, effort, appearance, health, even characteristics of one's spouse. Equity theory emphasizes that contributions (inputs) enter the employment exchange only when the individual recognizes them and perceives them to be relevant.

Quite a number of experimental studies have been made to test hypotheses derived from equity theory. (For reviews on equity research, see Lawler [1968]; Pritchard [1969]; Goodman and Friedman [1971].) Most of them attempt to manipulate the subject's perceptions of his qualifications (inputs). Subjects who are made to feel underqualified increase effort to achieve improved quality or quantity depending upon experimental conditions. But subjects tended to change their perceptions of the qualifications over time to bring them into line with their rewards.

A study by Andrews and Henry (1963) suggests that individuals with higher educational attainment consider this to be a relevant contribution in that they make different pay comparisons than others. Hamilton's (1966) study of attitudes toward pay held by a sample of public managers suggests that education, length of service, and effort were considered to be relevant contributions.

The authors of this chapter have conducted a series of equity studies in operating organizations. One series of studies attempted to determine the contributions (inputs) perceived as important by four occupational groups in one organization (Belcher and Atchison, 1970). All nineteen possible contributions were adjudged important but there were significant differences in importance assigned by different occupational groups. A number of unreported studies of other occupational and demographic groups in other organizations have found that all groups perceive a large number of contributions to be relevant to the employment exchange. The most difficult problem has been to devise a method of measuring employees' perceptions of relative importance of contributions.

Another unpublished study may provide a partial solution to this problem. The method developed by Kuethe and Levenson (1964) asks respondents to place appropriate salaries on an organization chart where only one box has an assigned salary. Kuethe and Levenson (1964) found that students agreed strongly on the importance of indirect over direct supervision and number of subordinates as contributions. The study enlarged the method by asking respondents to complete a number of separate organization charts on which material on possible contributions has been entered. The separate contributions presented to respondents were: education, job title, performance, job-related factors (experience, etc.), and personal characteristics (age, health, life-style). One hundred students and forty managers (second level and above with salary determination experience) were the respondents. Preliminary analysis shows that while students are quite consistent in their views of relevant contributions, managers are much more so. There was also surprising agreement between students and managers on the relative importance of the contributions. Students' rank order was education, job title, performance, job factors, and personal characteristics. Managers reversed the first two ranks. The results suggest that the contributions individuals believe relevant to the employment exchange are culturally determined before employment and confirmed during employment.

If equity theory and the results of studies made thus far are accepted, employees perceive a large number of contributions to be relevant to the employment exchange. One possible taxonomy of these contributions is job-related inputs, performance-related inputs, and personal inputs. Job-related inputs are those qualifications required by the job. Performance-related inputs are those perceived to be related to performance on the job and within the organization. (Perhaps the most obvious example is effort.) Personal inputs are those contributions not obviously required by the job but which the individual believes relevant as a contribution to the organization.

It is quite possible that the contributions considered relevant to the employment exchange by employees may not be so considered by the organization. Part of the conflict may be traced to employee perception that personal contributions are often considered in the initial hiring decision but do not enter the reward system. Much of the material in this section could be interpreted as evidence of this conflict. The most obvious is the organization whose individual wage incentive plan tells employees that the only contribution desired by the organization is effort. A less obvious but equally serious conflict exists under a rate range for managers where both the organization and the employee consider effort to be a relevant contribution but the organization does not reward it.

Belcher and Atchison (1970) attempted to measure the discrepancy between the weight employees believed should be attached to an input item and the weight they believed the organization actually attached to it. These discrepancy scores were found to vary by contribution and between occupational groups. When employees assign both high importance and high discrepancy to a contribution a conflict exists (at least in the eyes of the employee) between contributions rewarded by organizations and contributions valued by employees.

Dubin (1958b) has pointed out that one of the functions of early socialization is presumably to inculcate in the potential employee the appropriate rewards and contributions. It is quite possible that employing organizations in our society and the division of labor have become so diverse that explicit bargains are required.

What We Need to Know

Much more information is needed on the contributions employees expect to exchange for rewards in employing organizations. Needed also is knowledge of employees' current priority list—what do employees consider to be their most and least important contribution to the organization?

It will undoubtedly be found that employee groups differ on the contributions they want to provide organizations and be rewarded for. But it is important to know how groups differ. Some may differ by occupational groups, some by demographic groups. Some contributions may be important to all groups. Ideally, knowledge would exist on the contribution priority list for each occupational and demographic group. The sociological concept of situs (Morris and Murphy, 1959) would be of help in this.

It is equally important to know how employing organizations vary in the contributions they need and those they can accept. Certainly all organizations do not need total commitment from all employees but they need it from some employees. It also seems logical that the organization needs contributions other than effort, as many incentive plans imply. It seems essential that every organization think through and know the contributions it must have from each group of employees. It would also be useful to know what contributions beyond those required that it can accept. It may be that experience with Scanlon Plans (Slichter, et al., 1960; Goodman, et al., 1972) and productivity bargaining (Flanders, 1967; Rosow, 1972) would be useful in informing managers of the contributions at least some production employees want to make to organizations.

It would be equally useful to know more about the process by which employees acquire these beliefs concerning the contributions they will make to organizations and which organizations will reward for. Are they cultural values transmitted by the family? Are they, as Galbraith (1958) suggests, traceable to our affluent society?

Knowledge concerning this process would be useful in helping organizations and individuals in the employment exchange. Must organizations accept and reward the contributions that employees want to make? To what extent can organizations change employee beliefs and should they be permitted to do so? Or is the encouragement of self-selection by both the answer?

We are not unaware of the measurement problems involved in gaining the required knowledge concerning contributions. Nor should employing organizations be blamed for the unavailability of this information except that which would result from analysis of organization needs. Fortunately, both psychologists and sociologists are showing interest in measuring the components of the employment exchange.

Until solid information is available concerning the contributions employee groups want to make to organizations and the contributions organizations require and can accept from employee groups, bargaining seems to be the only acceptable solution. It seems inevitable that organizations will find it necessary to bargain with more employee groups on both contributions and rewards. Better information will permit it to be more rational, although it will not replace bargaining.

THE COMPARISON PROCESS

Exchange requires not only rewards and contributions but a comparison process in which the individual and the organization determine whether the exchange will be made and presumably also its equity. The comparison process contains some standard of comparison, a decision on what is to be compared, and a set of decision rules. The decision rules for both parties are: (1) maximize rewards and minimize contributions, (2) rewards must exceed contributions, (3) the exchange must be perceived as equitable and (4) increased contributions must yield at least proportionate increases in rewards.

What We Know: A Survey of the Literature

Some knowledge exists concerning the comparison process, but not very much. Some of it comes from studies of comparison practices of organizations and individuals. Some of it is inferential from observed behavior. But much of our information comes from theory that needs additional testing.

Organization comparison—standards and comparisons.   From the work of labor economists and from organization practices, we know that organizations use other organizations and internal relationships between jobs as comparison standards. Other organizations in the industry or area are the primary standard (Ross, 1957). Conditions in product and labor markets are also employed as standards as well as more general economic criteria such as cost of living, ability to pay, productivity, minimum budgets (Bullock, 1960).

Organizations primarily compare rewards, and the rewards compared are economic. Wage and salary surveys have been made or used by most organizations (Lester, 1948; Grigsby and Burns, 1962) and benefit surveys have been made by many (Belcher, 1974). Most benefit surveys are of prevailing practice rather than of benefit costs.

Wage and salary surveys imply a comparison of contributions in that data are collected by occupation and a major problem area is the comparability of jobs. Wage survey methods (Tolles and Raimon, 1952) and the manner in which the data are used (Groenkamp, 1967) suggest that occupational wages are collected to make economic rewards comparable, not to permit comparisons of contributions.

Interestingly, compensation practices with respect to professional employees have fostered organization comparisons of contributions as well as rewards. Salary surveys of professionals present salary rates by age (or years since degree) and performance level rather than jobs (Torrence, 1962). These maturity curves force organization attention to contributions not ordinarily considered. It may be that studies move in this direction when job comparability cannot be established. An interesting study of the compensation of engineering-scientific managers compared salaries and a number of contributions (Foster, 1969). It was found that contributions relating to both the position and the position-holder were required to predict pay level.

Internal comparisons made by organizations (job evaluation) are primarily of contributions. However, the contributions compared are typically limited to responsibility, skill, effort, and willingness to accept certain working conditions.

Thus organizations typically use pay and benefit practices of other organizations as comparison standards, limit comparisons to economic rewards, and pay little attention to contributions except when making internal comparisons. The contributions compared suggest that employers consider the employment exchange to be primarily an economic transaction.

Individual comparison standards and comparisons. In recent years, a great deal of attention has been focused upon the comparison standards of individuals and what they compare. The work of Elliott Jaques suggests that the employee uses a standard within himself (Jaques, 1961). Festinger's (1954) theory of social comparison processes suggests to Vroom (1964) that an individual employs his self-concept as a comparison standard and suggests to Weick (1966) that an individual uses an internal standard when objective reality is not available as a standard. Festinger's theory holds that people have a drive to evaluate themselves, that when objective means are not available people compare with other people, that objective standards are preferred, that subjective evaluations are based upon perceived similarity of comparison persons. Adams's (1965) formulation of equity theory postulates another individual or group as the comparison standard. Pritchard's (1969) review of equity research argues that the internal standard is more likely to be used in the employment situation.

Sociologists conceive of comparison standards as an application of reference group theory. Reference group analysis is concerned with the "determinants and consequences of those processes of evaluation and self-appraisal in which the individual takes the values or standards of other individuals and groups as a comparative frame of reference" (Merton and Kitt, 1950). Lipset and Trow (1957) have analyzed the "coercive comparisons" noted by labor economists in collective bargaining using reference group theory. They suggest that rationality, tradition, and rigidity of the social structure influence the choice of reference groups and that comparisons take on a moral tone. The following are hypotheses suggested by their analysis. Individuals or groups who are subordinate to the same authority are likely to use each other as reference groups but workers in a large "membership" structure are likely to use abstract status reference groups. In rigid social structures, intragroup comparisons are more likely than intergroup comparisons. Unions (and presumably employing organizations) can modify choice of reference groups but only in the direction of perceived legitimacy. They make a strong plea for studies empirically to determine reference groups, kinds of evaluations made, and the structural conditions making for these choices.

Some studies of comparison standards have been made. Patchen (1961) found that a comparison person could be identified and that he was somewhat similar to the evaluator. The comparison person varied, however, with the situation of the comparing individual and the weight he placed on the results of the comparison. Andrews and Henry (1963) and Hamilton (1966) found that managers at different levels vary in whether their choice of a comparison person comes from within the organization or without. Studies employing reference group theory found that manual workers choose comparisons close to their situation and very rarely compare themselves to nonmanual workers (Hyman and Singer, 1968). Some unpublished data obtained by the authors of this chapter indicate that different occupational groups vary in whether internal standards or comparison persons are employed. It was also found that there was a strong tendency by managers to compare their present situation with a previous one. Lawler and Porter's (1963) and Jaques's (1961) findings that managers on the same level had similar pay expectations imply that a standard internal to the individual is being employed. Weick and Nesset (1968) found that the choice of comparison standard varies with the result of comparison so that when inequity is perceived as inevitable, remote comparisons are preferred.

Economists assume that individuals compare economic rewards primarily with information from appropriate labor markets and also with rewards of others within the organization. Earlier empirical work by labor economists showed that benefits were unlikely to be compared (Reynolds, 1951), but more recent studies suggest that this is no longer true (Lester, 1967). Relative comparisons are assumed as likely to occur as absolute ones. This implies that contributions as well as rewards are compared.

Economists also tend to assume that individuals make money wage rather than real wage comparisons (Cartter and Marshall, 1972). Widely available information concerning inflation and changes in the cost of living may have changed the level of employee sophistication and made this assumption invalid.

The primary work on what individuals compare has been done by the psychologists. Equity theory (Adams, 1965) and the studies made to test it (see reviews by Pritchard, 1969; Lawler, 1968; Goodman and Friedman, 1971) have shown that an individual compares both contributions and rewards and that a long list of both is employed by the individual. Most of the tests have been made in a laboratory but the authors have found that individuals in organizations report about twenty contributions and an equivalent number of rewards as relevant and important (Atchison and Belcher, 1971; Belcher and Atchison, 1970).

Thus individuals use objective evidence, their self-concept, other individuals, and reference groups as comparison standards. They compare both rewards and contributions and a wide variety of each. Economic rewards and contributions are only a part of the considerations. Further, unlike organizations, individuals appear first to make comparisons within themselves, then with others with whom they come into direct contact, and finally with the external labor market. The difference between individual and organizational comparisons implies that the employment exchange will be differently viewed except by individuals attuned to the external labor market.

Organizations—comparison decision rules.   Economic theory and organization practice both imply that the decision rules followed by organizations in the comparison process involve economic decisions. In these terms the first decision rule—to maximize rewards to self and minimize contributions—becomes for the employing organization: maximize productivity and minimize wages. If employee productivity were the only reward organizations require, employing this decision rule would be functional for the organization. However, to the extent that the organization requires other rewards—employee concern for quality, employee cooperation in change, for example—focusing solely on productivity is dysfunctional to the organization. Likewise, to the extent that organizations have other potential contributions that employees consider rewards, limiting attention to wages is disadvantageous to organizations.

The decision rule that rewards must equal and preferably exceed contributions in economic terms is necessary for organization survival. This may account for the economic emphasis. Rewards and contributions are somewhat easier to match when translated into productivity and wages than when expressed more realistically. One of the functions of collective bargaining would seem to be the matching of rewards and contributions following this decision rule.

Organizations assume that the equity decision rule is met by comparing wages and benefits to those of other organizations (Belcher, 1964). Fortunately, however, this economic version of the equity decision rule is supplemented in most organizations by a second assumption underlying personnel policies and practices, i.e., to provide internal consistency in decisions affecting employees. In fact, some organizations have elaborate systems of due process to insure internal equity (Brown, 1960).

Organization practice (almost universal use of either rate ranges or incentive plans or both) assumes that additional rewards to the organization are invariably desirable and are attainable by providing additional economic rewards to employees. The first assumption may be questioned on logical grounds in any organization where coordination of outputs of interdependent units is problematical, or on practical grounds in organizations desiring to make optimum use of specialization of function (Moore, 1962). Although the consequences of neither rate ranges nor incentive plans is not fully understood, enough is known to question the universal applicability of the second assumption (Slichter, et al., 1960; Marriott, 1968).

Studies by labor economists have shown that noneconomic rewards and contributions are involved in the exchange (Reynolds, 1951), especially under conditions of collective bargaining (Taylor and Pierson, 1957). But the decision rules of the comparison process are almost always assumed to be measured in economic terms.

Individuals—comparison decision rules.   Whether or not the individual follows the decision rule of maximizing his rewards and minimizing his contributions has probably been the greatest point of difference between the economist and the human relationist. The economist derives his model of employee behavior from the theory of consumer preference and assumes a disutility of labor that must be offset by rewards. The human relationist assumes that (at least under the proper conditions) the individual seeks to maximize his contributions as well as his rewards (McGregor, 1960).

A good deal of theorizing by behavioral scientists supports the premise that individuals, in order to enter and continue the employment exchange, must perceive their rewards as at least equal to their contributions. The decision of the individual to participate in the organization (Barnard, 1938; March and Simon, 1958) is seen as involving a balance of inducements and contributions. The organization must maintain a positive balance of inducements (rewards) over contributions in the eyes of the individual. The greater the balance of inducements over contributions, the more stable the employment exchange will be, because the individual will not be motivated to search for a better exchange, and the individual more likely will allow the organization to control his behavior.

The decision rule that the exchange must be perceived as equitable is the attitudinal counterpart of the inducements-contributions decision. Equity theory and research provide considerable substantiation on this decision rule. An employment exchange must be perceived as fair by the individual. Jaques (1961) reports that any substantial deviation from "felt-fair pay" will be seen as unfair and will result in behavior to change the situation. Adams and others have shown that individuals can be experimentally induced to see the exchange as inequitable with behavioral consequences (Pritchard, 1969). These studies also show that an individual can be experimentally induced to change rewards or contributions to achieve equity. The authors have found it possible to measure employee perceptions of equity in organizations and discrepancy between actual and desired rewards and contributions (Atchison and Belcher, 1971; Belcher and Atchison, 1970).

Selznick's (1969) recent description of the development of due process in organizations may be seen as an attempt to secure equity. An important aspect of equity is employee perception that the system itself is fair and protects his interests. Scott (1965) points out that organizational justice involves both a method of distributing rewards and a method of correcting unfairness.

Collective bargaining and grievance procedures are mechanisms which validate the equity decision rule. Both labor economists (Kerr, 1964) and sociologists (Parsons and Smelser, 1956) have concluded that perhaps the major function of collective bargaining is to convince employees that the employment exchange is equitable.

The decision rule that additional contributions must be matched with additional rewards has been less carefully studied. March and Simon (1958) show that the employee's decision to perform is based upon a psychological construct that is quite different from the decision to participate in an organization. Porter and Lawler (1968) have developed and tested a model that shows that performance (additional contributions) requires that the employee: (1) want more of the reward or rewards that the organization offers, (2) perceive a high probability that additional effort will actually result in a net increase in rewards, (3) have the abilities and skills that could make his effort effective, and (4) have the proper role perceptions. The work of Locke (1966) on the effect of goals and intentions on performance suggests that (1) and (2) are the most important variables and that they operate through intentions. Lawler (1971) interprets the psychological research on pay as supporting expectancy theory.

This model postulates that to motivate good performance, the following conditions must exist:

1. employees must want the rewards the organization offers;
2. employees must believe that good performance does in fact lead to more of those rewards;
3. employees must believe that performance reflects their efforts;
4. employees must see more positive consequences from good performance than negative consequences;
5. employees must see good performance as the most attractive of all possible behaviors.

These findings clearly show the complexity of this decision rule and difficulties facing organizations attempting to achieve increased performance. It is quite possible, for example, that organizations may be offering additional rewards that employees do not want as much as they want more of other rewards. Or the employee may perceive that obtaining more of one reward (pay) will be offset by a reduction in other rewards (work group acceptance). Again, it is quite possible that the employee does not believe that there is a high probability that additional effort on his part will result in additional rewards.

A number of studies show that the "more pay for more performance" decision rule may conflict with the equity decision rule (Whyte, 1955). An incentive system that pays semiskilled high performers above highly skilled employees not covered by the plan is an example of the conflict.

Organization practices seldom give unambiguous signals on the relationship between rewards and performance. Lawler (1965) has studied the effects of keeping secret pay policies and practices in organizations and finds that one effect is that managers tend to underestimate the salaries of their bosses and overestimate the salaries of their peers.

The difficulties facing employees (and organizations) on the decision rule concerning additional contributions for additional rewards suggest the only viable solution is what Behrend (1957) calls the "effort bargain." Organizations are apparently going to have to be much more specific in the additional contributions they want and the additional rewards they offer and to bargain until credibility is achieved. Effort bargains for different occupational groups may be quite different and some may be neither possible nor needed by the organization.

What We Need to Know

Although a good deal of theorizing has been done on the comparison process, hard knowledge is quite meager. We need to know more about comparison standards, the factors compared, and decision rules employed.

We need to know what comparison criteria are employed by different groups. It appears that different occupational groups employ different standards but demographic or other variables may be operating.

It seems to be quite well established that rewards and contributions are the phenomena compared but little is known concerning which rewards and which contributions are compared. It seems likely that comparisons are made on the basis of available information with an emphasis on the quantifiable. If so, the concentration upon pay and benefits as the primary rewards and time and effort as the primary contributions is understandable.

If comparisons are made on the basis of available information, increasing the amount and quality of information should broaden comparisons (logically to the advantage of both employees and organizations). We need to know how additional information affects the comparison process. An unpublished study by the authors suggests that government employees, where economic matters are not secret, experience less internal inequity. Lawler's (1965) findings on the dysfunctional consequences of secrecy regarding pay suggest that organizations could enhance the employees' perception of equity with more information. The same conclusion seems to be available from the published record of the communications aspect of Boulwarism (Northrup, 1964). The frequency with which individuals make comparisons and individual differences in propensity to make more comparisons have not been systematically studied. The authors have noted in some of their studies that groups differ in both. In addition, the forces which increase or decrease the propensity to compare also need study.

We need to know how employing organizations and unions can and do influence the comparison process and the limits to their influence. It is quite possible that additional economic information has limited influence but additional information of a noneconomic nature would be accepted as relevant. Reference group theory appears to contain a large number of hypotheses regarding the influence of unions and organizations on comparison standards (Lipset and Trow, 1957).

We need to know the extent to which particular rewards relate to particular contributions and how this varies by groups. Gouldner's (1957) dichotomy of cosmopolitans and locals provides one model concerning professionals. Some items, such as responsibility, may be both a contribution and a reward to professionals and managers. Production and clerical workers may relate pay and benefits directly to time worked and effort expended. The probable relationships and similar ones need to be studied and any group differences established.

A related question is the inclusiveness of the employment exchange. To particular groups, to speak of the employment exchange may be equivalent to discussing their life and, to others, a very limited but specific exchange (Dubin, 1956; Argyris, 1973). We need to know more about how these two ends, of what is presumably a continuum, perceive the employment exchange. We also need to know how these views are changing.

Much of the theory and research reported in this section treats what we called the equity decision rule as the attitudinal equivalent of comparing rewards and contributions. While it seems conceptually reasonable to equate attitudes and behavior in the comparison process, knowledge of situations where people continue employment exchanges which they perceive as unfair and refuse employment exchanges although they perceive them to be more than fair lead us to believe that more study is needed to establish the equivalence. Perhaps the study of comparison standards will answer this question.

Further study of the comparison process should aid in understanding the concept of incentive. The concept of incentive is characterized in this section as a separate bargain, beyond the original employment exchange, involving more rewards for more contributions. More study of these bargains as perceived by different groups appears to be required. We need to know which organizations actually require such bargains and with which employee groups it is possible to make such agreements. Further, we need to know what must go into these agreements to preserve the concept of incentive.

RESULTS

The output of the exchange process is that the exchange is either made or not made or (if a previous exchange is still in effect) continued or not continued. Outputs are both behavioral and attitudinal and behavior and attitudes are interdependent.

In order to analyze the results of the exchange, it seems useful to examine the outputs separately from the viewpoints of the organization and the individual. The needs of organizations for results of the employment exchange in terms of the behavior and attitudes of employees must be matched with actual results.

Organizations

Because organizations have approached the employment exchange as an economic transaction involving purchase of a productive resource, they have assumed that the amount of the resource supplied is determined by the price paid. Organizations have also assumed that they want as many units of labor services as available for the price paid—that they wanted maximum performance on every job and would get it for the price paid and if more performance was needed it would be available for a higher price.

Organizations have been aware, of course, that human beings are a unique resource—not at all passive but almost infinitely reactive. They may also have been intuitively aware that the major advantage to organizations of human resources is their flexibility. They have also shown awareness of the influence of attitudes, but they have assumed that attitudes and performance were highly and positively correlated despite the negative empirical evidence (Vroom, 1964).

These beliefs have largely prevented organizations from perceiving that they require two quite different types of behavior from the employment exchange (Barnard, 1938; March and Simon, 1958). Organizations require participation (membership) and they also require performance. But the sources of these two quite different types of behavior are not the same. Also, the organization may not require nor be able to obtain both types of behavior from all employees.

Membership.   Members are required if the organization is to survive. Thus an unavoidable requirement for organization is that the employment exchange is made. But the organization does not require long-term membership of all types of employees. Some, perhaps most, are to be considered permanent. For others, the organization requires only short-term membership. But whether the result of the employment exchange required by the organization is long- or short-term membership, the requirements are the same. The member or potential member must perceive that the rewards at last equal and, if possible, exceed his contributions. Also, of course, the organization must view the contributions of the employee as greater than his rewards.

To obtain this result from the employment exchange, the organization must see that members get the rewards they want and are able to provide the contributions they want to make. These rewards and contributions should be expected to be different for different employee groups. Some groups may be expected to fit the economic model and want only economic rewards and want to provide only the agreed-upon contributions. Others, such as professionals and managers, will place strong emphasis on intrinsic rewards and may be inclined to make more than the agreed-upon contributions.

Organizations which require continued membership as a result of the employment exchange must insure that employees perceive rewards as exceeding contributions on a continuing basis. Otherwise employees may be expected to search for a better exchange and to limit their contributions. Because the employment exchange is dynamic, organizations must attend to changes in the environment that may affect the balance between rewards and contributions.

Any change in the environment that changes the perceived reward-contributions balance can weaken or strengthen the exchange (March and Simon, 1958: 100–106). An employee who perceives that his balance will be improved in another organization may leave. An employee who perceives that other jobs are not easily available may perceptually increase the value of his rewards and perceptually reduce the cost of his contributions.

All employment exchanges have positive and negative elements or costs (Homans, 1961). Because both rewards and contributions are perceptual, any change may result in a reevaluation of the balance. Thus a negative or positive change may have a cumulative effect. It seems useful to conceive of the continuing employment exchange as involving a set of frames like a motion picture. The original employment exchange affects the next and any change may have a continuing and exaggerated effect.

No distinction has been made in the above discussion between behavior and attitudes. Because the entire employment exchange is perceptual, attitudes and behavior must be treated as interdependent. It is, of course, conceivable that an exchange will be made or continued that is seen as unfair because no alternatives are available. But such exchanges must be unstable in that a process is set in motion to improve the balance or the exchange will be broken.

Jaques (1957) reports that his studies have established thresholds of fairness and unfairness. He finds that people feel they are fairly paid if they are within 10% of an internal norm, but the perception of fairness varies with whether the person feels under- or overpaid. He finds that a person must be overpaid by about 20% before he begins to feel injustice. Jaques (1957) reports that a feeling of being overpaid results in an euphoric state or psychological balance. This implies that the individual wishes to maintain the employment exchange as presently defined.

Adams (1963, 1965) has conceptualized the behavioral and attitudinal effects of perceived inequity. Building upon the concept of cognitive dissonance, he holds that because inequity is a situation that causes dissonance, the individual will seek to change the situation. A number of methods are open to the individual to change the situation. One is to make a change in: his inputs (contributions) or outcomes (rewards) or the inputs or outcomes of others with whom he compares himself. Following the first approach, he may ask for a raise or work less. The second approach might involve raising or lowering the inputs or outcomes of others through the enforcement of group norms.

Another method of changing the situation is for the individual to perceptually distort his own or others' inputs and outcomes. An example of this would be the individual who inflates or deflates the attractiveness of the task in response to inequity. Another is where the individual perceptually inflates or deflates the difficulty of the task.

A third method of changing the situation is to change the comparison standard. If the present comparison standard makes the individual look bad, he can change it. Both unions and management may attempt to influence employee choice of comparison standards, but since people are not completely malleable, any achieved change in comparison standards may turn out to be dysfunctional to both (Lipset and Trow, 1957).

Adams's conception of responses to inequity suggests that an individual will seek to change the situation by choosing responses in the order given. Thus, he will change behavior (inputs or outcomes). If behavior changes are blocked, he will change his attitudes (perceptually change inputs or outcomes or change comparison standards). Finally, if these changes are blocked, he may choose termination of the employment exchange (a behavior).

Laboratory experiments have shown that the individual does make changes in the situation when he perceives inequity (Pritchard, 1969; Lawler, 1968; Goodman and Friedman, 1971). Both over- and underpayment situations have been investigated. Also both behavioral and attitudinal changes are observed but the conditions under which each is chosen have not been determined. It would seem that the individual manipulates those variables over which he has most control and these appear to be attitudes. But perceived legitimacy of particular methods of changing the situation may also be operating. The emphasis given by organizations to economic variables in the employment exchange may give legitimacy to wage demands to correct inequity arising from any source.

Thus when individuals perceive the employment exchange as fair, the exchange is made or continued. Organizations get and keep members. Improvements to the employment exchange exist only in the eye of the beholder and may have either behavioral or attitudinal consequences. Employee groups may be expected to differ in the rewards they want and in the contributions they want to make. Organizations may not have the rewards that individuals want and may not be able to accept the contributions that individuals want to make. But if the organization is able to provide each employee group with a reward-contribution balance that each group considers fair, the organization reaps the results of the employment exchange—membership. However, only membership is guaranteed.

Performance.   Organizations also require performance from employees as a result of the employment exchange. As mentioned previously, obtaining performance involves different requirements from organizations than obtaining membership.

The simplest method for organizations to follow is to build performance into jobs. This method involves specifying the contributions as well as rewards in the employment exchange at the time the exchange is made. In this way acceptance of employment implies the contribution of the performance the organization needs. Many organizations follow this method without being aware of it. Employment exchanges resulting from collective bargaining have this result. Assembly lines and "white collar factories" have performance built into jobs whether unionized or not.

Another method of obtaining performance is available to organizations, however, if they can and wish to meet its rigorous requirements. This method, based on expectancy theory (Porter and Lawler, 1968; Graen, 1969; Lawler, 1971), involves (1) having available the rewards that individuals want and want more of, (2) tying these rewards to performance in such a way that individuals see that additional performance will result in more of the desired rewards, and (3) obtaining appropriate contributions from employees (abilities and role perception).

From the viewpoint of the organization, expectancy theory implies an additional employment exchange beyond the original one initiating membership. This second exchange must offer additional rewards of the kinds desired. It must also demand additional contributions of the kinds employees want to make. Further, the organization must convince these employee groups that additional contributions (performance) will in fact result in more rewards.

It is apparent that this second employment exchange may only be available from certain employee groups. Some may not want more of the rewards the organization has to offer, or the organization may not be able to offer more of the rewards certain groups want. Some groups may find that the additional contributions required offset the desirability of the increased rewards.

But perhaps the most difficult part of this second employment exchange is convincing employees that additional performance does result in more rewards. In many jobs, measuring performance is difficult and employees may not accept the measurements. More important, employees may see that the organization requires contributions not measured or rewarded that must be reduced to achieve the rewarded contribution. Finally, employees may not believe that additional performance results in additional rewards and convincing them may be difficult and expensive for the organization.

Individuals

Fortunately for the organization, individuals perceive only one employment exchange—the one resulting in membership. If the reward-contribution balance is perceived to be in their favor, they want to continue the employment exchange.

When the individual perceives that the reward-contribution balance is positive he expands his zone of indifference to organization demands (Barnard, 1938). When the balance is perceived as positive by both the individual and the organization, both want to make the employment exchange more inclusive. The individual is willing to contribute more than his time and energy when the employment exchange includes many valued rewards. The organization tends to increase its contributions to members who provide the most positive balance. Some groups want to expand the employment exchange and do so by providing more contributions in return for additional rewards (intrinsic) that they provide themselves. In this case, the organization is achieving a second employment exchange without being consciously aware that it is providing additional rewards.

Attempts by the organization to obtain a second employment exchange from groups who prefer to maintain the original exchange may be interpreted by these groups as an opportunity for continuous haggling over the terms of the agreement (Behrend, 1957). Attempts by the organization to obtain a second employment exchange from groups who wish to broaden and deepen the employment exchange will be welcomed and result in commitment to organizational goals (Argyris, 1957).

Organizations and individuals both influence the results of the employment exchange. Organizations can teach employees to value the rewards offered by the organization and that the contributions required by the organization are legitimate (Krupp, 1961:97). Individuals can influence organizations in regard to both the rewards to offer and to the contributions to accept.

However, the employment exchange is based upon perception and therefore is subject to misinterpretation on the part of either party. Considering the complexities of the exchange process, it is quite remarkable that the employment exchange works as well as it does. However, people do misinterpret the cues presented to them. Such misinterpretation results in unintended and often dysfunctional consequences both in terms of attitudes and behavior. Hampton (1970) and Ridgeway (1956) have illustrated some of these dysfunctions with respect to incentive programs and performance controls.

CONCLUSION

If our analysis is correct, compensation for work is a much broader subject than traditionally assumed. The employment exchange involves much more than a trading of economic goods and services; cultural, social, and psychological variables are also included. Further, it is much more than a simple trading relationship because typically the terms are unclear and the time period unspecified. We believe that this broader view of compensation needs to be recognized both in practice and theory.

Both research results and organization practice seem to have been restricted by a narrow view of compensation. While a good deal is known about rewards, less is known about contributions, and much less about comparison standards and results of the exchange.

The employment exchange appears to be becoming more inclusive. Both organizations and individuals seem to be demanding more from it. Even in economic terms, the expansion of benefits indicates a desire by individuals for a more complex reward package. Behavioral science research indicates that individuals expect much more than economic rewards. Organization demands for increased education show recognition of need for more contributions. Organization theory leads to the conclusion that organizations require many more different kinds of contributions than previously recognized.

Organizations must be prepared to make a greater variety of employment exchanges. The employee mix of organizations is changing and the work force is becoming more diverse, including more professionals, more women, more members of minority groups. The rewards that some of these employee groups expect are quite different from those expected by other groups. Organizations can be expected to respond with more differentiation of rewards between employee groups.

The differentiation of rewards for different employee groups creates a need for more sophisticated coordination of the reward process in organizations. In most organizations the responsibility for rewards is assigned to a number of separate organizational units and some rewards are no one's responsibility. It is essential that organizations develop several different reward packages for different employee groups and that the development of these reward packages be the responsibility of one particular person or organizational unit. The development of these packages should be based upon the characteristics of the work force of the organization.

Coordination of rewards into an integrated whole is essential if the organization is to gain maximum value from the rewards. It is not unusual in organizations with uncoordinated reward systems for individuals to receive contradictory signals from different rewards. When the responsibility for rewards is fragmented it is difficult to see these contradictions let alone to take steps to coordinate them.

It is equally important that rewards be integrated with contributions. The dearth of knowledge concerning contributions revealed by the analysis suggests that attention be devoted to the contributions required by the organization and the relationship for each group between desired rewards and desired contributions. It thus seems essential that job and organization design be integrated into the employment exchange. Further, it might prove useful to analyze labor contracts in terms of the employee contributions they imply.

The paucity of solid knowledge with respect to several parts of the employment exchange suggests that these exchanges are designed with crude tools and it is somewhat surprising that the process works as well as it does. Until more is known about the rewards different employee groups want (and the contributions they expect to make), the most logical course of action appears to be a considerable amount of bargaining. We suggest that the probable response to the changes envisioned will be: (1) more individual bargaining in the case of the highly educated professional; (2) more bargaining with diverse employee groups not usually unionized; and (3) a more careful spelling out of the employment contract at the time of hiring. Each of these implies different reward packages and a more complex compensation process.

However, hopefully bargaining is an interim solution. Bargaining is a rough-and-ready technique for achieving equity where information is limited. It is hoped that increased knowledge of the rewards and contributions different employee groups consider relevant, and of the comparison standards of these groups will serve to increase the likelihood that the employment exchange will be founded more on rationality than on power.

Improved knowledge of the employment exchange should improve the compensation process for the organization as well as employees. Organizations have limited resources and determining the optimum allocation of these resources to achieve organization goals is a crucial decision. Thus, the organization must determine the contributions it needs from each employee group and how it can best distribute its available rewards to attain them. This suggests that organizations should be willing to accept minimal performance and commitment from some employee groups while insisting upon high performance and commitment from others. Some work can be highly programmed requiring only that the individual maintain his membership at the minimum level of performance. For the groups involved, performance is built into the organization structure and the technology and rewards are primarily economic and defined explicitly.

Where, however, the organization requires that considerable discretion be exercised by the individual, more commitment is needed and this rquires that the individual see a connction between his actions, above the minimum level, and additional rewards. While these employment exchanges can probably never be completely specified, they can be expanded through further understanding of contributions relevant to both individual and organization and the availability of intrinsic rewards. These relationships are likely to be of longer duration and imply future contributions by the individual and additional rewards for efforts to develop them.

Our analysis of compensation for work has led us to wonder how the employment exchange works as well as it does and to speculate that organizations must be providing rewards not recognized as such. This suggests that organizations would do well to take a thorough inventory to determine why people work for them. This would enable the organization not only to correct deficiencies, but to reinforce the things it is doing unknowingly but correctly.

REFERENCES

Adams, J.S.
  1963　"Toward an understanding of inequity." Journal of Abnormal and Social Psychology (67) :422–436.
  1965　"Inequity in social exchange," in L. Berkowitz (ed.), Advances in Experimental Social Psychology. Vol. 2. New York: Academic Press, Inc.
Andrews, I.R. and M.M. Henry
  1963　"Management attitudes towards pay." Industrial Relations (October) :29–39.
Argyris, C.
  1957　Personality and Organization. New York: Harper & Row.
  1973　"Personality and organization theory revisited." Administrative Science Quarterly 18(June) :141–167.
Atchison, T.J. and D.W. Belcher
  1971　"Equity, rewards and compensation administration." Personnel Administration (July).
Atchison, T.J. and W. French
  1967　"Pay systems for scientists and engineers." Industrial Relations (October) :44–56.
Barnard, C.I.
  1938　The Functions of the Executive. Cambridge, Mass.: Harvard University Press.
Bauman, A.
  1970　"Measuring employee compensation in U.S. industry." Monthly Labor Review 93(October) :17–24.
Behrend, H.
  1957　"The effort bargain." Industrial and Labor Relations Review (July): 503–515.
  1959　"Financial incentives as the expression of a system of beliefs." British Journal of Sociology (June) :137–147.
Belcher, D.W.
  1960　"Employee and executive compensation," in Heneman, et al. (eds.), Employment Relations Research. New York: Harper & Row.
  1964　"Ominous trends in wage and salary administration." Personnel (September–October) :42–50.
  1974　Compensation Administration. Englewood Cliffs, New Jersey: Prentice Hall.
Belcher, D.W. and T.J. Atchison
  1970　"Equity theory and compensation policy." Personnel Administration (July–August) :22–33.
Bendix, R.
  1956　Work and Authority in Industry. New York: Harper & Row.

Blau, P.M.
   1963   The Dynamics of Bureaucracy. Chicago: University of Chicago Press.
   1967   Exchange and Power in Social Life. New York: Wiley.
Bowley, A. and T. Lupton
   1970   "Productivity drift and the make-up of the pay packet. Part II." The
          Journal of Management Studies (October):310–334.
Brown, E.H. and M. Browne
   1968   A Century of Pay. New York: St. Martin's Press.
Brown, W.
   1960   Exploration in Management. New York: Wiley.
Bullock, P.
   1960   Standards of Wage Determination. Los Angeles: University of Cali-
          fornia, Institute of Industrial Relations.
Campbell, J.P., M.D. Dunnette, E.E. Lawler III and K.E. Weick, Jr.
   1970   Managerial Behavior, Performance and Effectiveness. New York:
          McGraw-Hill.
Caplow, T.
   1954   The Sociology of Work. New York: McGraw-Hill.
Carpenter, W.H. and E. Handler
   1961   Small Business and Pattern Bargaining. Babson Park, Mass.: Babson
          Institute Press.
Cartter, A.M. and F.R. Marshall
   1972   Labor Economics. Homewood, Ill.: Richard D. Irwin, Inc.
Chamber of Commerce of the United States
   1970   Fringe Benefits. Washington, D.C.
Chambliss, L.A.
   1950   "Our employees evaluate their own jobs." Personnel Journal (Septem-
          ber):141–142.
Champoux, J.E.
   1971   "A test of the guide line method of job evaluation." Unpublished
          Master's Thesis. San Diego, California: San Diego State University.
Clark, J.B.
   1899   Distribution of Wealth. New York: The Macmillan Co.
Collins, O., M. Dalton and D. Roy
   1946   "Restrictions of output and social cleavage in industry." Applied An-
          thropology (Summer):1–14.
Corina, J.
   1965   The Development of Incomes Policy. London: Institute of Personnel
          Management.
   1970   Forms of Wage and Salary Payment for High Productivity. Paris: Orga-
          nisation for Economic Co-operation and Development.
Dalton, M.
   1948   "The industrial 'rate-buster': a characterization." Applied Anthro-
          pology (Winter):5–18.
Davis, L. and J.C. Taylor (eds.)
   1972   Design of Jobs. Middlesex, England: Penguin.
Davis, W. and L.M. David
   1968   "Patterns of wage and benefit changes in manufacturing." Monthly
          Labor Review (February):40–48.

Deci, E.L.
    1972   "Intrinsic motivation, extrinsic reinforcement, and inequity," Journal of Personality and Social Psychology (22) :113–120.
de Wolff, P.
    1965   Wages and Labor Mobility. Paris: Organisation for Economic Co-operation and Development.
Drucker, P.F.
    1973   Management. New York: Harper & Row.
Dubin, R.
    1956   "Industrial workers' worlds: a study of the central life interest of industrial workers." Social Problems (January) :131–142.
    1958a   Working Union-Management Relations. Englewood Cliffs, New Jersey: Prentice-Hall.
    1958b   The World of Work. Englewood Cliffs, New Jersey: Prentice-Hall.
Dunlop, J.T.
    1957   "The task of contemporary wage theory," in G.W. Taylor and F.C. Pierson (eds.), New Concepts in Wage Determination. New York: McGraw-Hill.
    1958   Industrial Relations Systems. New York: Henry Holt and Co.
Eckstein, O.
    1968   "Money wage determination revisited." Review of Economic Studies (April) :133–143.
Eckstein, O. and T.A. Wilson
    1962   "The determination of money wages in American industry." Quarterly Journal of Economics (August) :379–414.
Emery, F. and E. Thorsrud
    1969   New Designs for Work Organizations. Oslo, Sweden: Tannum Press.
Etzioni, A.
    1961   A Comparative Analysis of Complex Organizations. Glencoe, Ill.: The Free Press.
Executive, The (Wellington, New Zealand)
    1970   "Computer-assisted job evaluation." (March 1) :15–16.
Fellner, W., et al.
    1961   The Problem of Rising Prices. Paris: Organisation for European Economic Co-operation and Development.
Festinger, L.
    1954   "A theory of social comparison processes." Human Relations (May) : 117–140.
Flanders, A.
    1967   Collective Bargaining: Prescription for Change. London: Faber and Faber, Ltd.
Fogel, W.
    1964   "Job rate ranges: a theoretical and empirical analysis." Industrial and Labor Relations Review (July) :584–597.
    1965   "Wage administration and job rate ranges." California Management Review (Spring) :77–84.
Foster, K.E.
    1969   "Accounting for management pay differentials." Industrial Relations (October) :80–87.
Galbraith, J.K.
    1958   The Affluent Society. Boston: Houghton Mifflin.

Georgopoulos, B.S., G.M. Mahoney and N. Jones
  1957 "A path-goal approach to productivity." Journal of Applied Psychology (December) :345–353.
Gergen, K.J.
  1969 The Psychology of Behavior Exchange. Reading, Mass.: Addison-Wesley.
Goodman, P.S. and A. Friedman
  1971 "An examination of Adams' theory of inequity." Administrative Science Quarterly 16(September) :271–288.
Goodman, R.R., J.H. Wakeley and R.H. Ruh
  1972 "What employees think of the Scanlon Plan." Personnel 49(September–October) :22–29.
Gordon, T.J. and R. Le Bleu
  1970 "Employee benefits, 1970–1985." Harvard Business Review 48(January–February) :93–107.
Gouldner, A.W.
  1957 "Cosmopolitans and locals: toward an analysis of latent social roles." Administrative Science Quarterly (December) :444–480.
Graen, G.
  1969 "Instrumentality theory of work motivation: some experimental results and suggested modifications." Journal of Applied Psychology Monograph No. 2, Vol. 53, part 2:1–25.
Grigsby, O.R. and W.C. Burns
  1962 "Salary surveys—the deluge." Personnel Journal (June) :274–280.
Grinyer, P.H. and S. Kessler
  1967 "The systematic evaluation of methods of wage payment." Journal of Management Studies (October) :309–320.
Groenkamp, W.A.
  1967 "How reliable are wage surveys?" Personnel 44 (January–February) : 32–37.
Haire, M.
  1959 "Psychology and the study of business: joint behavioral sciences," in R.A. Dahl, et al., Social Science Research on Business: Product and Potential. New York: Columbia University Press.
  1965 "The incentive character of pay," in R. Andrews (ed.), Managerial Compensation. Ann Arbor, Mich.: Foundation for the Research on Human Behavior.
Haire, M., E.E. Ghiselli and L.W. Porter
  1963 "Psychological research on pay: an overview." Industrial Relations (October) :3–8.
Haire, M., E.E. Ghiselli and M.E. Gordon
  1967 "A psychological study of pay." Journal of Applied Psychology Monograph (August).
Hall, R.H.
  1969 Occupations and the Social Structure. Englewood Cliffs, N.J.: Prentice-Hall.
Hamilton, M.
  1966 "A study of public management attitudes toward pay." Unpublished Master's thesis. San Diego, California: San Diego State University.

Hampton, D.R.
   1970 "Contests have side effects too." California Management Review (Summer) :86–94.
Herzberg, F.
   1966 Work and the Nature of Man. Cleveland: The World Publishing Co.
Hildebrand, G.H.
   1963 "External influences and the determination of the internal wage structure," in J.L. Meij (ed.), Internal Wage Structure. Amsterdam: North-Holland Publishing Co.
Hinrichs, J.R.
   1968 "The components of job satisfaction." Personnel Psychology (Winter) : 479–503.
Homans, G.C.
   1961 Social Behavior: Its Elementary Forms. New York: Harcourt, Brace and World, Inc.
Hyman, H.H. and E. Singer (eds.)
   1968 Readings in Reference Group Theory and Research. New York: Free Press.
Jaques, E.
   1957 Measurement of Responsibility. Cambridge, Mass.: Harvard University Press.
   1961 Equitable Payment. New York: Wiley.
   1964 Time-Span Handbook. London: Heinemann.
   1967 Equitable Payment. Revised Edition. Harmondsworth, England: Penguin.
Johnson, T.L.
   1962 Collective Bargaining in Sweden. Cambridge, Mass.: Harvard University Press.
Jones, L.V. and T.E. Jeffrey
   1964 "A quantitative analysis of expressed preferences for compensation plans." Journal of Applied Psychology (August) :201–210.
Keat, P.G.
   1960 "Long-run changes in occupational wage structure, 1900–1956." Journal of Political Economy (December) :584–600.
Kerr, C.
   1964 Labor and Management in Industrial Society. Garden City, New York: Anchor Books.
Krupp, S.
   1961 Patterns in Organization Analysis. New York: Holt, Rinehart and Winston.
Kuethe, J.L. and B. Levenson
   1964 "Concepts of organizational worth." American Journal of Sociology 70(3) :342–348.
Lawler, E.E. III
   1965 "Managers' perceptions of their subordinates' pay and of their superiors' pay." Personnel Psychology (18) :413–422.
   1967 "Secrecy about management compensation: are there hidden costs?" Organization Behavior and Human Performance 2(May) :182–189.

1968 "Equity theory as predictor of productivity and work quality." Psychological Bulletin (December) :596–610.

1971 Pay and Organizational Effectiveness. New York: McGraw-Hill.

Lawler, E.E. and J.R. Hackman

1969 "Impact of employee participation in the development of pay incentive plans: a field experiment." Journal of Applied Psychology 53 (December) :467–471.

Lawler, E.E. III and L.W. Porter

1963 "Perceptions regarding management compensation." Industrial Relations (October) :41–49.

Lee, S.M.

1969 "Salary administration practices for engineers." Personnel Journal (January) :33–38.

Lester, R.A.

1948 Company Wage Policies. Princeton, New Jersey: Industrial Relations Section, Princeton University.

1957 "Economic adjustments to changes in wage differentials," in G.W. Taylor and F.C. Pierson (eds.), New Concepts in Wage Determination. New York: McGraw-Hill.

1967 "Benefits as a preferred form compensation." Southern Economic Journal (April) :488–495.

Levinson, H.M.

1966 Determining Forces in Collective Wage Bargaining. New York: Wiley.

Lewis, H.G.

1963 Unionism and Relative Wages in the United States. Chicago: University of Chicago Press.

Lipset, S. and M. Trow

1957 "Reference group theory and trade union wage policy," in Komarovsky and Mirra, Common Frontiers of the Social Sciences. Glencoe, Ill.: The Free Press.

Livernash, E.R.

1957 "The internal wage structure," in G.W. Taylor and F.C. Pierson (eds.), New Concepts in Wage Determination. New York: McGraw-Hill.

1970 "Wages and benefits," in W.L. Ginsburg, et al., A Review of Industrial Relations Research. Madison, Wis.: Industrial Relations Research Association.

Locke, E.A.

1966 "The relationship of intentions to level of performance." Journal of Applied Psychology (February) :60–66.

Lott, M.R.

1926 Wage Scales and Job Evaluation. New York: Ronald Press.

Lupton, T.

1969 "The management of earnings and productivity drift," in N. Farrow (ed.), Progress of Management Research. Baltimore, London: Penguin.

1970 Part I Introduction. Supplement to the Final Report. Paris: O.E.C.D.

Mabry, B.

1973 "The economics of fringe benefits." Industrial Relations 1 (February) : 95–106.

McGregor, D.

1960 The Human Side of Enterprise. New York: McGraw-Hill.

McKersie, R.
1963 "Wage payment methods for the future." British Journal of Industrial Relations (June):191–212.
Mahoney, T.
1964 "Compensation preferences of managers." Industrial Relations (May): 135–144.
Mangum, G.L.
1962 "Are wage incentives becoming obsolete?" Industrial Relations (October):73–96.
March, J.G. and H.A. Simon
1958 Organizations. New York: Wiley.
Marriott, R.
1968 Incentive Payment Systems. Third Edition. London: Staples Press.
Merton, R.K. and A. Kitt
1950 "Contributions to the theory of reference group behavior," in R.K. Merton and P.F. Lazarfeld (eds.), Continuities in Social Research. Glencoe, Ill.: The Free Press.
Moore, W.E.
1962 The Conduct of the Corporation. New York: Random House.
Morris, R.T. and R.J. Murphy
1959 "The Situs dimension in occupational structure." American Sociological Review (April):231–239.
Munson, F.
1963 "Four fallacies for wage and salary administrators." Personnel (July–August):57–64.
National Board for Prices and Incomes
1968 "Job evaluation." Report No. 83 and Supplement. London: H.M.S.O.
Nealey, S.
1963 "Pay and benefit preferences." Industrial Relations (October):17–28.
Nord, W.
1970 "Improving attendance through rewards." Personnel Administration 33(November–December):37–41.
Northrup, H.R.
1964 Boulwarism. Ann Arbor: University of Michigan, Graduate School of Business Administration.
Opshal, R.L. and M.D. Dunnette
1966 "The role of financial compensation in industrial motivation." Psychological Bulletin No. 2 (66):94–118.
Ozanne, R.
1968 Wages in Practice and Theory. Madison: The University of Wisconsin Press.
Parsons, T. and N.J. Smelser
1956 Economy and Society. New York: The Free Press of Glencoe.
Pasquale, A.M.
1969 A New Dimension to Job Evaluation. New York: American Management Association.
Patchen, M.
1961 The Choice of Wage Comparisons. Englewood Cliffs, New Jersey: Prentice-Hall.

Payne, B.
   1951   "Incentives that work." Proceedings of the Society for the Advance-
          ment of Management, November meeting.
Perry, G.L.
   1966   Unemployment, Money Wage Rates and Inflation. Cambridge, Mass.:
          The MIT press.
   1967   "Wages and the guideposts." American Economic Review (September):
          897–904.
Peters, L.H.
   1968   "The essential values of business," in L.H. Peters, Management and
          Society. Belmont, California: Dickenson Publishing Co., Inc.
Phillips, A.W.
   1958   "The relation between unemployment and the rate of change of money
          wage rates in the United Kingdom, 1862–1957." Economica (Novem-
          ber):283–299.
Porter, L.W. and E.E. Lawler III
   1968   Managerial Attitudes and Performance. Homewood, Ill.: Irwin.
Pritchard, R.D.
   1969   "Equity theory: a review and critique." Organization Behavior and
          Human Performance (May):176–211.
Reder, M.W.
   1958   "Wage determination in theory and practice," in N.W. Chamberlain,
          et al., A Decade of Industrial Relations Research, 1946–1956. New
          York: Harper & Row.
   1965   "Unionism and wages: the problems of measurement." Journal of
          Political Economy (April):188–196.
Rees, A.
   1962   The Economics of Trade Unions. Chicago: University of Chicago Press.
Reynolds, L.G.
   1951   The Structure of Labor Markets. New York: Harper & Brothers.
Richardson, R.
   1971   Fair Pay and Work. Carbondale: Southern Illinois University Press.
Ridgeway, V.F.
   1956   "Dysfunctional consequences of performance measurements." Adminis-
          trative Science Quarterly (September):240–247.
Ritti, R.
   1968   "Work goals of scientists and engineers." Industrial Relations (Febru-
          ary):118–131.
Robinson, D.
   1967   "The myths of the local labor market." Personnel (Great Britain)
          (December):36–39.
Rosow, J.M.
   1972   "Now is the time for productivity bargaining." Harvard Business Re-
          view 50(January–February):78–89.
Ross, A.M.
   1948   Trade Union Wage Policy. Berkeley, California: University of Cali-
          fornia Press.
   1957   "The external wage structure," in G.W. Taylor and F.C. Pierson (eds.),
          New Concepts in Wage Determination. New York: McGraw-Hill.

Roy, D.
  1952 "Quota restriction and gold bricking in a machine shop." American Journal of Sociology (March) :427–442.
Sayles, L.
  1973 "Job enrichment: little that's new and right for the wrong reasons." Proceedings of The Industrial Relations Research Association. Madison, Wisconsin.
Schein, E.H.
  1964 "How to break in the college graduate." Harvard Business Review (November–December) : 68–76.
Schuster, J.R., L.D. Hart and B. Clark
  1971 "Epic: new cafeteria compensation plan." Datamation (February 1) : 28–30.
Scott, W.G.
  1965 The Management of Conflict. Homewood, Ill.: Irwin.
Segal, M.
  1961 "Regional wage differences in manufacturing the postwar period." Review of Economics and Statistics (May) :148–155.
Seltzer, G.
  1961 "The United Steelworkers and unionwide bargaining." Monthly Labor Review (February) :129–136.
Selznick, P.
  1969 Law, Society and Industrial Justice. New York: Russel Sage Foundation.
Shultz, G.P. and R.C. Aliber (eds.)
  1966 Guidelines, Informal Controls and the Market Place. Chicago: University of Chicago Press.
Sibson, R.E.
  1974 Compensation. New York: American Management Association.
Skinner, B.F.
  1967 Science and Human Behavior. New York: Free Press.
Slichter, S.H.
  1941 Union Policies and Industrial Management. Washington, D.C.: The Brookings Institution.
Slichter, S.H., J.J. Healy and E.R. Livernash
  1960 The Impact of Collective Bargaining on Management. Washington, D.C.: The Brookings Institution.
Smith, P.C., L.M. Kendall and C.L. Hulin
  1969 The Measurement of Satisfaction in Work and Retirement. Chicago: Rand McNally.
Strauss, G.
  1970 "Organization behavior and personnel relations," in W.L. Ginzberg, et al., A Review of Industrial Relations Research. Madison: Industrial Relations Research Association.
Taylor, G.W.
  1957 "Wage determination process," in G.W. Taylor and F.C. Pierson (eds.), New Concepts in Wage Determination. New York: McGraw-Hill.
Taylor, G.W. and F.C. Pierson (eds.)
  1957 New Concepts in Wage Determination. New York: McGraw-Hill.

Tolles, M.A. and R.L. Raimon
  1952   Sources of Wage Information: Employer Associations. Ithaca, New York: Cornell University.
Torrence, G.W.
  1962   "Maturity curves and salary administration." Management Record (January):14–17.
Tumin, M.M.
  1967   Social Stratification. Englewood Cliffs, New Jersey: Prentice-Hall.
U.S. Department of Labor
  1970   "Area Wage Surveys, Selected Metropolitan Areas, 1968–69." Bulletin No. 1625-90, pp. 68–69.
Van Maanen, J.
  1972   " 'Breaking in': a consideration of organizational socialization," Technical Report No. 10 (August). Irvine, University of California, Graduate School of Administration.
Viteles, M.S.
  1953   Motivation and Morale in Industry. New York: Norton.
Vroom, V.H.
  1964   Work and Motivation. New York: Wiley.
Weick, K.E.
  1966   "The concept of equity in the perception of pay." Administrative Science Quarterly (December):414–439.
Weick, K.E. and B. Nesset
  1968   "Preferences among forms of equity." Organization Behavior and Human Performance (3):400–416.
Weintraub, S.
  1963   Some Aspects of Wage Theory and Policy. Philadelphia: Chilton Books.
Whyte, W.F.
  1955   Money and Motivation. New York: Harper & Row.
  1969   Organization Behavior. Homewood, Illinois: Irwin.

PART V

EXECUTIVES AND MANAGERS

INTRODUCTION—PART V

There are two very critical features of the management of work organizations that claim a great deal of the attention of managers and students of work behavior. Organization Development and managerial decision-making together account for a considerable bulk of the literature dealing with management.

Organization Development (OD) represents a major preoccupation with the ever-present problem of recruitment into the ranks of management a large and skilled enough cadre of persons capable of being the successor executives to those presently in positions of power. But OD has an even grander goal than adequate recruitment and training of future executives. There is also a widely held belief that the successor executives should be better than their predecessors. This belief adds a heavy burden to the recruitment function of OD: the responsibility to educate the new generation to be better than the old one. It may be resolved that these are not compatible goals, and until they are sorted out and separated, the OD movement will continue to face difficulties.

With respect to organizational decision-making, there are many ideas and models that provide some insight into the phenomenon. Admittedly, decision-making is a complex process. The subject, therefore, deserves the attention of imaginative scholars who have the courage to tackle large-scale problems head-on. We may never know all that we need to know about organizational decision-making. This is such a crucial function of management (even when it is shared with subordinates) that there will always be increased pressure to learn more in order to facilitate better decision-making.

CHAPTER **14**

Organization Development

George Strauss

University of California, Berkeley

INTRODUCTION

What has come to be known as Organization Development (OD) represents the most extensive current effort on the part of "behavioral scientists to apply knowledge (primarily sociological and psychological) to the improvement of business organizations" (Bennis, 1965:337). Indeed by the early 1970s OD and "behavioral science" were almost synonymous in many managers' minds, an impression somewhat reinforced by reading the movement's main journal, the *Journal of Applied Behavioral Science*. In the process, OD became big business: by 1969 one firm, Scientific Methods, Inc., numbered among its clients forty-five of the top one hundred U.S. corporations, conducted courses on every continent, and projected profits of $1.1 million (*Business Week*, 1969); and by 1973 there were an estimated 500 to 1,000 external OD consultants in the United States alone. "Today it is an international phenomenon" (Walton and Warwick, 1973).

The purpose of this chapter is to present a critical guide to this dynamic movement—as seen by a nonpractitioner—with an emphasis on the diversity of approaches and the main points of controversy. I will stress OD as depicted in the literature by leading author-practioners, rather than OD as it exists in practice. In so doing I run the risk of oversimplifying and perhaps overdramatizing complex issues. My biases will become obvious as the discussion proceeds.

Defining OD. As a rapidly evolving field, OD presents a moving target, making it difficult to define or criticize. Nevertheless, definitions abound (one of the best appears in French and Bell, 1973:7, 9). Some are "broad enough to include everything from market research to industrial espionage" (Kahn, 1974). Others are so narrow as to encompass only a single school of practice. At times it seems as if OD is merely a convenience term to cover a variety of activities, i.e., OD is what OD people do.

In writing this chapter, I have been helped by Chris Argyris, Douglas R. Bunker, John Drotning, Robert Dubin, Frank Heller, Raymond Miles, Leonard Sayles, Wallace Wohlking, and especially Peter Feuille and Arnold Tannenbaum.

617

Organizational development is not a concept, at least in the scientific sense of the word. The term organizational development is not precisely defined; it is not reducible to specific, uniform, observable behaviors; it does not have a prescribed and verifiable place on a network of logically connected concepts, a theory (Kahn, 1974).

Given these problems a fruitful approach to definition may be historical. Though OD is derived immediately from T-groups, it may also be viewed as a much enlarged version of what in the 1950s was called management development. As the change in name implies the years have brought about a substantial change in emphasis: the purpose now is to develop not just individual managers, but the organization as a whole. Further, OD means more than development in some passive sense; its objective is action—*planned change*, a coordinated attack on organizational interpersonal problems. In Argyris's (1971) terms, it is designed to generate "valid information" which will help the organization make "free choices" which will in turn assist not just in the solution of immediate problems, but also in the strengthening of problem-solving abilities.

OD, like older forms of management development, is designed to obtain change primarily (or at least initially) through altering attitudes and improving interpersonal relations (the term was once *human relations*). By contrast with representatives of other schools of management consultancy, an OD man is unlikely to recommend changes in accounting or compensation systems or organization structures, even though he may hope that the organization itself will eventually make these changes as a result of attitudinal changes he seeks to induce.[1] OD differs further from traditional consulting in that it is the client who generates the solution to the problem, not the consultant. The consultant's role is neither to "teach" behavioral concepts nor to prescribe behavioral or attitudinal changes. "Rather his role is that of managing learning opportunities—creating and capturing situations in which organization members can examine the implications of their actions and experiment with changed behavior" (Miles, 1975).

The unique contribution of the OD consultant is his interest in developing *process*, in helping the organization learn new ways of making change. "True" OD, as I would define it, does not prescribe the end result of the change process.

Because of their importance in OD's development, I will look first at older forms of management development and then at T-groups. Only after this introduction will I turn to OD itself.

---

[1] Because of OD's emphasis on attitudes and interpersonal competence, I am inclined to exclude from my definition of OD activities, such as the Kepner and Tregoe (1965) approach, that was designed primarily to improve analytic ability. I would also exclude Management by Objectives (MBO). Although MBO is in fact a form of planned organizational change (perhaps better planned and more organizational than most forms of OD), it is not bottomed in the assumption common to most OD: that the best way to improve organizational performance is to start with emotional and interpersonal competence.

It should be noted that as the term OD becomes more popular, the boundaries of the field become less precise. An increasing number of consultants engage in structural changes (e.g., MBO, job enrichment, or attempts to induce appropriate differentiation and integration, Lawrence and Lorsch, 1969), calling it OD. If this trend continues, my restrictive definition may be untenable. At the moment, I think it fairly describes the interests of a substantial number of people.

EARLY MANAGEMENT TRAINING

Though company training efforts for blue collar workers have a long history, systematic training programs for members of management became widespread only with World War II, with the "J" programs (e.g., Job Instruction Training), a remarkably well designed, standardized series of simple classes for new foremen. After the war, the spread of both human relations orientations and foremen's unions led companies to engage in foremen training more extensively, as a means both of persuading foremen that they were indeed part of management and of reducing the tyrannies that earlier had contributed to the growth of blue collar unions.

From this humble beginning, the focus of training moved upwards in the hierarchy. Foreman training was transformed into management training and then into Organization Development. Foreman training in anterooms off the factory floor gave way to laboratory training with top management in resort settings. Training techniques became considerably more sophisticated. As the limitations of older techniques became apparent, new techniques emerged. Some of these were merely fadish gimmicks, but even from these, lessons were learned.

Traditional Training Techniques

Among the traditional techniques used are the following, listed roughly in order of what might be called sophistication.

The *lecture* is still commonly used, especially in programs such as those offered by the American Management Association. Lectures may be suitable for imparting information regarding such subjects as changes in the tax law, but they are less useful in changing attitudes or behaviors. Further, being a form of one-way communication, lectures rarely achieve participant involvement, particularly at the emotional level.

The *guided discussion* or conference often times is little more than a form of not-too-subtle manipulation designed to induce the participants to arrive at the discussion leader's predetermined solution. Under these circumstances involvement is rarely obtained. On the other hand, loosely guided conferences may even devlop into forms of T-groups or OD.

The *case study method* at times achieves high involvement, but not necessarily at the emotional level. Although the case study method may inject realism to *university* classes, it is less real and more abstract than the problems *business* people ordinarily face. Practicing managers tend to look upon the case discussion as a sort of game in which they deal with problems in the *other* company. Too often there is little generalization to the problems back home, despite the fact that the case study method may develop skills in observing and diagnosing problems. And the case study method largely avoids the question of carryover from the classroom to the job.

The *business game* involves two or more teams, each of which takes the role of a separate business which competes against its rivals. Typically business games are used to develop both analytic abilities (especially in marketing and finance), and an appreciation of the interrelationships of factors such as research production and investment. The concern is with making decisions, not implementing them. However, modifications of the business game, which provide evaluation periods during which each team examines its interpersonal processes, have become an integral part of some OD programs.[2]

Role playing, in which the participants enact roles, such as foreman and worker, can engender a high degree of emotional involvement. Normally, however, it deals with problems formulated by the instructor, which may not necessarily be those bothering the trainee; the participants play other people's problems, not their own. Usually, too, the problem as presented is isolated from its context and so the impact is reduced. In general, structured role playing is used to develop skills, not to modify attitudes.[3]

All these techniques share a common characteristic: the problems they consider are presented by the trainer rather than the group, and therefore run the risk of being looked upon as not relevant to the trainee's own situation. Even if the program is meaningful and provides a certain amount of involvement, the participants tend not to become sufficiently involved (especially at the emotional level) to internalize changes in attitude or to develop insights concerning their own values and behaviors. Further, since the training process is normally encapsulated from the job, carryover is quite problematical. At best, skills and intellectual understanding are imparted, but attitudes and behaviors are hardly affected.

Because of the limited impact of traditional training, a number of companies turned to T-groups, the precursors to modern OD programs.

T-GROUPS

By the mid-1960s, the list of companies which had experimented with T-groups read like the blue book of American industry (and in the government it had spread even through the State Department and the Internal Revenue Service). T-groups seemed to be far more effective than traditional training. Certainly T-group members became emotionally involved—perhaps too much so! The problems which they dealt with were central to their interests (at least those of the moment).[4] T-groups also had a significant and immediately noticeable impact on attitudes and behaviors. Nevertheless, as we shall see, they also had some very definite limitations. But first, a few words of history.

A Bit of Background

Although some excellent historical essays have appeared, especially dealing with the early days (Bradford, 1967; Marrow, 1967; Bradford, Gibb, and Benne, 1964; French and Bell, 1973), still to be written is a full-scale analytic history of T-groups as a social movement (by far the best study to date is Back, 1972). Such

---

[2] Management games have also been used in management assessment centers as a technique for evaluating the behavioral and analytic skills of candidates for higher management positions. (Albrook, 1968).

[3] "Spontaneous role playing," developed by Moreno, makes use of problems developed by the participants themselves, but is more often used in psychotherapy than in organizational situations. (Wohlking and Weiner, 1971).

[4] In T-group terminology, the case study method emphasizes the "there and then"; T-groups, the "here and now." In traditional role playing you are playing someone else; in T-groups you are yourself.

a history would look at the tension in the early days between those who were interested in group dynamics chiefly as a form of research and those whose prime interests were in training. It would examine the growth period when the demand for professional trainers far exceeded the supply and would look at the conflict over whether professional certification also required adherence to some norm of orthodoxy (and which one?). Finally, the history might analyze the acceptance of the new technique as a case study of cultural diffusion.[5] As Back (1974:367) suggests, "we are looking here not at a development purely within psychology, but a social movement with its sects, ideologies, and polemics."

The fathers of the movement in 1946 (Lewin, Lippitt, and Benne, among others) were influenced by the then-current interest in participative forms of adult education, by Moreno's experiments with psychodrama, and especially by Lewin's early research on the dynamics of democratic groups. Nevertheless, they stumbled on the T-group format almost by accident (Lippitt, 1949) and were quite unprepared for the powerfulness of the forces which this new technique unleashed. Further, T-groups in the early days were somewhat differently designed than those of today[6] and their objective in large part was to train better committee chairmen and members. Certainly they were more concerned with group rather than individual factors.[7] Only gradually did the possibility emerge that T-groups could be used to make not just better conference leaders, but better managers and better people as well.

The early T-groups held at Bethel, Maine were as much concerned with research as with training, but by the mid-1950s, the two interests had split. The Research Group for Group Dynamics, which Lewin had founded, moved from MIT to the University of Michigan while the training function was assumed by what is now known as the NTL (National Training Laboratory) Institute for Applied Behavioral Science.

For the most part, T-groups' early clientele were educators and social workers, while companies were represented by personnel men more than by line managers. Then in the late 1950s, Shepard and Blake brought a modified T-group program into Esso Oil (Shepard, 1960; French and Bell, 1973). The idea caught on in industry. By 1966, twenty-five out of thirty-three leading firms were currently making some use of T-groups and another three had used them in the past (Campbell, et al., 1970:47). T-group trainers began to adopt the paraphernalia of professionalism, with NTL organizing training programs and a new organization established to certify competence, the International Association of Applied Social Scientists. And encounter groups, a poor man's form of do-it-yourself group therapy, sometimes without trained leaders, became a fixture (or a parlour game) in many communities, being prescribed among other things as a remedy for race differences or marital unhappiness.

---

5 For example, why did it spread so rapidly? Why did some organizations adopt it and not others? Who were the key individual "carriers"? Why have some companies continued to use it long after others dropped it? Such a history would also deal with how T-group training spread out into the community, especially into education, and how for some it became almost a religion, while for John Birchers it was a threat to the American way of life.

6 For example, T-groups around MIT in 1947–1948 had a formally assigned role of process observer, a role which was rotated among members of the group.

7According to my 1948 notes, the chief emphasis in T-groups was on the observable impact Mr. A might have on Mr. B. Only later the stress switched to how Mr. A felt about Mr. B or even (as in some encounter groups) to how Mr. A felt about himself.

Purposes and Forms

This is not the place to describe T-groups, neither will I develop their rationale at length. T-groups involve learning at the nonrational, emotional, even visceral level (though intellectual insight is gained as well). This learning is achieved chiefly through experiences obtained in a group setting, thus it is often called *experiential learning*. To use T-group terminology, the emphasis is on the *here and now* of the group, not the *there and then* of the participant's back-home setting. T-group training assumes that people have the power to grow and that they will respond positively to the often negatively oriented criticism they receive from their peers. It seeks to make participants feel freer in expressing emotions openly. It emphasizes both sensitivity to the attitudes and behaviors of others and the acquisition of skills in dealing with people. Together these developed traits are sometimes called *interpersonal competence*, and it is assumed that such competence gained in one situation will carry over into another.

Of course, T-groups are more than a training technique. As one author puts it (Alderfer, 1970:18):

> Laboratory education[8]—learning about human behavior through experiences in group activities—is simultaneously an evolving educational technology, a loosely defined philosophy, and a social movement. Most of its practioners believe that human interaction can be better understood and more effectively carried out, and, as a consequence, more gratifying to the participants. Thus, laboratory education offers the promise of radically changing the way we understand and act in human relationships.

T-groups may take a variety of forms. *Stranger* groups, as the name implies, consist of participants who have had little or no previous contact with each other. Normally, they come from different organizations. *Cousin* groups consist of people from the same organization, typically at the same level, who do not work closely together. A *family* group, on the other hand, includes a boss and his direct subordinates. A *diagonal* group consists of people at various levels in various departments, e.g., the boss of Department A and subordinates from Department B.

In the next few pages I will look first at the development of T-group training and then at some of the problems involved in its application as a means of management training. My purpose is to show how experiences with T-groups contributed to the development of OD—which presumably seeks to incorporate T-groups' strengths while minimizing its weaknesses.

Diverging Emphases

As of today, T-group training is far from a monolithic movement. As was the case with psychoanalysis in the 1920s, its advocates have split into wings with

---

[8] The terms "laboratory education," "T-group training," and "sensitivity training" are often used interchangeably. At one time sensitivity training referred to T-groups which gave relatively greater emphasis to individual rather than group factors. Laboratory education may be the broadest of the terms, since many laboratories include T-groups plus other forms of training, such as games and even lectures. Laboratories often consider relations *among* as well as within groups. There can even be laboratories without T-groups.

the major differences being over (1) the extent to which training should be structured, (2) the relative emphasis to be given rational as opposed to nonrational forms of training, (3) the depth of the intervention practiced by the trainer, and (4) the relative emphasis on individual, group, and organizational problems.[9]

At what might be called the right wing are those who are concerned with organizational, job centered problems. Right wing T-groups (which arguably are not T-groups at all) tend to engage in instrumented exercises, involve family groups, and deal with less deep problems than do left or center wing groups. Perhaps the best example of this form of training is the early stages of Blake's Managerial Grid. Since this form of training overlaps OD, I will postpone consideration of it until later.

What I classify as left wing groups are today increasingly called encounter groups.[10] Regardless of their name these groups are concerned chiefly with personal growth and personality change (Haigh, 1968:437). Allied to this wing (though not necessarily growing out of the T-group movement) are Synanon and Esalen groups, women's consciousness raising sessions, Alcoholics Anonymous, and the like.[11]

Typically, the left wing focuses on deep, individual feeling. At least compared to other types of T-groups, expression of emotion tends to become more important than understanding it. "The new left wing is emotive," Leavitt and Doktor (1970:178) put it. "When they 'feel,' they really *feel*. They do not 'perceive' or 'imagine.' " They engage in the "intentional subordination of intellective process to emotional release" (Lomranz, Lakin, and Schiffman, 1972:403). Many are active in "inventing important new techniques of inward migration" (Bennis, 1968:230) and have "experimented with the use of body movement, rhythm, form, color and similar interpersonally expressive and receptive modalities" (Tannenbaum, 1967). Physical contact, games (such as trying to break through clasped hands into a group) and even just plain screaming are among the techniques used to permit expression of feelings and the communication of nonverbal, nonrational experience—as are less dramatic modes, such as listening to music in the dark and swaying to it to "experience our bodies." In any case they are generally more concerned with the development of alternative life-styles than with better adjustment to contemporary organizations.

---

[9] In Harrison's terms (1970:185–187) the right wing is "instrumental process analysis," the center deals with "interpersonal relations," and the left is "intrapersonal analysis." Schein and Bennis (1965) draw the distinction between the "yogi" (left wing) and the "commissar" (right wing).

[10] Lieberman and others (1972) distinguish among ten varieties of encounter groups. Lomranz, Lakin, and Schiffman (1972) make use of factor analysis of group leaders' responses to questionnaires to reduce this number to three, according to their intervention strategies. "The learning-centered (A) trainer tries to highlight group and interpersonal conflicts rather than intra-personal conflicts. The remedial (B) leader's closest referent is group psychotherapy. The expanded experiencing (C) type is more diffuse in purpose, but more concrete in modeling sensory awareness" (p. 399). Variant A belongs to my center wing, variants B and C to the left wing.

[11] The professionally oriented NTL Institute has not been completely aloof from making an eclectic appeal. A *New York Times* ad for the Institute's 1971 weekend programs at Stony Point ("a stimulating new experience...and it even can be great fun!") lists as among the subjects, "Being a Liberated Woman..., Couples Interaction..., Organizational Development" and as, among the techniques, "encounter groups."

Occasionally left wing programs are nonstructured or even leaderless (Adler, 1967). Others are highly structured, even to the extent of having all instructions given by tape recorder (Klemesrud, 1970). And somewhere in between are programs which follow a somewhat loose structure, but with the trainer dominating the interaction.

Both right and left wings offer somewhat more formally structured forms of experiences than does the center, more orthodox wing which is concerned (as was Kurt Lewin, its godfather) primarily with the here and now behavior of the group.

CRITICISMS OF T-GROUP TRAINING

T-group training is highly controversial. As it is applied to industry at least four sorts of criticisms have been made: (1) it is unduly stressful and may trigger mental breakdown and violate norms of personal privacy; (2) because of the unrealistic nature of the T-group environment, the changes which occur in the group tend not to be carried back to the job; (3) the training teaches the wrong lessons—sensitivity and emotional freedom rather than, for example, decisiveness and logical analysis; and, finally, (4) T-groups seek to change attitudes when more effective and lasting change can be obtained through changing structure. The first two criticisms are discussed below. Since the last two pertain as well to OD generally, they will be discussed later on.

Stress and Privacy

The first issue relates to the charge that T-group training may be so stressful that it leads to mental breakdowns or at least violates norms of privacy. There is a danger that training of this sort may do a better job of tearing people apart than pulling them together (American Psychiatric Association, 1970).

A certain amount of frustration and tension is an integral (even essential) part of T-group programs and is relied upon to contribute to insight (Lippitt, 1969:233).[12] In a sense consultants manufacture stress. Presumably the trained leader can keep these stresses in bounds. In discussing the possibility that T-groups can "introduce strains that can have deleterious effects on the psychological adjustments of participants in such a program," McGregor (1967:170) concludes:

> Such possibilities do exist, but it seems to me important that we keep them in proper perspective. The possibilities of permanent harm to human beings from these methods of training—provided they are conducted by people who have *appropriate professional competence*—is

---

[12] Stress builds cohesion within the T-group and is somewhat the equivalent of the initiation period in many other organizations, e.g., the Marine boot camp, the religious novitiate, the young manager's first year with a company, or the PhD. prelim. Having successfully weathered stern trials together, T-group members (or most of them) feel a strong sense of group identification and euphoria. To what extent would the same results be obtained were the same individuals left in the wilderness, fifty miles from habitation, and forced to find their way out?

considerably less than that inherent in the conditions of everyday life in industrial organizations.[13]

The critical question is the one McGregor underlines. Unfortunately, the T-group movement has had its share of untrained leaders (and just plain kooks), particularly on its left wing. The leaders of the NTL are well aware of this problem and steps have been taken to introduce "professional standards" of training and ethics as well as to warn potential participants of possible risks. Presumably the trained leader is on his guard to protect individual members of his group from pressures greater than they can handle.

There is general agreement, too, that some sort of screening is desirable to weed out emotionally unstable participants. It may be true that anyone with the requisite fee is admitted to some groups (Odiorne, 1963; Maliver, 1971); however, given the well publicized nature of the risks, companies *should* be aware of the need for care in the selection of candidates to send to training. Whether such care is exercised in fact is another matter—the people who are sent to T-group training in some companies are those "who need it most"— frequently the most unstable.

Despite advances, several problems remain. Anyone can be a T-group practitioner, without certification or even training. Furthermore, differences within the movement as to what constitutes proper practice have precluded the development of tight standards.

Some T-groups, with their compulsive requirements of intimacy, may violate deeply felt concepts of privacy and tear down healthy psychological defenses (Drotning, 1966). In poorly controlled groups, the individual who is believed to withhold feelings may be subject to almost brutal attack.[14] "Invasion of privacy is an actual fact as well as a fantasized concomitant of the use of organizational change strategies of greater depth" (Harrison, 1970:194). Harrison argues that many consultants view their role as chiefly that of breaking down resistance to expression of emotion rather than dealing with the problems participants see for themselves. Harrison (1970:176) states:

> Consultants so oriented seem to take a certain quixotic pride in dramatically and self-consciously violating organizational norms. . . . The

---

[13] "The incidence of breakdown during laboratory training is substantially less than that reported for organizations in general . . . . One estimate is that the incidence of 'serious stress and mental disturbance' during laboratory training is less than one percent of participants and in almost all cases occurs in persons with a history of prior disturbance" (French, 1969:29, 34, citing Seashore, 1968:2). Similarly, a study of Posthuma and Posthuma (1973) indicates that psychological casualties in encounter groups are no greater than in control groups. On the other hand, a careful study of a sample of 209 Stanford students who completed one of a variety of laboratory or encounter group experiences found that 9.4% became "casualties" in that they "suffered some enduring psychological harm which was evident six to eight months after the end of the group" (Lieberman, Yalom, and Miles, 1972:42; see also Yalom and Lieberman, 1971). The casualty rates were greatest in groups with "charismatic, aggressive" leaders, most of whom were unaware of the harm these groups were doing to participants. But note, neither the Posthuma nor the Stanford studies involved work organizations.

[14] To be sure, T-groups, under some circumstances, can liberate people "to do their own thing," but suppose "their own thing" is to keep their private thoughts to themselves? The tyranny of the participative group sometimes breeds a new form of conformity, a 1984 in which private thoughts are verboten, with Big Brothers taking the place of Big Brother.

"marathon" T-group is a case in point, where the increased irritability and fatigue of prolonged contact and lack of sleep move participants to deal with each other more emotionally, personally, and spontaneously than they would normally be willing to do.

Something of an ethical question is involved here, especially since participation on the part of managers sent by their companies to T-groups is seldom truly voluntary.

At least as important as these two questions of emotional stress and privacy is the question of whether the degree of stress induced by the leader and the depth of intervention may actually be dysfunctional from the point of view of group learning. Certainly the relationship between anxiety and learning is unclear (Campbell and Dunnette, 1968). Harrison (1970) suggests that excessive stresses, especially working at a level deeper than the client really wants, result in rapid erosion of learning and little transfer from the group to the job. At times, the emotions engendered in training may be so threatening to some participants that they are more rigid than ever. Winn (1967) maintains "This fear of closeness may be particularly strong in the individual who goes through an all male lab, in which pressure of expression of feelings is prevalent with accompanying hugging and handholding." "The residual homosexual anxiety may freeze him from being close to another man, whether it be his superior, peer, or subordinate."

There are significant disagreements among respected T-group trainers as to the appropriate depth of intervention and the degree of relative weight to be given personal growth as against the development of interpersonal competence. Supporters of deep intervention argue that personal emotions must be dealt with if lasting change is to occur. Argyris (1968a), however, distinguishes carefully between what he calls competence acquisition and therapy. In a tactful but devastating critique (1967a; see also 1974), he suggests that some practitioners tend to confuse the two processes and to engage in personality analysis for which they are ill equipped. Therapy-oriented feedback, he argues, when given to people who do not need it, can lead to a sense of "psychological failure" and loss of trust in self (1970:129). Further, it makes the group too dependent on the leader and inhibits group members learning by themselves. Some trainers, "in their impatience—their almost anxious urge to open people up ... create conditions of coercion, failure, and loss of freedom" (1970:164). Thus the directive trainer who seeks to lead his trainees deeper than they wish to go may be using Theory X (McGregor, 1960) techniques for Theory Y objectives (Argyris, 1972).

Carryover

The second major charge against T-group training is that whatever changes occur in the group tend to fade out once the trainee returns to an unsympathetic environment where company policy and his boss's attitude may inhibit the exercise of his newly learned skills (Bolman, 1970, see also Buchanan, 1969:471). There is a need to move from the loving, permissive atmosphere which exists within the temporary social system of the laboratory to the harsh realities outside.

Advocates of T-group training as the sole approach to OD assume that what

is learned in the lab will be carried over to the job, that the openness of feelings which is permissible in the lab can be practiced in the real world.[15] The research evidence, "though limited, is reasonably convincing that T-group training does induce behavioral changes in the 'back home' setting" (Campbell and Dunnette, 1968:97); however, the amount of change after training is not very substantial, especially considering the dramatic events which occur during the T-group. It would seem that a number of factors tend to restrict successful carryover.

In the first place, the trainee may decide that the new skills and attitudes may be fine for the lab, but not appropriate for the organization, so he may make no effort to transfer them. "Laboratory values are so different from the values of most organizations that if individuals learned well at the laboratory they would probably tend to conclude that they should not use their new learning back home except where they have power and influence" (Argyris, 1967a: 163). At the end of training, according to a study of one T-group (Oshry and Harrison, 1966:197), the trainee has changed his diagnosis of "his interpersonal work world and his role in it," but "he sees no clear connection between his new perceptions and how he translates them into action." No wonder many participants complain of feeling let down once the training is over.

Nevertheless, a high percentage of trainees become sufficiently charged by their group experiences that they leave with a strong desire to apply their insights. Unfortunately, the trainee has changed (at least temporarily) but his environment has not. His training has taught him only how to get along with his fellow T-group members, not with the hard reality outside. His new repertoire of skills may be inconsistent with his past image (making it hard to convince others of the sincerity of his change) or inconsistent with the behavior or expectations of his peers and his immediate boss.[16] His attempts to express emotions openly, to be trusting and authentic on the job may be misinterpreted or rejected. Even if his new behavior is not actively squelched, it will not be rewarded. Many of his new skills will be extinguished, though a few which may be safe to practice, such as listening, may linger on.[17] The frustration induced by his T-group experience may even induce him to be more rigid than ever (House, 1968). Thus a trainee may undergeneralize, in that he makes no effort to apply what he learned on the job, or he may overgeneralize and seek to apply everything without making an appropriate translation. Neither alternative results in effective carryover.

One answer to these problems is to train an entire work group together, i.e., to have a "family T-group." But even if a group of managers go through a T-group together, it is unrealistic to expect that the larger organization will let

---

[15] "A lab affirms the possibility of a different world outside, and provides a partial model of what it could be like" (Shepard, 1970: 260). For a criticism of this view, see Argyris (1972) who suggests labs can be coercive and competitive.·

[16] A study by M. Miles (1965) indicates that changes in behavior after T-group training are correlated with security and authority on the job, thus suggesting that carryover is greatest among trainees who feel strong enough to implement their new ideas at work.

[17] "Many participants in 'stranger' laboratories are described by participants in back home situations as better listeners—more patient and more accurate perceivers of reality. All these skills can be used without openly violating the traditional pyramidal values which demand the suppression of much of what the individuals learn [in the T-group] to bring out in the open and solve." (Argyris, 1967a:163)

them live together in a tight little cultural island.[18] There is too much danger of "backfire" and of conflict with other interface groups (Bennis, 1966:174). Ideally, through interaction these individuals will spread their strain of what Dubin calls "organizational syphilis" to the rest of the organization; more likely the rest of the organization will combine to suppress the infection.

Left-wing groups, with their emphasis on personal development and self-expression make little provisions for organizational carryover. Even center-wing groups tend to punish reference to back home situations. Their emphasis on the "here and now" may prevent back home associations which would have helped transference. "The uniqueness of the T-group lies in its apparent disdain for back home and its almost exclusive focus on the immediacy of current experience" (Oshry and Harrison, 1966:186). The concern is with trying out new repertoires of behavior, not with testing their usefulness in the world outside the laboratory.

Of course, many lab programs (especially on the right wing) include special exercises to facilitate carryover and there is evidence that such exercises are effective (Friedlander, 1968). In fact, such organizationally oriented exercises are among the characteristics which distinguish OD from simple T-group training.

ORGANIZATION DEVELOPMENT: AN ADVANCE FROM T-GROUPS

Since the mid-1960s, in part because of the problems discussed above, there has been a distinct movement in management circles away from pure T-groups to a more eclectic approach with trainers (now often called "consultants" or "change agents"[19]) making use of a number of techniques (at times including T-groups). Collectively, these new forms of training have become known as OD. By and large OD is less threatening to participants than pure T-group training and is better designed to facilitate carryover.

Similarities and Dissimilarities

How does OD differ from T-group training? Generalization is difficult because of the many varieties of OD. Furthermore, the dividing line between right wing T-groups and OD is far from clear, and many OD programs include some variety of T-groups in their early phases.

The main difference, of course, is that OD's focus is organizational, not just interpersonal or intrapsychic. OD *claims* to be a systems approach: its objective is planned, managed change, and a coordinated attack on organizational problems. OD *presumably* deals not just with attitudes, structure, technology, or behavior alone, but with a combination of these (Friedlander and Brown, 1974). *In principle* it is concerned not just with the problems of a

---

[18] Another alternative is to put the entire organization through T-group training. Apart from other considerations, this may be terribly expensive. OD does deal with the organization as a whole, but the treatment is typically less intensive than sending everyone to T-groups.

[19] Probably a majority of OD consultants today have a strong T-group background. For the most part these men have not become disillusioned with T-groups per se, but look upon OD as a means of applying T-group principles in a broader context.

single department or a single organizational level, but the organization as a whole. (The italicized qualifiers are justified because OD often fails to live up to its promise and noninterpersonal aspects of the system tend to be slighted.)

T-groups seek to increase their participants' ability to be good group members in *any* situation; OD seeks actual improvement in interpersonal relations within a *specific* organization. T-groups are essentially artificial groups and they deal with tensions which arise in their own little world, tensions which in a sense are artificially created. OD, by contrast, is concerned with the real world, and it deals with tensions which arise on real jobs. It assumes as its bailiwick not just relations *within* groups, but also those *among* groups and even among organizations, for example, between unions and management (Blake, Mouton, and Shepard, 1964) or between countries (Walton, 1970).

Despite this major difference, the two forms of development have much in common. Their common point of departure is the individual, rather than the constraints within which the individual works. Although OD's ultimate goal is increased organizational effectiveness (which is a behavioral rather than an attitudinal measure) OD programs typically start with individual attitudes and utilize confrontation and experiences within groups as their primary learning techniques (as opposed, say, to lectures, individual coaching, or structural changes introduced from the top).

Both T-groups and OD give priority to changes in emotions, generally viewing these as important as more "objective" facts.[20] Both share a common faith in "interpersonal trust," in facing interpersonal problems directly, so that they can be solved, rather than trying to avoid, smooth over, or compromise them in a way which is not a true solution. But, by contrast with some forms of left wing T-groups, in OD emotional expression is merely a means toward an end, not an end in itself. Thus OD is generally less ego-threatening than some forms of T-groups.

Forms of OD

OD comes in a wide variety of forms. Some OD programs consist of little more than family T-groups. Others range from the flexible, ad hoc approach of Schein (1969) to the coordinated grand plan of Blake and Mouton (1969) or the integrated approach at Weldon which made use of a variety of approaches from T-groups to the discharge of incompetent workers (Marrow, Bowers, and Seashore, 1967)—the latter hardly OD.

At the risk of both confusing the reader and exaggerating the distinction between forms, at this point let me suggest two hopefully useful forms of classification, with other forms of classification to be presented later on. Table 1 illustrates my overall classification scheme, utilizing eight common forms of intervention (some arguably not OD). These classification attempts are rather arbitrary, especially with regards to "degree of consultant control." Please note that the column heads will make more sense as the discussion proceeds.

---

[20] In a context which equates laboratory training with OD generally, Bennis states, "Laboratory training...takes man's emotional life as its central issue...." (1969:62). The goals of OD are "effectuating a change in values so that feelings and similar non-intellectual expressions come to be considered a legitimate part of organizational life." (Bennis and Peters, 1966:7).

TABLE 1
TYPICAL INTERVENTION TECHNIQUES BY DIMENSIONAL CLASSIFICATION

Intervention techniques	"Step"*	Organizational level	Depth of intervention	Source of feedback	Degree of consultant control	Isolation from job
Stranger T-group (center wing)	1	Individual or with others	Interpersonal	Within group	Low	High
Simulation (business game) with family group	2	Within department	Interpersonal	Within group	Medium to high	Medium
TV observation of department meeting	3	Within department	On-the-job	Within group	Very low	Very low
McGregor (1967)	3	Within department	On-the-job	Actual vs. ideal	Medium	Low
Group feedback analysis (Heller, 1970)	3 & 4	Within department and intergroup	On-the-job	Within and without group	Medium	Low
Grid phase three (Blake and Mouton, 1969)	4	Intergroup	On-the-job	Without group	High	Medium
Michigan survey feedback (Mann, 1957)	3 & 5	Organization as a whole	On-the-job and reward systems	Without group	Medium	Low
Lawrence and Lorsch (1969)	5	Organization as a whole	Structure	Without group (to some extent actual vs. ideal)	Probably high	Low

*Step in illustrative coordinated OD program, as discussed in text.

The two classification dimensions which we will consider at this time apply to OD as a whole and deal with organizational level and depth of intervention.

Organizational level. OD programs focus on (a) the individual, (b) his relations with others, (c) relations within an interacting group or department ("team building"), (d) relations between groups, and finally (e) relations within the organization as a whole. Programs which dwell exclusively on the individual level obviously should not be called OD. On the other hand, as we shall see, relatively few OD programs really deal with the organization as a whole.

Depth of intervention. OD programs may also differ in the depth of the problems they deal with. Harrison (1970) lists five main intervention strategies. In order of decreasing depth (which he defines as relating to "how private [as opposed to 'relatively public or observable'] are the issues and processes about which the consultant . . . seeks to influence") these issues and processes are:

1. *Individual attitudes* (Harrison calls this "intrapersonal relations"), "values, and conflicts regarding (the trainee's) *own* functioning, identity, and existence"—often at a symbolic or fantasy level. (This is the focus of left wing T-groups.)

2. *Interpersonal relations,* e.g., the attitudes organizational members hold toward each other. Obviously this is directly related to interpersonal behavior and is the focus of center wing T-groups.

3. *On-the-job relations* (Harrison calls this "instrumental process"), "how a person likes to organize and conduct his work ... and the impact which this style or work has on others in the organization," including such factors as the extent of delegation.

4. *Reward systems,* "manipulation of individual performance" through personnel techniques such as salary administration, management by objectives, or rotational job assignments.

5. *Structure* ("role relations").

Most OD occurs at the interpersonal and on-the-job levels. Only a few programs deal with reward systems or structure even though the impact of deeper level changes may lead to consistent changes higher up.

Of course, there is considerable relationship between depth and organizational level. Individual level OD is typically more concerned with attitudes, and organization-wide OD, with structure. But this is not necessarily so: a change program (perhaps not called OD) might seek to restructure individual jobs or it might seek to change individual attitudes throughout the organization.

In practice, these categories are combined in a variety of fashions. Many OD programs move by steps, as their focus shifts typically from the individual to the organization, from isolation to dealing with the organization as a whole, and even from emotions toward structure.[21] For convenience of exposition, let me describe *one possible* sequence of techniques with the warning that OD rarely proceeds this smoothly.[22]

Step one might be a stranger T-group. Here the purpose, of course, is to help make participants more aware of their own emotions and those of others, to enable them to communicate "authentically," etc. In terms of overall OD design the intent is to open people up and to develop problem-solving and analytic skills which will be useful at later stages.

Step two (often a family lab) might involve an exercise of some sort—a case study or a simulation (such as a business game)—followed often by some kind of feedback and then a discussion of the interpersonal dynamics at work during the exercise. As with step one, this step is not focussed directly on the participant's actual work problems, although valuable insights will emerge which are applicable to the job. The purpose of step two is to permit the application of the skills developed in step one and also to permit their testing in a different kind of reality.

Step three could then deal directly with the on-the-job problems faced by the work team. It would permit application of the generalized skills developed in step one and the specific insights acquired in step two. Examples (to be discussed later): Schein's "process analysis" (1969), TV observation of on-going

---

21 Blake (1969), perhaps the most influential of the consultants, prescribes a six-step program, starting with a "Grid" (a combination of feedback and highly structured sensitivity training), running through teamwork and intergroup development, the development and implementation of a "Strategic Model," and ending with a systematic evaluation of progress to date.

22 No mention is made here of the entree process or possible diagnostic activity on the part of the consultant. This process will be discussed later.

groups, or the action planning stages of some OD efforts. Here the purpose is to make actual changes in on-the-job relations and to monitor their effectiveness.

Step four is much like step three, except that it deals with relations between groups, departments, work teams, or groups of superiors and subordinates. Examples: Blake's Phase 3, Heller's (1970) Group Feed-Back Analysis. In general, the purpose in this step is to reduce perceptional incongruity.

Step five involves going beyond strictly interpersonal relations and is concerned with what might be broadly defined as structural changes affecting the organization as a whole—changes not only in tables of organization and reporting relationships, but in job descriptions, evaluation programs, communication systems, and the like (Lawrence and Lorsch, 1969). Presumably the interpersonal trust developed in earlier stages permits problems at this level to be now confronted more realistically.

Few OD programs proceed in exactly this sequence. Some deal with only one step (though those which deal with step one or five alone I would exclude from my definition of OD). Very few cover all five steps; indeed a major criticism is that step five, the structural-organization-wide one, is often ignored altogether. And some programs stop at step two, without an institutionalized effort to obtain carryover or application to the job.

Furthermore, in recent years there has been an increasing tendency to begin OD efforts with on-the-job problems rather than simulations or T-groups and either to avoid the deeper, more personal levels altogether or to defer dealing with these until participants have become comfortable handling safer problems. A program jointly developed by Argyris and Bennis (Bennis, 1966:127) proceeded as follows: (1) discussion of survey feedback data; (2) weekly seminars on human relations; (3) T-groups; and (4) changes in the reward system, in this case, a Scanlon Plan. RCA utilized three techniques almost simultaneously: T-groups, Michigan type survey feedback, and a simulation. (As might be expected, the survey feedback seemed cold and uninteresting compared to the T-group. The mistake probably lay in improper sequencing.) Or a sandwich approach is possible. Bass (1967) suggests that it is possible to intersperse T-groups with business games. The frequently cited Medford case (Beer and Huse, 1972) began with job enrichment.

Regardless of whether OD programs follow the five-step model discussed above or whether they follow some other sequence, they must solve two problems, confrontation (information-getting) and carryover (action). Let us consider these in turn.

CONFRONTATION

Perhaps the main thing which distinguishes OD from other forms of consultancy or change-agentry is its imaginative use of "confrontation." The pages which follow are fairly involved but constitute an effort to make sense of this critical area. Please bear with me!

Broadly defined, confrontation is a diagnostic or information-gathering process in which organizational members obtain feedback as to their behavior in a form which will provide insights useful for improving their performance. Thus confrontation is change-oriented feedback.

The object of this feedback normally is to induce the participant to compare his (or the organization's) *actual* with his *idealized* concept of what his (or the organization's) behavior should be. [23] As we shall see, this comparison may be either explicit (as in the Blake grid) or implicit (as in many other forms of OD). In either case, the resultant "perceptual gap" (Heller, 1970) may serve a combination of purposes: (1) The comparison may reveal such a discrepancy between intended (or desired) and actual behavior as to disturb the previously stable psychological equilibrium and to introduce what Lewin called "unfreezing," or more specifically a desire for change or a "conviction of sin." (2) By bringing problems to the surface, confrontation can help diagnose (and even dramatize) their nature. (3) It can help the organization make informed and hopefully realistic choices as to possible behavioral changes. And, (4) it can be used to evaluate the effectiveness of changes, once these are under way.[24]

Thus confrontation should occur not just once, but can be repeated at every stage of the OD process. Indeed some observers say that a major purpose of OD is to make confrontation an organizational way of life.

Feedback must be provided in a form that is believable and which leads to action. Note that confrontation in itself does not automatically guarantee unfreezing. Instead it may easily lead to defensiveness and greater rigidity. The conditions under which confrontation will lead to unfreezing have been inadequately explored, but obviously the form and timing of feedback are important, as is the interpersonal environment in which it occurs. For feedback to be accepted it should be dramatic enough to induce disequilibrium but not so threatening as to lead to greater defensiveness. It should not be just a stunt, or intended just to shock. Feedback must also be provided in a form which increases rather than decreases interpersonal trust. Otherwise participants are unlikely to level with or learn from each other; neither will they feel as free to experiment with new forms of behavior.

Forms of feedback differ in the extent to which they are interpretative or evaluative. An interpretative comment, such as "The way you deal with people creates antagonism," can be threatening to the ego and can be ignored on the grounds that "that's just his opinion."[25] Implicitly interpretative feedback couched in "scientific" terms ("your group scores 2,2 on the Grid" or "behaves like Likert's System 2") may be harder to refute, but still may lead the group to suspect that it is being manipulated. Completely noninterpretative feedback, for example, the playback of a videotaped meeting, is more difficult yet to reject as biased; further it may be less ego-threatening since it is the individual con-

---

[23] Actually three kinds of discrepancy may be involved: between my actual and my ideal, between my behavior as I see it and as others see it, and between my present values (ideals) and what I decide they should be. (The last suggests that after confrontation I may change my values.)

[24] Even apart from the factors mentioned, it is one of the best established principles of learning theory that feedback facilitates learning (Annett, 1969).

[25] Experts may differ as to what is "evaluative." In commenting on suggestions made by members in a previous meeting that he might criticize their behavior, Argyris (1971: 41) says, "I have a hunch which I would like to test out with you. If you think that I might be evaluative and somewhat clobbering, and if I give no evidence to attribute this to me, maybe your fears are based on how you might deal with your subordinates....If you behave toward others the way that you felt I might behave toward you, it would greatly inhibit the effectiveness of your appraisal program." Argyris calls this type of feedback "non-evaluative." Arguably it is "clobbering."

cerned who provides the interpretation, not some outsider. On the other hand, as we shall see, one of the disadvantages of noninterpretative feedback is that it provides a relatively weak guide for behavioral change.

Forms of Confrontation

A wide variety of forms of confrontation are used. I have lumped these under four heads, primarily in terms of the subject matter of feedback.

Behavior as seen within the group. One category of confrontation involves feedback as to the training group's own internal dynamics and the behavior of its members *while in the group.* Confrontation of this sort may occur at any stage in the OD process, with stranger groups or family groups and with groups working on real or simulated problems. A good example is the T-group. Here feedback is typically provided by fellow group members, though on occasion by the T-group leader.

Raymond Miles has set up TV cameras to record regular staff meetings, with each staff member being given the opportunity to watch a playback of his of performance.[26] As a "process consultant" Schein (1969) comments on the interpersonal dynamics of on-going regular organizational meetings, thus confronting participants with "hidden agendas," personal rivalries and other factors which may be interfering with organizational effectiveness.[27] On the basis of his observations and/or listening to tapes of top management meetings Argyris raises questions relating "to the validity of some of the basic assumptions held by the clients ... and whenever possible, illustrated his view by relating it to actual behavior either on tapes or on here-and-now behavior during meetings" (1971:58–60).

A number of simulations have been developed which also provide an opportunity for confrontation (for example, Morton and Bass, 1964). Here the participants go through an exercise—such as running a mock company—or even constructing a building out of tinker toy pieces, and then analyze the interpersonal dynamics which occur in their group during the exercises; presumably by observing the limitations of their performance, group members are inclined to consider new patterns of behavior. Other simulations pit two teams against each other to illustrate the disadvantages of win-lose methods of competition.

One of the limitations of feedback generated within the group is that this form of confrontation precludes consideration of the impact of the group upon the larger organization. For example, members of top management may learn to function together quite well and still make decisions which are distinctly

---

[26] Miles and his associates have also measured the impact of TV feedback in experimental situations where groups of students engage in problem-solving exercises. This technique results in greater change in in-group behavior (measured in terms of Bales interaction categories) and self-acceptance than do T-groups (Weber and Miles, 1971). Miles argues that TV feedback provides most of the advantages of T-group training while avoiding some of its dangers. See also Alderfer and Lohdahl (1971) for an experimental study comparing the impact of T-groups with TV feedback.

[27] Note the difference between this approach and T-groups: (1) "real" not "artificial" groups are involved, and (2) the feedback role is concentrated in one individual, not distributed among group members. Schein also engaged in other forms of process intervention, for example consultation with individual managers.

harmful to their subordinates. At some stage external feedback is required as to the impact of the group on those outside its bounds.

Behavior as perceived by others. Here members of the trainee group receive feedback as to how their behavior (or overall group performance) is perceived by outsiders in their organization, especially by peers and subordinates. Since on-the-job behavior is involved, this form of confrontation is appropriate only for groups dealing with "back home" organizational problems. Such confrontation can be either face-to-face or indirect.

I utilized face-to-face confrontation in a training course designed to improve relations between union stewards and committeemen (the next step up in the union hierarchy). I had each group meet separately to list what they felt were the strengths and weaknesses of the relationship between their group and the other. Confrontation occurred when these lists were compared in a joint meeting. (Later meetings developed structural changes in grievance processing which helped reduce conflict.)[28]

More sophisticated versions of the same approach have been used by Blake and his associates to reduce union-management differences (Blake, Shepard, and Mouton, 1964), those between headquarters staff and division management (Griener, 1967b), and between superiors and subordinates (Heller, 1970), by Argyris in the State Department (1967b), and by Walton (1970) in an effort to reduce tensions between representatives of Kenya, Somalia and Ethiopia. (See also Golembiewski and Blumberg, 1967; Walton, 1969.)

Indirect confrontation involves the feedback of data collected from others (usually subordinates), with the consultant usually acting as collector. The data may be gathered either through interviews (Beckhard, 1966) or through attitude questionnaires. The latter approach is frequently used by the University of Michigan group, which calls it Survey Feedback (Bowers and Franklin, 1972).[29]

Regardless of its form, indirect feedback may be less stressful for the participants than face-to-face confrontation. Only overall *group* attitudes are transmitted, thus preserving individual anonymity and permitting greater frankness. On the other hand, the very impersonality of this form of feedback may lead participants to doubt its validity. Furthermore, face-to-face feedback permits two-way communications so that both groups learn; indirect feedback at best changes only the attitudes and/or behavior of the group which receives it.

To deal with these problems, Heller (1970) meets at first with groups of superiors and subordinates separately, providing each with indirect feedback (average opinions expressed in numerical terms) indicating how each group views itself and the other. Then, after separate discussion, he brings the groups together. Another interesting combination of face-to-face and indirect confrontation was developed by Bartlett (1967). In this case, superiors listened to

---

[28] The simple design worked in part because of a union tradition of uninhibited expression of feelings and because the union officers were less constrained by authority than are most company managers.

[29] Survey feedback is especially useful for dealing with organization-wide problems since it is possible to provide similar data to each organization subunit and to permit comparisons between the attitudes in one organization and "norms" developed in similar organizations elsewhere.

audiotapes of subordinates discussing their superiors, with the voices electronically filtered so as to be unidentifiable.

Actual vs. ideal. The confrontation here occurs between the manager's concept of an ideal managerial style and the style he actually practices on the job, i.e., it deals with the inconsistencies between his values and his behavior (Argyris, 1970).

McGregor (1967:172–175) developed a simple application of this approach in his work with Union Carbide. He presented members of a management team with a set of variables—items such as "Degree of Mutual Trust" (from "high suspicion" to "high trust") and "Communications" (from "guarded, cautious" to "open, authentic"). He then asked them to:

> Analyze your team (the group here in this room) by rating it on a scale from 1 to 7 (7 being what you consider to be ideal) with respect to each of these variables. Then (with the rest of the team) discuss in depth the situation with respect to each variable, paying particular attention to those for which the average rating is below 5 or for which the range of individual ratings is particularly high. Formulate some ideas about *why* these perceptions exist. The why are likely to be quite different for different variables.

The differences between the ideal and the actual provided a springboard for analysis (especially where there were differences among members of the group, indicating a divergence of perceptions regarding some vital questions).

Miles and Porter (1966) instruct managers to fill out an ingenious questionnaire designed to elicit a comparison of how they would like to be managed themselves with their philosophy of managing others. Almost invariably there is a wide gap between the two—a gap which most managers cannot defend on a rational basis. As a consequence they begin to re-examine their philosophy. The Michigan group sometimes makes similar use of Likert's System 1-System 4 model. Participants are asked to indicate the management profile they would like their organization to have—and then to answer questions indicating the profile as it actually exists. The difference, of course, indicates the area of needed change.

Participants in Phase I of Blake's Grid program first develop a model of ideal supervisory behavior (which usually turns out to be "9,9"—equal attention to production and people). They then engage in a simulation which reveals their actual behavior. The confrontation occurs between the actual and the ideal.[30] "You have to build a model," Blake puts it (*Business Week,* 1969):

> ...as if you had no past tradition, no past practices, cult or ritual. Then you see how lousy you really are in comparison with where you should be. So the ideal is a searchlight for seeing the real. You have to close the gaps once you see them. You can't live with contradictions.

---

[30] Blake finds that managers who have first developed a model tend to rate their own performance lower than those who have not gone through the model-developing exercise— thus suggesting that this exercise is instrumental in developing desire for change.

Note that each of these methods requires participants to develop (or at least make explicit) a philosophy of management *before* receiving feedback. Buchanan (1969:477) presents evidence suggesting that such an approach is more effective than confrontation alone.

Facing problems directly. This form of intervention involves confrontation in a much more limited sense. On occasion the consultant's intervention may consist merely of asking managers to list their problems in order of importance (Bennis, 1969). The primary OD technique at the Banner Company (Seashore and Bowers, 1963) was a series of meetings at various organizational levels called to deal with pressing problems, such as shift-rotation rules. Compared with other forms of confrontation, the problems in this case are more likely to involve content as opposed to process and certainly would be on a conscious as opposed to unconscious level.

Further Intervention Dimensions

We now return to the other dimensions listed on Table 1. Forms of confrontation differ not just in subject matter, but also in degree of control by consultant, isolation from organizational reality, and emotional depth.

Degree of consultant control. As T-groups gain experience, the form of feedback is determined by participants. By contrast, in many forms of OD, control over the form and timing of feedback is kept firmly in the consultant's hands (even if the group decides how to use the feedback after receiving it). Thus Heller, the Michigan group, the Grid Phase I, and many others quantify their feedback in certain preset categories, and Lawrence and Lorsch (1969:86) present feedback "not of raw data, but of data organized within a conceptual framework." (But group members may be allowed to participate in designing questionnaires to be used in survey feedback [Miles, 1969]).

Consultant control can be exerted in other ways. One of the technological innovations of recent years has been the development of structured or "instrumented" forms of OD. Blake's Grid Phase I is highly structured, with almost every group going through the same experience, filling out the same forms, and following roughly the same schedule. Culbert (1970) seeks to accelerate T-group learning by dividing the time spent in the group into a series of phases (such as "developing a climate of trust" and "exposure of individual differences") and asking participants to pay special attention to different questions in each phase. (See also, Myers, Myers, Goldberg, and Welch, 1969.)

Among the arguments in favor of consultant control is that it makes the change process quicker and more predictable, it prevents participants from going down blind alleys, and it reduces the danger that the group will get out of hand (for instance by generating pressures which harm individual members). Furthermore, the client may not have the knowledge or experience to determine what sorts of feedback are appropriate. Structure and consultant control—as in the case of the Grid or "Rational Training" (Ellis and Blum, 1967)—may reduce the kind of participant anxiety which inhibits learning (Gibb, 1964) and prevent proceedings from becoming excessively personal. An additional advantage of instrumented programs is economic; with instrumentation a program can be run with an untrained leader or none at all. Witness encounter groups in which participants receive instructions directly from tape recorders.

On the other hand, consultant control suggests a Theory X approach to Theory Y change. To be consistent with OD philosophy, some may argue that the group should participate in determining what data are to be gathered and in how they are to be obtained and used. Instrumentation may make the group feel that it is being manipulated; and it makes no provision for flexibility to meet special situations. Given the importance of modeling in learning theory, one may question what the participants learn in a situation where they have little control.

Isolation.   OD programs may differ in the degree of the isolation of the confrontation process from the realities of the job. At one extreme we have stranger T-groups which deal exclusively with the problems arising within the boundaries of their temporary "total institution." An example of the other extreme might be TV feedback of regular managerial meetings. In between are various forms of simulation in which participants deal with problems somewhat like those found on the job, but sufficiently different so the participants can feel they are not "playing for keeps."

Isolation may be obtained in a number of ways. The setting of OD may be a "cultural island," a resort setting, for example, where participants may presumably enjoy a "moratorium" from the pressures of immediate problems. Labs may consist of previous strangers who will separate for good once the problem is over. Status may be deemphasized through the use of first or nicknames rather than titles. Groups may concentrate on the "here and now" of their own development with mention of "there and then" problems back home being discouraged.[31]

The purpose of isolation is to create an atmosphere of psychological safety in which people feel free to express previously forbidden attitudes (or at least to reassess their present behavior) and to experiment with new forms of behavior without making any firm commitments for "keeps."

Isolation undoubtedly facilitates unfreezing and also permits deeper forms of confrontation. However, the greater the isolation, the greater the difficulty in obtaining carryover from the laboratory to the job (Schein and Bennis, 1965; Morton and Bass, 1964). The very factors which create psychological safety— being in cultural islands, temporary groups, not playing for keeps—also lead participants to engage in behavior which they may view as inappropriate for the job (Campbell and Dunnette, 1968). Skills learned in settings unlike those in which they are to be applied may not be easily recalled or utilized. Problems, such as how to deal with the boss, may be discussed at length but never resolved because the boss isn't there.

To put the dilemma another way: ideally, feedback should be relevant to work experience of the subject in order to obtain maximum carryover of learning to the job (Weick, 1965). But if the exercise is too realistic, the feedback may become so threatening that it is rejected—thus preventing unfreezing.

---

[31] The various forms of isolation do not necessarily go together. On-the-job problems may be discussed in resort settings. Family groups may deal exclusively with "here and now" of their own group, ignoring, for the moment at least, possible there and then applications back home. And so forth.

Are there solutions to this puzzle? Family groups are not entirely the answer. When a group of managers who normally work together on the job are brought together in a deep level training group, there is a danger that the antagonisms and tensions which flare up may remain unresolved and carry over back to work. Laboratory training may do a good job of tearing groups apart; they are not always successful in pulling them back together again.

Depth. The central issue here is whether it is necessary for the manager to experience some sort of personal unfreezing of his private values before he can unfreeze his on-the-job behavior or really understand the dynamics which lead to this behavior. Can there be effective team building without prior value changes? Can we deal with job adequacies without first dealing with personal inadequacies? Presumably OD leads eventually to greater self-confidence in handling day-to-day problems; is greater anxiety required during the confrontation period to obtain less anxiety later on?

Of course, we have run across these questions before, in our discussion of T-groups. On one side are those who argue that only through deep change can real change be achieved; since feelings interfere with on-the-job behavior, feelings must be changed first. Until confrontation of deeper problems occurs, confrontation of organizational problems is unlikely to be fruitful. According to Davis (1967) "confrontation without caring can be a rather destructive process" —and presumably caring ("authentic behavior") can best be developed in relatively deep level labs.

On the other side are these arguments: deep intervention may have more lasting impact on the *individual*, but the kind of change which occurs is highly personal; it is less likely to have an impact on those not directly concerned. Shallower forms of intervention may have a more lasting impact on the organization (Harrison, 1970). Deep intervention is personally more threatening, is more costly, is more likely to meet resistance (and to be concerned with tearing down resistance), and may lead to excessive dependence on the consultant. Finally, for some, the experience of deep confrontation may be so unpleasant that they reject less emotionally charged forms of OD, thus making carryover more difficult (Winn, 1967:9).

Harrison (1970) believes that intervention should be (1) "at a level no deeper than required to produce enduring solutions to the problems at hand" and (2) no deeper than the "client system's willingness to subject itself to exposure, dependency and threat."[32] He concludes that "with quite a few organization clients in the United States, the line of legitimacy seems to run somewhere between interventions at the instrumental level and those focused on the interpersonal relations."

There may be an analogy here with psychotherapy, where there is currently a sharp shift from psychoanalysis, isolation, and long-term therapies to shorter-term, situationally targeted, behaviorally oriented forms of treatment. "The old psychoanalytic ideal of attempting to change the basic character of the individual," Wohlking (personal communication, 1971) believes, "is being abandoned because of the difficulty of the task. Maybe OD people will find it ulti-

---

[32] But what happens when the two criteria conflict, when enduring solutions require intervention deeper than the client would accept without resistance? Presumably Harrison would choose the less deep alternative.

mately too difficult to change the basic character of the corporation," or even of the people within it.

The issues of isolation and depth of intervention are obviously intercon- nected. In practice the choice is often to provide confrontation on an emotion- ally deep level in cultural islands, as in T-groups, or on a less deep level with real organizational problems. The central dilemma, again, is that the deeper, more isolated forms of confrontation, while creating the conditions for more fundamental forms of personal change, may also make carryover more difficult. Carryover thus becomes a major problem.

CARRYOVER

Confrontation is just the first step (though some consultants seem to feel it is an end in itself). The next step is to develop skills which *can* and *will* (two sepa- rate requirements) be used on the job. Presumably the initial confrontation has led to an unfreezing of *attitudes*; carryover requires the participant to unfreeze his *behavior*, to develop new skills, or at least to consider alternative means of resolving the deficiencies revealed through confrontation.[33] The mode presum- ably changes from expression of emotions to experimentation with and utiliza- tion of new forms of behavior.

"The road from insight to implementation is a long and tedious one" (Winn, 1967). Carryover involves more than a single dimension. For OD to have a lasting effect, the participants must move (1) from confrontation to behavior, (2) from training group to work problems, (3) from intent to implementation (including structural change), (4) from sporadic action to routinization, and (5) to widen and permanize the entire OD effort.[34] Many of these processes occur simultaneously. And most involve continuing forms of new confrontation.

From confrontation to behavior.   Carryover is relatively simple if con- frontation has occurred at a job-related, less deep level. Presumably the feed- back has helped managers view their on-the-job problems in a new light. What is now required is that they consider and perhaps experiment with alternate solutions and adopt those which seem most useful. This process is sometimes called "action planning."

But, as suggested earlier, carryover becomes much more difficult when con- frontation occurs at a relatively deep and isolated level. When this happens, the new values and/or behaviors which have developed within the training group must be translated into forms which are relevant to the job outside.

Hopefully, in either case, the confrontation period has generated a sup- portive atmosphere in which the normal inhibitions on self-disclosure are re- duced and the participants in fact feel free to experiment with such new be- haviors, in effect trying them on for size before adding them as permanent parts of their repertoire.

---

[33] To put it another way: the perceptual incongruity induced by confrontation leads to stress; this in turn leads to search for methods to relieve the incongruity.

[34] Carryover may also require (1) the development of a new conceptual framework ("cognitive structure"), (2) the integration of this framework into individual thought patterns, (3) its application to on-the-job problems, and (4) its verification and reinforcement through experience (Dalton, 1970).

Changes in what direction? This brings up a parenthetical question largely ignored by the literature. Confrontation may create a desire for change, but what determines the direction of change? Recognizing a problem does not solve it. How do OD participants learn about the alternatives which are available, and how do they pick one over another? The manager who is used to supervising closely, for example, must learn alternative ways of obtaining organizational objectives (and spending his time).

Undoubtedly, there is a good deal of learning by trial and error. At first there may be oscillation from one extreme to another; eventually, by the process of elimination, the parties may pick a set of skills which fits them well in the lab. But trial and error is time consuming.

To determine direction, it is also likely that a certain amount of modeling (what Argyris calls mimicking) takes place, and OD participants copy the behavior of their consultants. Hopefully the values of openness, etc., which exist in the consultant-client relationship, provide "a microcosm of the organization they are trying to create" (French and Bell, 1973:178). (Whether OD consultants are the proper model for organizational managers is another matter.) Interpretative forms of feedback generally are suggestive of the direction in which change should go. Videotapes of "successful" groups can also provide models of behavior (Walter, 1975; Walter and Miles, 1974).[35]

Another powerful form of modeling is exemplified by the Blake Grid and Likert's System 4. Both set clear standards as to desired behavior. Indeed, as mentioned earlier, a number of confrontation forms require participants to adopt a philosophy of management *before* obtaining feedback. Lawrence and Lorsch (1969) go even further: they sometimes begin OD by putting their clients through the classical Harvard case method before beginning feedback proper. (Even T-groups are sometimes associated with "Theory Sessions.") Cognitive change may be more important than emotional awareness in facilitating organizational change (Buchanan, 1969).

The dilemma here is obvious. The more explicit the OD process is in suggesting solutions, the quicker the organization adopts the "right" answer, but the less likely it is to "own" it or to believe in it enough to persist in its implementation. There is a danger that some consultant's approaches (the Grid, for example) may be viewed as manipulative.

From training group to work problem. In some cases the same behavior patterns which have been developed within the training—for example, willingness to listen or to express feelings—can be tried out on the job. If these are further reinforced, presumably "refreezing" will occur, that is, they will be internalized, hopefully for good. Such changes may be fairly modest (for example, learning to listen).

More often, however, the skills developed in the isolated groups require translation and modification before they become job-relevant. Although simulations and the like are designed to be more realistic than T-groups, they can be perceived by participants as little more than a game unless they are tied into on-the-job problems. Indeed, some participants seem to resist using T-group learned skills even in simulations (Winn, 1967; Bolman, 1970). The importance

---

[35] For a survey of the literature dealing with various forms of modeling in group therapy, see Bednar and others (1974).

of making this tie-in between the job and the T-group is suggested by an important study (Friedlander, 1968) which suggests that the success of family T-groups in industry depends upon the "pre-work and post-work processes surrounding the laboratory" and upon the "emphasis upon work experience and concept utilization in the training process"—in other words that leaders of successful T-groups are concerned with making the groups relevant to on-the-job problems.

Certainly some mechanism is needed to "work through" OD knowledge in terms of practical day-to-day problems once the participants return to the job. Wagner (1965) had a group of managers play an Executive Decision Game immediately following a four-day T-group. As Campbell and Dunnette (1968:98) describe it, "During the first quarter of the game, considerable regression from T-group norms took place. After this was pointed out to the group members, they apparently overcompensated during the second quarter by becoming overly conscious of interpersonal factors. Only after a second critique session in which regression and overcompensation were both discussed did the group seem to make efficient use of its T-groups."

In order to assist in the "re-entry process," many OD programs go through one or more intermediate stages (my various "steps") which lead the participants from the hothouse atmosphere of the T-group stranger lab to the "planning and practice of specific activities back home" (Bunker and Knowles, 1967; Bass, 1967). Often these intermediate steps are called *team building*. At this stage, the emphasis shifts from generalized goals to specific work-place objectives. For example:

> Blake's Phase II (which follows Phase I's quasi-T-group) is concerned with work team development. The purpose here is the setting of individual and team standards of excellence, accompanied by the analyses of personal and organizational barriers, and the development of strategies to reach these standards. Ideally, the ground rules of openness and candor that were established in Phase I become the daily operating style in Phase 2 (Rush, 1969:54).
>
> The program at Sigma refinery began with a training program in which the objectives for the participants were the general goals of understanding the concepts and assessing their own present management style. Other meetings followed . . . to transfer the new concepts. . . to the operation of their own group. The objective became even more concrete as the men consciously tried to use some of their new problem-solving methods in working out a problem for reducing utility costs and in negotiating a difficult union-management contract (Dalton, 1970:241).

In an effort to introduce greater realism into the carryover process, Harrison (1972a) has members of OD programs engage in "role negotiations" in which participants make bargains with each other as to changes in behavior which will be mutually advantageous. "Each team member is expected to be open and specific" about the interpersonal processes in the organization which make his job more difficult and also to list his "expectations and demands" for changes in the behavior of others. "The process is essentially one of bargaining and negotiation in which two or more members each agree to change behavior in exchange for some desired change in the behavior on the part of the other." The process is impossible, of course, without the kind of "openness" typically generated in a T-group, but the goal is far more job-specific.

From intention to lasting implementation. Moving from feelings to behavior, from concept to agreement on action, is certainly a gain. But pledges as to job-related behavior change, made in the OD setting, are often forgotten once back on the job, and even if the new behaviors are tried on the job they often erode as participants become discouraged. The real test is whether carryover can be made permanent. Will "refreezing" occur? Can OD be made self-reinforcing? What can be done to prevent it from being a one-shot affair? ("We've got to charge 'em up once a year," one personnel man put it. "Otherwise they get stale.") [36]

I suspect that changes in attitude are not likely to persist unless accompanied by appropriate changes in structure, reward system, and interaction patterns (Dalton, 1970). For OD to become internalized, participants should enjoy the success experience of actually implementing short-run, specific organizational changes such as introducing a new production line, changing a promotion policy, and the like (Beer and Huse, 1972). More than this: for OD to continue as a lasting process, this implementation must be successful, that is, it must lead to directly observable (and preferably measurable) improvements, such as increased productivity, shortened lead-times, etc. (Beer and Huse, 1972). If OD is associated merely with "good feeling," it is likely to be viewed as an expendable luxury. It is argued that it is unrealistic to expect OD to provide quick results. But without quick results participants are unlikely to persist in their efforts.

Developing sustaining mechanisms. In some instances, perhaps, participants will be so completely changed by their OD experience that they will continue to practice their OD-learned skills on the job without further OD activity. Experience suggests, however, that unless sustaining mechanisms are developed, fadeout may well be rapid.

For successful, long-term OD, the participants must be prepared to reexamine their behavior almost continuously. They must look upon "perpetual diagnosis as a way of life" (Schein, 1969:125). There are reports of situations where the OD process has become so routinized, so much the norm, that no special mechanisms are required to keep it going. Here every man serves as the functional equivalent of a process observer and managers become accustomed to switching quickly and painlessly from substance to process, with perhaps only a buzz word or so ("aren't we 9-1?" or "let's green light this") to signal the change of mode (though there is the danger that such buzz words can become affectations without real meaning).

Thus OD can continue informally on the job. But job pressures being what they are, it often helps to institutionalize (formalize) the process, to provide for feedback on a routine basis.

---

[36] To put the issue in other terms, can OD be achieved as a steady-state condition, or should we view it as a series of kicks designed periodically to realert managers to the need for change? Can OD maintain a high pitch indefinitely, or is it more realistic to think of it as proceeding in spurts?

The State Department program began with T-groups and team-building and problem-solving sessions but associated with this program were outside "process observers" who sat in on regular Department meetings and would report back to each individual on his activities and how he came through to the group (Crockett, 1970).

Periodic attitude surveys seem to serve the same confrontation function, as do TRW's "sensing sessions" in which managers regularly meet to diagnose interpersonal problems which may be inhibiting organizational operations (Davis, 1967). This feedback function may be served by "social indicators" (such as accident or turnover figures—or even standard accounting data) and also by ombudsmen, the Scanlon Plan, representative structures (as at Glacier), and especially by unions.

Regular OD departments, which have been established in a number of companies, in effect are institutionalized lobbyists for human changes, just as R&D departments are lobbyists for product change. The problem with excessive reliance on OD departments is that line managers may conclude that OD is staff's responsibility, not their own. Thus strong OD departments may become counterproductive. The "ownership" of OD must be widely spread throughout the organization.

What about the consultant? There is an old saying that the job of every consultant, regardless of his field, is to work his way out of his job, but fortunately for his continued livelihood that he will never succeed. There is always plenty for the OD consultant to do, but it is likely that the value of the continued services of any given consultant will decline as time goes by. In the first place, if he is successful, the organization will have internalized the OD process. Continual feedback—both factual and emotional—will be a norm. Second, the extent that the consultant's initial impact depends on the novelty or even gimmickery of his approach will wear off fairly rapidly. After a while trainees may become inured to the shock effect of repeated confrontations. A new consultant, with a new bag of tricks, may be appropriate.

Toward new frontiers. In any case, it is far from clear whether OD can become sustaining if it is confined to a single work group or deals solely with interpersonal relations. The elaborate carryover efforts, just mentioned, may not be enough. For the delicate OD plant to grow vigorously, changes in overall organizational environment are required.

Certainly many OD programs provide for an intergroup stage (Blake's Phase 3) concerned with improving interdepartmental relations. And programs such as Blake's Phase 4 go beyond interpersonal relations and seek to re-evaluate overall organizational goals. Along the way structural questions may be considered. But more of this later.

In any case, it is reasonably clear that if OD is to meet its self-proclaimed goals of insuring continued organizational self-renewal, more than T-groups or even team building will be required. OD must continuously take on new challenges unless it is to lose its function as an instrument of *change*. Confrontation must deal with organizational problems, not just interpersonal ones, and OD must be viewed as useful for solving problems in marketing and finance, not just those involving personnel matters. Yet few OD programs get this far, not because the wrong carryover techniques have been used *after* confrontation but because too little thought has been given to the purposes for which OD has been introduced in the first place. For this reason we need to consider what is sometimes called the *entree problem.*

ENTREE

The issue of *entree* is somewhat ignored in the literature.[37] By entree I mean such questions as: Why do organizations engage in OD? What is the decision-making process by which they decide to call in a consultant (or establish an internal OD department)? What are the motives and expectations of the parties involved (for example, how do the consultant's expectations differ from those of the client)? How is OD structured in the eyes of the participants? Who is seen as "owning" OD (that is, in whose interests is the consultant seen as working)? Above all, how is entree best effected? Under what conditions is OD most likely to be successful?

Little research has been done on these questions; in any case, the subject is too complex to be treated here at length. But let me hint at a few problems.

Functions of the Entree Period

Some writers leave the impression that OD begins only after all the preliminary arrangements have been made. I would argue that the entree period should be regarded as an essential part of the OD process, perhaps the most significant one of all. The entree period should permit the client and the consultant to size each other up. The consultant (perhaps jointly with the client) can make a preliminary estimate as to which of the various forms of OD would be most appropriate for the given situation. Similarly the client can use this period to gain some sort of feeling for what the OD process is all about, to decide what kind of OD it wants, if any, and to test out whether the particular consultant being observed meets the bill.

Regretably, the parties are often unable to take sufficient advantage of their opportunities. A high percentage of consultants have but a limited repertoire and prescribe roughly the same form of OD, regardless of the client's special needs. And to complement this limitation, few clients are in a position to evaluate the consultant's proposals.

Expectations of the Parties

Obviously the expectations of the parties are critical to the success of the OD program. Frequently there is incongruity between the motives of the consultant and those of the client. Chances of failure are high if, for example, the consultant wishes to move the system as a whole toward a Theory Y approach to management, while top management expects the consultant to "work with" (i.e.,

---

[37] Among the studies are Sofer (1962), Griener (1967a) and Levinson (1972). Argyris (1970) discusses the issue at some length, but he is concerned chiefly with when the consultant *should* accept an engagement and how entry *should* be made. He says very little about the conditions under which OD normally *does* occur.

straighten out) a group of lower managers whose performance seems to be slipping, and the managers in question regard the process as a form of punishment or a "Mickey Mouse" waste of time.

Ideally, as Bennis suggests, OD should involve "mutual goal setting, an equal power ratio (eventually), and a deliberateness on both sides" (1965:341), as well as a "collaborative relationship ... a spirit of inquiry with data publicly shared, and equal freedom to terminate the relationship" (Bennis, 1965:343). But I suspect these conditions are satisfied in only a minority of cases and that in most instances consultants are brought in for a combination of the following four motives.

1. The conversion motive.   A key company individual learns about OD, perhaps through listening to a leading OD personality give a talk, through reading the literature, hearing it recommended by his counterpart in another organization, or even from his wife (see Rush, 1969:114). Alternatively, he may have participated in an OD experience himself (perhaps an executive seminar) and becomes so entranced that he wants everyone in his organization to share his experience. Insofar as this motive operates, there is little thought given to specific problems existing in the organization. The key individual is usually enthusiastic—he feels that he has been changed by the experience, or feels that it will be good for his subordinates—and that is enough.

A typical case involved a division personnel director who "got the word" from his counterpart in central headquarters that the executive vice president had "got religion" at a one week's T-group program and was full of excitement about its possibilities; as a consequence the personnel director felt "under strong pressure" to get a similar program going soon.

The training director of another organization said the way to "get your ticket punched" was to run the Grid. Top management was for it, there was money budgeted for it, and everyone went along.

2. The morale motive.   Here top management's motives are considerably more modest. OD is introduced as a means of raising morale.

A personnel director gave the following reasons for his OD program: "We don't expect to introduce any fundamental changes in this program, but it brings managers together from all over the country so that they can get to know each other and so that we can meet and observe them in something other than a purely social situation. And finally, it indicates that we are aware of their existence and interested in their future."

Few managers are this frank, but I suspect that motives of this sort are more common than generally admitted. Too often top management agrees to OD at the request of the personnel department in the hopes that it can do "some good," with OD being viewed primarily as a ceremony (Belasco and Trice, 1969) or a personnel gimmick on the order of the office party—rather than as an approach to management. OD is considered as a way of changing (improving) people—to make them function better within the present organization—rather than as a way of changing the organization.[38] In other words, top management signals that carryover must be kept within limits.

---

[38] Occasionally OD (or at least management development) is looked upon as a means of socializing lower-class supervisors into middle-class life-styles.

3. The handyman motive.   This is almost the direct opposite of the conversion motive. In this instance the client has a specific but limited problem and calls the consultant to fix it. Sofer (1962), for example, was hired for the purpose of defining the duties of a corporate secretary. Occasionally there is a considerable crisis. Nevertheless, to the extent that the OD consultant is called upon to solve a specific problem, the client may strongly resist the consultant's attempts to go beyond his assigned mission. Solving that problem—in isolation—is perceived as his only function.

4. The Mafia motive.   Here a consultant is brought in by one manager to "get" another manager or group of managers. As Raymond Miles puts it, the consultant acts as a hired gunman; after the smoke has cleared usually there have been some personnel changes made. Obviously those at the receiving end of the "planned change" have had little to say about it, even though there may be some trappings of democracy.

A typical case might be where top management invites "interventionists into their system to find ways to discharge or neutralize other senior executives" (Argyris, 1970:28). In one instance, the personnel department (the usual hirers of gunmen), with the approval of top management, brought in an OD consultant to "straighten out" the controller's office and to take it "off people's back." It was clear that no one in the organization (and particularly not the personnel department) had the courage to take on the unpleasant task.[39]

Sometimes top management has the best of intentions, as in the case of a newly selected superintendent of schools who brought in an OD team as a means of winning the support of his office's top bureaucrats for the progressive ideas which he wished to introduce.

Although the four motives may be overdrawn, certain elements of each seem to be present in many OD programs, even those run by the best consultants.

One of the country's top consultants was brought into a major hotel chain after the president had attended one of Douglas McGregor's workshops. Neither of the two articles on this case (Rush, 1969:106–112; Beckhard, 1966) make any mention of either the president or the consultant discussing the desirability of an OD program with any of the company staff until the first stage of the program was completed. In context the purpose of the program was quite clear: top management was trying to introduce common policies (greater centralization) into the newly established chain, but staff people at the local level were seeking to preserve their independence. OD was designed to improve channels of communications, i.e., reduce local autonomy (perhaps in return for increased influence at higher levels).

Thus the client's motivation is critical. It makes a big difference whether the consultant is being called in to deal with specific problems or just to provide "some OD training." It also makes a difference whether the contact man who brings the consultant in is seeking to develop more effective patterns of behavior for himself—or (as is more common) wants to change the behavior of others.

Should a consultant enter a situation where he perceives that the client's motives are inappropriate? Some consultants accept such assignments with the

---

[39] Another version of Mafia activity occurs when management induces the consultant to call a meeting "so that blacks could confront their 'white oppressors' and have a cathartic experience" (Argyris, 1970:23).

hope that, as OD proceeds, the range of questions dealt with will expand beyond the presenting symptoms. Still the question remains whether the consultant enters OD under false pretenses unless he makes a full disclosure of his intentions. For instance, the evidence is growing that successful OD is a long-term process, requiring at least several years before meaningful gains materialize (Friedlander and Brown, 1974). Given this, is it ethical for the consultant to accept a short-term assignment without making the limitations of such an assignment quite clear?

Should the consultant seek to confront the client's inappropriate objectives before the program proper begins? Too often the consultant and the client engage in a kind of "con" game. The consultant seeks to induce the client to make changes the client does not want to make; the client tries to persuade the consultant that he is really "sincere" in desiring change. (In many cases the consultant is far more deceived than the client.)

Client Participation

The foregoing discussion leads to a basic question: To what extent should a client participate in designing a program? Must there be explicit prior agreement between the client and the customer (a psychological contract) regarding the nature of the problems the consultant will work with and the techniques he intends to employ? Is it necessary at least to prepare the client for the role of the consultant and for the open examination of problems? Some writers say that if the client does not participate fully, a Theory X approach is being used to achieve Theory Y objectives, that OD's program of "caring and participation" may be completely incongruent with the techniques by which the program was introduced (Argyris, 1970:21).

But suppose the client is not familiar enough with OD to collaborate intelligently? Schein (1969:4) argues that it is not necessary to assume "that the manager or the organization knows what is wrong, or what is needed, or what the consultant should do." Indeed, the typical client needs a consultant precisely because he does not know what his *real* problem is (even if he is aware that something is wrong), and he can be expected to display unconscious resistance to dealing with it. Even the experienced consultant finds it hard to predict the problems that are likely to emerge as the OD process unfolds or to specify in advance the precise techniques which may be most useful for dealing with these problems.

Raymond Miles (1975) suggests that the way to get around this dilemma is for the consultant to educate the members of the client organization to become sophisticated OD consumers. Jointly the consultant and a key group of the clients' managers should explore (a) the nature of the client's problems and (b) the alternate OD methods available to deal with these.[40] The final decision, Miles insists, should be the client's—and the client should feel completely free to pick a different consultant, if after careful analysis, his skills better fit their needs. In any case, OD should move no faster than the client wants it to move, and he should be given numerous "backout points," which will permit him to avoid being carried by the momentum of the process further than he really wants to go.

---

[40] Indeed there may be a need for consultants whose specialty is helping clients pick consultants.

Top Management's Role

To what extent is top management support required? Must top management go through an OD experience before it can be extended to lower levels? Certainly this is what many consultants prefer. With top management setting the example, OD will be more accepted elsewhere in the organization (Schein, 1969:90). Furthermore, it is argued, unless top management changes its policies to make them congruent with OD values, OD participants at lower levels will be unable to practice their newly developed skills on the job and there will be little carry-over.[41]

Bennis suggests (1969:56), however, that under some circumstances OD can start in relatively autonomous groups. (See also Beer and Huse, 1972).[42] Nevertheless, there is the possibility—as one of Bennis's cases illustrates (1966:157–160)—that attempts to bootleg OD into the organization may turn out disastrously once top management finds out that such a "revolution" is occurring (Dalton, 1970:237). Top management involvement is required at least to the extent that any proposed change requires its support.

At the other extreme, there is a real danger that overly enthusiastic top management support will make lower management participation far from truly voluntary. This is one aspect of a more general dilemma: how does one work with the organization as a whole and still allow organizational subunits the freedom to decide whether to cooperate or not? At first at least, OD will not be viewed as equally "owned" by all participants.

How useful is it for top management to use "subtle pressures" to coerce lower management into OD? Arguably, to do so would be "unauthentic" and in violation of OD values. And yet, conceivably, forcing lower management to use Theory Y techniques may be no more "unauthentic" than forcing it to use Theory X. Further, Theory X techniques may be the only ones which some managers will understand.

Each time OD is extended to a new level in the organization, a new problem of entry is created. Ideally, in the entree period there should be free, unrestrained, and honest collaboration among all levels of the organization and between each level and the consultant. But if such "authentic" relations can be obtained before OD starts, why is OD needed at all?

Who Is the Client?

The OD consultant presumably owes an obligation to his client. But once he begins working with a number of organizational levels at once, the question arises who is his client? It is argued that for OD to be successful there must be a felt need for change. But who must feel the need? As Walton and Warwick (1973) point out, these are difficult questions, and they are particularly difficult when conflicting interest groups are involved, such as unions and management (Lewicki and Alderfer, 1973). When top management is the one to hire the con-

---

[41] The training effort was successful in one classic case which involved middle management—so successful that the bulk of these managers quit, upon seeing that top management would not change its ways (Sykes, 1962).

[42] It is also suggested that under some circumstances it is better to work with middle management, since middle management may be more receptive to change and will eventually act its own way when their new ideas can be put into effect. But this seems to assume that OD is concerned with people-training rather than organization-changing.

sultant initially, the consultant is likely to accept top management's definition of the problem. Furthermore, as we shall discuss below, complex ethical problems arise when potentially dangerous information is gathered, for example when a participant publicly admits serious personal weaknesses under the spell of a T-group. The consultant's interventions are bound to affect power relations in the organization. What are his responsibilities here? These questions have received relatively little attention.

Whole or Part?

Most consultants state a preference to work with the organization as a system—with all of its problems and all of its parts. Only in this way, they argue, can true change occur. But does not this place a terribly heavy burden on the consultant? And suppose the client is prepared to face only limited problems?[43]

Of course, the consultant's role can be defined so narrowly that he can accomplish nothing at all. However, it is clear that consultants can function (at least at first) dealing with only part of the system—provided this part is relatively isolated from the rest and free to make changes on its own. There is always the chance that once the consultant has demonstrated his success handling small problems, he will be permitted to handle larger ones. Further, those who have gone through OD can act as a "political pressure group" (Wilson, 1967) for further change. But this may mean that if OD is to spread past the point of entry, its results must become highly visible. OD may well be successful even when it is tried on only part of the organization, provided that the organization is relatively decentralized and its technology and structure are relatively fluid; however, OD's chances of success are somewhat less in highly centralized organizations, particularly when the technology is hard to change. In other words, the chances for OD may be better in "organismic," "open" organizations than those which are "mechanistic" and "closed" (Burns and Stalker, 1961; Argyris, 1970).

Crisis or Slack Period?

When is OD most likely to be introduced, when the organization is going through crisis, or when it enjoys organizational slack and can afford the luxury of re-examining its operations?

It is commonly argued that successful OD is likely to occur only when "the organization, and especially top management, is under considerable external and internal pressure for improvement..." (Griener, 1967a; see also French, 1969). In other words, dissatisfaction (conviction of sin) and recognition of need for change must be high before the organization will unfreeze its present values and behaviors and look for new solutions (Friedlander and Brown, 1974).

Regardless, my guess is that only companies with relatively minor problems are likely to call on the OD consultant (rarely the Lockheeds or Penn Centrals facing bankruptcy). Like psychoanalysis, OD may be the plaything of the wealthy; and like other luxuries, the OD business is highly dependent on the business cycle.

---

[43] Hornstein, Brunker, and Hornstein (1971) call this the "critical mass problem."

Though there is some interest in short-run "crisis intervention" (Goodstein and Boyer, 1972), there is also growing recognition that effective OD requires at least several years (Friedlander and Brown, 1974; Miles, 1974).

Setting Developmental Objectives

Probably the most important entree issue relates to goal setting: what kinds of problems is OD in the particular case designed to solve? By and large, managers who enter OD give too little thought as to its goals. Yet to a large extent, OD's success may depend on how well its goals are integrated into its process.

Just as product development may be viewed as a planned program of bringing in new products and management development as a planned program of developing managers, so organizational development should be looked upon as a planned program of organizational change (Miles, 1975). It rarely is. On the contrary, clients often buy OD as a "good" thing without much thought given to what precisely it is expected to accomplish or whether its goals are appropriate to organizational needs. Too often consultants will prescribe the same form of OD to every organization without regard to its particular needs.

Company A, a well-known consumer of OD services, has a large number of geographically separated operating units, each of which operates independently of the others, without any significant workflow or interdependence between units. Unit managers are controlled by a set of tight rules laid down by corporate headquarters and performance is measured by a series of statistics. Both technology and environment are reasonably stable. As a consequence, relatively little interaction is required between unit managers or between top management and unit managers. Why does this company engage in OD? To a considerable extent because one top manager is vitally interested in OD. And limited interviews (three to be exact) suggest OD objectives (and even procedures) here are almost exactly the same as in TRW (Davis, 1967), a firm with many highly interdependent functions existing in a turbulent environment.

I make no claim that the needs of company A have been misunderstood. But I do suggest that OD objectives deserve careful scrutiny.

WRONG OBJECTIVES

Does OD teach the wrong lessons? Critics argue that it (1) fosters soft, indecisive management, (2) stresses attitudinal over structural changes, (3) ignores power and assumes conflict to be a matter of misunderstanding, and (4) to the extent it deals with structure at all, opts for Theory Y, "organic" systems, even under circumstances where a more "mechanistic" bureaucratic approach might be appropriate.

Evaluation of these criticisms is difficult because there is little agreement among OD writers and practitioners. Some are concerned entirely with attitudes and interpersonal relations and so ignore structure (and even organizational efficiency) altogether.[44] Others look upon OD as a form of psychotherapy designed to help organizations confront problems in a more realistic manner with-

---

[44] There are some ex-T-group trainers who have shifted over into what they call OD without changing either their techniques or their values very much (Walton and Warwick, 1973).

out suggesting what the solutions should be.[45] Still others acknowledge that OD must face structural questions eventually, but insist that proper attitudes—"a climate of problem-solving rather than politics or buckpassing"—are required before managers can make realistic decisions of any sort. Only a limited number of OD writers (Bennis, 1966, for example) have written about structure at any length, and, in general, these are advocates of fluid, organic, Theory Y oriented systems. Among those who call themselves OD people, Lawrence and Lorsch (1969) stand out for their advocacy of an approach which takes into account differences in technology and environment.

With this caveat about the absence of any single, well defined OD position regarding structure, let me consider the criticisms in turn. As I see it, OD's sins are largely those of emphasis: excessive weight is given to attitudinal, interpersonal, and Theory Y oriented solutions to problems when these may constitute only part of the answer. As a consequence, OD often might be more appropriately entitled *people* rather than organization development. The first possible "wrong objective" relates to style of management.

Soft, Indecisive Management

Davis (1967:16) suggests that OD's objective should be to "develop an on-the-job culture within which we can relate to each other interpersonally just as we do in a T-group." Is this desirable? Or does OD make the manager so trusting, loving, so sensitive to the feelings of others, that he is incapable of acting decisively or of standing up for himself in real-life combat? Certainly there is a danger that people who have been exposed to T-groups may overvalue catharsis and consensus and undervalue definite roles and responsibilities. I have observed committees consisting of T-group trained people who seemed to talk for talk's sake, luxuriate in the expression of feelings, and so avoid making hard decisions.[46] But, whether this occurred *because* of their training is far from clear. Firm evidence in this area is limited and anecdotal evidence here is highly suspect. Every observer has stories to prove his point.

A questionnaire addressed to managers who had participated at sensitivity training at Dow Chemical (Anderson, 1971) indicates that at least 88 percent felt that such training led to increased understanding; on the other hand, less than 22 percent felt it contributed to "developing dynamic management with decision-making in depth." Harrison (1972) and Bass (1967:218) both agree that deeper forms of OD develop strong in-group loyalty, but fail to train participants to get along with other groups. Harrison also argues that managers have to learn how to bargain, even if this results in win-lose behavior. And Bass (1967) suggests that T-groups emphasize freedom (even anarchy) rather than responsibility or mutual predictability. He concludes that such groups may make more mature individuals, but less effective organizations. Miner (1965) implies that the effective manager behaves in a manner completely inconsistent with OD principles. He should "behave in accordance with what might be called

---

[45] Schein (1969:120) describes the process consultant as an "expert on how to help the organization learn, not on the actual management problems which the organization is trying to solve."

[46] There is a danger, in other words, of *overcarryover*. The ex-OD member may continue to behave on the job as he did in the last euphoric days of his laboratory group. Argyris argues that this is a sign of an inadequately designed OD program (1971:86–87).

the masculine role ... should impose their wishes on and direct their subordinates ... [and] should have a desire to compete and exercise power over people."

As Bunker (1967:230) puts it, the question is whether the unfreezing process is so severe as to destroy "one's confidence in authority structure and one's capacity to respond appropriately to organizational needs." Questions have been raised particularly about the value of complete openness under every circumstance. "As every husband [wife] and every therapist knows, in many circumstances it may well be better to suppress one's feelings in order to facilitate joint group accomplishment" (Levinson, 1967: 232).

OD supporters reject these arguments. They insist that OD is designed to help managers face problems, not run away from them. Maslow (1965:186; see also Bunker, 1967) suggests that since T-group training teaches people to behave more openly, with less defensiveness, it also teaches them not to fear to act in a forceful fashion if the situation requires. Davis (1967:4) rejects the "soft, mushy 'sweetness and light' impressions that some people feel are implicit in sensitivity training." Instead he feels OD values:

> ... have within them a very real toughness: In dealing with one another, we will be open, direct, explicit. Our feelings will be available to one another, and we will problem-solve rather than be defensive.

Argyris (1971) stresses that the dichotomy between soft and hard management is false. *Good* OD makes better managers, not softer.[47] He argues further (1967a:162) that "the laboratory approach does not value all openness. It values openness which helps the individuals involved to learn." Openness, he insists, is a relationship of trust between people which permits them to understand each other; it is neither "diplomacy" which hides problems nor irresponsible "honesty" which requires individuals to express their feelings without regard to their impacts on others (1971:18, 42).

According to Schein (1969) OD training is essentially training in how to make decisions effectively, and the OD-based decisions are tougher minded and take into account a wider range of human and nonhuman considerations than do those made by "interpersonally incompetent" people who have not had such experience. Above all, OD helps open communications channels and helps the organization recognize that there is a process aspect of all work.

> Acceptance or rejection of company data transmitted between people often depends upon the acceptance or rejection of each other as people, and how the people support, trust, and like each other. ... To get more facts flowing in a company people's feelings must be given full reign (Kuriloff and Atkins, 1966:68–69).

Thus, by eliminating "mutually reinforced blindness" (Argyris, 1971:33) and by providing a broader range of information, OD helps managers make better decisions. They become less decisive only in the sense that they now recognize the complex implications of seemingly simple problems.

Actually most of the criticisms are directed to deeper forms of intervention such as T-groups. Perhaps the real question is whether participants in OD can

---

[47] But those who have gone through *bad* OD learn only that directive management is unsuccessful, so withdraw rather than help others be active (Argyris, 1971:123–124).

pass through the stage of concern with purely interpersonal relations to the stage of realistic examination of organizational problems. Davis (1967) argues that such an examination will be "tough"—but what sorts of answers will emerge? Will structural questions receive insufficient emphasis? Will the one kind of structure be preferred over others even when not appropriate? Will questions of power be ignored? Let us consider these other possible "wrong objectives."

Attitude vs. Structure

Which comes first, changes in attitude (including values) or structure? By structure I mean reporting relationships, job descriptions, formal responsibilities (sometimes called prescribed roles, Brown, 1960), promotion and compensation schemes, work flow, and the like.

The alternate approaches have been called, by their opponents, "conversionist" (Chapple and Sayles, 1961) and "engineering" (Bennis, 1966). I will list the issues in the form of a debate, first, and then state my own views.[48]

For attitude change. The main argument here is that attitudinal or value changes are preconditions for either behavioral or structural change. Tannenbaum and Davis (1967) put it nicely, "Structure, function, and charters are not irrelevant, but ... they are less important and typically have less leverage in the early days of organizational development than does working with individuals and groups in a therapeutic manner."

OD not only helps managers make better decisions, but it makes decisions easier to implement. Certainly one of the lessons of early human relations is that change will be resisted if it is introduced by autocratic methods. To change behavior—whether dietary patterns, work routines, or the employment of older people—attitude changes are required and these are best induced by unfreezing (Coch and French, 1948; Lewin, 1947; Marrow and French, 1945). This holds just as true, so the argument runs, for the introduction of computers, decentralization, and new product lines. Without employee support, management cannot even get the information necessary to decide what structural changes are appropriate.

Changes in *managerial* skills will be especially resisted if just imposed from the top. "The development of skills without appropriate changes in values becomes, at best, an alternation whose lack of depth will easily become evident to others. Skills follow values; values rarely follow skills" (Argyris, 1962:135). The argument would seem to hold especially true if the proposed changes are Theory Y-oriented. Top management may be able to obtain tighter supervision at lower levels merely by engaging in tighter supervision itself. But to obtain more general, more participative supervision or to make matrix organization work may be impossible as long as managers are "interpersonally incompetent" or Theory X-oriented. Job enrichment or MBO programs, for example, are likely to fail unless the line managers are emotionally in tune with these programs' objectives. Argyris concludes "there is, to put it simply, very little empirically supported knowledge about how to change organizational structures

---

[48] It should be noted that this question of attitude vs. structure is closely related to the issue of depth of intervention, which has been discussed previously. For some it is also an ethical question: Is the consultant's primary obligation to the organization or to people?

or administrative controls" (1971:169). As a consequence, it is better to start by attitudinal change, a process about which presumably more is known.

Finally, OD supporters point out that their approach in fact does lead to structural change, for example, the introduction of the Scanlon Plan (Bennis, 1969:10), a reduction in the number of organizational levels (Beckhard, 1969:72), establishment of task force teams (Rush, 1969:120), better control of meeting agendas and clearer distinction between policy and operational details (Schein, 1969:180), and the like.

For structural change.   Structuralists charge that OD approaches the problem of change from the most difficult end, the human personality, when changes in structure (as broadly defined) can achieve results more economically and with less pain. "Conversion, or the achievement of 'insight' or 'understanding' by itself is not enough. . . . To obtain lasting change one does not try to change people, but rather to change the organizational constraints which operate on them" (Chapple and Sayles, 1961:201–202). Certainly it can be argued that to date, unions and computers, to take two examples, have had a far more important impact on organizational human relations than has OD.

The first point made is that structures are easier to change than values, particularly deep-seated values rooted in personality. *Lasting* value changes are extraordinarily hard to induce, particularly when they are not supported by preceding or simultaneous changes in structure. Attitude changes will persist only if the organization as a whole is changed—or at least the portion relevant to the individual in question (Whyte and Hamilton, 1964). Because of the difficulty in making attitudinal OD a self-perpetuating process, managers need constant retraining to keep up their enthusiasm; furthermore, new managers must be retrained from scratch. The trust painfully built up in one attitude-changing effort may be easily shattered by a change in management.

By contrast, structural change can change attitudes quite quickly and relatively permanently (Kahn, 1974). Certainly structural change (for example, in reward systems) can have a rapid *negative* impact: it can alter behavior (cause strikes), attitudes (lower morale), and perhaps even values (make people more distrustful and cynical). But fairly routine, structural changes, such as in job description,[49] work flow, payment systems, or reporting relations can also alter behavior and attitudes (if not values) in a positive direction, provided these changes are carefully thought out (with due consideration to presently existing attitudes) and introduced in an appropriate manner (management does not require OD to negotiate with a union or set up a system of consultation).

Those who put attitude change first tried to make the individual their unit of analysis. Structuralists would put the organizations first.

Treatment of friction.   The difference between the two viewpoints is illustrated by their treatment of interpersonal friction. The structuralist approach is to eliminate external causes of friction.

If Supervisor A has a tantrum whenever situation X occurs, his job can be changed so that the behavior that is difficult for him is not required.

---

[49] Some companies enlisted in the very popular job enrichment movement use straight Theory X techniques to impose "enriched" jobs on bottom level employees whether they like it or not!

It is unlikely that he will ever learn to tolerate situation X (Chapple and Sayles, 1961:191).[50]

To take a classic example, Whyte resolved frictions between waitresses and countermen in a restaurant by introducing a spindle to hold the waitresses' orders, thus reducing communications between the parties (Whyte, 1948).

OD people, on the other hand, stress the importance of helping the parties understand each other. Their starting point in Whyte's restaurant case would undoubtedly be some form of confrontation. Communications would be improved; after appropriate discussion the parties might eventually decide to adopt the spindle on their own.[51]

A balanced view. Upon reflection it seems clear that both views above overstate the case. Our everyday experience teaches us that changes in structure —the pressures under which we work, the tasks we are given, the rewards and punishments we receive—all lead to changes in attitudes and behavior (Colombolos, 1969), and even to neuroses and psychoses. Whether attitude changes can be induced without changes in structure and whether these attitudinal changes will persist and will lead to behavior changes may be more in doubt.[52] However, Miner (1965) has demonstrated that even short classes, using Theory X techniques to introduce Theory X attitudes, seem to succeed in creating long-range behavioral effects.[53]

I think it reasonably clear that attitudes, behavior, and structure are systems-related and changes in any one will lead to changes in the other two.[54] However, behavioral change is more likely to be achieved easily and be in a desirable direction if (a) attitudes and structures are changed simultaneously and in a consistent manner, or (b) either is changed alone, but in such a manner as to reduce previous inconsistency between the two.

Matter of overemphasis. The legitimate criticism of OD is not that it is ineffective but that it is one-sided. By and large, OD people seem to feel that

---

[50] Fiedler (1967) likewise argues that it is easier to change the nature of work or to select people with the right personalities than to engage in elaborate training.

[51] Structuralists might argue that this is a fairly involved way to solve a simple problem. Suppose that confrontation led to a massive blowup? Or suppose the group members never got around to thinking about a spindle? OD men, for their part, might ask how might the parties react to a spindle, if introduced in a Theory X fashion? Or suppose there were problems of which Whyte was unaware, problems which might require solutions other than the spindle?

[52] "Whether attitude change implies behavioral change is still a moot point, even when the total spectrum of attitude literature is considered.... There is virtually no empirical research linking attitudes and behavior, no matter what the content area" (Campbell and others, 1970:265; see also Ehrich 1969). Doubt has also been expressed as to whether attitude change can persist without concomitant changes in behavior (Wolhking, 1971).

[53] McClelland (1965) has apparently achieved the same results, but Wolhking (personal communication) points out that the efforts of both McClelland and Miner are consistent with predominant organizational values and reward systems. Theory Y oriented changes may be more difficult.

[54] Argyris (1971:167) concludes that either structural or interpersonal change should receive first emphasis, depending on the "set of conditions," with structural perhaps being more effective at lower levels in the organization and interpersonal higher up. Beer and Huse (1972) suggest it is best to start with structural changes in the actual situation.

attitudes are more important than structure and that most organizational problems are caused by distortions and misunderstandings. Of course, many writers acknowledge (tip their hat to?) the importance of structure; nevertheless, structure (and even behavior) still gets less attention in the literature (and perhaps in practice)[55] than do attitudes and values, though this is changing, as I discuss below.

Equally important, the analysis of behavior is largely in terms of face-to-face relations. The ideal organization is looked upon as an interlocking chain of smoothly functioning face-to-face groups. Yet I would argue that more than knowledge of the principles of small group effectiveness is required to make a complex organization work; it is not enough to look at individuals or in groups.

The heavy emphasis placed on nonstructural factors by some forms of OD may well lead its converts to believe structural changes unnecessary. To be sure, OD may soften managers up so that they can face structural problems more realistically. But if the only skills they have learned are interpersonal, attitude-oriented ones, they are unlikely to think in structural terms. Unless the consultant is prepared to offer a structural analysis of structure problems, why should his client? To put it another way, OD members may learn largely through modeling, yet the OD leader may provide a very anti-structurally oriented model (Bass, 1967:218).

My argument, in a nut shell, is that overemphasis on attitudinal and small group variables prevents most OD from being the systems approach it claims to be. Nevertheless, there are reasons for believing that the situation is rapidly changing.

1. Recognizing that face-to-face relations do not alone determine organizational effectiveness, some OD people have begun to stress "organizational climate." This is again an attitudinal variable, but it relates to the organization as a whole. Survey Feedback measures organizational climate and easily serves as a vehicle to consider organization-wide problems.

2. There has been an increasing interest in the development of forms of organizational structure in which people can operate more effectively. Friedlander and Brown's (1974) review of the literature looks at both "human processual" and "techno-structural approaches" to OD and lists under the latter heading both job enrichment and changes in technology. Other consultants have begun to consider the impact of personnel policies upon organizational behavior, especially those policies which affect reward and career systems. And in diagnosing organizational problems they are asking whether the informal and formal systems are consistent with each other.

3. The work of Lawrence and Lorsch (1967) has had a considerable impact on OD. A number of OD practitioners have begun to work with executives to help them analyze their organizations in terms of the Lawrence-Lorsch framework, with particular emphasis, for example, on how the integration function is performed. (See also Argyris, 1971:77.)

---

[55] Blake's Grid, for example, is supposed to make managers more decisive and to give equal attention to people and production. But the practice, at least in early stages, is to give greater emphasis to people (Dalton, Lawrence, and Griener, 1970:82–103).

And Lawrence and Lorsch themselves have written a book (1969) included in the well-known Addison-Wesley OD series.[56]

4. OD people have been showing increasing interest in another approach to organizational change which has roughly the same intellectual roots as T-groups—but is almost painfully structurally oriented—the work of those associated with the Tavistock Institute. Sofer, for example, makes it explicit that he is concerned with roles, not the improvement of relations (1962:103), with "questions of structure, rules, and relationships rather than on individual personality or individual competence" (p. 85). To be sure, Tavistock consultants do make comments on motives and resistance to change and in the process managers become psychologically more sophisticated, but these consultants see as the solution to organizational difficulties not greater ability to express feelings or face problems, but changes in job duties and work flow (Rice, 1963; Trist and others, 1963), selection and promotion systems (Sofer, 1962), compensation schemes (Jaques, 1961), and reporting and authority relationships and statements of responsibility (Sofer, 1962; Brown, 1960; Jaques, 1951). In Schein's terms, they are "expert" rather than process consultants.

5. Perhaps the most elaborately documented OD effort in the U.S. occurred at Weldon (Marrow, Bowers, and Seashore, 1967). Here, in an effort to straighten out a badly run organization, a host of human relations-OD and standard managerial-structural techniques were employed, ranging from group problem-solving and managerial T-groups through worker skill-training and the "weeding out" (discharging) of low earners. Given this attention, operator productivity rose 30%.

6. Contingency theory is receiving some recognition. French and Bell (1973) discuss it in their text, though they offer no suggestions as to the form of OD appropriate for those situations where the technology calls for a mechanistic approach. Harrison (1972b) says that there are some, but only some, "parts of organizations where it is both good for the individual *and* good for the organization for people to be independent and creative, self-directed. For the future, I want to work with those parts [which] are closely in harmony with my own goals" (Tichy, 1973:705–706). Hopefully other consultants will become equally realistic as to the relationship between their personal interests and organizational needs.

7. There have been several recent cases reported in which "orthodox" OD consultants began their intervention with a structural change: in one instance (Luke and others, 1973) it involved a shift from a functional to a product organization in a grocery chain, while in Beer and Huse (1972) the first intervention was to introduce job enrichment. The

---

[56] Note that the Lawrence and Lorsch approach is highly structural. Among their "change *methods*" are "new paper coordination methods, budgets, schedules, new official channels of communications, intensive educational programs, new divisions of labor and authority structure ... new selection criteria, replacement of incumbents" and these are used to obtain "change *targets*" such as different "interaction patterns ... role expectations ... orientations and values ... basic motives (achievement, power, affiliation, etc)" (1969:87, emphasis added). Thus, "replacement of incumbents" is a method used to obtain different "basic motives," changes in structure are used to obtain changes in attitude. Contrast this with mainstream OD!

process of introducing job enrichment or flex-time may provide a springboard for the re-examination of superior-subordinate relationships and thus, over time, may create a disequilibrium which leads to a re-evaluation of the relationships between these superiors and *their* bosses. Hackman (personal communication) reports a situation where job enrichment highlighted the existence of two unnecessary levels of hierarchy.

8. Finally, Tushman (1974:71-77) offers an interesting contingency approach. He concludes that effective organizational change requires both behavioral" (i.e., attitudinal) and structural change. Neither will do the job alone. But he suggests that, when organizations perform unpredictable, uncertain tasks, "behavioral" change should come first, followed by structural change. The reverse should occur when the organization performs predictable tasks. He argues that predictable tasks are usually accompanied by high centralization of decision-making and restricted availability of information. In such "mechanistic" (Burns and Stalker, 1961) environments subordinates are unlikely to have the information or the authority to make decisions, thus OD may merely create a desire for change which the OD participants themselves are unable to introduce. I would carry Tushman's analysis one step further. The stable bureaucracy which accompanies predictable tasks may be unconvinced of the need for change. Structural intervention may be required to shake them up and to provide the kind of "conviction of sin" which makes further OD possible.

Power and Conflict Ignored

Overemphasis on attitudes in some OD has been tied in with under-concern for power and conflict. Bennis (1969) laments the fact that OD "systematically avoids the problems of power, or the politics of change." As a consequence, the OD practitioner has no "model to guide his practice under conditions of distrust, violence, and conflict. Essentially this means that in a pluralistic power situation, in situations not easily controlled, Organizational Development may not reach its desired goals. . . . [It has] not met with success in diffuse power situations such as cities, large-scale national organizations, or the urban ghetto."

At least some versions of OD seem to assume that once the parties are imbued with sufficient trust and authenticity, they will renounce power advantages, and further, perhaps, this weapon of trust and authenticity will work even with those who don't accept these values.

Handling conflict. The handling of conflict may illustrate this problem. From reading the OD literature, one gets the view that much conflict is unnecessary and due primarily to immature, nonauthentic interpersonal relations. (It should be emphasized that OD theorists do not ignore conflict. As mentioned earlier, they argue that OD can bring conflicts out into the open and equip managers with the skills necessary to channel them in constructive directions.)

The common OD view is that if the parties approach conflict in terms of "problem-solving" rather than "win-lose," most problems turn out not to require zero-sum solutions (in which one party can gain only at the direct expense of the other). Further, OD people claim that approaching a problem as if it were a zero-sum-game involves a self-fulfilling prophesy: if the parties anticipate that a problem can be resolved only in a win-lose fashion, then hostilities will be engendered, constructive solutions ignored, and the parties will think in terms of gains and concessions rather than in terms of mutual interests.[57] Properly approached (with trust and authenticity) most problems yield to win-win solutions in which everyone gains.

Understandably, then, OD people tend to reject the use of power and of bargaining in interpersonal relations, characterizing them as "coercive" tactics which tend to polarize people into hostile, opposing camps. Unions are largely ignored and traditional collective bargaining is looked upon as a series of rituals which tend to magnify conflict.[58]

My own view is that many problems can be more easily solved if the parties understand each other better.[59] But it is too easy to fall into the trap that all problems are perceptual and can be solved through better understanding.[60] Certain early human relationists seemed to feel that industrial grievances could largely be eliminated by nondirective listening, just as there are those today who push marathon encounter groups as a means of eliminating racial discrimination. Black activists look with rightful scorn on social workers who seek to solve the problems of poverty through counseling. Confrontation helps bring out feelings, but there is a danger that the very intensity of the catharsis process may lull people into thinking that they are actively attacking the root core of their problems.

Recent developments. Fortunately for OD, recent years have seen a growing interest in power issues (see especially, Walton and Warwick's excellent article, "The Ethics of Organization Development," 1973). Walton (1969), for example, has dealt at length with the role of third-party interventionists in diffusing conflict. An entire issue of the *Journal of Applied Behavioral Sciences* (Chesler and Worden, 1974) has been devoted to "Power and Social Change" (unsuccessfully, in my opinion, because none of the articles really deals with the question of how power conflicts are to be resolved). Other articles (e.g., Berlow and Le Clere, 1974; Torczyner, 1972) suggest that the OD consultant cannot work with all groups with equal intensity; some groups will be more

---

[57] "Win-lose" is, of course, the main approach to our judicial system. Here truth is sought not by "problem-solving" but by the sharp and even exaggerated delineation of issues by opposing advocates.

[58] Blake, Shepard, and Mouton (1964) are among the few to deal with unions. They prescribe an intergroup training laboratory as a means of handling with union-management problems. Their "orientation is based on recognizing union and management disputes as symptoms of pathology in the problem-solving area, diagnosing the causes that produce the symptoms, and treating the causes directly" (p. 144). In context it is clear that the authors view the "causes" as interpersonal rather than economic. In other words, economic differences are caused by poor interpersonal relations, rather than the reverse. Lewicki and Alderfer (1973) were unsuccessful in an attempt to intervene in a labor-management dispute, largely because the union looked upon them as a management agent.

[59] Though I agree with many labor mediators that full disclosure at the beginning of a collective bargaining session may make final agreement more difficult (Garfield and Whyte, 1950; Walton and McKersie, 1965).

[60] It is also difficult to take protagonists out of their culture and presume that OD can induce lasting changes in behavior. Walton (1970) failed in his effort to resolve the Somalia-Ethiopian dispute in this manner. And I suspect OD attempts to resolve major labor-management disputes would be equally unsuccessful, for the closer the leaders of the two sides come to understanding each other, the greater the chance they will become alienated from their followers (Strauss and Rosenstein, 1970).

likely to support OD change objectives than others, and the OD consultant must pick his allies.

Theory Y Objectives

By and large OD's values are closely linked with those of McGregor's Theory Y and Likert's System 4: a belief that employees should enjoy high levels of participation and mutual influence (especially in goal setting), a stress on intrinsic rather than extrinsic forms of motivation, general rather than close forms of supervision, a de-emphasis of rigid rules, and the like. In general, these values add up to what Burns and Stalker (1961) call an organic system. Certainly many OD people argue for "temporary systems," what has been called the "adhocracy." Griener (1967b) suggests that OD's whole trust is to reduce power differentials and base decisions on information rather than on organizational roles. As he sees it, one of OD's major purposes is to demonstrate that there are means of motivating other than power.

The *universal* validity of Theory Y objectives has been questioned on a variety of grounds (Strauss, 1963, 1968, 1970), e.g., that Theory Y is inappropriate for a broad range of personalities, cultures, and technologies, and that in many circumstances the cost of redesigning an organization to make it consistent with Theory Y values (for example, abolishing the assembly line) may outweigh the gains in terms of increased motivation and organizational flexibility. Here let me deal with only one issue, technology.

A number of writers (Perrow, 1967; Lawrence and Lorsch, 1967; among others) argue that the appropriate structure varies with the work being done. Organic systems are best where the environment is uncertain and turbulent; more bureaucratic and mechanistic systems may be preferable where the environment is certain and stable. Arguably, then OD values and OD training will be more appropriate in the first case than the second (Sims, 1970).[61]

Some OD supporters seem to reject this view. They argue that in the future the environment will be, or at least should be, increasingly turbulent, thereby making mechanistic organization more and more anachronistic. Bennis (1966) argues that "Democracy [organic organization] is inevitable" because we are entering a "temporary society" of increasing technological change in which all relations will be turbulent. Argyris suggests (1971:20) that routine is not necessarily organizationally desirable; instead organizations should introduce "turbulence at least within the system," otherwise they will suffer from dry rot and be unable to react effectively to the stresses which will inevitably hit them; in other words, they should voluntarily engage in change now in order to avoid being "surprised by the environmental change" which will occur later on.[62] Since people function best in crisis, perhaps we should make crisis routine.

---

[61] Harrison (1970:191) argues that the less programmed the job, the deeper intervention (i.e., the greater the concern with people rather than procedures) should be. Perhaps with tongue in cheek, Pugh (1965) suggests the possibility that in a fluid, organic situation "only an immature, job-centered bastard can insensitively hack his way to achievement," while greater sensitivity may be required to add a human element to the rigidities required when the organization is mechanistic.

[62] Thompson (1969) states that OD tries to introduce what he calls "slack ... a lax, indulgent decision-making situation" which Thompson feels is essential to creativity. Note that this conflicts with another Theory Y concept, that organizations function best with "optimum undermanning."

Personally, I think both Bennis and Argyris overstate their position, though space prevents me from presenting my views in detail.

1. Whether work in the future will be more or less programmed is still open to considerable debate (and the evidence so far is mixed). Certainly it has been argued that in an age of automation both white and blue collar work will become more routine, while the computer will reduce the autonomy of all but the highest level of management (Leavitt and Whisler, 1958). In any case, new technologies rapidly become routine.

2. The strong case can be made that a major objective of organizations and indeed of human effort generally is to make routine, or at least predictable, what was previously turbulent and unpredictable. There are enormous advantages to both organizations and individuals in being able to know in advance how people and equipment will behave. Even OD is designed to increase the participants' ability to understand and control each other's behavior. Though high structure may reduce creativity, excessively little structure may induce anxiety. The scientific managers of the Taylor School may have been incorrect in suggesting that mechanistic organization is appropriate in all technologies—but the reverse is equally true.

3. What many organizations need—particularly small but growing ones—is more bureaucracy, more structure rather than less. These organizations are too informal, too open. They need written rules and standard operating procedures, better defined rules and more closely prescribed channels of communications. Not everyone in the organization can serve as a linking pin with everyone else.

The Banner Company (one of our few documented OD cases) was perhaps typical of many small companies which suffered from too little structure. Seashore and Bowers (1963:53–54) describe some of the problems involved in instituting OD here:

> Trial attempts at enlargement of involvement in decision-making were frustrated by uncertainty about respective areas of responsibility.... The problem was not one of conflict between formal and informal organization, but rather one of lack of stable organization of any kind.... Before the consequences of group-sustaining supervisory practices can be discerned, it is probably necessary to create a reasonably stable system of groups.... [Without this] it cannot be expected that more interaction will necessarily aid the decision-making process. It may add to the confusion.

Lawrence and Lorsch (1969:33–34) suggests that even in large firms greater interaction is sometimes harmful. They describe an electronics firm where there was "a heavy emphasis on participative management, with an extensive use of product teams for decision purposes. There was also careful planning of physical arrangements so as to facilitate interactions between groups." The nontechnical people liked this arrangement. The technical ones objected to all this enforced interaction as a violation of their freedom to do research work on their own. It was "concluded that the heavy emphasis being placed on securing integration through the use of group methods had not allowed the technical people enough of an opportunity to differentiate their role and orientation." A new set-up was devised which permitted greater isolation for technical people with an "integrator" to provide coordination with the rest of the organization.

OD supporters argue that since OD helps managers make more realistic decisions, it will also help them choose more realistically between mechanistic and open systems. But I am concerned that just as excessive emphasis on attitudes may lead to structural considerations being underplayed, so excessive emphasis on open systems may do management a disservice in cases where greater structure is required. Indeed, the manager who opts for the mechanistic approach would seem to be rejecting the thrust of OD teaching. And some forms of OD, I am afraid, teach no structure.

To conclude this section, OD authors differ among themselves, making criticism difficult, and OD practice corresponds only partly with the literature. OD need not make managers less decisive; it need not stress attitude over structure; it need not play down power and conflict; it need not prescribe an organic solution to every problem. It need not—but I suspect that very often it does. Despite recent articles suggesting some recognition of these problems, the OD literature as a whole still places people over organizations and fosters a hangloose attitude toward organizational functioning even when this is not appropriate.

If, as I suggest below, OD should be viewed as a *process* by which organizations learn to improve their abilities to make better choices, then the OD consultant may defeat his own purposes by influencing the nature of the choices themselves.

RESEARCH ON T-GROUP AND OD EFFECTIVENESS

So far there has been little mention of hard research findings regarding the effectiveness of OD under various conditions. The reason for this is that there is little such research available. There are many OD consultants who are strongly research oriented. However, research on OD is enormously difficult (Friedlander and Brown, 1974).

Research on T-groups

There has been considerably more research on T-groups than on broader forms of OD; indeed the effectiveness of T-groups has been probably subject to more research than any other alternative form of management training or social intervention.[63] But even research on T-groups is far from easy. At least three problems are involved.

The criterion problem. How is T-group effectiveness to be measured? Participant reports that they "found it very worthwhile" provide little help. Attitudinal questionnaires given before and after training may indicate only that the participant has learned to give the right answer, not that his behavior has changed. (In fact, with increased self-awareness participants may become

---

[63] Among the more significant discussions of the research literature are two surveys by Buchanan (1965 and 1969), House (1967), Campbell and Dunnette (1968), Campbell and others (1970), and Cooper and Mangham (1971).

more critical of their own deficiencies and so their self-ratings may go down.) Even observed behavior in a group may not continue on the job.

Change on the job is more relevant but also more difficult to measure. Self-reports, though used in some studies, are naturally subject to bias and a variety of more sophisticated techniques have been designed. A trainee's performance can be evaluated by his supervisor, by subordinates, or by fellow managers, and this evaluation may be made just before training, after training, and well after training (the last to see whether changes have persisted). Unfortunately, the fact that evaluators know that the trainees have gone through training may influence their judgments.

Usually such studies measure whether the trainee's behavior in dealing with people has changed. But to many members of management the crucial test is whether training increases efficiency and profits.[64] In practice it is extremely difficult to isolate the impact of training on organizational effectiveness, because so many other factors may be responsible, such as changes in technology or market conditions. Ideally, one should take a number of identical groups doing the same work under identical conditions and then train the managers of some of these groups and leave the others as controls. Yet in real organizations (as opposed to those created in the research lab) it is difficult to find groups that will remain identical (except for the characteristics being sudtied) throughout the research.

The Hawthorne effect.   Just as it is uncertain whether training leads to change, it is also uncertain whether observed change may be due to training rather than something else. The very act of answering questions or of being sent to any kind of training activity may change reported attitudes or even behavior. (Belasco and Trice, 1969, report one study in which the administration of a questionnaire produced greater change than did the conventional training program whose impact these questions were designed to measure.) Before and after testing normally involves taking the same test twice, and the resulting changes may be due merely to greater experience in test-taking. Finally, it is far from clear from most studies whether the changes presumably produced by T-groups might have been produced just as effectively (and less painfully) had the group spent *equal time* in some other form of training, or even on a group fishing trip enjoying the unfreezing effects of alcohol—just so long as interpersonal difficulties are discussed in a context removed from work.

Ideally, such problems might be resolved by the appropriate use of control groups, but developing such groups involves a host of difficult problems (Argyris, 1968b).[65]

Theory X techniques.   Another problem, suggested by Argyris (1968b) is that overemphasis on scientific rigor in research design may paradoxically lead to less rigorous results. He argues that conventional "mechanistic" research tech-

---

[64] Evaluation will be still more difficult if our criterion is not short-term profits and productivity but long-term measures such as organizational innovativeness and adaptability.

[65] In the absence of appropriate control groups, Campbell and others (1970) suggest the use of criterion measures taken before, during, and after training ("time series experiments"). A marked change in the trend of the data which occurs only during training may indicate that the training has had some impact.

niques treat subjects as if they were workers on the assembly line, giving them no opportunity to participate in evaluating evaluation procedures. The impact of being manipulated in this fashion may be to create hostility which can in turn interfere with the training process and also make the data obtained from research less valid.[66]

Evidence relating T-groups.   Given the problems listed above, research findings in this area must be viewed as highly tentative. Nevertheless, one must agree with Campbell and Dunnette's cautious conclusion that the evidence, "though limited, is reasonably convincing that T-group training does induce behavioral changes in the back home setting" (1968:97). Even though it is reasonably clear that there is lasting change for *some* people under *some* conditions, we have little evidence as to what sorts of people change most easily, the environmental conditions which are most conducive to change, or the direction in which change occurs. Clearly not everyone changes in the same way nor are all changes favorable in terms of organizational needs. Campbell and others (1970:295) conclude "about 30% or 40% of the trained individuals were reported as exhibiting some perceptible change." Limited studies (Buchanan, 1969) suggest that the people who change most on the job are those who (1) prior to training have already been described as open to new ideas and have highest levels of interpersonal trust (Friedlander, 1970); (2) participate most and change most in the T-group; and (3) have greater opportunity (power) to introduce changes on the job.

Research on OD

Research on OD involves all the problems faced by T-group research (controls, measurement of impact, etc.) plus others (for an excellent review see Friedlander and Brown, 1974). In the first place, since it is the organization which is being changed, a valid experiment would require two or more organizations which are roughly equal, not only in production processes, structure, and economic situation but which also have managers with identical initial values and personalities.[67] In practice, only the roughest approximations of this ideal have been achieved, with the closest approach being two cases which some might argue do not involve OD at all: (a) the classic Morse and Reimer (1956) experiment, in which two departments were induced to become more "hierarchically controlled" and two to become more "autonomous" and (b) Luke and other's (1973) report involving a primarily structural change in a grocery store. With these exceptions, the studies with which I am familiar provide at most before and after measures within a single organization.[68]

---

[66] For a debate on this issue between Dunnette and Campbell on one side and Argyris on the other, see the October 1968 issue of *Industrial Relations*. In my opinion, Argyris raises some important questions which should not be ignored and generally has the best of the argument. He argues for what he calls "organic" research in which the subjects are fully involved in research design (Argyris, 1970).

[67] The key difference between the organization which invites in an OD consultant and the one which does not may be in the mental set of the executive who invites the consultant in. But the organization with such an executive might have been more successful anyway.

[68] In the Weldon experiment (Marrow, Bowers, and Seashore, 1967), the Harwood plant was used as a control. However, substantial investments at Weldon tend to confound the results.

A second problem is that the OD change agent typically makes use of a range of techniques. Even though it is desirable to compare the relative effectiveness of these techniques, it is difficult to factor out the effects of any particular one. At Weldon (Marrow, Bowers, and Seashore, 1967) an imaginative attempt was made to develop statistics which could distinguish between the impact of the various change methods used. Nevertheless, in the process, a high degree of clinical judgment was required.

A final problem is neither clients nor consultants are likely to encourage publication of "failures"; thus success stories tend to be over-reported. Furthermore, these reports are often written by the very consultants whose success is being analyzed. The mixture of research and consultancy is difficult (Walton and Warwick, 1973). "Researcher/consultants serve two client systems whose requirements and criteria for evaluation are at least superficially incompatible" (Friedlander and Brown, 1974).

Findings regarding OD.   There are at least five studies suggesting that OD increases productivity and a much larger number indicating OD-associated improvements in various morale measures. Whether OD has a more positive effect than more conventional measures is still open to question, however. In the Morse and Reimer experiments, productivity increased in both hierarchical and autonomous divisions, but slightly more in the first than in the second. Similarly, a higher percentage of the productivity increases at Weldon were attributable to conventional managerial techniques (such as job simplification, time study, and "weeding out" of inefficient operators) than could be accounted for by more human relations, OD-oriented techniques. Morale related items improved at both Weldon and in the autonomous divisions, but fell dramatically in the hierarchically controlled.

At the Sigma oil refinery (Blake and others, 1964) a comprehensive OD effort was mounted stressing the Blake Grid. Self-reported managerial values were changed and net profits increased by 166%. A considerable portion of this latter increase was due to new equipment, layoffs, forced retirements, and changes in nonlabor costs. However, there were also substantial increases in productivity which are attributed to OD.

Two other OD efforts which led to measured increases in productivity both began with structural changes. At the Medford plant of Corning Glass (Beer and Huse, 1972), a comprehensive OD program, starting with job enrichment, was associated with substantial cost reductions and greater work flow efficiencies (however, there were no control measures). In the grocery chain (Luke and others, 1973) a shift from a functional to a product form of organization was followed by lower labor costs, this time compared with control groups elsewhere in the organization.

As yet, the hard research provides us with few guidelines as to the circumstances under which OD is most appropriate or as to the relative efficiency of alternative OD techniques. Griener (1967a) and Buchanan (1971) both analyze a series of OD efforts in an effort to explain the differences between successes and failures; for the most part, their studies deal with *how* the successes occurred rather than the preconditions to success. Bowers (1973) compared the impacts over time—as measured by a host of attitudinal measures—of four forms of OD intervention as opposed to two control treatments. In general, he found that Survey Feedback was most successful in changing both attitudes and organizational climate. "Interpersonal process development" (akin to team building) and one control treatment led to positive results when organizational climate was favorable; "task process consultation" (primarily structural change), laboratory training (T-groups), and one control treatment led to zero or negative change.

These studies represent a useful start. Further studies of all sorts are urgently needed: hard studies based on qualitative data and soft ones reporting anecdotal experiences; studies with rigid scientific controls and those involving action research and the close involvement on the part of "subjects"; studies by objective outsiders and those by concerned participants. Above all we need *comparative* studies, those which help us (1) distinguish between conditions which represent likely prospects for successful OD and those which do not, and (2) evaluate the relative value of alternative OD techniques under various conditions.

As Argyris (1971) suggests, OD is itself a form of action research. OD research should help us learn not only about how to change organizations but also more about the very nature of organizations themselves.

SOME RESERVATIONS

In the end, OD is likely to be evaluated in terms of gut reactions rather than by dispassionate research. After all, OD deals with emotions and it engenders emotional reactions. For some, it is almost a religion (Back, 1974). For my part, there are some aspects which bother me. Fortunately, these problems seem less serious in 1974, as I revise this chapter for final publication, than they appeared in 1971, when I wrote my original draft. Further, I am glad to report that the moral dilemmas which concern me are receiving increasing concern from other writers as well (e.g., Walton and Warwick, 1973; Friedlander and Brown, 1974; Miles, 1974).

The hard sell. For my taste OD has more than its share of evangelical hucksterism. As an academician, I am repelled by the cloying emotionalism and unsubstantiated claims which appear in *some* of the literature and much of the advertising. Of course, many OD practitioners are true believers and have little doubt as to the merits of their product. Further practitioners range from professors whose interest in OD is primarily research oriented to full-time consultants who measure OD's success largely in terms of its contributions to their firms' profits.

Which standards of evaluation should be applied here, those of academia or business? The question is suggested in Campbell's review (1971:135–136) of a major OD book:

> The object is to sell [one system of OD]; and for that purpose, the book is quite well done. For other subcultures in the audience, the book may not be quite so satisfying. There are no attempts to explore the pros and cons of the various issues. One gets the impression that [this system] works everytime and is the one best way to achieve the good life. As a persuasive device this is permissible, but as an educational device it is questionable.

Though considerable thought has been given to professional ethics, there are as yet no generally accepted codes of behavior. At present moral conviction combines with economic incentives to make some of the literature sound like a sales pitch.

Along with Walton and Warwick (1973), I am concerned by the tendency of some consultants to substitute salesmanship for diagnosis and to prescribe a single solution (their own) for any situation. "The practitioner who relies heavily on preprogrammed and prepackaged interventions may unwittingly define the problem in ways that meet his own constraints of time and competence" (p. 694). Too often OD is merely traditional training, wrapped up in a new package. "The image of consultant and client jointly defining problems and utilizing a wide range of behavioral science techniques . . . is more honored on the podium than in practice" (Miles, 1974:180).

Is it science?   To read some of the literature, one gets the impression that there is a vast reservoir of behavioral science findings just waiting to be applied and that OD is merely a transmission belt, a means of applying these truths. Even Bennis (1966:81) suggests:

> Planned change [OD] is a method which employs social technology to solve the problems of society. The method encompasses the application of systematic and appropriate knowledge to human affairs. . . . Planned change aims to relate to the basic discipline of the social sciences as engineering does the physical sciences or medicine to the biological disciplines. . . .

I think this overstates the case. OD techniques have been subject to some scientific research. But I think it a bit premature to conclude that OD is truly a scientific method or *the* "science based" approach. And, given the research problems previously discussed, it is downright misleading to suggest that OD's utility has been proved scientifically valid. (Remember how we smile today at the pretentiousness of scientific management.) At times OD is little more than abstract moralization masquerading as scientific theory. Even at best we have a theory of change-agent intervention, not a theory of planned change.

The T-group method was discovered almost by accident. The various OD techniques have been developed largely by trial and error, on the basis of sound clinical intuition rather than the careful scientific validation required, for example, in test development. Nor have the lessons which OD presumably teaches (e.g., the value of "authentic relations") necessarily been scientifically demonstrated.

I think Argyris, Bennis, and Haire are correct in stressing the importance of developing an applied social science. But I think there is a certain amount of jumping-the-gun on the part of those who imply that OD today involves the application of a significant body of behavioral science knowledge in the same way as engineers and doctors apply knowledge in their fields.

To take one example, the Blake Grid may well be the best known OD technique available. There is at least some evidence (Blake and others, 1964) that organizations which have gone through the grid program become more efficient. But I am unaware of any study which uses the grid as a research tool to determine whether 9,9 companies are in fact more efficient. The Ohio State dimensions, "initiating structure" and "consideration," come fairly close to Blake's two dimensions (concern for people and concern for production), yet extensive efforts to find consistent relationships between the two Ohio State variables and organizational efficiency make it clear that this relationship is highly complex (Korman, 1966; House, 1971). Despite our intuitive hunches, we still cannot make the scientific statement that 9,9 is the right direction for companies to go —particularly not under all circumstances.[69]

To date, only a limited body of behavioral science knowledge has accumulated which is useful to business, and OD makes use of only a small proportion of this limited stock. Indeed the manager who relies upon OD as his sole source of such knowledge is somewhat shortchanged.

A fad. To some extent, OD is a fad—at least in the sense that many organizations engage in OD because it is the popular thing to do without careful investigation of its merits. Such companies may well move on to other techniques as soon as the novelty wears off (and there is some evidence that this is occurring already). As of 1974, the reigning fad is transactional analysis (e.g., Luchsinger and Luchsinger, 1974).

American companies are suckers for gimmicks. Managers are too anxious to find short-cut solutions to complicated problems, particularly in the area of human relations. "The search for quick solutions, particularly to people problems, is a way of life in most organizations and is fueled by managers' need to demonstrate accomplishments rapidly in order to move on and up" (Miles, 1974:189). Companies try one attractive package after another, just as long as each promises a painless solution to their problems. Human relations, suggestions systems, the open door policy, brainstorming, zero defect programs—all have had their day. Each is tried in turn and then allowed to lapse gradually into oblivion.

Few managers recognize that the mere installation of a plan does not guarantee its success. Instead substantial change in a host of interrelated behavior patterns is required. When instant success is not achieved, there is a tendency to switch one's attention to other areas. And false expectations may lead to cynical disillusionment. As Miles (1974:189) put it:

> Ineffective OD may lead to what I have called the "inoculation effect"; that is, groups which engage in short-term ineffectual OD 'programs' will be unlikely to engage in more serious efforts in the future. This phenomenon is neatly summarized in a statement a manager made to me recently. "OD?" he said, "We went through that a couple of years ago."

Staff training men often contribute to fadism, even when they should know better. Staff effectiveness is not easily measurable and staff men must prove their worth by making contributions which are easily dramatized. The training director who is in his seventh successful year with the same program may not have the visibility of the man who introduces a completely new program with great fanfare each year.

Yet nothing is more guaranteed to insure OD's failure than the feeling on the part of management that it is something peripheral, something akin to a public relations gimmick.

---

[69] In fact, managers trained by Miner (1965) to be 9,1 oriented (purely concerned with production) have moved ahead in their companies significantly more rapidly than those not so trained.

Anti-intellectualism. In many respects, OD reflects the interests of its time. The popularity of OD in industry during the late 1960s was certainly influenced by the same currents which lead to the popularity of encounter groups, pot, and to hard-nosed managers growing sideburns. Bennis (1968:229) spoke of a "generation trying to assert itself and its strategy of truth through reliance on touch and feel and sight, rather than on words and numbers." Thus there was new romanticism (much like the romantic period of the 1800s), a period of innocence in which love solved all problems, a new conformity masked under the disguise of "doing your own thing."

Even today the emphasis in *some* OD (please note my qualification) is on feelings rather than facts, the medium rather than the message, on expression as an end in itself. There is a counterculture view of organization in which the goal is not more effective management, but a healthier life style.[70] And, for some, the measure of OD success is whether unfreezing ("turning on") is high, rather than whether tasks get solved. Both Alderfer and Argyris quite properly call this strain in the OD movement anti-intellectual.

Thus an analogy can be drawn between some OD and some Hippie communes. This version of OD attempts to provide a sense of community (and also spontaneity) through self-criticism; leveling and growth processes are used to generate commitment. I suspect that some team building takes on the character of a revival meeting, a sophisticated Billy Grahamism, in which each participant confesses his sins and thus avoids the necessity of examining the material (structural) sources of evil.[71]

Happily, as OD gains maturity, the anti-intellectual trend seems to be on the decline (perhaps reflecting a reaction against the emotionalism of the Johnson-Nixon period) and the recent literature suggests a somewhat more realistic consideration of organizational problems.

Essentially conservative. OD devotees may have oversold themselves as to the revolutionary impact of their movement. To the extent that OD seeks to introduce Consciousness III into industry, it is of course very radical. But in another sense it is very conservative. The "prepackaged corporate cultural revolution" (Henley, 1971:446) is imposed benignly from the top. In resolving conflicts between the individual and the organization, stress is placed on changing people, and most OD consultants seem able to persuade themselves that the process is in the interest of both parties.[72] The OD model "assumes and meth-

---

[70] "We should, then, bless T-groups," Perrow (1972:118) argues, "because they do for managers what pot, flower power, psychodelic experiences, encounter groups, and hard-rock music do for the far-out younger generation. The search for spontaneity and authenticity should be never ending, and if it must occur in the guise of better productivity in organizations, let it. The retrainees will return refreshed to the world of hierarchies, conflict, stupidity, and brilliance, but the hierarchies are not likely to fade away."

[71] Pages (1971) observed upon his return to Bethel in 1969 after a fifteen-year absence that there had been a marked shift in emphasis from "understanding" to "loving." He suggests that this emphasis was a means of avoiding the anxiety of facing hard problems.

[72] "The existing and profound idea" about OD, according to French and Bell (1973:xiii) is that: "it is possible for the people in an organization collaboratively to manage the culture of that organization in such a way that the goals and purposes of the organization are attained at the same time that the human values of the individuals within the organization are furthered."

odologically manufactures a compatability of individual and organizational welfare," Brimm (1972:104) puts it. "Thus the change agents have allied themselves with those groups who benefit from the existing distribution of power."
"Though most OD practitioners and researchers in some degree value both
organizational task accomplishment *and* human fulfillment, there is an organization press in favor of the former" (Friedlander and Brown, 1974:335).

Nevertheless, there is growing concern that OD is not power neutral
(Walton and Warwick, 1973). Earlier I discussed Miles' Mafia Model. Given the
fact that management is usually the group which hires the consultant, often he
accepts management's view of the problem. Thus OD is used at times to "cool
off" those who are hurt by organizational change—for example, to help a group
of demoted managers adjust to their new status (Golembiewski and others,
1972)—rather than to question the desirability of such change in the first place.

The recent literature reflects an increasing concern with "the practitioner's
ethical and value dilemmas arising from the need to be simultaneously a management consultant, with a primary concern for effectiveness, and a social re-
former, striving to increase humanistic values in the work-place" (Walton and
Warwick, 1973:683). There is even a small group which seeks to work with the
underdog against the organization (Torczyner, 1972; Gedicks, 1973). Pages
looks upon his job as helping "people destroy the organizational forms in which
they have become imprisoned" and calls Argyris "a really conservative, reac-
tionary social scientist . . . very dangerous" (Tichy, 1974:9). He adds (1971:280)
that "the training culture at Bethel performs the political function of preserving American society from internal and external disruption." And Ross (1971)
calls OD specialists "social scientists for hire," whose efforts on behalf of the
capitalist classes is a form of 'petit Eichmanism.' " I agree with these critics only
to the extent that I believe in practice, OD is often used as a technique for winning greater acceptance of a management's objectives on the part of lower participants—as are most personnel techniques.

Manipulation. Despite the somewhat manipulative flavor of the term
"planned change," most *theorists* try consciously to be nonmanipulative. Bennis
(1966), for example, wrestles with the dilemma of (1) moving people through
their *own* free will (2) in the direction desired by the trainer (such as toward
greater authenticity). Yet I suspect that in the hands of *some* practitioners, OD
involves a certain amount of slight of hand in that the consultant molds participants' attitudes (despite his protests that he does not). The pressures generated
in some confrontation processes come somewhat close to brainwashing.

It is sometimes argued that manipulation of this sort is morally more de-
fensible than that which normally occurs under Theory X management. But
giving orders, specifying behavior, and requiring outward conformity is very
different than trying to change values themselves. As Harrison suggests, OD is
most useful in circumstances where Theory X is insufficient. "It makes organizational sense to try to get a man to *want* to do something only when you cannot *make* him do it" (1970:194).

Violations of privacy. Earlier I suggested that T-groups may sometimes
violate individual rights to privacy, especially where participation is only semi-
voluntary. To a lesser degree, these same ethical problems apply to OD. As
Walton and Warwick (1973:689) point out, participants are rarely in a position

to give informed consent to their participation. Few consultants make "a serious effort to describe the process and range of consequences for the invitees." In any case, lower level managers "sense the implicit if not explicit powers of higher management behind the OD effort, and many persons are coerced into participation despite any tactic which the consultant may employ to prevent this" (Miles, 1975:186).

"A good OD practitioner is typically skilled in encouraging people to lower their defenses" (Walton and Warwick, 1973:689). Thus they may reveal information disadvantageous to themselves. "In the typical OD scenerio, such information is to be collected in an atmosphere of trust, where no one will be harmed by his honesty or by revelations made about him by others. But trust has its limitations and administrators are human" (p. 686). OD may be dangerous to people who surface their own inadequacies and also to those at the receiving end of hostile feelings. "Ethical questions arise when the participant is essentially seduced or pressured into self-revelations which he later comes to regret" (p. 692). Further, free expression may be harmful to those who are the butt of criticism. "The border between useful feedback and psychic battering is a fine one, and should be closely watched" (p. 693).

It is healthy for OD that such concerns are now being openly discussed (e.g., Friedlander and Brown, 1974:335); however, I am far from sanguine as to how they may be resolved without OD's sacrificing its practice of openness.

CONCLUSION

Undoubtedly some OD men are little more than hucksters or pitchmen. In some cases the value of OD is considerably overstated. For some managers OD is little more than a cheap psychological binge, an emotional orgy which relieves guilt and forestalls the necessity of hard thinking and decision-making about real organizational problems. OD is obviously not a complete management system, a complete personnel system, or even a complete system of management training. Nor is OD the only way to improve organizations.

Certainly it is easy to be put off by the gushy, gee-whiz attitude of much of the literature. Nevertheless, compared to traditional management training, OD is generally more meaningful, certainly leads to far more involvement, and also permits greater carryover from training locale to practice. Compared to the use of T-groups unaccompanied by other forms of OD, a comprehensive OD program is less likely to have problems with generalization and carryover and clearly runs less risk of being excessively stressful.

Despite the difficulties of research, it is now reasonably clear that *under some circumstances*, OD can lead to lasting organizational gain. More research is needed, of course, to specify what these circumstances are. Nevertheless, one can make some comments as to the major unresolved questions.

Depth of intervention. Are deep intervention techniques, especially T-groups, required for successful OD? On one side are those who argue that organizational change is impossible without prior change in individual values. On the other side are those who point to the dangers and difficulties inherent in deep intervention and who suggest that more superficial techniques, such as Schein's concern with meeting agenda, may yield higher payoff per unit of effort. My own view is that under *many* circumstances (note the qualification) and in the long run, deep intervention may have a beneficial effect, *provided* the organization and the individuals involved are willing and able to persist in the program through the long period of carryover. But too often, managers prefer deep (or at least attitude oriented) intervention because they see it as a means of getting people to work more effectively within current organizational constraints, rather than making fundamental changes in the organization itself.

Given the large number of aborted deep-intervention efforts, I would suggest that deep intervention be tried only after the organization has achieved some success with techniques which seek to obtain changes at a relatively modest level. Deep intervention is often entered into too cavalierly. T-groups, for example, may well get OD off on the wrong foot. It has been amply demonstrated that effective OD is possible without delving so deeply.

Too much sensitivity? The problem is whether the uncompromising honesty required in the T-group can be maintained in the organization, or whether it is better to set lower standards which are less inconsistent with organizational values. The T-group is an artificial social situation, and its conventions and values are not directly applicable to the real world. Despite imaginative efforts to develop new carryover techniques, the transition period is bound to be difficult. There are bound to be some who try to be completely honest, T-group style, in situations where this is inappropriate. There will be others who react, "It was a fantastic situation, and I learned a lot about myself. But I doubt if there is much I can apply on the job." And still others may be so disturbed by the T-group experience that they become afraid to try less intensive forms of OD.

Unless great care is given to carryover, T-group training should be reserved for *individual* development with *organization* development confined to less person-centered techniques. OD should be concerned with job inadequacies rather than personal inadequacies.

Carryover. This is still very much of a problem, especially after deep intervention. Carryover, as we have seen, involves movement on a number of dimensions, from training lab to the job, from "conviction of sin" to the development of alternative behavioral patterns, from a small "infected area" to the organization as a whole, and from OD as a temporary morale booster to OD as a way of life. Despite a number of innovative techniques to foster carryover, carryover is still less successful than confrontation. Insight is much easier to obtain than implementation.

Need for a systems approach. Although there is a strong recent trend among OD consultants toward giving greater weight to structure, by and large the OD movement (and especially its literature) still stresses questions of emotion, attitude, and face-to-face relations. Such an emphasis is natural, given OD's derivation from T-groups. Nevertheless, I suspect that the failure of OD people to give enough attention to formal structure may be as serious as that of management scientists who ignore attitudes. Attitudinal changes may cause temporary changes in behavior, but these are not likely to last unless accompanied by appropriate changes in structure. The two should move together in balance. Furthermore, OD needs to develop approaches to situations where "mechanistic" rather than "organismic" structure is appropriate.

My fundamental bias is that there are limits to what can be done with training and that it is often better to change the organization so that ordinary people can function well within it rather than to try to change the people themselves. Thus I sympathize with those who believe that the purposes of OD should be to induce managers to step back, not just to re-examine their interpersonal relations and emotions, but to take a fresh look at the organization as a whole, its goals, and its relationship to its environment. Only in this way can OD become the true systems approach which it aspires to become. Obviously this is a time-consuming process. Unfortunately, too often OD is either just people development or group development.

OD as an emphasis on process.   Although I criticize much OD for giving too little emphasis to structure, let me make my own position clear. I view OD's main contribution as being its concern with *process*—the means by which change is made. Effective OD occurs when organizational members learn *how* to diagnose what changes are required and *how* to make these with minimal pain and most lasting effectiveness—and also *how* to learn from this learning process, so that future changes can be made even more effectively and painlessly. If we adopt this view, then "leveling," "openness," job enrichment, or 9,9 management can all be viewed as possible alternative goals toward which the organization may decide to strive as a *result* of the OD process. They are not OD techniques in and of themselves (at least not according to the rather restricted definition I suggest here).

Choices among alternative training methods.   Few managers sponsoring OD recognize how much the sometimes mushy idealism of OD clashes with the dog-eat-dog values of everyday organizational life. Arnold Tannenbaum tells of a presumed OD program in a major company which combined the Grid with a Vince Lombardi movie preaching hatred of your opponent. Given this confusion regarding objectives, I wonder whether OD helps increase organizational effectiveness more than any other equally expensive and time-consuming effort which shows management's concern for its employees.

If, as Shel Davis insists, OD turns out not softer managers but better decision-makers, would equal results be obtained from programs specifically designed to improve decision-making (e.g., Kepner-Tregoe, 1965)? Dalton (1970) and Korman (1971) both argue that OD's key objective should be to raise self-confidence and esteem. If so, perhaps the answer is to provide training directly designed to alter levels of aspiration and aggressiveness—such as "rational training," the various programs designed by McClelland (Aronoff and Litwin, 1971) and Miner (1965), or those packaged under the title of "Behavioral Reinforcement."

We may have sold individual training short. The individual manager in many cases may have considerable freedom to bootleg "democratic" supervisory and interpersonal techniques, even in an autocratic environment. Training may well serve to provide the manager with a kit of alternative techniques which he can use on suitable occasions; it may also assist him in determining the particular situations in which each approach is most appropriate. (For an example of such an approach, see Vroom and Yetton, 1973.)

Actually what we need is a contingency approach—to adopt the techniques used to the specific client. As in psychotherapy, short-term treatments

with limited *behavioral* objectives may often be more useful than depth intervention. Cognitive, attitudinal, and structural changes are all important, individual, group, and systems-wide approaches should be used, but the particular
combination and sequencing should vary from client to client. "True" OD (by
the restricted definition just proposed) may not occur unless there is organizational learning which permits the organization to adapt better to *future* problems. However, "true" OD may be interspersed by other training techniques
with more limited objectives.

Towards the Future

How will OD stand up fifteen years from now? Will it have a lasting impact or
is it merely a fad? There is a real chance that the term itself will become as
anachronistic as "scientific management" and "human relations" are today. Yet,
like these earlier movements, which were also controversial in their time, OD
will have left its mark on managerial practice.

OD principles are not entirely new. Early human relations taught managers
to be considerate of their subordinates, to listen to them, to be concerned with
their off-the-job lives, and to recognize that much of their behavior was emotionally rather than purely rationally motivated. At the heart of *applied* human
relations was perhaps a single tool: nondirective listening as a form of feedback.

To what extent does OD go beyond this? It teaches that managers (as well
as workers) have feelings and that it is legitimate for these feelings to be expressed. It also teaches (though not especially effectively) that the organization
is a system in which the behavior of one part affects another. Finally, it has developed some effective means of feedback and confrontation.

To some extent the lessons of human relations have persisted, even though
nondirective listening as a technique is no longer popular. I would expect OD's
fate to be roughly similar. Specific programs, such as the Grid and even
T-groups, may become as passé as nondirective counseling is today. Nevertheless,
it may become slightly more legitimate for managers to express their feelings
openly (though there may be some fadeout over time). Further, some organizations may develop the tradition of periodically stepping back to reassess their
goals, tactics, and internal relations; they may be less concerned with *static*
analysis, where they stand today, and more concerned with *dynamic* analysis,
their ability to adjust to future problems. Finally, we may expect the growth of
institutionalized attitudinal feedback systems somewhat akin to (but given
somewhat less weight than) financial feedback systems.

These are modest advances, perhaps. But they are worth making, and
worth acknowledging.

REFERENCES

Adler, R.
   1967   "The Thursday group." The New Yorker 43(April 15):55–146.
Albrook, R.C.
   1968   "How to spot executives early." Fortune 78(July):107–111.
Alderfer, C.P.
   1970   "Understanding laboratory education: an overview." Monthly Labor
          Review 93(December):18–27.

Alderfer, C.P. and T.M. Lodahl
 1971 "A quasi experiment in the use of experimental methods in the class-
      room." Journal of Applied Behavioral Science 7(January):43–70.
American Psychiatric Association
 1970 Task Force Report: Encounter Groups and Psychiatry. Washington,
      D.C.
Anderson, S.D.
 1971 "Applied methods for evaluating research." Proceedings of the Twenty-
      Third Annual Meeting of the Industrial Relations Research Associa-
      tion. Madison, Wisconsin:232–239.
Annett, J.
 1969 Feedback and Human Behavior. London: Penguin.
Argyris, C.
 1962 Interpersonal Competence and Organizational Effectiveness. Home-
      wood, Ill.: Dorsey.
 1967a "On the future of laboratory training." Journal of Applied Behavioral
      Science 3(April):153–183.
 1967b Some Causes of Organizational Ineffectiveness Within the Department
      of State. Washington, D.C.: Department of State.
 1968 "Conditions for competence acquisition and therapy." Journal of Ap-
      plied Behavioral Science 4(April):147–178.
 1970 Intervention Theory and Method: A Behavioral Science View. Reading,
      Mass.: Addison-Wesley.
 1971 Management and Organizational Development. New York: McGraw-
      Hill.
 1972 "Do personal growth laboratories represent an alternate culture?"
      Journal of Applied Behavioral Science 8(January):7–28.
 1974 Theory in Practice: Increasing Professional Effectiveness. San Fran-
      cisco: Josey-Bass.
Aronoff, J. and G.H. Litwin
 1971 "Achievement motivation training and executive advancement." Journal
      of Applied Behavioral Science 7(March):215–219.
Back, K.W.
 1972 Beyond Words: The Story of Sensitivity Training and the Encounter
      Movement. Baltimore: Penguin Books.
 1974 "Intervention techniques: small groups," in M. Rosenzweig and L.
      Porter (eds.), Annual Review of Psychology, Vol. 25.
Bartlett, A.C.
 1967 "Changing behavior as a means to increased efficiency." Journal of
      Applied Behavioral Science 3(July):381–403.
Bass, B.M.
 1967 "The anarchist movement and the T-group: some possible lessons for
      organizational development." Journal of Applied Behavioral Science
      3(April):211–227.
Beckhard, R.
 1966 "An organizational improvement program in a decentralized com-
      pany." Journal of Applied Behavioral Science 2(January):3–26.
 1969 Organization Development: Strategies and Models. Reading, Mass.:
      Addison-Wesley.

Bednar, R.L., et al.
  1974   "Empirical guidelines for group therapy: pretraining, cohesion, and modeling." Journal of Applied Behavioral Science 10(April):149–165.
Beer, M. and E.F. Huse
  1972   "A systems approach to organization development." Journal of Applied Behavioral Science 8(January):79–101.
Belasco, J. and H. Trice
  1969   The Assessment of Change in Training and Therapy. New York: McGraw-Hill.
Bennis, W.G.
  1965   "Theory and method in applying behavioral science for planned organizational change." Journal of Applied Behavioral Science 1(October): 337–360.
  1966   Changing Organizations. New York: McGraw-Hill.
  1968   "The case study." Journal of Applied Behavioral Science 4(April): 227–231.
  1969   Organization Development: Its Nature, Origin, and Prospects. Reading, Mass.: Addison-Wesley.
Bennis, W.G. and H. Peters
  1966   Unpublished paper.
Berkowitz, N.H.
  1969   "Audiences and their implications for evaluation research." Journal of Applied Behavioral Science 5(July):411–427.
Berlow, D.W. and W.E. LeClere
  1974   "Social intervention in Curacao." Journal of Applied Behavioral Science 10(January):29–52.
Blake, R.R. and J.S. Mouton
  1969   Building a Dynamic Corporation Through Grid Organization Development. Reading, Mass.: Addison-Wesley.
Blake, R.R., J. Mouton, L.B. Barnes and L. Griener
  1964   "Breakthrough in organization development." Harvard Business Review 42(November):133–155.
Blake, R.R., H.A. Shepard and J.S. Mouton
  1964   Managing Intergroup Conflict in Industry. Houston, Texas: Gulf.
Bolman, L.
  1970   "Laboratory vs. lecture in training executives." Journal of Applied Behavioral Science 6(July):323–335.
Bowers, D.G.
  1973   "OD techniques and their results in 23 organizations: the Michigan ICL study." Journal of Applied Behavioral Science 9(January):21–43.
Bowers, D.G. and J. Franklin
  1972   "Self-guided development: using human resources measurement in organizational change." Journal of Contemporary Business (1):43–55.
Bradford, L.P.
  1967   "Biography of an institution." Journal of Applied Behavioral Science 3(April):127–143.
Bradford, L.P., J. Gibb and K. Benne (eds.)
  1964   T-Group Theory and Laboratory Method: Innovation of Reeducation. New York: Wiley.

Brimm, M.
1972   "When is a change not a change?" Journal of Applied Behavioral Science 8(February):102–107.
Brown, W.
1960   Explorations in Management. London: Tavistock.
Buchanan, P.C.
1965   "Evaluating the effectiveness of laboratory training in industry." In Explorations in Human Relations Training and Research, No. 1. Washington, D.C.: National Training Laboratories.
1969   "Laboratory training and organization development." Administrative Science Quarterly 14(September):455–477.
1971   "Crucial issues in OD." In H.A. Hornstein, B.B. Bunker, W.W. Burke, M. Guides, and R.J. Lewicki (eds.), Social Intervention: A Behavioral Science Approach. New York: Free Press.
Bunker, D.
1967   "Comment: the anarchist movement in the T-group." Journal of Applied Behavioral Science 3(June):228–231.
Bunker, D. and E. Knowles
1967   "Comparison of behavioral changes resulting from human relations training laboratories of different lengths." Journal of Applied Behavioral Science 3(October):505–524.
Burns, T. and G.M. Stalker
1961   The Management of Innovation. London: Tavistock.
Business Week
1969   "Grid puts executives on the griddle." (October 18):158–160.
Campbell, J.P.
1971   "Review: Addison-Wesley series on organization development." Administrative Science Quarterly 16(March):133–137.
Campbell, J.P. and M.D. Dunnette
1968   "Effectiveness of T-group experiences in managerial training and development." Psychological Bulletin (70):73–104.
Campbell, J.P., M. Dunnette, E. Lawler and K. Weick
1970   Managerial Behavior, Performance and Effectiveness. New York: McGraw-Hill.
Chapple, E.D. and L.P. Sayles
1961   The Measurement of Management. New York: Macmillan.
Chesler, M.A. and O. Worden (eds.)
1974   "Power and social change." Journal of Applied Behavioral Science 10(June):271–472.
Coch, L. and J.R.P. French
1948   "Overcoming resistance to change." Human Relations (1):512–532.
Colombotos, J.
1969   "Physicians and medicare: a before-after study." American Sociological Review 34(June):318–331.
Cooper, C.L. and I.L. Mangham
1971   T-Groups: A Survey of Research. London: Wiley-Interscience.
Crockett, W.J.
1970   "Team building—one approach to organizational development." Journal of Applied Behavioral Science 6(July):291–306.

Culbert, S.
    1970   "Accelerating laboratory learning through a phase progression model
            for trainer intervention." Journal of Applied Behavioral Science 6(Jan-
            uary):21–38.
Dalton, G.W.
    1970   "Influence and organizational change," in G.W. Dalton and P.R. Law-
            rence (eds.), Organizational Change and Development. Homewood,
            Ill.: Dorsey.
Dalton, G.W., P. Lawrence and L. Griener
    1970   Organizational Change and Development. Homewood, Ill.: Irwin.
Davis, S.A.
    1967   "An organic problem-solving method of organizational change." Jour-
            nal of Applied Behavioral Science 3(January):3–21.
Drotning, J.
    1966   "Sensitivity training: some critical questions." Personnel Journal
            45(November):604–606.
Ehrich, H.J.
    1969   "Attitudes, behaviors, and the intervening variables." The American
            Sociologist (4):29–34.
Ellis, A. and M. Blum
    1967   "Rational training." Psychological Reports (20):1267–1284.
Fiedler, F.
    1967   A Theory of Leadership Effectiveness. New York: McGraw-Hill.
Foreman, W.J.
    1966   "Management training techniques." Personnel Journal 45(October):
            548–552.
French, W.
    1969   "Organization development objectives, assumptions, and strategies."
            California Management Review 12(Winter):23–34.
French, W.L. and C.H. Bell
    1973   Organization Development. Englewood Cliffs, N.J.: Prentice-Hall.
Friedlander, F.
    1968   "A comparative study of consulting processes and group development."
            Journal of Applied Behavioral Science 4(October):377–400.
Friedlander, F. and L.D. Brown
    1974   "Organization development," in M. Rosenzweig and L.W. Porter
            (eds.), Annual Review of Psychology, Vol. 25.
Garfield, S. and W. F. Whyte
    1950   "The collective bargaining process: a human relations analysis." Hu-
            man Organization 9(Summer):5–10.
Gedicks, A.
    1973   "Guerrilla research: reversing the machinery." Journal of Applied
            Behavioral Science 9(September):645–651.
Gibb, J.
    1964   "Defensive communications," in H. Leavitt and L. Pondy (eds.), Read-
            ings in Managerial Psychology. Chicago: University of Chicago Press.
Golembiewski, R. and A. Blumberg
    1967   "Confrontation as a training design in complex organizations." Journal
            of Applied Behavior Science 3(October):535–547.

Golembiewski, R.T., S.B. Carrigan, W.R. Mead, R. Munzenrider and A. Blumberg
　1972　"Toward building new work relationships: an action design for a critical intervention." Journal of Applied Behavioral Science 8(March): 135–148.

Goodstein, L.D. and R.K. Boyer
　1972　"Crisis intervention in a municipal agency: a conceptual case study." Journal of Applied Behavioral Science 8(May):318–340.

Griener, L.
　1967a "Antecedents of planned organizational change." Journal of Applied Behavioral Science 3(January):51–86.
　1967b "Patterns of organizational change." Harvard Business Review 45 (May):119–130.

Haigh, G.V.
　1968　"A personal growth crisis in laboratory training." Journal of Applied Behavioral Science 4(October):437–452.

Harrison, R.
　1970　"Choosing the depth of organizational intervention." Journal of Applied Behavioral Science 6(April):181–202.
　1972a "Role negotiation: a toughminded approach to team development," in W.W. Burke and H.A. Hornstein (eds.), The Social Technology of Organizational Development. Fairfax, Va.: NTL Learning Resources, Inc.
　1972b "Understanding your organization's character." Harvard Business Review 50(May):119–129.

Heller, F.
　1970　"Group feedback analysis as a change agent." Human Relations 23 (August):319–333.

Henley, J.
　1971　"Review of Blake and Mouton, 'Building a dynamic corporation through grid organization development.'" British Journal of Industrial Relations 9(November):446.

Hornstein, H.A., B. Brunker and M. Hornstein
　1971　"Some conceptual issues in individual and group-oriented strategies of intervention into organization." Journal of Applied Behavioral Science 7(September):557–567.

House, R.J.
　1967　"T-group education and leadership effectiveness." Personnel Psychology 20(Spring):1–32.
　1968　"Leadership training: some dysfunctional characteristics." Administrative Science Quarterly 12(March):556–571.
　1971　"A path-goal theory of leader effectiveness." Administrative Science Quarterly 16(September):321–339.

Jaques, E.
　1951　The Changing Culture of the Factory. London: Tavistock.
　1961　Equitable Payment: A General Theory of Work. New York: Wiley.

Kahn, R.L.
　1974　"Organizational development: some problems and proposals." Journal of Applied Behavioral Science 10(October):485–502.

Kepner, C.H. and B.B. Tregoe
　1965　The Rational Manager: A Systematic Approach to Problem Solving and Decision Making. New York: McGraw-Hill.

Klemesrud, J.
  1970 "Having a wonderful encounter." New York Times Magazine. December (20) :8, et seq.
Korman, A.K.
  1966 " 'Consideration,' 'Initiating Structure,' and Organizational Criteria—A Review." Personnel Psychology 19(Winter) :349–361.
  1971 Industrial and Organizational Psychology. Englewood Cliffs, N.J.: Prentice-Hall.
Kuriloff, A. and S. Atkins
  1966 "T-group for a work team." Journal of Applied Behavioral Science 2(January) :63–93.
Lawrence, P. and J.W. Lorsch
  1967 "Differentiation and integration in complex organizations." Administrative Science Quarterly 12(March) :1–47.
  1969 Developing Organizations: Diagnosis and Action. Reading, Mass.: Addison-Wesley.
Leavitt, H.J. and T. Whisler
  1958 "Management in the 1980s." Harvard Business Review 36(November) : 41–48.
Leavitt, H.J. and R. Doktor
  1970 "Personnel growth, laboratory training, science, and all that: a shot at a cognitive clarification." Journal of Applied Behavioral Science (6): 173–179.
Levinson, H.
  1967 "Comments on 'The Anarchist Movement and the T-Group.' " Journal of Applied Behavioral Science 3(April) :232–233.
  1972 Organizational Diagnosis. Cambridge, Mass.: Harvard University Press.
Lewicki, R.J. and C.P. Alderfer
  1973 "The tensions between research and intervention in intergroup conflict." Journal of Applied Behavioral Science 9(July) :424–449.
Lewin, K.
  1947 "Frontiers of group dynamics." Human Relations (1) :5–42.
Lieberman, M.A., I.D. Yalom and M.B. Miles
  1971 "The Group Experience Project: a comparison of ten encounter group technologies," in L. Blank and M. Gottsegen (eds.), Encounter: Confrontations in Self- and Interpersonal Awareness. New York: Macmillan.
  1972 "The impact of encounter groups on participants: some preliminary findings." Journal of Applied Behavioral Science 8(January) :29–50.
Lippitt, G.
  1969 Organizational Renewal. New York: Appleton-Century-Crofts.
Lippitt, R.
  1949 Training in Community Relations. New York: Harper & Bros.
Lomranz, J., M. Lakin and H. Schiffman
  1972 "Variants of sensitivity training and encounter: diversity or fragmentation?" Journal of Applied Behavioral Science 8(July) :399–420.
Luchsinger, V.P. and L.L. Luchsinger
  1974 "Transactional analysis for managers, or how to be more OK with OK organizations." MSU Business Topics (Spring) :6–12.

Luke, R.A., P. Block, J.M. Davey and V.R. Averech
    1973   "A structural approach to organizational change." Journal of Applied
           Behavioral Science 9(September) :611–635.
McClelland, D.C.
    1965   "Achievement motivation can be developed." Harvard Business Review
           43(November) :6–24.
McGregor, D.
    1960   The Human Side of Enterprise. New York: McGraw-Hill.
    1967   The Professional Manager. New York: McGraw-Hill.
Maliver, B.L.
    1971   "Encounter groups up against the wall." New York Times Magazine
           (January 3).
Mann, F.
    1957   "Studying and creating change: a means to understanding social orga-
           nizations," in Arensberg and others (eds.), Research in Industrial
           Human Relations. New York: Harper & Bros.
Marrow, A.J.
    1967   "Events leading to the establishment of the National Training Labora-
           tories." Journal of Applied Behavioral Science 3(April) :144–150.
Marrow, A.J., D. Bowers and S. Seashore
    1967   Management by Participation. New York: Harper & Row.
Marrow, A.J. and J.R.P. French
    1945   "Overcoming a stereotype." Journal of Social Issues (1) :33–37.
Maslow, A.
    1965   Eupsychian Management. Homewood, Ill.: Dorsey.
Miles, M.B.
    1965   "Changes during and following laboratory training." Journal of Ap-
           plied Behavioral Science 1(July) :215–242.
Miles, M. B., et al.
    1969   "The consequences of survey feedback: theory and evaluation," in
           W.G. Bennis, K.D. Benne, and R. Chin (eds.), The Planning of
           Change. Second Edition. New York: Holt, Rinehart and Winston.
Miles, R.E.
    1974   "Organization Development," in G. Strauss, R.E. Miles, C. Snow and A.
           Tannenbaum (eds.), Organizational Behavior: Research and Issues.
           Madison, Wisc.: Industrial Relations Research Association.
    1975   Theories of Management: Implications for Organizational Behavior
           and Development. New York: McGraw-Hill.
Miles, R.E. and L.W. Porter
    1966   "Leadership training—back to the classroom." Personnel 43(July) :27–
           35.
Miner, J.B.
    1965   Studies in Management Education. New York: Springer.
Morse, N.C. and E. Reimer
    1956   "The experimental change of a major organizational variable." Journal
           of Abnormal and Applied Psychology (52) :120–129.
Morton, R.B. and B.M. Bass
    1964   "The organizational training laboratory." Training Directors Journal
           18(October) :2–18.

Myers, C.E., M. Myers, A. Goldberg and C.E. Welch
    1969 "Effect of feedback on interpersonal sensitivity in laboratory training groups." Journal of Applied Behavioral Science 5(April):185–197.

Odiorne, G.
    1963 "The trouble with sensitivity training." Training Directors Journal 17(October):9–21.

Oshry, B. and R. Harrison
    1966 "Transfer from here-and-now to there-and-then." Journal of Applied Behavioral Science 2(April):185–198.

Pages, M.
    1971 "Bethel culture, 1969: impressions of an immigrant." Journal of Applied Behavioral Science 7(May):267–284.

Perrow, C.
    1967 "A framework for the comparative analysis of organizations." American Sociological Review 32(April):194–208.
    1972 Complex Organizations: A Critical Essay. Glenview, Ill.: Scott, Foresman.

Posthuma, A.B. and B.W. Posthuma
    1973 "Some observations on encounter group casualties" Journal of Applied Behavioral Science 9(September):535–610.

Pugh, D.
    1965 "T-group training from the point of view of organizational theory," in G. Whitaker (ed.), ATM Occasional Papers, No. 2. Oxford: Basil Blackwell.

Rice, A.K.
    1963 The Enterprise and Its Environment. London: Tavistock.

Ross, R.
    1971 "Organizational development for whom?" Journal of Applied Behavioral Science 7(September):580–585.

Rush, H.M.F.
    1969 "Behavioral science: concepts and management application," in Studies in Personnel Policy No. 216. New York: National Industrial Conference Board.

Schein, E.
    1969 Process Consultation: Its Role in Organization Development. Reading, Mass.: Addison-Wesley.

Schein, E. and W.G. Bennis
    1965 Personal and Organizational Change Through Group Methods: The Laboratory Approach. New York: Wiley.

Seashore, C.
    1968 "What is sensitivity training?" NTL Institute News and Reports 2 (April).

Seashore, S.E. and D.G. Bowers
    1963 Changing the Structure and Functioning of an Organization. Survey Research Center Monograph No. 33. Ann Arbor, Michigan.

Shepard, H.
    1960 An Action Research Program for Organizational Development. Ann Arbor, Mich.: Foundation for Research on Human Behavior.
    1970 "Personal growth laboratories: toward an alternative culture." Journal of Applied Behavioral Science 6(July):259–266.

Sims, H.P.
  1970   "The business organization, environment, and T-group training: a new viewpoint." Management of Personnel Quarterly 9(Winter) :21–27.
Sofer, C.
  1962   The Organization from Within. Chicago: Quadrangle Books.
Strauss, G.
  1963   "Some notes on power equalization," in H. Leavitt (ed.), The Social Science of Organization. Englewood Cliffs, N.J.: Prentice-Hall.
  1968   "Human relations—1968 style." Industrial Relations 7(May) :262–276.
  1970   "Organizational behavior and personnel relations," in A Review of Industrial Relations Research, Vol. 1. Madison, Wisc.: Industrial Relations Research Association.
Strauss, G. and E. Rosenstein
  1970   "Workers participation: a critical view." Industrial Relations 9(February) :197–214.
Sykes, A.J.M.
  1962   "The effect of a supervising training course in changing supervisor's perceptions and expectations of the role of management." Human Relations 15(August) :227–244.
Tannenbaum, R.
  1967   "Reaction to Chris Argyris." Journal of Applied Behavioral Science (3) :205–206.
Tannenbaum, R. and S. Davis
  1967   "Values, man, and organization." Paper presented to the McGregor Conference on Organization Development.
Thompson, V.A.
  1969   Bureaucracy and Innovation. University, Ala.: University of Alabama Press.
Tichy, N.
  1973   "An interview with Roger Harrison." Journal of Applied Behavioral Science 9(November) :701–726.
  1974   "An interview with Max Pagès." Journal of Applied Behavioral Science 9(January) :8–26.
Torczyner, J.
  1972   "The political context of social change: a case study of innovation in adversity in Jerusalem." Journal of Applied Behavioral Science 8(May) :287–317.
Trist, W.L., G.W. Higgins, H. Murray and A.B. Pollock
  1963   Organizational Choice. London: Tavistock.
Tushman, M.
  1974   Organizational Change: An Exploratory Study and Case History. ILR Paperback No. 15. Ithaca, New York: New York State School of Industrial Relations, Cornell University.
Vroom, V.H. and P.W. Yetton
  1973   Leadership and Decision-Making. Pittsburgh, Pa.: University of Pittsburgh Press.
Wagner, A.B.
  1965   "The use of process analysis in business decision games." Journal of Applied Behavioral Science 1(October) :387–408.

Walter, G.A.
   1975   "Effects of video tape feedback and modeling on the behaviors of task
          group members." Human Relations. Forthcoming.
Walter, G.A. and R.E. Miles
   1974   "Changing self-acceptance: task groups and video tapes or sensitivity
          training." Small Group Behavior 5 (August) :356–364.
Walton, R.
   1969   Interpersonal Peacemaking: Confrontations and Third Party Consul-
          tation. Reading, Mass.: Addison-Wesley.
   1970   "A problem-solving workshop on border conflicts in eastern Africa."
          Journal of Applied Behavioral Science 6 (October) :453–489.
Walton, R. and R.B. McKersie
   1965   A Behavioral Theory of Labor Negotiations. New York: McGraw-Hill.
Walton, R. and D.P. Warwick
   1973   "The ethics of organization development." Journal of Applied Behav-
          ioral Science 9 (November) :681–699.
Weber, R.J. and R.E. Miles
   1971   "Comparison of the effects of sensitivity training and task group feed-
          back on interpersonal need orientation." Proceedings of the Academy
          of Management.
Weick, K.
   1965   "Laboratory experiments with organizations," in J.G. March (ed.),
          Handbook of Organizations. Chicago: Rand McNally.
Whyte, W.F.
   1948   Human Relations in the Restaurant Industry. New York: McGraw-Hill.
Whyte, W.F. and E.L. Hamilton
   1964   Action Research for Management. Homewood, Ill.: Irwin.
Wilson, A.T.M.
   1967   "Organization development and the integrative needs of the executive."
          Paper presented to the McGregor Conference on Organization Develop-
          ment.
Winn, A.
   1966   "Social change in industry: from insight to implementation." Journal
          of Applied Behavioral Science 2 (April) :170–184.
   1967   "Forbidden Games." Paper prepared for the McGregor Conference on
          Organization Development.
Wohlking, W.
   1971   "Management training: where has it gone wrong?" Training and De-
          velopment Journal 25 (December) :2–9.
Wohlking, W. and H. Weiner
   1971   "Structured and spontaneous role playing: contrast and comparison."
          Training and Development Journal 25 (January) :8–14.
Yalom, I.D. and M.A. Lieberman
   1971   "A study of encounter group casualties." Archives of General Psychia-
          try (25) :15–30.

CHAPTER **15**

Decision Processes:
An Analysis of Power-Sharing at
Senior Organizational Levels

FRANK A. HELLER

The Tavistock Institute of Human Relations

PART I: TOWARDS A MODEL OF DECISION-MAKING

Our understanding of decision-making in organizations has improved as a result of important theoretical and research contributions from diverse sources during the last fifty years. Nevertheless, it is still an underdeveloped subject and much in need of further theoretical refinement and subsequent validation. While such a sweeping statement could be made about many areas of business activity, not least about the oldest specialized discipline, economics, it may justify particular attention in this case. It may be asked whether the *act* of making a decision, defined in the manner described by the greater part of the literature on this subject, is really an important, recognizable managerial activity in modern organizations. The question is of some importance since the activity called decision-making has been endowed with a considerable amount of prestige and there has been a tendency to describe administration or management (particularly at senior levels) in terms of making decisions.

This chapter has two objectives. One is to present a theoretical framework for the discussion and evaluation of the decision-making process in organizations. It is an open system, multivariate approach and it stresses the *relative* rather than the *universal* importance of variables which contribute to the understanding of decision-making. For this reason the model will be called a contingency model to fit in with currently used terminology.

The second objective is to present some findings from field research at senior management levels to validate important aspects of this model. As a result of the gradually accumulating data, the model has been changed and, it is hoped, improved. The research, too, has expanded and it now covers seven

The following colleagues have read parts of the manuscript and made valuable comments: John Child, Robert Dubin, William Starbuck, George Strauss, Cecil Gibb, Cornelius Lammers and Eliezer Rosenstein. The many remaining inadequacies are due to the writer.

countries and will eventually draw on a multinational pool of results from several more. An important aspect of the presentation of the currently available results is to describe a relatively new method of research which has certain advantages for the model used here and for multivariate and multinational comparisons. The method enables one to collect simultaneously highly quantifiable data as well as in-depth qualitative information.

We have said that the activity called decision-making has been endowed with special importance and prestige. This is in part due to its close association with the concept of power and this has had an important effect on the description of organizational typologies such as line and staff functions. It is possible that the often rigid differentiation between giving orders and giving advice, which is so widespread in the classical description of organizations, is based on a misunderstanding of what happens when people say that a decision is being made. What really matters when a person gives an order or makes a recommendation is whether the substance of the order or advice is acted upon. In this sense, advice which is usually accepted is closer to decision-making than orders which are implemented after considerable delay and extensive changes. Accountants or Industrial Engineers may be staff specialists in theory, but if the Accountant's system of apportioning overheads and the Industrial Engineer's suggestions on preventive maintenance are acted on, they are indistinguishable from other decisions made by line managers. It can even be argued that line managers, particularly at senior levels, often *endorse* decisions which were really made much lower down in the organization.

This chapter will start with a theoretical analysis of the decision-making process and its relation to concepts such as influence and power, as well as to other dimensions of the environment surrounding the people who contribute to this process. Having developed the theoretical model we will describe the recent research project which sets out to test some of the assumptions of the model and which appears to validate them.

Some Important Contributions

Probably the most important contribution to our understanding of decision-making (DM) comes to us as a derivative of economic theory and is based on the work of Simon and his colleagues at the Carnegie-Mellon University. Simon (1957) successfully challenged two major assumptions made by traditional economics with its long history of building normative and deductive models of analysis. One is that DM is based on perfect knowledge, and the other is that man attempts to maximize his utilities or satisfactions. Simon's arguments go much further than simply reducing some of the over-rigorous elements of the normative model; he argues as a psychological realist to the effect that man's mind could *never* store and digest the complex information available. Man's rationality is not only bounded, it is also distorted by subjective processes which make him see *his reality* in a special perspective. Furthermore, man's search for alternatives is hampered by these perceptual and knowledge limitations as well as by his limited motivational stamina. Typically, man stops looking for alternatives when some minimum set of priorities is met fairly adequately. By chance, a particular choice could represent optimum conditions, but more usually *he is satisfied* with far less and looks no further. The model used by Simon and his followers stresses the need for empirical work to check on the formulated hypotheses, but like other economic models it is based on charting DM as a process of choice based on objective or subjective probabilities of outcomes. The new emphasis on subjective choices forged a fruitful alliance between statisticians working with Bayesian theories and psychologists exploring the phenomenon of thinking.

A second major contribution to this field, particularly to the analysis of power and its relation to DM comes from sociological theory and especially from the work of Weber (1947) and those who followed a structural-functional analysis of organizations. One can call this the institutional model, which like that of the classical economists, produced a logical and normative framework for explaining bureaucratic processes. Weber, however, centered his analysis around deliberately isolated logical categories called "ideal" types which were chosen to represent a selection of certain elements of reality, while at the same time avoiding the de facto reality of an empirical investigation.

Weber was interested in describing conditions which enabled the decision process to become operative and effective and he saw three major alternative forces at work: (1) rational beliefs based on a legal framework and effective bureaucratic machinery, (2) the force of traditionalism and the predictive stability it provided and (3) the forcefulness and exceptional qualities of leadership which enable some few people to impose their personal authority on the decision process. The orderly development of the bureaucratic process was seen to be helped by the existence of widely diffused values and by the recognition of self-interest in the legitimated decision procedure. Such a conceptual schema gets quite close to certain aspects of modern organization theory. Sociologists, however, usually avoid psychological explanations as carefully as psychologists avoid considering the impact of social structure and institutions on their preferred unit of analysis.[1]

Weber's analysis of bureaucracy and power has had a considerable impact on sociological and political thinking and fits in very well with the somewhat formal, legalistic and structural design of the European system of industrial relations. While Britain remains an exception, the European approach to DM has legitimated a formal division of influence and power which finds its apogee in the German legal code of co-determination based on a series of laws starting in 1951.

The third major impetus to the work on DM and power-sharing comes from the interpersonal analysis of social psychologists. Rensis Likert and many of his colleagues at the University of Michigan have worked on several different approaches in the late 1940s with investigations into supervisory styles of clerical work in insurance companies and manual work on the railways.

The long series of investigations have been summarized in a number of books (Likert, 1961, 1967; Tannenbaum, 1968) and the more experimental orientation of interpersonal DM and power-sharing was carefully reviewed by Cartwright (1965) and from a broader perspective by Vroom (1970). Most of this work is based on the view that decision styles can be adequately described

---

[1] Weber was not quite as doctrinaire in this respect as some sociologists who preceded and followed him. He did not see social structures or social institutions as collective wholes but insisted on looking for molecular explanations at the level of social interaction between industrial actors. The sociological schools that followed him usually failed to develop this eclectic trend.

by two modal categories, authoritarianism and participation (Lowin, 1968). As in the case of the economic and sociological models, the theoretical formulations concentrated on a universalistic position; that is to say, they tested propositions that would apply in most or all circumstances and conditions. Occasionally, exceptions were found and explanations to account for them were put forward (Likert, 1961; Fleishman, et al., 1955), but the view that decision styles are a function of known predictor variables related to the situation, technical factor, organization structure, etc. has been put forward only very recently (Fiedler, 1964; Heller and Yukl, 1969; Lawrence and Lorsch, 1967a; Wofford, 1971).

The three modes of DM analysis stemming from model-building in economics, sociology and interpersonal behavior have developed on autonomous lines and, with the notable exception of the Carnegie-Mellon work of March, Simon and Cyert have contributed little to each other. However, there are now signs that this isolation may soon break down under the influence of open systems thinking. The model to be described in this chapter certainly owes a great deal to a wide spectrum of work.

Our model started from the perspective of an interpersonal analysis of influence and power-sharing between dyads of senior managers. From the beginning, and in contrast with the bulk of the interpersonal work just mentioned, the model was designed to explore the effect of potential moderator and contingency conditions. The question was: How do these contingency variables affect each other and how do they relate to DM methods (the dependent variables)? The model was designed to make few explicit causal assumptions and to begin by studying independent variables that were thought to be psychologically and spatially close to the decision-makers.

Before describing our model and some examples of the supportive research evidence, it is necessary to take a close look at decision-making, which can be treated either as an event, a series of connected events, or as a flow process.

DM as a Series of Events

Most descriptions and definitions of DM concentrate on the modal point where a final *choice* is made (Vroom, 1964:19; Taylor, 1965:48; Applewhite, 1965:53; Brown, 1960:23; Tiffin and McCormick, 1942:500–502). This is particularly clear in all models using decision trees although in that case a number of modal points with a "go-no go" alternative describe a series of steps until the final outcome is reached. This concentration on *choice* based on a careful consideration of alternative utilities can no doubt be justified with many examples and it has certainly facilitated the building of mathematical models in which binary conditions are easily accommodated. Choice is an adequate description of DM when we focus on the activity of one person or on a group of people, such as committees making decisions in a limited time-span. However, organizational DM can only be described by a choice model if one makes a number of unrealistic assumptions and ignores the complex input of advice, recommendations and preferences which make up what eventually emerges as a decision.

The lack of reality is due to the assumption that, at the point where a person takes an action, he had a number of realistic alternatives from which to choose. As we shall show later, this is usually not the case. Nor does action in relation to alternatives require a decision; it often leads to an endorsement of someone else's decision or, more frequently, to a recommendation to be added to other recommendations that eventually lead to an outcome, such as the purchase of a machine.

The complexities of organizational DM have now been carefully documented in a number of case studies (Cyert, Simon and Trow, 1956; Dufty and Taylor, 1962; Cyert and March, 1963; Pettigrew, 1973). It is useful to draw a distinction between routine decisions, for which a computer program can be devised, and nonprogramed decisions which resemble one-off productions of prototypes with novel and unstructured variations. We will be concerned entirely with nonprogramed DM and with the *pattern of influence* which describes *how* decisions are made rather than *what* the decision is. This separation between the process and the content is somewhat artificial, since the former influences the latter and the nature of content also reacts on the process. Eventually, both aspects of DM will have to be described by means of a single model.[2]

In the meantime, we recognize the great value of case studies, since they make it possible to describe the process and content all at once, as well as to give some indication of the pattern of influence. This versatility of the case method is apparent in a well-known and detailed description of selecting a computer and EDP system (Cyert, et al., 1956). However, when the authors come to summarize what they call the "anatomy of the decision" within the constraints of a search-choice model they leave out all considerations of interpersonal relations and influence. This omission would make it very difficult for the model to predict outcomes, even where the decision content remained the same. The authors recognize this difficulty and try to deal with it intuitively by drawing an analogy with an engineering model transmitting and filtering information. Subordinates are said to be "information filters" who can secure a considerable amount of influence over a decision which is eventually made by their boss. The research to be described here measures information filtering in the sense used by Cyert, et al. (1956, 1963), but without using the engineering communication model.

Recommending Decisions or Deciding on Recommendations

Before we can explain our model, we must produce a realistic description of what a typical organizational decision is like. It is worth bearing in mind that when researchers have described what managers actually do during the course of an ordinary work day, they have rarely observed anything resembling the activity of making a decision. Carlson, the pioneer of managerial activity studies, actually concluded that in the judgment of most senior managers "they did not take part in so very many decisions and it was seldom that they gave orders" (Carlson, 1951:49). Most of the senior managers' time was taken up with advising other people and giving them explanations. Many other studies of managerial activities do not even mention decision-making (Stogdill, et al., 1956; Stewart, 1970; Marples, 1967). This strange contrast between one group of researchers who see DM as the truly major managerial activity and another

---

[2] We start by concentrating on the process, but since we are working with a contingency model, we are able to show how different types of content affect the process.

group who find very little trace of DM in the daily work diaries of managers has not yet been adequately explained. Different conceptual models and terminology are undoubtedly one aspect of this puzzling contrast, but there is also something more important. In our research, the main DM questionnaire consists of twelve decisions which were selected from a wide range of alternatives because they were typical of situations which most senior executives had to handle in their businesses. It soon became clear, however, that executives often "made" these decisions only very indirectly. Firstly, they "shared" the activity with various people: their subordinates, colleagues and their superiors. Secondly, it emerged that while they made *a* decision, the final authority could lie with somebody else and it was not always clear where the final decision emerged.

Thirdly, managers were often conscious that although they had the authority to make a final decision, they were in most cases unable and unwilling to reject the recommendations which had come to them. This situation of the decision-maker as the *endorser* of other people's recommendations has not often emerged in the literature, but has been eloquently described by Galbraith, who maintains that even presidents of large organizations such as General Motors "exercise only modest power over substantive decisions" (Galbraith, 1967:67–70). A similar situation of relative powerlessness at the top of the pyramid is noticed by Wilkins (1967) in the legal process. There is very little difference between a "decision" which could be countermanded at a later stage of the process and a "recommendation" which is almost invariably accepted.

DM as a Flow Process

The picture that emerges from these considerations is of a broad and lengthy process meandering its way up a pyramidal structure as in Figure 1. At various points in the DM process people search for facts, make suggestions, recommendations, write reports and make decisions. At a certain stage (called D/E on the diagram) a final resolution of the problem emerges. This can be either in the form of a final decision or an endorsement of recommendations which could have emerged from quite low levels of the pyramid (Blankenship and Miles, 1968).

An alternative way of describing the flow process is to describe a series of events as they relate to a business problem (Figure 2). Let us consider the problem of choosing a new manager for an important position. The process starts with a job description by person A, the previous manager of that job, who has just been promoted to another position. Person B, a relatively junior clerk in the personnel department, drafts the advertisement and suggests where it should be inserted. Person C, a senior member of the personnel department, revises the draft and slightly amends the list of advertising media (after consulting with G, the man who will be the new manager's superior). A short list of ten candidates is drawn up by D, the head of the personnel department and E, the adviser on management development. An outside consultant, F, has devised tests and the interview procedure through which he and D make the decisions on a short list of three candidates, one of whom is particularly highly commended. These three are interviewed by G, the senior manager, who decides on one of them.

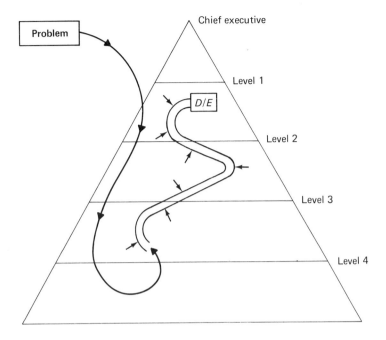

Figure 1. The decision process in a pyramidal structure.

Note: D/E = Decision or Endorsement.

In Figure 2 seven stages have been identified in the DM process in this particular and fairly simple problem. Although G appears to have made the final decision, there are clearly several other stages in the process at which important decisions were made. Only at Stage 7 does DM look like the classical tree choice situation, but in many important respects, G has less influence over who joins the company than several other people who contributed to the earlier stages. The usual questions: "Who made this decision?" "Who is responsible for it?" "Who has contributed most to the final outcome?" are all fairly meaningless. In order to improve the final outcome, namely the selection of the best possible candidate, a more useful question would be: "At which stage of the decision procedure should there be a change of time and money resources to improve the final outcome?" When the question is put in this way, several alternatives emerge which could lead to greater or reduced investment at any one of the seven stages. Just to make a discussion point, one could envisage a situation where the most junior of the eight contributors to the selection DM, namely the clerk, could be responsible for the most critical aspect of the whole process, namely the recommendation where and how to advertise. If substantially better candidates could be attracted at stages 2 and 3, then the subsequent stages of the process are affected by this change, and it is conceivable that none of the final trio who were selected at point 6 would have been sent forward to manager G. By treating DM as a flow process with various inputs of suggestions, choices and recommendations, the sobering conclusion emerges

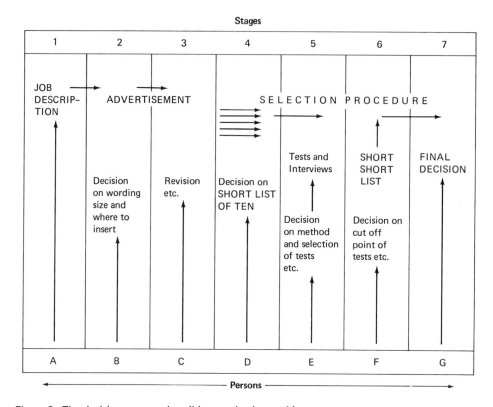

Figure 2. The decision process describing a selection problem.

that every stage of the DM process before the final "go-no go" choice may be more important than the final decision itself.

This example also shows why it is important to consider how much influence and authority (power) is exerted at each stage of the DM process. If we think that stages 2 and 3 are critical in this particular series of events, then we have to know how much influence B, C, and G have on the wording, size and location of advertisements. How do these three people interact in making their decision?

This brings us to a subject which textbooks describe as leadership and the styles of management and it is necessary to make an evaluation of its contribution to DM.

A Neutral Model of "Decision Styles"

The literature on decision styles and leadership methods is full of value assumptions which are so obtrusive that they are likely to influence the results. For instance, the standard research instrument developed by the Institute for Social Research of the University of Michigan uses a series of 4-point scales which are often headed by terms like "exploitive authoritative," "benevolent authoritative" (Likert, 1961:223). Even when these terms are replaced with more neutral terms such as System 1 and System 2 (Likert, 1967:4) the descriptions for each of the points on the scale are quite unequivocally positive or negative. For instance, "Have no confidence and trust in subordinates" as against "Complete confidence and trust in all matters" (Likert, 1967:4). Measurements on such a scale can be anticipated to produce results which will reflect people's values more than the actuality of the organization they are describing. When people are asked to describe on such a scale how they see the situation now and how they would like it to be later, the invariable result is a shift towards what are seen to be more positive or acceptable values (Likert, 1961:28).

There is therefore a need for a more realistic and neutral model of alternative decision methods. By this I mean a range of alternatives which are sufficiently well balanced to enable researchers to observe the empirical distribution of behavior without inviting response bias, resulting from a person's guess of what the "correct" or "desirable" response would be. The absence of such a neutral model is probably responsible for a fair proportion of the generalizations in the current leadership literature.

A neutral model of alternatives will enable us to collect evidence on the decision methods used by administrators in a variety of organizations and under a *range of different conditions*. We can then discover whether leadership styles are univariate or, alternatively, whether they vary in relation to predictable circumstances.

Research: The Influence-Power-Continuum

In our research model, the core variable is the DM process and this is obviously a very complex phenomenon. We have simplified our task by concentrating on how a decision is made rather than on the decision content.[3] Decisions are described in terms of the influence or power which a person or persons exert. We define these terms as follows.

Influence.   This is assumed to exist when a person has access to the decision process. Influence is legitimized when this access is formally recognized by the organization within which influence is exerted. As a result of this access, a person or group can make a contribution to decision-making with various degrees of impact. When the impact leads to acceptance of the contribution in the final outcome, it is called power.

Power.   This concept is defined as influence which has been incorporated in the decision process. When we talk about degrees of power, we attempt to assess or measure the relationship of a particular input to the total determination of all the other elements in the process of arriving at a decision.

Because we have conceptualized DM as a flow process with multiple inputs (as in Figures 1 and 2), we asked our managers to stretch the term *Decision to include advice-giving and recommendations*, as long as there is a high probability that the advice is accepted.[4]

---

[3] It must be repeated that we are aware that content and method are interrelated; we check on this, but concentrate on the latter.

[4] It would be preferable to use another word for DM described in this way, but so far no suitable term has come to mind.

Six positions can be identified on what is called an Influence-Power Continuum (IPC). Figure 3 describes the relationship graphically.[5]

- *Method 1: Manager's own decision without detailed explanation.* These are decisions made by *you* without previous discussion or consultation with other people in the organization. There are situations where the decision or recommendation communicates itself without special procedures.
- *Method 2: Manager's own decision with detailed explanation.* The same as above, but afterwards you explain the problem and the reasons for your choice in a memo or in a special meeting, etc.
- *Method 3: Prior consultation.* Before the decision is taken, you explain the problem to the other person(s) and ask for advice and help. You then make the decision by yourself. Your final choice may, or may not, reflect other people's influence.
- *Method 4: Joint Decision-making.* You and the other person(s) together analyze the problem and come to a decision. The other person(s) usually exerts as much influence as you. Where there are more than two in the discussion the decision of the majority is accepted more often than not.
- *Method 5: Delegation (short span).* You ask a subordinate or colleague to make the decision regarding a particular subject. You make it clear that you want to be kept informed on this matter, and that within a fairly short period you expect to review this decision with him.
- *Method 6: Delegation (long span).*[6] As above, but you do not ask to be kept informed and there is no short-term review. It is understood that even if you did not like the other person's decision, you would intervene only in exceptional circumstances. Some review or evaluation does take place in the long run. The time span will depend on a number of circumstances, such as role expectation, but principally on the nature of the work process and the budget review period.

The Concept of Power in Relation to DM

The concept of power occupies a very important place in the literature of sociology and political science. It is occasionally used in the description of organizational life (March and Simon, 1958; Simon, 1957; Whyte, 1969) and plays an important role through the use of related or overlapping concepts such as authority, control and participation. We have seen that purely organizational terms like *line* and *staff* rely heavily on an analysis of power and this is true of other terms such as *hierarchy* and *leadership*.

Definitions.   It is possible that the word "power" is *not* very widely used in the management literature because of its close association with politics on

---

[5] The IPC methods described here apply the DM process to subordinates, colleagues and superiors. The wording can be changed slightly if we want to study boss-subordinate interaction only as in our research project.

[6] In previous descriptions of the IPC, I used only one method of delegation and therefore only five points on the scale (Heller, 1971a:27–28). The research to be described here is also based on a five-point IPC. The advisability of introducing two modes of delegation arose from discussions during the feed-back stage of the research. The difference between positions 5 and 6 can be seen in time span of responsibility terms (Jaques, 1956).

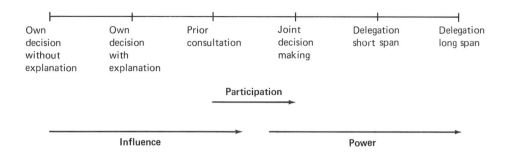

Figure 3. Influence power continuum.

the one hand and an almost medieval stereotype of dominant-submissive relationships, on the other. Terms like *line* and *staff*, *authority* and *control* appear
less tainted and do not offend current values with their emphasis on equality.
Against this background, it may be thought inept or at least unnecessary to
describe six alternative decision methods in terms of a distribution of power.
It can also be argued that if a term like power is used, then it should follow the
most widely accepted definitions, such as those of Weber or Dahl (1968). These
are weighty arguments and we must explain why we have not accepted
them.

    The first reason for not accepting the standard definition of power is that
if the six alternatives in Figure 3 correspond to the reality of the DM process
in organizations, and if we want to describe them as a continuum under a
single concept, then power or some synonym becomes the obvious choice. As has
already been said, most previous investigations have avoided this problem by
concentrating on a smaller range of methods, *excluding* delegation. This has
led to the possibility of seeing the range of alternatives in terms of authoritarian versus group-sharing methods and in this context *participation* is the
term most widely used. Faced with the necessity to choose the term power or
a less aggressive sounding synonym, it was thought that two considerations became relevant. One is the increasing tendency to draw on a wide range of social
sciences for the purposes of organizational analysis. Sociology, political science
and social anthropology have already made substantial contributions and use
the concept power in their analysis. Secondly, it is a question of whether the
realities of organizational life should be seen in sharp or soft focus either from
the point of view of a better understanding or in relation to democratic values.
It was decided that a sharp focus was more appropriate for descriptive as well
as normative purposes.

    The need for our definition of influence and power is more easily justified.
Almost all current definitions concentrate on the relationship between individuals, or between groups of individuals, or between individuals and groups. Our
own definitions *relate* the contribution of *people to a process.* In contrast,
French and Raven (1959) say that their "theory of social influence and power
is limited to influence on the person." Similarly, Dahl in his well-known article
on power (1968:407) states the case quite categorically: "... power terms in
the social sciences exclude relations with inanimate or even nonhuman objects."
Elsewhere, he defines power as determining the behavior of one social unit by

another. Alternatively he sees what he calls "agents" exerting influences, whether they are "individuals, groups, roles, offices, governments, nation-states or other human aggregates" (Dahl, 1957). It is possible, but not necessary, to see the decision process as a human aggregate; in many situations, in government bureaucracies, for instance, the process is best described and identified in relation to a file or set of papers that move from office to office for comment, endorsement or decision.

Weber has been the most influential person in this field and chose to conceptualize power in a classical but aggressive form. It is "the chance of a man or of a number of men to realize their own will in a communal action even against the resistance of others who are participating in the action" (Gerth and Mills, 1947:180). More briefly, he sees power as the "possibility of imposing one's will upon the behavior of other persons" (Bendix, 1960:294). The use of unequivocal German words like *Macht* and *Herrschaft* served to underline the coercive aspect of power which many writers have since followed.

Another important influence on the conceptualization of power is the possibility of relating it to causality (Dahl, 1957, 1968) or even more radically, of treating it as a special instance of causality (March, 1955; Simon, 1957). Our own model avoids causal conclusions and is even opposed to them.

Finally, there is the much debated question surrounding the *fixed* or *elastic* nature of power. The simpler and historically much more important view is to see it as fixed so that if one person obtains more of it, somebody else loses a corresponding amount. Parsons, however, has argued strongly against the dominant and erroneous "tendency in the literature that there is a fixed quantity of power in any relational system" (Parsons, 1963). Tannenbaum has taken the same position; he has operationalized a measure of *control* (Tannenbaum, 1957) and has shown that, by his definition, it is not a fixed amount so that one group of people can substantially increase the amount of control they have (or feel they have) without diminishing the amount held by other people in the same organization. In our description of the IPC (Figure 3), we probably approach zero sum game conditions at the two extremes of the continuum while Tannenbaum's definition applies to the middle ranges (to Methods 3 and 4).

These are the various reasons which have inclined us to define influence and power in an organizational rather than an interpersonal context. The particular organizational anchorage we have chosen is the decision process (Figure 1). Various gateways provide access to DM (our definition of influence) or beyond that, they facilitate incorporation (our definition of power). It must be emphasized that the organizational focus on power does not prevent it from being used in interpersonal power situations, as long as they relate to organizational variables. In our case the organizational variable is DM. For instance, interpersonal promotion and conflict problems may be analyzed as a part of the decision process and the definitions of influence and power given above apply.

A Contingency Model of DM

The next stage in the theoretical analysis of DM is to relate the IPC to a minimum number of variables which can be assumed to influence the styles of decision-making in organizations. From the very large number of conditions that could conceivably correlate with the IPC we have selected a number from the available evidence in the literature and from our previous research.[7] The contingency model on which the present research is based is expected to give way to a succession of simpler and empirically more accurate models under the guidance of the research findings; we will therefore talk of *transitional* models to stress our deliberate policy of revision.

Transitional models. The first transitional model (Heller, 1971a:xiii) is made up of systems of variables which are ordered by their assumed degree of immediacy and psychological proximity to DM (see Figure 4). The *alpha* system level is composed of variables of the person: age, experience, skill, attitudes, values, personal characteristics.

The *beta* system level describes situational variables close to the people making the decision, technology of the managerial job, job function, nature of the decision (to whom it is important), decision level (on whom does it act), job constraints.[8]

Micro structural variables surrounding the DM make up the *gamma* system level: span of control, number of authority levels, size of department, organizational constraints, policy and control procedures, centralization.

The *delta* system level includes the larger structural conditions: size of organization, relationship with other units, degree of competition in sector, turbulence of the immediate environment, technology of organizational workflow.

Finally, to complete the schema, one could consider the possible influence of the sociopolitical and cultural ecology of a geographic area where a business unit is located. The *omega* variables include: the trade union system, social class structure, education, political system and the economic policy emanating from it, state of economic development of the region or country, turbulence of the wider environment.[9]

One reason for expecting several transitional models is the uncertainty concerning the boundaries between the postulated system of variables. These boundaries are conceptual rather than empirical. Since our model is designed to measure patterns of interaction rather than cause and effect relationships, we do not expect that "boundary disputes" will seriously affect our work.[10]

---

[7] The 1967 US research used a number of variables which showed very little correlation with DM and were dropped in 1968. After pretesting, we added further variables in 1968 and again in 1970 and 1971. Some of the instruments were found to be very useful but could not be fitted into the two-hour maximum available for the field research. They will, however, be used for the "in-depth" studies which follow the broader field work. The identification of the various levels of the contingency model has been influenced by the sociotechnical systems approach (Trist, et al., 1951; Emery and Trist, 1960), by the conceptual scheme of Pugh, et al. (1963) and to some extent by Lawrence and Lorsch (1967b).

[8] We also measure how one level of management perceives the behavior or the requirements of another level. To identify such variables we could use terms like alpha-meta, beta-meta variables, etc. Meta is used here in its zoological meaning, signifying subsequent and more developed (shorter Oxford English Dictionary).

[9] Many omega system variables cannot easily be measured at this point of time, but it is important to consider these factors in the case of comparative organization research. Ajiferuke and Boddewyn (1970) have shown that eight indicators of socio-cultural, political and economic dimensions can be measured and correlated with attitudinal data (as the dependent variable).

[10] At the same time, various organization research projects will help to test our assumption. The work of Pugh and his co-workers has established a very carefully documented relationship between contextual variables and organization structure (Pugh, et al., 1963). These two groups of variables correspond fairly closely to our delta and beta levels of analysis.

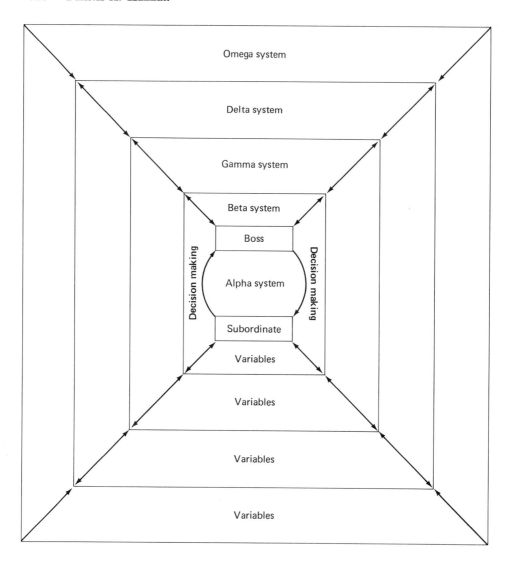

Figure 4. Transitional model: variables affecting decision-making.

It should not be thought, however, that in *any given situation* alpha variables will have a stronger effect on behavior than beta variables and beta variables more than delta variables. The assumption is simply that alpha variables will *normally* impinge on the DM process more continuously and possibly more directly than systems or variables that are at a greater sociopsychological distance from DM.

It will probably be argued that the five-level framework is too broad and complex to be handled in a single research project by means of existing statistical procedures. The purpose of the model, however, is long-term and is intended to achieve two objectives. One is to introduce the necessary amount of reality into the conceptualization so that, unlike the classical model of economic man, potentially critical variables are not left out even if they cannot all be measured at any one time. Secondly, it is expected that by successive stages and approximations, many variables will be eliminated because they are seen to make a small contribution to the problem under investigation, while other variables will be seen to be related to each other and together make a significant impact on our core variable.

The emergent theoretical model will almost certainly turn out to be very different from Figure 4 and may resemble a group of clusters as in Figure 5. Some clusters (for instance C_1) may be seen to make an independent impact on the core variables; others will have a certain amount of overlap (C_2 and C_3, C_4 and C_5).

In this way, the DM process will be described by a series of transitional models of increasing parsimony, measuring the major components which exert influence on the process in defined circumstances. For instance, it is hypothesized that the variable "tranquillity-turbulence" will be associated with low and high power centralization, but only at the extreme ends of the turbulence continuum, while the system of variables describing technical differences in tasks and the perceived existence of skills are expected to emerge as a cluster correlating with the Influence-Power Continuum at several points. It is conceivable that some of the clusters in Figure 5 will be made up mainly from variables described as belonging to one of the five levels in the first transitional model, while others will be made up of highly correlated items from several levels. The distance of each of the clusters of peripheral variables from the core variable is intended to describe the statistical contribution each makes to the total variability in the DM process. The specific hypothesis of interaction between DM and some of the variables in our model has been described in detail elsewhere (Heller, 1971a).

Vroom and Yetton have recently carried out a major research project on leadership styles which adopts contingency assumptions very similar to those reported here (Vroom and Yetton, 1973).[11] They use the term *situational variables* to cover the important circumstances which make leaders use different leadership styles and these styles are roughly comparable to the first four or five alternatives on our Influence-Power Continuum. A central hypothesis in their work is that no single leader-style (we would say decision method) is applicable to all situations and that the best way of testing this assumption is to look at the way managers solve particular problems.

While Vroom and Yetton use a different method of data gathering and different situational variables, their findings, like our own, clearly support the contingency framework and will be referred to later in this chapter.

Leadership Styles and Organizational Effectiveness

Discussion of leadership behavior has always looked for tangible criteria of effectiveness so that different leader methods could be judged by them. As

---

[11] The Vroom-Yetton research had been far advanced when our first report was published in 1969 and they were already writing up results when the first full report was published by Heller in 1971. Nevertheless, it has been possible to compare results. Many are sufficiently similar to strengthen the conclusions from both studies.

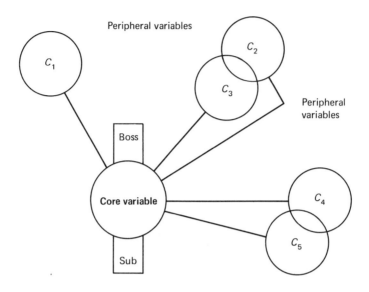

Figure 5. Second transitional model: clusters of variables accounting for observed variations in decision behavior.

the first flush of enthusiasm gave way to disappointment when personality factors did not predict leader behavior (Stogdill, 1948), mediating factors such as attitudes, motives and job satisfactions, were interposed between leader styles on the one side and effectiveness on the other. In recent years, this approach to leadership received a great deal of attention, and most models claimed causal relationships between the so-called styles of leadership and organizational effectiveness. Usually there was no provision for feedback loops or contingency conditions postulating that different circumstances would substantially affect the leader style. These models are now in some danger of following the demise of the earlier personality-behavior model. The difficulty is that the causal links are unreliable and have not been tested under a sufficient variety of conditions.[12] We still do not know what leader style makes for greater production or efficiency.

At one time it was thought that the critical link was the improved satisfaction of people who worked under the preferred (democratic) leader. This thinking has been incorporated into what can be called the Human Relations Model (Miles, 1965). It is illustrated in Figure 6.

The assumptions underlying this model turned out to be quite unreliable; sometimes they did predict correctly, sometimes they did not. The great debate since 1936, following on the Hawthorne studies, has never resolved the leader-

---

[12] As we shall show later, there must also be a serious doubt surrounding the global value-laden questions which serve as measuring devices in most current research on leader style (Likert, 1967; Marrow, et al., 1967; Blake and Mouton, 1964; Reddin, 1970).

Figure 6. Human relations model (After Miles, 1965).

ship question. What was responsible for the steady improvement in output of the relay assembly girls between 1927 and 1932? Was it a new style of supervision, the size of the groups, the incentive system, the special conditions of the room, or the famous Hawthorne effect itself?[13] The Human Relations school of thought tended to look for simple, causal relations and universalistic association between independent and dependent variables. With hindsight, it could be argued that a contingency model would have led to less consternation on the part of the Hawthorne investigators as they were faced with one surprise after another when the introduction of new independent variables and a return to previous conditions failed to affect the steady climb of the output curve.

The major blow to the simplicity of the Human Relations thinking came with the famous review studies of Brayfield and Crockett (1955), Herzberg, et al. (1957) and Miller and Form (1964), which noted very irregular relations between morale and output. So-called "good" leadership practices did not always lead to high morale, and morale could certainly not be relied upon to correlate with high output. It then became necessary to look for some new or additional factors. Likert has come to believe that more time is needed to allow a new leadership style (participation) to affect output. He estimates that if we measured all variables at least over three, and preferably over five years, we would stop getting inconsistent results (Likert, 1967:79–95). This may be so, but it is a difficult proposition to test.

An alternative idea, associated with the views of Likert, McGregor, Haire and others, has been well argued by Miles, who has called it the Human Resources Model (Miles, 1964, 1965). It is based on two assumptions which sharply differentiate it from the Human Relations school. One is the set of attitudes and beliefs which McGregor called Theory Y and which attribute positive qualities such as initiative, responsibility, self-direction and self-control to most people. A consequence of holding Theory Y beliefs is that you trust people.

The second characteristic of the new model is its stress on the hidden resources of skill which participative practices may evoke. Under the Human Relations Model, people might use participation simply to improve communications or to make people "feel" better (improve their morale). Apart from being relatively ineffective, at least with a sophisticated staff, it leaves the field wide open for manipulation and make-believe.

---

[13] By this is usually meant the effect of having a special extraneous factor such as an experiment or the feeling of the subjects that they are important enough to receive the "new" attention. There have been many interpretations and reinterpretations since 1949 when "Management and the worker" was published. One recent reinterpretation of the complete Relay Assembly study up to 1932 uses participative decision-making as the major explanation of the fluctuations in output (Blumberg, 1968).

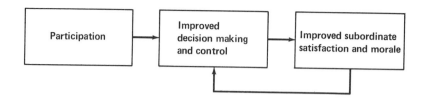

Figure 7. Human resources model (After Miles, 1965).

The contrast between the two models can be seen by comparing Figure 6 with Figure 7. In the Human Resources Model, participation is used because it is thought that better decisions would be made. The improved contribution to DM leads to improved satisfaction and morale and this in turn feeds back to the greater willingness to work and to take part in the decision process. Evidence from field research is now beginning to support this model (Ritchie and Miles, 1970; Miles, et al., 1968).[14]

It will not have escaped the reader's attention that we have recently started to use the popular term, "participation" when talking about leadership methods, while the previous discussion managed to do without this term. After this brief excursion into a description of the work of a very important school of thought, we will now return to our terms influence and power, because, in recent years, the term participation has become ambiguous and emotive.[15] It is also felt that the terms influence and power as defined for the purpose of the IPC enable us to make a very important extension to the participative model by including delegation. Delegation has been deliberately excluded from the Human Resources Model by Likert and his followers because they see a special virtue in group interaction which they cannot extend to a relatively solitary activity. However, it is difficult to reconcile this view with the Human Resources Model's stress on making the best use of a subordinate's opportunities and skills (Strauss, 1968). In this context, delegation is surely a potent alternative to consensus DM.[16] Delegation enables subordinates to show whether they have skill resources that can be used. Similarly, it is difficult to see why consensus and joint DM should be the optimum point on the Likert scale when that school of thought holds Maslow's self-actualization need and autonomy as major human goals. Both can be achieved at least as easily by handing over areas of power to subordinates (giving them an extended amount of autonomy) as by insisting on casting the very labor intensive interaction methods as the major stars of the model. For these reasons,

---

[14] As will be seen later (Figure 9) our own model allows for the interrelationship between effectiveness, satisfaction, DM and other variables. It must be admitted, however, that objective indeces of managerial effectiveness are not available at the present moment, at least at senior levels. This unsatisfactory position can change at any moment and we are therefore justified in including effectiveness in the model, although the research to be described later does not measure this factor.

[15] Furthermore, it is a difficult term to translate into some foreign languages. For a review of alternative approaches, see Walker (1974).

[16] Strauss (1963:58) was probably the first to treat delegation as an integral part of participation.

and a few others we will mention in a moment, we have found it necessary to produce an alternative Human Resources Model.

On the Lookout for Skills

Work in underdeveloped countries, where skilled people are irreplaceable, draws our attention to problems which industrialized countries have been able to overlook for a long time. One problem is the absence of any mechanism for identifying resources or capital other than land, machines, buildings or money. This is exacerbated by time-honored accounting procedures invented at a time when people were cheap and all other resources scarce. The lack of flexibility in the conventional accounting methods has been identified as an important obstacle to the better use of skills (Heller, 1964:1–2). These shortcomings have recently received very careful attention (Likert, 1967:Chapter 9; Pyle, 1970) and have been found to be as important in the highly industrialized United States as they were in underdeveloped areas (Heller, 1969a).

A second difficulty that showed up very clearly in underdeveloped countries was the absence of a concept such as *infrastructures* in organization theory. The term infrastructure is used by economists to draw attention to the differences between trees in the middle of a jungle and wood ready for shipment. Roads, airports, harbors, etc., are essential structural requirements for transforming potential resources into economic wealth.

Such a concept is as necessary in organization theory as it is in economics. The term organizational infrastructure has consequently been used to draw attention to the presence or absence of mechanisms, procedures, technologies and sociopsychological conditions which *facilitate* the use of existing human skills (Heller, 1969a). Several examples of business infrastructures have been given, from the communication system operating at board level to the method of training building workers. In each case, it was possible to show a connection between the wastage of human skills and the absence of certain infrastructure conditions. This extension to the Human Resources Model is illustrated in Figure 8. It describes relationships between an input of skill resources and motives at the upper end of a hopper and the various infrastructure conditions which facilitate their output or obstruct their passage. The hopper analogy enables us to describe a provision for storage since it would be quite unrealistic to assume that *all* available skill and motivational resources could or should be released into the operating system, that is to say, the work-place. Even if we restrict input to those skills which are related to work, we can presume that at least two conditions would result in *some* permanent storage or lack of output. One is the need for any two related dynamic systems, like the water supply to a city and that city's requirements for water, to keep a quantity in reserve. Secondly, one could assume that there would be some loss of effectiveness on the way through the hopper and the infrastructures. The more complex the structures, the more the loss of resources.

A second feature of the Infrastructure Model is its focus of attention on the *nature of the facilitating* or obstructing *quality* of the various channels which connect the hopper to the work system. These channels can describe technical, social or psychological factors. The communications procedure which made the board meetings in some companies more effective than in others was a technical procedure. A combination of dysfunctional status and a certain

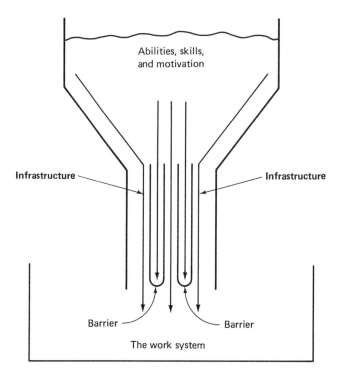

Figure 8. Infrastructure human resources model.

Note: Barrier is a negative infrastructure. An infrastructure is described as a facilitator of skill throughout, while a barrier prevents skills from entering the work system.

technique of writing, wasted the skill of highly trained secretaries (an example of a sociotechnical obstacle). The Theory Y attitudes described by McGregor (1960) are psychological facilitators because they give people a chance to show what they have in their skill hopper that could be applied at work (Heller, 1969a, 1971b). However, the Theory Y *Weltanschauung* is too wide and universalistic to fit into our contingency model; many real life situations do not permit the luxury of implementing managerial practices derived from a rigid adherence to Theory Y. In practice, the infrastructure model operates in relation to specified environmental circumstances (Figure 4) and this enables us to study *which* psychological beliefs, social and technical factors *are* facilitators in a given real situation.

One group of facilitators are of particular importance to our model; they are the various combinations of *influence* and *power* described in the IPC (Figure 3). It will be remembered that influence was defined as having access to the process of decision-making. Access can be thought of as a series of channels merging into the DM flow (as illustrated in Figure 1). The *sources of access* are very numerous and will not be discussed in detail here; they include the five bases of power described by French and Raven (1959), namely reward, coercion, legitimacy, identification and expertness. They also include the control a person may exercise over his environment in order to gain access to power and the Lewinian concept of social gatekeepers who control the access channels through which change may be accomplished.

In organizational terms, we can think of devices like committees and the numerous procedures or customs which decide who shall be members of such committees. Let us think of an organization which has a series of committees which shape policy and some that evaluate and control the ongoing work process. A subcommittee of the board shapes investment policies for the next three years and a lower level committee evaluates departmental cost performance against budgeted standards. When cost performance is off target, they recommend how to achieve a return to a desirable equilibrium. In company *A* the membership of these committees is based largely on seniority, in company *B* there is a deliberate policy of rotation and an emphasis on bringing in a proportion of younger people. It is clear that company *B* has more varied access channels and a greater spread of influence. Over a period of time one can see that, in terms of the model described in Figure 8, company *A* will have more barriers and company *B* more infrastructures.

Let us assume that in both organizations there are many people with knowledge, experience and innovative ideas on investment possibilities and the many factors that influence cost performance; we can then predict that the committee procedure of company *B* will make better use of existing skills, which in turn is likely to produce a higher level of motivation for a greater number of executives than in company *A*.

In the imaginary examples of company *A* and company *B* we have so far described two alternative arrangements relating to the *composition* of the committees.[17] The next step is to consider how each member of the committee relates to his subordinates and colleagues. Does he use methods 1, 2, 3 or 4? In this particular example, the committee members are not free to use delegation (methods 5 and 6) but they may consult or introduce joint procedures which would enable them to feed into the respective committee the opinions and experiences of noncommittee members or even consensus recommendations.

For the sake of the example, let us make the further assumption that committee members in company *B* will, on the average, use more influence-sharing methods with their subordinates and colleagues than company *A* managers. This would extend still further the range of infrastructure channels which tap available skill resources. If the people who are brought into the DM process by these means have skills to contribute, then it is reasonable to assume that the quality of the recommendations of the various committees in company *B* will be higher than in company *A*.

It follows that the analysis of DM methods and the various degrees of influence and power used by managers in solving work problems is an important ingredient of the "hopper" model. While our schema accepts the possibility that in *many* large organizations methods 1 and 2 (where the boss makes the decision on his own, see page 696, this chapter) will be used and may be appropriate in some circumstances, *these methods do not facilitate* the use of subordinates' or colleagues' skills. While these methods should not be condemned, as Likert condemns them, it is necessary to study (a) the extent to

---

[17] To simplify the description we have ommitted considering the method of DM inside the committees themselves and the role of the chairman, that is to say, his leadership methods.

which they are used, and (b) the sociotechnical circumstances which might legitimize them.[18] To make this point graphically; any business that, for whatever reason, were to use exclusively decision methods 1 and 2, would close many of the infrastructure channels in Figure 8 and this would lead to slow learning and poor quality DM.[19]

Skill Utilization as a Motivator

We may speculate for a moment on the relationship between skills, motives, infrastructures and organizational effectiveness. Economic infrastructures bring about a change from *potential* to actual physical resources and the same process of change can be studied with manpower resources. There is, of course, one important difference. Inanimate resources, such as machines and raw materials, do not *feel* underutilized; people do. Consequently, any scheme for using manpower resources must take account of the effect on people's satisfaction.

The behavioral science literature on satisfactions at work is very extensive and inconclusive but in relation to managerial satisfactions there has been a convergence of view between some major schools of thought (marred slightly by a bitter controversy over methodology). Maslow's famous hierarchy has at its peak a need called *self-actualization*, by which he means to "become more and more what one is, to become everything that one is capable of becoming" (Maslow, 1943). McGregor did not develop a formal theory of motivation, but in later life he became convinced that the major obstacle to man achieving satisfaction is the underestimation of other people's potential (McGregor, 1967:98). Various questionnaire studies on large samples of managers have obtained a rough corroboration of the self-actualization view[20] (Porter, 1964; Haire, Ghiselli and Porter, 1966; Heller and Porter, 1966). Alderfer reformulated Maslow's theory into three major groups of motives, one of which, *growth*, was described as satisfaction from utilizing one's capacity to the fullest extent. Alderfer claims that his ERG theory stands up very well to a preliminary empirical test (Alderfer, 1969:171, 1974).[20a] Moving away from the problems associated with covering large samples by distributed questionnaires, Herzberg asked people to describe critical work incidents during which their feelings about their jobs were either rated very high or low. *Achievement* feelings related to their work and receiving some *recognition* for what they had done always rank very high among positive elements and, of course, achievement and recognition are related, "they satisfy the individual's need for self-

---

[18] Legitimize in the sense of being formally acceptable to the people in the work system. We have, for instance, found many occasions when subordinates welcome centralized DM methods and complain when superiors resort to excessively time-consuming ways of consultation and group activity (Heller, 1971a:95–97). In this context one must strive to assess individual and role expectations. Expectations are subtle but powerful forces; they change over time and they are influenced by a variety of sociotechnical circumstances, including the research literature in our field.

[19] This is true unless we are to assume that subordinates and colleagues have no relevant experience and information to offer. But this would be quite an indictment of an organization.

[20] A recent factor analytic study of Maslow type questionnaires gives only moderate support to his *a priori* categories, but finds strong support for factors that can be called growth and recognition (Roberts, et al., 1971).

[20a] ERG stands for three components of motivation; needs of Existence, Relatedness and Growth.

actualization" (Herzberg, et al., 1959:114). While Herzberg has been severely criticized for an aspect of his theory, namely his claim to have isolated two orthogonal factors, this is not an issue that concerns us here, since we are interested only in the priority given to satisfactions.[21] More relevant to our argument is the circumstance that under-utilization of worker skill emerges as a major finding when Herzberg-type job enrichment schemes are applied in industry (Scott, 1964; Paul and Robertson, 1970). People can do more than they were previously expected to do and they like doing it. Furthermore, the findings on the possibility of redesigning jobs to make them fit in better with both technical and social requirements had been anticipated and substantiated by work at the Tavistock Institute of Human Relations (Trist and Bamforth, 1951; Emery, 1959; Herbst, 1962) and by Davis (1957).

The importance of having a large measure of autonomy in jobs, particularly managerial jobs, has been emphasized time and again, particularly in the evidence from questionnaire surveys. Some of this work has been done multinationally and the similarity in the motivational profiles in different national groups is surprising (Haire, Ghiselli and Porter, 1966; Sirota and Greenwood, 1971).[22] The need for autonomy and self-actualization was ranked highest in all fourteen countries studied (Haire, et al., 1966:100). A similar high priority for having considerable freedom to adopt their own approach to the job and to have work from which one gets a personal sense of accomplishment emerges from a recent research project with 13,000 managers and staff in one large, multinational corporation. The managers came from forty-six countries; the opportunity for training to improve skills, job challenge and job autonomy are ranked first, second and third (out of fourteen job goals) in this sample of salesmen, technical personnel and service staff (Sirota and Greenwood, 1971).

Taken together, the evidence, though inconclusive, supports the suggestion that *underutilization* of a person's *skill* could lead to two negative consequences. The first is identical to the loss sustained by underutilizing a machine or land: one simply fails to harness the available capacity. The second consequence arises only with human resources. It seems that people who have experience and skill feel dissatisfied when it is not used. This dissatisfaction could lead to further negative consequences such as low morale, high labor turnover or reduced efficiency. These tertiary dysfunctional consequences have not been established, they are simply a suitable subject for speculation and enquiry. However, even the primary and secondary effects of underutilization justify us in paying attention to the various infrastructure channels in our skill "hopper". One of these infrastructures, as we have seen, is the process of DM and the distribution of influence and power in the work system.

The model which contains the various components which we have described in the first part of this chapter is illustrated in Figure 9. Reading the model from left to right, we see that DM methods are influenced by various ecological variables surrounding the work. If, for whatever reason,

---

[21]See the critical reviews by Dunnette, et al., (1967) and Viteles (1969). Other criticisms could be more damaging (Vroom, 1964:127–129; Schneider and Locke, 1971).

[22] The similarity could be a sign of methodological weakness. It has been alleged that, although managers are assured anonymity, they still give the kind of answers they feel they ought to give.

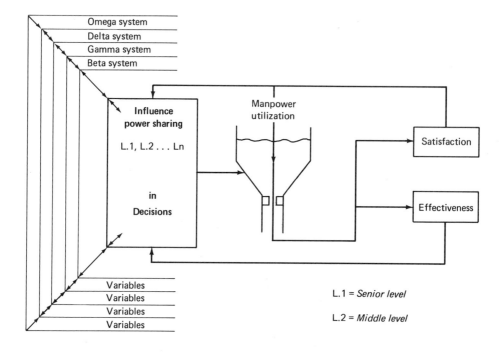

Figure 9. Contingency model of the decision process.

the DM methods are consistently low on the IPC, that is to say, if they fail to share influence and power with subordinates and colleagues, then they lead to an underutilization of the reservoir of available skills. This will tend to reduce satisfaction and to lower the quality or quantity of work. Various feedback loops are set up which reinforce, or moderate, the DM methods, contingency variables and manpower utilization.

Sociotechnical Remedies

One characteristic of the contingency model is to point to more than one possible remedy for a problem of skills wastage. Let us assume that high centralization of decision-making correlates with certain variables from the alpha to delta system, for instance, with the span of control. In such a situation, a change in the gamma system variable (span) might lead to less centralized decision behavior. This way of looking at the contingency model opens up the possibility that a change in organization structure could affect interpersonal relations.[23,24]

---

[23] This suggestion is not new, for instance, it is similar to that put forward by Fiedler (1967), although his theoretical and research approach are quite different. For a discussion on this, see Heller (1973:186–7).

[24] When structure is considered in relation to sociopsychological variables on a broad front, we can be said to have used an extension of the sociotechnical model. Structure becomes the equivalent of technology. We can postulate the need for a joint optimization of structure and sociopsychological variables.

The other alternative is the one which most current Organizational Development schemes champion, namely an attempt to change people's leadership values and decision-making styles directly by means of various organizational training and change agent procedures. We will not pursue this discussion further, since it has been well documented (Argyris, 1970; Heller, 1970, 1975).

In the second part of this chapter, we will present some preliminary evidence in support of a part of our contingency model. This evidence comes from a field research on fifteen large and progressive American companies and 260 senior managers. Supplementary evidence will be cited from a more recent study of a closely matched sample of British companies and over 300 British managers.

PART II: RESEARCH METHODS AND FINDINGS

From Theory to Field Research

While the model is multivariate in so far as it attempts to establish relationships between a considerable number of organizational and people-generated variables, it *starts* with people in interaction and then moves outward by stages to include more and more relevant ecological conditions. Other schemas start at the organization level and gradually move towards an inclusion of sociopsychological variables. Whether the movement is from micro to macro factors or vice versa is not important. However, there is an important distinction between open system multivariate models of this kind and the more self-contained research models which are preoccupied exclusively with variables within one level of conceptualization, be this psychological, sociological or ecological (Argyris, 1972).

While the ecological open systems approach claims advantages over simpler research designs, it must be admitted that it is, in practice, very difficult to implement. The difficulties are practical as well as conceptual; one needs a considerable amount of resources in time and staff to develop the research instruments, to test them and to obtain the willing cooperation of a reasonable sample of industry. Moreover, it is doubtful whether a single method of data gathering and data analysis is sufficient for a complex interactional approach of this kind. Data gathering must be differentiated from analysis. It is usual for data obtained from questionnaires to be analysed by a series of statistical procedures.[25] It is less usual for several different data gathering methods to be used on the same basic hypotheses and population.

In relation to the contingency model described in Part I of this chapter, it was thought advisable to rely on several kinds of data collection as well as on several statistical and qualitative procedures of data evaluation. These preferences were incorporated even at the micro stage of the research, that is to say, when the emphasis was chiefly on assessing sociopsychological variables. They have proved valuable and have been retained through the various extensions covering alpha, beta, gamma and delta system variables.

The main research method has been called Group Feedback Analysis (GFA). It is a multiple data gathering approach and will be described below.

---

[25] The analyses, however, tend to be either parametric *or* nonparametric, rather than a combination of both.

Other methods have since been added. There is, for instance, an extended interview with a chief executive to obtain more objective information on delta system variables, including what have been called contextual and structural variables (Pugh, et al., 1963) and turbulence of the environment (Emery and Trist, 1965). Unobtrusive measures (Webb, et al., 1966) are sometimes obtained and will be used for detailed case descriptions of individual companies. Finally an attempt is being made to use the Delphi method of convergent expert judgments (Dalkey and Helmer, 1963; Campbell and Hitchin, 1968). This method attempts to obtain an independent evaluation of measures of uncertainty and the rate of change facing different industrial sectors in the sample of companies represented in this research project. We want to see whether evaluation from the Delphi method coincides with the *felt* turbulence experienced by managers inside the organization.

Group Feedback Analysis for Gathering Field Data

While the method has been described elsewhere (Heller, 1969b, 1971a), it is convenient to summarize briefly the three main stages and to mention some of the reasons why Group Feedback Analysis (GFA) may be particularly appropriate for handling sensitive psychological and sociological data.

As the name suggests, the method is applied to a group of people who meet in an informal setting to produce the required data. In this particular case, the groups are managers and they are selected for their level and homogeneity. The senior level is made up of all the managers reporting directly to the chief executive of an organization. There are usually five to twelve in number, though larger groups are possible. At a later date, the same procedure is applied to an equal number of their immediate subordinates. Typically, the managers under observation are seated around a boardroom table. The three stages of the method are as follows:

Stage one. The research is introduced by means of a very brief statement by the researcher who also explains that the purpose of the tape recorder on the table is *in part* to standardize instructions for all the groups visited by the researcher. The tape recorder is then used to give a slightly more detailed explanation of the research objectives, including the feedback of results stage. It then gives the instructions for Form 1. The essence of the instructions is repeated on the form itself and, in the case of the more complex instruments, some verbal reinforcement is also given by the researcher. Each questionnaire is short (a maximum of three pages). At the beginning of each new instrument, the tape recorder gives a brief explanation and instructions; the time is used to collect the previous forms from the participants. While the group fills in the second form, the first one is checked for completeness or error. This stage lasts one hour.

Stage two. Some of the forms used in Stage one are submitted to a simple statistical analysis (means and an indication of variance). With the aid of a desk calculator, this takes about thirty to sixty minutes depending on the size of the group. These results are then fed back to the group from which they were taken. This feedback session sometimes takes place on the same day, after an interval for lunch, or anytime within one week.

Stage three. The purpose of the feedback session is—in part—to obtain the group's own interpretation of the results in the light of their knowledge of the situation. A group discussion based on the feedback information is stimulated. It starts off by being virtually unstructured; the researcher's question might be: "Well, these are *your* results, what do you make of them?" Later, more specific questions gradually structure the situation to give more quantifiable form to the discussion.

The tape recorder is on the table in the same position as before and again is used to give one part of the introduction to Stage three. Then, following the feedback, the group is asked whether it has any objection to the tape recorder to save the researcher the trouble of making elaborate notes on their replies. There has never been any opposition. Most of the ensuing discussions are then recorded; if the subject matter strays far afield, the machine can be switched off. The researcher uses the clock counter of the tape recorder to make very brief summary notes on the content of the discussion. This will save time in the subsequent content analysis.

The purpose of the third stage of this method is threefold: (a) to get a "group response" to questions that have previously been put to each individual in questionnaires, (b) to check on the validity of the hypotheses which form the basis of the inquiry, and (c) to deepen the understanding of the subject under inquiry beyond the specific questions asked in the research instruments during Stage one.

The method just described is a relatively novel approach to field research, although the particular ingredients it uses are all well known. Group Feedback Analysis claims to have a number of advantages over the widely used alternatives, namely the interview and particularly the self-administered questionnaire.

In essence, GFA uses the informants twice, for different objectives. During Stage one, we collect the usual questionnaire information, though it can be claimed that the reliability and validity of the results from the group setting are considerably greater than those from a distributed questionnaire. The main advantage is a uniform, undisturbed environment at which the speed of completing answers is controlled.

In Stage three, we use the same informants, and their experience in relation to the variables under discussion, as *interpreters* of the results. The group then analyzes the finer meanings of the research material and explains why the uniformity or heterogeneity has occurred and what specific organizational circumstances must be understood to explain the particular constellation of answers. Stage three is full of rich, often unsuspected depth, similar to the information one obtains from collecting case material. However, unlike case material, the base of the information consists of hard statistical data which can be analyzed by sophisticated multivariate procedures, if this is considered useful.

The Group Feedback Analysis method attempts to bridge the often very considerable gap between the so-called *hard* and *soft* scientific methods (Churchman, 1968) and to add their respective advantages without incurring any special penalty. It will be realized, for instance, that the standardized questionnaire answers are collected *before* the interpretative discussion and therefore remain unaffected by it. It is also worth pointing out that GFA is quite different from the often practiced combination of questionnaire and interview as separate methods of working on the same problem. It is not only that the methods remain separate, but by contrast with GFA they are usually carried out on different parts of the total sample and do not use the subjects to *interpret and enlarge on their own group responses.* The value of having a group interpret its own averages and frequency distribution can be considerable when the subject under discussion is a group or organizational phenomenon. This will be illustrated by the examples given later.

Variables, Measurements and Samples

The research was carried out at two senior levels. The most senior was made up of a group reporting directly to the chief executive and will be abbreviated: L.1. The other level was made up of their direct subordinates and will be abbreviated L.2. In America, the managers in the L.1 group were most usually called vice presidents. The American sample consisted of 260 managers from fifteen large and progressive companies.[26]

The *core variable* in Figure 5 and Figure 9 is the method of decision-making described by five alternative positions on the Influence-Power Continuum. The *Specific Decision Questionnaire* (Form 5) uses twelve decision situations which were selected so that most senior (L.1) managers in a considerable variety of business and industrial undertakings would be able to answer the questions based on their personal experience. In other words, each decision situation was of such a nature that the managers would be involved in it at least occasionally. The twelve decisions were:

1. To increase the salary of your direct subordinate.
2. To increase the number of employees working for your subordinate.
3. To hire one of several applicants to work for your subordinate.
4. To change the extension number of your subordinate's telephone.
5. To purchase for your department a necessary piece of equipment costing over an X amount of dollars.
6. To promote one of the employees working for your subordinate.
7. To give a merit pay increase to one of your subordinate's employees.
8. To increase the dollar allocation for your department during the preparation of the organizational budget.
9. To fire one of your subordinate's employees.
10. To change an operating procedure followed by your subordinate.
11. To assign your subordinate to a different job (on same salary).
12. The decision regarding what targets or quotas should be set for your subordinate.[27]

The items were selected after an extensive pilot survey and full use was made of items from an instrument that had previously been validated (Blankenship and Miles, 1968).

The answer to each question was given on a five stage cumulative percentage scale; each point represented one decision style:

1. Own decision without detailed explanation   _____%
2. Own decision with detailed explanation   _____%

---

[26] Where comparisons are made with the British research, they will be based on a sample matched firm by firm for industrial sector, technology, level, size and "progressiveness." Similar matched samples have been collected in five European countries.

[27] The following description is taken from Heller, 1971a.

3.   Prior consultation with subordinate   _____%
4.   Joint decision-making with subordinate   _____%
5.   Delegation of decision to subordinate   _____%

These five decision styles were carefully defined on a separate sheet of paper. There are two main methods of scoring the Specific Decision Questionnaire. The first makes full use of the five alternative styles, aggregating and averaging them across all respondents and producing an average frequency distribution of the preferred styles in each sample or subsample. The resulting percentage scale requires a forced choice, since high scores on one end necessarily require low scores on the other. This leads to a difficulty in interpreting the precise level of significance of correlation coefficients associated with the five-point scale. The second scoring method, which avoids this problem to some extent, produces an index called *decision centralization*. For this purpose the five decision styles are assumed to be separated by equal intervals on the IPC and scale scores of 5, 4, 3, 2 and 1 were assigned from left to right (delegation = 1). The frequency score, multiplied by the scale values divided by 100 gives the decision centralization index. The advantage of the index, for certain purposes, is that a single score summarizes the point on the IPC characteristic of a person's leadership style. A high score implies that a leader allows his subordinate little influence.

The same form was given to the subordinate managers who used it to describe their chief's decision behavior. Both levels described the *same decision behavior* and it was therefore possible to measure the *perceptual congruence* of matched pairs of boss-subordinates on this important variable.

Of the several *Alpha System* variables (Figure 5) two will be described here. The first measures skill requirements at two different levels and is called the *Skill Difference Questionnaire* (Form 2). The second assesses the time required for subordinates to reach the minimum skill requirements necessary for carrying out the senior job, and it is called the *Skill Acquisition Time Questionnaire* (Form 3). In both forms the questions revolve round the same twelve skills, abilities and personal characteristics:

1.	Knowledge of technical matters	7.	Decisiveness
2.	Closer contact with people	8.	Tact
3.	Knowledge of human nature	9.	Adaptability
4.	Imagination	10.	Forcefulness
5.	Self-confidence	11.	Intelligence
6.	Responsibility	12.	Initiative

These twelve items were chosen from a considerably longer list, for a variety of motives. One was to cover a range of frequently used job-description categories. Secondly, some of the "skills" had to be of a kind that made it reasonable to suppose that L.2 could require as much as, or more than, L.1. Thirdly, they had to be items that applied to all kinds of senior management jobs and were not specialized by function or type of industry. Several lists had previously been developed; six of the items came from Porter (Porter and Henry, 1964), four came from Heller (Heller and Porter, 1966), and two came from Miles (1964).

The Skill Difference Questionnaire asks for an assessment of the requirements of one's own job, compared with that of the other level. Most of the questions are worded as follows: "Does your own job require more or less knowledge of technical matters?" The answers are marked on a five-point scale from "very much more" to "much less." When L.1 managers answer the questions, they compare their job with their subordinates'; when the latter answer, they compare the job requirements at their level with the L.1 job. As a consequence of this arrangement, it is possible to measure the difference in job skills as seen by each level as well as to assess the difference in judgement between the two levels.

The *Skill Acquisition Time Questionnaire* asks the following question at the L.1:

> If you were promoted to another job today and your (named) subordinate were to step into your shoes tomorrow, how much time—if any —would he need to acquire the necessary skill?

The answers can be marked on a ten-point scale:

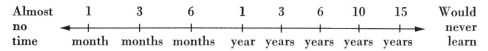

Almost	1	3	6	1	3	6	10	15	Would
no									never
time	month	months	months	year	years	years	years	years	learn

The subordinate is given a similar form but asked to consider how long he would take to acquire the "skills" necessary at the level of his immediate superior. The twelve skills, abilities, and personal qualities are the same as in the Skill Difference Questionnaire.

The *Beta System* is represented (Figure 5) by several variables: decision level, nature of the decision and job function. Only job function will be used in the present description; nine alternative categories are provided, using the standard alternatives from accountancy to personnel management.

The *Gamma System* is also included with several variables, of which span of control and size of department will be used in this chapter.

Some Basic Assumptions

In the original research formulation, twelve hypotheses were put forward and ten were supported by the statistical findings (Heller, 1971a). The present chapter is more concerned with the description of a theoretical model than with the analysis of research data. We will therefore present only sufficient findings to make out a case for the contingency multivariate model. This can be done by discussing seven assumptions which will be numbered in the same way as the original hypotheses:

H1.　Both levels of management believe that more skills are necessary in their own jobs than in those of the other level.

H2.　When L.1 and L.2 managers estimate the amount of time L.2 managers need to acquire the skills and qualities required at L.1, the senior manager's estimate will be larger than the subordinate's.

H3.　Subordinate managers see themselves as having more influence and power in relation to L.1 managers' decisions than L.1 managers believe to be the case.

H4.　Senior managers (L.1) who perceive a substantial gap between their own skill requirements and those relating to L.2 will use more centralized decision procedures than if the perceptual gap is small.

H5.　A large span of control (that is to say, the need to deal with a large number of people in one's department) will be associated with decision methods that save time (i.e., highly centralized or decentralized).

H6. Occupants of jobs that have a small degree of freedom (whose job environment exercises constraints on them) will use a centralized style of decision-making.

H9. Where decisions are more important to the business as a whole and to L.1 than to L.2, then centralized decision procedures will be used by L.1. Where the decision is more important to L.2, his superior will use more power-sharing styles.

These contingency hypotheses are supported by the American findings, and, where the same evidence was collected in the British research, the same trends emerge, sometimes with even greater statistical significance[28]

How Managers Evaluate Skills: Results

When managers judge the requirements of skills at their own level compared with that of the subordinate level, they attribute higher requirements to their own level. This would seem natural and probably accurate in view of the promotion and reward systems operating in most organizations. The twelve skills, however, were chosen so that some of them do not depend so much on rank, level or experience as on the nature of the task, and others could be more necessary at the subordinate level. The results as shown in Table 1 reflect these realities to some extent. Many managers at L.1 judged that their subordinate needed at least as much or more "technical knowledge" and this is reflected in the average shown in Table 1. By contrast, few managers doubted that the senior job required more or very much more "responsibility." The other judgments fell in between these two extremes.

A substantially different picture emerges when we look at the results for L.2 in Table 1 which describe how the subordinates describe the requirements at their own level compared with those of the senior level. The differences between the judgments of the two levels are substantial and in ten cases out of twelve are statistically significant. To interpret these results, it is important to know that the average age of the senior manager was 45.7 and that of the subordinate was 41 years. The L.1 manager had 9.3 years of experience in his company, the L.2 manager 7.2 years. In the British research, the age and experience differences were similar, but the difference in skill judgments was more extreme between levels.

Table 2 describes the results of the Skill Acquisition Time Questionnaire. It is worth remembering that the instructions ask both levels to estimate the amount of time the subordinate would need to acquire the minimum skills necessary to operate effectively at the senior level. The differences in judgement between the two levels are statistically very significant.[29] While the broad pattern in Tables 1 and 2 is similar, the divergence between the senior and

---

[28] An exception in the British sample relates to H9 which does not show the same trend as the American finding. In the British sample we collected other information bearing on this hypothesis which has not yet been analyzed.

[29] The reader should be aware that the subordinates were chosen by the senior level as being the most experienced and senior and this objective was probably achieved in most cases in assemblying the L.2 sample. However, this does *not* mean that the subordinates were chosen for their likelihood of succeeding the senior manager. In many organizations, successors would not necessarily be chosen from the subordinate group.

TABLE 1
SKILL DIFFERENCE QUESTIONNAIRE
US SAMPLE

Skills, abilities and job requirements	Means from a five-point scale*		Significance of difference
	Average L.1	Average L.2	
Knowledge of technical matters	3.1	3.4	NS
Close contact with people	2.9	3.5	.01
Knowledge of human nature	2.3	3.1	.01
Imagination	2.0	3.0	.01
Self-confidence	2.1	2.9	.01
Responsibility	1.6	2.1	.01
Decisiveness	2.0	2.8	.01
Tact	2.3	3.1	.01
Adaptability	2.4	3.3	.01
Forcefulness	2.2	2.8	.01
Intelligence	2.7	2.7	NS
Initiative	2.2	3.2	.01
Average Age	45.7	41.0	
Average Number of Years in Company	9.3	7.2	
Average Number of Years in Job	4.9	3.6	

Note: L.1 refers to level 1, the senior level of management immediately below the chief executive. L.2 is the level immediately subordinate to L.1.
* Scores below 3 indicate a judgement that the skill is more important for L.1 than for L.2. Scores above 3 indicate the reverse.

subordinate is considerably more pronounced in Table 2. The British results show even greater differences in judgments; the average for L.1 was 21.0 months and for L.2, 5.6 months.

During the feedback session, the average results from both these skill questionnaires and the frequency distribution are fed back to each group for discussion, but they receive only their own results, not those from the other level. Nevertheless, the discussions reveal a distinct feeling of unease as far as the L.1 managers are concerned. When they see the pattern of their results the majority of senior managers wonder whether they have not exaggerated the position. What seems to happen is that the managers whose own judgments have been less extreme than the average challenge their colleagues to say why subordinates should need so much time to prepare themselves for the senior

TABLE 2
SKILL PROMOTION QUESTIONNAIRE*
US SAMPLE

	Answer in months			
	Mean	SD		
Leader L.1	11.93	14.19	t = 3.88⁵	p < .001
Subordinate L.2	4.93	8.08	df = 76	

* Question Form: "If you were promoted today and your (named) immediate subordinate were to step into your shoes tomorrow, how much time—if any—would he need to acquire the necessary skill?"
(This is the L.1 version.)

job. "Did *we* have as much time as all that?" is a question often asked. In response to this kind of challenge, other managers admit that the results suggest that their management succession problems appear serious. Sometimes they suggest that their judgments may have been unduly hard.

The implications of these results for the contingency model will be discussed later; the first two hypotheses (H1 and H2) are confirmed.

How Managers Share Influence

The phenomenon of influence and power-sharing is difficult to measure since no objective visual indices are available. In group discussions involving problem-solving tasks in laboratory situations, an independent observer may make his own judgments, but there is no evidence that these estimates are more accurate than the judgments of the participants. In any case, real-life processes do not lend themselves to the outside observer method. Both for this reason and to introduce some element of control, we asked *both* levels to describe the behavior of the senior level on the given twelve decisions.

The average distribution of influence is shown in Figure 10. There is a highly significant difference in the way senior and subordinate managers de-

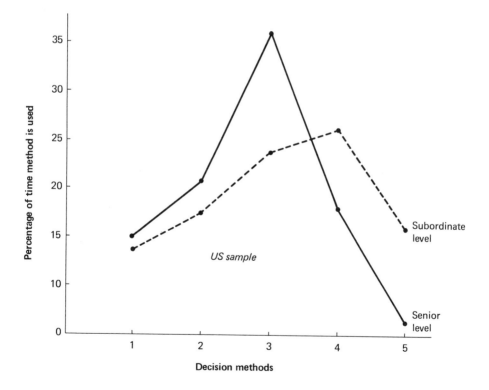

Figure 10. The style of decision-making as seen at two senior levels of management.

Note: The decision methods are those described in Figure 3 of the preceding section (Part I).

scribe the same behavior. The L.1 manager says that he uses "Prior consultation" over 35% of the time and that he delegates very little. The subordinate manager sees his boss using very much more "delegation" and "joint decision-making" and correspondingly less of the other methods. This result would appear to go against common sense. When one asks senior managers how they expect the subordinates to describe the senior's decision-making, they always guess that the shape of the curve would be displaced towards the more autocratic end of the continuum. Since the opposite is the case, it is important to report that the British results follow exactly the same curves and that German results also support this finding.[30]

Some Explanations. We cannot be sure what these results mean. At the moment, three explanations seem possible. One is in terms of the subordinates' wish-fulfillment and presupposes a high degree of motivation to exercise more power. It suggests that the motive leads to perceptual distortion. The second explanation also assumes that the subordinate is motivated to use more power, but that, in fact, he exerts more influence than his boss is aware of. Such an explanation makes sense if we accept the description of the decision process as a flow of events (as in Figures 1 and 2) rather than as a series of discrete choices on a decision tree. In such a situation uncertainties about the real extent of one's contribution or influence can arise. A decision is not a "go" or "no-go" act but a probability that a given piece of advice or other action is incorporated into the flow of events and influences it in some measure. In any case, both explanations of the perceptual gap presuppose the existence of motivations of which the senior managers appear not to be aware. This energy is an important ingredient in our skill "hopper" model (Figure 8). Together with the findings that senior managers have a lower estimation of their subordinates' skills and readiness to take on senior responsibilities, the present finding lends strong support to the possibility that the available human resources are not fully used. A third explanation suggests that the difference is due to a "positional perspective and somewhat comparable to the well studied phenomenon of perceptual illusion" (Wilpert and Heller, 1973).[31]

With the possibility of skill underutilization in mind we will now look at the relationship between a manager's perception of skills at the lower level

---

[30] The German results are reported in a paper by Wilpert and Heller (1973) and Heller and Wilpert (1974).

[31] Vroom and Yetton report a finding they consider to be inconsistent with ours (Vroom and Yetton, 1973:79). Managers were asked to rank order the frequency with which they employed the various decision methods. They were also asked to give the frequency with which these methods were used by their superiors. They report that "managers' superiors were typically seen as using much more autocratic styles than the managers themselves used." Vroom puts forward various explanations; we accept one and add another. In this part of his research, Vroom asked a *general* question about participation in all kinds of situations while we asked twelve questions describing specific decisions. The more specific the question, the less likely that stereotyped views of the *value* of participation will intrude in the judgments. Secondly, our research was carried out inside organizations and both levels knew that we would obtain data from the other. Anonymity was guaranteed, but the knowledge that both levels were to describe the same situation might have acted as a further limitation on the influence of value judgements. Vroom's finding is more in line with general common sense expectations. On the other hand, ours has now been obtained in four different samples (US, UK, Germany and a UK study in four government departments not yet reported). Further research is necessary to solve this issue.

TABLE 3
PERCEPTION OF SKILL RELATED TO
DECISION METHOD
US SAMPLE

METHOD OF DECISION-MAKING	How differently does L.1 see sub. skill from own skill:	significance level
1 Own decision without explanation	−.31	<.01
2 Own decision with explanation	−.17	NS
3 Prior consultation	.03	NS
4 Joint decision-making	.24	<.02
5 Delegation	.26	<.02

Note: A correlation in this table indicates a relationship between the following variables:
    (a) L.1's judgement of the differences in job skills between his own level and that of the subordinate level.
    (b) The frequency of L.1 using a certain decision style (frequency expressed as a percentage distributed over the five styles).

and his decision style (Hypothesis [H4.]). Table 3 produces some support for the assumption that managers who see less skill in their subordinates will use more centralized decision methods than managers who make more positive skill judgements.[32] The British and German results replicate these findings (Heller and Wilpert, 1974). Vroom and Yetton, using different methods and samples, arrive at the same conclusion (1973:83). This evidence can be interpreted in two ways. Either the senior manager's judgement of his subordinate's skill is correct, in which case his adjustment of decision style is logical. There is, after all, little point in spending time and effort on consultation or joint decision-making if the subordinate lacks the skill or qualities to make a real contribution to the process. Alternatively, if the senior's judgement is incorrect, and the subordinate has skills, etc., more nearly in line with his self-estimate, then the more centralized decision style could be a major factor in the under-utilization of managerial resources.

The Influence of Contingencies on Decision-Making

Hypotheses H5, H6 and H9 select three variables from the Beta and Gamma systems to test their predicted interaction with the decision process. To begin with, let us look at the interaction between a manager's span of control and his decision method. It is assumed that if a large number of subordinates act as a contingency variable, then they should influence decision-making by leading to methods which would save the senior man's time. A manager can save time by using either extreme of the decision continuum, that is to say, methods 1, 2 or 5. The other methods would seem to be more difficult to handle with many subordinates. Table 4 shows the results supporting this hypothesis. The result from the British research also supports this hypothesis.[33]

In the second place, it was thought that the technology of the managerial

---

[32] For further support, see Heller (1971a:78).

[33] The British results show a different pattern, the significant correlations showing that the tendency is to keep away from "prior consultation" and to lean slightly towards decentralization.

TABLE 4
RELATION BETWEEN SPAN OF
CONTROL AND METHOD OF DECISION-MAKING:
LEVEL 1

Methods	Correlation with span of control* Significance level
1 Own decision without explanation	<.01
2 Own decision with explanation	NS
3 Prior consultation	NS
4 Joint decision-making	NS
5 Delegation	<.05

* The larger the span, the more likely that Methods 1 or 5 will be used.

job would vary with the function of the work. Job function was therefore taken as a contingency factor and Figure 11 shows the relationship between six functions and the degree of decision centralization. The results show a clear relationship and an analysis or variance between the pairs of functions is statistically significant, confirming Hypothesis H6.[34]

The third contingency hypothesis postulated a relationship between the nature of the decision, for instance, its importance to the company, as a major

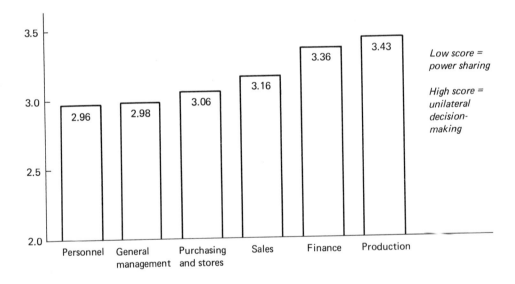

Figure 11. The relation of decision method to job function (US sample).

Note: The means are scores of Decision Centralization.

---

[34] The British results do not follow the same pattern and we have to await the results from further samples before reaching a conclusion.

influence on the decision method. Four different alternatives were envisaged:

1. Where the decision is of great importance for the subordinate.
2. Where the decision is about equally important for the company and the subordinate.
3. Where the decision is particularly important for the company.
4. Where neither the company nor the subordinate have a special interest in the decision.

The distribution of influence and power sharing on these four contingencies follows the curves of Figure 12. It can be seen that managers have no difficulty in differentiating the alternatives. Where the decisions are particularly important for the subordinate, the senior manager is prepared to give him a considerable amount of power. In sharp contrast, he retains most of the available decision power in his own hands when the company is the major interested party. When both parties are equally concerned, the power distribution approximates to a normal curve. When decisions are of relatively little importance to either, then the main preference is to avoid time-consuming procedures and to go straight for extreme "autocracy" or delegation.[35]

An Evaluation of Participation as a Style of Management

We have said earlier that we prefer to avoid the term "participation." It seems that in a large part of the literature on the subject, this term has become associated with various values which range all the way from the purely political to the sales talk of consultants who offer ready made packages of "how to do it" kits. In between these unsatisfactory extremes, participation is a term used by psychologists and sociologists to describe an organizational or interpersonal phenomenon based on power or influence. For this reason, it seems preferable to keep to an influence-power description and to avoid the emotional and usually vague term, participation. Throughout the research described up to now and in the definition of the five alternative decision methods, we have upheld this preference. A further reason for avoiding the term participation is that it does not lend itself to a description of the various types of delegation (see Figure 3). Delegation is, of course, a particularly important aspect of distributing power throughout an organization. If power were not "delegated" to various appropriate levels, there would be little genuine participation at lower echelons (that is to say, consultation, joint decision-making and consensus methods of various kinds). In the absence of a distribution of delegated power one would be left with "manipulative participation" which can be defined as a process that gives the appearance of distributing influence when no such influence is available. One is concerned here with the facts of the situation, not the reasons for them. Influence may not be available because the real decision has already been taken or because the key person in the process has no intention of allowing himself to be influenced, irrespective of the value of the contribution. We have said earlier that the reason why the major schools of thought on participative decision-making omit delegation from their range of alternatives is that they attach a particular value to group

---

[35] We put the term "autocracy" in quotation marks to signify that no negative implications should be attributed to the term; it is simply descriptive of a logical and possible appropriate alternative.

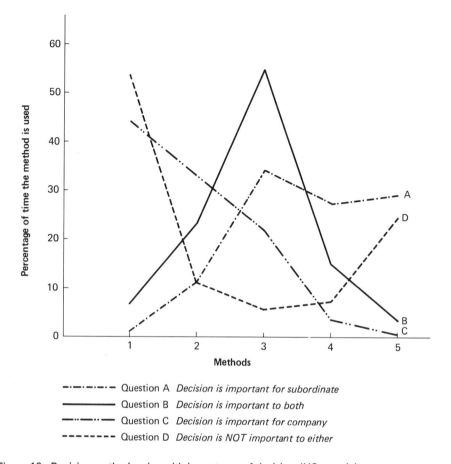

Figure 12. Decision method varies with importance of decision (US sample).

Note: For a description of the five decision methods, see Figure 3 and preceding section (Part I).

and interpersonal processes and that this somewhat doctrinaire position prevents them from including delegation.

Despite our preference, it must be recognized that practising managers in nearly all parts of the world have become accustomed to the term participation (Haire, Ghiselli and Porter, 1966). For this reason, we included this word on one of the fourteen questionnaires used in the present research. During the last ten minutes of the feedback discussion, we asked our group what managerial pay-off they expected from the use of the influence and power-sharing process which, in the literature, is often called "participation." The importance attributed to the various alternatives is scored and the results are shown in Table 5.[36]

The results are almost the same for both levels and show that managers

---

[36] In the first phase of the American research, the scoring was based on a method of content analysis of the tape recordings (Heller, 1971a). Later, a simple questionnaire was used, leading to a ranking of the five most important reasons.

TABLE 5
WHY MANAGERS USE
"PARTICIPATIVE" DECISION METHODS:
RESULTS FROM TWO SENIOR LEVELS

Reasons	Ranking L.1	L.2
To improve the technical quality of decisions	1	1
To increase satisfaction	2	3
To improve communication (understanding of problems)	3	2
To train subordinates	4	4
To facilitate change	5	5

Note: L.1 refers to Level 1, the senior level of management immediately below the chief executive. L.2 is the level immediately subordinate to L.1.

expect "participative" methods to be of most benefit in improving the quality of decision-making; secondly, in improving communication; thirdly, in increasing satisfaction and fourthly, in training subordinates. While behavioral scientists are particularly interested in "participation" as a powerful method of facilitating the introduction of change, managers give relatively little importance to it. The British results are identical to the American findings.

Finally a note about "management styles" and "democratic" management. As in the case of the word participation, these terms have strong emotive connotations and for the sake of accuracy and as a way of arriving at a description of organizational reality, it is best to avoid them. Instead of "styles," one can use the more neutral term "method;" this avoids the evocation that a certain "style" is fashionable or unfashionable, good or bad. Democratic management is a particularly inappropriate term since it has clear value implications.

However, beyond terminological preferences there is a very real question of how much influence and power is shared by different levels of management and how much of the senior man's influence is *seen* to be shared by his subordinates. We have two sources of evidence. One comes from the statistical summary of decision methods as seen by L.1 and L.2; this result is presented in two alternative ways in Table 6. In the first assumption, we define influence and power sharing by including "prior consultation." In the second, we include only the most powerful methods, 4 and 5. On the first assumption, both senior and subordinate see the distribution of power in roughly the same way, and over 60% report that Methods 3, 4 and 5 are used in their company. In making the more stringent assumption, differences of judgement between the two levels appear. The senior level reports 27% and the subordinate level 42% of power-sharing. Even this amount is considerable if we remember that several of the decision situations do not lend themselves to joint decision-making or delegation; it will be remembered, for instance, that Question 1 asks how L.1 decides about increases in the subordinate's salary.

If one relied on the statistical picture alone, one could well conclude that the average distribution of influence and power in this sample was very considerable. We will now look at other evidence.

A Reevaluation Based on Feedback Analysis

There are several reasons why the results from questionnaire enquiries alone may be inadequate, even if the research instruments have been carefully tested

TABLE 6
TWO INTERPRETATIONS OF
INFLUENCE AND POWER-SHARING
AS SEEN BY TWO SENIOR LEVELS

	As seen by L.1	As seen by L.2
INTERPRETATION 1		
Methods 1 & 2	36.2	33.6
Methods 3, 4 & 5	63.8	66.4
	100%	100%
INTERPRETATION 2		
Methods 1, 2 & 3	73.0	58.1
Methods 4 & 5	27.0	41.9
	100%	100%

Note: L.1 refers to Level 1, the senior level immediately below the chief executive. L.2 is the level immediately subordinate to L.1.

(Heller, 1969b). One problem relates to the bias due to expectations on a popular topic like participation or styles of management. Even if one avoids these value terms there is, at least in America, a constant stream of articles, books and public speeches which hammer home the point that certain styles of managerial behavior are better than others. Since the contingency framework has not yet gained much ground, the credo of "democratic" management in all circumstances has had no substantial opposition.[37] People take sides even before they think carefully. As a result of reading or attending courses, they have come to consider themselves as being a certain person, using a particular method of leadership and being judged as "avant-garde" rather than "old fashioned." This is, of course, a major reason for not using emotive trigger words. Thoughts like this lead one to question the value of enquiries which ask two questions: firstly, how much participation people experience now and secondly, how much they would like to have. Given that the stimulus word relates to a desirable experience, the answer to the second question is hardly in doubt, and tells us more about the nature of the response set than about the variable in question.

One of the major objectives of Stage three in Group Feedback Analysis (GFA) used as a method of field research is to delve into the real meaning of the statistical findings, to motivate managers to interpret their meaning and to reevaluate the results where necessary. The details of these reinterpretations and the content analysis used are described elsewhere (Heller, 1971a:59–68, 91–99) ; here we will describe only the main conclusions.

There is strong evidence that, as a result of the feedback discussion, one becomes conscious of two distortions in the statistical results. One is due to a substantial element of what we have called manipulative participation, particularly where managers have described themselves as using prior consultation. What typically happens in an L.1 feedback discussion is this:

---

[37] In the footnotes of the vast literature on this subject there are of course many caveats and the cumulative contribution of the work of Fiedler (1967), Woodward (1965), Burns and Stalker (1961), Lawrence and Lorsch (1967a), Trist, et al. (1963) is beginning to have an effect. For a review of these arguments, see Heller (1971a).

One manager has described himself as using prior consultation in 48% of his decisions, while others in the same group have put down figures varying between 20% and 35%. No names appear next to the results but every manager can recognize his own. A member of the group challenges the plausibility of 48% in the circumstances of their company. Two other managers identify themselves as having used much lower percentages. There is silence. Then Mr. Jones says that he "believes" he probably put down 48% but he would like to explain that he includes under that heading all the occasions when he meets his subordinate on a Monday morning to discuss performance against budgets for the previous week and the production plan for the following week. There is a pause and more silence. Then several colleagues challenge this interpretation; they point out that the budget targets are fixed a long time before and cannot be changed, and that the Monday morning meetings are almost entirely informational, since the plans have been hammered out between themselves (that is to say, the L.1 group) in the weekly review on Friday afternoon. Mr. Jones argues a bit about the possible interpretation of prior consultation; he says that he presents the plans as if they were for discussion, because his people like it that way. They refer to the written definition again and it is then agreed that only 25% or thereabouts was really appropriate under that heading; the remaining 23% should be divided between Methods 1 and 2.

This is an extreme case but the general trend of the re-evaluation is always in that direction. Unfortunately, there is usually not enough time to produce precise results as in the example above; the discussion tends to be in much vaguer terms and no worthwhile statistical readjustment of the original questionnaire results is practical.[38]

The second major distortion occurs in relation to Method 4, Joint Decision-Making. In discussion after discussion, it becomes clear that, in spite of the carefully prepared definition and verbal reinforcement by the researcher, a proportion of managers interpret Joint Decision-Making as describing situations that are more appropriate to Method 3 or to a point on the continuum close to Method 3. This seems to be due to the difficulty managers have in visualizing genuine consensus power-sharing situations in *specific circumstances*. They may be willing to talk about it in *general terms*, but when in the feedback discussion they are pinned down to actual examples, they readily admit that the formal definition of Method 4, where the "subordinate(s) usually has as much influence over the final choice" as the senior manager, is not feasible in the majority of cases.

We come back to the point that subjects like leadership, power-sharing or the pervasive "participation" cannot be described with complete objectivity. To a large extent *the reality of the behavior is the belief and the interpretation* of the parties concerned. One is therefore entitled to use judgments based on neutrally worded questions describing specific managerial behavior, backed up by careful definitions. This we do and the consequent results are probably as accurate as the questionnaire method alone permits. Group Feedback Analysis enables us to submit these results to further scrutiny but in the time available during the research described here, the conclusion must be put very tentatively. We estimate that in the American sample of senior managers, Methods 4 and 5

---

[38] If more time were available, and the number of questionnaires restricted, GFA could be used for a statistical reappraisal of results.

are used between 15%–20% of the time and Method 3 between 20%–30%. This would leave at least half the total decision behavior and possibly 65% to be described by Methods 1 and 2.

CURRENT RESEARCH EXTENSIONS IN EUROPEAN COUNTRIES

Following the American work, a British research with twenty large companies was carried out. Fifteen of these companies were carefully matched to the American companies in type of industry, technology, size and managerial level.[39] Between 1972 and the end of 1974, six other countries joined the project, five of them European.[40] The research now covers over 1600 managers in 100 companies.

The European work was an extension rather than a replication of the American research. In addition to the questionnaires used in the United States, nine further instruments were developed and validated. They were based on variables conceptualized in the alpha to omega hierarchy of contingencies (Figures 4 and 9) and will be briefly described.

- *Pressures and constraints questionnaire—Form 4*

  An assessment of the effect of constraints surrounding the managerial task. For instance, pressures and the amount of formal authority invested in a job limit a manager's choice of alternatives. A gamma level variable.

- *Lateral decision-making questionnaire—Form 6*

  Extended the IPC from the superior-subordinate level to an assessment of influence-power sharing among colleagues (an extension of the core variable).

- *Skill utilization measure—Form 8*

  A simple and very preliminary attempt to obtain a rough assessment of the perception of *underutilization* of skill at the two levels of management (skill hopper model Figures 8 and 9).

- *Turbulence and uncertainty questionnaire—Form 9*

  This is an attempt to measure a part of the theoretical concept of complexity and turbulence, discussed by Emery and Trist (1965). A variety of environmental variables which fall within the gamma and delta systems are included.

- *Expectation of change questionnaire—Form 10*

  While the turbulence questionnaire measures current conditions, here we assess expectation of the rate of change during the next five to ten years (delta system).

- *Formal skill qualification questionnaire—Form 11*

  This is the first attempt within the present research to obtain an ob-

---

[39] This work was done by the Tavistock Institute of Human Relations in London and supported by two grants from the Social Science Research Council (of Great Britain), including the European extension.

[40] The following European research centers are involved: The Erasmus University of Rotterdam supported by the Dutch Productivity Centre; The International Institute of Management, West Berlin; Centre d'Enseignement Superieur des Affaires, France; Economic Research Institute, Stockholm School of Economics; Instituto de Estudios Superiores de la Empresa, Barcelona; and the Leon Recanati Graduate School of Business Administration.

jective measure of the available skills of senior management at the two levels represented. It is designed to measure skills in the hopper model (Figures 8 and 9).

- *Work satisfaction measure*—Form 14

A simple questionnaire to measure the satisfaction and motivation variables described in Figure 9.

Finally, there are some organizational measures obtained through an interview with the chief executive of each company in the sample:

- *Aston measures of organization structure and context* as defined by Pugh, et al. (1963) and measured in a short scale (Inkson, et al., 1970). We have made slight adaptations to this scale and have included a simple assessment of organization effectiveness. This is part of the delta system of variables.

Further Assessments of Organizational Turbulence

Two similar measurements were attempted; first by interviewing the chief executive in each company and secondly by obtaining a panel of expert judges who knew the industrial sectors of our sample and who judged the relative degree of turbulence surrounding each of them. A form of "Delphi method" was used.[41]

Preliminary Results from Some European Research[42]

All field work was completed by the end of 1974 and most countries had analyzed a part of their results at that time. The following summary of some preliminary findings is based mainly on the British and German data.[43]

One of the simplest, but in terms of the contingency model very important, findings relates to the diversity of power-sharing methods used by senior man-

---

[41] The Aston and second stage turbulence measures were used only in the British sample.

[42] The statistical methodology for data analysis will not be described in detail since this falls outside the objective of this chapter. The basic outline will be mentioned to enable the reader to form a judgment about the eventual empirical validity in support of the contingency model. Each of the main variables described in this chapter has been factor analyzed to form composites of the dimensions in the model (Wilpert and Heller, 1974). The multivariate analysis was based on parametric methods in the first place (intercorrelation matrix of variables and composites; t-tests and one-way analysis of variance of noncontinuous variables such as comparisons between levels of management, indutrial sectors and countries). Multiple regression analysis and cannonical correlations were used to test the interaction between our peripheral and core variables. In the second stage the same data was treated nonparametrically. Contingency tables were constructed to test the main hypotheses; Kendall's tau and chi square tests were applied to three by three tables based on a high, medium and low trichotomization of all continuous variables. Multidimensional scaling was used on the British skill perception variables to compare with the factor analysis. Since many variables are not normally distributed, the main findings will be those that are confirmed by parametric as well as nonparametric methods. Finally, the tape recordings from the feedback discussions are being content analyzed in each country. It was agreed that the methods of content analysis would not be standardized since an idiographic rather than nomothetic result is aimed at.

[43] The West Berlin-based International Institute of Management has taken a leading part in the European research and its financial support. Dr. Wilpert, the chief German investigator, co-authored two papers with Dr. Heller presented at international research meetings in Canada during the summer of 1974. These papers are drawn on for the summary of results.

agers. There are two main trends in the leadership literature. The older approach, referred to earlier, was to see participatory or autocratic leadership methods as a function of *personality*. More recently, organizational psychologists have argued in favor of participatory methods in terms of a *normative* model. The norm became an organizational objective and managers were expected to converge to that norm irrespective of their personality.

It now seems that neither personality nor norm in fact decides the methods of decision-making used.[44] Managers change their method in relation to different *situations*. Both in Germany and Britain only one out of a hundred managers uses a single method of decision-making. 20% of the German managers and 30% of British managers use all five methods of the IPC on the twelve decisions described earlier in this chapter. Between 40% and 50% use four out of the five methods. This finding has considerable validity since the descriptions of both levels of managers agree and both levels describe the same behavior (Heller, 1973; Heller and Wilpert, 1974). The multiple use of styles by the same leaders is fully confirmed by Vroom and Yetton (1973), Bass and Valenzi (1973) and Hill (1973). The potential importance of situationally determined leadership has been discussed for a considerable time (Stogdill, 1948, 1956; Hemphill, 1950; Seeman, 1953; Wispe and Lloyd, 1955; Gibb, 1958; Argyris, 1964; Koreman, 1966), but it is only now that we are beginning to understand the nature of the specific contingencies which account for variations in leadership behavior (Fiedler, 1967; Lawrence and Lorsch, 1967; Heller and Yukl, 1969; Heller, 1971a; Vroom and Yetton, 1973; Bass and Valenzi, 1973; Hill and Hughes, 1974).

The major situational factors accounting for variations in managerial decision-making methods in the European research appear to be *task* and *skill*. Both come from the alpha and beta system of contingency variables. Task has been variously described as technology of the managerial job, job function and the nature of the decision. It is this last variable, measured by the twelve decisions described earlier in this chapter, which accounts for the greatest variance in decision method (Heller and Wilpert, 1974).

One particular way of differentiating task is to choose some decisions which apply to a whole group of people and compare them with decisions made only between a manager and one of his immediate subordinates. This difference is highly significant in the American, British and German samples (Heller and Wilpert, 1974).[45]

The second major contingency variable is measured by three indicators of skill. Two are attitudinal and judgmental, while the third presents the actual formal qualifications and skills of each manager (Form 11). The American results on the attitudinal measures have already been given (Tables 2, 3 and 4). The British and German results support these findings. On the basis of a sample of fifty companies and nearly 600 managers, it is now possible to argue as follows.

Managers who perceive a substantial difference between their own jobs and the jobs of their subordinates and/or between themselves and their subordinates (these are different judgments) tend to use centralized decision meth-

---

[44] A recent controlled laboratory research study confirms the relatively small contribution of personality factors in DM (Taylor and Dunnette, 1974).

[45] For other significant task dimensions, see Figures 11 and 12 (pages 722, 724).

ods. Small perceptual gaps on these dimensions are associated with participatory decision-making.

We cannot be sure that these perceptions of skill differences correspond to actual differences in every case, but the subordinate's judgments follow the same pattern.

An even stronger support for the hypothesis that skills and decision-making methods interrelate, comes from the measures of formal educational qualifications. British and German senior managers with high educational qualifications use participative decision methods. Those with lower qualifications use more autocratic methods (Heller and Wilpert, 1974).

The last specific finding to be mentioned here relates to the effect on decision-making of a complex and uncertain environment. In the present research, Form 9 is an attempt to operationalize Emery and Trist's (1965) ideas on turbulence of the environment.[46]

The hypothesis that a highly complex and turbulent environment is associated with decentralized decision-making is supported at both senior levels. The preliminary analysis suggests, however, that the relationship is weaker and less consistent than with the alpha, beta and gamma variables. If this turned out to be the case, it would support the hierarchical contingency assumptions. It will be remembered that turbulence was thought to be relatively peripheral to the decision act at these particular levels of management and was classified as a delta level variable (Figure 9).

It must be emphasized that this finding is very tentative since turbulence had not been explored in the earlier American research. A relatively low impact value of environmental turbulence would have to be reconciled with a considerable recent emphasis on the importance of this variable (Starbuck, 1972).[47]

PART III: A TENTATIVE OVERVIEW

Our main objective was to put forward a theoretical framework for an analysis of power relationships between decision-makers in organizations. There are three parts to the framework: infrastructures, flow process and contingencies. Some data were presented to provide a preliminary test of the dimensions incorporated in the theoretical framework. Other data are available in the literature referred to.[48]

---

[46] The instrument has nine closed and one open question. Repeat reliability and internal consistency are satisfactory. Construct validity is achieved by reasonable correlations with Form 4 (Pressures and constraints) and Form 10 (Expectation of change). Factor analysis yields two factors accounting for 44% of the variance, three factors 55%. The intercorrelations between perceived turbulence at the two levels are high and consistent.

[47] One argument which anticipates the possibility of low impact of environmental factors has been put forward by Child (1972). Child says that managers have a wide range of choices which are unlikely to be decisively constrained by a factor like turbulence. At the same time, we fully endorse Child's view that subjectively perceived turbulence is at least as important as objective measures. Since "coping with turbulence" rather than the uncertainty itself is likely to be the critical factor (Crozier, 1964; Hickson, et al., 1971), it is worth mentioning that the instructions used in our research instruments elicit judgments on the environmental impact on the here-and-now-work-situation. There is evidence that responses were in terms of "coping."

[48] For further examples of recent literature relevant to a flow analysis of DM, see Friend and Jessop (1969), Sadler and Barry (1970), Braybrooke (1974).

Decision Analysis

The flow process model of decision-making (Figures 1 and 2) departs from traditional approaches in several respects. The literature on decision-making tends to concentrate on solutions as choice between known alternatives. The decision process is usually thought of as going on in the mind of a single person and the objective is to work out an optimal solution within a set of constraints and a criterion of output. Much less attention has been paid to the dynamic interaction between people in arriving at a solution. In real life, this second situation is much more usual. Quite often, the constraints and alternative choices emerge only in the social interaction between people who represent different roles and positions of power.

In the area of industrial relations the inapplicability of the classic decision model is particularly clear. The outcome and the process of people-interaction are inextricably intertwined. The medium is the message and the outcome is the process, be it a strike or a compromise solution.

The present research on decision-making has concentrated on the people-interaction aspect and has left the question of alternative solutions to one side. Ultimately, these two branches of research will have to merge. For the time being, the area we are investigating and reporting on has been much less carefully developed than the other. This imbalance of knowledge about the socio-psychological compared with the cognitive side of decision-making has to be redressed before an integration of the two disciplines is possible.

Contingencies and Infrastructures

The second departure from tradition is the multivariate, multilevel contingency model which has been adequately described earlier. It developed gradually since about 1965, when work in the socioeconomic setting of South America demonstrated the difficulty of applying the then dominant theories of managerial leadership (Heller, 1973; Heller and Yukl, 1969). While there have been many additions and changes, it will be noticed that the term "transitional model" is still used and will continue under a new program of research currently in its early stages. The point to be underlined here is the deliberate provision for evolution and choice within the model itself.

The provision of choice among defined alternatives is also a feature of the contingency framework compared with an assumption of finality. A similar way of thinking about organizations has recently been described as the "equifinality principle." It is based on the finding that various dimensions of bureaucracy can be put together in several different arrangements which "appear to be equally viable strategies for the various sample organizations" (Reiman, 1973:402). By analogy with the bureaucracy example, one could say that different contingencies lead to decentralized power. According to our model, a devolution of influence and power could be a legitimate organizational objective since one of its outcomes is a higher utilization of skills. In such a case, the model would highlight a number of *alternative choices* for achieving the objective.

A possible disadvantage of such a model is the difficulty of reconciling its tentativeness and lack of finality with a change agent's demand for a normative theory. We recognize the apparent dilemma but wish to make two points. First, it could be argued that the premature, normative theories of the 1950s and 1960s may have been responsible for an ossification in managerial thinking about the subject of participation and "ideal" styles of leadership. We are still trying to recover from this in the 1970s.[49]

Second, we would not agree that a normative model is necessary for the practical purposes of helping organizations, their subunits or individual pairs of managers to improve their decision methods. A normative model may be useful for teaching or training purposes, but is not a requirement for action research.[50]

We can complete the description of the theoretical framework by pointing out that it differs from manpower models by its claim that the utilization of skill is a motivator. The infrastructure model (Figure 8) directs attention to various conditions which facilitate or inhibit the free flow of available skill resources.

The Macro-Micro Interface

The present application of the model focuses on individuals and small groups. That is to say, the micro level of organization. Even so, the micro level is assumed to interact with technical, structural policy and external sociopolitical events. In a sense, the model is designed to act as a bridge between micro and macro levels of analysis. It is rightly felt by some that this interface is one of the most neglected areas of theory and empirical study (Pugh and Phesey, 1968; Phesey, et al., 1971; Reiman, 1973; Leavitt, et al., 1974). Moreover, it seems likely that the transitional model can be adapted to work in other areas of organizational analysis, with a focus on organizational units or subunits instead of individuals. It can also be used for longitudinal studies of organizational processes.[51]

We should be aware of the limitations of narrow and specialized models and methodologies in a field of study as complex and controversial as power.[52] At a general level, this argument has been put very forcefully by Argyris, who

---

[49] A partial exception to our doubts about normative models is the recent and very sophisticated research of Vroom and Yetton (1973). They have produced a normative model which is a clear improvement on the theories of Likert (1967) and the training packages of Blake and Mouton (1964), Reddin (1970) and Kepner and Tregoe (1965). Even so, it is evident that the eight particular contingencies incorporated in the Vroom and Yetton model cannot claim to be the only or the major determining factors of leadership in the future. For instance, our own contingencies overlap with theirs only minimally, but both produce highly significant interaction patterns and account for a reasonable percentage of the total variance in behavior.

[50] While there is a wide range of different methods of introducing organizational change, we have argued elsewhere that "action research" should pay much more attention to the *research* part of the method than is usually the case (Heller, 1975). The search or research part of the change process benefits from having a flexible theoretical framework. A strictly normative model may mean that some predetermined "best solution" is the change agent's first and last choice. Very similar points have been made by Chris Argyris in his various writings (see, for instance, Argyris, 1970).

[51] The cross-sectional study reported in this chapter is now being followed up by a flow process analysis of decision-making and participation in Holland, Yugoslavia and Britain. The new study will pay special attention to the longitudinal interrelations between power and the use of skills. While the field methodology will be different, the basic structure of the transitional model is being used, at least to begin with.

[52] It must be remembered that as recently as 1964 Crozier drew our attention to the need to make power the central problem in studying bureaucratic organizations (Crozier, 1964: Chapter 6). Since that time there has been an enormous increase of research in this field (Participation and Self-Management, 1972–73).

criticizes sociological work on organizations for its neglect of the individual (Argyris, 1972). Curiously enough, this neglect is less clear in the special case of power which, since Weber, has usually been defined in terms of individual actors. This excessive psychological emphasis has been criticized by Perrow (1970). There is now some danger that we might overcompensate by depersonalizing power altogether. Argyris could also extend his strictures of subject specialization by pointing to his more traditional colleagues in industrial psychology who have striven hard to avoid many relevant and real issues because they fall outside the framework of interpersonal analysis.

EVALUATION

While it may seem natural that this chapter has stressed the more positive aspects of the model and research findings, there are important limitations and weaknesses. Most of the findings on both dependent and independent variables were collected at one moment of time and from only two levels of management. The one hundred organizations spread over eight countries and are not representative of the total population of companies, although they are fairly adequately matched to each other. While we went to a great deal of trouble to standardize the research administration in the various countries, differences have inevitably emerged.

More importantly, perhaps, we are very much aware that our resources and conceptual framework are not capable of dealing with all the subtle complexities of power and decision-making in organizations. We have not assessed most of the important omega level variables, nor what can be called meta power. Meta power is a description for various forms of control which limit the exercise of power at any one place and time (Buckley & Burns, 1974). Meta power is usually exercised one or more levels above the level which is constrained, although power cliques can exercise a similar effect by limiting the influence of their colleagues in a horizontal direction. The constraining influence of organizations on each other (banks on businesses; suppliers on manufacturers; professional associations or trade unions on businesses of various kinds) is an example of environmental turbulence but also, in many cases, of meta power. Other researchers have begun to work in these critical areas (for example Hickson, et al., 1971; Hinings, et al., 1974; Rus, 1974; Salancik and Pfeffer, 1974; Abell, 1975).

Finally, it must be said that we are aware of the limitation of findings derived from formal responses to formal questions. Even if one could produce an atmosphere in which respondents felt free to express their real views, one could not be sure that they accurately reflected their behavior (Argyris, 1965, 1976). The limitations of the stimulus-response method of enquiry led to the use of Group Feedback Analysis (GFA) which was described earlier. This method enables one to make some spot checks on the veridity of the statistical findings. As we saw, distortions occurred and we can make some rough allowance for them in our conclusions. However, we do not have a method for correcting statistical data for distortion of this kind.

Several of the problems we have described are too large to be tackled immediately. Others are due to the severe limitation imposed by studies that take a single "snapshot" and extrapolate from it to resemble real life. Snapshot research is economical and fully justified at certain stages of exploration, but we feel that a point has been reached when an understanding of power based on the contingency model described here (particularly Figures 1 and 2) requires studies in depth and over time. The challenge is to devise methods which will enable one to carry out longitudinal studies with reasonable objectivity.[53]

DISCUSSION AND CONCLUSIONS

We are moving into an era of hectic discussion of the case for and against "democracy" at the place of work. In Europe, this term is usually applied to power sharing with lower levels of organization, while in America, under the term "participation," it applies a little more to power-sharing at junior, middle and senior managerial levels. In Europe, the trend has been to underpin the movement by legislation, while in America, the emphasis has been on training in interpersonal skills.[54] The European structuralist and the American socio-psychological approach are beginning to merge in some Scandinavian countries.[55] These rapid increases in the application of power-sharing in different parts of the world throw up a number of questions:

- Can influence and power be shared in all circumstances?
- Which of the various methods of power-sharing are most effective?
- Are there limits to the distribution of influence and power?
- Is it possible to provide a feeling of participation without actually sharing power?
- What are the consequences of simulating power-sharing?
- Do people want to participate in most decisions or only in some?
- Can power-sharing be effectively used at only one level of a multilevel organization?
- Is democratic decision-making a function of personality, role, or situation?

Our research and the literature we have cited deals with a few of these issues but many more remain unanswered. Past experience suggests that the answers will depend substantially on the theoretical model used for the research. The choice of model is therefore important.

Udy (1965) has suggested that the search for *principles* of organizations can be contrasted with a *contingency* approch. The former is a search for constants and it seems that many writers who have followed this line have over-

---

[53] A pilot study for this new phase of research is currently under way in Britain and Holland supported by the Social Science Research Council (in Britain) and the Science Foundation (in Holland).

[54] For a guide to the very extensive literature on this subject see, for instance, Blumberg (1968), Participation and Self-Management (1972–73) and Walker (1974).

[55] Social scientists were at first very sceptical of mixing legal and sociopsychological remedies (Emery and Trist, 1960). It seems, however, that political and trade union pressures have coincided with a great shortage of skilled and semi-skilled labor. Workers have shown themselves unwilling to take on repetitive short cycle jobs. These factors have led to a great deal of experimentation with the redesign of jobs based on "democratic" decision-making procedures. The famous examples of Hunsfos, Saab and Volvo are based on sociotechnical theory (Trist and Bamforth, 1951; Emery and Trist, 1960; Davis and Taylor, 1972) and work through semi-autonomous groups. In addition, but more recently, the Norwegian and Swedish governments have legislated for worker participation at various levels, including the board of directors. Elsewhere, and particularly in America, more emphasis is placed on theories of motivation, job enrichment based on expert advice, and job satisfactions (Dowling, 1973).

structured and over-simplified the evidence to a point where it seriously departs from organizational reality. The opposite view is equally misleading; managers and critics of the behavioral sciences often argue that all situations are unique. This is the "it all depends" argument taken to an extreme. A contingency framework does not exclude the existence of organizational constants. It sets out to test the assumption very severely by assuming that these constants operate over a *limited area* of the phenomenon under investigation. The research is therefore directed towards an exploration of the limits within which a generalization applies. For instance, our investigation follows the assumptions made by previous research that power-sharing leadership styles can produce increased satisfaction and organizational effectiveness, but it tests power-sharing under a series of specified conditions. This enables us to conclude that power-sharing is limited by factors such as the size of the working group, the constraints imposed by the nature of the job, the importance of the decision, the available managerial experience and skill, etc. These and other contingency assumptions have now been supported by data from our samples in three countries.

There are some modern protagonists of power-sharing who hold the view that ethically correct procedures will always be effective. At the beginning of the century, management scientists took a different and more cynical view; procedures that could be shown to be effective were thought to be ethically correct. The second proposition is now widely discredited but the first is difficult to sustain.[56]

The approach we have used in this chapter and the evidence that has accumulated so far suggests an alternative position. We assume that participation and power-sharing are ethically and normatively acceptable to most people. According to our model, power-sharing methods are preferable to autocracy, "other things being equal." But why are power-sharing methods preferred? The answer (within the limits of our model) is that they lead to a better utilization of skills and there is some evidence that people like to use their skills. However, circumstances are not always equal. This is where the contingencies come in. In what circumstances is power-sharing not appropriate? As an example one can give the finding, also well substantiated by laboratory studies (Mulder and Wilke, 1970; Mulder, 1971), that a large difference in skill between people is associated with centralized methods of decision-making. What is an appropriate personal or organizational response to this situation? There seem to be at least four:

1. One can accept the position as it is and put up with the existence of differential power as a concomitant of differential skills.
2. One could try to rearrange the organization to produce a better match between boss-subordinate groups.
3. One can carry on as if this finding did not exist or did not matter. This is probably what actually happens in the majority of cases today. It explains the considerable amount of pseudo or manipulative participation one finds in real life and in the feedback discussions during our research (see our evidence above and Heller, 1971:97–98).
4. The organization, or individuals, could take deliberate steps to narrow the skill gap. One method of doing this "on the job" is by a more ex-

---

[56] A subtle analysis of the difficulty of reconciling some existing evidence on power sharing and efficiency is put forward by Lammers (1973).

tensive use of consultation, joint decision-making and delegation. In other words, power-sharing decision methods could be used as a means of increasing subordinate's experience and skill. Once this was achieved, power-sharing would make sense for a different reason; namely to use available resources.

Among the four alternatives mentioned, the last one is likely to be most acceptable from a humanistic point of view. It is also a realistic and practical solution from an organizational perspective. Our research has some data to test whether such a view receives any backing in present circumstances. Unfortunately, the answer is no. We have described the results of Table 5. Respondents were asked to say why participation was important. What were the consequences or results they expected? According to our respondents, "Training of subordinates" received a very low score, coming fourth out of five reasons. The results from equivalent groups of British and German managers gave the same low ranking. In all cases, "The improvement of the technical quality of decision" was given first rank.

This finding is not inimical to the use of participation since it shows that managers value the specific skill contribution subordinates can make. Moreover, they value participation for reasons that are "genuine" rather than "pseudo." Nevertheless we are left with the problem of a considerable skill gap. Senior and subordinate managers make significantly different judgments about their skills; this is likely to lead to unnecessarily centralized decision-making and to an under-utilization of skill resources.

Can anything be done about this? We believe that our research findings based on a contingency model, may facilitate the introduction of change in organizations. The existence of organizational choice (based on contingency thinking) should facilitate the task of organizational design (Clark, 1972; Kingdon, 1973) or redesign based on action research. Action research has two complementary objectives: one is to make new discoveries (or at least to obtain valid information) and the second is to use the discovered data to make a practical contribution to the solution of problems. If the conflictual perception of skill differences stands in the way of a more democratic pattern of leadership and a better use of skill, we have a problem. The nature of the problem can be explored by means of the data we have described. There is evidence that the use of suitable methods of feeding this information back to our respondents encourages a reexamination which usually leads to a shift in perception and eventually to a change in behavior (Heller 1970, 1975).

REFERENCES

Abell, P. (ed.)
  1975 "Organizations as bargaining and influence systems." Mimeographed. Imperial College of Science and Technology, London (To be published).
Ajiferuke, M. and J. Boddewyn
  1970 "Socioeconomic indicators in comparative management." Administrative Science Quarterly (15) :453–458.
Alderfer, C.P.
  1969 "An empirical test of a new theory of human needs." Organizational Behavior and Performance (4) :142–175.

1974   "The effect of variations in relatedness need satisfaction on relatedness desires." Administrative Science Quarterly (19) :507–532.

Applewhite, P.
1965   Organizational Behavior. Englewood Cliffs, New Jersey: Prentice-Hall.

Argyris, C.
1964   Integrating the Individual and the Organization. New York: Wiley.
1965   Organization and Innovation. Homewood, Illinois: Irwin.
1970   Intervention Theory and Method: A Behavioral Science View. Reading, Mass.: Addison-Wesley.
1972   The Applicability of Organizational Sociology. London: Cambridge University Press.
1976   "Problems and new directions in industrial psychology," in M.D. Dunnette (ed.), Handbook of Industrial and Organizational Psychology. Chicago: Rand McNally College Publishing Co.

Bass, B. and E. Valenzi
1973   "Contingency aspects of effective management styles." Technical Report 67. Management Research Centre, May.

Bendix, R.
1960   Max Weber: An Intellectual Portrait. London: Heinemann.

Blake, R. and J. Mouton
1964   The Managerial Grid. Houston, Texas: The Gulf Publishing Co.

Blankenship, L.V. and R.E. Miles
1968   "Organizational structure and managerial decision behavior." Administrative Science Quarterly (13) :106–120.

Blumberg, P.
1968   Industrial Democracy. London: Constable.

Braybrooke, D.
1974   Traffic Congestion Goes Through the Issue Machine. London and Boston: Routledge and Kegan Paul.

Brayfield, A.H. and W.H. Crockett
1955   "Employee attitudes and employee performance." Psychological Bulletin (52) :396–424.

Brown, W.
1960   Explorations in Management. London: Heinemann.

Buckley, W. and T.R. Burns
1974   "Power and meta power." Paper prepared for the 8th World Congress of Sociology, Toronto, August.

Burns, T. and G.M. Stalker
1961   The Management of Innovation. London: Tavistock Publications.

Campbell, R.M. and D. Hitchin
1968   "The Delphi technique: implementation in the corporate environment." Management Services (November–December) :37–42.

Carlson, S.
1951   Executive Behavior: A Study of the Work Load and Working Methods of Managing Directors. Stockholm: Strombergs.

Cartwright, D.
1965   "Influence, leadership, control," in J.G. March (ed.), Handbook of Organizations. Chicago: Rand McNally.

Child, J.
  1972 "Organizational structure, environment and performance: the role of strategic choice." Sociology (6) :1–22.
Churchman, W.C.
  1968 Challenge to Reason. New York: McGraw-Hill.
Clark, P.
  1972 Organizational Design. London: Tavistock Publications.
Crozier, M.
  1964 The Bureaucratic Phenomenon. London: Tavistock Publications.
Cyert, R.M. and J.G. March
  1963 A Behavioral Theory of the Firm. Englewood Cliffs, New Jersey: Prentice-Hall.
Cyert, R.M., H.A. Simon and D.B. Trow
  1956 "Observation of a business decision." Journal of Business (29) :237–248.
Dahl, R.A.
  1957 "The concept of power." Behavioral Science (2) :201–215.
  1968 Power. International Encyclopedia of Social Science. New York: Macmillan.
Dalkey, N. and O. Helmer
  1963 "An experimental application of the Delphi method to the use of experts." Management Science (9) :458–467.
Davis, L.
  1957 "Job design and productivity: a new approach." Personnel (33) :418–430.
Davis, L. and J. Taylor (eds.)
  1972 Design of Jobs. Harmondsworth, Middlesex, England: Penguin.
Dowling, W.
  1973 "Job redesign on the assembly line." Organizational Dynamics 51–67.
Dufty, N.F. and P.M. Taylor
  1962 "Implementation of a decision." Administrative Science Quarterly (7) :110–119.
Dunnette, M.D., J. Campbell and M. Hakel
  1967 "Factors contributing to job satisfaction and job dissatisfaction in six occupational groups." Organizational Behavior and Human Performance (2) :143–174.
Emery, F.E.
  1959 "Characteristics of sociotechnical systems." Unpublished. Tavistock Institute of Human Relations, Document Number HRC 527.
Emery, F.E. and E.L. Trist
  1960 "Sociotechnical systems," in C.W. Churchman and M. Verhulst (eds.), Management Sciences, Models and Techniques, Vol. 2. Oxford: Pergamon Press.
  1965 "The causal texture of organizational environments." Human Relations (18) :21–31.
Fiedler, F.E.
  1964 "A contingency model of leadership effectiveness," in Berkowitz (ed.), Advances in Experimental Social Psychology, Vol. 1. New York and London: Academic Press.
  1967 A Theory of Leadership Effectiveness. New York: McGraw-Hill.

Fleishman, E.A., E.E. Harris and H.E.E. Burtt
    1955   "Leadership and supervision in industry." Ohio State University, Bureau of Educational Research. Monograph No. 33.
French, J.R.P. and B. Raven
    1959   "The bases of social power," in D. Cartwright (ed.), Studies in Social Power. Ann Arbor, Michigan: Institute for Social Research.
Friend, J.K. and W.N. Jessop
    1969   Local Government and Strategic Choice. London: Tavistock Publications.
Galbraith, K.
    1967   The New Industrial State. Boston: Houghton Mifflin.
Gerth, H.H. and C.W. Mills (eds.)
    1947   From Max Weber: Essays in Sociology. London: Routledge and Kegan Paul.
Gibb, C.A.
    1958   "An interactional view of the emergence of leadership." Australian Journal of Psychology (10):101–110.
Haire, M., E. Ghiselli and L. Porter
    1966   Managerial Thinking. New York: McGraw-Hill.
Heller, F.A.
    1964   Integrated Manpower Development: A Successful Case Example. Buenos Aires: Argentine Productivity Centre.
    1969a "The managerial role in the effective use of resources." Journal of Management Studies (6):1–14.
    1969b "Group feedback analysis: a method of field research." Psychological Bulletin (72):108–117.
    1970   "Group feedback analysis as a change agent." Human Relations (23): 319–333.
    1971a Managerial Decision Making: A Study of Leadership Styles and Power-Sharing Among Senior Managers. London: Tavistock Publications.
    1971b "Social and technical aspects of manpower utilization." Management Education and Development (1):111–123.
    1973   "Leadership, decision-making and contingency theory." Industrial Relations (12):183–199.
    1975   "Group feedback analysis as a method of action research," in A.W. Clark (ed.), Experiences in Action Research. London. To be published.
Heller, F.A. and L.W. Porter
    1966   "Perceptions of managerial needs and skills in two national samples." Occupational Psychology 40(1, 2):1–13.
Heller, F.A. and B. Wilpert
    1974   "Limits to participative management: task, structure and skill as contingencies—a German-British comparison." Mimeographed. Tavistock Institute of Human Relations (SFP4146).
Heller, F.A. and G. Yukl
    1969   "Participation and managerial decision-making as a function of situational variables." Organizational Behavior and Human Performance (4):227–241.
Hemphill, J.K.
    1950   "Relations between the size of the group and the behavior of 'superior' leaders." Journal of Social Psychology (32):11–22.

Herbst, P.G.
   1962   Autonomous Group Functioning. London: Tavistock Institute of Human Relations.
Herzberg, F., B. Mausner, R.O. Peterson and D.F. Capwell
   1957   Job Attitudes: Review of Research and Opinion. Pittsburgh: Psychological Services of Pittsburgh.
Herzberg, F., B. Mausner and B. Snyderman
   1959   The Motivation to Work. New York: Wiley.
Hickson, D.J., C.R. Hinings, C.A. Lee, R.E. Schneck and J.M. Pennings
   1971   "A strategic contingency theory of intraorganizational power." Administrative Science Quarterly (16):216–229.
Hill, W.
   1973   "Leadership style: rigid or flexible." Organizational Behavior and Human Performance (9):35–47.
Hill, W. and D. Hughes
   1974   "Variations in leader behavior as a function of task type." Organizational Behavior and Human Performance (11):83–96.
Hinings, C.R., D.J. Hickson, J.M. Pennings and R.E. Schneck
   1974   "Structural conditions of intraorganizational power." Administrative Science Quarterly (19):22–44.
Inkson, J.H.K., D.S. Pugh and D.J. Hickson
   1970   "Organization context and structure: an abbreviated replication." Administrative Science Quarterly (15):318–329.
Jaques, E.
   1956   Measurement of Responsibility. London: Tavistock Publications.
Kepner, C.H. and B.B. Tregoe
   1965   The Rational Manager: A Systematic Approach to Problem Solving and Decision-Making. New York: McGraw-Hill.
Kingdon, D.R.
   1973   Matrix Organization. London: Tavistock Publications.
Koreman, A.K.
   1966   "Consideration, initiating structure and organizational criteria—a review." Personnel Psychology (19):349–361.
Lammers, C.
   1973   "Two conceptions of democratization in organizations," in E. Pusić (ed.), Participation and Self-Management. Vol. 4. Zagreb, Yugoslavia: Institute for Social Research, University of Zagreb.
Lawrence, P.R. and Lorsch, J.W.
   1967a "Differentiation and integration in complex organizations." Administrative Science Quarterly (12):1–47.
   1967b Organization and Environment: Managing Differentiation and Integration. Boston: Harvard Business School.
Leavitt, H., L. Pinfield and E. Webb (eds.)
   1974   Organizations of the Future: Interactions with the External Environment. New York: Praeger.
Likert, R.
   1961   New Patterns of Management. New York: McGraw-Hill.
   1967   The Human Organization. New York: McGraw-Hill.
Lowin, A.
   1968   "Participatory decision-making: a model, literature critique and pre-

scription for research." Organization Behavior and Human Performance (3):68–106.

McGregor, D.
  1960   The Human Side of Enterprise. New York: McGraw-Hill.
  1967   The Professional Manager. New York: McGraw-Hill.
March, J.G.
  1955   "An introduction to the theory and measurement of influence." Amer-
          ican Political Science Review (49):431–451.
March, J.G. and H.A. Simon
  1958   Organizations. New York: Wiley.
Marples, D.L.
  1967   Studies of managers—a fresh start?" Journal of Management Studies
          (4):282–299.
Marrow, A.J., D.G. Bowers and S.E. Seashore
  1967   Management by Participation: Creating a Climate for Personal and
          Organizational Development. New York: Harper & Row.
Maslow, A.H.
  1943   "A theory of human motivation." Psychological Review (50):370–396.
Miles, R.E.
  1964   "Conflicting elements in managerial ideologies." Industrial Relations
          4(1):77–91.
  1965   "Human relations or human resources?" Harvard Business Review
          (July–August):148–163.
Miles, R.E., K. Roberts and L.V. Blankenship
  1968   "Organizational leadership, satisfaction and productivity: a compara-
          tive analysis." Academy of Management Journal (11):402–414.
Miller, D.C. and W.H. Form
  1964   Industrial Society: The Sociology of Work Organizations. Second Edi-
          tion. New York: Harper & Row.
Mulder, M.
  1971   "Power equalization through participation." Administrative Science
          Quarterly (16):31–38.
Mulder, M. and H. Wilke
  1970   "Participation and power equalization." Organizational Behavior and
          Human Performance (5):430–448.
Parsons, T.
  1963   "On the concept of political power." Proceedings of the American
          Philosophy Society (107):232–262.
Participation and Self-Management
  1972   Six Volumes. Report of the First International Sociological Conference
  –73   on Participation and Self-Management. Institute for Social Research,
          Zagreb, Yugoslavia.
Paul, W.J. and K.B. Robertson
  1970   Job Enrichment and Employee Motivation. London: Gower Press.
Perrow, C.
  1970   "Departmental power and perspective in industrial firms," in M.N.
          Zald (ed.), Power in Organizations. Nashville: Vanderbilt University
          Press.
Pettigrew, A.
  1973   The Politics of Organizational Decision-Making. London: Tavistock
          Publications.

Phesey, D., R. Payne and D. Pugh
1971   "Influence of structure at organizational and group levels." Administrative Science Quarterly (16):61–73.
Porter, L.W.
1964   Organizational Patterns of Managerial Job Attitudes. American Foundation for Managerial Research.
Porter, L.W. and M.M. Henry
1964   "Job attitudes in management: perceptions of the importance of certain personality traits as a function of job level." Journal of Applied Psychology (48):31–36.
Pugh, D.S.
1969   "Organizational behavior: an approach from psychology." Human Relations (22):345–354.
Pugh, D.S., D.J. Hickson, C.R. Hinings, K.M. Macdonald, C. Turner and T. Lupton
1963   "A conceptual scheme for organizational analysis." Administrative Science Quarterly (8):289–315.
Pugh, D. and D. Phesey
1968   "Some developments in the study of organizations." Management International Review (8):97–107.
Pyle, W.C.
1970   "Monitoring human resources—on line." Michigan Business Review (July):19–32.
Reddin, W.
1970   Managerial Effectiveness. New York: McGraw-Hill.
Reiman, B.
1973   "On the dimensions of bureaucratic structure: an empirical reappraisal." Administrative Science Quarterly (18):462–476.
Ritchie, J.B. and R.E. Miles
1970   "An analysis of quantity and quality of participation as mediating variables in the participation decision-making process." Ann Arbor: University of Michigan. Mimeographed.
Roberts, K.H.
1970   "On looking at an elephant: an evaluation of cross-cultural research related to organizations." Psychological Bulletin (74):327–350.
Roberts, K.H., G.A. Walter and R.E. Miles
1971   "A factor analytic study of job satisfaction items designed to measure Maslow need categories." Personnel Psychology (24):205–220.
Rus, V.
1974   "The external and internal influences affecting industrial enterprises." Yugoslav papers presented to the 8th World Congress of the International Sociological Association at Toronto, August. Printed: University of Ljubljana.
Sadler, P. and B. Barry
1970   Organizational Development. London: Longmans Green.
Salancik, G. and J. Pfeffer
1974   "The bases and uses of power in organizational decision-making: the case of a university." Administrative Science Quarterly (19):453–473.
Schneider, J. and E. Locke
1971   "A critique of Herzberg's incident classification system and a suggested

revision." Organizational Behavior and Human Performance (6) :441–457.

Scott, M.M.
1964   "Who are your motivated workers?" Harvard Business Review (42) : 73–88.

Seeman, M.
1953   "Role conflict and ambivalence in leadership." American Journal of Sociology (18) :373–380.

Simon, H.A.
1957   "A behavioral model of rational choice," in H.A. Simon (ed.), Models of Man. New York: Wiley.

Sirota, D. and M. Greenwood
1971   "Understand your overseas work force." Harvard Business Review (January–February) :53–60.

Starbuck, W.
1972   "Organizations and their environments," Mimeographed. International Institute of Management, Berlin. Also in M.D. Dunnette (ed.), Handbook of Industrial and Organizational Psychology. Chicago: Rand McNally College Publishing Co., 1976.

Stewart, R.
1970   Managers and Their Jobs. London: Pan Books.

Stogdill, R.M.
1948   "Personal factors associated with leadership: a survey of the literature." Journal of Psychology (25) :35–71.

Stogdill, R.M., C. Shartle and Associates
1956   "Patterns of administrative performance." Ohio Studies Personnel Research Monograph No. 81.

Strauss, G.
1963   "Some notes on power-equalization," in H. Leavitt (ed.), The Social Science of Organizations. Englewood Cliffs, New Jersey: Prentice-Hall.
1968   "Human relations 1968 style." Industrial Relations (7) :262–276.

Tannenbaum, A.
1957   "The distribution of control in formal organizations." Social Forces (136) :44–50.
1962   "Control in organizations, individual adjustment and organizational performance." Administrative Science Quarterly (7) :236–257.
1968   Control in Organizations. New York: McGraw-Hill.

Tannenbaum, A., B. Kavčič, M. Rosner, M. Vianello and G. Wieser
1974   Hierarchy in Organizations. San Francisco: Jossey-Bass.

Taylor, D.W.
1965   "Decision-making and problem solving," in J.G. March (ed.), Handbook of Organizations. Chicago: Rand McNally.

Taylor, R. and M.D. Dunnette
1974   "Relative contribution of decision-maker attributes to decision process." Organizational Behavior and Human Performance (12) :286–298.

Thompson, J.
1967   Organizations in Action. New York: McGraw-Hill.

Tiffin, J. and E. McCormick
1942   Industrial Psychology. Englewood Cliffs, New Jersey: Prentice-Hall.

Trist, E.L. and K.W.Bamforth
  1951 "Some social and psychological consequences of the longwall method of coal-getting." Human Relations (4) :3–38.
Trist, E.L., G.W. Higgin, H. Murray and A.B. Pollock
  1963 Organizational Choice. London: Tavistock Publications.
Udy, S.
  1965 "The comparative analysis of organizations," in J.G. March (ed.), Handbook of Organizations. Chicago: Rand McNally.
Viteles, M.
  1969 "Critical evaluation of Herzberg's two factor theory." International Review of Applied Psychology (18) :5–10.
Vroom, V.H.
  1964 Work and Motivation. New York: Wiley.
  1970 "Industrial social psychology," in G. Lindzey and E. Aronson (eds.), Handbook of Social Psychology. Vol. 5. Reading, Mass.: Addison-Wesley.
Vroom, V.H. and P. Yetton
  1973 Leadership and Decision-Making. Pittsburgh: University of Pittsburgh Press.
Walker, K.
  1974 "Workers' participation in management—problems, practice and prospects." International Institute of Labour Studies (12) :3–35.
Webb, E.J., D.T. Campbell, R.D. Schwartz and L. Sechrest
  1966 Unobtrusive Measures: Nonreactive Research in the Social Sciences. Chicago: Rand McNally.
Weber, M.
  1947 The Theory of Social and Economic Organization. Glencoe, Ill.: Free Press.
Whyte, W.F.
  1969 Organizational Behavior. Homewood, Ill.: Dorsey Press.
Wilkins, L.
  1967 "Information and decisions regarding offenders." Paper presented at the National Symposium on Law Enforcement Science and Technology, Chicago, March.
Wilpert, B. and F.A. Heller
  1973 "Power sharing at senior management levels." Omega (1) :451–464.
  1974 "Decision-making in German and British companies." Paper to the 18th International Congress of Applied Psychology, Montreal, August.
Wispe, L.G. and K.E. Lloyd
  1955 "Some situational and psychological determinants of the desire for structured interpersonal relations." Journal of Abnormal and Social Psychology (51) :57–60.
Wofford, J.C.
  1971 "Managerial behavior, situational factors and productivity and morale." Administrative Science Quarterly (16) :10–17.
Woodward, J.
  1965 Industrial Organization: Theory and Practice. London: Oxford University Press.

PART VI

WORK AND SOCIETY

INTRODUCTION—PART VI

In the next two chapters some important relationships are examined to determine how the work institution is linked with the social structure and the political institution. We have grown accustomed to using the ideas of "power elite" and "military-industrial complex" as though the terms were self-explanatory, and required no further analysis as to the accuracy with which they define some feature of the social system.

The analysis of work in relation to social power and political behavior provides an opportunity to set forth some of the complexities of the articulation of major institutions with each other. New insights may be gained from this analysis, among the most important being the many contingencies that affect the institutional linkages. Most living things are very complex in the functional relationships among their separate parts and functions. A social system is just as complex, and is difficult to analyze because of its complexity. The whole society now comes into focus and attention turns to putting the work institution in its place within the larger social system.

CHAPTER **16**

Occupational Power

William H. Form
Joan Althaus Huber

University of Illinois,
Champaign-Urbana

INTRODUCTION

In traditional societies work is equivalent to the division of labor; hence, any analysis of work typically includes all productive functions (Richards, 1948). With industrialization, as the economy is increasingly monetized, the division of labor dichotomizes into paid occupations and unpaid work, a residual category usually excluded from socioeconomic analysis even though it has substantial value.[1] This essay examines only paid occupations because unpaid workers as a collectivity lack the resources to control their environment and extract material rewards from it.

The occupational structure of an advanced industrial society is difficult to comprehend. A highly complex network of related functions, it resembles a biological ecosystem in which different species find different niches in the struggle for scarce resources. Some species occupy secure but narrow niches, while others dominate wide areas. Some species must dominate an area exclusively while others tolerate or need symbiotic or parasitic relationships. Some species invade the niches of others, replacing them in the struggle for survival; others practice mutual aid. At any given time, the ecosystem may appear to be balanced, but slow or rapid shifts among species relationships are ubiquitous. Why some species grow or decline calls for an analysis of how well the properties of individual species serve them in the struggle for resources (Boulding, 1953: xvi–xxxiv). In this description, the word occupation may be substituted for species, occupational structure for ecosystem, and earnings for resources.

Much is known about occupations such as their functions, prestige, income, and the attainment process. The oldest research tradition describes specific

As coauthors, we are grateful to Anice Birge, Jim Faught, and Stanley Benecki for their assistance in preparing the manuscript.

[1] In 1964, for example, when median U.S. family income was $6,569, the average value of unpaid work was almost $4,000 per family, about 90% of it in the form of housework (Sirageldin, 1969).

occupational roles, the social system of work, and work culture, attitudes, and values (Nosow and Form, 1962; Hall, 1969). Later, many studies demonstrated that occupations constitute a stable system of prestige ranks (North and Hatt, 1947; Reiss, 1961; U.S. Bureau of the Census, 1963) although the methods for determining the ranks have been sharply criticized (Haug and Sussman, 1971). Davies' (1952) exhaustive review of this research showed that consensus on ranking was little influenced by the ranker's residence, occupation, social class, or other demographic characteristics. Moreover, the ranks tend to be stable over time (Hodge, Siegel, and Rossi, 1964) and cross-nationally (Hodge, Rossi, and Treiman, 1966). For thirty years, the U.S. Bureau of the Census and the Office of Business Economics have collected sufficient data to study income trends among occupations (Miller, 1966:2). Finally, in the last decade a sizable literature has documented the occupational attainment process with increasingly sophisticated measurement techniques (Blau and Duncan, 1967; Spaeth, 1970; Duncan, Featherman and Duncan, 1972; Sewell and Hauser, 1974). Yet little is known about occupational power: the struggle for income and environmental control.

How to classify occupations in order to study their power relationships is a problem that has no completely satisfactory solution. Narrowly defined categories force the analyst to deal with so many occupations that generalizing is difficult. Broadly defined categories include such a wide range of attributes (training, prestige, earnings) that variations within categories may be greater than variations between them. For example, a standard dichotomy is head versus hand work. While this distinction taps prestige differences, it serves little other purpose (Duncan, 1966:97). An arbitrary classification decision must be made. If we bear in mind how much overlap occurs with respect to income, work operations, social evaluation, and authority, we can usefully classify occupations into four major categories: (1) management, (2) blue collar, (3) clerical and sales, and (4) professional. In order to study the structuring of power within and between these four occupational families, it is first necessary to discuss in turn the concept of power, economic theories which account for differences in wage levels, types of occupational markets, and the relationship of the national political economy to the structuring of occupational power.

POWER, CONFLICT, AND CONTROL

If other factors would remain equal, then the impersonal forces of the market would determine wage levels and we could dispense with the concept of social power. But these other factors, the major variables of sociological and historical analysis, persistently vary—and they influence outcomes, leaving the analyst no choice but to confront the fact of power. Yet measuring power has proved exceedingly troublesome. Most attempts focus on the *agent*, using a variant of Weber's (1964:152) definition: the probability that one actor in a social relationship can carry out his or her will despite the resistance of others. Thus, power inheres in people who are reputed to be powerful, who win controversial decisions (cf. Gamson, 1966), or who perform certain essential and exclusive functions for organizations (Dubin, 1958:142). In an effort to break the bind of locating power in persons, Kaplan (1964:15–17) cited various external bases for power: coercion, reward, identification, legitimacy, and expertness. Similarly, Clark (1968:55–67) suggested ways to quantify the exchangeability of power resources. Yet no empirical study has successfully demonstrated the causal links between attributes, resources, and functions to outcomes, a fact which led March (1966) to declare that the concept of power was useless for the analysis of complex, long-run situations.

We have no magical solution for the study of power, but unlike most studies, we focus on the effects and processes of power rather than on its agents. Following Russell (1962:25), we define social power as the production of intended effects in a social system. We assume two effects as intended: increased income and control over conditions of work. We also assume that actions intended to produce such efforts must be directed to the regulation of the market, as Weber (1964:181–184) observed, through convention, law, and voluntary action. Thus, we expect that occupations use various social mechanisms to control supply and demand in order to protect or improve their income position and working conditions. The existence of occupational power is inferred from observed market effects. Obviously, this model is defective because other factors—such as the unplanned results of technological change—also affect market outcomes. The model's chief virtue is its focus on sociological rather than individual-psychological variables. Customary methods move from attributes, acts, and resources of persons or groups thought to be powerful, to the issues that arise, and from there to outcomes. We begin with outcomes—differentials in income and control over work environments—and infer that groups who benefit have power; we then examine the mechanisms they use to control their environments.

Occupational power, then, is the ability of an occupation, by using material or organizational resources, to defend itself against the incursions of others to obtain or maintain an advantage in the allocation of income. Occupational power may be so well consolidated that few may be aware that it is being exercised or that power may be conspicuously violent. In either case, a major occupational resource is the ability to withhold a necessary function either through a monopoly over a skill or its practice. This may involve the support of allies, the most useful of which is government. When groups institutionalize their control, people come to regard it as natural and legitimate.

The struggle over scarce goods between two or more groups is highlighted in conflict situations. Conflict may be highly institutionalized (as in collective bargaining) or it may run unrestrained (as in open warfare). An important variable is the social context of conflict. In a factory, authority, status, and wage differentials are stabilized, reducing conflict through a set division of labor. But conflict may be less structured among large work organizations where stratal relationships are amorphous—making it difficult to trace the intended effects of conflicting parties. Thus, labor, management, and professional societies bargain intermittently and do not exhibit clear power relationships (Form, 1968). The situation is even more obscure when large occupational sectors like business, labor, and government are involved in disputes. Yet power contests occur in all these areas and we shall describe them in highly rigid as well as in amorphous social structures.

THEORETICAL APPROACHES TO EARNINGS DIFFERENTIALS

Although income is a central reward in industrial stratification systems, social scientists have no occupational theory of income distribution that is both comprehensive and quantifiable. What we need is a theory that considers not just wage workers, but also salary workers, unpaid workers such as housewives and children, workers whose earnings derive from illegal activities, members of the armed services, prison inmates, the underemployed, and persons who live off their investments—in short, almost everyone. Such a theory should consider both impersonal market forces and the purposive forces of social power. But what we have are either elegant economic theories with so many factors held constant that they shed little light on the actual world or broad sociological theories with so many unmeasurable terms that they are not scientifically useful. Let us briefly review these theories about the market and social forces which affect occupational income distribution.

Economic Theories

Two kinds of economic wage theories may be distinguished. One explains earnings differentials among individuals or classes while another explains the share of national income that goes to the aggregate of workers. Both the oldest and most recent theories are addressed to individual and occupational differentials. The oldest wage theory is the prescientific doctrine of the just wage, which can be traced back to Aristotle. An ethical theory, it described the differentials needed if economic relations were to be just. Pay should equal the value of the work; hence, equal ability should receive equal pay. Workers had a right to maintain a status appropriate to their abilities, but their pay should be in line with community resources. The ambiguous clichés in the doctrine enhance its ability to justify almost any wage structure. In modern economics, people are governed by expediency, rather than ethics, but the doctrine survives to this day as a set of common sense principles in Britain (Fogarty, 1961:249; Routh, 1965:x) and as a conventional notion of an adequate wage in the United States (Reynolds and Taft, 1956:369).

Subsistence theory. Economic wage theories emerged during industrialization. The two oldest are concerned with aggregate shares. Subsistence theory, the oldest, was based on Malthus's population theory. It held that the price of labor would always approach the minimum needed for subsistence. If labor supply increased, wages would fall, leading to a decrease in labor supply. If wages rose above subsistence, population would increase till the labor supply forced wages down again. Smith, Ricardo, and Marx more or less adopted this theory.

Wages-fund theory. A second aggregate theory, the *wages-fund theory*, is associated with the name of John Stuart Mill. It held that wages derived from a fixed fund of capital and could rise only if that fund increased. Both of these theories assumed a relatively fixed demand for labor in economies that lacked means of credit creation; they have some applicability to preindustrial societies but are not useful in modern systems (Carrter, 1968:399).

The theory of marginal productivity. This theory appeared about 1870 as a product of the Austrian school. It explains wage or occupational differentials.[2] The basic ideas now seem obvious: value is not merely an attribute that

---

[2] Adam Smith (1937:100) earlier cited five principal reasons for wage differentials but his common sense principles were not easily quantifiable.

inheres in a thing but a result of the way people relate to that thing. The Austrians were the first to develop systematically the idea that a highly valued object had to be both useful and scarce, so that the conditions of valuation or choice had to be analyzed in order to explain value in exchange (von Hayek, 1968:459). Strictly speaking, the theory is not a wage theory, but a special application of the law of diminishing returns, expressing a direct functional relation between the quantity of a factor employed and its product (Carrter, 1968:399). The theory has two basic propositions: that employers will hire additional units of labor to the point where the cost per unit equals or exceeds the net contribution of that unit to the firm's revenue and that competition among employers seeking to maximize profits assures that they will bid wages up to the value of the marginal contribution of that class of workers to the firm's output (Lester, 1964:274–275). The employer will profitably expand employment till the equilibrium point between marginal cost and marginal revenue product of labor is reached. The theory rests on five assumptions: (1) that people are rational; (2) that producers choose among alternative factors, and consumers, among products; (3) that goods and services are highly mobile; (4) that information flows freely; and (5) that society is static. The first four are thought—to a degree—to characterize Western societies; the fifth is used to facilitate deductive reasoning (Chamberlain, 1958:323–324).

A main attraction of the theory is that its elements are readily mathematized but even many of its proponents readily admit that its rigid assumptions limit its applicability. In mass production, for example, the hundreds of operations in a single plant require hundreds of wage rates for which the market pricing mechanism is hopelessly inadequate (Machlup, 1952:381). Finkel and Tarascio (1971:53–56) review evidence showing that many entrepreneurs do not believe that they act in accord with the theory—they do not establish their price levels through a series of logical calculations. But the theory's staunch defenders (Dunlop, 1944) insist that it usefully explains long-term wage trends.

Socioeconomic Theories

Some social scientists have attempted to transcend the limitations of marginal theory, such as its inability to handle stratification problems.[3] One group includes institutional economists, power or bargaining theorists, and (from sociology) the functional theorists, all of whom explicitly or implicitly place economic theory in a sociocultural context. A second group, remaining firmly in the marginalist tradition, has long examined the adverse effects of imperfect competition (Dobb, 1968:452). By the 1960s, some of these economists began to study the economics of discrimination. At about the same time, some sociologists analyzed the social mechanisms which maintain economic discrimination. We shall discuss each of these developments in turn.

Economists who stressed the social context of economic analysis are typically "conflict" theorists. Best known are the institutional economists, an American school stemming from Veblen, who examine the economic system as part of human culture. Thus, they study the conflicts of business and labor in the political arena or between government and business concerning price fixing,

---

[3] Joan Robinson (1972) recently described the lack of a theory of income distribution as a crisis in economic theory.

monopolistic practices, and other efforts to manipulate economic variables. More recently, economists aware of the inadequacies of marginal theory have included sociological variables in a "power theory" of income. Wootton (1955:67, 104) claims, for example, that the most consistent feature of British wage structure is that those who give orders receive higher pay than those who must obey orders. Other work in the conflict context has been done by labor economists struggling to arrive at a bargaining theory of wages. Ross (1956), for example, stressed that labor union behavior must be understood as much in political as in economic terms. At least in the short run, specific wage rates in specific industries are determined by the bargaining strengths of unions and employers. One advantage of the bargaining model is that it illuminates bargaining strategy as a many-sided problem and provides a solution which is, at least in principle, determinate (Carrter, 1968:400). Some economists claim that even though marginal theory has a firmer conceptual framework and is hence a better point of departure for studying wage differentials, the results of starting with power or marginal theory may be the same (Pen, 1966:38).

Unlike economists, the sociologists who developed a theory of income inequality are "consensus" theorists. The Davis and Moore (1945) functional theory of stratification remains a rare attempt by sociologists to explain the differential rewards of occupations and individuals. The theory holds that society rewards certain jobs according to its needs. Thus, high paying jobs are the ones society needs the most: they require great skill which, in turn, can be acquired only with costly educational investment. Since such skills are scarce in a free market, high rewards are needed to motivate people to invest in training. To the extent that functional theory restates marginal theory—utility and scarcity determine price—it is quantifiable. But its sociological propositions ignore social organization. Who decides what society needs? Obviously, those who can pay for the services. A majority may have more important and pressing needs, but they are not defined as societal needs because people cannot afford to satisfy them.

Evidence to support functional theory tests only the variables of marginal theory. For example, Froomkin and Jaffe (1953) showed that scarce, semiskilled industrial jobs are classified as skilled in countries at lower levels of industrialization. As the skill becomes more plentiful with industrialization, such jobs exhibit downward mobility and are reclassified at lower levels. A similar argument holds that, as industrial bureaucracies grow, new positions of power emerge, such as plant manager, engineer, scientist, and superintendent. These positions must have authority and appropriate rewards if organizations are to achieve their goals. This argument legitimizes the incomes of the most powerful by defining their activities as equivalent to organizational goals; it does not explain how their power was won and consolidated. Finally, Abrahamson (1973) showed that incomes of military-related occupations tend to rise, relatively, in wartime, but this finding is explained by the relation of utility and scarcity; assumptions about the functional importance of military occupations to society are redundant.

The study of discrimination as a factor in wage and income differentials is of recent origin. In the United States, the most frequent criteria for discrimination have been ascribed statuses based on sex, ethnicity, race, and to an extent, age. Social scientists have studied race and ethnic discrimination more often than sex discrimination because, reflecting prevailing male attitudes (Stern,

1932:443), they perceived women's social position as a fact of nature. A number of European nationalities in successive waves suffered discrimination in the years following their migration, but today the chief targets of wage discrimination are women, blacks, and Spanish-speaking groups. We shall deal first with market discrimination and then with the more inclusive concept of social discrimination.

Market discrimination.   Although income differentials among status groups have been extensively documented in the last three decades, the existence of differentials does not *per se* constitute evidence of economic discrimination. In principle, members of certain groups could be more intelligent, highly trained, likely to stay on the job, and hence more valuable as employees. Economic discrimination occurs against members of a group whenever their earnings fall short of the amount "warranted" by their abilities (Becker, 1968:208).

Except for the neglected early work of Edgeworth (1922), the economic study of discrimination dates from the publication of Becker's (1957) classic study. Becker (1968:208) claims that economists failed to study it earlier because they were reluctant to interpret such phenomena as exploitation. The more recent interest of economists in discrimination was stimulated by an approach, based not on exploitation, but on considerations that involved an even sharper break with economic theory: the idea that members of a group earn less than their abilities warrant if others are willing to "pay" in order to avoid association with the target group. Hence, discrimination is economically irrational: it costs money to indulge in it.

Whether stimulated by Becker's approach or by the unrest of the 1960s, a number of studies have documented the degree of market discrimination against blacks (Lieberson and Fuguitt, 1968; Bergmann, 1971); about two-fifths of the earnings difference between nonwhites and whites is independent of the achievement of nonwhites (Siegel, 1965) and women (Fuchs, 1971; Bergmann and Adelman, 1973; Suter and Miller, 1973). A recent study reported the differential between men's and women's earnings to be about 20%, even after adjusting for such factors as education, work experience during the year and even lifelong work experience (U.S. Department of Labor, 1973:106).

Whether Becker's analysis is valid has been questioned. Fusfeld (1973: 60–62) points out that employers do not necessarily gain or lose from discriminating; the low incomes of minorities and women result from their being crowded into a small number of low-wage jobs while excluding them from high-wage or salary jobs. The gainers are workers in the majority population. The crowding hypothesis (Bergmann, 1971), like the theory of the split (Bonacich, 1972) or the dual labor market (Doeringer and Piore, 1971; Gordon, 1972; Bluestone, 1974) are variants of the older idea of noncompeting groups. The basic issue between Becker and his critics is whether discriminators profit economically.

Social discrimination.   A more inclusive concept than market discrimination, social discrimination assumes that abilities relevant to the labor market are fairly equally distributed among human populations. Discrimination can therefore be inferred when rewards among groups differ substantially and systematically for example, that women generally earned half to two-thirds the pay of men (Lydall, 1968:55), in Britain (Robertson, 1961:76–77), the United

States before the turn of the century (Long, 1960:104–107), and in this century (Reynolds and Taft, 1956:312). The primary indicator of social discrimination in the labor market is occupational segregation.[4] Dominant groups typically use one or a combination of six techniques to prevent other groups from competing for jobs.

The first and simplest technique excludes certain status groups by refusing to hire them even if they are qualified. A wealth of literature documents this for blacks (Ross and Hill, 1967; Ferman, Kornbluh, and Miller, 1968) and women (Astin, Suniewick, and Dweck, 1971). Since simple exclusion violates widely held ethical norms, target groups occasionally muster social support against such policies.

A second technique is the "buddy system" of transmitting information about job openings, which excludes persons who do not know the "right" people. Mangum's (1971:88–90) exhaustive review of labor research concluded that blacks had less access to informal networks than other groups. They relied instead on placement offices which rarely handled the best jobs. The buddy system generally excludes women from the professions (Rossi, 1965; Epstein, 1970) and management.

A third technique excludes certain status groups from the training needed for jobs. Female applicants have been typically excluded from formal skill training for the past 300 years (Clark, 1919), from colleges and professional schools even when they were more qualified than male applicants (Roby, 1973a), and from trade unions (Chafe, 1972; Lemons, 1973). Similarly, blacks have been excluded from schools and from labor unions (Hill, 1967, 1973; Strauss and Ingerman, 1968; Marshall, 1968; Lewis, 1974).

A fourth technique, credentialism (Miller, 1968) requires certification for skills not actually needed for the job, which, in turn, restricts opportunities of groups with limited training opportunities, typically blacks (Berg, 1970).

Fifth, responsibility for household and childcare has been used in industrialized societies to exclude women from effective job competition. Oppenheimer (1970:52) has shown that it is economic events which shape attitudes about whether women should work. In the early 1800s, women flocked to factories in the United States because land was cheap and farming was profitable. Industrial wages were not competitive with farming and it was cheaper to hire women than it was to hire men for factory work. Child and female labor was generally approved (Abbott, 1919:49, 59). Whenever economic conditions limited the number of jobs, women were forced out of the factories or into lower skilled industrial jobs (Holcombe, 1973:174). A variety of rationalizations were then offered about why they should stay at home. Probably the most effective rationale which kept women from occupying good industrial jobs was that their "natural" place was to be at home taking care of their children who otherwise would come to a bad end. Yet Sweet's (1973:3) review of the literature shows that no studies have isolated any effect of the working mother on the development of the child.

Yet when women's labor is needed (as during World War II), there is little

---

[4] The historical process of occupational segregation has been little examined; more is known about the degree of segregation. For example, Gross (1968) reports that from 1900 to 1960 the index of segregation by sex has increased slightly, to a little more than 68% (the proportion of women who would have to change jobs if their occupational distribution were to be the same as men's).

concern about how women meet their home responsibilities. Fully employed American married women typically spend a substantially greater proportion of their time on housework and children than do their husbands (Hedges and Barnett, 1972:10), and the effect of this burden on the long-term participation of women has remained fairly constant (Tsuchigane and Dodge, 1974:104). Even in the Soviet Union with its consciously egalitarian ideology, working women bear most of the burden of maintaining the home and childcare (Dodge, 1966: 94; Geiger, 1968:185), and this is accentuated among the poorer strata where women spend twice as much time on household chores as do the richest strata (Lipset and Dobson, 1973:154–155). Although existing American arrangements for childcare are remarkably wasteful (Bell, 1970:119), the shortage of institutional childcare facilities is increasing (Roby, 1973b), and little is known about the basic needs and financial costs of childcare (Rowe and Husby, 1973). Yet there are no current plans for a national study of childcare (Waldman and Whitmore, 1974:56).

A sixth device, restricting job competition, involves legislation and/or administrative rules limiting labor force participation on grounds of age or sex. For example, adolescents are restricted from working by compulsory school attendance and child labor laws; women, by laws which limit working hours— such as exclusion from night work—and conditions of employment; and the elderly, by compulsory retirement rules. When embodied in civil codes, such restrictions are collectively called protective legislation, which purportedly serves the best interests of target groups. Baker's (1925) early analysis showed that such legislation systematically excluded women from high wage jobs, and yet the current economic basis for opposition to the Equal Rights Amendment for women, which would end these legal restrictions on women's work, remains unexamined.[5]

Legal efforts to end race discrimination, such as fair employment legislation and presidential orders, date from the 1930s. Although there has been little analysis of the economic effects of such measures, evidence by states suggests that fair employment legislation somewhat increases both earnings and unemployment of minorities (Becker, 1968:208). Whether sex discrimination is unconstitutional is not clear, but the recent trend of legal decisions suggests that it might be (Sigworth, 1972:34). The Civil Rights Act of 1964 forbade sex discrimination in employment, but not until 1972 was it illegal in federally assisted education programs (Sandler, 1973:439); the impact of such laws on hiring practices and wage differentials is, at most, slight (Rossi, 1973). Some concern has been expressed that affirmative action programs will encourage hiring less "qualified" persons, especially in academia (Lester, 1974) but no data support this belief.

Legal Protectionism

Occupational groups use several devices to secure privileged sanctuaries *vis-à-vis* other occupations, the most effective of which is legal and governmental aid in

---

[5] Certainly some past opposition came from both trade unions and employers in lower-wage industries, such as the textile industry. The UAW has supported the ERA more than most unions. Not till October 1973 did the AFL-CIO Convention go on record in support of ERA (Raphael, 1974).

protecting or actually subsidizing the occupation. The courts or government may operate inconspicuously by granting an occupation or industry special tax advantages (Eisenstein, 1961). Legal codes may embody the very rules and regulations of an occupational association (Hughes, 1958; Rottenberg, 1962:3–20). Some professional bodies (Gilb, 1966:135) and skilled trades have succeeded in having their specific codes become the law through expert lobbying practices. An indirect device whereby interest groups obtain governmental protection is to place sympathetic persons to serve on regulatory bodies (Leiserson, 1942:11); in this way, government agencies are soon controlled by the very interests they were supposed to regulate (Hamilton, 1967:52). Publically supported universities help professions in various ways: they subsidize costly professional training, they restrict the number of trainees (thus controlling the supply of practitioners), and their faculties socialize students in the professional ideology which justifies monopolistic practices. If occupational groups such as labor unions, professional societies, trade associations, and private clubs are unsuccessful in obtaining government support, they try to build enough social solidarity and financial resources to control recruitment, training, promotion, conditions of work, pay schedules, and other benefits (Stinchcombe, 1965:164).

TYPES OF OCCUPATIONAL MARKETS

Occupations vary in their control over labor markets. Miller and Form (1964: 452–455) classified the following types: self-controlled, traditional, formally administered, contested, and free markets. Each type is described briefly.[6]

Self-controlled markets. These types of markets are found whenever occupational groups make decisions not only on their own incomes and conditions of work, but decisions for other employees. Owners, managers, and directors of large firms assign themselves high salaries and bonuses in the form of stocks, bonds, and noncash payments such as insurance policies, transportation, recreational facilities, retirement benefits, and so on (Pen, 1966:256–258). Typically, the larger the enterprise, the higher the incomes of the top echelon of management. While some competition exists for top executives in industry, the amount of job mobility for this group is low. Incomes of executives increase with hierarchical rank rather than corporate profits (Roberts, 1956) and even when losses are high, executive salaries may remain high. While data are sparse, it appears that managerial salaries are assigned by a small group of intimate peers who use traditional and particularistic guidelines.

Traditional market. Within this market, an occupation monopolizes certain skills and has an ethic for dealing with peers and clients. Included are such groups as independent professionals (doctors, lawyers), independent artisans (plumbers, carpenters), and some service workers (jewelers, watch repairers). Tenure in such occupations is long and generational recruitment is common. Strong occupational associations regulate recruitment, training, con-

---

[6] Parsons and Smelser (1965:146–156) derive three sub-types of labor markets: labor service at a low level of technical competence, executive services, and professional services. Increasingly removed from a competitive market, each has a more powerful grasp on the forces which affect its destiny.

ditions of work, fee structures, and client relations. Incomes, usually derived from fees for service, range from moderate to high and their level takes into account the client's ability to pay, traditional rates, and economic conditions. When these occupations are absorbed into large bureaucracies (government, education, business), their salaries and benefits tend to be reduced, but they parallel those found among independent practitioners. Incomes in both the private and bureaucratic sectors tend to be fixed by law or custom rather than by the market (Mills, 1956:112–141).

Administered markets.   These include such groups as white collar workers in government and military bureaucracies. A distinctive attribute is a finely graduated salary scale arrived at "scientifically" which parallels educational level and tenure. In order to be universal in recruitment and promotion, bureaucracies heavily rely on standard examinations (Weber, 1946:196–243). Despite efforts to fix salaries objectively, they tend to follow the wage patterns in the free market (Phelps, 1957:402–423), because both markets compete for a wide range of skills. An extended promotional ladder tends to prevent group solidarity, hence unionization (Dreyfuss, 1938).

Although salaries in administered markets are frequently lower than in other markets, they are more stable and secure. Until recently, employees in administered markets had advantages available only to management (pensions, sick leaves, paid vacations, pregnancy leaves, insurance, credit unions), but unions and professional associations have gained some of these advantages. Recent legislation permitting government workers to bargain collectively may reduce income differences between them and employees in smaller enterprises in the private sector.

Governments with planned economies include almost all workers in administered markets. Since rational determination of wage rates is difficult in the absence of an external yardstick (Dahl and Lindblom, 1953:372–385), traditional status requirements of jobs along with agency competition for scarce personnel, may affect wage levels. No satisfactory analyses have been made of markets for estate-like occupations (e.g., the military, clergy, teachers, and nurses) whose job security and prestige have been traditionally higher than their incomes. Perhaps, like teachers, all have suffered a relative decline as educational level has risen.

Contested markets.   These are associated with occupations which engage in formal collective bargaining. The extent to which bargaining, rather than the market, determines wages is a subject of considerable dispute and we shall discuss it in the section on blue collar occupations. Reynolds and Taft (1956:372) believe it is a mistake to think that the deficiencies in wage theory can be corrected by jettisoning economic theory and substituting a political theory of wage determination. Price-making by bargaining has not, however, received much attention from theoretical economics (Pen, 1959:113), nor is there an adequate sociological theory of the labor market (Chaplin, 1967). Carrter and Marshall (1967:369) think that tentative decisions, made at the level of the firm and the industry, are later ratified or altered at the macro-economic level. But labor unions fight at every level not only for higher wages, but for such guarantees as: control over hiring, promotion, and firing; sick benefits, cost of living adjustments, supplementary unemployment benefits, guaranteed annual wages, insurance, and retirement benefits. Success in reaching these goals pushes contested markets toward conditions found in administered markets.

The free or unstructured market. Classical economists describe this market as occurring when wages reflect only the supply of, and demand for labor (Polanyi, 1957:177). Low skill, lack of organization, and fluctuating demand push wages to very low levels for such occupations as small retailers, migratory laborers, domestic and casual workers (Fisher, 1951; Huber, 1974: 103–123). Probably about one-fifth of American families are headed by a person whose labor is sold in the free market.

SOCIETAL SETTING: THE POLITY-ECONOMY BALANCE

Scholars commonly assume that occupational controls of modern societies are conditioned by the relation between the economic and political institutions. If the state dominates the economy, the political elite has societal power; if the state does not exert control, then economic elites shape events. This generalization bears examination.

The economy may be briefly defined as the web of activities involved in the production of goods and services; the polity, as the activities which (ultimately) integrate and direct the society. In advanced industrial societies, it is difficult to distinguish the economic functions of government from the political functions of the economy because all governments operate enterprises, regulate industries, attempt to maintain full employment, and provide health agencies, employment bureaus, and social security services (McGuire, 1963:86–99). Even in governments which are dominated by socialist parties, large private enterprises exclusively control certain markets, strongly influence national economic planning, and regulate conditions affecting their operations. It is difficult in such cases to ascertain the extent to which governments control the economy and the extent that economic units constitute a private government (Hamilton, 1967:34–43). Because national economies are so complex, mechanisms must arise to insure their coordination. Whatever they are called, mechanisms which force coordination of economic and governmental units constitute a polity. When the economy-polity balance is closely examined, differences among industrial societies tend to diminish.

Two types of economy-polity structures may be distinguished, depending on the degree to which managers make interorganizational decisions. State ownership and operation of the economy constitutes a clear type, while the business-dominated system has two major variants. In multi-party systems, trade union officials, state agencies, and managers of public and private enterprises are involved in economic decisions, roughly constituting a representative pluralistic polity—as in Britain, Sweden, and the United States. In one-party states, labor, management, and government bureaucrats are dominated by party officials who make no attempt to assure a representative or competitive pluralistic polity.

The rhetorics of these systems are antithetical. In the state-dominated system, an organic idealistic rhetoric emphasizes the obligation of economic groups to grant priority to the state. Private property systems develop two rhetorics. One of them stresses the importance of individual freedom in economic life and the wisdom of the market in maximizing the common welfare. The other, especially in multi-party welfare states, emphasizes the importance of participative democracy and bargaining among economic groups to make economic policy and the need for the state to protect the interests of the unorganized.

These distinctive rhetorics tempt one to suppose that occupational power varies considerably among state or business-dominated polities, but trend data on the distribution of income do not support such a view. Bergson (1944:106) found that, despite a conscious drive toward equality, inequality in wages appeared to be approximately the same in the Soviet Union as in the United States. No adequate data support the belief that the welfare state in Great Britain (Titmuss, 1962) or the New Deal in the United States (Miller, 1964:37) substantially altered the distribution of income. We do not know, therefore, precisely how occupational power varies among these structures.

There are several reasons for thinking that variations in political economies are not as great as once believed. First, the integrative demands of complex economies fix parameters in the types of necessary controls. Second, the major participants in all systems are the same: government officials, the military, heads of large productive and service enterprises, heads of large labor unions and professional associations, and leaders in politics, education, and welfare. Third, both models may be evolving in a similar direction. Berle (1954) doubts that an historical comparison of capitalist and communist economic systems will reveal major structural differences. He feels that the political drive to industrialize in the Soviet system aimed at the same goals as in mature capitalist countries. Granick's (1961) study of Soviet managers highlights their similarities to managers in the United States. Fourth, the importance of technological development requires any government to pay primary attention to economic conditions. Fifth, the fact that very large bureaucracies (technical, governmental, and quasi-governmental) are involved in making major decisions may stimulate other parallels which have not been studied. This last point bears further examination.

Scholars of varying political stripe have long agreed that American society is dominated by economic giants (Boulding, 1953; Berle, 1954; Presthus, 1962; McGuire, 1963; Hacker, 1964; Zeitlin, 1970; Mermelstein, 1973). Drucker's (1950:263) slogan is apt: "The proper study of mankind is organization." With few exceptions (Mills, 1951; Miliband, 1969), most scholars have also adopted a pluralistic decision-making model of the relations among these giants. Each competes to achieve some of its goals, but no corporation or combination of corporations makes economic policy. While imperfect competition is acknowledged (Chamberlin, 1933; Robinson, 1933), the system is believed to have countervailing power built into it (Galbraith, 1956), assuring pluralistic decisions in the economic marketplace, similar to those found in the political sphere (Hacker, 1964:144).

Evidence to support this view is not available. While the American economy probably is not demonstrably controlled by a small directorate, the presence of giant corporate units makes for a special kind of pluralism, with "elephants dancing among the chickens" (Hacker, 1964:8). Unlike the situation in small enterprise capitalism, managers of giant enterprises control enormous resources, including concrete knowledge about the organizational environment of competitors, suppliers, and clients. American corporations use whatever means are appropriate to promote corporate goals: making a profit, expanding the market, eliminating competitors. Policies are evaluated by their results, and not in terms of political or economic philosophies.

In business-dominated polities, corporations freely locate plants, make investments, manufacture new products, fix prices and wages. Corporate free-dom is valued because it enables the corporation to maintain or expand profits. Should the government restrict corporate freedom but guarantee its profit and growth, the issue of freedom becomes less important (Melman, 1970). Tennessee Eastman and General Electric, for example, have built plants financed by the government, to government specifications, operated according to government regulations, to make products used exclusively by the government (atomic materials and space vehicles).

In conclusion, whatever the formal relations between economic and politi-cal institutions in advanced industrial societies, decisions are made by competing occupational elites who behave similarly (Rostow, 1954:182–189; Granick, 1961:201–205; Samuelsson, 1968:223–294). We shall now examine the debate concerning the power of single occupational elites to influence the political economy.

OCCUPATIONAL ELITES: THE MANAGERS

A persistent question in economic history is whether an industrial ruling class exists. In almost any complex society, a governing elite can be easily identified by locating those who occupy the top governmental posts. The two basic ques-tions are: how is the elite recruited and in whose interest does it rule? If a restricted occupation demonstrably made and directed economic policy for a nation, it would constitute an occupational elite which could control industrial facilities and receive the highest rewards. Such an elite would not necessarily be formally organized as a directorate, although such a possibility exists. Though the data permit no certainty about the existence of such an elite in the United States, perpetual questions and answers about it are proposed with each major change in economic organization.

Elites: the Past

Historical analysis suggests that the character of elites changes as technology changes. Knowledge of whether and how their "interests" become "vested" is as distant as it was in Sumner's day (Stinchcombe, 1965:167). Marxist theory points to changes in political control which accompanied shifts from agricul-ture, to commerce, to small industry, and finally, to large industry. Pirenne (1914) and Polanyi (1957) showed that capitalism itself is a changing system and that the composition of its leaders has changed with the size and organiza-tion of production, distribution, and marketing units. Such changes still occur in response to automation and rationalization in industry. A brief review of social thought concerning occupational elites in the United States shows the importance of economic and technological changes.

Prior to the Civil War, agriculture dominated the United States. Although small landholdings were the rule from the founding of the nation, large for-tunes were amassed by families which acquired vast landholdings. Early for-tunes were also made in shipping, commerce, and in urban real estate. Many of the great banking families acquired their original capital from shipping, commerce, and real estate. Myers (1937) showed that much of the large invest-ment required to build railroads and factories from the Civil War to World War I came from a few great fortunes. While this economic elite may not have been responsible for the majority of investments, it established giant industrial, business, and banking firms which to this day greatly influence economic events.

Manufacturing became critically important as a source of wealth from the Civil War to the present. Whether the Captains of Industry were more influential in determining the momentum and direction of economic growth than financiers is debatable; yet families accumulated vast fortunes in steel, railroads, utilities, oil, textiles, lumber, tobacco, munitions, chemicals, machinery, and other products. These giant enterprises, often managed by their founders, grew both by skillful reinvestment and borrowing. Industrialists became popular heroes in their own time, widely acclaimed as men who shaped America's destiny (Wyllie, 1954; Wohl, 1966).

While large, family-owned and operated industries continued to flourish, basic changes in the economy were thought to derive from other interests. Giant corporations grew with funds provided not by families but by banks and banking syndicates. Trusts established in manufacturing, commerce, and banking absorbed small competitors and directed company policies to maximize profits on investments, rather than to stimulate increased production, industrial growth, and efficiency (Veblen, 1923). Stocks in the large corporations increasingly were owned by persons and agencies with no knowledge of the businesses, which became so complex that teams of specialists in applied science, management, sales, and industrial relations were needed to run them. Three questions came to fore: (1) What occupations or interests were running the largest corporations? (2) Was the public (consumers and others) being best served by those in control? (3) If not, what ought to be the pattern of control?

The first major attack was directed toward the finance capitalists. Newspaper reporters (muckrakers) and some university professors charged that bankers rather than industrialists were running both the economy and government (Tarbell, 1904; Steffens, 1931; Lundberg, 1937). They accused bankers of stifling competition, creating trusts, manipulating stock and money markets, ignoring the welfare of workers, managers, and small investors, and creating economic crises which profited them at the expense of the general welfare. They also charged that financiers bought political protection or escaped government regulations. Responding to public pressure, Congress enacted many laws in this period to break the "stranglehold" of bankers on the economy.

If bankers were not to be most powerful, then who should be? Shortly after World War I, Thorstein Veblen proposed that the industrial engineers were and should be the functional elite of modern industry. He argued that, because the economy was comprised of interlocking sets of complex industries understood only by engineers and skilled technicians, it was no longer practical to leave it in the hands of businessmen whose interests were financial rather than technical and moral. Industry should be run only by those competent to manage it for the welfare of the community. "The industrial dictatorship of the captains of finance," Veblen (1940:82) concluded, "is now held at the suffrance of the engineers and is liable to be discontinued at their discretion.

Veblen's remedy was part of the social ideology of technocracy and pragmatism. The people's faith in the superior knowledge and morality of engineers was reflected in the election of Herbert Hoover, an engineer who was presumably above politics. The abortive technocracy movement was conspicuously unsuccessful in challenging the existing political order. Only in education did pragmatism, the ideology of applied science, take firm root. While many engi-

neers did in fact become managers of industry, they did not challenge propertied men's claim to their profits. Indeed, if anything, they accepted the prerogatives of capital by becoming capitalists themselves (Gerth and Mills, 1942).

The issue of who, in fact, was running the economy was kept alive by Berle
and Means' (1932) monumental work, *The Modern Corporation and Private
Property*. A few hundred corporations were responsible for half of national
industrial productivity; ownership of these corporations was widespread, but
the majority of the stockholders were not represented on the board of directors,
and the boards were in fact run by their managers. Corporate power was virtually unrestricted and not responsible to any group. They concluded that, if the
corporate system is to survive, the control of great corporations should develop
into a neutral technocracy, balancing a variety of claims in the community and
assigning to each a portion of the income on the basis of public policy rather
than private cupidity (Berle and Means, 1932:357).

The implication of Berle and Means' conclusion was the same as Veblen's:
despite changes in the economic structure, despite the functional dominance of
managers or engineers, the large corporations were in fact still run for their
owners.[7] However, the unanswered question still remained, "For which owners?"

Ten years after Berle and Means' work, Burnham (1941) proclaimed that
the issue of "who rules" had already been decided all over the world, but that
people were unaware of the silent managerial revolution which had taken place.
Managers of complex economic and political structures were in fact running all
countries, not only controlling instruments of production but also receiving
preferential rewards. While managers might not formally own corporations,
they had access to their resources through control of the state. In some places,
like the Soviet Union and Nazi Germany, the power of the managers was formally acknowledged as legitimate. In the United States, a burgeoning new ideology would legitimize the control of the managers over economy and polity
(Burnham, 1941:71–76).

Certainly Burnham's thesis is debatable. But he represented a school of
thinkers who felt that the most powerful occupation was that of the manager
who coordinated the activities of other men. Previous thinkers assumed that
managers had power because they were propertied or had technical knowledge
about industry. In a sense, Burnham was the culmination of a school of thinkers, including Weber (1946:196–244), who saw the growth of large bureaucracies to be the most significant trend in Western society, and he inferred that
their directors would be the most powerful. Earlier, Taylor (1911), Urwick
(1933) and many others had emphasized that management was a skill as technical as that of the engineer or applied scientist. Later administration theorists
saw management as a special profession devoted to maximizing the technical efforts of occupational strata in complex organizations. But Mayo (1945), Barnard
(1968), Roethlisberger and Dickson (1947), and others in the "human rela-

---

[7] In 1974, Zeitlin's exhaustive and painstaking study concluded that the empirical question
of the separation of management from owners was still open. Sheehan (1966:224) revealed that
possibly a score of firms with sufficient sales to qualify for *Fortune's* list of the 500 largest
corporations are controlled by one family. Moreover, Barlow, Brazer, and Morgan (1966:65)
found that in a national sample of high income respondents, one-third of the aggregate income
over $10,000 per year in 1961 went to persons who owned stock in a corporation in whose
management they were active.

tions" school emphasized that administrators must be skilled in motivating men to cooperative effort because morale was as important as technical skill in achieving organizational goals.[8] The emphasis on managers as motivators and coordinators rather than as technologists, distinguishes Veblen from Burnham, who explicitly excluded technical experts from the ranks of managers.

Following upon the increase of labor union membership during World War II, C. Wright Mills (1948) suggested another elite. If union leaders marshalled sufficient voting strength to place them in positions of governmental power, they might influence the industrial complex. A disciplined electorate voting for a particular political program could provide a greater resource than the property and knowledge available to industrial managers. But union growth following World War II was sluggish because the demand for labor increased most in sectors that are most difficult to unionize, and labor's power has not grown.[9]

Finally, some writers, following Veblen's lead, have proclaimed scientists as the new men of power (Klan, 1968; Price, 1965). Industry and government have become increasingly dependent upon research scientists and development departments to introduce technological innovations in industry and government. Faunce and Clelland (1967) and others have heralded the advent of a professional society wherein scientists would dominate both the economy and the polity. A scientific take-over would be a logical consequence of specialists in every area making both long- and short-run decisions.

Thus have changes in the technology and organization of the economy stimulated speculation about the possible dominance of elites. Power was seen to flow from small businessmen to owners of large industries, to finance capitalists, to engineers, managers, and scientists. Undoubtedly, the decision-making process became more complex and increasingly dependent upon the application of scientific knowledge in many fields. Indeed, Galbraith (1967:59–71) feels that complex, technically qualified occupations plan industrial life. This technostructure replaces earlier elites and directs the political economy as much for its own ends of growth as for owners, customers, government, or other groups. Similar technostructures occur in all advanced industrial societies regardless of their property systems.

Elites: Control

Yet modest evidence shows that something like an industrial elite exists to the extent that one occupational stratum exerts greater control over a range of resources. In any situation where elites compete, four resources are available: formal authority, material resources, skill or knowledge, and disciplined organization. In modern industry, management has the authority; the board of directors controls the money; the engineers or applied scientists control the knowledge; and the labor union officials control the disciplined workers. Management clearly has the most resources. Impressive evidence shows that management tends to control the boards of directors, hence material resources

---

[8] See Charles Perrow's (1972) penetrating analysis of the managerial ideologies of the human relations and subsequent movements.

[9] Recent unionization of public employees has revived speculation that a politicized labor might increase its power (Fogel and Lewin, 1974).

(Berle, 1965:87–102). Managers formally direct operations and decide if, when, and how to use expert knowledge. Finally, management is generally successful in containing collective bargaining within fairly narrow parameters and the union cannot discipline management's economic decisions.

The power of an industrial managerial elite can be surpassed only by a political elite which can legitimately use force. Whether a political elite controls the economy, is controlled, or shares control should be empirically determined. Scholars have not found a valid method of measuring control, although several arguments suggest that an industrial elite substantially influences the political economy. First, Miliband (1969; 1972) argues that, because business enterprise in the Western democracies is privately owned and because the smooth running of the economy is politically crucial, any measures to improve economic conditions must inevitably support private ownership. The fact that the higher positions in corporate management are available to those who retire from government may also enhance the favorable attitude of the political elite to business interests. Second, although pressure politics is one of the most controversial topics in the entire study of government (Hacker, 1962:367), studies of administrative regulation of business show that business interests have little difficulty in representing their views and in securing regulations acceptable to them (Leiserson, 1942). Third, owing to a climate of "liberal atomism," many occupational interests are not as well represented in government (Eckstein, 1960); similarly, small business, quite unlike large corporate business, is torn by so many cleavages that any sort of coherent pattern of attitudes and political activity is hard to imagine (Zeigler, 1961:65). Obviously, elites such as labor union officials would enhance their influence if they occasionally gained control of government as happens in Britain or Scandinavia. Yet the electoral victories of labor and socialist parties do not automatically lessen the influence of industrial managers (Miliband, 1969).

For whom and for what is corporate management power exercised? It is too easy to assume that organizations agree on a priority of goals and that managements allocate resources accordingly. In complex organizations, exchanges among many groups take place continually. The exchanges are not always equal; priorities in resource allocation are more visible in retrospect than in current plans. Galbraith (1967) has analyzed the question of who gets what in the mature corporate economy over the long run. Since management's first priority is to control the enterprise, it can best guarantee noninterference from the stockholders by assuring them a steady profit. On the whole, managers have both successfully maintained autonomy and made profits. Their third priority is to allocate resources to facilitate long-term planning. As part of the planning structure, managers give themselves the highest salaries, benefits, and amenities (Roberts, 1956). The cooperation of the technostructure is assured by management's granting resources for product development, research, and the next highest salaries. Wage demands, reflecting increased productivity, rise in cost of living, and a small share of profits, are met almost as routinely as dividend expectations. Other employees receive salaries based on formulae worked out with organized labor. Resource allocation follows the same pattern regardless of who is running the corporations, and regardless of the social composition of the managerial elite. Berle (1965), documenting changing patterns of corporation control, feels that corporations have a dynamic independent of who is in control. The growth of the technostructure and its increasing involvement in managerial decisions have not changed the pattern of resource allocation—first to management and stockholders, then to technicians, blue-collar workers, and white-collar workers.

Yet the most important question is whether industrial growth alters the pattern of rewards. Some theorists hold that the growth of large enterprise leads to increasing equality of reward (Dahrendorf, 1959:36–71; Parsons, 1953:122–128). They reason that increasing organizational size is accompanied by increasing division of labor which, in turn, promotes self-conscious occupational groups who know that their cooperation is essential to keep the system running. Moreover, managers know proportionately less of what they need to know to run the system (Lenski, 1966:313). Because each occupational stratum can withhold its collaboration, demands for rewards are legitimized on the basis of cooperation rather than the functional importance of the work. As enterprises become more efficient and the incomes of all strata rise above minimum needs, inequities are reduced in response to an ideology of fair share of system rewards. Some inequalities remain, but their magnitude decreases. This phenomenon is alleged to occur in the Western democracies and in socialist and communist countries as their industrial structures become more alike. Ideology declines everywhere as the problem of equity is resolved (Aron, 1968:92–183; Bell, 1960:43–67; Riesman, 1953:246–258).

But the idea that equality increases with industrialization is difficult to demonstrate because no country has adequate data showing trends in the distribution of income and wealth over time.[10] Better data is available on income than wealth, but even in the United States, the Census collected no income data on individuals and families until 1940. And these data do not cover fringe benefits which make considerable difference (Macaulay, 1959:14). Likewise, precise estimates of the effect of the tax structure are not available, although evidence indicates that the levelling of income produced by the graduated income tax (e.g., Heilbroner, 1968) is not nearly so great as generally supposed (Strachey, 1956:131–151; Eisenstein, 1961; Kolko, 1962:13–29; Stern, 1962; Bottomore, 1964:34–35; Schorr, 1968:275). Although social security systems increase income equality (Cutright, 1967a:189), state and local taxation has the opposite effect.

In addition to the problem of dealing with so many unknowns, recent data in the United States show no clear trend towards increasing equality. The narrowing of the income gap in the United States, apparent during the war years, stopped in the 1950s (Miller, 1964:46, 1966:84). Table 1 shows that the range of gains in annual compound growth rates by occupation was greatest from 1939 to 1950 and least from 1947 to 1968; managers made comparatively lower gains in the earlier period but in the later period they ranked first (U.S. Bureau of the Census, 1970a). Professionals were low in both, although physicians and lawyers (self-employed) made even greater gains than managers. These data

---

[10] Kuznets (1963:13), noting the inadequacy of income data, cautiously concluded that income equality was somewhat greater in developed than in undeveloped countries. Cutright (1967b:564), comparing eight economic sectors in fifty-two countries, found that sectorial inequality decreases with rising GNP; inter-sector income substituted for unavailable individual income data.

TABLE 1
ANNUAL COMPOUND GROWTH RATES, 1939 AND 1950 TO 1968:
WAGE OR SALARY INCOME OF ALL MALES FOURTEEN YEARS OLD AND OVER,
BY MAJOR OCCUPATION GROUP, FOR THE UNITED STATES

Occupation	1939-50	Occupation**	1939-68	Occupation**	1947-68
Farm laborers and foremen	11.1	Operatives	6.4	Managers	5.2
Service workers, except private household	9.7	Farm labor	6.2	Craftsmen	5.0
Laborers, except farm and mine	9.6	Laborers	6.2	Sales	4.9
Operators and kindred workers	9.5	Sales	6.2	Clerical	4.8
Craftsmen, foremen, and kindred	9.1	Craftsmen	6.2	Operatives	4.7
Sales workers	8.5	Service	6.0	Farmers	4.6
Professional, technical, and kindred workers	7.2	Professional	5.8	Professional	4.5*
Clerical and kindred workers	7.0	Clerical	5.5	Farm labor	4.4
Managers, officials, proprietors, except farm	6.3	Managers	5.4	Laborers	4.3
Farmers and farm managers	6.0	Farmers	4.2	Service	4.0

* Self-employed professionals, 5.4.
** See Column 1 for full occupational titles.
Source: U.S. Bureau of the Census, *Current Population Reports,* Series P-60, No. 69, "Income Growth Rates in 1939 to 1968 for Persons by Occupation and Industry Group, for the United States" (Washington, D.C.: U.S. Government Printing Office, 1970: 14–20, 53–57).

do not permit the conclusion that a marked leveling of occupational income is occurring because the occupations which show the greatest increase in growth rate are typically those which rank above median income.

The pattern of managerial rewards highlights the gaps in a purely economic explanation of income distribution. Their earnings are out of line with their level of education. In 1969 (U.S. Bureau of Census, 1973a), median income for males sixteen years and older was $7,620, and median education was 12.3 years (see Table 2). Median income for professional and technical workers was $10,617 and median education, 16.3 years; median income for managers and administrators was $11,012, median education, 12.9. Salaried managers in manufacturing had a median income of $14,829 and median education of 14.1. This income was higher than that of most professional and technical occupations even though the professionals had a substantially higher median education. The most plausible explanation is that managers have considerable power to determine their own incomes. Moreover, they can affect the working conditions and incomes of occupations under their authority. To equalize power, other occupations must create organizations independent of management's influence; these, whatever their names, are collective bargaining organizations.

OCCUPATIONAL ASSOCIATIONS AND COLLECTIVE BARGAINING

Although collective bargaining is a structural feature of industrial systems with huge corporate units and a high division of labor, it typically refers only to formal negotiations between management and labor unions. Yet any collective attempt by an occupation to compete with another for resources may be considered collective bargaining. Informal organization, the handling of grievances, the wildcat strike, and formal negotiations all illustrate bargaining and almost all occupations engage in it (Strauss, 1963). From a sociological perspective, the

TABLE 2
MEDIAN EARNINGS AND EDUCATION OF SELECTED OCCUPATIONS,
MALES 16 YEARS AND OLDER, U.S., 1969

	Median Earnings	Earnings as Percent of Total Median	Median Education
Total	$ 7,620	—	12.3
Professional and Technical Workers	10,617	139	16.3
College teachers	11,248	148	17+
Engineers	13,151	173	16.2
Physicians, dentists	19,337	254	17+
Lawyers and judges	18,870	248	17+
High school teachers	9,036	119	17+
Managers and Administrators, except Farm	11,012	145	12.9
College administrators	13,938	183	17+
Salaried managers, n.e.c.	11,914	156	12.9
Durable goods manufacturing	14,829	195	14.1
Finance, insurance, real estate	13,322	175	13.1
Bank officers, financial managers	11,742	154	15.0
Clerical and Kindred Workers	7,259	95	12.5
Sales Workers	8,447	111	12.7
Crafts and Kindred Workers	8,176	107	12.0
Operatives (except Transport)	6,737	88	11.1
Service Workers (except Private Household)	5,086	67	11.2
Laborers (except Farm)	4,614	61	10.4

Based on U.S. Bureau of the Census, *Census of Population: 1970,* Subject Reports, Final Report PC(2)-7A, "Occupational Characteristics" (Washington, D.C.: U.S. Government Printing Office, 1973: 1–11).

labor union, the professional association, the management club, occupationally-based fraternities, and trade associations are also collective bargaining agents.

This wider conception of bargaining forces the analyst to examine groups other than those formally recognized as opponents. Thus, a craft union may bargain with foremen, other unions in the factory, the employer, as well as other publics in the state or nation. Likewise, physicians may bargain with clients, other medical associations, government bureaus, and legislatures. Such full analyses of bargaining have rarely been done for single occupations (Freidson, 1970:105–164) and never for the occupational structure as a whole.

This section will examine the main contours of collective bargaining for three broad occupational families: manual workers, white-collar workers, and professionals.

Labor Unions

Labor unions, comprised primarily of middle-income manual, white-collar, and technical workers, typically bargain for a relatively narrow wage range of income; rarely does the highest paid member receive a wage double that of the lowest paid. Not all manual occupations are organized—63% of the skilled, 50% of the operatives, 38% of the laborers, and 20% of the service workers (Bok and Dunlop, 1970:45). Historically, unions first appeared among occupations with the highest degree of social cohesion and the most solidaristic informal organization, e.g., the skilled crafts. The creation of labor unions was thus an expression of an already existing solidarity (Commons, 1918).

Early labor unions were *ad hoc* organizations which lasted only long enough to call a strike and conclude it successfully. Up to 1900 about one-third of the strikes in the United States were sponsored by such groups (Ross, 1954:24). A few organizations survived the strike and later acquired full-time staffs, increased the range of bargaining issues, and united with other organizations to meet common problems in the industry. Less-skilled occupations, especially in smaller and scattered industries, organized more slowly. Semi-skilled workers in larger industries, exposed to similar work conditions and a common technology, were organized *after* the pattern of union organization was obviously viable. Even today, unions comprised primarily of unskilled and service workers get less membership support than craft unions (Sayles, 1958; Bok and Dunlop, 1970).[11] The technique of collective bargaining is now so well known and effective that other occupations are adopting it: clerical workers in large firms, government workers at all skill levels, and various levels of professional workers such as nurses, teachers, and airline pilots.

Increasing Labor's Share of Income

If labor unions have power, then one would expect them to increase labor's share of income and control over working conditions. The idea that unionization improves labor's share is widely held but it is unproved because of lack of data on a wide range of occupations in different industries. To what factor should labor's share be compared? In the days of Ricardo and Marx, it was compared to the share of the entrepreneurial class. But this class has been replaced by the salaried managers who are lumped together, statistically, with all white-collar workers.[12] Furthermore, some economic sectors use a much higher share of their income for wages than others. Changes in the relative size of sectors in the total industrial mix will consequently change labor's total share even if no changes occur within sectors.

Much support can be found for the view that, in the short run, unions raise money wages. Unions pull up very low wage rates by eliminating low-paying firms or forcing them to pay more, by holding up high rates against pressures for narrowing, and stabilizing other wages (Kerr, 1975b:192). But raising money wages in the short run is not the issue. The question is whether trade unions increase the real wages of labor as a whole in the long run (Machlup, 1952:395); i.e., whether the national income is redistributed in such a way that labor gets an increased share. Not all of the terms for an equation are measureable. The national income is the value of commodities and services produced by the economic system minus the costs of the commodities (raw materials and capital equipment) and of services of enterprises consumed in the production process (Kuznets, 1941:135). The total wage bill may refer to the aggregate income of wage earners, other employees, or employers and self-employed, or any

---

[11] Lipset, Trow, and Coleman (1956), Sayles (1958), Blauner (1964), and Meissner (1969) have demonstrated the relationship between skill level, technological environment, and patterns of work interaction such as spontaneous disruptions, the ability to present a united front to management, and degree of union loyalty.

[12] Kerr (1957a:297) argues that looking at functional shares of the income is a hangover from classical economics when wage workers owned little property and high income persons were rarely salaried workers. Today size distribution is more important than factor share distribution. Radical theorists take the same position (Gordon, 1972:103).

combination of these three (Phelps Brown, 1964:371), but it usually refers to wages and salaries (Pen, 1966:54). Although wage and salary data are available for a number of countries, they are usually so inaccurate or cover so short a period, or both, that they are not useful for this question (Kuznets, 1946:11; Kerr, 1957a:292). None of the standard American sources shows wages and salaries separately, over time, for all sectors, although in a few industries a breakdown is possible and the data are analyzed (Kuznets, 1941:251).

British data at first glance, seem more adequate to assess the relative shares of wages and salaries because the stability in the proportion of national income going to labor is well established (Clark, 1932:72; Keynes, 1939:48–49; Phelps Brown and Hart, 1952). Wages were 39% of the national income in 1870 and rose to 42% by 1950; wage earners constituted 84% of the occupied population in 1870, and 66% in 1950. But these facts do not answer our question because, first, the proportion of wage earners in the labor force varies. As industrialization begins, the number of wage earners rises in proportion to self-employed, family workers, and small entrepreneurs. As it continues, the proportion of wage earners falls while salaried workers increase. This shift reduces the share of wages in the national income and is related to internal shifts in each stratum. Wage earners move to better-paying jobs while the number of lower-paid salaried jobs increases. Second, over time, wage earners gained at the expense of rents and dividends, but the relation of wages to profits varied with market conditions. When the market was "repressive to price rises, union strength raised the share of wages and union weakness did not lower it; but when the market environment was conducive to price rises, wage rises did not increase the share of wages, and with union weakness, the share of profits rose" (Phelps Brown and Hart, 1952:274).

Wages and salaries, taken together, have increased as a proportion of national income in a number of countries. The ratio has risen from 55 to 75% in Britain, about 55 to 70% in the United States, and 35 to 60% in the Netherlands in the last half century (Pen, 1966:54). Estimates for the United States vary in detail but the general conclusions are similar: wages and salaries have risen at the expense of rent and dividends (U.S. Department of Commerce, 1956:52; U.S. Department of Commerce, 1958:46; Kuznets, 1941:262).

In the United States, labor's share of the national income, measured by total wage and salary compensation, has increased over time (Reder, 1957:426). When American wages are considered separately, economists are agreed that the real wage level has increased and also that labor productivity has increased. Economists agree on a further point: in spite of much intensive investigation by highly competent researchers, no one knows whether the share of wages in the national income has increased or not, and a relationship between union power and labor's share has not been demonstrated (Rees, 1962:77). That real wages have risen may be due to (1) the increase in the amount of capital; (2) market forces pushing up the wage rate as marginal productivity rises faster than average productivity; (3) the pressure of unions. But economists do not agree on the relative importance of these factors (Lewis, 1963).

Two statistical considerations make measurement difficult (Carrter and Marshall, 1967:365–371). First, the relative importance of various industries has changed over the past fifty years. Agriculture, with less than 20% of income paid out in wages, has declined; and manufacturing, with roughly 75% paid in wages, has increased. This fact means that the overall labor income share rises

without any necessary change within either sector. Second, when relatively organized categories of employment (manufacturing, construction, mining, transportation, and communication) are compared with relatively unorganized
(agriculture, wholesale and retail trade, finance, and service), the trend line
indicating labor's share is nearly horizontal in the organized sectors and
markedly upward in the unorganized. Even from 1945–1964 the increase is more
marked for predominantly unorganized sectors. In the long run, labor's share
reflects not only the relative wage rate but also the introduction of labor-saving
machinery. No adequate measure of such innovation exists and therefore we
do not know whether this factor has been more important in manufacturing
than in agriculture, finance, and trade, which showed gains without the benefit
of strong unions. Carrter and Marshall (1967:371) conclude that as long as the
level of employment and investment is privately determined, labor's share cannot be arbitrarily set through collective bargaining or public policy.

Among wage earners, however, unions appear to raise the average relative
wage position of the organized relative to unorganized workers by at least 10%,
except during periods of unusually rapid inflation (Lewis, 1963:191).[13] Although adequate time series data are not available, in certain periods it is known
that wage differentials between organized and unorganized workers vary widely
by occupation, from zero to 50%. The organized-unorganized differential has
been 50% for bituminous coal miners; 25% for skilled building craftsmen; 15%
for rubberworkers; 5% for unskilled laborers; and zero percent for men's clothing workers (Lewis, 1968:544). The level of wages reflects the market position
of industries much more than the qualifications of their work forces. Quasi-
monopolistic industries (such as the automobile) which are heavily organized
can pass high wage costs to consumers without difficulty, but industries whose
workers are as qualified but in more competitive markets (men's clothing, tobacco, furniture) must pay lower wages, even when workers are fully organized.
Bluestone (1970) points out that industries which are capital intensive, highly
profitable, and free from raging competition can pay higher wages most easily,
and these are the industries which are most easily unionized. In industries where
unions control recruitment and training and where owners are not themselves
strongly organized, as in home building, unionized workers also can secure
higher wages.

A related question is whether wage differentials by skill level have increased
or decreased. The bulk of research shows that they have decreased over time in
the United States, especially during and after wars, or when employment is high
(Ober, 1948; Reder, 1955; Keat, 1960), although Ozanne's (1962) comprehensive study of differentials over a one hundred-year period at the McCormick
works, shows the opposite. Wide skill margins are associated with low levels of
economic development (Reder, 1955) while developed economies remove the
aged, infirm, and children from the labor market so that ease of substitution
among skill levels increases. Keat (1960), reviewing factors which could cause
wage narrowing, eliminated race, sex, age. The effect of unions was thought to

---

[13] A recent study (U.S. Bureau of the Census, 1970b) shows that median earnings of male
labor union members was 1.29 times that of non-union males; if only year-round, full-time
male earnings are compared, then the ratio is only 1.06 in favor of unionized males. The ratio
was much higher for heavily unionized occupations (e.g., construction craftsmen, 1.50) than
for little-unionized occupations (e.g., clerical, 1.03).

be minor. Immigration, he concluded, possibly accounted for a substantial amount, but changes in the cost and time of education and training could conceivably explain much of the change.

Our conclusion on the power of labor unions to shift income to organized labor remains agnostic. Labor's share has remained so stable over time that one might suppose labor unions made little difference. On the other hand, Marx predicted that labor's share would decrease over time because competition among capitalists would force them to keep wages at a subsistence level. This has not occurred. Obviously the size of the pie to be divided has grown drastically and labor has enjoyed an enormous increase in real income, whether or not it has increased proportionately to other factors of production. Why did labor share in this increase at all? An obvious answer is that the wages must be high enough to buy the products that industrialists produce. Did capitalists grasp this point of macro-economics, were they motivated by humanitarian reasons, or were they worried about labor unrest in the closing years of the past century? We do not know. But we do know that organized workers have a small but decisive advantage over unorganized workers especially in industries where competitive forces are minimized.

Unions and Working Conditions

Labor unions have considerable impact on working conditions. Let us examine their behavior in (a) economically underdeveloped societies, (b) totalitarian societies where labor is a dominant force, and (c) private enterprise societies which have a mature industrial structure and a free labor movement.

In economically less developed countries which have recently become independent, labor unions are usually led by intellectuals or political elites who were active in the independence movement. After independence, union leaders attend to improving the income position of workers. The employer is often the government itself or private entrepreneurs supported by government loans. Moreover, industrial growth depends upon reinvestment of large profits, government loans, and foreign capital (Kerr, et al., 1960:134–140). Unable to compete with foreign industries, local industries push not only for a sheltered economic environment, but also for low wages in order to plow profits into capital expansion. Governments want industries operated full time in order to achieve national economic goals, so strikes and other forms of labor protest are discouraged (Morris, 1968). A militant labor movement may threaten the stability of the state. In such countries labor unions are not powerful allies of workers because they are concerned more with disciplining workers to help achieve national goals rather than with improving workers' well-being.

In some socialist nations, organized labor, formally incorporated into the political system, is a politically ascendant force, e.g., in Israel, Mexico, and Eastern Europe. Organized labor is thought to be so powerful that workers do not need independent unions to give them the control they are alleged to have. Unions independent of the state would be organizationally redundant where they are defined as administrative units of the state. The union therefore is not exclusively dedicated to increasing the workers' share where basic economic decisions are made by political organizations. At the factory level, unions are expected to cooperate with management because workers are most knowledgeable about production problems. Both unions and management are occupational specialties which must cooperate for the efficient operation of the enterprise. Evidence is clear that income inequalities exist among major occupational families, but evidence is scarce on whether income differentials have changed over time. One study shows that wage differentials increased in the Soviet Union from 1930 to 1956 and declined since that time, but these shifts seemed to result from changes in government policy decisions rather than changes in labor union power (Feldmesser, 1960; Yanowitch, 1963).

In the private enterprise economies of the West, important differences mark the strength of labor unions and their relations to the state. In England, France, Belgium, Germany and Italy, unions bargain autonomously though they are identified with specific political parties. Typically, they cannot support long strikes and they are not heavily involved with worker grievances. Union and management officials bargain on the national level for a series of related industries (e.g., metals, utilities), and the pattern is then applied locally. Unions typically engage in short disruptive strikes for one or two days and try to involve government agencies in the controversy. The agencies investigate and recommend changes—typically accepted—in wage and price policies. Lacking adequate data, we have no reason to suppose that unions have significantly increased labors' relative share of income. Union tactics seem to be more effective in reducing inequities arising from inflation and other factors *after* they have appeared (Lewis, 1963).

American labor union experience is somewhat different. Generally stronger financially than European unions, they have accumulated large treasuries, engaged in long strikes, and forced management to make sizable concessions for the short run. Moreover, they have generally operated without governmental intervention. But no evidence supports the belief that unions significantly restructure wage levels.

From these brief sketches, we can draw several conclusions. When labor unions emerge, they tend to be militant and they obtain short-run advantages for particular occupations. Whether unions or other forces are responsible for maintaining such advantages is open to question. But unions clearly institutionalize relationships with employers and resort decreasingly to strikes (Kerr, 1964:105–147), although some unions (coal, shipping, textiles), more militant than others, strike more frequently during prosperous than depressed economic periods. Union wages tend to increase predictably in response to inflationary trends and increases in productivity. Although no clear evidence supports the idea that unions increase labors' share in productivity, some evidence indicates that unions have a ratchet effect in stabilizing wages, for rarely do wages fall even during periods of deflation and unemployment.

The institutionalization of labor conflict results in the increased use of arbitration and mediation to solve problems. Unions reduce conflict at the local level, solve grievances on the plant floor, decrease the arbitrary authority of foremen, demand consultation on changes in wage rates, and secure adherence to seniority rules. In short, unions have forged a common law for everyday problems at the plant level and have institutionalized conflict in economic bargaining. Unions everywhere have stimulated governments to assume some of the burdens resulting from economic instability, such as unemployment insurance, old age benefits, medical insurance, and price stabilization (van de Vall, 1970:12).

Two other phenomena related to the labor movement need to be considered: the experience of labor parties in attempting to improve the economic position of workers when labor wins electoral victories, and the effort of unions to raise wages when they have formal equality of power with management to run enterprises, as in "co-determination."

Labor in Government: The Problem of Equity

Labor parties have controlled the government in England, the Scandinavian countries, Australia, and New Zealand but they have not successfully solved national economic problems nor altered labor's share of the gross national product. Indeed, labor parties, tending to win in times of crises, sometimes demand more of the workers than would conservative governments. The sacrifices that labor leaders urge workers to make perhaps benefit the economy in the long run, but workers sometimes view them as punishment from alleged friends.

Labor parties have controlled Sweden and New Zealand for a generation. These countries have reduced poverty and unemployment, removed slums, provided adequate medical service, trained workers for new jobs, and overcome some of the problems resulting from economic fluctuations. Although living conditions have been improved for all strata, it is not clear whether working people have obtained an increased share of the national income. Labor intellectuals have been dissatisfied with governmental efforts to reduce economic inequality and even party leaders have admitted that they had not reduced economic inequality. These countries retain free collective bargaining despite socialist and labor control of the government. Labor leaders have recently decided that profits and prices must be controlled in order to assign productivity increases more equitably.

Co-Determination and the Reallocation of Authority

Co-determination occurs when both workers and management direct the enterprise and allocate its resources and profits. Since this name has been applied to a wide variety of arrangements, it is difficult to generalize about the effect of reallocating authority. In most plans, elected representatives of the workers sit on the Board of directors and share responsibility for making basic policy. The workers' councils do not ordinarily engage in collective bargaining per se, but do join management in making the decisions which result from bargaining. The joint bodies typically have access to the technical, financial, and legal information needed to make policy decisions in every major area including technical innovation, capital funding, wage policies, pricing, and profit allocation. Although co-determination plans vary in the amount of authority given to joint bodies, corporate information is freely given in most plans and, sometimes, co-equal authority to the worker representatives (Sturmthal, 1964). Let us assess the effectiveness of these plans in reallocating authority and changing income distributions.

Co-determination is not widespread in the United States, nor do management or labor unions show much interest in it. It has a longer history in Europe and has been tried widely in both socialist and private enterprise economies. Reviewing worker participation in the control of industry in France, Belgium, England, and Germany since 1885, Myers (1958) concluded that the workers' council movement has not fulfilled the expectations of labor and, importantly, that the economic effects of such bodies were not discernible. But Myers believes that workers' councils will continue to spread because workers monitor management more effectively when they have access to information previously unavailable.

Probably the most effective case of co-determination has been the socialized steel industry of West Germany after World War II. McPherson (1955) reported that the anticipated split between management and worker representatives on the councils did not develop, that labor representatives on the strategic management council experienced no conflict of loyalties, and for the most part went along with management recommendations. Apparently management leaned heavily on labor representatives for information on hiring, transfer, and removal of redundant workers. The effect of worker representation on the issue of wage levels, while probably positive, was not dramatic. McPherson concluded that the most important effect of the plan was to reduce pressures to socialize industries in Germany.

Israel represents the most unusual test of the probable effect of workers' councils on authority and reward systems in industry. The Histadrut (the general federation of labor) owns and operates a substantial sector of industry. Derber (1963) concluded that, with the increasing professionalization of management, workers could provide only supplementary ideas where they had expert knowledge, e.g., conditions on the plant floor. Worker participation in management decisions was small, as in the United States or Britain. Significantly, Derber (1963:64) concluded that the workers' role was not markedly different in Histadrut and government establishments than it was in private establishments.

The effectiveness of workers' councils in socialist economies is similar to that in private enterprise economies. Two illustrations may be cited. Sturmthal (1961) described the rise of the workers' council movement in Poland as part of a protest movement against over-centralization. Councils were given wide powers, including discretion in setting wage schedules and determining the allocation of half of the profits earned beyond the plan and all profits earned from "side line" activities. One consequence was that production quotas were lowered so that large profits of "over-production" could be redistributed. A squabble promptly arose whether the distribution should follow an egalitarian or merit principle. No solution was found. Authority relations among management, worker representatives, and nonlocal governmental units remained unclear. The central government, slowly realizing that the Councils interfered with rapid industrialization, returned the party to control at the local level, making the councils advisory bodies to management and the party. No report was given of changes in ratio of income between management and workers.

A more mature decentralization pattern appeared in Yugoslavia. In an extensive analysis of councils in two Yugoslavian factories, Kolaja (1965) concluded that management proposed most of the technical, financial, and marketing decisions, which, in turn, were supported by the councils whose members felt incompetent to evaluate such decisions. Over time, the workers defined the councils as management-oriented but useful instruments to inform management of worker needs. Unfortunately the study did not analyze management-worker wage shares. Although the councils were concerned with the problem, they dealt with it less successfully than other matters (Kolaja, 1965:32). The ratio between the lowest and highest wage was not egalitarian; in one factory, 1:5; in another 1:7.

These studies suggest some tentative conclusions. Effective worker participation in management is limited by management's desire for such consultation and the technical ability of workers to provide useful information. Generally, management authority is retained but at the expense of spending more time in consulting worker representatives, who are most effective when they provide information on the adverse consequences of some decisions on worker cooperation. Scant evidence suggests that the ratio of earnings between skill levels or between management and labor are unchanged by co-determination.

Clerical and Sales Workers

When clerical workers were few, they were not thought to threaten managerial control. Often related to management by kinship or social origin, they were loyally pro-business. The situation today is quite different. Clerical and sales workers, the most rapidly growing sector of the labor force, represent a broad spectrum of low to high skills and status. At the turn of the century, they constituted 7.5% of the labor force in the United States; in 1970, 25%. In 1900, clerical workers were somewhat fewer than sales personnel but by 1970 there were twice as many clerical as sales workers. Reflecting the increasing bureaucratization of the labor force, the rapid increase of both office and sales workers was accompanied by a heavy influx of women into the labor force; today almost 70% of clerical workers are women in contrast to 24% in 1900. Both sales and office work have relatively high turnover because the pay is low at entry and increases only slightly with experience; women usually enter these occupations prior to child-bearing and re-enter after child-rearing, or work part-time.

The change in sex composition of these occupations was accompanied by an increase in the size and complexity of work organization. While the bookkeeper and/or secretary constituted the office force of most enterprises prior to 1900, today many different occupations are found in the offices of government, business, education, and industry. In retail sales, the traveling salesman has been largely displaced by the department store in which sales clerks do little more than take orders for customers who drift in. Although many small offices and retail stores still exist, offices increasingly look like factories, and stores, like rationalized bazaars (Mills, 1956).

The same forces which altered factory work have affected the office: mechanization, specialization, centralization, and bureaucratization (Crozier, 1964). Early office machines were simpler than most factory machines but recently a variety of machines invaded the office. Occupations which once covered a range of functions have narrowed as work has been simplified and standardized. While office automation has not produced massive unemployment (Hoos, 1960:102–112), it further rationalized work and created new occupations with a wider range of skills.

The earnings of clerical and sales workers have declined in comparison with those of skilled manual workers. In 1896 clerical workers in manufacturing and steam railroads earned more than twice the wage of all workers in a number of selected industries, but by 1926, they earned only about one-third more (Burns, 1954; U.S. Bureau of the Census, 1960:91). By 1959, among males, highly skilled manual workers earned slightly more than clerical and sales workers but if foremen, students, and males under 21 and over 59 are excluded, then clerical and sales workers earned more than highly skilled manual workers (Hamilton, 1964). By 1969, among males, sales workers' earnings topped those of craftsmen whose earnings, in turn, topped those of clerical workers (U.S. Bureau of the Census, 1973b). Probably more significant is the fact that the overlap in earnings between many white-collar and manual occupations may now be greater than the differences. Traditionally white-collar workers also enjoyed greater fringe benefits, paid vacations, holidays, and sick leave than manual workers. Between 1939 and 1956 this gap was almost completely eliminated (Blum, 1964: 38) by aggressive bargaining of industrial labor unions.

The relative decline in earnings of clerical and sales workers is the result of two factors: the increase of women in these occupations and the loss of a relative educational advantage as median education rose for all workers. Full-time women salesworkers earned 38% and clerical workers, 64% of the wages of comparable males in 1969, a relative decrease since 1959 (see Table 3). Female clerical workers had the same median education level as males (12.5 years) while the level of female sales workers was below that of males (12.2 vs. 12.7). A "rational" income theory cannot account for these differences.

Clerical and sales workers have also suffered a decline in work autonomy. Increasingly large numbers are under direct and constant supervision. Typing, accounting, bookkeeping, and filing have been mechanized and routinized. The office employee increasingly responds to bureaucratic controls and the sales person, to individual cost accounting. Both office and sales work become increasingly hierarchial so that workers must wait longer to gain more job autonomy and control (Dreyfuss, 1938:2). Although automation of the office has not in-

TABLE 3
MEDIAN EDUCATION AND INCOME OF CLERICAL AND SALES WORKERS BY SEX, 1969

	Male	Female
	Median Education	
Clerical	12.5	12.5
Sales	12.7	12.2
	Median Earnings	
Clerical	$7,259	$4,228
Sales	$8,447	$2,316
	Percent Working 50-52 Weeks	
Clerical	74	61
Sales	77	48
	Median Wage and Salary, Worked 50-52 Weeks	
Clerical	$7,936	$5,112
Sales	$9,264	$3,487

Based on U.S. Bureau of the Census, *Census of Population: 1970,* Subject Reports, Final Report PC(2)-7A, "Occupational Characteristics" (Washington, D.C.: U.S. Government Printing Office: 4, 5, 248, 504).

creased unemployment, clerical workers in industry have recently been subjected to almost as much unemployment as industrial workers. Despite their relative status and income declines, office workers report satisfaction with their work (Morse, 1953:77–92), but continued exposure to work routinization may stimulate them to organize.

White Collar Unionism

Relatively few white collar workers belong to labor unions in the United States and a widespread belief holds that they cannot be organized. Perhaps the most important barrier to unionism is the white collar workers' belief that they have good opporunity for upward occupational mobility. Elaborate office hierarchies with attractive titles provide some substance to their dreams (Dreyfuss, 1938: 133–135). Employers, recognizing the status concerns of office workers, attach more status symbols to jobs at higher levels. Bruner (1957) emphasizes that white collar workers dislike union rhetoric, preferring a professional model of an occupational association, which separates work from political problems.

The belief that white collar workers cannot be organized is patently untrue. About 70% of such workers in Sweden and 30% in Great Britain are unionized, in contrast to 11% in the United States. White collar unions are more prevalent in countries where unionism is stronger (Sturmthal, 1966:376). In the United States, about 3 million white collar workers belonged to unions in 1970, but only 15% of all union members were white collar workers. Solomon and Burns (1963:151–152) estimated that about one-eighth of the sales clerks and one-fifth of office clerks were unionized, in contrast to about half of the other workers. Only a tenth of unionized white collar workers belonged to industrial unions; about two-thirds were employed in government, utilities, and retail trade. The bulk of unionized workers are in the communications industry (telephone and telegraph), the postal service, other government agencies, and retail trade (large department stores). In short, most work in large enterprises is routine, manual-like, low status, and under tight discipline—conditions favorable to unionization.

Yet many white collar workers oppose joining unions. They are not so much antiunion, as supporters of the idea that unions are inappropriate for quasi-managerial and professional employees. Morse's (1953) study of white collar workers showed that, unlike industrial workers, they were not alienated from their work or from management, were satisfied with their jobs, and favorably disposed toward the enterprise. Another study (Opinion Research Corporation, 1957:8) revealed that three-quarters saw themselves as belonging more to management than to labor and more of them favored the Republican party or claimed an independent political position.

These generalizations may hide as much as they reveal because white collar workers are a heterogeneous lot, and most of the studies have ignored the sex stratification of such jobs. One exception (Mills, 1956:307) reports that those who are occupationally immobile tend to favor unions but this does not hold for women who tend to be apathetic because they feel their jobs are temporary. But when an occupation is successfully unionized, women quickly join. Many white collar workers are anxious not to be identified as manual workers. When they organize, they want their union modeled after a professional association.

Will more white collar workers be organized in the future? If industrial unions remain as unsophisticated in their approach as they have in the past, white collar unions will not prosper. Organizing workers in small offices and stores and workers with high skills will surely be expensive and difficult. Some people claim that since the era of union growth is over, white collar unionism will never expand. However, if industrial unions continue to raise wages for manual workers, white collar workers, especially during rapid inflation, may press employers to provide the same gains or face unionization.

We noted that many white collar workers aspire to the lifestyle of the professions. But are the professions also exposed to the same insecurities which have plagued white collar workers? Or has the prestige of the professions been sufficiently high to give them power without organization?

The Professions: the Power of Prestige or the Prestige of Power?

Scholars disagree whether calling some occupations "professions" helps or hinders sociological analysis. Hughes (1958:43–49) claims that the distinguishing feature of professions is their success in getting others to call them professions; they have succeeded in capturing a prestigious label. Others (Greenwood, 1957; Wilensky, 1964) insist that professions fundamentally differ from other occupations. Whatever the outcome of this controversy, the professions, as defined by the census, clearly comprise a family of occupations with more income, honor, and authority than most other occupations.

Historically, professions monopolized systematic bodies of knowledge (or skills based on knowledge) which required extensive training. Law, medicine, and divinity are some common examples. Such monopolies are maintained by the professions' control of the recruitment and training of their members and by the prevention of other groups such as clients, government agencies or even other related occupations from evaluating the effectiveness or cost of their services (Carr-Saunders and Wilson, 1944). Professions are occupations which have obtained either a mandate or an official license to practice (Hughes, 1959). The license represents a consolidation of power because governmental authorities legalize the monopoly over the selection and training of recruits as well as professional practice and they will punish trespassers of the occupational preserve. Lower status occupations such as plumbers, though licensed, are not widely considered as professionals because they do not have a systematic body of theoretical knowledge. Today, professional training typically requires a university degree.

Complex economies require increasing application of scientific knowledge for occupational practice. Some scholars (Hagstrom, 1965; Parsons, 1968) insist that control of all institutions by professionals is the overriding trend of this century. Since many occupations utilize scientific, technical knowledge, it is not surprising that they want to be identified as professionals. Wilensky (1964) insists, however, that the use of scientific, technical knowledge alone does not validate claims to professionalism; the service ideal, with supporting norms of conduct and ethics is also needed. Many occupations which are oriented to mass markets (e.g., advertisers, morticians, car dealers), do not, in Hughes' (1958) terms, get others to honor their professional claims.

While academicians argue whether particular occupations qualify as professions, they basically agree on the steps which established professions have taken to secure their status (Caplow, 1954:139). The first is to establish an association to exclude those unqualified to practice. Second, the name of the occupation is changed to break identification with a title in the public domain. The new title implies mastery of a body of technical information; for example, the office manager becomes a "systems engineer" and the undertaker, "a mortician." Third, to validate the titular revolution, education and training are specified, raised, and enforced. Fourth, a code of ethics is constructed which contains a rationale for protecting the public, the rules of professional conduct, the methods of enforcing standards and punishing violators. Last, the association agitates for exclusive legal right to a title, mandatory educational requirements, a regulatory agency, inspection mechanisms, and penalties for violating ethical codes. The American Medical Association is a model: it writes its own laws, names the members of its regulatory agencies, conducts inspections, and specifies penalties for violators (Yale editors, 1954).

Professions can also be classified by degree of success in securing a mandate and a license. Carr-Saunders (1955) noted four major types: the old established professions (religion, law, medicine, higher education); the new professions (chemistry, engineering, social science); semi-professions (nursing, optometry, pharmacy); would-be professions (funeral directors, sales engineers, hospital administrators). Reiss (1955) added a fifth type: marginal professions (laboratory technicians, draftsmen, interpreters). He showed that occupations nearest to the "established pole" had more formal education, higher social origins, higher rates of self-employment, and more stable work careers than those closest to the "marginal pole."

Professionals within the population.   Professional and technical occupations expanded to 16% of all workers between the ages of twenty-five and sixty-four in 1970 (U.S. Bureau of the Census, 1973b:1, 2, 242–243). Women at one time comprised slightly more than one-third of the professionals, a proportion which has declined steadily since 1930 as the job structure shifted toward male-dominated professions (Blitz, 1974). Two thirds of the women professionals are school teachers or nurses; men are much more diversified. Black women are much better represented in the lower-paying "women's" professions than black men are in higher-paying "men's" professions (Bock, 1969). School teachers—three-fifths of them women—are the largest single profession, followed by engineers, almost all of them men, found in large numbers across all industrial categories (Perrucci and Gerstl, 1969:2). Earnings of women professionals working full-time year round are 59% of men's (U.S. Bureau of the Census, 1973b:2, 243); a substantial differential persists even with workers in the same occupation. Highest median earnings go to physicians and dentists, followed by lawyers and judges, and airplane pilots. At the very highest income levels, self-employed professionals are almost entirely lawyers (Barlow, Brazer, and Morgan, 1966: 132).

Threats to Professionalism

The data on professions stress the danger of sweeping generalizations about such a diverse set of skills and technical knowledge. One common feature cited by most studies is the ubiquitous struggle for income. Rising availability of education has increased the supply in some occupations, resulting in a relatively decreasing income. This trend toward lower incomes can be thwarted if the profession itself controls entry. Two examples illustrate this point. As the proportion of persons graduated from high school and colleges increased, the ratio of teaching salaries to average wages in manufacturing shrank greatly from the years 1904 to 1953 (see Table 4). A full professor earned 3.61, the average wage in 1904, but only 1.73 times more in 1953, while the salary ratio of a high school teacher shrank from 2.88 to 1.36. Keat (1960:590) feels that these changes probably resulted from the decreased training differential between teaching and blue collar occupations.

TABLE 4
RATIO OF SALARIES IN SELECTED ACADEMIC OCCUPATIONS
TO AVERAGE WAGES IN MANUFACTURING (in percent)

Occupation	1904	1953
University president	776	407
Professor	361	173
Associate professor	271	138
Assistant professor	235	114
Instructor	144	91
High school principal, city 500,000+	641	226
High school teacher, city 500,000+	288	136
Elementary teacher, city 500,000+	158	119

Sources: Beardsley Ruml and Signey G. Tickton, *Teaching Salaries Then and Now*, Bulletin No. I, New York Fund for Advancement of Education, 1955, cited in Paul G. Keat, "Long Run Changes in Occupational Wage Structure, 1900–1956; *Journal of Political Economy 68* (December, 1960), p. 590.

An occupation which controls entry, however, can increase its relative income. Comparing differential incomes of physicians and dentists because the abilities needed are similar, Friedman and Kuznets (1954) found that the observed difference was 32%, in favor of physicians. The only measurable factor which could be responsible was the three years of additional training required for physicians. But this factor accounted for no more than 17% of the difference (Friedman and Kuznets, 1954:394). An important factor could have been the greater difficulty of entry into medicine, the result of a form of political-economic control that promised to become an increasingly important pattern of occupational power (Friedman and Kuznets, 1954:21).

Whether or not a profession typically works within a bureaucracy influences its income. A substantial majority of physicians and lawyers are self-employed; their incomes are much higher than those of salaried colleagues. Although salaried professionals increased at a faster rate than the self-employed, the increase in claimants to professional titles may decrease scarcity value and hence threaten established, self-employed professionals. Burgeoning scientific knowledge stimulates the formation of competing specialties, and even these are not secure, as in the mental health field where psychiatrists are challenged by clinical psychologists, counselors, and psychiatric social workers. Professional identity weakens when some professionals prefer to associate with those in their areas of competence rather than in their license areas, e.g., the preference of psychiatrists for social scientists rather than other physicians (Smith, 1958). These horizontal conflicts resemble jurisdictional disputes among the building trades, for each occupation claims an historical right to a monopoly, superior competency, greater public responsibility, and the exclusive right to evaluate performance (Gross, 1967).

Threats also come from lower-status occupations which are expanding their fields. The nurse with a Ph.D., the computer specialist, and the laboratory technician claim superior knowledge in some areas over physicians, professors, and engineers (Evan, 1964). Should the newer professions successfully establish their claims, older professions may become deprofessionalized by an erosion of their mandate and eventual removal of the license. More commonly, however, successful professional invasion creates a new niche in the division of labor.

Emerging Professions

Two other related threats to established professionalism are the rise of business professions and the growth of bureaucracies. As science is applied to business problems, business becomes the primary market for educated labor (Mills, 1954:134–141). Business management is professionalized and the professions are commercialized. Within business, intellectual tasks are bifurcated; some are simplified and passed to clerks while others are shifted to top management and professionals. In this process the mystery surrounding the professions is unmasked; salaries are fixed, work is rationalized, and autonomy is reduced. Among the salaried, top management emerges as the profession with the most authority, prestige, and income.

The entire professional market is affected by these trends. For the established professions, fees were once the primary source of income and, in the short run, the supply of professionals was inelastic, so that their incomes did not vary automatically with business cycles. When demand for services increased, its quality declined and income rose slowly, following long-term economic trends. Price competition was restricted by an established fee applied roughly according to the ability of the client to pay (Parsons, 1968).

The present situation for salaried professionals in business, government, and education is quite different. Salary scales are fixed and "rationalized" and the number employed and their earnings tend to fluctuate with economic conditions. In short, compared to the independents, salaried professionals are more exposed to market conditions and they tend to lose work autonomy in large organizations. Yet their training continues to stress traditional values of the independent and learned professions: gaining a broad range of expert knowledge and skill, exercising autonomy in selection of problems and clients, individual responsibility for work, and total commitment to an occupational lifestyle (Bucher and Strauss, 1961). Bureaucracy frustrates these values by forcing specialization to the point where work becomes technical and routine, by subordinating professionals to managers who do not respect their values, by reducing contact with clients thereby diminishing their sense of professional responsibility. This situation parallels the relationship between the engineer and the entrepreneur described by Veblen (1940): professional values are submerged to business values and the professional is reduced to a technician.

Scott (1966), Marshall (1939), Hall (1968), Clark (1963), and others reject this description as a caricature of a rare type. Conceding that professionals lose some autonomy in bureaucracies because they cannot perform *all* the tasks required of them, Scott (1966:270–5) describes four areas of role conflict: (1) resistance to bureaucratic rules, (2) resistance to supervision, (3) rejection of bureaucratic standards, and (4) conditional loyalty to the organization. In a professional bureaucracy (hospital, university, research organization), workers practice a wide range of skills, while in an industrial bureaucracy their skills tend to be segmented. The higher the prestige of the profession and the more central the skill to the organization, the more likely are professions to control their work and the less conflict they have with administrators. Hall (1968) also found that persistent conflict between administrators and professionals is not inevitable. Organizations vary widely in their bureaucratization and professions vary in their work values and structures. An equilibrium is reached in many situations; professional values and organizational styles penetrate bureaucracies and bureaucratic arrangements are introduced into professional practice.

Professional Associations

Despite these accommodations, the inability of professions to solve persistent problems creates turmoil. In addition to traditional struggles over licensing, training standards, accreditation, and violations of professional ethics, professional associations are interested in income maintenance and work prerogatives. The professions most exposed to bureaucratic controls (such as engineering, teaching, nursing) are most likely to experiment with new organizational tactics. Labor unions have made the greatest incursions into large professional bureaucracies. The experience of engineers, the largest single profession in private industry, illustrates the problems faced by other professions.

During and after World War II, large corporations such as aircraft manufacturing needed the services of many engineers who were typically assigned specialized parts of the task. But the demand for planes fluctuated. Although the industry wanted a ready pool of engineers to service new contracts, instability of employment could not be avoided. Consequently, prior to the early fifties, engineers' salaries failed to keep up with other professionals (Dvorak, 1963). Just before the passage of the 1947 Taft-Hartley Act, which prohibited unions comprised of both professional and production workers, the technicians in the aircraft industry organized labor unions and pressed the engineers to join them. To resist this threat, about twenty-five local and independent engineering unions were formed, some with the aid of the professional associations. The primary goals of these unions were to establish minimum salary scales, review procedures for merit increases, and specify grievance procedures (Goldstein, 1955).

Eventually most of these unions died. Engineers had backed into independent unionism in a desperate attempt to stave off absorption into unions dominated by lower-status occupations. Bargaining and grievance procedures of the engineering unions were ineffective because the engineers preferred an individual approach to their problems (Kuhn, 1963). Supervisors, often engineers themselves, tended to sponsor rather than squelch individual claims to higher management. In some disorganized situations, unions brought order to chaotic personnel policy, but despite pressure from older, downwardly-mobile workers to retain unions, the typical pattern was to revert to individual bargaining.

Teachers and nurses approached organizational problems differently than engineers. Professional associations after World War II were unable to deal with relative declines in income and increasing bureaucratization of work, so local units demanded new organizational forms. Three alternatives were open.

First, unions could displace professional associations, take over their functions, and become sole bargaining agents. Second, unions and professional societies could co-exist, dividing functions; the union would bargain at the local level while the association would deal with traditional professional problems (certification, standards, ethics, and training). Third, the professional association could bargain at the local level while continuing to perform its traditional tasks.

In an effort to stave off aggressive unionism, professional associations modified some union tactics to avoid violating the "professional sensitivities" of members. The third alternative, most commonly and effectively used by teachers, is the organizational solution of professions most exposed to bureaucratic pressures. The limited evidence points to modest gains by teacher organizations. Thornton's (1971) review of various studies concluded that collective bargaining increased teachers' salaries at a higher rate than for organized industrial workers, a finding corroborated by Moskow and Doherty's (1969) study of comparative earnings during 1950–65.

Three important questions on professional power remain: will the growth of professions in large organizations challenge management control? Will the professions recognize their common problems and begin to act in concert? What will be the political effects of the growth of professions? Only a cursory examination of each question is possible here. Goldner and Ritti's (1967) study of engineers in large industry suggests that professionals do not threaten management. Two routes to mobility are open: a series of steps on the professional ladder and the management ladder. But no matter how many steps it has, the professional ladder is rather short. The longer management ladder leads to real power. The professional ladder, open to those who fail to climb the management ladder, cools off failures and provides an alternative definition of success. The proliferation of occupational specialities in large organizations creates an atmosphere of pluralistic bargaining, but management continues to hold the, real power. Similar situations probably occur in all large organizations.

Will the professions become a solidary political force? A prerequisite is a high degree of self-awareness or a sense of common destiny, both of which are absent. The main thing professionals have in common is an uncommon amount of education and a sense of being above average in status. But important differences divide them: a wide gulf in educational attainment separates the learned from the would-be professions; enormous differences in earnings exist within the same sector, e.g., between physicians and nurses; social and occupational origins vary widely. More importantly, the conflicts among professional associations, e.g., nurses and physicians, are stronger than their conflicts with other groups, e.g., management and clients. The occupational values of independent practitioners, learned professions, business professions, and bureaucratic professions are not enough alike to provide a basis for collective action (Rosenberg, 1957). The traditional values of service, disinterest in money, work autonomy, and removal from politics—common to most professions—may serve as smokescreens for the pursuit of income and power (Mills, 1956; Berger, 1964). When threatened with their loss, professionals are as self-serving as other occupations.

Except for higher management, the professions have higher income, prestige, and autonomy than other occupational groups. While the professions as a whole tend to be politically conservative, business and independent professionals are adamantly so. The politics of other professions depend upon the issues they face and their social origins (Lipset and Schwartz, 1966). Thus, professionals recruited from the clientele they serve take on its political coloring, but some professions foster values which incline their incumbents toward a given political direction; social scientists and journalists tend to be liberal while the clergy and lawyers tend to be conservative.

Evidence is lacking that professionals have broader social vision and community concern than other workers. On the contrary, when professionals constitute the major occupation in the community, they press for facilities which advantage them most. Studies of communities populated by chemists (Clelland, 1970), atomic scientists (Holmes, 1967), and engineers (Hood, et al., 1970), reveal that when professionals dominate city councils and school boards, they press for expensive public services which benefit them most despite protests from less advantaged groups.

Evidence on political participation is contradictory. While all studies show that education is related to voting behavior, scientific professionals rarely engage in other forms of participation (Eiduson, 1961:227; Hagstrom, 1965:9; Wood, 1964:48), especially in community politics (Terman, 1955; Litt, 1966:14), but contrary evidence was found by Clelland (1970) and Zigmund and Smith (1969:448). The proposition that a scientific estate will increasingly direct national policy was proposed by Snow (1961) and Price (1962, 1965). Hall (1956) documented how congressmen were first awed by atomic scientists and frustrated by their inability to challenge them. While sufficient evidence for predicting the future political role of professionals and scientists is lacking, we believe that political and economic elites will use professionals in an advisory and technical capacity but will make the major decisions themselves (cf., Miliband, 1972).

CONCLUSIONS

Studying the power of occupational groups raises more questions than answers. Perhaps social scientists are not ready to present even tentative conclusions why some occupations have higher incomes than others. It is easy to assert that some occupations have more power than others, but the basic problem of measuring power independent of income remains unsolved. The task requires closer collaboration between sociologists and economists who have gathered massive data on wages, working conditions, and collective bargaining. Complex data explain wage rates and changes in the wage rates of manual workers, but comparable analyses are needed for clerical and sales workers, professionals, and managers. Most is known about the occupations most important to management, the unionized workers. Least is known about the most powerful of all occupations, management.

Changing industrial technology has spawned many new occupations, drastically altering the old occupational structure. Economists' explanations for differences in occupational earnings (e.g., marginal utilities, changes in educational in-puts) unfortunately fit the data poorly. Even where they fit reasonably well, other explanations appear equally cogent. For example, the reduction of the wage gap between skilled and unskilled workers over the years is said to result from the decreasing educational differentials. Yet during this period labor unions successfully organized unskilled and semi-skilled workers, thus responding to their demand to decrease income differentials. Since skilled work requires specific technical training, we are not certain that a rise in the general level of

education would inevitably affect skill differentials. Perhaps both rising education and unionization forces were at work, but the contributions of each cannot be isolated.

Similarly, income differences between white collar and skilled workers have
declined, and this too is ascribed to decreasing educational differentials. But
women's entry into white collar occupations, even though women were educationally qualified, depressed earnings in previously male-dominated occupations. Another example that resists a purely economic explanation is the income
difference between self-employed and salaried physicians. Here educational differences are minimal, but the two markets are organized differently, exposing
differences in the effect of organizational arrangements.

But organizational explanations are equally wanting. Thus, according to
sociological theory, unionized workers have greater control over factors affecting
their incomes and should, therefore, have substantially higher wages than unorganized workers. Yet the available evidence does not strongly support this position. Although obvious interaction effects occur between organized and unorganized markets, sociologists have not devised techniques to measure them,
partly because of inability to quantify organizational power.

However, sociologists can amplify and sometimes test economic explanations. For example, teachers' salaries have declined in this century relative to
wages of manual workers. Economic explanations stress decreasing educational
differentials between the two occupations and the increasing supply of teachers.
Yet other structural factors intervene, such as community effort to raise the
educational level of a larger segment of the population. In the past, the community provided higher education to a small stratum. Propertied interests
probably exerted pressure to hold salaries down when pressed to finance more
services for a less privileged population. The declining educational advantages
of teachers over skilled workers may be of less importance than the fact that
teachers' salaries derive from public taxes.

Both sociologists and economists find it difficult to explain why cumulative
changes in income differentials between occupational strata do not change the
total income profile. Economists have shown that income differences between
a number of occupations have declined: between skilled and unskilled manual
workers, clerical white collar workers and manual workers, salaried professionals and skilled manual workers, and so on. On logical grounds, these trends
should reduce income inequality and produce a burgeoning middle-income
society. Yet inequalities in the income profiles of industrial nations have remained remarkably constant.

Economists are inclined to accept given income distributions as inevitable
in economic systems which are not centrally planned. The failure to control
money, investments, prices, profits, and wages results in inequalities, as each
segment of the economy (e.g., occupations) seeks to maximize its rewards. Since
the government has limited economic powers (taxation, control of investments,
transfer payments), it cannot control the pattern of income and wealth. In
short, where centralized controls are inoperative, some occupations retain their
advantages. The task of sociology is to specify these advantages in organizational
terms.

Contrasting instances of centrally organized political economies may be
instructive. The scant data on income distribution for various occupational
strata in social democratic (socialist) polities such as Great Britain or Sweden

reveal, for example, a pattern similar to that in the United States; efforts to change income distribution have foundered. Thus the income levels of various occupations are quite similar in different economies. Only in the Soviet Union is there some evidence that income distributions have been changed as a result of national policy. Where both economic and organizational variables are controlled by a political directorate, an incomes policy can be enforced and occupational differentials can be reduced.

In a relatively free economy like that of the United States only the managers of the largest industrial corporations control such massive economic and organizational resources. These managers and owners have the highest incomes and the greatest control over their occupational worlds because they can manipulate the material and organizational resources of the corporation. Proprietors and managers of smaller enterprises are less able to do so because they have more competitors.

Unlike management, manual workers have limited economic resources but fairly strong organizational resources: labor unions. But even this resource is limited because a strike typically does not stop all of the economic activities of the large corporation nor endanger the earnings of its managers. Independent professionals differ from both corporate managers and unionized workers. Highly organized as a collegiate body, they encounter unorganized clients who are collectively unable to reduce their patronage in the face of rising fees. Thus professionals avoid confrontations with other groups and maintain control over their services. Clerical workers have fewer material and organizational resources than unionized manual workers. Their main weapon is to threaten management with unionization. Unorganized manual workers have fewest resources of all. They demonstrate the fate of those who are exposed to the forces of the open market. The study of occupational power must supplement economic analysis in order to understand the reward system of industrial societies.

REFERENCES

Abbott, E.
  1919 Women in Industry: A Study in American Economic History. New York: D. Appleton and Co.
Abrahamson, M.
  1973 "Functionalism and the functional theory of stratification: an empirical assessment." American Journal of Sociology 78(March):1236–1246.
Aron, R.
  1968 The Industrial Society. New York: Simon and Schuster.
Astin, H.S., N. Suniewick and S. Dweck
  1971 Women: A Bibliography on Their Education and Careers. Washington, D.C.: Human Service Press.
Baker, E.F.
  1925 Protective Labor Legislation: With Special Reference to Women in the State of New York. New York: Columbia University Press.
Barlow, R.H., E. Brazer and J.N. Morgan
  1967 Economic Behavior of the Affluent. Washington, D.C.: The Brookings Institution.

Barnard C.I.
  1968 The Functions of the Executive. Cambridge, Mass.: Harvard University
        Press.
Becker, G.S.
  1957 The Economics of Discrimination. Chicago: University of Chicago
        Press.
  1964 Human Capital: A Theoretical and Empirical Analysis with Special
        Reference to Education. New York: National Bureau of Economic
        Research (No. 80, general series).
  1968 "Discrimination, economic," in D.L. Sills (ed.), International Encyclo-
        pedia of the Social Sciences. Vol. 4. New York: Macmillan and The
        Free Press.
Bell, C.S.
  1970 The Economics of the Ghetto. New York: Pegasus.
Bell, D.
  1960 The End of Ideology. Glencoe, Illinois: The Free Press.
Berg, I.
  1970 Education and Jobs: The Great Training Robbery. New York:
        Praeger.
Berger, P.L.
  1964 "Some general observations on the problem of work," in P.L. Berger
        (ed.), The Human Shape of Work. New York: Macmillan.
Bergmann, B.R.
  1971 "The effect on white incomes of discrimination in employment." Jour-
        nal of Political Economy 79 (March–April) :294–313.
Bergmann, B.R. and I. Adelman
  1973 "The 1973 report of the President's Council of Economic Advisers: the
        economic role of women." American Economic Review 63 (Septem-
        ber) :509–514.
Bergson, A.
  1944 The Structure of Soviet Wages. Cambridge: Harvard University Press.
Berle, A.A.
  1954 The 20th Century Capitalist Revolution. New York: Harcourt Brace.
  1965 "Economic power and the free society," in A. Hacker (ed.), The
        Corporation Takeover. Garden City, New York: Doubleday.
Berle, A.A. and G.C. Means
  1932 The Modern Corporation and Private Property. New York: Macmillan.
Blau, P.M. and O.D. Duncan
  1967 The American Occupational Structure. New York: Wiley.
Blauner, R.
  1964 Alienation and Freedom. Chicago: University of Chicago Press.
Blitz, R.C.
  1974 "Women in the professions, 1870–1970." Monthly Labor Review
        97 (May) :34–39.
Bluestone, B.
  1970 "The tripartite economy: labor markets and the working poor." Pov-
        erty and Human Relations Abstracts (July–August) :15–35.
  1974 "The poor who have jobs," in P. Chalfant and J. Huber (eds.), The
        Sociology of American Poverty. Boston: Schenkman.

Blum, A.A.
  1964   Management and the White-Collar Union. New York: American Management Association.
Bock, E.W.
  1969   "Farmer's daughter effect: the case of the negro female professionals." Phylon 30 (No. 1) :17–26.
Bok, D.C. and J.T. Dunlop
  1970   Labor and the American Community. New York: Simon and Schuster.
Bonacich, E.
  1972   "A theory of ethnic antagonisms: the split labor market." American Sociological Review 37(October) :547–559.
Bottomore, T.B.
  1964   Elites and Society. New York: Basic Books.
Boulding, K.E.
  1953   The Organizational Revolution. New York: Harper & Row.
Bruner, R.
  1957   "Why white collar workers can't be organized." Harper's Magazine, 215(August) :44–50.
Bucher, R. and A. Strauss
  1961   "Professions in process." American Journal of Sociology 66:325–334.
Burnham, J.
  1941   The Managerial Revolution. New York: John Day.
Burns, R.K.
  1954   "The comparative economic position of manual and white-collar employees." The Journal of Business (27) :257–267.
Caplow, T.
  1954   The Sociology of Work. Minneapolis: University of Minnesota Press.
Carr-Saunders, A.M.
  1955   "Metropolitan conditions and traditional professional relationships," in R.M. Fisher (ed.), The Metropolis in Modern Life. Garden City, New York: Doubleday.
Carr-Saunders, A.M. and P.A. Wilson
  1944   "Professions," in International Encyclopedia of the Social Sciences. Vol. 12. New York: Macmillan.
Carrter, A.M.
  1968   "Wages I: theory," in International Encyclopedia of the Social Sciences. Vol. 16. New York: Macmillan and The Free Press.
Carrter, A.M. and F.R. Marshall
  1967   Labor Economics: Wages, Employment, and Trade Unionism. Homewood, Illinois: Richard D. Irwin.
Chafe, W.H.
  1972   The American Woman: Her Changing Social, Economic, and Political Roles. New York: Oxford University Press.
Chamberlain, N.W.
  1958   Labor. New York: McGraw-Hill.
Chamberlin, E.
  1933   The Theory of Monopolistic Competition. Cambridge, Massachusetts: Harvard University Press.

Chaplin, D.
 1967   The Peruvian Industrial Labor Force. Princeton, New Jersey: Princeton University Press.
Clark, A.
 1919   Working Life of Women in the Seventeenth Century. London: George Routledge.
Clark, B.A.
 1963   "Faculty organization and authority," in T.F. Lundford (ed.), The Study of Academic Administration. Boulder, Colorado: Western Interstate Commission for Higher Education.
Clark, C.
 1932   The National Income, 1924–1931. London: Macmillan.
Clark, T.N.
 1968   Community Structure and Decision-Making: Comparative Analyses. San Francisco: Chandler Publishing Co.
Clelland, D.A.
 1970   "Occupational composition and community structure." Unpublished Ph.D. dissertation. East Lansing: Michigan State University.
Commons, J.R., et al.
 1918   History of Labor in the United States. Vol. 1. New York: Macmillan.
Crozier, M.
 1964   The Bureaucratic Phenomenon. Chicago: University of Chicago Press.
Cutright, P.
 1967a "Income redistribution: a cross-national analysis." Social Forces (46):180–190.
 1967b "Inequality: a cross-national analysis." American Sociological Review (32):562–578.
Dahl, R.A. and C.E. Lindblom
 1953   Politics, Economics and Welfare. New York: Harper & Row.
Dahrendorf, R.
 1959   Class and Class Conflict in Industrial Society. Stanford: Stanford University Press.
Davies, A.F.
 1952   "Prestige of occupations." British Journal of Sociology (3):134–147.
Davis, K. and W.E. Moore
 1945   "Some principles of stratification." American Sociological Review (10):242–248.
Derber, M.
 1963   "Worker participation in Israeli management." Industrial Relations (3):51–72.
Dobb, M.
 1968   "Economic thought IV. Socialist thought," in International Encyclopedia of Social Sciences. Vol. 4. New York: Macmillan and The Free Press.
Dodge, N.T.
 1966   Women in the Soviet Economy: Their Role in Education, Science, and Technical Development. Baltimore: The Johns Hopkins University Press.

Doeringer, P.B. and M. Piore
  1971   Internal Labor Markets and Manpower Analysis: Lexington, Massa-
         chusetts: Heath Lexington.
Dreyfuss, C.
  1938   Ideology and Occupation of the Salaried Employees. Translated by
         E.E. Warburg. New York: Columbia University Press.
Drucker, P.F.
  1950   The New Society: The Anatomy of the Industrial Order. New York:
         Harper & Bros.
Dubin, R.
  1958   Working Union Management Relations: The Sociology of Industrial
         Relations. Englewood Cliffs, New Jersey: Prentice-Hall.
Duncan, O.D.
  1966   "Methodological issues in the analysis of social mobility," in N.J.
         Smelser and S.M. Lipset (eds.), Social Structure and Mobility in Eco-
         nomic Development. Chicago: Aldine.
Duncan, O.D., D.L. Featherman and B. Duncan
  1972   Socioeconomic Background and Achievement. New York: Seminar
         Press.
Dunlop, J.
  1944   Wage Determination Under Trade Unions. New York: Macmillan.
Dvorak, E.J.
  1963   "Will engineers unionize?" Industrial Relations (2):45–65.
Eckstein, H.
  1960   Pressure Group Politics. Stanford, Ca.: Stanford University Press.
Edgeworth, F.
  1922   "Equal pay to men and women for equal work." Economic Journal
         32(December):431–457.
Eiduson, B. T.
  1962   Scientists, Their Psychological Worlds. New York: Basic Books.
Eisenstein, L.
  1961   The Ideologies of Taxation. New York: The Ronald Press.
Epstein, C.
  1970   "Encountering the male establishment: sex status limits on women's
         careers in the professions." American Journal of Sociology 75(May):
         965–982.
Evan, W.M.
  1964   "On the margin—the engineering technician," in P.L. Berger (ed.),
         The Human Shape of Work. New York: Macmillan.
Faunce, W.A. and D.A. Clelland
  1967   "Professionalization and stratification in an industrial community."
         American Journal of Sociology (72):341–350.
Feldmesser, R.A.
  1960   "Toward the classless society. Problems of communism." U.S. Informa-
         tion Agency (9):31–39.
Ferman, L.A., J.L. Kornbluh and J.A. Miller
  1968   Negroes and Jobs: A Book of Readings, Ann Arbor: University of
         Michigan Press.
Finkel, S.R. and V.J. Tarascio
  1971   Wage and Employment Theory. New York: Ronald Press.

Fisher, L.H.
  1951 "The harvest labor market in California." Quarterly Journal of Eco-
         nomics 55 (November) :463–491.
Fogarty, M.
  1961 The Just Wage. London: Geoffrey Chapman.
Fogel, W. and D. Lewin
  1974 "Wage determination in the public sector." Industrial and Labor Rela-
         tions Review 27 (April) :410–431.
Form, W.H.
  1968 "Occupations and careers," in International Encyclopedia of the So-
         cial Sciences. Vol. 11. New York: Macmillan and Free Press.
Freidson, E.
  1970 Professional Dominance: The Social Structure of Medical Care. New
         York: Atherton Press.
Friedman, M. and S. Kuznets
  1954 Income from Independent Professional Practice. New York: National
         Bureau of Economic Research.
Froomkin, J. and A.J. Jaffe
  1953 "Occupational skill and socioeconomic structure." American Journal
         of Sociology (59) :42–48.
Fuchs, V.R.
  1971 "Differences in hourly earnings between men and women." Monthly
         Labor Review 94 (May) :9–15.
Fusfeld, D.R.
  1973 The Basic Economics of the Urban Racial Crisis. New York: Holt,
         Rinehart and Winston.
Galbraith, J.K.
  1956 American Capitalism: The Concept of Countervailing Power. Boston:
         Houghton Mifflin.
  1967 The New Industrial State. Boston: Houghton Mifflin.
Gamson, W.A.
  1966 "Reputation and resources in community politics." American Journal
         of Sociology 72 (September) :121–131.
Geiger, H.K.
  1968 The Family in Soviet Russia. Cambridge, Mass.: Harvard University
         Press.
Gerth, H.H. and C.W. Mills
  1942 "A Marx for the managers." Ethics (52) :200–215.
Gilb, C.L.
  1966 Hidden Hierarchies. New York: Harper & Row.
Goldner, F.H. and R.R. Ritti
  1967 "Professionalism as career immobility." American Journal of Sociology
         (72) :489–502.
Goldstein, B.
  1955 "Some aspects of the nature of unionism among salaried professionals
         in industry." American Sociological Review (20) :199–205.
Gordon, D.M.
  1972 Theories of Poverty and Unemployment: Orthodox, Radical and Dual
         Labor Market Perspectives. Lexington, Massachusetts: D.C. Heath.

Granick, D.
1961   The Red Executive. Garden City, New York: Doubleday.
Greenwood, E.
1957   "Attributes of a profession." Social Work (2):45–55.
Gross, E.
1967   "When occupations meet: professions in trouble." Hospital Adminis-
        tration (12):40–59.
1968   "Plus ça change...? The sexual structure of occupations over time."
        Social Problems 16(Fall):198–208.
Hacker, A.
1962   "Pressure groups," in A.F. Westin (ed.), The Uses of Power. New York:
        Harcourt, Brace and World.
Hacker, A. (ed.)
1964   The Corporation Take-Over. Garden City, New York: Anchor Books.
        Doubleday.
Hagstrom, W.O.
1965   The Scientific Community. New York: Basic Books.
Hall, H.S.
1956   "Scientists and politicians." Bulletin of the Atomic Scientists (12):46–
        52.
Hall, R.H.
1968   "Professionalism and bureaucratization." American Sociological Re-
        view (33):92–104.
1969   Occupations and Social Structure. Englewood Cliffs, New Jersey: Pren-
        tice-Hall.
Hamilton, R.F.
1964   "Income, class and reference groups." American Sociological Review
        (29):576–579.
Hamilton, W.
1967   The Politics of Industry. New York: Random House.
Haug, M.R. and M.B. Sussman
1971   "The indiscriminate state of social class measurement." Social Forces
        49(June):549–562.
Hayek von, F.
1968   "Economic thought VI. Austrian school," in the International Ency-
        clopedia of Social Sciences. Vol. 4. New York: Macmillan and The Free
        Press.
Hedges, J.N. and J.K. Barnett
1972   "Working women and the division of household tasks." Monthly Labor
        Review 95(April):9–14.
Heilbroner, R.
1968   The Economic Problem. Englewood Cliffs, New Jersey: Prentice-Hall.
Hill, H.
1967   "The racial practices of organized labor—the age of Gompers and
        after," in A.M. Ross and H. Hill (eds.), Employment, Race and Pov-
        erty. New York: Harcourt, Brace and World.
1973   "Anti-oriental agitation and the rise of working-class racism." Society
        10(January–February):43–54.
Hodge, R.W., P.H. Rossi and D.J. Treiman
1966   "A comparative study of occupational prestige," in R. Bendix and S.M.
        Lipset (eds.), Class, Status and Power. New York: The Free Press.

Hodge, R.W., P.M. Siegel and P.H. Rossi
  1964   "Occupational prestige in the United States, 1925–63." American Journal of Sociology 70(November):286–302.
Holcombe, L.
  1973   Victorian Ladies at Work: Middle-Class Working Women in England and Wales 1850–1914. Hamden, Connecticut: Shoe String Press.
Holmes, J.E.
  1967   Politics in New Mexico. Albuquerque: University of New Mexico Press.
Hood, T.C., J. Holmes and A. Elliott
  1970   "The scientist and his political activity." Unpublished manuscript. University of Tennessee.
Hoos, I.R.
  1960   "When computers take over the office." Harvard Business Review (38):102–112.
Huber, J.
  1974   "Mechanisms of income distribution," in P. Chalfant and J. Huber (eds.), The Sociology of American Poverty. Boston: Schenkman.
Hughes, E.C.
  1958   Men and Their Work. Glencoe, Ill.: The Free Press.
  1959   "The study of occupations," in R.K. Merton, L. Broom and L.S. Cottrell (eds.), Sociology Today. New York: Basic Books.
Jencks, C., et al.
  1972   Inequality: A Reassessment of the Effect of Family and Schooling in America. New York: Basic Books.
Kaplan, A.
  1964   "Power in perspective," in R.L. Kahn and E. Boulding (eds.), Power and Conflict in Organizations. New York: Basic Books.
Keat, P.G.
  1960   "Long-run changes in occupational wage structure, 1900–1956." Journal of Political Economy (68):548–600.
Kerr, C.
  1957a "Labor's income share and the labor movement," in G.W. Taylor and F.C. Pierson (eds.), New Concepts in Wage Determination. New York: McGraw-Hill.
  1957b "Wage relationships: the comparative impact of market and power forces," in J.T. Dunlop (ed.), The Theory of Wage Determination. New York: St. Martins Press.
  1964   Labor and Management in Industrial Society. Garden City, New York: Doubleday.
Kerr, C., J.T. Dunlop, F.H. Harbison and C.A. Myers
  1960   Industrialism and Industrial Man. Cambridge, Massachusetts: Harvard University Press.
Keynes, J.M.
  1939   "Relative movements of real wages and output." Economic Journal (49):48–49.
Klan, S.
  1968   The New Brahmins. New York: Morrow.
Kolaja, J.
  1965   Workers' Councils: The Yugoslav Experience. London: Tavistock Publications.

Kolko, G.
  1962 Wealth and Power in America: An Analysis of Social Class and Income Distribution. New York: Praeger.

Kuhn, J.W.
  1963 "Success and failure in organizing professional engineers," in Industrial Relations Research Association. Proceedings of the Sixteenth Annual Meetings. Madison, Wisconsin.

Kuznets, S.
  1941 National Income and Its Composition, 1919–1938. New York: National Bureau of Economic Research.
  1946 National Income: A Summary of Findings. New York: National Bureau of Economic Research.
  1963 "Quantitative aspects of economic growths of nations." Economic Development and Cultural Change (11):1–80.

Leiserson, A.
  1942 Administrative Regulation. Chicago: University of Chicago Press.

Lemons, J.S.
  1973 The Woman Citizen: Social Feminism in the 1920s. Urbana: University of Illinois Press.

Lenski, G.E.
  1966 Power and Privilege. New York: McGraw-Hill.

Lester, R.A.
  1964 Economics of Labor. Second edition. New York: Macmillan.
  1974 Anti-bias Regulations of Universities: Faculty Problems and Their Solutions. New York: McGraw-Hill.

Lewis, H.G.
  1963 Unionism and Relative Wages in the United States: An Empirical Inquiry. Chicago: University of Chicago Press.
  1968 "Labor unions IV. Influence on wages," in International Encyclopedia of the Social Sciences. Vol. 8. New York: Macmillan and The Free Press.

Lewis, J.D.
  1974 "Union activity and black income in central cities." Working Paper #7420 printed by the Program in Applied Social Statistics, Department of Sociology, University of Illinois.

Lieberson, S. and G.V. Fuguitt
  1968 "Negro-white occupational differences in the absence of discrimination." American Journal of Sociology 74(March):188–200.

Lipset, S.M. and R.B. Dobson
  1973 "Social stratification and sociology in the Soviet Union." Survey 88 (Summer):114–185.

Lipset, S.M. and M.A. Schwartz
  1966 "The Politics of Professionals," in H. Vollmer and D.L. Mills (eds.), Professionalization. Englewood Cliffs, New Jersey: Prentice-Hall.

Lipset, S.M., M.A. Trow and J.A. Coleman
  1956 Union Democracy. Glencoe, Illinois: The Free Press.

Litt, E.
  1966 "The politics of a cultural minority," in M.K. Jennings and L.H. Zeigler (eds.), The Electoral Process. Englewood Cliffs, New Jersey: Prentice-Hall.

Long, C.P.
  1960   Wages and Earnings in the United States, 1860–1890. Princeton, New Jersey: Princeton University Press.
Lundberg, F.
  1937   America's 60 Families. New York: Halcyon House.
Lydall, H.
  1968   The Structure of Earnings. London: Oxford at the Clarendon Press.
Macaulay, H.
  1959   Fringe Benefits and Their Federal Tax Treatment. New York: Columbia University Press.
Machlup, F.
  1952   The Political Economy of Monopoly: Business Labor and Government Policies. Baltimore: Johns Hopkins Press.
Mangum, G.L.
  1971   "Manpower research and manpower policy," in A Review of Industrial Relations Research. Vol. 1. Madison: Industrial Relations Research Association Series.
March, J.G.
  1966   "The power of power," in D. Easton (ed.), Varieties of Political Theory. Englewood Cliffs, New Jersey: Prentice-Hall.
Marshall, R.
  1968   "Racial practices of unions," in L.A. Ferman, J.L. Kornbluh and J.A. Millers (eds.), Negroes and Jobs. Ann Arbor, Michigan: University of Michigan Press.
Marshall, T.H.
  1939   "The recent history of professionalism in relation to social structure and social policy." Canadian Journal of Economics and Political Science (5):325–340.
Mayo, E.
  1945   The Social Problems of an Industrial Civilization. Cambridge, Massachusetts: Harvard University Press.
McGuire, J.W.
  1963   Business and Society. New York: McGraw-Hill.
McPherson, W.
  1955   "Codetermination in practice." Industrial and Labor Relations Review (8):499–519.
Meissner, M.
  1969   Technology and Work Group Behavior. San Francisco: Chandler.
Melman, S.
  1970   Pentagon Capitalism: The Political Economy of War. New York: McGraw-Hill.
Mermelstein, D. (ed.)
  1973   Economics: Mainstream Readings and Radical Critiques. New York: Random House.
Miliband, R.
  1969   The State in Capitalist Society. New York: Basic Books.
  1972   "Professor Galbraith and American capitalism: the managerial revolution revisited," in M. Mankoff (ed.), The Poverty of Progress: The Political Economy of American Social Problems. New York: Holt, Rinehart and Winston.

Miller, D.C. and W.H. Form
  1964   Industrial Sociology. New York: Harper & Row.
Miller, H.P.
  1964   Rich Man, Poor Man. New York: Crowell.
  1966   "Income distribution in the United States." A 1960 Census Monograph. Washington, D.C.: U.S. Government Printing Office.
Miller, S.M.
  1968   Breaking the Credentials Barrier. New York: Ford Foundation.
Mills, C.W.
  1948   The New Men of Power. New York: Harcourt, Brace & World.
  1951   The Power Elite. New York: Oxford University Press.
  1954   "The labor leaders and the power elite," in A. Kornhauser, R. Dubin, and A.M. Ross (eds.), Industrial Conflict. New York: McGraw-Hill.
  1956   White Collar. New York: Oxford University Press.
Morse, N.
  1953   Satisfactions in the White-Collar Job. Ann Arbor, Michigan: University of Michigan Press.
Morris, M.D.
  1968   "Labor relations: developing countries," in International Encyclopedia of the Social Sciences. Vol. 8. New York: Macmillan and The Free Press.
Moskow, M.H. and R.E. Doherty
  1969   "United States," in A.A. Blum (ed.), Urbana: University of Illinois Press.
Myers, F.
  1958   "Workers' control of industry in Europe." The Southwestern Social Science Quarterly (39):100–11.
Myers, G.
  1937   History of the Great American Fortunes. New York: The Modern Library.
North, C.C. and P.K. Hatt
  1947   "Jobs and occupations: a popular evaluation." Opinion News (9):3–13.
Nosow, S. and W.H. Form (eds.)
  1962   Man, Work and Society. New York: Basic Books.
Ober, H.
  1948   "Occupational wage differentials, 1907–1947." Monthly Labor Review (67):127–134.
Opinion Research Corporation
  1957   White Collar Loyalty. Princeton, New Jersey: Princeton University Press.
Oppenheimer, V.K.
  1970   The Female Labor Force in the United States: Demographic and Economic Factors Governing its Growth and Changing Composition. Berkeley: Institute of International Studies. Population Monograph Series, No. 5.
Ozanne, R.
  1962   "A century of occupational differentials in manufacturing." Review of Economics and Statistics (44):292–299.
Parrish, J.B.
  1974   "Women in professional training." Monthly Labor Review 97(May): 41–43.

Parsons, T.
 1953 "A revised analytical approach to the theory of social stratification," in R. Bendix and S.M. Lipset (eds.), Class, Status and Power. Glencoe: The Free Press.
 1968 "Professions," in International Encyclopedia of the Social Sciences. Vol. 12. New York: Free Press and Macmillan.
Parsons, T. and N.J. Smelser
 1965 Economy and Society. New York: The Free Press.
Pen, J.
 1959 The Wage Rate Under Collective Bargaining. Translated by T.S. Preston. Cambridge, Mass.: Harvard University Press.
 1966 Harmony and Conflict in Modern Society. New York: McGraw-Hill.
Perrow, C.
 1972 Complex Organization: A Critical Essay. Glenview, Illinois: Scott, Foresman.
Perrucci, R. and J. Gerstl
 1969 The Engineers and the Social System. New York: Wiley.
Phelps, O.
 1957 "A structural model of the United States labor market." Industrial and Labor Relations Review (10):402–423.
Phelps Brown, E.H.
 1964 "Labour," in J. Gold and W. Kolb (eds.), A Dictionary of the Social Sciences. New York: The Free Press.
Phelps Brown, E.H. and P.E. Hart
 1952 "The share of wages in national income." The Economic Journal (62):253–277.
Pirenne, H.
 1914 "The stages in the social history of capitalism." American Historical Review (19):494–515.
Polanyi, K.
 1957 The Great Transformation. Boston: Beacon Press.
Presthus, R.
 1962 The Organizational Society. New York: Knopf.
Price, D.K.
 1962 "The scientific establishment," in Proceedings of the American Philosophical Society.
 1965 The Scientific Estate. Cambridge, Massachusetts: Harvard University Press.
Raphael, E.E.
 1974 "Working women and their membership in labor unions." Monthly Labor Review 97(May):27–33.
Reder, M.W.
 1955 "The theory of occupational wage differentials." American Economic Review (45):833–852.
 1957 Labor in a Growing Economy. New York: Wiley.
Rees, A.
 1962 The Economics of Trade Unions. Chicago: University of Chicago Press.
Reiss, A.J., Jr.
 1955 "Occupational mobility of professional workers." American Sociological Review (20):693–700.
 1961 Occupations and Social Status. Glencoe, Illinois: The Free Press.

Reynolds, L.G. and C. Taft
  1956   The Evolution of Wage Structure. New Haven, Conn.: Yale University
         Press.
Richards, A.I.
  1948   Hunger and Work in a Savage Tribe. Glencoe, Illinois: The Free Press.
Riesman, D., N. Glazer and R. Denny
  1953   The Lonely Crowd. Garden City, New York: Doubleday & Co.
Roberts, R.D.
  1956   "A general theory of executive compensation based on statistically
         tested propositions." Quarterly Journal of Economics 20(May):270–
         294.
Robertson, D.J.
  1961   The Economics of Wages. London: Macmillan.
Robinson, J.
  1933   The Economics of Imperfect Competition. London: Macmillan.
  1972   "The second crisis of economic theory." The American Economic Re-
         view 62(May):1–10.
Roby, P.
  1973a "Institutional barriers to women in higher education," in A.S. Rossi
         and A. Calderwood (eds.), Academic Women on the Move. New York:
         Russell Sage.
Roby, P. (ed.)
  1973b Child Care—Who Cares? New York: Basic Books.
Roethlisberger, F.J. and W.J. Dickson
  1947   Management and the Worker. Cambridge, Massachusetts: Harvard
         University Press.
Rosenberg, M.
  1957   Occupations and Values. Glencoe, Illinois: The Free Press.
Ross, A.M.
  1954   "The natural history of the strike," in A. Kornhauser, R. Dubin and
         A.M. Ross (eds.), Industrial Conflict. New York: McGraw-Hill.
  1956   Trade Union Wage Policy. Berkeley: University of California Press.
Ross, A.M. and H. Hill
  1967   Employment, Race and Poverty. New York: Harcourt, Brace and
         World.
Rossi, A.S.
  1965   "Women in science: why so few?" Science 148(May):1196–1202.
  1973   "Report of Committee W, 1972–1973." AAUP Bulletin 59(June):171–
         175.
Rostow, W.W.
  1954   The Dynamics of Soviet Society. New York: Mentor Books.
Rottenberg, S.
  1962   "The economics of occupational licensing," in National Bureau of Eco-
         nomic Research, Aspects of Labor Economics. Princeton, New Jersey:
         Princeton University Press.
Routh, G.
  1965   Occupation and Pay in Great Britain, 1906–1960. London: Cambridge
         University Press.
Rowe, M.P. and R.D. Husby
  1973   "Economics of child care: costs, needs, and issues," in P. Roby (ed.),
         Child Care—Who Cares? New York: Basic Books.

Ruml, B. and S.G. Tickton
  1955   Teaching Salaries Then and Now. New York: Foundation for the Advancement of Education.
Russell, B.
  1962   Power. New York: Barnes & Noble.
Samuelsson, K.
  1968   From Great Power to Welfare State. London: Allan and Unwin, Ltd.
Sandler, B.
  1973   "A little help from our government: WEAL and contract compliance," in A.S. Rossi and A. Calderwood (eds.), Academic Women on the Move. New York: Russell Sage.
Sayles, L.R.
  1958   Behavior of Industrial Work Groups. New York: Wiley & Sons.
Schorr, A.
  1968   Explorations in Social Policy. New York: Basic Books.
Scott, W.R.
  1966   "Professionals in bureaucracies," in H.M. Vollmer and D.L. Mills (eds.), Professionalization. Englewood Cliffs, New Jersey: Prentice-Hall.
Sewell, W.H. and R.M. Hauser
  1974   Education, Occupation and Earnings: Achievement in the Early Career. Madison: University of Wisconsin, Department of Sociology.
Sheehan, R.
  1966   "There's plenty of privacy left in private enterprise." Fortune (74): 224ff.
Siegel, P.M.
  1965   "On the cost of being a negro." Sociological Inquiry 35(Winter):41–57.
Sigworth, H.
  1972   "The legal status of antinepotism regulations." AAUP Bulletin 58 (Spring):31–34.
Sirageldin, Ismail Abdel-Hamid
  1969   Non-market Components of National Income. Ann Arbor, Mich.: Institute for Social Research.
Smith, A.
  1937   The Wealth of Nations. New York: Modern Library.
Smith, H.L.
  1958   "Contingencies of professional differentiation." American Journal of Sociology (63):410–414.
Snow, C.P.
  1961   Scientists and Government. Cambridge, Mass.: Harvard University Press.
Solomon, B. and R.K. Burns
  1963   "Unionization of white-collar employees—extent, potential and implications." Journal of Business (36):141–165.
Spaeth, J.L.
  1970   "Occupational attainment among male college graduates." American Journal of Sociology 75(January):632–644.
Steffens, L.
  1931   Autobiography. New York: Harcourt, Brace.

Stern, B.J.
  1932 "Woman, position in society: historical," in E.R.A. Seligman (ed.), Encyclopedia of the Social Sciences. New York: Macmillan.
Stern, P.M.
  1962 The Great Treasury Raid. New York: New American Library.
Stinchcombe, A.L.
  1965 "Social structure and organizations," in J.G. March (ed.), Handbook of Organizations. Chicago: Rand McNally.
Strachey, J.
  1956 Contemporary Capitalism. London: Victor Gollancz.
Strauss, G.
  1963 "Professionalism and occupational associations." Industrial Relations (2):7–31.
Strauss, G. and S. Ingerman
  1968 "Public policy and discrimination in apprenticeship," in L.A. Ferman, J.L. Kornbluh and J.A. Miller (eds.), Negroes and Jobs. Ann Arbor, Michigan: University of Michigan Press.
Sturmthal, A.
  1961 "The workers' councils in Poland." Industrial and Labor Relations Review (14):379–396.
  1964 Workers Councils. Cambridge, Massachusetts: Harvard University Press.
  1966 White-Collar Trade Unions. Urbana: University of Illinois Press.
Suter, L.E. and H.P. Miller
  1973 "Income differences between men and career women." American Journal of Sociology 78(January):962–974.
Sweet, J.A.
  1973 Women in the Labor Force. New York: Seminar Press.
Tarbell, I.
  1904 History of the Standard Oil Company. Gloucester, England: Peter Smith.
Taylor, F.W.
  1911 The Principles of Scientific Management. New York: Harper & Row.
Terman, L.M.
  1955 "Are scientists different?" Scientific American (192):25–29.
Thornton, R.J.
  1971 "The effects of negotiations on teachers' salaries." Quarterly Review of Economics and Business 11(Winter):37–46.
Titmuss, R.
  1962 Income Distribution and Social Change: A Critical Study in British Statistics. Toronto: University of Toronto Press.
Tsuchigane, R. and N. Dodge
  1974 Economic Discrimination against Women in the United States. Lexington, Massachusetts: Lexington Books.
Urwick, L.
  1933 Management of Tomorrow. London: Nisbet Ltd.
U.S. Bureau of the Census
  1960 Historical Statistics of the United States: Colonial Times to 1957. Washington, D.C.: U.S. Government Printing Office.

1963 Methodology and Scores of Socioeconomic Status. Working Paper No. 15. Washington, D.C.: U.S. Government Printing Office.

1970a Current Population Reports, Series P-60, No. 69, "Income growth rates in 1939 to 1968 for persons by occupation and industry group, for the United States." Washington, D.C.: U.S. Government Printing Office.

1970b Population Characteristics, Current Population Reports. Series P-20, No. 202 (June 18, 1970), Washington, D.C.: U.S. Government Printing Office.

1973a Census of Population: 1970, Subject Reports, Final Report PC(2)-7A, "Occupational Characteristics." Washington, D.C.: U.S. Government Printing Office.

1973b Census of Population: 1970, Subject Reports, Final Report PC(2)-8B, "Earnings by Occupation and Education." Washington, D.C.: U.S. Government Printing Office.

1974 Current Population Reports, Series P-60, No. 93, "Consumer Income: Money Income in 1973 of Families and Persons in the United States." Washington, D.C.: U.S. Government Printing Office.

U.S. Department of Commerce

1956 Personal Income by States Since 1929. A Supplement to the Survey of Current Business, C.F. Schwartz and R.E. Graham, Jr. Office of Business Economics. Washington, D.C.: U.S. Government Printing Office.

1958 U.S. Income and Output. A Supplement to the Survey of Current Business, prepared in the Office of Business Economics under supervision of C.F. Schwartz and G. Jaszi. Washington, D.C.: U.S. Government Printing Office.

U.S. Department of Labor, Women's Bureau

1973 "The economic role of women," reprinted from The Economic Report, 1973. Washington, D.C.: U.S. Government Printing Office.

van de Vall, M.

1970 Labor Organizations. London: Cambridge University Press.

Veblen, T.

1923 Absentee Ownership. New York: B.W. Huebsch.

1940 The Engineers and the Price System. New York: The Viking Press.

Waldman, E. and R. Whitmore

1974 "Children of working mothers, March 1973." Monthly Labor Review 97(May):50–58.

Weber, M.

1946 From M. Weber: Essays in Sociology. Translated by H.H. Gerth and C.W. Mills (eds.). New York: Oxford University Press.

1964 The Theory of Social and Economic Organization. Translated by A.M. Henderson and T. Parsons. Glencoe: The Free Press.

Wilensky, H.L.

1964 "The professionalization of everyone?" American Journal of Sociology (70):137–158.

Wohl, R.R.

1966 "The rags to riches story: an episode of secular idealism," in R. Bendix and S.M. Lipset (eds.), Class, Status and Power. New York: The Free Press.

Wood, R.C.

1964 "Scientists and politics: the rise of an apolitical elite," in R. Gilpin and

C. Wrights (eds.), Scientists and National Policy Making. New York: Columbia University Press.

Wootton, B.
1955   The Social Foundations of Wage Policy. London: Allen & Unwin, Ltd.

Wyllie, I.G.
1954   The Self-Made Man in America: The Myth of Rags to Riches. New Brunswick, New Jersey: Rutgers University Press.

Yale Editors
1954   "The American Medical Association: power, purpose and politics in organized medicine." Yale Law Journal (63):938–947.

Yanowitch, M.
1963   "The Soviet income revolution." Slavic Review (22):683–697.

Zeigler, H.
1961   The Politics of Small Business. Washington, D.C.: Public Affairs Press.

Zeitlin, M. (ed.)
1970   American Society, Inc.: Studies of the Social Structure and Political Economy of the United States. Chicago: Markham.

Zeitlin, M.
1974   "Corporate ownership and control: the large corporation and the Capitalist class." American Journal of Sociology 79 (March):1073–1119.

Zigmund, J., II and R. Smith
1969   "Political participation in an upper-middle-class suburb." Urban Affairs Quarterly (4):443–458.

CHAPTER **17**

Work and Political Behavior

Erik Allardt

University of Helsinki

INTRODUCTION

On first glance, work and politics appear to be the two most important realms of man's life in industrial society. It is mainly through political participation that members of social groups collectively pursue goals, and according to powerful traditions of thought, man's worklife is the most crucial single factor influencing political behavior. According to Karl Marx, man's position in the production process provides the crucial life experience, determining his political as well as other beliefs (e.g. Marx and Engels, 1939). Other great representatives of the sociological tradition also place a heavy emphasis on the role of work. In Max Weber's historical analyses, one of the most profound elements in his concept of modernization is the change in the meaning of work: the medieval concept of religious vocation is transformed into a conception of a secular vocation demanding high and total commitment (Weber, 1958; Berger, 1964: 211–241).

A study of existing research results, however, shows that great caution is called for when assessing the role of work in the modern world. There is evidence that for a majority of the industrial workers, the central life-interests are not related to work and the work-place, and that their most intimate relationships and rewarding forms of social participation occur outside the world of work (Dubin, 1956:131–141). This result, however, lends itself to different interpretations. That preferred primary relations are located outside work can be taken as a natural and irreversible result of the fact that efficiency in industrial society is related to work in huge bureaucratic organizations. A conference in the 1950s also concluded that "the problem of creating an industrial civilization is essentially a problem of social invention and creativity in the nonwork aspects of life" (Dubin, 1956:141). The same tendency, however, may be seen as indicating man's alienation and spiritual isolation in modern society. In light of the alienation tradition, modern factory technology and bureaucratic organizational life have deprived employees of a human relationship to their work with a resulting loss of initiative, freedom and creativity (e.g. Blauner, 1964).

Whatever the answer to the dilemma posed above, work is obviously related to most factors known to influence political commitments and behavior. Man's political behavior is influenced by many factors outside his work life but these factors are strongly related to the rewards and positions he obtains from his work. What Gross has to say applies very well to the relationship between work and politics: "... it is through his work that man is most intimately implicated in the human drama. It may not be his central life interest, but how he goes about it or even tries to avoid it tells us much about him" (Gross, 1964:619). Therefore, an analysis of the relationship between work and politics calls for a specification of different features of work. At least the following broad categories can be differentiated: (a) the economic position of the individual as determined by his earnings and position in work, (b) the individual's social status as influenced by his occupation and work, (c) the occupational structure of the community, (d) the external, physical conditions of work, and (e) the human relations in work. The three first mentioned may be labeled indirect effects while the two latter ones are direct effects. The above-mentioned categories are analytically separable but in actual research practices it has mostly been very difficult to assess the specific effects of any one single factor. The distinction between work and nonwork applies to modernized groups and occupations existing in an industrial society but it is less valid when considering rural populations in traditional societies. Throughout history, peasants have formed and joined in many political movements but the term peasant and peasantry refer to a total life situation rather than to the nature of work.

Politics and political behavior are not unambiguous terms. The term politics is sometimes understood in a very general sense denoting all kinds of use of, or fight for, power and control (Greer and Orleans, 1964:808). In this sense, political reactions and behavior exist in all kinds of groups and organizations, e.g. in the family as well as in huge bureaucratic organizations. Conflicts between staff and line managerial officers (e.g. Dalton, 1967:159–171), a salient topic in industrial sociology, would be an example of work-related political behavior. It seems reasonable, however, to use the term political in a more restricted sense. Since the time of Max Weber, most political scientists and sociologists have adopted the view that politics is concerned with the exclusive control over the legitimate use of force in a territorial state or community (Weber, 1946:78–79). Politics is thus always related to power vested in the state, and this power rests ultimately on the control of the legitimate use of force. All behavior which is conditioned by, can lead to, or is opposed to actions based on the legitimate power of the state can be labeled political. The competition for informal leadership in a work group is in this sense not political *per se*, although the outcome under some circumstances may have political consequences. If the same work group starts a wildcat strike, its actions may be defined as political since these actions are clearly related to the legitimate power of the state. There are, however, many borderline cases for which it is a matter of interpretation whether an action should be classified as political. In any case, the main focus in this chapter will be on the relation of political behavior to national politics and the total political system.

Lack of Work: Political Consequences

Explanations of political behavior are usually based on the assumption that men act politically in order to satisfy their needs, or as reactions to deprivations of basic needs. On the other hand, available evidence indicates that an extreme deprivation of physical needs does not lead to political expressions at all. J.C.

Davies points out that the search for satisfaction of the need for food, shelter, clothing and health is carried out mainly by social but nonpolitical means. When these means are nearly unavailable people become apathetic and passive. As Davies (1963:16–17) formulates it, "Extreme physical need destroys politics for the needful." This formulation conforms to Knupfer's famous description of the Underdog: economic underprivilege is psychological underprivilege and leads to a circular pattern. Underprivileged people are passive because they lack opportunities, and they lack opportunities because they are passive (Knupfer, 1947:114).

Some available evidence on the effects of prolonged unemployment strongly supports the generalizations by Davies and Knupfer. In the now classical studies by the Lazarsfeld and others in Warsaw and the Austrian village of Marienthal during the Great Depression, it was shown that general unemployment has led to a widespread resignation and apathy. No political action whatsoever could be reported, and the feeling of belonging together in a community had completely broken down (Zawadski and Lazarsfeld, 1935:224–251). The use of mass media indicated a shift of interest away from politics to entertainment (Jahoda-Lazarsfeld and Zeisel, 1932:35–37). Results of a similar kind have also been found elsewhere (Lipset, 1960, 1963:192–193).

Despite the evidence for a negative correlation between unemployment and political participation, it is obvious that the effects of unemployment is contingent upon both the preceding and succeeding development. Also, the lack of political participation does not exclude the possibilities of violent reactions of a political nature. This seems to be particularly true when a period of rising expectations is followed by a short period of sharp reversal, as described in the J-curve theory of revolutions (Davies, 1969:690–691). A more important consideration, however, is the fact that wide-scale unemployment of the kind that existed during the Great Depression is unlikely to be found today in industrialized and developed nations. All Western societies have a more planned economy today than they had in the 1920s and 1930s, and the governments are more able to arrange work and make other provisions for the unemployed. In most countries, however, there exist structurally or technologically conditioned patterns of seasonal or periodic unemployment.

Unemployment and the Life Situation

For some groups, periodic unemployment is a part of a general lower-class life situation. In his work, *Political Man*, Lipset (1960, 1963:243–248) clearly shows how insecurity of income strongly tends to increase leftist voting and radicalism in lower-income groups. Among occupational groups riddled by periodic unemployment and with histories of high rates of leftist voting, Lipset especially mentions miners and lumbermen. Miners in Great Britain, France, Germany and United States display by and large the same over-all pattern. They have been exposed to heavy unemployment, and they have also been among the strongest leftist groups. In the same fashion, as data from Sweden, Finland and the United States indicate, lumber workers have often suffered from cyclical fluctuations in the economy, and also have shown a voting record of support for radicalism on the left.

A number of ecological studies indicate how past unemployment may influence voting in the present. Findings from Great Britain show how unemploy-

ment during the Great Depression still seemed to have effects on the voting patterns in the full employment year of 1950. The districts which showed the least
decline in the vote for Labour were also the ones worst hit by unemployment in
the 1930s (Nicholas, 1951:297–298). In Finland, the areas with high rates of
unemployment in the early years of the 1930s have, after World War II, had a
strong Communist vote. Survey studies support the conclusions from the ecological studies. The Communist working class voters in Finland have experienced
unemployment much more often during their life-time than the Social Democratic voters (Allardt, 1964:100–110). Results of a similar kind have been reported from France (Lipset, 1960, 1963:247–249). In none of the mentioned
studies has it been possible to isolate clearly the effects of unemployment from
other effects. Experiences of unemployment, however, have formed a part of a
general, lower-class life situation, tending to increase support for Leftist politics.

Data about the effects of unemployment among middle-class groups are
more scarce than those concerning the working class. This seems to be due both
to greater job security in middle-class groups and to the absence of clearly political reactions in middle-class occupations. Middle-class groups are often less
concentrated locally, and as a result are usually harder to organize politically.
The history of the rise of Nazism in Germany shows how middle-class unemployment was related to support for the Nazis (Lipset, 1960, 1963:148). It is,
however, hard to generalize from this single, although historically important,
case. It is difficult to say whether white collar or middle-class groups, if hit
severely by unemployment today, would support the Radical Right or not.

As seen from the results mentioned above, the findings about the political
effects of unemployment are not entirely consistent. With a certain amount of
caution, however, it seems reasonable to state that present unemployment often
tends to make the working class individual passive and apathetic whereas the
experiences of unemployment afterwards when conditions have changed for the
better, tend to have a radicalizing effect.

Dual Attachment to Work and Union

There exists along side evidence of how the lack of work and employment tends
to make the individual politically passive, other findings showing how strong
integration with the work and the work milieu has a politically activating effect
within that milieu. The internationally famous study indicating such a relationship is *Union Democracy* by Lipset, Trow and Coleman (1956). It was shown
how within the International Typographical Union, many factors integrating
the workers to their work and work environment also contributed to political
activity and the maintenance of organizational democracy. In the ITU, an
obvious relationship existed between interest in work and interest in the trade
union activity. It is interesting to note that this generalization stating a positive
relationship between interest in work and interest in union activity was found
almost at the same time in other countries independently of Lipset, et al.
(1956). In a Swedish study by Segerstedt and Lundquist (1955:215) passive
workers within the organizational life, have a significantly lower work morale
(as estimated by the foremen) than organizationally active workers. In a
Finnish study, Seppänen showed that workers active within the trade unions
were more interested in improving their occupational skills, less willing to
change to another factory, more apt to make suggestions, and more often rated

as good workers, than the passive workers. In the same vein, they were also much more apt to criticize the management than the passive workers (Seppänen, 1958:35–58). It seems correct to conclude that a strong attachment to the work environment tends to increase at least such political activity which is related to existing organizations.

ISSUES RELATED TO WORK AND POLITICAL REPRESENTATION

The findings reporting political apathy among the unemployed represent cases in which occupational groups with specific and concrete grievances lack adequate political representation. In the Marxist tradition, this is assumed to be true for more or less all lower class groups until, conditioned by the physical concentration of large masses of people, they begin to organize and articulate their interests. Until then, the workers will form, as Marx's famous saying goes, "a class against capital but not yet a class for itself" (Marx, no date:145–146). Although it has been necessary to revise many of Marx's definitions, his basic assumptions about the effects of class interests have strongly influenced modern political sociology. It has to a large extent been dominated by a stratification aspect. This stratification aspect is, for instance, a dominant theme in Lipset's *Political Man* (1960, 1963). A basic assumption by Lipset is that in every democracy, conflicts between social groups are expressed through the party system which at the core represents a democratic transformation of the class struggle. True, he points out that the gulf between social classes is not the only cleavage that is expressed through the political parties; nevertheless it can be said that the main thread in the book deals with the question of how political behavior to a large extent can be explained by reference to social class. Lipset points out how in all developed states, the low income groups tend to vote with the left and the high income groups with the right. The exceptions to this rule are also seen in the light of a stratification aspect. Lipset cites the aphorism "Each country has its South," and thereby contends that the exceptions to the tie between social class and political behavior only occur in underdeveloped areas that have not yet been modernized. In such areas one can encounter not only political passivity but often also strong support for Conservative parties and traditionalist values. With the exception of some new trends which have been observable at the end of the 1960s and which will be discussed later, the most typical cases of conservative voting among lower income groups have been found among farmers and other rural occupations.

The Worker-Collectivity

The dilemma whether certain occupational groups have an adequate political representation can hardly be discussed without explicit references to values and cannot be solved by scientific methods alone. It has nevertheless spurred many interesting research efforts. Whether parties, unions, and occupational organizations actually represent the groups they pretend to represent is a real dilemma with many practical consequences. One of the most seminal contributions is Sverre Lysgaard's study on the "worker-collectivity" in a Norwegian factory (Lysgaard, 1961). By worker-collectivity, Lysgaard means the system of informal values, norms and expectations existing among the workers in an industrial shop. The worker-collectivity, however, is much more comprehensive than what usually has been described as the informal social organization or what Homans has labeled the "internal system." The worker-collectivity cannot be described as the totality of all work groups and other small groups existing in the factory but is deeply rooted in the culture of the local community. One of the main functions of the worker-collectivity is the defence of the individual worker against the demands of the formal-technological system of the factory. It also contains boundary-maintenance mechanisms intended to keep a clear demarcation between the last mentioned system and the worker-collectivity. There is a complicated relationship between the worker-collectivity and the labor union but the unions have had difficulties (in practice) representing the worker-collectivity since the latter's main idea is to maintain a front against all formal excessive management demands and relations, whereas the activities of the labor union focus on formalized and explicit relations with the formal-technological system of the factory. Successful union-management relations are shown to require close contacts between union leaders and management and lead to routinization and professionalization of these relations (Dubin, 1957:60–81).

The idea of a worker-collectivity is helpful in understanding the phenomenon of wildcat strikes which, although reliable comparative statistics are lacking, have been very frequent in many countries in the late 1960s. High rates of wildcat strikes have not only been common in Western countries but also in Yugoslavia which is said to have the most comprehensive system of workers' self-management in the world. Analyses of wildcat strikes usually show that official settlement of labor disputes (by collective bargaining, etc.) have left the basic tensions underlying the disputes untouched. Furthermore, the settlement may have tended to increase the bureaucratic mechanisms which in any case are resented by the worker-collectivity. This is basically the pattern described by Alvin Gouldner in his study about a wildcat strike (Gouldner, 1954, 1965). Sayles indicates that although wildcat strikes sometimes have been used as a deliberate tactical weapon by labor unions, it is nevertheless primarily a rank-and-file phenomenon (Sayles, 1954, 1967:498). Wildcat strikes are, in fact, a typical expression of actions formed within the worker-collectivity. One of the latter's most outstanding traits is that it does not recognize leaders. One of its norms is that no one should be regarded as more important than others (Lysgaard, 1961:244).

Representation

· *Working-class representation.*   The discussion about the nature of representation has a long tradition, and it has always posed a particular dilemma for parties and organizations of lower-class groups. As early as 1911, Robert Michels formulated "the iron law of oligarchy" thereby stressing that organization and formal delegation always lead to oligarchical patterns (Michels, 1949). Another type of dilemma is captured by the term "co-optation," first coined for sociological purposes by Philip Selznik (1949). In his study on the TVA, he used co-optation to denote those mechanisms by which a dominant group ties subgroups and subordinated collectivities to the goals of the organization and the ongoing enterprise (Selznik, 1949). Another dilemma is that numerous studies show how leaders within organizations are drawn disproportionally from the higher social ranks (Bell, Hill, and Wright, 1961). With the emergence of the New Left, the discussion about the nature of political representation became

extremely lively during the latter half of the 1960s. In a challenging and provocative analysis of class divisions in Great Britain, Robin Blackburn tries to
show that industrial conflict is structurally rooted in the existing factory conditions and property relations. He argues that in most cases, the trade unions have
not functioned as adequate expressions of the class interests of the workers, and
demands that "an authentic trade union must be, politically as well as indus-
trially, militant" (Blackburn, 1969:282–283). There is hardly one and only one
correct answer to the problem of representation but the dilemma continues to
be one of the most crucial and research-provoking questions in the border area
of industrial and political sociology.

Middle-class representation. Whereas the problem of authenticity of
representation has been a core dilemma in the working-class, the sheer willingness to organize and to form politically representative bodies has been a problem within middle-class occupations and occupational groups. The nonmanual
labor force is becoming increasingly important not only on the labor market
but also in evaluations of national politics. In some countries, the nonmanual
labor force already clearly outnumbers the manual one, and in all industrialized, Western countries the nonmanual labor force has in the last decades been
strongly increasing, whereas the proportion of industrial workers has been decreasing. International comparisons show that almost everywhere the majority of
white collar workers reject the idea of being placed in the same political camp
as the trade unions for manual workers. This pattern has been attributed both
to the status aspirations and the sense of higher status in nonmanual occupations
as well as to certain factors in the work environment. Individuals in white collar
jobs or middle-class occupations are often not concentrated as a mass in the
same work-place, and they often work closely with managers and also identify
with them. White collar occupations to which these conditions do not apply
have, in many countries, joined the working class trade union movement (Lipset, 1967:525–548). The picture, however, is very scattered. In many countries,
middle-class occupational groups which are large in number can function effectively as unions without any clear ties to the general trade union movement.
For example, this has been true of teachers, nurses, and airline personnel. In
some countries, the employees in nonmanual work have joined in a strong
trade union movement of their own.

Nonmanual occupational groups often form strong and solidary organizations which were not originally organized as trade unions. They may or may not
function as such. In most countries, this is particularly true of professional
groups representing a clear upper-class tradition such as medical doctors. In
such groups, the combination of specialized professional skills, relative insu-
lation and high rewards tends to produce a conservative political outlook combined with a tendency to avoid party politics (Glaser, 1960:230–245). On the
other hand, professional bodies of such occupational professional groups often
function as strong pressure groups in matters regarding their special fields of
interest.

Representation and the political system. The problems and conflicts related to representation are, of course, not only dependent upon the structure
of the occupational groups, but upon the society which contains the groups.
First, problems of representation are often different in different political sys-

tems. Second, different stages in the technological development demand extremely different types of skill from their group members.

Concepts which are of central importance in market economies such as collective bargaining, strikes, settlement of disputes, industrial democracy, etc., hardly carry the same meaning in Socialist or Communist states. In the Soviet Union, the state and the management are viewed as organs of the working-class no less than the trade unions themselves. This different view also means that conflicts are discussed in very different terms than in Western market economies (Spyropoulos, 1969:319–320). Most likely, these differences have not been analyzed at length in a scientific manner because attempts to analyze usually are strongly partisan. It is also apparent that the problems of representation and labor relations in general take a very different shape in the developing nations than in industrialized states. Trade unions and collective bargaining can hardly develop as long as the economy is basically rural, and the main loyalties are tribal or related to kinship. It has been argued that occupational organizations and trade unions emerge at a rather late stage of development (Epstein, 1958).

Despite differences related to the nature of the political system, some problems seem to arise everywhere with the industrial development. Zygmunt Bauman reports some interesting findings from a study of the party activists and party executives of all the great industrial enterprises in Poland (Bauman, 1964:203–216). The investigation showed that there had been a considerable increase in the number of persons both with relatively high educational achievements and with specialized vocational skills. Simultaneously, important changes had occurred in the institutional and behavioral standards prevailing in the factory party organizations. There was a remarkable shift from predominantly ideological to mainly technical and managerial preoccupations. The new men were often from outside the community, their position was an episode in their career, and they tended to consider the national problem of economic growth as the primary issue rather than the settlement of local grievances. The pattern described by Bauman can probably be found in all industrialized Socialist and Capitalist countries. Likewise, the new trend has been met almost everywhere with resistance not only among the old and ousted party workers and trade unionists but also among the rank-and-file members of parties and unions. The modern world requires technological skills from decision-makers but at the same time, these demands create problems of political representation and raise the issue of the "power of the technocrats."

Problems of representation are related to other concepts such as "responsibility," "delegation of authority," "workers' participation in management," etc. The terms selected often reflect the degree to which matters are considered primarily political. All these terms have been used in the very lively debate about "industrial democracy" and the workers' participation in management. It can hardly be denied that many of the issues raised in the debate about "industrial democracy" are related to the very structure of the enterprise and to the laws and rules regarding private property.

The greatest structural changes are of course brought about through nationalization of industries and enterprises. Abolishment of private property leads to many other kinds of structural changes as well. In the Soviet Union, and the peoples' democracies in Eastern Europe, private property has been replaced by a centrally planned economy, a single party and single trade union movement. Nevertheless it has resulted in rather diversified systems of management. In the Soviet Union, the manager of an enterprise bears sole responsibility (although crucial powers of co-decision are given trade union committees in personnel matters) and arrangements are made for enabling workers' participation in the preparation and execution of plans for the enterprise. In Yugoslavia, a system of workers' self-management has existed since 1950, and all workers have the right to participate through elected delegates (see Chapter 20). Since 1963, this has been a fundamental right according to the Yugoslav Constitution. Poland and Romania have also instituted self-management systems.

In market economies, different systems of co-management have been tried. West Germany passed an act in 1951 according to which a co-management system was instituted in its coal-mining and iron and steel industries (de Givry, 1969:6–10). Many private industries have experimented with different systems and many forms of advisory councils have been tried. Especially in Western Europe the debate about "industrial democracy" or about workers' self-management and co-management has been extremely lively during the 1960s. Many serious research projects have been planned and executed. Sociological studies of the matter have to some extent been hampered by the fact that the political nature of the problems have not been discussed explicitly enough by researchers.

The system of workers' self-management in Yugoslavia has been considered the most comprehensive and has also drawn the attention of many scholars in the Western countries. Yet, it is hard to find any conclusive findings in the literature both in regards to the Yugoslavian situation and to the conditions in other countries. It is typical that the Yugoslavian case sometimes is discussed in a fairly critical tone (e.g., Kolaja, 1965) and at other times in a very appreciative manner (Riddell, 1968:47–75). It can hardly be overstressed that it is very hard to find conclusive research findings in regards to the effects of workers' self- and co-management. The decisions in these matters will be political, and it will take time before the results can be properly evaluated. Nevertheless, this is one of big issues in studying work and politics.

FEATURES OF WORK RELATED TO POLITICAL BEHAVIOR

There is an abundance of results showing how men react to the conditions of their work-places. On the basis of recent research, however, it seems reasonable to somewhat de-emphasize the role of the internal work environment as a condition forming the attitudes of the workers. Reference has already been made to results showing how the industrial workers' "world" and "central life-interests" to a large extent focus on the nonwork environment. Among industrial workers in the United States, Dubin found that only 10% of the workers thought of the work as the source of their most important relationship. Their friends were, as a rule, not fellow workers. Three out of four did not regard their work and place of work as a central life-interest (Dubin, 1956:131–141).

Job Satisfaction

A British study, conducted at Vauxhall's Luton factory, has shed additional light on the subject (Goldthorpe, 1966:230–233; Goldthrope, Lockwood, Bechhofen, and Platt, 1968). Goldthorpe and his co-workers showed that the car-assembly workers had a prior orientation to their work, and that this orientation was not a product of the conditions at the job. They had brought their orientation with them, and their prior attitudes crucially influenced their perceptions of their job. Their past experiences in life such as family background, geographical location, patterns of community living, social and geographical mobility, etc. formed their expectations and attitudes. The researchers strongly stressed the instrumental orientation of the workers. The auto workers were not worried by the pressures of the assembly line nor by the lack of stimulants in their work. They did not enjoy the repetitive work on the assembly line but their main attitude was calculative: they wanted to make as much money as possible.

According to Goldthorpe's, et al., descriptions, the working conditions in many shops were filthy and hazardous for the health but were often accepted as a matter of course. This is an important point in reviewing many research results in regards to the influence of the working conditions on political attitudes and behavior. Many lower-class groups which have shown radicalism in their political attitudes have worked in unsatisfactory working conditions. This, however, has in most cases been only a part of a general lower-class environment. Lipset also states that "whether job satisfaction and creativity contribute independently to political behavior over and beyond differences in status and economic conditions is still, however, not proved" (Lipset, 1960, 1963:148–149).

The problem here is that most studies of satisfaction in work only indirectly provide information about political reactions and attitudes. Most studies have focused on the conditions under which workers perceive their work as satisfactory or unsatisfactory, and since this is an important goal in itself, systematic evidence about the political effects has not been searched for. There is an American counterpart to the Goldthorpe, et al. (1968) British study on the conditions in the Vauxhall factory. Blauner's large (1964) study on alienation, based on a survey in four industries, gives partly similar, partly dissimilar results to those found in Vauxhall. Of the four industries studied by Blauner, workers in the automobile industry appeared to be most alienated. In previous studies (Chinoy, 1952:453–459) it has been pointed out that the anonymity of the job of the auto-workers has had a strongly negative effect on the level of aspiration among the workers. The auto workers work mostly on the assembly line, which often has been considered as the very symbol of the oppression of the human element in industrialized society (see, e.g., Walker and Guest, 1952; Touraine, 1955:183). For the workers in both Blauner's and Goldthorpe's studies, however, the work was mainly considered as a means to satisfy needs which lie outside the work and the work environment. According to Blauner, monotonous work often does not create feelings of powerlessness precisely because the aspirations of the workers lie outside the work (Blauner, 1964). There are, however, differences in the interpretations given by Blauner (1964) and by Goldthorpe (1966). According to Blauner, the workers have often not learned nor been socialized into such needs and adopted such values that they would be apt to require self-actualization in their work. Blauner still stresses the importance of the alienative influences in work and work arrangements. He denies, however, that this has any political effect on the behavior of the workers, for instance, on their attitudes concerning ownership of the means of production. Goldthorpe stresses to a greater degree that alienation among the workers is a result, not of the working conditions, but of the general societal conditions. It is very difficult to say whether the differences between Blauner and Goldthorpe are due to differences between the U.S. and Great Britain, or are due to different views concerning human nature and society. A core problem with the whole concept of alienation, which later will be somewhat more systematically referred to, is that its applications apparently are strongly dependent on basic assumptions about human nature (Israel, 1968:61–65).

Political-Industrial Traditions

On the whole, as indicated, it is very difficult to find conclusive results in regards to the political effects of working conditions. It is apparent that some political attitudes are results of political socialization but it is often impossible to isolate the effects of this factor. From André Siegfried on, political ecologists have been able to show how political traditions differ according to region. Although these studies do not permit inferences about individuals they strongly suggest that political organizations, parties and institutions have independent effects. In Finland where the Communist party has a strong following in the working class, observers have often distinguished between an Industrial and a "Backwoods" Communism. The latter is particularly related to present hardships and unemployment whereas the former is even more strongly related to grievances in the past. It is quite obvious that the working class voters classified under the heading of Industrial Communism are socialized into specific views concerning matters related to alienation and their living conditions (Allardt, 1970:55–57). It has not, however, been possible to analyze these effects independently of the effects of other conditions.

In very extensive analyses, Stein Rokkan has shown how political mobilization and polarization varied widely in Norway, and that politics in the peripheries are still largely determined by regional tensions rather than by economic conflicts (Rokkan, 1969). Similar patterns of political traditions, degree of mobilization and the nature of political socialization can exist between industries and factories but no results in regards to the effects of political institutions can be considered conclusive. There are good studies of the propensity to strike in different industries but there are no clear findings regarding the interaction effects of workers' conditions and political action and propaganda (Kerr and Siegel, 1954:189–212). Studies of the relationship between work and political behavior have mainly been conducted either by economists or political sociologists who have been inclined to regard politics only as a dependent variable. Political scientists are more apt to regard politics and political phenomena as well as independent variables. They have rarely focused their attention on industrial relations.

Despite the difficulties in isolating specific effects, some factors related to working conditions nevertheless correlate consistently with specific political reactions. One factor of importance is the sheer size of a shop. Among manual occupations, the tendency has been rather clear: the larger the shop, the more often the workers' political attitudes have been radical in nature. It is, however, very difficult to say precisely through what kind of mechanisms size exerts its influence. According to the alienation tradition it can be assumed that size often is related to depersonalized and monotonous work. Alienation would in this case be a kind of intervening variable between size and the political reactions. Size and the geographical concentration of many individuals with a similar social position also facilitate intercommunication which in turn make for joint political action. Political parties are also able to concentrate their activities in large plants where in one stroke they can reach many individuals.

The political effects of good channels of communication among people with similar interests and living conditions have been demonstrated in numerous studies. Good channels of communication facilitates the organization of people with similar interests but organizations, have in their turn, effects on the patterns of communication. In Lazarsfeld's classic Erie county study, the effects of memberships in organizations on voting was clearly substantiated, and the same result has been replicated many times since then. In the Erie county study, membership in organizations tended to strengthen the tendency to vote for Republicans among middle- and upper-class people. Among lower-class people, on the other hand, there were clear differences between trade union members and others. The latter voted more often Republican, and the former more often for the Democrats (Lazarsfeld, Berelson, and Gaudet, 1944:146–147). According to Lipset, both size of the plant and size of the city (in Western Europe) have been correlated with Leftist voting (Lipset, 1960, 1963:263–264). In a similar fashion, large plants and large cities facilitate intra-class communication. Also data from the U.S. show that tensions between working and managerial or owning groups are higher in cities than in rural areas. This has been explained by the fact that working classes in the cities have opportunities to develop their own leadership and organizations (MacRae Jr., 1955; Lane, 1959, 1965:266–267). High population density seems to increase both political activity and political tensions.

Data about occupational groups have generally supported the inferences made about the relationship between facilities for good communication and political behavior. One-crop farmers, miners, lumbermen and fishermen not only suffer from insecurity of income but are also often in very close contact with each other, either in their place of work or on the community level. The one-crop farmers are dependent on the world market or the national market rather than the local market, they are easily hit by business fluctuations, and they have been apt to maintain contact with others in the same occupation. In contrast to these groups, Lipset particularly mentions the employees in service occupations. They scatter among well-to-do groups which they serve, and they meet all kinds of people in their jobs. They are likely to be both politically passive and rather conservative in their political outlook (Lipset, 1960, 1963:224 and 263).

Another occupational group which, according to many studies in the past, has tended to be conservative was the small farmer working in traditional manner with diversified crops. His traditionalism and conservatism was usually interpreted as a result of his isolation and structural position. This view has had a long tradition in sociology. It goes to a large extent back to Marx's assumption that traditional farmers, despite their poverty, do not develop class-consciousness because they are isolated by their class position in social structure. Peasants (small land-holders) were, according to Marx, a typical example of a "class in itself" which was unlikely to develop into a "class for itself." Hence, Marx stated his famous prediction that proletarian revolutions would be likely in highly industrialized but unlikely in rural societies. Sociological studies of industrialized societies have tended to enforce this conclusion and interpretation. In fact, however, proletarian revolutions have occurred only in rather clearly rural societies in which the peasants have played a decisive, revolutionary role. This is true for Mexico, Russia, Viet Nam, China, and most recently Cuba. It seems also to be true that Latin American revolutionaries increasingly place their hopes in the peasantry as the bearer of revolution. A recent study indicates how Allende's victory in the Chilean presidential elections to a large extent was due to the increasing class consciousness of the agricultural proletariat (Petras and Zeitlin, 1968:254–270).

This rather new emphasis on peasants and small land-holders as a revolutionary class puts the earlier reported results related to size and intra-class communication on one hand and political behavior on the other, in a somewhat new light. It was often assumed that size, and structural conditions for easy communication, were factors which *per se* created a certain political climate and specific political actions. Today one cannot be sure of whether this was mainly due to the fact that the working-class movements in the Western world followed the path indicated by Marx. Organizational efforts were concentrated in urban areas, large plants, and large cities. In any case, the difficulty of isolating the effects of political training, socialization and propaganda hinder any attempts to make conclusive statements. Again we may note that the importance of political action as an independent variable often has been neglected by both industrial and political sociologists.

SOCIAL CLASS, OCCUPATIONAL STRUCTURE AND POLITICAL BEHAVIOR

Members of the lower-classes tend to support the left whereas middle- and upper-class individuals tend to support Bourgeois parties or at least tend to be located more toward the Right than the lower classes. This is a loosely formulated but nevertheless consistent generalization presented in innumerable studies of particularly Western European nations. Social class can, of course, be defined in many ways. Theoretically, probably the most important distinction is between strata usually defined by status and prestige, and classes defined by economic power or simply by power and authority (Dahrendorf, 1959:74–77). Whatever the definitions are, the above generalization has been supported by many kinds of research findings. This is of course due to the fact that different criteria for stratification almost always are positively correlated although the value of the correlation varies. Whatever the theoretical reasoning on the nature of stratification and social classes is, the most commonly used operational criteria have been related to occupation and occupational ranking. This is partly due to the easy accessibility of data about occupation by pollsters, for instance, but the fact is that in stating the above generalization about the correlation between social class and political behavior, occupational differences are the first to be considered.

There are, to be true, many exceptions to the generalization mentioned above but they are usually presented only as exceptions to a general rule. This is also the reason why Lipset has been able to characterize elections as an expression of democratic class struggle (Lipset, 1960, 1963:230–278). As has been indicated in some occupational groups, the general tendency is strengthened by special grievances or by conditions facilitating class politics. For instance, in the lower-classes this is true for miners, lumbermen, fishermen and one-crop farmers.

The exceptions are, of course, often very important and show the independent effects of certain political factors. In order to obtain satisfactory explanations, we must in many cases resort to political traditions which are deeply imbedded in the political organizations themselves. Philip Converse has pointed out that when one wants to predict how a person in France will vote, his attitude towards religion is a considerably safer criterion than all known and accessible criteria of social class (Converse, 1964:248–249). Thus there are also other cleavages in developed countries that are often as important as social class. Many political scientists as well as many political sociologists have studied the British Tory working-class voter. The findings point definitely to the independent effects that political organizations have on political behavior. Whether or not the British worker has contacts with the trade unions seems to be decisive for his political preferences (Blondel, 1963). Since the days of Disraeli, the Tories have made conscious efforts to keep in touch with the working-class voters. Two American researchers, Denton Morrison and Keith Warner, have shown in an analysis of militant farmers in Michigan and Wisconsin how factors that are connected with political organization explain the militancy of the farmers considerably more effectively than all available indicators of economic status (Morrison and Warner, 1971:5–19). Hence, there exists a whole raft of studies that show how political organization and political traditions that are passed on by political organizations have independent effects on political behavior.

Class Polarization and Political Behavior

There are international variations regarding class polarization in political behavior. Robert Alford has used sample survey data to study political behavior in four countries—the United Kingdom, Australia, the United States, and Canada—and estimated the degree to which party preferences are a function of social class. He found that class polarization was greatest in Britain and least in Canada with the United States and Australia in the intermediate positions. Class polarization may be reduced by many factors such as regional and religious factors, weakness of labor unionism, etc. (Alford, 1963). Others who have used the measurements developed by Alford have shown that class polarization in politics tends to be higher in some smaller countries in Europe (such as the Scandinavian countries) than in the four English-speaking countries (Lenski, 1970).

Some of the theoretically most interesting exceptions to the straightforward association between social class and political behavior have been analyzed with the related concepts of "status crystallization," "status consistency," "rank equilibration," etc. (e.g. Bennoyt-Smullyan, 1944:151–161; Lenski, 1954:405–413; Malewski, 1963:9–20; Anderson and Zelditch, Jr., 1964:112–125, and Galtung, 1966:121–161). In all these studies, it is assumed that persons can occupy different ranks on different status variables or rank dimensions, and that the lack of consistency in an individual's ranking usually is perceived by the individual as something unpleasant and avoidable. He will try to equilibrate his rankings, and his efforts to rank equilibration often lead to political actions. Thus, a person ranked high according to occupation and education but low on ethnicity (race, color, or ethnic origin) may try to change the structure of the society in order to eliminate ethnicity as a rank criterion and in such a fashion get his ranks equilibrated. Although the efforts have been theoretically important they have not led to any consistent results as regards the association between the degree of status crystallization (rank equilibrium, status consistency) and political behavior. One provocative generalization is that persons who are ranked high on achieved status variables (occupation, education) but low on ascribed status variables (ethnicity, and in some societies generally social origin) tend toward radicalism on the left. Similarly, individuals ranked high on ascribed status variables but low on achieved status variables would tend to support the Radical Right. The empirical results, however, are inconclusive. At the present stage of research, we have predominantly theoretical deductions, and they differ from author to author depending on the nature of their basic assumptions. This subfield of social stratification studies is, however, important in studying the effects of the occupational structure on political behavior.

Changes in Class Occupation and Politics

The middle-class. During the 1960s many authors writing on the relationship between social class, occupation and politics had stressed signs of the emergence of new allegiances and new patterns. These changes have mainly been attributed to the strong increase in white collar jobs and middle-class occupations. Some occupational groups such as farmers, farm laborers, unskilled labor and servants have sharply declined in number whereas others (such as professional and technical managers, clerks, sales personnel and foremen) have increased substantially in most industrialized countries. Robert Lane argues that because the declining occupational groups have been associated with low, and the increasing occupational groups with high political interest, the result has, among other things been a clear increase in electoral participation (Lane, 1959, 1965:333–334).

The working-class. Many have speculated about the political consequences of the sharp rise in educational opportunities in a large number of industrialized countries. Nevertheless, there are more numerous research findings on the changing allegiances among the industrial workers. In 1958, Mark Abrams pointed out a gradual trend toward middle-class values and support for the Tories among British skilled manual workers (Abrams, 1958:543–547). Many others have since then made similar observations, and Bottomore (1965, 1969) has made an apt summary of some of the research findings. He cites findings from the U.S. (Zweig, 1961:134), France (Andrieux and Lignon, 1960: 189), Germany, and Great Britain. In a German study of the steel workers in the Ruhr, it was found that the steel workers had a strong class consciousness built around the distinction between manual and nonmanual workers. On the other hand, those who thought in Marxist terms and believed in a victory of the working-class and a classless society were in a small minority (Popitz, Bahrdt, Jüres, and Kastig, 1957). In another German study, Bednarik has reached similar conclusions as has Dubin (1956) : that the workers were strongly oriented toward their private life (Bednarik, 1955).

A more general analysis of the same trend has been made by Goldthorpe and Lockwood, who used the term "embourgeoisement" to capture the changing attitudes both in the working- and the middle-class. They refer to the observation that in Western industrial countries, there has been a convergence between "the new middle-class" and "the new working-class" leading to a distinctive new view of society. Both the radical individualism of the old middle-class and the comprehensive collectivism of the old working-class is refuted. According to this new view, collectivism is widely accepted as a means but not as a goal. The authors indicated that the increasing trend toward unionization of white collar occupations is a sign of the first-mentioned emphasis on collectivism as a means, whereas the decreasing feeling of class allegiance shows how collectivism has weakened as an end in itself (Goldthorpe and Lockwood, 1963:133–163). The two British sociologists also stress the same point as Dubin (1956): the workers are predominantly concerned with their families and their own private lives.

Bottomore (1965, 1969:527) also discusses the working-class as a revolutionary force:

> in all the advanced industrial countries the violence of class conflict has greatly diminished over the past few decades, and the working-class parties which still regard their aims as likely to be achieved by the use of force are few in number and insignificant.

The New Left and the student revolt. The over-all picture and the interpretations given changed somewhat in the last years of the 1960s because of the activities of the New Left and the international student revolt. However, the new situation hardly influenced commentaries on the trends within the working-class. Rather, it has led to an increasing interest in trends within the middle-class.

The analyses of the student revolt have varied greatly both in content and quality. Some facts, however, are repeated in most studies: (1) In most countries, the most radical and Leftist protesters have been students rather than members of the working-class. (2) The members of the New Left frequently have been much more concerned with grievances of other, often more distant groups, than with their own welfare. In this situation, the traditional generalization according to which the working-class supports the Left, and the middle- and upper-classes the Right becomes questionable.

One serious problem in interpreting political trends is that the voting pattern in many industrialized states contains a strong element of habit and tradition. Considerable changes in the voting patterns occur often in crisis situations only. Such a crisis occurred in France after the so-called May revolution in 1968, and Inglehart and Lindberg have made a challenging analysis of the results of the French elections held shortly after the unrest had ceased. In these elections, the parties on the Left lost about 5% of their total vote whereas the Gaullist coalition increased by 14%. The greatest loss was suffered by the parties in the Center which lost over one-fifth of their vote. Analyzing the data from a nation-wide sample, the authors show that the former voters for the Center moved as often to the Left as to the Right. The new Gaullist strength was mainly due to previous nonvoters, and to former Communist and Socialist voters. The analysis shows quite clearly that the election results by no means can be attributed to increased class polarization. On the contrary, it is evident that on the whole, the working-class moved toward the Right whereas the middle-class voters moved toward the Left. Age was an important factor, and the younger members of the middle-class produced nearly as large a Leftist vote as did the older working-class (Inglehart and Lindberg, 1970).

Inglehart and Lindberg discuss whether the trend so clearly observable in the French elections will be something typical for what they call "the post-industrial society." The student activists and the left-voting members of the middle-class are characterized by the term "post-bourgeois," and by this is meant that they no longer are primarily motivated by economic concerns. Survey data give substantial support to such an interpretation.

The trend so vividly observed in the French elections can also be observed to some extent elsewhere. There is evidence for the fact that the middle-class element in movements of the Radical Right has been on decline whereas the working-class proportion has increased. Data about the neo-Nazi Party (NPD) indicates a predominance of manual occupations among its supporters. It has been suggested that this is due to increasing middle-class consciousness or "embourgeoisement" of the newly propertied skilled workers (Liepelt, 1967:tables 23 and 24). At the same time, particularly the younger members of the middle-class have become moved by other considerations, as Inglehart's and Lindberg's term "postbourgeois" indicates (Inglehart and Lindberg, 1970). The observations do not yet permit conclusive statements but it is apparent that the same trends can be observed in many other countries.

The Need Hierarchy

The generalization about the tendency for the working-class to support the Left and for the middle- and upper-classes to support the Center or the Right has not only summarized facts about voting patterns and political attitudes, but has also been based on an assumption that the frustration and deprivation of economic motives or physiologically based material needs create support for the political Left. Yet for the first time in history, many countries are now in such a position that the majority of their population cannot be regarded as deprived of the basic physiological, material needs. This "need theory" may still be useful in explaining extremist political behavior, on the basis of need deprivation, but it has been increasingly suggested that in the industrial societies needs other than the material ones are most often frustrated (Davies, 1963:8–63). The work of Abram Maslow (1943:370–396) has recently gained in popularity, and his need hierarchy is also referred to in Inglehart's and Lindberg's analyses. Maslow argues that man's basic needs are arranged in a sequence, from the most to the least powerful. The most powerful are the physiological material needs but when they are reasonably well-satisfied, man concentrates on the next need in the hierarchy, namely the safety needs. The next order needs are the love (solidarity) needs, the esteem needs, and finally the need for self-actualization. It is suggestive to say that different social groups have their main frustrations located in different stages in the need hierarchy. If the new middle-class (and especially its younger members) are motivated by frustrated needs, it also seems reasonable to assume that the frustration does not concern the first-order physiological needs related to material welfare.

The present and the future.   Whatever the interpretations are, it seems reasonable to say that in the mid-1970s, we are moving toward new political allegiances. Some cautions regarding interpretations are, however, in order. It has already been said that voting in industrial society to a large extent is habitual. Ideological trends have proven to be extremely difficult to study. This is particularly complicated by the ideological resurgency in many countries of which commentators only recently spoke about "the end of ideology" (for an analysis of this notion, see Himmelstrand, 1970:89–92). Recent research also indicates how very difficult it is to pinpoint ideological beliefs. Most of the orientation in man's values appears to be based on idiosyncratic personal experiences although class and especially occupational experience appear to have some effects (Kohn and Schooler, 1969:659–678). A challenging study by Form and Rytina (1969) shows that whatever the income or educational background of the respondents in their study, very few of them possessed a consistent or sophisticated ideology. It has often been assumed that the better educated have more consistent political beliefs, but in the Form and Rytina study, especially, the richer and better educated were subject to strong conflicts between normative and existential beliefs. They did not appear more systematic than the lower strata (Form and Rytina, 1969:19–31).

In any case, statements regarding the ideology and the form of ideology in different classes and occupational groups appear to have low reliability. Ideological beliefs also change easily over time. The problem of the degree of authoritarianism, for instance, in different groups or classes such as the working-class has been debated extensively and the whole issue is still problematic (Lipset, 1960, 1963:87–115; Miller and Riessman, 1961:263–376; Lipsitz, 1965: 103–109). The main problem lies in the difficulty of assessing whether the differences in findings and interpretations are due to different ideological beliefs of the researcher, faults in the methods used, or to actual changes or differences in the groups studied.

WORK, ALIENATION AND POLITICS

The concept of alienation has already been referred to in the discussion of the studies by Blauner (1964) and Goldthorpe et al. (Goldthorpe, 1968). One problem is that the term has been used in almost innumerable senses. It is also hard to conclude how much it has helped to bring forward reliable results regarding the relationship between work and political behavior. It has, however, clearly served as a useful sensitizing concept and certainly contributed to the presentation of many useful and challenging insights. As already has been said, the concept of alienation rests very much on certain assumptions about human nature and society, and the way a researcher uses the concept tends to tell much about his basic assumptions.

Alienation: A Brief History

As is well-known, the concept alienation came from Hegel via Marx into the sociological vocabulary. For Marx, work and man's self-realization through his work was central in the discussion of alienation. It is hard to describe Marx's views briefly but with some justification it can be said that he particularly stressed two conditions for alienation: (1) private ownership of the means of production, and (2) the division of labor in industrial society. He regarded alienation in the first instance as the process by which a human being comes to be regarded as a commodity. This process led to other processes of which the most important has been captured by the term "reification" or in German *Verdinglichung* meaning by and large that all human relations are regarded as commodities or things which can be subject to exchange. These sociological processes led in turn to psychological processes such as the elimination of creativity, feelings of estrangement from the products of one's work, self-alienation, etc. (Israel, 1968; Lukács, 1923).

Since Marx, the literature on alienation has taken on voluminous proportions, and during the latter half of the 1960s, it has had a renaissance in the sociological literature. Despite the numerous specific meanings attached to the concept, it seems justifiable to distinguish two major uses of the term. Authors who have tried to stay true to Marx and certainly those who explicitly have represented a Marxist position have stressed alienation as a social process and fact. Strongly empirically oriented researchers have been inclined to emphasize the psychological aspects of alienation such as feelings of rootlessness and powerlessness. The latter interpretation can be said to have been dominant in American empirical sociology. For Melvin Seeman (1959:753–758) who has presented the most widely used classification, alienation is related to psychological processes. He presents a five-fold classification: (1) feelings of powerlessness, (2) meaninglessness, (3) isolation, (4) normlessness, and (5) self-estrangement. The discussion in terms of psychological processes is related to Marx since Marx treats both social and psychological processes.

Contemporary Theories of Alienation

It seems practical to delimit the discussion of alienation only to those studies in which clear references are made to the nature of work and the work environment. C.W. Mills (1951, 1962) discusses alienation from a theoretical view and also applies ideas about alienation to empirical descriptions. Mills strongly stresses that alienation and job satisfaction, in the sense this latter term has been used in industrial sociology, are quite different phenomena. Mills also stresses the point that alienation can exist in environments where the standard of living is high. He also criticizes Marx and indicates that Marx's ideas cannot be applied to most work of importance in the industrialized society. Marx's point of departure was the work performed by craftsmen, but (according to Mills) the cratfsman ideal cannot be applied to the industrial worker. In the modern society, the kind of work done by craftsmen is mostly related to leisure time and hobbies. According to Mills, the concept of alienation is useful even if one does not accept Marx's assumption that only through his work can man realize himself. In his book *White Collar* Mills analyzes the kind of alienation found mostly in industrialized societies. White collar individuals have to sell their personalities; they suffer from "status panic"; they remain anonymous in large bureaucratic organizations, and they have to get used to the idea that everything can and has to be marketed (Mills, 1951). Mills does not discuss the political consequences in detail, but the implications are clear enough. Personal political reactions are apt to become rare. In white collar groups, the goal is to make a good impression and to sell oneself on the personality market.

Mills' analysis of the white collar groups is not very different from those made by many American scholars without any explicit interest in Marx and Marxism. David Riesman's description of the "other-directed" personality contains many of the traits attributed by Mills to the white collar groups (Riesman, 1950). Riesman and Glazer have argued that the extent of political apathy is underestimated if we only consider formal criteria and overt measures of political activity such as voting. They, too, imply that there is a wide spread apathy, especially in the middle-class, and that this apathy mainly is due to the need to appear pleasant and to conform (Riesman and Glazer, 1950).

The most comprehensive analysis of work-life in which alienation is the key concept is Blauner's (1964) study. Yet he does not make very explicit inferences about the political consequences of alienation. He argues that even if alienation is widespread, the industrial workers are not particularly interested in questions related to the ownership of the means of production (Blauner, 1964:16–18). One reason for the absence of results concerning political attitudes is, of course, the fact that alienation very often is assumed to be associated with apathy and passivity. Some studies have indicated that feelings of powerlessness influence the turnout in political elections but not the voters' choices (Aberbach, 1969:86–99).

Many interpretations indicate that alienated individuals can be aroused to extreme and violent political reactions under some specific circumstances. This contention has been very much the central theme in the analyses of the so-called mass society. Theories of the mass society, however, usually place its core emphasis on factors outside the work-life. Feelings of rootlessness along with easily mobilized individuals are to be found in societies and groups in which secondary groups and communal bonds are weak and few (Kornhauser, 1959:227–230).

The sociologists in the Socialist states in Eastern Europe have made important and interesting contributions to the discussion of alienation. The debate was triggered by the Polish scholar, Adam Schaff, who contended that there are forms of alienation also in Socialist states. While Schaff accepts the Marxist assumption that alienation is something intrinsic in Capitalist society, he contends that alienation can occur in conditions imposed by the state bureaucracy and that it also exists under Socialism although in other forms than in Capitalist states (Schaff, 1970). Schaff's theses created lively debates in Poland as well as in other Socialist states (see Chapter 19). The Hungarian scholar M. Almasi expressed views similar to those of Schaff and contended that the differentiation of the division of labor and the technological development have created alienation which is hard to eliminate under present circumstances (Almasi, 1965). The sociologists from the Socialist countries in analyzing alienation have generally placed heavy emphasis on industrial enterprises and working conditions as possible causes. On the other hand, they have not presented systematic empirical data in their analyses of alienation.

In the meantime, alienation continues to be an intriguing and fruitful sociological concept. It is fruitful in the sense that it has sensitized many researchers to questions related to the consequences of working conditions in industrial and (if the expression is permitted) in post-industrial societies. It is, however, hard to find any clear research findings which have been replicated and supported in consecutive studies.

CONCLUSION

Although the relationship between work and political behavior almost could be regarded as a key question in debates and analyses on industrial society, it is apparent that there is scarcity of conclusive evidence. In one sense this is hardly surprising. The relationship between work and politics is the key question in Marxism, and the whole area has strongly invited partisan interpretations. One particular difficulty is that in most sociological analyses, work has been considered the independent variable, or explaining factor, whereas political behavior has been the dependent variable. Very few serious analyses have been done on the influence of politics, political institutions, and patterns on work behavior. To a certain extent, this could be regarded as a Marxist heritage in much of political sociology. This is, however, a one-sided picture. There are political sociologists interested in studying how political institutions change and transform the society. There are also Marxist schools which explicitly stress how political and symbolic actions influence behavior, and that the economic conditions primarily define only some terminal conditions (Althusser, 1966).

Another difficulty has been that the influence of work on politics often is very difficult to isolate from other factors. It is, as Lipset has stated, difficult to assess whether unsatisfying work explains political behavior independently of factors related to the general social and economic situation (Lipset, 1960, 1963: 148–149). Unsatisfying work is often only one indication of a general lower-class situation.

More research has been done on industrial workers than on other groups. Today the number of people in middle-class occupations is greatly increasing but it is hard, because of their diversity, to predict the political consequences of this development.

REFERENCES

Aberbach, J.D.
   1969   "Alienation and political behavior." American Political Science Review (63) :86–99.
Abrams, M.
   1957   "Press, polls and votes in Britain since the 1955 elections." Public
   –58   Opinion Quarterly (21) :543–547.
Alford, R.R.
   1963   Party and Society. Chicago: Rand McNally.
Allardt, E.
   1964   "Patterns of class conflict and working class consciousness in Finnish politics," in E. Allardt and Y. Littunen (eds.), Cleavages, Ideologies and Party Systems. Helsinki: The Westermarck Society.
   1970   "Types of protest and alienation," in E. Allardt and S. Rokkan (eds.), Mass Politics. New York: Free Press.
Almasi, M.
   1965   "Alienation and socialism," in H. Aptheker (ed.), Marxism and Alienation: A Symposium. New York: Humanities Press.
Almond, G.A.
   1958   "A comparative study of interest groups and the political process." American Political Science Review (52) :270–282. Reprinted in H. Eckstein and D.E. Apter (eds.), Comparative Politics. New York: The Free Press, 1965.
Althusser, L.
   1966   Pour Marx. Paris: Maspero.
Anderson, B. and M. Zelditch, Jr.
   1964   "Rank equilibration and political behavior." European Journal of Sociology (5) :112–125.

Andrieux, A. and J. Lignon
  1960 L'Ouvrier d'aujourd'hui. Paris: Marcel Rivière.
Bauman, Z.
  1964 "Economic growth, social structure, elite formation." International So-
        cial Science Journal (16):203–216. Reprinted in R. Bendix and S.M.
        Lipset (eds.), Class, Status and Power. Second Edition. New York: The
        Free Press.
Bednarik, K.
  1955 The Young Worker of Today: A New Type. Translated from the Ger-
        man. London: Faber and Faber.
Bell, W., R.J. Hill and C.R. Wright
  1961 Public Leadership. San Francisco: Chandler.
Bendix, R.
  1956 Work and Authority in Industry. New York: Wiley.
Bennoyt-Smullyan, E.
  1944 "Status, status types and status interrelations." American Sociological
        Review (9):151–161.
Berger, P.L. (ed.)
  1964 The Human Shape of Work. New York: Macmillan.
Blackburn, R.
  1969 "The unequal society," in H.P. Dreitzel (ed.), Recent Sociology I.
        London: Collier-Macmillan.
Blauner, R.
  1960 "Work satisfaction and industrial trends in modern society," in W.
        Galenson and S.M. Lipset (eds.), Labor and Trade Unionism. New
        York: Wiley.
  1964 Alienation and Freedom. Chicago: University of Chicago Press.
Blondel, J.
  1963 Voters, Parties and Leaders—the Social Fabrics of British Politics.
        Harmondsworth, Middlesex: Penguin Books.
Bottomore, T.B.
  1965 Classes in Modern Society. London: Allen and Unwin. A Condensed
        summary published in C.S. Heller (ed.), Structured Social Inequality.
        London: Collier-Macmillan, 1969.
Chinoy, E.
  1952 "The tradition of opportunity and the aspirations of automobile work-
        ers." American Journal of Sociology (67):453–459.
Converse, P.E.
  1964 "The nature of belief systems in mass publics," in D.E. Apter (ed.),
        Ideology and Discontent. Glencoe, Ill.: The Free Press.
Dahrendorf, R.
  1959 Class and Class Conflict in Industrial Society. Stanford, Ca.: Stanford
        University Press.
Dalton, M.
  1950 "Conflicts between staff and line managerial officers." American Socio-
        logical Review (15):251–342. Reprinted in R. Dubin (ed.), Human Re-
        lations in Administration. Englewood Cliffs, New Jersey: Prentice-Hall,
        1951, and in W.A. Faunce (ed.), Readings in Industrial Sociology. New
        York: Appleton-Century-Crofts, 1967.

Davies, J.C.
  1963 Human Nature in Politics. New York: Wiley.
  1969 "The J-curve of rising and declining satisfactions as a cause of some
        great revolutions and a contained rebellion," in R.D. Graham and T.R.
        Gurr (eds.), The History of Violence in America. New York: Bantam.
Dubin, R.
  1956 "Industrial workers' worlds: a study of the 'central life interests' of in-
        dustrial workers." Social Problems (3):131–141.
  1957 "Power and union-management relations." Administrative Science
        Quarterly (2):60–81. Reprinted in W.A. Faunce (ed.), Readings in
        Industrial Sociology. New York: Appleton-Century-Crofts, 1967.
Engels, F.
  1958 The Condition of the Working Class in England. Translated from the
        German. Stanford, Ca.: Stanford University Press.
Epstein, A.L.
  1958 Politics in an Urban African Community. Manchester, England: Uni-
        versity Press.
Etzioni, A.
  1968 The Active Society. New York: Macmillan.
Form, W.H. and D.C. Miller
  1960 Industry, Labor and Community. New York: Harper & Row.
Form, W.H. and J. Rytina
  1969 "Ideological beliefs and the distribution of power." American Socio-
        logical Review (34):19–31.
Galtung, J.
  1966 "International relations and international conflicts: a sociological ap-
        proach." Transactions of the Sixth World Congress of Sociology. Lou-
        vain: International Sociological Association. (1):121–161.
Givry, J.de
  1969 "Developments in labour-management relations in the undertaking."
        International Labour Review (99):1–35.
Glaser, W.A.
  1960 "Doctors and politics." American Journal of Sociology (66):230–245.
Goldthorpe, J.H.
  1966 "Attitudes and behavior of car assembly workers: a deviant case and a
        theoretical critique." British Journal of Sociology (17):227–244.
Goldthorpe, J.H. and D. Lockwood
  1963 "Affluence and the British class structure." Sociological Review (11):
        133–163.
Goldthorpe, J.H., D. Lockwood, F. Bechhofer and J. Platt
  1968 The Affluent Worker: Industrial Attitudes and Behavior. Cambridge,
        England: Cambridge University Press.
Gouldner, A.W.
  1954 The Wildcat Strike. New York: Antioch Press. Reprinted as paperback,
        New York: Harper and Row, 1965.
Greer, S. and P. Orleans
  1964 "Political sociology," in R.L. Faris (ed.), Handbook of Modern Sociol-
        ogy. Chicago: Rand McNally.

Gross, E.
  1964   "Industrial Relations," in R.L. Faris (ed.), Handbook of Modern Soci-
         ology. Chicago: Rand McNally.
Himmelstrand, U.
  1970   "Depolitization and political involvement," in E. Allardt and S. Rok-
         kan (eds.), Mass Politics. New York: Free Press.
Inglehart, R. and L.N. Lindberg
  1970   "Political cleavages in post-industrial society: the May Days in France."
         Madison: University of Wisconsin. Mimeograph.
Israel, J.
  1968   Alienation: Från Marx till modern sociologi. Stockholm: Rabén and
         Sjögren. Published in English, Alienation: From Marx to Modern
         Sociology. New York: McKay, 1971.
Jahoda-Lazarsfeld, M. and H. Zeisel
  1932   Die Arbeitslosen von Marienthal. Leipzig: Hirzel.
Kerr, C. and A. Siegel
  1954   "The industrial propensity to strike," in A. Kornhauser, R. Dubin and
         A. Ross (eds.), Industrial Conflict. New York: McGraw-Hill.
Knupfer, G.
  1947   "Portrait of the underdog." Public Opinion Quarterly (11):103–114.
Kohn, M.I. and C. Schooler
  1969   "Class, occupation and orientation." American Sociological Review
         (34):659–678.
Kolaja, J.
  1965   Workers' Councils: The Yugoslav Experience. London: Tavistock.
Kornhauser, W.
  1959   The Politics of Mass Society. Glencoe, Ill.: The Free Press.
Lane, R.E.
  1959   Political Life. Glencoe, Ill.: The Free Press. Reprinted as a paperback,
         Glencoe, Ill.: The Free Press, 1965.
Lazarsfeld, P.F., B. Berelson and H. Gaudet
  1944   The People's Choice. New York: Duell, Sloan and Pierce.
Lenski, G.
  1954   "Status crystalization: a non-vertical dimension of social status." Amer-
         ican Sociological Review (19):405–413.
  1970   Human Societies. New York: McGraw-Hill.
Liepelt, K.
  1967   "Anhänger der neuen Rechtspartei: Ein Beitrag zur Diskussion über
         das Wahlerreservoir der NPD." Politische Vierteljahresschrift, Heft 2.
Lipset, S.M.
  1950   Agrarian Socialism. Berkeley: University of California Press.
  1960   Political Man. Garden City, New York: Doubleday. Reprinted as paper-
         back, Garden City, New York: Anchor, 1963.
  1967   "White collar workers and professionals—their attitudes and behavior
         toward unions," in W.A. Faunce (ed.), Readings in Industrial Sociol-
         ogy. New York: Appleton-Century-Crofts.
Lipset, S.M. and S. Rokkan
  1967   "Cleavage structure, party systems and voter alignments," in S.M. Lip-
         set and S. Rokkan (eds.), Party Systems and Voter Alignments. New
         York: Free Press.

Lipset, S.M., M. Trow and J. Coleman
  1956   Union Democracy. Glencoe, Ill.: The Free Press.
Lipsitz, L.
  1965   "Working class authoritarianism: a re-evaluation." American Socio-
         logical Review (30):103–109.
Lukács, G.
  1923   Geschichte und Klassenbewusstsein. Berlin: Der Malik Verlag.
Lysgaard, S.
  1961   Arbeiderkollektivet. Oslo-Bergen: Universitetsforlaget.
Macrae, D., Jr.
  1955   "Occupations and the Congressional vote 1940–1950." American Socio-
         logical Review (20):332–344.
Malewski, A.
  1963   "The degree of status incongruence and its effects." The Polish Socio-
         logical Bulletin 1(7):9–20. Reprinted in R. Bendix and S.M. Lipset
         (eds.), Class, Status and Power. New York: The Free Press.
Marx, K.
  n.d.   The Poverty of Philosophy. Translation from the German. New York:
         International Publishers.
Marx, K. and F. Engels
  1939   The German Ideology. Translation from the German. New York: Inter-
         national Publishers.
Maslow, A.
  1943   "A theory of human motivation." Psychological Review (50):370–396.
Michels, R.
  1949   Political Parties. Translation from the German. Glencoe, Ill.: The Free
         Press.
Miller, S.M. and F. Riessman
  1961   "Working class authoritarianism: a critique of Lipset." British Journal
         of Sociology (12):263–276.
Mills, C.W.
  1951   White Collar. New York: Oxford University Press.
  1962   The Marxists. New York: Dell.
Morrison, D.E. and W.K. Warner
  1971   "Correlates of farmer attitudes toward public and private aspects of
         Agricultural organization." Rural Sociology (36):5–19.
Nicholas, H.G.
  1951   British General Elections of 1950. London: Macmillan.
Petras, J. and M. Zeitlin
  1968   "Agrarian radicalism in Chile." British Journal of Sociology (19):254–
         270.
Popitz, H., H.P. Bahrdt, E.A. Jüres and H. Kastig
  1957   Das Gesellschaftbild der Arbeiters; Soziologische Unterschungen in
         der Hüttenindustrie. Tübingen: Mohr.
Riddel, D.S.
  1968   "Social self-government: the background of theory and practice in
         Yugoslav socialism." British Journal of Sociology (19):47–75.
Riesman, D., et al.
  1950   The Lonely Crowd: A Study of Changing American Character. New
         Haven, Conn.: Yale University Press.

Riesman, D. and N. Glazer
  1950 "Criteria for political apathy," in A. Gouldner (ed.), Studies in Leader-
         ship. New York: Harper and Brothers.
Rokkan, S.
  1969 Citizens, Elections, Parties. New York: McKay.
Sayles, L.R.
  1954 "Wildcat strikes." Harvard Business Review (32):42–52. Reprinted in
         W.A. Faunce (ed.), Readings in Industrial Sociology. New York:
         Appleton-Century-Crofts, 1967.
Schaff, A.
  1970 Marxism and the Human Individual. Translated from the Polish. New
         York: McGraw-Hill.
Seeman, M.
  1959 "On the meaning of alienation." American Sociological Review (24):
         783–791.
Segerstedt, T. and A. Lundquist
  1955 Människan i industrisamhället I-II. Stockholm: Studieförbundet när-
         ingsliv och samhälle.
Selznik, P.
  1949 TVA and the Grass Roots. Berkeley: University of California Press.
Seppänen, P.
  1958 Tehdas ja ammattiyhdistys. With an English Summary: Dual Alle-
         giance to Company and Union. Helsinki: WSOY.
Spyropoulos, G.
  1969 "An outline of developments and trends in labour relations." Interna-
         tional Labour Review (99):315–348.
Svalastoga, A.
  1965 Social Differentiation. New York: McKay.
Titmuss, R.M.
  1962 Income Distribution and Social Change. London: Allen and Unwin.
Touraine, A.
  1955 L'Évolution du travail ouvrier aux usines Renault. Paris: Centre Na-
         tional de la Recherche Scientifique.
Walker, C.R.
  1962 Modern Technology and Civilization. New York: McGraw-Hill.
Walker, C.R. and R. Guest
  1952 Man on the Assembly Line. Cambridge, Mass.: Harvard University
         Press.
Weber, M.
  1946 "Politics as a vocation." Translated from the German and reprinted in
         H. Gerth and C.W. Mils, From Max Weber: Essays in Sociology. New
         York: Oxford University Press. Issued as a paperback, 1958.
  1958 The Protestant Ethic and the Spirit of Capitalism. Translated from the
         German. New York: Scribners.
Wilensky, H.L. and C.N. Lebaux
  1958 Industrial Society and Social Welfare. New York: Russell Sage Foun-
         dation.
Zawadski, B. and P. Lazarsfeld
  1935 "The psychological consequences of unemployment." Journal of Social
         Psychology (6):224–251.

Zeitlin, M.
   1967   Revolutionary Politics and the Cuban Working Class. Princeton, New
           Jersey: Princeton University Press.
Zweig, F.
   1961   The Worker in Affluent Society. Heinemann Books on Sociology. New
           York: Free Press.

PART VII

WORK IN DIFFERENT SOCIAL SYSTEMS

INTRODUCTION—PART VII

A rapid way to overcome parochialism in outlook is to encounter the same analytical problems in widely differing settings. That is one of the purposes of this section of the Handbook.

The first chapter emphasizes the role of rising expectations as they have an impact on the development of social movements to achieve these expectations. And in this context a labor movement fits the analytical scheme. This analysis of social movements draws heavily on historical as well as contemporary examples.

The next four chapters deal with entire societies. Two socialist societies are represented in the chapters dealing with Poland and Yugoslavia, which, as is well known, are also different from each other. It becomes evident that many of the problems of organizing work and managing the enterprise are by no means unique to capitalist enterprises, for the same problems emerge in socialist systems.

The chapter on Japan reveals the strong hold that traditional social relations have on practices in the industrial sector. We know, of course, of the enormous success of the Japanese economy. This may suggest that there are some lessons to learn about how the social practices of an earlier period are adaptive to new conditions, but still manage to retain some of their traditional features. In the case of Israel another type of social system is revealed to have problems that are not unlike those encountered in the West.

It is sobering to discover that there is no perfect design for an industrial system; that some problems are common in all societies; and that every society has its unique successes and difficulties that can only be understood by first knowing something about the society's character.

CHAPTER 18

Labor Movements, Social Movements and Social Mobility

Henry A. Landsberger

University of North Carolina at Chapel Hill

I. INTRODUCTION

Purpose

This chapter has two objectives: one at the empirical level, the other at the conceptual and theoretical levels.

At the empirical level, we hope to demonstrate that the histories, characteristics and major dilemmas of working class movements have been and are likely to be similar in many respects to those of all movements of low status groups. We shall illustrate this mainly by showing similarities between the histories of working class and peasant movements. However, parallels from the movements of black people in the U.S.—from their origins in the late eighteenth century to the present—could equally well have been used, and so could movements for women's equality.

Evidently, there are substantial differences between labor and peasant movements (and between these two and the movements of black people and of women). But then, too, there have always been differences between one kind of labor movement and another, both within different societies and among them. Yet the analysis of these differences (e.g., why were the European labor movements more socialist oriented than those of the United States?) has always been regarded as capable of shedding much light on each movement. So, too, will systematic differences that might be found between the social movements of industrial labor and those of peasants illuminate each of these movements separately. To give but one example: the lesser organizational and even psychological cohesion of peasant movements is likely to be due, in part, to the greater geographical dispersion of the peasantry. This points up, by implication, the general importance of physical propinquity for social movements, and its impor-

This chapter was made possible by the award of a Simon Visiting Professorship by the University of Manchester, England, during the Spring of 1972. Stimulating discussions with faculty and students of the Department of Sociology, and with Professors Peter Worsley and Clyde Mitchell, were particularly helpful.

tance when accounting for differences *within* the labor movement (Kerr and Siegel, 1954).

The evidence we shall use to make our points will be mainly illustrative and not systematic and comprehensive. Short of analyzing the content of at least a sample of encyclopaedic histories of all labor and peasant movements (no such universe of histories exists), systematic and comprehensive evidence is not possible. Nor is it scientifically necessary in order to demonstrate the existence of crude, though very important and obvious similarities.

At the conceptual level, labor movements, and all movements of low status groups, will be regarded as falling within the analytical field of social stratification, and more specifically, into the subfield of social mobility: since the avowed purpose of such groups is that of raising the status of their members. In our consideration of labor and peasant movements, we intend to apply concepts from the field of stratification and mobility to these movements: if not to replace other models from collective behavior, at least to supplement them.

Definition

We define "movements of low status groups" as those movements which are composed of low status individuals, whose members are reacting in a *similar* fashion to their low status and are partly *influenced* (consciously or otherwise) by the fact that others are also suffering from low status and have reacted to it.

A more complete discussion of the complex reasons for and the implications of this definition may be found elsewhere (Landsberger, 1969a, 1972, 1973) but we may summarize them for purposes of the present chapter.

1. Movements which are *composed* of low status persons (e.g., some religious movements, certain nationalist movements) may be *more or less* affected by their members' reactions to their low status. Some movements—e.g., the labor movement—will be almost entirely based upon that reaction, but other movements will be less so. Thus, being a "low status movement" is, in our sense, itself a quantifiable characteristic, a variable dimension. It is not an either-or issue. Why certain religious movements are more suffused with this reaction and others less so, despite similarity in membership, becomes itself something to explain, and its differential effects become matters to be studied.

2. This chapter revolves around movements which are predominantly *goal-oriented and instrumental,* and more narrowly have as their explicit and chief goal the raising of their members' status. Trade unions and workers' parties are prime examples, but so are peasant movements and, for instance, the NAACP which has sought to raise the legal, educational and political status of blacks.

However, emotional-expressive reactions to low status may be "functional equivalents" or in other ways intimately related to goal-oriented ones. They are therefore in principle included in the field of study, since the choice of one may sometimes be better understood as in part a rejection of the other.

Moreover, "goal-oriented—instrumental" vs. "emotional-expressive" are only analytically mutually exclusive, as the originators of these concepts emphasized (Parsons, Bales and Shils, 1953). For example, revival-like meetings and labor songs, so typical of certain sectors and epochs in the history of the U.S. labor movement, are an indication of the mixture of the instrumental *and* the expressive. Indeed, some theorists of the labor movement, both friendly and skeptical (Mayo, 1945) have felt that unions primarily represented a search for a lost emotional "Gemeinschaft" of diffuse personal relationships. On the other hand, neither labor nor peasant movements can exist solely for the purpose of expressing affect, whether positive (intermember) or negative (against the enemy: landowner, employer, tax or rent collector, etc.). Movements dominated by the expression of violence—the French peasant *jacquerie* of the mid-fourteenth century; the British industrial Luddites who destroyed the new employment-robbing machinery in the early nineteenth century—never gained many adherents, nor did they last long. This illustrates the well-known Parsons, Bales and Shils thesis that all social relations, if they are to persist, must make allowances for both expressive and instrumental elements, even though they may emphasize one or the other (Parsons, et al., 1953).

3. The matter of "collective" reaction is likewise a variable, indeed, two. Organizations or incipient organizations are formal manifestations of collective reaction, but the field of "collective reactions to low status" is much broader. At the other end of the continuum may be relatively individualistic, goal-oriented reactions. An example is migrations which are influenced by the fact that others, too, are leaving, but are not otherwise coordinated (though some migrations are indeed coordinated, as when whole villages of East European or Russian peasants moved across the ocean, or within Russia, in the centuries preceding the twentieth). Indeed, it seems best to think in terms of two separate dimensions under the general heading of "collectivization":

1. The *"extensiveness"* of the movement. Here the measure is: of all those individuals who are *potentially conscious* of a common and shared grievance over their low status and might be reacting to it, what is the proportion who are *in fact conscious* and reacting in that knowledge? What determines that proportion and what are the effects of it?

2. The *"degree of organization"* of the movement. Here the measure is: of those who are at all conscious and reacting similarly, what is the proportion *deliberately coordinating* their actions? Here one would weight efforts more heavily in which primary groups are coordinated with each other to form *complex organizations*, and weight less the separate, uncoordinated existence of various isolated, but internally structured groups in order to arrive at a measure of what might be termed, "degree of organization."

Table 1 illustrates the possible combinations of the extensiveness and the degree of organization of a movement.

Some Examples of the Similarities of Low Status Movements

Empirically, movements of low status people of all kinds which have had as their goal the changing of that status, and which have attempted to act collectively to do so, have had much in common. The commonality will be greater, the larger the role which low status has played in the formation of the movement and in determining its goals.

Let it be noted how easy it is to pick, at random and without effort, various issues common to these movements. Note the extent, for example, especially in their earliest phases, to which they have sought to restore a lost past. In the case of peasants, this has taken the form of demands for the return of communal land and common rights: a demand in Mexico in the early twentieth century

TABLE 1
THE "EXTENSION" AND "ORGANIZATION" OF LOW STATUS MOVEMENTS

	Low Organization	High Organization
Low Extension	Only few are even aware of grievances; protest spontaneous and unorganized: early phases of peasant and worker protest	Working class movements in developing countries: "islands of strength" in railroads, mines, etc.
High extension	Generalized peasant discontent but little organization (e.g. Peruvian peasantry 1963; British industrial workers 1815–1820).	Working class movements in N. Europe today: Percentage of unionized workers very high

(White, 1969); in England after the breakdown of feudalism (Landsberger and Landsberger, 1974). In the case of industrial workers, it took the form of demands for governmental wage setting by eighteenth century British trade unions (Pelling, 1969); or a return to Africa on the part of U.S. blacks from the 1780s onward (Draper, 1970). Note the discussion about whether evangelical movements held back or strengthened the movements of peasants in Latin America; or of workers in England, e.g., Methodism in the early nineteenth century (Thompson, 1964). Often the senior clergy of established churches looked askance at these movements, while lower-level priests came to their support. This was the case with the worker-priest movement in the industries of France after 1945 (Siefer, 1964) and it is the case of many young priests in Catholic churches of various Latin American countries today, in both the industrial and rural sphere (Turner, 1971).

We can also note the extent middle-class aid has been helpful, and to what extent it has been diversionary and divisive, especially the aid of middle class intellectuals. Russian peasants rebuffed the *narodnikii* in the 1870s; Russian workers rejected them in 1905 (Landsberger, 1973:374). To what extent—re ferring, for a change, to an internal, organizational problem—is the mass of the membership inevitably "apathetic"? And is there an almost inevitable tendency to bureaucratize which enhances the members' tendency toward apathy and the leaders' toward oligarchy (Michels, 1959) if the movement of industrial workers, or of peasants, manages to establish itself and crystallize into an organization?

To what extent will these movements become truly revolutionary, or at least, be used temporarily by urban intellectuals for revolutionary purposes, even if the spontaneous inclinations inside a movement are reformist or even backward looking? How unified are the members of the group: can one really speak of a group or a class—whether of industrial workers, or of peasants? Or are the interests of various subgroups within each of these classes so different and even conflicting that any single movement is subject to severe strains? Thus, the major union in the U.S. auto industry has had problems keeping skilled and unskilled workers satisfied; while in both pre-coup (1973) Chile and Mexico— to cite but two countries among many—landless laborers became restless after peasants with better luck obtained land and began to employ labor just as the old "patrones" had in the past. Under what circumstances do the established elites yield and coopt (employers, or landowners, and the upper strata generally) and under what circumstances do they resist to the finish? If the latter: when, if ever, does their resistance collapse?

These issues have been debated among analysts of both working class and peasant movements. Our concern at this point is not, of course, to attempt to continue this discussion. It is to assert that the common appearance of these issues in the analysis of both movements (and of all movements of low status groups whose purpose is to raise their status) is an indication that there are, empirically as well as analytically, important problems common to them.

Precisely because these questions, by their very nature, are not common to the study of many other so-called social movements, there is a substantial analytical distinction between the study of the movements of low status groups and all other social movements. Most of the above questions simply would not be appropriate to the study of messianic movements, the Women's Christian Temperance Union, and other "social movements" commonly analyzed by sociologists.

Some Key Issues in the Study of Low Status Movements

Before we turn to some of the major issues which have arisen in the conceptualization (and hence empirical investigation) of class and mobility, let us first list more systematically some of the key issues which have interested those who have studied such movements. This list differs in some important respects from Smelser's analytic scheme (Smelser, 1963). In particular, our list implicitly emphasizes the importance of the rational element in low status movements, while Smelser makes the irrational a part of his definition of all collective behavior, including social movements. The following are key issues in the analysis of labor, and peasant movements.

What *societal changes* preceded the establishment of low status movements? This issue corresponds roughly to Smelser's two categories of "Structural Conduciveness" and "Structural Strain," but our terminology purposely emphasizes our belief that movements arise out of *changes* in structure, rather than conduciveness in a static structure. These changes may be either objective or subjective. Examples of *objective* changes are the social and economic ramifications of a decline of the traditional industrial commercial structure prior to the Industrial Revolution, without which the labor movements as we know them are inconceivable; and on the agricultural side, the decline of the traditional *haciendas* and *hacendados* in the face of the rapid rise of more commercialized agriculture in Latin America. Changes of this kind occurred in Mexico before the Revolution (White, 1969) and in Peru before the 1960s (Craig, 1969).

These changes may also be *subjective:* an increase in the expectations of Africans exposed to industrial civilization during World War I, but especially after World War II, giving rise to labor movements in many European colonies in Africa and to more general independence movements to which the new unions were often, but not invariably, linked (Davies, 1966). The rise of expectations may also occur on the side of high status groups, leading to increased pressure on those subordinate to them, thereby resulting in the formation of movements. Thus, landowners may begin to desire city luxuries as the English did prior to the peasant revolt of 1381, and the French aristocracy prior to 1789. Middle-class intellectuals may have aspirations for power, resulting in their search for a mass organizational power base, as in the case of Russia, among the peasants and then—influenced by Marx from the 1880s onwards—among the working class (Daniels, 1961).

We have so far refined the concept of social change—at least, change relevant to the formation of movements of low status groups—in two ways. We have distinguished between (a) objective and subjective changes, and between (b) those changes affecting the low status group itself vs. those affecting other groups of relevance, or the state, which then puts pressure on low status groups (Mousnier, 1960). But there is also: (c) a useful distinction between long term changes—the rise of industry; the decline, for various reasons (including changes in military technology) of the lower aristocracy as in Germany in the fourteenth and early fifteenth centuries (Franz, 1965)—and more immediate, precipitating events, perhaps the imposition of a tax, or a lowering of wages; and (d) a distinction between economic-technical changes and political changes. Indeed, insofar as the latter distinction is concerned, we shall see in our discussion of class and mobility that in addition to economic and political factors, status in the narrow sense of "prestige," as well as access to cultural goods (education, for example) are also of relevance. It has been recognized for a long time, that class and status are multi-dimensional, hence so are *changes* in them. This fact plays a considerable role in understanding the movements of low status groups, as we shall demonstrate below.

A second major question of concern to all those who have studied labor, but also peasant and other low status movements is: who are the *participants* in the movement, and what conditions hinder or facilitate their organization? Participation in a movement by potential recruits is never total and uniform. Hence questions have invariably arisen as to who are the first, and who are the most likely to band together: skilled workers or unskilled; rich peasants or poor? This question can be asked at two levels: at that of the aggregate—what types of industries and what kinds of communities are more susceptible to organization? It can also be asked at the level of the individual: within any group what kind of individual (defined in both sociological and psychological dimensions) is more susceptible?

What are the *goals* of the movement? Three separate issues are evident. (a) With respect to how many sectors of society does the movement have goals—the economic exclusively; the political; the educational; or the religious? And, (b) how profound are the changes the movement is seeking? The latter might be termed the radicalism or depth and profundity of its goals; the former, their breadth. (c) The objectives sought by a movement are often part of an explicit *ideology* concerning the history and the future of society as well as its present characteristics. Such ideologies, where they exist, will be studied as part of the exploration of "goals".

What *means* are employed by the movement? Here, as in the case of goals, there is a link with ideology, which again influences (a) the breadth of means considered—political, economic action, education, propaganda, etc., and (b) the "radicalism" of means in each of these areas. Is sabotage of machines and occupation of land included among economic means; or are violence and revolution among political means?

The organizational cohesiveness and structure of low status movements has invariably been problematical. Peasant movements have often been said to have failed because of parochialism. Differences over the importance of accepting a combat-type discipline and authority has been a central issue dividing Marxists of various kinds (e.g. orthodox Leninist communists from Castroites and followers of Guevara, who believe that action comes before monolithic organization both in industry and in rural areas).

Allies and enemies of the movement: who are they, and under what conditions do they act? No more is needed here to illustrate the centrality of this issue than to point out that key writers, including Lenin and Mao, often were deeply concerned about such questions as: the possibility of workers and peasants forming some kind of alliance, the role of intellectuals vis-à-vis each of these groups, whether or not it is essential for at least some parts of the bourgeoisie to participate to gain an ultimate working-class victory (and vice versa, in the case of the earlier, bourgeoisie revolution).

What are the *conditions of success and failure?* Being by definition low in economic, political, cultural, and prestige resources and in power, there is, logically at least, a built-in likelihood for the movements of low status groups to fail to improve their status, at least when relying upon their own efforts alone. The question of the circumstances under which the weak become stronger and the poor richer is therefore a particularly intriguing one. Indeed we might ask whether, and in what sense, such movements have ever been successful in elevating the status of members, particularly in the long run.

With this all-too-sketchy enumeration of issues known to be of interest to students of low status groups, we shall now attempt to do two things. First, we shall look at some critical debates in stratification and mobility theory, and demonstrate how they parallel some of these major issues in the analysis of low status movements. Second, we shall consider at least some of the remaining key issues, insofar as they have not already been elucidated, and deliberately attempt to reformulate them in mobility and stratification terms never, we hope, doing violence either to data or concept. Implicit in the above is that there are interesting conceptual parallels between individual mobility and the mobility of entire groups and, further, that there are empirical and conceptual relationships between the two levels. Whether or not individuals see themselves as having a chance to be mobile at either level affects the degree to which they might throw their energies into mobility efforts at either level. We shall now elaborate on all this.

II. INDIVIDUAL AND CLASS MOBILITY

Comparison of the Concepts

Preoccupation with the mobility of individuals, or of their children, from one stratum and class to another, has tended to obscure the fact that the mobility of entire strata or classes relative to each other is both conceptually and pragmatically a form of attempted mobility, as well.

Definitions will highlight the contrast between the two kinds of mobility. *Individual mobility* occurs when individuals move to class positions which have different rewards from the positions they are leaving (or which their fathers are occupying, in the more usual case of intergenerational mobility). The reward attached, however, to each position remains unaltered. *Collective or position mobility* occurs when the rewards of positions are altered—absolutely or relative to each other—while the individuals remain in their original group.

Table 2 illustrates that individuals as well as groups can strive either for collective mobility (elevating the rewards of the position) or for individual mobility (individual's moving to a higher position).

TABLE 2
SCHEMATIC REPRESENTATION OF COLLECTIVE MOBILITY VS. INDIVIDUAL MOBILITY BETWEEN POSITIONS; AND INDIVIDUAL VS. GROUP EFFORT TO ACHIEVE EITHER OF THESE

	Individual Effort	Group Effort*
Individual Between-position mobility	Individual seeks to rise in the economic system, or to facilitate his or her child's mobility, e.g., by personally financing the child's schooling A	Unions seek improvement in and opening of educational system as a whole so that as a group, members' children will no longer be limited to blue-collar work. Also: union fights for improvement of promotion opportunities for all within the organization B
Collective Mobility of the Position	C Individuals seeks to improve e.g., wages of his or her position. Unlikely to succeed on a mass basis unless facilitated by structural circumstances (shortage of labor).	D Unions negotiate better wages and working conditions; Labor or Peasant parties strive for political power or for worker participation in management.

* As discussed in the text: just as the aggregate success of individual mobility, i.e. mobility in quadrants A and C is attributable *both* to changes in the structure of society and to the "openness" of society, so, too, the success of group efforts (B and D) will depend on structural changes as well as on group effort. Indeed the extent of group effort will itself, in part, depend on structural changes; see text.

Smelser and Lipset briefly noted the existence of collective or, as one might also call it, position mobility. "The phenomenon of 'collective mobility' has been little analyzed by social scientists" (Smelser and Lipset, 1966:18) they stated in their introduction to a collection of readings devoted to the relationship between economic development and individual mobility. The place of *organized efforts* to alter the rewards of low status positions is the focus of this chapter. It is what movements of low status groups are all about.

"Individual mobility is frequently substituted for collective mobility" (Smelser and Lipset, 1966:12). It is, however, at least as true that the reverse occurs: that collective mobility is sought because individual mobility is blocked. It may be argued that the more individual mobility is blocked—e.g. in ex-feudal Europe as compared with the U.S. (at least, so ran the myth: see, Lipset and Bendix, 1959)—the more likely it is that organized group mobility efforts will take place. The phenomenon is by no means confined to industrialized societies (Hutton, 1946:41–61, 97–100, as cited in Smelser and Lipset, 1966:8–9).

The points to be emphasized are first, that the two methods—individual and collective—are alternative methods of mobility. They may represent a real choice for the individual because the end result is the same for him. Second, the existence of that real choice may explain some of the characteristics both of low status movements and of individual mobility efforts. The misappropriation of funds by movement officials, for example, or their collusion with the other side —employers, landowners, conservative political parties or "the white power structure"—are phenomena encountered especially in the early phases of the movements both of workers and of peasants. These actions become more explicable when one realizes that individual mobility is one of the most important motivations of those who participate in low status movements, including persons who become movement leaders. It is of course not the only motive, and without altruism (in Parsonian terms, "collectivity orientation") on the part of many leaders and followers, most movements would not have been established and could not survive.

As already noted, other remedies for low status, apart from mobility within the society, may be sought either individually or collectively. Among these are individual and collective expressive reactions or physical and psychic secession (physical migration, psychic retreatism). The existence or nonexistence of these alternatives, too, affects the characteristics of collective mobility efforts, and of efforts at individual mobility within the society.

History of the Concept of "Class" or "Position Mobility"

As is to be expected in view of their more global approach to society and social change, nineteenth century and early twentieth century analysts were more likely than we are today to cast their theories in terms of the movement of classes. Marx's entire sociology was built around precisely such conceptions: the growth but progressive economic emiseration of the working-class; the decline of the lower middle-class; the increased wealth but shrinking size of the propertied groups; to be followed by the political dictatorship of the proletariat and, subsequently, the abolition of classes. Marx analyzed not only modern capitalism and the future in this fashion, but also the birth and decline of ancient empires and, of course, the growth and decay of feudalism.

Marx was neither the first to do so (Ricardo, for example, thought in terms of the increasing wealth of landowners), nor after him were Marxians the only ones to think in these terms. Schumpeter gave the title, "The Rise and Fall of Whole Classes" to the fourth section of an essay originally written in 1927: "Social Classes in an Ethnically Homogeneous Environment" (Schumpeter, 1951). Although Schumpeter addressed himself only to the rise and fall of two elites (the rise of the bourgeoisie and the decline of the aristocracy during the transition from feudalism to capitalism) his approach is, in principle, that which we would like to see made co-equal to that of the study of individual mobility. Interestingly enough, his theory was far more uncompromisingly functionalist than even Davis and Moore some thirty-five years later:

> Every class has a definite function. . . . Moreover, the position of each class in the total national structure depends, on the one hand, on the significance that is attached to that function, and, on the other hand, on the degree to which the class successfully performs the function. Changes in relative class position are always explained by changes along these two lines, *and in no other way.*" (Emphasis added.) (Schumpeter, 1951:40.)

By implication, Schumpeter would seem to be sceptical of deliberate efforts—through the creation of movements of workers or peasants—to raise their status, unless "objective conditions" (as Marxists would say) are ripe for it. Later analysts of the efficacy of the trade union movement to raise real wages over a period of time, have debated that very point. Many analysts believe that the efforts of such movements are fruitless unless structural changes bring about improvements in any case (Chamberlain, 1965).

Schumpeter applied his theory to only two elite groups. He symbolized (it would be inaccurate to say "influenced") the tendency for most sociologists since that time to analyze the collective mobility of *either* elites *or* lower status groups, but only rarely to see the system as a whole in perpetual flux, and certainly not to formalize the problem of class (collective) mobility systematically.

Sorokin, imaginative in this as in other fields, did briefly deal with one aspect of the problem of class mobility. He devoted a chapter in his *Social and Cultural Mobility* to "Fluctuations of the Height and the Profile of Economic Stratification" (Sorokin, 1964:36–67). That chapter discusses the now familiar topics of the distance between the bottom and the top of the income distribution; the shape of the distribution; and the changes through time in both parameters. Sorokin, too, was a functionalist: too much equality leads to

> catastrophic destruction of the economic life of the society; and will generally be avoided; and social catastrophe occurs if the profile becomes too steep." (Sorokin, 1964:59.)

But apart from the size of the economic gap between top and bottom, Sorokin does not deeply enter into the problem of class mobility. In particular, he is not overly concerned with causes, implicitly because he regards inequality as functionally so self-evidently necessary that it needs little elaboration. The overall emphasis of his book is, however, chiefly on individual mobility from one class to another though here he does recognize three dimensions: economic, political, and occupational.

From the mid-1930s on, separate literatures began to grow dealing with relative class mobility either at the "top" or at the "bottom," but with little reference to each other, and with no general concept of class mobility. Concerning the top, there has been discussion whether managers were displacing owners (see, for example, Burnham, 1941), or whether both were giving way to classes stratified on the basis of competence (Young, 1959), or whether the concept of a single ruling class or a single elite in the sense in which Pareto and Mosca thought of them, might not better be given up for that of a group of strategic elites (Keller, 1963).

Concerning the "bottom," there has been not only a continuous debate over whether there is a single, relatively conscious working class, or whether there are several, each perhaps, with limited self-awareness. There has also been discussion of whether the working-class, or working classes, are moving up toward the middle-class: the phenomenon of "embourgeoisement" (Goldthorpe and Lockwood, 1963; Goldthorpe, Lockwood, Bechhofer and Platt, 1969; Berger, 1960; and the later writings of these and other authors.) This is the kind of phenomenon in which we are interested.

Few authors seem to have an image of society as an entire class system whose parts are constantly moving in relation to each other while the shape and height of the whole may be changing simultaneously. In this image, individual mobility is micromovement of a quite different order. Authors who do have such a vision are generally those with a socialist or radical orientation working within a European tradition which tended to see class as defined by opposition to class.

C. Wright Mills in his *Power Elite* had perhaps the most comprehensive vision of some groups (local elites, independent professionals and white collar groups) which were moving down, albeit from very different starting points, while other groups (managers and owners, whom Mills saw as melding into the "corporate rich") were fusing and still other groups (the military, for example) were rising (Mills, 1956). Bottomore (1966) and Dahrendorf (1959) are also among the few writers analyzing the relationships among various levels of the class structure. In his *Power and Privilege*, Lenski, perhaps more than any other author, presents empirical material bearing on the mobility i.e., changing rewards of a great diversity of occupational, economic, political, educational and other groups (Lenski, 1966). In addition, Lenski makes the very provocative point that conflict may be not only vertical, between strata, but also horizontal: between those who would like to see more weight given to educational than to economic criteria, or to occupational standing as opposed to political power (Lenski, 1966:81).

Let us now analyze the empirical issues which have arisen in the histories of working class, and of peasant movements, using the conceptual tools of stratification and mobility theory, both as they apply to individuals, and as they apply to collectivities.

III. THE APPLICATION OF MOBILITY CONCEPTS TO MOVEMENTS OF LOW STATUS GROUPS

The multi-dimensionality of class positions and mobility

Marxist revisionists like Bernstein, a major theorist of class relationships from the 1890s onward (Bernstein, 1898), and even Marx himself recognized that political status did not coincide perfectly with economic status. Further, Marx recognized that this status incongruity or lack of status crystallization, as sociologists call it today, would affect the nature of working-class movements: their aims, their estimate of the point which they had reached, etc. For example, Marx accepted in 1871 that possession of universal suffrage, "the equivalent of political power for the working class of England," would have there the "inevitable result ... (of) the political supremacy of the working-class" (*The Civil War in France*, as cited in Bottomore, 1966:39). In other words: the upward political mobility granted to the working classes of England, a dramatic semi-revolutionary change in their status, would necessarily affect the British working-class movement, and especially its goals.

It has long been accepted, therefore, that the position of individuals and of groups in society is affected by their standing in various, and not just a single dimension. These dimensions are analytically quite distinct, but conceptual as well as empirical research centers precisely on elucidating how and to what extent they are statistically and causally interrelated. In the case of workers, and of peasants, whose role is by definition first and foremost in the economy, it seems helpful to subdivide "economic status." We believe this is best done in such a way that the subdivisions are applicable to other dimensions of statuses as well.

The subdivisions which Almond and his colleagues have employed to analyze political systems (Almond, et al., 1960) seem applicable to the economic system also, and to status in other sectors as well. It is an analysis couched in terms of "inputs," "transformation" and "outputs." Thus, as far as the economic status of workers and peasants are concerned, one would measure: (1) the *extent* to which and the *security* with which they have effective control over "inputs" (ownership of industry; ownership of land or easy access to land rented for long periods); (2) the extent to which they have decision-making power over the "transformation" process (i.e. over production matters—which workers theoretically can, and in practice in certain countries do, have without owning the inputs); and (3) their share in the output of the economic system (and the security of that share).

This division is certainly meaningful in measuring economic and political status (where Almond, et al. first employed it), and to a somewhat lesser but still highly useful degree in measuring status in other realms e.g., that of education and even religion. In education, low status groups increasingly want not only more "output" for their children (i.e. a higher level of education, such as easy access to college) but also control over the "transformation process" (how school systems are run).

Distinguishing, as we attempted to do in Table 2, between individual mobility and collective mobility and between individual and group efforts to achieve either, becomes particularly fruitful in exploring changes over time in mobility efforts. At least at the level of officially proclaimed doctrine, the trend among people of low status all over the world, including peasants and workers, is to emphasize collective rather than individual mobility and to attempt achievement of it at least in part through collective efforts, through movements of workers and peasants.

But most significant has been the changed emphasis in the subdimensions along which mobility is sought. Thus in Western Europe, as well as in countries such as Chile (before the 1973 coup) and Peru, the trend has been for a relatively rapid growth in the demand for participation (i.e. "transformation" decisions) and "input" decisions (nationalization), in addition to the traditional demand for an increased share of "output." In many parts of the world, this sharing in decision-making power is now being viewed as a profound human right, indeed, as a powerful, logical extension into the economic realm of the principle of political equality.

The demand for participation in production decisions has been difficult to accept for both centralized socialist systems and late capitalist ones—i.e., those upon whom the demand is made to give up or at least to share power. The fact holding special interest for us in the context of this chapter is that trade unions or their officials have often been reluctant to push this new demand. Under many codetermination schemes, the trade union is shunted aside in favor of direct participation by the individual worker or else the scheme envisages single plant or company-based worker organizations (Sturmthal, 1964) in potential rivalry with the established union. Not only is the trade union reluctant; there is an interesting question about the extent to which the entire effort to raise status along "transformation" and "input" dimensions is more a goal set by middle-class intellectuals, i.e. by "allies," than by members of low-status groups themselves. The latter have shown a more spontaneous interest in obtaining a larger share of "output." Lenin long ago recognized this. Who sets the goals of

low status movements is an intriguing question.[1] But regardless of who sets them, the new goals of participation is also to be found with respect to the status of workers and other low status groups in other sectors of society: above all, the educational, but even the religious, where there is now more lay participation than ever before (especially in the Catholic Church).

Approaching status as "multidimensional" helps us to clarify a second set of issues, also in the area of goals and means of low status movements. It has long been recognized that individuals take different avenues to increase their status. Education may be sought first. It is often recognized as the means to elevate other statuses of the self or of one's children. On the other hand, it may be wealth that is sought first, in the belief that the rest, including benefits for one's children, will come with it. Within low status movements important debates and profoundly weakening divisions have occurred over precisely this issue.

Marx, the economic determinist, believed that the proletariat's ownership and control over the means of production was the most important long-term goal of the working-class movement: at least, its goal prior to achieving the really ultimate goal of total equality of status for all: the classless society. But to attain economic dominance, Marx believed that a political revolution would be necessary. Hence he saw the more proximate goal as being that of arousing the political awareness and achieving the political organization of the working-class, and believed that the crisis of the system would facilitate this. Indeed, the breakdown of the system was seen as an indispensible condition for successful organizational efforts. To achieve such political organization, he recognized that trade unions in the economic sphere, as well as a Communist Party in the political, would be necessary. Marx saw the utility of trade unions as training workers for class struggle and making them aware of the nature of the system opposing them, with less importance attached to the union's role in obtaining higher wages (a goal in the consumption, or "output," sector of the economy). Struggles to improve wages and working conditions would be, he thought, a useful means to achieve such working-class consciousness, provided it was not regarded as an end in itself. Marx believed in a subtle interplay of the two status dimensions, the economic and political, both as means and as intermediate goals of the working-class movement.

In this he differed from Ferdinand Lassalle, his early German rival, who wished to concentrate all energies on increasing the political influence of the working-class over the state. On the other hand, the French anarcho-syndicalists wanted to forgo politics altogether, believing that direct economic action, the general strike, would be enough to bring down the system and put the working class in command in all sectors of society. In short, there have been major policy differences for more than a century over whether the economic or the political dimension of status constituted the more fruitful road to elevate low status groups. And the choice between these two has not been the only one posed.

From the first Social Encyclical, Leo XIII's *Rerum Novarum* of 1891, and onward Catholic trade unionism has always placed a great deal of emphasis on the education of workers as a prerequisite to gains in other dimensions. Only in part was this an attempt to divert unions from engaging in class conflict, a concept which was anathema to Catholic doctrine (Landsberger, 1969b:257–265).

---

[1] For a bibliography of the entire issue of worker participation, see International Institute of Labour and Social Studies (1971).

It was to be a special kind of education—religious, character building—totally different from that conceived of by Marx.

It is only appropriate, however, to recognize that in addition to Catholics, many others who have sought to lead workers and peasants, have regarded education as crucially important, but more than just indoctrination in whatever the ideology might be, whether catholic, marxist, or other. The broader view of education includes improved literacy and the sense of self-respect and the prestige that often accompanies it, together with an understanding of how the modern world functions. Educators like Paulo Freire in his approach to Brazilian peasants in the 1960s can be compared in purpose with the highly developed educational efforts of the early German and British Labor movements. The kind of education which would facilitate *intra*generational mobility with which movements of low status groups frequently concern themselves has, therefore, been an important issue for debate in these movements. In addition, the relative importance of education as compared with other means of elevating status has also been an issue of debate. The *analytical* controversy so familiar to sociologists, over which dimension of status ultimately holds the key to the remainder, has been a major element, therefore, also in the *empirical* history of many labor and peasant movements. It has been of particular importance in the development of the divisions and rivalries of which so much of their history consists. G.D.H. Cole's extensive *History of Socialist Thought* is the best single reference to this complex field (Cole, 1952).

The relative importance of seeking political power—i.e. an improvement of the political status of the worker or peasant, whether individually (the vote) or collectively (the party) has been a universally controversial issue. Note, for example the argument in the United Kingdom at the end of the last century: whether workers should eschew parliamentary politics altogether; should work within the Liberal Party, or should establish a new and separate Labour Party (Pelling, 1969). East European peasants were similarly very ambivalent in the inter-war years about whether the parliamentary politics created, as they perceived it, by an effete urban bourgeoisie, could be of utility to them in elevating their status. They did not perceive engaging in parliamentary politics as a useful means toward, nor as a desirable characteristic of the society they ultimately hoped to establish (Jackson, 1974 and more fully in Jackson, 1966).

Another profound division within working class and peasant movements has been over whether or not revolution would be necessary to achieve collective mobility, or whether reform of the present system would be sufficient. Within the revolutionary position, there are in turn further divisions that can be reformulated as alternative social and social psychological theories. An example is the Ché Guevara-Moscow argument over whether revolutionary consciousness can be created in the working-class and peasantry in the absence of an objective breakdown of the existing system. Guevara, and others before him, have said it could be, orthodox communists thought not. Though a matter of tactics for revolutionaries, it is obviously a matter of great empirical and theoretical interest for sociologists.

The German labor movement of 1900–1933 was the best known example of the split over reform vs. revolution with the climax reached during the Spartacist uprising of January, 1919. But the division could be found anywhere in Europe and, indeed, wherever there was a sizable labor movement, such as

Chile before the coup, Mexico and Argentina, as well as in India and Japan. At first glance, there appears to be no exact parallel at the level of individual mobility for this issue. But such a judgement would be erroneous. Movements consist ultimately of individuals, and the existence of a revolutionary movement —insofar as low status persons are involved as well as intellectuals—implies that at least some individuals perceive the societal situation as one in which individual mobility through individual effort is useless and/or undesirable. Such individuals have individually chosen as the appropriate path that of collective, position mobility ("the dictatorship of the working class") through collective means of a certain kind (revolution).

These have been the great alternative means and pathways for group mobility: collective education; collective economic action (the withholding of products and of labor in the role of producers) and collective political action inside and outside parliament. The choice among them has faced all movements of this kind. Internal debate has not often been able to settle a necessarily difficult question, and division has been the result.

Status Crystallization, Incongruity and Related Concepts

Once the multi-dimensional nature of status is recognized, the way is open to see that individuals may suffer from inconsistency; that though they enjoy a relatively high position on one dimension (education, for example) their status may be incongruously low on another (income, or prestige). The importance of such incongruity in determining the individual's political views and his other attitudes has been recognized and has been the subject of much research (Lenski, 1966).

Our interest here is to point out that *shared* incongruities of status are sometimes the bases of movements of low status groups. Peasant uprisings have occurred in part because of status incongruities. When the peasantry's lot has been improving in some respects, the remaining disabilities sometimes have been felt even more painfully. This was the case in the English Peasant Revolt of 1381. It occurred at a time when in the long run, the feudal system was clearly breaking up and the lot of many peasants had greatly improved. Yet the remaining disabilities, such as the payment of certain dues and the requirement to grind corn at the mill of the lord of the manor (Landsberger and Landsberger, 1974), were keenly felt for precisely this reason.

Parallel events in the trade union field have been the drive to organize among engineers (Kuhn, 1971:86, et seq.) and teachers (Wildman, 1971:131, et seq.). The organizing drives among these groups were a reaction to their declining prestige and decision-making power so much at variance with their high educational attainments and their previous status on these dimensions. In the case of engineers, it occurred through being submerged in the bureaucracy of large organizations; for teachers, through being asked to do low-status clerical and custodial tasks, as well as losing power to educational bureaucrats and, more recently, to parents and community representatives.

Thus, both at the group level—the susceptibility to collective action on the part of peasants and various urban groups—and at the level of the individual (what kind of person is readily recruited into a movement, what kind of person becomes a leader), the concept of status inconsistency has explanatory value.

Absolute vs. Relative Position Mobility

Expanding on work begun in the 1940s and 1950s, the exploration of how, and with what results, individuals concerned about their status engage in comparison processes with other persons became a central focus of sociological literature in the 1960s. These processes involve notions of equity and justice, as the individual, engaged in an "exchange" with his environment, compares what *he* or *she* receives with what *others* receive, in relation to their inputs and outputs. These others may be in the same position, or they may be the persons with whom he or she "exchanges": the employer, for example (Adams, 1966; Blau, 1968; Homans, 1961; Runciman, 1967). We will discuss in another section what Davies would call "relative deprivation" (Davies, 1962), since his concept involves reflection about the individual's past and his future hopes and expectations, rather than comparisons with others.

In many countries today, the U.S. and the U.K. not least among them, elevating the income of the poor is being discussed in terms which essentially involve moving their positions (we may regard the poor as today's successors of the once underprivileged working-class which has now achieved considerable gains). What is being debated is how to move permanently upward the entire block of positions at the bottom of the income ladder. Two policies are being advocated involving conceptualizations of poverty in absolute and in relative terms respectively. While these are predominantly not discussions among the poor themselves, let alone among organizations of the poor, the argument over absolute vs. relative mobility sheds light on a variety of issues in the history of movements of the underprivileged themselves.

In the United States today, some think in terms of elevating low income groups up to some minimum absolute income, whether it be a modest $2,400 per year for a family of four as suggested by the advisors of former President Nixon, or a more generous figure of $6,000 or higher, as advocated by the National Welfare Rights Organization. This is the "absolute" mobility approach. There are others, however, who would not regard poverty eliminated through any kind of absolute minimum, however high, but only when no one had an income, for example, of less than half the median income. The purpose then, is to move people up *in relation* to others. In countries other than the United States, the permanent elimination of the role of "the poor" and/or greater equality of wealth and of income, have for long been among the most important aims of those associated with movements of the underprivileged. That aim is increasingly coming to the fore, as witnessed, for example, by a new set of Fabian essays in England (Townsend and Bosanquet, 1972). The concern for relative mobility has assumed two very different forms and has been propagated by very different groups. One is that of middle-class intellectuals, allies rather than members of lower-class movements, who have generally focused upon inequality at the societal level. Examples are R.H. Tawney's influential *Equality* (Tawney, 1931), or the slogan adopted by Marx: "From each according to his ability, to each according to his need."

Trade union members and their working class leaders, however, have generally had a far more limited approach to issues of relative mobility. When engaged in collective bargaining, one approach has been to focus specifically and in an *ad hoc* manner upon short term movements in the profits of their particular industry, as compared with movements in the wages paid by that industry over the same period of time. At least as frequently, however, emphasis has been on the wages received by members of a particular union as compared with the wages or wage increases of other workers. The dramatic coal strike in Britain early in 1972 turned substantially, and quite explicitly, on the drop of miners from their previous position at, or near, the very top of all wage earners, to the tenth position. In the United States, the officers of major unions keep a very sharp look-out on the percentage increases obtained by other unions, lest their members think they are less effective than leaders of other unions.

Even within unions, particularly industrial type unions, there are political strains on union officials resulting from inter-job comparisons. To keep skilled members happy they must maintain percentage skill differentials of a substantial and steady kind, without making the absolute differences between skilled and unskilled so large that the mass of unskilled members become embittered. This caused a problem for the United Auto Workers Union (UAW) in the 1950s which obliged the UAW to set up a Skilled Trades Department. Divisions between older and younger workers are also common. The former are interested in fringe benefits, especially pensions, while younger members feel that this is of no advantage to them and that their interests are being "neglected." Indeed, invidious comparisons between departments and job classifications in a factory over wages and earnings often make the life of a union leader extremely difficult (Sayles and Strauss, 1967).

All of these instances indicate that the peculiar interplay between absolute and relative mobility of individuals and subgroups has a profound effect upon the organizations and movements of low status groups. These sensitivities often have the effect of weakening and dividing the organizations.

Comparison processes are not confined to setting the goals of a movement. They also affect the choice of means for improving status. In its milder form we see this in groups which by law or custom are prohibited from striking, or even from organizing. Civil servants, utility workers, policemen, firemen, doctors and teachers are increasingly asking why their right to bargain, let alone strike should be limited if others are free to organize and strike. And increasingly, these rights are being granted where they do not already exist.

Much more dramatically, the use of direct violence has increasingly been justified by those low in power. Here we may perhaps briefly use an example from recent U.S. racial history. Certain groups, especially of young blacks, have sought to justify the use of violence morally (which is not to say that they have necessarily used it) by pointing not to groups comparable to themselves, but to their opponents. Police-caused fatalities and heavy prison sentences among the black population, as well as high infant mortality rates resulting from inadequate health services and nutrition—these have been reconceptualized as "institutionalized violence," if not genocide. If the power of those in high status positions permits them to exercise these forms of violence in their dealings with those in low status, then, it is argued, why should those in low status not adopt whatever methods of violence are open to them in their struggle upwards?

Again, therefore, comparison processes are critically involved. It has long been known that perceived exploitation and loss of status have resulted in completely unorganized *individual* acts of sabotage, especially at the beginning of the process of industrialization (Kerr, et al., 1960). Comparison processes with respect to violence as a means are equally important at the level of *organized* upward mobility efforts.

"Sponsored" vs. "Contest Mobility"

Some years ago, Turner drew attention to the fact that the mobility of individuals could involve either the process of a "contest," or that of "selection and sponsorship" of lower status persons by those already enjoying higher status (Turner, 1960). With the English educational system in mind (as contrasted with that of the U.S.), he speculated that sponsors of superior status might elevate those beneath them on the basis of how to make the best use of the talents of society. C. Wright Mills likewise had a sponsorship process very much in mind when attempting to explain how individuals found their way into higher social positions. Not only did they have roughly the same background, but they were further assessed by the critical gatekeepers as to how well they would fit in, and "sponsored" only if their values and assumptions were in consonance with those of the elite (Mills, 1956). The concept of "sponsorship" is a useful supplement to the idea that those who are upwardly mobile are successful only because they win in a competitive "contest" with their competitors. The concepts of "contest" and "sponsorship" are equally useful in attempting to understand the fate of movements of low status groups. "Sponsorship" is useful to cover the relation between these low status groups and other, superior groups who are willing to help them elevate the status of their position. It is one of the answers to the riddle of how groups, who by definition are "low" in economic and political resources, ever come to improve upon their condition when, almost by definition, they lack the means to do so. As in the case of individuals, the group's own efforts in the struggle to rise may be less important than the sponsorship of those who wish to see it rise.

The help of superior classes has been of particular importance in the early stages of the development of movements of low status groups. Even elements of the upper-class, who might be thought to be hostile, have at times supported measures which would improve the position of those low in status, for example, by sponsoring protective factory legislation (as did Lord Shaftesbury in 1844), or by introducing social security legislation as in Imperial Germany in the 1880s or in Chile in the 1920s (Morris, 1967). Often—as in the case of Bismarck—the specific aim was to raise the status of workers in order to reduce their desire to organize themselves independently and in opposition to the existing system. Efforts such as Bismarck's are, in the terms of Kerr, et al., the hallmark of the "realist" elements of the dynastic elites (Kerr, et al., 1960:52–55). Kerr's *Industrialism and Industrial Man*, while perhaps now somewhat out-of-date, remains one of the most stimulating in the realm of how different elite sponsorship groups seek to structure the trade union movement and deal with worker discontent.

Marx, and all later generations of Marxists, clearly understood the need for mutual exchange between workers and other classes, and the need, too, for sponsorship. Lenin estimated that the Russian bourgeoisie would recognize that it was by itself too weak in the early twentieth century to make a revolution against the decaying feudal order of Russia, and would therefore seek the support of the working-class (Hammond, 1957). The middle-class of England courted labor to some extent in order to obtain political power (which it began to obtain with the passage of the 1832 Reform Act) and even after that point, to obtain cheap duty-free food imports. These were desired by workers and middle-classes alike but resisted by land-owning Tories. The aim was achieved with the repeal of the Corn Laws in 1846.

The most usual situation is one in which some group of what might be termed higher than low but lower than high status takes a critical view of the ongoing economic and political system as a whole. In part, its motivation may be patriotic, or more broadly, altruistic and humanistic. But in part, the motivation will also be to receive for itself increasing economic, prestige and political rewards, i.e., to see their own positions be upwardly mobile. Needing mass support, such groups of intermediate status sponsor the demands of peasants, workers and other low status groups, be it for better welfare services, trade union rights and minimum wages, land reform or the abolition of discrimination. Even relatively progressive sections of the army may forge such alliances with workers and/or peasants—as happened in Bolivia in the late 1930s and in Venezuela and Argentina in the 1940s. In each case, however, the phenomenon was much more complex than being merely a "progressive alliance." The existing oligarchy is the common enemy; on the details of what is to follow its downfall, there is usually far less agreement. Thus, all the earlier, and some of today's marxist-type parties have had to mask their belief in state-controlled farms (and factories and trade unions) in order to obtain peasant and worker support. In some countries—in Latin America most recently, especially in Chile and Brazil, and in Western Europe long before that—certain sectors of the established churches or of their lay membership, may sponsor the elevation of the poor (de Kadt, 1970; Landsberger, 1970).

In exchange for such sponsorship (insofar as it is not purely altruistic), support is expected in whatever "currency" the sponsor seeks: loyalty to church and doctrine; voting for the party; or demonstrating "power capability" (Anderson, 1967) through strikes, street demonstrations and symbolic or real acts of violence in order to obtain concession from the existing regime.

The role of "intellectuals" in this process of sponsorship needs particular analysis, both in Western Europe and in the developing countries (Millen, 1963). Daniels, an authority on Russia, and perhaps overly harsh, draws attention to its changing nature—from what he calls the early, mid-nineteenth century creative "literary intelligentsia" to the later "quasi-intellectuals" whom he sees as intellectually second rate, hence failing and frustrated, and therefore advocating policies whose implementation would clearly leave them at the top of the new hierarchy of power (Daniels, 1961). Some have no credentials to be intellectuals at all, but are small-town traders and minor officials (Seton-Watson, 1967). The personal mobility motivation of some of the intellectual politicians became so apparent in their opportunistic switching of sides, that some parts of the early working class movements, e.g., the syndicalists of France (Lorwin, 1954) wanted to have nothing to do with them.

The role of the middle-class and particularly of intellectual sponsors of the lower classes, has therefore been a subject of lively discussion within the movements themselves. The first and most famous Workers' Councils in Russia, those of St. Petersburg in 1905, sought to exclude intellectuals altogether, despite the fact that Trotsky, an intellectual *par excellence*, played a key role in the Councils (Anweiler, 1958). European movements discussed their role vigorously (Brin, 1928); and intellectuals themselves have often been caustic about their fellows (Perlman, 1928).

Lack of Sponsorship: "Parochialism"

Among the most important crises in the movements of low status groups are those induced by the failure for "sponsorship" to occur from groups from which one would expect it. The failure of the skilled and relatively well-paid workers of the American Federation of Labor (AFL) to be concerned with the growing army of semi-skilled workers in the mass production industries led to the establishment of the Congress of Industrial Organizations (CIO) in the mid-1930s: a debilitating breach which was not healed, if indeed it has ever been, until some twenty years later. This was merely a repeat of British working-class history of the nineteenth century, when certain "labour aristocratic" elements showed no interest in helping dock and transport workers in the 1880s. Marx, once again, became aware quite early of the dangers of this aristocratic parochialism, both within the working-class movement of any one country, and between the entire working-class of the more advanced countries, such as England and their less fortunate brethren in other countries, especially in the colonies (Lozovsky, 1935).

An analysis of peasant movements (including an analysis of black rural cooperatives in the Southern United States in which the author was recently engaged), likewise reveals again and again that a successful group in one area often does not help a struggling group in the next and, more systematically, that those strata which have gained some advantage will not help strata below them. An important example today is that of the Mexican *ejidatario*, once he has his parcel of land. He may well exploit the ever-growing army of landless laborers of whom he, or his father, were once members. Far from helping them establish their own organizations, he seeks to stifle such organizations (Landsberger and Hewitt, 1970). Before the 1973 military coup, the same problem was beginning to appear in Chile in areas where some peasants had benefited from land reform, and others had not.

This "parochialism" has long been noted with disappointment by Marxists and other observers of movements of this kind. It is, of course, not confined to the "better off" abandoning the "less well off." It has also shown itself in countless failures to aid striking fellow-workers at roughly equal levels. Some of these cases are well known, as is that of the British coal miners left to their fate at the end of the General Strike of 1926 (Pelling, 1969). The single most dramatic instance of "parochialism" is considered by many to have been the failure of the workers of France and Germany jointly to resist their governments as they went to war with each other in 1914. The fact that they did go to war was not solely emotionally "expressive" of their patriotism. It represented also, among many complex factors, a realistic estimate by each group of leaders that the interests of their own movement would be best served, or least harmed, by supporting their own governments, who would no doubt show themselves duly grateful. Once again, such behavior becomes more readily understandable when it is recognized that seeking improvement in the position of movement members from those who have the power to deliver it, e.g., the government, is one of the main determinants of the tactics of this kind of organization. "Parochialism" is the inevitable result of such a goal whatever the rhetoric of working-class, or peasant, solidarity may proclaim.

Disappointed Expectations

Davies' well known theory of "relative deprivation" (Davies, 1962) is perhaps better called one of "disappointed expectations." The rather special case in which Davies is interested is the following: a long-term objective improvement in a group of positions has led their occupants to expect continued improve-ment, so that, when a short-term deterioration occurs for certain random rea-sons, a revolutionary mood is produced. (Let us note that revolutions as such, as distinct from revolutionary moods, can never be explained by such a theory, since the resistance of existing elites, and many other factors, not only the mood of potential revolutionaries, plays a crucial role in whether or not a revolution is attempted and, if attempted, is successful.)

There is no question that such disappointments have caused the kind of bitterness upon which movements are based: for example (and apart from the cases cited by Davies), in the instance of the Pugachev revolt in Russia in the late eighteenth century (Longworth, 1974). But there is no reason to think that disappointment over the failure to continue a long period of objective improve-ment in their. status alone produces moods conducive to movements of low status groups. In some cases, a serious objective deterioration has caused peas-ants to revolt, as in the case of the French *jacquerie* of 1358 (Luce, 1894). In other cases, even continuous objective improvement did not forestall a move-ment for the understandable reason that the expectations to achieve total equal-ity rose even faster (Banfield, 1968).

Thus, many combinations of objective and subjective (expectation) trends may produce conditions for a movement. The important element, as Gurr has pointed out, seems to be a widening gap between the two, however it is pro-duced, but necessarily due to some *change* in the relation between objective conditions and subjective expectations (Gurr, 1970).

In summation.   Problems of status disequilibrium between different dimen-sions of the same group; tensions over relative position as between groups; and problems of temporal expectations unusually out of balance with objective con-ditions and/or expected conditions, all have fed into the creation of—but have also created internal problems for—movements of low status groups.

Structural vs. Intended Mobility

So far, this chapter has no doubt conveyed the impression that any gains made in the status of low status positions are due to the collective reactions of those who have sought them. Yet here, too, there is an illuminating parallel from the study of individual mobility. The parallel suggests valuable questions pertinent to the relative efficacy of deliberate efforts to achieve group mobility vs. other causes of "class mobility."

Since Rogoff's famous contribution in the early 1950s (Rogoff, 1953), it has been recognized that the degree to which a society is "open" to individual mobility (especially intergenerational mobility over substantial periods of time) can only be judged *after* allowance is made for changing occupational structures. If unskilled jobs are declining and the number of white collar jobs expanding, the sons of many of the former will necessarily rise into the ranks of the latter. The "supply" of jobs, or demand for labor, needs to be allowed for before measuring genuine vertical mobility opportunities.

Change in the demand for labor also affects the status and rewards of a given position, i.e., the mobility of the position, not only the flow into it. Indeed, economists have expressed this in the following terms. As the demand for white collar workers goes up, an increase in the rewards of the positions stimulates the flow into them, and in any case, such a flow would be quickened by the sheer availability of positions and the absence of alternatives.

Our point here is to draw attention to the fact that these supply and demand factors (a) directly affect the rewards (the status mobility) of positions; and (b) that they also condition the efforts, and the success and failure of the efforts, of low status movements.

The trade union movements of Britain had their beginnings in the efforts of certain crafts to maintain their position in the face of threats from new technologies and expanding markets. When their jobs became easier to perform while the demand for them declined, these artisans sought to protect their status by limiting the number of apprentices and formulating work rules (Pelling, 1969:24–25). This desire to counter structural trends continued in the post-Napoleonic period, with the destruction of machines by the "Luddites" who again were responding to threats to their position emanating from technological changes. It has continued until today, when dockers have resisted, or insisted on compensation for, the introduction of labor-saving machinery, and railway engineers have sought to maintain certain levels of manning which were appropriate for steam locomotives, but unnecessary with automated diesel equipment.

There are other instances, where the goal of an industrial labor or peasant movement has been not so much that of preventing the downward mobility and possible elimination of the position threatened by structural changes as it is to cash in on the possibility of raising status by preserving the scarcity of positions in a situation of rising structural demand. Doctors (not exactly a low status group) have sought to limit training opportunities. But so, too, have craft unions, even when there has been no danger of a decline in rewards.

In the short run, in the face of a threatened decline in position-reward due to the downswing of the trade cycle, unions have attempted to fight back, including use of the strike (Rees, 1954), but generally unsuccessfully. Labor strife is also intense when the trade cycle is in its upward phase and at such times, the efforts of unions have been much more successful, both in terms of increasing rewards and in terms of expanding the union organization. Union effort is the same in both the upswing and the downswing of the trade cycle, but it is effective only in the former case. What then, determines success? The effort or the structural situation?

In the case of the peasantry, movements have very frequently been spurred by encroachments on the status of their members. Sometimes, the defense has concerned newly won status, as in the case of the Peruvian *arrenderos*, in the *La Convencion* valley, who sought to protect the recently won privilege of growing coffee (Craig, 1969). In other cases, there were attempts to preserve the status of ancient standing, as in the case of Zapata's villagers in Morelos,

Mexico in 1910. The factors of "status disequilibrium" and "relative depriva-tion" or "disappointed expectations" are in a sense no more than secondary aspects of a more general unsettling of established statuses. These may be due to more general economic and technological changes, or to the slow permeation of new values like egalitarianism and humanitarianism.

The case of blacks in the United States is also one in which it is difficult to disentangle whether change did not, at least, *begin* well before mass movements began. The argument could be made that their day of genuine emancipation had "about come" in the late 1950s and early 1960s. This can be seen in Su-preme Court decisions going back to the late 1930s and in Presidential Exec-utive Orders of the 1940s (Woodward, 1966), making the Civil Rights move-ment more of a dramatic push over-the-brink, taking advantage of increasingly strong ideological commitments to equality and democracy following the de-pression and, especially following World War II.

Similar questions have been raised about what actually have been the long term effects of trade unions on the position of wage earners. Have the status gains been due to union efforts, or would they have come about regardless due to structural reasons? Many analysts are inclined to think that possibly the only permanent effect of the movements of low status groups has been to widen the gap *within* the working-class (or peasantry) between the organized and unorganized, rather than that of closing the status gap separating them from higher strata. Others have expressed doubts that trade unions have had any appreciable effect whatever on wages (Chamberlain, 1965:468–484).

Long term forces affecting the rewards of positions are, perhaps, only rarely under the control of movements of *low status* groups. On the other hand, higher status groups—the more affluent farmers of Western Europe and the United States, and the military and bureaucracies of the developing nations—are, by contrast, fully capable of stemming and distorting changes which would be healthy in their societies, e.g., stemming the tendency toward diminishing the rewards accruing to their own positions.

IV. STRATIFICATION WITHIN LOW STATUS GROUPS

Stratification and Differential Susceptibility to Organization

The general issue of internal stratification has already been encountered at sev-eral points in our discussion, especially so in the section on relative mobility. The phenomenon is so important that it affects almost all issues faced by low status movements. This has been recognized particularly by those who have been practically concerned with these movements. The issue can be phrased in this question: which substratum among those of low status is more capable of becoming mobilized?

Theorists espousing populism were often content to envision a homoge-neous peasantry and/or a homogeneous working-class, perhaps even to dream of each of these uniting permanently with the other against the middle- or upper-classes. In one guise or another, this was essentially the view of the Social Revolutionaries in Russia, and of the agrarian parties in post-1918 Europe (Jackson, 1974).

Marxists like Lenin and Mao Tse-tung, far less sentimental and romantic than the populists, recognized that the peasantry was highly stratified. They built their entire revolutionary strategies around this fact (Rochester, 1942:17, 28 et seq.; Schram, 1969:236–246). Less activist-orientated analysts of peasants, like Wolf (1969) and Moore (1966), have also been concerned with precisely the same questions as Lenin and Mao: who is more readily organized, the poor, the middle, or the rich peasant? Who is more revolutionary? Are there systematic changes over time—does one group become more revolutionary while another becomes less so?

The Marxists, of course, envisaged the richer peasants as ready to partic-ipate in the first revolution, the one against the remnants of feudalism, just as skilled workers were the first to unionize, and better-off blacks were more in-volved in the early stages of the Civil Rights movement. All of them, Marxists fear, are likely to become conservative rapidly thereafter. Hence, it would be only the poorer peasantry who could later be relied upon to help in the coun-tryside to bring about the final proletarian revolution, together with the urban working-classes, on whom Lenin placed prime emphasis, Mao far less. Wolf and Moore, however, are skeptical about the revolutionary potential of the lowest strata of the peasantry and place more confidence in the middle group (Wolf, 1969:290–292; Moore, 1966:455). In the case of the working-class, the same doubt as to whether the bottom strata—the "Lumpenproletariat"—had revolu-tionary potential divided Bakunin (who thought it had) from Marx.

Goals, Means and Social Change

The concepts developed so far will be utilized to formulate propositions con-cerning the "mobilization" of the different strata of low status groups, their "goals" and their "means," and the relation of these three to social change. The reader will recall that we have distinguished between goals and means and their respective breadth and radicalism. We have also made distinctions be-tween status incongruity, relative deprivation and disappointed expectations. Changes in the position and expectations of other groups play a large role when we regard the movements of low status groups as merely one part of broader social changes. Finally, in the matter of goals, we distinguish between those arising from a look back toward some previously existing state, and those which are couched in terms of future utopias. However, the novelty of the latter is a matter of degree: elements of a supposed previously existing egalitarianism and a return to a primitive lack of specialization are often major features of utopias presented as "new."

Some Propositions

Concerning *societal changes*, we propose:[2]
1. Encroachment upon previously existing rights will understandably lead to feelings of real declining status, i.e., to feelings of *disappointed ex-pectations* for at least continuity of status. Encroachment may be prompted by negative pressures on the elites which the elites then pass

---

[2] This section draws in part on several points made in the introductory chapter in Lands-berger, 1974 and in Landsberger, 1973.

downwards, like competition or temporary depression, or by positive incentives such as the elites' desire to take advantage of new commercial or technical opportunities. Or they may be caused by rising consumption aspirations of the owners of the means of production, or by governments seeking to defray the costs of war (frequently a cause of medieval peasant uprisings but also dramatically operative in causing working-class unrest in early 1917, leading to the abdication of the working-class unrest in early 1917, leading to the abdication of the Czar).

2. The rise of new groups in growing urban and commercial centers results in the creation of new industrial working classes; or migration to towns, and seeing for the first time new standards of living: these changes will give rise to feelings of *relative deprivation* as established peasant or working-class groups compare themselves with other, newer, "reference" groups.

3. Rapid changes of any kind—the breaking up of a feudal system, the rapid spread of automation in industry or agriculture, the rise of new professions—will result in feelings of *status incongruity*. Rapid change is likely to be uneven, causing some aspects of status to improve more than others.

4. The diffusion of new general ideologies (visions of an egalitarian or socialist society) and of ideas about specific rights (e.g., relative to education and material standards of living) give rise to the discontent of *insufficiently met rising aspirations*.

Propositions concerning *goals and ideologies* of the movements resulting from the above sentiments include the following.

1. Encroachment on existing rights and the consequent disappointed expectations (see number 1, above) will lead initially to relatively *narrow*, specific, *backward* looking demands for the preservation or restoration of a *status quo*. If these demands are not met, more radical demands, blending old and new, will be formulated and their corresponding ideologies welcomed. Examples of this are to be found in rural Mexico of 1910, and in industrial Britain, 1810–1840.

2. Relative deprivation due to the rise of new classes (see number 2 above) will lead to the formulation of *comprehensive*, though still *backward* looking demands and the acceptance of supporting ideologies. This occurred among the peasantry in the face of rising urban classes in interwar Eastern Europe (Jackson, 1972; 1966) and with the French utopias for industrial workers during the 1820–1860 period. (Moore [1966] refers to this as "catonism.")

3. The break-up of a feudal society and a halting change in the direction of an individual, private property system (see number 3 above) will lead to relatively specific, *narrow forward* looking demands for the universal establishment of individual property rights and the abolition of remaining feudal impositions. Examples occurred in rural France in 1789 and are visible today in the demands of Latin American peasants for private property.

4. The diffusion of new ideologies (see number 4 above) will, by definition, stimulate movements to make *specific or general* demands, *depending on the nature of the ideology*. There seems to be no agreement

on the circumstances under which new ideologies spring up except that they flourish at times of change and strain. And of that there seems to be no lack at any stage in history.

Additional propositions regarding goals and means may be formulated in the following fashion.

5. The spontaneous demands made by workers and peasants are usually specific, limited to their own situation rather than embracing society-wide changes, and are not overly "radical."

6. Initially, too, collective reactions also are not violent, i.e., they are not "radical," in means.

7. Prolonged frustration will, however, radicalize all low status groups, probably more with respect to means than goals. Only a small group within a movement will have visions of a "new society." A larger proportion may tacitly support violent means.

8. It is possible that the lower strata (owning no property) of each group are more easily radicalized with respect to *means*. This was precisely the case of Marx's "Lumpenproletariat," in whose ideological long-term commitment he had no confidence—but in whom Bakunin had confidence in so far as immediate violent *action* was concerned. The higher substrata within the generally low strata, on the other hand, when they do become radicalized at all, are more likely than the Lumpenproletariat to become radicalized with respect to goals. By virtue of education, the higher strata are more likely to grasp the interrelations among institutions and recognize the need to change them simultaneously.

9. The more interconnected are the various institutions opposing the low status group, the more likely that demands will be broad and comprehensive. Thus European labor, facing a post-feudal society in which property, church and state were often still intertwined in various degrees (as in nineteenth century France and Germany) produced movements with broader goals than was the case in the U.S. Early peasant movements, which generally occurred in societies with highly interconnected institutional sectors, almost invariably had political and religious as well as economic goals. This was even more true of their middle-class intellectual sponsors, often heavily tinged with anti-clericalism (as in Spain before 1936 and in Mexico until 1940).

10. Demands for a comprehensive and profound restructuring of the reward systems of society (i.e., broad and radical goals) insofar as they are genuinely sustained by low status groups themselves, seem to be more typical of early than of later stages of industrialization in the case of workers (Kerr, et al., 1960) but to be more typical of late than of earlier stages in the case of peasant movements.

11. De-radicalization of the working-class and increased radicalization of the peasantry is based on structural developments. Industrial workers tend to grow in number and strength as industry grows and workers cannot be replaced. Hence concessions to them must be made and as a result, they become less radical. Peasants, on the other hand, become proportionately, and finally even absolutely, less important through technical changes in agriculture. As bargaining strength de-

clines, their demands continue to be frustrated. As a result, they may tend to become more radical over time.

Factors Other Than Stratification Affecting the Establishment of Low Status Movements

The utility of a stratification and mobility approach in understanding low status movements has been emphasized deliberately in this chapter. However, just as we know that the individual's behavior is influenced by factors which either reinforce or cut across class factors, so too in the case of collective mobility efforts, do factors other than those related to stratification reinforce or impede such efforts.

In the previous two sections, attention has been drawn to the various effects of internal stratification on collective mobility efforts. Other factors internal to these groups are also important in determining their potential for organization. This is quite apart from the many *external* factors which affect these movements, especially (1) "sponsorship," (2) position-change produced by changes in the economy and the political structure and, above all else in our opinion, (3) the attitude and repressive or diversionary power of the ruling elite.

These internal factors include the following:

1. Whether a web of community relationships—*Gemeinschaft*—supports cohesion based upon the more limited interest in group mobility. While a community base and its traditional exchange and cooperative mechanisms may not necessarily serve as a good model for more goal-oriented cooperation (cf. Dore, 1971), on the whole it is helpful. Working-class militancy has been related to this condition, as in their own isolated communities among miners and dockers (Kerr and Siegel, 1954); and the civil rights movement in the U.S. clearly gained much from its base in closely-knit rural communities, or urban ghettos, with their "shared grievances," as Kerr and Siegel have called them.
2. The presence of cleavages which cut across and divide classes is harmful to organization. Race and differences in ethnic background have weakened the organizational unity of the U.S. labor movement until recently; religious differences have divided the labor movements of Holland and other West European, as well as Latin American countries; while nationality differences divided the Croatian from the Serbian peasant in the interwar period, and Slovak from Czech (Jackson, 1974).
3. The presence of cleavages in the society other than class, but paralleling it, will tend to strengthen the possibility of organization. In preindependence Africa as well as in India, trade union formation was reinforced by the fact that the employer was often not only of a different race but, politically, also a conqueror. In China and in Yugoslavia, as in all of Eastern Europe before 1918, the organization of peasants into a truly radical force was likewise reinforced by the presence of a national enemy who at the same time acted as a class oppressor or was allied with the class oppressor (Johnson, 1962).
4. The exposure of the population to egalitarian ideas and to experiences with organization—especially to service in the armed forces—often ex-

ercises a mobilizing effect. Many Mexican peasants had been to the U.S. before the Revolution of 1910 and had compared its relatively more liberal spirit with that of Mexico, while service in the disastrous Chaco War helped to mobilize Bolivian peasants. Service in the Allied armies stimulated African workers both after World War I and, especially, after World War II (Davies, 1966).

5. Cultural differences in values between societies—in the intensity with which equality is desired and with which ascriptive criteria are rejected—may greatly affect the nature of movements. This point has been elaborated by Lipset in his contrast of U.S. and European working-class movements (Lipset, 1967:Chapter 5).

6. What some call value differences and some label personality traits have been related to the "culture of poverty." The difficulty experienced by some of the "lower classes," as Banfield calls them, in postponing gratification, and in their lack of trust, have been said to make it difficult for peasants (and lower-class blacks) to organize (Banfield, 1968). This was said at an earlier period about the lower working-class. But today, in the case of the affluent society, the value problem for their organizations, the trade unions, is seen to lie in the increasingly individualistic mobility strivings of their members rather than in the old-fashioned vices of incontinence (Goldthorpe, et al., 1969). Whether or not there are personality traits characteristic of peasants, in particular, thereby differentiating them from the urban working classes and making their organization more difficult, is certainly a hotly debated issue and worthy of serious research rather than the kind of poorly supported charge and countercharge which has characterized the argument so far.

V. SUCCESS AND THE FUTURE OF LOW STATUS MOVEMENTS

Moving to a discussion of the determinants of the success of low status movements and taking a look at what the future may hold for them, we can draw the following conclusions from the preceding discussion. To succeed, a low status movement needs one or more of the following external conditions in *addition to* certain conditions within the low status group itself:

1. The silent help of objective conditions which, through an increase in demand (whether for their labor or their political vote), increase the rewards of their positions, i.e., raise their status;

2. The help of sponsors;

3. An opposition which either chooses not to resist to the finish, as was true in the United Kingdom and the United States, or is too weak to do so and is therefore pushed aside, as was the case with the pre-revolutionary governments of China and Russia and the classes supporting them. The crucial importance, for the success or failure of revolution, of weaknesses in the ruling classes has long been recognized (Brinton, 1938). We postulate the same for the success and failure of collective mobility efforts.

These are severe conditions, and lead us to believe that the future of these movements, taking the world as a whole, is more likely to be dark than bright.

In industrialized countries, industrial labor movements did not achieve their aims, and did not even become firmly established, until the major break-through to industrialization itself had occurred. Increasing the living standards of, and obtaining political power for, the working classes came at the end of the nineteenth century or the first quarter of the twentieth, even though organized efforts to achieve these goals had been started over one hundred years earlier. For many workers in the U.S., it did not come until World War II. The goals of the movements were not reached for some time, and the movements themselves were weak. There is much reason to think that the countries presently attempting to industrialize—the so-called "developing," third world countries—will, in essence, also seek to curb their labor movements, and not satisfy their goals, just as the governments of the presently industrialized countries did in their time. "Supply" and "demand" conditions in both an economic and a political sense are frequently such as to enable the elites, and even post-revolutionary governments in developing countries, to repress or assure that independent labor and peasant movements will remain weak.

Fundamentally, those on top, even when benevolently inclined, do not want political rivals, or to have their plans for economic development exposed to the buffeting of yet one more pressure group. This is especially true for mass groups, the satisfaction of whose consumption demands would severely affect development plans. Where certain labor groups are in a strong bargaining position in a third world country—and we find islands of strength, such as the Chilean copper workers—their petitions for economic betterment, more education and prestige, and even political power, may have to be granted. But strong, independent organized groups of workers on a large scale have lower chances of developing.

The Soviet Union, in its early development may serve as a typical example. It put an end to the independent power of trade unions and organized workers as represented by the so-called "Worker Opposition" in the early 1920s. That policy decision was symbolized by the crushing of the 1921 Kronstadt rebellion. Immediately succeeding events within the Communist Party indicated that though the new government might act for the ultimate benefit of workers, it did not want them to make policy nor to exert pressure for higher consumption. This has been the policy of all socialist governments, with the possible exception of Yugoslavia. This failure of workers to have the right to participate in decisions was true of Cuba, a fact which has drawn severe criticism recently from a spate of marxist intellectuals (cf. Huberman and Sweezy, 1969).

Refusal to permit the existence of effective organizations of low status groups is true of all right wing governments: at the time of this writing, those of post-coup Chile, Guatemala, Brazil and the Dominican Republic may be used as examples. It is true even of those military governments with some claim to having a "modernizing" leftist bent. The Peruvian military regime, for example, has not permitted independent union militancy in its mines, nor among teachers, sugar workers and other erstwhile well organized groups (Quijano, 1971).

Perhaps most intriguing is the fate of trade unions in those developing countries where it looked for a time as if such movements would flourish. We refer to the ex-colonial countries of Africa and Asia in which nationalism, not socialism or communism, was the guiding ideology. Working-class movements originally seemed to show strength there. In their early stages, they were often nourished by the labor movements of the metropolitan countries: Great Britain,

France, and Holland. Even more importantly, they were stimulated by those essentially middle-class groups who were fighting for independence and needed well organized mass support. The group mobility aspirations of these middle-class elements, often lower level civil servants and professionals, should not be overlooked as an element underlying their more idealistic nationalism. During the 1940s and 1950s, Tunisia, the British African colonies and mandates (Ghana, Nigeria, Kenya and Tanzania), French West Africa, Ceylon, Indonesia, and India all showed a very considerable degree of working-class organization despite the fact that these countries were and are primarily agricultural, and even though structural weaknesses in their movements were detectable (Millen, 1963; Galenson, 1959).

Today it is clear that the exigencies of development in a setting of poverty, and the need to achieve national integration in the face of centrifugal forces, are leading most of these countries to some form of one-party centralized and even dictatorial government. Generally, their political history seems to be divisible into three stages: the exhileration and freedom of independence; followed by a tightening of controls under a charismatic nation-founding leader (Nkrumah, Sukarno, Bourguiba, Ben Bella); and most recently followed by a wave of military regimes. While not much information is available on the precise status of trade unions under the new regimes, the general impression is that their power and importance is far less than it was in the last few years of the colonial regimes. For example, making a year-by-year comparison of entries under "Trade Unions" in the annual index of "West Africa" (a weekly periodical) makes this dramatically clear. In the last few years, the number of entries has declined dramatically. Their power turns out to have been transitory; dependent on the unique combination of the relative tolerance in the declining years of the colonial authorities on the one hand and the temporary need which certain middle-class elements had for mass organizations until they could seize power under the doctrine of nationalism, on the other (for Africa, see Davies, 1966).

Much the same can be asserted about peasant movements, with even fewer reservations. The few peasant movements which do exist at all in the developing countries are generally government controlled, Mexico being the outstanding example. If there is a competitive political system—as there used to be in Chile—the competing peasant federations could not survive without (middle-class) party support. The rural cooperatives set up in Africa in the 1960s, and in Eastern Europe after World War I, are and were substantially part of a government production plan, and a plan for rural development. While there may be some elements of local self-government, there is no question of their becoming independent forces, sufficiently powerful to exert effective pressure for the elevation of the status of their members beyond that envisaged in government plans. The lack of complete compatibility between development, especially investment policy, and the existence of strong mass movements claiming economic and political improvements has long been recognized (Galenson, 1959; Kerr et al., 1960; Millen, 1963). Today the claim even to cultural elevation is being questioned, as the impossibility of meeting the cost of universal education becomes recognized.

This leaves us with the movements in the developed countries of the latter-day capitalist variety. As for the European "peasant" of yesteryear: the position of low status farmers and of their movements is clearly being eroded, as the decisions of, and the strains within, the European Economic Community make clear. In the United States, similarly, only high status, large scale farmers are doing well.

Trade unions as organizations are probably maintaining their power for the time being in the West, but they no longer represent the poorest and lowest status sectors of their societies. In many countries—France is an example—they are increasingly involved in governmental economic decision-making. But even here, the growing spread of automation and its displacement of workers as individuals, threatens to be one of those impersonal, structural drifts which will simply eliminate low status positions rather than raise them. This will weaken the unions representing them. It will mean also that individuals of low status (youth looking for jobs, for instance, or, in the case of Europe, immigrant labor from Southern Europe and North Africa) will be unemployed to a substantial extent and thus, as individuals, lose status.

Over the years since the industrial revolution, the working classes of the developed countries have increased in status. This has been due as much to the operation of impersonal forces or to the efforts of other groups interested in the welfare of the working-class as through their own organized efforts, though these of course did play a part. However, their organizations—labor parties and trade unions—are ceasing to possess the distinctive characteristics of low status movements to the extent they once did: understandably so, since the goal of raising status has been achieved. In the case of the political parties, they cannot and do not remain pure in class membership. (We refer to the Social Democratic Party of Germany, Britain's Labour Party, etc.) They would decline in size as shrinkage takes place in the proportion of blue collar workers. And such shrinkage is occurring even if we include all those of lower rank in any organization, whether blue or white collar, as Dahrendorf (1959) would have us define class.

The trade unions, the economic manifestation of the working-class movement, have few characteristics today basically differentiating them from the organizations of other economic groups concerned with pay, working conditions, job security and the limitation of entry rights. Admittedly, trade unions maintain some superficial distinctions in that they are often larger than other bodies of this kind. They do press their economic claims more explicitly in highly visible negotiations with highly visible employers and industries. Unlike entities such as the American Medical Association and the Natonal Education Association, unions do not pretend to perform professional functions apart from those of defending and increasing the economic status of their members. Their members do continue to be among those with lower status. In all this, the trade union movement is still to a limited extent different from associations of other job holders who are seeking to protect or improve the status of their positions. But these differences are matters of degree, not of principle.

The characteristics which once distinguished the working-class movements in the United States and in other western countries, are no longer present or are present only in highly attenuated form. A high degree of "involvement" of those who were members, both behaviorally and in terms of enthusiasm and emotional pitch; a low degree of bureaucratization, of centralization and hierarchy in organization; the feeling of being part of a larger movement whose purpose was to change some of the basic values and institutions of society; the sense of being a movement in mortal combat; occasional visions of substantial changes in the structure of society: all these have given way to the so-called "mature" union described by some and mourned by others (Ross, 1964).[3] In terms of sheer militancy, at least as measured by strike statistics, there has been a very substantial decline indeed (Ross and Hartman, 1960:Chapter 5). And an increasing percentage of strikes are unauthorized by the union, and are in part a rebellion against the union, particularly by its lowest status members, as in the case of "wildcat" strikes by black assembly-line workers in the auto industry in the U.S. or by North African workers in the auto plants of France.

This "embourgeoisement" of the organization is paralleled by the "embourgeoisement" of the individual worker. As we have just noted: there are admittedly sectors of the working-class which continue to be disaffected, some parts of the black working-class, for example. In the auto industry, black unions rivaling the UAW have sprung up in certain localities, and studies of unemployed black workers are particularly poignant in portraying their continuing disaffection (Leggett, 1968). There may also be occasional eruptions of militancy: France in the summer of 1968 is often cited, but six years later nothing on that scale has happened again. There may also be eruptions of white working-class backlash against black claims, but this is an indication that these white workers are defending a privileged position against the less privileged.

A class conscious working-class movement with revolutionary potential, of the kind envisaged in the early part of this century, is over and done with: atrophied by success in economically developed societies; subject to repression by governments of all political colors in the developing nations. As Goldthorpe and his colleagues have correctly pointed out, this by no means implies that unions as such will disintegrate in the capitalist countries, nor that working-class people will become precisely like others in life-styles and values (Goldthorpe et al., 1969). But clearly, what remains is not "the movement" in the old sense.

We must conclude that it was only in the relatively liberal, capitalist and, of course, rich countries of the West that movements of some low status groups were given ample scope for limited periods of time. In economies of scarcity, and in polities of instability, including post-revolutionary ones, such movements would likely not be allowed to thrive.

The central issue of this chapter has been the elevation of those positions which are low in status. The organizations and movements of low status people is only one means to achieve upward mobility. Liberal-capitalist governments permit such movements. But in the long run, these systems may not be most effective in structuring society to accomplish the basic aim of rapidly and lastingly elevating the economic, political, prestige, and cultural status of the least privileged. Indeed, it may be that different forms of government are differentially effective in each of these areas: the socialist countries more efficient in some respects, and for some groups, the predominantly capitalist societies more for others. But in neither type of society are classical working-class, or peasant movements, likely to play a powerful role over any lengthy period of time.

---

[3] Footnote three of Ross' article contains references to those who "mourn," such as Paul Jacobs, Sidney Lens, Paul Sultan, B.J. Widick, and others.

REFERENCES

Adams, J.S.
  1966 "Inequality in social exchange," in L. Berkowitz (ed.), Advances in
        Experimental Social Psychology. Vol. 2. New York: Academic Press.
Almond, G. and J.S. Coleman, et al.
  1960 The Politics of the Developing Areas. Princeton, New Jersey: Prince-
        ton University Press.
Anderson,C.W.
  1967 Politics and Economic Change in Latin America. Princeton, New Jer-
        sey: Van Nostrand.
Anweiler, O.
  1958 Die Raetebewegung in Russland, 1905–1921. Leiden, Holland: E.J. Brill.
Banfield, E.C.
  1958 The Moral Basis of a Backward Society. Glencoe, Ill.: Free Press.
  1968 The Unheavenly City. Boston: Little, Brown and Co.
Berger, B.
  1960 Working Class Suburbs: A Study of Auto Workers in Suburbia. Berke-
        ley: University of California Press.
Bernstein, E.
  1898 Evolutionary Socialism: A Criticism and Affirmation. 1961 Edition.
        New York: Schocken Books.
Blau, P.
  1968 "Social exchange," in International Encyclopedia of Social Sciences.
        Volume 7. New York: Crowell-Collier and Macmillan.
Bottomore, T.B.
  1966 Classes in Modern Society. New York: Pantheon.
Brin, H.
  1928 "Zur Akademiker und Intellektuellen-frage in der Arbeiterbewegung."
        PhD Dissertation, Faculty of Philosophy. Basle: University of Basle.
Brinton, C.
  1938 Anatomy of Revolution. 1965 Edition. Englewood Cliffs, New Jersey:
        Prentice-Hall.
Burnham, J.
  1941 The Managerial Revolution, New York: John Day.
Carr, E.H.
  1952 The Bolshevik Revolution, 1917–1923. Volume II. Baltimore: Penguin
        Books.
Chamberlain, N.W.
  1965 The Labor Sector. New York: McGraw-Hill.
Cole, G.D.H.
  1952 History of Socialist Thought. London: Macmillan.
Craig, W.W.
  1969 "Peru: the peasant movement of La Convencion," in H.A. Landsberger
        (ed.), Latin American Peasant Movements. Ithaca, New York: Cornell
        University Press.
Dahrendorf, R.
  1959 Classes and Class Conflict in Industrial Society. Stanford, California:
        Stanford University Press.

Daniels, R. V.
 1961   "Intellectuals and the Russian Revolution." American Slavic and East
        European Review 10(April) :270–278.
Davies, I.
 1966   African Trade Unions. Harmondsworth, Middlesex, England: Penguin
        Books.
Davies, J.C.
 1962   "Toward a theory of revolution." American Sociological Review. (27) :
        5–19.
Dean, L.R.
 1954   "Social integration, attitudes and union activity." Industrial and Labor
        Relations Review 8(October) :48–58.
Dew, E.
 1969   Politics in the Altiplano. Austin: University of Texas Press.
de Kadt, E.
 1970   Catholic Radicals in Brazil. London and New York: Oxford University
        Press.
Dore, R.F.
 1971   "Modern cooperatives in traditional communities," in P. Worsley (ed.),
        Two Blades of Grass: Rural Cooperatives in Agricultural Moderniza-
        tion. Manchester, England: University of Manchester Press.
Draper, T.
 1970   The Rediscovery of Black Nationalism. New York: Viking Press.
Franz, G.
 1965   Der Deutsche Bauernkrieg. Darmstadt, Germany: H. Gentner.
Fuchs, V.R.
 1967   "Redefining poverty and redistributing income." The Public Interest
        No. 8 (Summer) :88–95.
Galenson, W. (ed.)
 1959   Labor and Economic Development. New York: Wiley.
Goldthorpe, J.H. and D. Lockwood
 1963   "Affluence and the British class structure." Sociological Review 11
        (July).
Goldthorpe, J.H., D. Lockwood, F. Bechhofer and J. Platt
 1969   The Affluent Worker and the Class Structure. Cambridge, England:
        Cambridge University Press.
Gurr, T.R.
 1970   Why Men Rebel. Princeton, New Jersey: Princeton University Press.
Hammond, T.T.
 1957   Lenin on Trade Unions, 1893–1917. New York: Columbia University
        Press.
Homans, G.C.
 1961   Social Behavior: Its Elementary Forms. New York: Harcourt, Brace
        and World.
Huberman, L. and P.M. Sweezy
 1970   Socialism in Cuba. New York and London: Monthly Review Press.
Hutton, J.H.
 1946   Caste in India. Cambridge, England: Cambridge University Press.
International Institute of Labour and Social Studies
 1971   Labour Participation in Management: Selected Bibliography, 1950–
        1970. Geneva: International Institute for Labour and Social Studies.

Jackson, G.D.
  1966   Comitern and Peasant in East Europe, 1919–1930. New York: Columbia University Press.
  1972   "Peasant political movements in Eastern Europe," in H.A. Landsberger (ed.), Rural Protest. London and New York: Macmillan.
Johnson, C.
  1962   Peasant Nationalism and Communist Power. Stanford, Ca.: Stanford University Press.
Keller, S.
  1963   Beyond the Ruling Class. New York: Random House.
Kerr, C., J.T. Dunlop, F.H. Harbison and C.A. Myers
  1960   Industrialism and Industrial Man: The Problem of Labor and Management in Economic Growth. Cambridge, Mass.: Harvard University Press.
Kerr, C. and A. Siegel
  1954   "The interindustry propensity to strike: an international comparison," in R. Dubin and A. Ross (eds.), Industrial Conflict. New York: McGraw-Hill.
Kramer, R.
  1969   Participation of the Poor. Englewood Cliffs, New Jersey: Prentice-Hall.
Kuhn, J.W.
  1971   "Engineers and their unions," in A.A. Blum, et al., White Collar Workers. New York: Random House.
Landsberger, H.A.
  1969a "The role of peasant movements and revolts in development," in H.A. Landsberger (ed.), Latin American Peasant Movements. Ithaca, New York: Cornell University Press.
  1969b "Chile: a vinyard workers, strike," in H.A. Landsberger (ed.), Latin American Peasant Movements. Ithaca, New York: Cornell University Press.
  1970   "Time, persons, doctrine: the modernization of the Church in Chile," in H.A. Landsberger (ed.), The Church and Social Change in Latin America. Notre Dame, Indiana, and London: Notre Dame University Press.
  1972   "Trade unions, peasant movements and social movements as voluntary action," in D.H. Smith and R.D. Reddy (eds.), Voluntary Action Research. Lexington, Mass.: D.C. Heath and Company, Lexington Books.
  1973   "Labor and peasant movements as sources of voluntary organizations and instruments of class mobility," in D.H. Smith (ed.), Voluntary Action Research: 1973. Lexington, Mass. and London: D.C. Heath and Company.
  1974   "Peasant unrest: themes and variations," in H.A. Landsberger (ed.), Rural Protest: Peasant Movements and Social Change. London and Geneva: Macmillan and International Institute for Labour and Social Studies.
Landsberger, H.A. and C.H. de Alcantara
  1971   "From violence and pressure-group politics and cooperation: a Mexican case study," in P.M. Worsley (ed.), Two Blades of Grass: Rural Cooperatives in Agricultural Modernization. Manchester, England: University of Manchester Press.

Landsberger, H.A. and C.H. Hewitt
  1970 "Ten sources of weakness and cleavage in Latin American peasant movements," in R. Stavenhagen (ed.), Agrarian Problems and Peasant Movements in Latin America. Garden City, New York: Anchor Books, Doubleday.
Landsberger, H.A. and B.H. Landsberger
  1974 "The English peasant revolt of 1381," in H.A. Landsberger (ed.), Rural Protest: Peasant Movements and Social Change. London and Geneva: Macmillan and International Institute for Labour and Social Studies.
Leggett, J.C.
  1968 Class, Race and Labor: Working-Class Consciousness, Detroit. New York: Oxford University Press.
Lenski, G.
  1966 Power and Privilege. New York: McGraw-Hill.
Lipset, S.M.
  1967 The First New Nation. Anchor Books. Garden City, New York: Doubleday.
Lipset, S.M. and R. Bendix
  1959 Social Mobility in Industrial Society. Berkeley: University of California Press.
Longworth, P.
  1974 "The Pugachev revolt," in H.A. Landsberger (ed.), Rural Protest: Peasant Movements and Social Change. London and Geneva: Macmillan and International Institute for Labour and Social Studies.
Lorwin, V.R.
  1954 The French Labor Movement. Cambridge, Mass.: Harvard University Press.
Lozovsky, A.
  1935 Marx and the Trade Unions. New York: International Publishers.
Luce, S.
  1894 Histoire de la jacquerie d'après des documents inédits. Revised Edition. Paris: H. Champion.
Marx, K.
  1964 "The chartists," New York Daily Tribune, August 25, 1852 as cited in T.B. Bottomore, Elites and Society. New York: Basic Books.
Mayo, E.
  1945 Social Problems of an Industrial Civilization. Boston: Graduate School of Business Administration, Harvard University.
Michels, R.
  1959 Political Parties. First Published in English in 1915. New York: Dover Publications, Inc.
Millen, B.H.
  1963 The Political Role of Labour in Developing Countries. Washington, D.C.: The Brookings Institution.
Mills, C.W.
  1956 The Power Elite. New York: Oxford University Press.
Moore, B., Jr.
  1966 Social Origins of Dictatorship and Democracy: Lord and Peasant in the Making of the Modern World. Boston: Beacon Press.
Morris, J.O.
  1967 Elites, Intellectuals and Consensus: A Study of the Social Question and

the Industrial Relations System in Chile. Ithaca, New York: New York State School of Industrial and Labor Relations, Cornell University.

Mousnier, R.
1960   Peasant Uprisings in Seventeenth Century France, Russia and China. New York: Harper and Row. Also published in London by Allen and Unwin, 1971.

Moynihan, D.P.
1969   Maximum Feasible Misunderstanding. New York: Free Press.

National Advisory Commission on Civil Disorders
1968   Report of the Commission. New York: Bantam Books.

Olsen, M.
1968   The Logic of Collective Action. New York: Schocken Books.

Parsons, T., R.F. Bales and E. Shils
1953   Working Papers in the Theory of Action. Glencoe, Ill.: Free Press.

Pelling, H.
1969   A History of British Trade Unionism. Harmondsworth, Middlesex, England: Penguin Books.

Perlman, S.
1928   A Theory of the Labor Movement. New York: Macmillan.

Quijano, A.O.
1971   "Nationalism and capitalism in Peru: a study of neo-imperialism." Monthly Review No. 3, 23 (July–August) :1–122.

Rees, A.J.
1954   "Industrial conflict and business fluctuations," in A. Kornhauser, R. Dubin and A. Ross (ed.), Industrial Conflict. New York: McGraw-Hill.

Rochester, A.
1942   Lenin on the Agrarian Question. New York: International Publishers.

Rogoff, N.
1953   Recent Trends in Occupational Mobility. Glencoe, Ill.: The Free Press.

Ross, A.M.
1964   "Labor organization and the labor movement in advanced industrial society." Virginia Law Review (50) :1359–1385.

Ross, A.M. and P.T. Hartman
1960   Changing Patterns of Industrial Conflict. New York: Wiley.

Runciman, W.G.
1967   Relative Deprivation and Social Justice. Berkeley: University of California Press.

Sayles, L.R. and G. Strauss
1967   The Local Union. Revised Edition. New York: Harcourt, Brace and World.

Schram, S.R.
1969   The Political Thought of Mao Tse-tung. Revised Edition. New York: Praeger.

Schumpeter, J.
1951   Imperialism and Social Classes. Clifton, New Jersey: Augusta M. Kelley, Inc.

Seton-Watson, H.
1967   Eastern Europe Between the Wars, 1918–1941. New York: Harper and Row.

Siefer, G.
   1964   The Church and Industrial Society. London: Darton, Longman and
          Todd.
Smelser, N.J.
   1963   Theory of Collective Behavior. New York: Free Press of Glencoe.
Smelser, N.J. and S.M. Lipset (eds.)
   1966   Social Structure and Mobility in Economic Development. Chicago:
          Aldine.
Sorokin, P.A.
   1927   Social and Cultural Mobility. 1964 Edition. New York: Macmillan.
Sturmthal, A.
   1964   Workers' Councils: A Study of Workplace Organization on Both Sides
          of the Iron Curtain. Cambridge, Mass.: Harvard University Press.
Tawney, R.H.
   1931   Equality. 1964 Edition. London: Allen & Unwin.
Thompson, E.P.
   1964   The Making of the English Working Class. New York: Pantheon.
Townsend, P. and N. Bosanquet (eds.)
   1972   Labour and Inequality. London: Fabian Society.
Turner, F.C.
   1971   Catholicism and Political Development in Latin America. Chapel Hill:
          University of North Carolina Press.
Turner, R.H.
   1960   "Sponsored and contest mobility and the school system." American
          Sociological Review 25(December):855–867.
White, R.A.
   1969   "Mexico: the Zapata movement and the Mexican revolution," in H.A.
          Landsberger (ed.), Latin American Peasant Movements. Ithaca, New
          York: Cornell University Press.
Wildman, W.A.
   1971   "Teachers and collective bargaining," in A. Blum, et al., White Collar
          Workers. New York: Random House.
Wilkie, R.
   1971   San Miguel: A Mexican Collective Ejido. Stanford, Ca.: Stanford Uni-
          versity Press.
Wolf, E.R.
   1969   Peasant Wars of the Twentieth Century. New York: Harper and Row.
Woodward, C.V.
   1957   The Strange Career of Jim Crow. Galaxy Books. New York: Oxford
          University Press.
Worsley, P. (ed.)
   1971   "Introduction," in P. Worsley (ed.), Two Blades of Grass: Rural Co-
          operatives in Agricultural Modernization. Manchester, England: Man-
          chester University Press.
Young, M.
   1959   The Rise of the Meritocracy. New York: Random House.

CHAPTER **19**

Industrial Relations in Japan

Bernard Karsh

University of Illinois, Urbana–Champaign

Japanese industrial relations are characterized by one salient fact: a stratification system based essentially upon non-occupational criteria. This in turn has
given rise to three major characteristics of Japanese employment relations: (1)
a so-called "life-long employment" system, (2) payment of wages and retirement
benefits according to age, education, and length of service (*Nenkō*) rather than
job distinctions reflecting workers' direct production contributions, and (3) a
trade union system which organizes workers primarily into single entity unions,
co-extensive with the enterprise which employs them. The combined effect of
these factors suggests that Japan's system of industrial relations is notably different from that of other industrial countries. This chapter will examine each of
these characteristic features.

THE TRADITIONAL STATUS SYSTEM

Rank by *social* position rather than occupational criteria is deeply rooted in all
aspects of Japanese life—in the family, society, community, and employment.
Human relationships are defined and evaluated on the basis of status related to
group membership. With the head of the family on top, ideally, relationships
between husband and wife, between parents and children, among brothers and
sisters, have always been framed in terms of superior and subordinate in social
or traditional rank. Parents by definition and irrespective of all other considerations rank higher than children and husbands higher than wives. Though primo-
geniture was officially abolished following World War II, the oldest son still has
superior rank, both in the distribution of family properties and in the succession to an occupation. Younger sons and daughters have always been in subordinate and neglected positions in the family, as well as in their status in the larger
society.

I am grateful to M. Tsuda, Professor of Economics, Hitopsubashi University, Tokyo;
H. Kawada, Professor of Economics, Keio University, Tokyo; and N. Funabashi, Professor of
Economics, Hoshi University, Tokyo, for substantial aid in providing basic materials upon
which this chapter is based. For a more extensive discussion of the topic, see Okochi, Karsh
and Levine (1974).

In community life, the social ranking and status of warrior (*samurai*-farmer-artisan-merchant [*shi-no-ko-sho*]) established in the feudal era has since been maintained and had great influence upon both rural and urban life. In addition, there have been kinds of rank, such as the old boss-controlling (*oya-bun-kobun*) system which still prevail in political, social, and even in industrial and labor relations, as well as in business. Thirty-four different ranks and grades characterized the modern Japanese Army until its reorganization in the 1950s along the lines of the American Army ranking system with seventeen formal status ranks.

The source of identity for Japanese workers is not the job or the occupation as is common in Western countries and particularly in the United States. Rather, it is the firm, the enterprise to which he belongs. Thus, one does not ask a Japanese, "What do you do?" or "What kind of work are you in?" One asks, "What company do you work for?" The Japanese word *uchi* is commonly translated as house or one's home or the whole family. It symbolizes the intimacy of group relations and not the physical structure. However, the perception of the group leads a Japanese to say *uchi-no* (my house) when referring to the workplace, the company, or the office to which he is attached. The company is not perceived as an objective entity such as a business enterprise with which one has some kind of contractual relationship. Rather, the company for which "I" work is always perceived as "my" or "our company."[1] The traditional household (*ie*) and the system by which households were linked in kin-confederations (*dō-zoku*) were other basic expressions of the corporate group.[2]

The extension of the family idea to industry also leads the Japanese worker to refer to the person of his employer and often to his immediate superior as *oyaji*, literally a term used by an adult son to refer to his father.

Thus, ideally, social rankings within and between relatively closed corporate groups rather than occupation or job is at the base of Japan's stratification system. Under this system based on age, education, and length of service, industrial relations in Japan has acquired its particular characteristics and stability.[3]

However, there has always been a large gap between the ideal and reality. Industrial relations as a concept at first was based on the relationship of superior-inferior, at least after 1870 and up to the 1930s. Compassion and obedience based on paternalism were considered most ideal. This was clearly a kind of human relations that rested on the ranks of ruler and ruled, and derived from premises quite contrary to the idea that all human beings were created equal, as stated by Fukuzawa Yukichi (1948) in the early period. The belief apparently was that industrial relations in Japan could be stabilized only by ordering

---

[1] For elaboration, see Nakane (1967b:32–33). However, the idea of *uchi* as translated has been abbreviated and in some ways distorts the original Japanese meaning as given here.

[2] For good summaries of many of the interpretations of the role of *ie* and *dōzoku* in Japanese organization, see Nakane (1967a) and Fukutake (1967).

[3] The family analogy may lead one to conclude, as Abegglen (1958) does, that Japan's industrial system is unique. However, the contemporary arrangements which are consistent with the idealized tradition are a relatively recent development and did not commonly exist in the feudal era. Further, as both Cole (1971b) and Taira point out, these apparently unique patrimonial industrial relations forms have clear functional equivalents in the U.S. and probably in other industrial societies as well. See Cole (1971a) and Taira (1970). However, the one factor of Japanese industrial relations which does appear to be unique, namely, a stratification system not based on occupation, is not dealt with either by Cole or Taira.

human relations according to high and low rank. At the time, the Factory Law (adopted in 1911) was being discussed in Japan. The major point of discussions was how to avoid running the risk of disturbing traditional social relationships or, in other words, of upsetting the order of control of labor in terms of social status.

There was considerable interest in the question of what the industrial relationships should be. Intellectuals in Japan thought that the labor movement then spreading over Europe and the resulting unstable industrial relations could be attributed entirely to the egalitarian ideas which were widely disseminated. The whole of Japanese business society believed in guarding against the enforcement of the new Factory Law and in maintaining traditional human relations. This opposition was in great part based on the surmise that enforcement of the Law might bring about the rise of industrial relations based upon egalitarian ideas. In substance, there was strong hope for an industrial relationship of a unique Japanese type, linked with traditional social relations, and for labor-management stability based on "paternal warmheartedness between master and servant." However, the more intense this hope became, the more difficult it was for actual social relations in industry to be placed within a concept of hierarchical rank, especially after the end of the World War I and the development of the International Labour Organization.

THE EMERGENCE OF "LIFE-TIME" EMPLOYMENT

Through the Meiji and Taisho Eras, that is, from the 1860s to at least 1918, workers in Japan were highly mobile. The more skilled the worker, the more frequently he moved. Since at that time, a worker's only chance to obtain higher wages and promotion to higher rank was to get a new job, whether old or young, skilled or unskilled, he moved if he had the opportunity. In effect, there were actually open, horizontal labor markets according to occupation. To move from one job to another was quite a natural and even respectable way of living, and those who would not move were regarded as unable and below average in skill. As the terms "drifting artisan" or "wandering" craftsman, generally used in those days, indicate, a worker in the Western sense of free labor was free only insofar as he drifted and wandered.

Undoubtedly, there were some differences in labor mobility, depending on whether the occupation was a traditional Japanese craft or was a skill based on Western technology. However, it is clear that the rate of labor mobility was especially high, particularly among male workers.

Moreover, this mobility was closely associated in many ways with the life of workers. For each occupation, "horizontal" wage rates based on skill and experience existed in labor markets which were wider than an individual factory or enterprise. Older workers did not necessarily receive higher wages as in the present wage system. Rather, wage rates were determined by the ranking of an occupation or by the grade of skill within an occupation without relationship to years of service in the same firm and without a necessary relationship to age. As a worker's years of service increased, he might be promoted, for example, from Class C to Class B in the skill classification of a specific occupation, and, with such a promotion, he might be paid a higher wage rate. But as long as he worked in the same occupation and his job remained in the same skill rank as that of his fellow workers, his wage was also the same and was not related to his years of service in the same rank. Thus, until the early 1920s, Japan's wage system closely resembled the Western model.

If there were differences in wage rates by enterprise for the same occupation, or if there were dissatisfactions within a skill group, the workers commonly moved. They suffered no disadvantages by moving as they were paid according to their ability or skill, wherever they might go. Mobility not only strengthened their sense of independence and self-respect, but it also resulted in the maintenance of wages at a reasonably high level. Average wages, except for female workers, were much higher than was the case after the mid-1920s. An indication of the prevailing wage level was in the common expression, "fifteen-days of work maintains you for a month." Although wages then were clearly lower than in Western countries, they were high enough for a skilled worker to maintain a sizable family.

With mobility so encouraging their spirit of independence and pride, workers believed that wherever they might go, the sun and rice were waiting for them. In a sense, they enjoyed much more freedom than they did later when the practice of life-long service centering on new school graduates had developed in large enterprises. From an employer's point of view the more skilled the worker, the more difficult he was to handle since mobility gave rise to greater independence.

After World War I and during the period of the postwar depression, the structure of Japanese industry underwent a very substantial transformation. There was a rapid introduction of new production facilities in the name of "rationalization" centering in the large enterprise. New equipment and new production processes were introduced with the objective of escaping from the postwar recession, recapturing domestic markets, and recovering a larger share of world markets. Automatic machines, assembly-line mass production and product standardization were the results. Rationalization by cutting costs, lowering prices, strengthening competitive power, and stimulating mass purchasing power was considered the only way to weather the critical postwar situation.

As production processes in the large firms were divided into simplified jobs through the use of belt conveyors and assembly lines, the all-around skilled workers who had occupied key positions during the Meiji and the Taisho Eras became increasingly unnecessary. In their places, trained workers were needed as production operatives. Since workers of this type were entirely different from the old type, large enterprises in Japan rapidly developed personnel policies centered on acquiring and training their own new labor forces. This was carried out with considerable success.

If the old-type skilled craftsmen were doomed for gradual extinction the pressing need was for young operators trained in one-skill repetitive small operations. Moreover, these operators would require formal education in elementary, higher elementary, or junior high schools, and a record of good conduct. Thus, new school graduates replaced the older and more independent skilled craftsmen with high mobility, relatively high wages, and family responsibilities. The young workers were employed as unskilled laborers immediately upon graduation rather than at some other time of the year as jobs opened. Thus, the method of recruitment changed, with industry hiring only new school graduates through the schools at a specified time.

The recruits, upon completing their formal education (in most cases six years of compulsory education), were no longer trained under masters as before, but were hired directly as production workers in the large factories. Factory management assumed the responsibility for their acquisition of skills. Training of operatives for the new equipment actually was beyond the ability of the skilled workers of the master-craftsman type, so that each enterprise or factory established its own training facilities for new employees within the organization. Management then selected only those trainees who became proficient in skills, remained in good health, and were taken to have "sound" thoughts. Workers so selected gained the status of "regular" or "permanent" employees.

Since regular employees were trained intentionally as single-skill operatives for a particular type of equipment, that is, with largely nontransferable skills, needless to say they could no longer move from one work-place to another at any time they wished. The status of a permanent employee was based on the tacit understanding that the new school graduates, following their skill training within a factory, would continue to work as employees at that factory or enterprise for an indefinite period of time.

Thus there emerged a new type of labor force based on regular recruitment of new school graduates, training within industry, a permanent employment system, wages based on seniority and length of service, and welfare facilities provided by the big enterprises. As the new system developed among the large firms, workers ceased moving and horizontal labor markets gradually disappeared except in the small and medium-sized enterprise sector.[4]

Although the new system completely revamped previous employment practices, the guarantee of life-long employment was achieved, in practice, only gradually. However, the high turnover previously experienced now ceased, and older skilled workers were dismissed. When the workers gave up their mobility based upon their skills, they understandably demanded employment security in their work-place. In fact, even today the ideal of life-long employment has not been fully settled among the medium and small-scale enterprises, since the financial obligations involved are often considerably beyond the economic capabilities of such relatively small firms.

After the end of World War II, the norm of life-long employment spread not only among large enterprises but also among small and medium-sized businesses. Further, unlike the pre-1940 period, the rule is now applied generally not only to all sorts of white collar workers but to blue collar workers in production as well. The single exception is women employees. Since the 1870s, female workers were young, temporarily employed and from poor peasant families. After working for two or three years, most of them returned home, married, and for the most part, never appeared again as factory workers. As a result, from the beginning they had no attachment to a "life-long employment" system. It is notable that in the spinning, silk, and textile industries, which were the center of the industrial structure through the formative period of Japan's industrialization, 90% of the workers were women from poor peasant families. Later, beginning in the 1920s when the females worked in offices of governmental agencies and private companies, their employment also was of very short duration. It was common practice for the young women to work for a few years after graduation from elementary or junior high schools until they married. Even though the average number of years of employment for females has increased

---

[4] For elaboration, see Taira Koji (1970).

considerably since the end of World War II, it still remains quite short compared with averages in other countries. Consequently, life-long employment is still only applicable to male workers.

Employment security is relatively costly and was made economically feasible by the gradual introduction of the so-called seniority wage system (*Nenkō*). Throughout the prewar period, however, the system of periodic wage increases was not firmly established even in the large enterprises. Although in the case of white collar workers, as a rule, wage increases based on job rank were becoming common (following the practice for paying salaries of public employees), blue collar workers had no system of periodic wage raises. However, as permanent employment began to be fixed, it was inevitable that private industry would introduce a system of periodic wage increases to assure security for the labor force. Thus wages began to be paid to "regular" employees not on the basis of job, occupation, or skill level, but according to amount of education and years of service. Although the desirability of this wage system is not argued here, clearly it was the beginning of today's so-called seniority wage system.

Retirement allowances also were only gradually introduced for regular employees in the large enterprises. Finally, in order to secure the foundations of life-long employment, seasonal and year-end bonuses, and various types of welfare facilities such as company housing, recreation, medical care, and educational activities, which are financed by the employer were steadily adopted in the large enterprises. These were new, especially for male employees.

As mentioned, wages of skilled male workers of the craftsmen type had been relatively high during the Meiji and Taisho Eras. Wages had to be large enough to maintain the average worker with an average family. The high degree of labor mobility at that time made this possible. In contrast, the young recruits trained within the enterprise beginning in the 1920s were all single males, so that, as in the case of the temporary migrant women workers during the Meiji and Taisho periods, they were paid barely enough money to maintain themselves as unmarried persons. Undoubtedly, it was in order to prevent turnover and to encourage attachment of these workers to the enterprise that wages were gradually raised on a regular basis and various fringe benefits were devised. As a whole, however, the low starting wages of Japanese workers, together with the system of regular wage increases, took root in the large enterprises. In this manner, then, the so-called "household wage" previously provided was dissolved into a "single wage." One result often was the resort to home work by wives, children, and aged who earned small amounts to supplement the wages of the chief bread-winner thereby making it possible for a whole family to achieve a subsistence level of income. This was the origin of the so-called "multi-employee" household, an additional effective device for preventing worker turnover.

As the skilled craftsmen were being eliminated from the large enterprises, some were employed as labor relations staff people in enterprises, some, because of their all-around skills, found jobs in subcontract factories, and still others became active local leaders or bosses of labor unions. The last mentioned group dropped out of sight after the China-Japanese Incident of 1937, but in 1945 they often re-emerged, sometimes as elder advisors of the new postwar labor movement or as Socialist Party members of the Diet.

With the lack of mobility between the large and small and medium sized firms, only within the latter sector did workers move from factory to factory. In fact, once a worker began his work career in a small factory, he usually had to wander from one small firm to another for all of his working life and thus had a high rate of mobility. Young workers in small and medium size factories commonly did not settle down, faced as they were with low wages, no prospects for promotion and retirement benefit, and also no welfare facilities. They were constantly subject to the control of left-wing agitators or militant union leaders, or they withdrew from the labor force owing to the difficulties which they faced daily in trying to earn a livelihood.

PLANT-LEVEL STRATIFICATION SYSTEM

The elaboration of status distinctions carries over to the factory a substantially more elaborate formal status system than is found in American industry. White collar distinctions are immediately noted.

The job function of the white collar staff (the *shokuin*) is to carry out the policies established by and under the supervision of top management (Yoshino, 1968:Chapters 7, 8 and 9). This, of course, is not different from any modern management organization. However, Japanese white collar workers are formally superior to blue collar workers (*kōin*) in both status and function, and there is a well-defined gulf which the latter hardly ever bridges. This gulf is defined and reinforced in a number of ways.

First, there is a vertical status system for both the *shokuin* and the *kōin*. For example, the status system for the *shokuin* at one typical large-scale manufacturing company begins with the *minaraiin*, or apprentice staff, and continues upward through the *junkōin* (semi-junior employee), the *kōin* (junior employee), the *junshain* (semi-senior employee), and the *shain* (senior employee) ; above the *shain* are the positions of *fukusanji* (vice-councilor) and *sanji* (councilor), the highest position or status for the *shokuin*.

Kōin positions begin with the *minarai kōin*, or apprentice worker, at the lowest level and continue up the status ladder to third-class, second-class, first-class, and the upper-class *kōin* or worker. It is possible for a few competent second-, first-, and upper-class workers to be promoted to *kōin* positions in the *shokuin* category upon recommendation and under a merit-rating system.

Second, the *shokuin* are paid monthly salaries, whereas the *kōin* receive wages computed at a daily rate. Before World War II, only the *shokuin* received semiannual seasonal bonuses.

Third, there is a clear-cut difference between the *shokuin* and *kōin* in terms of location and size of residence which a company builds and provides for its employees. Many companies, in fact, provide residences only for the *shokuin* and have separate assembly and dining halls for the *shokuin* and *kōin*.

This distinction between the two functional groups has always been based upon the employees' level of formal education. Before World War II, this distinction was so well-defined that it corresponded almost completely with the pyramid-type structure of formal education levels. Those who received only six to ten years of education were doomed to stay at the *kōin* status throughout their lives, whereas those who received education beyond this level were employed as *shokuin*. Under the present educational system, most people who complete nine years of compulsory education or junior high school are employed as *kōin* or blue collar workers; persons with more education (high school or college) are hired for the clerical staff or *shokuin*.

The distinction between the *shokuin* and *kōin* by education level corresponds to a job function distinction in the industrial organization. At the company referred to earlier, both the president and the vice-president at the headquarters have the status of *sanji* (councilors). Under them are the department heads (*buchō*) at the company's headquarters, and the plant superintendents (*kojōchō*), all of whom have the status of vice-councilor (*fuku-sanji*). At each plant there are assistant superintendents (*jichō*), section chiefs (*kachō*), subsection chiefs (*kakarichō*), and subsection staff (*kakariin*). All of these are *shokuin* positions.

Under the *kakarichō* are *kōin* positions in each workshop, in the following order from the top down: the *kōchō*, chief worker, the *fukukōchō* or assistant chief worker, and the *kōin* or manual workers. In other companies, the *kōchō* and *fukukōchō* are often called *kumichō* (group chief), *gochō* (assistant group chief), and *hanchō* (crew chief). After World War II, one of the targets for which the labor movement strove was the abolition of job status discrimination, and as a result it disappeared in many companies. However, in the period of economic growth after 1952, it returned, and since 1965 it has developed into a job qualification system.

The several different employee positions within the *shokuin* and *kōin* groups vary in status and remuneration, and each position has particular characteristics. For the *kōin* there are four positions.

1. *Regular kōin employed following graduation from school.* A *kōin* may be classified as a regular employee, a temporary worker, or an outside worker. The regular employee group is further divided, one segment being composed of regular *kōin* who enter the group upon graduation from school. Compulsory education (elementary school) is the requirement for those who entered the labor force before World War II and junior high school for those who began work since the War. There are no variations in the educational requirements for factory workers. The regular *kōin* who are employed upon graduation from school are expected to work for the company for forty years, starting from age fifteen when they graduate until age fifty-five when they retire. Because of this expected long service, they are generally assumed to be the "key" workers in the factory.

2. *Regular kōin employed according to company needs.* Another type of regular employee is one who formerly worked for another company or who was hired by the company for the first time, depending on its need, and at a time other than following school graduation. Large enterprises tend to hire this type of personnel away from the small and medium sized companies, the medium sized companies tend to hire them away from the smaller ones, and the small firms hire them from each other. These factory workers who move from one company to another usually have particular occupational experience and thus are different from workers who are employed directly from school. These workers are called *chūtosaiyōsha*, for which there is no equivalent English word but which means literally "mid-term employee." This literal translation will be used here to identify these workers. In Western countries, workers of this type are usually considered to be regular employees, but in Japan they are regarded as irregular and inferior in

status to those who were employed immediately after their graduation from school.

3. *Temporary workers.* In addition to regular *kōin*, the enterprise employs temporary workers, also depending on the company's need. According to the definition in Article 21 of the Labor Standards Law, a temporary worker is one who is employed on a day-to-day basis or whose employment contract is for two months, subject to renewal. In actual practice, however, some temporary workers are employed by a company for many years. The work rules for temporary workers are quite different from those for the regular *kōin*, and although their job duties are similar to those of the regular workers, they can be discharged or laid off at any time. These temporary workers are usually hired from smaller firms or from farming villages.

4. *Outside workers.* The outside worker is not by definition an employee of the company; rather he is an employee of a subcontracting firm and therefore is paid by the latter, although he works in the parent company and uses its production equipment. In shipbuilding, these outside workers usually work in a crew under the regular *kōin*, although both groups work together in the shipyard.

Unfortunately there are no nation-wide statistics on the distribution of these four types of factory workers. According to a partial survey of several chemical companies, the proportion of regular workers employed by the companies varied from 11.4% to 62.7% (Fujita, 1965). An incomplete nation-wide survey conducted regularly by the Ministry of Labour, reports that temporary workers compose about 6% of the total manual labor force in manufacturing (Ministry of Labour, 1965), but as temporary workers employed for more than two months are excluded from the statistics, it is impossible to get a true picture of the percentage of temporary workers from these data. In reality, there may be far more temporary workers than the reported percentage implies. Nor are there any statistics on the number of outside workers. In the shipbuilding industry, the proportion of outside workers is greater than that of regular *kōin*. In any case, it is essential to note that "life-time employment" does not guarantee anyone a job for life, that it extends *only* to *regular* workers, estimated at not more than 35% of all workers in large scale industry and that is not the norm in medium and small scale enterprises.

The job hierarchy of the *shokuin* is based not only on the method of employment, as in the *kōin* category, but also on educational level. As a rule, these employees are graduates of high schools or of colleges and universities. The expectation is that the college graduates will eventually be promoted higher than merely to middle management, and they are carefully assigned to tasks where they will have special training on the job and will become familiar with various functions. High school graduates are expected to remain within the lower management staff to do certain types of clerical work. Female employees who have completed high school are not expected to work for the company for many years, and therefore most of them are assigned to lower grade clerical work or to a receptionist's job. Some clerical workers are hired temporarily according to the company's need, but use of this type of personnel is rare. They are usually assigned to cleaning, and other custodial work.

In Western countries, personnel administration policies are designed mainly for management and not much attention is paid to workers as an integral part of the industrial elite. In Japan, however, manpower development policies cover not only the managerial elite but also the *kōin* elite. This *kōin* elite is composed of the regular factory workers who are employed following their graduation from school and who are trained and given favored treatment by the company. The personnel administration policies described below are designed for regular factory workers.

Life-Time Employment

Workers who are employed following their graduation from school are designated regular employees and as a rule work continuously for the company until they reach retirement age. When the number of employees needs to be reduced for some reason, the temporary and outside workers are the first to be discharged; if more reduction is absolutely necessary, the mid-term employees are then dismissed. In this way the company protects the employment security of its regular employees. Life-time employment security is not explicitly written into labor contracts, work rules, or any other employment contracts, but it is a traditional employment practice which has been upheld by the courts in a series of decisions since 1955. If a regular employee is inadvertently placed on the discharge list, other regular employees raise strong objections and the incident often develops into a serious conflict between labor and management. As the mid-term employee *is* a regular employee, he too usually is eligible for life-time employment, but he is not as firmly established and protected as those who became regular employees upon school graduation.

Successive Promotion

When young people are employed upon school graduation, they have neither the occupational knowledge for the jobs nor any occupational experience, since compulsory education in Japan does not include training for specific vocations. Thus the company which hires new school graduates must train them. The large and medium-sized enterprises usually train employees for up to two years at the company facilities.

Employees enrolled in a company training program are regarded as students or apprentices and are supposed to acquire the necessary knowledge in the classroom and through practical experience in the training shop. Many of the training programs in operation within large enterprises qualify as schools officially certified by the Ministry of Education. When an employee completes his training, he is assigned to the lowest position in the workshop; his place in the job hierarchy is determined by the year he completes his training. The job to which he is assigned may be determined to some extent by any aptitude he demonstrates during his training course, but in many cases it is decided by the company's production management. A regular employee tends not to reject jobs or occupations in order to pursue a preferred job or occupation. Rather, he is always ready to move from one job to another, at the will and request of the company.

The new employee starts out on a simple job, under the guidance of senior employees; later he moves up to more difficult tasks. Therefore, length of service can be an index of his achievement, and the skill he acquires is not transferable to any other workplace or to any other company. This kind of occupational skill is quite different from the industrial skills in Western countries; it may be called the *nenkō* skill (skill improvement under the *nenkō* system).[5]

These regular employees are assigned to jobs with the assurance that they will progress from one job to another as they improve their skills, but their place in the hierarchy of regular employees and, therefore, the timing of their promotions is determined by the length of their service, not by the importance of their job duties or occupations. There are two types of promotion—status promotion and occupational promotion—and the two are well integrated. In both, length of service is the decisive factor. For example, in one company, a regular *kōin* assigned to his first job is given the status of a third-class worker. After more than six years of service, as a rule he moves up to become a second-class *kōin*; in ten years he becomes a first-class *kōin*; and after 25 years he is eligible to be promoted to upper-class *kōin* status. A *fukukōchō* (assistant chief worker) is appointed from among the second- and first-class *kōin*, and a *kōchō* (chief worker) from the upper-class *kōin* group. Thus regular factory workers employed upon their school graduation are guaranteed successive promotions to these higher positions on the basis of their years of service.

Progressive Wage Increases

As previously discussed, length of service also determines a worker's economic status. The initial wage rate of a regular employee and the increases he may expect depend upon the date of his school graduation. Thus any occupational experience that a midterm employee acquired before he was employed by the company tends to be discounted in his wages.

Before World War II, when large enterprises usually found new workers through personal contacts, there was considerable variation in beginning wage rates. After the War, the number of job-seekers who had completed middle school decreased, so that the labor market came to influence the beginning rate. However, the wage increase curve still varies greatly among companies.

The wage rate being discussed here is a daily rate for the *kōin* and a monthly salary for the *shokuin*; it is not an hourly rate for a specific job or occupation. Nor does it follow that employees with the same length of service receive exactly the same amount of pay. Instead there is a wage range based on a merit-rating system.

The wage level of employees reflects their positions in the job hierarchy. Regular employees hired upon their school graduation tend to be guaranteed wages higher than the wage-increase curve as their service to the company lengthens.

Retirement Allowance for Life-Time Support

The yearly wage increase makes it possible for the income of regular employees to keep pace with increases in their household expenses related to marriage, child-bearing, education, and so on. In this sense, wages are not an economic reward for service but rather are company support for the sustenance of em-

---

[5] For added details in English, see Tsuda (1965a, 1965b).

ployees and their families. The retirement allowance completes the company's support of its employees. Before World War II, children were required, under civil law, to support their parents, and the retirement allowance was sufficient for a retiring employee to rent land and build his own home. It was the ideal for a retired worker to build a house and live in it with his children, with the children providing the support for the parents. After the War, however, the family system changed, and children tended to become independent of their parents. Furthermore, the price of land rose enormously, as did home construction costs. Under these circumstances, companies now are unable to provide a lump-sum retirement allowance sufficient for an employee to build a suitable house, but the allowance still is important as a part of the company's life-time support of an employee and it is assumed to be sufficient to cover expenses for him and his wife for the rest of their lives. The allowance increases in proportion to length of service; it is far less for mid-term employees than for regular employees.

Welfare Facilities

The company usually provides dormitories for single employees and houses for married couples, dining halls, discount shops for commodities, assembly halls, gyms, recreational facilities, and cultural and study facilities. The cost of these facilities is not small. Although many companies have such welfare facilities, the number and extent vary with the size of the company; even small companies with less than 100 employees often have rather broad welfare programs.

Before World War II, these welfare facilities were provided primarily for regular employees, and although they have expanded since the War, they still benefit regular employees exclusively. Company houses are usually available only for long service.

Corporate-Group Ideology

Both Robert Cole (1971a:12–15) and Ezra Vogel (1967:107–111) have noted the strength of corporate groups in Japanese industry. Comparing Japan to other industrialized societies, Vogel (1967:107–108) remarks that "Japanese society is still composed of tight-knit groups with relatively few channels for contact and movement between groups. The commitment of an individual to his own group is much stronger than any commitment to a transcendant value system or to a professional, occupational, or union organization tying him to others occupying the same position in other groups." Cole, who worked in a Japanese factory, found it remarkable that his co-workers associated only among themselves during the lunch recess, despite the plant's location in a crowded factory area. Cole (1971a:13) states: "They knew none of the workers in the factory across the narrow street although for years they had been having baseball catches side by side at noon."

Personnel administration in Japanese industry operates to preserve these group distinctions. Yet the different employee groups must be integrated by some kind of ideology. The traditional family system provides this.

Though it is not necessary here to detail the Japanese family system, it is necessary to note that there were two Japanese family systems in the preindustrial period. One had a family ideology based on Confucianism which was wide-spread among the elite group constituting the warrior class. Under this system, the family members were subordinate to patriarchal authority. The other family system was rooted in village life and governed peasant families. Patriarchal authority existed but was not as strong as in the warrior class, and a cooperative relationship among the family members was dominant.[6] Thus, the Japanese family system has always emphasized patriarchal authority combined with co-operative relations. Traditional values of familism, unity of the social group, emphasis on place rather than individual qualification all emphasize the impor-tance of the corporate group in Japanese tradition (Nakane, 1970).

In the early stages of industrialization, the family ideology of the warrior (*samurai*) class prevailed in the personnel administration of government enter-prises. In the 1900s, after modern Japanese industry was established, the two ideologies were combined to create a family-nationalistic view (*kazoku-kokkakan*) which integrated the idea of subordination to authority with the idea of cooperation. Applied to industrial life, the idea of *keie-kazoku-shugi* or company-familism became the ideology which integrated the many subgroups comprising the work force in a Japanese factory.

A modern industrial establishment cannot be staffed and run exclusively by members of only one family. Accordingly, the family ideology, if it is ap-plied to a modern company in Japan, must be replicated by the employers. The kinship relation in a family appears as the life-time-employment commitment to workers, which is limited to employees actually hired by the company and does not include a guarantee of employment to their children. If the children are qualified to work for the company, they receive preferential treatment in the hiring process, thus reducing or eliminating the problem of manpower re-cruitment for the company. Furthermore, the patriarchal support of the house-hold appears again in the employer's commitment to lifetime sustenance of the regular worker and his family—more concretely, the *nenkō* wage and retire-ment allowance. In addition, the various kinds of welfare facilities serve this purpose. Successive promotion based on length of service is comparable to the fixed seniority order of a family about which an individual member can do nothing.

The system has its deficiencies. First, as mentioned, it applies completely only to regular employees hired upon school graduation—the "key employees." The mid-term employees enjoy some of the benefits of the system, but tempo-rary and outside workers are excluded and probably are the victims of a system which supports the employment security of others. Even those regular blue collar workers benefitted by the system cannot, however, bridge the status gulf between themselves and the *shokuin* because of their lower educational level, and they almost always are required to remain beneath the *shokuin* class. One way that a few able workers can achieve the higher status is through examina-tion, although here, too, the status gulf seems to be more consolidated than eliminated. Those who are fortunate enough to be promoted to a higher posi-tion are given the status of mid-term employees in their new positions, and this

---

[6] For a detailed discussion of these two types of family ideologies, see Kawashima (1950). For discussions of the importance of the corporate group in Japanese society, see Hall (1962) and Vogel (1967).

discrimination tends to discourage competition among employees for status or class promotion. The status system is reinforced by wide differentials in employment conditions among the large, medium-sized and small companies and by the fact that the employment conditions of temporary workers in large companies often are better than those of regular employees in small companies.

A second deficiency in the *nenkō* system stems from the family ideology of subordination to authority and cooperation. Before World War II, employees who violated work rules suffered severe penalties, the main purpose of which was to rid the company of those employees who offended the subordination principle. Key employees were protected by the system which controlled the promotion schedule and the number of openings in each category. Therefore, those employees rarely violated the rules or the principle. On the other hand, the mid-term employees had little expectation of promotion to higher positions, however long they might serve the company, and as a consequence they often were actively critical of the employer. Under this discriminatory system, the company could maintain the normal pyramid-type hierarchy simply by replacing employees, and a massive displacement often occurred in a large company on the occasion of a strike, an action which "offended" the family ideology. A postwar reaction to this discriminatory arrangement was that most of the active leaders of the new unions came from the ranks of the mid-term employees, and among their first demands were the abolition of the status system and dismissal of personnel managers who had been in their positions since prewar days and who were rigid in their personnel policies.

Under the system, company personnel administration typically does not consider employees as separate individuals; they exist only as members of the enterprise which is supported by the family ideology, and as long as they submit to the principle of subordination to authority and cooperation, their future livelihood is protected by the company. If they are loyal to senior employees or to persons in higher positions, they learn to perform their jobs and their efficiency increases. The system is the realization of two management goals: production efficiency and maintenance of order in the work-place. The phrases *kigkō ikka* (one-enterprise family) or *kigyō wa unmei kyōdōtai de aru* (the enterprise and its employees share a common destiny) denote integration of the family ideology and the *nenkō* system. Thus, personnel administration under the system may be said to be based on the collectivity rather than the individual.

The definition of the term as it is used here leads to a discussion of a third possible deficiency of the *nenkō* system. Japanese industrialization developed individualism as well as the family ideology among industry personnel. The system in modern industry requires that employees meet only two conditions: the specified educational level and employment directly from school. Once these conditions are met, ambitious employees are provided with opportunities for promotion to higher positions, for which they compete vigorously. Thus individualism functions within the framework of the group.

An individualistic ideology could not appear in a distinct form in the Japanese industrial milieu, but ability and ambition of individual employees emerge in subgroups or cliques of employees within the company. Cliques are formed on the basis of a commonality of education level, place of birth, the year individuals entered the company, as well as the ambition of individual employees. These groups often compete for leadership in the workshop, the department, the factory, or the company as a whole. They criticize each other for disrupting the order of the company and for inefficiency—a reflection of the "family" integrity of an enterprise and the dynamic situation produced by interfirm competition in the product market, where no rules are explicitly established. In this respect, the existence and function of cliques have often encouraged the growth and development of an enterprise under the system. At the same time they have created severe internal struggles, which might be considered a deficiency (Cole, 1971a).

ENTERPRISE UNIONISM

If Japanese labor unions are judged in terms of the experience and concepts of Western industrial relations systems, they may be very much misunderstood (Karsh, 1965:55–69). The local union in the U.S. does not correspond to the "unit union" in Japan. Nor is the American national union the equivalent of the Japanese "industrial union." Although by 1970 the rate of organization among Japanese wage and salary earners was among the highest in the non-Communist world, it would be misleading to conclude that the strength of Japanese unions is equal to that of unions in Western countries. Japanese unions are relatively weak as collective bargaining organizations; they still lack a strong voice in determining standard employment conditions on either a local or an industrial basis.

The most important feature of Japanese unions is "enterprise unionism." A *kigyōbetsu-kumiai* (enterprise union) is organized autonomously by workers within a given enterprise. They are widespread and dominant not only in large private industry and the public sector but also in the small and medium industries. More than 90% of all unions in Japan are organized on an enterprise basis and they number more than 60,000 unit unions.

Though these unit unions may be affiliated with a higher level industry-wide or national organization, each is virtually autonomous in the conduct of those affairs which relate to the employer or firm. The characteristics of an enterprise union are:

1. It includes all *regular* employees in a single enterprise or industrial establishment regardless of occupation or job status. In many cases, it embraces both blue and white collar workers and lower-level management. Immediately after the close of the Pacific War, when the labor movement mushroomed, even the middle management people were included.

2. Since membership of the enterprise unions in most cases is confined to regular employees, temporary and subcontract workers are usually excluded.

3. Regular employees automatically join even where there is an open shop, and their union dues are usually collected through automatic check-offs.

4. Union offices and other administrative facilities are commonly provided by the company.

5. Leaders of enterprise unions are elected from among the regular employees in the enterprise. Those elected officials usually maintain their employment relationship with the enterprise while devoting themselves

to union activities. Becoming a union officer does not mean giving up promotions in the enterprise. On the contrary, it often leads to promising careers within management.

6. The organizational structure of the enterprise union inevitably corresponds to the organization of the enterprise, facilitating the maintenance of the union's organizational integrity, but at the same time, making the union readily subject to employer intervention.

A number of reasons can be offered to explain the predominance of this form of unionism. First, "paternalism" remains among firms of all sizes. It is persistent on the part of employers, while workers expect the benefits as a matter of course and respond by being strongly conscious of the closed "communities." Since before World War II, employers in large-scale industry have tried to confine employee organization to single enterprises and have developed labor-management consultation systems and employee welfare facilities based on the enterprise. During the war both labor and management were forced to cooperate with each other for war production. During the postwar inflation and shortage of goods, as workers spontaneously and rapidly organized labor unions with the help of Occupation policies, they inevitably organized on an enterprise basis as a result of their experience.

A second reason why the unions could not be organized on a basis other than the enterprise was the very wide variation in working conditions and employment security among firms. Interfirm differentials made it especially difficult for workers to unite industry-wide.

Third, there have been deficiencies in public investment in a social security system, housing development programs, and the like. As a result, workers in both large private industry and the public sector have been seriously concerned about guaranteed livelihoods and have demanded such guarantees from their employers.

The Development of Enterprise Unionism

Efforts of Japanese workers to organize themselves for purposes of dealing with employers reach back to the 1860s and 1870s when large-scale industry was first developed to make munitions for defense and textiles for foreign exchange. For the most part, these undertakings were built with substantial amounts of foreign technical assistance. However, worker self-help organizations, as "friendly societies" for mutual cooperation and assistance or labor unions designed to function along the lines of American models, were hardly successful. Continual employer and government harrassment, the absence of legal rights and protection to organize and the lack of worker job or class consciousness frustrated these efforts. Though there were encouraging signs of growth in the 1920s and very early 1930s, not more than 8% of the industrial work force joined unions at the high point of organization in the mid-1920s. The rise of the militarists to power in the mid-1930s and the Great Depression severely impeded further growth. Political factionalism and fragmentation deepened existing splits between left and right tendencies. In 1937 the left wing Japanese Council of Labor Unions was declared illegal. Even earlier, in 1934, the right-wing labor federation, *Sodomei*, embraced union-management cooperation. In 1940, the government outlawed all unions while establishing a "labor front," the *Sangyō Hōko-*

kukai, popularly known as *Sampo*. Thus, independent trade unionism ceased to exist.[7]

Immediately after World War II it became possible for the leftist unions to reach the masses of workers and to organize them effectively in enterprise-wide unions. What emerged was *Sanbetsu*, or All-Japan Congress of Industrial Labor Organizations, a national center of unions organized by industry. *Sanbetsu's* rule that persons from outside of the enterprise work force should be excluded from union leadership as far as possible was well accepted by leaders within the enterprises. These leaders also were encouraged to be sympathetic to and to join the Communist Party, and they were soon assigned to party "factions" within the unions. Thus many union leaders at the enterprise level were induced to organize along Communist Party lines, and they were successful in promoting radical worker movements for several years after the war. The result was that the Communist Party began to visualize a revolution for Japan and to mobilize masses of workers in an effort to develop radical political struggles.

However, there was a limit to such a radical movement in large enterprises because many workers, having been trained by and committed to the company over a long period, could not bring themselves to engage in revolutionary activities. These workers, especially clerical employees who closely identified with the employer, gradually dropped away from the radical movement. As a consequence, there remained only those who had been ill-treated by the company during the war or were Communists or Party sympathizers. When the Occupation mounted the "red purge" in 1949, there was a drastic change in the direction of the workers' movement and the successful development of the *Minshuka Dōmei*, the National Liaison Council for Democratization (Levine, 1958:69–76).

Nevertheless, the premodern status system and other traditional practices that persisted in and outside industry gave rise to a revolutionary ideology among workers. Accordingly, *Sōhyō*, the General Council of Trade Unions of Japan, organized after the "red purge" as a moderate national center, has continued to be critical of Japanese conservatism and capitalism and to support the Socialist Party. While it is true that the majority of workers are committed to the enterprise, when they are organized on an industrial or national basis, they also tend to be critical of the existing society.

The Japanese labor movement is based mainly on exclusive organization of employees in large private and public corporations and in the government who are highly conscious of belonging to their enterprises. Should the union become independent of the enterprise and engage in radical "class struggles" against the enterprise, it usually faces opposition from its own members as well as from the employer. Therefore, unions at this level move from a radical towards a moderate position. How to attain sustained organizational autonomy within the enterprise framework is a very serious question for Japanese unionism.

In 1973, union membership reached 12,097,848 or about 36% of the total number of wage and salary earners in Japan. There were more than 60,000 unit unions (*tan-i kumiai*), the smallest labor union organization in a plant-wide basis with its own constitution and independent activities. When the unit unions

---

[7] Several good histories of this period are available in English. However, the most complete dealing with labor is Okochi (1958). For the most authoritative, over-all discussion of the re-emergent Japanese labor movement, see Levine (1958).

in the same enterprise are combined, the result is a total of just over 30,000 entity unions (*tan-itsu kumiani*). The average union membership is only 180 per unit union (Ministry of Labour, 1970:310). Given the organizational basis of unions, labor union size corresponds closely to enterprise size. According to a survey of the Ministry of Labour in 1969, union membership in enterprises with 500 or more employees was about 63% of the total, excluding public employees. If the latter were included, the proportion increased to over 77%. In the manufacturing industry alone, it was 76.5% (The Japan Institute of Labour, 1970: 155).

96% of all enterprises with 1,000 or more employees recognize their labor unions, but the rate of recognition is less among the smaller enterprises: 22% in enterprises with fifty to ninety-nine workers, 11% for the thirty to forty-nine group, and 1.4% for those with one to three employees. Union organizing in the small and medium-sized firm is unlikely, due primarily to the paternalism in that industrial sector, lack of understanding of unions, insecurity of employment, lack of able leadership, and poor financing of union administration. The absence of craft unionism is a significant indication of these conditions. Since the mid-1950s, however, the national centers have become active in organizing workers in the small industry sector, but their successes have been slow in coming and meager. Therefore, it can be said that the Japanese labor movement has been led by unions in the large enterprises and in the public or government sectors.

Extent of Worker Organization

In 1970, about 36% of all union members were in manufacturing industry; 18% in transportation and communication, where public corporations play a dominant role; 13% in services including education; and about 10% in local and national employment. Construction accounts for not quite seven-tenths of 1% of all union members, perhaps the lowest unionization rate for this sector among all industrial countries. The balance is distributed between mining, wholesale and retail trade, finance and insurance, real estate, and other industries, no one of which accounts for as much as 1% of the total membership (Ministry of Labour, 1970:309–316). Generally, the more an industry is concentrated, the more likely it is that the workers are organized. Where public or government employees are involved in an industry, there is likely to be a labor union. As large enterprises employ more workers, the rate of organization among them in most cases goes up as a result of union shop practices. From 1960 to 1970, the rate of organization in the declining coal and metal mining industries fell from near 80% to almost 50%. On the other hand, the rate of organization increased in transportation, communication, and public utilities about 4% to near 72%, in manufacturing from 31% to about 38%, in public and government services from 60% to 65%, and in commercial trades about 14% to almost 27%.

Reflecting the practice of overcommitment in employment for regular workers (*honkō*), labor unions composed exclusively of regular workers comprise 85% of all labor unions and 82% of the total membership. Labor unions organized with both regular and temporary workers (*rinjikō*) together comprise nearly 12% of the total membership, while unions exclusively organized by temporary or daily workers comprise only 0.4%.

In principle, many unions claim to have eliminated discrimination with regard to employment conditions between regular and temporary or subcontract workers (*shagaikō*). In practice, however, a wide gap remains. Because temporary and subcontract workers function as a safety valve for adjusting employment to business fluctuations, it is very difficult for enterprise-level unions of regular workers to admit temporary and subcontract workers into their organizations. The labor shortage in recent years, however, has helped to promote temporary workers to regular worker status or to substitute subcontract workers. Despite these changes, the labor movement has been predominantly in the hands of regular workers closely committed to the enterprise for their life-times and therefore reluctant to open their unions to others whose employment situation is less secure.

Male union members make up 72.7% of the total. Of the females, the majority are unmarried and young; middle-aged female workers are very rare, although their number is increasing gradually. Female members are in the majority, however, in the government monopoly tobacco industry, textiles, garment manufacturing, and medical services, a reflection of the important role of female labor in these industries, dating to the pre-1930s when women comprised the majority of the industrial labor force.

The laws protecting the right to organize in Japan are different for private and public sector industries. Public workers are divided into public service and government corporation employment, and public service is further divided into national and local service employment. Collective bargaining by public employees is partially restricted by law, while strikes by public employees are prohibited. Despite these restrictions, public employee unions are organized on a national basis and play a leading role in the Japanese labor movement. In 1970 the number of organized public employees, including national railways, electric power and education as well as local and national government, was 29.1% of the total union membership.

Types of Labor Unions

In prewar Japan, there were some craft unions, but none was strong enough to set wage standards for the crafts in the labor market. Furthermore, by the time of World War II, all labor unions were forced to dissolve and reorganize into the Industrial Patriotic Association, as part of the wartime mobilization. After the war, labor unions organizing all the workers within an enterprise sprang up in great numbers.

The few craft unions in Japan which correspond to craft unions in Western countries are found among carpenters, plasterers and other building trades, dye workers, harbor workers, and female domestics. These unions function primarily as labor-supply centers since private employment exchanges are prohibited by law. However, there are several unions based on a specific craft line, such as the locomotive engineers and machinists, but they restrict their bargaining to single employers. In this sense, they may hardly be called craft unions. Moreover, wage earners and the self-employed in construction, restaurant, barbershop, and other service industries organize trade associations which are far from being labor unions. Such associations are often sponsored by conservative politicians as a means for obtaining votes in elections. On the other hand, recent technological changes have had a significant impact on craftsmen and their organizations. As craftsmanship has become less important in industry, the traditional organizations based on master-servant relationships have been reorganized gradually into modern labor organizations.

When workers are employed in enterprises too small for them to be able to form labor unions on an enterprise basis, they sometimes establish unions outside the firms but within a given area. This type of organization, called *gōdō rōsō* (combined unions), developed before the war and produced many of the well-known union leaders of that time. They have again become common since about 1955 due to the organizing activities of national centers and industrial unions through local branches of the latter. However, their growth has been very slow because of the gulf between this type of worker organization in the smaller-sized industry and the unions in large enterprises. The experience of the latter is not always helpful to the former. Worker organizations in small-size industry are inevitably handicapped by financial difficulties due to business fluctuations and bankruptcies. There is also considerable mobility among workers from small company to small company, hardly creating solid ground for the development of a strong and competent leadership from their own ranks.

There are three types of *gōdō rōsō:* industrial, occupational (craft-based), and general. The general *gōdō rōsō* organizes workers in various types of industries and occupations, but since there are few common interests among the members, it is difficult to maintain organizational integrity. Industrial and occupational *gōdō rōsō* have succeeded in bargaining collectively with individual employers or their associations in some cases. They have common grounds for negotiation with employers and may become more widespread in the future.

Unions of the Unemployed

As previously mentioned, there is also a union of workers registered at the Employment Security Offices throughout the country who work as casual day labor on unemployment relief programs. Most are repatriates, war widows, and discharged workers. In spite of the placement service of the Employment Security Offices, many of these workers remain casual laborers continually dependent on work relief projects. Their union bargains with the offices for wage increases and bonus payments.

For the labor movement as a whole, enterprise unionism has had a number of consequences:

1. As all employees in an enterprise are organized together, frequent internal conflicts of interest tend to arise within the enterprise union. Such conflict often leads to splits between those workers who stand firm against the employer and those who are more cooperative with the employer, or between blue collar workers and white collar employees.
2. New employees who automatically join the union upon employment in the enterprise are generally indifferent to the union and have no clearcut consciousness of being a union member. Consequently, the union tends to be an instrument solely for the leadership.
3. Union leadership tends to change frequently so that there is little possibility for experienced, competent, and responsible leaders to emerge or develop.
4. When the union is organized in a small firm, it is apt to be weak and inactive.
5. Since the union organization is confined within an enterprise, the scope of union activities tends to be narrow.

6. Because of the nature of the enterprise union organization, it is rather ineffective for determining wage rates of individual union members, and once general base-ups are agreed upon, individual wage-rate determination is usually left to the employer's discretion.
7. As there are no distinctive occupational demarcations among union members, it is rather easy for the employer to transfer workers at will.
8. Since the union is so closely attached to the enterprise, it is sometimes very difficult for an employer to merge his business with another. Merger is less difficult when the unions involved belong to the same national center or industrial union, but when they do not, intense strife between the unions often occurs.

Although there are an increasing number of exceptions, many regular workers still come from farm areas after school graduation, are employed through careful selection and personal connections, and are assigned to training in the corporation's school or to training on the job. Usually after spending three to five years in acquiring occupational skills, they adapt to the enterprise's occupational hierarchy based on education level and length of service and commit themselves to the enterprise for an indefinite period. At the same time, the enterprise provides its employees with a variety of welfare facilities and special allowances such as housing, recreation, cultural facilities, medical care, semi-annual seasonal bonuses, and retirement allowances and pensions based on age and length of service. Many large companies and agencies also provide substantial discounts in house rent, utility charges, commodities, lunches, haircuts, movies, and so forth. Thus, for most regular employees in these enterprises, family life is a kind of extension of the work-place and is closely tied to the enterprise. All of these benefits tend to encourage worker loyalty to the enterprise. As a consequence, employees in large private and public corporations or government service enjoy far more employment security and higher wages than workers in small business or in daily or temporary work.

Workers' consciousness tended to vary, depending upon age, occupational status, etc., but there was no significant difference among them in answers to questions about their interest in their jobs, sense of being worthwhile, and worker loyalty. On the other hand, young workers were more concerned than older workers about having a happy family life, and they tended to view their jobs as a means to achieving this goal. This tendency among young workers may be due to drastic changes in their values in the postwar period, away from the ideas of obedience to the sovereign and filial love and duty (*giri-to-ninjō*) of the prewar days.

In small business, the employer in many cases has to function as a worker as well as a manager, and he tends to work along with his family employees. Even when he employs persons other than family members, they usually live at his residence like members of a family. In this situation, hired employees work for the employer at the latter's discretion while learning occupational skills on the job and they often change employers in order to take advantage of opportunities to acquire skills in the least amount of time.

Small business usually is labor-intensive, and what little capital it has usually is in the form of obsolete machinery. These firms are highly subject to business fluctuations, and they maintain themselves by keeping labor costs low. Members of the employer's family working in the business receive no regular wages or salaries, and there tends to be no distinction between business and household accounts. The hired employees generally expect little in the way of wages and benefits, but look forward to becoming independent managers in the future. For this reason, a majority of young workers in small businesses tend to find this work interesting, in spite of the poor employment conditions.

Under these circumstances, workers in small business have little interest in unionism and little commitment to a given employer. Their rate of mobility is high, and the ratio of organized workers is quite low in this industrial sector.

Temporary and subcontract workers also have little employment security, as they may be discharged at any time. Although they often are employed by large enterprises, they receive less length-of-service benefits than regular workers, and they are only poorly protected by fringe benefits and welfare facilities. Minimum wages, agreed upon by employers, provide them with hardly more than the unemployment benefits of public relief workers. Their employment conditions are comparable to those of workers in small business.

Daily workers, of which there are three types, make up still another group. First are the traditional craftsmen, common in the building trades and in the longshore industry, whose current employment status emerged from the labor boss system which broke down under the impact of technological and social change. Many craftsmen are organized in either craft-type unions are in gōdō rōsō (combined unions), among small and medium-sized industries. Second are the common laborers, unskilled workers, and janitors, and the third group is composed of persons unemployed as the result of being repatriates, war widows, divorced women, or unsuccessful self-employed and family workers. Daily workers of the second and third types find it difficult to obtain jobs and therefore come to the Employment Security Offices for unemployment relief or casual jobs on relief projects. Workers in the third category have been organized by the All-Japan Day Workers' Union, Zennichijiro, to bargain collectively with the public Employment Security Office.

SUMMARY AND CONCLUSIONS

The Japanese life-time employment system, a merit system based upon age, education, and length of service, and a trade union structure which consists overwhelmingly of worker organizations limited to the enterprise which is the locus of employment are the three cornerstones of the structure characterizing Japanese industrial relations. In turn, these characteristics reflect a more basic fact describing Japanese society: stratification system which is rooted in corporate-group membership rather than status derived from occupation or job.

These factors do not stand as independent characteristics. Rather, they are mutually re-inforcing so as to produce a highly integrated and functional set of arrangements. Personnel practices in the firm and the seniority-oriented organization principles based upon the norm of employment for life for "regular employees" provide the economic and social basis for the formation of the enterprise union. The continuation of the enterprise union in turn preserves the management system based on seniority and the life-time employment system.

Yet, the very rapid economic growth of Japan over the past fifteen years to the point where it has now emerged as a colossus rivalling the U.S. and the U.S.S.R. suggests that the whole structure is being subjected to substantial tensions. The projected long-term labor shortage stemming from population stabilization has created substantial problems for continued economic growth. While in the past technological advances have off-set labor shortages in the quest for increased production, in many industries, particularly manufacturing industries, there appear to be no or only very limited possibilities of continuing large-scale technological innovations. Thus, increasingly employers search for new sources of labor and their competitors or other sectors of the economy appear more and more attractive as potential sources of new workers.

However, hiring new employees from other firms, however skilled or experienced, directly threatens the wage and reward system based upon the practice of hiring only new school graduates as "regular workers" and increasing their rewards as their length of service (and age) increase. Meshing into the existing reward structure, newly hired and even experienced "outside" workers creates a difficult problem for Japanese employers as long as the basic reward system remains as it has been. However, to change the reward system to a job classified wage system, such as in the U.S. and much of Western Europe, shifts the source of social identity away from the traditional ideal of group membership and in the direction of job-related achievement criteria. This kind of shift represents a disjuncture in the fabric of Japanese social relations. It would also substantially strain the enterprise union structure which more than anything else secures the employment status of the regular workers who form its membership. By definition, newly hired experienced (outside) workers or temporary and contract workers cannot be "regular workers." There is no clear evidence that union members and leaders are prepared to substitute the seniority based wage system for job classified wages, to admit "outside workers" to membership, and to bargain away the employment security of their members. To do so would be to dissolve the whole trade union structure or to risk reducing it to virtual ineffectiveness.

Yet, the present system which has developed as a reflection of rapid economic growth, vigorous inter-enterprise competition for skilled workers and an ideology supporting patrimonial relations in industry, will increasingly face testing. The economy confronts increasing international competition and the combined effects of the labor shortage and higher and higher costs of achieving smaller and smaller increments of technological advantage put greater and greater strain on the existing system of allocating workers and rewarding them.

REFERENCES

Abegglen, J.
    1958   The Japanese Factory. Glencoe, Ill.: Free Press.
Cole, R.E.
    1971a Japanese Blue Collar. Berkeley: University of California Press.
    1971b "Functional alternatives, economic development and historical explanation." Paper No. 2. Ann Arbor, Mich.: Center for Research on Social Organization.
Fujita, W.
    1965   "Kagaku" ("Chemical industry"), in K. Okochi (ed.), Sangyobetsu-Chingin Kettei-no-Kikō (Wage-Determining Mechanisms in Industry). Tokyo: Rōdō Kyōkai.
Fukutake, T.
    1967   Japanese Rural Society. Translated by R. Dore. Toronto: Oxford University Press.

Hall, J.
  1962 "Feudalism in Japan: a reassessment." Comparative Studies in Sociology and History 5(October).
Japan Institute of Labour, The
  1970 Japan Labour Statistics. Tokyo: The Japan Institute of Labour.
Karsh, B.
  1965 "The exportability of trade union movements: the Japan-U.S. trade union 'cultural exchange' program," in, The Proceedings of the International Conference on the Changing Patterns of Industrial Relations, The Changing Patterns of Industrial Relations. Tokyo: The Japan Institute of Labour.
Kawashima, T.
  1950 Nihon Shakai no Kazokuteki Kōsei (Family Structure in Japanese Society). Tokyo: Nihon Hyōronsha.
Levine, S.B.
  1958 Industrial Relations in Postwar Japan. Urbana: University of Illinois Press.
Ministry of Labour
  1965 Rōdō Ryoku Chōsa (Manpower Survey). Tokyo: Ministry of Labour.
  1970 Rōdō Tokei Nempō (Yearbook of Labour Statistics). Tokyo: Ministry of Labour.
Nakane, C.
  1967a Kinship and Economic Organization in Rural Japan. London: University of London Press.
  1967b Tate Shakai no Ningen Kankei: Tan'itsu Shakai no Riron (Human Relations in a Vertical Society). Tokyo: Kōdansha. Published in English as, Japanese Society. Berkeley: University of California Press, 1970.
Okochi, K.
  1958 Labor in Modern Japan. Tokyo: The Science Council of Japan, Economic Series No. 18.
Okochi, K., B. Karsh and S.B. Levine (eds.)
  1974 Workers and Employers in Japan. Princeton, New Jersey: Princeton University Press.
Taira, K.
  1970 Economic Development and the Labor Market in Japan. New York: Columbia University Press.
Tsuda, M.
  1965a Basic Structure of Japanese Labor Relations. Tokyo: The Society for the Social Sciences, Mushashi University.
  1965b "The Japanese wage structure and its significance for international comparisons." British Journal of Industrial Relations Vol. 3.
Vogel, E.
  1967 "Kinship structure, migration to the city and modernization," in R. Dore (ed.), Aspects of Social Change in Modern Japan. Princeton, New Jersey: Princeton University Press.
Yoshino, M.Y.
  1968 Japan's Managerial System. Cambridge, Mass.: The MIT Press.
Yukichi, F.
  1948 Autobiography of Fukuzawa Yukichi. Translated by Eiichi Kiyooka. Tokyo: The Hokuseido Press.

CHAPTER **20**

Work and Management in Poland

Alexander Matejko

University of Alberta

In Eastern Communist Europe there is an unavoidable and permanent contradiction between the democratic and the authoritarian interpretation of the system. It is, as Brzezinski says, a struggle between sectarianism and universalism (Brzezinski, 1970:192). With the general progress towards industrialization and universal education, which is an undoubted achievement of Communist ruling elites, the authoritarian style of management becomes more and more outdated (Zielinski, 1973). There is a growing awareness not only among intellectuals, but also among the rank-and-file workers, that some kind of participatory democracy is the only solution to the dilemma.

CRISIS OF AUTHORITARIAN MANAGEMENT

One of the main difficulties in progressing towards participatory democracy in Eastern Europe (except in Yugoslavia) is of a doctrinaire nature. Officially there is participatory democracy in all fields of social life, and especially in the area of work. Therefore, why look for something new? If under socialism there is no longer alienation, then why join Western social scientists (Blauner, 1964; Blumberg, 1968; Pateman, 1970; Likert, 1967, etc.) in studying various ways of overcoming alienation? In many Eastern European studies conducted from the Marxist orthodox viewpoint, it is just taken for granted that nationalization of means of production leads automatically to overcoming alienation (e.g., Osipov, 1966).

The basic traditions of the Eastern European intelligentsia have a lot to do with their skepticism about simplifying the whole issue. First of all, it is against the scientific orientation of many Eastern European intellectuals to accept the doctrinaire interpretation without reservation. This acceptance is evidenced, for example, in Poland (Gella, 1970, 1971; Hertz, 1942, 1951; Matejko, 1969a). Second, under bureaucratized regimes the intelligentsia suffers status incongruence to such an extent that a growing interest in alienation becomes unavoidable (Matejko, 1966). Third, among members of the intelli-

---

This chapter is based on two articles written by the author (Matejko, 1971a, 1971b). A more extensive treatment of the subject can be found in Matejko (1974).

gentsia there is a feeling of responsibility for the fate of the nation. This feeling leads to a search for some solutions to the problems of alienation.

Among all the Eastern European countries, Poland has the most influential intelligentsia, which inherited (Chalasinski, 1946; Gella, 1971; Zajaczkowski, 1961) not only several elements of the social culture of the gentry, but also its high sociopolitical aspirations. This inheritance explains to a large extent why there appears in Poland on many occasions, a widespread criticism of a highly bureaucratized model of management. This was the situation in 1956 as well as in 1970 when workers' uprisings shook the whole system.

Among Polish intellectuals, there are many who are very critical of the existing model of a highly centralized administrative command which is monopolized by the top of the hierarchy. According to this type of economic model, the command originates at the Central Committee of the Party, goes down to the ministry, then to the industrial corporation (which is responsible for a particular group of enterprises) and finishes on the level of an individual enterprise. The upward communication is cumbersome and ineffective because all administrative levels above the enterprise select and even distort information according to their own vested interests.

Corporations (in Poland they are called associations) are under strong triple pressure: from the ministries and central party authorities, as well as from the enterprises. At the top there is a tendency to treat the staff in corporations as objects of manipulation. At the bottom there is a constant attempt to bargain for all kinds of benefits and privileges. Under such conditions it is very difficult for people in corporations to establish their own authority and to play an active middle role. It seems easier to limit responsibility just to the transmittal of orders down the hierarchy. On the other hand, corporations are financially poor and they do not have enough resources to extend their activities and to hire additional specialists (Sadownik, 1971).

It is quite obvious to critics of the state bureaucracy (that is currently imposed upon the entire nationalized economy of Poland) that the growing needs and necessities of the Polish nation can not be satisfied effectively without giving much more freedom to management. At present, initiative is discouraged; contributions are not rewarded; decisions are based on distorted and belated information; feedback does not work. Administrative means become ends in themselves, while improvements are piecemeal (Zielinski, 1973). Detailed interference in the running of an enterprise reduces it to a mere bureaucratic office. As Lipinski (1971a:3) states: "Desperate clinging to old methods of administration or government in the face of a new situation which demands that changes be brought, leads to the application of preemptory pressures on the one hand, and resistance and crisis on the other."

The control of technical progress in hands of high level bureaucrats becomes just one more manipulative device which stimulates the worker orientation more toward some external show effects than real efficiency.[1] For

---

[1] For example, in 1970, of all TV and radio sets delivered by the manufacturer to dealers, 31% were rejected at the wholesale level. Of these sets which were later delivered to the retail stores, every fourth TV set and every sixth radio had to be repaired before being sold to customers. Among sets sold to clients, the manufacturer had to repair every TV set under the guarantee about three times, and every radio at least once (Kilbach, 1971:5).

example, in the mining industry, application of modern equipment is dictated by bureaucratic commands supported by attractive bonuses established especially for managers and the technical personnel. Instead of looking for real economic effects, local "supporters" of technical progress create artificial conditions in which new equipment provides some short-term pseudo-attractive effects, but in reality harms the long-term interests of the enterprise (Kraus, 1968).

Trade unions are expected by the Party to mobilize workers and employees for the fulfillment of production targets,[2] organize various cultural and social activities, administer recreation centers and sports. Trade unions embrace 95% of all workers and employees, but it is a well known fact, recognized even by some union officials, that unions are unable to defend the vital interests of their membership. According to one union officer, trade union authorities

> in their majority have taken versus the state administration the position of a client instead of a partner. On the other hand, the bureaucratic leadership of trade unions has eliminated democratic principles from the daily practice. Subservient and loyalistic functionnaires have been much better accepted than energetic, critical and courageous people (Kucharski, 1971:4).

This may be due in part to the fact that trade union leaders are older men. For example, among chairmen of local trade union committees located at workplaces, in the early 1970s only 11% were less than thirty years old; among members of executive committees of individual unions, only 0.6%, and among chairmen of regional trade union boards, only 1% (Urban, 1971:4).

A survey conducted in 1966 and 1967 in seven industrial enterprises showed that manual workers engaging in socialist work competition, sponsored officially by the Party, expected such practical outcomes as higher work output (59%), better wages (51%), bonuses (37%), and improvement of personal technical qualifications (22% of all surveyed workers). In reality, however, workers often became disillusioned with what was really offered to them. Quite often, they viewed officially sponsored Party competition just as one of several managerial devices which were beyond their own control. Most of the surveyed workers showed deep distrust for the method of distributing rewards used by management and local Party authorities (Nicki, 1969).

Numerous Polish economists and sociologists support relaxation of the authoritarian system of management (Zielinski, 1973). Kurowski is outspoken in arguing for activation of market forces, introducing widespread competition among enterprises, and stimulating a businesslike orientation among managers (Kurowski, 1970). Lipinski expressed his view on many occasions that it is necessary to leave a lot of freedom to the industrial managers instead of limiting their initiative. On the other hand, he maintains that

> the socialization of private property can only be made a reality by the participation of every member of the community in the business of decision-making. Only thus can the worker cease to be an isolated

---

[2] Unions and youth organizations sponsor teams of workers who promise to achieve higher production targets.

and alienated individual, subordinated to forces which he himself has created (Lipinski, 1971b:129).

The late O. Lange was in favor of granting autonomy to enterprises and managers even if only within the framework of "mobile" central planning (Kowalik, 1971:13). According to J. Szczepański (1971:2) bureaucratic commands which flow from the top just

> blur the responsibility for bad organization, defects, wastage, stifle all initiative, submerge the chances of rational management in a flood of unnecessary activity which is either demanded by the regulations or just by the need to maneuver around them

According to Podgórecki (1971) formalism is one of the main faults. It consists in

> proliferation of standing orders, out of all proportion to the actual objectives of the institution which by deterring management from taking any legitimate risks curbs all initiative (Podgórecki, 1971).

The main issue of all eventual reforms is how to transform industrial corporations and work-places from subordinated administrative units into real enterprises able to exercise entrepreneurship. Jakubowicz (1971), for example, suggests a highly elastic grouping of nationalized enterprises into corporations centralized or decentralized depending upon the nature of particular economic needs and necessities.

The ruling elite is afraid to restrict central planning, much less eliminate it. According to the view widely held by members of the elite, the market economy would lead to: monopoly exercised by the most successful enterprises, growth of inequalities, and, in the final outcome, to the abandonment of socialism. Some influential economists support this view. Pajestka (1971:11) says that

> the whole point of socialist planning is rationality on a national scale, that is, to arrive at the options which represent the general socio-economic optimum over a longer time scale. Such rationality cannot be achieved without safeguarding the proper role of central planning and making sure it is performed as well as it conceivably can be.

Pajestka belongs to the category of influential Party economists who want to improve the whole system, but only within the limits of a benevolent autocracy. According to them, power

> should belong to those who, by virtue of their grasp of the whole brief (that is to say, their command of the essential facts, their ability to proceed on them, their mastery of the broader issues and their positive motivation) can do the job best (Pajestka, 1971:15).

In practice it always means the preservation of total power and decision-making in the hands of the same people who reached high positions in the political establishment several years ago and who do not want to lose power and privileges. They just appreciate themselves as those who "can do the job best."

Development of the managerial model in Poland will lead either toward some kind of industrial democracy or toward strengthening an authoritarian centralism, depending on several external and internal factors. The most important external factor is in the field of international relations, and particularly the role of the Soviet Union in Eastern Europe. We will deal here only with internal factors. There is now plenty of sociological data on Poland and we would like to utilize it in order to analyze the changing nature of the Polish labor force.

DISLOCATION OF THE LABOR FORCE

Two-fifths of the population of Poland in the late 1960s was located in urbanized and industrialized areas which constitute 9% of the Polish territory. In these areas, only 8% were employed in agriculture (Eberhardt, Herman and Leszczycki, 1971:1). Due to progressing industrialization and urbanization, the percentage of the population earning a living mainly by nonagricultural work has grown in Poland from 40% before the Second World War to 53% in 1950 and 70.2% in 1970.[3] On the other hand, among the rural population the percentage of those who have nonagricultural sources of livelihood has grown from 23% in 1950 to 46% in 1973. In rural areas, of 8.3 million people economically active in 1970, one-sixth worked in agriculture as a secondary occupation, in addition to their basic employment outside of agriculture, and a similar portion (1.5 million) were not in agriculture at all. On the other hand, 64% of all farm income came from trade with the state, and only 15% came from the free trade not directly controlled by the state.

In the decade 1960–1970, the proportion of people in rural areas who treat farming as a secondary occupation has grown by 88%, and the number of people who live in the countryside but are employed outside of agriculture has grown by 48%. On one of every two farms, there is one person who is gainfully employed outside agriculture, and on one of every five farms there are two people who, in addition to farming, have jobs somewhere else (but not in agriculture).

In 1973 there were nineteen million people in the potential labor force of Poland (men 18–64 and women 18–59), and sixteen and a half million were economically active: 5.4 million in agriculture and forestry (4.4 million on private farms since only a small percentage of farms are collectivized or owned by the State); 4.7 million in industry; 1.3 million in construction; 1 million in transport, etc. For every three people gainfully employed, there is one person on pension, welfare or scholarship.[4] At the beginning of the 1970s, there were approximately three-tenths of the labor force involved in agriculture, four-tenths in industry and in the building trade and the remaining three-tenths in service occupations. Agriculture is underinvested and split into many small private farms. Consequently, its contribution to the gross national income (15% in 1973, when service occupations are excluded) is lower than its participation in the labor force. The regime has pushed forward industry and construction

---

[3] In Poland 50% of the total population of 34 million (1975) is economically active (47% in cities and 53% in rural areas in 1972).

[4] The average pension in 1973 was 1304 zl per month (1672 zl employee pension, 1117 zl disability pension and 1016 zl widow pension), far from being satisfactory.

(their participation in the gross national income has grown from 50% in 1960 to 63% in 1973 when service occupations are excluded) but at the expense of services which are evidently underdeveloped. The bureaucratic machine is very large and grows constantly in some fields, e.g., in the construction enterprises, from 1965 until 1970 the percentage of white collar employees has grown from 18% to 21%. However bureaucratic services, instead of contributing to the development and improvement, became to a large extent just a commonly recognized nuisance.

The Polish labor force is still underqualified, although the government invests considerable money and effort to raise the general level of training and education. Only one-fourth of all labor force members have some sort of diploma or certificate. Among those active in the nationalized economy, 63% have no more than an elementary education or the basic vocational school. In the period 1958–1968 the proportion of workers who did not complete elementary school diminished from 43% to 24.5% (in industry, 20.5%). On the other hand, the proportion of workers with vocational education (elementary or higher) had grown from 9% to 18% (in industry, 22%). Among workers who have elementary vocational education, one-third completed it after starting their employment; the same is true for two-thirds of workers with vocational secondary education, and one-fourth of the workers who completed the general high school (Zagorski, 1971:2). Some 70% of workers work just with their own hands. According to data from 1969 in the electromechanical industry, there was the following breakdown of production-worker jobs: 4% automated jobs, 10% fully mechanized jobs, 45% partially mechanized jobs, 40% manual jobs. 58% were skilled workers (Zagorski, 1971:2).

The large proportion of manual jobs even in industry, not to mention under-invested agriculture and services, puts a limit on demand for skilled workers. On the other hand, there is a constant rise in the educational level of new generations among traditionally lower strata. Even if there is still some obvious social inequality in entering higher levels of education, the children of workers and farmers now have relatively large opportunities for educational advancement.[5] The proportion of Polish youth aged 14–17 attending any secondary schools has grown from 14% in 1938 to 87% in 1972–73, and the number of students in higher education per 10,000 people has grown in the same period from 14 to 110. About 5% of the young people in the age group 18–24 are enrolled as regular students of higher education (daily courses) (Zegzdryn, 1971). These figures are quite low in comparison with the U.S.A., but it is a significant advance in comparison with prewar Poland.

Still, many jobs are filled in Poland by people who are not fully qualified for them. According to data from 1964, 20% of the jobs which necessitate higher education were filled by people who did not have it, while jobs which necessitate at least high school graduation had only 31% as qualified (Krol, 1970). With progress in educational opportunity, the situation has undoubtedly improved since 1964. Of course, practitioners who lack an adequate education feel endangered by newly arriving graduates and defend their posts with all available means. The generation gap in Poland is based to a large

---

[5] For example, the participation of the youth from rural areas (mostly of peasant descent) declines considerably the higher the level of education; from 55% in elementary education to 34% in secondary education, and 21% in higher education (Zegzdryn, 1971).

extent on conflicting interests between older people, anxious to preserve their privileged positions, and young people competing with them.

The relative proportion of youth in the Polish society has grown in the last decade from 14% in 1960 to 20% in 1970 (the age group 15–24), which leads to their growing pressure on the labor market as well as in the political field.[6]

Structure of the Labor Force

Manual workers constitute 41.5% of all gainfully employed Poles; most of the workers are concentrated in industry and construction. Almost one-quarter of all manual workers are employed by the manufacturing, power and electronic industries. Their general level of education is higher than among other workers with 30% to 40% having completed vocational education (Zagorski, 1971:2).

In the period 1971–1980, the labor force will grow by approximately 3,250,000 people and there will be a need to provide jobs for them.[7] On the other hand, any substantial progress in agriculture will inevitably lead to an even higher emigration rate from the country villages to the towns. The pressure of the young, trained workers will continue to exert itself on the older, less-trained workers.

Women constitute two-fifths of the work force. The employment status among women (as among all workers) depends, as in other countries, upon their education even to a larger extent than among men. According to data from 1960, among urban women 18–29 years old, 88% of women with higher education were employed, but only 55% with elementary education were employed.

The Polish economy is under increasing pressure from young people and women both of whom expect the fulfillment of some basic promises. Peasants who moved from the country to urban areas did so for better material conditions and opportunities for further advancement for their children. People who attained an education expect to enlarge considerably their labor and life horizons.[8]

The transformation of all these pressures into a contribution to the gross national product depends on several conditions. One of them is a degree of labor mobility which would not be detrimental to the economy of the country. Human resources have to be mobile, but not too mobile.

LABOR MOBILITY

Lack of employment opportunities to match the rapid population progress was, for many years, one of the most difficult social problems in Poland. The progress in agricultural technology and in sanitary conditions (resulting in dimin-

---

[6] During the widespread strikes, demonstrations and riots at the seashore in December, 1970, of 2882 arrested persons, 70% consisted of people below the age of 25.

[7] One of the difficulties consists in matching education to the labor demand. Even in a highly centralized economy it is quite a difficult task which puts a heavy burden on planners. Several serious failures have been committed in this field, e.g., one-third of all the young people who completed vocational education could not find jobs in their own fields of specialization (Wawrzewska, 1971:3).

[8] The newly married couples still find it difficult to find housing for themselves even though the congestion in existing housing resources has diminished from 1.66 persons per room in 1960 to 1.37 in 1970. In 1973 there were 722 newly constructed flats for 1000 newlyweds (1029 in urban areas but only 371 in rural areas).

ishing child death rates), in addition to the abolition of traditional serfdom in the nineteenth century contributed to the growing surplus of labor in agriculture. The urban population grew from the early 1920s to the outbreak of the Second World War by only 4% (from 33% to 37%; compared to 22% in 1810). Cities were not able to offer enough jobs and housing. Only after the Second World War was there a fast growth of urbanization (urban population has grown from 32% in 1946 to 54% in 1973) due to the intensive industrialization of the whole country by the new regime. About one-third of the population lives in areas in which at least 65% of the people are employed in non-agricultural occupations (Dziewoński and Jerczynski, 1970:166). On the other hand, in Poland, as in other Eastern European countries, a considerable part of the urban population consists of rural migrants (Poland, 26%; Yugoslavia, 45%; Bulgaria, 42%; Rumania, 21%; Hungary, 18%; Czechoslovakia, 13%; East Germany, 9%).[9]

The population migration is still quite substantial in Poland in spite of severe restrictions and housing shortages in moving to big cities. Starting immediately after the Second World War there was a major movement from the east to the west of the Polish territory, and from rural villages to urban areas. However, even later, segments of the population continued migrations. People preferred to settle in large cities (100,000 inhabitants or more).

In the period from 1951 to 1970 about 23 million people[10] moved from one location to another (changes within the same town or village are not included here), which means a considerable mobility averaging about a million and a quarter a year. There was some evident decline of that mobility in the 1960s in comparison with the 1950s, thanks to the growing stability of the economy. People have moved mostly from one village to another village or from the rural areas to the cities and their mobility is closely related to the progress of industrialization. The migration is now oriented mostly to large cities (Stipczynski and Szeliga, 1971:1–3).

Mobility of the population has contributed to a very considerable socioeconomic upgrading of some lower social strata, especially peasants. Substantial transformations of Polish peasants after the Second World War were based first of all upon their gradual move to towns to become industrial workers in the nationalized economy (Turski, 1970). Those remaining in agriculture faced a growing demand for agricultural products which increased their economic (and hence social) position; however, they were very often older people; in 1960, 24% of all economically active in farming were 60 years old or older (Kowaleski, 1970:92), and the proportion was undoubtably higher in more recent years.

The successful adaptation to the Polish urban environment of rural newcomers depends first of all upon their ambition, supplemented by education and occupational or political commitment, and the exposure to external stimuli (e.g., the kind of acquaintances is quite important in this respect). The length of residence in urban life is less important (Siemienska, 1969:357). One must remember that the past industrialization of Poland has created a very substandard demand for labor power.

People who remain in rural villages even while working outside of agriculture, may still maintain to some extent the village style of life and some

---

[9] The estimation for 1965 done by J. Kowaleski (1970:90).

[10] The population of Poland has grown from 25 million in 1950 to 34 million in 1975.

local traditions. Therefore, in Poland, it is quite common to find semitraditional villages occupied mostly by workers and office clerks. Still to be found in such villages are the traditional practices of marrying, inheriting land, relatively little migration of women, much mutual help and division of work between the busy wife on the farm and the husband who commutes to the place of his employment (Pietraszek, 1968; Turski, 1965). As long as village people are able to stay at home and continue at least part of their traditional close neighborhood and family connections, they do not become socially and culturally uprooted.[11]

Among the younger generation of blue collar workers (thirty-five years and younger) there are two-fifths who are of peasant descent. This is a higher percentage than among older workers (e.g., among workers over 50 years old one-third are of peasant descent and over one-half are of worker descent). There is a smaller proportion of peasant descent among skilled industrial workers (36%), than among unskilled (42%), or among skilled construction workers (48%). One-tenth of all workers started their occupational careers in agriculture (Zagorski, 1971).

Among white collar employees, one-fourth are from families of the intelligentsia, one-third are of worker descent and over one-fourth are of peasant descent (Zagorski, 1971:2). One-fourth of all white collar personnel started their careers as manual workers. Over 45% of all white collar employees completed their education while gainfully employed.

Over nine-tenths of the functionaires of the local state authorities (people's councils) are of worker or peasant descent. From 17% to 37% of these functionaires started their careers working as manual workers (Zagorski, 1971:2).

Data from sociological studies done in the 1960s show that there is not much basic material inequality among the following socioeconomic groups: intelligentsia, technicians, clerical staff, foreman, craftsmen, and manual workers (skilled, semiskilled and unskilled). The differences are less in basic incomes, and even in life style, than in general level of education and opportunities which are opened because of it. Moonlighting is more common among some categories of white collar employees. Thus many earn more than others due to the fact that they have greater opportunities for securing second jobs.[12]

Conditions of Employment

Manual workers in Poland spend 46 hours per week on their jobs (on Saturdays, six hours and on weekdays, eight hours). However, in the early 1970s, 12% of them enjoyed a shorter work week averaging forty-one hours. About 15% of the nonagricultural labor work less than eight hours per day (e.g., miners work 7.5 hours per day, teachers and scientists work seven hours per day, steelmakers on four shifts work forty-two hours per week).

Vacations depend on the length of employment; fourteen days after one year of employment, seventeen days after three years, twenty days after six years, twenty-six days after ten years; in 1970, the average vacation leave was

---

[11] There are many such villages, e.g. in Silesia. One of them was studied by Olszewska (1969).

[12] According to the survey data from three Polish cities, moonlighting was most common (27%) among people with the highest incomes (more that 4000 zl per month) (Wesolowski, 1970).

21 days per manual worker (in 1955 it was only fifteen days) (Paradysz, 1971:2). Among manual workers, approximately two-fifths have 14 to 17 work days of annual vacation leave (only 8% among white collar employees) and one-half have 26 work days or more (among white collar employees, four-fifths). Only 12% of manual workers and 7% of clerical workers spend their leave being gainfully employed instead of enjoying full leisure (Krysiak, 1971:2).

Polish industrial enterprises work an average of twelve hours per day (in 1969 an average of 1.6 shifts). In 1973, among all employed industrial workers, 61% worked on the morning shift, 27% on the afternoon shift and 11% on the night shift. By introducing more shifts it would be possible to produce more at lower unit costs and provide more employment. However this situation would eventually limit the extent of extra paid overtime for workers. In 1973 there was about 76 hours per year of overtime per worker in all industries, and 152 overtime hours per year per worker in power industry. In 1970 about one-third of all manual workers worked overtime and they spent an average of 2.5 hours per week for that purpose. On the other hand, 3 hours per week were lost from normal work time for absenteeism (part of it justified by sickness, education, political activism etc.) (Paradysz, 1971:2).

One of the persistent problems of Polish industry has been the high mobility of personnel. Working people in Poland are accustomed to moving from one work-place to another looking for better conditions. For example, in 1955, 40% of industrial workers voluntarily left their work-places. In the last few years, there is much less of this kind of labor mobility; in 1973, 20% of industrial workers (24% among men and 15% among women) left their jobs for new ones. However, there are still difficulties with keeping people on their jobs.

Polish work establishments must rely to a large extent on people who quite often live far from their work-places and have to spend considerable time traveling to and from work in congested trains and buses. About 20% of all people employed in the nationalized economy travel to work from another village or town. Commuters spend an average of 2 hours per day travelling, with 40% spending more than 1.5 hours (Oledzki, 1967; Lijewski, 1967). The improvement of public transportation is one of the most evident needs in Poland.

The average net income in the nationalized economy has grown from 1867 zl per month, in 1965 to 2798 zl in 1973.[13] There are differences in this respect depending on the branch of economy (e.g., in forestry, 2388 zl; and in construction, 3471 zl), status of job (more than 5000 zl earned by 3% of manual workers and 5% of white collar employees), and qualifications. Managers earn a basic salary which is 2 to 2.5 times higher than the average salary, and in addition to it receive 40%–70% in a bonus if they fulfill planned tasks (Galinowski, 1971:9).

---

[13] In the early 1970s, official exchange was 24 zl for 1 U.S. dollar, however on the black market, dollars have an exchange rate of four or five times higher. The exchange value in terms of comparative prices of goods is approximately 1 U.S. dollar for 40 zl to 50 zl. Starting in January 1975, foreign tourists as well as local Poles receive in the state bank 33.2 zl for one U.S. dollar. The prices of basic foodstuffs are kept frozen by the government, but the new merchandise enters the market at higher prices. In any event, inflation in Poland is much slower than in the West.

Complaint about low salaries is common in Poland. To illustrate, in the early 1970s, the average yearly minimum for a family of 4 people[14] in Warsaw is 12,300 zlotys per capita (for a single male, 18,000 zl), of which about 51% goes for food (Tymowski, 1971:4). Table 1 shows the per capita income and distribution of expenditures. As may be seen, there is a growing, progressing evaluation of the living standard of people who belong to various special strata, traditionally being apart from one another. However, in all families, the food expenditure still dominates the budget. Even though housing is inexpensive because it is heavily subsidized, the average income available does not support a higher level of discretionary expenditures. About two million people moonlight because they find it difficult to maintain themselves just from one job.

TABLE 1
COMPARISON OF AVERAGE FAMILIES AMONG WAGE EARNERS AND
AMONG WHITE COLLAR EMPLOYEES AND FARMERS (1969)

Subject	Wage Earners	White Collar Employees	Farmers*
Average number of people in household	3.3	2.9	4.0
Yearly income per capita in zl (thousands)	14.5	18.5	12.8
Foodstuffs as percent of total expenditure	49%	42%	49.5%
Clothing and footwear as percent of total expenditure	17%	17%	17%
Culture, education, sports and tourism as percent of total expenditure	7%	10%	5%
Radio sets per household	0.8	0.9	0.7
TV sets per household	0.6	0.7	0.3
Laundry machines per household	0.8	0.8	0.5
Refrigerators per household	0.2	0.5	0.1
Sewing machines per household	0.5	0.4	0.4
Motorcycles per household	0.1	0.1	0.3
Bicycles per household	0.3	0.2	1.0

* They are better off in comparison with average peasants because of more modern ways of farming.
Source: Budżety rodzin (1971) and Rocznik Statystyczny 1970 (1970: 242, 503–517) ; Concise (1974:69) ; Rocznik (1974:154, 160).

Occupational Status

In comparison with the prewar situation, differentials in earnings is at the present time much smaller. The spread between wages and salaries also has been substantially reduced (See Table 1).

The average net monthly income of industrial workers was 2765 zl in 1973 in comparison with 3989 zl for the technical staff and 2768 zl for the administrative staff working in industry. The highest net average monthly income was for workers in the coal industry (4424 zl), and the lowest in the textile industry (employing mostly women), porcelain-faience industry, paper industry, and clothing industry (all well below 3000 zl).

According to Kalecki (1964), during the period 1937–1960, there has been

[14] The size of an average household in cities is 3.1 members (in villages, 3.9 persons).

a considerable rise in the living conditions of the working population. It is the result of an over two-fold increase in the real incomes of manual workers and a certain drop in those of salary earners. This increase in the standard of living is to a considerable extent a result of the increase of employment; the average rise per employee is much lower. It remains high for manual workers, but in the case of salary earners there has been a fall of about 25%. However the index for manual workers amounts to only 145 when the prewar 'pariah' group, that is domestic servants and artisans' laborers, is excluded. This rise is a result of a 55% increase for industrial workers and an approximately 30% increase for workers employed in other branches of the economy (excluding domestic servants and artisans' assistants) . . .

The ratio of salaries to wages per employed individual in the nonagricultural sector for all employed Polish persons was 2.80 in 1937, but only 1.18 in 1960. If we exclude domestic servants and artisans' apprentices, that ratio was 2.20 in 1937, but only 1.12 in 1960. Members of intelligentsia have much less reason than the workers to be satisfied with the present equalization of incomes, especially in regard to members of the intelligentsia engaged in the performance of tasks of special importance (e.g., factory engineers promoting technical progress). According to research done by Nowak in 1961, there is a significant difference in predilection for egalitarianism between blue collar workers and intelligentsia (Nowak, 1964). Among white collar workers there are quite strong tendencies against egalitarianism (Wisnewski, 1963).

The present social structure in Poland favors a certain egalitarianism, which is also inherent in the Marxist ideology. The rapid industrialization brought many basic changes, abolishing previous distinct strata and groups marked by skill (skilled workers, semiskilled workers, unskilled workers), branch (heavy industry, small industry), ownership (state workers, private business workers), nationality (dominant nationality, minorities), religion, etc. Many of those differences continue to exist, but to a much lesser extent than there used to be before the Second World War.

The high inter- and intragenerational vertical social mobility, as well as an advanced equalitarianism concerning earnings and living conditions, favor to some extent the strengthening of the workers' positions. According to research done in Poland (Sarapata and Wesołowski, 1961) the hierarchy of socio-occupational status is as follows:

1. intelligentsia
2. skilled workers
3. private farmers
4. private enterprise
5. white collar workers
6. unskilled workers

The social prestige of the worker has risen in comparison with the prewar time, especially in occupations like mining, construction, and plumbing. But at the same time aspirations are rising even faster. Workers no longer desire to perpetuate their occupation among their children. They are eager to help their children into the ranks of intelligentsia. A study of the late 1950s shows that

... the models for desired occupational careers among the manual and nonmanual workers are the engineer and medical doctor for boys and the medical doctor and teacher for girls; the tailor is also a model among the manual workers (Sarapata and Wesołowski, 1961).

In that respect, the aspirations of workers do not differ very much from the typical aspirations of the white collar professional groups. The same is true for evaluations of the occupational structure.

The progress in improving working conditions and opportunities to gain an attractive employment is not fast enough to really satisfy the workers.

> The workers are still hired labor. The socialist revolution does not change the relation of the worker to the machine, nor does it change his position within the technological system of the factory. It changes his position in the social and economic system of the industry or factory. But his relation to the machine and the organizational system of work requires his subordination to the foreman and the management of the factory. He receives wages according to the quantity and quality of work performed, and he must obey the principles and regulations of work discipline. Thus, the status of workers is to some degree inconsistent, being at the same time that of hired laborers and that of co-owners of the means of production (Szczepański, 1970:125).

It is hardly necessary to add that this kind of status incongruence unfavorably influences workers' morale.

Working Women

One of the important problems in Poland is the status of working women. In 1972, they constituted 78% of the work force in public health, 76% in banking and insurance, 70% in trade, 72% in education, 45% in science, 56% in public administration, and even 38% in industry.[15] Women constitute 41% of total employment in the nationalized economy (1972). One of the main problems of the working woman is how to combine jobs with household duties and eliminate the possible adverse effects on family life, child bearing and household management (Strzeminska, 1970). Only 2% of the married women have part time jobs.

According to the statistical survey done in 1968–1969 on the time budget of families in which there is at least one person employed in the nationalized economy, working women have less leisure time than working men or non-working women (See Table 2). The burden of working women is very heavy.

In the Polish textile industry, women constitute about three-fifths of the work force. Many of them have small children. According to the 1960 sample data for the families of textile workers in Lodz, 54% of the wives were gainfully employed: 61% in families with one child, 50% in families with two

---

[15] For the teaching profession, 70% of all teachers are women (in 1966 in elementary schools, 77%). Among students of teachers colleges, the percentage of women is even higher (Worach-Kordas, 1970:126).

TABLE 2
TIME BUDGET IN POLISH FAMILIES (1968–1969)
IN HOURS AND MINUTES

		Work and Commutation	Household	Physiological Needs	Leisure
Working men	Sunday	—	}2:27	11:29	8:48
	Saturday	8:14		9:12	4:27
	Other day	9:21	2:32	9:30	3:34
Working women	Sunday	—	4:59	11:32	6:43
	Saturday	7:40	5:22	8:59	3:00
	Other day	8:44	4:36	9:21	2:26
Nonworking women	Sunday	—	5:00	11:49	7:22
	Saturday	—	}8:50	10:36	4:09
	Other day	—		11:00	3:49

* Source: Zycie Gospodarcze (1971, Vol. 2:9).

children, and 45% in families with three children or more. Two-thirds of the families consisted of three or four members. When husband and wife both were gainfully employed as textile workers, the family monthly income was approximately 4200 zl, or 1050 zl per person in a family of four members. The average family spends about 53% on food, 10% on clothing, 5% on shoes, 11% on household investments. The situation was quite difficult among one-third of the families in which the monthly income per family member was very low, or who live just in one room flats (30% of the sample). However, in general there was a considerable percentage of families which owned small washing machines (86%), sewing machines (36%), vacuum cleaners (32%), refrigerators (25%), TV sets (58%), bicycles (7%), motorcycles (8%), and of course radio sets (83%) (Marczak, 1970:78).

The life situation of working women as textile workers depends on several factors: the work shift (until the 1970s, 42% of them had to work on the night shift), regularity of supply in food stores (determining the length of time spent finding and waiting in lines to buy food), the length of the yearly leave (22 days was average among textile workers in 1970), supply of kindergartens and nurseries, and mutual help among family members, etc. There is some improvement in all these respects, and working women now have more free time (half of them have 1.5 to 3 hours of free time daily) than they used to have before, but clearly, the progress does not seem to be satisfactory.

In general, women occupy lower paying jobs and still are very much underrepresented in managerial posts. By the end of the 1960s, women constituted almost two-fifths of all employees with higher education and half of all employees with only secondary education. Women constitute two-fifths of the graduates of higher education, almost half of the graduates of vocational schools (secondary level), and more than two-thirds of the graduates of general high schools (1969). On the other hand, according to data from 1958, only 2% of business executives were women (in the USSR in 1961, 6%). 3% of the university chairmen were women (1962), while 13% of the members of parliament were women (1958) (Sokołowska and Wrochno, 1965:152–155). There is a growing pressure among Polish women to have not only a formal equality, but also an appropriate share in salaries and promotion opportunities.

Workers' Morale

Human relations in industrial enterprises is under the impact of two opposed patterns. One of them is based on local cultural traditions of mutual help and moral support, which is supplemented by traditions of craftsmanship (Pomian, 1969:135). The second pattern is based on a pressure coming from the top of the bureaucratic hierarchy. Managers reward quantity not quality, give priority to negative sanctions not positive ones (there is a serious penalty for being absent from work, but there are at the same time few incentives to commit oneself to the well being of the factory), impose a formalistic approach, and prefer a blind loyalty over any initiative. Such an approach is dictated not only by authoritarian preferences of managers, but even more by the nature of the system in which they are located. In Poland there is a long tradition of a positive approach to the issue of managing people. One of the leading Polish specialists in the scientific organization of work (Adamiecki, 1970), stimulated creative thinking in that field. However, under the historic regime of authoritarianism and bureaucracy, obstacles existed to the transformation from dependence on command and blind obedience on one hand, to dependence on human good will on the other. Only in 1971, after the takeover of political power in Poland by a technocratically oriented elite, has some movement begun toward a more up-to-date approach.

There are several factors which have to be taken into consideration with respect to the workers' morale in Poland. First of all, in the 1950s and 1960s, the great demand for labor quite often necessitated hiring people who were uneducated and ill adapted to work in industry. The low morale of newly recruited workers was especially evident in the industrial establishments that were erected during the late 1940s and the early 1950s. At the present time, the most difficult period in that respect is over. However, there are problems with absenteeism and labor turnover. The average industrial worker in 1973 missed without a good reason 17 hours of work annually in the excavating industry and 25 hours in construction—a little over 1% of the total work period. There is a yearly turnover in industry of approximately one-fifth of all workers (it was two-fifths in the 1950s). In addition, work input is lost due to illness. The number of paid lost work days, due to illness, has grown from 66 per one hundred employed people per month in 1960 to 89 in 1973 (130 industry and 101 in construction in 1972).

It is not uncommon for people to "call in" sick, just because they do not want to come to work. For example, peasant workers are especially "sick prone" during the harvest time. In 1958, the government introduced a regulation which limited the number of sickness benefits (pay for sick leave) allowed in the enterprises. In addition, industrial doctors receive bonuses for keeping this number relatively low. However, it is possible to say that most workers who go to doctors are really sick. Many of them even hide their sickness and continue to work in order not to lose a portion of their income (piece work is quite common).

On the other hand the accident and sickness rates are quite often caused by hazards related to work or by poor working conditions in old fashioned plants and industries. In coal mines, for example 31% of crews work in unusually dangerous conditions. From 1960 until 1966 the number of work days lost per one hundred employees because of accidents had grown from 187 to 229 (Sokołowska, 1969:280, 294).

In the official propaganda offered for external as well as for internal use, there is emphasis on workers being proud of their work. However, this propaganda so far has not been very effective. Work as a social value is not deeply rooted in the Polish society. According to the survey carried out in 1961, there appears to be an inclination among Polish people to evaluate human behavior more according to the social and ethical criteria, than according to the criteria of efficiency and material success. Very important in this respect is the impact of the sociocultural traditions created and maintained by the gentry, which constituted around 15% to 20% of the total population in the eighteenth and early nineteenth century (Zajaczkowski, 1961). The younger generation attaches a growing importance to work as a social value, but in general this value is still not in the ascendancy. Honesty was chosen as an important value in a survey by 46% of urban respondents and by 51% of rural respondents, but the corresponding percentages for thoroughness were only 16% and 15%; for inventiveness, 16% and 12.5% etc. "A job well done," and especially its components, such as thoroughness and motivation, are not values that are universally held in high esteem (Sufin and Wesołowski, 1964). This is the reason why the people do not react vigorously against their colleagues who are busy at work with personal affairs during working hours, or who feign illness and remain at home.

The full employment policy enables people to choose their jobs quite freely and to change them at their convenience. Until recently their was a substantial mobility of the industrial crews in the socialized enterprises. The percentage of workers having seniority less than five years was rather substantial in 1962: 41% in industry and 52% in construction.

The smooth functioning of the enterprise, its efficient organization, and the regular supply of raw materials usually seem to be the decisive factors in creating workers' satisfaction with their work and in stimulating their morale. According to the survey data from 1961, a considerable portion of workers was dissatisfied with the irregular supply of tools (72% of respondents in the manufacturing industry), the poor quality of the tools (55% in the manufacturing industry and 44% in the electronics industry), the irregular supply of raw materials (from 28% to 59% in different industries), the poor quality of the materials (from 38% to 49% of respondents in different industries), the poor organization of work (from 7% to 32% in different industries), and with the poor treatment of the foremen (from 36% to 61% in different industries). The young workers were inclined to be more critical than their older colleagues, especially in modern branches of industry. Most of the young and skilled workers were satisfied with their choice of occupation and they would like to practice good workmanship. The deficiencies of an inadequate work organization made them angry because it impeded the proper execution of work (Wesołowski, 1962).

The dissatisfaction of workers with the inefficiency of the economic system has grown for years. In addition there has been a widespread awareness that under the current regime there would be little to do in order to improve the whole situation. According to the survey from 1960, 35% of the respondents among workers and employees did not believe they had any influence on what happened at their work-places. Only less than one-half of the respondents believed that it was resonable to criticize the mistakes of their supervisors and that such criticism could bring positive changes (survey done by the Polish Centre of Public Opinion Polls).

The lack of belief in practical usefulness of adapting an active attitude, supported by obstacles in bringing a smooth internal communication in the factory, is detrimental to the employee's morale.[16] The survey done by the weekly journal *Polityka* among its readers (see Table 3) showed that the level

TABLE 3
DEGREE OF SATISFACTION REGARDING WORKING AND PAYMENT
CONDITIONS AMONG VARIOUS OCCUPATIONS, IN PERCENT OF RESPONDENTS
(SURVEY OF *POLITYKA* 1971 [FIKUS, 1971])

Subject of Evaluation	Manual Workers	Foremen	Technicians	Graduate Engineers
Happy with present work-place	70	85	75	75
Feel that the present income from work is adequate	56	61	50	65
Regard human relations highly	15	26	23	19
Feel that they have influence on what happens at the work-place	9	32	21	28
Are trying to contribute to improvement at the work-place	45	75	..	67
Feel totally restricted in improving work and functioning of their work-places	79	71	..	57

of work satisfaction differed, depending upon the occupational and administrative position of respondents. In general, people were quite happy with their work-places, but on the other hand, moving down the hierarchy increased the proportion who felt restricted, helpless and discriminated against. When asked about their promotion opportunities, 61% of the workers and 58% of the graduate engineers answered that they were very limited (among all respondents one-half felt the same). People look for better income (70% of all respondents), autonomy (27%), and stability (18%)—more than for promotion (13% of all respondents). At the same time one-half of all respondents believed that there was no honest way to be promoted, and the only possibility was to look for private sponsors, or to push strongly in selling oneself to the management. Among graduate engineers, only one-fifth believed that promotion depended upon the qualities of an individual (Fikus, 1971).

---

[16] According to the study of Surmaczynski (1965) done in five factories, there were several deficiencies in the communication process between the bottom and the top of the factory hierarchy. One-half of all respondents did not accept official arguments used by the factory authorities. The percentage of people convinced by those arguments was much higher among the Party members (80%), than among the people not belonging to the Party (58%). The percentage of people convinced by official arguments was lower among the rank-and-file than among people in higher ranks.

ASPIRATIONS OF WORKERS

The rapidly rising sociocultural aspirations of the new workers' generation are beginning to play an important role in present Poland, creating several social problems of great importance for the regime. First of all, there is a substantial increase in the absolute numbers of young people entering the labor force. There is little inclination for workers' sons to follow their father's occupation. The young generation breaks very easily with the tradition of occupational inheritance and is strongly supported in this tendency by the parents. The education level of the peasants' offspring migrating into the towns and cities has been rising, as have their aspirations. A general decline of migration from the rural areas of individuals with modest aspirations and still more modest requirements (as to the conditions of work and nature of the job) is an obvious result of all those factors. The young migrants from the countryside do not have reason anymore to accept passively the fact that they would be eventually treated as inferiors by urban workers. There no longer exist basic differences in educational level and culture between them and their colleagues of a blue collar descent. Universal education and the mass media (radio, TV, cinema) popularize the same patterns of thinking and behaving in the countryside as in the urban areas.

In principle, the governmental full employment policy gives a guarantee for younger people to find a place to work and live (Rajkiewicz, 1965); however this place is quite often not up to their aspirations and expectations. The transition from a permissive school environment to the average work environment is not an easy one for young people. They must come to grips with several hardships. First of all they must overcome the negativism and defensiveness of the older generation who feel themselves to be challenged by their less experienced but better educated young colleagues.

The participation of the wage earning class in the educational system has changed substantially in comparison with the prewar situation (Matejko, 1969a, 1974b). In secondary education, during the late 1960s this participation (38.3% in 1966–67 in comparison with 33% in 1960–61) was more or less satisfactory. However, there are many more workers' offspring in basic vocational schools (49%) and in vocational technical secondary schools (37.5%) than in general secondary schools (28%), whose students are children of white collar parents (44%) (Nowakowska, 1970). In 1973–74 among college students, the workers' offspring constituted 30% (in comparison with 52.3% of white collar offspring), but there was a much higher participation of them among evening class students (59%) and students taking extension courses (45% compared to only 22% of the white collar origins) (Matejko, 1969a).

Regarding their own educational level, today's workers have advanced a great deal, as one can see from the comparison of the educational level of the workers with that of their parents. Such a comparison among Polish industrial workers showed one-half of the fathers and three-fifths of the mothers did not complete their elementary education, while only 27% of their children did not (Sarapata, 1965c).

Young workers are interested in continuation of their education, but are quite often critical about the attitude of their supervisors towards training and education. In a case study done in one of the industrial communities, one-third of the young workers were critical about the failure of their employers to support their educational interests and efforts (Herod, 1969:248). The problem of education is especially acute among young single workers who come from the country and settle temporarily in workers' hostels. They have a lot of free time after working hours and they do not know what to do with it.[17]

Frustrated Expectations

Relatively light work, good working conditions, gentle treatment, opportunity for advancement, permissive discipline, and a standard of living much higher than that of the parents—these are the values for which the young generation of workers strives. For the older generation of workers who experienced the difficult interwar period (unemployment, the war and the German occupation), the generation which has suffered need and often primitive living conditions as the unemployed in the towns or the landless and impoverished redundant hands in the villages, it was satisfying to get steady work in the state-sponsored industry and a place to live in the town (Zweig, 1944; Matejko, 1974a). Their social aspirations were thus gratified to a large extent, and their hopes were more easily transferred to their children. The old generation's hope was that the young generation would advance further on the social ladder and would obtain better conditions of work, finally breaking with hard physical labour.

Workers, especially the younger generation, demand further advances in abolition of social differences, separating the workers from higher social strata. According to research done by Nowak, 53% of skilled workers and 44% of unskilled workers would like to see the social differences disappear entirely in the future, as compared to 38% of the creative intelligentsia holding the same postulate (Nowak, 1964).

This does not mean, however, that the workers are for the full equalization of incomes. A research done in Poland in 1959 by Sarapata showed that the Polish people universally regarded differentiation of earnings as the status quo and that representatives of different occupational groups constructed different wage hierarchies. The steel workers, miners' wives, and manual workers, surveyed by Sarapata, put in the first four ranks of the occupation ladder, classified according to the "proper rate for the job," such occupations as university professor, cabinet minister, mechanical engineer and physician (there was relatively little difference in that respect in the opinions of workers and representatives of other occupational groups). Such occupations as actor, priest, building laborer, nurse, spinner, and recreationist were given much more variable rankings compared to the four above mentioned professions (Sarapata, 1963).

The same research showed also, that the level of earnings postulated by workers as desirable for their own occupational groups did not exceed the level of actual earnings to a great extent. Workers were realistic enough to postulate for themselves one-fifth to one-fourth more than their actual incomes. At the same time, they were interested in limiting the highest possible incomes to the maximum wage typical for highest paid blue collar workers. Quite different in that respect were opinions of highly skilled professionals. Their level of

---

[17] According to the survey done in the period 1956–58 in Nowa Huta one-half of the inhabitants of workers' hostels had five hours or more of free time per day and three-fourths had at least two hours (Siemienski, 1961).

income expectation was much higher. There were several reasons for this: the incomes of these professionals often were relatively higher before the war, there was a tendency (much stronger than among workers) to compare ones' own incomes with salaries paid in other countries (e.g. in East Germany and in the West), there was a conviction that one's real contribution was much greater than real income, etc.

A moderately high percentage of workers covered by the quota sample of the total male urban population studied by Nowak define their social status as lower than average: 66% among unskilled workers, and 45% among skilled workers. The lower the educational level and also the lower the income of a blue collar respondent, the more unfavorable his evaluation of his own social status. It is also worth mentioning that workers, especially unskilled ones, were —in comparison with higher social strata—less optimistic with regards to the possible future diminishment of distinctions between members of different social groups in Poland. Income, education, and managerial or nonmanagerial positions—were perceived by workers in the first place as sources of permanent division of society.

The political and social advancement of the working class (workers comprise about 40% of the members and candidate-members of the Polish United Workers' Party) is another fact which stimulates workers' aspirations. About two-thirds of all industrial executives are of worker or peasant origin (Najduchowska, 1969b). Many of the ruling Party elite were workers at one time or were of blue collar origin. According to the research data from 1960, 74% of all great industrial enterprises had a Party membership between 9% and 21%. Two-thirds of all Party members in the industrial, transport and building enterprises were manual workers (Bauman, 1962). Party membership is relatively much more common among male workers than female workers, among skilled workers than among unskilled workers, among people with seniority than among people without seniority.[18]

Activity of workers and employees in Party organizations is greater the higher the occupational status of a particular category of employees.[19]

> Degree of militancy is relatively highest among engineers and technicians, and lowest among unskilled workers (exactly seven and a half times less than among the engineers). This personal skill which as a rule is correlated to the position of engineer predestines him, more than others, to behave in such a way as is accepted as a measure of Party militancy. Exactly the opposite is the case with the unskilled manual workers.... The percentage of Party militants among the factory personnel with a secondary education is relatively four times more than among those with a primary education (Bauman, 1962:59–60).

---

[18] In Poland, as in other Eastern European countries, seniority plays only a limited role.

[19] Survey data from 1970 shows that the interest for political issues correlates with the Party membership. For example, among Party members 49% and among nonmembers only 19% read more or less regularly the sociopolitical literature. There are in that respect also some important differences depending on the educational level. Four-fifths of Party members with higher education read that literature (only 16% among nonmembers at the same educational level), but one-third of Party members with no more than elementary education and 57% with no more than secondary education (Gospodarek, 1971:249–251).

According to some recent research, differentials in activity were as follows: technical staff—every third person; foreman—every fifth, clerical staff—every seventh, skilled workers—every eleventh, unskilled workers—every twenty-fifth (Krall, 1970).

The same phenomenon appears concerning the activity of workers in the Workers' Councils created in 1956. In spite of the fact that these Councils were supposed to represent mainly the manual (blue collar) workers (Widerszpil and Owieczko, 1970), the latter show relatively less interest in them than do the members of higher occupational strata. In the research done in 1958

> it was discovered that there was a connection between extent of interest on the one hand, and the level of qualifications on the other. At the one end, the unskilled workers showed the least interest. . . . The main adverse criticism was directed toward the fact that, in the respondents' opinion, the Councils failed to act as representatives of the workers on the management (Szostkiewicz, 1962).

It seems important to add here that social research done later also showed a very limited worker interest in Workers' Councils. Only 5% of the workers in the machinery and metal structures industry and 19% of the workers in the leather industry in 1961 said that according to their judgment, Workers' Councils really represented interests of blue collars (survey of the Polish Centre of Public Opinion Polls). In another study, 40% of the respondents among workers could not say anything about the activity of the Workers' Council in their own enterprise, and 86% of the respondents did not know anything about the last session of that Council (Morawski, 1969:259).

Not only in Poland but also in other Eastern European countries the social and political activity among workers increases, according to the research data, along with their educational level, importance of work done and seniority. There is also a significant difference in this respect between the two sexes. Men are much more active in industry than women, which relates not only to tradition, but also to their higher degree of skill, better education, and smaller commitment to the family care.

Work Satisfaction Among White Collar Workers

Socialist economies primarily need engineers and technicians in the white collar ranks. White collar workers filling clerical positions are of secondary importance. However, it seems even justified to say that all white collar employees are put in a situation in which they have to follow the bureaucratic pattern. The state machine tends to give the bureaucratic content to all kinds of jobs. The Party apparatus shows deep appreciation for technology, not so much because of its crucial importance for the Party ideology, but because of its contribution to the fulfillment of Party goals.

Immediately after the Second World War there was such a great demand for white collar workers (22% of the total population were killed by Nazis, mostly Jews and intelligentsia) that all kinds of candidates were admitted to salaried posts, especially when it was in interest of the Party to have loyal and reliable people socially advanced from lower ranks in industry. According to survey data, 40% of clerical staff used to work previously as manual workers, and nine-tenths were of blue collar descent (Lutynska, 1965:55–56). These people owed everything to the Party and many of them were active Party members. On the other hand, their salaries were low as was the social prestige of the clerical staff. In the Polish society there was a common distaste for clerks as a bulwark of the highly bureaucratized state machine.

> Lower-echelon employees become the scapegoats of any and all short-comings and deficiencies in the present order. They are blamed for bureaucratic distortions, and the populace very often holds them responsible for any inconveniences, shortages of goods, and so forth (Szczepański, 1970:123).

Therefore, the advancement into the clerical ranks is not particularly attractive for the young generation of a blue collar descent. This fact contributes substantially to the general dissatisfaction of clerks with their professional image.

The clerical staff is, to a large extent, publicly believed to be responsible for the inefficiency and inhumanity of bureaucracy. However in reality most clerks have little impact in this regard. Two-thirds of lower and middle clerical positions even in industry are occupied by low paid women. Among the clericals, there is a very considerable percentage of people with relatively low education as well as people of manual worker descent (Lutynska, 1965; Janicki, 1968). Their incomes are much lower than incomes of technicians and quite often below wages of workers.

There is a common feeling among the clerical staff in industry, as well as in other branches that their position is inferior, that they are very much underpaid, and that it is not worthwhile to be a clerk. In a study of employees in trade, about 70% of sale clerks as well as store managers surveyed felt they would not like their children (male or female) to enter into the same profession (Altkorn, 1963:29). Only 24% of sale clerks and 33% of store managers said that were they to start over again, they would choose again the same profession (Altkorn, 1963:37).

For clerks and even more for their supervisors, the practical solution for low status is to strengthen their position by joining the Party. There is a certain eagerness among people from clerical and administrative ranks to become accepted into the Party. However, the presumedly worker's Party is endangered by this inflow into its ranks of bureaucrats widely disliked or even hated by the great majority of the members. Therefore, from time to time there is a purge among Party ranks directed mostly at clerks.

Technicians, and especially engineers, are welcomed into the Party as specialists. For the most part they are also people who are indebted to the regime for their social advancement. The share of engineers, technicians and managers in the total ruling Party's membership has grown in the period of 1960 to 1973 from 8% to 11%. According to data from a 1965 sampling of nine industrial enterprises located in various parts of the country, among the technical personnel, two-thirds consist of people originally from the lower social strata (24% from peasant origins and 41% from blue collar origins) (Preiss, 1967). The technical personnel are not very far from the blue collar workers in their basic characteristics, and thus they do not practice the kind of "splendid isolation" which was a barrier preventing the traditional intelligentsia from committing themselves to the ruling elite (Matejko, 1974a). In Poland, political activity increases with higher position in the hierarchy.

People who were educated under the rule of the present regime have less restraints than their fathers about joining the Party, and secure some concrete advantages from doing so. As long as the percentage of young people ideologically committed to religion is decreasing and the number of people who lack any ideological concern is growing, there are no reservations about becoming members of the Party, especially if it seems necessary to support one's own professional career.[20] This explains why the percentage of Party militants

> is highest among comparatively young engineers and technicians, who have been Party members for 6–10 years, and who have been working for 3–5 years in the same place of employment, and who have a fairly high level of education (Bauman, 1962).

It does not mean, however, that by becoming active in the Party, engineers just strive for a managerial career. For them the promotions to administrative posts almost always mean the neglect of their own professional qualifications. Instead of pursuing what they learned in technical colleges, engineers promoted to managerial positions must commit themselves entirely to tasks of an administrative character for which they were never professionally qualified (Pasieczny, 1968). This is the main reason why a promotion to managerial ranks is not particularly attractive for engineers. Among 215 of them surveyed by Grzelak only 10% said they would choose a job which would open the way to managerial promotion, while 71% chose a technically interesting job. On the other hand, less than one-third (28%) were interested in production as a type of occupational career (Grzelak, 1965).

This is closely related to the type of professional training which young engineers receive at technical universities. The study of adaptation of young engineers to their first job, done in 1960, shows that most of them were not prepared to assume any managerial responsibilities (Matejko, 1962).

Engineers prefer to move from industry to design bureaus or research and development institutes. In the case of a sample studied by Grzelak, two-thirds of surveyed engineers mentioned poor human relations and one-half mentioned poor work organization as serious shortcomings of their work-places. This was significant because the political and managerial system which existed at that time in Poland left engineers feeling helpless in dealing with such shortcomings. In a study of chemical engineers, one-half of them did not believe in the possibility of improving the situation by their own action nor did want to act, and only one-tenth felt personally responsible for what happened in their work-places (Kowalewski, 1962). A survey of engineers employed in heavy industry in Warsaw showed a very high level of dissatisfaction especially with the organization of work (81% of engineers being dissatisfied), salaries (77%),

---

[20] The study of students at the Technical University in Warsaw conducted by Nowak and Pawełczyńska in 1958 and in 1961 shows the considerable diminishment of religious commitments, the slow gain by Marxist materialists and the rapid growth of people without any commitment (neutral). The Polish censorship did not allow the entire study to be published, but some of the data has appeared in articles (Nowak, 1962; Pawełczyńska and Nowak, 1962; Jozefowicz, Nowak and Pawełczyńska, 1958: Nowak, 1960). See also Kasinska (1970) and Wilder (1964).

attention paid by the employer to the vital interests of people employed by him (72%), prospects of advancement (60%), climate of work performance (51%), etc. Among engineers there were significant proportions who wanted to change their jobs: 70% in enterprises, 62% in design bureaus, and 58% in research institutes. The negative evaluation of the existing work organization was given by 81% of engineers in industrial enterprises and 68.5% of engineers in design offices and institutes. The very positive opinion about organization was expressed by only 3% of the engineers in enterprises and 4% of the engineers in bureaus and institutes (Hoser, 1970:156). In comparison with these above mentioned aspects, the climate of human relations was evaluated much more favorably. This means that it was primarily the formal organization imposed by the higher authorities which provided the basic source of dissatisfaction.

In a work situation characterized by an ossified and dehumanized formal organization imposed arbitrarily from outside of one's own work-place, the only support for legitimate grievances may be provided by friends. Engineers surveyed by Hoser were asked who would defend their interests if necessary. In reply to this question, 12% of them mentioned the management of their respective factories, 10% the Party (or other political institutions managed by it), 16% the professional associations, 18% said that nobody would help them, and the largest portion, 41%, mentioned just friends. This means that informal ties play a much more important role than any formalized safeguards (Hoser, 1969:119).

It is very significant that the dissatisfaction with formal organization did exist even among engineers who occupied managerial positions (Hoser, 1969:137). There was some reduction of dissatisfaction when going up to managerial ranks but the drop did not seem to be great enough to make the picture entirely different. Under the current highly centralized systems of management, all engineers at the level of work-places, whether occupying managerial positions or not, felt dissatisfied.

The same data, related to engineers employed in 1963 in heavy industry, show some basic differences in their opinions about the current system of incentives. People who held managerial positions appeared to be more pessimistic in their judgment (Hoser, 1969:136). Almost half of all surveyed engineers were employed in research development centers and one-third in factories (Hoser, 1969:118). A study of engineers in electro-technical industry lead Pasieczny to the conclusion that the currently applied "system of financial rewards in general does not stimulate a motivation which would favor technical progress" (Pasieczny, 1968:352).

It seems that Polish engineers and technicians mostly followed a purely pragmatic approach in their orientation toward the Party. In order to achieve something fruitful it was necessary to gain personal acceptance by the Party. Even if there is not very much to be trusted it just seems practical to cooperate. Such an interpretation is consistent with the general, present-day Polish utilitarian approach to principles. According to survey data from 1970, only 23% of all Poles felt that one should always follow moral principles, 40% declared themselves in favor of flexibility in that respect, and 30% took a purely pragmatic approach (7% did not answer). In another survey, the majority of respondents declared themselves as preferring good human relations over effective work (Podgórecki, 1971). On the other hand, there is an evident tendency in the younger generation to give priority to some concrete tasks over all kinds of political loyalties and commitments. Among students surveyed recently about their ideals, more than one-half had positive commitment to work, but only 19% declared themselves in favor of loyalty to state authorities (13% among students of worker descent), and only 14% chose political commitment (Przeclawska and Sawa, 1971:11).

RED EXECUTIVES

Immediately after World War II, the Party was eager to tolerate all kinds of specialists in executive positions, because they were badly needed for the reconstruction of the whole economy and administration. However, even from the start in 1945, there was pressure to promote the people from lower social strata to higher positions. Being dependent upon the political establishment for everything they had achieved, those promoted people seemed to be much more loyal and politically reliable than the old intelligentsia. During the period 1949–1955, this pressure became dominant even though it led to a general decline of qualifications.[21]

The doctrinaire Marxist approach to the economy was introduced in Poland on a broad front in the early 1950's. Exactly at that time the new kind of executives started their careers. They were promoted not on the basis of their professional qualifications but on account of their unreserved commitment to the Party cause. Most of the well known Polish economists were shocked by what happened to the economy. The whole array of newly appointed executives blindly followed orders coming from the Party headquarters and secured their future careers in this way. It was at that time that executives became equal to apparatchiks. The Party established the institutionalized register, called nomenclature, of reliable people chosen to fill all executive positions in the whole country. It became a common practice to move these people from one executive slot to another according to the changing plans and whims of top Party officials. Executives included in the nomenclature enjoyed a relative security in the sense that it was rather unusual to fire them. As long as they were politically reliable and blindly committed to the current Party line, they could be sure of at least some kind of executive position.

This practice was stopped to some extent in 1956 but the whole process once started was in reality irreversible under the current political conditions. The regime was vitally interested in promoting people who could be totally reliable. At the same time people from the lower strata, advancing educationally and socially, looked for better positions for themselves, their friends, relatives, etc.

According to data on 1541 executives in 1965, only one-fifth were from the white collar stratum (Najduchowska, 1969a). This was much less than in most of the Western countries. "Approximately 60% of the samples of the business elite in Britain, the Netherlands, Sweden and the United States have businessmen as fathers" (Lipset and Bendix, 1967:40). Only about one-half of Polish executives who came from lower social strata had higher education; quite a number of them were just transferred from the ranks of the Party, army, or secret police.

With the progress towards higher levels of industrialization in Poland, just

---

[21] In the sample of forty enterprises studied by Najduchowska (1969b) for only one year (1948–1949) the ratio of executives with higher technical education has fallen from one-half to less than one-third.

as in other socialist countries (Parkin, 1969; Matejko, 1974a), there was increasingly more emphasis on formal qualifications. The pressures of rapid industrialization made this inevitable (Matejko, 1974b). The analysis of 1541 industrial executives (manufacturing, light industry, chemistry, mining, power, foodstuffs) in 1965 showed that the most common practice was to recruit them from the ranks of technical personnel. Three-fifths of them were originally from the manual workers' stratum (Najduchowska, 1969b:195). Two-thirds had a technical education and one-sixth had an economic education. This means that most of those executives were trained in technical disciplines (39% were graduates and 18% were on the level of secondary technical education) and only a very few had some background in humanities.

According to data on 127 business executives (industry, construction, communal services and trade) gathered in 1964 by Sarapata, it can be shown that Polish executives in comparison with executives in Britain, West Germany, Italy, the U.S.A., France and Sweden, feel much less secure in their positions, far more limited in achieving some self-actualization (even if their ambitions in this respect are lower than in other countries) and that they place more emphasis on gaining autonomy (Sarapata, 1970). Expectations of Polish executives are clearly shaped, but their satisfaction is far from being fulfilled. Data on occupational and professional prestige among the Polish population show that there is an evident social disagreement in Poland about the status of executives. Some people rank this status very high and some others put it relatively low. Even if the comparative study, 1959–1968, done by the Polish Center of Public Opinion Polls shows some progress in improving the social prestige of executives, they are still very far from establishing their social position in society. It seems obvious that without a reform which would give local industrial executives much more power, their position will remain shaky and ambiguous[22] (Zielinski, 1973).

Executives in general work from ten to twelve or even fourteen hours per day, sometimes even longer, which means two to six hours longer than regular office hours. Their daily effort is split into many, often sixty or more, activities which do not balance one another.[23] Industrial executives work even longer hours. Most of their activities are very short in time (7 to 10 minutes) and do not allow them to focus attention on selected issues. Executives are busy all the time with details of governing their units and preventing the whole organizational order from collapsing. The manager who would not spend all his time and effort on the current issues almost unavoidably would expose himself

---

[22] What kind of reform is possible in the Polish economy under the current political conditions is always an open question. It is necessary to remember that bureaucracy on the one hand, and privately owned agriculture on the other, provide considerable room for the petit bourgeois mentality. For orthodox Marxists, therefore, the same question that was acute under NEP in Soviet Russia still exists: "how long the communist government, which was bound to represent the ideal of the class of industrial workers, could survive before being engulfed in this petit bourgeois sea?" (Swaniewicz, 1969:73). The same reason which pushed Soviet Marxists to the dramatic intervention in agriculture, now prevents Polish Party officials from committing themselves to any wide spread reform of the total economy in the sense of giving more freedom to local initiative. It is a long established tradition of communism that leaders should be tough in dealing with all orientations towards growing consumption among the masses.

[23] There are several research data in this respect. See a summary of them in Kowalewski (1970).

to the accusation of being lazy and negligent. The only way of avoiding the negative appraisal by bosses is to spend as much time as possible in the office at the expense of his family and his private life.

Subordinates expect their supervisor to take as much formal responsibility as possible. Because of the narrow salary ranges they are not able to gain substantially by taking risks, and the heavy responsibility put on them discourages any initiative and gives a premium to just playing safe. It leads to a situation in which the executive has to spend most of his time merely controlling his own subordinates (to whom he is not able to pass full responsibility), and being in contact with various authorities of a political or bureaucratic character.

Under the constant pressure of deciding on issues forced upon him either by subordinates or by superiors, the executive has little opportunity to prepare and to conduct actions originated by himself. Instead of steering the enterprise he is in fact constantly pushed around by current events. People below him avoid taking responsibility and therefore they overburden the executive with various kinds of petty issues. But at the same time, being personally responsible to political authorities for all kinds of shortcomings, even in minor cases, the executive has to concern himself constantly with details. By displaying continuous activities he constructs a defense against diverse accusations of negligence and laziness. As there are always many other people vitally interested in seeing him removed from his present position and taking it over for themselves, he has to be extremely careful in his overt behavior.[24]

Executives are so busy with bureaucratic aspects of their jobs that they do not have much time for social aspects. According to a time budget study of executives in some industries, conducted in 1958–1960, only 4% of their time was spent in dealing with the problems of employees. But, according to research data, executives spend from one-third to two-thirds of their time on various conferences and only a small part of their work time is spent on effective work in their own office (Rupinski and Taubwurcel, 1961:47, 65–69). In reality much of the effort is spent on meeting various people; more than forty per day. For conceptual work there is less than one-hour per day, and for one's own study— only a few minutes per day.

Executives as a distinct social category within the society, are exposed to sociocultural trends and influences which dominate the national scene. It seems fully justified to say that Poland is a country dominated culturally by the intelligentsia now more than before World War II. Even when executives are much closer to the new group of political leaders than previously, they are still under the pressure of intellectual values. Political leaders, including executives, "are to some degree interpenetrated by traditional intellectuals, but the latter have rather limited influence on political decisions" (Szczepański, 1962: 419).

Executives and apparatchiks, although isolated from the rest of the popu-

---

[24] The study of local bank executives conducted in 1964 and 1967 by Kiezun shows a very high bureaucratic rigidity of decision making. Executives are personally responsible for fulfillment of many detailed commands which flow perpetually from higher levels of the centralized authority, but they do not have time and resources to follow these commands. The only reasonable solution is to merely pay lip service to most of the commands, follow only some of them, and construct effective defense mechanisms, which excuse the neglect of others (Kiezun, 1968–69, 1968, 1969).

lation, still are exposed to pressures and influences of an informal nature. The values and norms of the intelligentsia play the main role in this respect: traditions of an intellectual openness and tolerance, genuine political and cultural interests, strong emphasis on the idea of honor, but on the other hand also some pretentiousness and lack of a sense of reality, distaste for working just in order to earn money, and lack of appreciation of business and calculation (Ossowska, 1973). "The 'personal model' (ideal type) of the intelligentsia was created by poets, writers, historians, and artists rather than businessmen and technocrats" (Gella, 1971:17). However, under the bureaucratic model of communism, executives did not have any real opportunity to develop their own ethics and their own sociocultural identity.[25] Because of the progressing ritualization and formalization of the official ideology, there has not been any real commitment to it. Under the pressure of the ruling Party elite, suspicious about any potential rivalry, there has been no opportunity for independent social forces and institutions to develop their own sociocultural patterns. The Catholic church, as the most dangerous rival of the Party was always kept away by the ruling Party from the power structure in which executives were located.

However, by promoting education (Matejko, 1969a), art and culture, science and mass media, the ruling Party had to accept the services of intelligentsia. Because of industrialization, bureaucracy and general sociocultural progress, the share of white collar employees and their families in the Polish society has grown almost four times in comparison with the interwar period. For most of these people, the patterns of thinking developed by the traditional intelligentsia are still very attractive. The ruling Party failed in trying to redirect in this respect the new arrivals to intelligentsia from the workers' and peasants' ranks (Chalasinski, 1958). Executives in their leisure time follow the only patterns which do exist and which have been originated by the intelligentsia. The social gatherings arranged by them are attended by members of the intelligentsia. Children of executives choose careers which follow the ideals and values of the intelligentsia. In order to impress their friends and acquaintances, the executives have to pay at least some lip service to what is dear to the heart and mind of a typical member of the intelligentsia.

Subject to the constant pressure of two opposite patterns: the orthodox pattern of the Party dogmatism, and the liberal pattern of the intellectual tolerance, the executives in order to survive and gain some success develop tactics based primarily on evasion.

The typical executive has several good reasons to be suspicious about intellectuals. First of all he avoids all kinds of utopias which, according to Feuer (1964:88) "illuminate the unconscious stirrings and direction of the intellectuals." Second, he does not share the doubts and frustrations of the intellectuals. Third, he suspects them of a superiority complex of a more or less authoritarian nature. Fourth, it is very difficult for him to appreciate a way of thinking which does not culminate in action. Fifth, his sense of reality prevents him from becoming too involved in abstract concepts of a doctrinaire character.

However, the main obstacle built into the role of executives in Poland has

---

[25] It is very significant that in the Soviet Union only in the last few years there has been a tendency to treat management as a separate problem, and not just as one of the issues of Party functioning. The necessity to appreciate sociological and psychological aspects of management was emphasized in 1966 by Gvishani (1966) and from that time it became politically acceptable to deal with them.

been related, at least until 1971, rather to the low intellectual level of the ruling elite than to the conflicts with intellectuals. Before World War II, the communist Party was insignificant and not sufficiently influential to attract the better educated people. The Party was illegal in Poland and the few committed intellectuals fled to the Soviet Union where most of them became victims of the great purge arranged by Stalin who was especially suspicious of Polish communists. People who formed the new elite which took power under the Soviet guidance in 1944–1945 consisted mostly of either low rank local agitators and leaders, or new careerists who looked for personal advantages. In both cases the level of education and sophistication was very low. What matters even more, these people developed some vested interest which discouraged a significant change even later. "In a party apparatus composed of some 7,000 officials, in 1964 only 1,275 and even by 1968 only around 2,000 had completed their higher education" (Bromke, 1971:486).

Dilemma of Bureaucratic Management

After the fall of the Gomulka regime in 1970 under the pressure of working class masses, a new era started in the field of management in general and industrial management in particular. For the first time in the history of communism, political leaders were driven from office because the public did not accept them. The leaders who assumed control at the end of 1970 have to face a new sociopolitical situation in which the purely authoritarian style of management simply is obsolete.

There is a growing awareness among the Polish establishment that in order to improve the economy it is necessary to overhaul the whole style of management. The current bureaucratic structure puts a premium on security and stability. Within the bureaucratic structure it is easier to do little and to risk nothing than to do much and run the risk that something will happen that deviates from the existing set of regulations (Matejko, 1975a). In order to create some show-effects and to secure their own positions, bureaucrats constantly contrive regulations. Instead of taking risks by making administrative decisions, they hide themselves behind the regulations, even if these regulations do not help to fulfill the tasks (Matejko, 1973a, 1975b). As a result of these bureaucratic activities the whole structure of action becomes so ossified, and rigid, that in order to achieve something it becomes necessary either to look for indirect ways of dealing with things or to break the existing legal order by relying on influence ("string pulling" power). In order to achieve its goals the Party must constantly break the bureaucratic status quo by directly applying its power. The law of the land applies only to the weak and underprivileged who do not have the direct access to power centers.

The behavior of an administrator in all kinds of work establishments is greatly influenced by the contradictory expectations of the higher authorities. On the one hand they expect him to cooperate closely with all kinds of institutionalized bodies like the local Party organization, the local trade union committee, the workers' council, etc. On the other hand he is not allowed to share his responsibility with anyone and his decisions should be of an authoritarian nature. In case something goes wrong, no one else but he would be responsible.[26]

---

[26] There are similar problems for Soviet executives as discussed in Granick (1961), Berliner (1957) and Richman (1965).

Therefore, most administrators develop a specific style of management based on a dialectic contradiction between collective and authoritarian approaches. The administrator attends numerous meetings and consults continually with his political and professional partners. But in reality the purpose of all these activities consists primarily in manipulating all of them according to his own will and vested interests. He knows what higher authorities expect him to do but it would not be in his interest to reveal it to the partners. By pretending to consult them, he in fact imposes his own goals upon them. Moreover, consultation provides a means to share at least part of the responsibility with them. Should trouble arise, it is much more advantageous for the administrator to be able to reveal that the wrong view has been shared by a larger number of people. Being subjected to a shared accusation they would have to support the administrator to protect themselves (Kiezun, 1969).

In the highly centralized economy of a Soviet model, executives have to develop a special ability in bargaining with people around them without really making it an open issue. In relation to central authorities there is the problem of obtaining "the smallest possible target of production for the largest possible allocation of manpower, raw materials, and investment funds" (Swaniewicz, 1968:472). In relation to labor there is the problem of satisfying their growing need with available scarce resources (how to distribute them in a way which would secure a maximum of subordination and commitment). In relation to other executives and their enterprises, there is the problem of securing their cooperation even if they do not have any particular interest in quotas imposed by the central plan.

In order to achieve goals and to appear successful, the executive has to rely on clever manipulation. For example, the whole concept of workers' councils in Poland was dictated, at least to some extent, by the inability of executives to bargain effectively with their own bosses in corporations, ministries and Party bodies. Appointed by the higher levels of the state and Party bureaucracy, the executive was very limited in his ability to achieve favorable conditions for his enterprise. By establishing workers' councils it was possible to exercise at least some pressure on the higher authorities without exposing the executive and the local Party secretary to sanctions against them. Representatives elected to the workers' councils are not directly dependent on the authorities located above the enterprise and therefore they are able to show some courage and initiative in defending vital interests of their enterprise. Chairmen of workers' councils take part in the advisory committees at the level of the corporation and they can be quite helpful to executives in their struggle for a better position of the enterprise versus the corporation (Morawski, 1969:249–252).

It seems quite obvious that the executives and the leaders of workers' councils are vitally interested in cooperating against the higher echelons of the bureaucracy. Therefore, it seems necessary to look on workers' councils more as local pressure bodies adding some strength to executives than as real self-government of workers. It is very significant in this respect that workers asked in public opinion polls in 1961 whose interests were being represented by workers' councils answered in many cases (41% of respondents in electronics and 47% in manufacturing) that these councils represented in reality the interests of executives. Only 8% of respondents in electronics and 5% of respondents in manufacturing felt that workers' councils, in fact, represented the interests of the manual working class (Wesołowski, 1962).

It is in the interest of a manager to bargain for tasks that are as easy as possible, and for the maximum of resources available for him and his enterprise. There are several tasks on which bonus depends and therefore the manager selects some of them, neglecting others. In order to stabilize his income, which derives to such a large extent from his bonus, the manager from the beginning arranges everything in a way which would assure him a safe play. The most common device is to hide all kinds of resources in order to have the stronger bargaining position versus bosses (Zielinski, 1973; Feiwel, 1965).

Managers on all levels of the hierarchy are exposed to tensions originated by the strong pressure of the Party to accomplish things and the strong resistance of bureaucracy to accept any kind of innovation. The Party does not want to destroy the bureaucracy and thus allow the existing "law and order" to collapse. The monopolistic position of the Party is buttressed by the bureaucratic order. However, at the same time the Party does not want to forego its ambitions for rapid ecnomic and social growth. Even if the bureaucratic machine is usually able to produce only some show-effects which may temporarily satisfy the Party bureaucrats, the international competition is always something real and the Party therefore cannot accept any considerable slowing down of the progress.

The mass demonstrations of blue collar workers in 1970 and strikes which followed them introduced into the situation an entirely new internal factor which did not exist before. In Poland industrialized democracy becomes not a dream to be suppressed to some degree by authorities, like it used to be before, but an urgent necessity which appears to many people an important development to overcome current economic and political difficulties (Matejko, 1973b). On the other hand, it seems almost impossible to practice industrial democracy without accepting some basic political freedoms of citizens. Even if it is difficult to say in which direction Poland will go, it seems obvious that the commitment to the authoritarian style of management has been seriously undermined, and that the political establishment in future has to look for some new styles (Matejko, 1973a, 1973b).

CONCLUSIONS

The soviet model of state socialism in Poland very strongly emphasizes the necessity of making citizens active and committed. The rulers of Poland are aware that the smooth interaction between the set of norms, interpersonal relations and available resources is of crucial importance if the ability of the system is to establish an effective performance structure, i.e. the processes which deal with tasks, control, coordination, decision-making, communication, maintenance, adaptation, and conflict. The rulers pay special attention to the local network of groups that comprise a complex bargaining system, to the conflicting claims on available resources, and to the unavoidable incompatibility between any formal structure designed to achieve limited economic goals and the expression of potentialities of those who work within it.

Obedience to authority may be secured by custom, material incentives or concern. In Eastern Europe this last factor is still very important. Depending on the more or less effective establishment of authority, the manifest functions of power relations may be more or less dominant and successful in comparison with latent functions. For example, the impersonal character of a formal organization consists, among others, in a manifestly strong discipline. However, the latent function of impersonality will consist in the development of informal groups with their increased flow of emotional responses, opportunity for status, independence and security, relief from monotony, boredom and fatigue. In Eastern Europe, and particularly in Poland, the informal structure so far seems to be extremely important and effectively prevents achievement of a satisfactory performance of the formal structure.

Social systems in Eastern Europe (including Poland) are more or less effective in terms of achieving their objectives, problem-solving, and utilization of human resources. However, a common lack of internal congruence in various fields of systems compliance leads to a shaky authority. Various types of authority are based on legitimacy, position, competence, social attraction or personality, may either support one another or be in mutual contradiction (Peabody, 1964). Because of a widespread bureaucratization in Poland, the occupants of authority positions show a limited interest so far in their personal acceptance by the public. Their power, based on control of key party positions, may disintegrate because of the depletion of their prestige. It has happened in the past with Gomulka (to cite one example).

The authoritarian style of power execution in Poland is gradually undermined by the progressive sophistication of the masses on one side and of technology (in a very large sense of the word) on the other. It is very significant that the communist regimes in East Europe are now eager to promote management sciences in order to improve the general quality of supervision. The real issue, however, is not one of making the manager a better manipulator, but one of avoiding constant displacement of goals[27] (lack of public control[28] and weakness of market mechanisms) and organizational ineffectiveness.[29] There is the major problem of adequate utilization of human resources in all sorts of workplaces. The internally negotiated order as "a pattern of relationships among

---

[27] Displacement of goals, methods, and functions in several establishments (Industrial enterprise, accounting center, bank, and a trade organization) was studied a few years ago by Witold Kiezun (1971) in Poland. He found that such displacement was originated by pressures of groups or individuals vitally interested in using this displacement to serve their interests. A unit survives even when it is no longer needed, because there are people who want to continue their employment. The number of managers grows beyond the demand for them because there are so many candidates for managerial positions. People who should work to a great extent in reality do very little because "lazy" people have more power at hand. There is, it would seem, an obvious misuse of authority. In all these cases the formal organization does not place any limitations on deviancy because within it there are no groups able to countervail actions that would prevent "deviants" from achieving their ends.

[28] This is a common problem of bureaucracies all around the world. In India, for example, "Many of the evils associated with the Indian bureaucracy-misuse of power, abuse of discretionary authority, collusion with the ministers—are partly the result of the absence of effective public scrutiny of the actions and decisions of the civil servants" (Bhambhri, 1971: 271).

[29] The effectiveness of organizations, according to Mott (1972:20), expresses itself in (a) *productivity,* as mobilizing of power resources to the efficient creation of products satisfactory quantitively as well as quantitatively; (b) *adaptability,* as anticipating problems in advance and developing satisfactory and timely solutions to them and as staying abreast of new technologies and methods applicable to the activities of the organization (symbolic adaptation), as well as prompt and prevalent acceptance of solutions (behavioral adaptation); and (c) *flexibility,* as organizing centers of power to cope with temporally unpredictable overloads of work.

people improvised, either individually or collectively, by them in response to problems" (Mott, 1972:10) is based too much on a status or compliance-orientation and too little on a genuine task-orientation (Matejko, 1970b).

Organizational flexibility and environmental adaptability of formal structures in Poland is handicapped to a great extent by formal rigidity. Communist leaders responsible for management and organization insufficiently understand that the main question is not how to find an optimal formal way of coordinating things, but "what are the criteria determining the optimal combination of formal and informal problem-solving for different organizations at different times, in order to optimize productivity and adaptability" (Mott, 1972:11).

There is still a strong belief among the ruling elite in Poland that any public control must be equalized with the Party control. The bureaucratized Party apparatus, however, is no longer able to represent adequately the broader public interest. The organizational goals of Party leadership compete with the interests of the rank-and-file as well as with the ostensible goals of work places.[30] Under such circumstances, a real collectivistic spirit is much less probable in communist work-places than in voluntary communes elsewhere.[31] Authoritarianism has been justified semipublicly by the leadership in terms of efficiency, but the latter is also meager, even though the public control cannot be blamed for the low level of work output.

The democratization of the whole Polish system becomes a very tempting solution. However, it seems almost impossible to reconcile the authoritarian political system, based on a single ideology and one-Party rule, with the local self-government and freedom of collective initiative. Any reform oriented towards stimulation of entrepreneurship and public will becomes effectively challenged sooner or later by the totalitarian aspects of the whole system. In several cases, local democracy just does not work because nobody really bothers to confront the blueprint with the reality. Designers of a particular project are just too delighted with the product of their imagination and therefore neglect to study how it will work in social practice. The elected or nominated representants have vested interests in gaining as much power as possible without bothering with the common will. People at the bottom of the hierarchy keep quiet because they fear that things will turn worse.

> By its very nature, the bureaucracy destroys social initiative since its rule is based on a monopoly of social organization and the atomization of independent social forces (Kuron, Modzelewski, 1965:23).

---

[30] It is possible to say that within organizations in general "the pursuit of organizational maintenance and enhancement induces group leaders to seek stability and predictability in their relations with the leaders of other groups, including those groups with which they are supposedly in bitter conflict... All participants in the political process are therefore faced with what is essentially the same problem: tame their environment and make it safe" (Kwavnick, 1972:2).

[31] In Israeli communes, for instance, "Collective settlement organization is such that for orderly decision-making and harmonious social life members must be of the same ideological persuasion. At the very least there must be preparedness to shelve political differences, so as to enable decision-making to continue on the basis of direct democracy. Compromise is especially significant because economic, productive and work-assignment decisions are made collectively. Clearly defined ideological factions which act separately in all matters can quickly immobilize the life of the collective..." (Medding, 1972:23).

Self-government on the community level and in the work-places presents a problem of importance that increases with rising qualifications and aspirations of the Polish blue and white collar workers, with developing tendencies among Polish experts to improve the planned economy by giving the enterprises more freedom, and with progressing stabilization of Polish management personnel. Some of the difficulties in making workers' participation effective may be related directly or indirectly to the under-development of the factors mentioned above. Thus, in the factories using workers who have come from the countryside (the first industrial generation) among the crew, there is often only slight interest in self-governmental activity and also a relatively low level of elementary qualifications for participating in management of the factory. The knowledge and the practice necessary for self-government are especially low among uneducated workers (Meister, 1964; Kolaja, 1965). The more highly educated strata of the work force (especially economists, engineers and technicians) are also the most active participants in self-government (Slejska, 1965).

The level of organizational motivation is formally high in Poland. In 1973, there was almost 15 million members of the co-ops, in it 640,000 members of the nonagricultural productive co-ops, and 46,000 members of the agricultural productive co-ops. 642,000 people took active part in various co-operative boards and committees, 135,000 people participate as councellors in the municipal councils, 11,160,000 people are members of the trade unions, 2,322,500 are members of the ruling Polish United Workers' Party (twice as many as there were in 1960).

In the Polish nationalized enterprises, there are numerous committees and productivity meetings. Activists comprise only a small percent of the total work force, but their role is essential because the attainment of production and other goals by the enterprise depends largely on them. They tend to come from the ranks of those blue collar workers who are more highly skilled and have better positions. The activists are more interested in demonstrating their skills in order to advance their careers; while the Party and other organizations in the workplace wish to strengthen their positions by having competent and effective supporters.

When dealing with social reality, and not just the normative model, one must distinguish among the various types of activists: those who wish to further their careers; those who have been forced into participation by a greater or lesser degree of pressure; and finally, those who do not take "activism" seriously. As Kulpinska says in Szczepański (1969:275) about Polish activists,

> the motives of activism frequently relate to the opportunities for contact with management during meetings and campaigns at a level of relative "equality." Linked to this motive is usually that of gaining promotion or other privileges. Activism is treated as the means of advancement in the organizational hierarchy.

People frequently engage in activism only for a limited period of time to achieve a specific goal: in order, for instance, to gain enough credit to become eligible for staff housing. Some, however, treat their activism very seriously and place themselves in trouble by obstinately fighting for lost causes or by annoying influential superiors.

It is obvious that neither "activism" as understood in this way, nor to an even greater extent, the above-mentioned forms of the ostensibly self-governing system, are sufficiently functional. This model of workers' activism has remained largely unchanged since Stalinist times. The fact that it is unsuited to the real situation was ignored for a number of years by the Party elite. In Poland, Gomulka (1967:10) once said that

> we have never had a situation in which the working class and the individual work forces of enterprises were completely deprived of opportunities to participate in the running of the national economy and of their work-places, and in which they did not make use of these opportunities.

It is obvious that Gomulka identified the working class with Party action groups, and that in addition he did not wish to acknowledge the totalitarian essence of Stalinist communism.

REFERENCES

Adamieeki, K.
    1970 O nauce organizacji. (On the Knowledge of Organization). Second Edition. Warszawa: Państwowe Wydawnictwo Ekonomiczne.
Adamski, F.
    1965 "The steel workers occupation and family." The Polish Sociological Bulletin (1):103–107.
    1966 Hutnik i jego rodzina (Steelworker and His Family). Katowice: Śląski Instytut Naukowy.
Altkorn, J.
    1963 "Identyfikacja pracowników handlu z zawodem" (Identification of trade employees with their profession). Handel Wewnetrzny (5).
Bauman, Z.
    1962 "Social structure of the party organization in industrial works." The Polish Social Bulletin 3 (4):50–64.
Bhambhri, C.P.
    1971 Bureaucracy and Politics in India. Delhi: Vikas Publications.
Berliner, J.S.
    1957 Factory and Manager in the U.S.S.R. Cambridge, Mass.: Harvard University Press.
Bielicki, W. and K. Zagorski
    1966 Robotnicy wczoraj i dżiś (Workers Yesterday and Today). Warszawa: Wiedza Powszechna.
Blauner, R.
    1964 Alienation and Freedom. Chicago: University of Chicago Press.
Blumberg, P.
    1968 Industrial Democracy: The Sociology of Participation. London: Constable.
Bochenski, A.
    1970 Rzecz o psychice narodu polskiego (On the Psychology of the Polish Nation). Warszawa: Państwowy Instytut Wydawniczy.
Bromke, A.
    1971 "Beyond the Gomulka era." Foreign Affairs (49).

Brzeżinski, Z.
 1970 Between Two Ages: America's Role in the Technetronic Era. New
       York: The Viking Press.
Budżet czasu rodżin pracowniczych (Time Budget of Working Families)
 1970 Warszawa: Główny Urząd Statystyczny.
Budżety rodżin pracownikow zatrudnionych w gospadorce uspolecznionej poza
 rolnictwem i leśnictwem 1969 r (Family Budgets of Nonagricultural Employees of the National Economy in 1969)
 1971 Warszawa: Główny Urząd Statystyczny.
Chalasinski, J.
 1946 Społeczna genealogia inteligencji polskiej (Social Genealogy of Polish
       Intellegentsia). Lodz: Czytelnik.
 1958 Przeszlosc i przyszlosc inteligencji polskiej (The Past and Future of the
       Polish Intelligentsia). Second Edition. Warszawa: Ludowa Spółdzielnia
       Wydawn.
Concise Statistical Yearbook of Poland
 1973 Warsaw: Central Statistical Office.
Daniluk, W.
 1968 "Organizacyjne i psychospołeczne aspekty pracy sprzedawców" ("Orga-
       nizational and psychosocial aspects of salesclerk's work"). Studia
       Socjologiczne 4(3):385–410.
Dobrowolska, D.
 1965 Górnicy salinarni Wieliczki w latach 1880–1939. Studium historyczno-
       sojologiczne załogi robotniczej (The Salary Workers of Wieliczka in
       the Period 1880–1939: An Historical and Sociological Study of a
       Worker's Crew). Wroclaw: Ossolineum.
Dyoniziak, R.
 1967 Społeczne warunki wydajności pracy (Social Conditions of Work Effi-
       ciency). Warszawa: Książka i Wiedza.
Dziecielska-Machnikowska, S. and J. Kulpinska
 1967 "Women's promotion. Women in managerial posts in Lodz industry."
       The Polish Sociological Bulletin (1):85–93.
Dziewoński, K. and M. Jerczynski
 1970 "Urbanization in Poland." Studia Demograficzne Vol. 22 No. 23:161–
       171.
Eberhardt, P., S. Herman and S. Leszczycki
 1971 Polska 2000 (Poland in the Year 2000). Polityka-Statystyka (5).
Feiwel, G.R.
 1965 The Economics of a Socialist Enterprise: A Case Study of Decision
       Making. New York: Praeger.
Feuer, L.S.
 1964 "Marxism and the hegemony of the intellectual class." Transactions
       of the Fifth World Congress of Sociology, International Sociological
       Association (4):83–96.
Fikus, D.
 1971 "Dlaczego tak pracujemy?" ("Why do we work like this?") Polityka
       (32).
Galdzicki, Z.
 1967 Pracownicy przedsiębiorstwa elektronicznego. Studium socjograficzne

załogi Wroclawskich Zakładów Elektronicznych ELWRO (Workers and Employees in an Electronic Establishment: A Sociographical Study of the Crew of the Electronic Works in Wroclaw ELWRO). Wroclaw: Ossolineum.

Galeski, B.
1963   "Farmers' attitude towards their occupation." The Polish Sociological Bulletin (1) :57–68.

Galinowski, K.
1971   "Placa zasadnicza—podstawa ("Basic Salary as a Principle"). Zycie Gospodarcza (13).

Gella, A.
1970   "The fate of Eastern Europe under 'Marxism' ". Slavic Review (29): 187–200.
1971   "The life and death of the old Polish intellegensia." Slavic Review (30) :1–27.

Gniazdowski, A.
1969   "Zwartosc małych zespolow roboczych" ("Cohesiveness of small work teams"). Studia Socjologiczne (2) :225–248.

Gomulka, W.
1957   "Przemowienie." Nowe Drogi (6).

Gospodarek, T.
1971   "Z badán nad kulturą polityczną w zakładach wielkoprzemysłowych" ("Studies on political culture in big industrial establishments"). Studia Socjologiczne (2) :235–252.

Granick, D.
1950   The Red Executive: A Study of Organization Man in Russian Industry. Garden City, New York: Doubleday.

Grzelak, A.
1965   "Problemy adaptacji młodych inżynierów" (Adaptational problems of young engineers"), in M. Hirszowicz (ed.), Problemy kadry przemyslowej (Problems of Industrial Personnel). Warszawa: Wydawnictwo Zwiazkowe CRZZ.

Gvishani, D.M.
1966   "Problemy upravlenija socialisticzeskój promyszlennostiu" ("Problems of managing industrial enterprises"). Voprosy Filosofii (11).

Herod, C.
1969   "Opinie młodych robotników na temat ksztalcenia się" ("Views of the young workers about their learning"). Studia Socjologiczne (3) :237–252.

Hetrz, A.
1942   "The social background of the prewar Polish political structure." Journal of Central European Affairs (July) :145–160.
1951   "The case of an Eastern European intellegentsia" Journal of Central European Affairs (11).

Hoser, J.
1969   "Inżynierowie w przemyśle" ("Engineers in Industry"), in J. Szczepański (ed.), Przemysł i społeczeństwo w Polsce Ludowej (Industry and Society in People's Poland). Wroclaw: Ossolineum.
1970   Zawód i praca inżyniera. Kadra inżynierska w świetle ankietowych

badań socjologicznych (Profession and Work of an Engineer. A Sociological Survey of Engineers). Wroclaw: Ossolineum.

Jakubowicz, S.
1971 "Organizacja to nie schematy" ("A nonformalistic approach to organization"). Zycie Gospodarcze (20).

Janicki, J.
1968 Urzędnicy przemysłowi w strukturze społecznej Polski Ludowej (Industrial Clerks in the Social Structure of People's Poland). Warszawa: Książka i Wiedza.

Jarosinska, M.
1964 Adaptacja młodzieży wiejskiej do klasy robotniczej (Adaptation of Rural Youth to the Working Class). Wroclaw: Ossolineum.

Jarosz, M.
1967 Samorzad robotniczy w przedsiębiorstwie przemysłowym (Worker's Self-Government in an Industrial Establishment). Warszawa: Państwowe Wydawnictwo Ekonomiczne.

Jozefowicz, Z., S. Nowak and A. Pawełczyńska
1958 "Students: myth and reality." Polish Perspectives 3(4).

Kasinska, B.
1970 "Student activism in Poland: 1968." Unpublished MA Thesis. Calgary: University of Calgary, B.C.

Kiezun, W.
1968 Dyrektor (The Executive). Warszawa: Ksiazka i Wiedza.
1968 "Niektóre zagadnienia formalizacji w biurokracji" ("Some problems
–69 of formalization in management"). Prakseologia (30).
1969 "Style kierownictwa na tle zadań organizacyjnych" ("Styles of management and organizational tasks"), in A. Matejko (ed.), Socjologia kierownictwa (Sociology of Management). Warszawa: Państwowe Wydawnictwo Ekonomiczne. 117–154.
1971 Autonomizacja Jednostek Organizacyjnych. Ź patologii organizacji (Alienation of Organizational Units. The Organizational Pathology). Warszawa: Państwowe Wydawnictwo Ekonomiczne.

Kilbach, D.
1971 "Kary, reklamacje i co z tego wynika" ("Penalties, complaints and their consequences"). Zycie Gospodarcze (10).

Kolaja, J.T.
1960 A Polish Factory: A Case Study of Workers' Participation in Decision-Making. Lexington, Kentucky: University of Kentucky Press.
1965 Workers' Councils. London: Tavistock.

Kowaleski, J.
1970 "Niektóre konsekwencje demograficzne migracji ludnośći wiejskiej do miast w europejskich krajach socjalistycznych—1950–1965" ("Some demographic consequences of the migration of rural population to urban areas in socialist countries of Europe—1950–1965"). Studia Demograficzne (21):81–97.

Kowalewska, S.
1962 Psychospoleczne warunki pracy w przedsiębiorstwie przemysłowym (The Psychosocial Work Conditions in an Industrial Establishment). Wroclaw: Ossolineum.

Kowalewski, S.
1970   Przełozony—podwładny (Supervisor—Subordinate). Second Edition. Warszawa: Państwowe Wydawnictwo Ekonomiczne.

Kowalewski, Z.
1962   Chemicy w Polskiej Rzeczypospolitej Ludowej. Studium o pozycji społecznej i kulturalnej inteligencji technicznej (Chemists in People's Poland: Study on Social and Cultural Position of Technical Intellegencia). Wroclaw: Ossolineum.

Kowalik, T.
1971   "Oskar Lange. His influence on Polish economics." Polish Perspectives (6):9–17.

Krall, H.
1970   "Pobieżny szkic do portretu klasy" ("Essay on the working class"). Polityka—Statystyka (5).

Kraus, G.
1968   Społeczne aspekty wdrazania postępu technicznego w górnictwie węgla kamiennego (Social Aspect of Applying Technical Progress in Coal Mining). Katowice: Slaski Instytut Naukowy.

Krawczewski, S.
1970   Zawód nauczyciela (Teacher's Profession). Warszawa: Książka i Wiedza.

Krol, H.
1970   Postęp techniczny a kwalifikacje (Technical Progress and Qualifications). Warszawa: Książka i Wiedza.

Krysiak, J.
1971   "Jak wykorzystujemy urlopy wypoczynkowe?" ("How do we spend our leaves?"). Polityka-Statystyka (2).

Kucharski, W.
1971   "Związki zawodowe—ale jakie?" ("Trade unions—but what kind?"). Polityka (10).

Kuron, J. and K. Modzelewski
1965   "An open letter to the Party." New Politics Vols. 2 and 3.

Kurowski, S.
1970   "Granice usprawnienia systemu planowania i zarządzania" ("The limits of the reform of the system of planning and management"). Gospodarka Planowa (4).

Kwasniewicz, W.
1964   Czytelnictwo prasy w Nowej Hucie—jego podłoże i funkcje społeczno-kulturowe (The Press Reading in Nowa Huta—Its Background and Sociocultural functions). Krakow: Osrodek Badan Prasoznawczych.

Kwavnick, D.
1972   Organized Labour and Pressure Politics. Montreal: McGill-Queen's University Press.

Lane, D. and G. Kolankiewicz (eds.)
1973   Social Groups in Polish Society. New York: Columbia University Press.

Latuch, M.
1970   Migracje wewnętrzne w Polsce na tle industrializacji—1950–1960 (Internal Migrations in Poland and Industrialization). Warszawa: Państwowe Wydawnictwo Ekonomiczne.

Lijewski, T.
  1967 Dojazdy do pracy w Polsce (Transportation to Work in Poland).
        Warszawa: Państwowe Wydawnictwo Naukowe.
Likert, R.
  1967 The Human Organization. New York: McGraw-Hill.
Lipinski, E.
  1971a "Czwarta śiła wytwórcza-zarządzanie" ("The fourth element in the
        forces of production-management"). Zycie Literackie (4).
  1971b Marks i zagadnienia współczesnośći (Marx and Contemporary Prob-
        lems). Warszawa: Państwowe Wydawnictwo Naukowe.
Lipset, S.M. and R. Bendix
  1967 Social Mobility in Industrial Society. Berkeley: University of Cali-
        fornia Press.
Lutynska, K.
  1964 "Office workers' views on their social position." The Polish Sociological
        Bulletin (1):79–83.
  1965 Pozycja społeczna urzędników w Polsce Ludowej (Social Position of
        Clerical Staff in People's Poland). Wroclaw: Ossolineum.
Madej, Z.
  1963 O funkcjonowaniu gospodarki narodowej (Operation of the National
        Economy). Warszawa: Książka i Wiedza.
Majchrzak, L.
  1965 Pracownicze przestępstwo gospodarcze i jego sprawca (The White
        Collar's Crime and the People Responsible for It). Warszawa: Wiedza
        Powszechna.
Marczak, J.
  1970 "Warunki rodzinne i socjalno-bytowe włokniarek lódzkich" ("Family
        and living conditions of working women in the textile industry in
        Lodz"). Studia Demograficzne (21):69–80.
Markiewicz, W.
  1962 Społeczne procesy uprzemysłowienia (Social Processes of Industrializa-
        tion). Poznan: Wydawnictwo Poznanskie.
Matejko, A.
  1962 Kultura pracy zbiorowej (The Culture of Teamwork). Warszawa:
        Wydawnictwo Zwiazkowe CRZZ.
  1964 Hutnicy na tle ich środowiska pracy. Wyniki badań socjograficznych
        w czterech poliskich hutach (Steelworkers Upon Their Work Environ-
        ment. Results of Sociographic Studies in Four Polish Steel Mills).
        Katowice: Slaski Instytut Naukowy.
  1966 "Status incongruence in the Polish intelligentsia." Social Research (4):
        611–638.
  1967a "The organization and stratification of scientific workers in Poland."
        Sociology of Education (3):367–376.
  1967b "Workers' aspirations." Polish Perspectives (10): 29–37.
  1968 Socjologia pracy. System społeczny zakladu pracy (Sociology of Work.
        Social System of Work-Places). Warszawa: Państwowe Wydawnictwo
        Ekonomiczne.
  1969a "Planning and tradition in Polish higher education." Minerva (4):
        621–648.

1969b Socjologia kierownictwa (Sociology of Management). Warszawa: Państwowe Wydawnictwo Ekonomiczne.

1969c Socjologia zakładu pracy (Sociology of Work-Place). Second Edition. Warszawa: Wiedza Powzechna.

1969d "Some sociological problems of socialist factories." Social Research (3):448–480.

1969e Wieź i konflikt w zakładzie pracy (Cohesion and Conflict at the Work-Place). Warszawa: Książka i Wiedza.

1970a "A newspaper staff as a social system," in J. Tunstall (ed.), Media Sociology. London: Constable.

1970b "Task versus status." International Review of Sociology (1–3):329–354.

1970c Usłovia tvorczeskogo truda (Conditions of Creative Work). Moscow: Izdatelstvo Mir.

1971a "The executive in present day Poland." The Polish Review (3):32–58.

1971b "From peasant into worker in Poland." International Review of Sociology (3).

1972 "Sociologists in-between." Studies in Comparative Communism (2–3): 277–304.

1973a "Industrial Democracy." Our Generation (1):24–41.

1973b "The self-management theory of Jan Wolski." International Journal of Contemporary Sociology (1):66–87.

1974a Social Change and Stratification in Eastern Europe: An Interpretative Analysis of Poland Among Her Neighbors. New York: Praeger.

1974b Social Dimensions of Industrialism. Meerut: Sadhna Prakashan.

1975a "Dilemmas of hierarchial organizations and of industrial democracy." Paper presented at the Second International Conference on Self-Management. Mimeographed. Ithaca, New York.

1975b Overcoming Alienation in Work. Meerut: Sadhna Prakashan.

Medding, P.Y.
  1972 Mapai in Israel: Political Organization and Government in a New Society. Cambridge, England: Cambridge University Press.

Morawski, W.
  1969 "Funkcje samorządu robotniczego w systemie zarządzania przemysłem" ("Functions of workers' self-government in managing industry"), in J. Szczepański (ed.), Przemysł i społeczeństwo w Polsce Ludowej (Industry and Society in People's Poland). Wroclaw: Ossolineum.

Mott, P.E.
  1972 The Characteristics of Effective Organizations. New York: Harper & Row.

Mrozek, W.
  1965 "Social transformations of family relations and environment of coal miners in Upper Silesia." The Polish Sociological Bulletin (1):108–112.

  1966 Rodzina górnicza (The Miner's Family). Katowice: Slaski Instytut Naukowy.

Najduchowska, H.
  1969a "Drogi zawodowe kadry kierowniczej" ("Professional careers of executives"). Studia Socjologiczne (3):253–269.

  1969b "Dyrektorzy przedsiębiorstw przemysłowych" ("Industrial executives"), in J. Szczepański (ed), Przemysł i społeczeństwo w Polsce

Ludowej (Industry and Society in People's Poland). Wroclaw: Ossolineum.

Nicki, H.
1969   "Niektóre społeczne problemy socjalistycznego współzawodnictwa pracy w świetle badań opinii pracowników" ("Some social problems of socialist work competition in the opinion of the workers"). Studia Socjologiczne (2):203–224.

Nowak, S.
1960   "Egalitarian attitudes of Warsaw students." American Sociological Review (25):219–231.
1962   "Social attitudes of the Warsaw students." The Polish Sociological Bulletin (1).
1964   "Changes of social structure in social consciousness." The Polish Sociological Bulletin (2).

Nowakowska, I.
1970   "Struktura społeczna młodżieży szkolnej" ("Social structure of the school youth"). Kultura i Społeczenstwo (3).

Nowicki, M.
1968   "Adaptacja młodych robotników w zakładach przemysłowych" (Adaptation of young workers in their industrial establishments"). Studia Socjologiczne 3(4):365–384.

Oledzki, M.
1967   Dojazdy pracy. Zagadnienia społeczne i ekonomiczne (Commutation to Work. Social and Economic Problems). Warszawa: Książka i Wiedza.

Olszewska, A.
1969   Wieś uprzemysłowiona. Studium społecznosći lokalnej w powiecie opolskim (The Industrialized Village. A Study of the Local Community in the Opole District). Wroclaw: Ossolineum.

Osipov, G.V. (ed.)
1966   Industry and Labor in the USSR. London: Tavistock.

Ossowska, M.
1973   Etyka rycerska (Ethos of Knights). Warszawa: Państwowe Wydawnictwo Naukowe.

Ostrówski, K.
1968   "Funkcja mobilizacji w działalnosći związkow zawodowych" ("The function of social mobilization in the activity of trade unions"). Studia Socjologiczne 3(4):137–151.

Pajestka, J.
1971   "Streamlining the economy." Polish Perspectives (2):7–22.

Paradysz, S.
1971   "Ile naprawdę pracujemy?" ("How effectively do we work?"). Polityka -Statystyka (8).

Parkin, J.F.
1969   "Class stratification in socialist societies." British Journal of Sociology (4):355–374.

Pasieczny, L.
1968   Inżynier w przemyśle. Studium polityki zatrudnienia i płac (The Engineer in Industry. Study on Employment and Salaries Policy). Warszawa: Państwowe Wydawnictwo Ekonomiczne.

Pateman, C.
    1970   Participation and Democratic Theory. Cambridge, England: University Press.
Pawełczyńska, A. and S. Nowak
    1962   "Social opinions of students in the period of stabilization." Polish Perspectives (2):38–50.
Peabody, R.L.
    1964   Organizational Authority. New York: Atherton.
Pietraszek, E.
    1966   Wiejscy robotnicy kopalń i hut. Dynamika przemianspołeczno-kulturowych w sierszańskim ośrodku górniczym w 19th i 20th wieku (The Rural Workers in Mines and Foundries. The Dynamics of Cultural Change in the Siersza Mining Centre in the 19th and 20th Centuries). Wroclaw: Ossolineum.
    1968   "Żrożnicowanie a typologia wsi robotniczych" ("The differentiation and typology of workers' villages"). Studia Socjologiczne (2):111–139.
Piotrowski, W.
    1966   "Life and work of rural migrants in urban communities." The Polish Sociological Bulletin (2):149–158.
Podgórecki, A.
    1966   Zasady socjotechniki (Principles of Sociotechnique). Warszawa: Wiedza Powszechna.
    1968   Socjotechnika. Praktyczne zastoswania socjologii (Sociotechnique. Practical Applications of Sociology). Warszawa: Książka i Wiedza.
    1970   Socjotechnika. Jak oddziaływać skoteczinie? (Sociotechnique. Principles of Effective Influence?). Warszawa: Książka i Wiedza.
    1971   "Swiadomosc prawna Polakow" (Law consciousness of Poles"). Polityka (13).
Pohoski, M.
    1964   Migracje ze wśi do miast (Migrations from Villages to Towns). Warswaza: Państwowe Wydawnictwo Naukowe.
Pomian, M.
    1969   "Robotnik jako pracownik i jako kolega—wzory zachowań społećności robotniczej" ("Worker as an employee and mate—patterns of behavior in the workers' community"), in S. Kowalewska (ed.), Z zagadnien kultury pracy robotnikow przemysłowych (Selected Problems of the Work Culture Among Industrial Workers). Warszawa: Wydawnictwo Zwiazkowe CRZZ.
Preiss, A.
    1967   "Robotnicy a pracownicy inzynieryjno-techniczni" ("Workers, technicians and engineers"). Socjologiczne Problemy Prsemyslu i Klasy Robotniczej (2):19–42.
Przeclawska, A. and J.K. Sawa
    1971   "Studenckie idealy" ("Student ideals"). Polityka (20).
Rajkiewicz, A.
    1965   Zatrudnienie w Polsce Ludowej w latach 1950–1970 (Employment in People's Poland in 1950–1970). Warszawa: Książka i Wiedza.
Rawin, S.J.
    1969   "The manager in the Polish enterprise: a study of accommodation under conditions of role conflict," in R.A. Webber (ed.), Culture and

Management. Text and Readings in Comparative Management. Homewood, Illinois: Irwin.

Richman, B.M.
 1965   Soviet Management. New York: Prentice-Hall.
 1970   Rocznik Statystyczny (Polish Statistical Yearbook). Warszawa:Główny
 –74   Urzad Statystyczny.

Rupinski, G. and S. Taubwurcel
 1961   Elementy organizacji zarządzania przędsiebiorstwem (Elements of
        the Management Organization in Enterprises). Lodz: Zaklad Prod.
        Skyrptow Politechniki Poznanskiej.

Sadownik, H.
 1971   "Miejsce zjednoczenia" ("Placement of industrial corporation in na-
        tional economy"). Zycie Gospodarcze (17).

Sarapata, A.
 1963   "Justum pretium." The Polish Sociological Bulletin (1):41–56.
 1970   "Motywacje i satysfakcje dryrektorów—studium porównawcze" ("Mo-
        tives and satisfactions of executives. A comparative study"). Studia
        Socjologiczne (3):61–89.

Sarapata, A. (ed.)
 1965a Socjologia zawodów (Sociology of Occupations and Professions).
        Warszawa: Książka i Wiedza.
 1965b Socjologiczne problemy przedsiebiorstwa przemysłowego (Sociological
        Problems of Industrial Enterprises). Warszawa: Państwowe Wydawnic-
        two Ekonomiczne.
 1965c Studia nad uwarstwieniem i ruchliwoscią społeczną w Polsce (Studies
        on Stratification and Mobility in Poland). Warszawa: Warszawa, Książk
        i Wiedza.
 1968   Płynnosc załóg (Labor Turnover in Industrial Crews). Warszawa:
        Państwowe Wydawnictwo Eknomiczne.

Sarapata, A. and W. Wesołowski
 1961   "The evaluation of occupations by Warsaw inhabitants." The American
        Journal of Sociology (66):581–591.

Sicinski, A.
 1966   "Expert—innovator—adviser." The Polish Sociological Bulletin (1):
        54–66.

Siemienska, R.
 1969   Nowe zycie w nowym mieście (New Life in a New Town). Warszawa:
        Wiedza Powszechna.

Siemienski, M.
 1961   Z badań nad działalnością kulturalno-óswiatowa w Nowej Hucie (Stud-
        ies on Educational and Cultural Activities in Nowa Huta). Wroclaw:
        Ossolineum.

Skorzynski, Z.
 1965   Między pracą a wypoczynkiem. Czas "zajęty" i czas "wolny" mieszkań-
        ców miast w świetle badań empirycznych (Between Work and Leisure.
        Results of a Survey on the Time Budget of the Urban Population).
        Wroclaw: Ossolineum.
 1967   Socjologiczne aspekty kształowania się socjalistycznego przedsiębior-
        stwa (Sociological aspects of development in socialist enterprises).
        Warszawa: Państwowe Wydawnictwo Naukowe.

1966 Socjologiczne problemy przemyslu i klasy robotniczej (Sociological
–67   Problems of Industry and Working Class). Vols. 1, 2. Warszawa: Pań-
      stwowe Wydawnictwo Naukowe.

Slejska, L.
1965 "Prace i rizeni." Sociologicky Casopis Vol. 2.

Sokołowska, M.
1966 Kobieta współczesna. Z badań socjologów, lekarzy, ekonomistów,
      pedagogów i psychologów (The Present Day Woman. Studies of So-
      ciologists, Physicians, Economists, Educationalists and Psychologists).
      Warszawa: Książka i Wiedza.
1969 "Funkcjonowanie przemysłu a zdrowie" ("Health and Functioning of
      Industry"), in J. Szczepański, Przemysł i społeczenstwo w Polsce
      Ludowej (Industry and Society in People's Poland). Wroclaw: Osso-
      lineum.

Sokołowska, M. and K. Wrochno
1965 "Pozycja społeczna kobiet w świetle statystyki" ("Social position of
      women from the statistical viewpoint"). Studia Socjologiczne (1).

Strzeminska, H.
1970 Praca zawodowa kobiet a ich budżet czasu (Women's Employment and
      Their Time Budget). Warszawa: Państwowe Wydawnictwo Ekono-
      miczne.

Sufin, Z. and W. Wesołowski
1964 "Work in the hierarchy of values." The Polish Sociological Bulletin
      (1).

Surmaczynski, Z.
1965 "Informacja w zakladzie przemyslowym" ("Information in the indus-
      trial enterprise"). Studia Socjologiczno-Polityczne (19).

Swaniewicz, S.
1968 "World economic growth and the Soviet challenge." The Review of
      Politics (4):455–475.
1969 "The impact of ideology on Soviet economic policy." Canadian Slavonic
      Papers (1):66–81.

Szczepański, J.
1962 "The Polish intelligentsia. Past and present." World Politics 14(April).
1969 "Pracownicy administracyjno-biurowi" ("The clerical staff"), in J.
      Szczepański (ed.), Przemysł i spoleczenstwo w Polsce Ludowej (In-
      dustry and Society in People's Poland). Wroclaw: Ossolineum.
1970 Polish Society. New York: Random House.

Szczepański, J. (ed.)
1961 Studia nad rozwojem klasy robotniczej (Studies on Development of
      the Working Class). Vols. 1, 2. Lodz: Państwowe Wydawnictwo Nau-
      kowe.
1967 Socjologiczne problemy industrializacji w Polsce Ludowej (Sociolog-
      ical Problems of Industrialization in People's Poland). Warszawa:
      Państwowe Wydawnictwo Naukowe.
1969 Przmysł i społeczeństwo w Polsce Ludowej (Industry and Society in
      People's Poland). Wroclaw: Ossolineum.

Szczepański, J. and G.W. Osipów (eds.)
1970 Spoleczne problemy pracy i produkcji. Polsko-radzieckie badania

porownawcze (Social Problems of Work and Production. The Polish-Soviet Comparative Studies). Warszawa: Książka i Wiedza.

Szostkiewicz, S.
1962 "Two researches in industrial sociology." The Polish Sociological Bulletin (1–2).

Tulski, J.
1971 Młodzi robotnicy w zakładzie przemysłowym (Young Workers in an Industrial Establishment). Warszawa: Książka i Wiedza.

Turowski, J.
1964 Przemiany wśi pod wpłyem zakładu przemysłowego (Changes of Villages Under the Impact of an Industrial Establishment). Warszawa: Państwowe Wydawnictwo Naukowe.

Turski, R. (ed.)
1970 Les transformations de la campagne polonaise. Wroclaw: Ossolineum.

Turski, R.
1965 Między miastem i wsią. Struktura społeczno-zawodowa chłopów-robotników w Polsce (Between Town and Village. Sociooccupational Structure of Peasants—Workers in Poland). Warszawa: Państwowe Wydawnictwo Naukowe.

Tyszka, A.
1971 Uczestnictwo w kulturze. O różnordonośći stylow zycia (Participation in Culture. On the Variety of Life Styles). Warszawa: Państwowe Wydawnictwo Naukowe.

Urban, J.
1971 "Związki zawodowe" ("Trade Unions"). Polityka (5).

Wawrzewska, B.
1971 "Poszukuje pracy..." ("They are searching for jobs"). Polityka (37).

Wesołowski, W.
1962 "Robotnicy o swojej pracy i o zakładach" ("Workers about their work and their employers"). Studia Socjologiczno-Polityczne (12).

Wesołowski, W. (ed.)
1970a Zróżnicowanie społeczne (Social Differentiation). Wroclaw: Ossolineum.
1970b Struktura i Dynamika Społeczenstwa Polskiego (Structure and Dynamics of Polish Society). Warszawa: Państwowe Wydawnictwo Naukowe.

Widerszpil, S.
1965 Skład polskiej klasy robotniczej. Tendencje zmianw okresie industrializacji socjalistycznej (Structure of the Polish Working Class. Changes During the Period of Socialist Industrialization). Warszawa: Państwowe Wydawnictwo Naukowe.

Widerszpil, S. and A. Owieczko
1971 "Management and workers' control." Polish Perspectives (1):7–16.

Wilder, E.
1964 "Impact of Poland's stabilization on its youth." Public Opinion Quarterly (3).

Wisnewski, W.
1963 "Tolerance and egalitarianism." The Polish Sociological Bulletin (2).

Worach-Kordas, H.
1970 "Problem feminizacji zawodu nauczycielskiego" ("Feminization of the teacher's profession"). Studia Demograficzne (21):119–127.

Woskowski, J.
  1964 "Primary school teachers and their social position in People's Poland."
        The Polish Sociological Bulletin (1) :84–89.
Zagorski, K.
  1971 "Robotnicy w strukturze społecznej Polski" ("Manual workers in the
        social structure of Poland"). Polityka-Statystyka (7).
Zajaczkowski, A.
  1961 Główny elementy kultury szlacheckiej w Polsce. Ideologia a struktury
        społeczne (Basic Characteristics of the Gentry Culture in Poland.
        Ideology and Social Structures). Wroclaw: Ossolineum.
Zakrzewski, P.
  1969 Zjawisko wykolejenia społecznego młodżieży na terenach uprzemy-
        sławianych wyniki badań w Nowej Hucie (Social Deviance among
        Youth in Industrializing Areas. Survey in Nowa Huta). Warszawa:
        Wydawnictwo Prawnicze.
Zegzdryn, R.
  1971 Studenci studiów dziennych. Rok szkolny 1969–70. Rozmieszczenie
        terytorialne (Students of Regular Courses. Academic Year 1969–70.
        Territorial Distribution). Warszawa: Główny Urzad Statystyczny.
Zielinski, J.G.
  1973 Economic Reforms in Polish Industry. London: Oxford University
        Press.
Ziomek, J.M.
  1964 Absencja w pracy (Absenteeism at Work). Warszawa: Państwowe
        Wydawnictwo Ekonomiczne.
Zweig, F.
  1944 Poland Between Two Wars. London: Secker and Warburg.

CHAPTER **21**

The Industrialization of
a Rapidly Developing Country — Israel

Theodore D. Weinshall

Tel Aviv University

INTRODUCTION

In several senses, Israel could be considered a social science laboratory. The country is a newly created Jewish nation, composed of a pluralistic society originating from a variety of cultures. This, however, is only part of the socio-cultural scene of Israel; the other part consists mainly of an Arab minority to which, after the Six Day War, a large Arab population was added. The latter, until then, had been separated from the Israeli Arabs, and had little contact or intermingling with the Jewish population for a period of twenty years.

ENVIRONMENTAL ASPECTS OF SOCIAL STRUCTURE

In this chapter, we shall be concerned with the Jewish population of Israel because the number of Arabs in industry and business, unlike the number in agriculture, is comparatively low. Let us mention several phenomenal aspects of the social development of the Jewish population in Israel. Listing them according to their chronological appearance on the Israeli scene, they were:[1]

1. *The Kibbutz and the Moshav*—two forms of communal social structures, which developed initially in agriculture and subsequently spread their activities into industry. The kibbutz, which was founded first, is the more closely knit communal structure of the two where almost no private ownership exists; the kibbutzim (plural for kibbutz) in 1970 contained 3.5% of the Jewish population of Israel. Similar to the Kibbutz, the Moshav is a cooperative organization, but with less communal sharing. Members of the Moshav have cooperative selling and buying

---

[1] The term "Israel" is used in this chapter as the name of the country which used to be called "Eretz Israel" (the Land of Israel) and "Palestine" during the British Mandate (1918–1948) and which constituted the southern part of the Turkish Empire during the first period of the renewal of the Jewish population (1870–1918). A short historical survey of Israel from 1960 to 1970 appears hereafter.

services and own jointly the larger investments in agriculture and industry, but have separate ownership of the small farms around their
houses where they live with their families. The Moshavim (plural for
Moshav) encompassed 5.1% of the Jewish population in 1970.

2. *The Histadrut's (Federation of Trade Unions) ownership of industry
   and business*—the Histadrut[2] was founded in 1920 and soon started its
   own civil engineering contracting firm. Today it invests about 16%[3]
   of the total industrial and business investments in the Israeli economy
   and operates in almost every field. The dual role of the Histadrut, as
   the largest single owner and as the dominant trade union, sometimes
   creates ambivalent situations for its decision making processes.

3. *Zahal (the Israeli Army)*—Zahal performs special functions in the social structure of Israel which make it an exception among armies for
   two reasons. First, because of Israel's special position in the Middle
   East, the great majority of Israelis (males between the ages of eighteen
   and fifty-five and females between the ages of eighteen and thirty-six,
   except those who have children) are very much part of the army—if
   not in regular service, they are apt to be called annually for over one
   month of active service. Second, Zahal has assumed special educational
   and social roles which are unusual for an army: running elementary
   schools (for all new immigrant soldiers who have not completed their
   elementary education), trade schools in various fields, etc., which serve
   both as a democratic melting pot and as a training center for civilian
   work and life.

4. *The geopolitical position of Israel*—Since 1948, Israel has been under
   siege, cut off from the rest of the world except by way of air or sea
   communication. This isolation has had a considerable effect on the
   sociocultural structure of the Jewish population. Lately, this factor
   has had a greater effect than all the other special aspects of the Israeli
   social structure previously mentioned. Unfortunately, it has been studied
   less than other aspects and one still awaits a major research effort to
   explore the effects of isolation on a nation.

THE DEVELOPMENT OF MODERN ISRAEL

Let us now turn to the recent historical development, which led to the present
demographic and geopolitical situation of Israel. The history of Israel during
the last 100 years could be divided into three main periods: (1) the Turkish
rule, (2) the British Mandate and (3) the State of Israel.

The Birth of a New Homeland (The Late Ottoman Period, 1870–1918)

For more than seventeen centuries, the Land of Israel (Eretz Israel, at the time
commonly referred to as Palestine) was a country at a standstill. The last

---

[2] *Histadrut*—"voluntary organization" in Hebrew. For all practical purposes this is the
only trade union organization in Israel.

[3] 16% for the period of 1966–69. In 1969 the Histadrut invested 225 million Israeli Liras
($64 million) as compared to an overall investment in the Israeli economy of 1,450 million
Israeli Liras ($415 million). The share of the Histadrut's industrial holdings in 1959 was
23.3% out of the total Israeli industry (Eisenstadt, 1967:75).

Jewish revolt against the Romans (A.D. 132–135) had resulted in the disappearance of organized Jewish communal life in the country, while subsequent conquerors had been, for the most part, nomads incapable of maintaining progress throughout the ages. Whatever had existed at the time, mainly in agriculture, was gradually destroyed. Failure to prevent soil erosion, for example, is the reason why large tracts of the country are barren today and cannot serve the same agricultural purposes for which they were used two thousand years ago.

There had been Jewish attempts to return to the Land of Israel during all these years, but it was only in the nineteenth century that systematic resettlement of the country was undertaken. The earliest new Jewish settlements were established after 1870, and remained for about forty years under Turkish rule. Two waves of immigration—the first towards the end of the nineteenth century and the second during the first decade of the twentieth—provided the foundation for the resurrection of the old homeland. Both immigrations originated from Eastern Europe, mainly from Russia, and consisted of people who had no roots in either agriculture or industry. Their first ideal was a return to agriculture. Professional people, on one hand, and religious scholars, on the other, turned to the land and to farming.

The Prestate Era (The Mandatory Period, 1918–1948)

The foundation on which the State of Israel was later based had been established during the British rule (under a League of Nations Mandate entrusted to Great Britain after the First World War). It was during this period that the two main pre-State immigration waves entered the country, one (in the 1920s and early 1930s) mainly from Poland and the other (in the mid- and late 1930s) from Germany. These immigrants introduced industry into the country. By the end of this period, immigrants of the four waves and their descendants accounted for more than one-third of the country's population west of the river Jordan.

The Independent State (The State of Israel after 1948)

Emergency (1948–1952). Within a short period of four years, the new state faced two challenges. The first was the War of Independence (1948–1949), which was accompanied by some 600,000 Arabs abandoning areas which then formed the boundaries of Israel, and by the precipitate withdrawal of the British without any attempt at an orderly transfer of administration.

The second challenge was the in-gathering of about 1,000,000 immigrants, survivors of the Nazi catastrophe in Europe, where over 6,000,000 Jews had perished during the Second World War. This meant an increase of some 130% over the existing population of about 650,000 Jews and about 150,000 Arabs.

Thus, within this short period, the main task to be encountered was absorption of the newcomers, at least on a temporary basis, combined with the establishment of a working government charged with planning the country's economy and securing its frontiers against ever-present physical dangers.

The Investment Period (1952–1962). Within a period of ten years, some 2,500 million dollars were invested in Israel. The main sources for these investments were the United States, and German reparations. Distribution of such funds during the years 1955–59 was as follows:

Agriculture and Irrigation	19%
Industry and Mining	16%
Transportation	13%
Electric Power	6%
Commerce and Services	13%
Building for Housing	33%
	100%

One of the major problems during this period was the adjustment of the man-power factor with a view to economic expansion. While it has been Israel's proclaimed policy to enable any Jew who desired to immigrate to do so, planned immigration has been ruled out as beyond the country's control. This is the main reason why the country faced widespread unemployment at the outset of the Investment Period, while during its second half, the situation was reversed to one of over-employment; i.e., a condition in which there are many more jobs available than people to fill them, resulting in a significant manpower shortage.

Economic problems (1962–1967).   This period could be divided into two parts. During the first part of this period (1962–1965) Israel experienced an over-employment situation accompanied by an economic boom. This produced escalating wages and salaries, declining discipline and effectiveness, high inter-organizational mobility, increased absenteeism, etc. During the second part of this period (1966–1967), the economy was confronted with unemployment and recession. This came about because of governmental steps to stop the escalating "boom" by economic measures.

Post Six Day War Period (after 1968).   The Six Day War of June, 1967, changed the situation in two ways. First, it left the whole area between west of the Jordan up to the Suez Canal, with an additional Arab population of 750,000, under the jurisdiction of Israel. Second, it induced a further economic growth period, with increased immigration and full employment.

ISRAELI INDUSTRY AND BUSINESS

Having briefly described the environmental and historical setting of the Jewish population in Israel, we can now describe the social structure of Israeli in-dustrial and business organizations. One may refer to the state of the social structure of Israeli organizations as a state of flux. Everything that could affect industrial and business organizations happened at once—physical and techno-logical growth, waves of immigration and fluctuation in employment and the hostility surrounding Israel (which included an Arab economic blockade and the French arms embargo).

The "state of flux" has probably been both the cause and the effect of the prevailing political-economic structure. The concentrated regularization of eco-nomic activities by the Ministry of Finance commenced immediately after the establishment of the State of Israel. The concentration of economic power was mainly a consequence of the large amounts of funds streaming to Israel from foreign sources (mainly from the U.S. government, American Jews and German Reparations). These funds were mainly regulated by the Ministry of Finance. Such a concentration of economic power is similar in some ways to the ones existing in several developing countries where ownership and political power are concentrated in the hands of a few families. In many other ways, it is quite different, however. Israel began at a relatively high level of industrialization as compared to other developing countries created after World War II. It has been populated mainly by people with stronger democratic traditions and inclinations than one would find in other newly created countries. Israelis, therefore, generally rejected any type of a highly controlled bureaucracy, even in the midst of war periods. Consequently, an ambivalent situation was created in Israel; on the one side there was a very strong centralization of economic decisions, in which the Minister of Finance could directly intervene in the decision-making processes of individual industrial firms, while on the other side there was a complete absence of a totalitarian system, linked to a tightly controlled bureaucratic structure. The main means of control are through a personal network of relationships among the several hundred top executives, and their personal acquaintance with and awareness of the Minister of Finance. Thus, the control of the execution of the centralized policies and decisions is performed through the Israeli social structure, where managers are much better acquainted with each other than they are in countries with populations similar in size to that of Israel. This is mainly so because of Israel's geopolitical position, its relatively isolated and self-centered economy, and its business managers being associated with each other in different social systems, primarily in their service in Zahal's reserves. However, such an informal control system cannot deeply penetrate into the grass roots of the economy. This is one of the main reasons why few medium or long range policies survive in Israel. This informal control system, indeed, is also how the concentrated, nontotalitarian, political-economic structure of Israel—which is caused to a large extent by the "state of flux"—is simultaneously directly contributing to the maintenance of such a "state of flux."

Let us see how the social structure of Israeli organizations was affected by the above and other factors. We shall analyze organizational behavior in terms of different sociological phenomena: (a) social and organizational stratification; (b) interorganizational mobility of management and workers; (c) the integration of various ethnic groups in the social structure; (d) the effects of the general employment situation on organizational behavior; (e) the effects of technological development on individual and group behavior; (f) organizational size and structure; and (g) values and norms of management, workers and trade unions.

SOCIAL AND ORGANIZATIONAL STRATIFICATION

Israeli society, based as it is on a combination of Zionist, Socialist and pioneering ideals, has emphasized and practiced equalitarianism from its very beginning. Equalitarianism assured accessibility to various occupational positions to everyone through the comparative homogenity of educational and cultural facilities and by the dependence of all groups on external economic and political resources (Eisenstadt, 1967). Israeli society is typified by a complete absence of outward class symbols as found in other societies. Special forms of addressing people belonging to different "walks of life" are almost nonexistent in Israel. People address each other usually by their first names, or occasionally by their family names with or without the title of Miss, Mrs. or Mr. Any differences in the forms of address rarely have any relevance to the social position of the person addressed.

The integration of immigrants from various countries with different languages and cultures has been achieved partly by the pluralistic nature of the society. Thus the adoption of the Hebrew language as the official language of the country was finalized after the Second World War. However, sociocultural integration has been a slower process, but has accelerated since the Six Day War. The melting of the Jewish population into a homogenous Israeli society was accompanied by additional pressures of equalitarianism, such as the increased perceived political and physical danger and the more extensive length of service in the Israeli armed forces. The army provides a strong bulwark against social stratification, not only because of the relatively democratic nature of the Israeli army, but also because of the status incongruence it introduces for many Israelis between their professional and other status positions and their position in the army.

In 1964, mobility patterns in Israel were investigated by interviewing 643 male residents of Haifa, aged 25–54 (Zloczower, 1968). The same population exhibited extensive intergenerational and intragenerational mobility. Intergenerational mobility was found to be considerable in both directions and was explained largely as a function of educational qualifications. Thus, for example, Table 1 shows that the Inequality Index of 172 of this Israeli sample is by far the lowest compared to a variety of other countries. Indices range from 234 to 1598, with a Median Index (not including Israel) of 284. It is interesting to note that the country with the next lowest Inequality Index is Great Britain. The relative equality in Israeli society is also shown by the distribution of income among the population. Figures 1, 2 present the curves representing actual income distribution in Israel and the United States. We can see that Israel had, in 1965, a curve typical of industrializing nations, but that in 1969 it drew closer to the U.S. income curve of 1950. Recent research on the inequality of income distribution in Israel (Yuchtman and Fishelson, 1970) revealed the four following trends: (1) The inequality between salaried personnel and self-employed grows; (2) A widening gap in the distribution of income as a function of skill (there has been however no change in the gap as a function of the level of education); (3) A lessening of the direct influence of the country of birth and the length of service, although it is still present to a considerable degree; and (4) less inequality in the general distribution of education, with a much narrower education gap between immigrant groups of different origin.

The relatively high degree of equality income has its parallel in organizational structures and behavior in industry and business organizations. In a study carried out on thirty Israeli plants in various manufacturing areas covering three main types of production systems, three types of ownership, and employing from 150 to 4500 persons (Samuel and Mannheim, 1970), it was found that none of the six types of bureaucratic profiles which were discovered were "highly bureaucratic in all the structural areas. None were found to approach the Weberian ideal type of Bureaucracy." There was a tendency for the bureau-

TABLE 1
INEQUALITY IN OPPORTUNITIES IN VARIOUS COUNTRIES

Country	(1) Non-Manual Worker Sons of Non-Manual Worker Fathers %	(2) Non-Manual Worker Sons of Manual Worker Fathers %	(3) Inequality Ratio
Australia (Melbourne)	62.9	24.1	261
Belgium A*	91.1	5.7	1598
Belgium B	96.6	30.9	313
Brazil	81.5	29.4	277
Denmark	63.2	24.1	262
Finland	76.0	11.0	691
France A*	79.5	30.1	264
France B	73.1	29.6	247
Great Britain*	57.9	24.8	234
Hungary	72.5	14.5	500
India	73.1	27.3	268
Italy	63.5	8.5	747
Japan	70.3	23.7	297
Holland	56.8	19.6	290
Norway	71.4	23.2	308
Puerto-Rico	57.3	14.3	401
Sweden	72.3	25.5	284
U.S.A. A	80.3	28.8	279
U.S.A. B	77.4	28.7	270
U.S.S.R. (refugees)	85.0	34.9	244
West Germany	71.0	20.0	355
Israel (Haifa)	55.5	32.3	172

* After correction of calculating mistakes in the original source.
Source: (Goode, 1966:585).

cratic structures to have relatively few levels. There is reason to believe that the perceived degree of equality in industrial organizations has a limiting effect on the development of the organizational structures. Samuel and Mannheim (1970) say that their findings should not be interpreted as a final typology, generalizing all possible profiles and all types of formal organizations, because "the small size of the sample and the contextual variables selected were severely limiting factors, dictated to a great extent by the industrial situation in Israel."

Indeed, this may mean that if the organizational structure has to change, in order to absorb technological innovations and growth (Weinshall, 1971), the Israeli organizations are restricted in their ability to adapt themselves to structures which are not based on a high degree of perceived equality.

INTERNATIONAL MOBILITY OF MANAGEMENT AND WORKERS

The term *interorganizational mobility* covers the movement from one organization to another by groups such as managers, workers, customers, shareholders, etc. When the movement of one group is discussed in interorganizational terms, managerial mobility is warranted. Interorganizational mobility is essential if Israeli organizations are to adapt their organizational structure for growth, and to be able to absorb innovations and new technologies (Weinshall, 1971). When individual organizations are large enough to become multistructural, i.e.,

TABLE 2
INCOME DISTRIBUTION IN ISRAEL AND THE U.S.

Annual Gross Income Group	ISRAEL (% Income and Number of Families)*							U.S. (% Number of Families)**					
	1960	1965			1969			1950		1960		1965	
	% Income	% income	No. of Families %	Accum. %	% Income	No. of Families %	Accum. %	%	Cum. %	%	Cum. %	%	Cum. %
Less than 2,000	24.6	20.7	40.1	40.1	14.3	31.5	31.5	30	30	20	20	17	17
2,000 to 2,999	27.7	27.6	29.1	69.2	22.6	27.9	54.4	30	60	19	39	16	33
3,000 to 4,999	29.9	33.5	23.5	92.7	34.4	27.0	86.4	20	80	22	61	18	51
5,000 to 6,999	10.2	14.8	5.8	98.5	19.7	10.7	97.1	13	80	22	61	18	51
7,000 to 9,999	7.6	3.4	1.5	100.0	9.0	2.9	100.0	13	93	21	82	24	75
Over 10,000								7	100	18	100	25	100
Total	100.0	100.0	100.0		100.0	100.0		100		100		100	

* Data for 1960 From "The Report of the Committee for the Examination of the National Income in Israel" (December 1960, Treasury). Table 12, Page 54: "Division of Income of All Assessees 1960/61."
1965 and 1969 data from "'Statistical Yearbook of Israel 1970"—Table F/7. "Jewish Urban Employees', Families and Their Total Money Income by Annual Gross Income Group (1965–67)."
In order to compare with U.S. figures—the Israeli Liras were converted to Dollars according to the rate of exchange of that year and the percentages were divided proportionately in order to equate the Israeli distribution to the salary brackets of the U.S. distribution.
** From "The American Challenge" Page 64. Data for 1950, 1960 and 1965 (Servan-Schreiber, 1967).

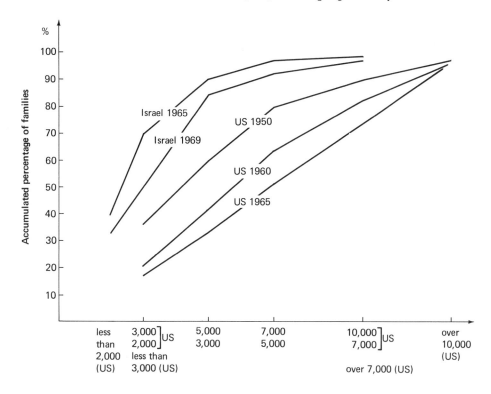

Figure 1. Accumulative income distribution curves for Israel and the US.

a structure composed of a conglomeration of different combinations of the three basic types of structures—entrepreneurial, functional and decentralized— managerial mobility could occur within a single organization, from one type of structure to another (Weinshall, 1971). However, as long as organizations in Israel are too small to aspire to a multistructural managerial level—the only hope of Israeli organizations for survival in open market conditions of Israeli integration in the world economy—is to have interorganizational mobility, at the managerial and worker levels.

Interorganizational mobility is often associated with physical mobility from one geographical location to another. Historically Jews were accustomed to the latter type of mobility. This is probably the reason Israelis do not have a strong social value against interorganizational mobility of the sort found in most Western European countries. An apparent reason for the relative absence in Israeli society of what one could refer to as "the golden watch after twenty-five years of service" norm, is the pluralistic nature of the society. On this point, the Israeli population is closer to the U.S. population, which is also composed of a variety of ethnic origins. Thus, while in European cultures the attitudes towards interorganizational mobility possibly originated from the life-long service in the army, the church and the government, the relative absence of such a norm in the U.S. as well as in Israel could be attributed to the pluralistic society composed of communities of people from a variety of origins, who voluntarily abandoned their previous cultural environments and became absorbed in a

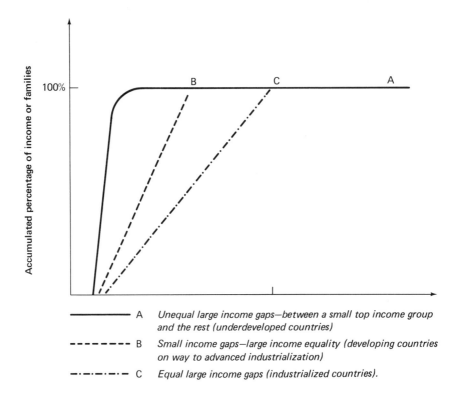

Figure 2. Three schematic patterns of income distribution.

new culture. Such newly created cultures, even when they are constructed on the basis of a fallen culture, are closer to the present needs of survival rather than to past, historical needs.[4] Let us consider rates of interorganizational mobility among three groups of Israeli employees: workers, lower management and top management.

Worker Mobility

A survey carried out in the period 1958–1964 (Israel Productivity Institute, 1965) found that the average rate of worker mobility declined as the age of the workers and the length of their service in an organization increased. The survey was carried out in a period of full and even over-employment. As we shall see later in this chapter, in such a period, interorganizational mobility is higher than during periods of unemployment. Furthermore, in a situation of full and over-employment, there is a tendency for workers to leave sectors of the economy with relatively more difficult working conditions and to be replaced by other workers, usually less qualified. This is why the movement, indicated in Table 3, in and out of sectors like "Mines and Quarries," "Building and Public

---

[4] E.g., in the Soviet Union, where on the whole, like in the U.S., interorganizational managerial mobility is regarded positively.

Works," and "Electricity, Water and Sanitation Services" was higher than for, say, "Commerce, Banking and Insurance." The lowest figures for sector mobility were those for workers moving in and out of Agriculture, which is one of the areas of employment associated with difficult working conditions. There are two possible, and closely related, ways of explaining this apparent contradiction. The first is that Israel differs from other developing and industrialized countries in that Israeli society accords high status to agricultural occupations. Second, the greater part of those working in Agriculture are members of Kibbutzim or Moshavim, that is, they are members of cooperatives and may not own their own farms (in fact, in the case of most kibbutzim, members do not even have private ownership of some of their personal belongings). Therefore there are both ideological and practical reasons for the low rate of movement from collective farms in comparison with other sectors of the economy.

The average rate of movement "towards" all sectors of the economy was 13.06% higher than the figure for "moving out" (11.29%). The reason for this discrepancy is the annual increase in the size of the labor force. However, the net figures for sector mobility are evidence of the process of industrialization. Thus we see that the sector which had the second highest figures for net mobility (+4.29%) was the Manufacturing Sector, and a similar positive trend was found in all the Service Sectors (5.01%, 3.53%, 3.45%, 3.04% and 2.66%). The lowest figures for net mobility were in Building and Public Works (+2.22%), Mines and Quarries (+2.20%) and Agriculture, the only sector in which the net mobility was negative, that is to say in which, over time, more people were moving out of the sector than into it (−1.73%).

TABLE 3
RATES OF MOBILITY IN THE MAIN SECTORS OF THE ISRAELI ECONOMY
(AVERAGE NUMBER OF MOVES PER EACH 100 YEARS OF WORK IN THE SECTOR)
(1958–1964)

Sector	Away from the Sector	Towards the Sector	Net Mobility
Agriculture	5.75	4.02	−1.73
Mines and Quarries	17.47	19.67	+2.20
Manufacturing	8.87	13.16	+4.29
Building and Public Works	15.19	17.41	+2.22
Electricity, Water and Sanitation Services	12.87	16.32	+3.45
Commerce, Banking and Insurance	7.66	10.70	+3.04
Transport, Freight, Storage and Communications	6.73	10.26	+3.53
Public and Personal Services	7.09	9.75	+2.66
Other Services	11.18	16.19	+5.01
Irregular Employment	20.10	13.09	−7.01

Middle Management Mobility

Two separate studies carried out by the Israel Productivity Institute (1965) and by Simmons, et al. (1962), make possible a comparison of two types of middle management—foremen, and "production technicians" (Time-Study men and

Methods Improvement technicians). It was found that, while the foremen had a comparatively low rate of interorganizational mobility, the production technicians had a high rate. The I.P.I. researchers suggested some reasons for this difference between managers with a typical staff function.

They noted that production technicians are professionals in that they have a broad formal education which can be utilized in many different types of organizations. In Israel it is required that such technicians should be graduates of secondary schools and should complete a specialized course in industrial engineering of several months duration. Foremen, on the other hand, were found to have a rather limited education—29% of those studied had only completed elementary education (i.e., a maximum of only eight years of schooling), and only 13% had some form of higher education.

It was also discovered that production technicians had been through one or more periods of readjustment to new social conditions. This experience resulted in establishing relationships with people both above and below them in the organizational hierarchy. The foremen, on the other hand, in spite of being in constant communication with their superiors, had very few social contacts with them. Fifty-seven percent of the foremen in Simmons', et al. sample were socially oriented towards workers, rather than managers.

Another factor which this research brought out was the importance of having access to information on opportunities for employment outside their own organizations. Production technicians often met their peers at reunions and managerial post-experience programmes and study periods, while foremen generally lacked these opportunities for acquiring information on employment possibilities.

Production technicians further differed from foremen in being more psychologically prepared for change because of their backgrounds. While the production technicians were accumulating new experiences with a variety of problems, people, and situations, foremen were usually confronted in their working experiences with the same problems and people.

Finally, it was discovered that relative to foremen, production technicians were younger and more eager to change their positions for better ones. In the foremens' case, they had usually been promoted from the ranks of the factory workers, and were older than the production technicians with an average foreman being about 42 (and with some 72% of those studied being over 36).

Top Management Mobility

A recent study of Israeli chief executives (Margalit, 1971) furnished similar results to those found in earlier studies of Presidents (Chief Executives) in six European countries (Hall, de Bettignies and Amado-Fischgund, 1969). Table 4 presents the relevant findings for interorganizational mobility. Indeed, if we define the total Mobility Rate as the percentage distribution weighted by the number of companies in which the Chief Executives were previously employed,[5] the ranking order of Israel, U.K., Belgium, France, Italy and Germany is close to the ranking by Inequality in Opportunities in Table 1 (Israel, Great Britain, France, Germany, Italy and Belgium).

---

[5]E.g., Belgium: $(15.1 \times 0) + (9.4 \times 1) + (41.5 \times 2) + (34.0 \times 3) = 194.4$

TABLE 4
INTERORGANIZATIONAL TOP MANAGEMENT MOBILITY
(NUMBER OF COMPANIES IN WHICH PRESIDENTS WERE EMPLOYED)
IN SEVEN EUROPEAN COUNTRIES

Number of Companies in Which Presidents Were Previously Employed*	Distribution of Chief Executives Studied in Every Country (%)						
	Belgium	France	Germany	Holland	Italy	U.K.	Israel
0	15.1	18.4	40.9	12.8	26.3	18.9	8.1
1	9.4	20.8	20.4	29.8	16.2	11.9	17.0
2	41.5	27.8	29.0	17.0	23.2	23.8	28.5
3 and more	34.0	31.0	9.7	40.4	34.3	45.9	46.4
SOURCES	(Hall, de Bettignies, Amado-Fishgrund, 1969)						(Margalit, 1971)

* In addition to the one in which he was employed as President (Chief Executive) at the time of the study.

Adjustment of New Immigrants to Industrial Patterns

Some sociological work in Israel has been devoted to the problems of integrating ethnic groups and their adaptation to the Israeli bureaucracy (Eisenstadt, 1954; Katz and Eisenstadt, 1960; Shuval, 1963). However, the problem of adjustment to industrial work has received only limited attention.

During the first years after the establishment of the State of Israel, there was a general tendency to divide Jewish communities of varying ethnic origins along the dichotomy, Eastern-origin and Western-origin. This division was based on the assumption that, with respect to certain characteristics, the similarities inside each of the two communities were greater than the similarities between the Oriental and Western communities. One early study (Bonne, 1956) found that the Oriental immigrants, coming from societies in which agriculture was the main source of livelihood, brought with them the norms of a preindustrial society which stressed economic and social security for the individual and the value of leisure and traditionalism. This contrast created some problems for the newcomers.

In their first contact with a new country, immigrants may suffer what amounts to a "cultural shock," provoked in part by the new set of values they encounter. Their personal abilities to adjust, together with the social factors governing such adjustment, determine the ease with which they take up their new occupations which require new technical skills as well as specific values.

A study of the values of immigrant workers (Bar-Yosef, 1965) distinguished between the adaptive and the integrative systems of an enterprise.[6] One-third of the workers sampled were from Europe and were familiar with industrial production processes. The remaining two-thirds came from countries where

---

[6] The *adaptive system* includes the technological, skilled and professional sectors and the exchange (manpower) sector. The *integrative system* includes the cooperative sector, the administrative sector, the trade union sector and the informal relationships sector.

methods of production were largely nonindustrial. Work within Israeli industry required an occupational change for some 92% of the labor force investigated. The remaining 8% had been factory workers before. The assumption, therefore, was that the industrial behavior of this type of new immigrant as well as the measure of their adjustment would undoubtedly be affected by both the cultural background of their countries of origin and the new set of values they encountered in Israel.

Bar-Yosef (1965) found that there was a strong link between a worker's general job satisfaction and the satisfaction with the adaptive system. In the adaptive system, wages are the critical factor which decisively determine satisfaction with the work itself and its conditions. In her investigation, Bar-Yosef (1965) found that 75% of the workers were satisfied with their jobs. This is an interesting finding in view of the fact that industrial work was relatively new to them. However, bearing in mind that at the time of the research, Israel was in the grips of unemployment, this finding is understandable.

A further variable that was discovered and added yet another facet to the ethnic group fabric was the immigration process itself. This included such factors as the motives for immigration and the degree of distintegration of the immigrant community. It has been argued (Eisenstadt, 1967) that the immigrant's very motives, whether messianic, utopian, or merely pragmatic, have an impact both on his predisposition to change and on the outcome of such a change. In Eisenstadt's view, it is this very predisposition to change that forms the immediate basis for successful adjustment to new situations. He regards it as a function of the primary group structure and of the immigrant's secureness of status.

Eisenstadt holds that the immigrant's concepts and aspirations take shape when he comes face to face with the demands of Israeli society as presented to and imposed on him by its official and unofficial representatives. The smaller the gap between his aspiration and reality, and the more long-range his expectations, the better his chances for personal adjustment.

A summary of studies concerning the adjustment processes of immigrants in Israel was conducted by Bar-Yosef (1968). The study regarded them as processes of desocialization and resocialization and concluded as follows:

> It was the intention of this paper to analyze immigration and adjustment as processes of desocialization and resocialization. The disturbance of the role system caused by immigration was seen as the main factor of desocialization. Resocialization is then the tendency to re-establish the role-set, to rebuild the connection between the self-image and the role-images and to achieve a real and acceptable social status. Disintegration and reintegration appear as parallel processes. It was assumed that a certain measure of desocialization is necessary in order to allow restructuring within the cultural and social context of the absorbing society. Successful adjustment was seen as a dynamic balance of desocialization and resocialization, where the desocializing tendencies are slowly eliminated while the resocializing forces expand. It seems important that the transitional period should be defined as such by the absorbing society and the immigrant should be free during this time from pressures towards binding institutional commitments.

Bar-Yosef pointed out that absorption is not a well ordered temporal sequence of phases of adjustment, but a fluid exchange between the immigrant and the society. In this exchange, the inputs are determined not only by the social situation but also by the changing receptivity of the immigrant. The process involves the dissolution of old patterns and the rebuilding of new patterns and the intermediary product is often distorted and meaningless if judged from the viewpoint of the settled society.

Field research carried out in Israeli factories at various technological levels (Tenne 1969) found a significant correlation between the workers' origins and the complexity of their jobs. While the workers originating from Oriental countries (Asia and North Africa, etc.) were found to work in manual and unskilled jobs, those of Western origins and Israeli born workers were occupied mainly in the highly skilled and professional jobs. It was likewise found that the percentage of European, Anglo-Saxon and Israeli-born workers in the more advanced technological factories, was considerably higher than that of workers originating from North Africa and Asia. However, Tenne's findings show no significant difference between workers originating from the West and Israeli born workers, most of whose families originated from Oriental countries. This last finding indicates that the difference between immigrants from the East and the West tend to disappear among second generation workers in Israel.

A more recent study compared the incomes of various wage earning groups according to their continents of origin (Yuchtman and Fishelson, 1970). They found that both the continent from where the immigrants originated and their length of stay in Israel had a considerable effect on the level of income in all the years shown in Table 5. Yuchtman and Fishelson specifically mention four trends in the data in Table 5: (1) The comparative income of natural-born Israelis is rising. (2) The income of Afro-Asian immigrants is lower than the total national average income, but changes occur in their comparative income the longer they stay in Israel. (3) The income of natives of Europe and America who immigrated before 1955 has been higher than the total average income and there is an upward trend in the income of those from these countries who have immigrated since 1955. (4) The increase in income of the workers who originated in Europe and America, who have immigrated since 1955 has been faster than the increase in income of Afro-Asian workers who immigrated during the same period of time.

Yuchtman and Fishelson found that when they allowed for differences in age and education (i.e., they measured the segregated, pure effect of the continents of origin), although the Israeli-born workers earned higher incomes than the Afro-Asian-born workers, the gap between the two groups had substantially diminished from 1957–58 to 1966. On the other hand, the income gap between the Israeli-born workers and the European and American-born workers had been steadily increasing in favor of the latter, even when allowing for differences in age and education.

The Effects of the General Employment Situation on Organization Behavior

The Israeli economy has witnessed sharp and frequent fluctuations in the conditions of the manpower market. There were two studies which explored the effects of the general employment situation on organizational behavior during the period of 1962–69 (Niego, 1964; Blustein, 1970). Until World War II, unemployment had been a permanent phenomenon of the economy. During the World War, the country profited, due to the war situation, but was not

TABLE 5
THE EFFECT OF CONTINENT OF ORIGIN AND LENGTH OF STAY IN ISRAEL ON
THE INCOME LEVEL OF IMMIGRANTS AND ISRAELI-BORN WORKERS
(IN PERCENTAGES COMPARED TO THE TOTAL AVERAGE IN EACH YEAR)

	1957/58	1963/64	1966	1968
Total Average	100%	100%	100%	100%
Israeli-Born	99	107	131	127
Afro-Asian Born:				
Immigrated before 1948	100	79	76	75
" 1948–54	72	83	76	76
" 1955–60	47	68	61	67
" 1961–67				60
European- and American-Born:				
Immigrated before 1948	129	134	143	133
" 1948–54	102	114	101	108
" 1955–60	62	82	85	101
" 1961–67				90

affected by it except as a supply and service base to the war effort. Then came a long period of unemployment, which culminated with the large immigration of 1949–51. From 1958, the ebb turned to flood, which reached its peak in 1964. During 1965–67, Israel suffered a sudden period of unemployment which turned into full employment in 1968, and in 1970, into slight overemployment. Table 6 gives the variations in a number of economic variables together with some unemployment statistics for 1962–69.

Despite the favorable economic situation and the increased demand for manpower during 1962–65, the percent unemployed never dropped to less than 3.3% (which occurred in 1964, at a time of overemployment). It would appear, therefore, that the 3.5% are permanently unemployed, i.e., the marginal labor force which is unemployable, because of lack in basic skills and training, or else too old or physically handicapped. These people subsist mainly on

TABLE 6
VARIATIONS IN ECONOMIC INDICES, POPULATION AND EMPLOYMENT INDICATORS
1962–1969

Item	Year 1962	1963	1964	1965	1966	1967	1968	1969
Local Gross Investment*	12.5%	4.5%	22.5%	−1.5	−17.0	−28.5	45.0	21.1
G.N.P.*	11.5%	12.5%	10.5%	8.0	1.5	2.0	14.0	13.4
Total Population (in thousands)	2,332	2,430	2,526	2,598	2,657	2,774	2,841	2,919
Population of Working Age (in thousands)	1,514	1,592	1,656	1,727	1,793	1,839	1,928	1,978
Labor Force (in thousands)	808	846	883	911	943	927	970	990
Unemployed (% of Labor Force)	3.8	3.4	3.3	3.7	7.5	10.4	5.9	5.0

* Variation in % for each year as compared to the previous year's figures.
Source: Israeli Central Bureau of Statistics.

social welfare or on the specially initiated public works projects of the Ministry of Labor.

The analyses of Niego and Blustein were based on three clinical research studies of a number of organizations which were selected for this purpose. The first field research, which was carried out in 1963, comprised eleven organizations of which nine were industrial plants. The second (1965–67) restudied six out of these nine industrial organizations while in the third (1968–69), the same six organizations were studied again, together with five additional industrial organizations. It follows that between 1963 and 1969 six industrial organizations were investigated at times of full employment, of unemployment, and again of full employment. The findings of each of these periods may be considered separately.

The effect of full employment, 1962–64. From 1961 on, the Government Labor Exchanges were no longer able to meet the plants' demands for employees, in spite of the influx of new immigrants and the natural increase in population. In most cases the only available labor was the unemployable who were either unsuitable for the jobs offered, or would not accept them. These workers would arrive at the plant, stay a day or two, and then leave of their own accord, or be dismissed. Out of the total number of workers taken on, only a handful stayed on, in some cases as few as 10%.

The plants most affected by this transient state of affairs were those which employed fewer permanent employees, either because they were newly founded or because they depended heavily on seasonal and temporary labor. This applied to firms in the canning industry, to building and construction companies, and the like. Also, firms where the work was difficult or dirty—foundries, tire manufacturing plants, etc.—found it hard to get the necessary steady labor. The research findings clearly indicated that both the employment of substandard labor and the constant turnover led to lowered input in the plants involved. In some, the output dropped measurably; in others, expected expansion planned on the basis of newly expanded and potential markets, failed to materialize. In the wake of lowered output came the inability to meet delivery dates and deadlines. This was especially evident in building companies, and somewhat less so in industrial firms. Orders had to be turned down for fear that they might not be filled in time. The study points out, however, that the process plants and the chemical industry were not affected by this trend.

Absenteeism statistics in a number of plants clearly pointed to an upward trend. A similar upward trend could be observed in labor turnover in certain firms. Turnover was highest, in absolute terms, in newly founded enterprises or in those undergoing expansion.

Labor turnover and "labor reserves," created in order to meet seasonal and eventual expansion needs, caused some increase in production costs in most plants but the main source of the increase was the rise in wages and social benefits. Organizations had to give in to pressures for increasing wages over and above the wages agreed contractually with the Histadrut. Wages rose most sharply in privately owned and small firms. Arabs and Deruzes were employed especially for the harder types of physical jobs.[7] Similarly, an in-

---

[7] Arabs and Deruzes are a Mid-Eastern religious sect living primarily in Syria and Israel. This religion, although monotheistic, is different from other monotheistic religions and customs.

crease occurred in the number of youths employed. Woman labor began to be used in jobs which hitherto had been the province of males. In many firms, the elderly and the disabled were employed, usually with conspicuous success. Some companies went so far as to bring in workers from abroad to make up for the shortage on the local market, but only in a limited number of cases and involving only a few hundred workers.[8] The geopolitical situation of Israel made the employment of foreign workers difficult for reasons of cost, security and social cohesion. In some firms, more effective use of available manpower was achieved through longer working hours and overtime. Others tried to increase the level of mechanization but, these attempts usually were ill-conceived and were difficult to introduce because of the conditions created by the over-employment itself.

A marked change took place in labor relations. Workers who realized that they were a much "sought-after commodity" gained in power, inasmuch as they felt they no longer needed the backing of their trade union to retain their job, or to obtain improved working conditions. Not infrequently, management and trade union leadership were on one side of the fence with the workers facing them in opposition. In turn, a slackening of work discipline and morale could be observed in nearly all plants.

The effect of unemployment, 1965–1967.   The outcome of inflation and other consequences of the manpower shortage was the introduction of severe cuts, referred to as a "slow-down" in the government development budget. This was probably the main reason for the recession which started in Israel towards the end of 1965. Economic activity was slowed down considerably and the demand for many commodities dropped sharply. Most affected were the building trade and allied industries as well as plants which only supplied the domestic market. Export industries, by their very nature, were less affected by the reduced local demand.

Blustein (1970), when analyzing the data of 1965–67, found that affected companies were forced to cut back production and lay off some of their work-force. In all, in the firms investigated in 1966 (as compared with 1965) an average of 14% of the labor force was dismissed, with some percentages varying from 5% to 19%. However, various other steps usually preceded any such dismissals in an effort to avert them. No new workers were taken on, overtime was abolished, the working week was cut from six to five days, premiums were reduced, and workers were asked to take their paid vacations. Only when all of these steps failed were workers dismissed, generally according to the principle of last in first out. Thus, the relatively high unemployment which marked the two years of the economic slow-down and recession was the direct outcome of these dismissals. Only a handful of firms took advantage of the situation to recruit some of the available skilled labor.

Labor turnover which had been so high during the period of full employment vanished almost entirely. The prevailing feeling of job insecurity was accompanied by tighter work discipline, fewer instances of absenteeism, higher

---

[8] The only area in the Israeli economy where the employment of foreigners reached the thousands was in shipping. The Israeli merchant navy became a manpower buffer, as the merchant navies of larger maritime countries are—absorbing national labor in periods of unemployment and returning it in periods of full and over-employment.

productivity per worker, a slight drop in the number of work accidents, and greater readiness by the labor force to accept inter-job and inter-department mobility when requested by management to do so. A complete wage-freeze set in where it had formerly been common practice to press for wage increases at the time of signing of the newly negotiated contracts. The customary annual salary advancement for professional and managerial staff became a thing of the past and the number of strikes was reduced to nil.

Some firms made the most of the situation to introduce improvements at work; for example, by investment in new equipment, by improving methods in existing work processes, by the modification of inappropriate work standards, by the reorganization of teams, and by abolishing redundant labor. In two of the investigated firms even the top management team was completely changed during this period. Management also invested considerable effort in trying to find new export markets and in expanding existing ones. A comparative study of Israeli exports with those of Holland, Denmark and Switzerland (Hirsch, 1970), in five industrial export fields—food, textiles, chemicals, machinery and electrical-electronics—established that Israel was lagging considerably behind the other three countries, especially in machinery and electrical-electronics. Hirsch found, however, that during the period 1966–69, the proportion of these five industrial fields in the total exports of Israel had increased considerably. He likewise found that during these years (1966–1969) the difference between the export structure of Israel and that of three European countries had diminished. According to Blustein, firms which were successful in this respect laid off fewer people and produced almost the same amount.

The effect of full employment, 1968–1969.   The Six Day War of June 1967, had three major effects on employment. First, the mobilization considerably reduced the number of people available for employment. A similar effect in a much milder form was produced when the average annual length of service in the reserves was increased and the conscription was raised to three years for males and to almost two years for females. Second, until the Six Day War a substantial part of the armaments of the Israeli Defence Forces (Zahal) had been considerably restricted, mainly because of the French Embargo, and Israeli industry had to take over. The industrial expansion created by the Zahal was carried over to civilian production, not unlike the effect that NASA orders by the U.S. Government had on manufacturing for civilian use. The Six Day War and its economic consequences swung Israel around to a period of economic boom and over-employment.

The third effect of the Six Day War helped somewhat to overcome the severe manpower shortage. The territories held by Israel since the Six Day War were populated by large numbers of Arabs (about one million, including Arabs who were Israeli citizens before June 1967). The over-employment in Israel drew upon available Arab workers to the extent that more or less full employment conditions existed in all Israeli-held territories. It was found (Blustein, 1970) that the economic recovery reduced and almost eliminated unemployment in 1968, culminating in full employment in 1969.

The effect of full employment on the six companies in the study was not unlike the effect in 1962–1964. Skilled and well-trained labor became hard to obtain, and not infrequently workers were hired whose qualifications fell somewhat short of the functions they had to fulfill. This lowered the output per worker, and caused higher material costs because of loss by spoilage and de-fective production and, therefore, led to a greater need for training. Given the manpower shortage, the desperate economy once again drew upon potential sources of unused labor. Women, elderly people, youngsters, and above all, members of the Israeli minorities (Arabs and Deruze) as well as Arabs from the administered territories, were called in. This again resulted in a lowering of work standards in the different plants, because minority labor was chiefly employed in unskilled jobs.

Blustein also found that the increased demands for manpower caused a greater number of workers to change their places of work for better paying jobs. As firms learned to value their skilled and qualified personnel and offered them better terms to keep them, the labor available on the market sharply declined in quality and skills. To fill the growing number of vacancies, often unsuitable labor had to be employed, only to leave soon after. As a result, labor turnover in some firms reached alarming proportions. Similarly, ab-senteeism rose. Absences almost doubled as a consequence of the widespread call-up of reservists for military duty which was necessitated by the vastly ex-panded post-Six Day War security requirements.

Blustein found that in order to prevent job-hopping of highly qualified personnel and to attract well-trained workers, quick career advancements were being offered once again. Salaries and wages rose, as did social benefits. In turn, labor costs as a component of the overall production costs rose steeply.

Blustein pointed out that output was the chief casualty of the manpower shortage, with supplies badly lagging behind demand. To offset employment of inexperienced and untrained hands, increasingly longer hours and more shift-work had to be used. Firms took to relying more heavily on subcontract-ing, and, wherever the quality of their work force made it possible, intra-plant mobility. Yet despite these measures, delivery dates could not be kept. In an effort to achieve a balance between the growing demand and the lagging pro-duction, most of the firms investigated embarked on expansion projects includ-ing the introduction of highly mechanized and automated equipment to replace existing labor—intensive machinery. Yet once again, their implementation came up against the stumbling block of inadequate manpower both in the in-stallation and in the operation of the new facilities.

Industrial relations, on the whole, continued to be satisfactory, with only a few minor labor disputes erupting here and there. At the same time, however, a change could be observed in employee attitudes. This found expression in a general slackening of discipline, more tardiness, increased absenteeism, non-compliance with instructions, and basically rude behavior towards superiors. Yet management, fearful of losing any of its previous staff, was powerless to combat such behavior in an effective manner.

The Utilization of Female Labor

Having reviewed the effects of the employment market on organizational be-havior as a whole, let us now consider one aspect of the social consequences of the employment conditions, the role of women in the economy. The utiliza-tion of women employees in industrial and other types of organizations has come to assume a special importance in a country like Israel where, except for the two years of 1966 and 1967, a prolonged period of full and even over-employment, has existed since 1958. The shortage of manpower during 1958–65 was counteracted by the employment of women. Indeed the Zahal had women in its compulsory service from the start. It offered women as well as men, training in various occupations which help the young person on leaving the army to find a job in civilian life. Training as nurses, secretaries, wireless operators, key punch operators, programmers, teachers and the like, together with the practical work within the compulsory service of two years (as compared with three years conscription for males), provided many women with a trade. Also, a few women served as officers and thus became eligible for managerial positions.

However, while in the Zahal, the role and status of women is established in advance by military manpower planning and procedures, their full utilization in nonmilitary organizations, however, encounters one major difficulty— the problem of equality between men and women employees. To describe the role and status of women in Israeli organizations, we turn to the findings of two research studies. The first (Barad and Weinshall, 1967) dealt with the status of women managers in Israeli organizations, while the other (Rosner, 1965) was devoted to the role of women in the Kibbutz. Both studies placed emphasis on comparing the status of women to that of men in the same type of job.

Despite the considerable difference in the way of life in a Kibbutz and in urban society, it was found that both had a lot in common in terms of patterns of thought and the true state of women employees. It therefore seems relevant to give a brief outline of the ideology behind the problem of the sexes in both the city and the Kibbutz.

Ideas about the role of the women in the Kibbutz have changed. Rosner (1965) states:

> In the beginning of the Kibbutz movement an extreme conception predominated, according to which all differences between the sexes were blurred where social functions were concerned. Today it has already become clear that this conception which held that women were to perform even the most arduous physical labor ... is a thing of the past.

As a second generation of Kibbutz-born children grew up, a differentiation process occurred in respect to a woman's inclinations, ambitions, and even of some of her qualities. Still, the idea of a qualitative equality held sway. While the physical disparity between the sexes and the implications of women's biological function came to be recognized, the belief in a fundamental equality in intellectual capacity and basic psychological traits persisted. Throughout it was held that, by educational efforts and suitable organizational and institutional means, the inherent differences in inclinations and aspirations between the sexes could be overcome.

It was Aristotle who stated that a man's relation to woman is by nature such that he is the superior being and she the inferior one, he the ruler and she the ruled. Today, although most of the sting has by now been taken out of Aristotle's dictum, it is still safe to assume that in modern urban society the battle of the sexes continues to rage! Support for this assumption emerges from a research on the status of women in management (Barad and Weinshall,

1967). They showed that men disliked being subordinated to women. Both Rosner, and Barad and Weinshall found that the condition of Israeli women in both the Kibbutz and the urban setting is far from equalling that of men.

In keeping with Kibbutz ideology, a woman member is almost entirely relieved of her own household duties to be free to take over communal tasks and participate in social activities. There is no conflict between the demands of home and the job for parents with children. In the city, by contrast, no satisfactory solution has been found to this problem. Barad and Weinshall found that the urban woman continues to be torn between family responsibilities and her devotion to her outside job, and that this in turn makes employers reluctant to engage women and has hampered their advancement in relation to men. Let us now consider the two studies separately.

Rosner interviewed a sample of men and women from twelve Kibbutzim which differed in age, size and country of origin. He found a considerable disparity between the attitudes of men and women regarding the nature, capacities, and inclinations of each of the sexes. For, although both perceived both sexes as intellectually equal, their perception of the spheres of interest and social roles of each sex revealed an increasing tendency to differentiate according to the characteristic inclinations of the sex. Certain fields of activity were declared more suited to one sex or the other. Rosner's interviewees generally considered that "womanly duties" require more "compassion and gentleness." Women, it was held, make more patient listeners, show greater sympathy for and understanding of certain problems, and, have a certain intuition. Rosner consequently found that certain areas of activity within the Kibbutz become the sole province of women. The perceptual image of woman's and man's different characteristics helps members of the Kibbutz to rationalize the allocation of specific jobs to one sex or the other.

The urban study was based on total populations and random samples from among university graduates with degrees in engineering, economics and education. All women graduates up to and including those of 1961, with B.Sc. degrees in Civil Engineering and Chemical Engineering from the Israel Institute of Technology and B.A. degrees in Economics from the Hebrew University, were approached. In addition, a random sample of graduates with degrees in education from the Hebrew University was approached. A matched sample of men was drawn; in this way, the women's progress in the four professional fields was compared to that of men in the same professions, from the time they graduated up to the period of the research. Before we proceed with the results of this second study, some clarification of the point of departure of the comparison between women of the Kibbutz and of an urban society is required. It must always be remembered that the conditions which make it difficult for urban women to assume jobs outside their homes (child care, housework, etc.) do not apply in the Kibbutz. Indeed, Barad and Weinshall found that a higher percentage of women than men in managerial positions, claimed that marriage impeded a professional career of their own.

The advancement of a professional woman in Israeli industry was slower than that of a man with a comparable training. The slower advancement was measured by both their status (types of managerial roles, achieving managerial authority, etc.) and their rewards (salary, salary increases, company-sponsored further training, etc.).

Barad and Weinshall found that within the first ten years of a person's

TABLE 7
MANAGERIAL AND PROFESSIONAL JOBS IN TEACHING FOR WOMEN AND MEN

Sex	Primary Schools		Secondary Schools	
	% Among Teachers	% Among School Principals	% Among Teachers	% Among School Principals
Women	68.0	19.3	39.0	7.4
Men	32.0	80.7	61.0	92.6

employment, a steadily widening gap exists between the status of male and female employees. After ten years, the level of advancement of women approaches that of men in respect to salary and functions such as "supervision of performance and administration." But even then, the gap between the status of male and female employees, regarding achievement of managerial authority, still persists. Barad and Weinshall concluded on the other hand, that Israeli women tend to prepare themselves less than men for managerial careers. There was a smaller proportion of woman graduates in engineering and economics (the two principle fields were found to lead toward managerial functions), than in other higher education areas, (e.g., liberal arts, behavioral sciences, law and teaching), despite the fact that they were found to do just as well as men, both at school and at the university. The proportion of women and men in teaching and in principal roles in Israeli schools, show that women in that profession turn from managerial authority and supervisory duties. Hence, it may be inferred that only a minority of women really wish to achieve equality of status in employment (as compared to men) by being ready to override any obstacle (child raising as well as prejudices of employers or fellow employees) on their way. It seems that women in the engineering and economic professions can be looked upon as part of the above category of women who in addition to their natural aspirations, also prepared themselves theoretically for a managerial career.

Thus we see that although, by and large, employment opportunities in Israeli urban society were the same for both men and women, there was a tacitly admitted inequality between the sexes for the reasons outlined above. Women tended to look for the type of job that would alleviate the recognized difficulties. In the Kibbutz, on the other hand, women had, *a priori*, fewer spheres of activity open to them. As part of a work rationalization process, a more restricted number of peripheral occupations are considered suitable for women.

Having seen the effects of the general employment situation on the employment of women, who form one part of the "employment reserve" of the country, let us now turn to another aspect that has a relationship with the general employment situation—the technological development and level of mechanization of the industry.

THE EFFECTS OF TECHNOLOGICAL DEVELOPMENT ON INDIVIDUAL AND GROUP BEHAVIOR

The main problem of Israeli industry is probably competition on equal terms (i.e., without tariff barriers) with products of other countries, whose standards of living are closest to Israel's standard. The two areas in which Israel has to meet world competition are productivity and the quality of its industrial output (Weinshall, 1967).

The reasons for Israel's relative weakness in industrial quality and productivity are several. First, Israel entered industry and other economic fields only in this generation, or at the earliest, in the last generation. When mechanization started to penetrate Israel on a large scale after World War II, Israel by and large had neither the expertise nor the tradition in industry and other fields.

The second reason for the lack of high quality and productivity was the relatively low level of skill brought in by immigrants. The third reason was a shortage in the required types of managers (Weinshall, 1969); Israel has always been in need of able and knowledgeable managers. The contribution of the big immigration of 1949–53 to the managerial strata of Israel was very low. University training in industrial management began in Israel in 1953 and the first graduates in management and business administration (with M.B.A.'s, M.Sc's, or the equivalent) from Israeli universities, concluded their studies only in the early 1960s.

The fourth circumstance affecting productivity and quality was the negative effect of the over-employment periods of 1963–65 and since 1969. The introduction of more advanced technology was considered as a solution to the problem of productivity and quality, enabling Israel to be more competitive with and within the industrialized countries. However, the technological development which has taken place in Israeli industry (see Table 8) evidently had to be accompanied by structural changes in behavior within the industry.

TABLE 8
INDUSTRIAL PRODUCTION IN TEN COUNTRIES,
INDEX NUMBERS OF INDUSTRIAL PRODUCTION
(BASE YEAR 100 – 1965)

Country	1953	1958	1962	1965	1966
Australia	—	76	93	112	116
Belgium	64	74	93	109	111
Canada	61	75	94	118	128
France	56	79	95	109	116
West Germany	48	73	96	115	116
Israel*	42	52	88	125	127*
Italy	42	60	92	107	119
Sweden	59	71	94	119	—
U.K.	74	84	97	111	112
U.S.A.	73	75	95	115	126

* The total annual gross value of production from April 1965 to March 1966 was Israeli Lira 5,852,000,000 (equivalent to $1,950,000,000 at the rate of exchange at the time).
Source: All the above figures appear in the U.N. Statistical Yearbook (New York, 1968). The figures of the above table on pages 155–168 (Table 50) and the additional information about Israel (*) on pages 210–224.

A field research on 138 workers in nine industrial plants explored their attitudes toward their work group, the job and the industrial organization—at different levels of mechanization (Tenne, 1969). The sample was divided into three groups as follows:[9]

---

[9] According to Bright (1958).

Level 1	Hand Control Level of Mechanization (Stages 1–4)	78 workers
Level 2	Mechanical Control—Signal Response (Stages 5–11)	30 workers
Level 3	Variable Control—Action Response (Stages 12–17)	30 workers

Tenne followed and compared her findings with several studies in other countries. Her population, however, had some characteristics which should be borne in mind when comparisons are made. Tenne's interviewees were only a small part of the work force of every one of her nine plants. The plants as a whole were not necessarily at the same advanced level of technology as plants of the workers that Tenne interviewed. Thus, their attitudes do not necessarily represent the average attitudes of the whole plant. In each of her three groups, she combined workers operating at the same mechanization levels, but who may have belonged to plants which predominantly operated at a different level of mechanization.

Another point to stress is that while Bright (1958), for example, when referring to the "changing contribution required of operators, with advances in levels of mechanization," had in mind the operators who directly attended the same piece of equipment during most of their time within the plant, Tenne included among her interviewees people who were responsible, among their functions, for repairs and maintenance and other technical functions related to the equipment.

Tenne found that the lower the level of mechanization, the stronger the awareness of patterns of work group interaction and communication. 25% of the workers in Level 1 had a comparatively high preference for the social objectives and aspects of communication patterns in the work group, as compared with only 7% of the workers in Levels 2 and 3. On the other hand, only 62% in Level 1 gave a comparatively high preference to the functional and job objectives of the communication patterns, as compared to 84% who expressed the same attitude in Levels 2 and 3. It was likewise found that while in the two higher levels, the workers evaluated their colleagues according to their work proficiency, in the lowest level they judged their peers, to a large extent, by their personal characteristics and their social behavior. Similar tendencies were found outside Israel (Marek, 1967).

Tenne also found that the higher the level of technology, the higher the percentage of workers who aspire toward more autonomy and who attribute more importance to intrinsic rewards (i.e., an interesting job, a job with responsibility and authority, etc.). On the other hand, workers in the lowest level of mechanization put more emphasis on the importance of instrumental rewards (i.e., wages and working conditions). This agrees with Blauner's findings (Blauner, 1964). Another finding of Tenne's was that the higher the level of mechanization, the more the worker thinks that his job contributes to the overall success of the plant. On the other hand, Tenne found that the higher the mechanization, the smaller the percentage of those who thought that the worker himself is the predominant factor in the success of the job (50%—Level 1; 43%—Level 2; 27%—Level 3). She found that the percentage of those who thought that the quality of the equipment and the proficiency of the worker equally establish the success of the job was larger in the two higher levels (38%—Level 1; 67%—Level 2; 54%—Level 3).

In the higher levels of mechanization, the workers felt that the equipment dictated the speed of their work (27% in Level 1; 47% in Levels 2 and 3). Tenne also found that in the higher levels of mechanization, the workers expressed more interest in the work of other departments in the plant and better knowledge of the other phases of the production process. These findings coincide with the work done in the sociotechnical area (Blauner, 1964; L.E. Davis, 1962; Emery and Marek, 1962; Marek, 1967; Mann and Hoffman, 1960).

Tenne also examined the clarity of the promotional ladder and the degree of satisfaction in the various levels of mechanization. Her findings corroborated that of previous writers in this field (Walker and Guest, 1952; Bright, 1958; Blauner, 1964; Turner and Lawrence, 1965). She found that the higher the level of mechanization, the higher the degree of general satisfaction as well as the satisfaction from the job. The correlation between these two types of satisfaction (general and job) was found to be highly significant. The highest correlation found between these two types of satisfaction and satisfaction from other factors was with the following three factors:

1. Degree of interest in the job
2. Authority and responsibility on the job
3. The management of the plant

It could be deduced from the findings that the correlation between the worker's satisfaction from his job and the intrinsic and immediate rewards of the job was more significant than the correlation between his satisfaction and the instrumental and external rewards. This agrees with Herzberg's findings regarding the motivation to work (Herzberg, et al., 1957, 1959).

Kibbutz Industry

In 1969, a number of American professors expressed their impressions of the Kibbutz in Israel in the following terms:[10]

> The kibbutz is a voluntary socio-economic community, an egalitarian society which provides complete economic, social, and cultural services for its members.
> There are no police in any kibbutz. Crime and delinquency are very rare in the usual meaning of those terms. Instead social control of deviant behavior is exercised through standards of self-discipline. Its members obey its unwritten laws which embody the opinion of the majority. Moral compulsion and appeal to the force of conscience have largely replaced material incentives and coercion.
> There is less formal stratification and privilege, and life is based upon direct democracy. The kibbutz is a unique, small scale social system. Solidarity and informality are the expected bases of member-to-member relationships. It is a system viewed by its members as morally right and bound together as a big family is bound together—by ties

---

[10] From a report to the American Council for the Behavioral Sciences, in the Kibbutz Management and Social Research Center (1969).

of common values, common experience, common past, common fate, and mutual aid.

The kibbutz community is a family-oriented society. The family has an important role in shaping public opinion of the community and in the socialization of children.

The kibbutz always provides the economic needs of aged members. There is a system of gradual retirement of aged members: a decreasing number of hours worked per day according to age and sex. Every member when he reaches this age may have the right to work less. However, some members prefer to continue working to give more meaning to their lives and they, of course, may do so.

The kibbutz community structure integrates two subsystems: the *economic*, consisting of farming and manufacturing and services; and the *social*, consisting of education, health, culture, defense, etc.

The general assembly, consisting of adult members, is the supreme authority in the kibbutz. It enables the individual member to express his opinions and cast his vote. It provides a platform on which public opinion can make itself felt on all issues.

Below the General Assembly in the structure, there is a network of functional and coordinating committees. The coordinating committees are the policy making bodies. They integrate the system by deciding on crucial and boundary issues between and above functional committees. The coordinating committees are: the Executive Committee which is at the top of the social subsystem and the Management Committee which is at the top of the economic subsystem. Within the coordinating committees are located the four key office holders in the system structure: (1) the *General Secretary* is the chief executive coordinator of the social subsystem and the chairman of the executive committee; (2) the *Top Manager* is the chief coordinator of the kibbutz economic subsystem and the chairman of the Management Committee; (3) the *Treasurer* is responsible for the finances of the kibbutz and a member of the Management Committee; (4) the *Manpower Manager* is in charge of the allocation of manpower.

These four key office holders occupy complementary roles which coordinate the kibbutz system as a whole. Their role definition is very diffused, thus giving every key leader a chance to maximize his contribution in those specific situations where he is most competent.

The economic subsystem is organized into branches which carry out the work of the community. Members are allocated as workers of teams in branches in farming, industry, and services. They have maximum autonomy with decision-making involving their work situation. The branch teams are the foundation blocks of the economic subsystem of the kibbutz and they utilize group processes to increase performance. Every team elects its branch coordinator (supervisor) who plays a major leadership role in his team's performance. He serves as a link between the branch team and kibbutz committees and office holders.

The kibbutz system is based on planned rotation of office holders. Between one-half and one-third of the kibbutz members serve on committees. They are elected and about half of them are rotated every year. Key office holders and branch coordinators are elected for one to four years and then rotated. The kibbutz uses a system of planned rotation in order to be consistent with its democratic values, to maximize member involvement in the system, and to minimize stratification.

The kibbutzim consist of 4% of the whole population of Israel. The number of members per kibbutz ranges from 100 to 1000 (average about 200), and the total population including children is from 200 to 2000 (average about 400). There is an annual growth of about 3% in the population of the kibbutzim.

Until the end of the Second World War, the Kibbutzim in Israel had been based entirely on agriculture. Subsequently, some members in various Kibbutzim made the point that it was necessary to introduce industrial enterprises into the Kibbutzim in order to solve the following two problems:

1.   Finding useful employment for the elderly, the handicapped and the infirm who could not be absorbed in the various branches of agriculture. This was based on the assumption that in an industrial enterprise it would be possible to find suitable employment for handicapped members or elderly parents.

2.   Creating a regulating factor to cope with the seasonal fluctuations especially in respect to manpower, in the various branches of farming. Those advocating the introduction of industry into Kibbutzim assumed that such industrial enterprises would be able to absorb members who had temporarily become redundant in agriculture by reason of seasonal fluctuations or other factors. Once there was again a demand for them in agriculture, these members could be transferred back from industry.

However, once industry was introduced into the Kibbutzim it was discovered that neither of these two problems could be solved by it. Industry was found to be even less flexible than agriculture had been, regarding the type and skills that manpower required and regarding the working capital.

A study on the participation of workers in the decision-making process in industrial plants was carried out in ten Kibbutz plants (Tannenbaum, et al., 1974). The participation was measured by several different research tools; for example, in decision-making and its effects on attitudes and communication, Likert's scheme (Likert, 1961) was followed. Other related questions asked the respondents as to their opinions regarding the desirable degree of worker participation in decision-making and of their supervisor's participativeness. Finally, the participation was measured by means of the degree of control in the plants (Tannenbaum, 1968), the bases of power and by rewards and sanctions.

The Israeli Kibbutz findings were compared to those in industrial plants in Italy, Austria, the United States and Yugoslavia. The conclusion of Tannenbaum, et al. (1974) was that the Kibbutz and Yugoslav plants included in this study were not only highly participative according to their formal charters, but also in their actual operations. This was particularly true of the Kibbutz plants. According to the respondents in these plants, members participated substantially in decisions related to the plant as well as to their own work. Participation also appeared to pervade relations between superiors and subordinates. Superiors in Kibbutz plants were receptive to the ideas and suggestions of those under them, and they were helpful and supportive in relations with their subordinates. Kibbutz plants were also characterized by a relatively flat, power equalized distribution of control—although the slope of the control curve was negative, as in the typical industrial organization. Furthermore, the character of control and the bases of power in the Kibbutz plants reflected a participative managerial style. Members acceded to the influence of superiors largely because of a sense of commitment to the organization. Rewards for good work and sanctions for bad were dispensed through social approval and disapproval by coworkers as well as supervisors. Although the Kibbutz plant was highly participative, it was not as participative as its formal charter implied, nor as participative as members would have liked it to be. Nonetheless, Tannenbaum, et al. (1974) point out that the discrepancy between the ideal and the reality in Kibbutz plants was small compared to that in other organizations. The Yugoslav plants also corresponded to the participative model, although not as closely as the Kibbutz plants. The American, Austrian and Italian organizations were not as participative as the Kibbutz or Yugoslav plants in terms of most criteria.

ORGANIZATIONAL STRUCTURE

Organizational structure generally is consistent with "the scope of the managerial decision-making process in order to ensure the cooperation of all the human factors (e.g., workers, suppliers, customers, shareholders, bankers, trade union and government agencies, etc.) without which the organization cannot survive" (Weinshall, 1971). According to this view, the managerial structure has to be adapted to the size (i.e., the scope of the decision-making process) in order to allow for the absorption of new technologies and innovations.

Although structure is not easily measured, some surrogate measures are possible. One of them is the system of production, which was found to be correlated with the managerial structure (Woodward, 1958, 1965). Another study found that both technology and product, as well as area diversification, can be good indicators of structure, since both correlate with the managerial structure (Stopford, 1968). On the basis of Woodward's findings, it could be said that until recently Israel has not been very advanced in its production systems. According to Woodward, an average of twenty-five subordinates to a first line supervisor is indicative of a unit and small batch production system. An Israeli study of 650 supervisors (478 of whom were first line production supervisors), in 100 plants, with at least fifty employees in each, covering all industrial areas, reported the number of subordinates per first line production supervisor (Simmons, et al., 1962). Comparing Simmons' findings with those of Woodward (see Table 9), it is evident that the profile of Israeli first line supervisors, as regards span of control, is the closest to that of Unit Production supervisors and farthest from that of Mass Production in Woodward's study. This finding was corroborated in a later research (Shor, 1969) which studied various departments in an automobile assembly plant. Although one would assume that in such a plant the span of control of first line supervision would be close to Woodward's average for Mass and Large Batch Production (forty-five subordinates), Shor actually found an average of twenty-four subordinates per supervisor, which is Woodward's average for Unit and Small Batch Production.

Indeed when Shor studied more closely the actual behavior of the production supervisors, he found that their leadership behavior was what one would expect of foremen in a Unit Production plant in that they were usually active on the floor rather than being desk foremen (i.e., they were managing their departments in an entrepreneurial structure, informally, rather than formally, as in a more bureaucratic structure). When correlating the behavior of the supervisors with their ranking according to Fleishman's scales (Fleishman, et al., 1955), Shor found that the better the foreman ranked according to Fleishman's scales,

TABLE 9
SPAN OF CONTROL OF FIRST LINE SUPERVISION
COMPARISON BETWEEN BRITAIN AND ISRAEL

Average No. of Subordinates of first line Supervisor	BRITISH PLANTS						TOTAL			
	Unit Production		Mass Production		Process Production		British Plants		Israeli Supervisors	
	No.	%	No.	%	No.	%	No.	%	No.	%
41 and over	4	–	22	74.2	–	–	26	33.2	72	15.2
31 – 40	4	17.3	5	16.2	2	8	11	14.2	69	14.9
21 – 30	8	34.7	2	6.2	5	20	15	19.2	85	18.0
11 – 20	6	26.1	1	3.2	12	48	19	24.3	145	30.7
10 or less	1	4.4	–	–	6	24	7	8.9	101	21.2
Total No. of Plants (or supervisors)	23	100%	30	100%	25	100%	78	100%	472	100%
SOURCE	(Woodward, 1958, 1965)								(Simmons, et al., 1962)	

the more he maintained direct contact with his department to accomplish his job.

The entrepreneurial (informally centralized) and functional (formally centralized) structures of Israeli industrial organizations are at present adequate to cope with their scope of decision-making processes. It is now clear why in a study on bureaucratic structures in Israeli plants, as has been previously mentioned, more types of structures have not been found (Samuel and Mannheim, 1970). The Israeli culture would, however, facilitate the future growth of companies, the establishment of new types of managerial structures and interorganizational managerial mobility. The Israeli culture and its norms and values are much closer to those of the U.S. than to those of Western European continental countries.

There is, however, another organizational behavioral characteristic in which Israeli managers are closer to Anglo-American managers than to continental European ones—oral or written communication. Several communication studies on self-recorded perceived interactions (Weinshall, 1966, 1970; Tzirulnitsky, 1969) found that (see Table 10) while the average daily number of interactions per person (face-to-face and by telephone, but not written communication) in two business organizations in the U.S. and the U.K. were almost identical, the averages for two French industrial organizations were five to ten times less. The Israeli study, which was performed in an Army ordnance unit, gave an average of 2.6 daily interactions per person, only about one half of the U.S. and U.K. averages. Assuming that in army organizations there is on the average more written communication than in business organizations, average perceived interactions per person in Israeli industrial organizations would probably be found to be even closer to the U.K. and, especially, the U.S. figures. Indeed, Tzirulnitsky drew attention to Table 10, emphasizing that the Israeli figures, with regard to the percentage of interactions by telephone and face-to-face, as well as the consensus as to Type of Interaction (i.e., instruction, information, advice, etc.), are almost identical to those of the U.S. corporation.

TABLE 10
COMPARISON OF SELF-RECORDED INTERACTION STUDIES
IN FIVE ORGANIZATIONS IN FOUR COUNTRIES

Data Studied / Type of Organization Country Year	Industrial Chemical U.S. 1959	Marketing- Chemical- Consumer U.K. 1966	Industrial- Electronic Components FRANCE 1966	Industrial Aircraft Productions FRANCE 1966	Army- Ordnance ISRAEL 1969
No. of Managers Approached	50	60	26	21	48
Participated	34	50	26	21	41
Length of Study (No. of days)	10	10	10	10	10
Oral Interactions Total Reported	1,708	2,639	128	215	672
% Mutually Perceived	26%	14%	17%	21%	7%
Daily Average Per Person	5.0	5.3	1.0	0.5	2.6
% of Interactions By Telephone	22%	45%	73%	29%	19%
Face to Face	78%	55%	27%	71%	81%
Consensus as to Type* In Mutually Perceived Interactions	47%	35%	46%	73%	50%
Source	(Weinshall, 1966)	(Weinshall, 1970)			(Tzirulnitsky, 1969)

* Type of Interaction—e.g., Instruction, Information, Advice, Compliment, Reprimand, etc.

VALUES AND NORMS OF MANAGEMENT AND WORKERS

One of the most difficult processes to which the State of Israel has been subjected since its inception is the change-over from the noneconomic dogma embedded in the ruling ideology of pre-State days to the principles of economic rationality governing modern economy and administration. With changing circumstances and Statehood, the driving force of, "if you will it, it is no dream,"[11] which had served the short-term targets of early colonization proved ineffective for long-range objectives (Eisenstadt, 1967; Gilboa, 1965).

A characteristic example of this process was the sharpening conflict between the traditional tenets of the cooperative movement and the cooperatives' adaptation to technological change and individualism. What compounded the conflict was the rising importance of materialism against the declining power of the ideology. Both the General Federation of Labour (Histadrut) and its Co-operative Centre have been putting up a vain struggle against deviations from the fundamentals of production cooperatives.

---

[11] From Theodore Herzl's futuristic novel, *Altneuland*.

Let us consider an analysis of the impact of the changing values of the Israeli society upon the principles of the cooperative as experienced in one manufacturing cooperative (Feldman, 1968). The study was carried out in one of the largest cooperatives in Israel, comprising three geographically dispersed plants manufacturing complementary products. Feldman investigated if the four cardinal principles of the cooperative stood up against under the realities of the enterprise. In addition, he examined the cooperative's organizational structure which violated cooperative principles by employing hired labor as well as members.

Feldman found that the principle of equality was highly rated, as revealed in the attitudes of members of the cooperative. Some of the cooperative's members thought that the principle of equality had an adverse effect on the organizational structure. Still, most members were opposed to any modifications in the equality of wages (80% of the members were against professional and skill wage differentiation; 70% were against granting additional financial allowance to holders of administrative posts, and 80% claimed that a uniform wage scale had to be maintained at all costs). The only exception concerning attitudes towards wage equality occurred with regards to premiums for higher productivity. 59% of the members favored personal productivity premiums, to be paid over and above their equal wages. Members held that distribution of profits was to be on a profit-sharing basis. However, the principle of equality was abandoned with respect to sharing assets. Members thought that the length of their membership in the cooperative should determine the individual's share.

Unequal opportunities for advancement for hired labor and members (with most of the senior executive and management posts being held by the latter) was considered by the heads of the Histadrut to be exploitation of the hired workers. Nevertheless, some 55% of the cooperative's members were in favor of having properly trained men from within their ranks take over key posts in management that were held by hired personnel. However, in their actual behavior they demonstrated little inclination to do so and were not really prepared to accept such responsible duties, which may have been because the responsible jobs were paid the same as the less responsible jobs they held. The hired personnel, on the other hand, were interested in joining the cooperative as fully pledged members. The main reason given for wanting to become a member was that it would spell advancement (33%), that it would give one a secure future (15%), and that as members they would draw higher wages (13%). The members of the cooperative, however, were ready to admit only a limited number of hired personnel as new members. Half the cooperative members studied by Feldman threatened either to leave the cooperative or to fight for wage differentials, if they had to admit all hired employees as fully pledged members.

One of the basic values of the new Israeli society, since its early formation a century ago, was called "sanctity of work." For many centuries, until middle of the 19th century, the Jews had been almost exclusively traders and scholars. As a reaction to this heritage, the new Jewish pioneers put a strong emphasis on agricultural work or on manual work in general (Eisenstadt, 1967). The practice of the "sanctity of work" value was studied by Blecher, et al. (1961) by measuring absenteeism among Israeli employees. It was found that absenteeism was no different in Israel than elsewhere in Western industrial society, but it was lower when the net income was high, and when the employees were paid a salary rather than a wage, and it was higher among male wage earners than female wage earners (see Table 11). Furthermore, it was shown to be lower among employees of Western European origin than among those of African or Asian origin, reflecting, as one might expect, the differing cultural values of these regions.

Table 12 presents data on comparative absenteeism by country of origin and by type of absence. While "illness" and "accident" rates of absence had declined from 1959–60 to 1963–64 for employees by all countries of origin, the rates for "annual leave" and "other reasons" had risen for all origins. Another phenomenon is that the rates of absence for the employees from various countries drew closer to each other on all types of absence, except for "other reasons," over the period 1959–60 to 1963–64, which means that the modes of behavior of people from various countries of origin drew closer together.

The value system shared by many of the immigrants since the beginning of this century led to the establishment of the Histadrut as a means for "the formation and development of a working class, nation building through pioneering and land development, the creation of a just and egalitarian society and development of a high standard of living for the growing Jewish community" (Rosenstein, 1970). These aims led to the dual role of the Histadrut which turned into the only influential trade union federation of Israel, with fifty national trade unions, as well as the largest single holder of business assets and, therefore, employer. The industrial holdings of the Histadrut are divided into those which are directly controlled by the Histadrut's management (53% of the industrial employees of Histadrut-held enterprises) and those which are governed by themselves—consisting of the kibbutz industries (28% of the employees), production cooperatives (14%) and others (5%).

It was within the 17,000 employees of the industrial holdings (directly controlled by the Histadrut) that all the efforts to implement worker participation in management were made (Rosenstein, 1970). The drive for participation had its origin in both the egalitarian ideologies of Histadrut leaders and the fact that the Histadrut members owned the plants in which they worked. However, it should be realized that a plant in which 700 employees work is owned by all 700,000 Histadrut members, which is a structure not too dissimilar to a publicly owned industrial corporation in the U.S.

The notion that the workers own their factories originally led the Histadrut to seek promotion of efficient economic units based on functional and hierarchical division of labor, in which all profits should be reinvested for the purpose of further development. Workers, on the other hand, demanded better wages and working conditions. These issues caused unofficial strikes in Histadrut's enterprises in the 1940s. This reaction of the workers, as well as other Histadrut failures to induce them to identify themselves as managers or owners, supports Barnard's theory of cooperation (Barnard, 1938) which conceives each of the human factors of the organizational decision-making process (i.e., workers, owners, suppliers, customers, trade unions, government, etc.) as cooperating with the organization only as long as it suits its "egoistic" interest, while the management is the only "altruistic" human factor of the organization, responsible for its survival by way of ensuring the cooperation of all the human factors of the decision-making process with the organization (Weinshall, 1971).

According to Rosenstein, there have been four major experiments for achieving worker participation in management. The first mechanisms through

TABLE 11
RATE OF ABSENCES FOR WHATEVER REASON, ACCORDING TO NET INCOME AND SEX

| | TOTAL | | MEN | | | | WOMEN | | | |
| | | | Daily (Waged) | | Monthly (Salaried) | | Daily (Waged) | | Monthly (Salaried) | |
Income	No. of People	Rate of Absence	No. of People	Rate of Absence	No. of People	Rate of Absence	No. of People	Rate of Absence	No. of People	Rate of Absence
		%		%		%		%		%
Up to 199	569	11.6	272	12.5	31	5.3	234	12.1	32	8.8
299	1004	12.0	642	13.3	67	9.7	293	9.9	56	10.0
399	1418	11.4	1154	11.7	142	10.0	59	9.7	63	10.3
499	1081	10.6	817	10.9	211	9.9	13	8.4	40	9.0
Above 500	1263	9.5	739	10.2	500	8.5	9	5.3	15	6.2
Unknown	97	10.5	55	11.5	26	9.0	13	9.7	3	10.2
TOTAL	5432	10.9%	3679	11.5%	977	9.0%	567	10.6%	209	9.45%

Table 12
COMPARATIVE RATE OF ABSENCES BY COUNTRY OF ORIGIN
(ALL REASONS) 1959/60–1963/64

Country of Origin	Period of Survey	Rate of Absence (%)				
		Total	Illness	Accident	Annual Leave	Other* Reasons
Anglo-Saxon	1959/60	10.78	2.94	0.74	5.29	1.81
& Europe	1963/64	10.14	2.76	0.54	4.62	2.22
Africa &	1959/60	10.97	3.47	1.07	3.88	2.55
Asia	1963/64	11.48	3.00	0.72	4.07	3.68
Israel	1959/60	10.50	2.92	0.71	3.80	3.07
	1963/64	10.98	2.64	0.50	4.40	3.40
Not known	1959/60	11.04	3.30	0.86	4.97	1.91
	1963/64	11.30	3.07	0.58	5.17	2.48

which worker participation was sought were the "worker committees" which are, in Israel, the shop steward committees, i.e., the trade union body at the plant level.

The second effort to securing worker participation was the Joint Production Committee (JPC), which was introduced in 1945, and was similar to such consultative management-worker committees in other countries (e.g., Britain). Rosenstein says that "the most interesting point for our discussion is the irrelevance of enterprise ownership—the functioning of the JPCs in the Histadrut enterprises has not differed from that in the private sector" and adds that "the failure of these committees to reduce worker alienation left many Histadrut intellectuals disappointed, and prepared the way for plant councils."

The third experiment, the "Plant Council" program, started in 1956 and its main feature was that every plant should be governed by a council composed of two-thirds of workers' representatives and one third of management representatives. The Council had jurisdiction over all the decision-making processes concerning all the human factors (customers, owners, etc.), except for the major problems of wages and working conditions, concerning the workers themselves. Decisions approved by two-thirds of each side (worker representatives and management representatives) were meant to be binding on management and the workers.

The fourth experiment in the efforts to achieve worker participation was the joint management program. This was attempted both at the plant level and in the central management of several plants, i.e., at the holding company level. The "joint management at the plant level" called for a management committee, composed equally of representatives of the whole work force and of top management under the chairmanship of the general manager. Rosenstein stresses that "it should be noted that the scheme provides merely consultation" for top management. Emphasis was put on separating trade union representation (i.e., workers' committees) from the joint management program. Although there was also an effort to introduce profit sharing, this did not occur.

The participation of workers in the central management did not fulfill expectations. First, as Rosenstein puts it, "the rank and file in the plants know little about the work of the representatives and expect little from them. Often, the representatives demanded for themselves or for their colleagues an appointment to the small managing group, e.g., a full time position as a director." This indeed is why the professional managers of the Histadrut welcomed this scheme which, according to Rosenstein,

> brought representatives of the trade unions—the "other side" with whom the central management negotiate—closer to the center of managerial decision-making. The prospects of co-opting the representatives into management while at the same time limiting their influence undoubtedly caused many managers to welcome such a plan.

However, Rosenstein says that by and large

> the activities of the worker-directors have failed to promote a feeling of satisfaction among the rank and file. The hope that a programme would cause an improvement in the work atmosphere in the enterprises, or that it would cause workers to identify more with their workplace, has not materialized.

An attitude survey carried out in 1966 on 567 employees (managers and workers) in sixteen industrial enterprises owned by the Histadrut (Tabb and Goldfarb, 1970) found that:

- About three-quarters of all interviewees understood by "participation" that workers' representatives participate in the management of the plant and in its decisions without dissociating themselves from the general work force.
- A much higher percentage among workers than among managers expected participation to bring about positive results in the areas of economic conditions of the plant, labor relations, morale, and discipline. Managers by and large did not expect participation to improve the workers' material rewards. Most workers, on the other hand, did expect such a result.
- Nine out of ten secretaries of workers' committees favored participation, while 55% of the managers opposed it. Among the work force 54% favored participation, 16% opposed it, and 30% thought that it was impractical.
- Enterprises with a low percentage of supporters were those that had the most unsatisfactory experience with previous forms of participation. By contrast, the highest percentage of support came from enterprises that either had no experience with participation or where there was relatively little management opposition.
- To most respondents, the failure of participation programs was due neither to reasons intrinsic to the idea of participation nor to the numerous practical problems, but rather to the Histadrut's method of handling such programs. This suggests the existence of a participation credibility gap between the leadership of the Histadrut and employees in the plants.

Rosenstein concludes that "the history of workers participation in Histadrut-owned enterprises reflects not only a strong motivation by the political leadership of the labor organization to change the status quo, but also the lack of success in achieving that desired change. This lack of success can be explained by: the official ideology of the Histadrut; the power of the Histadrut managerial elite; and the reactions of both managers and workers to the various participation programmes." The failures in worker participation in management in Israel are compatible with both present day managerial decision-making theory (Weinshall, 1971) and with the findings regarding similar experiments in countries like Yugoslavia, Sweden, Germany, etc. (Strauss and Rosenstein, 1970).

Another type of "participation" which was studied in Israel was the amount of information about the industrial organization which is diffused by management to the workers and its influence on motivation for achievement, affiliation, accomplishment and motivation maintenance. The Israeli study followed the pattern of a similar study in the U.S. (Davis, 1967). The interviewees in the Israeli study included managers and 167 workers in a random sample of thirty plants in the Tel Aviv area, each employing more than fifty employees (Kaly, 1970). It was found that the longer the service of the workers, the less positive the attitudes; this finding was contrary to a study of the management of a U.S. industrial organization where it was found that the longer the service the more positive the attitudes (Weinshall, 1960). Eliminating the effect of the length of service, Kaly found that the wider the knowledge of the workers about the organization, the more positive their attitudes. He likewise found correlations between the workers' attitudes and several characteristics of their managers. The attitudes of workers were more positive when the managers were older, had longer service in the organization, and had been a shorter time in Israel.

SUMMARY

This chapter has described the industrialization of a new society in a rapidly developing country. One has to realize that this new society, although to a large extent Jewish in its religious and cultural heritage, is also a pluralistic society, integrating communities which had brought with them the cultures of their countries of origin. Israel has experienced, along with the processes of industrialization and integration of people arriving from diverse origins, the process of fighting for its physical survival. In a way, these three processes are a national parallel to a simultaneous struggle for the achievement of four out of the five needs of individuals according to Maslow's hierarchy (Maslow, 1954)—the physiological, security, social, and self-actualization needs.

The most notable phenomenon that emerges out of this struggle is, possibly, the high degree of egalitarianism and relative absence of social stratification both in the society as a whole and inside industrial organizations. Along with this phenomenon, we have witnessed the gradual disappearance of differences between the various communities, originating from a variety of countries, and the emergence of a new culture, with mores and values more closely in line with the needs of a small industrial nation, which simultaneously has to achieve national integration and physical survival, on the one hand, and international recognition and economic survival on the other.

REFERENCES

Barad, M. and T.D. Weinshall
    1967   "Women as managers in Israel," in Israel Institute of Public Administration, Public Administration in Israel and Abroad in 1966. Jerusalem: Israel Institute of Public Administration.

Barnard, C.I.
  1938   The Function of the Executive. Cambridge, Mass.: Harvard University
         Press.
Bar-Yosef, R.
  1965   "The adjustment of new immigrants to industrial employment." Un-
         published PhD Dissertation, Department of Sociology. Jerusalem: The
         Hebrew University of Jerusalem.
  1968   "Desocialization and resocialization: the adjustment process of immi-
         grants." International Migration Review (3):27–45.
Blake, R. and J.S. Mouton
  1965   The Managerial Grid. Houston: Gulf Publishing Co.
Blauner, R.
  1964   Alienation and Freedom: the Factory Worker and His Industry. Chi-
         cago: University of Chicago Press.
Blecher, R., et al.
  1965   Worker's Absenteeism in Israeli Industry. In Hebrew. Tel-Aviv: Israel
         Productivity Institute.
Blustein, M.
  1970   "The effect of employment situations on the organizational behavior
         of certain industrial enterprises, 1965–1969." In Hebrew. MBA Dis-
         sertation. Tel-Aviv: Graduate School of Business Administration, Tel-
         Aviv University.
Bonne, A.
  1956   "The adjustment of Oriental immigrants to industrial employment in
         Israel." International Social Science Bulletin (8):15.
Bright, J.R.
  1958   "Automation and management." Published Paper. Cambridge, Mass.:
         Division of Research, Graduate School of Business Administration,
         Harvard University.
Crozier, M.
  1964   The Bureaucratic Phenomenon. London: Tavistock Publications.
Davis, K.
  1967   Human Relations at Work—The Dynamics of Organizational Behavior.
         New York: McGraw-Hill.
Davis, L.E.
  1962   "The effects of automation on job design." Industrial Relations (2):53–
         71.
Eisenstadt, S.N.
  1954   The Absorption of Immigrants. London: Routledge and Kegan Paul.
  1967   Israeli Society. London: Wiedenfield and Nicholson.
Emery, F.E. and J. Marek
  1962   "Some socio-technical aspects of automation." Human Relations (15):
         17–25.
Feldman, Y.
  1968   "The impact of hired labour and members of the organisational struc-
         ture of the cooperative." In Hebrew. Unpublished MSc Dissertation,
         Department of Industrial and Management Engineering. Technion:
         Israel Institute of Technology.
Fleishman, E., et al.
  1955   "Leadership and supervision in industry." Monograph No. 33. Colum-
         bus: Ohio State University, Bureau of Educational Research.

Gilboa, M.
   1965   Changes in Workers' Companies and Cooperatives. In Hebrew. Jeru-
          salem: Culture and Education Publications.
Goode, W.J.
   1966   "Family and mobility," in R. Bendix and S.M. Lipset (eds.), Class,
          Status and Power: A Reader in Social Stratification. New York: The
          Free Press.
Hall, D., H.-Cl. de Bettignies and J. Amado-Fischgund
   1969   "The European business elite: an exclusive survey." European Busi-
          ness, No. 23 (October).
Herzberg, F., et al.
   1957   Job Attitude Review of Research and Opinion. Pittsburgh: Psychologi-
          cal Service of Pittsburgh.
Herzberg, F., B. Mausner and B.B. Snyderman
   1969   The Motivation to Work. New York: Wiley.
Hirsch, S.
   1970   "Anatomy of five export fields in European countries and Israel." In
          Hebrew. Economic Quarterly (65–66):3–14.
Israel Productivity Institute
   1965   Worker Mobility. Tel-Aviv: Israel Productivity Institute.
Kaly, J.
   1970   "Correlations between the amount of workers' knowledge about the
          operation of the organisation employing them and their attitude
          toward the organisation. Unpublished MBA Dissertation. Tel-Aviv:
          Graduate School of Business Administration, Tel-Aviv University.
Katz, E. and S.N. Eisenstadt
   1960   "Observations on the response of Israeli organisations to new immi-
          grants." Administrative Science Quarterly (5).
Likert, R.
   1961   New Patterns of Management. New York: McGraw-Hill.
Mann, F.C. and L.R. Hoffman
   1960   Automation and the Worker: A Study of Social Change in Power
          Plants. New York: Henry Holt and Co.
Marek, J.
   1967   "Technological development, organisation and interpersonal relations."
          Acta Sociologica (10):224–257.
Margalit, Y.
   1971   "The Israeli presidents." In Hebrew. Unpublished MBA Dissertation.
          Tel-Aviv: Graduate School of Business Administration, Tel-Aviv Uni-
          versity.
Maslow, A.H.
   1954   Motivation and Personality. New York: Harper and Brothers.
Niego, S.T.
   1964   "The effect of full employment on what goes on in industrial enter-
          prises." In Hebrew. Unpublished PhD Dissertation. Technion, Israel:
          Department of Industrial Management and Engineering, Israel Institute
          of Technology.
Rosenstein, E.
   1970   "Histadrut's search for a participation program." Industrial Relations
          (9):170–186.

Rosner, M.
  1965 Summaries of Research on Women in the Kibbutz. In Hebrew. Givat
       Haviva, Israel: The Institute of Research on Kibbutz Society.
Samuel, Y. and B.F. Mannheim
  1970 "A multidimensional approach toward a typology of bureaucracy."
       Administrative Science Quarterly (15):216–228.
Servan-Schreiber, J.J.
  1967 Le Défi Américain. Paris: Denoel.
Shor, Z.
  1969 "The status of the foreman in the organisational structure of an in-
       dustrial enterprise." In Hebrew. Unpublished MSc Dissertation. Tech-
       nion, Israel: Department of Industrial Engineering, Israel Institute of
       Technology.
Shuval, T.
  1963 Immigrants on the Threshold. New York: Atherton Press.
Simmons, I., et al.
  1962 Foremen in Israeli Industry in 1961. Tel-Aviv: Israel Productivity In-
       stitute.
Stopford, J.M.
  1968 "Growth and organizational change in the multi-national firm." Un-
       published PhD Dissertation. Cambridge, Mass.: Graduate School of
       Business Administration, Harvard University.
Strauss, G. and E. Rosenstein
  1970 "Workers' participation: a critical view." Industrial Relations (9):
       197–214.
Tabb, J.Y. and A. Goldfarb
  1970 Worker Participation in Management: Expectations and Experience.
       Oxford, England: Pergamon Press.
Tannenbaum, A.S.
  1968 Control in Organizations: New York: McGraw-Hill.
  1974 Hierarchy in Organizations: An International Comparison. San Fran-
       cisco: Jossey-Bass.
Tenne, R.
  1969 "A worker's relationship pattern with his fellow workers, his function
       and industrial organization at the mechanised and automated level."
       In Hebrew. Unpublished MSc Dissertation. Technion, Israel: Depart-
       ment of Industrial and Management Engineering, Israel Institute of
       Technology.
Turner, A.N. and P.R. Lawrence
  1965 "Industrial jobs and the worker: an investigation of response to task
       attributes." Published Paper. Cambridge, Mass.: Division of Research,
       Graduate School of Business Administration, Harvard University.
Tzirulnitsky, D.
  1969 "Quantitative and qualitative measurement of the elements affecting
       the organisational structure of the 'Matzlah' military unit." In He-
       brew. Unpublished MBA Dissertation. Tel-Aviv: Graduate School of
       Business Administration, Tel-Aviv University.
Walker, C.R. and R.H. Guest
  1952 The Man on the Assembly Line. Cambridge, Mass.: Harvard Univer-
       sity.

Weinshall, T.D.

1960 "Effects of management changes on organisation relationships and atti-
      tudes." Unpublished PhD Dissertation. Cambridge, Mass.: Graduate
      School of Business, Harvard University.

1965 The Role of Automation in the Future of Israel. Fontainebleau: Euro-
      pean Institute of Business Administration (INSEAD).

1966 "The communigram," in J.R. Lawrence (ed.), Operational Research
      and the Social Sciences. London: Tavistock Publications.

1968 Organisational Behaviour in Israel and the West. Tel-Aviv: Tel-Aviv
      University.

1969 "Managerial training in Israel." In Hebrew. Organisation and Admin-
      istration (15):21–29.

1970 "Some uses of the communications pattern research," in B. Roig-Amat
      (ed.), La Empresa Multiactional: Algunos Aspectos Importantes. Bar-
      celona: EUNSA (Ediciones Universidad de Navarra).

1971a "Two conceptional schemes of organisational behaviour." Management
      International (11):43–64.

1971b "Applications of two conceptual schemes in case study and organisa-
      tional research. Papers in Management Studies. Hertfordshire, En-
      gland: Ashridge Management College.

Woodward, J.

1958 Management and Technology. London: H.M.S.O.

1965 Industrial Organisation—Theory and Practice. New York: Oxford Uni-
      versity Press.

Yuchtman, E. and G. Fishelson

1970 "The problem of the inequity of income distribution in Israel." In
      Hebrew. Economic Quarterly (65–66):3–16.

Zloczower, A.

1968 "Mobility patterns and status conceptions in an urban Israeli setting."
      Published PhD Dissertation. Jerusalem: The Department of Sociology,
      The Hebrew University of Jerusalem.

CHAPTER 22

Self-Management Systems in Yugoslavian Enterprises

Janez Jerovšek

Faculty for Sociology, Political Science and Journalism
University of Ljublana

The economic system of Yugoslavia is substantially different from that of any other socialist country. The central difference lies in its organization: while centralization is the prevailing mode of organization in most socialist countries, that of Yugoslavia is a market system. The centralized system is perhaps most efficient in a simple and undeveloped economy, where the subsystems are not highly interrelated or interdependent. It is less efficient as the economy becomes more complex, and the operation of individual subsystems more determinate of the efficiency of each other and the whole. It is for this reason that the industrial organizations of Yugoslavia operate on a market system, with efficiency measured in terms of profit and growth.

SELF-MANAGEMENT

In the Yugoslavian market system, all organizations are largely autonomous, and the responsibility for decisions regarding planning, production targets, investment, prices, and wages is vested in the individual organization. The question is, who makes these decisions within the organization?

The formal system which has been instituted follows a participative model. "Participative," in this sense, refers to a structure of organization in which the legitimacy of all decisions stems from the participation of all employees in the decision-making process. In practice, the workers vote on all important policy decisions, and set the fundamental aims of the enterprise. The workers also elect the top managers of the organization, and the management is responsible to them. The Yugoslavian system of participation is to be distinguished from the traditional Western "human relations" approach. In the latter, the emphasis is placed upon transforming executives from a task to a human orientation, without any real power sharing with subordinates. The Yugoslavian system does involve power sharing between executives and workers.

The operation of this system is accomplished through the Workers Council, an elected body composed of about thirty or more members, depending on the size of the enterprise. About 70% to 80% of the Workers Council members are workers; the rest are top managers, middle managers, supervisors, and professionals. The council meets once or twice a month and votes on all important decisions concerning growth, prices, wages, expansion of the enterprise, the incentive system, safety provisions and, in general, the internal operations of the enterprise.

The self-management concept was introduced in Yugoslavia as a system which had previously been untested. It was defined and instituted on the assumption that self-management would produce the greatest efficiency in organizations, with a high degree of democracy in operating procedures. Scientists from the field of organizational science were aware that an untested participative model was being introduced about which no research data had been collected. The task of the organizational scientist, then, was to investigate the results of this implementation.

Organizational scientists were confronted with the invention of a new organizational system whose counterpart was not to be found elsewhere in the industrial world. There was, therefore, a great deal of interest generated as to how this social system worked in practice; its level of efficiency and democracy; and which structural and operating features were unsuitable or inadequate.

Attention was directed to some central questions, including the following: (1) How well is the system of collective responsibility working? (2) What is the relationship between leadership and self-management? (3) What are some of the pressures and conflicts surrounding the position of general manager? (4) What are the sources of power within the enterprise? (5) Who bears the risks of decisions? (6) How does the system of financial incentives operate? It was necessary to answer these and other questions in order to be in a position to evaluate the Yugoslavian system of self-management and to modify and improve those features found to be inadequate.

The self-management concept was introduced and formally institutionalized by government fiat. Where this system was implemented in organizations already operating on a bureaucratic or prebureaucratic basis, problems of incoherency and structural inconsistency arose between the old and new systems. The self-management system, as implemented, was rather complicated, and the tasks and relations within it were only loosely defined. The ensuing complications and lack of coherence resulted in informal modification of the system within individual organizations. As a consequence, there existed inconsistencies between the formal system, with its provisions of ligitimate decision-making, and the actual system in operation. One of the critical tasks of the applied organizational scientists was to discover how to modify the formal structure so that formal and informal structures and processes of the enterprises would become more compatible.

The following listing of the advantages and disadvantages of the system will clarify the problems that have arisen. Some of the advantages of self-management include the following.

1. The self-management system produces an increase in cooperation and involvement in working toward organizational goals.
2. The self-management model facilitates the spread of information through the organization, resulting in greater identification of the workers with the enterprise, and a greater opportunity for participation in decision-making.

3. The self-management model provides opportunities for mutual influence and control; improving communications, stimulating production, and generally allowing more flexibility within the organization. The organization is then more able to adapt to those outside influences, such as market, economy, and technology, which affect its progress and development.

4. All employees participate directly, or through the Workers Council, in the allocation of financial resources. This procedure encourages the idea that responsibility for the success or failure of the organization rests mainly with the members of the enterprise, and not with outside groups.

5. The value system in the wider society is based on participative ideals, which enhance the feelings in all employees that they are the legitimate source of power.

6. The discrepancy between individual and organizational needs is not obviated; however, it is not as great as is common in typical hierarchical organization. Individual needs, especially those of lower echelon employees, are satisfied to a much greater extent. In such a participative organization, there is a greater probability of differential reward than in the classical organization.

Balancing the clear advantages of the self-management system are some of the problems which accompany it. Major disadvantages and problems include the following.

1. The self-management scheme was institutionalized from the top downwards, by the implementation of an extensive system of laws. When autonomous action is viewed as going beyond the framework of the formally permissible, it tends to be labelled disruptive by those managing the top of the formal organization. There follows an attempt to bring the autonomous behavior within the rules of the formal organization, or to make more rules that will limit the outburst of such behavior in the future. There may develop excessive rules and regulations that greatly narrow the motivational foundation of participative management.

2. The model of self-management is partly based upon the assumption of common interests. A work organization is a social and status system in which a variety of organizational and socioeconomic groups, occupying different positions in the enterprise (and having different education, aspirations, responsibilities and incomes) interact to run and operate the organization. All these differences lead to conflicting interests. The interactional processes are not always complementary, and the individual actors do not always accomodate their expectations and actions to those of other actors.

3. The existing model of the self-management organization encompasses two different structures: a hierarchical one functioning within the daily work process, and a non-hierarchical (participative) one functioning only at designated times.

A decrease in efficiency may be expected when these two systems operate according to disparate principles, and are relatively independent of each other. The more these two subsystems are merged, and the more they operate on similar principles, the greater the expected efficiency of the work organization.

Prior to the introduction of the self-management system, the Yugoslavian economy was strictly decentralized by policies (systems of planning) which limited the autonomy of working organizations. With the introduction of self-management, not only was the social system within organizations changed, but also the political and economic policies of the government. As a result of these changes, the effectiveness of working organizations, and of the wider society, increased. The Gross National Product increased by 12% per annum, placing Yugoslavia among those countries with the most intensive and rapid economic development in the world.

It is difficult to quantify the extent to which this development is attributable to abolition of centralization or to the establishment of the self-management system. We do know that the centralized system imposed substantial limitations upon individual initiative, and the self-management system has loosened those limitations to a great extent. There is little doubt that self-management created a more flexible organization, capable of rapid adaptation to changes in the environment.

Yugoslavia is thus a unique subject for the study of the participation system, both to the theorist concerned with organizational behavior, and to the policy maker concerned with the problems of economic development. There is evidence that the participative system in Yugoslavia is a viable one, worthwhile for comparative and cross-cultural studies, although few generalizations are justifiable at this point due to the changes and modifications which are still taking place.

The studies which have been carried out, and their results, give us a clearer picture of how the self-management system actually works in practice.

INFLUENCE

One of the main goals of the self-management system was a wide distribution of influence among all employees. Since the workers represent the majority of any industrial organization, it was intended that they have a larger amount of influence than the executives.

One of the first tasks of industrials sociologists in Yugoslavia was to determine the actual distribution of influence in industrial organizations. The introduction of a democratic organization formally altered the distribution of power, as prescribed in a series of laws and regulations for all organizations. The question posed most often was to what extent the actual distribution of influence followed the prescribed distribution. Numerous empirical studies have been undertaken, using the same methods and measurement, with almost identical results.[1]

The compiled data cover the six years from 1964 to 1970 in which the actual (perceived) and the desired distributions of influence are given.[2] The purpose of measuring the desired influence was to ascertain the extent to which the desired distribution differed from that formally prescribed. We measured

---

[1] We used methods developed by Tannenbaum (1968) and applied in his research.

[2] We could not at this time, go into a lengthy methodological discussion of whether or not the perceived distribution corresponds to the actual; but our research has been based on the assumption that there is no substantial difference between actual and perceived distribution. There is methodological evidence to justify this assumption.

aspirations to participate in two different time periods. In Figure 1, we can see what changes have occurred in desired distributions of influence over the six year time period (Jerovšek, Možina, and Rus, 1970:183).

In Figure 1, we can see that changes in distribution of influence did not occur as had been predicted. The actual distribution is somewhat similar to classical hierarchical distribution. The top managers have the greatest amount of influence, and the workers the least. (There was, however, one significant change; the Workers Council, elected by all employees, is a very influential body.) Nevertheless, other data indicate that the greatest influence within the council rests with the top managers and professionals, despite the fact that they represent a small minority.

Again, from Figure 1, we can see that the desired distribution of influence in the earlier period was consistent with the formally prescribed distribution, and inconsistent with the actual distribution. At that time, it was expected that the curve representing the actual distribution would gradually conform to that of the desired distribution. The results, however, show that the desired distribution has adjusted to the actual. We do not have sufficient data to explain this change in aspirations. Possible explanations are (1) that employees have become disappointed with any real possibility for participation, or (2) that the content of aspirations has changed considerably.

In comparing the structure of influence in more and less efficient organizations, we found the distribution of influence to be identical in the two types of organizations. There was, however, a difference in the total *amount* of influence; in more efficient organizations, the total amount of influence was somewhat larger.

Several factors may be considered as possible explanations for lack of change in the influence distribution. We offer two possible explanations for

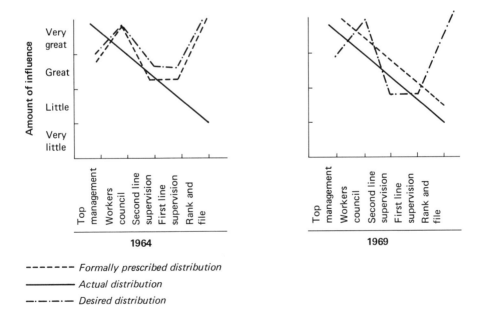

Figure 1. Amount of influence exercised in industrial organizations.

the influence distribution remaining hierarchical. First, there is the situation in which the executives possess the most crucial information pertaining to strategic decisions adopted by the Workers Council. Second, executives prepare and elaborate all the possible alternatives for these decisions; they explain proposals to the Workers Council and are responsible for the interpretation and execution of those adopted. The executives exert great influence in all phases of the decision-making process, despite the fact that the legal authority rests with the Workers Council.

Further consideration may be given to the ideas presented by Županov (1969:109):

> Wherever a system of activity exists, based on division of labor, there must be individuals directing and coordinating the actions of the other individuals toward a certain aim to be realized by the cooperative system. These individuals are called leaders. To the extent we talk about permanent, everyday activity which is characteristic of economic organization, the importance of those directing and coordinating the different activities is even greater. It is the importance of this role for the functioning of the collective activity we call work organizations which gives the occupants of this role power within the framework of the system. A fund of information indispensable for the organization, which the leaders receive from the organization itself, or from political–administrative resources, contributes to the perpetuation of leadership positions and, further, strengthens their power. Thus, the position of leaders is linked with a great amount of social power because of its strategic position in the functioning of the organization as a system of activity. This explains why the power does not depend on the amount of *formal* authority given to the leading positions because the amount of authority vested in them in no way changes the character of these positions for the system of activity. (Italics in original)

In the last fifteen years, we have tried to increase the influence of workers by transferring the formal authority to make all important decisions to the Workers Council. The Council members decide on all matters, even those about which they have little information or technical understanding. The evidence suggests that the acquisition of formal authority does not, in itself, result in an increase in influence.[3]

There is some empirical evidence that workers are more interested in being informed about matters and events directly concerning their situations, than in just having the formal authority for making decisions (Mozina, 1968). It appears that we cannot satisfactorily explain the operation of the social system in work organizations by the concept of formal authority alone. The system of communication, and access to information appear to be important factors in understanding this type of organizational system.

The introduction of self-management, then, has not measurably changed the distribution of influence. The top managers are still the most influential, although their influence is not entirely legitimate within the formal system.

---

[3] It is important to note that in the United Kingdom, the distribution of influence in nationalized plants is almost the same as in private ones. See Flanders (1966).

This does not mean, however, that some decisions might not be made more democratically. We do have some evidence that in decisions which are not technical, but deal with the inner operation of the enterprise, the Workers Council can and does exercise considerable influence.

Although the distribution of influence tends to be autocratic, the style of leadership is generally democratic. Managers who still practice autocratic style of leadership are often brought into conflict with the workers or their representatives, the party, and the unions. Autocratic styles of leadership are successful in cases where management is considered to be extremely efficient. They may also function successfully under the following conditions.

1. When the work force is comprised of workers from rural areas.
2. When the workers have no background in an industrial tradition.
3. When the level of education of the work force is very low.

Traditionally, management was not considered a profession which required special knowledge or training. There has been a visible change in orientation toward management. The field is now considered more and more as a profession which requires special training. It is to be expected that with this change in orientation, the social system of work organizations will operate more efficiently. However, there is some concern that this new manager will acquire more control in the organization, control which the workers have at this time.

Management has already exceeded its legitimate power. With more professional training, managers may be capable of further enlarging it. The problem is that this power, being informally held, carries no formal responsibility with it. There is the possibility, then, that management could take great risks without being responsible for failure. However, it is expected that management will meet many difficulties in striving to enlarge its power. The first is the political barrier stemming from the larger social system which advocates democratic values, and the second difficulty would be the workers, who are opposed to an extreme type of leadership.

RESPONSIBILITY

The most controversial issue, in theory as well as practice, is the problem of responsibility. How can the problem be solved in cases where the decision-making process is democratic? Who should be held responsible for the outcome of a strategic decision when it has been adopted by the Workers Council? It is very likely that in a democratic decision-making system, everyone would be responsible for an outcome which causes damage or financial loss to the organization, and, in fact, no one would be answerable.

This problem has yet to be solved despite the fact that an intensive search for theoretical and practical solutions has been going on for many years. The problem appears to be almost insurmountable since this is a systemic issue. It is impossible to solve the problem of responsibility in isolation since it is both linked to, and dependent upon, other crucial organizational variables.

The classical solution to this problem is one in which all responsibility for strategic decisions rests with the managers who adopted them. This solution is not acceptable to Yugoslavian industry for three reasons.

1. It would involve the abandonment of the self-management system.
2. There is fear that a managerial elite would have too much power within the organization as well as in the wider society. True democracy

is always in danger when one group has too much power and that power is not checked or counterbalanced by another powerful group. Fear of a powerful managerial elite is, in Yugoslavia, substantial, and this fear is to some extent justified, since managers are already the most influential group—despite the fact that their power is not entirely legitimate.

3. Returning to a classical hierarchical decision-making system is not a satisfactory solution since even in such a system the principle of unity of command is incompatible with the principle of specialization.

Warren G. Bennis also argued that a variety of factors, including rapid technological change, make obsolete the traditional emphasis on a well defined chain of command (Bennis, 1966).

In the system of classical theory, there will always be irresponsibility and confusion when the principle of unity of command is not followed. Dual supervision, which is functionally necessary for organizations operating in a complex and heterogeneous environment, is incompatible with the principle of unity of command. The classic hierarchical system, then, does not offer a satisfactory solution to the problem of responsibility, especially in an unstable or heterogeneous environment where the completion of nonroutine and complex tasks is involved.

The task at present is to modify the system to effect a distribution of responsibility according to the skill and power of the individuals in the organizational structure. There exists a constant effort to allocate more effectively the responsibility for important decisions.

The problem of responsibility has been explored by research, the results of which are presented in Table 1. In the survey, we attempted to determine how the mechanism of responsibility operates in ten more efficient, and ten less efficient organizations. We asked the respondents how sanctions were applied and distributed when decisions resulted in financial loss to the organization.[4] We then compared the allocation of responsibility with the distribution of influence. Our assumption was that in a structurally consistent organization, the amount of influence a group has corresponds with its amount of responsibility. In cases where the relationship between the two did not correspond, the assumption was that the organization was structurally inconsistent, and incapable of achieving maximum efficiency. The data in Table 1 demonstrate a higher correspondence between influence and responsibility in more efficient organizations, although some inconsistency was observed at certain hierarchical levels.

From Table 1, we can see that in more efficient organizations there exist six organizational groups having a high degree of responsibility, and in less efficient organizations, there are only two such groups. The data also indicate that in less efficient organizations there is a greater inconsistency between influence and responsibility.

In the same survey, we measured the desired distributions of influence and responsibility and found no structural inconsistencies between them.

We have some case study data which indicate that the search for an adequate and efficient solution to the problem of responsibility in the frame-

---

[4] The question was: who will suffer the consequences if a wrong decision has caused financial losses? The consequences are dismissal, demotion, or lower wages.

TABLE 1
ALLOCATION OF INFLUENCE AND RESPONSIBILITY,
IN MORE EFFICIENT AND PARTICIPATIVE ORGANIZATIONS AND
LESS EFFICIENT AND PARTICIPATIVE ORGANIZATIONS

Organizational Groups	More Efficient and Participative Organizations		Less Efficient and Participative Organizations	
	Will Suffer Consequences	Influence	Will Suffer Consequences	Influence
Members of Workers Council, and Management Board	0.53	3.39	0.38	2.98
Unskilled and Semiskilled Workers	0.74	1.97	0.83	1.88
Skilled and Highly Skilled Workers	0.73	2.45	0.82	2.32
Clerical Workers	0.65	2.22	0.65	2.03
Professionals	0.79	3.95	0.51	3.92
General Manager	0.78	4.80	0.54	4.64
Department Heads	0.83	4.13	0.59	3.79
Foremen and Supervisors	0.73	3.20	0.65	3.19
Secretary of Party Organization in the Plant	0.51	2.92	0.38	2.92

LEGEND

DISTRIBUTION OF RESPONSIBILITY
Scores 0.00 to 0.49—no responsibility
Scores 0.50 to 0.69—little responsibility
Scores 0.70 or more—great responsibility

DISTRIBUTION OF INFLUENCE
Scores 1.0 to 2.9—little influence
Scores 3.0 to 3.9—moderate influence
Scores 4.0 to 5.0—great influence

work of a democratic organization is not in vain. The data suggest that there is a strong, positive relationship between feelings of responsibility and participation.[5] Participation is a more significant factor in great responsibility than is education (Rus, 1970:748).

> This connection between responsibility and participation show us that the participative democracy is a condition for responsibility among employees; without it we cannot imagine a balance in a society in which private property is abolished.

EFFECTIVENESS OF SELF-MANAGEMENT SYSTEM

We will limit this section to the presentation of some empirical data and indicators which demonstrate, indirectly, that the operation of the self-management system has created a vital social dynamic in work organizations.

---

[5] Rus employed a definition of responsibility, which was introduced by Županov who characterizes the personal responsibility as the responsibility which is manifested with the feeling of responsibility, and the organizational responsibility as the responsibility which is manifested as the ability of organization to accord the behavior of individuals and groups with the normative system existing within organizaton (Županov, 1969:10).

The operation and effectiveness of the self-management model has been examined in a study (Možina and Jerovšek, 1969). We based the study, in part, on the organizational theory of Likert and Tannenbaum. Likert distinguishes among four different systems of organization: (1) exploitative authoritative, (2) benevolent authoritative, (3) consultative, and (4) participative. The following descriptions of systems 1 and 4 have been partly adapted to the conditions of our study.

System 1—Exploitative Authoritative

Within this system, management has responsibility and authority for decision-making and policy, while the workers are viewed as units of the organizations who are paid for work, but have no management responsibilities or influence. Coercion is the primary means for controlling workers' output and functioning within the organization. The flow of communications is in one direction: from the top downwards.

Decisions regarding aims and policy of the enterprise are made by top managers only, and often on the basis of inaccurate and inadequate information. As the lower echelon employees do not participate in decision-making, they do not feel responsible for carrying out these aims and policies. Responsibility is found only at the top of the organizational structure. Since managers depend primarily on coercion, there is little voluntary cooperation or interpersonal influence. Changes are carried out with difficulty because resistance to management is strong. There are many conflicts and they are difficult to solve. In such a social system the dissatisfaction of lower echelon members is significantly high.

System 4—Participative

Within this system, all those employed are treated as important parts of the organizational structure. Managers are responsible for decisions, but the opinions and suggestions of all participants are considered. Communications flow vertically, in both directions, and horizontally, and are rapid and effective. There are effective interpersonal relations. The differentiated reward system, which provides that greater and higher quality production is rewarded, and poor performance is not, increases motivation. With mutual control and influence, a highly coordinated, cohesive, and tightly knit system is established. The formal organization of this system is such that everyone is simultaneously an object of control, and exercises control over others. Responsibility is not located with one particular group, but distributed throughout the organization. The degree of responsibility is linked to the power which the individual, and group, possesses. There are fewer conflicts in system 4 than in system 1, and the level of employee satisfaction is higher. Changes are more easily introduced because those concerned with implementing changes are active participants in their formulation.

We have described only systems 1 and 4 to illustrate the extremes in organizational systems. Systems 2 and 3 differ primarily in degree. While system 4 is labelled participative, it has also been defined in terms of motivation, communication, interaction, responsibility, change, efficiency, etc.

For the purposes of our study, we assume that work organizations are managed on the basis of different social systems, and that the efficiency of those systems varies. The hypothesis was that those work organizations closely fitting system 4 would be more efficient than those operating on the basis of systems 1 or 2. For these reasons, we selected twenty enterprises, ten highly efficient and ten less efficient. We selected one of each level of efficiency from each industry branch we studied.

The following criteria was used to determine the level of efficiency in each organization:

1. average personal income per employee
2. profit per employee
3. funds per employee
4. investments per employee
5. increase in number employed over last three years
6. increase in number of professionals employed in the last three years.

These criteria are interrelated. Average income was, in more efficient organizations, high, and in less efficient ones, low. In the three years of the study, profit has increased in the more efficient organizations and stagnated in the less efficient ones. Funds per employee grew in more efficient organizations over the three year period, while in less efficient ones they decreased. In 1966 and 1967, investments grew in the more efficient organizations and decreased in the less efficient ones. Over the three years, the numbers of employees and professionals employed increased in more efficient organizations and decreased in their less efficient counterparts.

Since this study was based on comparing two groups of enterprises distinguished from each other by their level of efficiency, we will make comparative statements with reference to each other. When it is found that one group is characterized by more or less of some feature, it is only in relation to the other group that this comparison holds.

In selecting the organizations for study, we were also concerned with the social system that characterized them. We found that all the highly efficient organizations could be classified within system 3, and the less efficient ones in system 2. In Figure 2, this difference is revealed, and the differences are statistically significant.

In highly efficient organizations, superiors expressed trust in their subordinates, while in less efficient enterprises, trust was low. In highly efficient organizations, subordinates felt relatively free to discuss their problems with their direct superiors; in less efficient organizations, they felt correspondingly less freedom. In highly efficient organizations, superiors often sought the ideas and opinions of their subordinates in solving problems; in less efficient enterprises, this was done far less often. This type of influence is of primary importance since other studies (Rus, 1968) have shown that employees favor participation in determining their own working conditions, where their knowledge and experience is greatest, but are not as concerned with participation in those decisions concerning the entire enterprise, about which they have little information. It is very likely that workers will be less concerned with these significant decisions in the enterprise as long as their influence in the working processes, where their knowledge is most useful, is low.

In highly efficient organizations, employees were motivated to participate more than in less efficient organizations. Nevertheless, we established that on

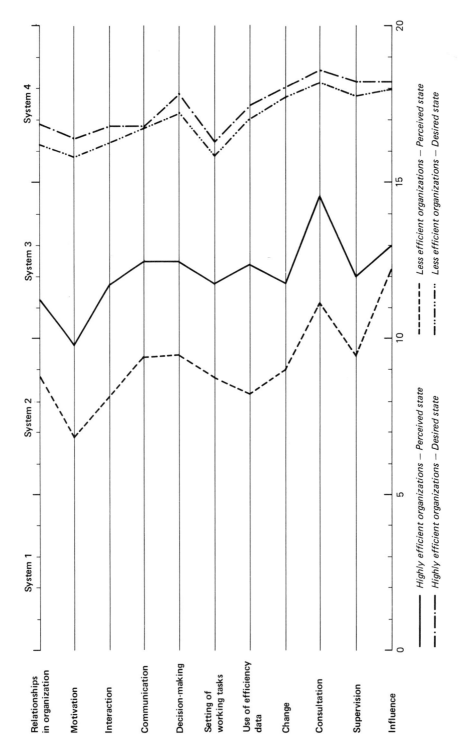

Figure 2. Profiles of organizational characteristics of highly efficient and less efficient organizations.

this variable, highly efficient organizations approached system 2. This means that human potentialities were not being fully utilized, even in the highly efficient organizations. Concerning the interaction variable, we established that in highly efficient organizations there were many contacts and exchanges of opinion among employees when solving working and organizational problems. In less efficient organizations, there were fewer such exchanges. Further, in highly efficient organizations extensive use was made of teamwork, while in less efficient organizations little use was made of this work process.

We also found that in highly efficient organizations the vertical communications flowed both ways; in less efficient enterprises the majority of communications were from the top down. In more efficient organizations, employees receive information with confidence and trust, while in the less efficient enterprises, skepticism greeted information from management. Information flowing upwards was, for the most part, accurate in efficient organizations, while in the less efficient, information was screened before it moved upwards. Supervisors tended to be well acquainted with the working problems of their employees in the efficient organizations, and less so in the inefficient.

We found that in highly efficient organizations, decisions were made at the top, but with considerable delegation of authority in their formulation. In less efficient organizations, decisions were both formulated and made at the top. The decision-making group, in the efficient organizations, was usually better informed than its counterpart in the inefficient enterprises.

Working tasks were defined and distributed through group discussion and decision in the efficient organizations. Inefficient organizations did not regularly make use of this practice.

In highly efficient organizations, data on operations, expenses, income and productivity are used to a much greater extent than in less efficient enterprises.

Systems 3 and 4 are not characteristically loose organizations; in these two systems, there is intensive supervision. Our data demonstrated that in highly efficient organizations, there was more supervision of all organizational groups than in less efficient organizations. Not only were all groups more closely supervised, but they were also more differentially supervised. From other studies (Leavitt, 1968) we know that those groups and organizations with more differentiated reward systems and structures of influence are more efficient than those with more egalitarian reward systems. Our data also leads to the conclusion that a more differentiated system of supervision is related to higher efficiency.

Although members of organizational groups are more closely supervised in highly efficient organizations than otherwise, they are considerably more satisfied. We found that when supervision is more extensive, in efficient organizations, there is a more effective utilization of working time. The difference in degree of satisfaction is substantial. In less efficient organizations, 84.1% of respondents answered that they were not particularly, or not at all, satisfied with the current operation of the enterprise; in highly efficient organizations, only 12.5% of respondents were of the same opinion.

In our study, we found that all highly efficient organizations fell into system 3 and all less efficient organizations into system 2. At the same time, we asked respondents (top managers and members of the Workers Council) in which system they would prefer to operate. In Figure 2, it can be seen that for several variables, all respondents, in more *and* less efficient organizations, preferred system 4.

CONCLUSIONS

Self-management system, as it has been defined, cannot be effectively implemented from the top. Institutionalization does facilitate the introduction of a social system which appears to maximize efficiency, however, a system characterized by maximum utilization of human resources cannot be realized through laws or institutionalization alone. A participative social system can be formally introduced into bureaucratic structure, but it is possible that the formal self-management organization will remain, in reality, bureaucratic and autocratic.

Within the framework of a bureaucratic organization, the style of leadership can be democratic, motivating workers and stimulating productivity. On the other hand, the style of leadership in a self-management social system may be autocratic, lowering the level of satisfaction, morale, and productivity. In our study of self-management enterprises, we found that work organizations operating on the basis of a participative model were highly efficient; those employing autocratic principles were less efficient, and thus did not maximize profitability.

It appears that the philosophy of management differs between these two groups of organizations. We found in interviews that the general managers of highly efficient organizations define effectiveness as the expansion of their organizations. General managers of the less efficient organizations, on the other hand, defined effectiveness as simply staying in business. For the latter, then, effectiveness is defined as the existence of the enterprise, and not its expansion.

The fact that highly efficient organizations have different social systems leads us to the supposition that this is a result of differing philosophy and practice. Managers, primarily those in less efficient organizations, often asserted that their low levels of efficiency were the result of changes continuously introduced by the environment. These changes, they maintained, were often unjustified, inconsistent, and frequently discriminatory. While these claims had some basis in fact, they were quite exaggerated. If they were completely accurate, it would leave unexplained the existence of both high and low efficiency in organizations in the same branch of industry. Economic policy may have discriminatory effects between branches, but not within a particular branch.

We found, from our study, that the main difference between the high and low efficiency organization was the type of social system within which they operate. We would now ask: who creates the different social systems, and who contributes most to the system operating with high efficiency? There is no empirical evidence to provide an answer to this question, but a possible hypothesis is reasonable. There is a possibility that the social system is the creation of those who exert the greatest influence within the organization, i.e., the general manager and top managers immediately below him. If this is the case, then it follows that the degree of democracy in an organization depends to a great extent on the outlook of top managers. The education of managers, and the recruitment policy of the enterprise then become of primary importance.

Our research was not undertaken with such hypotheses in mind, but the results have more clearly defined the actual operation of the self-management model, as well as suggesting hypotheses which may be tested in future studies.

Although we are aware that the structure of working organization is inseparable from the particular culture and environment of which it is a part (Lawrence and Lorsch, 1967), the experiences of Yugoslavia in introducing the self-management organization may be useful for those who would experiment in the same area.

REFERENCES

Bennis, W.G.
  1966 "The coming death of bureaucracy." Think (November–December).
Flanders, A.
  1966 "The internal social responsibilities in industry." British Journal of Industrial Relations No. 1.
Jerovšek, J., S. Možina and V. Rus
  1970 "Sociologija organizacije." Višja šola za organizacijo dela Kranj.
Lawrence, P.R. and J.W. Lorsch
  1967 Organization and Environment: Managing Differentiation and Integration. Cambridge, Mass.: Harvard University Press.
Leavitt, H.J.
  1968 "Unhuman organization," in H.J. Leavitt (ed.), Managerial Psychology. Chicago: University of Chicago Press.
Rus, V.
  1968 "Status strokovnega in vodstvenega kadra glede na komuniciranje, moč odgovornost." Moderna organizacija No. 5.
  1970 "Odgovornost in sistemi sankcioniranja." Teorija in praska No. 5.
Simon, H.A.
  1969 "The proverbs of administration," in A. Etzioni (ed.), Readings on Modern Organization. Englewood Cliffs, New Jersey: Prentice-Hall.
Tannenbaum, A.
  1968 Control in Organizations. New York: McGraw-Hill.
Županov, J.
  1969 Samoupravljanje i društvena moč. Biblioteka Naših tema.

PART VIII

POSTINDUSTRIALISM

INTRODUCTION—PART VIII

It is usually understood that the term "postindustrialism" means the kind of society that enjoys all the material rewards of a high level industrial regime, but with some of its more negative features eliminated. Postindustrialism does not mean a return to an idealized primitive world.

It is not necessary to introduce the concluding chapter of this volume for its task is obvious from the chapter title. It is evident that this chapter envisions the impact of shifts in social values as the engine that will drive society into the postindustrial era.

CHAPTER **23**

Toward a Postindustrial Culture

Eric Trist

Management and Behavioral Science Center, Wharton School,
University of Pennsylvania

There has not yet emerged a set of values congruent with the needs of the postindustrial society despite the fact that postindustrialism is structurally very much in evidence. Let me ask what are the salient cultural patterns today compared with thirty years ago; more particularly, those related to our core values, whether personal, organizational, or political? The answer can only be that despite superficial appearances, they are still very much the same. Therefore, is it surprising that we are witnessing a mounting crisis of alienation whose manifestations increase in variety and intensity, whether expressed as withdrawal or protest? Maladaptive trends are only too plain in many of the more extreme contemporary subcultures which represent short-circuiting strategies, self-limiting attempts at complexity reduction. It is not to say that adaptive trends are nowhere to be discerned, but that they are nearer the horizon than the main sky overhead.

THE NATURE OF RELEVANT EMERGING VALUES

A Three-Dimensional Cultural Model

If I ask what kind of new values can be regarded as appropriate, my answer can only be in terms of the following criterion: they must be values which enhance our capability to cope with the increased levels of complexity, interdependence and uncertainty which characterize the turbulent contemporary environment (Emery and Trist, 1965). Evidence is mounting that the individual by himself, or indeed the organization and even the polity by itself, cannot meet the demands of these more complex environments. A greater pooling of resources is required; more sharing and more trust. Appropriate emergent values will need to be congruent with Emery's (1967) second design principle— the redundancy of functions as opposed to the redundancy of parts. They may be expected to be communal rather than individualistic regarding access to amenities; cooperative rather than competitive regarding the use of scarce resources; yet personal rather than conforming regarding life styles and goals.

The direction of new values will be opposite that which value-formation

1011

has taken in industrial societies, molded as these have been by the Protestant Work Ethic (Weber, 1947). One may, therefore, expect resistance to and diffusion of their establishment. Such resistance, which is both conscious and unconscious, is responsible for a good deal of the cultural lag which has prevented more extensive cooperative action concerning problems of the urban environment.

Though the emergent patterns to be described may all be said to exist as cognitive orientations, they nontheless function as motivators of behavior for only relatively small numbers of people and are embodied in the practices of only a few organizations. They are perceived in widely differing ways in different groups. Our concern is with the extent to which such new patterns have properties which are likely to aid in the adaptation to complex environments.

Before describing them, however, it will be convenient to summarize the four environmental types introduced by Emery and Trist (1965) (elaborated in their subsequent book [1973]) and the extension of systems theory on which they are based. The four environmental types are listed below.

1. A main problem in the study of organizational change is that the environmental contexts in which organizations exist are themselves changing at an increasing rate, under the impact of technological change. This means that these environmental contexts demand consideration for their own sake. Towards this end, a redefinition of the causal texture of the environment is offered at a social level of analysis. This concept was first introduced by Tolman and Brunswik (1935).

2. This redefinition in terms of causal texture requires an extension of systems theory. The first steps in systems theory were taken in connection with the analysis of internal processes in organisms, or organizations, which involved relating parts to the whole. Most of these problems could be dealt with through closed-system models. The next steps were taken when these wholes had to be related to their respective environments. This led to open-system models, such as that introduced by von Bertalanffy (1950), involving a general transport equation. Though this enables exchange processes between the organism, or organization, and elements in its environment to be dealt with, it does not deal with those processes in the environment itself which are determining conditions of the exchanges. To analyze these, an additional concept—the causal texture of the environment—is needed.

3. The laws connecting parts of the environment to each other are often incommensurate with those connecting parts of the organization to each other, or even those which govern exchanges. Dangers and difficulties arise when there is a rapid and gross increase in the area of relevant uncertainty, a characteristic feature of many contemporary environments.

4. Organizational environments differ in their causal texture, in regard to the degree of uncertainty and in many other important respects as well. A typology is suggested which identifies four "ideal types" of organizational environments, approximations of which exist simultaneously in the "real world" of most organizations, though the weighting varies enormously. The typology of organizational environments follows.

Type 1. The Placid Randomized Environment. In the simplest type, goals and noxiants (i.e., desirable and undesirable features) are relatively unchanging in themselves and randomly distributed. This may be called the placid, randomized environment. A critical property (from the organization's viewpoint) is that there is no difference between tactics and strategy, and organizations can exist adaptively as single, and indeed quite small, units.

Type 2. The Placid Clustered Environment. The next type is also static, but goals and noxiants are not randomly distributed; they hang together in certain ways. This may be called the placid, clustered environment. The need then arises for strategy as distinct from tactics. Under these conditions, organizations grow in size, becoming multiple and tending towards centralized control and coordination.

Type 3. The Disturbed-Reactive Environment. The third type is dynamic rather than static. It consists of a clustered environment in which there is more than one system of the same kind, i.e. the objects of one organization are the same as, or relevant to, others like it. Such competitors seek to improve their own chances by hindering each other, each knowing the others are playing the same game. Between strategy and tactics there emerges an intermediate type of organizational response—what military theorists refer to as operations. Control becomes more decentralized to allow these to be conducted. On the other hand, stability may require a certain coming-to-terms between competitors.

Type 4. The Turbulent Environment. The fourth type is dynamic in a second respect; the dynamic properties arising not simply from the interaction of identifiable component systems but from the field itself (the "ground"). We call these environments turbulent fields. The turbulence results from the complexity and multiple character of the causal interconnections. Individual organizations, however large, cannot adapt successfully simply through their direct interactions. An examination is made of the enhanced importance of values, regarded as a basic response to persisting areas of relevant uncertainty, as providing a control mechanism, when commonly held by all members in a field. This raises the question of organizational forms based on the characteristics of a matrix.

Tables 1, 2, and 3 represent a model of seventeen key social patterns persisting from industrialism (column one in each Table). Contrasted is a set of recently emergent patterns (column two in each Table) which, though their hold is precarious, may be regarded as congruent with postindustrialism and therefore likely to gain in salience.

Cultural Values

These social patterns are grouped in three domains: (1) cultural values carried by the individual as a member of the social aggregate; (2) organizational philosophies embodied in the practices of the formal organizations to which he belongs in various task environments; and (3) strategies of "social ecology" through which governments and interest groups (at any level) seek to regulate the contextual environment of society. Events and processes in the three domains influence each other: if in the same direction, then a self-consistent and

TABLE 1
CHANGES IN CONTENT OF CULTURAL VALUES
IN THE TRANSITION TO POSTINDUSTRIALISM

Industrial Era	Postindustrial Era
1. Achievement	Self-actualization
2. Self-control	Self-expression
3. Independence	Interdependence
4. Endurance of distress	Capacity for joy

coherent ethos may be expected to arise; if contradictory, then maladaptive social defenses may be expected to increase (Emery, 1967).

Under "cultural values" (Table 1) are listed four corner-stones of industrial morality; achievement, self-control, independence, and endurance of distress (grinning and bearing it). But while psychologists are busy giving tests to discover how "need achievement" is progressing in developing countries, planners concerned with the advanced countries might be better advised to design the "habitats" of the future from the postindustrial list. This would include self-actualization, self-expression, interdependence and a capacity for joy. The new list will not replace the old but will gain in relevance and centrality. It will produce a re-structuring. The new items, like the old, are interrelated among themselves. As a set, they will come out differently through emerging on the background of the prevailing items. Postindustrial values represent retrievals, rediscoveries of preindustrial values which have been diminished, or lost, in industrial society. The gestalt which includes both will be new.

Self-Actualization

Self-actualization is a concept associated with the need hierarchy introduced by Abraham Maslow (1954, 1967). It states that the more that elementary needs are satisfied, the more matters of personal growth become central. There could scarcely be a more thorough postindustrial value. Though scientific theories about personal growth are contemporary, the concept itself is found in religions and philosophies which were born and matured in the preindustrial world. It became marginal in the industrial world where the achievement emphasis was fostered by the Protestant Work Ethic. Today, subcultures focusing on the retrieval of self-actualization often utilize Eastern religions and philosophies which have not been transformed by industrialism for the purpose of fostering self-actualization.

Yet even within Western tradition, Italian medieval literature contains a supreme exponent of self-actualization. Dante, at the age of thirty-five, went into the "dark wood" to work through his mid-life crisis. He describes this process in *The Divine Comedy* as he passes from the *Inferno* through the *Purgatorio* and into *Paradiso*. The idea that personal development (as distinct from personal achievement) stops at adulthood is purely an industrial concept. One had to become an adult to do the job but it became the job rather than oneself that an individual then developed and improved upon. Achievement is a closed-system, biophysical concept—as instanced in Freud's theory of genitality—rather than an open-system, biosocial idea. But Erikson's work

(1968) on identity has shown there are later identity crises than those of adolescence. This whole line of thought was foreshadowed by Jung's concept (1953) of individuation. Weathering the mid-life crisis was postulated as a critical process of self-renewal which determined the capacity for forward movement in the "third quarter of life." Recent developments in psychoanalysis concerning the working through of conflicts associated with the paranoid and schizoid positions, regarded as continuous throughout life, have increased understanding of later as well as earlier possibilities for development (Klein, 1948; Jaques, 1965). The positive theory of madness advanced by R.D. Laing (1967) recovers the "lost tradition" in a more recent socioexperiential idiom. Industrial society has not kept pace with new developments regarding the more profound needs of man.

In the preindustrial tradition, capacity for personal growth beyond the attainment of psychosexual maturity was assumed to be a rare capacity reserved for those few with inborn (or God-implanted) gifts in the arts, religion or philosophy. It was generally viewed as an aristocratic capacity. Maslow's research convinced him that this was widespread. The democratization capacity of the value is the postindustrial phenomenon. Market researchers have been forecasting increasing percentages of self-actualizing people in the American population in 1975, 1985 and, of course, in the year 2000!

Self-Expression

In regard to self-expression, Friedmann and Miller (1965) report data obtained by the Stanford Research Institute showing that fifty million Americans now participate in some form of amateur art activity. "Doing your own thing," a recent preoccupation which has since reached epidemic proportions, represents a reaction against being forced to do someone else's "thing"—being coerced at work by narrowly prescribed roles, especially within a large organization; being faced as a consumer with the choice of only mass-produced goods; and being expected as a social individual to conform to one or other of a very limited set of life styles. Yet as fate would have it, it is precisely this affluence of the much criticized technological society that is producing a greater scope for choice (Toffler, 1970). Self-expression is also concerned with trying out unused capacities, with discovering unsuspected potential. As far as the search for self-expression increases the variety and range of the individual's response repertoire, it may be seen as aiding adaptation to more complex environments. But it cannot proceed far without raising questions about the identity of the self which is seeking "expression." Is this the true self, or "am I my false self?" Psychoanalysts have found that a great deal of the work in character analysis—and character analyses have become the most common type of psychoanalytic undertaking—consists of the undoing of a false self (Winnicott, 1958; Deutsch, 1942). Denial of the deeper aspects and ordeals of self-actualization and self-expression will lead to the "trivialization" of these values. Evidence of this is abundant in the cultism at present surrounding them.

Values of self-actualization and self-expression could lead to a solipsistic personalism were they not balanced by the other two values of the emerging set. Angyal (1941, 1966) regards the life process as consisting of two underlying, opposite, but complementary trends—which he calls autonomy and homonomy. Autonomy expresses the individual's need to separate himself from others, to establish his own domain and to expand this vis-à-vis his environment. Homonomy expresses his need to relate to others and to become part of something larger than himself, to do "more than his thing," because after all, he is not self-sufficient but belongs to a "universe" which includes both himself and his environment. Self-actualization and self-expression embody the trend towards greater autonomy as do achievement and self-control. But the first two emphasize expansion of the person's being, rather than of his field of action, as do the second pair. Independence and endurance of distress continue the trend towards autonomy, whereas interdependence and capacity for joy assert the countervailing trend to homonomy. The industrial values emphasize autonomy and the action frame of reference; the postindustrial values emphasize homonomy and the existential frame of reference. The adaptive requirement of the future is a cultural system which embodies a balanced configuration of them all.

Interdependence

In developing a socioexperiential theory of human interdependence which recognizes the reality of the other as well as the self, Laing (1962) remarks that the word "you" does not occur in Freud. So far as the ego has an id and a superego, all of which are contained within the person, he is right about the conceptual scheme which Freud developed. But he is wrong about the process of psychoanalysis since it requires the presence of a real other in the person of the analyst. The development of child analysis by Melanie Klein (1948) and Winnicott (1958) has increased the emphasis on an object-relations approach which recognizes the importance of the real object, or other, as well as the phantasized object, or other, and the interplay between them. For there can be no denying the importance of the real mother to the child in the situation of infantile dependence, the psychological understanding of which has been extended by Bowlby (1969) from an ethological standpoint. Growing up, as Fairbairn (1952) puts it, is the conversion of dependence into interdependence. Capacity for interdependence will carry an ever higher premium in the postindustrial society given that higher levels of complexity and uncertainty can only be met by the greater adaptive resources brought into being by self-regulatory collaborative endeavor.

Capacity for Joy

Interdependent life styles need to be founded on a high level of trust, which raises the question of the positive element in relations with, and feelings about, others. One cannot have good feelings for others unless one has a fund of good feelings in oneself. This means being on better terms with oneself than most people are—being less alienated from one's real self by a false self. When society may be construed as hostile and the work one must do for a living is replete with "unpleasure," when one's relations with others are competitive while the injunctions of the superego are forbidding; then a philosophy of combative or stoical endurance is congruent with one's experience and needs. Tomkins (1962–63) points out that we are more experienced in regulating negative than positive affects. The culture of the work-addicted industrial society has been elaborated to aid adaptation to a negative affective life. When life is earnest we can deal with it; when it is not we are at a loss. The Grateful Dead (the quintessential San Francisco rock group) not only gave their 1969 album a symbolically postindustrial title, *The Working Man's Dead*, but included a lyric the burden of which is "having a hard time living the good life"—which would seem to be the core problem "at the frontier."

The prospect that the traditional distinction between work and play, made extreme in the industrial society, will be replaced by a new modality in which the reality and pleasure principles "cooperate" is both incredible and terrifying. The infrastructure of distress, which has a numbing effect on the rest of the affective life, has functioned as a defense against the degree of self-encounter required to meet this challenge. What capacity does one have for joy when the world created by "the dismal science" (the queen discipline of the industrial society) has issued an injunction against finding out?

Some of the contemporary subcultures assume that mere assertion of the capacity to love is enough to create at least a subworld of joy—with badness and hate banished and displaced onto the "brutal society" (even though Woodstock has had to reckon with Altamont, and the McCarthy idealism with Weatherman terrorism). Gross projection carrying the assumption that we can enter our own heaven by getting rid of our own hell is indicative of the type of splitting which Emery (1967) calls superficiality. Moreover, hippie colonists and protesting extremists have been encouraged to be superficial by none other than the existential sages. Sartre himself has proposed that hell is other people. The new humanists (Maslow included) denounce the pessimistic world-view propagated by psychoanalysts, supported, it would seem, by the Judeo-Christian tradition (the establishment of the invention of "sin"). Marcuse's (1956) doctrine of the conspiracy of repressive tolerance constitutes a social interpretation of Freud which is paranoid.

The fallacy regarding the positive affects is to suppose that love has a simple hedonistic basis—the pleasure principle. This leads to a sensate theory of the positive affects which can only end in solipsism. The experience of "excitement" now becomes the *summum bonum*. Whether induced by another person, oneself, or a drug is irrelevant; the sensation matters, the relationship does not; it becomes an instrument to be used, not an object to be cherished. This value has obtained wide currency and is currently in favor with some futurists (Kahn and Wiener, 1967). So far as this "pleasure principle" prevails, joy cannot become linked to interdependence and allow homonomy to balance autonomy in a new value configuration.

Reparation. If the version of psychoanalytic theory current before World War I supported a simple hedonistic theory of the positive affects, the version which began to develop in the interwar period corrected this by the introduction of a new concept aimed toward a new understanding of "self": *reparation* (Klein and Riviere, 1937). This concept states that the first dilemma of the child is to love and hate the same needed, but frustrating, maternal object. The child's most primitive defence against the pain of his ambivalance is to split his mother (both in phantasy and in his actual behavior) into an idealized, good, fulfilling mother and a denigrated, bad, frustrating mother. In so doing he splits himself. Moreover, in his greed for the good mother he exhausts her (to the point of losing her life in his phantasy, her patience in reality). Then the child turns her into a useless and, therefore, bad object, who will revenge herself on him for what he has done to her. As the child's growing cognitive structure enables him to separate an external world from himself he begins also to realize that his good and bad mothers are parts of one real whole other person and his good and bad feelings parts of himself— another real whole person. The pain of this discovery is complicated by his having to admit that the goodness he so desperately needs and wants is hers not his (as he had assumed when innocent i.e., in his original state of undifferentiated omnipotence). This arouses the deepest and most difficult to deal with of all the negative affects—envy. The child launches an envious attack on the goodness of the mother because the goodness is hers not his (to do what he likes with and to have always "on tap"). Only through recognition of his predatory aggressions can the child find his sense of guilt and only through this his need to make reparation to the good mother he has begun to destroy (and will, in his anxieties, lose). But in making reparation he finds goodness in himself, in his good feelings for her, and in his gratitude for what she has given him. He cares for her and wishes to put her right. The elucidation of the envy-gratitude dynamics came very late in psychoanalysis (Klein, 1957). This insight shows that the source of feelings of one's own goodness is in the experience of good feelings towards the other. This in turn involves recognition that the source of one's need satisfaction is in the other who has good feelings towards oneself. The experience of positive affects is founded on the recognition and experience of interdependence. These give the conditions for the person's realizing his independence; as he can only become whole (can only undo his own psychological splitting) by recognition of the contribution of the other.

Physical pleasure may be a component in good feelings but it does not bind their meaning. If good feelings are associated with sexuality, whether at the oral or the genital level, sexuality is an expression of interdependence and belongs to the homonomous rather than the autonomous trend. Goodness is discovered in the encounter with badness, not through its denial. Moreover, because good feelings are associated with making the other whole, they have an aesthetic component which is the basis of innovation (cf. Ackoff, 1969a). And innovation will be in demand more than ever in the postindustrial society. Plato excluded poets from the Republic because they were change agents. The need of a changing society is to strengthen these innovative capabilities in as many people as possible.

To achieve this higher level of self-actualization, we must grow up; that is, become more mature in the psychosocial as well as the biophysical sense. Continued personal growth is indeed what is required but it can only come about by a working through of the deep ordeals which have always belonged to the human condition to a far greater extent and by far more people than in previous societies. We need more self-actualizing adults, not more self-indulging children.

All this means that the psychosocial price of survival in complex fast-changing environments is going up. We are not going to get away too much longer with having rather bad societies composed largely of rather immature people. To produce a better world turns out to be the hard job it is because it means becoming better oneself. To maintain the "negative therapeutic reaction," not to change, is more comfortable. To remain in hell—where one lives a somewhat dreary life in a rather inhospitable atmosphere—is to remain on psychological easy street (however Satanic, or productive, the mill).

To go further means a more thorough working through of the anxieties of the depressive position but it is this which releases the positive growth process. Such working through is unlikely to attain a new general level unless a new social context emerges, for the present level is a function of the present context. The regulation of positive effects requires the identification of new values and the formation of new norms. We need to find ways of going beyond the super-ego without falling back on the pleasure principle. In the making of a new society the psychologist's job is to go on showing that there is no salvation in the cultivation of superficiality as the basis of personal values. A society based on a denial of the deeper—and darker—aspects of the human psyche will be more one-dimensional than the present and there will be no joy in it.

TASK AND CONTEXTUAL ENVIRONMENTS
FOR NEW PERSONAL VALUES

New values will become salient only if experience in all parts of the life-space consistently supports their emergence. Therefore, what is happening in organizations has particular importance in that it will affect the character of the task environments in which the individual is likely to find himself.

Organizational Philosophies

Column one of Table 2 summarizes classical organization theory and pre-vailing management practice, column two the emerging ethos. It is in complex science-based enterprises, the most postindustrial, where the attitudes and values of column two are beginning to take hold.

TABLE 2
CHANGES IN EMPHASIS IN ORGANIZATIONAL PHILOSOPHIES
IN THE TRANSITION TO POSTINDUSTRIALISM

Industrial Era	Postindustrial Era
5. Mechanistic forms	Organic forms
6. Competitive relations	Collaborative relations
7. Separate objectives	Linked objectives
8. Own resources regarded as owned absolutely	Own resources regarded as society's

Burns and Stalker (1961) showed the gathering influence of what they called the organismic pattern of management in the electronics industry as this sought to establish itself after World War II in Scotland in an area in which were ingrained the autocratic and bureaucratic traditions of the first industrial revolution. The impact of McGregor's (1960) Theory Y in a number of countries on managers endeavoring to further the second industrial revolution illustrates the key importance of clarifying an emergent value. A new ideology arose in organization theory during the 1960s which sought to identify a new organizational archetype—the trans-bureaucratic modality. Likert (1961) classified enterprises according to the number of steps taken in management style away from the traditional exploitative and authoritarian form (System 1). Likert's System 2 continued to be based on one-to-one relations between superior and subordinate but its autocracy was benevolent rather than exploitative. In System 3, an element of consultation entered, with subordinates now also being treated as a group. System 4 could be considered participative in that decisions emerged from the joint work of superior and subordinates. Groups at all levels behaved similarly so that the organization became a hierarchy of overlapping group decision systems with the leader at each level performing a "linking pin" role with the members of the next. A wide range of organizational variables was examined in order to show the high degree of consistency within each of the four styles. Likert (1967) has since been amassing evidence that this system of overlapping group hierarchies yields the best payoffs in organizational performance.

Argyris (1964) identified two steps "further out" than Likert's System 4 by considering first the project form of organization which spread from research and design into production in the aerospace industry, and next the need to renew sanction from a "constituency" group when ground rules were changed. Bennis and Slater (1968) considered capability to belong, rapidly and effectively, to *temporary systems* not only as an organizational but as a life style congruent with a more mobile world.

Social perception of the trans-bureaucratic mode as "good" and of the bureaucratic mode as "bad" would, as a posture, appear to be ahead of changes in practice. Likert thought it might take ten to fifteen years for a large organization to change its norms from System 1 or 2 to System 4. There is considerable danger that value change may not take place at the pace required. Even though "systems management" has become very much the "in mode," unfortunately, systems management still tends to be apprehended in a technical rather than a sociotechnical frame of reference, suggesting that very little underlying value change has yet taken place.

Competitive strategies appropriate to Type 3 disturbed-reactive environments predominated in what Galbraith (1967) has called the "New Industrial State" where, especially in the advanced industries, a few large firms, to varying degrees multinational, vie with each other under conditions of an oligopoly. Yet, as he points out, there are many indirect ways of calling off what would otherwise be a fight to the death without getting into the kind of trouble with the Anti-Trust Laws which fifteen years ago befell General Electric and Westinghouse. This incident was a warning, belated rather than early, that a Vickers (1968) type of limit had been reached.

For the student of emergent processes, it is not so much the growth of take-overs (a Type 3 environmental phenomenon) which has been of interest during the last decade as the increasing tendency of large firms across the world to undertake "joint ventures." Joint ventures often combine public and private capital. Participants in a scheme recently put forward to develop a petro-chemical and shipyard complex in a part of Newfoundland included the Provincial Government, the Federal Government of Canada, a British firm (B.P.) which is part public, part private, and various American private interests, including Litton Industries. Such undertakings involve a strategy of "shared parts" which is a Type 4 environmental process. They involve substituting for an order based on the competitive challenge of superior power, a *negotiated order* based on mutual accommodation of interests all considered to be legitimate. The term "negotiated order" is surfacing in many fields at the present time: in the hospital world—concerning the relations of medical and other staff categories (Strauss, 1964); in the prison world—concerning staff-inmate relations (Rutherford, 1969); no less than in the labor-management world from which it came (Walton and McKersie, 1965). Vickers (1970) has contrasted "negotiation" with "containment" (by the use of coercive power) in the political evolution of industrial England. The idea of a negotiated order is congruent with the need to develop a greater capability to manage interdependence through cooperative rather than competitive relations, (though not without confrontation).

The question of linked vs. separate objectives is also best approached by considering what has been happening to it in the leading part of the industrial field. In the values of the industrial society, it was presumed that an enterprise had, and should have, an exclusively economic objective. The economic sector thrived best when its independence from other sectors was maximized. Though this idea was challenged many years ago in the management literature (Berle and Means, 1932) it received scant attention in practice until very recently. But the urban crisis in a country such as the United States is bringing home to corporations, whose business inextricably binds their fate to the inner city, that social losses can undermine economic gains. Externally, they have little option but to become actively concerned about the quality of the environment, just as internally they have to be actively concerned about the quality of work-life and career opportunity offered to employees at all levels. While most responses to all this are arrested at the level of tokenism, here and there more thoroughgoing changes are beginning to take place.

The issue is closely linked to that of attitude to ownership of resources which became a central topic in a project on company objectives and management philosophy which the Tavistock Institute began during the mid-1960s with Shell (U.K.) Limited, and which has recently been reported by C.P. Hill (1971).

The company stated publicly that it regards its resources, both material and human, as belonging to society as well as to itself and has undertaken to manage these resources in accordance with this principle. The public statement was made only after the implications had been worked through over an eighteen-month period in a large number of residential conferences involving employees at all levels from the Board to the shop floor. Are employees to be regarded as owned absolutely (like slaves) or conditionally—and if the latter, what are the conditions? Who are the claimants (other than oneself—or the stockholders)? What are their rights? How are they reconcilable? The claimant or holder theory of the firm, involving multiple interest groups, has been put forward to answer questions of this kind (Perlmutter, 1965; Ansoff, 1965).

This whole set of issues involves the concept of a negotiated order and the values—and competences—of interdependence. The following hypothesis seems warranted: *that so far as a negotiated order evolves it will reduce segmentation.*

Strategies of Social Ecology

Signs of a new and adaptive trend are hard to discern in the contextual environment. This includes the wider world of large interorganizational and interurban clusters. Yet the world of these clusters is sufficiently established in postindustrial societies for the systems of social ecology they compose to be regarded as their critical contextual element. The appropriateness of the strategies through which ecological as distinct from organizational systems are regulated becomes decisive in determining the adaptive effectiveness of the culture of postindustrialism.

In column one of Table 3 is the prevailing pattern, which reflects the persistence of an industrial concept of ecological regulation based on a combination of bureaucratic and laissez-faire principles. Column two contrasts it with a very different pattern which only in the last few years has begun to take shape. The list contains two subsets, items 9–13 being concerned with policy, and items 14–17 with administration.

TABLE 3
CHANGES IN EMPHASIS AMONG STRATEGIES OF SOCIAL ECOLOGY
IN THE TRANSITION TO POSTINDUSTRIALISM

Industrial Era	Postindustrial Era
9. Responsive to crisis	Anticipative of crisis
10. Specific measures	Comprehensive measures
11. Requiring consent	Requiring participation
12. Dampening conflict	Confronting conflict
13. Short planning horizon	Long planning horizon
14. Detailed central control	Generalized central control
15. Small local government units	Enlarged local government units
16. Standardized administration	Innovative administration
17. Separate services	Coordinated services

The clue to policy-making under industrialism is in the first item which discloses the passive mode of adaptation. A negative system of government was held to be the necessary counterpart of a positive system of enterprise. Intervention took place only when it became undeniable that a particular corrective was needed so that the specific measure became the unit of legislative action. Consent expressed in the vote of a simple majority of elected representatives (themselves chosen every four or five years by a similar method) constituted sufficient sanction, even if the majority was narrow. One did not mind being in the minority on some items and on some occasions so long as one could be in the majority on others. The pattern of an open series of specific measures restricted in scope, introduced piecemeal and sanctioned by a simple majority, dampened conflict by allowing it to be absorbed in repeated small doses. This pattern was inherently that of a "non-planning" system. One kept accounts and saw that they balanced (deficit financing in any circumstances is still frowned upon in pre-Keynesian circles) but the budget year was the limit of the planning horizon. To look further ahead would have been to interfere with the future which was dangerous and immoral.

All this worked tolerably well so long as the main regulator at the ecological level—the market—was working autoregulatively. The worst that could happen was a bad trade cycle swing. That of the Great Depression of the 1930s was so bad that it caused even the most laissez-faire societies to seek some form of economic regulation. Since then, purely economic regulation has proved insufficient. Other dimensions of value concerning the quality of life have come to the fore. But these have been creating incompatible demands which are increasing the dissociation of social sectors at a time when the need for them to become interdependent is increasing by internalizing the "externalities."

So long as mixes of Type 1 and Type 2 environmental conditions prevailed in the market place, the relation between negative politics and positive economics could be maintained in balance. Increased salience of Type 3 conditions subjected this arrangement to increasing imbalance. Tactical accommodation has consisted of step-by-step intervention leading to jungle growth in the Administrative subset of Table 3. As Type 4 conditions become salient this model can be stretched no further.

Treasury control as traditionally exercised in Britain typifies the detailed item by item supervision imposed by the key department of a central government over others. An increase in the use of block grants to autonomous bodies, such as the University Grants Committee or to local authorities, represents a move away from this. The "new federalism" to be practiced by Washington bureaucracies in allocating resources to fifty states is a belated declaration of intent to reverse the centralizing trend of recent decades, though attempts to implement it are likely to be fraught with considerable difficulties.

In most advanced countries in North America and Western Europe, local government units based on the city and the country have been breaking down. In the United States, bankrupt cities deteriorate beside prospering surburban counties. The incompatible interests of City and State have been symbolized in a number of mayor-governor feuds. A proposal has been made out of desperation to make major metropolitan areas directly responsible to the Federal Government. A Maritimes Union and a Prairies Union would make good sense in Canada; but these have not yet been deemed politically feasible (though proposed by Mr. Bennett, the former Premier of British Columbia). France and Britain, each in their own manner, are proceeding to regionalize themselves and to extend the boundaries of local governments within regions. But unless this is done in ways perceived as meaningful, little can be expected regarding participation. Yet people in these nations need a sense of more effective control over some relevant proximal "realm"—experienced as valid and with which they can identify—the more so as they become confronted with supranational European institutions.

Related to all this is the extreme standardization which has characterized administrative procedures. Whether the aim has been to maintain fairness or to prevent abuse, homogenization of treatment for increasingly specified classes of claimants and the limitation of the discretion of officials have depersonalized the relations of the administered and the administrators. Yet as Donald Schon (1971) has pointed out, the center-periphery model cannot meet the rising complexity. The "provinces" will have to make policy as well as execute it. Government agencies will have to transform themselves into "public learning systems" in order to cope with the faster change rate. The proliferation of separate services, each jealously guarding its own turf, is an expression of the same legacy. They compete and cultivate their own power bases in ways which substantially distort the pattern of public expenditure. Whether the recent unification of health and social services in Britain under one Ministry will turn out to be more than nominal, despite recognition of their interpenetration, remains to be proven. Nevertheless, the intent is in the right direction.

Reform at the administrative level in the direction of column two is impossible, beyond a modest limit, without reorientation in the same direction at the policy level. But this requires new and widespread understanding of the underlying issues. It may be doubted whether the present culture of politics considered as a medium for the ecological regulation of society has the capability without substantial modification to achieve this reorientation. Should we start to behave consistently in terms of the policy items of column two (see Table 3) we would have already changed our political character, even though we would not have rewritten the constitution.

The familiar alternatives to democracies of the Western type are totalitarian regimes. These may be traditional in form, combining a coercive political system with a stagnant economic system—as in preindustrial societies—or they may be established as the result of revolutions when they endeavor to combine coercive government with economic growth. Regimes of the first type have registered successes in delaying industrialization; regimes of the second in accelerating it. But these latter are societies beginning industrialization. There is no evidence that totalitarian regimes can provide a safe passage to postindustrialism for advanced industrial societies. One may expect increasing social political disturbances in totalitarian countries, the more complex they become.

The Function of a Common Ground

If political democracies of the Western type break down and if totalitarianism is even less able to meet complexity, in what direction may an answer lie? It would seem to lie in the direction of *social pluralism*. The question then becomes how much pluralism is containable, without further dissociation, unless a unifying element is also identifiable? One aspect of currently emerging pluralism is loss of the paramountcy of economic values. Other dimensions of value are reasserting their claims. Even in the enterprise itself, Lawrence and Lorsch (1967) have shown that better overall performance arises from an ability to accept a diversity of internal management climates appropriate to different functions. This is analogous to the acceptance of different life styles. Both involve increasing the range of one's directive correlations, to use the concept of adaptation introduced by Sommerhoff (1950, 1969).

If we must learn to accept a variety of figures is there a common ground? We have not been accustomed to look at the "ground." Our training has made us figure-focused. But we may not find a common figure; common ground we may. The following hypothesis may be advanced: *the capacity to accept the greater degree of pluralism that is characterizing the transition to postindustrialism and which involves loss of paramountcy in any one value or "figural" societal system will be a function of the extent to which a unifying ground can become established.*

Marshall McLuhan (1964) can be of assistance in furthering our understanding of how this might be possible. He has shown how the new media consequent on the second industrial revolution are changing the sociocultural "ground forces" in a common direction whatever the differences between individuals, groups and organizations. The conditions obtaining in Type 4 environments lead us to expect the emergence of more powerful ground forces than in simpler environments. These may produce unregulable disturbance as envisioned by Vickers (1968). They may also produce a new type of background cohesiveness. In McLuhan's view, they are altering the "sense-ratios" from the dominance of visual to a re-emphasis of aural-tactile experience. They are altering simultaneously our cognitive structures from domination by an analytic approach, to acceptance of a synthetic approach (Ackoff, 1974). We are learning to think and feel in terms of fields and simultaneity processes, as well as in terms of elements and causal trains. This is congruent with modern physics. Rational and nonrational modes of experience are not inherently incompatible.

Noticeable are the extent to which popular folk music is establishing itself as a *lingua franca* across a large part of the world and the unifying influence of the transnational youth culture. McLuhan adds that television, being a "cool" medium, increases involvement and decreases detachment.

Such processes have the effect of strengthening the trend towards homonomy. They do so by acting on the ground both in the environment and in ourselves rather than on the figures on which we focus. In this they are ecological. In time they may influence "figural" appreciations in ways likely to be adaptive to postindustrialism. They are congruent with the forces impinging on the individual from other parts of his life-space which have been tending to produce the emergent values which have been described. It may be hypothesized that *the establishment of more common ground will reduce dissociation.* Current experience, thence expectation (outside a narrow range of social encounter) of a lack of common ground inhibits exploration and increases isolation.

This potential for congruence may be noticed without our ceasing to notice also the disturbing effects of ground forces of another kind—those through which the limits of regulation are being reached. The appearance of a trend towards more background coherence constitutes a necessary but not a sufficient condition of successful adaptation to complex (Type 4) environments. Active and constructive use will have to be made of it if one of the better of the alternative futures is to be attained. The communications technology of the second industrial revolution is available. As Emery (1967) has said the consequential change which has taken place in intraspecies communication is "a greater mutation than if man had grown another head." According to what we do with them, the new media may work for us rather than against us and increase the diffusion rate of new values at a level not previously possible. At least they may prepare the ground.

FROM PLANNING TOWARDS THE SURRENDER OF POWER

The structural-cultural mismatch which has been examined, together with the nature and direction of the emergent adaptive processes, has led to a restatement of Emery's position—that we must take an active, intervening rather than a passive, respondent role in regulating the welfare and development of society. This means facing the planner's dilemma. How can planning be carried out under conditions of accelerating change and rising uncertainty? What style of planning, if any, provides a field of maneuver for getting out of ecological traps?

Planning as Process

For most people, planning conjures up the idea of comprehensive planning, technocratically devised and centrally imposed. Such planning rests on two assumptions:

    1. That there was once a steady state and that there will again be an-

another steady state—and that the way to get from the first to the second is to produce a complete plan which supposes that the principal future states of the system can be foreseen.

2.   That implementation can be carried out with resources completely under one's own control.

This represents closed system thinking, the machine theory of organization, the maximization of power—everything which the encounter with higher levels of complexity and uncertainty has shown to be unworkable. Yet a relapse into nonplanning is equally unworkable. A form of anticipation and regulation has to be found which will match the realities of rapidly changing Type 4 environments.

Fortunately, an approach to planning which has some of the requisite characteristics has begun to make an appearance in theory and in practice. It is an open-ended type of planning which takes account of the emergent, allows for the unforeseeable and follows strategies of interdependence rather than independence in the mobilization of resources. It has acquired various names: innovative planning (Friedmann and Miller, 1965; Friedmann, 1973); interest group planning (Chevalier, 1968) and adaptive planning (Ackoff, 1969b). The "disjointed incrementalism" proposed by Hirschman and Lindblom (1962) would be regarded by many as a first conceptual move in this direction though to the writer it seems too much like a "reaction formation" against comprehensive planning. As such it becomes indistinguishable from "muddling through" which worked only when auto-regulative processes were functioning at the ecological level and the specific measure could remain as the unit of legislative action. The type of planning now required must be able to give direction and to set standards in the sense asked for by Frank (1967) while at the same time being flexible and always remaining incomplete.

In France.   Thanks to Monnet, some French planners began fifteen years ago to put the above type of planning into practice based on recognition of a simple but fundamental truth: that planning is not so much a program as a process. However technical many of its aspects may be, in underlying nature, planning is a social process. Moreover, it is continuous. Phases of formulation, implementation, evaluation and modification succeed and interact with each other without reaching a final limit. It is also participative. All those concerned must contribute in appropriate roles. Or else, one might ask, regarding continuity "What of the plan, now that circumstances have changed?" and, regarding participation, "Who is making plans about what for whom?"

Michel Crozier (1966) carried out a sociological study of the decision-making process of the Vᵉ Plan, as brought into being by the *Commissariat du Plan*. He has shown that the most important effect of French planning lies not so much in the achievement of the targets as in the social learning released in the innumerable commissions which take part in making, carrying out, and revising "the plan." Each of these commissions represents a particular coalition of interests, often never brought together before, or previously too antagonistic to cooperate. In the planning context, however, they became progressively more able to undertake joint problem-solving. This whole process, whatever its shortcomings (it has been criticized as too elitist—even though it is in reality cross-elitist), was initiated during the Fourth Republic when the party political system was collapsing and the Algerian War was dividing the country. It has continued during the Fifth Republic. De Gaulle had to take the need for more involvement into account during *les événements mai* of 1968. The nature of the emergent social processes, however, remained unrecognized. A regressive characterization was made in terms of old "images" which presented the choice as either preserving order by retaining the familiar "bourgeois" society or facing chaos and thence the rise of "communism"—rather than taking innovative steps in the transition towards postindustrialism. A moment of opportunity was lost (though promises were made) to begin genuinely innovative educational reform in the thorough-going way the society required to advance further into the transition.

No attempt was made to find a possible new meaning in the unusual and precarious coalition which emerged between students and workers during *les événements mai*. This was discussed in an interview given by Sartre to Cohn-Bendit. Sartre took the position that because being a student represented a temporary status while being a worker represented a permanent status, there could be no coalition. Cohn-Bendit pointed out that in the on-coming society, being a student would indeed become a permanent status because learning had become life-long, while all workers would need the opportunity to continue learning. Though Sartre took the point, the implications were lost in an ideological jumble which mixed Trotskyism, Maoism and Dadaism and in which the past is easier to discern than the future.

Nevertheless, the more planning, as a continuous and participative activity, becomes organically linked to the open-ended political process of a society, it would seem to become more "robust"—more able to survive the knocks and shocks of rapidly changing environments. The hypothesis is advanced that *the planning process (not the plan) can become the basis of a new "culture" of politics*. This new political culture will involve continuous dialogue, painful confrontation, "animation sociale," hard bargaining and multiple interest group accommodation. But these are the processes which can lead to innovative joint problem-solving as experience is gained and greater trust is established. The new culture will also demand a full technical "input" from the planning professions and their supporting sciences at all stages and levels. There is likely always to be a certain dissonance between the technical and the participative aspects, and the "planner's dilemma" is never likely completely to be resolved, though attendant conflicts, we may hope, will on the whole be benign rather than malign (in Boulding's sense [1966]).

Pluralism

The task of the new politics will be the regulation of ecological systems undergoing rapid but uneven change. One of the troubles is that there is a galaxy of such systems which overlap in various dimensions. Somehow we must find a way of reducing both systems and dimensions to a manageable set–though neither by opportunistic circumscription nor over-centralized control. A greater coherence in the "ground forces" will strengthen capability to tolerate a greater degree of social pluralism in "figural" systems. *It is hypothesized that the development of social pluralism may represent a method of complexity reduction without regressive simplification.*

To succeed in a problem-continuing environment, postindustrial politics must become both more informed and more participative than the politics of industrialism, more devolved and open to more rapid and continuous feedback. Postindustrial man will spend more of his time in politics than industrial man and more in the planning processes associated with it. In all likelihood, he will have the leisure time to spend in such activities.

A Required Dissociation

The United States—with superpower responsibilities, a population of 200 million and an heterogeneity which has made extreme the processes of internal fragmentation, segmentation and dissociation which to varying degrees have affected all advanced countries—is a society too complex to tolerate much innovation in the social present in the political engagement of the planning process. A country like Canada is better placed, being a very advanced country yet out of the storm center of world politics, and possessing a highly educated but relatively small population. These conditions make more manageable some of the problems critical for the transition to postindustrialism. However severely Canada may be challenged by problems, such as that of Quebec and the position of the French speaking minority, these problems do not seem as intractable as many in other parts of the world. In recent decades, the Scandinavian countries have been responsible for several social and cultural innovations in the European context. All may not be affluent in these countries but poverty has been eliminated. The stability and coherence of the ground has permitted such figural innovations as industrial democracy in Norway (Emery and Thorsrud, 1969), the containment of pornography and the megafamily in Denmark (in which the Church played a leading part), prison reform in Sweden, and an aesthetic renaissance in architecture and design which has spread through all these countries. Canada has some of the properties of a North American Scandinavia. Social innovations in the U.S., though multiple, have so far been more restricted regarding the groups they affect.

The suggestion may be made that some of the smaller advanced countries may become social laboratories from which others may learn in the transition to postindustrialism. One reason for this is that they are experienced in not exercising political power on the world stage, while remaining economically competent in the world market. They proclaim the viability of a dissociation between two elements on whose association the major states not only of the industrial but the preindustrial period have been founded. To amass power has been the strategy of choice in adapting to a world in which Type 3 environmental conditions have been salient. *To surrender power is a necessary condition for survival in a Type 4 environment.* The Great Powers and the Superpowers have found (and find) themselves obliged to spend unduly large proportions of their resources and energies in elaborating and maintaining specialized control systems (military and other)—in accordance with Emery's first design principle. Sooner or later (as the history books never tire of recounting) this weakens their core societies. By contrast, the smaller advanced countries are closer to Emery's second design principle of self-regulation. They have preserved a core identity while maintaining themselves transnationally. They have successfully cultivated well selected capabilities in the economic field which embody cultural traditions which have grown out of their whole ecological setting and in which they have comparative advantage.

In certain respects the world of the postindustrial society, if this manages to establish itself, will recover some of the properties of the Type 2 environment. Anthropologists, perhaps, see this more clearly than others. Lévi-Strauss (1960) has spelled out the argument in his inaugural lecture on being elected to the first Chair of Social Anthropology at the Collège de France:

> So called primitive societies, which we might define as "cold" in that their internal environment is on the zero of historical temperature, are, by their limited total manpower and their mechanical mode of functioning, distinguished from the "hot" societies which appeared in different parts of the world following the Neolithic revolution. In these, differentiations between castes and between classes are urged increasingly in order to extract social change and energy from them.

> ... When, on the morrow of the Neolithic revolution, the great city-states of the Mediterranean Basin and of the Far East perpetrated slavery, they constructed a type of society in which the differential statuses of men—some dominant, others dominated—could be used to produce culture at a rate until then inconceivable and unthought of. By the same logic, the industrial revolution of the nineteenth century represents less an evolution oriented in the same direction, than a rough sketch of a different solution: though for a long time it remained based on the same abuses and injustices, yet it made possible the transfer to *culture* of that dynamic function which the protohistoric revolution had assigned to *society*.

> If—Heaven forbid!—it were expected of the anthropologist that he predict the future of humanity, he would undoubtedly not conceive of it as a continuation or a projection of present types, but rather on the model of an integration, progressively unifying the appropriate characteristics of the "cold" societies and the "hot" ones. His thought would renew connections with the old Cartesian dream of putting machines, like automatons, at the service of man. It would follow this lead through the social philosophy of the eighteenth century and up to Saint-Simon. The latter, in announcing the passage "from government of men to the administration of things," anticipated in the same breath the anthropological distinction between culture and society. He thus looked forward to an event of which advances in information theory and electronics give us at least a glimpse: the conversion of a type of civilization which inaugurated historical development at the price of the transformation of men into machines into an ideal civilization which would succeed in turning machines into men. Then, culture having entirely taken over the burden of manufacturing progress, society would be freed from the millennial curse which has compelled it to enslave men in order that there be progress. Henceforth, history would make itself by itself.

This statement, which at one and the same time presents an analysis and a vision, conceives the viable future as an achievement of societal self-regulation made possible by the culture of the second industrial revolution. This would bring to an end the epoch we have known as history and have called civilization. Yet there can be no simple return to a Type 2 world in which large numbers of small societies existed independently; rather will there come into being a matrix in the interdependent networks of which values will be such that pluralism can be tolerated. But, if diversity is to be internalized and to become figural, similarity will be needed as external support in a common ground. The coolness which McLuhan discerns in the new cultural media may enable coldness as conceived by Lévi-Strauss to re-enter society. Somehow the heat has to be taken off and the self-exciting systems described by Vickers brought under regulation. If planning processes are to be a principal means by which this is brought about, planning would, as Ackoff has suggested, work itself out of a job—if ever an ideal state of self-regulation could be reached in the world as a whole.

REFERENCES

Ackoff, R.L.
1969a "Institutional functions and societal needs," in E. Jantsch (ed.), Perspectives in Planning. Paris: OCED.
1969b A Concept of Corporate Planning. New York and London: Wiley.
1974 Redesigning the Future. New York: Wiley.
Angyal, A.
1941 Foundations for a Science of Personality. Re-issued 1958. Cambridge, Mass.: Harvard University Press.
1966 Neurosis and Treatment. New York and London: Wiley.
Ansoff, I.H.
1965 Corporate Strategy. New York: McGraw-Hill.
Argyris, C.
1964 Integrating the Individual and the Organization. New York and London: Wiley.
Bennis, W.G. and P.E. Slater
1968 The Temporary Society. New York: Harper and Row.
Berle, A.A., Jr. and G.C. Means
1932 The Modern Corporation and Private Property. New York: Macmillan.
Boulding, K.
1966 "Conflict management as a learning process," in A. de Reuck (ed.), Conflict in Society. London: Churchill.
Bowlby, J.
1969 Attachment and Loss. Vol. 1: Attachment. London, New York: Basic Books.
Burns, T. and G. Stalker
1961 The Management of Innovation. London: Tavistock Publications.
Chevalier, M.
1968 "Interests group planning." PhD Dissertation, Philadelphia: University of Pennsylvania.
Crozier, M.
1966 "Attitudes and beliefs in national planning," in B.M. Gross (ed.), Action Under Planning. New York: McGraw-Hill.
Deutsch, H.
1942 "Some forms of emotional disturbances and their relationship to schizophrenia." Psychoanalytic Quarterly 2:301–321.
Emery, F.E.
1967 "The next thirty years: concepts, methods and anticipations." Human Relations (20):199–237.

1969   Systems Thinking. Harmondsworth, Middlesex, England: Penguin Books.

Emery, F.E. and E. Thorsrud
1969   Form and Content in Industrial Democracy. London: Tavistock Publications. Norwegian Edition, 1964, Oslo University Press.

Emery, F.E. and E.L. Trist
1965   "The causal texture of organizational environments." Human Relations (18):21–32. (Reprinted in Emery [1969]).
1973   Towards a Social Ecology. London and New York: The Plenum Press.

Erikson, E.H.
1968   Identity, Youth and Crisis. London: Faber and Faber.

Fairbairn, W.R.D.
1952   Psychoanalytic Studies of the Personality. London: Tavistock Publications.

Frank, L.K.
1967   "The need for a new political theory." Daedalus 96(August):809–816.

Friedmann, J.
1973   Retracking America: A Theory of Transactive Planning. New York: Anchor Press/Doubleday.

Friedmann, J. and J. Miller
1965   "The urban field." Journal of American Institute of Planners (31): 312–320.

Galbraith, J.K.
1967   The New Industrial State. Boston: Houghton Mifflin.

Hill, C.P.
1971   "Towards a new philosophy of management." London: The Gower Press.

Hirschman, A.O. and C.E. Lindblom
1962   "Economic development, research and development, policy making: some convergent views." Behavioral Science (7):211–222.

Jaques, E.
1965   "Death and the mid-life crisis." International Journal of Psychoanalysis (46):502–514.

Jung, C.J.
1953   "Two essays in analytical psychology," in C.J. Jung, Collected Works. Vol. 7. London: Routledge and Kegan Paul.

Kahn, H. and A.J. Wiener
1967   The Year 2000. New York: Macmillan.

Klein, M.
1948   Contributions to Psychoanalysis: 1921–1945. London: Hogarth.
1957   Envy and Gratitude. London: Tavistock.

Klein, M. and J. Riviere
1937   Love, Hate and Reparation. London: Hogarth.

Laing, R.D.
1962   The Self and Others, Further Studies in Sanity and Madness. London: Tavistock Publications.
1967   The Politics of Experience. Harmondsworth, Middlesex, England: Penguin Books.

Lawrence, P.R. and J.W. Lorsch
1967   Organization and Environment. Boston: Division of Research, Graduate School of Business Administration, Harvard University.

Lévi-Strauss, C.
  1960 The Scope of Anthropology. Translated from the French by S.O. Paul and R.A. Paul, 1967, 1968. London and Atlantic Highlands, New Jersey: Cape, Humanities Press.
Likert, R.
  1961 New Patterns of Management. New York: McGraw-Hill.
  1967 The Human Organization: Its Management and Value. New York: McGraw-Hill.
McGregor, D.
  1960 The Human Side of Enterprise. New York: McGraw-Hill.
McLuhan, M.
  1964 Understanding Media. New York, London: McGraw-Hill, Routledge and Kegan Paul.
Marcuse, H.
  1956 Eros and Civilization. London: Routledge and Kegan Paul.
Maslow, A.H.
  1954 Motivation and Personality. New York: Harper & Bros.
  1968 Toward a Psychology of Being. Second Edition. New York: Van Nostrand Reinhold.
Perlmutter, H.
  1965 Towards a Theory and Practice of Social Architecture. London: Tavistock.
Rutherford, A.
  1969 "Towards a bargaining model." New Haven, Conn.: Yale University Law School. Unpublished manuscript.
Schon, D.A.
  1971 Beyond the Stable State. New York, London: Random House, Temple Smith.
Sommerhoff, G.
  1950 Analytical Biology. London: Oxford University Press.
  1969 "The abstract characteristics of living systems," in F.E. Emery (ed.), Systems Thinking. Harmondsworth, Middlesex, England: Penguin Books.
Strauss, A., et al.
  1964 "The hospital and its negotiated order," in E. Friedson (ed.), The Hospital in Modern Society. New York: The Free Press.
Toffler, A.
  1970 Future Shock. New York: Random House.
Tolman, E.G. and E. Brunswick
  1935 "The organism and the causal texture of the environment." Psychological Review (42):43–77.
Tomkins, S.S.
  1962 Imagery, Affect, Consciousness. 2 Vols. New York: Springer.
  –63
von Bertalanffy, L.
  1950 "The theory of open systems in physics and biology." Science (3): 23–29.
Vickers, G.
  1968 Value Systems and Social Process. London, New York: Tavistock, Basic Books.

1970   Freedom in a Rocking Boat. London, New York: Allen Lane (The Penguin Press), Basic Books.

Walton, R.E. and R.B. McKersie
1965   A Behavioral Theory of Labor Negotiations: An Analysis of Social Interaction Systems. New York: McGraw-Hill.

Weber, M.
1947   The Protestant Ethic and the Spirit of Capitalism. London: Oxford University Press.

Winnicott, D.W.
1958   Collected Papers. London: Tavistock.

Name Index

Subject Index